A STUDY OF
HISTORY

VOLUME XII
RECONSIDERATIONS

CONTENTS

XII. RECONSIDERATIONS

C. RECONSIDERATIONS OF PARTICULAR TOPICS . 223

CONTENTS

XII. RECONSIDERATIONS

INTRODUCTION

IN publishing a book a writer is deliberately exposing his work to 'the wreckful siege of battering days'. This is his own doing. He has been under no compulsion, except an inner one. But, having once published, he must then choose between two alternative policies. He can say, 'What I have written, I have written', and spend the rest of his working life on trying to maintain his previous positions—for no better reason than that he happens once to have occupied them. Alternatively, he can think again; see whether or not he has changed his mind on this or that disputed point; publish the results of these second thoughts; and explain why, after reconsideration, he has in fact changed his mind in some cases and held to his previous opinion in others.

At a meeting of the Royal Geographical Society at which a critique of Ellsworth Huntington's work and mine had been presented by O. H. K. Spate, the Chairman is reported[1] to have remarked, at the close of the discussion: 'I always wish there was some way in the scientific world of retracting what one has said in the past.' Surely there is. *Solvitur ambulando.*

Justice Holmes once wrote that 'to have doubted one's own first principles is the mark of a civilized man'.[2] In quoting this passage a philosopher, M. R. Cohen, comments that men like Socrates and Einstein 'never outgrow a childlike curiosity about the Universe and continue, as long as they live, to ask questions of the World and to revise mistaken views'.[3] The choice between following their example and following Pilate's is not a difficult one to make.

Pilate's stand would indeed be a particularly unreasonable one for me to take about the first ten volumes of this book. One of my critics has called it 'an intellectual autobiography'.[4] A number of them have pointed out that, in the course of writing it, I have moved from one position to another at least once. If I had not, I should feel uneasy, for that would have meant that my mind had stood still during the thirty-three years (1921–54) that passed between my making of a first sketch for a plan of the book and the publication of volumes vii–x. In this last batch of volumes 'a hardening of the categories' has, indeed, been detected by one critic;[5] and obviously it is probable that I may show

---

[1] *The Geographical Journal*, vol. cxviii, Part 4 (December, 1952), p. 428.
[2] O. W. Holmes: 'Ideals and Doubts' in *Collected Legal Papers* (New York 1921, Harcourt Brace), p. 307.   [3] M. R. Cohen: *The Meaning of Human History*, p. 175.
[4] R. P. Blackmur in *The Kenyon Review*, Summer, 1955, pp. 357–90.
[5] 'These last four volumes reveal an aspect of Toynbee which is inevitable in any scholar who has worked at a chosen subject for over a generation. It is what has been called a hardening of the categories. These four volumes are constructed on the framework made familiar in the previous six. . . . All of these concepts were introduced earlier as tentative, hypothetical ideas to be tested out to see how far they could serve in organizing the synoptic historian's material. Now, in the last volumes, they are all taken for granted as having been proved and established—as being, in fact, the framework within which the events of history do actually arrange themselves. What was once a subjective suggestion is now objective fact' (F. H. Underhill in *The Canadian Historical Review*, vol. xxxvi, No. 3 (September, 1955), pp. 222–35).

symptoms of this intellectual malady. But the verdict of other critics makes it also probable that, during those thirty-three years, my mind did move considerably, and, if it did, I am glad of this. That means, however, that, if I now tried to maintain all my previous positions, I should find myself at war with myself as well as with my critics. It is more profitable to try to learn from one's critics than to try to fight them; and the avowal of one's own inconsistencies and changes of view is a small price to pay for the liberty that this gives one to try again and to attempt to do better. One reviewer of the first ten volumes has generously given me credit for changing my views and citing my critics.[1] This testimony is worth having. I shall do my best to continue to deserve it. If there is any treatment that can rejuvenate one's categories, it is the exercise of keeping one's mind open and making a habit of thinking again. Another reviewer has said that this book is my education.[2] I want to carry this education farther. To stop it would feel, to me, like committing intellectual suicide. So I do not quarrel with this reviewer for going on to say that I have not found my port.[3] Another reviewer has called my work a 'quest' (*zetema*).[4] He feels that my latest position, in the volumes published hitherto, is not a final one,[5] and he finds a 'tension between the immanent logic of the *zetema* and Toynbee's unwillingness to pursue his search to the end'.[6] I mean to go on pursuing my search, but I do not expect it to bring me to an 'end', and if I found myself 'in port' I should be distressed. Man's quest is really an attempt to probe to the heart of the mystery of the Universe, and I do not believe that human beings can attain that goal in this life. If a port on this side of death is unattainable, it is best to keep the seas. One does this, of course, at one's peril. 'Es irrt der Mensch, solang er strebt.'[7]

The present volume therefore makes no pretension to finality. It is merely a report of second thoughts. If the English-reading public still tolerated Latin titles, I could not find a better one for this piece of work than Saint Augustine's word *retractationes*. This means 'reconsiderations', not 'retractions', though it is unlikely that a writer will not retract some of his previous propositions if he has reconsidered them genuinely.

The first ten volumes of this book need to be reconsidered now because of the new knowledge and new thought that have been accumulating since the autumn of 1954, when volumes vii–x were published. Some of the new knowledge is new for everybody. During the intervening years there have been important archaeological discoveries and important current events. Some of it is new only for me. I have made good a few of the innumerable gaps in my own knowledge, mainly by travelling round the World and seeing, at first hand, a number of countries that I had previously known only from maps and descriptions.[8]

[1] F. Neilson in *The American Journal of Economics and Sociology*, supplement to vol. xiv, No. 3 (April, 1955), p. 3.
[2] A. Hourani: 'Toynbee's Vision of History' in *The Dublin Review*, vol. 229, No. 470 (December, 1955), p. 386.   [3] Ibid., p. 400.
[4] E. Voegelin in *The Intent of Toynbee's History: A Cooperative Appraisal*.
[5] Ibid.   [6] Ibid.   [7] Goethe: *Faust*, l. 317.
[8] See A. J. Toynbee, *East to West* (London 1958, Oxford University Press). I have been able to make this journey, and others, thanks to a grant from the Rockefeller Foundation to my wife and me.

Meanwhile, current events have been following each other thick and fast. A reviewer, commenting in April 1955 on what I have written in volume ix about the prospects of the Western Civilization, remarks that 'perhaps it was written too soon'.[1] This is always true of all attempts at interpreting contemporary history, at whatever date they may have been written. The best that one can do in this field is to go on producing interim reports, and to take care, each time, to put one's provisional findings tentatively. Meanwhile, there has been progress in thought, and some of this, again, has been progress for everybody, while some of it has been peculiar to me. The public progress has been most striking, I should say, in the field of psychology; my private progress has been mainly owing to the critiques of my first ten volumes that have appeared since these were published. I have read, and thought about, as many of these criticisms as I have been able to track down, and have done my best to reconsider with an open mind those things in my work that the critics have questioned, challenged, or disputed. The ideal would be to be able to take one's second look at one's own work as if it were someone else's, and as if one were making one's first acquaintance with it for the purpose of reviewing it. This is the state of mind at which one should aim in order to draw the maximum profit from other people's criticisms. But, since an author is also a human being, it is unlikely that he will succeed in even approaching this degree of detachment.

I have tried especially to take to heart those criticisms in which there has been something like a consensus among critics who differ widely from each other in their temperaments, outlooks, and intellectual equipment. The most important point, I should say, that has been almost unanimously contested has been my claim that my method of inquiry has been an empirical one. Most of my critics evidently have the impression that it has been just the opposite. They feel that I have worked out an *a priori* scheme that is too clear-cut and too rigid to be likely to correspond to reality, and that I have then tried to force the phenomena to fit into this arbitrary framework at the cost of distorting the truth. This is, it seems to me, the most fundamental, and therefore the most serious, of all the criticisms of my work; so I have discussed it as fully and frankly as I have known how to do. I have also reconsidered with special care the other points that have drawn a converging fire; for example, my construction of the course of what I have called 'Hellenic' history to include the history of Rome (a number of critics have objected that the role which I have assigned to Rome is too subordinate a one); my use of this construction of Hellenic history as a pattern or key or 'paradigm' for analysing the histories of other civilizations (this has been cited as an instance of my tendency to force the facts); my construction of the course of what I have called 'Syriac' history, and my consequent handling of Islam and of the Jews.

If it is a good working rule for an author that, where he finds two or more critics agreeing, he should prick up his ears, I must also take notice of an impression that I have evidently made on some critics' minds. This is that I have sought to set myself up as a 'prophet', or,

[1] Neilson, op. cit., p. 57.

short of that, that I have lapsed into playing the prophet unconsciously.

The word 'prophet' has, of course, two distinct meanings, owing to
the fact that two different roles have sometimes been played simultaneously by the same person. The ordinary current meaning of the
word in present-day English is someone who predicts the future, and
on this head I have no need to try to exculpate myself. For one thing,
prophecy in this sense is considered to be quite respectable when it is
practised by students of the non-human sciences. Astronomers, for
instance, prophesy boldly and successfully with impunity. In the second
place, I myself believe that prediction is not possible in the field of
human affairs. I believe that the outcomes of human choices, purposes,
and plans are unpredictable intrinsically, however fully we may be
informed about the relevant past facts up to date. And I also believe
that these intrinsically unpredictable plans, purposes, and choices play
a large enough part in every human situation to invalidate predictions
based on other elements in human affairs that might perhaps be predictable if ever they could be isolated. I have set out my views on this
explicitly in previous volumes[1] and need not go over the same ground
again here. There is, however, also another meaning of the word
'prophet' in which the original Greek preposition 'pro' signifies not
'fore' but 'out'. The prophet in this other sense is not someone who
predicts the future; he is someone who speaks out or promulgates the
word of God. The prophets of Israel and Judah and the two gentile
prophets Zarathustra and Muhammad have been *the* prophets in this
sense. It is the official doctrine of Judaism, Christianity, and Islam
alike that this series of promulgations of God's will has long since been
closed; and, anyway, anybody who set up in the present-day world to
be a prophet in this sense would rightly be treated as a figure of fun.[2]
The imputation is difficult to deal with, because the next most ridiculous thing to saying 'I think I am a prophet' would be to say 'I really
don't think I am.' Perhaps the best answer is not a verbal but a practical
one. A readiness to believe that one may have been mistaken in the
views that one has expressed is surely incompatible with believing that
they are not one's own, but God's. So I hope this volume of reconsiderations may effectively dissipate the spectre of 'Toynbee the
prophet'.[3]

---

[1] For instance, in i. 299–302, and in ix. 167–405.

[2] I admire Dean Inge, nevertheless, for having had the courage to write: 'The philosopher ought to be a prophet' ('The Place of Myth in Philosophy' in *Philosophy*, vol. xi,
No. 42 (April, 1936), pp. 131–45, ad fin.).

[3] Pieter Geyl, at any rate, seems to hold that playing the prophet and paying attention
to criticisms are incompatible. In a critique in which he says that my work is vitiated by
my thinking that I have a 'message' (M. F. Ashley Montague: *Toynbee and History*,
p. 360), and that I am not an historian but a prophet (ibid., p. 370), he complains that I
do not reply to my critics and that I never will reply, because I am impervious to
criticism (ibid., pp. 375–6). I take this argument of Geyl's to hold good in reverse: in
this volume I *have* replied to my critics; therefore I cannot be a prophet after all. Geyl is
not implacable. In another critique, published in the same volume (p. 68), he says that
my '*method*, at any rate, is not intended to be that of the religious prophet'. He also lets
me off rather lightly when he says (in *Toynbee and History*, pp. 372 and 377) that, if I
labelled myself 'prophet' instead of 'historian', he would have no quarrel with me.
Indeed, he goes so far as to say that, 'as a prophet, as a poet, Toynbee is remarkable'
(P. Geyl, *Debates with Historians*, p. 143).

At the same time I am now uncomfortably aware that, without my having been conscious of this, there must have been things in the previous volumes of this book that raised this spectre in the minds of several critics.[1] One such thing may have been my declared belief that a study of human history up to date reveals a certain number of recurrent patterns. 'All cyclical theorists', H. Stuart Hughes says,[2] 'play the role of intuitive seers.' I need not repeat that I am not a determinist. I do not believe that any of these past recurrences were inevitable, nor do I believe that any of them, or any others, are bound to repeat themselves in the future. But my belief that I have descried recurrences in the past may have given me the air of being a 'seer', if Hughes is right. Another possible source of this impression is my belief—mentioned already in this chapter—that Man's quest cannot stop short of trying to probe the heart of the mystery of the Universe. But, if following this quest is tantamount to setting up as a prophet, then this offence is committed by every human being who passes through this life; for following Man's quest is, I believe, an inescapable part of being human.

A third possible source of the impression has been mentioned by Hourani.[3] In volumes vii–x of *A Study of History* Hourani is conscious of 'a strange, exalted, excited note, more fitting to prophecy than to science'; and Sir Ernest Barker[4] uses almost identical words. I write, he says, 'on a high and strained note'. Geyl too finds me 'high-strung'.[5] I am conscious of this myself, and I think the explanation is not far to seek. It has, indeed, been detected by more than one of my critics. These four volumes were written after the atom bombs had been dropped on Nagasaki and Hiroshima. The note heard in volumes vii to x was already audible in volumes v and vi, which were written between the Italian invasion of Abyssinia and the outbreak of the Second World War. In reviews of volumes iv–vi Sir Maurice Powicke noted that my mind struck him as being not a 'cool' one,[6] and Sir Llewellyn

---

[1] Besides Pieter Geyl, who has been cited in the previous footnote, W. den Boer (in *Toynbee and History*, p. 238) and Albert Hourani (in loc. cit., pp. 399–400) record the same impression. F. H. Underhill finds that I escape from being caught in Spengler's determinism 'by soaring above history to become a metahistorian, a prophet, a theologian', and that it is my 'system-making, with its prophetic overtones of doom to come', that makes me 'attractive to the general public of the last ten or fifteen years' (*The Canadian Historical Review*, vol. xxxii, No. 3 (September, 1951), pp. 201–19. Underhill gives me to same label ibid., vol. xxxvi, No. 3 (September, 1955), pp. 222–35). H. Trevor-Roper seems to think that I set myself up as a prophet in both senses of the word (*Toynbee and History*, p. 122). J. F. Leddy thinks that I oscillate between behaving like a prophet and claiming to be an empirical historian (*The Phoenix*, vol. 11 (Toronto 1957, University of Toronto Press), pp. 140–1). Father L. Walker, O.P., feels that I have not 'been content with being just a historian but have tried also to be a prophet and teacher' (*Toynbee and History*, p. 146). E. E. Y. Hales says: 'In reality he is a religious prophet, who uses his wide knowledge of history to exemplify and reinforce his religious teaching' (*History Today*, May, 1955, p. 322). This is L. C. Stecchini's impression too. 'Toynbee', he says, 'has gone so far as to try to reclaim for the historian the right to prophesy' (*Midstream*, Autumn, 1956, pp. 84–91). On the other hand, Crane Brinton finds that this book 'is not a prophetic work in the specific sense that word has in the Judaeo-Christian tradition' (*The Virginia Quarterly Review*, vol. 32, No. 3 (Summer, 1956), pp. 361–75). T. S. Gregory reports that, 'more or less deliberately, Mr. Toynbee refuses to be "the prophet of the World's final causes" ' (*The Dublin Review*, vol. 220, No. 440 (Spring, 1947), pp. 74–87). A. L. Guerard pronounces that 'Spengler is a prophet; Toynbee is an inquirer' (*The Herald-Tribune*, 28th October, 1934).
[2] H. Stuart Hughes, *Oswald Spengler: A Critical Estimate* (New York 1952, Scribners), p. 164.   [3] In loc. cit., pp. 399–400.   [4] In *Toynbee and History*, p. 93.
[5] Ibid., p. 373.   [6] *The Manchester Guardian*, 29th September, 1939.

Woodward that 'deep and genuine' emotions were manifest in my work.[1] Woodward pointed out, in the same context, that these volumes had been 'written, like the *De Civitate Dei*, under the strain of immediate social catastrophe'. Kohn has noticed[2] that the difference in outlook between volumes vii–x and volumes i–vi is a reflection of the course of public events between 1939 and 1954. Hofer makes the same point in general terms. He points out that the questions put to history by me, like those put by Alfred Weber, are no longer of the same kind as Ranke's questions. 'In their study of history (*Geschichtsbetrachtung*) they are consciously seeking to be serviceable to the needs of the time in which we are living by being of some help to it in its grave spiritual and political crisis (*Lebensnot*). One might put it that their recognition of the urgency of this crisis was the stimulus by which their questions were originally evoked.'[3] Anderle observes[4] that, in Tangye Lean's account of my work,[5] 'the prophetic note is not taken as being an aberration, as it is by Geyl, Barnes, and others. Lean presents Toynbee as the exponent of a given cultural situation, the embodiment of the anxiety of the age over the existential issue (*Verkörperung der Existentialangst der Epoche*), its obsession with the spectacle of decadence in the face of death, and its burning desire in some way or other to transcend transitoriness and to make sure of achieving immortality.'

The consequent note of urgency and anxiety may be unscientific, but I do not find it at all 'strange' in the circumstances. On the contrary, I think it would have been strange if I had not felt deeply enough about these tragic and ominous public events for my feeling to come out in what I was writing at the time. To be sensitive to what is going on in the World is, I should say, a mark just of being human. It ought not to put one under suspicion of setting up to be a prophet, but it may perhaps have contributed, all the same, to the creation of this impression about me. Anyway, all but, possibly, one of those critics who have indicted me for the offence of setting up as a prophet have, I am sure, made the charge in good faith. If anyone is at fault, it is I, for having unwittingly given them cause for misunderstanding me.[6]

The educational value of any critique depends on its spirit and its method. A few critics write with an animosity which suggests that their first concern is to draw blood from the colleague whose book they are reviewing. This spirit surely militates against the purpose for which books are given out for review. This purpose is the correction of error and the increase of knowledge and understanding. It is an impersonal purpose and one that the reviewer shares with the writer whose work he

[1] *The Spectator*, 18th August, 1939.
[2] H. Kohn in *Der Monat*, Berlin, August, 1955.
[3] W. Hofer: *Geschichte zwischen Philosophie und Politik*, p. 129. Lewis Mumford, too, sees in *A Study of History* a piece of action—but, as he sees it, it is action that leads, like Reinhold Niebuhr's, to an 'other world' (*Toynbee and History*, p. 143).
[4] In an unpublished paper.
[5] In *Toynbee and History*, pp. 12–38, especially pp. 35 seqq.
[6] In reviewing vols. iv–vi of this book Sir Llewellyn Woodward remarked: 'It is, of course, impossible for a historian to insulate himself from the present, but at least he ought to be on his guard against putting himself in deliberate and unnecessary contact with lines of thought highly charged with emotion' (*The Spectator*, 18th August, 1939). There is justice in this counsel, and I recognize that it is good advice for me.

is appraising. To serve this purpose effectively, a review must, of course, be severe if severity is called for in the reviewer's judgement. I have profited particularly from reviews that have been severe without being hostile. The value of a review also depends on the reviewer's way of working. Some critics work with the road-metal-worker's hammer. Sometimes it is the stone that breaks, sometimes, perhaps, the hammer-head. In either case the result is on the small scale, and its value, while appreciable, is limited. A more creative kind of criticism is the kind that blows in like a sand-laden wind from the desert; for this usefully transforms the landscape. It finds out the softer rocks and scours them away, and it grinds down the harder rocks' sharp edges. Anything that still stands after this wind has done its testing work will be that much nearer to reality.[1]

Books are expendable, like the man-hours that go to the making of them. A book that has been weathered away will have served its purpose if it provokes other minds to write other books that may perhaps prove less vulnerable. The one thing that matters is that inquiry shall go on; for, so long as it continues, there is hope that it may also get further.

I am, of course, a reviewer myself, besides being an author. Almost every writer is constantly alternating between the two roles. When I am playing the role of a reviewer I find it a useful rule to remind myself of the indubitable truth that a reviewer inevitably reviews himself, too, in the act of reviewing the author whose book lies on his dissecting table. Whenever a reviewer is tempted to treat an author as a dart-board he should remember that the missile which his hand is itching to lance is not a dart but a boomerang. Reviewing, as well as writing, is, in fact, a dangerous trade. But a reviewer can reduce the danger to which he is exposing himself. He can avail himself of safeguards that are at the same time virtues worth cultivating for their own sakes. These tutelary virtues are humility and generosity. The point has been put by H. J. Morgenthau in a critique of my work.[2]

'We can judge what others have tried to do and have done only if we ourselves have tried to do, or at least have dreamt of doing, what they have done.'

---

[1] I owe this simile to J. F. Leddy. The article, cited in footnote 1 on p. 5, ends as follows: 'His work might well remind us of one of those colourful outcroppings of rock to be seen sometimes in flat country, once much larger but still raising a sharp silhouette against the sky. As time has passed, the winds have eroded the softer layers of rock, crumbling them away, and so projecting the more durable veins of granite into greater prominence. Such may be the . . . fate awaiting Toynbee's . . . study when once the winds of criticism have worn away those lines of thought which do not deserve to remain, . . . and so have left in plainer view the . . . outlines of his reduced but still massive structure.' [2] In *Toynbee and History*, p. 191.

A

PHILOSOPHICAL CONSIDERATIONS

I. THE INADEQUACY OF OUR MEANS OF THOUGHT

I. APPREHENSION THROUGH ANALYSIS AND CLASSIFICATION

A PHILOSOPHER will probably find little in this chapter except truisms and elementary errors, if he finds anything at all that is not a meaningless misuse of words. All the same, at my peril, I have to write it, because some of my critics have been philosophers who have taken issue with me on philosophical grounds. I exposed myself to this by raising philosophical questions. I did not seek these out. I found them arising out of a study of history. This is, I should say, to be expected, because, as I see it, the study of human affairs is really one and indivisible. The conventional academic dismemberment of the vast subject into 'disciplines' is a convenient, and perhaps unavoidable, educational device, but it is an arbitrary surgical operation, and this makes it a serious impediment to the gaining of knowledge and understanding.[1] It is true that any one mind can make itself thoroughly familiar with no more than some patch of the great forest. Yet, unless it also dares to venture out into the surrounding stretches that, for it, happen to be *terra incognita*, it cannot hope to understand the nature even of its own narrow beat.

All study, whether of human affairs or of non-human nature, is subject to the limitations of human thought; and the first and greatest of these is that thought cannot help doing violence to Reality in the act of trying to apprehend it.

For all that we know, Reality is the undifferentiated unity of the mystical experience. We cannot know whether it is or is not, because we cannot know anything without being in a state of consciousness, and we cannot be conscious without our mental image of Reality—or Reality's image of itself, mirrored in a human mind[2]—being diffracted or articulated into subject and object.[3] This is the first link in a chain of articulations that we forge as fast as we go on thinking.

Our human consciousness, after its self-generating—or Reality's

---

[1] See further pp. 128–32.

[2] 'The consciousness of each of us is evolution looking at itself and reflecting' (Father Pierre Teilhard de Chardin, S.J.: *The Phenomenon of Man* (London 1959, Collins), p. 221).

[3] 'Almost incurably subject and object tend to become separated from each other in the act of knowing. We are continually inclined to isolate ourselves from the things and events which surround us, as though we were looking at them from outside, from the shelter of an observatory into which they were unable to enter, as though we were spectators, not elements, in what goes on' (Father Pierre Teilhard de Chardin, S.J., op. cit., p. 220).

generating—articulative act, goes on to dissect Reality farther into the conscious and the subconscious, soul and body, mind and matter, life and environment, freedom and necessity, creator and creatures, god and devil, good and bad, right and wrong, love and power, old and new, cause and effect, and so on. Such dichotomies are indispensable categories of thought; they are our means of apprehending Reality, as far as this is within our power. At the same time they are so many boundary-marks indicating the limits of human understanding, since they misrepresent Reality by breaking up its unity in our apprehension of it. They are as baffling as they are enlightening. We cannot do without them, yet cannot do with them either. We cannot afford either to discount them completely or to take them at their full face value.[1]

We cannot think about the Universe without assuming that it is articulated; and, at the same time, we cannot defend the articulations

[1] It is, no doubt, difficult to use categories as instruments for trying to grasp Reality without falling into the error of treating them as if they were absolute realities in themselves. I have evidently fallen into this error myself. At least five critics have censured me for succumbing to dualism: Lewis Mumford (in *Diogenes*, No. 13 (Spring, 1956), pp. 22–23, and in *Toynbee and History*, p. 145); J. K. Feibleman (in *T'ien Hsia Monthly*, vol. xi, Nos. 1 and 2 (1940), pp. 13–14); Albert Hourani (in *The Dublin Review*, vol. 229, No. 470, p. 377); W. Altree (in *Toynbee and History*, p. 270); and Father L. Walker, O.P. (in *Toynbee and History*, p. 344). In Mumford's eyes this dualism has involved me in 'profound Augustinian pessimism' (*Diogenes*, loc. cit., p. 11) and in an unresolved contradiction between this mood and an incompatible 'thisworldliness' (ibid., p. 21). Feibleman, in the passage cited above, writes that Toynbee 'sets up primary categories which immediately involve him in an ontological dualism, an epistemological subjective idealism, and a theological transcendentalism. The first is precarious and tentative, the second partial and tenuous, and the third total and absolute; all three are nominalistic.' In particular, he objects to my dichotomy between 'spirit' and 'matter', and adds, with justification, that I ought to have defined my use of these terms, but have failed to do this. Altree, too, objects to this dichotomy. Walker objects to my dichotomies between reason and the subconscious and between truths of science and truths of religion. Mumford finds that I have dug a gulf between the world of Nature and the world of Spirit. This gulf, he insists, must be closed (*Diogenes*, loc. cit., p. 24); I ought to rise to a holistic standpoint (*Toynbee and History*, p. 146). Feibleman deplores my 'old-fashioned kind of ascetic transcendentalism' (loc. cit., pp. 147 and 152) and urges me (ibid., p. 142) to embrace the doctrine of immanence, which, as he points out on p. 157, I have, in fact, adopted in one passage (*A Study of History*, vol. iv, p. 647). Richard Pares feels that I have gone too far in dissecting the mind into different layers (*The English Historical Review*, vol. lxxi, No. 279 (April, 1956), p. 258).

These charges of dualism might seem, at first sight, to be cancelled out by charges that, in my conception of history, 'the Deity becomes almost entirely immanent and loses *all* transcendent qualities' (C. B. Joynt in *The Australasian Journal of Philosophy*, vol. 34, No. 3 (December, 1956), p. 201); that 'Toynbee either fails to make necessary distinctions or blurs them' (M. A. Fitzsimons, in *The Intent of Toynbee's History: A Cooperative Appraisal*; that I have 'a passion for unity' (Fitzsimons in the same context, and Sir Ernest Barker in *Toynbee and History*, pp. 94–95); and that I have an impulse to push the process of synthesis and schematization farther than is warranted by the phenomena (e.g. Sir Ernest Barker in *Toynbee and History*, p. 95; K. D. Erdmann in *Archiv für Kulturgeschichte*, xxxiii. Band, Heft 2 (1951), pp. 242–3; R. L. Shinn in *Christianity and the Problem of History*, p. 227; H. A. L. Fisher in *The Nineteenth Century and After*, December, 1934, p. 671; J. B. Vogt in *Saeculum*, No. 2 (1951), pp. 557–74; G. Weil in *Toynbee and History*, p. 285; A. Hourani in *The Dublin Review*, vol. 229, No. 470 (December, 1955), p. 381; J. K. Feibleman in *T'ien Hsia Monthly*, vol. xi, Nos. 1 and 2 (1940), p. 23).

Though these two errors (if such they are) are in contrary directions, I think I have, in fact, probably fallen into both of them. But I also think that, if I have, this illogical commission of two contradictory offences is not peculiar to me, but is a weakness that is a consequence of the nature of thought. A human mind seeks unity, but cannot approach it without paving its path with dichotomies. 'Segmentation is humanly inevitable, i.e. essential to sane observation'; 'the problem of causation is . . . merely one aspect of the wider problem of individuation' (M. R. Cohen: *The Meaning of Human History*, pp. 107 and 108).

that we find, or make, in it against the charge that these are artificial and
arbitrary, that they do not correspond to anything in the structure of
Reality, or that, even if they do, they are irrelevant to the particular
mental purpose for which we have resorted to them. It can always be
shown that they break up something that is indivisible and let slip
something that is essential. Yet, without mentally articulating the Universe, we ourselves cannot be articulate—cannot, that is, either think
or will. And we cannot go on thinking or willing if we regain the unity of
the mystical experience. So we have to dissect—and, in dissecting, misrepresent—Reality in order to be able to apprehend Reality sufficiently
to be able to act and live in the light of the truth as far as we can discern
it. Our inability to apprehend Reality completely is, of course, not
surprising. It is a paradox that one part of a whole should be able to
distinguish itself from the rest and should then be able to achieve even
a partial apprehension of the whole, including itself. This feat is
miraculous, however imperfect. How far it does fall short of attaining a
true mental image of Reality it is impossible for a human mind to tell.
'We have a kind of knowledge, but it is of a kind which can be corrected
or perfected.'[1]

Thought has no sooner set itself going by mentally breaking Reality
up than it gets to work to put Reality together again. After having
analysed, thought operates by classifying: that is, by identifying a
number of different objects as being specimens of one and the same
kind.[2] These objects between which the mind finds sufficient resemblance to allow it to bring them mentally under some single head are no
more than particular facets of phenomena.[3] The facets of any phenomenon are innumerable, as is demonstrated by our ability to classify
one and the same phenomenon in innumerable different ways, each
corresponding to some different facet that it displays.[4] So any one
classification apprehends no more than a fraction of each of the phenomena that it brings together; and, when we have classified the same
phenomenon under as many different heads as it displays facets whose
like we can detect in other phenomena, we are still left with an un-
identifiable residue.[5] This residue is of unknown magnitude.

The human mind's mental categories are thus 'incomplete tools'.[6]
'No conscious experience can grasp any object, not even ourselves, in all
its completeness. . . . There is no knowledge, no matter how abstract,
which does not point to some *it*.'[7] This 'it' is not something positive
that we can apprehend as being a phenomenon's 'essence'. It is the

[1] Father M. C. D'Arcy, S.J.: *The Sense of History*, p. 46. Cp. pp. 138–9.

[2] '*All* mental phenomena—sense perceptions and images as well as the more abstract
"concepts" and "ideas"—must be regarded as acts of classification' (F. A. Hayek: *The
Counter-Revolution of Science*, p. 47).

[3] '*All* thought must be to some extent abstract. . . . All perception of Reality, including the simplest sensations, involves a classification of the object according to some
property or properties' (ibid., p. 68).

[4] See ibid., pp. 68–69 and 70.

[5] 'The human mind can never grasp a "whole" in the sense of all the different aspects
of a real situation' (ibid., p. 70). On the other hand, C. B. Joynt contends, in a letter of
14th August, 1959, that 'any object has a certain unity or wholeness which characterises
it'.

[6] R. L. Shinn: *Christianity and the Problem of History*, p. 19.

[7] M. R. Cohen: *The Meaning of Human History*, p. 42.

residue of a phenomenon that has eluded all classification. This is wha we mean when we say that in every phenomenon there is something 'unique'. This word 'unique' is a negative term signifying what is mentally inapprehensible. The absolutely unique is, by definition, indescribable.[1] In fact, the unique element in a phenomenon is like the intractable core of a Palaeolithic flint-knapper's nugget, which defies his skill after he has struck off flake after flake and blade after blade. These flakes and blades fly off in familiar standard shapes. The residual core's shape is all its own; no other core's shape is identical with it.

Why does a human mind employ a method of operation which is bound, by its very nature, to yield incomplete and imperfect results? Perhaps the answer is to be found in our minds' nature, which is finite, and in their purposes, which are primarily practical. Though the human brain is so superbly built and so cleverly packed into its case that it can register the maximum number of permutations and combinations of mental associations that is possible for an instrument of its volume, this number, though very great, must be finite, whereas the number of phenomena with which a mind has to deal is infinite. It is only by classifying this infinite host of phenomena under heads that the mind can attempt to cope with them. The price of classification is, no doubt, some degree of misrepresentation. But the alternative to the payment of this price would be intellectual paralysis; and, for most minds' usual purposes, the price is not inordinately high because the misrepresentation is not frustrating. It may be frustrating and even exasperating to minds, like my critics' and mine, that want knowledge for its own sake, are insatiable in seeking it, and cannot rest content while any residue of reality remains unknown to them. Such restless minds, however, are a small and almost freakish minority. Most minds do not want knowledge for its own sake; they want the minimum doses of knowledge that are sufficient for guidance in taking action in particular circumstances. Knowledge beyond that quantum is a matter of indifference to them. Indeed, besides being superfluous, it would be a positive impediment to them owing to its irrelevance.

'In theory we could describe every site on the Earth's surface as a unique thing-in-itself, as in strict logic it is. But, even if this were practically feasible, it would take us nowhere: the mere bulk of facts could not be grasped by the human mind; we must classify, and that implies evaluation.'[2]

'All description is necessarily selective.'[3]

Suppose that a human mind were to set itself to grasp every

1 Cohen, op. cit., p. 84. Philip Bagby points out in *Culture and History*, pp. 33–34, that this is demonstrated by the inability of historians ever to describe a unique event exhaustively. The logic of the mind's method of operation is put by Bagby, ibid., p. 58, as follows: 'Absolute difference would eliminate all possibility of comparison. Absolute similarity would reduce all difference to identity and leave us nothing to compare.' The same point is made by R. Redfield in *The Primitive World and its Transformations*, p. 100. 'Absolute chaos is inconceivable. The notion of regularity, of what is called law, is inescapable. Yet it is probably also true that every world view combines with the idea of law or regularity the idea of capriciousness.' See also the present volume, p. 73.
2 O. K. H. Spate in *Geographical Studies*, vol. iv, No. 1 (1957), p. 2.
3 K. R. Popper: *The Poverty of Historicism*, p. 77.

phenomenon exactly in its unique entirety, without misrepresenting it by introducing any reference to, or mental association with, any other phenomena. It would be burdening its powers of memory with a Psyche's task—as if someone were to set himself to memorize the visual shapes of all the myriads of Chinese characters without deigning to make use of the radicals under which the characters have been rather artificially and arbitrarily grouped. And then, supposing that this illimitable and therefore impossible feat of memorization had been accomplished, of what practical use would it be? The normal purpose of trying to apprehend a phenomenon is not just to know it; it is to deal with it. And how can one deal with a phenomenon that one has come to know so perfectly that one has inhibited oneself from referring it to, or associating it with, any other phenomenon? A knowledge that was as theoretically complete as this would be equivalent to complete ignorance for practical purposes.

It seems as if one might almost say that the mind is an effective instrument for its usual purposes just because it is an imperfect one. Then how is a scholar to use this instrument for his peculiar purpose of study for study's sake? The obvious line for him to follow first is the line of least resistance; and the line of least resistance is to keep in step with the innate operational movement of the mind as far as the inquirer finds that this line will carry him. This is the policy that has been followed, with cumulative success, by students of non-human nature. Physical scientists 'are concerned . . . with formulating general propositions about the patterned interrelationships of . . . events', and 'science is the study of observed regularities'.[1] Have we any warrant for not following the same intellectual procedure when human nature is the object of our study? If it is contended that the drawing of an analogy between the processes of human history and those of non-human nature is inadmissible[2] or, short of that, hazardous,[3] and that I, in particular, have applied to thought about human history a method appropriate to thought about non-human nature,[4] it may be admitted that 'the simple repeatable patterns of physics or physical laws have not been discovered in human affairs',[5] but, nevertheless, it must be pointed out that a human being possesses only one mind, and that this mind operates in only one way—that is, the analytical and classificatory way—whatever kind of phenomenon its owner may set it to work on. The onus of proof lies on those who deny the reality of the uniformity that is found in Reality by the analysing and classifying human mind.[6] If the analytical and classificatory method that works well when we are studying non-human nature is to be ruled out when it is a question of studying human

---

[1] P. Bagby: *Culture and History*, pp. 4–5 and 84. He goes on to point out that 'comparative study' involves showing not only similarities but also consistent differences. These differences also constitute a kind of regularity (ibid., p. 183).
[2] Geyl in P. Geyl; A. J. Toynbee; P. A. Sorokin: *The Pattern of the Past: Can We Determine It?*, pp. 84–85.
[3] P. Geyl: *Debates with Historians*, p. 132.
[4] A. Hourani in *The Dublin Review*, vol. 229, No. 470 (December, 1955), p. 382. This is the charge that I myself have brought against the modern Western historians at the very beginning of this book.
[5] M. R. Cohen: *The Meaning of Human History*, p. 116.
[6] R. Caillois in *Diogenes*, No. 13 (Spring, 1956), pp. 2–3.

nature, we are left without any method for proceeding. Surely it is common sense to make a start in the study of human affairs by continuing to follow the mind's innate method, and to find out, by exploration, how far this method will carry one in this field. If and when we find ourselves brought to a standstill, with still unconquered ground ahead of us, we shall then be in the best possible position for examining whether any change of method is practicable, and, if it is, what our new method should be.

This is the policy that I myself have followed in the first ten volumes of this book. In Part XII I have tried to find the locus of a frontier dividing the realm of human affairs between a province of necessity and a province of freedom,[1] after having concentrated, in the preceding parts, on making as exhaustive an inquiry as I could into the regularities, uniformities, and recurrences that human affairs display. In the earlier of these two successive sections of the book I have deliberately pushed my exploration of regularities in human affairs to the limit; and, since, by temperament, I am, I believe, intellectually rash, I am willing to take it from my critics that I have not only reached the limit but have passed it. In a benevolent review of the first three volumes of the book, H. A. L. Fisher says that 'the generalisations are sometimes overdriven'.[2] Lewis Mumford says[3] that I do not make enough allowance for what is non-repetitive and unique. K. D. Erdmann finds[4] that, in my petrified schematization, I have come near to losing sight of the individuality of events.

2. THE HISTORIANS' PURSUIT OF THE UNIQUE

These excesses of mine—if I am guilty of excesses—evidently deserve the notice, and the reproof, that they have received. But my plan of work has not only drawn reasoned criticisms of the way in which I have carried it out; it has also provoked strong, and even violent, hostility among a considerable number of my fellow historians. It has been noted[5] that in the United States I was ill received by extremely distinguished reviewers—e.g. Charles A. Beard and Lynn Thorndike—in the important professional journals. This reaction has not been peculiar to American scholars; I am conscious of an even stronger current of hostile feeling among British and Dutch scholars, and also of a more aloof distaste and disapproval among French scholars. This vein of emotion has surprised and puzzled me. At first sight it seems uncalled-for in an intellectual argument; for in this field emotion is not only irrelevant but is notoriously inimical to clear thinking. On consideration I have come to the conclusion that—when full allowance has been made for the annoyance that my way of working evidently gives to scholars with a different temperament—the personal hostility that I have unintentionally drawn on myself is only a minor cause of the hostile

---

[1] A criticism, by C. B. Joynt, of my Biblical conception of the circumstances in which human wills have some freedom of choice is cited on p. 43, footnote 4.
[2] H. A. L. Fisher in *The Nineteenth Century and After*, December, 1934, p. 671.
[3] In *Diogenes*, No. 13 (Spring, 1956), p. 25.
[4] In *Archiv für Kulturgeschichte*, xxxiii. Band, Heft 2 (1951), pp. 242–3.
[5] By E. T. Gargan in *The Intent of Toynbee's History: A Cooperative Appraisal.*

emotion that the publication of my work has evoked. If the distinguished scholars who have hurled thunderbolts at me had merely felt annoyed with me personally, they would have just ignored me, which would have been a more effective way of trying to dispose of me than the policy of anathematizing me which they have actually adopted. I believe that the strength of their feeling reveals that they felt themselves to be fighting about something much more important than anything merely personal. They are, I think, up in arms in defence of the uniqueness of historical events and human personalities. This is, in their eyes, a treasure of supreme value; and my work has been a red rag to them because they have taken it as a symbol of an attack on the principle of respect for the element of uniqueness in history which they value so highly.[1] As a matter of fact I, too, value it; but at the same time I am conscious that, besides the element of uniqueness in human affairs, there is also an element of uniformity, and that, of the two, this is by far the less difficult for human minds to apprehend. This is, I think, why I have been misread as if I were denying the unquestionable truth that an element of uniqueness is to be found in human affairs.

A high valuation of this element of uniqueness within the realm of human nature is evidently what has made its status a burning question in the study of human affairs, while it is not one in the natural sciences. This also perhaps explains why it is that, among the various schools of students of human affairs—philosophers, theologians, logicians, psychologists, anthropologists, sociologists, historians—it is the historians who have made it their business to be not only the exponents of the element of uniqueness, but also its champions. The most obvious definition of an historian is to see in him a student of human affairs as these present themselves in motion through time; but a different definition has been proposed by A. L. Kroeber. The essence of the historian's approach, Kroeber suggests, is not the vision of human affairs as temporal events; it is 'the endeavour to achieve a conceptual integration of phenomena while preserving the integrity of the phenomena'.[2]

'The attachment to contiguity in space and time, to continuity of the spatial and temporal relations of the phenomena, coupled with attachment to the phenomena themselves, is what gives the historical aspects of phenomena their semblance of immediate reality. It is also the factor which prevents the historical approach as such from attaining to "laws", to general theory, to exactness of measurable findings, and to genuine verifiability by experiment. It is also what gives historical findings their quality of uniqueness, their individuation, their physiognomic property.'[3]

---

[1] W. H. McNeill notes, in *The Intent of Toynbee's History: A Cooperative Appraisal*, that I have 'the habit of mind which strives in the face of all the diversity of experience and of history to arrive at the interconnectedness of things—to see multiplicity and discrepancy reduced to unity and order, to see the whole in the parts, the One in the Many. This is, indeed, the most basic and fundamental quality of Toynbee's mind, a quality perhaps unusual in an historian, who is normally liable to be arrested and intrigued by the variety and multiplicity of things and take the data of history more or less for what they are—infinitely various, changeable, shifting, and interesting.' The Rev. E. R. Hardy Jr. finds, ibid., that 'the composition' of this book 'is remarkably unified'. He generously adds that my 'central themes are really central'.
[2] A. L. Kroeber: *The Nature of Culture*, p. 70. Cp. pp. 63, 102, 127.
[3] Kroeber, op. cit., p. 101.

'All recorded history [is] a series of objective unique events whose significance lies in their organisation into distinctive patterns and not in ill-defined formulas or generalised denominators.'[1]

The same characteristic of history is singled out by F. A. Hayek and by Alan Bullock as being distinctive of it.

'In the social field [as contrasted with the fields of most of the natural sciences] a particular or unique event is often of such general interest, and at the same time so complex and so difficult to see in all its important aspects, that its explanation and discussion constitute a major task requiring the whole energy of a specialist.'[2]

'What the historian finds fascinating is to come as close as he can to the concrete and the individual, to try to get inside the skin of *the* man or group of men, . . . to trace the causes, the connections and consequences of this particular revolution . . . or a particular series of events. . . . History is always an attempt to explain the sequence and connection of events.'[3]

Bullock is careful not to overstate his point.

'The moment the historian begins to explain, he is bound to make use of general propositions of all kinds. . . . The historian gives a false account of his activity if he tries to deny the part that general ideas and assumptions play in his work. There is, however, a difference between the historian on the one hand and the metahistorian, seeking for patterns of historical evolution, or the sociologist, seeking for general laws, governing human development, on the other. This difference lies in their purpose and in the use that they make of such generalizations. What the metahistorian and the sociologist are trying to do is to clear away the confusion of facts and reveal the pattern, or establish the law, which lies beneath. But this is not the historian's purpose; what he wants to know is what happened. For him, general propositions are both necessary and illuminating, but they are not the essential purpose of his work.'

Joynt and Rescher make a point that bears out Bullock's thesis. 'Historians', they point out,[4] 'tend to formulate, not general laws, but restricted generalizations, limited by spatio-temporal considerations, but fully valid and law-like within them.' Conversely, a sociologist, Michael Postan, commends me, in a review that is otherwise mostly critical, for pursuing historical information, not for its own sake, but for the purpose of using it as scientific evidence.[5]

The historians' approach to the study of human affairs, which Postan here deprecates, has merits to which Kroeber draws attention. Science, in pursuing its method of abstraction, resolves phenomena into 'metaphenomenal' formulas.[6] But the higher the level of the phenomena under consideration, the more recalcitrant they are to this scientific treatment

---

[1] Ibid., p. 86.   [2] Hayek, op. cit., p. 68.
[3] Bullock in *History Today*, February, 1951, pp. 5–11.
[4] C. B. Joynt and N. Rescher: 'On Explanation in History' in *Mind*, vol. 68, No. 271 (July, 1959), pp. 383–8.
[5] M. Postan in *The Sociological Review*, vol. xxviii (1936), p. 53 (see further pp. 225–7). K. D. Erdmann, on the other hand, is critical of my treatment of history as a series of examples (*Archiv für Kulturgeschichte*, xxxiii. Band, Heft 2 (1951), p. 203).
[6] Kroeber, *The Nature of Culture*, p. 101.

that is designed to discover uniformities and repetitive regularities as a basis for prediction. On the other hand, phenomena of the higher kind yield readily to historical treatment.[1] My own approach to history is criticized by H. Frankfort[2] on the ground that

'his use of "species" and "genus" obscures the fundamental fact that science can study individuals as members of a species only by ignoring their individual characteristics. The historian, following this course, would defeat the very purpose of his work. In fact, Toynbee's vaunted empiricism is an attempt to transpose the method of the natural sciences, where experiment is essential and experience is reduced to figures, to history, where experiment is impossible and experience subjective.'

The historical outlook (*Historismus*) involves

'the recognition that a consideration of history that is obtained by factual research does not enable one to extract from it any consistently intelligible picture of universal history. So far from throwing light on concrete situations and events, interpretations of the general course of history that are based on theological or rationalist dogmas actually themselves require to be interpreted historically. In reaching this conclusion, the historical outlook has won for itself a standpoint of its own which is distinct not only from that of physical science but also from that of metaphysical and natural law.'[3]

'In recognizing the uniqueness of its subject matter and in failing to reduce it to instances of a law, the procedure of history differs from that of science.'[4]

Historians

'are convinced that the differences between civilizations are more significant than their likenesses, and that standardised causal patterns cannot logically be deduced from the facts of history'.[5]

This point has been driven home by Christopher Dawson:

'It is [the] mysterious and unpredictable aspect of history which is the great stumbling-block to the rationalist. He is always looking for neat systems of laws and causal sequences from which history can be automatically deduced. But history is impatient of all such artificial constructions. It is at once aristocratic and revolutionary. It allows the whole world situation to be suddenly transformed by the action of a single individual like Mohammad or Alexander.'[6]

---

[1] Kroeber, op. cit., pp. 122–3.
[2] In *The Birth of Civilization in the Near East*, p. 26.
[3] K. D. Erdmann: 'Das Problem des Historismus in der Neueren Englischen Geschichtswissenschaft' in the *Historische Zeitschrift*, Band 170 (1950), p. 73. Cp. E. F. J. Zahn: *Toynbee und das Problem der Geschichte*, p. 6.
[4] M. C. Swabey: *The Judgment of History*, p. 113.
[5] L. Stone in *Toynbee and History*, p. 111.
[6] Chr. Dawson: *The Dynamics of World History*, ed. by J. J. Mallory, p. 257. Ibid., p. 90, Dawson writes: 'There is an unknown quantity in religious change which defies the most careful historic analysis'; and in illustration of his thesis in its application to religion he cites, here too, the epiphany of Islam and also the conversion of the Roman Empire to Christianity.
I myself believe that, in human affairs, something that we may well call 'creativity', in default of a more revealing word, is perpetually at work, and that this is constantly producing novelties that have not only not been predicted but have been intrinsically unpre-

These are impressive justifications for the historian's approach. At the same time this approach is open to challenge on two grounds. Its critics may contest the value of the element of uniqueness in human affairs, which historians prize so highly. And they may contend that, whatever its value may be deemed to be, the unique is not apprehensible by human minds.

The value of phenomenal human selves and of their experiences in the media of time and space has been rated low in Indian thought since at least as early as the sixth century B.C. This low valuation was common ground between the Buddha and the contemporary school of Indian philosophy with which he took issue. Both schools put their treasure in Absolute Reality. The school that the Buddha was opposing conferred value on phenonemal human selves by identifying them with Absolute Reality and giving them the good tidings that they could experience this truth for themselves by an act of intuition. The Buddha took the more radical line of analysing phenomenal human selves into discontinuous series of successive psychological states kindled by desire and kept alight

dictable. Thus I agree with Dawson in the point that he is making in the two passages here quoted. At the same time, I do not think that the cases which he has cited here really illustrate his thesis. I do not believe that either of the revolutions headed respectively by Muhammad and by Alexander can properly be described as 'the action of a single individual'. Surely both were the result of the interaction between a leader and his followers in a particular set of circumstances. Without the circumstances and the followers, the leader would not have found his opportunity; and, given the followers and the circumstances, the opportunity would have been found and taken by some leader or other, if Muhammad and Alexander had never been born. If Muhammad, for instance, had failed, Maslamah would have found his opportunity. This question of the relation of leading individuals and minorities to the rest of society is discussed further on pp. 125–7, 148–50, and 305–6. As for the circumstances, the conquests of the Roman and the Sasanian Empire by Muhammad's successors and of the Achaemenian Empire by Alexander were surely not mysterious nor even unpredictable. In retrospect, both these revolutionary events look as if they had been more or less inevitable. When once the Achaemenian Empire had tried and failed to conquer the Hellenic World, it was probable that there would be an Hellenic counter-offensive, and that this would be successful as soon as it was made by the Hellenes' united forces under a single command. Similarly, the successful over-running of the south-eastern provinces of the Roman Empire by the Arab transfrontier barbarians might have been predicted from the previous success of the Teutonic and Eurasian Nomad barbarians in over-running the western provinces. The simultaneous overthrow of the Roman and the Sasanian Empire by the Arabs is explained by the exhaustion of the two empires as a result of their long series of wars with each other, culminating in the two particularly long-drawn-out and devastating wars of A.D. 572–91 and A.D. 603–28. The epiphany of Islam is explained by the radiation of the Syriac Civilization into Arabia during the preceding 2,000 years, and of the Hellenic Civilization during a period of about half that length. The attitude of Islam towards Hellenism had been foreshadowed in the attitudes of Monophysite and Nestorian Christianity. The rise of Islam is discussed further in Chapter XIV below, on pp. 461–76. As for the conversion of the Roman Empire to Christianity, this may no have been foreseen by Roman statesmen till half way through the third century of the Christian Era, but it was surely foreseeable long before that and had in fact been foreboded in the second century by Celsus. It was indeed the culmination of a victorious advance of Oriental religions into the Hellenic World which had begun at least as early as the fourth century B.C.—within a hundred years of the beginning of the Hellenic Time of Troubles.

Alexander illustrates Dawson's point not by the range and rapidity of his conquests but by the prematureness of his death. If Alexander had had as long a life as, say, his companion Ptolemy son of Lagus, who lived to be 84 and died in 284 B.C., the course of history might indeed have been different from what it has been. Yet the earliness of Alexander's death, though not inevitable, was also not mysterious and was even not unpredictable. If Alexander had truthfully filled in a life-insurance company's proposal-form at Susa in 324 B.C., the actuaries would certainly not have rated his expectation of life very high in the light of the way in which he had been taxing his stamina during the preceding ten years.

by action, and he prescribed for his disciples a course of ascetic spiritual exercises designed to burn these impurities away till nothing should be left but Absolute Reality in its negative aspect of 'extinguishedness' (*Nirvāna*). It is no accident that in India, where all indigenous schools of thought have agreed in disparaging the element of uniqueness in human affairs, there has been no notable indigenous school of historians. The first attempts, of any consequence, to write the history of India have been made by her Muslim and Christian invaders with their Judaic tradition of finding significance and value in temporal events. It is only in very recent times that, under Western inspiration, a Hindu school of historians on the present-day Western model has tardily come into existence.

Considering that some of the greatest historians who have made their appearance at any time and place have been Hellenic, it is remarkable that history should have been held in as low esteem in the Hellenic World, in theory at any rate, as it has been in India, and here, too, because of a contempt for what is unique.[1] This commonly accepted Hellenic view has been put pointedly by Aristotle in a famous passage.

'It is not the function of the poet to relate what *has* happened, but what *may* happen—what is possible according to the law of probability or necessity. The poet and the historian differ not by writing in verse or in prose. The work of Herodotus might be put into verse, and it would still be a species of history, with metre no less than without it. The true difference is that one relates what has happened, the other what may happen. Poetry, therefore, is a more philosophical and a higher thing than history; for poetry tends to express the universal, history the particular. By the universal I mean how a person of a certain type will on occasion speak or act, according to the law of probability or necessity; and it is this universality at which poetry aims in the names she attaches to the personages. The particular is—for example—what Alcibiades did or suffered.'[2]

After the renaissance of Hellenism in the modern Western World, this Hellenic attitude of mind survived Hellenism's discomfiture in the seventeenth-century 'Battle of the Ancients and Moderns' and was taken as a matter of course by the eighteenth-century school of Western philosophers. Though they had adopted the optimistic Confucian confidence in the perfectibility of human nature and had accordingly made a belief in 'progress' in human affairs into one of their cardinal doctrines, these eighteenth-century Western philosophers saw progress in terms solely of an impersonal movement on the grand scale. In their eyes the element of uniqueness in human affairs was something irrational, barbarous, and, above all, irrelevant. They regarded historians with the impatience that astronomers might feel towards geographers if these were to contend that it is more important to map out the mountains, valleys, and other minute irregularities in the conformation of the Earth's surface than it is to follow up the astronomical corollaries of the discoveries that our rough-coated planet is approximately spherical in

[1] This Hellenic attitude is touched upon again on pp. 124–5.
[2] Aristotle: *Poetics*, chap. 9 (1451 a–b), S. H. Butcher's translation (in his *Aristotle's Theory of Poetry and Fine Art*, 3rd ed. (London 1902, Macmillan), p. 35).

shape and that its orbit round the Sun describes a well-known mathematical figure.

This disparagement of uniqueness and irregularity, in favour of recurrence and uniformity, has been inherited from eighteenth-century Western philosophers by nineteenth-century and twentieth-century Western students of non-human nature. Natural science today has a great and growing prestige, and the method of analysis and classification, as opposed to the method of description and narrative, is now being applied to the study of human affairs in one province after another. Two distinguished living students of the archaeology of Nuclear America have declared that the ultimate purpose of archaeology is 'the discovery of regularities that are in a sense spaceless and timeless', and that the regularities investigated by archaeologists and by anthropologists are of one and the same order.[1] The method has even been winning converts in the historians' own camp. W. F. Albright has declared[2] that 'the historian of human culture . . . is just as much interested in discovering general laws as is the natural scientist, since every single phase of past—and present—culture has its own pattern of constituent elements'. It is not surprising that, at the present time, Western historians should be on the defensive, and should therefore be sensitive to any movement that looks to them like a fresh attack on their position with an eye to a further encroachment on the dwindling domain that still remains exclusively theirs.

At the same time they have to face the question whether their quest for the unique is a feasible one for human minds with their 'built-in' analytical and classificatory method of operation. Geyl insists[3] that historical events are invincibly unique and asks[4] whether the logic of class and instance is applicable to historical phenomena. This question has been answered conclusively in a report by the American Social Science Research Council's committee on historiography. 'Every historical event, however similar to others, is in some respects unique', because it has its own particular position in time. But,

'if every historical event were literally unique, history as science would be inconceivable. . . . No generalisations whatever would be possible; history and actuality would *mean* nothing, and any attempt to *understand* the past would be entirely futile.'[5]

This must be so, because

'To perceive is to assign to a familiar category; we could not perceive anything completely different from everything else that we have ever perceived before.[6] . . . All the unique objects of history which [the historian] studies are in fact either constant patterns of relations or repeatable processes in which the elements are of a generic character.'[7]

---

[1] G. R. Willey and P. Phillips: *Method and Theory in American Archaeology* (1958), pp. 2–3.
[2] W. F. Albright: *From the Stone Age to Christianity*, 2nd ed., p. 114.
[3] In *Toynbee and History*, p. 69.   [4] Ibid., p. 48.
[5] Social Science Research Council's Committee on Historiography's Report (1954), pp. 24 and 25.
[6] Hayek, op. cit., p. 47.   [7] Ibid., p. 72.

'It is . . . only through some continuity and identity in the process that we are able to understand what the past is like. Some common ground inevitably serves as our bridge of interpretation.'[1]

Geyl agrees[2] that 'the greatest function of the historian is to interpret the past'. Kroeber too points out[3] that history aims at preserving the complexity of individual events 'while also constructing them into a design which possesses a certain coherence of meaning'. Deutsch points out that communications engineering 'does not transfer events'; it transfers information in the shape of 'a patterned relationship between events'.[4] 'What interacts, has structure; and what has structure, can be known.'[5] So

'Every historian has a philosophy of history, no matter how insipid or self-contradictory it may turn out to be if explicitly stated. . . . From the use of this kind of hypothesis [the vulnerable kind] no historian is or can be free, although historians differ in their awareness of their particular frame of reference.'[6]

'Any discipline of knowledge, whether theoretical or historical, can deal only with certain selected aspects of the real world.'[7]

'Like the natural sciences, history must be selective unless it is to be choked by a flood of poor and unrelated material. . . .'[8]

'Aiming at objectivity [the historians] feel bound to avoid any selective point of view; but, since this is impossible, they usually adopt points of view without being aware of them. This must defeat their efforts to be objective; for one cannot possibly be critical of one's own approach, and conscious of its limitations, without being aware of it.'[9]

'Uncritical analogies are the peculiar plague of the historian, and all too often insinuate themselves as ruling assumptions without the author's being aware of their dominance—hovering in the background of language beyond clear-cut intellectual or empirical check.[10] . . . Views of causal relations, social dynamics, and of the springs of human action tend to linger

---

[1] M. C. Swabey: *The Judgment of History*, p. 19. In Swabey's view 'the basic sameness in history which makes cross-reference possible would seem to be relational, a matter of scale and proportion, rather than of literal sameness of facts' (op. cit., p. 9). 'What appears as uniformity may be characteristic of the statistical method rather than characteristic of the individual originating phenomena' (ibid., p. 91). In the study of human affairs 'sooner or later retreat seems inevitable from empirical recurrence to relational common factors' (ibid., p. 91). 'It is because the World involves a unity of logical structure, a formal invariancy through its varying content, that knowledge has power to survey and to connect the different domains of history' (ibid., p. 91). It will be seen that Swabey finds her uniformity in relations between phenomena, not in the phenomena themselves, and in the mind's procedure for dealing with these relations mentally rather than in an external world. But Swabey remains a believer in the reality of some kind of uniformity, nevertheless.

[2] In P. Geyl; A. J. Toynbee; P. A. Sorokin: *The Pattern of the Past: Can We Determine It?*, p. 84.

[3] A. L. Kroeber: *The Nature of Culture*, p. 79.

[4] K. W. Deutsch in *Philosophy of Science*, vol. 18, No. 3 (July, 1951), p. 241.

[5] Ibid., p. 231.

[6] W. H. Coates: 'Relativism and the Use of Hypothesis in History' in *The Journal of Modern History*, vol. xxi, No. 1 (March, 1949). Cp. the passage quoted from Hales on p. 26. C. Trinkaus seems inclined to think that I am an exception to Coates's rule. In my work, he finds, 'a purely negative critical method was pursued that had as its result a theory of the universal incomprehensibility of the past, and hence of its eternal sameness' (*Science and Society*, vol. xii, No. 1 (1948), p. 221). Yet Trinkaus debits me with having a 'theory' of a sort.   [7] F. A. Hayek, op. cit., p. 69.

[8] K. R. Popper: *The Poverty of Historicism*, p. 150.

[9] Ibid., p. 152.   [10] M. C. Swabey: *The Judgment of History*, p. 105.

in the background unaccredited and unannounced, while operating to control the narrative.'[1]

The truth is that 'no description of any individual object or event can dispense with predicates or abstract repeatable traits',[2] and that therefore 'no statement about the past can avoid some element of generality'.

'If . . . there is genuine novelty in the Universe and if events occur that have never occurred before, history must be an incomplete explanation of the present. In order to learn from the past there must be recurrences and similarities both throughout the past and between it and the present. There are enough recurrences and similarities to enable history to give us some account of the past and some explanation of the present. Thus our choices are at least partially illuminated and enlightened.'[4]

Change, novelty, and creation in human affairs are manifestations of the element of uniqueness in them, and one of the most cherished aims of historians is to catch creation, novelty, and change in their mental grasp; but they have to employ an instrument of thought which can analyse and classify points of likeness, but cannot cope with elements in phenomena that display no relation with any others. In seeking to apprehend what is unique, historians are, in fact, trying to swim against the current of the operational movement of the intellect.[5] The gallantry of this endeavour deserves our sympathy, and its romance does not convict it of being a forlorn hope.

'Historical events and conditions are often unique simply in being different from others with which it would be natural to group them under a classification term—and different in ways which interest historians when they come to give their explanations. . . . It is thus misleading to say without qualification that the historian's use of classificatory words supports the thesis that, if historical events are to be explicable, they must be recurring phenomena.'[6]

If this is true, it is good news; for, if the historian's goal is an attainable one, this opens up a prospect of extending the bounds of human knowledge and understanding, by an intellectual *tour de force*, in a field that cannot be conquered by the straightforward scientific method of using the human mind's classificatory method of operation for classificatory purposes. It has been claimed that, at any rate since the turn of the nineteenth and twentieth centuries, human studies (*die Geisteswissenschaften*) have liberated themselves from the shackles of the natural sciences' method of thinking.[7] Whether this claim is justified

---

[1] Swabey, op. cit., p. 110.
[2] M. R. Cohen: *The Meaning of Human History*, p. 42; cp. Bagby: *Culture and History*, p. 53.
[3] Cohen, op. cit., p. 47.
[4] Cohen, op. cit., pp. 289–90. Cp. Bagby, op. cit., pp. 53–54.
[5] 'The uniqueness of historical data poses a fundamental problem for the historian. His task is to describe and interpret. But to describe adequately he must necessarily understand what he wants to describe, and he cannot understand that which he cannot truly describe' (W. Altree in *Toynbee and History*, p. 243).
[6] W. Dray: *Laws and Explanation in History*, pp. 47 and 48.
[7] E. F. J. Zahn: *Toynbee und das Problem der Geschichte*, p. 6. Cp. Erdmann in the passage quoted on p. 16.

or not, for practical purposes there is everything to be said in favour of acting as if it were. As Kroeber has wisely observed,[1] the historical approach and the scientific approach are both alike applicable to any kind of phenomena in principle. And our human intellectual equipment is not so lavish that we can allow ourselves the luxury of forgoing any possibly efficacious method of using it. 'For the understanding of any concrete phenomenon, be it in nature or in society, both kinds of knowledge . . . the historical and the theoretical . . . are equally required. . . .[2] Theoretical and historical work are . . . logically distinct but complementary activities.'[3] The historical-minded student of human affairs and his scientific-minded confrère are really indispensable to each other as partners in their arduous common undertaking. Sir Maurice Powicke[4] has counselled his fellow historians to face 'the discomfort of the historic generalisation'. This is surely good advice; and conversely the scientific-minded student of human affairs should be advised to face the discomfort of the quest for what is unique.[5]

3. THE MIND'S QUEST FOR EXPLANATION

If it is agreed that historians, as well as scientists, are bound to make generalizations—even though this may not be the historians' aim—because making them is of the essence of thinking, whatever may be the object of our thought, the next question that presents itself is: How, in fact, are generalizations made? Dilthey is quoted[6] as saying that

'part of the method of those studies that are concerned with human affairs is to maintain a constant reciprocal action between experience and concept. In these studies, the consciousness should not entertain any concept that has not arisen from an exhaustive historical resuscitation of past experience. It should accept no generalisation that is not an expression of the inwardness of some historical reality.'

This is a statement of an ideal but not a prescription for achieving it. So I will start *ad hominem* by declaring, as accurately and candidly as I can, the process by which I believe that I myself have arrived at the numerous generalizations that I have made about human affairs. Usually, I think, the process has started by my noticing some striking and interesting apparent resemblance between two or more events, situations, institutions, or other phenomena. These now present themselves as instances of the generalization that has been made on the strength of them. The next step is to survey as wide a range as possible of other cases that seem likely to be relevant. The purpose of this survey is to

---

[1] A. L. Kroeber: *The Nature of Culture*, p. 101.
[2] Hayek, op. cit., p. 66.   [3] Ibid., p. 73.
[4] F. M. Powicke: 'After Fifty Years' (1st January, 1944), in *Modern Historians and the Study of History* (London 1955, Odhams Press). The sentence here quoted will be found on p. 234.
[5] C. B. Joynt comments, in a letter of 14th August, 1959: 'The "unique" school is on the same footing as the "law" school *at the level of epistemology*. The question as to which describes situations more adequately is an empirical question. Until we know more about human culture and behavior, the former will be able to score easy debating triumphs. *The future lies with those who realize that you do not have to choose between these two approaches. They are not and cannot be mutually exclusive.*'
[6] In a paper by Otto Höver, of which he sent me a copy in typescript.

ascertain whether this widening of the field of evidence bears out or conflicts with the generalization drawn from the original instances. This account of my own procedure and experience agrees, as far as I can see, with a description of the nature of historical research that has been cited in a report by the American Social Science Research Council's committee on historiography:

'Historical Research consists essentially in application of empirically derived hypothetical generalisations and in testing the closeness of the resulting fit, in the hope that in this way certain uniformities, certain typical situations, and certain typical relationships among individual factors in these situations can be ascertained.'[1]

If there is any truth in these two virtually identical accounts of the process of generalization,[2] it would appear that the detection of connexions is what makes generalizations possible.[3] But how do we detect them? 'By what right do we ever generalise from our experience? And how can we tell when we have a right to do so?'[4] It is easy to tell when we have not a right. 'An empirical generalisation is at once overthrown by a contradictory instance.'[5] One is enough.[6] One instance will disprove a proposition. On the other hand, no finite number of instances will prove it.

It is obvious that there is no logical cogency in an enumeration of affirmative instances that is not, and does not profess to be, complete.[7] Most, if not all, of my own numerous surveys of historical phenomena, made with a view to ascertaining whether some hypothetical generalization of mine will or will not hold water, have been incomplete—or, as logicians call them, 'simple'—enumerations; and it has been correctly pointed out by many critics that such incomplete surveys are not demonstrative, even if they have brought no contradictory instances to light.[8] It is also true, though this is perhaps not so obvious to laymen, such as me, at first sight, that there would be no logical cogency in a complete enumeration either. 'Induction by complete enumeration, if the conclusion be understood as a genuinely universal judgement, and not as an enumerative judgement about all of a limited number of things, has the character of induction by simple enumeration.'[9] Conclusions based on complete enumeration 'would not be universal truths at all in

---

[1] American Social Science Research Council's Committee on Historiography's Report (1954), p. 156, quoting A. Gerschenkron: 'Economic Backwardness in Historical Perspective', in *The Progress of Undeveloped Areas*, ed. by B. A. Hoselitz (Chicago 1952, University of Chicago Press), pp. 3–4.
[2] The process is discussed further on pp. 41–45, 158–66, 243–6.
[3] See H. W. B. Joseph: *An Introduction to Logic*, 2nd ed., p. 427.
[4] Ibid., p. 400. [5] Ibid., p. 531.
[6] R. B. Braithwaite: *Scientific Explanation*, p. 14.
[7] Joseph, op. cit., p. 392, footnote 1. 'The discovery of instances which confirm a theory means very little if we have not tried, and failed, to discover refutations. For, if we are uncritical, we shall always find what we want: we shall look for, and find, confirmations, and we shall look away from, and not see, whatever might be dangerous to our pet theories. In this way it is only too easy to obtain what appears to be overwhelming evidence in favour of a theory which, if approached critically, would have been refuted' (K. R. Popper: *The Poverty of Historicism*, p. 134).
[8] 'His laws are not universally true, and his proofs of them not convincing' (A. Hourani in *The Dublin Review*, vol. 229, No. 470 (December, 1955), p. 382).
[9] Joseph, op. cit., p. 530.

the proper sense, but only truths about the whole of a limited number of particular facts'.[1] If complete enumeration of instances is held, as it was held by Aristotle, to be the only possible way of establishing general propositions, then 'we can never prove anything by reasoning until we already know it by direct experience'.[2] Anyway, there cannot be exhaustive enumeration where the units constituting the instances are individuals (individual things or persons or events or situations or institutions), not sub-classes of some class of individuals.[3] All generalizations have the same status, whether their subject is human affairs or is physical nature. 'All scientific hypotheses will be taken to be generalisations with unlimited numbers of instances.'[4] And, when the instances with which we are dealing are of a kind in which the number is apt to increase with the passage of time, we have to reckon, all the time, with an unknown future.

'It is a historic fact that the inductive policies of good scientific repute are effective-in-the-past policies; it is a general hypothesis that they are effective as well as being effective in the past.'[5]

This distinction is one of capital importance in any field of investigation —and therefore, among others, in the field in which the phenomena with which we are concerned are human affairs. I myself have never believed, and never contended, that the regularities, uniformities, and recurrences that, in my belief, are discernible in our record of the course of human affairs up to date are bound also to recur in the future. The most that I would infer from their past occurrence is that they *may* recur; we cannot, I believe, infer from it that they *must*. We must bear in mind all the time the possibility that

'an inductive policy . . . may fail in the future, either by its past successes turning out to be failures after all or by its failing to have future successes.'[6]

These considerations bring out the limitations of the scientific method, in whatever field it may be applied, as a strategy for trying to arrive at the truth about Reality.

'The imperfection attaching to the conclusions of inductive science— conclusions which are said to be reached by 'imperfect induction'— springs from the defective analysis of the instances cited, not from the failure to cite every instance; and it is a mistake to suppose that "perfect induction", if it could be employed—as it is acknowledged it cannot— would remove the defect of certainty attaching to scientific generalisations. For science seeks after the necessary and the universal, not after the merely exceptionless.'[7]

Joseph goes on to point out two of the weaknesses of scientific explanation:

[1] Joseph, op. cit., p. 504.   [2] Ibid., p. 381.   [3] Ibid., p. 384.
[4] Braithwaite, op. cit., p. 14.   [5] Ibid., p. 268.
[6] Ibid., p. 268.
[7] Joseph, op. cit., p. 504. Philosophers of a different school might here comment that, if science does seek after the necessary and the universal, it is in quest of something that is unattainable.

'It often starts with principles or truths or laws which are neither accounted for nor in themselves self-evident,[1] but only warranted by the success with which they account for the facts of our experience; and these principles are not absolutely and irrefragably proved, as long as any others which might equally well account for the facts are conceivable.'[2]

Accordingly, while conceding that 'it would be foolish to let these considerations engage us in a general and indiscriminate distrust of scientific principles', Joseph concludes that 'it must be allowed that the scientific account of Reality cannot be the ultimate truth'.[3] Braithwaite likewise finds that '"the quest for certainty" is, in the case of empirical knowledge, a snare and a delusion'.[4] 'A scientific "law" merely states probabilities.'[5]

The truth seems to be that 'the empirical evidence of its instances never proves the hypothesis . . . in the sense that the hypothesis is a logical consequence of the evidence.[6] . . . Induction must be considered, not primarily as induction by simple enumeration, but as the method by which we establish hypotheses within scientific systems.'[7]

'The use of . . . particulars is, not to serve as the proof of a principle, but to reveal it. . . . They are the means used because some countable material is necessary in order to realise the general truth; but the general truth is not accepted simply because it is confirmed empirically by every instance.'[8]

'The reasoning which infers general truths from the analysis of a limited number of particulars does not rely on enumeration and is not an operation of the same kind as that which proceeds by complete enumeration. . . . [What it relies on is] an attempt to establish connexions of a causal character by analysis and elimination.'[9]

The 'apprehension of the necessary relation between . . . two terms, which our familiarity with particulars makes possible, . . . is the work of the intellect'.[10] But the torch that the intellect has snatched out of the senses' incompetent hands is snatched away, in turn, by another faculty of the psyche. In the act of establishing general propositions, 'an incommunicable intuition takes the place of any process of reasoning'.[11] 'The induction is now a psychological rather than a logical process.'[12]

Under the guidance of practised logicians we have cursorily examined the nature of inductive reasoning and have noted the formidable difficulties which it encounters in its attempts to arrive at cogent demonstrations. On our way we have now caught a glimpse of the possibility

---

[1] 'The first or fundamental principles of science are themselves insusceptible of scientific explanation, and they usually also do not appear to be self-evident' (Joseph, op. cit., p. 503). 'We give reasons if we can, and turn to empirical laws if we must' (W. Dray: *Laws and Explanation in History*, p. 138). C. B. Joynt points out, in a letter of 14th August, 1959, that to demand demonstrations of initial assumptions would involve an inquirer in an infinite regress. In a letter of 16th September, 1959, he makes the point that 'the laws of physics or of history must be irreducibly contingent logically'.

[2] Joseph, op. cit., p. 505.   [3] Ibid., p. 505.

[4] Braithwaite, op. cit., p. 163.

[5] Social Science Research Council's Committee on Historiography's Report (1954), p. 89.   [6] Braithwaite, op. cit., p. 14.   [7] Ibid., p. 11.

[8] Joseph, op. cit., p. 383.   [9] Ibid., p. 504.

[10] Ibid., p. 385. Cp. p. 391.   [11] Ibid., p. 385.   [12] Ibid., p. 384.

that proof, even of the uncontestedly cogent kind which it has been claimed that deductive reasoning produces,[1] may not, after all, be the human mind's main objective. The goal of human thought may turn out to be, not proof for its own sake, but explanation. 'A scientific problem, as a rule, arises from the need for an explanation';[2] and, in the study of human affairs, 'the scientific function involves not only identifying and describing temporal sequences; it also involves explaining them'.[3] '*Some* explanation, implied or stated, is firmly planted in every history',[4] for example. And the search for explanation is a quest for intelligibility.

'All thinking is an attempt to make experience more intelligible, and, so far as it is not intelligible, we assume our account of it to be untrue. It is for this reason that we are always recasting in thought the account of what appears in our experience.'[5]

When we are confronted with something that we do not understand, we try to make it intelligible to ourselves by tracing a connexion between it and something else that we believe we understand better.[6] Explanation is essentially an act or process of reference.[7]

One step towards explaining a phenomenon is to find its context. 'Research into meaning cannot be free from synthesis, for only by putting anything into a wider context can its meaning be seen.'[8] A fact cannot be established or made intelligible unless it is related to other facts or is part of a larger system.[9]

If I may venture to illustrate this point from my own work, I should say that volumes i–x of *A Study of History* hinge on two attempts to find 'an intelligible field of study' as a framework for a narrower field that I had found unintelligible when taken by itself without looking beyond its limits. The starting-point of the inquiry was a search for a more or less self-contained field of historical study of which the contemporary Western historians' customary national units of study would turn out to be parts. I had felt these national units to be unsatisfactory

[1] As Joseph sees it, inductive reasoning differs from demonstration in not making connexions intelligible (Joseph, op. cit., pp. 398–9). But he holds that a general proposition can be established *either* by 'insight into the necessity connecting the terms of the system of nature' *or* by 'appeal to particular facts' (ibid., p. 399); so, on his view, deductive and inductive reasoning are different without being contrary (ibid., pp. 396–7). The difference itself ceases to be clear-cut if even mathematical axioms (e.g. Euclid's) turn out not, after all, to be self-evident, as they have traditionally been taken to be.

[2] K. R. Popper: *The Poverty of Historicism*, p. 122.

[3] Social Science Research Council's Committee on Historiography's Report (1954), p. 86.

[4] E. E. Y. Hales in *History Today*, May, 1955, p. 323. Cp. the passage quoted from Coates on p. 20.

[5] Joseph, op. cit., p. 486, footnote 1.   [6] Ibid., p. 502.

[7] Presumably the act of referring something to something else implies that one has a better understanding of this other thing. The Israelites explained history to themselves by finding a meaning for it in God's purposes and in the action taken by Him for bringing about their fulfilment (R. L. Shinn: *Christianity and the Problem of History*, p. 33). This was perhaps, as is claimed by L. C. Stecchini (in *Midstream*, Autumn, 1956, pp. 84–91), the earliest of any attempts to explain history that have been made anywhere. In a rationalist's eyes it is an explanation of *obscurum per obscurius*. In a trans-rationalist's eyes it is a recognition of the presence of a Reality that is only partially revealed in the phenomena. The usage of the terms 'rationalist' and 'trans-rationalist' in this volume is explained on p. 72, footnote 3, and on pp. 75–76.

[8] Cohen, op. cit., p. 33.   [9] Ibid.

because they seemed to me to be un-self-contained, which would mean that they must be fragments of something larger. I found this larger unit of study in a species of society that I labelled a 'civilization'. Civilizations proved, so it seemed to me, to be intelligible units of study so long as I was studying their geneses, growths, and breakdowns; but when I came to study their disintegrations I found that, at this stage, their histories—like those of the national subdivisions of the modern Western World—were no longer intelligible in isolation. A disintegrating civilization was apt to enter into intimate relations with one or more other representatives of its species; and these encounters between civilizations gave birth to societies of another species: higher religions. At the beginning of the inquiry I had tried to explain the higher religions, like the national and other varieties of parochial states, in terms of civilizations. The last stage of my survey of the history of civilizations convinced me that this way of looking at the higher religions did not, after all, give anything like an adequate explanation of them.

It was true that the higher religions had served as 'chrysalises' in which disintegrating civilizations had undergone a metamorphosis and from which new civilizations of a younger generation had emerged. It was also true that this had been the higher religions' role in the histories of civilizations. But, in the histories of the higher religions themselves, this role turned out to have been not only an incidental one but actually an untoward accident in the sense that it had been apt to divert them from their proper task of carrying out their own missions. If I was to continue to pursue my search for some intelligible field of study that would provide an adequate context, and therefore a satisfactory explanation, for units of other species than nations and of other magnitudes—for instance, an explanation of civilizations—I now had to ask myself whether I ought not to reverse my previous plan of operations. If one species of society was to be explained in terms of another, ought not the civilizations of the first and second generations to be explained as preliminaries to the rise of the higher religions? These second thoughts about the identification of 'the intelligible field' of historical study, to which I had been led in the course of my inquiry, gave me a new point of departure; and the change of outlook, demanded by the necessity for a change of explanation, was a radical one. Christopher Dawson is right in defining it as a change from a cyclical system to a progressive system.[1] It was indeed so radical that many critics have been struck by it and some of them have suggested that, at this point, I ought to have wound up my original comparative study of civilizations and to have started a new inquiry into the meaning of human history in terms of religion.[2]

---

[1] Chr. Dawson in *Toynbee and History*, p. 131. K. W. Thompson, ibid., pp. 207–12, traces my change of standpoint in greater detail. See also W. H. McNeill in *The Intent of Toynbee's History: A Cooperative Appraisal*. Geyl sees it (in *Toynbee and History*, p. 360), 'the new system springs naturally from' the old one.

[2] See, for example, Hourani, in loc. cit., pp. 387–8 and 384–5; A. G. Bailey in *Queen's Quarterly*, vol. lxii, No. 1 (Spring, 1955), pp. 100–10; E. Voegelin in *The Intent of Toynbee's History: A Cooperative Appraisal*; K. D. Erdmann in *Archiv für Kulturgeschichte*, xxxiii. Band, Heft 2 (1951), pp. 228, 234–8, 241, and 247; H. Werner in *Deutsche Vierteljahrsschrift für Literaturwissenschaft und Geistesgeschichte*, 29. Jahrgang,

In explaining something in terms of its context one is explaining it in terms of another thing that is more intelligible in virtue of its larger scale, but not necessarily in virtue of being of a different and intrinsically more intelligible nature. An explanation of this second type is evidently more illuminating. 'To explain a law is to exhibit an established set of hypotheses from which the law follows.'[1]

In this more illuminating type of explanation there are any number of possible gradations of achievement. At the bottom of the scale of intelligibility are those generalizations that rest merely on induction. 'From an empiricist point of view, all explanations of actual events or features of experience take the form of showing that what is to be explained is, in itself or with some of its attendant circumstances, an example of a regularly recurrent pattern of events or aspects of events.'[2] But 'inductive conclusions are never seen to be intrinsically necessary, but only to be unavoidable'.[3] Accordingly, they 'present . . . a blank wall to our intelligence'.[4] However, 'having explained some event or feature of an event as an instance of some recurrent regularity, it is always legitimate to go on and ask for an explanation of that regularity';[5] and one may succeed in explaining it in terms of another regularity that is wider in its range or more lucid in its degree of intelligibility or has both these explanatory features.[6] 'Complete explanation would only come if the law which the facts had forced us to recognise should, when considered, appear self-evident.'[7] This ideal is most nearly approached in mathematical propositions. In these the necessity of the relations has been held to be transparent,[8] and, even if this view of them is contested, it will probably be agreed that they stand at the top of the scale of intelligibility. Most of my own explanations of historical phenomena are of the comparatively opaque inductive kind. 'An historical pattern has been shown, but not a logical cause.'[9]

Mathematical relations are apparently transparent because mathematical entities are not phenomena but abstractions. Abstractions can be made simple and precise in the degree in which they eliminate the

---

xxix. Band (Stuttgart 1955, Metzler), p. 530; R. Pares in *The English Historical Review*, vol. lxxi, No. 279 (April, 1956), p. 264; O. F. Anderle, unpublished paper; L. Mumford in *Diogenes*, No. 13 (Spring, 1956), p. 11; Rabbi J. B. Agus in *Judaism*, vol. 4, No. 4 (Fall, 1955), pp. 320 and 331; M. Savelle in *The Pacific Historical Review*, vol. xxv, No. 1 (February, 1956), pp. 55–67; A. N. Holcombe in *The American Political Science Review*, vol xlix, No. 4 (December, 1955), pp. 1151–4; T. A. Sumberg in *Social Research*, vol. 14, No. 3 (September, 1947), pp. 267–84; K. Löwith: *Meaning in History*, pp. 12–17; G. Masur in the *Historische Zeitschrift*, Band 177 (1954), pp. 521–2; R. V. Chase in *The Partisan Review* (Winter, 1944), p. 51; B. D. Wolfe in *The American Mercury*, No. 64 (1947), pp. 755–6; G. Weil in *Toynbee and History*, pp. 285–6; and Anderle, commenting on Weil, in op. cit. See further p. 94, footnote 1, p. 100, footnote 3, and Chapter II, Annex, pp. 649–51.

[1] Braithwaite, op. cit., p. 343.

[2] P. Bagby: *Culture and History*, p. 130. 'To explain with the aid of a theory is to do indirectly what the historian perhaps painstakingly and piecemeal . . . does directly: reduce what is puzzling to what is not' (W. Dray: *Laws and Explanation in History*, p. 81). [3] Joseph, op. cit., pp. 551–2.

[4] Ibid., p. 437. [5] Bagby, op. cit., p. 133.

[6] e.g. Newton's laws, which were once believed to be all-inclusive, are now seen to be included in the theory of relativity.

[7] Joseph, op. cit., p. 417. [8] Ibid., p. 547.

[9] J. K. Feibleman: 'Toynbee's Theory of History' in *T'ien Hsia Monthly*, vol. xi, Nos. 1 and 2 (1940), p. 141. Cp. p. 16. Cp. also W. Dray, op. cit., pp. 61, 69, 97.

unique essence of Reality. In mathematical abstractions this process of
elimination is carried to extremes. By comparison with mathematical
abstractions, phenomena, even those of the non-human kind, are complex and elusive. Human phenomena are more complex and elusive still.
Bagby observes[1] that, in the comparative study of civilizations, 'qualitative rather than quantitative considerations play a primary role'. *Ad
hominem*, it is not surprising that J. K. Feibleman is struck by 'the low
abstractive level' of my work in earlier volumes of the present book.
'The result', he pronounces, 'is not the highly abstractive logical and
quantitative structure which it ought to be, but something still qualitative and indeed almost literary in its approach.'[2] I do not question
Feibleman's report, but I do demur to his requirement. What he is
demanding is, I believe, a counsel of perfection for a student of human
affairs. In attempts to explain human affairs, complete transparency is
most unlikely to be attainable. I agree with another philosopher's dictum
that we should be underestimating the limitations of finite human minds
if we were to claim that our minds can find the whole of human history
intelligible, even if we help ourselves out by trying to explain history in
terms of God's sovereignty, instead of confining our horizon to the
field of human action.[3]

4. THE RELATIVITY OF EXPLANATION TO OUTLOOK

It will be seen that the objective of both 'explanation' and 'demonstration' is intellectual satisfaction, and that the achievement of this is
the warrant that the objective has been attained. In this sense 'demonstration', as well as 'explanation', is a subjective experience. On the
other hand, 'demonstration', in contrast to non-demonstrative 'explanation', is objective in the sense that we do not regard a demonstration as
being valid and authentic unless an identical intellectual satisfaction is
found to be experienced by all minds that have followed out the particular train of reasoning in question,[4] whereas an explanation may give
different degrees of intellectual satisfaction to different minds and may,
indeed, give full satisfaction to some minds while giving none at all to
others, so that 'explanation' is not only subjective but is also relative.[5]

[1] In op. cit., p. 164.
[2] J. K. Feibleman in *T'ien Hsia Monthly*, vol. xi, Nos. 1 and 2 (1940), p. 20.
[3] R. L. Shinn: *Christianity and the Problem of History*, p. 45. Cp. C. B. Joynt in *The
Australasian Journal of Philosophy*, vol. 34, No. 3 (December, 1956), pp. 195–202.
[4] 'Scientific proof is public, not private' (J. Needham: *Science and Civilization in
China*, vol. ii (Cambridge 1956, University Press), p. 515). 'The burden of demonstrating
the significance of the pattern he has selected is on the historian. . . . Empirical hypotheses are not private visions but public assertions' (C. B. Joynt in *The Australasian
Journal of Philosophy*, vol. 34, No. 3 (December, 1956), p. 202). In a letter of 14th
August, 1959, Joynt points out that the meteorologist's and the shaman's explanations
of a thunderstorm, cited below, differ in the point that the meteorologist's explanation is
testable, whereas the shaman's is not. Even, however, if the meteorologist's explanation
passes all tests available at the moment to the satisfaction of all minds that have followed
this train of reasoning, its validity is still no more than provisional, as we have seen.
[5] W. Dray insists on this point that explanation is *not* equivalent to prediction and
verification (*Laws and Explanation in History*, p. 59). K. R. Popper appears to be making
the same point when he says, with reference to the historians' approach to the study of
human affairs, that 'there is necessarily a plurality of interpretations, which are fundamentally on the same level of both suggestiveness and arbitrariness' (*The Poverty of
Historicism*, p. 151). In Popper's terminology, however, 'interpretation' and 'explanation' are not synonymous, and the word 'explanation' seems to be used (see ibid.,

This point is illustrated by the plurality of satisfying explanations of a thunderstorm. Minds educated to adopt the intellectual outlook that is customary in the present-day Western World will accept the explanation in terms of the regular and predictable working of inanimate physical forces—temperature, barometrical pressure, electricity, and so on—that is offered in a meteorological observatory's report. Perhaps only one layman in a thousand really understands the meaning of an explanation of this scientific kind; but the other nine hundred and ninety-nine accept it with little less confidence by taking it on faith. People living in a society with a non-scientific outlook will likewise take on faith the explanation of the same thunderstorm that is given to them by authorities who are the experts in their eyes. They will take it from these interpreters of the phenomenon that the thunderstorm is produced by the capricious and unpredictable whim of a god riding on the clouds, and that the 'thunderbolt' is this god's physical weapon with which he visits his anger on mankind. The meteorologist's explanation would seem not merely unilluminating but incredible to the shaman's clientele, just as the shaman's explanation would seem not merely incredible but ridiculous to the meteorologist's public. Here we see two incompatible explanations of the same phenomenon respectively giving intellectual satisfaction to two sets of human beings that share our common human nature but happen to have been brought up in two different cultural milieux.

It will be noticed that the relativity of intellectual satisfaction to the cultural milieu of the inquiring mind is something inherent in the human situation common to all men, and that this common mental limitation cannot be overcome by any increase in intellectual sophistication, however great.

'Even the physical sciences start with some assumptions concerning the nature of things.[1] Still more does any treatment of history. Empirical operations in history are always limited by the intellectual presuppositions of the author, and there is no escape from this rule.'[2]

5. THE EXPLANATORY USE OF ANALOGY

The relativity of the value of an explanation, in terms of giving or not giving intellectual satisfaction to different publics, or, for that matter, to different minds in one and the same cultural milieu, is also illustrated by differences of opinion about the explanatory value of the use of analogy.

Analogy, like all other kinds of attempts at explanation, is an interpretation of something that seems comparatively obscure in terms of

pp. 122–3) to mean something more cogent than 'interpretation'. In Popper's view 'the use of a theory for *predicting* some specific event is just another aspect of its use for *explaining* such an event' (ibid., p. 124) and 'there is no great difference between explanation, prediction, and testing' (ibid., p. 133). I am using the word 'explanation' to mean what Popper means by 'interpretation'.

[1] Cp. Joseph, quoted on pp. 24–25. C. B. Joynt, in a letter of 14th August, 1959, points out that presuppositions, assumptions, and hypotheses are, all alike, provisional, expendable, and replaceable.

[2] C. A. Beard in *The American Historical Review*, vol. xl, No. 2 (January, 1935), p. 309.

something else that seems comparatively transparent. Joseph brackets analogy with 'simple enumeration'. 'Both point to a general principle which, if it were true, would account for the facts from which we infer it.'[1] 'Neither', he continues, 'prove its truth.' But nevertheless he endorses a dictum of J. S. Mill's that 'there is no analogy, however faint, which may not be of the utmost value in suggesting experiments or observations that may lead to more positive conclusions'.[2]

The weakness of analogy as a method of thought seems to lie, not in the nature of the method itself, but in the nature of most of the phenomena to which it is applied. In mathematics the argument from analogy is accepted as being valid.[3] Indeed, 'the most fruitful developments of modern mathematics can almost all be analysed into the application of old ideas to new fields'.[4] This is because the entities with which mathematical thought operates are simple and precise abstractions, and the use of analogy in the sense of finding 'proportion' between different sets of such entities cannot lead the user intellectually astray. The possibility of error arises when the entities between which he is drawing an analogy are not mathematical abstractions but are observed phenomena. Two or more phenomena may have facets which genuinely correspond with each other and between which analogies can therefore properly be drawn. Here we may fall into error by failing to abstract the genuinely corresponding features precisely,[5] or by making the unwarrantable assumption that an analogy which holds good just for these facets is also applicable to the phenomena in their entirety; for this means treating the non-comparable facets of these phenomena as if they too were comparable, when they are not.

A case in point is the kind of explanation of non-human phenomena of which my imaginary shaman's explanation is one example. Human beings find themselves buffeted by forces, some of which are exerted by their fellow human beings and others by non-human phenomena. Since the exertion of force is a common activity of both kinds of agency, and since, of the two, the human kind is the more familiar, and therefore seems the more transparently intelligible to human minds that have not been initiated into the science of psychology, people living in a non-scientific-minded cultural milieu explain the action of a thunderstorm, torrent, or bull in terms of the action of a strong and angry man. Their error, of course, lies in their uncritical assumption that all the external forces that they encounter are forces of one single kind, obeying one single set of laws, and that these universal laws of force are identical with the particular laws with which they are most familiar, namely the laws of the behaviour of human beings of like passions with themselves.

From the standpoint of those of us who have been brought up in a scientific-minded cultural milieu, this reading of human behaviour into the action of inanimate nature, and even the reading of it into the action of creatures that are alive but are not human, is an unwarranted use of

---

[1] Joseph, op. cit., p. 540. Cp. p. 541.
[2] J. S. Mill: *System of Logic*, III. xx. 3 *med*.
[3] Joseph, op. cit., p. 532.
[4] Cohen, op. cit., p. 249.
[5] Joseph, op. cit., p. 532.

analogy that makes nonsense of these phenomena.[1] We have labelled this error 'the pathetic fallacy' and the practice of it 'mythology'. But if we maintain that mythology is an erroneous use of analogy to which non-scientific-minded people are prone, we must also admit that there is an inverse error—let us call it 'the apathetic fallacy',[2] and call the practice of it 'counter-mythology'—which consists in interpreting human conduct in terms of the action of non-human animals and of inanimate nature.

This is an error into which we are prone to fall in our modern Western World. We have been dazzled by the successes of our men of science in explaining phenomena to us and in justifying their explanations by successfully bringing the phenomena under human control as a result of handling them on the assumption that the explanations correspond to the realities. The earliest successes of our modern Western scientists in finding explanations that proved to be keys to establishing control were in the field of inanimate nature. They then extended their operations to the study of the material structure and working of living organisms. Finally they have applied their method to the study of the spiritual constitution and conduct of human beings—the study of human affairs, as I have called it in this book. As a result of this course that the development of modern Western science has taken, the most familiar kind of phenomenon for a modern Western scientist is the inanimate kind. It is this kind that he has succeeded in explaining to himself the earliest, and also the most to his own satisfaction. It is therefore natural that, when he ventures into the, to him, comparatively unfamiliar field of human affairs, the scientist, like the shaman, and indeed like any other human being, should try to illuminate what is less familiar to him by putting it in terms of something that he feels he understands better. He is tempted to use his physiological, biological, chemical, physical, and mechanical terminologies for interpreting social and cultural phenomena, and this misuse of analogy is no less misleading than the shaman's. The obscurity of human affairs is intensified, instead of being clarified, when they are described in non-human terms—however familiar these terms may be and however well they may have served their users when they have been applied in their own proper contexts.[3]

---

[1] K. W. Deutsch in *Philosophy of Science*, vol. 18, No. 3 (July, 1951), pp. 230–52, points out on p. 231 that the use of a human society as a model for non-human nature leads to the practice of magic.

[2] See the present book, i. 7–8 and 271.

[3] The classic example—dating from long before the rise of modern Western science—of an analogy applied to human affairs from a different level of phenomena is the description and explanation of society in terms of physiology. I myself believe that this particular analogy is wholly misleading (see pp. 268–9 and 271–2). In a letter to me of 8th January, 1936, F. J. Teggart writes: 'One of our habits of thought—and it is part and parcel of our intellectual make-up—is the use of the organic analogy in dealing with the problems of culture and society. The use of the analogy is as old as the beginnings of European thought; this is *not* a demerit, but the employment of the analogy means that our outlook on the world (of culture) is restricted to one way of looking at things.'

A sharp critique of the apathetic fallacy in the work of one school of recent Western historians will be found in M. C. Swabey: *The Judgment of History*, pp. 93–95 and 108–10. 'Who ever heard . . . of a mechanism without any consciously invented machinery? Of selection without purposive choice? Of warfare without cognisance or intent? Discredit is brought upon history by such wholesale borrowing from the blind, inhuman world for

Of course the conscientious use of human terms for describing human affairs is not, in itself, a safeguard against falling into error through a misuse of analogy. For instance, the hypothesis of a primordial 'social contract' as an explanation of the origin of human society is misleading, in spite of its being an interpretation of a human affair in human terms, because it seeks to explain an obscure event in one kind of social milieu by reference to an institution that is non-existent in this kind of milieu and is to be found only in a different one that happens to be more familiar to the inquirer. The making of contracts between human beings is possible only when these are already in social relations with each other and when their society has become well enough established and sophisticated enough to have inaugurated the reign of law over human relations. To project this rather mature social situation back into a pre-social state of affairs as an account of how society came into existence is an attempt to explain society's origin in terms of one of its eventual products. This is evidently an erroneous analogy from a social state of human affairs to a supposed pre-social state of them. It does not give the explanation that it purports to give. Yet the error involved in this misleading account of the obscure origin of human society in terms of a social contract is at any rate far less gross than the error involved in the 'counter-mythological' attempt to explain the same event by the use of terms applicable only to inanimate nature, such as 'gravitation', 'attraction', 'fusion', 'conglomeration', 'crystallization'.

A classical illustration of the 'counter-mythological' variation on the misuse of analogy is the conjuring up of the pseudo-science of astrology through the drawing of an unwarranted analogy between the movements of human affairs and those of the heavenly bodies. In Babylonia in the eighth century B.C. astronomers made the discovery that the relative positions of the Sun, the Moon, and the five then known planets in regard to each other at a particular moment recur regularly at a uniform interval of time which the discoverers labelled 'the Great Year'. This mighty manifestation of regularity, uniformity, and recurrence in the movements of the stellar cosmos was so impressive and exciting that its makers jumped to the conclusion that they had found the key to the workings of everything in the Universe. They would not have been far wrong if they had been content with concluding that everything—or almost everything—was subject, like the heavenly bodies, to some kind of 'law' in the sense of 'laws of Nature': that is, apparent regularities that have been revealed by observation, and, so far, have not been shown by it to be illusory. This has been the finding of modern Western science, and it has been found to hold good not only in the case of non-human nature but in the case of the sub-conscious element in human nature too—if we accept the findings of the newly fledged science of psychology. Where the Babylonians went astray was in their further assumptions that there was nothing in the Universe that was exempt from the rule of 'the laws of Nature', and that these laws were all

the interpretation of human happenings. . . . How much better, says common sense, for historians to choose their analogues from human life rather than from inhuman, impersonal worlds, thus avoiding far-fetched comparisons' (pp. 109-10).

comprised in a single code which governed all kinds of phenomena alike. Actually, it is non-proven that the apparent partial freedom of human consciousness, purpose, and will is illusory; and, in so far as human nature may be partially subject to 'laws', there is no warrant at all for assuming that the laws of psychology and the laws of physics are identical with each other or even similar to each other, or, short of this, that they are geared together in some mechanical way. So far from that, it looks as if the realm of 'laws of Nature' were articulated into a number of different provinces, each with its own provincial code of laws, so that, while the whole realm is under the reign of law of some kind, different codes of law are valid simultaneously in different areas.[1] The Babylonian astronomers who became the fathers of astrology went wrong, not in drawing their analogy, but in pressing it to unwarranted lengths.

Notwithstanding these monitory examples of the misuse of analogy, it is nevertheless true that a prudently discriminating use of it can be fruitful even in perilous fields as well as in the safe field of mathematics. One daring and, no doubt, hazardous use of it for the extension of the range of thought and language has been justified by its continued and cumulative success. As far as we can guess, the original vocabulary of human speech must have been limited to a number of ejaculations supplemented by a few imperatives and even fewer indicatives, and the earliest essays in these parts of speech must all have been expressions of an experience of those phenomena that are immediate data of the senses. In societies which have risen above the primitive cultural level and have started on the enterprise of civilization, this original nucleus of Man's vocabulary has been buried under the vast successive additions that have been made to it. We have built up our vocabulary—and, with it, the thoughts that it expresses—into a huge inverted pyramid, and the new materials for this invaluable mental structure have been produced by the use of analogy.

Our ideas of, and our words for, spiritual presences, actions, and experiences are derived from words and ideas denoting material things, sensations, and events. Our ideas of, and words for, abstractions are derived from concrete objects from which the abstractions have been elicited by an intellectual *tour de force*. In thinking and talking about what is abstract in terms of what is concrete, and about what is spiritual in terms of what is material, we must have been drawing an unwarranted analogy and therefore must have been exposing ourselves to the risk of misrepresenting and misunderstanding those elusive spiritual and abstract aspects of Reality that we have represented to ourselves in imagery borrowed from material and concrete aspects of it that are immediate data of the senses. This enormous extension of the range of human language and thought is, in fact, a product of analogy; yet, in this crucially important instance, the resort to analogy seems to have justified itself by its results. For example, we successfully make mathematical calculations with mental tools originally fashioned for other uses. The very word 'calculation' means playing about with pebbles as counters. Yet, in making the abstractions required for calculation, we

[1] See E. F. J. Zahn: *Toynbee und das Problem der Geschichte*, pp. 9–11.

have not lost touch with Reality, as is witnessed by the effectiveness of the application of mathematics in technology and also, far more convincingly, by the impression of self-evident truth that mathematical reasoning makes on our minds.

Cohen points out[1] that 'the number of available analogies is a determining factor in the growth and progress of science'.

'The ancient doctrine of atoms led to plausible speculations but became a useful scientific idea when the development of mechanics enabled us to apply the analogies of billiard balls and statistics to groups of atoms.'[2]

Cohen also reminds us that our mental picture of the internal structure of an atom is an analogy drawn from our knowledge of the solar system. We have constructed our theory of gases on the analogy of capillary action. The structure of star clusters has given us a clue for developing the electron theory of electricity. We have successfully explored the behaviour of electricity by thinking of it in terms of the behaviour of a fluid. We have discovered some of the physical properties of the planet on whose surface we live by thinking of it as if it were a magnet or the needle of a compass. Our notion of the independence of the biological cell and our theory of genes are analogies from our atomic theory. Our notion of the way in which natural selection 'works' is an analogy from our knowledge of the way in which a human breeder of animal livestock works.[3]

In this last instance we are taking the personal work of a human being endowed with a consciousness, a will, and a purpose as a clue for understanding the character of 'work' of another kind. This other kind of 'work' is, in the modern Western scientist's view, *ex hypothesi* something impersonal, unconscious, and unpurposive, in opposition to the Jewish-Christian-Muslim belief in acts of creation by a God conceived of in the likeness of an almighty human being. The analogy from a human breeder to an impersonal 'breeding force' may or may not bring us nearer to the truth[4] than the older analogy from a human breeder to a superhuman 'creator', but this older analogy at least has the advantage of being the less far-fetched of the two, and it may be doubted whether the new analogy would have been attainable by human minds if they had not previously provided themselves with this older and nearer one to serve as a stepping-stone for their striding imagination.

To continue our recital,

'The discovery of the circulation of the blood by William Harvey was at any rate partly inspired by the known relation of the Sun to the meteorological water circulation cycle.'[5]

But Harvey also partly found his way to his discovery by thinking of the heart, arteries, and veins in terms of man-made pumps and valves. And other human artefacts have given clues for explaining, not only the

[1] Cohen, op. cit., p. 249.   [2] Ibid., p. 252.
[3] All these examples of fruitful analogies in the field of science are given by Cohen in op. cit., p. 250.   [4] For an adverse verdict on it, see Swabey, op. cit., p. 109.
[5] J. Needham: *Science and Civilization in China*, vol. ii (Cambridge 1956, University Press), p. 298.

physical 'structure' and 'working' of living organisms, but also the ways of Man and even the ways of God. Analogies have been drawn from the wheel to explain the revolutions in human affairs as well as those in the movements of the heavenly bodies. The clock has been taken as a model not only in astronomy and physiology but also in political science and theology. Schiller wrote of 'the watch-spring of the Universe'. Tom Paine called God 'the first mechanic'. The Pyramids have provided a sensuous image of a hierarchical social structure. The potter has served as a prototype for a creator god. A pair of scales has become a symbol for justice. The weaver's thread and web have become symbols of Reality (*Wirklichkeit*) itself.[1]

At the present moment we can watch the advance of technology once again giving Man the craftsman a new clue to a better understanding of his own psychic nature. Since the nineteen-forties 'a new science about an old subject' has made its appearance under the name of cybernetics. Today there is

'a growing division of labour between human minds and an ever-growing array of electronic or other communications, calculating, and control equipment. . . . By continuing to make . . . equipment which fulfils . . . functions of communication, organisation, and control, we cannot help in the long run but gain significant opportunities for a clearer understanding of those functions themselves. . . . [Cybernetics] uses the facilities of modern technology in order to attempt to map out, step by step, the sequence of actual events in getting these operations accomplished. . . . As simplified models, [calculating machines] can aid our understanding of more complex mental and social processes. [What this may give us is] a generalised concept of a self-modifying communications network or "learning-net".'[2]

No doubt, each time that we resort to the method of analogy, we are courting the risk of misapplying it.[3] Yet the use of analogy has certainly been a fruitful device, and perhaps an indispensable one, for Man in his sustained mental endeavour to take his bearings in the mysterious Universe into which he finds himself born. He has wrested valuable results not only from analogies between kindred phenomena, but also from the more far-fetched 'mythological' analogies drawn from human conduct to the behaviour of non-human animals and to the processes of inanimate nature, as well as from 'counter-mythological' analogies drawn from the processes of inanimate nature to human affairs. I agree, for my part, with M. C. Swabey's dicta[4] that, 'since all knowledge proceeds through the detection of resemblances, in dealing with objects largely beyond empirical check, analogy must be appealed to', and that, 'despite the pitfalls of analogy, history has its roots in it'.

[1] All but the first of the examples cited in this paragraph are given by K. W. Deutsch in 'Mechanism, Organism, and Society: Some Models in Natural and Social Science', in *Philosophy of Science*, vol. xviii, No. 3 (July, 1951), pp. 232–4.

[2] Ibid., pp. 239–41.

[3] 'The [analogical] method . . . comes from a dangerous and subtle form of mysticism which has been widespread in all ages. It makes it possible to prove and to believe almost anything. One of the best-known examples of its use was the proof of a whole cosmogony and religion from the analogy of a watch' (L. S. Woolf in *The New Statesman and Nation*, 23rd September, 1939).

[4] In *The Judgment of History*, p. 75.

In the history of modern Western science there is one instance of the use of a 'mythological' analogy which is as famous as it has been fertile. Darwin has recorded that, at a stage in his inquiry into the origin of species at which he was making no further progress in the direct approach to his problem, he happened to read one of Malthus's works expounding his theory that, in human society, there is a tendency for the growth-rate of the population to forge ahead of the growth-rate of its food supply, and that this results in a struggle for life. In this celebrated economic hypothesis Darwin found the clue that led him to his own still more celebrated biological hypothesis. Conversely, Deutsch, the exponent of the new science of cybernetics who has been quoted just above, claims for it that it is a promising line of inquiry because it is throwing light on the working of human minds from the working of Man's latest artefacts. He finds that 'the striking parallels and suggestive insights' into the working of human affairs that are offered by concepts drawn from human history have 'remained empty of inner structure'. For example, my own ' "creative minorities" are unanalysed vessels of a creativity which itself has no intrinsic details that could be described and understood'. Deutsch finds Joseph Schumpeter's concepts of 'creativeness' and 'innovation' in the field of economics likewise unfruitful for the same reason. Schumpeter and I, he suggests, have drawn blank because we have taken human society itself as our model for explaining processes of human organization.[1] Deutsch's point may be expressed analogically as the doctrine that, in the use of analogy, as in the process of evolution and in the practice of the breeder's art, inbreeding makes for sterility, cross-breeding for fertility.

Whether or not this particular analogy is justified by the evidence of results, I myself have been commended by some critics and censured by others on the ground that I have in fact used analogy in the cross-fertilizing way that Deutsch recommends.[2] I have also been censured for using analogy to excess,[3] for using it in its mythological form

---

[1] Ibid., pp. 237–8.

[2] H. Kuhn notes in *The Journal of Philosophy*, 28th August 1947, pp. 489–99, on p. 497, that I use analogy both 'horizontally' (i.e. in the in-breeding way) and 'vertically' (i.e. in the cross-breeding way). 'Vertical' analogy, as Kuhn defines it, 'puts together phenomena of different types or of different structural levels'. He pronounces that 'denying the legitimacy of this second kind of analogical reasoning would be tantamount to denying the possibility of philosophy'. At the same time he stipulates that, 'in order to be legitimate, . . . the use of vertical analogy must strictly observe the rule of hierarchy'. On the other hand, Richard Pares (in *The English Historical Review*, vol. lxxi, No. 279 (April, 1956), p. 271) remarks that, 'if Dr Toynbee rejects mechanical analogies, he falls victim to the far more dangerous biological analogies'. O. H. K. Spate (in *The Geographical Journal*, vol. cxviii, Part 4 (December, 1952), p. 419) warns against 'the danger . . . of anthropomorphising nature'. C. A. Beard (in *The American Historical Review*, vol. xl, No. 2 (January, 1938), p. 309) objects that 'the introduction of analogies from biology and physics into historical thought (a practice which most of us are guilty of) does violence to the actuality of history and adds to confusion rather than to knowledge'. K. R. Popper quotes a passage of the present book (vol. i, p. 176) as an example of the misapplication of terms taken from physics to sociology (*The Poverty of Historicism*, p. 112). L. S. Woolf (in *The New Statesman and Nation*, 23rd September, 1939) objects to my fondness for 'comparing the phenomena observable in the growth or disintegration of civilizations to the phenomena observable in radiation or in the diffusion or diffraction of light'. On the other hand, John Strachey, in a letter to me of 3rd August, 1950, writes: 'I like best of all your "radiation" way of putting it.'

[3] Analogies: 'Handle with caution' (P. Geyl in *Toynbee and History*, p. 66). Toynbee ought to chasten his metaphors and prune his analogies (Sir Ernest Barker, ibid., p. 97).

concurrently with the scientific method of reasoning,[1] for using it as a substitute for reasoning,[2] and using it, in its mythological form, at all.[3]

Poetry, myth, and metaphor are over-used (M. S. Bates in *Christianity and Crisis*, vol. 15, No. 4, 21st March, 1955, pp. 27–30 and 32). There is too much intuition, mythology, and argument from analogy in Toynbee's work (O. H. K. Spate in *Toynbee and History*, p. 291, and in *The Geographical Journal*, vol. cxviii, Part 4 (December, 1952), p. 407). Toynbee goes too far in trusting analogy (Kuhn, in loc. cit., p. 492). 'Some analogies one feels to be strained or even false' (R. T. Clark in *The Nineteenth Century and After*, November, 1941). His use of analogy is an illustration of the reckless-ness of his ways of thinking (O. H. K. Spate in *Toynbee and History*, p. 303). Cp. A. Eban ibid., pp. 330 and 331, and Sir Llewellyn Woodward in *The Spectator*, 6th July, 1934.
    [1] Toynbee drives science and poetry in double harness (K. W. Thompson in *Toynbee and History*, p. 201). Zeus is not evidence (G. J. Renier, ibid., pp. 74–75). Toynbee ought not to mix myth with scientific thinking (E. F. J. Zahn: *Toynbee und das Problem der Geschichte*, p. 36). 'Arguments which . . . have a curious way of coalescing with their imaginative illustrations so as to form philosophical myths' (Kuhn in loc. cit., p. 489). One cannot be historian and philosopher simultaneously (D. B. Richardson in *The Thomist*, vol. xx, No. 2 (April, 1957), p. 164). 'His determination to mix genres' (W. Kaufmann in *Toynbee and History*, p. 306). 'In Toynbee's interpretation of history there is an uncertainty which in a way seems to mirror the mind of the author, who is at the same time both a mystic and a scholar proud of the capacity of the human intellect' (H. Holborn in *The Saturday Review of Literature*, 31st May, 1947). 'His myth of history' (E. E. Y. Hales in *History Today*, April, 1955, p. 322). 'There can be no com-promise on such a vital point. Either we have history or we have myth. No half-way house is possible' (C. B. Joynt in *The Australasian Journal of Philosophy*, vol. 34, No. 3 (December, 1956), p. 200). According to O. F. Anderle in an unpublished paper nine-tenths of the criticism of my work is directed against my reunion of science with myth. In Anderle's own view, true myth embraces everything, including science. See further p. 130, footnote 3.
    [2] 'At times . . . the constructive artist in him . . . triumphs over the carefully weighing historian.' A simile or metaphor may become an end in itself and be taken as an ex-planation or a 'law' into which facts can be forced (G. Weil in *Toynbee and History*, p. 282). There is an ambiguity between the use of analogy as illustration and the use of it as argument. Ought metaphors to be allowed to persuade and control, besides just illuminating? In Toynbee's work 'the form and the content are organically related. . . . Thus every aesthetic aspect of the work involves the question of truth' (E. Fiess, ibid., pp. 282–3). Toynbee's images 'seem sometimes for their author to take on an indepen-dent life and vitality of their own' (W. H. McNeill in *The Intent of Toynbee's History: A Cooperative Appraisal*). 'Analogy is not proof' (R. H. Tawney in *International Affairs*, November, 1939, p. 802). Toynbee's simile of the hedgehog illustrates but does *not* prove the continuity of the history of the Syriac Civilization (A. L. Kroeber: *The Nature of Culture*, p. 376). 'Analogy is essential in history, but we all historians judge by analogy alone' (Pares, in loc. cit., p. 268). Visual images 'are often used, not as embellish-ments, but as structural parts of the arguments, not as aids to exposition, but as sub-stitutes for thought' (M. Postan in *The Sociological Review*, vol. xxviii (1936), p. 57). 'Again and again, beginning with a suggestive simile or metaphor, he ends by accepting the metaphor as proof of identity' (L. S. Woolf in *The New Statesman and Nation*, 23rd September, 1939). 'His lavish metaphors and similes, allegories and parables, suggestive as they sometimes are, are too often assumed to possess evidential value' (R. K. Merton in *The American Journal of Sociology*, vol. xlvii, No. 2 (September, 1941), pp. 205–13). Toynbee systematically falls into the confusion of historical illustration with historical proof (S. Hook in *The Partisan Review*, June 1948, p. 693). 'He is . . . doing what he censures in Spengler: that is, setting up a metaphor and then proceeding to treat it as a basis for argument' (A. R. Burn in *History*, February–October, 1956, p. 11). 'The exposition proceeds by analogies, by parables, and by quotations from philosophy and poetry. This method can never prove anything, for other parables, analogies, and quota-tions can, in the same way, prove the opposite' (O. Handlin in *The Partisan Review*, July–August, 1947, pp. 171–9). Toynbee has turned history into mythology (T. J. G. Locher in *De Gids*, May, 1948, p. 21).
    [3] Toynbee deals in myths (G. J. Renier in *Toynbee and History*, p. 74). In the present age people who take myth seriously are derided (Anderle, unpublished paper). 'Whatever else history is, it is not myth. The essence of mythology is an effort to state by means of metaphors and analogies experiences which transcend the senses. There can be a history of myths but there can be no history which consists of myths as part of its structure of meaning. At such a point, history becomes metaphysics, religion, or poetry' (Joynt in loc. cit., p. 201). This uncompromising view is not, however, taken by all rationalist-minded critics. For instance, F. H. Underhill generously declares (in *The Canadian*

I have also been offered an acquittal on condition of my agreeing to be labelled a poet, or even a musician, rather than an historian.[1]

I plead guilty to having carried my use of analogy to excessive lengths. I should have guessed that I might have made this mistake, even if I had not been accused of it by a convincing consensus of critics. I am conscious that 'going too far' is a standing temptation for me, and that too often I have succumbed to it. I agree that analogies are not explanations, but are heuristic devices for seeking explanations.[2] I also confess myself in error if it has been proved against me that I have used mythological analogy as a substitute for scientific reasoning (i.e. used it in contexts in which scientific reasoning would have been not only feasible but also more enlightening). This would be wrong, because science and mythology are two different ways of trying to explain phenomena, and they ought not to be confused with each other or used in each other's place. Up to this point my critics and I agree. But some of them will certainly disagree with me when I go on to express my belief that neither of these two approaches can do duty for the other, and that scientific reasoning cannot serve as a substitute for mythology. In earlier passages of this chapter I have touched upon the universally admitted limitations of the human reason's power to apprehend Reality by its analytical and classificatory method of working. The method of mythological analogy is, no doubt, a still more imperfect instrument for trying to apprehend Reality

---

Historical Review, vol. xxxii, No. 3 (September, 1951), pp. 201–19) that Toynbee's 'profusion of colourful and stimulating metaphors and similes, his skilful use of myth and poetry, philosophy and religion, to throw light on the past experience of Man in society, all this has reminded us that Clio is a muse and not merely a pedestrian statistical social scientist'.

1 Is Toynbee's use of myths meant to be merely confirmatory or is it meant to be evidential? The historians are left guessing. 'Is the historian's loss the poet's gain? . . . It is *not* a work of history. . . . Taken as a whole, it is a huge theological poem' (E. Fiess in *Toynbee and History*, pp. 380 and 383). 'The historian is a poet and the history is his poem' (T. S. Gregory in *The Dublin Review*, vol. 220, No. 440 (Spring, 1947), pp. 74–87). 'His . . . insights are not those typical of the historian, but rather those of the prophet, the seer, the poet, the mystic' (F. H. Underhill in *The Canadian Historical Review*, vol. xxxvi, No. 3 (September, 1955), pp. 222–35; cp. vol. xxxii, No. 3 (September, 1951), pp. 201–19). 'His Approach is poetic, intuitive' (Chr. Hill in *The Modern Quarterly*, Autumn, 1947, p. 295). 'His habit of mind is poetic, and it would be a mistake not to recognize his book as a prose epic, whatever else it may be besides' (W. H. McNeill in *The Intent of Toynbee's History: A Cooperative Appraisal*). Toynbee's work is 'an imaginative vision of history having the same relation to fact as has poetry' (A. Hourani in *The Dublin Review*, vol. 229, No. 470 (December, 1955), p. 382). 'Toynbee is writing history fundamentally as a poet and moralist and not as a scientific historian' (Hook in loc. cit., p. 692). 'At his best his theory is a kind of wild and tragic poetry softened by an ill-defined but clearly amiable religious faith and charity' (D. G. Macrae in *The Literary Guide*, January, 1955). 'The secret of Toynbee's greatness is that he is a poet and something of a mystic' (David Thomson in *The News Chronicle*, 14th October, 1954). 'As a poet, Toynbee is remarkable' (P. Geyl in *Debates with Historians*, p. 143). 'A . . . revival of . . . "the Christian Epic"' (H. E. Barnes in *An Introduction to the History of Sociology*, p. 719). 'Is Toynbee perhaps preparing the way for some future poet to write a new *Divina Commedia* or *Faust?*' (K. D. Erdmann in *Archiv für Kulturgeschichte*, xxxiii. Band, Heft 2 (1951), p. 236). Toynbee's history is a mythological drama (J. K. Feibleman in *T'ien Hsia Monthly*, vol. ix, Nos. 1 and 2 (1940), p. 172). The intelligible unity that Toynbee finds in history is the unity of a drama (McNeill, op. cit). 'He writes like a musician, developing his motifs in a series of academic variations' (R. H. S. Crossman in *The New Statesman*, 8th March, 1947). Crossman evidently does not think that this should earn me an acquittal; and M. Savelle concedes that there is poetry in history without conceding that an historian can be granted poetic licence (*The Pacific Historical Review*, vol. xxv, No. 1 (February, 1956), pp. 55–67).

2 This distinction is drawn by C. B. Joynt in a letter of 14th August, 1959.

than scientific reasoning is; the gleams or hints given to us by mythology are unverifiable; but, in compensation for its greater weakness, mythology has a wider reach than science and a deeper penetrative power.[1] Moreover, if there is truth in the account, given above, of the part played by the use of analogy in the progressive extension of the range of language and thought, then it is no accident that mythology has arisen earlier than science as a means of explanation, and poetry earlier than prose as a vehicle of expression. It also seems likely that mythology has a role to play, as a means of explanation, always and everywhere, not only in fields which science has not yet succeeded in entering, but also in those in which science has now established itself. For, even in long-since occupied territory, science's hold is never more than partial and incomplete.[2]

I therefore join issue with critics who take me to task for driving science and mythology in double harness. So long as we recognize and advertise that this mental equipage is a carriage-and-pair and not a one-horse shay, I believe that we can use it without misleading either ourselves or the public. I also believe that the two steeds, side by side, can carry us farther than either steed can by itself, and that a reconnaissance made by this method will not turn out to be a wild-goose-chase. The method is Plato's,[3] and his practice of it accounts for almost everything in his work that has proved to be of high enduring value. The Platonic conception of the place of myth in philosophy has been admirably expressed by Dean Inge:

'When the mind communes with the world of values, its inevitable language is the language of poetry, symbol, and myth. . . . Philosophy has to deal with a number of irreducible surds which cannot be rationalised. . . . Our reason . . . has reached its limits. We are driven to mythologize, confessing that we have left the realm of scientific fact.'[4]

As for being labelled a poet, I should be glad to be convinced that I deserve the title,[5] but I should not take this as acquitting me of the charges made against me that I have cited. What matters is not the name by which one is called but the extent of one's failure or success under any name or none. In the study of human affairs one cannot afford to neglect any approach. One must be free to resort to the different methods of the poet, the historian, and the scientist in turn, according to the nature of each piece of the task;[6] and, in order to enjoy this free-

[1] Like Vico, Toynbee has 'an understanding of myths as containing the essential truths of history' (J. K. Feibleman in *T'ien Hsia Monthly*, vol. xi, Nos. 1 and 2 (1940), pp. 165–6). Bagby allows that 'myths seem to be an essential part of the fabric of social life', and his proviso that 'they should not be allowed to stand in the way of a more rational understanding of history' will not be disputed—at any rate, not by me. See P. Bagby: *Culture and History*, p. 2.

[2] O. F. Anderle suggests that true myth embraces everything, including science (unpublished paper, cited already on p. 38, footnote 1).

[3] W. H. McNeill observes that my use of myth and metaphor is in the Platonic tradition (*The Intent of Toynbee's History: A Cooperative Appraisal*).

[4] W. R. Inge: 'The Place of Myth in History' in *Philosophy*, vol. xi, No. 42 (April, 1936), p. 131.

[5] I have never written poetry in the formal sense in any other languages than Greek and Latin.

[6] 'Historians must be both researchers and artists' (K. W. Thompson in *The Political Science Quarterly*, vol. lxxi, No. 3 (September, 1956), p. 367).

dom to use all the methods, it is best not to be tied to any of the corresponding names.

6. THE HEURISTIC USE OF HYPOTHESES

In the act of thinking we inevitably make two unprovable assumptions. One is that our thought apprehends, if only partially and imperfectly, a Reality that exists independently of it and is not just the mind's own mental construction.[1] Our second assumption is that Reality has some meaning for us which is accessible to us by the mental process of explanation.[2] We assume that Reality makes sense, even if perhaps not completely. That is to say, we assume that there is at least a certain amount of order and regularity in the relations between the myriad phenomena into which our image of Reality is dissected in our consciousness. 'We cannot treat the World as a mere succession of events.'[3] 'Science and sanity postulate a World in which there are certain fixed characters.'[4] 'All induction *assumes* the existence of connexions in Nature, and . . . its only object is to determine between what elements these connexions hold.'[5] Two expressions of this assumption are the beliefs in the uniformity of Nature[6] and in causation. Since this is true of all thought, it is true of thought about human affairs. 'The historian employs concepts and hypotheses because of the general assumption that underlies all social science: history is not exclusively chaos or chance: a degree of observable order and pattern, of partially predictable regularity, exists in human behaviour.'[7]

The assumption of the uniformity of Nature underlies all inductive reasoning—and much more of our stock of beliefs is based on inference than on experience. This assumption is not verifiable from experience. If we ask what justification we have for making it, all that we can say is that to deny the uniformity of Nature is to resolve the Universe into items that have no intelligible connexion with each other.[8]

One of the reasons why science has made unprecedented progress in modern Western hands is the practice, by scientists of this school, of virtues that are moral quite as much as intellectual. They have had the courage to create hypotheses for explaining the phenomena, the honesty to give their hypotheses up when these have not been borne out by the results of the investigations in which they have been used,[9] and the versatility to exchange them for others when, without having been refuted, they have been utilized up to the limits of their usefulness. All

[1] 'The choice among rival lines of division is an essential part of the process of rational inquiry. But, once such choice has been made, it is the nature of the pie or the Universe that determines the content of each part or division' (Cohen, op. cit., pp. 67–68). Scientists act on 'a belief that the Universe is rational, not derived from experience, but controlling the interpretation of experience' (Joseph, op. cit., p. 506).

[2] R. L. Shinn makes the point that meaning is the basis, not the conclusion, of thought and definition (*Christianity and the Problem of History*, p. 16).

[3] Joseph, op. cit., pp. 404–5. Cp. p. 426.

[4] Cohen, op. cit., p. 86.   [5] Joseph, op. cit., p. 401.

[6] Joseph points out ibid., pp. 402–3, that a belief in the uniformity of Nature is not inconsistent with a belief in Nature's variety.

[7] Social Science Research Council's Committee on Historiography's Report (1954), p. 95.   [8] Joseph, op. cit., pp. 401 and 424.

[9] A classic example (cited by Bagby in op. cit., p. 3) is Kepler's abandonment of Plato's *a priori* hypothesis that the orbits of the planets must be circular.

our currently accepted propositions, generalizations, and 'laws' are merely hypotheses that have not been discredited by experience so far.[1] 'All theories are trials: they are tentative hypotheses, tried out to see whether they work; and all experimental corroboration is simply the result of tests undertaken in a critical spirit, in an attempt to find out where our theories err.'[2] But 'theory is not necessarily bad because it is hypothetical, tentative, and not yet conclusively demonstrated or rejected'.[3] And 'theory that runs beyond the established data is the source of fertility in cumulative scientific analysis'[4]. The formation of an hypothesis may be likened to an act of artistic creation[5] or to the manufacture of a tool.

'A calculus is an artefact, and the interpretation of a calculus is a resolution to employ this artificial tool in a particular way.'[6]

Kroeber uses the word 'tool' to describe his key-concept, 'culture', and adds that the word applies to every concept.[7] One significant characteristic of tools is their number and variety.[8] Each of them is designed for doing a particular job. No tool is omnicompetent. There is no such thing as a master-key that will unlock *all* doors.[9] If we treat an hypothesis as a mental key, we shall discard it if we find that it unlocks no doors at all, and put it down for the moment in order to try another if, after having successfully opened a number of doors with its aid, we eventually come to a door into whose lock it does not fit.[10] But, when we do lay aside a well-tried key, we must not forget that it did unlock the previous doors. While it is true that there is no hypothesis that explains everything, this does not mean that each of our hypotheses is not good as far as it goes.[11]

This is what is meant by saying that the value and validity of hypotheses, and of those organized systems of hypotheses which we call

---

[1] 'The effectiveness of a[n inductive] policy is an empirical proposition which does not logically follow from the policy's effectiveness-in-the-past' (Braithwaite, op. cit., p. 269). This consideration governs the question of the validity of predictions made on the strength of scientific laws. 'The function of a scientific law . . . is . . . that of organising our empirical knowledge so as to give both intellectual satisfaction and power to predict the unknown. The nature of scientific laws cannot be treated independently of their function within a deductive system. The World is not made up of empirical facts with the addition of the laws of Nature: what we call the laws of Nature are conceptual devices by which we organise our empirical knowledge and predict the future' (ibid., p. 339). [2] K. R. Popper: *The Poverty of Historicism*, p. 87.
[3] Social Science Research Council's Committee on Historiography's Report (1954), p. 139. [4] Ibid., p. 137.
[5] Joseph, op. cit., p. 525. It is noteworthy that this simile should have been adopted by an austere-minded logician. [6] R. B. Braithwaite, op. cit., p. 69.
[7] A. L. Kroeber: *The Nature of Culture*, p. 118.
[8] Joseph, op. cit., p. 459, points out that we need alternative classifications for different purposes; Cohen, op. cit., pp. 67–68, that we need to choose between alternative classifications for each particular purpose.
[9] For instance, Geyl points out that it is impracticable to think of history exclusively in terms of the units that I call civilizations, and that this is demonstrated by my own practice of citing instances from the histories of smaller units, notwithstanding my contention that civilizations are the smallest units that are intelligible fields of study (*Toynbee and History*, pp. 71–72).
[10] Romein rightly insists that one ought to be prepared to drop a theory as soon as it has fulfilled its function (ibid., p. 348).
[11] Braithwaite, op. cit., p. 269, points out that there may be an exhaustion of the field for the profitable exploitation of a policy without the policy's past successes being impugned on this account.

sciences, is no more than 'heuristic' (i.e. exploratory)[1] and 'operational' and 'instrumental'. For instance, the usefulness of dialectical patterns, such as 'thesis-antithesis-synthesis' and 'challenge-and-response', is 'heuristic and operational; it must depend on their effectiveness in suggesting new fruitful questions, experiments, or techniques in dealing with problems'.[2] In Deutsch's expectation, modern control engineering may give us other patterns that will be more fruitful and suggestive.[3] 'An operational theory is one that is stated in such a way that it can conceivably be proved false by reference to empirical evidence.'[4] The theories used in social science 'are not statements of eternal and immutable truths; they are, rather, statements that may possibly provide valid explanations'.[5] 'Concepts are instrumental. They are formulated for the purpose of enlarging human understanding and are themselves subject to growth and change.'[6] 'The formulation of a law is arrived at with the "implicit proviso to modify it on the basis of later experiences".'[7] 'For the historian, . . . generalizations are hypotheses which he can use to open up a subject and suggest lines of approach, discarding, adapting, or continuing with them, as they prove fruitful.'[8] 'The only ultimate test of such provisional instruments of thought is neither their clarity nor their truth, but whether they lead to any useful results.'[9] 'No theory is definitive; every theory is provisional only. A theory will have yielded the best performance of which it is capable if it has kept going the flow of research.'[10] 'To study history in terms of *problems, some* theoretical framework and *some* working hypotheses are unavoidable.'[11] The purpose of putting forward heuristic hypotheses is

---

[1] See Chapter VII, pp. 243–6, and Chapter II, Annex: *Ad Hominem*, pp. 641–2.

[2] Deutsch, loc. cit., p. 245. Cp. Zahn, op. cit., p. 9.   [3] Deutsch, ibid.

[4] Social Science Research Council's Committee on Historiography's Report (1954), p. 28. In the same passage, Spengler's theories and mine are denied the benefit of this definition. 'Their theoretical structures should not be taken as examples of the use of social science methods' (ibid., p. 28. Cp. pp. 92–93). 'Toynbee's generalisations . . . must be elaborated to be testable propositions—an elaboration that the author does not provide' (ibid., p. 109). As O. F. Anderle puts it in his paper, my theorizing runs ahead of my verification of it. My verification of my hypotheses, he finds, is my obvious weak point. In K. R. Popper's view, this weakness is inherent in the historians' approach to the study of human affairs. 'As a rule, . . . historical "approaches" or "points of view" *cannot be tested*. They cannot be refuted, and apparent confirmations are therefore of no value, even if they are as numerous as the stars in the sky' (*The Poverty of Historicism*, p. 151). Here Popper is applying to the case of the historians a general proposition of his that has been quoted already on p. 23, footnote 7. An instance of a thesis that is intrinsically untestable, and is not merely so far untested, is found by C. B. Joynt in my Biblical conception of the freedom of human wills as being a freedom to obey or disobey 'laws of God' (*The Australasian Journal of Philosophy*, vol. 34, No. 3 (December, 1956), pp. 195–202).

[5] Social Science Research Council's Committee on Historiography's Report (1954), p. 91.   [6] Ibid., p. 19.

[7] G. Buchdahl in *The Australasian Journal of Philosophy*, vol. 34, No. 3 (December, 1958), p. 170, quoting M. Schlick: *Gesetz, Kausalität, und Wahrscheinlichkeit* (Vienna 1948, Gerold), p. 22.

[8] A. Bullock in *History Today*, February, 1951, pp. 5–11.

[9] G. A. Birks in *Philosophy*, October, 1950, pp. 336–40. *Ad hominem*, P. Kecskemeti observes, in *The Modern Review*, vol. 1, No. 4 (June, 1947), pp. 308–13, that 'the real test of Toynbee's theory is heuristic and empirical'. Kecskemeti judges that I am justified in my method, but that my basic concepts are too few to bear, without strain, the load that I have put upon them.   [10] Anderle, op. cit.

[11] Social Science Research Council's Committee on Historiography's Report (1954), p. 132. Bagby, in op. cit., p. 202, assigns this status to his 'conceptual framework'. Anderle points out, in his unpublished paper, that some of my critics do not seem to

to make approaches towards the attainment of new knowledge and understanding by a dialectical interplay of intellectual action and reaction.[1]

have realized that, in the activity of thinking, hypotheses have a role that is not merely legitimate but indispensable. 'It is', he writes, 'astonishing to find—especially in Geyl and critics of his school—that they apparently dispute an inquirer's right to be convinced of the validity of his own observations, conclusions, and proofs and to build these into the process of his thinking. Criticism can, of course, demonstrate that this or that point is untenable and, in doing so, sometimes bring to the ground an entire theoretical structure. But criticism cannot object to the procedure in itself, since, without this procedure, there can be no progress in scientific thinking. In the criticism of Toynbee's work, a particularly great part has been played by the reproach that he has anticipated his conclusions (*der Antizipationsvorwurf*).... Yet not a single participant in the debate has gone into the underlying epistemological problem. All the critics who bring up against Toynbee the reproach that he works with "anticipatory schemas" (*antizipierende Schemata*) seem to be quite unconscious of the fundamental importance of this function of *all* thinking—including, of course, their own. They appear to hold the naïve view that complex ideas are arrived at by the additive process of stringing together ideas of a more or less elementary kind. This is a point of view that has been left behind long ago in the modern psychological study of thought. The field of inquiry has shifted to the discussion of heuristic and verificatory method. The criticism directed against anticipating results seems to have overlooked this development, at any rate when it has been turned against Toynbee. Consequently it has missed fire.'

In another passage in his paper, Anderle makes the point that 'any man of learning is within his rights in arranging the material known to him in accordance with his theory, in order to see how far this will carry him. He has a right to do this without taking into consideration, for the moment, the possibility that contrary instances may come to light in the course of his researches.'

Of course, the inquirer ought to test the validity of his hypothesis or 'model' (see pp. 22–23 and 158–66) by applying it to all the apparently relevant evidence on which he can lay hands, and seeing whether it does or does not fit the phenomena. But, to apply an hypothesis or a 'model', one must have it in hand; one cannot have it without having first constructed it; and the materials out of which one constructs it cannot embrace all the evidence to which it is going to be applied after it has been constructed (see pp. citt.).

The line of criticism that Anderle criticizes may be illustrated by some examples. What Geyl says of me is that 'he introduces into his argument his own theoretical construction as an established datum' (*Toynbee and History*, p. 56). In M. A. Fitzsimons' view, my 'philosophy of history even dictates the organisation and selection of material' (*The Review of Politics*, October, 1957, pp. 554–5). In T. R. Fyvel's view, my work seems 'in the end frustrated, because it had always to be fitted into a pre-conceived brief' (*The Tribune*, 21st March, 1947). H. Werner finds in my work an 'external application of pre-fabricated schemata' (*Deutsche Vierteljahrsschrift für Literaturwissenschaft und Geistesgeschichte*, No. 29 (1955), pp. 528–44). J. K. Feibleman compares 'the iron rigidity' of my system to 'the medieval torture device of the iron woman' (*T'ien Hsia Monthly*, vol. xi, Nos. 1 and 2 (1940), p. 23). Patrick Gardiner compares my work to a jigsaw puzzle whose parts interlock only because they have been constructed to do so (*Time and Tide*, 30th October, 1954). See further p. 246, footnote 6.

On the other hand, Father M. C. D'Arcy holds that 'every great historian begins with a theory, and, though he modifies it in the face of evidence, he is nevertheless driven by it to select his evidence and marshal his facts' (*The Sense of History*, p. 60). 'The function and gift of the historian is to ask questions' (ibid., p. 59). E. E. Y. Hales holds that I am justified in contending 'that *some* interpretation, implied or stated, is firmly planted in every history' (*History Today*, May, 1955, p. 323). Father D'Arcy, too, maintains that 'history uses interpretation; it seeks for an intelligible pattern or whole' (op. cit., p. 23). The true historian has a theme and finds significance (ibid., p. 16). M. R. Cohen observes that 'philosophies of history are none the better for being held and transmitted unconsciously' (*The Meaning of Human History*, p. 5; cp. p. 35) and points out 'the essential role of ideas or hypotheses in the activity of the historian' (ibid., p. 68; cp. p. 78). 'Effective investigation demands some previous division or classification' (ibid., p. 65). 'The mere accumulation of facts will not indicate their significance. Some general idea or anticipatory hypothesis is necessary to define our field of investigation and to determine what facts are relevant to our inquiry' (ibid., p. 204). 'Men generally observe only what their ideas have prepared them to observe' (ibid., p. 204). In other words, if we did not have these antecedent ideas, we might fail to see anything at all; at the same time, we must be on guard against the danger that they may also limit our horizon.

[1] On this dialectical procedure, see further the Annex to Chapter II, pp. 641–2; E. F. J. Zahn in *Toynbee und das Problem der Geschichte*, p. 15; H. Marrou in *Esprit*, July, 1952, p. 124. Zahn and Marrou are referring particularly to my treatment of civilizations. In Marrou's view (expressed ibid.) civilization looks more like a real entity in

This purpose presupposes a readiness to modify or abandon an hypothesis if sufficient cause for doing so has been shown as a result of the test of debate.

But, if the use of hypotheses is indispensable, it also has at least one besetting danger: 'the habit of treating a mental convenience as if it were an objective thing'—an error that, in academic language, is called 'the hypostatisation of methodological categories'.[1] This is a confusion into which it is notoriously easy to fall unconsciously, because hypotheses and generalizations and concepts are, after all, realities, though they are realities of a different order from that of the phenomena which they are designed to apprehend, handle, and explain. This is, of course, a failure to distinguish between tools and their products or, to use broader terms, between means and ends.

In this connexion I have been accused of introducing into my argument my own theoretical construction, not just as a working hypothesis, but as an established datum,[2] and also of having 'an anthropomorphic conception of civilizations'.[3] I confess to having frequently written of them in anthropomorphic language, but this is not because I conceive of them in anthropomorphic terms. I think of them as operational concepts—'intelligible fields of study'—which are useful for exploring and explaining some important provinces of the domain of history, though not the whole domain. I also think of them as institutions: that is, as networks of impersonal relations between human beings. It is possible for them to be both these things at once. But of course neither concepts nor institutions are persons.

The reason why I do, nevertheless, use anthropomorphic language in dealing with civilizations is because I am driven to it by the poverty of the English language so far—a poverty that it shares, I believe, with all other languages up to date. Even the most sophisticated languages hitherto evolved have continued to be prisoners of all language's sensuous and mythological past, and consequently have failed almost entirely to equip concepts and institutions with vocabularies of their own,

a still-life cross-section tableau than when we look at it on the move. 'The essential point is that one should not make what is really a label or a classificatory concept into an idea or an ontological principle.'

[1] P. Geyl: *Debates with Historians*, p. 133. Cp. R. Pares in *The English Historical Review*, vol. lxxi, No. 279 (April, 1956), pp. 257–8; H. Tingsten in *Dagens Nyheter*, 16th January, 1949; A. R. Burn in *History*, February–October, 1956, pp. 2–3; W. O. Ault in *The Journal of Bible and Religion*, April, 1955.

[2] P. Geyl in *Toynbee and History*, p. 56 (quoted already in footnote 11 to p. 43); F. H. Underhill in *The Canadian Historical Review*, vol. xxxvi, No. 3 (September 1955), pp. 222–35 (quoted already in the Introduction to this volume, p. 1, footnote 5). Cp. E. E. Y. Hales in *History Today*, May, 1955, p. 320: 'He writes as though the principles he thinks he perceives were laws in the Newtonian sense.' A. L. Guerard, in a review of vols. i–iii of this book in *The Herald-Tribune*, 28th October, 1934, writes that Toynbee 'seems to forget, and he makes us forget, that his "laws" are valid only as hypotheses and approximations'. The same indictment has been made against H. T. Buckle by M. C. Swabey. 'Loose generalisations are quickly converted into premises for arguments, and the mere plausibility of conjectures is taken for their substantiation' (*The Judgment of History*, p. 84).

[3] W. Kaufmann in *Toynbee and History*, p. 310. H. D. Oakeley observes that 'there is a tendency in his work to "personify" civilization or treat it as something more than the individuals who, like many Atlases, "bear it up"' (*Philosophy*, vol. xi, No. 42 (April, 1936), p. 191). M. R. Cohen observes that to ascribe conscious purpose to groups is mythology (*The Meaning of Human History*, p. 125).

referring distinctively and exclusively to these two orders of reality. In the study of biological evolution, for example, the creation of a non-anthropomorphic vocabulary has been proving difficult, though it has been one of the main concerns of scientists in this field to dispense with the hypothesis of a creator god. The linguistic situation is even worse, if that is possible, in the field of human studies; but here the difficulty of avoiding the use of anthropomorphic language in writing about civilizations is, I should say, neither greater nor less than when one is writing about other institutions: states, peoples, churches, religions, classes, professions, and so on. I do not believe that any historian has, so far, ever managed to write more than a page or two of narrative without using 'anthropomorphic' or some other form of 'hypostatical' language in some degree. If I can be confronted with an instance to the contrary, I will admit that this verbal misrepresentation of the realities is avoidable and that, in so far as I have failed to avoid it, I deserve to be taken to task.

One test of whether the user of a concept or an hypothesis does think of it as being something more than a mental tool will be the degree of his readiness or unreadiness to drop it. In an appraisal of my work Kroeber writes, with characteristic generosity:

'His formal scheme presumably will mostly go the way of sociologic fit-alls. Actually, however he himself may regard it, this scheme has served him well as a scaffold from which to rear a most stimulating structure of further comparative interpretation of a large part of human history.'[1]

Another critic has given the correct answer to Kroeber's query. He has reported that I do not claim to have discovered any absolute, universal laws.[2] Anderle, in his survey of criticisms of my work, has found that some critics have ignored my recognition of the truth that all historical work is no more than provisional.[3] But at least one critic has testified in my favour on this point.

'One has the feeling that Toynbee, unlike Spengler, is really trying to subject his historical laws to empirical tests, and that he would have the integrity and the modesty, if given sufficient reason, to modify or abandon his laws.'[4]

I have done, and shall go on doing, my best to justify this good opinion of my intellectual honesty. In the first ten volumes of this book I have already given proof of my good faith in an instance which I apologize for mentioning again, after having cited it already, earlier in this chapter, in a different context. I laid aside my original hypothesis about the historical relation of 'higher religions' to 'civilizations' when I found that, while this might serve to explain the transition from an

---

[1] A. L. Kroeber: *The Nature of Culture*, p. 378. Cp. R. Caillois in *Diogenes*, No. 13 (Spring, 1956), p. 1.
[2] Father L. Walker, O.P., in *Toynbee and History*, p. 389.
[3] O. F. Anderle in his unpublished paper.
[4] W. H. Coates: 'Relativism and the Use of Hypothesis in History' in *The Journal of Modern History*, vol. xxi, No. 1 (March, 1949), p. 27, footnote 14.

earlier civilization to a later one, the role of higher religions as 'chrysalises' for civilizations was, in their own histories, no more than an
incidental one that did not explain their true mission. Accordingly, I
tried a new hypothesis about the relation of civilizations to higher religions, to see if this would be more illuminating as an explanation of
the higher religions' histories. This change of tools is, I should say, an
indication that I have a greater respect for the historical evidence than
I have for any particular hypothesis that I happen to have picked out of
my tool-bag. A large part of the present volume is occupied by similar
reconsiderations of concepts and hypotheses used in volumes i–x. I have
reviewed my previous notions and, where I have found reason, have
gone on to modify or abandon them. I have aimed at treating my own
past work no more tenderly than I should have treated anyone else's.
How far I have succeeded in achieving this ambitious aim will, no doubt,
be easier for my critics to judge than it is for me.

II. THE RELATIVITY OF A HUMAN OBSERVER'S APPROACH TO HUMAN AFFAIRS

AT the beginning of the preceding chapter we have taken note of
Reality's feat of looking at itself through a part of itself in the
shape of a conscious human mind. This feat is achieved through a
mental self-articulation of Reality into subject and object in the diffracting mind of a human observer. This is an indispensable condition
for attaining consciousness and for thinking. 'It is methodologically impossible to dispense with the viewpoint of *some* observer.'[1]

If this diffracting mental operation could have the effect of dividing
Reality itself into two really separate entities, our human enterprise of
finding our way about the Universe would be easier than it is. The supposedly actual division in Reality corresponding to the mental dissection
of Reality in our consciousness would then be like the pane of glass in
the window of a conning-tower. By looking out of its mental window the
mind could observe the objective world; by turning round and looking
inwards it could also observe itself; and it could conclude that, after having
taken its observations in both directions, it had obtained an accurate
picture both of itself and of external Reality. Unfortunately, in making
our assumption that there is an effective division in Reality corresponding to our dissection of it, we are, as we know, doing violence to the very
Reality that we are trying to apprehend. The pane of glass in our simile
cannot really be an insulator. It is an inseparable part of the same Universe as the adjoining atmosphere in the landscape beyond its outer face
and in the room inside its inner face. The glass, by its interposition,
makes a link, not a break; and, if the glass is really there, this is evidence that room and landscape are both really parts of one and the same
Universe, while, if the apparent presence of the glass pane between
them is an hallucination, in that case they are still more obviously one

[1] H. and M. Sprout: *Man-Milieu Relationship Hypothesis in the Context of International Politics*, p. 65.

and indivisible. The observing mind is, in fact, itself part of the Universe that it is trying to observe.[1] And this reading of our simile is borne out by everyday experience in a world in which there are more observing minds than one. Each mind is a subject only from its own individual standpoint. From the standpoint of every other mind, it is one of the objects in each of these other minds' objective world. And, if we found ourselves not being regarded by other minds as being objective realities, we should be astonished, affronted, and, even more, alarmed.

What are we to make of this undeniable truth that an observing human mind is itself part of the Universe, in spite of the Universe's appearing, as the mind surveys it, to lie outside the mind and, conversely, appearing to be observed by the mind from a mental standpoint outside the Universe? This truth means that the problem of observation is not an easy but a difficult one, and that, though it seems to be solved for practical purposes in the act of observation, this practical solution cannot be more than partial and imperfect. One necessary condition for perfect observation might appear, at first sight, to be that, during the act of observation, both the observer and his object should remain constant, without either of them being modified by the other or by any third agent. On second thoughts, however, it becomes evident in the first place that this condition is actually unattainable and in the second place that, if one could imagine it to have been attained, it would have defeated its own object by making the act of observation impossible to carry out. There cannot be observation without interaction between the observer and the object under his observation, and in interacting they are bound to affect each other reciprocally.[2] In terms of our simile of the conning-tower, the observer posted in it affects the degree of visibility in the landscape outside when he turns his searchlight on it, and the vision of the landscape given by this illumination of it affects the image obtained by the observer's eye. Moreover, if this reciprocal disturbance of both parties' previous state did not take place, there could be no observation, because the disturbance is set up—and this unavoidably—by the establishment of communication, and it is only through this disturbing operation that the act of observation is achieved.

The logical puzzle here brought to light is also illustrated by another of the mind's dissections of Reality: the dichotomy between creatures and their creator. In seeking to explain to themselves how the phenomenal world can have come into existence, some human minds in some societies have been led to propose the hypothesis that there must have been a creator. But a creator must, *ex hypothesi*, be outside his handiwork, as a potter is outside his earthenware, while at the same time he must be in contact with it, as the potter has to be with his clay. This logical dilemma has caught on its horns the inquirers into the riddle of cosmogony when they have become sophisticated enough to begin to philosophize. A god who is credited with having been the creator of the phenomenal world has to be banished from it by being relegated into a state of transcendence; yet, when once he has been thus placed in a

---

[1] See the passage quoted from Teilhard de Chardin on p. 8, footnote 3.
[2] This point is noted by Bagby in op. cit., p. 60.

possible position for performing the work of creation, he has thereby been deprived of the possibility of carrying the operation out. A complete insulation will have made him impotent, not omnipotent. If he is to create the Universe, he must be in contact with it. If he is to create it out of previously existing materials, he must be inside the same world as these; they themselves cannot be his handiwork; and their previous existence has then to be accounted for. On the other hand, if the creator has to create the phenomenal world out of nothing but himself, then in reality it will still remain a part of himself and the phenomena will be no more than unaccountable hallucinations in human minds that will also be unaccountably conscious.

Accordingly, the intellectual struggle with the problem of creation has made speculative minds first push God out of the phenomenal world and then pull Him back into it again. When He has been conceived of as being transcendent, He must also be conceived of as being immanent. If He is Brahmā, He must be Vishnu as well. But God Incarnate in an avatar cannot be the creator of a Universe of which He has revealed himself to be a part, while, on the other hand, if it is one of the inalienable attributes of divinity to be parked quite out of contact with the phenomenal world, somewhere in inter-stellar space (Epicurus's hypothetical *intermundia*), then it follows inevitably that the gods cannot either affect or be affected by mundane affairs. The difficulty that is encountered by a would-be observer is, in fact, inherent in the nature of the genus of which the activities of observation and creation are two species. Both these kinds of activity are relations, and every relation sets up a mutual disturbance of the parties to it.

For a would-be observer of the phenomenal world this difficulty is aggravated by one of the World's apparent characteristics. Phenomena have the appearance of being on the move through time and space; and, since the observer himself is one of these apparently travelling phenomena that he is surveying, he must do his intellectual work in a fellow traveller's never stationary driving-seat. For example, in the astronomical province of the mental field in which the general object of study is the physical cosmos, human observers are at present confined to the surface of one of the travelling stars; and our astronomers will not find themselves in any better position for taking their observations if they manage, one day, to make their way to the Moon or to Mars or to some planet in another solar system than ours or even in another galaxy. As athletes, they will have been as clever as Baron Munchhausen was when he jumped off the cannon's mouth on to the cannon-ball that had just come whizzing out of it, and when he then changed cannon-ball mounts in mid-air. But like the Baron the astronomers will still be travelling inside the realm of time and space whose physical phenomena they are studying, and the relativity of their own physical track through time and space to the tracks of the heavenly bodies that they are observing will still be affecting their scientific findings. It must, indeed, be affecting these at each successive configuration of the perpetually changing network woven by the respective space-time points through which each of the heavenly bodies, including the observer's own vehicle, is passing. It was a marvellous feat of intellectual imagination to realize that the actual astronomical observer, being imprisoned in space and time, could never take observations from the illusory vantage-point of an hypothetical observer inconceivably posted outside them. But thanks to Einstein's genius the point is now obvious to ordinary minds. It should be still more obvious when the phenomena that we are trying to observe are not the movements of the stars but are human affairs.

In this field of observation it is surely manifest that the observer himself is being carried, all the time, farther down the stream whose upper reaches he is attempting to survey from the crow's-nest on his travelling mast-head. The past course of the river of human history does not shift its bed. When once events have happened, they remain unchanged in fact. But they keep on changing their appearance because there are unceasing changes in the observer's own momentary position, which is the only position from which he can ever look back at the past.[1]

'In the sciences of Man, the rational core, common to all science, is diminished, obscured, and distorted by the inevitably partial perspective of the observer.'[2]

This is why, for the last two hundred years or so, each successive generation of modern Western historians has rewritten the history of the Hellenic World. The facts of Greek and Roman history have remained, throughout, what they always were, and our information about these

---

[1] 'The history of history eludes historical inquiry (*Die Geschichte der Geschichte entzieht sich der Historie*). There can be no scientific pronouncement about the whence and whither of history. One has to be inside history for any such question to be possible.' The sense of freedom comes from a conscious questioning of the past and the future, and this presupposes that human souls, as we know them, are already in existence (K. D. Erdmann in *Archiv für Kulturgeschichte*, xxxiii. Band, Heft 2 (1951), pp. 237 and 240). The historian is an observer who stands inside the framework of the events that he describes (K. W. Thompson in *The Political Science Quarterly*, vol. lxxi, No. 3 (September, 1956), p. 367). 'The meaning of the past is seen in the present, and, as the present changes, so does the meaning that we see in the past' (Social Science Research Council's Committee on Historiography's Report (1954), p. 23). This last point is also made by Bagby in *Culture and History*, p. 41.

[2] H. J. Morgenthau in *Toynbee and History*, p. 193. In the same context, Morgenthau points out that 'scientific' history is 'unproblematic in detail but a problem in its very conception of history'. It is, he suggests, an epistemological impossibility to study one civilization objectively from an observation-post in another civilization. If Burckhardt's idea of history is right, 'the great achievement of Mr. Toynbee as a historian lies in that very subjectivity that is the horror of scientific historiography'.

The would-be scientific and objective historians have, it would seem, been caught in a trap. Their pursuit of scientific objectivity has led them, as we have seen, to insist on the uniqueness of the human phenomena that they are studying. But, as Erdmann points out, a belief in the uniqueness of individuality implies a denial of the belief in the uniformity of human nature, and this denial, in its turn, leads to an affirmation of relativity that applies to the personality of the historian himself. 'Historiography becomes its own subject-matter (*Die Geschichtsschreibung wird sich selbst zum Gegenstand*)'—as it has become for Gooch and Butterfield and Collingwood, for instance. ' "Historism" (*Historismus*) and "existential" philosophy are expressions of the same intellectual process in two different provinces of study' (K. D. Erdmann in *Archiv für Kulturgeschichte*, xxxiii. Band, Heft 2 (1951), pp. 178–81).

In the same article (on p. 182) Erdmann remarks that the naïveté of my approach to history has saved me from inhibiting myself by 'ruminating in a broad way about the "ifs" and the "buts" of the [epistemological] problems involved in an undertaking like' mine. I admit to the naïveté of my first approach, and I agree with Erdmann's ironical comment that it gave me the hardihood to rush in where a philosophically sophisticated angel might have feared to tread. Now that my naïveté has allowed me to produce ten volumes, I can afford, in the present volume, to let myself consider the epistemological problem of relativity.

facts has not changed to anything like the extent that would be required if this change in our modern Western knowledge of the facts was to be taken as explaining the successive changes in the appearance of these facts to our modern Western eyes. There have been no losses of knowledge; we have preserved all our previous knowledge intact; and, in spite of our archaeologists' magnificent achievements in bringing to light buried buildings, works of art and technology, and inscriptions, the consequent additions to our knowledge have not been very great—at any rate not great enough to account for the continual changes in our view of Hellenic history. The changes in the appearance of the picture have been brought about, not by changes in the historical facts or in our knowledge of them, but by successive changes in the position of the modern observer. The only light that we can throw on the past is the light of our own experience. Any historian will inevitably be living and working in a particular social milieu at a particular stage of its development, and his own situation will make him sensitive to some features in a past situation and blind to others. In recent centuries our experience in the West has been changing, from one generation to another, sufficiently to produce appreciable changes in the distribution of our sensitive spots and our blind spots. Nineteenth-century Western students of Hellenic history were sensitive, for instance, to the constitutional aspect of Greek and Roman political life, and particularly to manifestations of democracy; their twentieth-century successor's eye is caught by the economic facet of Greek and Roman life and by manifestations of bureaucracy and dictatorship. Different features of an unchanging landscape appear to be the salient features in each successive generation. In each case these things that seem to stand out from the rest are things whose significance has been brought home to the historian by his own experience in his own day.[1]

Westerners of the present generation feel that, in these recent centuries, the Western way of life has been changing at a pace that has been accelerating until it has now become uncomfortably fast. Yet the West has been singular, and fortunate, in having been free to move at its own pace. No outsiders have been setting its pace for it. In contrast to the Western peoples, all other peoples in the World have been having their pace set for them, during these same recent centuries, by the West. They have been having to try to catch up with the West in the field of the West's own special achievements in order to hold their own against the West. So in recent times the non-Western World's pace,

---

[1] This point has been well taken by Bagby. 'Every human activity must find its origin in present human needs' (op. cit., p. 48). 'Each generation must find its own interpreters, the historians who will show how the past can be related to the new needs and problems of the day' (ibid., p. 49). In other words, 'all true history is contemporary history' (B. Croce: *Teoria e Storia della Storiografia* (Bari 1917, Laterza), p. 4). F. A. Hayek, too, holds that 'we . . . study particular events because they have contributed to create the particular environment in which we live, or because they are part of that environment' (*The Counter-Revolution of Science*, p. 70). At the same time, Hayek rightly contests the doctrine that all historical knowledge is *necessarily* relative. 'The kernel of truth in the assertion about the relativity of historical knowledge is that historians will at different times be interested in different objects, but not that they will necessarily hold different views about the same object' (op. cit., p. 70). Yet, though this is not inevitable, it can happen and has, in fact, happened frequently.

by comparison with the West's pace, has been revolutionary. This means, among other things, that in our day a Russian or a Muslim or a Hindu or a Chinese or a Japanese has been having to make far more drastic revisions of his view of the past—particularly his own society's past—than any that a Westerner has had to make in his view of the Hellenic past. The facts of Russian, Muslim, Indian, and East Asian history have not changed, any more than the facts of Hellenic history have changed. But the modern African or Asian or Russian observer has had to move still faster and farther, between one generation and another, than the contemporary Western observer has.

This inherent relativity of the historical kind of observation has been brought to our attention by the world-wide acceleration of the pace of social and cultural change in the current age. But this is not the first instance within our knowledge. We know of previous revolutions that have produced comparable changes between the pre-revolutionary and the post-revolutionary view of the past. After the 'epoch-making' overthrow of the Achaemenian Empire by Alexander the Great and the consequent incorporation of Egypt and South-West Asia in the Hellenic World, Hellenic historians—for example, Polybius and Diodorus among those whose works have partially survived—looked back on the pre-Alexandrine age of Hellenic history with different eyes from Thucydides' or even Herodotus's. Herodotus had a lively curiosity about the ways of life in the regions that Alexander was subsequently to bring under Hellenic domination, but the pre-conquest and post-conquest Hellenic pictures of these non-Hellenic civilizations were not the same. After a subsequent religious revolution in the Hellenic World, Hellenic converts to Christianity conflated the traditional Hellenic picture of world history, as presented in the works of pre-Christian post-Alexandrine Hellenic historians, with the traditional Jewish picture of world history, as presented in the Jewish holy scriptures, which the Christian Church had incorporated in its Bible, and they transformed both these pictures not only by conflating them but also by reinterpreting them in terms of the Christian conception of God's plan leading from the Creation to the Last Things. After yet another religious revolution of comparable magnitude, Christian and Zoroastrian converts to Islam similarly reinterpreted in Islamic terms the traditional picture of pre-Islamic history that they had inherited from their non-Muslim forebears. At the present day we can watch converts to Communism at work on reinterpreting in Marxian terms the traditional pictures of past history that have hitherto held the field in the West and in the domains of the other living civilizations.

These kaleidoscopic changes in the appearance of the past illustrate the problem of relativity which besets historians, anthropologists, sociologists, economists, and other students of human affairs—not least, perhaps, the psychologists. It is the same problem that besets astronomers, physicists, and other students of non-human nature. Whatever the nature of the object that is under observation, a human observer is incapable of seeing it with the imaginary detachment of an inconceivable outsider. If his study is physical science, he can see the physical cosmos only with the eye of one mobile human participant in an apparent network of physical events that is perpetually changing its configuration in time-space. If he is a student of human affairs, he can see these only as a perpetually unfolding human drama. In every case his view of the past will be conditioned by the ever-changing position of his own present observation-point. Relativity is a limitation that is imposed on human studies in all fields by the very nature of the situation in which a conscious human mind finds itself; and it is a situation from which there is no escape.

In this matter of relativity the student of human affairs is in the same boat as the student of non-human nature; but the boat is partitioned by a bulkhead, and, on the humanist's[1] side of this, there are two holes in the boat's hull, not just one. Like the physicist, the humanist has the problem of relativity to cope with, but he has also to cope with the problem of bias; and from this the physicist seems to be exempt.

The physicist has to contend with the difficulty that the measurements which he registers of objects, events, or relations between objects or events in the physical cosmos will vary according to the speed with which he and his measuring-instrument are approaching towards, or receding from, the thing that he is trying to measure. This fluctuation that complicates the physicist's work is a mental occurrence, but it occurs only at the observational and interpretative level, that is to say at the intellectual level. The unavoidable play of relativity makes the physical objects of his study intellectually elusive for the physicist, as it also makes human affairs elusive for the humanist. But the physical scientist does not also have to contend, as the student of human affairs does, with discriminatory judgements of value and with partisan reactions of feeling for or against the objects of his study. In the physical scientist's field the objects are non-human, even when they are not inanimate, and this means that, in the psyche of a human student of them, they do not evoke 'affective' feelings or value judgements. The physical scientist is unlikely to catch himself admiring or loving this or that nebula, solar system, molecule, atom, or electron and despising or hating this or that other one. It requires quite a feat of scientific engineering to bring a remote nebula or even a close-up electron within the field of the observer's perception. Any specimen is welcome grist to his intellectual mill; but all specimens leave him emotionally and morally indifferent. On the level of feeling and valuation they are all one to him. By contrast, the student of human affairs has an ethical and emotional problem

---

1 The word 'humanist' is used in this volume in its literal meaning of a 'student of human affairs', without the implication, which it sometimes carries, of a belief, in the humanist's mind, that human affairs can and ought to be studied in exclusively human terms, without taking account of religious beliefs in the existence and intervention of a spiritual presence or presences higher than Man. To describe this point of view, I shall be using the words 'rationalism' and 'rationalist'. Of course, a humanist can be a rationalist as well, just as a 'Germanist'—the German term for a student of Teutonic antiquities —can also be a holder of the belief that the Teutons are 'the master race' (*Herrenvolk*). The Germans' English fellow Teutons find this German belief quaint (though some English people actually hold it with an un-German unselfconsciousness). But if Teutonolatry is ridiculous, can anthropolatry escape the same charge? Does the notion of a *Herrenvolk* become any less fantastic when it is extended to the human race at large instead of being confined to the Teutonic fraction of it?

as well as an intellectual one to contend with. The objects of his study
are human beings of like passions with himself. And it is impossible for
one human being to think about another human being, present or
absent, living or dead, without also having feelings about him and
passing judgements on him. He either likes him or dislikes him; regards
him as being either beneficent or maleficent; feels him to be either a
friend or an enemy; judges his actions to have been either right or
wrong; and appraises his character as being either good or bad, either
righteous or wicked.[1]

We may say with our lips that, when we are making an historical study
of our fellow human beings, we suspend our moral judgements and
suppress our feelings; but, if we fancy that we can do that, we are deceiving ourselves.[2] 'All interpretations of human events which profess to

---

[1] *Ad hominem*, the Rev. E. R. Hardy Jr. notes that my 'historical and ethical judgments interlock. He is sure, for instance, that earthly militancy ruins a religion. As moral
theologian he is sure that it ought to, and as historian he notes that it usually has'
(*The Intent of Toynbee's History: A Cooperative Appraisal*). T. A. Sumberg observes
that, 'by . . . yielding to the pressure of his personal predilections, Toynbee makes his
reader acutely aware of how time and space limit a historian's vision—a fact which he
laments so audibly with respect to other historians' (*Social Research*, vol. 14, No. 3
(September, 1947), pp. 267–84). F. Borkenau, too, criticizes me for moralizing (in
Commentary, May, 1955, pp. 241–2). A. L. Kroeber finds my mind old-fashioned 'in
founding its system of the ultimate interpretation of human history on explanations
through character and morals. Therefore the distinctive and differential qualities of his
civilizations are largely missed or ignored' (*Style and Civilizations*, p. 127).

On the other hand, Father M. C. D'Arcy draws the distinction that I have drawn
above. 'In science the subject matter does not call for moral judgment, and the emotions
of the scientist are not engaged. But the subject matter of history is human conduct.
Moreover, the historian cannot divest himself entirely of his feelings and beliefs; and, if
he were to try to do so, he would blind himself to what is the nature of human action'
(*The Sense of History*, p. 167).

Robert Redfield, too, holds that we cannot study human conduct without placing
values on it (*The Primitive World and its Transformations*, pp. 139–41). 'It is easy enough
to be objective towards objects; but the human individual refuses to be only an object.
When he is there before you, he insists on being judged as human beings are judged in
life, if not in science' (ibid., p. 152). Redfield's view is derived from his own experience
as a field anthropologist. 'In the very necessity to describe the native, one must feel for
him—or perhaps against him. The feelings are mixed with valuations. In Indian communities in which I have worked, I have found myself constantly liking and disliking
some people as compared with others, and some aspects of the total culture as compared
with others. . . . Objectivity . . . requires me to become aware of the values I have that
may lead me in one direction rather than another. . . . But I do not think that it asks me
that I divest myself of the human qualities, including valuing. I could not do my work
without them' (ibid., p. 154). 'In me, man and anthropologist do not separate themselves sharply' (ibid., p. 165).

On this point, M. C. Swabey takes the same view as Father D'Arcy and Robert Redfield. 'To a far greater extent than in science . . . the historian's compilation of facts
reflects the social background and preferences of the compiler. Not only is he, like the
scientist, part of the physical world, but in a far more intimate way he is part of a particular society' (*The Judgment of History*, p. 233). 'In a sense, history is always concerned
with the preservation of values. . . . Everywhere scales of preference and importance are
woven into its accounts' (ibid., p. 55). The role that is characteristic of the historian is the
judicial one (ibid., p. 238). In Swabey's view, however, valuation is an inseparable concomitant of study even where the object of study is non-human nature. She pillories
'the falsity of trying to exclude values from the method and content of knowledge' (ibid.,
p. 241). 'Valuation . . . is omnipresent in experience. . . . All alleged knowledge (not
excepting the scientific) is essentially evaluative. . . . Acceptance of a framework of values
as authentic presuppositions is the condition of natural knowledge' (ibid., p. 250).

[2] 'The approach to history which will be advocated here is essentially aesthetic rather
than moral. It involves a sympathy with things as they are, rather than as they ought to
be. It is the point of view of the scientist or the saint as opposed to that of the political
or religious reformer' (P. Bagby: *Culture and History*, p. 48). In the present writer's
judgement, Bagby usually fails to live up to this claim when he touches on the subject of

exclude ethics actually smuggle in uncritical ethical judgments.'[1] Feelings and judgements are inherent in all relations between one human being and another.[2] This is, of course, generally recognized in the case of relations that are competitive: e.g. personal rivalries, business competition, litigation, political contests, war. Perhaps there is an element of competition in all the relations of practical life. But it may be asked whether it is really impossible to be unemotional and uncensorious in one's attitude towards one's fellow human beings when one's relation towards them takes the form, not of action, but of study. Is not this a relation in which the observer's personal interests are not engaged, even if the people whom he is studying are his living contemporaries? *A fortiori*, if they are now dead, and have been dead for hundreds or thousands of years, cannot the historian study them with the emotional and ethical indifference that comes so easy to the physicist in his study of his electrons and his galaxies?[3] This question is answered in the

religion. In these passages there is an animus showing through a cloak of irony; Bagby has not really got rid of the religious reformer in himself; he has turned him inside out, but he is still transparently the Old Adam.

The approach attempted by Bagby is also proposed by G. A. Birks in a letter to me of 23rd January, 1949. He suggests 'eliminating all values' on the ground 'that they are irrelevant in any connexion in any scientific inquiry, and harmful both to the pursuit of truth and to its acceptance. Other sciences have found it difficult to eliminate them, but have found new vitality after doing so: e.g. chemistry (long preoccupied with the "precious" metals) and astronomy (with its former bias towards "perfect" circular motion).' It is undoubtedly true that, in the study of non-human affairs, the introduction of human values is out of place and that there is everything to be gained by getting rid of this incongruous and confusing importation. But it does not follow that human values can similarly be eliminated from the study of human affairs. In my belief the suggested analogy of the sciences dealing with non-human nature does not hold good on this point.

However, Trinkaus has criticized me on the ground that I have achieved what appears to me to be Bagby's aim. According to Trinkaus, the comparative method of study that I have followed has broadened the view of history, but this at the cost of taking the element of value and purpose out of our view of ourselves (*Science and History*, vol. xii, No. 1 (1948), p. 221). This judgement seems hardly compatible with Sumberg's cited on p. 54 in footnote 1. One of the two must surely be mistaken. I myself agree with Sumberg.

1 M. R. Cohen: *The Meaning of Human History*, p. 287.

2 Frederick Schuman is recognizing this truth when he commends me (in *The Nation*, 6th November, 1954) for 'boldly making judgments and seeking no refuge in specious detachment'.

3 Sorokin seems to imply that we can achieve this scientific detachment in studying human affairs, for he criticizes my account of the rises and falls of civilizations on the ground that I have presented evaluative formulae of progress and regress but not true formulae of change (P. A. Sorokin in *Toynbee and History*, p. 180. Cp. p. 183). Yet it is not easy to find formulae of change that do not carry connotations of value. In my series of four terms—'genesis', 'growth', 'breakdown', 'disintegration'—the last three, at any rate, obviously imply that the changes described by them involve gains or losses in value. In applying this scheme to Egyptiac history, I applied my term 'breakdown' to the stage in which 'the Old Kingdom' went to pieces, and my term 'disintegration' to all that followed after—labelling 'the Middle Empire' and 'the New Empire' as 'rallies' which temporarily arrested the process of 'disintegration' but did not ultimately reverse it. This application of my scheme has been courteously but firmly rejected by J. A. Wilson in *The Burden of Egypt* (Chicago 1951, University of Chicago Press), p. 32, footnote 12. Wilson is one of the foremost living authorities on the Egyptiac Civilization, and, in the light of his criticisms and others, I have reconsidered and revised, in the present volume, my previous view of the structure of Egyptiac history. At the same time, I find that Wilson's own picture of this resembles mine in carrying with it connotations of value. In Wilson's morphology of Egyptiac history, the two periods of political disunity between 'the Old Kingdom' and 'the Middle Empire' and between 'the Middle Empire' and 'the New Empire' are labelled respectively 'the First Intermediate Period' and 'the Second Intermediate Period'. These labels are, of course, correct in the sense that these two periods of political disunity were in truth intermediate between three periods of political unity. But it is equally true that those three periods of political unity were intermediate

negative by the evidence of a classical test case in which the conditions have been as favourable to the possibility of indifference as they could ever conceivably be. It is also answered in the negative by a consideration of the nature of Man and the consequent nature of relations between human beings.

This identical finding of deductive reasoning and empirical observation cannot, I believe, be gainsaid. But, if it cannot, that is not the last word; it is an indication that we are face to face with a problem that we can neither evade nor ignore. If we come to the conclusion that feelings and judgements cannot be eliminated from human relations, even when these take the relatively anodyne form of a scholar's academic exercise, this does not constrain us also to conclude that there are no steps that we can and ought to take for coping with this particularly awkward feature of the human situation. There are possible steps that can be at any rate partially effective; and we must consider these, with the earnest intention of taking them. But we shall be in a better position to do this when we have fully faced the difficulty of the task.

Let us examine, as our test case, whether it has actually proved possible to be emotionally and ethically indifferent when one is studying, and writing about, some controversial personality. Let us rule out the living: Mr. Khrushchév, for instance, and Mr. Nixon and Pandit Nehru and Colonel Gamāl 'Abd-al-Nāsir. The negative answer to our question would be obtained too easily on these tests. Let us also rule out the recently dead: John Foster Dulles, for instance, and Franklin D. Roosevelt, Stalin, and Hitler. These personalities still arouse the feelings and evoke the judgements that they aroused and evoked in their lifetimes. Let us even rule out controversial figures that have been dead now for some time, but whose souls go marching on: such posthumously potent personalities as John Brown and Karl Marx and Calvin and Luther. Let us take the Egyptian Pharaoh Ikhnaton, who lived and died in the fourteenth century B.C., and let us remind ourselves of his extraordinary history.

Ikhnaton stood for a revolution[1] in every important sphere of cultural and spiritual life: in literature, in art, and, above all, in religion. This made him an acutely controversial figure in his lifetime; and, when his opponents regained the upper hand after his death, they vented their hatred of him by chiselling out his name from his inscriptions and

between four periods of political disunity. Thus it would have been equally logical to label the periods of unity 'intermediate', and to call the periods of disunity by some descriptive name: let us say, 'periods of local liberty'. Why has Wilson chosen to call these periods of local liberty 'intermediate' and given descriptive names to the intervening periods in which local liberty was restricted or even suppressed? Surely his terminology has been determined by an unspoken value-judgement. Wilson evidently thinks of the periods of political unity as being the 'great' periods of Egyptiac history, and thinks of the periods of political disunity as being temporary lapses from the ideal.

[1] It is best to use this form of words, because it avoids begging the question whether Ikhnaton was the real author and initiator of the revolution associated with his name and his reign, or whether he was a stalking-horse, figure-head, or puppet who was manipulated and exploited by other people. The evidence for answering this question with certainty may never come into our hands. But it is certain that Ikhnaton became the symbol of the revolution in the minds of both his collaborators and his opponents, and this undisputed fact is all that is needed to make his history a relevant test case for our present purpose.

by blackening his memory. Ikhnaton was remembered vividly in his own world as an arch-criminal so long as the Egyptiac Civilization lasted. But it did not last for more than about sixteen hundred years after Ikhnaton's death. In and after the third century of the Christian Era, people in Egypt began to forget how to write and read any of their traditionai scripts. The memory of the whole history of Pharaonic Egypt was almost entirely lost; and, for the next sixteen hundred years, there was no one alive in the World who knew that such a person as the once notorious Ikhnaton had ever existed. Then, in the nineteenth century, modern Western scholars deciphered the Egyptiac scripts, and in the eighteen-eighties they dug up Ikhnaton's archives and published them. So, after having been buried in oblivion for sixteen centuries, Ikhnaton became notorious again; and, as soon as this happened, the challenging personality that he had been, or at any rate had been taken to be by his contemporaries, quickly aroused something of the same passion, for him and against him, among modern scholars in Western countries as it had aroused in his lifetime in Egypt.

This example—and it is only one of a number that could be cited—shows that the problem presented to students of human affairs by feelings and judgements is not a problem that is solved automatically by the mere passage of time. We do not find it surprising that a challenging personality like Franklin D. Roosevelt's should still be arousing passionate feelings when the hero or villain has been dead for no more than sixteen years. But, if we assume that such feelings were then still haunting his memory simply because he had been in the land of the living so recently, we are not facing the problem of bias squarely. The case of Ikhnaton indicates that this problem will always dog the historian, however remote in time and place the human object of his study may be.

But we do not have to depend on an induction from historical evidence to convince us that, in the study of human affairs, the elimination of feelings and judgements is impracticable. The cogent proof of this proposition lies in the consideration that, if we did succeed in making ourselves emotionally and morally indifferent to a human being whom we were studying, we should have thereby made it impossible for us to go on studying him as a human being. To be human means being morally responsible and therefore responsive to moral judgements—other people's judgements and one's own judgements—about oneself. It also means being emotionally sensitive to feelings about oneself—one's own feelings and other people's. However exasperating or crushing other people's feelings and judgements about oneself may be, it is not so painful to have to bear them as it would be desolating to be relieved of them; for, however hostile and unfavourable they may be, they are certificates that one is still being regarded as human by one's fellow human beings; and, so long as one really is human, life would be intolerable if these certificates of one's humanity were to be withdrawn.

Human beings smile when they see a dog vindictively break his teeth on a stone against which he has stubbed his toe. Only a poor brute beast, we reflect, would be so irrational as to mistake an inanimate object for a responsible agent who could be taught a lesson or at least be made to pay for his offence. Xerxes has earned undying derision by his canine folly in flogging the waters of the Dardanelles as a punishment for their having carried away his bridges. Such childishness, we feel, is beneath a grown-up human being's dignity. Human adults do not bite stones or flog waves. And, if they are attacked by a non-human living creature—a shark, say, or a man-eating tiger, or a bacillus—they do not feel the anger and indignation that they would feel if they were being attacked by a human assailant. They just try to save their lives, as they would if they were being imperilled by a fire or a shipwreck or an avalanche. Again, they do not think it reasonable to resent or condemn the behaviour of a fellow human being who has gone out of his mind or become senile, and they feel that allowances ought to be made for infants and invalids.

These attitudes are rational and humane, but they are not complimentary. They imply a recognition that the fellow human being who benefits by them has permanently or temporarily lost, or has not yet gained, the priceless gift of being completely human. As the invalid recovers and the infant grows up, the indulgence granted to them is progressively withdrawn, and its withdrawal is not an act of inhumanity; on the contrary, it is the recognition of the recovery or attainment of full human moral stature, with its corollary, full human moral responsibility. The spectacles of lunacy and dotage are harrowing because here there is no expectation of recovery; and, for human beings, the continuance of mere physical life without human rationality and responsibility is a fate far worse than physical death. Perhaps I have now demonstrated my thesis that complete emotional and moral indifference towards a human object of study would enable this study to become entirely objective at the cost of making it utterly impossible. It would mean that the object of study had ceased to be human in the student's eye, and this, in turn, would mean that there was no longer a human relation between the two parties. If, on these terms of emotional and moral indifference, the study could continue at all, it could only be on the basis of treating the object of study as an automaton, and this would surely deprive the study of all further significance and value.

How, then, are we to cope with our feelings and judgements about human beings whom we are trying to study, when we have faced the truth that we cannot cope with feelings and judgements by eliminating them? Clearly we cannot be content just to take note of this question without trying to find an answer to it. We must try, because these feelings and judgements that it is impossible to eliminate are not, on that account, necessarily justifiable. Perhaps they might be if the rationality that gives dignity to human nature were complete and all-pervasive. Unhappily, as we well know, rationality is only one facet of a human psyche; another of its facets is its self-centredness, and this is a vice which is capable of vitiating any feelings and judgements and which therefore renders all feelings and judgements suspect.

For example, a person's feelings and judgements about another person with whom he happens to be in competition or in conflict are rightly suspect in the eyes of everyone else, and also in the eyes of the person who is experiencing the feelings and making the judgements, if he has any capacity at all for introspection and reflection. It is a sound working rule to presume, unless and until convincing evidence has been produced to the contrary, that a human being is self-centredly prejudiced in his own favour. But self-centredness in the singular is not the only form of the vice. There is also self-centredness in the plural.[1] In Arabic there is a word for it: *nahniyah*, which, in Western languages that draw on Latin to extend their vocabularies, can be translated literally by coining the word 'nosism', as a plural for the singular word 'egotism' which is already well established. Self-centredness is perhaps even more difficult to cope with in its plural form than it is in the singular, because in the plural it is both more insidious and more potent.

It is more insidious because, when a human being is acting self-centredly, not solely on his individual account, but in the name of his family, parish, nation, state, or church, he can delude himself into imagining that he is acting on behalf of something that is not only greater than himself but is outside himself, and that therefore he is acting altruistically and even self-sacrificingly—as, for instance, when he risks, and perhaps loses, his life by serving his country as a soldier. In reality, of course, when I have expanded my singular 'me' into our plural 'us', my singular is still contained in our plural. The act of changing the grammatical number of my self-centredness has not disengaged me from it; it has actually made it more difficult for me to cope with by giving me a plausible ground for imagining that I have disengaged myself from it, though I have not.

Self-centredness is also far more dangerous in the plural than it is in the singular. Someone who is pursuing his singular self-interest may be checked by a guilty conscience and a sense of shame in himself, even before he draws on himself the disapproval and opposition of his neighbours, who, collectively, are likely to be able and eager to keep him within bounds. Someone who is pursuing a plural self-interest will be more prone to feel self-righteous; he will also have collaborators whose fellow feelings will confirm his confidence in the righteousness of his cause; and the collective power that he and they can jointly apply for putting their self-centred aim into action will be immeasurably stronger than the power of each of them acting individually.

If it were conceivable that Man's pre-human ancestors could have become fully human without having become social beings in the process, a completely human but at the same time utterly solitary individual would be one of the weakest of living creatures, because, in isolation, he would not be able to take much advantage of the potentialities of power latent in the freedom and the grasp of his hands, in the stereoscopic vision of his co-ordinated pair of eyes, and in the intelligence of his exquisitely organized brain. Robinson Crusoe managed to bring

[1] This important point has been well taken by M. C. Swabey. 'Egoism . . . is by no means lacking in social scope, since a man's self-interest tends to be as wide as the circle on which he depends' (*The Judgment of History*, p. 230). 'Social consciousness is never free from self-love, and experience plainly shows how a man may be "socialised" in the service of a group without at all relinquishing self-love as his supreme value. . . . A great gulf separates our fellow-feeling for the existent members of our society from respect for the dignity of Man' (ibid., p. 142).

ashore with him, out of the wreck, a fair sample of the material equipment that was the cumulative product of human co-operative enterprise up to date, and he also inherited the accumulated knowledge of the use of such tools as he had. Thus, even when marooned on his island, he was by no means isolated in reality; he was isolated only in the present; he still shared in the common heritage from the past. Yet, even so, he was constantly finding that the absence of present companions set disconcerting limits to his power—as, for instance, when he had used his tools and his skill successfully to build a big boat in the well-timbered interior of his island, without having remembered that it would need the muscle-power of more human beings than one to move the completed boat down to the water's edge.

Co-operation enormously increases the possibility of turning to account Man's potentialities for exerting power. Accordingly, a human being's self-centred pursuit of self-interest can be far more effective, besides being likely to be less conscience-stricken and therefore less hesitant, when the first person of the active verb is in the plural number. This consideration applies to relations of all kinds between human beings: to the study of human affairs no less than to the so-called practical kinds of human social activity. This point is particularly pertinent to our present inquiry, because so large a part of the study of human affairs is concerned with Man in the plural, not in the singular.

How are we to deal with these feelings and judgements that always assert themselves in us when we are studying human affairs, however apparently remote these may be from ourselves and from our own interests? We cannot afford not to do battle with our self-centredness in both the singular and the plural. The degree to which we succeed in extricating ourselves from it gives the measure of the level of our knowledge and understanding of a universe which, in reality, does not centre on us.[1] The first step is to try to drag our feelings and judgements up into the full light of our consciousness and to try to see them as they are.[2] The effort demanded by this undertaking is a moral as well as an intellectual one. Unless we can bear self-mortification, we shall not be able to carry self-examination to the necessary painful lengths. Without humility there can be no illuminating self-knowledge. In fact the moral and the intellectual effort must go hand in hand, and, in both aspects, the enterprise is difficult and strenuous. However able, open-minded,

---

[1] See M. C. Swabey: *The Judgment of History*, pp. 5–6.
[2] The need for such self-examination has been widely recognized. See, for instance, the passage quoted on p. 20 from K. R. Popper's *The Poverty of Historicism*, p. 152. 'A perfect objectivity is, no doubt, impossible, but it must always be our goal, and we should do well to become fully conscious of our individual biases in order to be able to discount them ourselves and to help others to do so' (Bagby, op. cit., p. 4). 'The safeguard against bias is not to indulge in useless resolutions to be free from bias but rather to explore one's pre-conceptions, to make them explicit, to consider their alternatives, and thus to multiply the number of hypotheses available for the apprehension of historical significance' (Cohen, op. cit., p. 80. Cp. p. 115). 'The need for awareness of bias . . . rests on the widely accepted psychological theory that selectivity in the individual's response to any stimulus is unavoidable. The remedy proposed by psychologists is not to strive to eliminate the element of selectivity, not to assume that by careful attention one can become an objective recording machine, but rather to define the basis for selection' (Social Science Research Council's Committee on Historiography's Report (1954), p. 85).

and humble-hearted an inquirer may be in analysing himself, many of his fundamental prejudices—and these are the most warping prejudices of all—are likely to escape detection, just because they are buried at so deep a level of the subconscious abyss of the psyche. There are limits to a human being's ability to read the secrets of his own heart, however sincerely and valiantly he tries. So the enterprise of self-examination can never be carried through to complete success. This, however, is no argument for refraining from making the attempt; for it is not a case of all or nothing. Even the smallest advance in self-knowledge is so much to the good.

In any inquiry it is wise to make one's approach by starting from what is least obscure. On this principle the most promising starting-point for an attempt to examine oneself would be to consider how one's outlook has been affected by one's education. The word 'education' should, of course, be construed in a broad enough sense to include, not just formal schooling, but the whole influence of one's total social and cultural environment since one's birth: the civilization, country, parish, and family into which one happens to have been born; one's mother-tongue;[1] one's parents' religion, social class, and profession; one's personal education, in the narrower sense of the word,[2] and profession in after life; and the extent of one's acquaintance with other social and cultural milieux besides the one in which one has been brought up. One would then have to consider one's reactions to these divers influences. Has one accepted them unquestioningly and uncritically, or has one welcomed them enthusiastically, or has one resisted them, even to the extent of 'leaning over backwards' in a determination not to be governed by them? At this point one would be trying to observe the interaction between education and innate temperament. This interaction is so constant and so intense that it is not easy to distinguish and disentangle the two factors. As far as one could succeed in doing this, one would be able to insulate one's temperament and analyse it. This would obviously be the most difficult part of the inquiry. These psychological phenomena are obscure in themselves, and they concern the inquirer so intimately that, even if he were trying bona fide to bring them to light, he might misinterpret them unintentionally.

A self-survey on some such lines, however inadequate, would be likely to suggest several useful reflections. It would immediately make one aware of the relativity of one's outlook to one's temperament and one's environment. One's temperament is the product of a particular combination of genes from one's parents' respective genetic heritages. The number of alternative possible combinations was very great, and each one of them would have produced a different temperament from that with which one happens to have been endowed by Nature's

---

[1] Bagby points out that 'our own ideas and values are embodied in our language, and yet our language is the only tool we have with which to describe alien ideas and values' (*Culture and History*, p. 191).

[2] If one has had the 'classical' education that, in most of the civilizations, has been the usual form of higher education till quite recently, one would have to take account of the effect of an acquired classical language or languages on one's ideas and values, besides the effect of one's mother-tongue. On this, see further the Annex, *Ad Hominem*, to Chapter II, pp. 575–605.

mathematical game of permutations and combinations. One's actual temperament, which is the foundation of one's personality, has been allotted to one casually by a biological mechanism which, from the human product's standpoint, is a blind throw of the dice; and it has been singled out of a host of various possibilities ranging, perhaps, over most of the gamut of Theophrastus's characters and Jung's psychological types.

The allotment to one of one's social and cultural environment might, at first sight, seem less capricious. A child is the offspring of parents who must have been living in some particular environment at the time when the embryo was conceived; and, since most children are brought up by their parents, most of them also grow up in their parents' environment as a matter of course. This, however, is merely normal without by any means being inevitable. In the grim age through which people of our generation have been living since A.D. 1914, there have been many children in the World who, in early infancy, have lost their parents and have grown up as orphans, waifs, and strays, in quite different social and cultural surroundings from those in which their parents brought them into the World. It is a well-known fact that these changelings have been moulded by the actual environment in which they have grown up to just the same extent as their contemporaries who have grown up in the same environment, not in consequence of a catastrophe, but for the normal reason that this was their parents' environment. The Russian-born child of Russian-born parents that has been transported in early infancy to Portugal, and has been brought up there without any subsequent contact with parents and native land, will speak Portuguese as if that were its 'mother-tongue' and will take it for granted that Roman Catholic Christianity is the only true and saving faith. Conversely, the Portuguese-born child of Portuguese parents that has been transported in early infancy to Russia and has been brought up there in insulation from its Portuguese origins will speak Russian as if that were its 'mother-tongue' and will take it just as much for granted that the true and saving faith is Communism.

When once one has realized that one's own standards, values, and outlook are the product of one's heredity and one's environment, and that they could and would have been different if a different heredity and environment had fallen to one's lot, it becomes impossible to maintain a child's naïve assumption that its feelings are right, its judgements just, and its beliefs true in some absolute sense. This recognition of the relativity of any set of human standards and values—whether it is common to a group or is peculiar to an individual—should make one more distrustful and critical of one's own set and at the same time more charitable and open-minded towards the sets that we find in other people. This may lead one to try to examine alien outlooks, values, and standards as dispassionately as one will have tried to examine one's own in the first stage of the inquiry.[1] One will now inquire, as one will have

---

[1] Bagby, in op. cit., p. 3, submits that 'our personal prejudices, even if expressed in the form of moral judgments, are poor guides to the understanding of anything whatsoever'. This dictum is true if, for the word 'whatsoever', we substitute the words 'except oneself'. If we can detect our personal prejudices and face them, they will give us a clue

inquired in one's own case, what the circumstances were in which these standards were acquired, and one will probably find that the circumstances explain the standards to us by revealing to us why they seem right and just and reasonable to the people whose standards they are.[1]

Any such change of attitude towards ourselves, and consequently towards our fellow human beings too, would evidently make for an improvement in human relations of all kinds. When the relation is an intellectual one—a study of human affairs by a human mind—it would be true to say that a recognition of the implications of relativity is a prerequisite for achieving any results at all. 'Moralising is incompatible with historic insight.'[2] So long as one is taking one's own standards as an absolute norm to which other people's standards must measure up, one cannot begin to see these other people as they really are, or to appraise their standards at their real worth.[3] This is evident when one is trying to make a comparative study of two or more persons other than oneself, or of two or more societies, cultures, or religions other

to the distortions in our mental picture of phenomena, and this clue will give us a means for trying to see the picture in something more like the true perspective.

The same point is made by Bagby in *Toynbee and History*, p. 108. Bagby's contribution to this volume originally appeared in *The Times Literary Supplement* and was therefore published anonymously in accordance with the usual practice of the *T.L.S.* On the day of publication, Bagby himself told me, at a public meeting, that he was the writer of the article. So I am free to make it known that this article comes from the same hand as *Culture and History*.

[1] 'If one man wishes to understand and predict another's behaviour, he does not consider his own preferences; he tries rather, in the common phrase, "to look at things from *the other man's* point of view", to appreciate and sympathise with *his* likes and dislikes rather than to project his own' (Bagby, op. cit., p. 3). In another passage (ibid., pp. 45–46), Bagby acutely discerns the limits of this possibility. 'We may be able to describe more or less objectively the behaviour or even the motives of others to which we are indifferent; if we wish to *feel* their emotions, we must inevitably project into them something of ourselves. For this reason, our knowledge of human beings in the past, and for that matter in the present, is necessarily limited. We are inevitably outsiders and must resign ourselves to that fact.' Bagby also points out, however, that our own mental processes, including our ways of feeling as well as our ways of thinking, do provide us with a 'model' for interpreting the mental processes of other people (ibid., p. 66). It goes without saying that this 'model' which is derived from one's own picture of oneself must be used discriminatingly and cautiously if we are to avoid being misled by it.

[2] W. den Boer in *Toynbee and History*, p. 240. Cp. p. 242.

[3] This point is perhaps easier to take when the intellectual and moral misdemeanour is being committed, not by oneself, but by someone else. We rightly feel that a trick has been played on us when we discover that the only surviving account of some dead person or extinct people presents them, not as they really were, but as they have been portrayed by some vocal third party who has 'made a corner' in the telling of the tale and has innocently or deliberately taken advantage of this opportunity to blacken the face of his dumb neighbour in the picture of him that he has handed down to posterity.

Two classic examples are the Athenian picture of the Boeotians and the Israelite picture of the Philistines that have been transmitted to the Western World and have given the words 'Philistine' and 'Boeotian' uncomplimentary connotations in modern Western languages. The Philistines seem to have little chance of redress. Our modern archaeologists have not yet succeeded in giving us much independent evidence about them to set against the ugly picture given in the Old Testament. The Boeotians—branded by the Athenians as 'Boeotian swine'—have managed to bequeath to us some telling evidence on their own behalf. Read Pindar's odes and Plutarch's biographical and philosophical essays, and look at a collection of graceful terracotta Tanagran figurines in some modern museum, and you will be astonished that, in the teeth of this evidence of the true nature of Boeotian culture, the Athenians should have succeeded in establishing their *fable convenue*. What the Athenian fable truly tells us is, not what the Boeotians were like, but what their enemies the Athenians wished us to believe about them.

Another example is the Achaeans' picture of the Aetolians, as painted in the surviving parts of Polybius's work. The Aetolians' case has gone by default. There is no surviving picture, either of the Aetolians themselves or of their Achaean rivals, from an Aetolian pen.

than one's own.[1] And there is a valid and pertinent sense in which all study of human affairs is comparative study, for implicitly the inquirer is, all the time, comparing his human objects of study with his human self, singular or plural. Open-mindedness, charity, and sympathy are not only signs of grace; they are priceless virtues. But, if one manages in some measure to acquire these virtues and to practise them, they lead one to the threshold of a problem for which they themselves do not provide any automatic solution. For it is not true that 'tout comprendre est tout pardonner'.

Suppose that one has now recognized the fallibility of one's belief in the absolute rightness of one's own standards and in the consequent absolute wrongness of other people's conflicting standards, one is confronted with Pilate's question, 'What is truth?' It is clear that the two conflicting sets of standards cannot both be absolutely right, but this is no proof that either of them is absolutely wrong, and all standards cannot be absolutely wrong; for if they were there would be no such thing as truth and therefore no possibility of judging between one set of standards and another. Indeed, it seems impossible, *ex hypothesi*, that any set of standards can be totally wrong if it is the actual guiding rule of a group of human beings, or even just of one solitary individual. However perverse it may look in the sight of the rest of mankind, they cannot judge it to be totally wrong without judging the people who live by it to be insane, or in other words non-human and therefore incapable of having any standards of a human kind. This must, it would seem, be so; for to lack any recognizable moral standard would be tantamount to lacking the sense of a distinction between right and wrong; and this sense is surely part of the essence of being human. A sane human person will still retain it, even if his standards strike other people as being preposterously wrong, and even if he deliberately and consciously violates his own standards, such as they are.

It will be seen that the recognition of the relativity of human outlooks, standards, and values raises a difficult question. When one has admitted that his own standards are relative, can he have any intellectual basis or moral standing for passing judgements on someone else's standards? Logic answers this question in the negative; but experience rules this negative answer out by pointing to the unquestionable fact that Man is a social being; for there could be no human society if human beings had no capacity and no right to pass judgements on each other and, what is more, to put their judgements into action—and we should be inhibited from doing either of these things if we did not believe, or rather take for granted, that our own standards represent, however imperfectly, a generally valid standard, common to us and to our fellow human beings. If we believed that our own standards represented nothing but personal caprice or, at the widest, tribal custom, we should not have the face to make and execute judgements on the strength of them. This is obvious in the field of practical affairs; a belief in the general validity of moral standards is one of the necessary conditions for social relations; but it is also a necessary condition in the field of study; for study too is action in

[1] See A. L. Kroeber: *The Nature of Culture*, p. 6.

a social setting.[1] It is true that we cannot study our fellow human beings' standards intelligently unless we recognize that these have a value of their own which we should be misrepresenting if we insisted on interpreting it in terms of ours. But it is also true that, if our recognition of the relativity of all sets of standards were to lead us to the conclusion that we are not entitled to pass judgements on any of them, we should be debarring ourselves from making any study of human affairs. 'The problem of the validity of any historical classification involves a question of values and cannot be solved on purely logical or metaphysical grounds.'[2] We can regard each other, and study each other, as fellow human beings only on the assumption that, underlying the equivocal differences between our relative points of view, there are some fundamental common standards in virtue of which we recognize each other as being members of one and the same human race.

'When we speak of Man, we necessarily imply the presence of certain familiar mental categories. . . . It follows, indeed, from the nature of the evidence on which all our historical knowledge is based, that history can never carry us beyond the stage where we can understand the working of the minds of the acting people because they are similar to our own. Where we cease to understand, where we can no longer recognize categories of thought similar to those in terms of which we think, history ceases to be human history.'[3]

'Just as facts cannot be divorced from some interpretation, so it seems impossible to divorce history from the imputation of values that are objective.[4] . . . Only by assuming an enveloping, transcultural pattern of values can we explain how judgments of praise and censure from ancient Egypt or Rome can be veridically comprehended by our contemporaries.'[5]

In what cases ought we to pass judgement on the strength of our belief in the existence of such common human standards, and in what cases ought we to suspend judgement in deference to our recognition that some human standards, including some of our own, have only a relative validity? Here there is no *a priori* rule to guide us; we can only feel our way; and, all the time, we are perpetually being forced into taking a line by the pressure of events. Were the Roman authorities justified in forcibly suppressing the practice of human sacrifice in North-West Africa, or the Spanish authorities in forcibly suppressing it in Middle America? Were the British authorities in India justified in suppressing infanticide, suttee, and the self-immolation of the devotees who used to throw themselves under the wheels of Juggernaut's car? From the point of view of the Punic, Aztec, and Hindu addicts to these rites, their alien conquerors were misusing their military power to

---

[1] Bagby, in op. cit., p. 3, makes the point that 'it is only when some action is required that' one 'finds it necessary to judge other men's behaviour, and his action is all the more effective if he has first understood this behaviour in as cold and rational a manner as possible'.
The second statement in this sentence is indisputable; the preceding statement is uncontroversial if it is recognized that action takes more than one form, and that one of its forms is study.   [2] Cohen, op. cit., p. 66.
[3] F. A. Hayek: *The Counter-Revolution of Science*, pp. 79 and 78–79.
[4] M. C. Swabey: *The Judgment of History*, p. 242. Read the whole passage, pp. 242–54.
[5] Op. cit., p. 75.

suppress religious practices whose significance and value these aliens did not understand. Ignorant prejudice militant is certainly an ugly thing, and the Aztec citizens of Tenochtitlan can have seen nothing but an outrageous act of sacrilege in the overthrow of their gods' images and altars and the slaughter of their priests by Cortés's indignant soldiers. On the other hand, Cortés and his companions saw nothing but an atrocious barbarity in the tearing of human hearts out of living human bodies by priests whose locks were matted with their victims' blood. And the Spanish intruders had to take a line. Now that they were in Mexico and in power there, they must either suppress the local practice of human sacrifice or else condone it. How is the voice of humanity to decide between Spaniards and Aztecs in this case? Perhaps it has delivered its verdict already. If not, it will surely deliver it in time. A verdict that is both unanimous and enduring is the only conceivable last word that can be spoken in judgement between one relative set of human standards and another. And in our day the possibility of such unanimous judgements is only just coming within sight, for it is only in our day that mankind is beginning to grow together into a single family. 'The fundamental criterion . . . is generality.'[1] Generality is rooted in reasonableness.[2] And an all but unanimous consensus among people who recognize each other as being reasonable can be taken as being decisive, even if there are still some dissenting voices.[3]

It is not only conquerors and rulers who have found themselves forced to pass summary judgements on the respective merits of their own standards and those of alien peoples. Anthropologists and historians are in the same plight. Their hands too are forced by the relation into which they have entered with the human objects of their study. They cannot study without finding themselves also compelled to judge.[4]

---

[1] N. Rescher in *The Journal of Philosophy*, vol. lv, No. 6 (13th March, 1958), pp. 243–55, on p. 252.   [2] Rescher, ibid.

[3] Rescher in loc. cit., p. 254. Ibid., p. 255, Rescher points out that this criterion is not absolute. Justification in ethics is always reasoned, but it is not deductive. 'We are able to bring to light in a "dialectical" manner an increasingly firm basis of reason in justifying our moral judgments.'

[4] Kroeber, in *The Nature of Culture*, p. 6, expresses the opinion that value judgements are possible as between the values of different cultures. Redfield holds that they are inevitable and desirable. 'It cannot be proved, from the proposition that values are relative, that we ought to respect all systems of values' (*The Primitive World and its Transformations*, p. 147). He recalls that the United Nations commission on human rights did not adopt a suggestion, made to them by American anthropologists, that they should recognize the right of men to live in accordance with their own traditions (ibid., pp. 147–8). Redfield testifies that anthropologists implicitly assume that civilization is better than primitive life (ibid., p. 158), and he explicitly makes this standpoint his own. 'I simply could not look neutrally at the ideas that move in history towards a more humane ideal and practice' (ibid., p. 141).

In an article under the title 'Are Moral Problems Genuine?' in *Mind*, New Series, vol. lxv (1956), pp. 166–83, D. H. Munro raises the question whether 'there are several alternative ethical systems, each equally valid' (p. 176), and comes to the conclusion that we cannot escape asking and answering the question: Which of two ways of life is the better? (p. 179).

In an important article under the title 'Ethical Relativity: Sic et Non', in *The Journal of Philosophy*, vol. lii, No. 23 (10th November, 1955), pp. 663–77, Clyde Kluckhohn draws attention to, and gives his own blessing to, a current turn of the tide of anthropological opinion against the extreme relativist position. As he puts it, ethical relativity still stands in certain contexts, but 'the areas of indeterminacy' have been narrowed (p. 663). 'There are pan-human universals as regards needs and capacities that shape, or could rightly shape, at least the broad outlines of a morality that transcends cultural difference'

The conclusion to which the foregoing discussion seems to point is that, in our dealings, academic as well as practical, with our fellow human beings, we must try to maintain all the time a difficult balance between two attitudes, both of which are indispensable on the evidence of experience, though they may be mutually exclusive in logic. On the one hand we have always to treat our neighbours' standards and values with the respect and tolerance that we crave for our own, notwithstanding our recognition of our own standards' relativity. On the other hand we have sometimes to pass judgements in the name of standards deemed by us, at our peril, to be common to all men. Such judgements are so hazardous that we should pass them only reluctantly and tentatively, but we must not flinch from making them in the last resort; for the price of refraining from them in all circumstances would be to break the moral bond of common humanity which is the necessary framework for any relations, academic or practical, with our fellow human beings. I therefore join issue with a scholar who maintains, without qualification, that 'we shall never be able to understand' history 'unless we first put aside all moral considerations' and that these 'must be as firmly put aside as in the study of physics and biology'.[1] In the study of non-human nature there is no question of putting moral considerations aside, because here these do not arise. In the study of human affairs it is impossible to ignore them, because they are inherent in the human observer's relation with his human subject; and there is no clear and simple rule for dealing with them. We shall go wrong if we refuse to make them, at our peril, when they do arise in this field, and we shall also go wrong if, in making them, we undiscriminatingly apply the relative standards of our own civilization, country, class, family, in our own personal version of them, as if these were identical with, and not, as they are, only approximations to, the fundamental common standards implicit in our having a common human nature.[2] I am sure that I myself have fallen into this error. Several critics have concurred in convicting

---

(p. 666). Cultures are not isolated monads, and some valid comparisons between them are possible (pp. 670–1). 'While the specific manifestations of human nature vary between cultures and between individuals in the same culture, human nature is universal' (p. 676). There are some moral standards that are 'altogether universal' (e.g. the distinction between 'murder' and killings that are felt to be justifiable) (pp. 671–2). 'Both within and between cultures moral behaviour in specific instances and in all its details must be judged within a wide context but with reference to principles which are not relative' (p. 674). 'The position of radical cultural relativity' is 'untenable' (p. 673).

These considerations against unmitigated relativism and in favour of a circumspect universalism are impressive. On the other hand, in *Toynbee and History*, Sir Ernest Barker (on pp. 101–2) and Philip Bagby (on p. 110) deprecate the condemnation of Man's past labours. A. J. P. Taylor finds (ibid., p. 121) that I am guilty of this offence. 'He lacks . . . the historian's characteristic piety towards the past.'

[1] Bagby in *Culture and History*, p. 3, and in *Toynbee and History*, p. 108. Cp. the passages quoted from Bagby and Birks on p. 54, footnote 2.

[2] Bagby points out, in *Culture and History*, p. 140, that modern Western psychologists have not entirely succeeded in making this necessary discrimination in their attempt to apprehend human nature in the sense of 'universal psychological traits hereditary in origin and present in every human being'. 'The formulations of the psychologists are based on their observations of their neighbours, that is, on the behaviour of bearers of Western European culture, and undoubtedly are largely tinged by the peculiarities of that culture. There can be no assurance that these generalizations apply to all mankind until all the immense variety of human behaviour has been studied.'

me of it.[1] At the same time, I believe that I should have erred no less if I had gone to equal lengths in putting moral considerations aside.

III. THE RELATIVITY OF A HUMAN OBSERVER'S APPROACH TO RELIGION

1. THE ISSUE BETWEEN TRANS-RATIONALISTS AND RATIONALISTS

IT will have become apparent, if it was not already, that a human observer's inescapable relativity is even more embarrassing for him when the object of his study is human affairs than when it is non-human nature. In the humanist's field, feelings and judgements, standards and values, assert themselves importunately and gravely complicate the inquirer's task. But this is only one of two complications that the humanist has to reckon with. For the knowledge of good and evil, with the attitudes and actions that follow from it, is one of two faculties that distinguish Man from all other creatures known to him. Since his second distinctive faculty is a controversial subject in the present-day world, perhaps the least controversial description of it will be a negative one. One may describe this second faculty as being a capacity for feeling that Man himself is not the highest spiritual presence in the Universe in which he finds himself. In fact, in entering the field of observation, Man does not come unaccompanied. He brings with him an intimation of the existence of a spiritual presence higher than his.

'There is a sense of significance beyond our feelings, of discovering something distinct and other than human experience. If consciousness means what it claims to mean, not everything of worth in the World is traceable to an origin with Man, reference to Man, or application to Man's use. The view which makes Man the measure of all things falsifies our attitudes in valuation.'[2]

To call this sixth sense a 'consciousness' or 'assurance' would be to beg the question, which is in dispute today, whether there is in truth a reality with which Man's religious sense puts Man in touch. The evidence is a matter of private individual experience. It cannot be verified by public observation, as we can verify the findings of physical and even social science. Yet the unverifiable findings of Man's religious sense give rise to attitudes and actions that have played at least as important a part in human affairs as the attitudes and actions arising from Man's moral faculty.

---

[1] Hourani, for instance, in loc. cit., p. 383, says that I have 'a moral vision of history'. Geyl, in *Toynbee and History*, p. 373, reproaches me for my 'spate of moral judgments'. Christopher Dawson notes that, in the earlier volumes of this book, 'the moral absolutism' of the author's 'judgements' clashes 'with the cultural relativism of his theory' (ibid., p. 13). Geyl (ibid., p. 372) finds that 'every age and every civilization is judged by a standard foreign to it'. This may be true in the sense that an historian cannot ever jump completely clear of the standards of his own time and place. But this is true of all historians, including Geyl himself.

[2] M. C. Swabey: *The Judgment of History*, p. 242. Illustrations of the point here made are given on pp. 185–7.

Thus Man's entry into the field of observation complicates the observer's vision of the Universe by introducing into it the vista of religion beyond the vista of ethics; and, if the problem of ethics is enigmatic, the problem of religion is more so. There is, indeed, no limit to the commitment incurred by the inquirer who ventures to be a student of human affairs, for, whether he has foreseen this or not, he has committed himself, in the act, to becoming a theologian too. In consternation he may try to beat a retreat from this perilously exposed position into the dead ground of 'comparative religion', in the hope that he can escape from theology under the scientific camouflage of anthropological research. But theology is an incubus that a humanist can never shake off. He may seek refuge from theism in atheism or from animism in materialism. But after each desperate twist and turn he will find himself committed to some theological position or other. Theology is inescapable, and it is dynamite. It will betray its identity through the camouflage by exploding in the end.

In most chapters of the histories of most of the human societies of which we have a record up to date, the position in regard to religion has been not unlike the position in regard to ethics. In the field of ethics, as we have seen, the differences between partially conflicting local standards and values have evoked violent feelings and sweeping judgements. The respective champions of the different sets of standards have each been apt to see in their own set the fundamental common standards of mankind, without recognizing the play of relativity or facing its implications. In this blind self-assurance and self-righteousness they have sometimes gone so far as to claim that their own code of morality was the only right one, and that variant codes were no true codes at all. But none of the belligerents in this intellectual warfare has ever denied that there is a distinction between right and wrong and an obligation to do right that is incumbent on all men *ex officio humanitatis*: they have merely denied the validity of any code of conduct except their own. In the greater part of the World for most of the time as far as our records go back, the position in regard to religion has been similar. There have been conflicts between different local practices and beliefs, and, since the first appearance of higher religions and philosophies in and after the last millennium B.C., claims have been made that this or that one of these is the only true and saving faith. But the fanatics who have denied that there is any truth or saving grace in any religion except their own, have, of course, never dreamed of denying the truth and efficacy of religion itself. So far from that, they have been eager to convert the rest of the human race to 'the true religion', with which their own religion is synonymous for them.

At this point, however, the history of religion and the history of ethics have diverged. So far there has been no known human society in which the distinction between right and wrong, and the obligation to do right, have been denied. But in more than one society, at some stage in its history, there have been sceptics[1] who have broken with the world-wide

---

1 The word 'sceptic' is used in this volume in the meaning of 'disbeliever' in the tenets of religion and in the existence of the spiritual presence or presences, higher than

traditional belief that religion—at any rate one's own religion—is true and valuable. These sceptics have denied the reality of the spiritual presence or presences whose existence is the presupposition of all religions, lower or higher, including those religions that are 'false' in the eyes of some rival religion's adherents. This loss of belief in the reality of some trans-human presence or presences in the Universe leads to the conclusion that religion itself is either an hallucination or a fraud or else that it is the product of an unedifying interplay between false pretences and naïve credulity. A sceptic is bound to regard religion as a misapprehension or misrepresentation of Reality which hinders human minds from seeing and facing Reality as it is. He will, in fact, see in it 'an opiate of the people'.

Since sceptics, like other human beings, including believers, may be either idealists or cynics, their common disbelief in the tenets of religion and in the reality of religious experience will not make them all agree on the question of what their policy towards religion ought to be. Sceptical idealists will feel that religion is a scandalously fraudulent and obscurantist institution and that it is the duty of all enlightened and honest-minded men to do their utmost to liberate their fellow men's minds from the pernicious influence of this sinister social evil. A classical exposition of this point of view is the Roman Epicurean philosopher Lucretius's poem *De Rerum Natura*. Lucretius's missionary zeal to cure men of the belief in religion of any kind is as sincere and intense as a Buddhist, Christian, or Muslim missionary's zeal to convert unbelievers to his own religious faith. On the other hand, sceptical cynics may feel that the fraudulence and obscurantism of religion make this institution a convenient instrument for keeping in order such irrational and ill-behaved social animals as human beings are. A classical exposition of this point of view is the attitude and policy towards traditional Roman religion that is attributed to the Roman governing class in the second century B.C. by the Greek historian Polybius.[1] For the immediate purpose of our present inquiry, however, this difference between alternative policies to which scepticism may lead is of secondary importance compared to the intellectual problem that the phenomenon of scepticism itself creates for the student of human affairs when he has to reckon with it—and this he must do whenever and wherever scepticism asserts itself; for in this situation the humanist will either be a sceptic himself or will have to face sceptical criticism if he is a believer.

Man, which religion postulates. The word can also be used to mean a disbeliever in the whole of Man's mental image of Reality and in any possibility of apprehending Reality mentally by the use of the analytical and classificatory intellectual procedure that we call reasoning. Few philosophers have ever tried to be sceptics in this absolute sense, and none, perhaps, have ever succeeded. So far from being disbelievers in the reasoning powers of human minds, most disbelievers in religion have been convinced rationalists. These rationalist-minded disbelievers in religion have taken exception to religious beliefs, not because they have been sceptical about the possibility of any apprehension of Reality, but because they have believed in the efficacity of the human reason and have thought that the effective exercise of the reason was inexpediently inhibited by religious faith. In their eyes the objects of faith are figments of the imagination because they are data of private personal experience and therefore cannot be verified by the test of public observation and examination (see also p. 72, footnote 3, below).

[1] Polybius: *Historiae*, Book VI, chap. 56, quoted in v. 646–7.

This issue between sceptics and believers looms larger in the present-day world than in any other known society in any previous age as far as our records go back. Previous accesses of scepticism did not spread beyond rather narrow circles within the societies in which they made their appearance, and they were also relatively short-lived by comparison with the duration of those societies themselves. Each time, after a certain number of generations or centuries, this uninfectious minority would die out, and society would revert to its usual state of almost universal and unchallenged belief in the reality of the objects or object of religious faith. In retrospect, however, from the standpoint of the present day, these previous cases take on significance as premonitory symptoms of a sceptical movement which started in the modern Western World in the seventeenth century of the Christian era and which, since then, has not only gone from strength to strength on its native ground but has spread over the rest of the World in the train of the Western Civilization's recent world-wide expansion. This modern Western sceptical movement originated in a moral reaction against the *odium theologicum* that had provided fuel for the so-called 'Wars of Religion'. *Tantum religio potuit suadere malorum.*[1] Men of good will deliberately took their treasure out of religious controversy and put it into scientific research, which seemed to promise to be a more innocent and also more fruitful activity. Since then, the findings of scientific research have seemed to undermine the intellectual foundations of traditional religion; and this second blow, following on the moral discredit that the Western Wars of Religion had brought upon religion itself, has now carried religious belief to a perhaps unprecedentedly low ebb.

The present-day world is divided by an intellectual barrier between the minds of believers and unbelievers which is as effective an insulator as 'the Iron Curtain' which divides a Communist from an anti-Communist ideological camp.[2] And we cannot tell how long this modern schism between believers and unbelievers is going to last or what its eventual outcome is going to be. It would be unwarrantable to assume that the modern sceptical movement is going to be as short-lived as its predecessors, and equally unwarrantable to predict that, if it persists, it will extinguish religious belief universally. Nor can it be foreseen what may happen eventually if unbelief and belief continue to coexist. It is conceivable that eventually both attitudes of mind might be superseded by some third outlook which would embrace both belief and unbelief and consequently exclude them both at the same time. It might, for example, come to be held, as a result of some advance in human powers of understanding, that the antithesis between 'reality' and 'unreality',

---

[1] Lucretius: *De Rerum Natura*, Book I, line 101. 'Such was the enormity of the evil that religion could make men do.'

[2] These two lines of division do not, of course, coincide. The ideological barrier runs along a sharply demarcated frontier between states of opposite ideological colours, yet even the 'Iron Curtain' has not completely sorted out the sheep from the goats Non-Communist and Communist minorities are still to be found on what, from both standpoints, is the wrong side of the line. As for the barrier between believers and unbelievers, it does not correspond, even approximately, to any line that could be plotted on a map. All over the World today, believers and unbelievers are to be found living side by side in the same society, country, and even household.

which is a useful, or at least an unavoidable, category of thought for dealing mentally with our experience of phenomena, is inapplicable to experience of the religious kind. However that may turn out to be, the mental gulf between the believer's and the unbeliever's outlook is one of the unquestionable realities of the present-day world, and it therefore creates, for the present-day student of human affairs, a problem of relativity that is as unavoidable as it is acute.

The problem is acute because the sceptical-minded and the religious-minded student of human affairs are both living in the same world and addressing themselves to the same public, while at the same time the outlook of each of them seems, from the other's standpoint, to make human affairs unintelligible. For the religious-minded inquirer religion is the highest form of human activity. It offers Man the greatest opportunity of gaining insight into Reality, and of entering into contact with It, that is open to him in this life.[1] For anyone who holds this view, life is robbed of its purpose, and Reality of its meaning, by the sceptic's contention that religion is the shadow cast by an illusion.[2] Conversely, for the sceptical-minded inquirer a rational understanding of Reality is made impossible by the believer's contention that the essence of Reality is a spiritual presence which, from the rationalist's[3] point of view, is imaginary, considering that its reality is vouched for only by a private personal experience that can never be verified by the test of public observation and examination.[4]

Can we find any common ground between two points of view when the assumptions in which these are respectively grounded are concerned with the very essence of Reality and at the same time appear, to human minds within the present limits of their powers of understanding, to be in diametrical opposition to each other? Perhaps a bare foothold of common ground can be obtained if we can win a concession from either side.

Believers might be asked to meet rationalists part-way by agreeing to leave the trans-human presence or presences, in whose existence and potency they believe, out of account when they are engaged in the common enterprise of trying to explain the course of human events and to analyse the structure of human society and the configurations of human culture. It is true that, in the pre-rationalist age, historians, as well as poets, treated the reported occurrences of allegedly 'supernatural' phenomena on a par with reports of human actions. Accounts of omens, miracles, and the epiphanies and physical intervention of gods were interwoven with accounts of human debates, decisions, agreements, conflicts, achievements, and failures, as if these two elements in the

---

[1] See, for example, Dawson, *The Dynamics of World History*, pp. 169, 171, 173.

[2] The Rev. E. R. Hardy Jr. counts it as a merit in me that I recognize 'that religion cannot be studied purely as an objective phenomenon' (*The Intent of Toynbee's History: A Cooperative Appraisal*).

[3] The word 'rationalist' is used in this volume in the meaning of someone who believes in the efficacy of human reasoning powers to apprehend Reality at least to some extent and disbelieves in any alleged explanation of phenomena, or of the Reality underlying them, that is non-rational in the negative sense of not being vouched for by the findings of reasoning, as well as in the positive sense of being contradicted by these (see p. 69, footnote 1 above).

[4] See, for example, Bagby, op. cit., pp. 2, 57, 149–50, *et alibi*.

pre-rationalist historians' picture of the course of events were, in principle, equally credible. The reality of the 'supernatural' element was simply taken for granted. But, when once the rationalists have challenged this assumption, the onus of proving it surely lies on the shoulders of the believers. They need not be asked to repudiate their traditional assumption; they need merely be asked to refrain—unless and until they can prove it—from continuing to make it when they are engaged in recording, examining, and analysing human affairs.[1]

As a matter of fact this concession has been made, in practice, by historians who have not renounced their belief in the existence and potency of trans-human spiritual presences. The reports of miraculous occurrences in terms of polytheistic religious beliefs were repudiated by Jewish, Christian, and Muslim historians long before the modern Western rationalist movement started. Since then, modern historians who have continued to be believing monotheists have tacitly taken to treating the miraculous element in their own religions' picture of human affairs as they have long since treated it overtly in the polytheistic presentation of it. Without repudiating their own belief in the existence and potency of a spiritual presence higher than Man, they have given up their former practice of introducing, into their accounts and explanations of human affairs, elements of a 'supernatural' order: that is to say, elements that cannot be observed, verified, and explained by the use of human reasoning powers.

The reciprocal concession to believers that rationalists might be asked to make is to recognize that rational explanation is imperfect and incomplete not merely in practice but intrinsically. We have seen in the preceding chapter that thought operates by classifying phenomena according to their recognizable similarities. It follows from this, as Bagby points out,[2] that, while it is true 'that some order, some recurrent features, must occur in any homogeneous and interrelated field of events', it is also true 'that such a field of events cannot be fully ordered; there must be some features of it which are arbitrary, undetermined, and inexplicable', and 'these consequences arise from the very notion of comparison, which requires both similarity and difference'. Thinking is an attempt to apprehend Reality by catching it in a conceptual net, and a net is able to serve its purpose in virtue of having a texture which leaves gaps between the meshes. It is this open texture which gives a net its fling. If the net were made, not of an open network, but of a tightly woven cloth, the material would be too heavy to allow a net made of it to be effectively extensive. But the price of having a texture which makes it possible to catch something in the net's meshes is the inevitability that something else will slip out of the net through the gaps.

This paradox is the crux of the intellectual procedure of rational analysis and explanation. The objective of rational thought is to discover in phenomena an intelligible system of regular and therefore

[1] This is all that is demanded on behalf of rationalism by, for instance, Bagby in *Culture and History*, pp. 148–9, or by M. Savelle in *The Pacific Review*, vol. xxv, No. 1 (February, 1956), pp. 55–67.

[2] In op. cit., p. 58. See also the passages quoted from Bagby, op. cit., and from Redfield on p. 11, footnote 10.

predictable uniformities and recurrences. But the very nature of the intellectual procedure by which this objective has to be pursued makes it inevitable that any system established by this procedure will not, after all, be really closed but will stay untidily open. And Heaven knows what may or may not slip out—or in—through the yawning gaps between the meshes of intelligibility. There are, in short, more things in Heaven and Earth than are dreamed of in the rationalist's philosophy,[1] and he cannot be sure that the draught which is let through by the chinks in his system may not be the importunate wind which bloweth where it listeth,[2] and which, though it may be invisible to the rationalist's eyes, makes in the believer's ear a sound that, for him, fills the World. It looks as if the believer may fairly ask the rationalist to meet him to the extent, not of renouncing his rational objective, but of making the negative concession of recognizing that human history 'is impatient of' the 'neat systems of laws and causal sequences' for which the rationalist 'is always looking', and that the 'mysterious and unpredictable aspect of history' is a genuine and irremovable 'stumbling-block' for him.[3]

On the other hand, I think that an inquirer who holds, as I myself hold, that rationalism is not enough ought, none the less, to follow the rationalists' good example of recognizing that the human reason's mental net is binding in so far as it is truly effective in apprehending Reality. If I stand convicted (and I have no doubt that I do) of having sometimes lapsed from reasoning into mythologizing when reasoning would have been capable of doing the job, I admit that I have been at fault. At the same time I am alive to the limitations of human reasoning power, and I am convinced that there are questions which reasoning cannot answer but which human beings are nevertheless bound to ask, because one would be less than human if one did not ask them and did not go on to try to answer them, even though one's answers to such 'trans-rational' questions will be, by definition, unverifiable.

Questions of this sort—and they are the most momentous questions with which human beings find themselves confronted—bombard us through the gaps between the meshes of reason's net. I do not believe that these gaps can be plugged, and, as far as I know, rationalists do not imagine that they can; so this is not one of the points in dispute between rationalists and 'trans-rationalists'. There are, however, rationalists who, while recognizing that they cannot plug the gaps, imagine that they can dispose of them by ignoring their existence and turning a deaf ear to any voices that may sound through them. With rationalists who adopt this 'know-nothing' policy I am in disagreement. Whether they can dull their senses successfully or not, I do not know. But I do feel sure that, if they did succeed, they would be defeating their own purpose of trying to comprehend Reality. They would have succeeded in preserving their cherished picture of Reality as a closed system, transparent to the human reason through and through, but, in the act, they

---

[1] One of these things is the entry of human souls on to the scene of this planet. Is a biological mutation sufficient to account for this? This question, which is a searching one, is asked by K. D. Erdmann in *Archiv für Kulturgeschichte*, xxxiii. Band, Heft 2 (1951), p. 237.   [2] John iii. 8.
[3] Chr. Dawson: *The Dynamics of World History*, p. 257, quoted already on p. 16.

would have been shutting their eyes to another vision of Reality that is, perhaps, likely to be rather less remote from the truth. Part of the truth about Reality, as it appears to the 'trans-rationalist' in his glimpse of it, is that it is boundless and mysterious and, for human eyes, not all of a piece. From this 'trans-rational' point of view, Reality looks like a house of many mansions, and our human reason's mansion does not seem to be self-contained, or, indeed, even semi-detached.

The point of view here described is, of course, a personal one,[1] but I have ventured to describe it, nevertheless, because I think that it brings out the point on which the current controversy between rationalists and 'trans-rationalists' turns. I am, myself, an ex-believer who first became a convert to rationalism with no reservations and has since become a convert to a 'trans-rationalist' standpoint with two reservations. One of my present reservations is in regard to rationalism. I am now more alive than I once was to the limitations of human reasoning powers. I believe that the answers to the questions that matter most to us can be found only beyond the reason's limits, if they can be found at all. So I am no longer entitled to call myself a rationalist if the label commits one to holding that human reasoning powers are capable of answering all questions that one needs to ask (capable of proving, for instance, or disproving, the existence of an absolute spiritual Reality beyond the phenomenal world). My second present reservation is in regard to religious belief. I do not think that unverifiable religious beliefs can stand against the findings of the reason within the field in which human reasoning powers are effective. So, if belief, in the religious meaning of the word, were to commit one to holding that the reason could and should be overridden on its own ground by an irrational faith, then I should be entitled, perhaps, to claim that I had become a 'trans-rationalist', but not to claim that I had again become a believer.[2] My present state of mind is, as far as I can judge, a common and characteristic one in the Western World in the generation into which I happen to have been born. It is an open state of mind, and the necessary price of this intellectual and moral boon is a partial break in one's vision and a certain tenseness in one's feelings. Finding myself in this situation does

[1] My point of view is personal in the sense that I cannot demonstrate its validity to someone who does not share it; but it is not personal in the other sense of being peculiar to me. It is, for example, identical with the point of view expressed in the following passage of a letter written by Gilbert Murray to Lord Russell on 26th July, 1954: 'Then about faith. What I wrote about beauty, physical and moral, was, I think, based on some sort of faith: that is, on a strong consciousness that, beyond the realm of our knowledge, there was a wide region in which we had imperfect intimations or guesses or hopes. Most of the so-called faiths are these intimations worked up into the form of definite myths or dogmas, almost all of them anthropomorphic. The myth is mostly invented, but the faith at the back of it has at least a good deal of probability about it. . . . It is in some ways the most interesting part of life, the great region in which you must be agnostic, but nevertheless you must have something like conviction.' The full text of this letter will be found in *Correspondence between Gilbert Murray, Lord Russell, and Bernard Shaw* (this has not yet been published). The passage here quoted will also be found in *Gilbert Murray: An Unfinished Autobiography* (London 1960, Allen & Unwin), p. 218. I am grateful to Sir Stanley Unwin for his permission to me to print the passage here.

[2] H. Kohn, in *Toynbee and History*, p. 354, notices that I do not believe in the feasibility or desirability of a return to traditional religious dogmas and institutions. I am, in fact, an agnostic in the sense in which the word is used by Gilbert Murray in the passage quoted in footnote 1. See further p. 98, footnote 2.

not strike me with dismay, because I do not feel that it puts me out of tune with Reality in so far as I have any intimation of what Reality may be like. I am also not aggrieved, because I feel grateful for the dark and broken glass that lets through to me my human glimmer of light. No doubt, a perfect lens would be better to have than a cracked one, but it is very much better to have a cracked one than not to have any lens of any kind. The mind's cracked lens is mankind's greatest treasure.

I have been trying to find terms for a 'gentlemen's agreement' between religious-minded and rationalist-minded participants in our present-day world-wide human society. This is probably the nearest approach that they can hope to succeed in making towards each other for the present. As far as one can see ahead, there seems to be no prospect of their being able to close the great gulf that has been opened between them by the relativity of their respective points of view to fundamental presuppositions that are in such stark disagreement as theirs are. But a gulf that cannot yet be closed can perhaps be bridged provisionally by a *modus vivendi* which may make it possible for the two parties to communicate, and even perhaps co-operate, with each other. The test of a bridge, of course, is its ability to bear the traffic. Let us now see whether the *modus vivendi* that I have suggested will hold firm or will break down if we try to make it serve as common ground for the study of human affairs in the particularly controversial field of the study of religion.

In setting out together on this inquiry, religious-minded and rationalist-minded explorers can at least find a common point of departure. For, differ as they may and will in their interpretations of the significance of religious experience, they will agree that the practices, beliefs, and institutions to which this experience has given rise always have been, and still are, a most important element in human affairs.[1] A test of whether they can travel together farther than just the first step will be their respective answers to two questions about the relation between religion and culture. If the rationalist asks the religious-minded party whether he agrees that religion is a part of human culture, this question, I should say, ought to receive the answer 'yes'. If the religious-minded party then asks the rationalist whether he agrees that religion is not only a part of culture but is also something more than that, the answer ought to be 'yes', I should say, again. If the two parties can both bring themselves to give their answers in the affirmative, they will be able to go on being travelling companions, and, what is more, they will, I should say, be taking together the road that leads towards a better understanding of Reality.

What do we mean by 'culture'? Let us use Bagby's clearly thought-out definition of it as 'regularities in the behaviour, internal and external, of the members of a society, excluding those regularities which are

---

[1] They can, of course, still differ in their estimate of religion's relative importance. For instance, Geyl, in *Debates with Historians*, pp. 138–9, maintains that I pay too much attention to religion and show too little concern for social betterment. In Geyl's opinion, my belief in the outstanding importance of religion is subjective: it cannot be proved by history or be disproved by it.

clearly hereditary in origin'.[1] Religious practices and institutions, and, by implication, also religious beliefs and experiences, are certainly a part of culture as thus defined, and in another passage[2] Bagby explicitly mentions religion, together with art, technology, and social structure, as examples of the elements of which culture consists. We can agree that religion is one of these elements without needing to try, at this point, to give either a complete list of them or a systematic account of their relations to each other.

Sorokin seems to hold that the culture elements that one finds present simultaneously in the participants in a society, collectively and individually, are merely casual conglomerations,[3] but here he is surely flying in the face of the evidence presented by the phenomena. In the light of this evidence most sociologists and anthropologists hold that one of the intrinsic properties of culture is that its component elements are integrated in some degree—that culture has, in fact, what Kroeber has called 'configurations'. No doubt there are any number of possible degrees of integration in any number of possible varieties of pattern. In all cultures some of the elements may be more closely tied than others to each other and to the culture itself in virtue of their respective natures. Religion and art, for instance, have often been closely associated with each other, and art, at any rate, seems to be one of the clearest and most precise expressions of a culture's distinctive character. If one is trying to ascertain the duration of some particular culture and its geographical distribution at different times, the presence or absence of its distinctive style of art is one of the surest and most accurate clues. By contrast, technology is less informative. The partakers in some particular culture have sometimes made revolutionary changes in their technology without this having produced any immediate change of comparable magnitude in the culture as a whole or in any of its non-technological parts. It looks as if a culture's technology sits more loosely to it than its art sits. And, in fact, in the technological field there seems always to have been a great deal of give-and-take between different cultures. In whatever culture a technique may have originated, it has been apt to spread beyond the parent culture's limits, and the history of technology can perhaps be understood best by regarding technology as having been, from the start, a common achievement and possession of all mankind, and also one which, so far, has improved progressively while cultures, as integrated 'configurations', have been coming and going.

Thus different parts of culture seem to display intrinsic differences in the degree of their integration with each other and with the total configuration of the particular culture in question. There are, no doubt, also differences in the degree of overall integration as between one culture and another, and also as between one phase and another in the history of some single culture. In an agricultural village community or in a pastoral nomadic tribe, we should expect to find a more highly integrated state of culture than in a great cosmopolitan city at an advanced

---

[1] Bagby: *Culture and History*, pp. 84 and 95; cp. pp. 93–94. See further pp. 272–3 of the present volume. [2] Bagby, op. cit., p. 93.
[3] Sorokin in *Toynbee and History*, pp. 180–1, 182, 188.

78 PHILOSOPHICAL CONSIDERATIONS

stage in the history of a civilization. It is here, if anywhere, that Sorokin's description of a culture as being a conglomeration of casual elements might come nearest to being a convincing account of the phenomena. Again, when an 'age of faith' begins to give way to an 'age of reason', as it did in the Hellenic World in the fifth century B.C. and in the Western World in the fifteenth century of the Christian Era, art tends to dissolve its traditional association with religion and to strike out on an independent course of its own.

Religion is certainly one of those parts of culture that have usually been closest to the heart of it and also most closely associated with other parts; and this generalization becomes more clearly valid the farther we look back into the past. In all societies, including civilizations of the first and second generations, down to the rise of the 'higher religions' in and after the last millennium B.C., religion has been intimately connected, not only with art, but also with social structure, political organization, and economic activities. The connexion with economics seems to have come earliest. Before Man had gained the upper hand over non-human nature, the elements in his environment from which he was wresting a precarious livelihood were the medium through which he felt himself to be in touch with the spiritual presences, higher than himself, in whose existence and potency he believed.[1] It has been only in societies in which a considerable, and influential, minority of the population has been living an urban life for a considerable time that the worship of gods manifest in Nature has fallen into the background; and then, when Man has become confident enough in his own powers to begin to divest Nature of her aura of divinity, he has come to find a more impressive manifestation of the godhead in his own social organization and in the collective power which he has acquired through this. In this next stage religion comes to be connected with politics more pronouncedly than with economics. The gods who now inspire the strongest feelings of awe, fear, and love are manifestations of divinity seen through the medium of states. The god of the city-state of Nippur or goddess of the city-state of Argos now overshadows the storm-god or the corn-goddess; and Athene holds her worshippers' allegiance as the divinity manifest in Athens rather than as the one manifest in the olive-tree.

Eventually the advent of the higher religions brings with it a new vision of the trans-human spiritual presence. Whether this is experienced as being immanent or as being transcendent, as being personal or as being impersonal, in every mode it is now experienced direct, and not through either an economic or a political medium. But the higher religions have so far had to incorporate almost as much as they have been able to abolish in the traditions of the earlier religions that they have sought to supersede. In the annual cycle of the liturgy of the Christian Church, as this is still observed in many of the Church's present branches, the underlying annual cycle of agricultural operations is manifest. The most conspicuous manifestation is in the thanksgiving

---

[1] 'Even in primitive nature-worship, the object of religious emotion and worship is never the natural phenomenon as such, but always the supernatural power which is obscurely felt to be present and to be working through the natural object' (Chr. Dawson: *The Dynamics of World History*, p. 173).

service for the harvest. Again, when in a Christian place of worship a *Te Deum* is sung to celebrate the victory of one professedly Christian state in a battle with another, the god to whom the thanks are given is manifestly the 'god of battles' who is the symbol of the collective power of a local political community, rather than the One True God who, according to Christian doctrine, is the common god not only of all Christians but of all human beings and all other created things.

It will be seen that, in the past, the association of religion with other parts of culture has been intimate. There has, it is true, been a tendency, in the histories of some civilizations, for art to part company with religion, and an inverse tendency, in the history of mankind as a whole, for religion to part company with economics and politics. But these dissociative movements have been tardy and gradual, and religion seems to have been less successful in achieving independence than art has been. The judgement that religion is a part of culture is confirmed and fortified by the evidence of religion's ancient and persistent connexion with other parts of culture whose status as such is not in dispute. If religious-minded students of human affairs can agree with their rationalist-minded confrères on this point, they will have found a piece of common ground. But this agreement on one important question of fact will have had the disconcerting effect of widening the area of their disagreement on a question of interpretation.

Let us suppose that they had been able to agree, instead, that religion was *not* a part of culture and was *not* connected with other phenomena that *are* parts of culture beyond dispute, then the disagreement between them over their respective interpretations of the significance of religion would have been confined to the topic of religion itself, and they could have agreed without reservation or ambiguity that culture, minus religion, is an exclusively human phenomenon that can be interpreted as such without any dispute over the question of the existence or non-existence of trans-human spiritual presences. On the other hand, when it has been agreed that, in the past, religion has not only been a part of culture but has been a highly pervasive part, intimately connected with a number of other parts, the dispute over the interpretation of the significance of religious experience extends itself, *pari passu* with religion's pervasive influence, over the whole field of culture. So the gulf between the two points of view yawns wider than ever; and this is, after all, only what is to be expected; for the cause of the gulf is the relativity of the two points of view to their respective fundamental presuppositions, and the conflict between these presuppositions will not have been overcome by an agreement on one question of fact. The only effective way of overcoming—or, short of that, of mitigating—this conflict is for each party to make the moral and intellectual effort to examine, analyse, and criticize his own bias.

The barrier of relativity—persisting, as it does, so long as it is left unanalysed—alienates the religious-minded and the rationalist-minded inquirer not only from each other but also from some of the common human objects of their study, since some of these will be in the opposite camp to the inquirer's, whichever of the two inquirers he may be. For both inquirers this is an obstacle to achieving the sympathy without which there can be no understanding. But up to the present this handicap has been less formidable for the religious-minded student of human affairs than it has been for the rationalist, simply because, up to date, the vast majority of human beings have been religious-minded, whereas the rationalists, into whose state of mind it might be difficult for the religious-minded inquirer to enter sympathetically, have been comparatively few and far between. By contrast, the rationalist-minded humanist has to study a world of men with whom he is out of sympathy with the exception of a few kindred spirits that catch his eye here and there.

A classical example of the un-self-critically rationalist-minded observer's handicap is the limitation which this state of mind imposed on the achievements of so great a genius as Gibbon. Gibbon's case is an outstanding one, because he was a genius who was rationalist-minded to an almost naïvely un-self-critical degree and who chose for his field of study an epoch of history in which a temporary access of rationalism was engulfed by a resurgence of religious faith. In Gibbon's eyes the spirit of Hellenic rationalism was identical with the spirit of the Western rationalism of Gibbon's own day. It was the same intellectual light dispelling the same darkness of ignorance and superstition; and Gibbon's subject was the submergence of Hellenic rationalism by the rise of Christianity. He saw his theme as the story of a catastrophe. What had happened was shocking because it had condemned civilization to undergo a long-drawn-out eclipse, and it was also inexplicable because it was not consonant with the rationality which, as Gibbon saw it, is not only part but the whole of what is distinctively and creditably human in human nature.

In approaching this subject from this standpoint Gibbon could hardly help seeing almost all the characters on his stage in one or other of the two roles of fool or knave. If they were not cheats, they must be dupes. *Ex hypothesi*, a rational human being could not really believe in religion, so, if someone who was unmistakably rational professed to believe in it, he must be an imposter who was seeking to deceive his fellow men for his own self-interested purposes. Conversely, if someone was an unmistakably sincere believer, he must be an irrational fool. The psychological barrier that the relativity of Gibbon's outlook interposed between the historian and the great majority of the figures passing across his stage prevented Gibbon from entering into the true motives and feelings of many of these actors, and therefore also prevented him from gaining a really penetrating insight into the meaning of the play. Gibbon's failure in these two respects—and the two points are both crucial—strikingly illustrates the seriousness of the handicap imposed by relativity when this is not corrected by self-criticism; for Gibbon's mind was surely the most powerful and most lucid one that has appeared so far in the whole distinguished company of Western historians up to date.

2. THE HIGHER RELIGIONS' DECLARATION OF INDEPENDENCE AND ITS IMPLICATIONS

The un-self-critically rationalist-minded humanist is likely to run into still greater trouble if he is not content to have a consensus that religion is a part of culture, but goes on to insist that religion is merely this and nothing more. Romein and Bagby appear to take this second position if I have rightly interpreted their meaning.[1] It is a position that gets its holders into difficulties when they come to deal with cultural and social morphology; for, in this field, it is only, it seems to me, by forcing facts and begging questions that one can stow away all specifically religious institutions entirely inside the framework of other institutions which may have a tincture of religion in them, but which are not themselves primarily institutions of a religious kind. The impracticability of this procedure may not be apparent at first if one approaches one's morphological studies in historical order, starting with pre-civilizational societies and going on to civilizations. The difficulties come to light when one comes to higher religions.

The problem of morphology presents itself because 'culture' and 'society' are abstractions. It is possible to define them; 'Culture' can be defined, as we have seen, as 'regularities in human behaviour',[2] and 'society' perhaps as 'the total network of relations between human beings'.[3] They can be defined, but the subjects of these definitions cannot ever be met with in real life. What we do meet with and are able to observe and examine are not 'culture' and 'society' but 'societies' and 'cultures'. Particular cultures are observable as regularities in the behaviour of human beings who are participants in particular societies, besides being partakers in the cultures that are respectively characteristic of these. A society, with its cultural expression, and a culture, in its social setting, are institutions that have structures. What is the relation of religion to these social and cultural structures? In the singular number 'religion', like 'society' and 'culture', is an abstraction. What we meet with in real life is not 'religion' but 'religions'; and 'religions', like 'societies' and 'cultures', have institutional structures. The question that arises is: Are these religious institutional structures nothing more than parts of other institutional structures that are not religious structures exclusively or even primarily? Can all the religious institutional structures that are now in existence, or are known to us from the historical record, be classified and explained satisfactorily as being parts of

---

[1] In *Toynbee and History*, p. 348, Romein writes: 'From my viewpoint, all religious phenomena are part of the social whole, a product, an important product, no doubt, perhaps the most important, but nevertheless a product only of society itself.' Ibid., p. 107, Bagby writes: 'It [religion] is merely a part or aspect of civilization, one of those systems of practice and belief which go to make up a way of life. It cannot be isolated from its social and cultural context and turned into a primary agent.' In *Culture and History*, p. 175, Bagby writes: 'Religion is ... only one aspect of culture and cannot give its name to the whole; we are no more and no less entitled to speak of "Christian civilization" than of "Democratic" or "Monarchical civilization" or, for that matter, of "Tea-drinking civilization". These terms do not cover empirically discoverable entities; they are rather classes into which we put various cultures because they share a single culture-trait or complex.'
[2] See further pp. 272–3.
[3] See further pp. 271–2.

other institutional structures of other kinds? Or are there some religious institutional structures, at any rate, that can be classified and explained only as being representatives of a separate and independent institutional category?

Let us try the policy of treating religious practices and institutions simply as parts of the culture of some society, or some community within a society, that is not primarily, or at any rate not solely, religious in character. This policy seems to work so long as we are dealing with pre-civilizational societies and civilizations of the first generation. In these societies, as we have seen already, religion is closely connected, not only with art, but with economics, and, later on, with politics, and further inspection shows that religion also enters into almost every other kind of activity in which the participants in these societies engage: for instance, war, education, and recreation. These societies do, in fact, seem to be highly integrated and more or less self-contained; and their religious horizon seems to coincide with their boundaries on other planes.

This is obvious in the case of the political divinities; their respective realms do not even embrace the whole of the society in which their worshippers participate. A political god's writ runs only within the frontiers of the local state whose collective power he or she symbolizes; and, even in those rare cases in which a local state—say Babylon or the Thebaid or Rome—expands into a universal state, the realm of the presiding god or gods—Marduk or Amun or Dea Roma and Divus Caesar—expands only up to the limits of the worshippers' empire. It might seem, at first sight, as if the older gods, in whom the super-human spiritual presences manifest themselves through the medium of non-human nature, must, like this medium, have a more or less world-wide range. Olives grow in other countries besides Attica; Mother Earth yields corn at other places besides Eleusis; and the sea has no bounds. So how can the Attic olive-goddess Athene and the Eleusinian Earth-goddess Demeter and the Corinthian sea-god Poseidon be merely local divinities? Demeter of Eleusis did, as a matter of fact, extend her realm beyond Eleusis and beyond Attica to embrace the whole Hellenic World; but in this she was exceptional. Local nature-gods who reigned in principle wherever their natural media—sea, corn, olive-trees, and so on—were to be found, were in fact conscripted by their local worshippers to concentrate their attention on meeting local economic needs. In fact, economic as well as political divinities were community-bound. There were as many of each of them as there were communities to require their services. Even the goddess whose medium was the boundless Earth was not allowed to be one and indivisible. Every economically autarkic territory had, under some name or other, a Demeter of its own.

So long as the horizon of religion is thus bounded by the borders of regional societies, or even by the frontiers of states into which such societies are divided up or unified politically, it remains possible to treat religion just as a part of culture and as nothing more. But the possibility of continuing to take this line becomes doubtful and disputable when the 'higher religions' make their appearance.

Higher religions, as a class, may be defined by characteristics of theirs which are revolutionary new departures. They catch a new vision of the spiritual presences, higher than Man, in which these presences are no longer seen through the medium of human economic and political needs and activities but are seen direct as powers that are not implicated *ex officio* in their local worshippers' human concerns.[1] These powers may reveal themselves to human beings either as transcendent or as immanent in the inward experience of sensitively attuned human hearts. But, whichever way they choose, they make their presence felt as an act of grace towards human beings to whom they owe no obligation and on whom they are not in any way dependent. If the trans-human spiritual presence is experienced, not in Its personal aspect as God, but as an impersonal state of spiritual being, as It is in the experience of a Buddhist spiritual athlete, the quest for Nirvāna requires the arhat to extricate himself not only from society but from self-hood. In either case there is a disengagement of the trans-human spiritual presence—and, with It, of Its worshippers—from the highly integrated life of some particular local community, and this disengagement has the consequence that the presence's realm now comes to be thought of as being coextensive, not with some local state or some regional civilization, but with the entire Universe, while Its worshippers come to feel themselves members of a church that, in principle and in intention, embraces all men.

In short, the higher religions are entitled to their distinctive name because they have a vision of the godhead as being sovereignly self-sufficient and omnipresent, instead of any longer thinking of It, in traditional terms, as being indentured to the service of local worshippers, being tied down to their territory's soil, and being debarred from breaking bounds by the presence, in adjoining territories, of other local divinities of the same order, who have corresponding rights and duties on their own no less narrowly and jealously circumscribed home ground. If the trans-human spiritual presence, when It is experienced direct, is seen, as in the Buddha's vision of It, no longer as a personal godhead but as an impersonal Nirvāna, then Its disengagement from the traditional configurations of the particular culture of some particular society will be more radical than it will be if the direct vision of the presence does not obliterate the traditional anthropomorphic image of It as a divine person. Yet, even if the personal aspect of the presence survives the new experience of It, this new experience will have the revolutionary

[1] In the Weltanschauung of primitive societies, Man, Nature, and God are not differentiated from each other (R. Redfield: *The Primitive World and its Transformations*, p. 104). 'Neither an absolutely unconditioned God nor a wholly secular description of natural law is conceivable in a savage or barbaric settlement before the rise of cities' (ibid., p. 102). A spiritual tension over the difference between what is and what ought to be seems to have made itself felt first as a result of the experience of 'the First Intermediate Period' in both Egypt and Sumer (Chr. Dawson: *The Dynamics of World History*, p. 116). The revolutionary spiritual event was the experience (authentic or illusory) of the establishment of direct communion between individual human souls and an Absolute Spiritual Reality transcending the world of Nature (and also the world of human society); and this dates from the last millennium B.C. (ibid., pp. 117–18; cp. p. 177). 'It was in India that the decisive step was first taken, and it was in India that the new view of Reality was followed out unwaveringly in all its practical implications' (ibid., p. 118).

cultural and social effect of breaking up the previous comprehensive cultural integration of the society in which the new vision is attained. In fact, the epiphany of a higher religion splits an integrated culture in a way that is comparable to the splitting of undifferentiated Reality by the awakening of consciousness.

If this is the higher religions' nature and effect, it will be inherent in their nature that they should find their social expression in independent organizations of their own and that they should engage in missionary activity. When the trans-human spiritual presence is seen direct instead of through the medium of human social needs and activities, human beings who have attained this new vision will be impelled to act on it in two new ways. They will want to enter into a new association with each other, independent of their traditional social ties; and they will want to communicate to the rest of mankind the saving truth about Reality that has been revealed to, or been discovered by, the adherents of the new religion in their belief. The emergence of this impelling sense of mission, with nothing short of the whole World for its field, raises the question whether the histories and institutions of the higher religions can really be stowed, like those of older religions, within the frameworks of the histories and institutions of particular pre-existing societies of a kind that is not primarily religious. May it not be found that the higher religions must be treated as societies of a new species, and must therefore be regarded as phenomena which cannot be dealt with in terms of any other species than their own if they are to be dealt with adequately—that is to say, intelligibly? This question can be brought into sharper focus. Can the higher religions be dealt with as if they were simply parts of the cultures of the civilizations, which were the highest species of society in existence at the time when the higher religions emerged? Can each of the higher religions be regarded as being one of the products and expressions of some particular civilization, and as being nothing more than that?

An orderly rationalist mind will be reluctant to be convinced that this question cannot be answered in the affirmative; for, if it can be, without doing violence to the phenomena, this will be a victory for simplicity and for clarity.[1] It will make for simplicity because it will allow the student of human affairs to go on dealing with human history, since the emergence of the earliest civilizations about five thousand years ago, in terms of a comparative study of this species of society and this one only. The subsumption of higher religions under civilizations will also make for clarity, because it will make it possible to go on treating religion simply as a part of human culture. It will make it possible still to avoid grappling with the controversial question whether the spiritual presence higher than Man, that is vouched for by unverifiable religious experience, is Reality itself or is a prodigious illusion. The powerful appeal of this rational quest for clarity and simplicity got the better of me, for one, when I was working out my original plan for this book. I decided to try to bring the whole field of human affairs,

---

[1] 'We are inclined to believe that the ultimate laws of Nature are not only few but simple' (H. W. B. Joseph: *An Introduction to Logic*, 2nd ed., pp. 506–7).

since the appearance of the earliest civilizations, within the framework of a comparative study of civilizations.[1] And, before I started to put this decision into action, I was reassured by the publication of the first volume of Spengler's work, in which I found that my own intended plan of operations had been anticipated, with apparently complete assurance, by an inquirer who was obviously a man of genius. The same plan of operations has since been followed by Bagby;[2] and I should guess that he, too, was attracted to it by the promise of clarity and simplicity that this plan appears to hold out before one has begun to put it to the test of applying it to the phenomena. This empirical test raises the question: Do the phenomena allow of this apparently clear and simple solution of the problem presented by the appearance of the higher religions? This is a difficult question to answer, because it is difficult to find anyone who is in a position to approach it impartially, without *parti pris*. The most that anyone can do is to get to grips with the phenomena in as open-minded a mood as he can muster up.

3. THE HIGHER RELIGIONS' STATUS IN THE LIGHT OF THE PHENOMENA

If we start by looking at the three oldest of the higher religions— Judaism, Zoroastrianism, and Hinduism[3]—we may be inclined to judge that these can each be subsumed under a particular civilization more or less legitimately.

It is true that all three, like other representatives of the new species of religion, conceive of the godhead as being sovereignly self-sufficient and omnipresent. Brahmā, Ahuramazda, and Yahweh reign, each of them, over the whole of mankind and the whole of the Universe.[4] They are not just the respective communal divinities of the Hindus, the Parsees, and the Jews. It is also true that the followers of all three religions have shown concern to propagate their faiths. The Jews converted to Judaism the royal family of the kingdom of Adiabene (in what is now

---

[1] Here, I think, I was committing the sin of pride of which several critics accuse me (see Chapter II, Annex: *Ad Hominem*, p. 638). I stand convicted, I am afraid; and this is, I also fear, presumptive evidence of conceitedness. The only defence that I can plead is that I have since changed my plan as a result of my experiences in trying to carry it out in its original form. [2] In *Culture and History.*

[3] For the purpose of the present argument, I am using the word Hinduism in its more usual sense as meaning the indigenous religion of India from the close of the interregnum following the dissolution of the Indus Culture down to the present day (the religion of the Indus Culture remains unknown to us so far, save for a few flashes of light that have been thrown upon it by some of its disinterred artefacts). In vols. i–x I have provisionally confined my usage of the word to mean only the post-Buddhaic indigenous religion of India. This usage of mine has been disputed, together with the chronological caesura, tentatively drawn by me in Indian history, with which it is connected. These points are discussed in the present volume on pp. 182–4, below.

[4] Ahuramazda's omnipotence is, of course, contested by his adversary Angramainyush; Yahweh's omnipotence is defied by his adversary Satan; and Brahmā is made manifest to men in the form of a host of emanations, who, looked at historically, are survivors from a previous polytheism with which Hinduism has never made a break. On the other hand, in the Hindu vision of the godhead, its personal facet, Brahmā, has a complement in an impersonal facet, Brahman. And Brahman is more remote and farther withdrawn from implication in human affairs than either Yahweh or Ahuramazda, who have never been followed beyond the range of personality in their worshippers' vision of them.

'Iraqi Kurdistan), in the first century of the Christian Era, and the royal family of the Turkish Khazar horde, on the steppe between the Lower Volga and the Lower Don, in the eighth century; and, in the fastnesses of the Caucasus and of the Semyen Mountains in Abyssinia, there are today highland clans professing the Jewish religion whose ancestors must have been converted to Judaism by Jewish missionary enterprise. Zoroastrianism, again, was propagated in the time of the Achaemenian Empire (550/525–331 B.C.) to Cappadocia, and, in and after the time of the Sasanian Empire (A.D. 224–651/2), from Iran and the Oxus-Jaxartes Basin across the Great Eurasian Steppe to Northern China. As for Hinduism, it was propagated eastwards from India as far across Indonesia as the island of Bali and, on the mainland, as far as what is now Southern Vietnam.

These three religions thus display the two distinctive marks of their class; 'an ancient civilization was transmuted by a series of challenges into a universal religion';[1] yet none of the three ever took the new road decisively; all three remained straddled ambiguously with one foot on either side of the line marking the new departure. In their conception of the role of Almighty God, their adherents became arrested in a state of double thinking which, to Christian and Muslim minds, seems paradoxically inconsistent. After they had come to think of God as the omnipresent lord of the Universe, they went on thinking of Him at the same time as still being the peculiar local god of the society or community in which He had originally been worshipped as such. Thus, each of these three religions, in becoming a higher religion, still also continued to be a part of the integrated culture of a particular community or society; and it has never become feasible to be converted to the Jewish, the Zoroastrian, or the Hindu religion without at the same time having to become a naturalized member of Jewish, Zoroastrian, or Hindu society.[2] Conversion to Judaism or Zoroastrianism has involved submission to a system of law[3] in which religious observances are inextricably intertwined with what, to Christian and Muslim minds, would seem like purely secular regulations. Conversion to Hinduism has involved incorporation in a caste and submission to the restrictions that the Hindu caste system entails.[4] This explains why conversions to these three religions have been rare, and why their adherents have been no more than half-hearted in their efforts to bring gentiles into their jealously guarded folds.[5] The source of the perennial ill-feeling between

[1] Rabbi J. B. Agus, in *Judaism*, vol. 4, No. 4 (Fall, 1955), p. 332.
[2] In Jewish history 'there resulted in the post-Biblical period a unique combination of a perfectly universalistic religion with an intensely nationalistic ethnic group' (Agus, in *Judaism*, 1956, p. 30).
[3] 'To accept Judaism without accepting the Mosaic Law is a contradiction in terms' (E. Berkovitz: *Judaism: Fossil or Ferment?* p. 76).
[4] All the same, when Hinduism was propagated into Indonesia and into continental South-East Asia, 'the Indian social structure, with its caste system, was less thoroughly absorbed than was the religious' (H. G. Quaritch Wales: *The Making of Greater India* (London 1951, Quaritch), p. 20).
[5] Agus holds that ethnic loyalty diverted the Jews from missionary efforts, in spite of the fact that 'the Jewish religion was as universalistic in its teaching as Christianity or Islam. . . . The Talmud operates consistently on the supposition that a deep line of distinction must be drawn between the rights of Jews and non-Jews' (Agus in *Judaism*, 1956, p. 45; Cp. Juvenal: *Satura XIV*, ll. 101–4). At the same time Agus points out that, in

Jews and gentiles, and of the tragedies and atrocities in which this has repeatedly come to a head, is the inability of both gentiles and Jews to tell whether being a Jew means being an adherent of a religion or whether it means being a partaker in the culture of a community that, even in dispersion, has retained its original ethnic character.[1]

The question whether Judaism is part of the culture of a community or whether it is a religion that can be embraced by anyone, whatever his ancestral culture or his local nationality may be, is the question that was at issue, in the first generation of Christianity, between the Jewish Christian church and the gentile Christian church created by the missionary work of Saint Paul. And it is significant that the secession of the Christian Church from Jewry, which followed in spite of Paul's and Peter's unanimous desire to avoid the breach, was not the only case of its kind. Six hundred years later another new religion inspired by Judaism, namely Islam, parted company with Jewry, as Christianity had done, on a mission to convert the gentiles to the saving truth which the Jews themselves had been keeping to themselves,[2] like the talent

the Gospels, the Pharisees are described as being eager to make converts. See, for example, Matt. xxiii. 15.

[1] The ambiguity of the attitude of some Jews, at any rate, on this point is illustrated by the following set of passages in M. Samuel's *The Professor and the Fossil*: 'When a Jew considers his Americanism or his Englishhood as a substitute for Judaism and a replacement for his feeling of participation in the Jewish peoplehood . . . he secularizes himself out of his Jewish identity' (p. 180). 'Neo-Zionism was an instinctive counter-move against the threat of assimilation presented by specific modern conditions' (p. 197). At the same time, Samuel maintains that to say that the Jewish êthos was incompatible with the functions of modern citizenship would be to declare the Jewish êthos immoral—'a point of view not worth arguing with' (p. 196).

To judge by these passages, Samuel's position seems to be that a Jew would be failing to do his full duty towards Judaism if he were to decide to do his full duty as a citizen of the gentile country of which he is a citizen *de jure*, but that it would be offensive in a gentile to point out that a Jew who took this line was deliberately assuming two incompatible obligations and was trying to have the best of both worlds.

In another passage (p. 263), Samuel suggests that being a good Jew, in his sense, may be incompatible, not only with being a good citizen of a gentile state, but even with being a good human being. 'I have asked myself whether a strong feeling of history within one's own people makes it impossible to share in the general sense of history; whether this kind of belonging and inclusion must lead to a proportionate not-belonging and exclusion; whether, in short, this is a form of egocentricity destructive of one's all-human consciousness.'

If Samuel may be taken as being representative of one of several present-day Jewish states of mind, these passages suggest that, in some Jewish minds today, there is a still unclarified ambiguity on the questions what it means to be a Jew and what attitude towards gentiles this entails. If so, it is perhaps natural that some present-day gentiles—including, for instance, me—should also be somewhat in the dark on these points. Rabbi Agus is right in saying of me that 'his judgment derives from an ambiguity in the use of the term Judaism. At times he equates Judaism with the ethnic culture of Jewry; at other times he thinks of the Jewish faith as a separable pattern of ideas which is included more or less in our modern Western culture' (*Judaism*, vol. 4, No. 4 (Fall, 1955), p. 321). 'He tends to lose sight of the distinction between Judaism and "Jewishness" or the national-cultural civilization of Jewish People' (*The National Jewish Monthly*, November 1956, p. 40).

[2] Rabbi J. B. Agus explains the secessions of Christianity and Islam from Judaism in terms of one of the ideas put forward by me in the present book (viii. 10): it was a case of barbarians capitulating to a superior culture by adopting it and at the same time still asserting their own cultural distinctiveness by adopting the superior alien culture in an heretical form (*Judaism*, 1956, p. 41). The combination of Jewish monotheism with Jewish nationalism inevitably produced this gentile reaction. In Christianity and Islam 'the [Jewish] message was twice accepted, but the messenger was twice rejected' (ibid., p. 39. Cp. E. Berkovitz, *Judaism: Fossil or Ferment?*, pp. 45–46 and 48–49).

Agus criticizes (ibid., pp. 19–20) Klausner's view—shared by Dubnow and by contemporary Christian scholars, e.g. Wellhausen—that the reason why Jesus was rejected

wrapped in a napkin and buried in the earth by the servant in one of Jesus's parables. In the history of Zoroastrianism it has been the same story. During the age in which Zoroastrianism was the established national religion of the Sasanian Empire, Manichaeism seceded from it in the third century of the Christian Era and Mazdakism in the fifth century; and in the following age, when the Sasanian Empire, as well as half the Roman Empire, had been conquered by the Muslim Arabs, the new regime's Zoroastrian subjects in Iran were converted to Islam much more rapidly than were its Christian subjects in 'Iraq, Syria, and Egypt. In the history of Hinduism again, Buddhism and Jainism seceded in the sixth century B.C.

These portentous secessions are evidence of an unresolved tension in the bosom of the Jewish, Zoroastrian, and Hindu societies between a will to transform the ancestral religion of one people into a religion for all men and a reluctance to cast before swine the pearls that were the spiritually privileged people's heirloom. The tension resulted in repeated secessions because, in each of these three cases, a people that had seen the vision of a higher religion could not bring itself to go the whole way either in accepting the consequences or in rejecting them. It shrank from paying the price of collective self-abnegation that has to be paid by a 'Chosen People' if they are to become the missionaries of a world-wide faith; yet, at the same time, it could never turn its back on this vision when once it had seen it. This indecision condemned each of these three peoples to become a house divided against itself.

This infirmity—common to Judaism, Zoroastrianism, and Hinduism —of hovering on the borderline between two different ideals makes it just possible for a systematist to treat each of these three religions as being no more than the religious component (or part of this) in the culture of one of the civilizations. The same tendency to relapse from a universal into a communal outlook can also be observed in the histories of Buddhism, Christianity, and Islam. For instance, in Tibet, until the other day, the ecclesiastical institutions of Buddhism were being employed to serve as the political machinery for a national government. In Western Europe, for nearly a thousand years ending in the nineteenth century, many local states besides the Papal States were governed as prince-bishoprics. Trent, Salzburg, Passau, Mainz, Cologne, Trèves, Liége, and the County Palatine of Durham are examples. Conversely, there are still today a number of countries in which Christianity has been

by the Jews was because his teaching was supra-national. Klausner admits that all the *logia* attributed to Jesus appear in the rabbinical literature too; and the Pharisees, Agus here points out, were universalists, whereas at least one passage in the Gospels, Matt. xv. 21–28, is more contemptuous of gentiles than any passage in the Talmud. As Agus sees it, Jesus was rejected, not because he was not a nationalist, but because, in the eyes of contemporary pharisees, he did not make good his claim to be the Messiah.

On this showing, the true founder of Christianity, in its historic form as a universal religion, would be, not Jesus, but Paul, when he won his point that membership in the Christian community need not carry with it an obligation to observe the rules of the Mosaic Law.

Agus (ibid., pp. 30–31) cites Y. Kaufman's thesis that the reason why Christianity failed to convert the Jews—whereas it did convert the World—was because the World needed monotheism, whereas the Jews already had it. According to Kaufman, 'the Jewish religion maintains automatically the wall of ethnic alienation between Jew and Christian', and therefore the Jews cannot accept assimilation wholeheartedly.

reduced to the status of a national religion incorporated in the establishment of some national government. This is, for instance, still the status of Episcopalian Protestantism in the Kingdom of England, minus Wales, and of Eastern Orthodox Christianity in every country, except those now under Communist rule, in which this form of Christianity is prevalent. In the Islamic World, again, the Shi'ite sect of Islam is today still the established national religion of the Kingdom of Iran; and a consideration of the early history of Islam, during the first century and a half after the opening date of Muhammad's preaching at Mecca, suggests that Islam as a whole nearly lapsed into becoming the national religion of the Arabs—a fate which would have prevented it from being, as it has been, a missionary religion with a world-wide appeal.[1]

Is it possible, then, to dispose of Islam, Christianity, and Buddhism in the way in which it might conceivably be just possible to dispose of Judaism, Zoroastrianism, and Hinduism? Can each of these other three religions, likewise, be assigned by a systematist to this or that civilization and be labelled as the religious component—or as part of the religious component—of the container-civilization's culture? Spengler has taken this line uncompromisingly. In his morphology of human affairs since the emergence of civilization, the higher religions find a place only as elements in the structures of the civilizations and as incidents in the histories of the civilizations' rises and falls. Bagby, in his prolegomena, follows Spengler's lead, apparently without misgivings. I took the same line myself till I was pulled up short by the intractability, as I saw it, of the phenomena when, in carrying out my plan of operations, I reached the point at which I had to come to grips with the problem of the higher religions' place in human affairs. Bagby would have been confronted by the same problem if he had lived to reach the same point in the testing of his original hypotheses.

In his prolegomena Bagby gives the same list of six higher religions that I have given in the present chapter, and he fits each of them into the framework of some one or other of the nine major civilizations in his list of civilizations.[2] Buddhism, as well as Hinduism, is taken as

[1] See Chapter XIV, pp. 470–1.
[2] The form of words which he uses is that these six religions each 'originated within a major civilization' (*Culture and History*, p. 173). This would be true and indisputable if, for the sake of the argument, we were to recognize the existence of Spengler's 'Magian Civilization', which Bagby has adopted under the name 'Near-Eastern Civilization' (see ibid., pp. 167 and 168), and if we were also to concede Bagby's postulate (ibid., p. 173) that the 'inventions' of Judaism and Zoroastrianism in or about the eighth century B.C. are to be attributed to the 'Near-Eastern Civilization', on the ground that these 'inventions' were 'premonitory developments prior to the rise of the Near-Eastern Civilization' —an event that Bagby dates some eight hundred years later, in about the first century of the Christian Era. Bagby holds, however, if I have read him correctly, not only that each of the higher religions *originated* within some single civilization, but also that none of them, at any stage in its history, was anything more than a part of the culture of some single civilization or other. This is implied in his thesis (see *Toynbee and History*, p. 107) that religion is merely a part or aspect of civilization, not a primary agent. In accordance with this thesis Bagby abstains from giving the higher religions any separate place of their own in the morphology of human affairs that he outlines in *Culture and History*. In his view the study of human affairs since the emergence of civilization is wholly covered by 'the comparative study of civilizations' that figures in the sub-title of his book, and he sets himself to fit all six higher religions into this morphological scheme.

being simply part of the Indian Civilization. The other four—Judaism,
Zoroastrianism, Christianity, and Islam—are packed into a veritable hold-
all for unwanted religions: the hypothetical 'Near-Eastern', alias 'Magian',
Civilization that Bagby has taken over from Spengler.[1] The hypothesis
that there has been, and still is, a real civilization corresponding to this
label is a disputable one. This question is discussed at a later point in the
present volume.[2] Undoubtedly it presents the most difficult of all the
problems that confront anyone who tries to identify the civilizations that
have arisen so far and to disentangle them from each other. My own
attempt to solve this problem by the hypothetical construction of a
'Syriac Civilization' has drawn heavy fire from my critics. In the present
volume I am making a second attempt to grapple with this problem,[3]
and I am in no mood to be censorious about other people's different
approaches to it. Anyway, in this chapter we are not concerned with this
problem on its own account. We are concerned with it here only in its
bearing on the general question of the relations between civilizations
and higher religions.

It should be noted that Spengler's and Bagby's system of cultural and
social morphology takes for granted their thesis that each of the higher
religions is wholly contained within one or other of the civilizations and
that each of them is also wholly explicable in terms of its container-
civilization. The system and the thesis on which it is based stand or fall
together. If Spengler and Bagby found themselves forced, by the historical evidence, to admit that one of the higher religions had, at one or
another time and place, been in some relation with two or more civilizations without ever losing its own identity, they would then be bound to
admit that this particular higher religion was not, after all, wholly contained in one single civilization and wholly explicable in terms of this.
To vindicate the validity of their morphology they must demonstrate
either that each of the higher religions has run its course, so far, within
the channel of some single civilization's history, or, alternatively, that,
if a higher religion has apparently been in relations with more civilizations than one, this apparent historical datum is illusory. What has
transcended the limits of a single civilization is merely a common name,
with no common substance corresponding to it. The religion associated
with each of the two or more different civilizations in question will, in
Spengler's and Bagby's view, be found on inspection to be in reality a
separate and different religion from any that is associated with any other
of these civilizations. Even if it does bear the same name, the common
label will prove to be incorrect and misleading.

In *Culture and History* Bagby does not go into this point in his re-
ference to Buddhism,[4] but in the light of his morphological analysis of
Christianity we may assume, I think, that he regards the Buddhism of
Eastern Asia (China, Korea, Japan, Vietnam) as being, in effect, a new
religion that has nothing beyond the name in common with the earlier
Buddhism of India. It is true that every higher religion—Christianity,
Buddhism, Islam, or whichever it may be—tends both to retain some-

---

[1] See the preceding footnote.   [2] See pp. 443–6.
[3] See pp. 446–61.   [4] On p. 173.

thing of the distinctive colour of the social and cultural environment in which it has originated, and also to take on something of the colour of any other environment into which it may subsequently have made its way. This is to be expected, since the higher religions, whether or not they are 'of' the World, are unquestionably 'in' it, and 'the World' means, in this context, some particular regional culture. But when this has been granted it remains to be proved that the transforming effect upon a higher religion of the experience of entering a new cultural province is so radical as to produce a break with the migratory religion's own past that amounts to a change in its identity.

The test-case for Bagby's thesis, as presented in his published work up to the date of his untimely death, is his analysis of the relations between Judaism, Zoroastrianism, and Christianity and his hypothetical 'Near-Eastern Civilization'. In recognizing[1] that the origins of Judaism go back to the eighth century B.C., Bagby is implicitly identifying it as part of the culture of the Syro-Phoenician civilization that figures[2] in his list of 'secondary' civilizations. This identification is obligatory if we apply Bagby's own morphological principles. This, however, would involve him in admitting that Judaism had been in relations with more civilizations than one, since he reckons present-day Jews as being partakers in the 'Near-Eastern Civilization'.[3] His solution[4] is to identify the religion of Israel and Judah, from the eighth century B.C. onwards, and Zoroastrianism too, from whatever the date of its origin may be, as 'premonitory developments prior to the rise of the "Near-Eastern Civilization"'. In doing this, he is setting back the origin of the 'Near-Eastern Civilization' itself by 800 years, to the eighth century B.C. from the first century of the Christian Era. This changes his 'Near-Eastern Civilization' from being one that arose *after* the intrusion of the Hellenic Civilization into South-West Asia and Egypt into being one that, like my 'Syriac Civilization', originated in South-West Asia before the intrusion of Hellenism there and survived the millennium of Hellenic domination there that was inaugurated by Alexander's overthrow of the Achaemenian Empire.

I do not quarrel with Bagby for doing this, but I do notice that, as a result of his effort to bring Judaism within the compass of a single civilization, he falls into an inconsistency with himself. A few pages farther on,[5] in a criticism of my construction of a 'Syriac Civilization', he reasserts the separateness of his 'Syro-Phoenician Civilization' and his 'Near-Eastern Civilization' from each other. In this he may be right; but, if so, his previous modification of his own scheme so as to include his 'Syro-Phoenician Civilization' in his 'Near-Eastern' one, just for the sake of packing Judaism inside a single civilization only, suggests that here he may be forcing the facts; and this suggests, in turn, that the thesis for the sake of which he allows himself to fall into an inconsistency may not stand up to the test of being confronted with the historical phenomena.

This doubt becomes more insistent when we also find Bagby follow-

---

[1] In op. cit., pp. 167 and 173. [2] Ibid., p. 169. [3] Ibid., p. 167.
[4] Ibid., pp. 167 and 173. [5] On pp. 178–9.

ing Spengler[1] in treating Christianity in the Western World since the eleventh century of the Christian Era as being a different religion, in spite of the common label, from Christianity in the West before that date and from Christianity elsewhere down to the present day.[2] This contention is surely a paradoxical one; for surely Christianity, in all its later forms, bears not only a common name but a common character impressed on it by the experiences and achievements of the Christian Church during the first four and a half centuries of its existence. This age—the age of the Apostles, Martyrs, Fathers, Anchorites, and Creeds —has manifestly been the formative one. Compared to the decisive developments that occurred within that period, all subsequent developments in Christianity as a whole or in any of its branches have been no more than minor variations on the original theme; but the manifest formative period of Christianity was over, and the distinctive character of Christianity was firmly set, more than five hundred years before the emergence of the Western Civilization according to Spengler's chronology, which Bagby adopts.

Why then do Spengler, and Bagby following him, exert themselves to prove that Christianity in the West since the eleventh century is a new thing? The explanation is to be found in their inventory[3] of the contents of their 'hold-all' civilization: the 'Magian' or 'Near-Eastern', whichever of the two labels may be preferred. This receptacle is so capacious and so elastic that they have managed to pack into it all peoples and communities that have ever professed Christianity down to the present day, with one single, and awkward, exception. After having packed in, along with the rest, the Christians of Western Europe from the conversion of Constantine down to the eleventh century, they have had to recoil from

---

[1] See Spengler: *Der Untergang des Abendlandes*, vol. i, p. 256. 'The penchant towards the infinite was present in the Northern landscape, in a state of deep slumber, long before the first Christian set foot there; and, when the Faustian soul awoke, it re-shaped both primitive Teutonic heathenism and western Christianity into conformity with its own primordial symbol. It did this just at the time when the German, French, English, and Italian nations emerged, as unities, each with a strongly characterised physiognomy of its own, out of the fugitive forms of the Goth, Frank, Lombard, and Saxon peoples. The Edda has preserved this earliest religious expression of the Faustian soul. It attained its inner completion just at the moment when Abbot Odilo of Cluny initiated the movement that transformed the Magian Christianity of the Oriental-Arab World into the Faustian Christianity of the Western Church. Round about the year 1000 there were two possible ways in which a Faustian religion could take shape. It could either adopt and re-interpret the Magian Christianity of the Fathers or it could develop the Teutonic forms. The Edda is evidence for what the second of the alternative possibilities was.'

[2] In Bagby's own words (in *Culture and History*, p. 175), Christianity 'was adopted by the Teutonic kingdoms of Western Europe along with a number of other features of Near-Eastern Civilization. When these kingdoms began to develop a distinct major civilization of their own around the beginning of the second millennium, they retained Christianity but modified it profoundly in accordance with their new ideas and values. . . . In accordance with the development of Western Europe, Western European Christianity has been even further modified and has now taken a secular and rationalist cast in accordance with the character of the present age. Though many of the forms of belief and practice, especially among Catholics, are similar to those of Oriental Christians, the spirit—the basic ideas and values—is quite different. . . . To an outsider it must be evident that Christ and his disciples were Near-Easterners, not Western-Europeans.' This last of the points here made by Bagby is certainly correct, but it does not prove that Christianity in the modern West is not still the Christianity that took shape during the first four and a half centuries of the Christian Era.

[3] See Spengler: *Der Untergang des Abendlandes*, vol. ii, chap. i B, pp. 49–51, especially p. 50, and chap. iii, pp. 225–399; Bagby, op. cit., p. 167.

trying to do the same with those earlier Western Christians' descendants. The Christianity of Western Europe from the fourth century to the eleventh can be labelled as part of the culture of a 'Near-Eastern Civilization' without creating a startling impression of incongruity. But it would be almost prohibitively incongruous to pack the Westerners of the last nine centuries into the same mixed bag as the Byzantines, Muslims, Armenians, Jews, Copts, Maronites, Parsees, and Nestorians—the more so, when the Abyssinians and the Russians have been tied on to the hold-all's outside.[1]

It is hardly possible to label the culture of the modern West 'Near-Eastern'. But, when once it has been conceded that there are two different civilizations—first a 'Near-Eastern' Civilization and then a Western one—with which Christianity has been in relations, it must be argued, on Spengler's and Bagby's hypothesis, that there are two different Christianities—a separate religion to fit into each separate culture-frame. If this is not demonstrated it will have to be admitted that Christianity has been in relations with two different civilizations with no change in its own identity; and this, in its turn, would mean that Christianity is a phenomenon which cannot be classified in terms of any particular civilization and which must therefore be a representative of some different species of society.

This last-mentioned alternative is, I myself believe, the correct conclusion to draw from an examination of the difficulties into which Spengler and Bagby run when they attempt to deal with higher religions entirely in terms of civilizations. I ran into difficulties myself when I was taking the same line, and I concluded from my own experience that I had been on the wrong tack. One's recognition of an error is more convincing when the work in which one detects it is one's own and not somebody else's.

I, too, originally tried to account for the higher religions simply in terms of the civilizations. I took my cue from the relations, as I interpreted them, between the Christian Church on the one side and the Hellenic, Byzantine, and Western civilizations on the other, and I took this set of relations as my 'model' for interpreting the historical roles of other religions of the 'higher' species. I still think that, in the case that I took as my prototype, my interpretation was not incorrect as far as it went; and I think this case does throw some light on the way in which the transition between an earlier and a later civilization takes place when there is an historical connexion between them. At the same time, I now think that I went farther than is warranted by the historical phenomena in applying my prototype case to other cases.[2]

Following my clue, I saw a higher religion as a mechanism by which the species of society called civilizations had provided for its own repro-

---

[1] See Bagby, op. cit., pp. 167, 171, 174. In terms of my classification, as revised in the present volume, Spengler's and Bagby's procedure might be salvaged by ruling that the whole of the crop produced by a common Syriac–Hellenic culture-compost (see pp. 446–61) constitutes a single civilization. But this ruling would debar the West from being counted as being a distinct and separate civilization from the rest.

[2] A reconsideration of my previous procedure will be found in the present volume on pp. 170–86.

duction. I thought of higher religions as being 'chrysalises' into which a disintegrating civilization entered in the last stage of its dissolution, and from which a new civilization subsequently emerged. This view of the historical role of the higher religions was, I now think, a variation on the same fundamental error that I see in Spengler's and Bagby's view. It assumed that the higher religions were significant solely on account of their serviceableness to societies of a different kind from their own.[1] Starting from my own taking-off point, I arrived at different findings from Spengler's and Bagby's over some points of detail. Instead of thinking that a higher religion always originated inside some single civilization, I thought that it always originated from an encounter between two civilizations or more, and that this encounter was always preceded by the breakdown and disintegration of at least one of the parties to it. One of the outward visible signs of social breakdown, as I saw it, was the spiritual secession of a proletariat from a ruling minority that could no longer maintain its dominant position by anything better than sheer force. I saw that in several cases the seceding minority met and mingled with fellow proletarians seceding from some other civilization, and I thought that higher religions were the offsprings of encounters between civilizations at this social level. Seeing Christianity as the offspring of an encounter between the Hellenic and the Syriac Civilization, and judging that both civilizations were in disintegration when this happened, I applied the same formula rightly, perhaps, to the history of the Mahayanian form of Buddhism,[2] and wrongly, as I am

---

[1] In retrospect I think that this mistake (as I now believe it to be) in my original diagnosis of the role of the higher religions in history was a consequence of my general outlook at that time. I readily fell into thinking of the higher religions' role as being simply a means towards a non-religious end because I was sceptical about religion in general. This attitude of mine is evidently apparent in earlier volumes of this book; for several critics have noticed it. John Strachey, for instance, in an unpublished critique of vols. i–vi, finds that my arguments for a return to religion are utilitarian and that I come near to thinking that religion is man-made. Lord Hailsham concurs with this criticism of Strachey's in a letter of 4th December, 1949, written to Strachey after he had read Strachey's critique of my attitude. J. K. Feibleman, in *T'ien Hsia Monthly*, vol. xi, Nos. 1 and 2 (1940), p. 146, footnote 10, finds that my argument in favour of other-worldliness is a pragmatic one, on the lines of the fable of Solomon's choice. J. H. Nichols, too, suspects that, in the churches, and indeed in religion in all its manifestations, I see a means to a worldly end. This makes on Nichols' mind an unpleasant impression of utilitarianism, and reminds him of the spirit of the age of the restoration after the French Revolution and Napoleon (*The Journal of Religion*, No. 28 (1948), pp. 99–119; *Studium Generale*, No. 4 (1951), pp. 175–182, ad fin.).

My original approach to the relation between religion and the secular side of life may, I fear, have given some justification for these criticisms. Since then my attitude has changed, as has been noticed by the critics cited on p. 27, footnote 2, p. 100, footnote 3, and pp. 649–51. If my attitude towards religion was formerly utilitarian, it is not so now. In any case, whatever the judgement on my present attitude may be, I agree that the utilitarian attitude towards religion is a wrong one. Religion is an end in itself, because it is concerned with things that matter more to human beings than anything else in the world. This is the discovery—or revelation—that was the origin of the higher religions. The utilization of a higher religion to serve non-religious purposes is a reversion to a primitive state of affairs in which religion is an integral part of the total configuration of culture. This social reversion seems to me to be also a spiritual regression.

[2] The Mahayana seems to have arisen in India, contemporaneously with the rise there of the modern form of Hinduism, after there had been an encounter between the Indic Civilization and the Hellenic. This encounter seems comparable to that between the Syriac Civilization and the Hellenic after the overthrow of the Achaemenian Empire by Alexander the Great. India's Hellenic conqueror, Demetrius of Bactria, overran India in and after 183 B.C., just after the Maurya Empire had been overthrown by a usurper.

now convinced, to the history of the worship of Osiris[1]—to take, as illustrations, two cases out of a number that I tried to identify, analyse, and interpret. These differences of detail do not acquit me from the charge that, in the earlier stages of my inquiry, I was making the mistake into which, as I now see it, Spengler and Bagby, too, have fallen. The view that I now hold has been exactly expressed by Dawson:

'The great civilizations of the World do not produce the great religions as a kind of cultural by-product; in a very real sense, the great religions are the foundations on which the great civilizations rest. . . . We shall never create a living religion merely as a means to an end.'[2]

Religious faith comes by grace, not by will. Religion cannot be called to heel, like a dog, to suit human convenience.[3] At certain times and places living religions have been tempted or driven into serving as means to non-religious ends; but to take these episodes of their history as being their *raison d'être*, as I have done in the past, is to misunderstand and misinterpret their mission. So far from this service of secular purposes being a fulfilment of their mission, it is a diversion from it; and, whenever a higher religion has allowed itself to be shunted into this side-track, there has always been a spiritual-minded minority among its adherents who have remained faithful to their religion's true purpose.

When, in the Roman Empire, the Christian Church was not only granted toleration but was made virtually a department of state, the anchorites withdrew into the Desert, and the Donatists, Nestorians, and Monophysites successively seceded from a church which the Monophysites branded as 'Imperialist' (Melchite). When, in the West, a

The Mahayana played the role of a 'chrysalis' during the interregnum in the history of China that followed the fall of the Han Dynasty at the turn of the second and third centuries of the Christian Era. In this series of events, the pattern of my prototype—the relations between the Hellenic and Syriac civilizations, Christianity, and the Western and Byzantine civilizations—is, I think, recognizable, though perhaps I have exaggerated the points of resemblance between the two episodes. The role of the Mahayana in Chinese history is reconsidered on pp. 176–80.

[1] See further pp. 184–5. Our pictures of the civilizations that have been rescued from oblivion by the work of modern archaeologists are apt to change more rapidly and more radically than our pictures of others—for example, the Hellenic—of which the memory has never been lost and from which we have a large body of surviving literature that gives us not only a record but a key to interpreting this. Our knowledge of the Egyptiac Civilization has no such solid body of evidence to stabilize it, and the reading of Egyptiac history by the Egyptologists therefore not only changes rapidly but also fluctuates disconcertingly. My original account of the worship of Osiris in i. 141–4 was given on the authority of J. H. Breasted's book *The Development of Religion in Ancient Egypt*, published in 1912. Breasted had been one of the leading Egyptologists of his generation, and in 1930, when I was writing those pages, it was not unreasonable to follow him with confidence. Breasted held that 'the worship of Osiris was a popular religion' (op. cit., p. 29) and that one of the results of its triumph was 'the democratisation of blessedness beyond the grave' (ibid., p. 252). This view of Breasted's has now been discarded by his successors (see, for example, pp. xi–xii of the introduction, dated March, 1959, by J. A. Wilson to a new edition of this book of Breasted's: New York 1959, Harper Torchbooks), and we have no guarantee that their view will stand the test of time any better than his has stood it. Meanwhile, the helpless outsider has to take it from the diadochi that the worship of Osiris was not a popular religion at all. The future opinion of the epigoni is anybody's guess.

[2] Chr. Dawson: *The Dynamics of World History*, pp. 128 and 168.

[3] These points are made by H. J. Morgenthau (in *Toynbee and History*, pp. 198–9), among other people.

resuscitated imperial government tried to reduce the Roman See, and the rest of the Church within its reach, to the state of subordination to which the 'Melchite' Orthodox Church had already been reduced in the East Roman Empire, this secular challenge to the Church's freedom evoked the mighty resistance movement that was carried to a victorious conclusion, under the Papacy's auspices, in the eleventh and twelfth centuries. This was the original issue in the conflict between the Empire and the Papacy. When the Papacy had successfully asserted against the West Roman Empire its claim to be the presiding institution in the medieval Western Christian Commonwealth, its assumption of this quasi-political power provoked first the Conciliar Movement and eventually the Protestant Reformation. The Lutheran and Anglican Protestants jumped out of the frying-pan into the fire. They fell straight into the jaws of autocratic parochial princes; and the Calvinists, where they survived, avoided the fate of becoming the slaves of parochial governments only by resorting to Muhammad's expedient of acquiring political control. After the Anglican Protestant Church had been successfully reduced to subordination by the English Crown, the Church's true role was upheld in England by the secession of the Free Churches from the Establishment. Even in Eastern Orthodox Christendom, where the Church has been deprived of its independence more continuously than in any other part of the Christian World, there has been at least one great country, Russia, in which the movement of nonconformity has been as vigorous as it has been in the English-speaking countries.

Such assertions of a claim to independence, and refusals to acquiesce in seeing the Church being made to serve non-religious purposes, have not been exceptional incidents in the Christian Church's history; they have been vindications of the rule against exceptional breaches of it. The Hildebrandine movement in Western Christendom in the eleventh century was not the inauguration of a new religion. So far from being a breach with the spirit of the primitive Christian Church, it was a revival of this. And the nonconformist movement in Protestantism has not been a flash in the pan. Today England and Scotland are the only English-speaking countries in which there are still established churches; in all the rest, including the United States, all Protestant churches, as well as the Roman Catholic Church, are free from control by the state; and in Russia, since the Communist Revolution of 1917, the boon of hard liberty, that had previously been the dearly-bought privilege of the Russian nonconformists, has been thrust upon the Eastern Orthodox Church by a hostile political regime whose intention, in disestablishing the Church, was, no doubt, not a benevolent one. Through adversity even more than through prosperity, the free churches, Protestant, Catholic, and Orthodox, have been gaining ground in our day, while the established churches have been receding.[1]

---

1 This is not, of course, the last word on the relative merits of the Christian churches that are carried on the establishments of states and those that are free from this servitude; for the political status of churches is not the only measure of their prosperity and adversity. Another measure—and one which is no less informative—is the average level of the wealth and power of a church's individual members; and the readings on this gauge

The subordination of higher religions to states or other secular institutions is a relapse into the ancient dispensation—prevalent before the first emergence of higher religions—under which religion was an integral part of the total culture of some pre-civilizational society or early civilization. On the other hand the independence re-achieved by the Roman Catholic Christian Church since the eleventh century and, in more recent times, also by the free Protestant and free Eastern Christian churches is in the main line of advance, not only of Christianity itself, but of the higher religions as a class. For example, the establishment of the Shi'i form of Islam as the official religion of a Persian national state in the sixteenth century of the Christian Era has been followed, in the nineteenth century, by two secessions from the Shi'ah in Persia. The Babi movement, and its offspring the Baha'i movement, are missionary religions which address themselves not only to all Shi'is and to all Muslims but to all human beings of all religious denominations.

4. THE LIMITS OF PRESENT POSSIBILITIES OF AGREEMENT

The higher religions are bound always to strive to keep themselves disengaged from secular social and cultural trammels because this is an indispensable condition for the fulfilment of their true mission. This mission is not concerned directly with human beings' social or cultural relations with each other: its concern is the relation between each individual human being and the trans-human spiritual presence, of which the higher religions offer a new vision. We may believe that this vision is an hallucination or we may believe that it is a revelation or discovery of Reality; our choice between these two interpretations of the phenomena will be determined by, and relative to, our fundamental presuppositions. But, whichever interpretation we adopt, we can perhaps agree upon accepting four propositions about the phenomena themselves. The first of these surely uncontroversial propositions is that the believers in the higher religions are convinced that their religious experience is not illusory. The second is that this conviction, whether justified or not, has given them the faith to move mountains. The third proposition is that the deeds which the adherents of the higher religions have done, and the institutions which they have built up, loom large in the panorama of human affairs since the date when religions of this kind first appeared on the scene.[1] The fourth proposition—which has, I hope, been demonstrated more or less convincingly in this chapter— is that, in a study of human affairs, the higher religions cannot be dealt with intelligibly simply as products or parts of particular civilizations.

do not necessarily coincide with those on the other. A politically 'free' church may become the preserve of a privileged class, and may even become an instrument for protecting and promoting this class's worldly interests. The 'free' Protestant churches in the English-speaking countries and the Roman Catholic Church in France have, in our time, become, to some extent, the preserves and instruments of the Western middle class. Conversely, an 'established' church may be a seed-bed, not only for worldliness, but for spirituality. In England, since the Reformation, spiritual prowess, insight, and leadership have not been confined to adherents of the 'free' churches.

[1] But see p. 76, footnote 1.

They require to be dealt with, at least on a par with civilizations and with pre-civilizational societies, as primary phenomena that cannot be reduced to terms of anything other than themselves.

A rationalist-minded student of human affairs can, I believe, accept these propositions, including the fourth of them, without compromising his philosophical position or being untrue to his convictions. Acceptance still leaves open the question whether the unverifiable experiences, from which the higher religions have sprung, are or are not true insights. At the present day we cannot bring our conflicting answers to this question into agreement. This is beyond our power, because these various answers are relative to a still unreconciled difference in our fundamental presuppositions about Reality.

Indeed, there is disagreement not only between rationalists and 'trans-rationalists', but also inside the 'trans-rationalist' camp. This domestic disagreement among 'trans-rationalists', is, as I see it, a family quarrel. The differences of view from which it arises are conspicuous, but I do not believe that they are irreconcilable, because I do not believe that they are fundamental. But this, of course, is precisely the point of contention between orthodox adherents of the historic higher religions and ex-believers who have come again to believe that Man is not the highest spiritual presence in the Universe, yet have not returned to this belief in any of its traditional forms.[1] Such agnostic[2] 'trans-rationalists', of whom I am now one, are perhaps even fewer in number than the rationalists in the present-day world. At present we cannot tell whether one or other of these two present minorities, or the huge present orthodox majority,[3] or some other sect, as yet not visible above the horizon, is 'the wave of the future'.

The unclosed rift between orthodox believers and unorthodox 'trans-rationalists' is not, of course, the first schism that there has ever been within the ranks of those who do not find in rationalism a convincing explanation of Reality. There are also the schisms between the different orthodoxies themselves, and these go back to the first appearance of the higher religions on the scene. Each of the Judaic higher religions has always been intolerant of all others, besides being intolerant of religions of the older 'pagan' kind; and this, though tragic, is not surprising; for intolerance is the defect of the higher religions' virtue. The direct

---

[1] See pp. 75–76.

[2] I say 'agnostic' (see p. 75, footnote 2) because Father Walker (in *Toynbee and History*, p. 343) and Strachey (in his unpublished critique) are right in their judgement that I do not hold the traditional view of revelation as being a 'release' by God of information telling the truth about Reality in some absolute sense. I believe that the Buddha's experience of enlightenment through His own spiritual exertions was as valid as Muhammad's experience of enlightenment through God's instructions dictated to him by the Archangel Gabriel. If the origin of the experience of enlightenment is divine, it is so, in my view, in a sense in which the same epithet can be applied, with equal truth, to all the rest of our experience. My belief on this point is exactly expressed in the following comment, by one of the contributors to the collected papers of the Hippocratean school of medicine, on the 'Holy Sickness': 'I too hold that these phenomena are divine, but I also hold that everything else is likewise, and that nothing is either more divine or more human than anything else. Each phenomenon has its own nature, and none occurs in any but a natural way' (*Effects of Differences in Atmosphere, Water, and Location*, chap. 22).

[3] The orthodox adherents of historic higher religions are still in an overwhelming majority in the World as a whole; in a rather smaller majority in the West; and in a minority perhaps only in Western intellectual circles.

vision of Reality that each of them has caught is so much more convincing and inspiring than the older religions' vision of it that the adherents of each higher religion have jumped to the conclusion that their own religion is a unique discovery, or revelation, of absolute truth and a unique means of salvation. Only the adherents of higher religions of Indian origin have kept their minds open to the possibility that there may be more facets of truth and more ways of salvation than one.[1] The reason why they have remained comparatively tolerant is that they have made less sharp a break than the higher religions of the Judaic group have made with previous forms of religion; for the virtue of 'pre-higher' religion's defects is its readiness to 'live and let live'.[2]

It is, of course, impossible that each of the higher religions can be right in believing that it has a monopoly of truth and salvation, but it is not at all impossible that all of them should have found alternative roads to salvation and should have seen truth, 'through a glass, darkly', in one or other of truth's different facets. This is what I myself have come to believe. This belief does not necessarily involve the further belief that all the higher religions have seen the truth in equal measure and have found roads to salvation that are equally good. Nevertheless, I fear that Dawson will have been right in his forecast[3] that orthodox theologians would find my position unacceptable. A belief in the relative truth and relative saving-power of all the higher religions alike will seem tantamount to unbelief in the eyes of an orthodox believer in any one

[1] In this context Dawson observes, in *Toynbee and History*, p. 135, that the religions of the Indian group and those of the Judaic group are as allergic to each other as oil and vinegar, and that, in the course of history up to date, the acid Judaic religions have been gaining ground at the milder Indian religions' expense.

[2] The comparative tolerance of the spirit of 'pre-higher' religion is noteworthy, considering that, as we have seen, the dominant divinities of 'pre-higher' religion in its latest phase have been apt to be associated with their worshippers' collective political power, and the parochial states, with which these political divinities have been associated, have by no means been willing to 'live and let live' in their political and military relations with each other. They have habitually gone to war with each other, and these fratricidal wars have tended to become more intense and more devastating until, in the end, all competitors but one have been wiped off the map by a sole surviving victor. It might have been expected that a victorious state would treat the gods symbolizing the collective political power of its conquered adversaries as ruthlessly as it has usually treated the political structures in which this power has been embodied. But, so far from that, the victor, in the age before the rise of the higher religions, has usually shown a prudent discrimination in giving differential treatment to his human enemy and to the enemy's national gods. He has taken it for granted that the enemy's gods, in their domain, are as living and as potent and as legitimately sovereign as the victor's own gods are in theirs; and the military defeat of the human enemy has not, in the victor's view, entailed the consequence that the enemy's gods have either lost their potency or forfeited their rights. A politic victor in this epoch has therefore usually treated the enemy's gods with consideration and even with deference. The Romans, who were past masters in the art of conquest, used to make it their practice, before delivering their final assault on the enemy's military defences, to address an invitation to the enemy's gods to come over to the Roman side, and the invitation was usually accompanied by the offer of attractive terms for admission to the Roman pantheon.

[3] In *Toynbee and History*, p. 134, Dawson forecasts that I shall be as unpopular with theologians as I am with historians. J. F. Leddy finds that, though I exalt religion, my form of it is not agreeable to the orthodox (*The Phoenix*, vol. 11, No. 4 (1957), pp. 141–2). K. Löwith finds that I am 'neither an empirical historian nor a good theologian' (*Meaning in History*, p. 14). Anderle reports, in his unpublished paper, that my approach to religion is too lay-minded to suit the theologians' taste, and too theological to be of much interest to the historians, sociologists, and philosophers.

of them.[1] A reverence for them all will seem to him to be what Taylor has nicknamed 'the religion of mish-mash'.[2]

It is sad to find oneself at variance with fellow human beings with whom one believes—notwithstanding their contrary belief[3]—that one

---

[1] 'To advocate religiousness is one thing; to advocate religious eclecticism is another' (H. J. Morgenthau in *Toynbee and History*, p. 197). As a result of not rejecting any of the religions, Toynbee remains outside them all. 'Toynbee is sensitive to the word of God in so far as it has become historically tangible in dogmatic symbols and ecclesiastic institutions, but . . . he does not hear the word as spoken to him personally' (E. Voegelin in *The Intent of Toynbee's History: A Cooperative Appraisal*). The Rev. E. R. Hardy Jr. is, I think, making the same point as Voegelin when (ibid.) he judges that, 'in the religious field, Toynbee is not sufficiently aware of his own limitations'. L. C. Stecchini (in *Midstream*, Autumn, 1956, pp. 84–91) points out that the 'essence' of Christianity, as I see it, is, in effect, the element that Christianity has in common with the Mahayana. Dawson (in *Toynbee and History*, pp. 134 and 130–1) finds my notion of 'philosophical equivalence' even more questionable when applied to higher religions than in its application to civilizations. As Dawson sees it, 'it is necessary to accept the Christian faith in order to understand the Christian view of history, and those who reject the idea of a divine revelation are necessarily obliged to reject the Christian view of history as well' (*The Dynamics of World History*, p. 235). I agree. Löwith (op. cit., p. 16) points out that I do not see history in its Christian framework (e.g. B.C.–A.D.).

In Dawson's opinion (*Toynbee and History*, loc. cit.), I am arguing that the living higher religions are identical with each other and in thus arguing, I am forcing the evidence. I agree that I should be forcing it if I were, in truth, arguing what Dawson thinks I am. On this point, he has not caught my meaning—I am sure, not through his fault but through mine, for having failed to express myself clearly enough. I do believe that all the higher religions, and, indeed, religions of all kinds, have in common an inkling of an identical truth about Reality and of an identical goal of salvation for human beings. But I do not hold that the religions themselves are identical; and, for as far into the future as we can see ahead, I do not expect that they will agree to make a merger of their different doctrines, practices, and institutions, in which their common spiritual treasure is diversely presented.

[2] A. J. P. Taylor in *Toynbee and History*, p. 117. Taylor's disapproval of my catholic piety towards the historic higher religions seems inconsistent with his accusation that I lack 'the historian's characteristic piety towards the past' (see footnote 4 to p. 66).

[3] e.g.: 'Toynbee does not mean what the Church means at all' (Father L. Walker, O.P., in *Toynbee and History*, p. 341). 'It is necessary . . . to stress the radical unorthodoxy of Toynbee's position in terms of any of the established sacramental Christian churches' (Crane Brinton in *The Virginia Quarterly Review*, vol. 32, No. 3 (Summer, 1956), pp. 361–75). In *Wissenschaft und Weltbild*, 2. Jahrgang, Heft 4 (October, 1949), pp. 268–9, F. Engel-Janosi maintains that my dualism—as revealed in my adoption of the myth of God's encounter with the Devil—is incompatible with Christian doctrine. The idea that God needs the Devil's help in order to create is not compatible with the idea of creation *ex nihilo*. I think H. Baudet is making the same point in *Historie en Metahistorie*, p. 53, when he says that I have 'historicised', 'biologised', and 'secularised' an antique piece of mysticism by turning the Devil into a ubiquitous insect: i.e. into Nature trying to reassert herself against culture. In the same passage Baudet also says that I have replaced God by the Christian Church, 'which is of greater practical use in virtue of its social qualities, on which' I lay 'so much stress'. J. H. Nichols, too (see the *Journal of Religion*, No. 28 (1948), pp. 99–119, on pp. 118–19, and *Studium Generale*, No. 4 (1951), pp. 175–82, on p. 182) finds that I identify the Kingdom of God with the Church and thereby reduce Christianity to ecclesiasticism. R. L. Shinn finds that 'Toynbee's dangerous ecclesiasticism threatens to subdue his deeper insights' (*Christianity and the Problem of History*, p. 241). Toynbee, contrary to his intentions, sometimes mistakes a universal church for religion, the institution for the spirit (M. C. Swabey: *The Judgment of History*, p. 223). In T. A. Sumberg's view, in *Social Research*, vol. 14, No. 3 (September, 1947), pp. 267–84, 'some of the insidious virus of modern paganism has penetrated the soul even of our modern historian'. Father G. F. Klenk, S.J., in *Stimmen der Zeit*, No. 145 (1949/50), pp. 376–84, on pp. 382 seqq., demurs to my explaining the rise of Christianity as a natural event—a result of syncretism—and thereby wiping out Christianity's supernatural character. Joynt remarks that 'in some ways the Toynbee view of the meaning of history is odd even by theological standards. The traditional Christian view is that the ultimate meaning of history is eschatological, i.e. it lies beyond itself. Toynbee claims to have used empirical methods, and produced not only "laws of Nature" but "laws of God" as well. In other words, the ultimate meaning of history is to be found in history. In this conception the Deity becomes almost entirely immanent and loses *all* transcendant qualities' (*The Australasian Journal of Philosophy*, vol. 34, No. 3 (December, 1956),

is really in agreement over the heart of the matter at issue. But I am anchored in my present moorings by two convictions that will not let go of me. I am convinced that the spiritual presence that is higher than Man is merciful and compassionate[1] in Its aspect in which It presents Itself to us as a person and in which we see It as God. And I am convinced that every human being is capable of catching a vision of the trans-human presence and of entering into communion with It, whether he finds It in Its personal aspect as Brahmā or in Its impersonal aspect as Brahman or as Nirvāna. Each of these two convictions can stand by itself; yet though they are independent they give each other mutual support; for each of them implies the other; so, if either of them is a true insight into Reality, the other cannot be a delusion. Together they give, for me, an assurance that the presence behind the phenomena is not capricious, and that the capacity to enter into communion with It is of the essence of human nature. I therefore believe that there never has been, and never will be, a 'chosen' people or sangha or church invested with a monopoly of truth and salvation. Any such monopoly, if it were conceivable (and it is not conceivable to me), would be invidious both for the recipient and for the donor of the privilege. It would not be consonant either with Man's nature or with God's nature as I see them. And, as long as I continue to see them as I do, I shall also continue, as

p. 201). Brinton in loc. cit., and J. H. Nichols, in *Studium Generale*, No. 4 (1951), p. 182, find that I am a Pelagian. The Rev. E. R. Hardy Jr. finds that I am a semi-Pelagian (*The Intent of Toynbee's History: A Cooperative Appraisal*.

If the reader cares to compare the passages cited in this footnote with those cited on p. 27, footnote 2, p. 94, footnote 1, and pp. 649 and 656), he will see that my attitude and beliefs in regard to religion have been criticized, on a number of points, on grounds that are not merely different from each other but are diametrically opposite and are therefore presumably incompatible. I have been classified as being both a Pelagian and an Augustinian. I have been censured both for seeing God as more immanent and for seeing Him as more transcendent than is right in the critic's judgement. My attitude has been denounced as being both unduly 'otherworldly' and unduly 'thisworldly'. I have been charged both with valuing religion for utilitarian purposes and with denying value to the secular and material side of human life except in so far as this serves as a means to religious and spiritual ends. In H. E. Barnes's eyes I am 'a devout Christian mystic', and my 'imagination is primarily centred on the second coming of the Lord under Anglican auspices' (*An Introduction to the History of Sociology*, pp. 718 and 736). More discern-ingly, the Rev. E. R. Hardy Jr. finds that my interpretation of world history is, in the last analysis, a devout one, but that, 'from the Christian point of view, the trouble with Toynbee's "true religion" is that it is too purely spiritual' (*The Intent of Toynbee's History: A Cooperative Appraisal*).

Some of these mutually contradictory criticisms seem to cancel each other out. In so far as they do not, this must mean that there are inner contradictions in my position, or in my critics' positions, or in both. My position has certainly changed while I have been writing this book (see p. 27 above, and pp. 649–51 below). I have also, perhaps, been imprecise, in places, in setting out what my position is. At least, several critics have taken me to task on this account. I can only say that I am neither orthodox nor rationalist, and that my 'trans-rationalist' position, between these two poles, is clear to me, at any rate. In any case, whatever light my critics may or may not have thrown on my position, they have thrown much light, I should say, on a far more interesting point. They have brought out the truth that, at the present time, the Western World is a house divided against itself on the fundamental issue of religious attitude and belief.

I am all the more grateful to E. I. Watkin for the concluding paragraphs of his review of vols. iv–vi of this book in *The Tablet*, 12th August, 1939. 'Professor Toynbee's book', he generously writes, 'is a challenge to us [Catholics]. . . . Rather, it is the challenge, not of this book, which does but display it, but of history itself. . . . May he communicate to the readers of his . . . work the vision he has seen with the faith and hope which it inspires.'

[1] 'Misericors et miserator Deus'; 'Allāh ar-Rahmān ar-Rahīm'. This testimony from the harsh Judaic religions is impressive.

far as I can foretell, to remain in the theological position in which I now find myself.

This stand of mine may put me out of communion with the orthodox adherents of each of the higher religions (at any rate, each of those in the Judaic group). It lies with the orthodox, not with me, to decide whether, in their eyes, I am within their pale or am beyond it. But it lies with me, not with them, to feel the feelings that I, too, feel towards those sublime figures that are revered and adored by me as well as by their orthodox followers or worshippers. No human writ of excommunication can come between those saviours and me. My knee bows, like every Christian's knee, at the deed of self-sacrifice, done for love of us men and for our salvation, that is recited by Saint Paul to the Philippians.[1] For me, the doer of this deed is one presence in more than one epiphany. It is Christ, and, because it is Christ, it is also the Buddha and the bodhisattvas.

[1] Phil. ii. 10.

B

RECONSIDERATIONS OF STRUCTURAL PROBLEMS

IV. THE PROBLEM OF QUANTITY IN THE STUDY OF HUMAN AFFAIRS

1. THE INEFFECTIVENESS OF TEAM-WORK IN INTELLECTUAL OPERATIONS

THE problem of quantity arises in the study of human affairs because it besets all intellectual inquiry, whatever the field. It is a consequence of the conjunction, in the structure of human minds, of two inescapable limitations. A mind has to operate by the method of analysis and classification, because it has no other method at its disposal. A mind has also to do whatever it is going to do within a single lifetime, and, what is more, within that span of it in which the mind is neither infantile nor senile. Thinking by means of analysis and classification takes time, and the process of apprehending Reality in this way breaks up the undifferentiated unity of the mystical experience into an innumerable host of phenomena. The quantity of the phenomena is out of all proportion to the capacity of any single mind to deal with them in a single working lifetime. *Ars longa, vita brevis.* This lapidary statement of the common human experience of the mind's inadequacy for carrying out its ambitious enterprises comes from the pen of an Hellenic student of medicine.[1] As soon as people began to try to make a systematic study of any fraction of the boundless field of the phenomenal universe, they found that they had set themselves Psyche's task.

Cannot her task be accomplished, and the problem be solved, by co-operation? Though the phenomena may be innumerable, human beings, too, are numerous—even though the number is limited, for practical purposes, to the roster of living participants in some particular society. Man is a social animal; co-operation has become a second nature to him; and, though practical co-operation has hitherto been limited to fractions of the whole living generation of mankind, it has nevertheless done marvels. Team-work has been the means by which Man has accomplished his enormous achievements in technology, economics, politics, war, and even religion on its institutional side. Could Man not obtain comparable results by resorting to the same device in other activities? The answer is that, up to now, creative acts in the fields of thought, art, and the personal side of 'higher religion' (as defined in this book) have been the achievements of single minds; and we do not yet know whether, in these fields, team-work is or is not

[1] ὁ βίος βραχύς, ἡ δὲ τέχνη μακρή (Hippocrates: *Aphorisms*, i. 1).

possible. As far as we know at present, only single minds can think thoughts and express them. The squads, gangs, crews, and committees that have done, and are doing, so much of the World's work have never yet succeeded in doing this part of it. There have never been such things as collective thinking and collective writing. Any document that purports to be the product of a committee will prove—if it makes any genuine contribution to knowledge and understanding—to be the unacknowledged work of some anonymous single draftsman.[1] Accor-

---

[1] 'As every person with experience of committee work knows, its fertility is limited to what the best mind among its members can master; if the results of the discussion are not ultimately turned into a coherent whole by an individual mind, they are likely to be inferior to what would have been produced unaided by a single mind' (F. A. Hayek: *The Counter-Revolution of Science*, note 82 on p. 218). This is also my own considered belief. It was the starting-point of this book, and, on reconsideration, I find myself as firmly convinced of its truth as I was in 1925, when I wrote what are now the first pages of vol. i. I have been encouraged by finding that I share this belief with Father M. C. D'Arcy. Team-work, Father D'Arcy, too, holds, 'can never take the place of the great historian' (*The Sense of History*, p. 57). This is, however, a controversial belief, and my declaration of it in i. 4 has drawn the following comment from Sir George Clark in a paper on 'The Origin of the Cambridge Modern History' in *The Cambridge Historical Journal*, vol. viii, No. 2 (1945), pp. 57–64. 'The more we regard historical study as a methodical search for truth, the readier we must be to dispense with the smooth readable continuity which only an individual author can give to a whole work; and, if we look at *The Cambridge Modern History* from this point of view, we shall be impressed, not by the splitting up of the work among many authors, but by their thoroughness. The system is the exact opposite of industrialism; each writer made a fully articulated and finished piece of history which might have been published by itself. They worked like medieval craftsmen, some of them even grinding their own colours' (p. 58).

I agree, of course, with Sir George Clark's account of what has been achieved in *The Cambridge Modern History*—as well I may, considering that he is making my point for me. What he and I are both saying is that historical thought, like all thought, is the work of single minds, and that, when you put a number of minds to work on different sections of some epoch of history, what you get is a number of separate self-contained pieces of work—so effectively self-contained and separate that (to repeat Sir George's words) each piece 'might have been published by itself'. What you do *not* get by this division of intellectual labour is an organic whole in which the individual writers' contributions fall into place as integral parts of a unified structure. Each of the contributions may be a unity in itself, but they do not make a unity when they are strung together. Sir George's contributors are like performers in an orchestra who have each played a tune of his own, instead of executing an allotted part of some work by a single composer. As I see it, structural unity is the property with which the editors and writers of *The Cambridge Modern History*, and other symposia of the kind, have been ready to dispense, and in my view this readiness is a serious error.

In a work of thought, as in a work of art, of architecture, or of engineering, structural unity ought, I should say, to be one of the chief objectives, and this not only because it is an important end in itself, but even more because, in default of it in an intellectual enterprise, it is probable that some of the most important issues, problems, questions, and topics that ought to have been under consideration will have been passed over. This is likely because the most important points are usually general points. These do not come into view unless one takes a comprehensive survey of the whole field; and this is what will be lacking in a volume that is not a book but is an assemblage of booklets, each of which might just as well have been published separately. This point has been made by Polybius in the passages quoted here on p. 138, footnote 2.

For this reason I am not ready to dispense with the structural unity that can be produced only by a single mind (as is illustrated by the fact that each of the contributors to *The Cambridge Modern History* has successfully made a structural unity of his own contribution). I am as ready as Sir George and his contributors are to dispense with 'smooth readable continuity', and I am impressed, as Sir George is, by 'the laboriousness, the "factual" knowledge', and 'the mechanical skill' of the contributors (I am repeating the words that I used in the passage that he cites). But I am still more impressed by the inability of an intellectual engineering enterprise to achieve, by team-work, the result that mechanical engineering enterprises do achieve by it. A product of mechanical engineering team-work—a bridge, dam, liner, battleship, or skyscraper—is a structural unity. In work done by an intellectual team, the contributions of the single minds do not produce a structural unity, as Sir George himself points out.

The reason for this difference between the two results is to be found, I believe, in a

dingly, for as far as we can see ahead, the problem of quantity in intellectual work will continue to be one with which single minds must grapple as best they can. The enterprise courts failure and therefore requires audacity. In this field audacity is a virtue, not a vice. It does not, in itself, convict the intellectual adventurer of the self-centred sin of *hybris*. Being human, he may, of course, fall into this. But in plunging into the jungle he is performing a perilous public service. For the problem of quantity in intellectual inquiry is one that is not just personal to the inquirer; it is one of the important problems of society; and society's need to see this problem faced, and, if possible, solved, is a need that, at least for the present, only single minds can meet.

2. THE INORDINATE INCREASE IN THE QUANTITY OF INFORMATION ABOUT HUMAN AFFAIRS

The problem of quantity in intellectual inquiry is as old as human society itself. A society is a network of relations between individual human beings, and, even in the smallest and simplest society, the quantity of these relations is innumerable. Moreover, an individual human being is not 'individual' in the literal sense of being an unfissionable psychic unit. A personality is a network of relations between psychic events, and the quantity of these relations, too, is innumerable. So the intellectual problem of quantity has always been there. It has not, however, always been so strikingly and formidably manifest as it is in the present-day world. It is true that, at all times and places, including the present, the best-informed and wisest individual's knowledge and understanding of the phenomena, within his own psyche and outside it, is infinitesimally small compared with the infinite quantity of the myriad things that are demanding to be known and understood. But it is also true that, for practical purposes, the range of an individual's ignorance and knowledge is relative not so much to the infinite extent of the whole potential field as to the actual range of ignorance and knowledge in the culture in which this particular individual happens to partake. The extent of this common store of knowledge that is at the individual's disposal is, of course, like the extent of the individual's personal knowledge, always infinitesimal by comparison with the extent of mankind's universal and perpetual ignorance. At the same time, it varies enormously as between different cultures, and, within a single culture, as between its different phases, by comparison with the maximum capacity of an individual mind. This variability of the extent of the common store of knowledge is a point of great practical importance, because a society's common store of knowledge 'only exists in the dispersed, incomplete, and inconsistent

difference in the meaning of the word 'team' in the two contexts. The same word is being used as the label for two quite different social structures. An editor's 'team' is a number of independent creators; an engineer's or architect's team is like a composer's orchestra: it is a number of disciplined executants, each playing his allotted part in the performance of a piece previously composed by a single mind. Even the clerk-of-the-works, *alias* conductor, is merely an executant-in-chief. An editor's 'team' are not executants of the work of a single mind; each man is his own composer and is the executant of his own separate piece only.

form in which it appears in individual minds';[1] and it becomes coherent and consistent only in so far as some single mind succeeds in comprehending and unifying it.

If we may use the terms 'knowledge' and 'ignorance' in the second, and more practical, of the relative usages of their intrinsically relative meaning, it would be true to say that, in most societies at most times up to date, relative omniscience has not only been possible; it has been a normal attainment of any mind whose cumulative acquisition of knowledge has not been cut short by an early death. As Marcus Aurelius puts it,[2] 'any man of forty who is endowed with moderate intelligence has seen—in the light of the uniformity of Nature—the entire past and future'. This dictum was hardly true of the Hellenic World in Marcus's own day. Marcus himself, as his writings reveal, was the heir of a culture that, by his time, had been accumulating experience and knowledge over a period of more than twelve hundred years. Marcus's dictum would have been truer of the pre-Hellenic cultural interregnum. Relative omniscience will have been within men's reach in an age in which the art of writing in the Minoan scripts had been lost, and in which the Hellenes had not yet learnt the use of the Alphabet from the Phoenicians. Relative omniscience came within reach, again, during the post-Hellenic cultural interregnum in what, in Marcus's day, had been the western provinces of the Roman Empire. This time, it is true, the art of writing was not lost even in this culturally backward western penumbra of the former Hellenic World. But the common store of culture did dwindle, here and then, to a compass that made it possible for an individual to master the whole of it; and here it was some time before the achievement of this relative omniscience was made impracticable once more by the gradual rise of the Western Civilization. The whole of the common store of Western knowledge could still be known in the eighth century of the Christian Era by Bede and Alcuin, and almost the whole of it, even as late as the thirteenth century, by Saint Thomas Aquinas and Dante. We present-day Westerners, however, like the Hellenes in Marcus's day, have at our disposal a fund of experience and knowledge that has been accumulating for more than twelve hundred years, and this present-day Western fund is also at the disposal of the whole human race, since the Western Civilization has now grown to a stature at which it is offering itself as an initial framework for a future world-wide culture. So, today, both in the West and in the World as a whole, the individual once again finds himself living in the times of ignorance, in the sense that, in the present-day world, the common store of knowledge is vastly greater than the maximum that an individual can assimilate. In this sense a problem that is universal and perpetual is also peculiarly ours. In our case it has been aggravated to a degree that is perhaps without precedent.

This increase in the amount of what there is to know is overwhelming, even if we confine our horizon, for present purposes, to the field of human affairs. This dichotomy between what is human and what is

---

[1] F. A. Hayek: *The Counter-Revolution of Science*, pp. 29–30.
[2] Marcus Aurelius Antoninus: *Meditations*, Book XI, chap. 1. Cp. Book VII, chap. 49.

non-human has, of course, always been arbitrary. Its arbitrariness is being shown up in our time by the rapid advances in the two sciences of psychology and biology. Advancing from opposite quarters, they are bridging the traditional gulf between soul and body, spirit and matter, organic and inorganic, animate and inanimate; and they are already pointing towards a future stage of understanding in which it will no longer be intellectually tolerable to diffract the concrete unity of psycho-somatic phenomena. In fact, a day is now in sight at which the minimum 'intelligible field of study' will be nothing less than the whole of the phenomenal world in all its aspects.

Meanwhile, in the present psychic as well as in the present physical province of knowledge, there has been a sudden revolutionary increase in the quantity of data as the result of a great feat of analysis. The word 'individual' means in Latin what the word 'atom' means in Greek. It means a unit that cannot be subdivided and that therefore offers a solid foundation for research into the structure of the Universe. In our time this once supposedly solid ground has given way in both provinces of knowledge. While the physicists have been splitting 'atoms', the psychologists have been analysing 'individuals'. In both fields the former basic unit has been found, not merely to be fissionable, but to be a universe in itself: a microcosm that is as complex as the macrocosm built of hosts of these miniature worlds. The material atom has been proved to have an internal structure resembling a solar system, and the human individual to have an internal structure resembling a society. Like a society, an individual is a network of relations, and the individual's internal psychic relations have, in common with his external social relations, the awkward property of being innumerable.

This is not, of course, a new state of affairs; it is not even a new discovery. In the Indic World in the sixth century B.C. the Buddha made the discovery that the supposed indivisibility of an 'individual' personality was an illusion. With the discerning eye of intuition, He diagnosed a personality as being a fleeting series of innumerable successive psychological states. Each of these states, as He saw them, was discontinuous with both its predecessors and its successors. Two forces, and two only, held them together: the wind of desire, which drove them along in company like a herd of hurrying cloud-racks, and the load of *karma*—the cumulative balance of the self-recording moral profit-and-loss account to which desire gives rise in its vain attempt to satisfy itself. Modern Western psychology, approaching its subject of inquiry by the circuitous route of analogy from the procedure of modern Western physical science, has arrived at the Buddha's discovery about 2,400 years after the date at which the Buddha achieved it intuitively. Buddhists and modern Western psychologists agree in seeing the internal psychic structure of an individual human personality as a network of relations between innumerable psychic events and in finding that this net has some kind of structural pattern. But the objectives of these two schools of inquiry have been widely different, and consequently an identical discovery has not had the same effect, in the two cases, on the intellectual problem of quantity.

The Buddha's aim was austerely practical. He had no inclination to count or measure or classify the psychic cloud-racks; and He had no inclination, either, to study the texture and pattern of their relations with each other except to the minimum extent necessary for dissipating them. He was convinced that they could be dissipated by strenuous spiritual exertions, and He prescribed a plan of operations, based on His own spiritual experience and achievement. The goal was the liquidation of *karma* and the extinction of desire, and the reward for attaining it was that it would bring with it an exit from sensuous life into a state of 'extinguishedness' (*Nirvāna*). The spiritual residue, after the flame of desire had burnt out, would be immune from the malady of reacquiring personality in the form in which we know it, since it would be immune from being born again into this world. The Buddha's paramount concern, after His enlightenment, was to teach His fellow sentient beings the way of release that He had found for Himself. Since the way was hard and forbidding, He was vigilant in seeing to it that His disciples should not find excuses for diverging into easier paths. One insidious temptation, for which He was always on the look-out, was that of yielding to intellectual curiosity about the psychic landscape that was the setting of the spiritual enterprise on which He and His disciples had embarked. In the Buddha's eyes such curiosity was no better than camouflaged escapism, and He always firmly refused to satisfy it. His attitude towards knowledge was like that of a present-day Western civil servant, not like that of a present-day Western professor. The information that He gave about the fleeting psychological states and the way of release from them was the minimum amount needed for taking the necessary action. Accordingly, His discovery of the individual human being's inner psychic universe did not lead, in His world, to any revolutionary increase in the amount of what there was to know.

In the present-day world, on the other hand, the repetition of the Buddha's discovery has brought with it a revolutionary expansion of the intellectual horizon, because the aims and methods of modern Western psychologists have been unlike the Buddha's. The purpose that has inspired them has not been to help a human personality to extinguish itself; it has been, on the contrary, to help it to keep itself in psychic repair for the term of its natural life. The only things in common between this aim and the Buddha's are a disinterested compassion for the sufferings of fellow human beings and a benevolent concern to bring them relief. But, since there is a polar opposition between the Buddha's conception and a modern Western psychologist's conception of what it is that suffering souls need to be relieved of, it is no wonder that the two schools should have put an identical psychological discovery to entirely different uses. Since the modern psychologist's prescription for getting rid of suffering is not the radical Buddhist remedy of getting rid of oneself, but the mild palliative of preserving oneself by getting rid of one's psychic disorders, the modern psychologist is eager to know as much about the psyche's inner universe as possible. The maximum, not the minimum, amount of knowledge is what he needs for the pursuit of his un-Buddhist objective; and the duty of acquiring as much knowledge of his subject as he can is enjoined upon him, not only by his approach to the practical problem of suffering, but also by his scientific method of work, which he has taken over from the older branches of modern Western science that are concerned with non-human nature. The modern Western school of science has been led by its experience to take up an attitude towards intellectual curiosity for its own sake which is the inverse of the Buddha's attitude. So far from looking on curiosity as a specious excuse for shirking present practical tasks, modern scientists look on it as a key to future practical successes; and this favourable view of theirs has certainly been justified by their experience during the last three centuries.

For these reasons the rediscovery, in our time, of the individual personality's inner psychic universe has already had the effect of vastly extending the range of what there is to know about human affairs. If it were practicable to make an exhaustive record of all the psychic events, sub-conscious and conscious, emotional and intellectual, that are now known to take place in a single psyche within the shortest span of time that a human mind can register, 'the World itself could not contain the books that should be written'.[1]

While there has been this revolutionary increase, in our time, in the quantity of things to know about Man's psychic microcosm, there has also been a contemporaneous increase in the quantity of things to know about his social macrocosm. Indeed, the increase in this field, too, would have been sensational if the increase in our knowledge of the psychic universe had not put it in the shade. The multiplication of the volume of social data has been proceeding rapidly in several directions, and in all these directions it has been due to one or other of the many consequences of the unprecedented technological advance of the Western Civilization in its recent 'late modern' and its current 'post-modern' age.

One of these consequences has been to give the Western peoples an ascendancy over the rest of mankind. This ascendancy has been something abnormal, and it now looks as if it were going to be no more than a temporary episode in the World's history. But transitory events can produce lasting effects, and one effect of the recent world-wide Western ascendancy has been to knit together the whole habitable and navigable surface of the planet, with the air above it, into 'one world'. This effect seems likely to last, because it is a product of the Western technological achievement of 'annihilating distance'; and Western technology, unlike Western domination, does not look as if it were going to be ephemeral. So far from that, it looks as if it were going to become a common possession of the whole human race. This knitting together of all mankind into a single world-wide society is still only in its early stages. But already it has produced a vast increase in the amount of things to know about human affairs.

In the past, until quite recent times, a human being's horizon was more or less closely confined to the particular civilization in which he happened to have been born and brought up. Even if he had become

[1] John xxi. 25.

one of a small highly educated minority, the classical education that was the standard form of higher education in most civilizations till the other day would have expanded his horizon in the time dimension only. He would have acquired some familiarity with the culture of his own society in some earlier phase of its history, or with the culture of some earlier society to which his own was affiliated. This historical background might have been broadened and deepened if the civilization in which he was a participant had grown up under the aegis of one of the higher religions. He would then also have been instructed in this religion's tenets and history. But he would still have remained more or less ignorant of the rest of the contemporary world outside his own civilization and his own religion, and also ignorant not only of the present characters but of the historical backgrounds of the other civilizations and higher religions—not to speak of the pre-civilizational cultures—among which the rest of the human race was distributed. At the other extreme, if he happened to have been born and brought up in a society that was still in the pre-civilizational stage, his intellectual horizon would, of course, have been far more narrowly circumscribed than that.

This traditional state of mutual ignorance had at least one important intellectual advantage for human minds. It set some limits to the quantity of things to know. But these limits have been swept away by the revolutionary unification of the World as a consequence of its Westernization. One section of mankind after another has been constrained, by this levelling of previous barriers, to widen its mental horizon to embrace the whole World.

The first to be affected have been the people in leading positions in the non-Western civilizations. The force of the West's impact has compelled them to acquaint themselves with Western technology, Western languages, and, to some extent, also with Western manners and customs. They have had to do this if their country has been subjugated by some Western state, because they have had to accommodate themselves to the alien ways of their new Western rulers. But they have had to do the same if they have saved themselves from falling under Western rule and have been bent on continuing to preserve their independence; for the West's technological superiority has been so manifest, and has also so manifestly been the cause of the West's military and political ascendancy, that it has quickly become obvious that the only effective way of resisting the West is to do it with Western weapons, spiritual as well as material. This has meant, not merely acquiring these weapons, but also learning how to use them, service them, and make them; and that, in turn, has meant serving an apprenticeship in Western arts. Sooner or later it has become apparent that these arts cannot be mastered if one approaches the task from a narrowly utilitarian point of view. To acquire the Western art of war involves acquiring one element of Western culture after another, until the only practicable course comes to be the adoption of the Western Civilization in its entirety. This bitter pill may be sweetened by labelling the importunate alien civilization 'modern' instead of 'Western', and coming to look upon it as a common achievement and possession of all mankind rather than as something imposed, either directly or indirectly, on the majority by an all-powerful Western minority. Whether sweet or bitter, the pill has had to be swallowed. It has been no more possible for non-Western diehards to reject the Western Civilization than it has been for non-Western defeatists. This Westernizing movement in the non-Western World began among the Eastern Orthodox Christian peoples—Greeks, Serbs, Rumans, and, above all, Russians—towards the end of the seventeenth century, in the generation of Peter the Great. During the quarter of a millennium that has elapsed since then, the movement has gathered momentum and has become world-wide. By now it would be near the truth to say that there is no longer any living society, however primitive, that has not been drawn into the Westernizing movement, at least to some extent.

This Westernizing movement among the non-Western majority of mankind has had its counterpart among the Western minority in an impulse to learn something about the rest of mankind. This movement in the inverse direction has been slower in getting under way. In any encounter between parties that are signally unequal in strength, the weaker party always has to come on to the stronger party's ground faster and farther than the stronger party finds it necessary to come on to the weaker party's. As the West progressively loses its temporary ascendancy, we may expect to see its approach towards the rest of the World gain in impetus.[1] Meanwhile the West has already gone far in making itself acquainted with the non-Western societies and their cultures. It has been impelled partly by practical needs; for the stronger party, too, has to know at least something about the party with which it is dealing. Without some knowledge of its weaker neighbours, it cannot trade with them or govern them or even make war on them efficiently. Such practical considerations, however, have been notably reinforced, in the West, by a disinterested intellectual curiosity that has been one of the cardinal virtues of the modern Western scientific movement. This curiosity has inspired a distinguished company of Western Orientalists, Americanists, and anthropologists. Between them they have won for the West an increasing knowledge of the higher religions (which are all Asian in origin), the non-Western civilizations of the Old World, the pre-Columbian civilizations of the Americas, and the surviving pre-civilizational cultures all over the globe. The West's own store of knowledge has naturally been the first to be increased by this Western intellectual enterprise. But the new knowledge of non-Western religions and cultures that the West has won has quickly become the common possession of all men and women who have had a higher education on Western lines, including the Westernizing element among the leaders in the non-Western societies. In our generation some of these Westernizers are already looking at their own civilization and its historical background with new eyes, and are making original contributions

---

[1] Already, in Great Britain today, Oriental studies are being supported financially out of the public purse on a markedly more generous scale than in the days when what are now the independent states of India, Pakistan, Burma, and Ceylon were being garrisoned by British, or British-officered, troops and were being governed by British officials in the higher ranks of the administrative hierarchy.

to the study of it by Western methods. Even Chinese scholarship, which has a critical tradition of at least two thousand years' standing, has probably gained much by adopting modern Western critical methods as a second string to its bow.

Thus, by our day, a knowledge of all the living religions and cultures and their backgrounds has become accessible to all 'modern-minded' people in all parts of the World.[1] This world-wide panorama of human affairs, which is now accessible to everyone, had not been within any-one's reach before. But the widening of our new common horizon in the field of human affairs has gone still farther than this. The new know-ledge acquired by the Orientalists, Americanists, and anthropologists has reached back into the past no farther than the farthest reach of the living societies' unbroken traditions. But, in the meanwhile, the archaeologists have been acquiring knowledge of 'dead' civilizations that have no living heirs to keep their memory green.

Some of these 'dead' civilizations had been lying in complete oblivion for centuries or millennia, until modern Western archaeological enter-prise brought them to light again. Others had been known to have existed without being known for what they really were. Memories of them had survived in second-hand accounts of them that were so ill-informed as to be misleading; or the remains of their monuments, still standing above ground, had gathered round them legends that were screens for ignorance. The retrieval of these long-lost civilizations was begun in earnest by the French scholars who accompanied Napoleon in his invasion of Egypt in 1798. Within the subsequent century and a half, archaeological excavations, conducted with ever greater technical skill, have thrown floods of light on the Egyptiac and Sumero-Akkadian civilizations, which had always been known of at second hand through the Bible; on the Hellenic Civilization, which had been far better known through the continuous currency of a surviving remnant of its literature; and on the pre-Columbian civilizations of Middle America and Peru, whose last phases had been placed on record by the Spanish conquerors who put an end to them.[2] But archaeology has made still greater addi-tions to knowledge by disinterring civilizations of which only the faintest memory, if any, had survived: for instance, the Hittite Civilization in Anatolia; the pre-Hellenic Minoan-Helladic-Mycenaean Civilization in the Aegean; the pre-Aryan Indus Culture in North-Western India; the pre-Chou Shang Culture in Northern China.[3] These archaeological additions to knowledge have also become the common possession of

[1] A. L. Kroeber points out that the whole contemporary and whole past world of art is now playing upon each single field of contemporary regional art (Style and Civiliza-tions, p. 50).

[2] In the rediscovery of the pre-Columbian civilizations of the Americas, archaeology is playing an overwhelmingly important part—partly because the Spaniards destroyed most of the destroyable indigenous records, and partly because these records, even before the Spaniards made havoc of them, were rudimentary by comparison with those of the literate civilizations of the Old World. The pre-Columbian civilizations of the Americas reveal themselves mainly through their artefacts; and, for this reason, every Americanist has to be something of an archaeologist, and usually to be an archaeologist first and foremost.

[3] Excavations carried out by Chinese archaeologists at Anyang, the capital of the Shang dynasty during the century or two before its overthrow by the Chou, have demon-

all modern-minded people; and already the present-day inhabitants of the countries in which the 'dead' civilizations once rose and fell are beginning to produce archaeologists trained in up-to-date archaeological technique and eager to take a share in bringing to light buried civilizations with which their own society is linked by the geographical bond of having a common home.

It will be seen that the quantity of things to know about human affairs has been increased in the social field—on a scale almost comparable with the increase in the psychic field—by the contributions to mankind's new common pool of knowledge that have been made by the Orientalists, Americanists, anthropologists, and archaeologists. As if this were not enough, there has been a vast simultaneous increase in the facilities for making and preserving documents, owing to the combined effects of several recent Western inventions—particularly the invention (or rather, in this case, re-invention) of the art of shorthand, which has made it possible to dictate letters, memoranda, and books instead of laboriously writing them by hand, and the invention of the typewriter, which has carried with it the device of automatically producing, in one operation, a number of carbon copies in addition to the 'top copy'. The first of these two inventions has led to a sharp increase in the volume of documentation, since, in dictating to a shorthand typist, to be long-winded requires less concentrated mental effort than to be concise, whereas in the old days, when even a grandee had to write his ukases with his own hand, his very sense of self-importance might prompt him not to waste his time by running to prolixity. The automatic multiplication of typewritten documents in carbon copies, some of which are likely to be filed in different registries in different places, now gives a document, once produced, a much greater chance of survival—perhaps even in an age of atomic weapons—than the unique hand-written original exemplar of a document ever had in the past.

Already, before these recent inventions gave the production of documents a sudden new impetus, documents had been piling up in increasing quantities and at an accelerating rate in the Western World. The archives of the Vatican had been supplemented by those of medieval Italian city-states, modern national states, aristocratic houses, private commercial and industrial corporations, and smaller business firms. Some of this material has, of course, already perished—partly through natural accidents, such as damage from fire or from damp, and partly through the wars and revolutions in which Man, the indefatigable builder, gives vent to his counter-impulse towards destructiveness. Up to date, however, a vast quantity has survived. Before the invention of atomic weapons it would have been thought safe to say that Man's capacity for producing documents had definitely won its age-old race with Man's and Nature's combined capacity for destroying them. In inventing atomic weapons we have armed ourselves with the means of disposing of our own vast documentation as the contents of the Library of Alexandria were eventually disposed of, according to the story, in the

strated that the Chinese classical tradition, in which the Shang figure as the Chou's predecessors, is not legend but is authentic history, on this point at least.

furnaces of the local public baths. So far, however, we have had the sense, or the grace, to refrain from getting rid of our gigantic archives by a method that would condemn us to getting rid of ourselves, too, in the process. The mass of documents has increased and is increasing. We do not hold that it ought to be diminished. At the same time we have not yet discovered how to cope with it.

The formidableness of the problem was brought home to me by hearing Sir Keith Hancock talk on the subject at a conference on the documentation of the Second World War that was held in Holland not long after the restoration of peace. Hancock spoke with authority, for he was in charge of the writing of official histories of the war-time acts of the departments of the Government of the United Kingdom. He also spoke with a wit that drove his point home. His point was that the scale of the war-time production of documents was unprecedented. One of the illustrations of this that he gave was that the volume of official documents produced by the United Kingdom Government and its agencies during the six war years 1939–45 equalled, in cubic content, the volume of all previous archives of the United Kingdom and of its constituent kingdoms England and Scotland that had survived down to the date of the outbreak of war in 1939. Another of his illustrations was the calculation that, if all the files produced in one particular ministry during the six war years were to be stacked on edge, jacket pressing against jacket, in a single continuous row, the length of this row would be seventeen miles. His comment on this was that the first thing needed by an historian nowadays was a motor-bicycle to cover the ground.

3. ATTEMPTS TO BRIDGE THE GAP BETWEEN OUR KNOWLEDGE OF PSYCHIC AND SOCIAL PHENOMENA AND OUR KNOWLEDGE OF THE ACTS OF INDIVIDUAL HUMAN BEINGS

This astonishing increase in the number of things to know, and in the quantity of information about them at an inquirer's disposal, has had a disconcerting effect on the relations between so-called 'individual' human beings and the myriad psychic and social actions and interactions in which each individual is involved. It is conceivable that an individual human being's existence consists in his serving as a node, or point of intersection, in two networks of relations between events: an 'inner' psychic network and an 'outer' social one. Events of both these kinds have now come within our cognizance in numbers that are legion; but in the process a great gulf has opened between the individual and both the 'inner' and the 'outer' events in which he is implicated. This consequence of our great increase in knowledge is paradoxical; for the individual is not merely 'implicated' in these events; his existence is bound up with them, and (in Buddhist terms) detachment from them would spell extinction for him. Gossamer threads, charged with coursing energy, must really extend, across both the psychic and the social gulf, between the individual and the innumerable psychic and social phenomena that are now visible to an observer's eye. Can the connecting threads, in both directions, be brought into visibility too? Unless and until they can, it will be difficult to make much sense of human affairs.[1]

On the psychological side this problem of tracing connexions is a new one. In the modern West the fleeting psychic cloud-racks, discerned long ago by the Buddha's inward eye, have only just begun to be charted. Till yesterday this inner psychic universe was beyond our Western science's horizon, and our ignorance of its existence exempted us from the task of trying to analyse its structure. It is to be expected that the psychologists, now that they have revealed the gulf, are going to bring to light the system of psychic relations by which it is bridged. Several hypotheses about the configuration of the human psyche have already been advanced. But these hypotheses conflict with each other, and the science of psychology itself is still too young for there to have been time yet for the debate between opposing schools to have produced even a minimum consensus. At the present moment, speculation as to how this gulf is eventually going to be closed would probably be premature even for psychologists, and would certainly be unprofitable, as well as presumptuous, if attempted by an outsider. It may be more profitable to concentrate our attention, for the present, on the gulf between individual human beings and social phenomena. Our awareness of this gulf is of longer standing; and the problem of tracing the connexions betwen social phenomena and the actions and interactions of individual human beings is the crux of the study of human affairs on its social side.

There is no difficulty about discerning social phenomena; it would, indeed, be difficult to ignore them, considering that their impact on each of us makes itself felt all the time and, at times, makes or mars an individual's fortunes. Each of us finds himself virtually at the mercy of the social setting in which he has been placed by the accidents of birth and upbringing.[2] Yet we know very well that these titanic social forces that bear down on each of us, apparently from outside, have no other origin than the acts of individual human beings,[3] and no other source of energy than these individuals' respective psychic power-houses.[4] Granting, as we must grant, that these obstreperous social phenomena are realities of some kind, we are aware, at the same time, that this kind of reality is of a different order from the reality of the puny human beings whose innumerable actions set these huge social forces in motion. We can also see that, by comparison with the reality of a human being, the reality of a social phenomenon is of a secondary order. A social phenomenon is a network of relations between human beings. Remove the

[1] 'Unless the specific structure of the social field is analysed and the mode of the relations between individuals, the actions of individuals . . . are incomprehensible accidents' (C. Trinkaus in *Science and Society*, vol. xii, No. 1 (1948), p. 229).

[2] 'While the source of action is in Man, the nature of human actions is determined by definite historical social structures within which men act' (Trinkaus in loc. cit., p. 228).

[3] Cultures 'do not do anything; only people do things' (P. Bagby: *Culture and History*, p. 116).

[4] H. D. Oakeley rightly insists that, if there is one principle that shows itself to be absolute, it must lie in the nature of personality (*Philosophy*, vol. xi, No. 42 (April, 1936) p. 189). 'The deepest experiences of personality cannot be transferred to a group of persons as such' (ibid., p. 192). 'A group is essentially a set of interacting persons and their relationships, without the necessity of any tertium quid' (Social Science Research Council's Committee on Historiography's Report (1954), p. 64).

human beings, and the social phenomenon generated by their relations will vanish into thin air. But remove the social phenomenon, and the human beings that have been the authors of its existence will still be there. Being social animals they will not, of course, be able to go on existing in a complete social vacuum; but, if they are forcibly deprived of some particular social institution, or if they themselves forcibly liquidate it in disgust with it, they will live to equip themselves with some new institution to fill the gap. This seems to indicate that the reality of a human being is a reality of a more fundamental kind than the reality of a social institution. Yet social phenomena and their vicissitudes are visible to the intellect's naked eye,[1] whereas nearly all the actions and interactions of individuals, from which these phenomena and their vicissitudes arise, are invisible even under a sociologist's mental microscope.

For instance, in the event of a parliamentary general election we have no difficulty in ascertaining which party received a majority of the electors' votes; but, if we try to study the election in individual terms, instead of being content just to register the institutional result of it, we find ourselves groping in the dark. We know that the casting of the votes was determined by an interplay of thoughts and feelings in each individual elector's psyche, and that this psychic interplay was, to some extent, determined, in its turn, by social relations between each of the electors and other people. But so far it has been quite beyond our intellectual resources to trace, in detail and with precision, how the result of the election, in terms of the casting of votes, is related to the actions and interactions of all the individuals concerned. We know that the resulting social phenomenon is a resolution of these forces that have been exerted by individuals, but we do not know how to conduct an investigation that would bring to light, exactly and completely, how the single conspicuous resultant social phenomenon has been produced by the innumerable obscure generating actions of individual human beings. Similarly, in the event of a battle, we have no difficulty in ascertaining which side won, and we know that the military decision was the result of an interaction of the psycho-physical performances of each of the soldiers actively engaged on the two sides. But we do not know how to trace the relation between the military decision and the way in which each of the combatants conducted himself. This inability of ours to state the results of a battle or an election in terms of the actions and interactions of individuals, which were the real forces whose interplay made the battle or the election turn out as it did, is paradoxical but not exceptional. Whatever kind of social phenomenon we take, we shall find ourselves baffled in

---

[1] Trinkaus finds (in loc. cit., p. 228) that, in my account of human affairs, 'society disappears as an active structure'. If by 'an active structure' Trinkaus means an agent that takes the initiative, he is stating my view correctly here. On this point I agree with the authorities cited in the preceding footnote. It looks to me as if Trinkaus has fallen into the fallacy of anthropomorphism that is attributed by some other critics to me. I admit to having sometimes written about society and some of its component institutions in anthropomorphic language (see pp. 45–46). With the vocabulary that is at one's disposal, this is sometimes almost impossible to avoid. But my belief is that institutions are not active forces. At the same time, I believe that they are realities —though realities of a different order from human beings. I do not think that there is any contradiction between these two beliefs of mine.

the same way if we try to analyse the phenomenon in terms of the individual human beings who brought it about. 'The number of separate variables which in any particular social phenomenon will determine the result of a given change will, as a rule, be far too large for any human mind to master and manipulate them effectively.'[1]

Here is a problem that has confronted all investigators of social human affairs since the moment when investigations were first attempted in this field. Our inability to trace the connexions between the social events that we observe and the actions of individuals by which we know that these events were generated is a gap in our knowledge and understanding that has always been there and has frequently been recognized. This gap has not been created by the recent multiplication of the social phenomena within our ken; it has merely been enlarged. But the enlargement of the gap has brought the problem to a head and is compelling us to face it.

How, in the past, have inquirers into social affairs managed to cope with this crucial hiatus in their intellectual operations? The hiatus is so paralysing that it seems a wonder that they should have succeeded in operating at all. In so far as they have 'got by', they have achieved this by papering over a gap that they found themselves unable to close. They have resorted to two makeshifts. They have made intuition serve in place of investigation, and mythology serve in place of analysis.

Intuition—whatever the nature of this mysterious mental faculty may be—has sometimes served inquirers well in a number of different fields. Intuition enabled the Buddha to anticipate modern Western science's discovery of the psychic universe within an 'individual' human being, and it enabled Democritus to anticipate the discovery of the physical universe's atomic constitution. Yet the results of intuition remain provisional and precarious until they are verified by investigation. As for the use of mythology, it would hardly be possible for a sociologist to write a line of description, or for an historian to write a line of narrative, without resorting to mythological language. Mythology, in the sense in which the term is being employed in this volume,[2] means a particular use of the mental operation that we call analogy. It means thinking and talking about phenomena that are not human beings as if that was what they were. In giving an account of social phenomena, an historian or a sociologist is constantly slipping into treating them as if they were persons, instead of rigorously treating them all the time as the enormously complex relations between an enormous number of persons which is what institutions really are, but which is also something beyond the human mind's present capacity to apprehend.

This procedure is as misleading as it is difficult to avoid. It is misleading because there is not, I believe, really any illuminating analogy between the psycho-somatic organism that we call a human being and the network of relations between human beings that we call a social phenomenon. If they have any points of likeness at all, they certainly have many more points of difference. Nevertheless, we talk glibly about

[1] F. A. Hayek: *The Counter-Revolution of Science*, p. 42.
[2] See pp. 250–2.

the actions[1], reactions, feelings, thoughts, intentions, and plans of governments, states, peoples, churches, and other institutions, as if 'legal personalities' were what they purport to be, instead of being the mental fictions that they are.[2] To ascribe conscious purpose to groups of human beings is mythology.[3] We talk and think about institutions in these personalizing mythological terms because that is the nearest intellectual approach that we have been able to make to the elusive realities that lurk beneath these wraiths.

However, in our day we are being compelled to look for more efficient methods of coping with this intellectual problem because of the sudden great widening of our horizon. In the study of human affairs this challenge has had the same stimulating effect as it has had in the study of the physical universe. Physical 'science . . . has been obliged . . . to take account of parts of the Universe, the enormously great and the enormously small, which transcend the range of sizes for which the Newtonian world-picture was constructed'.[4] In the field of social human studies a corresponding revolution in our vision of the phenomena has led sociologists to go in for minute analysis, and historians to go in for statistical 'prosopography' ('study of persons'). Each of these experiments is an attempt to bridge the great gap between social phenomena and human beings by a pontoon made of intellectually more respectable materials than intuition and mythology. Sociologists are trying to dissect the web of social relations, under a microscope, into smaller and smaller constituent parts, in the hope that these progressive diminutions in the scale of the investigator's observations will eventually bring into view the actions and interactions of individual human beings and, by displaying these in their social context, will reveal, in its concrete continuity, the whole of the hitherto obscure process by which the texture of social phenomena is woven out of raw materials of the personal

[1] See W. Dray: *Laws and Explanation in History*, p. 140.
[2] These fictitious personifications of non-personal social phenomena are least likely to mislead their users when their fictitiousness is conspicuous. Accordingly, the least objectionable form of this verbal trick is to describe the effects of an institution—say, a state—as acts of a god in whose name the institution is symbolized: 'Amun chastised the barbarians', 'Asshur triumphed over his enemies', and so on. The next least objectionable procedure is to personify the name of the state itself: 'Egypt', 'Assyria', 'Sparta', 'Athens', 'Rome', 'France', 'Britain'. To say 'the Lacedaemonians did it' or 'the Athenians did it' is a more insidious formula, because it implicitly lays claim to a non-existent knowledge of the process by which the resultant effect is related to the thoughts, feelings, and acts of all the individual Lacedaemonians and Athenians. Still more specious are such constitutional formulae as 'King Philip and the Macedonians' or 'the Roman Senate and People'. They purport to analyse the actors into their constituents, whereas in fact they leave the gap between social effects and individual originators of these effects still wide open. The most unsatisfactory usage of all is to ascribe political events to the personal action of an individual human being: 'Pharaoh', 'Caesar', 'the Queen'. This language might really mislead users of it into imagining that political events are the personal acts of the human being to whom they are ascribed; and that, of course, would give a wholly misleading idea of how political institutions work. The social operations that constitute the government of even the smallest and most simply organized state immensely exceed an individual human being's maximum capacity for action, however domineering, decisive, energetic, industrious, intelligent, physically strong, and long-lived the person in question may be. Of all the acts that are attributed to a ruler, only a small fraction can ever be genuinely his own; the majority of the acts done in his name will, in truth, have been the acts of other people. This is as true of a ruler who is theoretically an absolute autocrat as it is of one whose powers are constitutionally limited.   [3] M. R. Cohen: *The Meaning of History*, p. 125.
[4] J. Needham: *Science and Civilization in China*, vol. ii, p. 339, following Nils Bohr.

order of reality. From the opposite bank of the river of ignorance historians are trying to span the gap in the reverse direction. Starting, not from social phenomena, but from human beings, they are trying to trace how the ascertainable actions and interactions of individuals build up into social phenomena, and thus to find a way of describing, discussing, and explaining these phenomena in terms of human realities, in place of the language of social mythology, with which historians have hitherto found themselves unable to dispense.

On the sociological side one distinguished living authority, Michael Postan, goes almost to the length of identifying the miscroscopic method of sociological inquiry with sociology itself.

'What makes a question sociological is not only the nature of the problem it raises, but also the nature of the answer it requires. It is the great virtue of some questions that they can only be answered in a sociological way, by the laborious and painful process of social analysis, by defining and classifying social groups and institutions, by counting and measuring the differences in social arrangements from place to place and from time to time. . . .

'Sociological treatment . . . involves a difference in scale. . . . The scale of the social scientist is . . . infinitesimally small compared with that of Professor Toynbee's book. . . . He does not intend to solve the problems of civilization and society by a frontal attack on the massed evidence of all the historical societies. All he hopes to do is so to organise the study of his minute topic as to be able to answer, by the light of its evidence, at least some of the problems which are common to society in general. In this, he differs not only from the antiquarian, who is interested in his patch but has no questions to ask, but also from the philosophical historian like Professor Toynbee, who has all the questions in the world to ask but no patch on which even a single satisfactory answer can be raised.'[1]

Will the sociologists succeed in carrying their pontoon from its taking-off point in the field of social phenomena to the farther shore, which they will have reached if and when they succeed in describing and explaining social phenomena in terms of the acts of individual persons? Their intellectual engineering technique of building each successive section of their pontoon of a shorter length than the preceding section might seem, to a lay spectator, to be unpromising. The problem with which they are contending is that of dealing with 'the enormously great', and they are seeking to solve this problem by a technique of *diminuendo*. This looks rather like courting the fate met by Achilles in the famous logical puzzle of his race with the tortoise. The logical conditions laid down for registering the runner's progress deny to him, *a priori*, the possibility of ever reaching his goal. The exclusive use of the microscope, on the unconvincing assumption that this, or any other, instrument is an omnicompetent tool, is, I should say, the fundamental and permanent weakness of sociology, if this assumption is really of the essence of its operational creed, as Postan seems to hold that it is. This is also a particularly serious weakness in an approach to

[1] M. Postan in *The Sociological Review*, vol. xxviii (1936), pp. 62–63.

the study of human affairs at a time when the problem of quantity is the major problem in this field. This point has been neatly put by Bagby.

'It would be a great thing if someone could invent a "macroscope", an instrument which would ensure that the historian would see only the larger aspects of history and would blind him to the individual details. It is only by remaining at this higher level of abstraction that we can hope to decipher the principal patterns of historical change, to identify the "forces", whatever they are, that have made the World what it is today. . . . It is the very broadest regularities for which we should first search, since these are likely to be necessary for the explanation of any smaller phenomena.'[1]

These precepts apply, of course, not only to historians but to all students of human affairs, including sociologists.

Contemporary sociologists and social anthropologists have also been criticized by Bagby on several other grounds. One of these is that their

'studies have been primarily static in nature, more concerned with social structure in the present than with its development in time. Yet [as Bagby justly comments] it is precisely the developments, the changes in the lives of many human beings over the course of centuries, which are of major interest to the student of history.'[2]

They are, indeed, of major interest to all students of human affairs, under whatever label they happen to do their work, since human affairs are never visible except as being on the move, whatever may be the angle from which one is looking at them.

Bagby goes on to point out[3] that the studies undertaken by contemporary sociologists 'are dependent on direct observation and tend to neglect some of the important aspects of group life', and that, 'in addition, while their science theoretically deals with the structure and functioning of all societies, in practice their studies have very largely been confined to European societies or those of European origin', and that 'their concepts and methods are therefore not, on the whole, designed for universal application'. All these observations of Bagby's may be valid as criticisms of current sociological practice. But there is not anything, inherent in sociology itself, to prevent sociologists from remedying the present defects in their work that Bagby criticizes. It is open to them to enlarge the scope of their operations. Bagby himself mentions[4] that 'Max Weber . . . saw the necessity of comparing the social structure of our own with those of the other civilizations if we are to be able to make generalizations valid for all mankind', and that, although Weber's 'initial studies have never been followed up by the sociologists, . . . the social anthropologists . . . have begun to examine Chinese and Indian social structure in the last decade or two', and, 'in addition, . . . have made many synchronic [i.e. static] studies of this kind among individual primitive peoples'. It looks, in fact, as if sociology needed only the necessary time to extend its geographical horizon

1 P. Bagby: *Culture and History*, pp. 128 and 158.   2 Ibid., p. 8.
3 Ibid., pp. 9–10. Cp. p. 185.   4 Ibid., p. 185.

from the West to the World as a whole. There also seems to be no reason why it should not replace the rather abstract method of studying social phenomena in cross-section by the more realistic one of studying them in time-depth. The crucial question for sociology would seem to be whether it is or is not indissolubly wedded to the use of the mental microscope as its exclusive instrument. It is to be hoped that it is not, since the study of human affairs cannot afford to see any of the present approaches to it stultified.

On the historical side the problem of bridging the gap between human beings and social phenomena in our intellectual comprehension of human affairs has been attacked in the present generation by a method which seems promising in itself and which has, in fact, been vindicated already by some brilliant successes. This 'prosopographical' method tries to bring social mythology down to earth by taking, for its initial units in a study of some social phenomenon, as large a number of the relevant acts of as large a number of participating individuals as the state of the extant information allows.[1] In this approach the ideal would be, presumably, to make an exhaustive survey of all relevant acts of all individuals concerned, and then to give an account of the social phenomenon in view in terms of generalizations from these data. But, apart from the philosophers' doubts about the logical validity of induction by complete enumeration,[2] it is, in practice, impossible, in any investigation into human affairs, to survey these exhaustively. Even where one is dealing with a small and more or less closed circle of *dramatis personae*, and where also the accessible information about each of them is comparatively copious, what remains undiscovered will still far exceed what has been brought to light, even if we have conducted our researches with the utmost possible skill and industry. Accordingly, when the prosopographical historian has built the first section of his pontoon to the maximum length allowed him by his supply of *personalia*, he has to prolong it by a different form of structure. If he is to give himself any chance of reaching the other side of the gap between the personal acts of individuals and social phenomena, he must extend the reach of his information about personalities by generalizing from this with the aid of such devices as sampling and statistics.

In this procedure the prosopographical historian's technique is the inverse of the sociologist's. It is one, not of *diminuendo*, but of *crescendo*.

---

[1] *Ad hominem*, I myself have been gently criticized in *The Japan Chronicle*, 29th July, 1934, for not having made enough use of this approach. 'If fault is to be found with Mr Toynbee's work, it is that he does not seem to give sufficient value to the individual element. . . . The individual merits the attention of the historian as well as the society of which he is an eminent unit.' I myself would go so far as to say that, even when he is not eminent (and the great majority of us are not), he still merits the historian's attention if the historian can lay hands on evidence about him and his acts and their effects. It seems likely that, in this book, I may have paid too little attention to individuals, since my first (though not my exclusive) concern here has been to try to trace regularities and uniformities in social phenomena. If I have been guilty of this neglect in practice, I have been failing to live up to my own principles. In principle, I hold that human beings are the source of all social phenomena, and are therefore realities of a higher order than these are. I believe that my contemporaries who have taken the prosopographical approach to history have chosen a promising (though not the only promising) line of work. And I much admire their achievements.

[2] See pp. 23–24.

The method would appear to be a more promising one, in itself, for grappling with the problem of quantity by which the historian and the sociologist are both confronted. It is also more promising because of the fortunate coincidence that, at the very time when historians have been taking to a method that has led to their seeking help from the procedures of sampling and statistics, these procedures have been gaining in potency through the acquisition of new experience and new equipment. In the present generation the art of sampling has been applied to human affairs in many fields—for instance, in the study of the preferences of consumers of goods and casters of votes with a view to trying to predict what their future choices are going to be. Contemporaneously, the science of statistics has been developing its mathematical apparatus and has been supplying itself with ministering *jinns* in the shape of electronic computers. These electronic 'brains' cannot, it is true, serve as substitutes for human minds. They cannot take the initiative in propounding questions or in formulating problems. But when once a problem has been formulated by a human mind in the terms of binary arithmetic—giving the machine the simple choice of answering 'yes' or 'no'—the *jinn* can perform the calculations demanded of him by his human master on a colossal scale in almost no time. Thanks to the sudden rise of the new science of cybernetics, it now looks as if human ingenuity, with the leviathan-power of an electronic Briareus at its command, may eventually succeed in bridging the gap between social phenomena and the acts of individual human beings by starting from the prosopographical historian's point of departure and using the contrivances of sampling, statistics, and electronically-operated computers to carry the human mind across the gap between the two banks.

For making the prosopographical approach to the problem of bridging the gap between human beings and institutions, the most favourable situations are obviously those in which a relatively small minority of the participants in a society, constituting a more or less strictly closed social circle, control between them one or more of their society's more important institutions, or even the society's whole life. The smaller the number of both the human beings and the institutions that are involved, the simpler the prosopographical researcher's task will be, and this for several reasons. The number of the units, of both the personal and the institutional order of reality, with which the researcher will have to deal, is then likely to be manageable; and the persons concerned, being all of them privileged and some of them eminent, are likely to be fairly well documented. Prosopography lends itself, in fact, particularly well to the study of the management of social affairs by oligarchies—military, political, economic, or ecclesiastical. It has been applied, for instance, with notable success, to studies of the eighteenth-century political oligarchy in the United Kingdom and of the Roman aristocracy during the last two centuries of the republican regime, especially the final decades that are documented by Cicero's letters and speeches and by an increasing flow of Latin inscriptions. In these two fields brilliant pioneer work has been done in England by two scholars, born elsewhere, Sir Lewis Namier and Professor Sir Ronald Syme, who have paid England the compliment of settling there and doing their life-work in an English intellectual environment. Two other oligarchies that have been studied in a comparable way are Alexander the Great's officers and the Prophet Muhammad's companions. The Venetian oligarchy and the Roman Curia would, no doubt, lend themselves to the same method of historical research. The richest mine of all is probably the series of Chinese dynastic histories, since these are on the grand scale and are organized partly on 'prosopographical' lines. A considerable section of each of them is allocated to biographical notices of distinguished persons, and these not only in the political line. A beginning has already been made with the use of these Chinese materials for a prosopographical approach to the study of Chinese social phenomena. The development of the relations between the Topa barbarian invaders of North China and the Confucian gentry within their domain has been studied in this way by W. Eberhard,[1] and the materials for a similar study of the corresponding relations of the Confucian gentry with the Manchu invaders have been sorted out and published by A. W. Hummel.[2]

Perhaps most human institutions, communities, and societies, at most times and places, have been managed by minorities of the total number of human beings concerned, even when and where the institutions have been officially democratic. Oligarchy has been common because the two antithetical human tendencies to take a lead and to follow one seem to be unevenly distributed as between different individuals, even though there may be something of either tendency in everyone.[3] This question of leadership is discussed further at other points in this volume.[4] Without needing to adopt any particular conclusion about it, we can see that, while a considerable sector of the total field of social affairs has been oligarchically managed in the past, there is also a large sector in which oligarchical management is at any rate less conspicuous. Moreover, this more democratic sector seems likely to increase relatively in the future, as hereditary privilege is progressively whittled away by the graduated taxation of wealth and by the free education of ability. Furthermore, even in the most oligarchically, or indeed monarchically, managed society, in which the material and spiritual amenities of culture are withheld from the majority of the participants in the society in question, every one of these obscure individuals will, nevertheless, make his or her influence felt, in some infinitesimal degree, in the shaping of social events by human action. Accordingly, if oligarchy were a necessary condition for making an episode of human affairs a suitable subject for prosopographical treatment, this method would not be an effective one for dealing with human affairs in general. Fortunately it is at this point that the new mathematical and electronic aids to the art of sampling and to the science of statistics will come to the prosopographer's rescue. They will enable him to cope with units in far greater

[1] W. Eberhard: *Das Toba Reich Chinas* (Leiden, 1949, Brill); *Conquerors and Rulers* (Leiden 1952, Brill).
[2] A. W. Hummel (ed.): *Eminent Chinese of the Ch'ing Period* (vol. i, London 1944, Kegan Paul; vol. ii, Washington D.C. 1945, U.S. Government Printing Office).
[3] See p. 149.   [4] On pp. 125–7, 148–50, and 305–6.

numbers than could ever be handled by single human minds that did not have this Briarean apparatus at their command. Present scientific and technological progress in this sphere makes it not unreasonable to expect that the prosopographical study of human affairs, after its brilliant start in a field in which the numbers are small enough to be manageable without the use of apparatus, will prove able, with the help of apparatus, to extend its operations into fields in which, without this help, the numbers would be unmanageably great.[1]

It looks, then, as if there were fairly good prospects of bridging the gap between human beings and social phenomena from the prosopographical side, if not from the sociological side. In any case, whether the prospects are good or bad, we cannot afford to abandon our attempts to solve this problem, for that would mean abandoning the study of human affairs, and we certainly cannot afford to do that. To conduct this study successfully, we have to pursue three studies in conjunction: the study of human beings, the study of social affairs, and the study of the relations between these two different orders of reality. So we must resist any suggestion for abandoning any one of the three, whether the motive inspiring the suggestion is defeatism or is prejudice. We must resist the historians' prejudice against the analysis of social phenomena and the investigation of regularities and uniformities in these. Equally we must resist the social philosophers' prejudice against the narration of particular events and particular acts of particular individuals. Both lines of inquiry are indispensable; the two can, and in fact do, co-exist; and, unless they are simultaneously pursued, it will be impossible to make the study of human affairs intelligible; for these will not become intelligible till human beings and social phenomena have been brought into an intelligible relation with each other by either the prosopographical approach or the sociological approach or both.

4. THE DISTORTING EFFECTS OF DEVICES FOR REDUCING THE QUANTITY OF INFORMATION

Hellenic thinkers despised particulars in principle as being intellectually contemptible, and esteemed generalities as being intellectually admirable. In their practice they were more catholic than in their theory;[2] for they produced a galaxy of great historians, including eminent exponents of the prosopographical method, such as Plutarch, who presented the whole panorama of Graeco-Roman history in his series of parallel lives, and the 'doxographers', who recorded the doctrines of the Hellenic philosophers in their personal contexts. The Hellenic theory

---

[1] *Ad hominem*, I have been criticized (in the most friendly terms) by Lord Samuel, in *John o' London's Weekly*, 5th January, 1935, for having 'touched little upon the standards of life and thought of the average man' in vols. i–iii, and again by a reviewer in *The Economist*, 6th November, 1954, on the score that 'the common people do not receive the place or proportion' in my 'scheme of things which must surely be theirs on any transcendental view of history'. I admit the charge and plead, in my defence, that this grave omission on my part has been due to a lack of means, not to a lack of will. 'Give us the tools, and we will do the job.' Besides the modest motor-bicycle for which Sir Keith Hancock indents, every historian nowadays needs an electronic computer.
[2] This Hellenic attitude has been touched on already on p. 18.

on this issue was introduced into the modern Western World at the Italian Renaissance and was not jettisoned when Hellenism in general suffered its defeat in the seventeenth-century 'Battle of Ancients and Moderns'. The Hellenic prejudice against taking account of particulars and individuals in the study of human affairs was maintained by the Western philosophers of the eighteenth-century French school; and it was not killed by the reaction against it in the nineteenth-century Romantic Movement. It has still found active and able representatives in the present generation. Philip Bagby, for instance, suggests, in his prolegomena to the comparative study of civilizations,[1] that

'it is perfectly possible to admit that occasionally individuals do affect culture and still to maintain that the elucidation of cultural processes and the broader features of experience which affect them is the most promising method of making historical events intelligible. From this point of view, the part played by individuals will be seen as a random or inexplicable element.'

Bagby argues[2] that, though individuals may affect *what* other people do, they do not affect *the way in which* they do it. He also emphasizes the social, as opposed to the individual, contributions to inventions. It is well known that the last step in making an invention is often taken almost simultaneously, and apparently independently, by several individuals,[3] and the reason is that all of them alike are really drawing much more on a collective and cumulative advance in knowledge and understanding than on their own individual genius. Cultural growth releases individual genius that is always potentially present.[4] 'The man of genius . . . is, in an even more intimate sense than the ordinary man, the product of a society and a culture.'[5] 'The dichotomy between great men and social forces is a false one. . . . Great men are precisely the points of intersection of great social forces.'[6] 'The appearance of a succession of great philosophers, musicians, or artists in a given country and century appears to be an amazing coincidence unless we recognise the social character of these achievements, the social fund of knowledge, techniques, and aspirations which reach their summits in the careers of a few outstanding individuals.'[7] 'Granted that gifts are individually congenital, it is the cultural setting into which they are born which makes or prevents their realisation.'[8] 'What we are wont to call "great men" are those among many more individuals of above-average ability who happen to get born in a time and place and society the patterns of whose culture have formed with sufficient potential value and have developed into sufficient

[1] P. Bagby: *Culture and History*, p. 156.
[2] In op. cit., pp. 150–7.
[3] This is illustrated and discussed by A. L. Kroeber in *The Nature of Culture*, pp. 43–44, 45, and 128.
[4] Kroeber, ibid., p. 8.
[5] Chr. Dawson: *The Dynamics of World History*, p. 57. Cp. pp. 51–52.
[6] M. R. Cohen: *The Meaning of Human History*, pp. 220–1. The same point is made, in almost the same words, in the Social Science Research Council's Committee on Historiography's Report (1954), p. 64.
[7] Cohen, op. cit., p. 222.
[8] Kroeber: *Style and Civilizations*, p. 61.

ripeness to allow the full capacities of these individuals to be realised and expressed.'[1]

Kroeber points out[2] that there is 'a correlation between realised genius and opportunity given by stage of a civilization's development'.[3] If an individual genius does make a discovery for which society is not ready, this discovery will be ignored, as Mendel's was, till society has caught up with the genius intellectually.[4] 'Watt's invention of the steam engine fitted into the practical needs of British industry in the eighteenth century far more than Hero's invention into the economy of Hellenistic or Saracen culture.'[5]

A. R. Burn suggests[6] that the reason why the prophets of the 'Axis Age' made their appearance and won their followings more or less contemporaneously was that, by that time, large populations had been detribalized as a result of the development of towns in the Bronze Age, while traditional beliefs had been discredited by the subsequent decline and fall of the bronze-age civilizations. 'It was not the personalities of these great men that were unique, but the opportunity. If they had lived earlier, they could have been poets, but not the prophets that they were. The effectiveness in society of even the most original individual thought is a social achievement. The thought of a prophet cannot be preserved without disciples; and every gospel requires a *praeparatio evangelica*.' Burn goes on to suggest[7] that 'the only two recorded higher religions to emerge in "primary" civilizations . . . were "abortive" . . . because the traditional polytheisms were not yet sufficiently discredited'. These two higher religions had been deliberately invented by two kings, the Pharaoh Ikhnaton and the Inca Viracocha, as responses to the challenge of their individual situations. At the beginning of the process of detribalization, 'among the first men to feel acutely the stresses, the loneliness, and the need for heroism in their position as individuals were kings and chiefs'. In these two cases the lonely individual's isolatedness defeated his attempt to cure his loneliness by communicating a consciousness of the same distress to his fellow human beings and persuading them to adopt a common remedy of his devising. 'Any fool can devise a more consistent system than exists, but even a despot rarely can institute one.'[8]

In general Bagby argues that the influence of so-called 'great men' on public affairs has been much exaggerated—e.g. the role of revolutionary leaders and military commanders.[9] The Social Science Research Council's Committee on Historiography goes with him to the extent of reporting[10] that 'to-day it is generally agreed that leadership is a relation to which the leaders, the followers, and the requirements of the

[1] Kroeber: *The Nature of Culture*, p. 128.   [2] Ibid., p. 128. Cp. p. 403.
[3] Kroeber here gives the answer to Father G. F. Klenk's question how we are to explain the breakdowns and disintegrations of societies, considering that the capacities of individuals continue to be what they always have been (*Stimmen der Zeit*, No. 145 (1949/50), pp. 376–84).   [4] See Kroeber, op. cit., pp. 44–45 and 158–9.
[5] Cohen, op. cit., p. 256.   [6] In *History*, February–October, 1956, p. 9.
[7] Ibid., p. 10.   [8] Kroeber, op. cit., p. 130.
[9] Bagby, op. cit., pp. 126–7.
[10] The Social Science Research Council's Committee on Historiography's Report (1954), pp. 64–65.

situation, including the traditions of the group, all contribute'. This is of course, true.[1] We seize upon the actions of 'great men' as explanations of social events because some of their acts are on record and are ascertainable, whereas most people's acts have passed into oblivion. To reduce the role ascribed to individuals to its true proportions is a valuable intellectual exercise. The distinction between an individual and his social and cultural environment is, in truth, an arbitrary and artificial one,[2] though the drawing of it is also the essential first step towards beginning to think about human affairs at all.[3]

In Bagby's mind an eighteenth-century depreciation of the role of individual human beings in social and cultural human affairs is reinforced by a twentieth-century pessimism about the practicability of coping with the problem of quantity if once the study of individual persons and particular events has been admitted to be necessary.

'It is . . . impossible as a practical matter to trace all the influences which have led to the formation of the character of an individual in the past. The evidence is simply not available. And, similarly, . . . the task of tracing individual interactions anywhere but in the very recent past far exceeds our powers.[4] . . . We simply do not have sufficient evidence to establish the sequence of events at this level and, even if we had, we should not have the time to study it in all the necessary detail. . . . This is probably the major reason why history has proved unintelligible up to date. Our inveterate and natural habit of conceiving [of] human events at an individual level has led us to persist in a hopeless undertaking.'[5]

The undertaking is not truly a hopeless one if there is any force in the considerations that have been set out in the present chapter; and, if we were to be so faint-hearted as to abandon the undertaking, we should be landing ourselves in a truly hopeless situation. Bagby's solution for the problem of quantity in the study of human affairs is to exclude individual human beings from his purview.

[1] This point is made wittily in an anecdote recounted by Herodotus in Book VII, chap. 125. 'Timodemus of Aphidna was nagging Themistocles about his embassy to Lacedaemon, and was saying that it was for Athens' sake, not for his own, that the Lacedaemonians had paid him such honours. Timodemus kept on nagging like this, till at last Themistocles said to him: "Look! Certainly I would not have been treated with such distinction by the Spartans if I had been somebody from Belbina; but you, Sir, would not, in spite of your being an Athenian."'
The same anecdote is recorded by Plutarch in his *Life of Themistocles*, chap. 18, in a different version: 'A man from Seriphos once said to him that he owed his fame not to himself but to his country. "You are right", replied Themistocles. "I should not have become famous if I had been a Seriphian, but you would not if you had been an Athenian."'
[2] This is equally true of the distinction between an individual—or a group of human beings—and mankind's physical environment (see pp. 146–8 and 314–27).
[3] If Bagby had confined himself to these empirical considerations, he would have been on strong ground. But he cuts this ground from under his feet by deliberately subordinating Reality to the exigencies of the pattern in his own mind. The explanation of culture by the actions of individuals is excluded, Bagby says, not by the fact that it is 'not sufficiently well-formulated, but by the nature of our theory, by the way in which we conceptualise the data. . . . We are engaged in theory-construction. . . . Individual actions are excluded *a priori*.'
I have some sympathy with Bagby in his commission of this intellectual sin. I have committed it myself, and have been censured for doing so by my critics—Bagby among them. It is a sin nevertheless. If Bagby had lived, perhaps he would have repented of it.
[4] P. Bagby: *Culture and History*, p. 54. [5] Ibid., p. 150.

'What we are talking about are regularities in the behaviour of groups of human beings, ways of doing things. . . . Individuals and their actions are abstractions on a different level from that on which we propose to conduct our investigations.'[1]

Individual human beings and social human phenomena are certainly alike in being abstractions from Reality, and different in being abstractions from it on different levels. The making of abstractions is, as we have seen, of the essence of the activity of thinking. But this operational necessity brings with it distortions in our mental picture of Reality which we must be striving perpetually to correct, and we can correct them only in so far as we can achieve the intellectual *tour de force* of recombining what we have distortingly put asunder. We are depriving ourselves, in advance, of the possibility of performing this needful but particularly difficult intellectual operation if we rule out any one of our abstracted facets of Reality from further consideration. Historians are making this mistake if they propose to rule out the study of regularities and uniformities in social phenomena. Bagby is making the same mistake in reverse in his proposal to rule out individuals and their actions. Any inquirer, following any line of approach, is free—or it might be nearer the truth to say 'bound'—to make any abstraction that seems to him promising for operational purposes; but, if the investigation that he is trying to conduct is to be fruitful, he must eventually reassemble the fragments into which, for temporary working purposes, he has mentally dissected the really seamless web of human affairs.

Proposals to leave human beings out of account or to leave social patterns out of account in the study of human affairs are not the only variants of the idea of trying to cope with the problem of quantity by a recourse to intellectual surgery. There is also an old habit of cutting the study up into separate 'disciplines', and there have been a number of suggestions for cutting it down by cutting out of it all but some single one of Man's major activities, or all but one single track in mankind's multiple movement through space-time. All such attempts at a solution by simplification are defeatist in their spirit and distorting in their effects.

Ad hominem, I have noticed, in surveying criticisms of my own work, that a number of critics have used up a number of lines of print in discussing, in all earnestness, whether I am justified, as an historian, in dealing with theological, philosophical, and sociological issues, and conversely whether, if I do behave like a theologian or perhaps like a poet, I am entitled to call myself an historian.[2] These solemn discussions seem to me to make no sense apropos of intellectual work. They imply, I think, the tacit drawing of an analogy between intellectual work and public administration. As I see it, this analogy does not hold; and scholars who fancy that something is gained by drawing it are, I should say, convicting themselves of being intellectual mandarins. I speak from some experience of both worlds, since, in the course of the First and Second World Wars, I have spent nearly ten years of my working life, all told, as a temporary civil servant.

[1] Ibid., p. 150.
[2] Examples of such criticisms have been cited on pp. 37–41.

In this, to me, alien world I have had an experience that has been common to many outsiders who have had an inside glimpse of it. I have been partly amused and partly exasperated by the civil service's occupational disease of 'departmentalism'. 'This business is—or is not—our—or your—department's affair'; 'this file is—or is not—for my—or for your—attention'. Though officially just a department of one almighty sovereign state, each department is *de facto* an independent 'great power', and this not only in Japan, but also in the United States and the United Kingdom. Even over trivialities, and this even in war-time, departments conduct diplomatic negotiations with each other with portentous gravity and at extravagant length. Perhaps this departmentalism may have something to be said for it in public administration on an elephantine scale. On this scale orderliness is genuinely so important that it is not altogether paradoxical to argue that form matters more than substance and that the approved procedure must be followed even when this thwarts the achievement of desirable results. Short of admitting this, it is perhaps plausible to suggest, in the light of a formidably large dossier of experience, that this state of mind, which seems characteristically and reprehensibly 'bureaucratic' to outsiders, is in any case inevitable in a world of professional administrators on a large scale. My quarrel is not with the civil servants; it is with scholars who gratuitously import the bureaucratic state of mind into the field of intellectual inquiry.

In this field the bureaucratic approach is not only incongruous; it is obstructive; for, in intellectual inquiry, freedom is the breath of life and formalism is, not a safeguard, but a shackle. There is nothing to be said for breaking up the study of human affairs into the so-called 'disciplines'. These have grown up haphazard, independently of each other. In consequence there are overlaps between them and also gaps that are covered by none of them. The relations between them have never been reviewed or revised on a rational plan.[1] Indeed, any suggestion that this should be done would be likely to arouse hot opposition. The feeling between the votaries of the different intellectual disciplines is almost as bad as it is between the adherents of the different higher religions. There are historians, for instance, who do not admit that sociology is a legitimate form of study, or who, if they do admit this, do so only on the proviso that the two disciplines are to be deemed to have nothing to do with each other—a fantastic notion, considering that history and sociology are concerned with the study of the same affairs.[2] There are

---

[1] The best suggestion that I know is A. L. Kroeber's. He suggests that anthropology is the study of cultures, sociology that of societies, psychology that of individuals, history that of events (*The Nature of Culture*, p. 104). This is logical. Yet in practice it would be difficult to work in any of these four disciplines without trespassing on the fields of the other three as here defined.

[2] A common-sense verdict on this benighted feud has been pronounced by A. L. Kroeber. History, as Kroeber defines it, deals in phenomena, science in process. An interest in phenomena and an interest in process are both necessary. Which of the two a particular inquirer should concentrate on is a matter of temperament (A. L. Kroeber: *The Nature of Culture*, pp. 63 and 62). 'It is as one-sided, and ultimately sterile, to be exclusively occupied with structure as with function' (ibid., p. 88). M. R. Cohen shows the same wisdom in observing that 'history is *one* [italics mine] of the ways of organizing human knowledge' (*The Meaning of Human History*, p. 41).

philosophers, again, who take up a corresponding attitude towards psychology.

Such attitudes are not only absurd but obscurantist if it is true that dialectical debate is the source of advances in knowledge and understanding,[1] and that, the wider the field of discussion, the greater the chance of striking out fruitful new ideas. When each discipline draws in its horns and tries to turn itself into a Leibnizian 'monad', intellectual progress is being sabotaged; for there can be no exchange of ideas between the inmates of windowless houses; and the cutting of interdisciplinary communications is the more damaging because the traditional boundary walls between the disciplines are unplanned and arbitrary. 'If we throw aside . . . administrative considerations and look at the problem itself, we see that the difference between the philosopher and the historian can only be one of degree and emphasis.'[2] These conventional barriers are particularly cramping at a time, such as that through which we are now living, in which knowledge and understanding are in flux, and in which successive increases in both of them are making repeated revolutionary changes in the configuration of the whole of our intellectual landscape.

What is needed now is a ruthless demolition squad, armed with the intellectual equivalent of atomic artillery, to batter the traditional interdisciplinary dividing walls down to the ground. This would restore the natural unity of the field that has been cut up, for so long, by these encroaching enclosures. No doubt, at all times and in all intellectual situations, the huge field of human studies needs to be parcelled out for operational purposes. But the partitions should be provisional only, and they should be demarcated by transferable hurdles, not by embedded stone walls. Or, if we think of the study of human affairs as being a house of many mansions, we should construct it, not like a Western house, but like a Japanese house, in which the internal arrangements can be given any number of alternative configurations, interchangeable at a moment's notice, because the interior is divided up by movable screens, not by walls that are 'permanent fixtures'.

Meanwhile, among some followers of each of the existing disciplines, there seems to be an increasing assertion of each discipline's claim to separateness and independence, and an increasing desire to keep their own discipline's monadic blank walls erect along their traditional alignments.[3] This rising temper is significantly like that of some of the

---

[1] See pp. 41–45 and 641–2.

[2] M. R. Cohen: *The Meaning of Human History*, p. 7.

[3] This monadic-mindedness has entered into some of the criticisms of my work (see p. 38, footnote 1). Critics representing this school have taken the trouble to report that I am, or am not, this or that—apparently in the belief that the word written on the label of a jar has some power to affect the quality of the contents.

L. Stone would like to disallow my claim to be an historian because so much of the contents of vols. vii–x of this book is the kind of thing that requires a metaphysician, not an historian, to review it (*Toynbee and History*, p. 111). 'The questions Dr Toynbee asks are largely irrelevant to their [his "professional" colleagues'] concept of the proper study of history, which consists in studying the past for its own sake, in attempting to understand and differentiate, to arrange and classify, the discoverable facts about the nature of a given society in a given period. They are convinced that the differences between civilizations are more significant than the likenesses, and that standardised causal patterns cannot logically be deduced from the facts of history' (Stone, ibid.). 'If it is

nationals of each of the contemporary local states. On the plane of politics, states are counterparts of disciplines on the plane of intellectual inquiry. So perhaps this common temper gives the key to the anxiety that is being shown to preserve the traditional intellectual partitions from being demolished. This anxiety is manifestly perverse in an age in which these traditional partitions have become obvious impediments to the advancement of knowledge and understanding; and at first sight such perversity seems strange. It may be accounted for in the diehard champions of the departmental disciplines, as it certainly is accounted for in those of the parochial states, by a dread of the unknown situation that awaits them, out in the open, in boundless space, if the familiar walls of the present voluntary prison houses are torn down. This anxiety may be natural, but it is neither rational nor expedient. It offers no basis for a constructive policy. It needs to be combated and overcome. 'Specialisation has . . . prepared the way for a new universalisation, but there is not yet any recognition of this truth, and hardly any use is yet being made of this opportunity.'[1] The objective has been defined by

true that Mr Toynbee has tried to generalise Gibbon's inquiry, he has failed to notice that, in doing so, he has ceased to be an historian, except incidentally. . . . His comparative study of the rises and falls of civilizations should be taken as a contribution, not to history, but to "Social Dynamics". . . . His true predecessor here is not Gibbon but Auguste Comte' (W. H. Walsh in *Toynbee and History*, p. 126). 'When Mr Toynbee discusses questions about the meaning and point of the historical process as a whole, he writes, not as an historian or even a sociologist, but as a metaphysical philosopher. If in his early volumes he is in effect a successor of Comte, his models here [i.e. in vols. vii–x] are such writers as Vico, Herder, and Hegel' (Walsh, ibid., p. 127). In proposing to present history as, in the end, a theodicy, 'it is surely clear that . . . he has travelled far . . . from what any normal historian would regard as history proper' (Walsh, ibid., pp. 126–7). 'It is not objective, or even interpretative, *history*. It is theology' (H. E. Barnes: *An Introduction to the History of Sociology*, p. 729). E. Berkovitz, too, finds that my work is not history but a philosophical and theological interpretation of history (*Judaism: Fossil or Ferment?*, p. 9). G. J. Renier's pronouncement on my work is that 'it is the supreme embodiment of what I [i.e. Renier, not Toynbee] call "left-wing deviationism"', the confusion between history and the philosophy of history' (*Toynbee and History*, p. 73). W. Kaufmann feels that my 'determination to mix genres' makes it enormously difficult to do me justice (ibid., p. 306).

Critics of this school are, it seems to me, paying too much attention to labels, which, in my belief, are not either interesting or important. This preoccupation of theirs offers their human target an easy way of putting them out of action. He has merely to read the label on the critic's hat and affix a different label on his own. He will then be able, with impunity, to talk as much nonsense as he likes, as far as this particular critic is concerned. However outrageously he behaves, he can count on the critic's simply registering 'not my subject'.

Fortunately, there are other critics who rate labels at their true zero value and see human affairs as the unity that they really are. W. H. McNeill, for instance, after noting that 'Toynbee has felt himself free to connect his studies of history with ultimate philosophical and theological questions', suggests that this is a challenge to other presentday historians (*The Intent of Toynbee's History: A Cooperative Appraisal*) H. Kohn dismisses the criticisms of the present book that censure it for not being history. He submits that I am not trying to write history here, though I have done that in other books of mine, e.g. *The Survey of International Affairs* (*Der Monat*, August, 1955, p. 464). K. W. Thompson suggests that I must be judged both as an historian and as a philosopher of history (*Toynbee and History*, p. 201). E. Fiess finds that the present book 'is not a work of history' and, 'a fortiori, not a work of archaeology, sociology, philosophy, theology, or even of all these combined; it enters into each one of these fields, but no man can be an authority in all of them. Taken as a whole, it is a huge theological poem in prose' (ibid., p. 383). This last sentence of Fiess's has already been quoted on p. 39, footnote 1.

I like being called a poet. I do not suppose that any real poet would acknowledge me as being his confrère. Nevertheless, I will make no objection to having this label affixed to me by non-poets, if this will induce my critics to give up the unprofitable game of debating which, if any, of the 'disciplines' is my legal domicile.

[1] E. R. Curtius in *Merkur*, 1. Jahrgang, Viertes Heft [Heft 4] (1947), p. 493.

A. L. Kroeber in language that is less militant and more statesmanlike than mine. Kroeber believes 'the time to be near when efforts for closer federation in the united sciences may well come from students of culture'. 'This great unity', he declares, 'is the true study for the student of Man.'[1]

If partition is a wrong way of trying to deal with the problem of quantity in the field of human studies, so is omission; and this applies equally to both the main devices for lightening the human mind's fast-increasing cargo. One of these is to pick out one of Man's plural activities—say, politics or economics or technology or religion—and to give this the status of a 'master-activity', with the implication that the other activities may and should be ignored except in so far as they can be treated as being subordinate to the single activity that has been given pride of place. This device would certainly simplify the problem of quantity by drastically reducing the number of phenomena to be taken into account.[2] It involves us, however, in insuperable difficulties as soon as we try to carry it out. These difficulties are discussed in the annex to the present chapter,[3] so we need not go into details here. The other device is as old as human nature itself, or indeed as life, since it is a patent reflection of the self-centredness that is inborn in every living organism. It is based on the assumption that the inquirer's own religion, civilization, community, or parish in the inquirer's own generation is the culmination of all human history, without even adding the proviso 'up to date'.[4] On this scheme the inquirer gives himself licence to ignore everything in human affairs that does not lead up to his own 'here and now'. This egocentric device would, of course, reduce the number of the phenomena as effectively as the 'master-activity' device would; but, like that device, this one, too, is impracticable. Now that all the histories of all the societies, in all ages and in all parts of the World, have been pooled in one all-inclusive intellectual heritage, accessible to the whole human race,[5] it is no longer possible to present history as a single-track line reaching its terminus in the short-lived contemporary generation of a 'Chosen People'.

5. THE NEED FOR SIMULTANEOUS CULTIVATION OF PANORAMIC AND MYOPIC VISION

If the problem of quantity cannot be eluded by any device—not, for instance, by trying to narrow the field, and not by trying to subdivide it—we have to grapple with the stark difficulty of overcoming the disparity between the overwhelming mass of the data and the limited

---

[1] A. L. Kroeber: The Nature of Culture, pp. 10–11 and 19. Kroeber's suggestion that the anthropologists may be the pioneers in a coming general study of human affairs is taken up by Bagby. 'A future science of history must at first rely heavily on anthropology both for concepts and methods' (Culture and History, p. 20).
[2] This is why the 'master-activity' device is tempting (see Chr. Dawson: The Dynamics of World History, pp. 24–25).   [3] See pp. 658–63.
[4] F. Engel-Janosi observes that historians of the single-track school always think of themselves as being on the threshhold of the Last Things (Wissenschaft und Weltbild, 2. Jahrgang, Heft 4 (October, 1949), p. 270).   [5] See pp. 110–13.

capacity of a single human mind. There is no escape from the formidable requirement that we must each of us attempt to take a panoramic view of the whole field;[1] and, considering how vast this is by comparison with our intellectual powers, we have to face the truth that our panoramic view is bound to be a superficial one.[2] Superficiality is a defect about which we cannot afford to be complacent, because it exposes us to the risk of misconstruing Reality,[3] and the whole purpose of intellectual inquiry is to come as near as possible to seeing Reality as it is. How are we to correct our superficiality? The defeatist remedy is to avoid it by renouncing the panoramic view that exposes us to it; but this means renouncing the endeavour to arrive at any understanding of human affairs. A more constructive remedy is, not to seek to avoid superficiality at this prohibitive price, but to try to counterbalance it by aiming at thoroughness in some fraction of the total field.[4] This fraction must be

[1] This point is well made by P. Bagby: *Culture and History*, p. 158. Ranke declared his belief that 'the final goal—not yet attained—always remains the conception and execution of a history of mankind' ('Das letzte Ziel, ein noch unerreichtes, bleibt immer die Auffassung und Produktion einer Geschichte der Menschheit'). This passage occurs in a fragment, written by Ranke in the eighteen-sixties and left by him in manuscript, which has been printed by A. Dove on pp. xiii–xvi (the passage just quoted is on p. xv) of his preface to the Ninth Part, Second Section, of Ranke's *Weltgeschichte* (published in nine parts, Leipzig 1881–8, Duncker and Humblot). As Ranke sees it, 'to comprehend the whole without failing to meet the requirements of exact research will, of course, always remain an [unachieved] ideal. It would entail a solidly grounded understanding of the entire history of mankind' ('Das Ganze zu umfassen und doch dem Gesetz der Forschung gerecht zu werden, bleibt freilich immer ein Ideal: es würde das Verständniss der gesammten Menschheitsgeschichte auf festem Grund und Boden in sich schliessen') (ibid., p. xvi). 'In conversation with intimate friends, I have often considered the question whether there is any possibility of composing a world history on these terms. The conclusion was that to satisfy the highest demands is, no doubt, not possible, but that it is imperative that the attempt should be made' ('Im Gespräch mit vertrauten Freunden habe ich öfter die Frage erwogen, ob es überhaupt möglich sei, eine Weltgeschichte in diesem Sinne zu verfassen. Der Schluss war: den höchsten Anforderungen zu genügen, sei wohl nicht möglich, aber notwendig, es zu versuchen' (Ranke's own introduction to his *Weltgeschichte*, First Part, p. ix).
[2] J. K. Feibleman notes that a large picture of world history is bound to be based on secondary sources of dubious validity (*T'ien Hsia Monthly*, vol. xi, Nos. 1 and 2 (1940), p. 18). The Rev. E. R. Hardy Jr., too, observes that 'the impossibility of being equally expert in everything is a limitation that the universal historian must accept and work with. But', he continues *ad hominem*, 'I do feel that in the religious field Toynbee is not sufficiently aware of his own limitations.' 'In the field of religion it is not really possible to know more than one religion from the inside.' Toynbee has 'a sound text-book knowledge of Hinduism, Buddhism, and Islam; but is that really enough for writing with authority about their historical significance?' (*The Intent of Toynbee's History: A Cooperative Appraisal*). Apropos of my treatment of Indian history, culture, and religion, L. Renou sums up a friendly critique by pronouncing that I get at an external truth, but not at the 'vision' which comes from first-hand knowledge (*Diogenes*, No. 13 (Spring, 1956), p. 79).
[3] For instance, Owen Lattimore points out, in *The Atlantic Monthly*, vol. 181, No. 4 (April, 1948), pp. 104–5, that 'dependence on secondary sources implies loss of an absolutely sure touch in distinguishing between the best secondary authority and an inferior authority, or in discriminating between the strong and weak points of a secondary authority who is on the whole good. One of the foredoomed limitations of scholarship, unfortunately, is that, when a bold and adventurous thinker like Toynbee takes over not only the facts but the ideas of a secondary authority, and projects them further, the projection is apt to reveal the flaws and weaknesses of the adopted ideas more than it enhances their strength.' Lattimore illustrates his point from my use of some of Ellsworth Huntington's ideas about the relations between the Nomadic culture and its physical environment.
[4] I am grateful to Michael Postan for giving this good advice to me. In reviewing the first three volumes of this book, Postan remarks that 'the bulk of his new inventions are too wide and too vague to lead to a true sociological discovery, while the few which happen to provide openings for a truly original and a perfectly definite enterprise are left

small enough for us to be able to achieve thoroughness here without having to devote so much of our energies to this that we have not enough left over for taking even the most superficial panoramic view as well.[1] 'Critical method, objective approach, and comprehensive synthesis can and must go together.'[2] 'Critical research on the one side and comprehensive understanding on the other side can be counted on to give each other mutual support.'[3]

If we agree that the solution of the problem of quantity lies in combining the panoramic with the myopic view, perhaps we shall also agree that, in the present state of intellectual knowledge, understanding, and technique, we must be prepared to go to extremes in each of these two antithetical lines of attack on our problem. Considering the vastness of the current increase in the amount of what there is to know, our panoramic view must have the sweep of the view caught from the window of an aeroplane aloft in the stratosphere. Considering the minuteness of the current work that is being done by both the sociologists and the psychologists, our counterbalancing view must penetrate to the depth that is reached by a well-drilling apparatus. Since the radius of our panorama will be almost infinitely long, that of our drill-hole will have to be almost infinitesimally short. After all, when one is using a power-drill in quest of oil or water, it is a matter of course that one's drill-hole should have a shorter diameter than the shaft of a spade-dug well.

This counterbalancing intellectual activity of doing microscopic work on a minute area ought to be an effective insurance against succumbing to the danger inherent in the panoramic view's inevitable superficiality. If we know, from practice, what thoroughness is, we shall not mistake superficiality for it; and, if we see our superficiality for what it is, we shall at least be on our guard against the misconstruction of Reality to which it lays us open. Conversely, in our microscopic work, we shall be put on our guard, by our concurrent use of the telescope, against the misconstruction of Reality to which we are exposed by myopia. The crux of microscopic work is that its thoroughness within its own tiny area does not give the inquirer any information about the relations between this area and its setting in the general field of which it is a part;

---

unexplored'. Postan concludes that, 'until he writes a work of sociology'—meaning, as the context shows, a work of the microscopic kind—'he will not be able to rid himself of his vague images or to meet the challenge of his fruitful ones' (*The Sociological Review*, vol. xxviii (1936), pp. 56 and 63).

The same point is made in the Social Science Research Council's Committee on Historiography's Report (1954), p. 109. 'Toynbee's generalisations . . . must be elaborated to be testable propositions—an elaboration that the author does not provide.'

[1] It is, of course, a difficult question of judgement for an inquirer to decide, in the light of his particular objective, how much of his energy he should spend on telescopic work and how much of it on microscopic work. Christopher Dawson finds that there is too much telescopic work and too little microscopic work in the previous volumes of this book (*Toynbee and History*, p. 139). L. Mumford finds that I have 'succeeded better than most scholars in combining the methods of the specialist with those of the "generalist"' (*Diogenes*, No. 13 (Spring, 1956), p. 12).

[2] 'Kritik, objective Auffassung und umfassende Combination zusammengehen können und müssen' (Ranke: fragment written in the eighteen-sixties, printed in *Weltgeschichte*, Ninth Part, Second Section, p. xvi).

[3] 'Die kritische Forschung auf der einen, das zusammenfassende Verständniss auf der anderen Seite können einander nicht anders, als unterstützen' (Ranke: *Weltgeschichte*, First Part, p. ix).

and, unless and until one sees the object of one's study in its setting, one does not know or understand the object itself, however thoroughly one may have analysed its internal anatomy. An oil-prospector does not sink capital in a boring until he has made a wide geological survey of the whole region for which he holds a prospecting option. If he made a boring at random, and tried to judge its prospects exclusively on the materials brought to the surface by the drill out of this single narrow hole, he would soon lose his employer's money and his own job. A three-dimensional test would be a reckless undertaking without the guidance of a previous two-dimensional survey—just as, conversely, the two-dimensional survey would yield no precise knowledge of the contents of the sub-soil if it were not followed up by a three-dimensional test.

This means that the panoramic and myopic approaches do not only benefit, both alike, by being made concurrently, but need each other's complementary services so much that no inquirer can afford to neglect either of them. Either approach has its own inherent weaknesses; but the remedy for these weaknesses is, not to abandon the approach in which they arise, but to pursue the other approach as well. If we pursue both approaches at once, we shall be giving ourselves a chance of bringing the strong points of each of them to the rescue of the weak points of the other. On the other hand, if we sought to get rid of a weakness by abandoning the approach in which it arises, we should end by abandoning both approaches and consequently abandoning all inquiry.

This, in turn, means that inquirers who concentrate on the bird's-eye view and those who concentrate on the fly's-eye view are, not natural enemies, but natural, and indeed indispensable, allies. As Ranke puts it, 'research cannot be damaged by being brought into relation with a universal standpoint. Without the universal, research would lose its fire; without research, conception would degenerate into fantasy.'[1] If the specialist and the generalist were inevitable enemies, each would have to fight himself, as well as his colleague, since we have seen that, whichever of the two approaches may be the more attractive to a particular inquirer, he must also learn to follow the other approach, too, to some extent, as a means of insuring against falling into his preferred approach's pitfalls. Which of the two approaches is to be preferred by each of us is a matter of personal choice, and each of us will make his choice in accordance with his temperament. There is room, and need, for any number of inquirers of both schools. The one thing for which there is no room is civil war between them and within the bosoms of each of them. This necessity for concord and co-operation seems to be better understood, and better practised, at present by the students of non-human nature than it is by humanists. On this point, we humanists would be well advised to follow the good example set by inquirers in other fields.

[1] 'Die Beziehung auf ein Allgemeines kann der Forschung keinen Eintrag thun: ohne jenes würde diese erkalten, ohne diese die Auffassung in ein Hirngespinnst ausarten' (Ranke: fragment written in the eighteen-sixties, printed in *Weltgeschichte*, Ninth Part, second section, p. xvi).

V. THE NEED FOR A COMPREHENSIVE STUDY OF HUMAN AFFAIRS

THE demand for a comprehensive study of human affairs is inspired by several motives. Some of these are permanent and some temporary; some are disinterested, some self-regarding. The strongest and most estimable of these is curiosity. This is one of the distinctive traits of human nature. No human being seems to be altogether without it, though the degree of its strength varies enormously as between different individuals. In the field of human affairs, curiosity prompts us to seek a panoramic view in order to gain a vision of Reality that will make it as intelligible as is possible for a human mind. 'History certainly justifies a dictum of Einstein, that no great discovery was ever made in science except by one who lifted his nose above the grindstone of details and ventured on a more comprehensive vision.'[1] A panoramic view will at any rate be a less misleading reflection of Reality than a partial view.[2] And, while it is true that in the search for knowledge and understanding, as in all human activities, human achievements are never complete, it is one of Man's virtues that he has the intelligence to be aware of this and the spirit to go on striving, with undiminished zest, to come as near to his goal as his endowment of ability will carry him.

Another motive for the quest for a panoramic view of human affairs, and indeed of the whole of the phenomenal universe, is more self-regarding. The phenomena appear to be innumerable, and the Universe infinite, to the diffracting human mind; and this experience of being adrift in a boundless sea, without chart or compass, is terrifying for a being whose powers are finite. In this disconcerting human situation our first recourse is to make believe that the ocean is not as big as it looks; we try to play on it those tricks of partition and omission that have been noticed in the preceding chapter; but, in playing them, we see through them, and then the only recourse left to us is the formidable one of trying to fling our mental net over the Universe as a whole. Needham points out[3] that 'one of the greatest stimulatory factors of primitive science' was 'the need for at least *classing* phenomena and placing them in some sort of relation with one another, in order to conquer the ever-recurring fear and dread which must have weighed so terribly on early men'. In the Sinic World this universal human response to the psychological challenge of the consciousness of infinity took the form of the development of a set of symbols—eight trigrams and sixty-four hexagrams—generated by working out all the possible permutations and combinations of sets of lines, some unbroken and some broken. These lines seem to have represented sticks—some short, some long— that had been used originally for magical operations. 'Originating from what was probably a collection of peasant omen texts, and accumulating a mass of material used in the practices of divination', this scheme of

---

[1] M. R. Cohen: *The Meaning of Human History*, p. 210.
[2] See E. E. Y. Hales, quoted on p. 647.
[3] J. Needham: *Science and Civilization in China*, vol. ii, p. 336.

visual configurations, in its canonical presentation in the classic called *The Book of Changes* (*I Ching*), 'ended up as an elaborate system of symbols and their explanations'.[1] 'What seems to show through' a number of passages in the commentaries on the *I Ching* by Chinese philosophers

'is the effort made by the School of Naturalists and the Han Confucians to erect the figures made by the long and short sticks into a comprehensive system of symbolism containing in some way all the basic principles of natural phenomena. Like the Taoists, they were looking for peace of mind through classification.'[2]

Primitive societies are not the only societies, and the Sinic is not the only civilization, in which an anxiety in the presence of infinity has spurred human minds to try to bring infinity under mental control. In the rise of Hellenic science, as in the rise of its Sinic counterpart, one of the stimuli was the urge to set bounds (*perata*) to a Universe that presented itself as boundless (*apeiron*). In the modern Western World the same anxiety has been rekindled on the academic level since the introduction of the Chinese system of grading intellectual ability by the test of written examinations—the more so because this innovation in Western education coincided in date with the sudden rapid increase, discussed in the last chapter, in the amount of what there was for examinees to know. A Westerner nowadays may have been educated, during fourteen or fifteen impressionable years, with the immediate object of passing successive examinations, and he may emerge from this ordeal in the state of mind of a perpetual examinee with an infinite number of things to learn and only one working lifetime before him for learning them—a hopelessly short term for acquainting himself with infinity, even if he were to make this his exclusive life-work.

Ad hominem, I still vividly remember my discomfort in emerging in this state of mind, in the summer of 1911, from the final examination at Oxford for the School of *Literae Humaniores*. I immediately started out to read all the surviving sources for Hellenic history in the Greek and Latin languages that I had not read already while I was preparing for the examination that I had now passed. I soon realized that, even if I succeeded in reading every word that there was to be read about Hellenic history both in Greek and Latin and in the languages of the modern Western World, I should be chasing a receding horizon that would lead me on, beyond Hellenic history, into the histories of all the other human societies within Western knowledge. This time the term of my penal servitude would be, not just two and a half years or fourteen; it would be the rest of my life, with the culminating examination postponed to the other side of death. Must I really spend the rest of my life living in fear of a post-mortem examination by Rhadamanthus? This was a melancholy state of mind to have fallen into on the threshold of adult life. I was delivered from it unexpectedly by finding myself making something out of the new knowledge that I was taking on board.

In the course of my post-examinational reading I had been comparing

[1] Ibid., p. 304.   [2] Ibid., p. 328.

facts and figures mentioned in Xenophon's continuation of Thucydides' history with facts and figures mentioned by Thucydides himself. These were data about the numbers and organization of the Lacedaemonian army at successive dates. I had been looking at these data synoptically, trying to make out the relation in which they stood to each other, and I now found that I had been unconsciously producing the nucleus of a paper on 'the Growth of Sparta'. This was something that I had never done before, and the realization that I had been doing it gave me immediate psychological relief. In doing something with the innumerable phenomena, I had 'fixed' them in the American usage of the verb 'fix' as well as in its literal meaning. I had found a pattern in the apparent flux, and, in finding this, I had made the flux less menacing to me. Of course, the little batch of data that I had managed to deal with in this way covered only a tiny patch of the boundless field of human affairs, but I had made a beginning. Now that I had 'fixed' one bit, I need not despair of being able to do the same with the rest. Without knowing it, I had taken the first step towards producing, not only a paper on Sparta, but the present book.

This anxiety in face of the phenomena spurs human minds, always and everywhere, into 'fixing' the phenomena by finding a pattern in them; but it has been accentuated in the present-day world as a result of the World's sudden unification by means of modern science and technology. The same unprecedented scientific and technological advances that have unified the World by 'annihilating distance' have put it into mankind's power to annihilate itself by making war with atomic weapons. We are now waking up to the truth that we have unintentionally put ourselves in a new position in which mankind may have to choose between the two extreme alternatives of committing genocide and learning to live henceforward as a single family.[1] The human race's survival is now once again in doubt for the first time since Man established his ascendancy over non-human nature—a feat that he achieved part way through the Palaeolithic Age. This time it is human nature that threatens mankind with extinction. The recurrence of the ancient threat from this new quarter is a challenge to all human beings to subordinate their traditional parochial loyalties to a new paramount loyalty to mankind itself. The recurrent threat's source in human nature is a challenge to us to study human affairs in order to bring them under control.

In a world that has been unified in both space and time, a study of human affairs must be comprehensive if it is to be effective.[2] It must

---

[1] Among many other contemporary observers, J. Romein testifies that, in our day, 'one world or none' is the truth about our situation (*Toynbee and History*, p. 350).

[2] This point has been made by Polybius in several telling, though perhaps unnecessarily polemical, passages of his *Oecumenical History*. Book I, part of chap. 4, Book III, chap. 31, and Book VIII, chap. 2, have been quoted in the present book already (in iii. 317, footnote 5, and x. 65–66). The whole of Book I, chap. 4, may be quoted here. 'The coincidence by which all the transactions of the World have been oriented in a single direction and guided towards a single goal is the extraordinary characteristic of the present age, to which the special feature of the present work is a corollary. The unity of events imposes on the historian a similar unity of composition in depicting for his readers the operation of the laws of Fortune on the grand scale, and this has been my own principal inducement and stimulus in the work which I have undertaken.

include, not only the whole of the living generation, but also the whole of the living generation's past. In order to save mankind we have to learn to live together in concord in spite of traditional differences of religion, civilization, nationality, class, and race. In order to live together in concord successfully, we have to know each other, and knowing each other includes knowing each other's past,[1] since human life, like the rest of the phenomenal universe, can be observed by human minds only as it presents itself to them on the move through time. Historical forces can be more explosive than atom bombs.[2] For our now urgent common purpose of self-preservation, it will not be enough to explore our common underlying human nature. The psychologist's work needs to be supplemented by the archaeologist's, the historian's, the anthropologist's, and the sociologist's. We must learn to recognize, and, as far as possible, to understand, the different cultural configurations in which our common human nature has expressed itself in the different religions, civilizations, and nationalities into which human culture has

'I have also been influenced by the fact that no contemporary writer has attempted to put together a comprehensive account of world affairs. If there had been anyone else in the field, I should have felt far less urge to enter it myself. Actually, however, I see many specialists writing works about local wars, including some of the political transactions connected with these, but, so far as I know, nobody even attempting to make a general examination and synthesis of the configuration of contemporary events by tracing these back to their origins and explaining how they reached their consummation. This spectacle has made me feel an imperative call not to leave unrecorded, and not to let slip unheeded, a transaction that is surely the foremost and the most beneficial of all that stand to Fortune's credit. No doubt she is never tired of innovating and is continually putting her spoke in the wheel of human affairs. But the *tour de force* that she has achieved in our time is quite without precedent; and it is also something that could never be gathered from a study of the works of the specialist historians.

'What should we say of somebody who visited the World's famous cities one by one—or, if you like, just took a look at separate pictures of them—and then immediately assumed that, by this process, he had acquired a knowledge of the physiognomy of the whole World, including its entire layout and structure? People who are convinced that historical specialisation will give them a fairly good synoptic view of the whole of history are, it seems to me, suffering from a delusion. They remind me of people who have taken a look at the *disjecta membra* of an organism that was once alive and beautiful, and who then imagine that they have had a first-hand view of this creature in all its activity and beauty. We have only to suppose that someone promptly rehabilitates the creature, body and soul, in its original unity and perfection, and then displays it again to the same spectators. Surely these would all then admit that, at the first view, their vision of the object had fallen far short of the reality and had been more like what one sees in a dream. The truth is that the part may give us a notion of the whole, but will never give us a genuine knowledge or an accurate appreciation of it.

'On these analogies, we must conclude that the work of the specialist historians makes a singularly small contribution to an intimate and trustworthy insight into history as a whole. The only way of arriving at this is to grasp the mutual inter-connexions and inter-relations of all the phenomena, together with their likenesses and differences A panoramic view of this kind enables one to find utility as well as enjoyment in history.'

[1] This point is made by Diodorus of Agyrium in the following passages (Book I, chaps. 1 and 3) of the Preface to his *Library of Universal History*: 'We are indebted to these authors [i.e. the authors of universal histories] for their efforts to marshal the whole human race, who are all members one of another, in spite of the barriers of space and time, in one magnificent array. In attempting this, they have constituted themselves nothing less than the servants of Providence. God, in His Providence, has related in a single system the evolutions of the stars of heaven and the characters of men, and maintains them in perpetual motion to all eternity, imparting to each the lot which Destiny assigns; while the authors of universal histories, in their works, record the general transactions of the World as if it were a single community, and pass the works of Providence through the grand audit of their clearing-house. . . . In short, the superiority of this branch of history over the rest is to be measured by the superior utility of the whole to the part and of continuity to discontinuity.'

[2] L. C. Stecchini in *Midstream*, Autumn, 1956, pp. 84–91.

come to be articulated in the course of its history. 'All of human history is relevant to present and future human needs.'[1] 'The knowledge of the history of mankind should be one of mankind's common possessions.'[2]

We shall, however, have to do more than just understand each other's cultural heritages, and more even than appreciate them. We shall have to value them and love them as being parts of mankind's common treasure and therefore being ours too, as truly as the heirlooms that we ourselves shall be contributing to the common stock. Without the fire of love, the dangerous fissures in mankind's social solidarity cannot be annealed. Danger, even when it is as extreme as ours is today, is never a sufficient stimulus in itself to make men do what is necessary for their salvation. It is a poor stimulus because it is a negative one. A cold-blooded calculation of expediency will not inspire us with the spiritual power to save ourselves. This power can come only from the disinterested pursuit of a positive aim that will outrange the negative one of trying to avoid self-destruction;[3] and this positive aim can be given to men by nothing but love.

In mankind's present situation a demand for a comprehensive view of human affairs is to be expected. Indirect evidence that this demand is, in fact, being made today comes to light incidentally in some of the critiques of earlier volumes of the present book. Some of this evidence carries conviction, because it is the testimony of critics who hold that the book has had a more favourable reception than it deserves. They explain this lack of judgement, as it seems to them, on the public's part by suggesting that people are now making this demand for a comprehensive view and that they have welcomed my work uncritically because they feel that it is at least giving them something of what they want.

R. V. Chase, for example, suggests[4] that 'persuasive theorists do not . . . exert their strongest influence because of the logical air-tightness of their theories, but rather because they fill an unconsciously felt vacuum with the force and urgency of their moral passion'. Tangye Lean sees[5] me performing the role of an exponent of a particular cultural situation, embodying my contemporaries' anxiety over the problem of existence, their obsession with the spectacle of decay, which brings them face to face with death, and their burning desire to find some way of overcoming their own transitoriness and securing immortality. As A. G. Bailey sees it,[6] 'clearly this book answered a deep-felt need of people beset with the anxieties and uncertainties of the twentieth century'. Christopher Dawson suggests[7] that one reason why my work has found some accept-

---

[1] R. Coulborn in *Phylon*, 1940, offprint, p. 62.
[2] 'Die Erkenntnis der Geschichte der Menschheit soll ein Gemeingut der Menschheit sein': a fragment, written by Ranke in the eighteen-sixties, printed on pp. xiii–xvi of A. Dove's preface to the Ninth Part, Second Section, of Ranke's *Weltgeschichte* (Leipzig 1881–8, Duncker and Humblot, 9 parts). The passage here quoted is on pp. xv–xvi.
[3] In a critique of my work, J. Romein judges that I am right in thinking that the unity of the World is now in the making. As Romein puts it, world unity has been created by the technicians; we have now to raise this technological unity to the level of creativity (*Toynbee and History*, p. 350).
[4] In *The American Scholar*, vol. 16, No. 3 (Summer, 1947), pp. 281–2.
[5] In *Toynbee and History*, pp. 35 ff., as summarized by O. F. Anderle.
[6] In *Queen's Quarterly*, vol. lxii, No. 1 (Spring, 1955), pp. 100–10.
[7] In *Toynbee and History*, p. 129.

ance is because it is a study of the civilizations. These have now become realities that cannot be ignored. J. F. Leddy suggests[1] that it is because people in our time want to see the World as a whole and to find some meaning in its history. J. Romein says[2] that my work is valuable in giving a real world-view, and that I have done something to help in overcoming the opposition between East and West. H. Kohn says[3] that a sense of unity will be my contribution to an understanding of things. T. J. G. Locher finds[4] that 'our age is asking for a total vision, now that the World has grown together into so close a unity. This super-human task is the one at which Toynbee has tried his hand.'[5] Other critics, too, have made the point that I have tried to take a comprehensive

[1] In *The Phoenix*, vol. 11, No. 4, p. 140.

[2] In *Toynbee and History*, pp. 349–50.

[3] Ibid., p. 359. [4] In *De Gids*, May, 1948, offprint, p. 30.

[5] If Pieter Geyl ever reads this page, the passages here quoted from observations made by some of his fellow critics of my work may throw light on something that has apparently puzzled him. He, too, has noticed that my work has been not badly received by the non-professional public, and this seems to have left him perplexed. 'This chorus of praise', he remarks, 'is a chastening reminder of the very restricted influence exercised by professional criticism' (*Toynbee and History*, p. 377). If the 'chorus of praise' has been evoked by my attempt to take a comprehensive view of history, this gives Geyl his cue. He and my other critics have only to try their hands at the same enterprise, and the chorus will give them the same grateful welcome, even if they make no more of a success than I have made of the effort to see human affairs as a whole and to find some meaning in them.

This suggestion, will, I fancy, draw from some of these critics the retort that they do not want praise from the public at any price, and certainly not at the price of doing anything so unprofessional as to take a panoramic view of things. In their eyes popularity is incriminating. My kind interpreter Crane Brinton has done his best to exonerate me from this imputation. 'It is quite clear', he testifies, 'that his fame is everywhere confined . . . to high-brows and middle-brows, and has not reached the low-brows, as it would have to do if he is to do the work of a major prophet. It is very hard indeed to think of Toynbee effectively translated to the many, as Marx has certainly been translated' (*The Virginia Quarterly Review*, Summer, 1956, pp. 361–75). Marx is vulgar indeed. His shamelessly panoramic view of human affairs has caught the *profanum vulgus*'s imagination all over the World. I have not incurred that damning degree of popularity, anyway. Yet I fear that even a modest popularity among the high-brow and middle-brow fraction of the public is enough to ruin my reputation with the professionals. E. Fiess notes disapprovingly that 'popularity is no substitute for understanding', though he does concede that 'all discourse is in some sense a simplification' (*Toynbee and History*, p. 378). H. J. Morgenthau and A. J. P. Taylor draw attention (ibid., pp. 196–7 and 115) to the contrast between a popularity that they ascribe to me with the public and the condemnation that I have received from my fellow historians. Both of them assume, without arguing the point, that, on any issue between public and professionals, the professionals must be right. Morgenthau chivalrously testifies that I am not being popular on purpose. 'This popularity is unjust', he writes, 'to Mr Toynbee's intent, but it illuminates the weakness of his achievement' (ibid., p. 197). It is true that I have never set out to win popularity, any more than I have sought to avoid it. When I am writing, the reception that is awaiting me is not in my mind. I write as the subject moves me. But surely the truth about popularity is that, in itself, it is no evidence of merit or demerit. One must know the reason why a book is popular before one can judge whether, in the particular case in point, popularity damns the author or does him credit. Morgenthau evidently holds that popularity, whatever its cause, damns an author and his work automatically. This dogma seems to rest on two assumptions: that the judgement of the public must always be wrong, and that the judgement of the professionals must always be in conflict with it.

If these are the doctrines of a professional, they are unfortunate. In what we vaguely call 'the public', there are many different levels of intellectual cultivation; and, if a professional despises all these levels indiscriminately, he is putting himself in jeopardy, for at the higher levels he is likely to find his intellectual equals, and may even find his superiors in the field outside the contemptuous specialist's own chosen province. What is more, the contemptuous specialist is doing a disservice to the culture that ought to be common to the cultivated public and to him. When professional intellectual work becomes esoteric, this is a sign that culture is in a bad way. Culture flourishes only when there is an active and constant intellectual intercourse and exchange of ideas between cultivated people of all kinds.

view of history, without going into the question whether my work has been well received, or whether, if it has been, its attempt at comprehensiveness is what has won it favour. The purpose for which the point is made by most of them is to go on to say—as Locher does in the passage from which I have just quoted—that, in attempting this, I have obviously attempted the impossible, or that, for whatever reason, I have failed to achieve my aim.[1] If the critics quoted in the present paragraph are right in holding that my work has been well received and that its attempt at comprehensiveness accounts for this, then the other testimonies to this attempt at comprehensiveness indirectly give further support to the view that there is a genuine demand for such attempts in the present-day world.

One of my critics has compared earlier volumes of this book to a 'palace' in which 'the rooms . . . are over-furnished to the point of resembling a dealer's warehouse'.[2] This reviewer must also be a thought-reader; for I have often thought of myself as a man moving old furniture about. For centuries these lovely things had been lying neglected in the lumber-rooms and attics. They had been piled in there higgledy-piggledy, in utter disorder, and had been crammed so tight that nobody could even squeeze his way in to look at them and find out whether they were of any value. In the course of ages they had been accumulating there—unwanted rejects from a score of country houses. This unworthy treatment of these precious pieces came to trouble me more and more; for I knew that they were not really junk; I knew that they were heirlooms, and these so rare and fine that they were not just provincial curiosities; they were the common heritage of anyone who had any capacity for appreciating beauty in Man's handiwork. At last I found that I could not bear this shocking situation any longer, so I set my own hand to a back-breaking job. I began to drag out the pieces, one by one, and to arrange them in the hall. I could not pretend to form a final judgement on the order in which they should be placed. Indeed, there never could be a final judgement on this, for a number of attractive different orders could be imagined, each of them the right order from some particular point of view.[3] The first thing to be done was to get as many of the pieces as possible out into the open and to assemble them in some order or other. If once I had them parked down in the hall, I could see how they looked and could shift them and re-shift them at my leisure. Perhaps I should not have the leisure; perhaps the preliminary job of extracting these treasures from the lumber-rooms and attics would turn out to be as much as I could manage with my single pair of hands.[4] If so, this would not matter; for there would be plenty of time afterwards for other people to rearrange the pieces, and, no doubt, they would be doing this again and again as they studied them more closely and came to know more about them than would ever be known by me.

[1] See the passages quoted in the Annex to Chapter II, p. 647.
[2] *The Listener*, 19th October, 1939, in a review of vols. iv–vi.
[3] See further p. 168.
[4] 'His work is a gigantic labour—the labour of a comprehensive attempt to put things in order (*Die Riesenarbeit seines Werkes ist eine umfassende Ordnungsarbeit*)' (H. Werner in *Deutsche Vierteljahrsschrift für Literaturwissenschaft und Geistesgeschichte*, 29. Jahrgang, xxix. Band (1955), p. 544).

This furniture-shifting job is, of course, David's kind of work, not Solomon's; and the time when Solomon's achievement will be feasible is now only just dawning.

'There is as yet no history of humanity, since humanity is not an organised society with a common tradition or a common social consciousness. All the attempts that have hitherto been made to write a world history have been in fact attempts to interpret one tradition in terms of another, attempts to extend the intellectual hegemony of a dominant culture by subordinating to it all the events of other cultures that come within the observer's range of vision.'[1]

This has certainly been true up to now. It is true, for instance, of the presentation of world history in the Old Testament, in Hellenic literature, in the Chinese dynastic histories, and in Western historians' works. If a Western historian does not fall into the egocentric error of making all history lead up to the point reached in the West in his own generation, he is likely to fall into another error, only one degree less egocentric, with which I, for instance, have been charged, with some justice, by a number of my critics.[2] He is likely to use Hellenic history, which lies in the background of his own Western history, as an exclusive 'model', not just as one out of a number of alternative possible models, for elucidating the configuration of history in general in the current age of the civilizations.

Since the World is now being unified as a result of Western inventions, and therefore, initially, within a Western framework, one or other or both of these characteristic Western distortions of the true picture of world history are likely to persist for some time and to die hard. Nevertheless, it is already possible to look forward to a time when these Western distortions of the true picture, and all other distortions of the kind, will be replaced by a new vision of the past seen from the standpoint, not of this or that nationality, civilization, or religion, but of a united human race. If mankind does respond to the challenge of its present self-imposed ordeal by saving itself from self-inflicted genocide, this will have been the reward of a common effort to transcend all the traditional divisions and to live as one family for the first time since mankind made its first appearance on this planet. This *union sacrée* in the face of imminent self-destruction will be, if it is achieved, Man's finest achievement and most thrilling experience up to date. From the new position of charity and hope which Man will thereby have won for himself, all the past histories of the previous divisions of the human race will be seen, in retrospect, to be so many parts of one common historic heritage. They will be seen as leading up to unity, and as opening out, for a united human race, future prospects of which no human being could have dreamed in the age of unfettered parochialism.

1 Chr. Dawson: *The Dynamics of World History*, p. 273.
2 See p. 161, footnote 1.

VI. THE PROBLEM OF ORGANIZING A COMPREHENSIVE STUDY OF HUMAN AFFAIRS

I. THE USE AND ABUSE OF SIMPLIFICATIONS

THE enterprise of trying to organize a comprehensive study of human affairs is still in its pioneering stage. The pioneer's task is to open up the jungle by blazing trails. If he does this well, he will have opened the way for his successor the surveyor.

To do well in this preliminary reconnaissance work means satisfying two requirements. The trails must follow the lie of the land, and the blazing must be clear enough to give guidance to the next comer. The trails must link up the key points in the landscape by the shortest practicable routes. The blazing must be unmistakable. If the pioneer is literate, he will chart his trails and his blazes on a sketch-map; and as a map-maker he enjoys a licence. His task is the practical one of ensuring, as far as may be humanly possible, that the next comer shall not miss the way that the pioneer has found and has opened up. Therefore, in drawing his sketch-map for the next comer's use, the pioneer may take it upon himself, at his own discretion, to simplify the pattern and to exaggerate the prominence of the outstanding features of the landscape. He may take these liberties legitimately on two conditions. The first is that he must limit these deliberate cartographical distortions of Reality to the minimum necessary for his purpose of giving plain guidance. The second condition is that he must not try to pass his sketch-map off as being anything but what it is. He must make it clear that it is a sketch, not a survey, and that it is therefore not definitive but provisional. He must, in fact, note on it a warning for all future users that it not only may be superseded, but will be, and will be soon. It will be superseded the sooner, the better the pioneer has done his work; for, the better he has done it, the faster the legion of surveyors will be able to follow his reconnaissance up by triangulations that may prove to be at least 'semi-permanent'.

Pioneers are not the only map-makers to whom the pioneer's licence is customarily allowed. It is also granted to the modellers of relief-maps, though these, unlike pioneers in the wilderness, have all the resources of science and technology at their disposal in their workshops. Relief-map modellers sometimes deliberately misrepresent Reality by presenting altitude out of scale to area, and they do this for the reason that leads a pioneer to misrepresent Reality on his sketch-map by simplifying it. Their first concern, like his, is to give the users of their map clear guidance; and a relief-map that did not exaggerate altitude out of proportion to area would give little more guidance than a two-dimensional map would give. It is well known that a model of the globe, with the unevenness of its surface reproduced in scale with the extent of its area, would look no rougher than an unpealed orange. The differences in altitude between mountains and valleys, plateaux and plains, would be difficult to discern without the aid of a powerful magnifying-glass and would be less legible to the finger than the embossed lettering in a braille book. The heights and depths must be exaggerated, quite out of scale with the area of the globe's surface, if a relief-map is to be serviceable. It is therefore mere common sense to model a relief-map in these disproportionate dimensions. This is, however, legitimate only if the modeller takes care not to leave the prospective user under any misapprehension. He must make a declaration of the scale on which the heights and depths are shown in his model, and of how this stands to the scale as it is in Nature; and he must display this schedule prominently enough for it to be impossible for a user to overlook it.

In previous volumes of this book I have allowed myself the pioneer's and relief-map modeller's licence, and I make no apology for this. If I had not done it, I should not have been able to find my own way, not to speak of giving myself a chance of providing guidance for anyone else. I do, however, plead guilty to not having signalled to my readers what I was doing. I was hardly conscious of this myself, since my mind was all the time intent, first and foremost, on bringing out the salient features in the vast landscape that I was trying to explore. I have paid the penalty of being censured, both in general and over particular points, for having tacitly made the features more salient in my model than they are in Nature.

No doubt all thinking is a mental fission of a unitary Reality.[1] J. Romein recognizes[2] that 'every theory is simplifying and contracting', and E. Fiess, in still wider terms, that 'all discourse is in some sense a simplification'.[3] But C. Trinkaus pronounces[4] that the simplifications in my formulae are too crude; and T. J. G. Locher likewise finds[5] that my presentation is too simple, one-sided, and subjective, and that I push my points too far. E. I. Watkin passes the same judgement[6] with a philosopher's discrimination.

'We believe that there are patterns in human history, and we are convinced that Professor Toynbee has discerned a pattern, a rhythm which does in fact exist, and has assigned many true causes at work to produce it. But we also think that the complication of factors in human history is so great that no pattern is repeated so regularly and is so clearly discernible as Professor Toynbee maintains. . . . In many respects we prefer Mr Dawson's simpler scheme. . . . That is not to say that we think Christopher Dawson's scheme, or indeed any other, is to be simply accepted in place of Arnold Toynbee's. None is wholly false, none wholly true. All are more or less partial views of a pattern more complex than any, but also, for that very reason, more imperfect.'

I will give some examples, noticed by my critics or by me or by both, of distinctions, contrasts, or turning-points that come out sharper, in my presentation of them, than they are, perhaps, in reality.

The primordial dichotomy is the distinction between consciousness and the subconscious level of the psyche. It is primordial because it is

---

[1] See Chapter I, *ad init.*   [2] In *Toynbee and History*, p. 347.
[3] Ibid., p. 378.   [4] In *Science and Society*, vol. xii, No. 1 (1948), pp. 218–39.
[5] In *De Gids*, May, 1948, offprint, p. 15.
[6] In *The Tablet*, 12th August, 1939.

consciousness that generates our awareness of the phenomenal universe. It would seem, then, that the frontier of consciousness ought to be delineated firmly, but 'firmly' is not, of course, the same thing as 'sharply'. The border between consciousness and the unconscious or subconscious may be, in reality, more like a threshold (*limen*) than like a demarcation line (*limes*). M. Savelle observes[1] that the line between subconscious impulse and purely intelligent choice or planning is not, in truth, a sharp one. M. R. Cohen notes[2] that we must not ignore either the unconscious or the states intermediate between unconsciousness and consciousness.

In applying the myth of challenge-and-response[3] I may sometimes have drawn too sharply the distinction between the two parties to the encounter. I have, though, taken account of the truth that the parties are not necessarily in reality the separate individual personalities that they are represented as being when they are brought on to the stage as *dramatis personae* in a mythological drama. I have cited[4] Saint Paul's *Epistle to the Romans*, chapter vii, verses 24–25, as an example of the drama's taking the form of an encounter between conflicting spiritual forces within a single soul. If we depersonalize the word 'encounter' by calling it 'dialectical interaction',[5] it is evident that this can take place between two or more entities of a number of different kinds. It seems, indeed, to be one of the fundamental rhythms of Reality as this presents itself to human minds. It is also, I believe, characteristic of the pattern of dialectical interaction that it should be serial—one transaction leading on to another, and this to another again—and that, if and as the chain of dialectical interactions prolongs itself, there is a tendency for the field of action to be transferred from the outer to the inner world of the party responding to this succession of challenges.[6]

One of the types of encounter to which the myth of challenge-and-response applies is the interaction between Man and his environment, both human and non-human.[7] M. Postan observes[8] that the notion of challenge-and-response 'might have enabled Professor Toynbee to proceed much farther than the biologists and sociologists have so far done in abolishing the artificial abstraction of the object from the environment'. J. K. Feibleman remarks[9] that I have discovered, in discussing the geneses of civilizations, that 'human society is only for certain narrow purposes a valid isolate', but that I then drop this discovery and try to explain all human affairs from inside. O. H. K. Spate makes the same criticism with greater precision. '"Environment taken by itself" is a meaningless phrase; without Man, environment does not exist.'[10]

---

[1] In *The Pacific Historical Review*, vol. xxv, No. 1 (February, 1956), pp. 55–67.
[2] M. R. Cohen: *The Meaning of History*, p. 123.
[3] My usage of this term is discussed and explained on pp. 254–63.
[4] In i. 294.
[5] See pp. 43 and 641–2.
[6] See iii. 174–217.
[7] This is discussed further in Chapter VIII, pp. 314–27.
[8] In *The Sociological Review*, vol. xxviii (1936), p. 60.
[9] In *T'ien Hsia Monthly*, vol. xi, Nos. 1 and 2 (1940), p. 25.
[10] *The Geographical Journal*, vol. cxviii, Part 4 (December, 1952), p. 419. The same point is made in the Social Science Research Council's Committee on Historiography's Report (1954), p. 119. 'No product of Nature can be considered a natural resource until

There is a danger of setting up a false duality and so creating chicken-and-egg questions of priority.[1] Toynbee and Ellsworth Huntington 'both fall into the fallacy that there is, or can be, such a thing as environment "taken by itself"'.[2] 'The facts of geography are the facts as they are approached. . . . This world, without Man, is not environment, is not our world'[3]—and, in illustration of this point, Spate cites[4] the 'piscine geography' so brilliantly and amusingly sketched by Rupert Brooke in a poem in which the key-note line is: '"There shall be no more land" say fish.' In reality, as Spate points out,[5] 'environment' always means 'the environment of people x', 'and x is a variable, even if the environment is not'.[6] 'The environment affects us through the idea formed of it.'[7]

Spate's critique is penetrating and conclusive. It immediately calls to mind a number of dramatic illustrations of its truth. For example, the nineteenth-century diplomatists' idea of a desert was that it was a region of no economic or political value because it was incapable of supporting life. Accordingly, while they were prepared to haggle, and, in the last resort, to go to war, over a few square metres in Alsace or Oregon, they amicably partitioned the Arabian Desert and the African Sahara by blithely drawing straight lines of enormous length across small-scale maps. In this cavalier way they disposed of the sovereignty over vast areas which, in the atlases of the day, were the 'perfect and absolute blank' commended as the ideal kind of map by the Bellman in Lewis Carroll's *The Hunting of the Snark*. During the late-nineteenth-century partition of Africa between European states there was an occasion on which Lord Salisbury—under fire in the House of Commons at Westminster for having acquiesced in the annexation of startling numbers of African square kilometres by France—made the celebrated reply that most of this territory that he had let slip was 'very light soil'. Some of it, however, was the soil under which the French oil-prospectors have recently discovered what they believe to be rich oil-bearing strata; and the time has long ago passed when diplomatists negotiating international frontiers in either the Sahara or Arabia were carefree. The desert-girt Buraymi oasis is at this moment an object of acrimonious dispute between the governments of Sa'udi Arabia and Great Britain. The 'idea formed' of a desert has in fact been transformed—in regions in which deserts overlie an oil-bearing subsoil—by the late-nineteenth-century discovery of the economic value of mineral oil and the twentieth-century development of techniques for tapping it at ever greater depths below surface-level. The Arabian desert is just as inhospitable to life today as it ever was, yet it has now become a key part of the environment of the peoples of Western Europe. Similarly, in the second

Man wants it for his use and has techniques for exploiting it. Thus rich, swampy land is not a natural resource unless men can drain it and cultivate it; nor were coal, gold, or uranium ore of any importance until Man worked them and had means of using them.'

[1] *The Geographical Journal*, vol. cit., p. 419.
[2] Ibid., p. 419. H. and M. Sprout also make the point that 'environment is a relative term, not an absolute one' (*Man-Milieu Relationship in the Context of International Politics*, p. 17). [3] Spate, loc. cit., p. 419.
[4] Ibid., p. 419, footnote 2. [5] Ibid., p. 411.
[6] Ibid. [7] Ibid., p. 423.

century B.C., the forest-clad Po Basin, which had been a wilderness for Gallic squatters in its glades, was transformed into a new Italy by Roman peasant pioneers who approached it with the tools and the will to cut down the trees and plough the fertile soil that the Romans' Gallic predecessors had never dreamed of disputing with the native oakwoods.[1] This Old-World tale has been repeated in North America within the last three centuries. The forests in which the pre-Columbian human fauna had been content to cultivate the glades, and the prairies on which they had been content to hunt the buffalo, have been brought under the plough by Roman-hearted West European invaders. In truth, 'unto everyone that hath shall be given, and he shall have abundance; but from him that hath not shall be taken away even that which he hath'.[2]

In reality, then, the distinction between a challenging environment and the people challenged by it is a fiction of mythology. 'The facts are as approached.'[3] The environment is not just another name for its material constituents. It means these material constituents as they appear to human beings who have—or have not—the will and the means to master them. Everything within a human being's physical reach and mental range is part of that human being. His self is, in fact, potentially coextensive with the Universe.[4] If Man's environment were really distinguishable as a separate entity from Man himself, Man's mastery of his environment—an achievement on which his existence depends— would never have been a possibility, any more than a human mind could apprehend phenomena, or God create the World, if there were really a great gulf fixed between the parties to these two other kinds of encounter. Logically, then, I have been put in the wrong. To draw the vulgar distinction between Man and his environment is scientifically inadmissible. I confess my sin, but must continue to commit it, and this for the reason that compels Spate himself to commit it in company with me. The reason is that, in the study of geography, as in all other kinds of thinking and creation, to tell the absolute truth about Reality is to say the last possible word, and therefore to debar oneself from all further research, discovery, and increase in understanding. Man and his environment are fictitious products of an unwarrantable mental fission of a monolithic Reality. This may be the truth, but the declaration of it puts a full stop to all further thinking about human affairs. In fact, the proof of Spate's proposition is double-edged. *Quod erat demonstrandum* turn out also to be *quod est absurdum*. The truth is that 'segmentation is humanly inevitable, i.e. essential to sane observation'.[5]

Five other distinctions that I have drawn too sharply—as I have now come to believe, on reconsideration—are those between leading minorities and the masses, between minorities that are creative and those that are merely dominant, between creativity itself and uncreativeness,

---

[1] See Polybius: *Historiae*, Book II, chaps. 15 and 35.
[2] Matt. xxv. 29. Cp. Matt. xiii. 12; Mark iv. 25; Luke viii. 18; and Luke xix. 26.
[3] Spate in loc. cit., p. 423.
[4] H. and M. Sprout point out, in *Man-Milieu Relationship in the Context of International Politics*, p. 18, that a single human being is the ultimate 'environed unit'.
[5] M. R. Cohen: *The Meaning of Human History*, p. 107.

between inspiration and mimesis, and between originality and diffusion. These distinctions, too, are, I believe, indispensable instruments for mental operations with human affairs.[1] I also believe that they are valid as far as they go, but I admit to having sometimes pushed them farther than is legitimate.[2] The differences between individuals in point of character and ability are evidently great enough to be a factor of capital importance in the determination of the course of human affairs. But all magnitudes are relative; and I could not maintain with any conviction, even if I wanted to, that the magnitude of these innate differences between individuals is so great as to require us to sort out mankind into what, in effect, would be two or more different species.[3] I believe in the uniformity of human nature, as well as in the uniformity of Nature in general, and I hold this belief in two senses. I believe that the likenesses between the 'finest' and the 'crudest' specimens of the *genus homo*—supposing that we can define what we mean by 'fine' and 'crude' in this context—are greater and more pertinent to the conduct of social relations than are the differences between them. I also believe that these innate individual differences, such as they are, are distributed evenly, on the average, among all the so-called races into which mankind has been classified on the basis of physical criteria.[4] It goes without saying that they are distributed evenly as between the members of different social classes;[5] as between the partakers in the different cultures; and as between the adherents of the different higher religions. I also admit that

[1] E. F. J. Zahn judges that, in my handling of 'creative minorities', I have fallen into the error of 'hypostatising an heuristic principle' (*Toynbee und das Problem der Geschichte*, p. 28). C. Trinkaus holds that I take refuge in 'the myth of creative personalities' and give 'no real analysis of social relations based on historical data' (*Science and Society*, vol. xii, No. 1 (1948), pp. 218–39).

[2] C. Trinkaus makes a general indictment of the sharpness of my distinction between 'creative' and 'uncreative' in loc. cit. H. Becker judges that I give too much prominence to individuals and to minorities (*The Annals of the American Academy of Political Science*, vol. 210 (July, 1940), p. 161). A. H. Hanson rejects my concept of 'creative minorities' *in toto* (*Science and Society*, No. 13 (1949), pp. 118–35). Chr. Hill notes that the true creators are 'the inventors and artists whose brains [the] ruling class picks' (*The Modern Quarterly*, Autumn, 1947, p. 299).

[3] E. F. J. Zahn, commenting on Henri Bergson, *Les Deux Sources de la Morale et de la Religion*, p. 300, justly observes that there is dimorphism, in Bergson's meaning of this word, in each of us: i.e. each of us has something in him of the capacity to lead as well as of the capacity to follow (Zahn, op. cit., p. 28, footnote 62). I agree with R. Coulborn (in *Phylon*, 1940, reprint, pp. 35–36) that there is no sharp distinction between leaders and followers. Coulborn attributes to me (ibid., p. 57) 'the false premise that ordinary men lack the power of creation'. I agree that this premise is false. I have never entertained it. But I may sometimes have used language that made it look as if I did. Coulborn is justified in asking (ibid., p. 28) what I mean by saying that creative individuals 'are superhuman in a literal and no mere metaphorical sense' (iii. 232). Here I was echoing—but, in the act, exaggerating—Bergson's dictum that 'the apparition of each of these souls has been like the creation of a new species' (Bergson, op. cit., pp. 96–97)—and this dictum is itself an exaggeration, as, on reconsideration, I now believe (see p. 568 of the present volume, footnote 2). I have thus exposed myself to suspicions that I am a fascist, though, of all current ideologies, fascism is the most odious to me, and I entirely agree with Coulborn (ibid., p. 58) in seeing, as the ideal, 'the maximum freedom for the creative urge of all men and the strongest unity of spirit between men'. Trinkaus, for instance, finds, in my theory of mass-mimesis, 'a disguised theory of social domination' (loc. cit.). F. Engel-Janosi, too, catches a fascist note in my accentuation of the role of minorities (*Wissenschaft und Weltbild*, 2. Jahrgang, Heft 4 (October, 1949), p. 269).

[4] This point is made by A. L. Kroeber in *The Nature of Culture*, p. 42, and by W. Altree in *Toynbee and History*, p. 269.

[5] R. Coulborn makes the perhaps rather obvious point that creativity is not confined to people who happen to be at the top of the social hierarchy (*Toynbee and History*, p. 182).

no minority that has taken a lead has ever succeeded in doing this solely in virtue of its creativity and through the charm exerted by the attractiveness of this. Even the least domineering leadership has never been able to dispense entirely with some element of force,[1] though it is also true that, conversely, even the most domineering leadership has never been able to maintain itself by force alone without some minimum degree of consent on the part of the governed. In previous volumes of this book I have, I think, underrated the effect of force in human affairs.[2] I need not go into this point here, as I deal with it in another place in this volume.[3] For the same reason, I also need not here go into my anthitheses between 'inspiration' and 'mimesis'[4] and between originality and diffusion, except to mention, by anticipation, that both antitheses have been bridged by a middle term: A. L. Kroeber's suggestive concept of 'stimulus diffusion'. This, too, is dealt with in this volume in another place.[5]

I have also drawn too sharp a dividing line between 'civilizations' and 'primitive societies'[6] and have confounded with each other, under the sweeping term 'primitive', different kinds of societies that have as good a claim as the civilizations have to be treated as distinct species.[7] The development of human culture has, in fact, been a movement in which there have been more than just two steps. Civilization has been heralded in the Old World by a Neolithic type of culture, and in the Americas by a 'Formative' type, that were transitional between earlier types of culture and the civilization into which the Neolithic and the 'Formative' culture respectively blossomed.[8] It might be judged—though such judgements are inevitably subjective—that the cultural transformation through which the Neolithic and the 'Formative' culture came to be superseded by the culture that we call 'civilization' was less revolutionary than the previous transformation through which these transitional cultures themselves had emerged from the Palaeolithic. The sharpness of the transition from the Neolithic culture to the Old-World civilizations of the first generation was mitigated by an intermediate culture, the Chalcolithic; and both the Old-World Neolithic culture and the

---

[1] I have been criticized for underrating the role of force in leadership by G. Masur in the *Historische Zeitschrift*, Band 174 (1952), pp. 269–86, and by M. Watnick in *The Antioch Review*, No. 7 (Winter, 1947–8), pp. 587–602.

[2] A. H. Hanson submits that violence has been coeval with civilization (*Science and Society*, No. 13 (1949), pp. 118–35).

[3] See the Annex to Chapter II, pp. 612–15.

[4] O. Handlin rejects this antithesis (in *The Partisan Review*, July–August, 1947, pp. 371–9); and R. Coulborn makes the point that it is an unreal one (*Toynbee and History*, pp. 152–3). 'The whole art of moral education', he justly remarks, 'is to inspire and drill simultaneously.' We are all, all the time, seeking examples and at the same time serving as examples to other people (Coulborn in *Phylon*, 1940, offprint, pp. 21–30). My comment on this is that two different activities are not proved to be one and the same as a result of its being shown that they are carried on side by side.

[5] See pp. 343–5.

[6] See Chr. Dawson: *The Dynamics of World History*, pp. 423–4, and *Toynbee and History*, p. 137; A. L. Kroeber in *The American Anthropologist*, vol. 53, No. 2 (April–June, 1951), pp. 279–83; C. Trinkaus in *Science and Society*, vol. xii, No. 1, p. 238.

[7] I agree with P. Bagby (*Culture and History*, p. 159) that the distinction between 'civilized' and 'primitive' needs clarifying. J. K. Feibleman justly criticizes me (in *T'ien Hsia Monthly*, vol. xi, Nos. 1–2 (1940), p. 24) for having ignored the possibility that there may have been an intermediate stage between primitive societies and civilizations.

[8] See Chapter IX, pp. 327–43.

American 'Formative' culture were certainly more akin to the civilization by which they were followed than either of them was to the Early Palaeolithic Culture.[1] At this point again, however, the transition was not sharp. Between the Early Palaeolithic and the Neolithic culture there were at least two intermediate types: the Late Palaeolithic and the Mesolithic; in the Americas the Old-World Mesolithic culture has a counterpart in the 'Archaic' culture;[2] and at this stage the pace of cultural change—measured in terms of the average time-span of a single human generation—was immensely slower than it was at the stage in which the Neolithic culture was turning, through the Chalcolithic, into civilization.[3]

Measured in terms of this standard unit of the generation, the pace of cultural change has, in fact, been accelerating—and this at an accelerating rate of acceleration—since the earliest stage of human history so far known to us from disinterred relics of Man and his artefacts. In our generation the rate of acceleration has been keyed up to an unprecedented pitch; and we are having to face the questions whether there may not be a limit to the amount of cultural change to which human nature can adapt itself within a single lifetime, and whether we may not be approaching this limit or perhaps exceeding it.

In the past the impact of cultural change has been softened by a persistent survival of the old, side by side with the new. Each successive new type of culture has been embraced whole-heartedly and thoroughly by no more than a minority, and, even within this minority, ancient cultural habits have held their own. Hunting, for instance, which was one of Palaeolithic Man's two staple ways of winning his livelihood, has survived into the age of civilization as a highly appreciated form of 'sport'; and in the form of fishing, which has proved to be its most efficient and least rapidly exhaustible form, hunting has remained a staple part of Man's economy. Even now we are only just beginning to replace hunting in the sea by the method of deliberate cultivation that we have been following on the land since the Old-World Neolithic and the American 'Formative' age.[4]

In more general terms it may be said, with truth, that, although all but a tiny fraction of mankind is to be found today within the ambit of one or other of the living civilizations, the so-called 'dead' civilizations still survive in the legacies that they have bequeathed to the living civilizations and in the 'renaissances' that they have evoked in the

[1] A. R. Burn points out that 'there is no case on record of what we may perhaps call truly primitive societies, that is pure "food-gatherers", being successfully brought within the orbit of a civilization, whereas so-called primitive peoples who have passed through the agricultural revolution often have so been. Food-gatherers find the strain of such forcible integration into an alien society too great, and die out, like the West Indian islanders and most of the North American Indians; while African slaves are successfully—from the invaders' point of view—introduced to replace them' (*History*, February–October, 1956, pp. 7–8). Burn cites other pertinent examples.

[2] According to Willey's and Phillips', as opposed to Spinden's, usage of the term 'Archaic' (see pp. 340–3).   [3] See further Chapter IX, pp. 327–43.

[4] Examples of this substitution of cultivation for hunting are the institution of hatcheries for fish, the laying-down of oyster-beds, and, in Japan, the cultivation of both oysters and edible seaweed on the grand scale on rafts moored in the sea in sheltered inlets. This Japanese pioneering enterprise in cultivating the sea may perhaps foreshadow what may become Man's main source of food if the planet's total human population ever reaches the numbers that have been forecast.

histories of these.[1] More than that, the Neolithic culture of the Old World and the 'Formative' culture of the Americas still survive in the living civilizations or—it might be more accurate to say—under their surface.[2] Something between two-thirds and three-quarters of the living generation of mankind is accounted for by a peasantry that is still in the Neolithic state of mind and is virtually still leading the Neolithic way of life,[3] notwithstanding the fact that they have long since learnt to use some of the metal tools and other pieces of Post-Neolithic equipment that have been invented in the nurseries of civilization within the last five or six thousand years.[4] Again, it may be said, with truth, that, though all but a tiny fraction of the living generation of mankind is to be found today within the ambit of one or other of the higher religions, even the minority that is not still living virtually in the Neolithic or 'Formative' age is virtually still living in the age of civilization as it was before the higher religions made their appearance. The higher religions have suffered many backslidings in their attempts to shake themselves free from the lower religions out of which they have sprung, and, in relapsing to this lower level, they have relapsed into being integral parts of societies that are not exclusively, or even primarily, of a religious nature.[5] The effect produced on the majority of mankind by the higher religions, during the two and a half millennia of their existence up to date, has perhaps been still slighter than the effect of the civilizations during their five millennia.[6]

All the same, the influence of the civilizations and the higher religions has made up to some extent for its superficiality up to date by the speed and range of its diffusion. This point is illustrated by the very widespread present use of metal tools among a peasantry that is otherwise still Neolithic. Since a very early stage in the successive rises of civilization and higher religion, each of these two ways of life has made an impact on all surviving earlier ways, and has influenced all of them in some degree, without yet having completely put any of them out of

[1] P. A. Sorokin makes the point that many elements of civilizations that are customarily written off as being dead are, in truth, alive today (*Toynbee and History*, p. 184).

[2] This point is discussed further in the Annex to Chapter II, pp. 602–4. It is made in general terms by R. Coulborn in *Phylon*, 1940, offprint, p. 53. In the particular case of the Maya province of the Middle American Civilization it is debated by S. F. de Borhegyi in *American Antiquity*, vol. xxi, No. 4 (1956), pp. 343–56, and by G. R. Willey in *The American Anthropologist*, vol. 58, No. 5 (October, 1956), pp. 777–82.

[3] This point is made by C. S. Coon in *The History of Man*, p. 151.

[4] L. Mumford criticizes me for ignoring the primitive elements that survive in the living civilizations (*Diogenes*, No. 13 (Spring, 1956), p. 14).

[5] See pp. 85–97. There is this much justification in R. Coulborn's charge that I have drawn too sharp a line between 'higher religions' and others (*Toynbee and History*, pp. 155–6). It is true that in religion, as in everything else, the distinctions drawn by human minds are necessities of the process of thinking which misrepresent, to some extent, the Reality that we are trying to apprehend. In reality there are gradations and interpenetrations, not sharp dividing lines or clean cuts. All the same, the epiphany of the higher religions is, I should say, the most outstanding event in recorded human history up to date; and, if I am right in holding this controversial opinion, then the distinction that I have drawn between 'higher' and 'lower' religions will be a closer approximation to Reality than a view of religion in which different levels or species of it are not distinguished.

[6] Chr. Dawson justifiably questions a suggestion of mine that the rise of the higher religions might lead to the civilizations withering away (*Toynbee and History*, p. 133). R. L. Shinn asks whether a church can really take the place of the civilizations (*Christianity and the Problem of History*, p. 233).

action. Human culture is, in fact, now stratified, like the surface of the planet on which it subsists, in a heap of layers that still remain distinct enough from each other to provide a decipherable record of a series of passages of history. It has still to be seen whether our current 'post-modern' civilization, with its unprecedented penetrative power, will be able to perform the unprecedented feat of fusing all the diverse strata of society into a single homogeneous social magma with the consistency, and perhaps the savour, of processed cheese. Meanwhile, it is evident that the different strata of culture have not only been more numerous than I have allowed for, but have also been less sharply divided. They have coexisted with each other, and there has already been much mutual interpenetration. My over-simplified antithesis between just one age of primitive culture and just one succeeding age of civilization has to be corrected accordingly.

I have also been criticized for having exaggerated the sharpness of the demarcation between one civilization or higher religion and another. Here, I think, it is my critics who are in error. They have mistaken an operational procedure of mine for a definitive account of my view of Reality, and they have fallen into this error in spite of my having, in this case, certainly made it clear what I was doing. In introducing my notion of a civilization as being 'an intelligible field of study', and in illustrating this idea by taking the Hellenic example of a civilization as my working 'model', I took note, at the very beginning of this book, of the relativity of the separateness, in reality, of any unit that one might pick out. I noted, for instance, at this early stage, that the Hellenic and the Western civilizations were related to each other by a link which I labelled 'apparentation-and-affiliation'. I noted that the Christian Church had played something like the role of a chrysalis in the transition from the disintegration of the Hellenic Society to the genesis of the Western. I noted that Christianity itself had arisen out of an encounter between two civilizations, the Hellenic and the Syriac. I noted that, in modern times, the Western Civilization had had encounters with almost every other living civilization and pre-civilizational culture. I gave a plan of the whole book in which I showed that I did not intend to confine myself to a comparative study of civilizations in which I should be treating these, provisionally, not only as if they were so many specimens of their species, but also as if each specimen were entirely self-contained and therefore entirely intelligible if studied by itself. I announced my intention of going on to study the contacts between civilizations—both those between contemporaries and those between non-contemporaries that are commonly described as being renaissances of a 'dead' civilization in the course of the history of a living one. And I did eventually carry out this intention in volumes viii and ix. It is true that some of the charges against me, on the ground that I had treated civilizations as closed systems, were made in reviews of the first two batches of volumes. But in each batch the plan of the whole book was printed and displayed conspicuously, and this ought, I think, to have led the critics to suspend judgement on this point, pending the publication of the promised discussion of 'contacts'. On this point, therefore, I feel no conviction of sin.

I have also been criticized—in this case, rightly, I think—for having painted in too strong colours the contrast between the state of a civilization in its growth stage and its state after it has broken down, if it happens to be one of the civilizations that have come to grief. E. I. Watkin[1] and C. Trinkaus[2] contend that I distinguish these two stages from each other too sharply, and P. A. Sorokin[3] that my 'uniformities of growth and decline . . . are largely fantastic and are not borne out by the facts'. A. R. Burn contends[4] that 'there is no real distinction between' my "'growing" and "broken-down" civilizations in point of brutality or "radiation by charm"'. He illustrates this contention from Hellenic history.

'The seventh and sixth centuries, the period of the most rapid growth of Greek culture, are known in political history as the "Age of the Tyrants": a period of violent, often bloody, and at times atrocious class-conflict and revolution, affecting precisely those cities which took the most active part in the transformation of Greek society, and in the efflorescence of a new art.'[5]

Richard Pares, too, contends[6] that periods of growth are not, in fact, periods of harmony; and other critics have made the same point with regard to particular features in my picture.

W. Altree observes,[7] with regard to Sinic history, that the spirit of the Sinic Civilization was militaristic and aggressive throughout the Shang and Chou periods, and that the intensification of warfare in and after the seventh century B.C. was due, not to any spiritual change from bad to worse, but to an increase in the means of making war and in the prizes to be won by it (the introduction of iron tools, draft animals, irrigation, and manure strengthened the economic sinews of war by increasing productivity and so providing a larger surplus, beyond the requirements of bare subsistence, for expenditure on war, while the growth of cities created a market economy which, in its turn, accumulated stores of grain large enough to be worth raiding). M. Watnick contends[8] that creative and uncreative minorities are not confined respectively to periods of social growth and periods of social disintegration in the senses in which I use these terms. J. K. Feibleman remarks[9] that the social maladies, and the attempted remedies for them, that I depict, are not confined to periods of social disintegration. O. Handlin makes the same point, with regard, in particular, to archaism and futurism.[10] A. H. Hanson makes the point that disturbances, unrest, and revolutions are normal elements in the process of history at all times.[11] P. A. Sorokin,[12] R. H. S. Crossman,[13] and A. R. Burn[14] point out

[1] In The Tablet, 12th Augus , 1939.
[2] In Science and Society, vol. xii, No. 1 (1948), pp. 218–39.
[3] In Toynbee and History, p. 185.
[4] In History, February–October, 1956, p. 5.   [5] Ibid.
[6] In The English Historical Review, vol. lxxi, No. 279 (April, 1956), p. 259.
[7] In Toynbee and History, pp. 257–8.
[8] In The Antioch Review, No. 7 (Winter, 1947–8), pp. 587–602.
[9] In T'ien Hsia Monthly, vol. xi, Nos. 1 and 2 (1940), p. 29.
[10] O. Handlin in The Partisan Review, July–August, 1947, pp. 371–9.
[11] A. H. Hanson in Science and Society, No. 13 (1949), pp. 118–35.
[12] In Toynbee and History, pp. 185–6.   [13] In The New Statesman, 8th March, 1947.
[14] In History, February–October, 1956, p. 4.

that barbarians have not been assimilated peacefully by expanding civilizations when these were in their growth-stage—for instance, not by the Hellenic Civilization before 431 B.C. Barbarians have always resisted attempts to subjugate or expropriate them, in whatever state the aggressive civilization may happen to have found itself at the time. This is true, and Burn is right in saying[1] that

'the hostility of the barbarian west towards Greek expansion, even while it continues to import and to be stimulated by Greek works of art, culminates in the "barbarian reaction" of the sixth century, in which members of every unconquered people with which the Greeks were in contact take part, as allies or hired warriors, in the concerted efforts of Carthage and the Etruscans to halt the Greek colonists . . . and to expel them.'

Burn here puts his finger on a distinction that I have missed, though it is essential for a proper presentation of the point that I have been trying to make about the difference in the attitude of the barbarians towards a neighbour civilization in different phases of this civilization's history. The point is that people feel and act differently on the cultural and on the political plane. The common experience of sharing, or appreciating, the same culture does not deter different political communities from fighting each other, and, conversely, fighting each other does not deter them from sharing, or appreciating, the same culture. Englishmen who were fighting Germans in the First and the Second World War did not lose their love of German music or cease to think of it as being *their* music; and Germans who were fighting Englishmen in the same wars did not lose their love of Shakespeare's plays or cease to think of these as being *theirs*. Similarly, the barbarians who resisted Greek aggression by force of arms in the 'growth-stage' of the Hellenic Civilization continued, as Burn testifies, to feel the attraction of the civilization and therefore went on Hellenizing themselves voluntarily. On the eve of Hellenism's fifth-century catastrophe, Ducetius, the Sicel patriot who had led his Sicilian fellow barbarians' last forlorn hope in their struggle to throw off the yoke of the aggressive colonial Greek city-state Syracuse, went into exile at Corinth, Syracuse's mother city in Continental Greece, and eventually returned to Sicily in order to found in his own country a city-state on the Hellenic pattern.

Other barbarians fought the Hellenes, as Ducetius fought them, from beginning to end of the long history of the Hellenic World's relations with its barbarian neighbours; but the Hellenic Civilization did not captivate all barbarian leaders of resistance movements in all chapters of the story, as, in the earlier chapters, it had captivated Ducetius and his predecessors. There came a time when barbarians became unwilling to receive the Hellenic Civilization without giving it a distinguishing twist of their own, or even unwilling to receive it at all. This change in the barbarians' attitude towards Hellenism is, I believe, a verifiable historical event, and an important one. I also believe that it was due, not to a change in the barbarians' own spirit, but to a change in the character of

[1] Ibid.

the Hellenic Civilization with which they were in contact. This change
was, in fact, the change for the worse that I have sought to indicate in
coining my terms 'growth' and 'disintegration'. On the level of feeling,
the difference in the state of things before and after this change has been
well put by D. B. Richardson.[1] Participants in a growing civilization
feel, he notes, an 'exultation', based on their religious sense, which may
be described as 'exultation'. On the other hand, there is an absence of
exultation among participants in a civilization that is in decline.

Besides being criticized for having drawn a distinction between
'growth-periods' and 'disintegration-periods', or at any rate for having
painted the contrast between the two in excessively strong colours, I
have been criticized for trying to determine too precisely the moment at
which the change that I call the 'breakdown' of a civilization occurred.
In general, Pieter Geyl, for example, finds the sharpness of my demarcations between different phases of history unconvincing.[2] In particular,
I have been criticized—for example by H. Michell,[3] P. A. Sorokin,[4] W.
den Boer,[5] J. F. Leddy,[6] M. S. Bates,[7] D. M. Robinson,[8] and A. R.
Burn[9]—for having picked out the year 431 B.C. (the date of the outbreak
of the Great Atheno-Peloponnesian War) as a moment at which the
Hellenic Civilization brought upon itself a 'breakdown' from which it
never succeeded in recovering. I have come across only one reviewer
(J. Vogt)[10] who has endorsed this date of mine, and he has endorsed it
only after much hesitation.

Are 'epoch-making' events realities, or are they figments of the
imagination? I do not know what has been the experience of other
people, now alive, who were grown-up at the time of the outbreak of
the First World War in August 1914. For me that moment has been
'epoch-making' ever since. My lifetime, viewed in retrospect, is still
divided into a 'pre-1914' and a 'post-1914' period as sharply as the
traditional Western scheme of chronology divides all history into 'B.C.'
and 'A.D.' At the moment of the outbreak, in 1914, of a great and evidently fateful war in the society into which I happened to have been born, I
felt myself suddenly understanding what (it seemed to me) Thucydides
must have felt at the moment of the outbreak of war in his society in
431 B.C. Leddy suggests[11] that I have been too much impressed by
Thucydides' point of view and that this is what has led me to make too
much of the date 431 B.C.—as, in Leddy's opinion, I have done. Actually,
it was my own experience in A.D. 1914 that made me appreciate what
Thucydides had felt in 431 B.C., and made me endorse Thucydides'
view of the importance of the great war whose history he resolved, there
and then, to write. Whatever may be the verdict of posterity on the
historical importance or unimportance of the year A.D. 1914 in Western

---

[1] In *The Thomist*, vol. xx, No. 2 (April, 1957), pp. 169–70.
[2] In P. Geyl, A. Toynbee, and P. A. Sorokin: *The Pattern of the Past: Can We Determine It?*, pp. 73–74.   [3] In *Toynbee and History*, p. 83.
[4] Ibid., p. 184.   [5] Ibid., p. 24c.
[6] In *The Phoenix*, vol. 11, No. 4 (1957), p. 149.
[7] In *Christianity and Crisis*, vol. 15, No. 4 (21st March, 1955), pp. 27–30 and 32.
[8] In *The Intent of Toynbee's History: A Cooperative Appraisal*.
[9] In *History*, February–October, 1956, pp. 4–5.
[10] In *Saeculum*, No. 2 (1955).   [11] In loc. cit., p. 149.

history, I remain convinced, on reconsideration, that the verdict of history has already justified—and this conclusively—Thucydides' judgement of the importance of what happened to the Hellenic Civilization in the year 431 B.C. Moreover, 431 B.C. and A.D. 1914 are far from being the only dates that have been singled out by contemporaries and by posterity as being 'epoch-making'. Alexander's passage of the Hellespont, the nativity of Jesus, the *hijrah* of Muhammad, the first landfall of Columbus in the Americas, and the landfall of the *Mayflower* are a few of the more celebrated cases in point.

The criticism of my practice of singling out a definite date to mark the 'epoch-making' event of the 'breakdown' of a civilization has also been put in more general terms. Richard Pares castigates[1] my 'habit of pinning a long and complicated process to one or two salient events in order to dramatise it'. A. H. Hanson also objects[2] to my treating long chains of events as being consequences of particular decisions taken by particular individuals at particular moments. It is, for instance, an inadmissible simplification, Hanson considers, to trace back to something done by Pope Gregory VII in the year 1075 the character of all subsequent Western history.

'If one is prepared [he sums up] to reduce the complexity and variety of history to such a single cause-and-effect stream, any important decision can be made into the "first cause" of a whole series of events, within the category to which it applies.'

In a similar vein Sir Ernest Barker asks[3] whether the West can really have been on the wrong track, as I suggest that it may have been, since the time of the Emperor Frederick II Hohenstaufen. J. F. Leddy pronounces[4] that it is fantastic to suppose that events in the time of the Roman Empire could have been determined by things that had happened hundreds of years earlier. E. Dyason comments[5] that, when one is called upon to regard, as the cause of the 'breakdown' of civilization in Egypt, events that occurred 1,700 years before its final dissolution, it is difficult to give the weight which Toynbee gives to their evidence. Philip Bagby enunciates[6] a general law of historical causation to the effect that a cause must be proximate as well as adequate, and, like Leddy, he finds in this a ground for questioning my view that what happened in the Hellenic World in 431 B.C. exercised a continuing effect on the whole subsequent course of Hellenic history.

Bagby's law would seem to be difficult either to validate or to apply because of the intrinsic relativity of the key word 'proximate'. Its meaning depends entirely on the chronological horizon that we happen to choose, and we have a choice between any number of alternatives: there is no criterion for deciding that any one of these is the proper horizon, and that the others are inadmissible. If we take for our horizon

[1] In *The English Historical Review*, vol. lxxi, No. 279 (April, 1956), p. 260.
[2] In *Science and Society*, No. 13 (1949), pp. 118–35.
[3] In *Toynbee and History*, pp. 96, 100, 101.
[4] In *The Phoenix*, vol. 11, No. 4 (1957), p. 145.
[5] In *The Australian Outlook*, March, 1949, p. 59.
[6] In *Toynbee and History*, p. 107.

the beginning of the Modern Age of Western history, then only those events will be proximate that have been remembered and recounted to us by our grandparents, and this will limit the maximum run of historical causation to something like one hundred years. If we take the rise of the earliest civilizations some five thousand years ago, then any event since the emergence of the Western Civilization, some twelve hundred years ago, will be proximate for Westerners of the present generation. If we think in terms of the estimated age of life on Earth, then any event in human history since the first appearance of *homo sapiens* will be proximate. If we think in terms of the age, up to date, of this galaxy, then any event in the history of this planet will be proximate in this astronomical context. Each of these usages of the word 'proximate' is as legitimate as every other, because each of them depends directly on a particular choice of the time-span that is to be taken as our standard of measurement; and the choice is arbitrary because it is completely free. If, for the particular purpose of studying human affairs, we decide to choose for our standard one of the shorter time-spans—say, the age-of-civilization span or the age-of-mankind span—we shall get more closely to grips with Reality if we drop the inconclusive word 'proximate' and think of the time-factor in human relations in terms of an indefinite number of different definite time-scales, each governing some particular kind of relation at some particular level.

'In a civilization there are definite time-lags involved in the communication of knowledge and emotions between the thousands or millions of individual persons belonging to the commonwealth. . . . There are dialectics of ideas or concepts that ravel or unravel themselves in years, decades, and centuries. All these various time-lags are rather independent of the reason and the free will of Man.'[1]

The Buddha's concepts and precepts, for example, are still actively communicating themselves to millions of His fellow human beings today, two and a half millennia after the date of His Enlightenment. What is more, the influence of every one of the forgotten human beings who have ever lived is still affecting everyone in the living generation to some infinitesimal degree.

2. THE UNAVOIDABLENESS OF COMPARATIVE STUDY BY MEANS OF MODELS

However, the problem of the nature and range of historical causation (if causation is the right word here) is not, I believe, the main question at issue between my critics and me in our debate about whether it is legitimate to draw sharp lines and to lay on strong colours when one is attempting to give a panoramic exposition of human affairs. The main question is whether one is justified in attributing to particular events a significance for the understanding of the course of events as a whole. Pares suggests, in a passage quoted above, that I pick my particular events out because they are 'salient', and that I do this in order to

[1] D. B. Richardson in *The Thomist*, vol. xx, No. 2 (April, 1957), p. 183.

'dramatise' a long and complicated process. I myself would maintain that I pick them out, not because they are salient, but because they seem to me to be illuminating, and that my objective, when I use this device, is explanation, not dramatization. My 'key' events, dates, periods, plots, and processes serve me as symbols: that is, as landmarks which, like a pioneer's blazes on tree-trunks, have a meaning that points to objects beyond themselves. These objects may be distant; a single blaze may guide a traveller who takes note of it to some spring, ford, pass, or shelter many days' march away. The token does not, of course, exhaust the meaning of the thing betokened by it; but, if it is well chosen, it will work as a key to turn a lock and thereby open a door.

An example of this intellectual operation is my use of the three-masted square-rigged sailing-ship as a symbol of the Western Civilization in its modern age (*circa* A.D. 1475–1875). John Strachey[1] has objected that the invention of this new type of ship in the West in the fifteenth century is only one among the factors which account for the West's acquisition, in this age, of an ascendancy over the rest of the World. He points out that the relation between these many various factors was intricate, and that to ascribe the whole result to the invention of the 'ship' would be to give a misleadingly simplified account of a process that was really very complicated. I should have been guilty of this error if I had sought to present the 'ship' as being the sole and whole cause of the West's rise, in the modern age, to a position of world-wide hegemony. My intention, however, was not that. For me the 'ship' is not so much a cause as a symbol—the most illuminating one within my knowledge—of the new spirit which made the West's modern triumphal progress possible.

Of course, this new spirit also manifested itself in a thousand other outward and visible signs, and some of these, too, could be used, and have been used, as symbols of it. It is in the nature of a symbol that it has no monopoly. It has none because it is not identical or coextensive with the object that it symbolizes. If it were this, it would be, not a symbol of the thing, but the thing itself. A critic is falling into an error if he supposes that a symbol is intended to be a reproduction of the thing that it is really intended, not to reproduce, but to illuminate. His shafts fly wide of the mark if they are launched under this misapprehension. The test by which a symbol stands or falls is not whether it does or does not faithfully reproduce the object to which it points; the test is whether it throws light on that object or obscures our understanding of it. The effective symbol is the illuminating one, and effective symbols are an indispensable part of our intellectual apparatus. This is the meaning of the at first sight paradoxical dictum that, in order to grasp the real context, we have to construct an unreal one.[2] Of course, the constructor of a symbol does not introduce unreality into it out of perversity. In so far as a symbol does depart from Reality, it falls into danger of defeating its constructor's purpose by becoming misleading. In my attempts to construct symbols in this book, I am sure to have made errors of this

---

[1] In unpublished correspondence.
[2] Max Weber, cited by J. Romein in *Toynbee and History*, p. 347.

kind. Some of these have, in fact, been pointed out by my critics. Having to make a symbol unreal at the risk of making it misleading is one of the awkward necessities of thought. It is necessary because, if a symbol is not simplified and sharpened to a degree that reduces it to something like a sketch-map of the piece of Reality on which it is modelled, it will not work as an instrument for intellectual action.

When a symbol is used as an instrument it becomes a 'model', in the sense in which this word has come to be used apropos of scientific investigation.

'Men think in terms of models. We may think of our thought as consisting of symbols which are put in relations or sequences according to operating rules. Together, a set of symbols and a set of rules may constitute what we call a calculus, a logic, a game, or a model. It will have some structure, i.e. some pattern of distribution of relative discontinuities, and some "laws" of operation.'[1]

Whether a model resembles anything in the outside world can be discovered only by verification.[2] When we verify a model by testing how far it does or does not correspond to the phenomena, this is, of course, not an end in itself but only a means to an end. Our ulterior purpose is not to learn whether the model is or is not valid; it is to get new insight into the structure and nature of Reality by applying a model that is valid and is therefore an effective tool. How far the model is or is not valid is not a matter of any intrinsic interest in itself. As Bagby puts it,[3]

'It seems best to look on models as a heuristic device rather than as the goal of our studies. In so far as the models appear to be valid, we might look on them, not indeed as a description of the events, but as a description of the interrelationships of certain factors present in the events. A full understanding of the events would involve the elucidation of all the other factors present, factors which we may not be able to identify.'

In this context Bagby suggests that it might be useful to set up a model for the development of a major civilization. This is what I have done in previous volumes of this book, though I have done it without being altogether conscious of what I have been doing, and indeed without knowing, until recently, the current term of art for this intellectual operation. I have constructed my model from the pattern of Hellenic history and the pattern of its relations with the histories of Christianity and of the Western Civilization, as these patterns present themselves to me. The extensiveness of my use of this model has been noted by a number of my critics.[4] A majority of them, in noting this, have pro-

---

[1] K. W. Deutsch in *Philosophy of Science*, vol. 18, No. 3 (July, 1951), p. 230.
[2] Ibid.   [3] P. Bagby: *Culture and History*, p. 201.
[4] For instance, R. T. Clark in *The Nineteenth Century and After* (November, 1941); A. J. P. Taylor in *Toynbee and History*, p. 115; K. W. Thompson, ibid., p. 215; W. den Boer, ibid., p. 226; Granville Hicks, quoted by E. Fiess, ibid., p. 380 (Hicks, as here quoted, speaks of my Hellenic 'paradigm'); J. K. Feibleman in *T'ien Hsia Monthly*, vol. xi, Nos. 1 and 2 (1940), p. 20; C. Trinkaus in *Science and Society*, vol. xii, No. 1 (1948), pp. 224 and 237; K. D. Erdmann in *Archiv für Kulturgeschichte*, xxxiii. Band, Heft 2 (1951), p. 191; Paul M. Sweezy in *The Nation*, 19th October, 1946; J. A. Tor-

nounced that I have worked this model to death or have made of it a bed of Procrustes into which I have fitted the histories of other civilizations by doing violence to them.[1] These criticisms would have led me to reconsider my use of this model, even if I had not felt myself moved to do so spontaneously. I am going to do this in the present chapter; but first I must explain why I believe that a model, or a set of models, is an indispensable instrument for anyone who is trying to organize a comprehensive study of human affairs.[2]

In setting out on this large enterprise the explorer can find guidance for the first stage of his course in a pair of instructions. He must recognize the truths that, since he is a human being, his standpoint will be a relative one and his attitude a self-centred one, and he must take account of these two truths in his policy for action. He must accept the limitations of relativity by starting operations, consciously and deliberately, from his own time and place. He must reject the limitations of self-centredness by seeing to it that he does not end up at the point from which he has started. One's own time and place are clearly not the culmination of all history.

I have tried to follow this pair of instructions in my own work. I am a Westerner born in A.D. 1889, so I took as my starting-point the recent Western practice of making all human history culminate in the Western inquirer's own country in his own time. If I had been an Englishman of an earlier generation—a contemporary of the Venerable Bede's or even

modsen and G. C. Wasberg in *Samtiden*, vol. 58, hefte 12 (Oslo 1949), pp. 647–60; H. Frankfort in *The Birth of Civilization in the Near East*, pp. 21–22 and 26–27; W. H. McNeill in *The Intent of Toynbee's History: A Cooperative Appraisal*; the Rev. E. R. Hardy Jr., ibid.

As Erdmann puts it, 'the Hellenic Civilization is', in my vision, 'not an exemplar, but an archetype.... It might be still truer to Toynbee's intent to say that, running through Hellenic history, the completed archetypal career of a civilization becomes visible, and that this civilization serves as a transparent medium through which the phenomenon of civilization itself can be apprehended in its archetypal form (*Die Antike . . . ist, nicht Vorbild, sondern Urbild. Oder vielleicht wird man der Absicht Toynbees noch gerechter, wenn man sagt, dass durch sie hindurch ein urbildlicher Kulturablauf abgeschlossen sichtbar werde, dass sie transparent sei für das Urphänomen der Kultur*).'

[1] For instance: Sir Ernest Barker finds that my analogies with Hellenic history are sometimes fanciful (*Toynbee and History*, p. 92). Chr. Hill finds that I devote 'enormous ingenuity to the task of discovering other "societies" which will fit into' my 'plan, and to working out parellels between them and' my 'norm' (*The Modern Quarterly*, Autumn, 1947, p. 292). W. den Boer finds that I force other civilizations into the framework of the Hellenic Civilization by Procrustean methods (ibid., p. 226). H. E. Barnes finds that my use of the Hellenic model constrains me frequently 'to squeeze' my 'facts into a pattern and framework which they do not always fit' (*An Introduction to the History of Sociology*, p. 721). The same judgement is passed by J. K. Feibleman (*T'ien Hsia Monthly*, vol. xi, Nos. 1 and 2 (1940), p. 20); A. Hourani (*The Dublin Review*, vol. 229, No. 470 (December 1955), p. 381); W. Gurian (*The Review of Politics*, vol. 4, No. 4 (October, 1942), p. 512); T. J. G. Locher (*De Gids*, May 1948, offprint, pp. 6–8); K. D. Erdmann (loc. cit., pp. 224–5), with particular reference to my use of the Roman Empire as a model for universal states; F. Hampl (the *Historische Zeitschrift*, Band 173, Heft 3 (1952), p. 458); R. K. Merton (*The American Journal of Sociology*, vol. xlvii, No. 2 (September, 1941), pp. 205–13); Hajo Holborn (*The Saturday Review of Literature*, 31st May, 1947), with particular reference to my use of the Roman Empire; J. A. Tormodsen and G. C. Wasberg (*Samtiden*, vol. 58, hefte 12 (Oslo 1949), pp. 647–60; J. Bishko (*The Richmond News Leader*, 21st October, 1954); H. Frankfort (*The Birth of Civilization in the Near East*, pp. 24, 30–31, 99).

E. Fiess declares that my Hellenic paradigm 'persuades as it pervades'. But Fiess is in a minority.

[2] Vico, for instance, found a model in the history of Italy, as Engel-Janosi points out in *The Intent of Toynbee's History: A Cooperative Appraisal*.

of Saint Thomas More's—I should, no doubt, have made history culminate, not in England, but in Western Christendom; for, at any date from the conversion of the English to Christianity down to the Reformation, the consciousness of being an adherent of the Western Christian Church would have overshadowed the consciousness of being a subject of the English Crown in the thoughts and feelings of an inhabitant of the Kingdom of England—or, rather, of one or other of the Roman Patriarchate's two arch-dioceses of Canterbury and York. The priority of ecclesiastical over political allegiance was symbolized locally in the shrine of the martyr Saint Thomas Becket, until King Henry VIII plundered and desecrated this shrine and sent another Saint Thomas to his death. If I had happened to live in an age in which the Western Christian Church, not the Kingdom of England, would have been my natural starting-point, I should have had a different experience in the later course of my explorations.[1] I should not have been pulled up short, and compelled to change my plan of operations, by finding, as I did find, that the higher religions could not be dealt with adequately within the framework of a comparative study of civilizations. On the other hand, I might then have found that the framework of a comparative study of higher religions, which I should have adopted if I had been doing my work in the eighth century or in the early decades of the sixteenth, was not entirely adequate for dealing with the civilizations, not to speak of the pre-civilizational societies.

However, I happened to be born in 1889, so, for me, there was no question of taking my ancestral religion as my starting-point. As a matter of course I took my native country. I then duly rejected the self-regarding hallucination of mistaking the England of my time for the culmination of history. I found that England, taken by itself, was not, in fact, an 'intelligible field of study' either in my time or at any earlier date since the time when such a thing as England had first become discernible on the political map. I therefore went in search of the minimum unit, of which England is a part, that might be found intelligible if treated as being self-contained, and I found this in the Western Civilization. Having thus identified my native specimen of a species of society that not only was larger than a nation-state but also was more intelligible, in virtue of approaching nearer to being self-contained, I became aware of the presence of the other living civilizations with which the West was in contact in my day. Between them, they and the West account for all but a fraction of the whole living generation of mankind. But, for the purpose of a comprehensive study of human affairs, the civilizations in this set have a common property which greatly detracts from their usefulness. Just because they are still alive, their histories are not yet finished; and at least one complete specimen of the history of a civilization is a necessary first piece of material evidence for a study of the species.

I therefore probed backwards in time, towards the origins of my own native Western Civilization, till I struck the latter end of an earlier one, the Hellenic, to which the Western Civilization is affiliated through

---

[1] This point is taken up again on p. 218.

the Christian Church. The history of this Hellenic Civilization was a complete specimen of its kind. It had certainly come to an end, for in my day there was no longer any Hellenic Civilization in existence. It had long ago been superseded by two successors: the Western Civilization and the West's sister and contemporary, the Byzantine Civilization. The history of the Hellenic Civilization also certainly did not extend backwards in time beyond our ken, for it was known to have had, not only successors, but also a predecessor, the Minoan-Helladic-Mycenaean Civilization. Here, then, in the history of the Hellenic Civilization, was the specimen history of a civilization for which I was looking. It had one general merit and two special merits for a Western inquirer. Its general merit was its completeness. It had an identifiable beginning and end, and the whole story, in between, was on record, at least in outline. Its special merits for a Western inquirer were its link with Western history and its familiarity to a Westerner. Even if he had not been educated in the Greek and Latin classics, he would be likely to know more about Hellenic history than about the history of any other civilization outside his own.

Now that I had found my complete specimen of the history of a civilization, how was I to use it for my purpose? This purpose was to explore ways and means of organizing a comprehensive study of human affairs; and, from the start of my inquiry, I had rejected the customary presentation of history that leads the whole of it up to the inquirer's own time and place. This means rejecting a single-track chart of history; for it is only by making it all lead up to oneself that one can persuade oneself that history runs along a single line. From any non-self-centred standpoint it will be evident that history must run simultaneously along two separate lines as a minimum. Two is the minimum for the history of living beings of any species in which the mode of reproduction is the sexual one; and any such species that was actually represented by no more than one specimen of each sex would be, of course, on the verge of extinction. In order to have a reasonable prospect of survival, a species must have dozens of representatives or millions; and, whatever may be the species that we are studying, the number of representatives of it with which we shall have to reckon is sure to be of the plural order of magnitude, not the dual or the singular. In fact, a single-track chart of the history of anything whatsoever will be a false picture of Reality: a picture of it in which the truth has been distorted by the observer's uncorrected egocentricity. A multiple-track chart is the true picture of the movement of the phenomenal universe or of any part of it. This finding applies, of course, to the study of the histories of civilizations and of higher religions. It is impossible to force all the known specimens into a configuration that makes them all culminate in some single point-moment.

If we try, for instance, to make the histories of all the known civilizations lead up to the West in our time, we shall not be able to find any place for the Byzantine and Islamic civilizations at any date before the West impinged on them in the Crusades, or for the civilizations in India, Eastern Asia, and the Americas at any date before the landfalls of

Western ships on their coasts in and after the last decade of the fifteenth century. Alternatively, if we try to make them all lead up to China in our time, we shall not be able to find any place for the Indian, Islamic, Byzantine, Western, or pre-Columbian American civilizations. A single-track chart of history leading up to present-day China will be able to take account of Indian history only since the first century of the Christian Era, when Buddhism made its first lodgement on Chinese soil. It will be able to take account of Islamic history only since the thirteenth century, when Islam gained a foothold in north-western and south-western China in the wake of the Mongol conquest. It will be able to take account of Western history only since the sixteenth century, when the first Portuguese ships reached Chinese ports. Moreover, in so far as any of the alternative possible single-track charts does have to take account, however fragmentarily, of the parallel histories of contemporary civilizations, it is confessing its own invalidity; for it is admitting the existence of civilizations whose histories cannot be accommodated on its own single track.

Corresponding difficulties would arise from the use of a single-track chart if we were taking the histories of the higher religions as our units of study. For example, the traditional Christian chart of mankind's religious history makes the whole of it lead up to Christianity via Judaism from Abraham and via Abraham from Adam. But this Christian chart is, of course, unacceptable to the adherents of all the other higher religions. It is unacceptable to Muslims because their chart makes the whole lead up from Adam via Abraham to 'the pure religion of Abraham': that is to say, Islam. It is unacceptable to Jews because, for them, the single track reaches its divinely appointed terminus in themselves, and they reject, as preposterous, the Muslims' and the Christians' rival claims to have superseded the Jews in the role of being God's 'Chosen People'. Finally, the Christian chart is unacceptable to Zoroastrians, Hindus, Buddhists, Taoists, and Confucians because it completely ignores their existence. But, if we were to try to appease feelings wounded by the Christian chart by substituting the Confucian or the Buddhist chart for it, we should run into the same trouble in reverse. We should be wounding the feelings of the adherents of all three religions of the Judaic family. In short, whether the units in terms of which we are thinking are higher religions or civilizations or entities of any other kind, single-track charts of history will not work. Multiple-track charts are the only kind that will fit the phenomena as we find them.

In a mental picture, fitting the phenomena is a supreme merit. It tells decisively in favour of multiple-track charts as against single-track charts. But the price of the intellectual gain won by rising from the singular to the plural is the consequent presentation of an intellectual problem that a single-track chart does not raise: the problem of organizing the data.

So long as one is following a single track, no problem of organization arises. The observer has merely to take events as he finds them; he finds them in a sequence; and a sequence can be reproduced in a narrative. But, as soon as he refuses to keep to a single track any longer, the observer finds himself with a number of simultaneous phenomena on his hands. These cannot be dealt with in a single narrative, because they do not constitute a single sequence. A number of different narratives have now to be brought into some kind of relation with each other, and *ex hypothesi* this relation cannot be the narrational one, since it is not possible to be telling more than one story at a time. When we have to establish a relation between two or more series of concurrent events, this requires us to take a synoptic view of them, and that, in turn, requires us to study them comparatively. For example,

'The situations in from 13 to 48 states cannot be adequately described in a unified narrative; to have meaning, they need to be seen in an analytical structure.'[1]

And we can have a history of particular monarchies or a sociology of monarchy, but not a history of monarchy.[2] The history of European literature, too, can be studied only analytically—that is, comparatively.[3] In more general terms,

'An approach that uses the concepts of structure and process leads us to ask questions that cannot be answered merely by identifying the succession of events. Events are of the moment, episodic; process and structure have duration in time, recognisable patterns, and a high degree of continuity.'[4]

A comparative study of a number of specimens means noting their likenesses and differences with a view to discovering whether or not there is a standard type to which they conform, notwithstanding their individual peculiarities. But in order to make our comparison with any assurance we have also to satisfy ourselves that the specimens which we are proposing to compare are properly comparable.[5] Here are two intellectual operations that are required of us as soon as we adopt a multiple-track chart of the phenomena in place of the self-regarding and misleading single-track one; and this is where the construction of a model can, I believe, serve us in good stead. My own use of my Hellenic model has been criticized by Erich Voegelin[6] in the following terms:

'The construction of type-concepts, which should be based on the civilizational courses, slides over, in the practice of the operation, into the entirely different task of identifying societies as members of the species through the application of the type-concepts, developed from the limited basis, to data which are assumed to be fragments of civilizational courses of the same type.'

I do not dispute Voegelin's account of what I have done, but I do dispute the suggestion—if I am right in detecting this—that what I have

---

[1] Social Science Research Council's Committee on Historiography's Report (1954), p. 161.

[2] A. L. Kroeber: *The Nature of Culture*, p. 97.

[3] E. R. Curtius in *Merkur*, 1. Jahrgang, Viertes Heft [Heft 4] (1947), p. 496.

[4] Social Science Research Council's Committee on Historiography's Report (1954), p. 97.

[5] This obvious but fundamental point is made by H. E. Barnes in *An Introduction to the History of Sociology*, p. 732.

[6] In *The Intent of Toynbee's History: A Cooperative Appraisal*.

done is not intellectually legitimate. What Voegelin is describing is, I should say, the normal heuristic use of an hypothesis, and, if this is the use that I have made of my Hellenic model, as I believe it is, then I do not think that my practice needs reconsideration or revision.

It is true that the operation of constructing a model is different from the operation of testing whether it fits the phenomena.[1] But, so far from its being proper to dissociate the two operations from each other, it would seem to be impossible to obtain sure results from either of them if they are not carried out in conjunction. The model has to be constructed out of only a fraction of the total body of data, or we should never be able to mount it for use in investigating the remainder. But, just on this account, the structure will remain tentative and provisional until it has been tested by application to all the rest of the data within our knowledge.[2] Conversely, our picture of the data as a whole will remain chaotic until we have found a model that brings out in them a pattern of specimens of a species. Unless we bring these two operations into conjunction with each other by conducting them simultaneously and interdependently, we cannot tell whether or not our provisional model provides a genuine clue to some principle of order in the apparent chaos, or whether this particular model must be modified or supplemented or discarded in favour of another. Nor can we tell whether the items in a particular conglomeration of data that we have picked out of the chaos, like a child picking spillikins out of a heap, have any significant common features, or whether they merely happen to have hung together accidentally. In performing each of the two operations, we have provisionally to anticipate the results of the other operation. The untested results of each provide a test—and this the only test at our disposal—of the other operation's validity. This reciprocal checking and counter-checking of unchecked assumptions may or may not be a form of arguing in a circle; but, even if it can properly be convicted of being that, it is useless to condemn the procedure on that account, because it is impossible to renounce it without renouncing the whole activity of thinking.

There is nothing unfamiliar about this mental procedure. It is the analytical and classificatory procedure which, as has been noted at the beginning of this volume, is the human mind's fundamental mode of operation and is consciously and deliberately followed in scientific inquiry,[3] including the scientific study of human affairs. This is, indeed, the only way in which our minds can work either in the scientific field or in the practical one, since in all fields we have to cope with simultaneous phenomena in large quantities. This problem of dealing with large quantities besets the student of human affairs when he is approaching them as an historian no less than when he is approaching them as a

---

[1] G. Buchdahl, in *The Australasian Journal of Philosophy*, vol. 34, No. 3 (December, 1956), p. 168, quotes a dictum of Newton's about Newton's own method of work: 'In this philosophy, propositions are deduced from phenomena and afterwards made general by induction.' Buchdahl labels Newton's first step 'the inductive process' and the second step 'the inductive inference'.

[2] I hold (see pp. 41–45 and 244–6), as Bagby holds, that 'we shall only be able to judge our scheme when we have applied it to the actual facts of history and seen what results it gives us' (*Culture and History*, p. 202).   [3] See pp. 9–13.

sociologist or a psychologist. Why, then, do some historians feel a repugnance, which psychologists and sociologists do not share, to applying the analytical and classificatory procedure to human affairs? The reason for this repugnance is apparent if Kroeber is right, as I believe he is, in holding[1] that the essence of the historian's approach is a concern to preserve the integrity of events, in all their individual complexity, in his way of presenting and explaining them. In any case the repugnance is both unquestionable and characteristic. It is illustrated, for example, by a comment of Sir Ernest Barker's on my work.

'With the passion of unity there naturally goes a zest for schematization: a zest for seeing history and the whole past in abstract general terms: a zest, if the phrase may be used, for "botanising" history[2]—for classifying in *genera* and *species* all its multitudinous data. I am inclined to call this zest by the name of "Linnaeanism". Dr Toynbee imposes patterns on history, and gives the patterns names, much as Linnaeus classified and named plants. But this raises the question whether history is really like botany.'[3]

Barker's answer to this question is, like Hourani's,[4] in the negative, and he gives his reason. 'Plants have a general uniformity'; history 'is infinitely multiform'. This distinction is surely disputable. The truth surely is that all phenomena—plants, human affairs, or whatever they may be—are both multiform in some respects and uniform in others as they present themselves to human minds, and that this is the problem of knowledge and understanding with which the mind always has to cope, no matter what may be the nature of the phenomena with which it happens to be dealing in any particular case. If this is correct, the crucial question is whether history is really unlike botany in respect of the epistemological problem with which the inquirer's mind has to wrestle, and the right answer to this question is in the negative in my belief.[5] In the paper here quoted, Barker lets this question go by default. After denying the legitimacy of applying the method of science to human affairs, he does not go on to make any suggestion for an alternative method to which a student of human affairs can resort when—as, in practice, is always the case—the quantity of simultaneous phenomena exceeds the capacity of a single narrative to carry the freight. It is just because the data of history are 'multitudinous' (to quote Barker's own word) that a resort to the method of classification, in addition to the method of narration, is, as I see it, unavoidable. If the inquirer is unwilling to resort to it, his only alternative is to accept defeat and to

---

[1] See the passages quoted on pp. 14 and 20.
[2] Cp. C. A. Beard in *The American Historical Review*, vol. xl, No. 2 (January, 1935), pp. 307–9; also F. S. Marvin in *The Hibbert Journal*, July, 1935, p. 623: 'The general plan of the work, as far as it is revealed in these first three volumes, is to collect, classify, and compare all the main types of civilization which his travel and study have brought to light; and then, as the result of this classification and comparison, to draw what conclusions are possible as to the laws of growth, spread, mixture, decay, and disappearance of the various species—treating, in fact, each separated and classified civilization much as a botanist or zoologist treats a species of animal or plant.'
[3] Sir Ernest Barker in *Toynbee and History*, p. 95.   [4] See p. 12.
[5] I am not alone in holding this belief. W. F. Albright, for instance, likewise holds that 'there is . . . no basic epistemological difference between *comparable* fields of history and of science' (*From the Stone Age to Christianity*, 2nd ed., p. 115).

renounce all attempt even to present the phenomena, not to speak of trying to give some explanation of them.

This is not, of course, to say that the comparative study of human affairs is as plain sailing as the comparative study of flora or even fauna.[1] While it is not evident that human affairs are 'multiform' in some sense in which plants are not, it seems indisputable that they are more intricate than plants are; and, the greater the intricacy of the phenomena, the more difficult the quest for a model becomes. E. Voegelin observes[2] that adequate descriptive type-concepts are more difficult to arrive at for civilizations than they are for botanical specimens; and M. R. Cohen warns the inquirer[3] that the 'single repeatable patterns of physics or physical laws have not been discovered in human affairs'. Sir Llewellyn Woodward has acutely pointed out that

'we know so many facts which lend themselves to arrangements in patterns that we can make any number of such patterns; but we do not know enough to judge between these patterns or to be sure that we are doing more than pick out chance or superficial resemblances'.[4]

Applying this consideration to my work, he justly comments[5] that

'it would be possible to make an entirely different selection of facts and, as a result, to give an entirely different version of the development of Western Civilization during the last fifteen centuries'.

The same point is made by K. W. Thompson:[6]

'The cauldron of history is so immense and limitless that the individual historian can serve up but a tiny spoonful, and whether this can symbolise or represent the full mixture of history is always a most doubtful issue.'

This embarrassing wealth of alternative possible choices besets the student of human affairs when dealing with phenomena of the lower orders of magnitude. On the other hand, when dealing with phenomena of higher orders of magnitude—for instance, with civilizations or with 'higher religions'—he is embarrassed by a problem arising from the

---

[1] In spite of the evident difficulty of the enterprise, I feel fortified in my determination to persevere in it when I notice the line taken, on this issue, by a critic who has not treated me so benevolently as Sir Ernest Barker has. Philip Bagby concedes (in *Toynbee and History*, pp. 106 and 108) that 'there certainly seems to be some evidence for Dr Toynbee's (and Spengler's) thesis that there is a regular pattern of development of civilizations' and that 'a morphology of cultural and social forms and a general theory of culture-change may serve to reduce many of the puzzling phenomena to order'. In his own book, *Culture and History*, he says: 'I shall have one primary end in view, one particular problem which I wish to attempt to solve. It is the same problem which has chiefly engaged the attention of recent philosophers of history such as Spengler and Toynbee: that is, whether there is any regularity in the development of civilizations, in their slow growth and their sometimes rapid decline.' Towards the end of this volume of 'prolegomena to the comparative study of civilizations', in a chapter in which he examines some examples of similarities in the development of civilizations, Bagby takes the history of the Hellenic Civilization as his principal model. He applies this model first to the history of the Western Civilization up to date (pp. 205–10) and then to the other civilizations on his list (pp. 212–17).
[2] In *The Intent of Toynbee's History: A Cooperative Appraisal.*
[3] M. R. Cohen: *The Meaning of Human History*, p. 116.
[4] Sir Llewellyn Woodward in a letter of 25th July, 1952, to the writer of this Study (quoted in ix. 211, footnote 3). Cp. R. L. Shinn: *Christianity and the Problem of History*, p. 15.   [5] In *The Spectator*, 18th August, 1939.
[6] In *Toynbee and History*, p. 219.

paucity of his data at this level.[1] J. Madaule notes[2] that the specimens with which I am working are more scarce, besides being more complex, than a botanist's, and that the margin of error in my comparative study must be proportionately greater. It is true that the maximum number of civilizations that I originally believed I had identified is less than thirty, and for operational purposes the figure may have to be reduced considerably for various reasons. The 'arrested civilizations', as critics have pointed out,[3] are a rather arbitrary selection; and two of them—the Spartan and the Ottoman—are also included in other civilizations on my list. The development of both the 'arrested' and the 'abortive' civilizations breaks off short at so early a stage that their utility for purposes of comparison is slight. And so is the utility of several of the civilizations that the archaeologists have disinterred—in this case, not because of evidence that they prematurely went to pieces or became petrified, but because the material debris of their culture, which the archaeologists have brought to light, do not enable us to reconstruct their spiritual or even their political history.

The number of specimens will be further reduced if my critics are right in contesting one of the results of my application of my Hellenic model. This model shows an earlier civilization, the Hellenic, being succeeded by a later one, the Western, that is 'affiliated' to it through a 'higher religion', Christianity, which serves as a 'chrysalis' out of which the new civilization emerges. Applying this model to Eastern Orthodox as well as to Western Christendom, I have assumed that the civilization of the Byzantine World, as well as the civilization of the medieval and modern West, is not a continuation of the Hellenic Civilization but is a successor to it with a separate identity of its own. Again, on the analogy of the role played by Christianity as a 'chrysalis', I have assumed that the same role has been played by Christianity's sister religion, Islam, and that the Islamic civilizations in the Iranic and Arabic worlds are therefore two more separate civilizations, on a par with the two Christian civilizations of Byzantium and the West. When the Hellenic model is applied to the history of civilization in India and China, it brings to light counterparts of itself there too, with the Mahayana playing Christianity's role in China and the post-Buddhaic form of Hinduism playing it in India. In previous volumes I have assumed that in these two subcontinents there has been a succession of civilizations, on the analogy of the series at the western end of the Old World. I have also assumed that there has been a similar succession in the Tigris-Euphrates basin and in Middle America, though in these two areas the break in the continuity of history was not signalized by a religious revolution. I made this series of assumptions tentatively and provisionally, in order to test how far it was borne out by the facts.[4] Now that it has been tested by me in previous volumes and has been contested by a number of my critics,[5]

---

[1] See ix. 210–11 and the present volume, p. 234.
[2] In *Diogenes*, No. 13 (Spring, 1956), pp. 33–34.
[3] See p. 548, footnote 5, and pp. 553–4.   [4] See i. 117–18, 133–6, 146.
[5] For example, my analysis of the histories of India and China into the histories of two distinct civilizations, one following the other in either case, has been rejected by M. Savelle (*The Pacific Historical Review*, vol. xxv, No. 1 (February, 1956), pp. 55–67)

I must experiment with the alternative policy of assuming that in Middle America, the Tigris-Euphrates basin, India, and China, and perhaps in the domains of Byzantine Christendom and Islam as well, there has been, not a succession of civilizations, but a single continuous civilization in each case, as I have assumed that there has been in the Andean area down to the Spanish conquest and in Egypt down to its conversion to Christianity. After having operated with the maximum number of civilizations, it will be a useful check on the results of the manœuvre to repeat the operation, this time with the minimum number. But this drastic reduction in the quantity of the specimens reinforces Madaule's point that the paucity of the data for the study of civilizations is a difficulty, besetting this study, with which botany, for example, does not have to contend.

The number of effective specimens would be reduced still farther if Dawson is right in challenging[1] my postulate of the 'philosophical equivalence' of all the civilizations, and my corresponding postulate in regard to the higher religions. In spite of my respect for Dawson's judgement, I should be reluctant to defer to it on this point. A specimen is a specimen, and, if we are satisfied that we have verified a particular specimen as being a genuine one, it seems hazardous to draw distinctions between this and other specimens on the ground of differential valuations that will inevitably be subjective and therefore disputable.[2] All civilizations and all higher religions alike, up to date, have fallen infinitely short of their ideals; all alike have risen far above the level of older species of human society. In this perspective it seems prudent to treat all specimens of each species as each other's equals.

3. A RETRIAL OF THE HELLENIC MODEL FOR CIVILIZATIONS

Under the new and more exacting conditions to which I have just committed myself, I will now repeat the experiment, made originally near the beginning of this book, of applying my Hellenic model to the rest of the field of the histories of civilizations. Before applying it, I will dissect it, and will then apply the component parts one by one. This procedure seems likely to be illuminating, because we shall find that

and by E. I. Watkin (*The Tablet*, 12th August, 1939) in respect of both cases; by N. C. Chaudhuri in respect of the Indian case (in an unpublished communication to the writer); by W. Altree (*Toynbee and History*, p. 266), by E. C. Dyason (*The Australian Outlook*, March 1949), by M. S. Bates (*Christianity and Crisis*, vol. 15, No. 4 (2nd March, 1955), pp. 27–30 and 32), and by P. L. Ralph (in the *Saturday Review*, 16th October, 1954, p. 19) in respect of the Chinese case. Watkin also rejects (in loc. cit.) my distribution of the history of Islam between the histories of two series of civilizations, the Syriac followed by the Arabic and the Iranic. Chaudhuri regards civilization in India from about A.D. 1000 down to the beginning of the impact of the Western Civilization on India as being, not a new civilization, but a 'folk civilization' into which the previous classical civilization of India (the 'Indic' in my terminology) had lapsed.

An open-minded examination, by a specialist in Chinese history, of my analysis of this has been made in *The Pacific Historical Review*, vol. viii, No. 4 (December, 1939), under the title of 'A Bisection of Chinese History', by M. E. Cameron. After pointing out the number and importance of the strands of continuity in Chinese history, Cameron agrees (p. 411) that my '"Far Eastern Civilization" does have a real character of its own as distinct from that of Chinese antiquity', though evidently she would not go as far as I have gone in drawing this distinction.

[1] In *Toynbee and History*, pp. 130–1 and 134. Cp. L. Mumford in *Diogenes*, No. 13 (Spring, 1956), p. 17.   [2] This point is taken up again on pp. 551–3.

different parts fit the phenomena in different degrees and in different numbers of instances. I shall keep in mind M. R. Cohen's counsel: 'Give special note to those facts that fail to fit into preconceived patterns.'[1]

My Hellenic model comprises more than the internal history of the Hellenic Civilization. It also includes this civilization's relations with contemporary civilizations whose participants it annexed to its internal proletariat; its relations with Christianity; and finally its relations, through Christianity, with the subsequent Orthodox Christian and Western civilizations. This configuration of historical events can be analysed into the following elements.

One element is the configuration of the Hellenic Civilization's own political history. At the earliest stage of Hellenic history of which we have any record, there is a sharp contrast between the cultural unity of the Hellenic World and its political disunity. We find it divided up politically into a number of sovereign independent states whose citizens recognize that they are all partakers in a common culture yet are not inhibited by this from going to war with each other. In the course of time these fratricidal wars become so devastating that they bring the civilization to grief. When it is on the point of dissolution it wins a reprieve through the belated political unification of the Hellenic World in the Roman Empire. This brings temporary peace and order, but at the prohibitive price of a series of 'knock-out blows' ending in the overthrow of all political powers except for the one surviving victor. By the time when the Hellenic 'universal state' is established by Rome, the Hellenic World is already so seriously exhausted and demoralized that it proves incapable of maintaining its universal state in perpetuity; and the break-up of the Roman Empire spells the Hellenic Civilization's dissolution.

A second element is the configuration of the Hellenic Civilization's social history after its 'breakdown'. The leading minority in the society comes to depend more and more on force, and less and less on attraction, for maintaining its ascendancy. This change in the character of its relation with the majority alienates both the dominant minority's subjects within the Hellenic Civilization's domain and the primitive peoples beyond its borders who have previously been attracted towards it. These two classes turn respectively into an internal and an external 'proletariat' (in the sense of a class that is 'in' society but not 'of' it). The internal proletariat is swollen in numbers by the addition of barbarians from the external proletariat and of representatives of foreign civilizations who are forcibly incorporated in the Hellenic Civilization's internal proletariat through military conquest.

A third element is the configuration of the Hellenic Civilization's religious history in the same phase. The internal proletariat creates a higher religion, Christianity,[2] that draws its inspiration from one of the

---

[1] *The Meaning of Human History*, p. 114. The same advice is given by W. Kaufmann in *Toynbee and History*, p. 311.

[2] The proletarian origin of Christianity has been contested. K. D. Erdmann, for instance, maintains that it was never a mass movement (*Archiv für Kulturgeschichte*, xxxiii. Band, Heft 2 (1951), pp. 225–6).

non-Hellenic civilizations whose representatives have been incorporated in the Hellenic internal proletariat. Christianity converts the Hellenic World and also its barbarian invaders. An attempt to organize a counter-religion, Neoplatonism, professedly drawing its inspiration from native Hellenic sources, is a failure. The Christian Church, in which the Christian religion has taken social form, serves as a chrysalis out of which two new civilizations, the Eastern Orthodox Christian (*alias* Byzantine) and the Western Christian, eventually emerge after a cultural interregnum.

A fourth element is the part played by 'the external proletariat' (the barbarians). Their creativity expresses itself in epic poetry, and their nationalism in the adoption of Christianity in heretical forms (e.g. Arianism and Islam). The barbarians conquer the Hellenic universal state militarily and establish successor-states on its domain. But their contribution to the creation of the new civilizations is slight compared to 'the internal proletariat's' contribution. The matrix of the new civilizations is the Christian Church, not the Roman Empire's barbarian successor-states.

A fifth element is a series of 'renaissances' of the Hellenic culture in the course of the histories of the two 'Hellenistic' civilizations: the Byzantine and the Western. These renaissances are attempts to draw inspiration from Hellenism direct, and not merely indirectly through the medium of the Hellenic element in Christianity.

Bagby has arrived at much the same results as mine in constructing a model out of a stage-by-stage comparison of Hellenic history with Western history up to date.[1] But he has also included one important further element. He sees the course of each of these two civilizations as exhibiting 'a gradual process of "rationalisation"', which 'seems to come in two pulses or phases, two ages, one of Faith and one of Reason'.[2]

'Essentially this movement is one of growing rationalism and individualism. It reaches its creative peak in the seventeenth century in France (the Age of Louis XIV) and the fifth century in Athens (the Age of Pericles). This is the period when faith and reason are perfectly balanced, the period of the great triumphs of art and thought, when the basic forms of the civilization are laid down once for all.'[3]

It will be seen that if Bagby's schematization is superposed on mine his 'creative peak' of Hellenic history comes shortly before my 'breakdown', which I equate with the outbreak of the Great Atheno-Peloponnesian War in 431 B.C. It corresponds, in fact, with 'the Half Century' (*pentekontaetia*) that ended in this catastrophe and that had opened with the triumph of Hellenism over the Persian invaders of Continental European Greece in 480–479 B.C.

Let us now see how far these several elements in my Hellenic model fit the histories of civilizations other than the Hellenic.

The combination of cultural unity with political disunity, which we find in the Hellenic World at the dawn of its history, appears to be widespread. It is the situation in all known living pre-civilizational

---

[1] *Culture and History*, pp. 205–10.   [2] Op. cit., p. 209.   [3] Op. cit., p. 207.

societies, according to Bagby.[1] Its frequency is not surprising, for, after all, there are only two possible alternatives: if a society is not united politically, it is necessarily divided. So political disunity, taken by itself, is too general a feature to have much significance. The significant political configuration in my Hellenic model is the revolutionary change from disunity to unity as a result of a series of ever more devastating wars which have brought the civilization to grief before the political unity is achieved. And, in the histories of the civilizations, this configuration is a frequent one. For instance, it occurs—in unmistakable counterparts of the Hellenic pattern—in the histories of the Andean and Middle American civilizations (if we now regard civilization in Middle America as being continuous and unitary, and see the Aztec Empire as its universal state in the making). The same pattern is also unmistakable in the histories of the Syriac, Sinic, Indic, and Sumero-Akkadian civilizations, the Eastern Orthodox Christian Civilization in Russia, and the Far Eastern Civilization in Japan. Syria was unified politically in the Assyrian Empire and its successors the Neobabylonian Empire and the Achaemenian Empire, China in the Ch'in (Ts'in) and Han Empire after the period of 'the Contending States', India in the Maurya Empire after a similar period of fratricidal inter-state warfare, the Sumero-Akkadian World in the Empire of Agade and in the subsequent empire established by the Third Dynasty of Ur and re-established momentarily by Hammurabi, Russia in the Muscovite Empire, Japan in the unitary regime established by the Tokugawa Shogunate.[2] In the anatomy of Indian history the thesis that, since the end of the Indus Culture of the third and second millennia B.C., there has been a succession of two civilizations in India is supported by a second occurrence, in Indian history, of the Hellenic political configuration. From the eighth to the sixteenth century of the Christian Era India was divided politically, except for an ephemeral unification under Muslim rule in A.D. 1318–36, among a number of contending states, as she had been during the age before the establishment of the Maurya Empire in the fourth century B.C. In the sixteenth century of the Christian Era India was united politically in the Mughal Raj, and in the nineteenth century this political unity was re-established in the form of the British Raj.

We have now found, on reconsideration, that the political configuration of our Hellenic model is plainly discernible in nine other instances. There would be a tenth instance if I have been right in assuming, as I have assumed in volumes i–x, that there was a second occurrence of this pattern in the history of the Tigris-Euphrates basin, as well as in the history of India. In these earlier volumes I cast the Neobabylonian Empire for the role of universal state of a Babylonic Civilization affiliated to the Sumeric, but this attribution is perhaps dubious. The Neobabylonian Empire was only one of four successor-states of the Assyrian Empire, and it was not even the largest and most powerful of these. It lived in fear of its neighbour the Median Empire, which had taken the

---

[1] Op. cit., p. 101.
[2] The role of the Tokugawa regime in Japanese history is discussed further on p. 207, footnote 2.

metropolitan provinces of Assyria as its share of the Assyrian spoils. Then should the Assyrian Empire itself be regarded as the universal state of a Babylonic Civilization? It was larger and longer-lived than any of its immediate successor-states, and its provincial administration was highly organized. Yet even the Assyrian Empire did not include the whole of the Babylonic World. It never succeeded in conquering the rival Empire of Urartu, which was a convert to the Babylonic culture. The Assyrian Empire has more in common with the abortive empire of the dynasty of Agade than it has with the Third Dynasty of Ur's and the First Dynasty of Babylon's Empire of Sumer and Akkad, which I have identified with the universal state of the Sumeric Civilization. To find a convincing universal state for a hypothetical independent Babylonic Civilization, we must wait for the Achaemenian Empire, and this, even if it started its career as a vehicle of the Babylonic Civilization, had become the vehicle of a different civilization, the Syriac, before its overthrow. It will be seen that we cannot identify a Babylonic universal state with confidence, and this tells against my earlier thesis that there was a Babylonic Civilization, separate from, and successive to, the Sumero-Akkadian. An interpretation of the civilization of the Tigris-Euphrates basin at this later stage as being a continuation of the Sumero-Akkadian Civilization might be less open to question.

In the history of the Egyptiac Civilization the political configuration of our Hellenic model can be identified if it is accepted that there was a period in which the nomes (cantons) of Egypt were so many sovereign independent states, perpetually going to war with each other, and that this was followed by a period in which first Upper Egypt and then the whole of the Nile Valley below the First Cataract was united politically in the so-called 'Old Kingdom'.[1] This configuration conforms to the Hellenic model, but the chronology does not. In the history of the Hellenic Civilization the revolutionary change from disunity to unity on the political plane came in the last chapter of the story, after the warfare between the contending states had not only brought the Hellenic Civilization to grief but had carried it to the verge of dissolution. In the history of civilization in Egypt there was the same revolutionary change, but it came at the very beginning. The age, if there was one, of the contending Egyptian cantons was 'prehistoric' in the sense of being 'pre-civilizational'. In Egypt political unification was simultaneous with the dawn of civilization, and it was followed by the most creative period of Egyptiac history instead of being followed by dissolution and preceded by breakdown and disintegration, as it was in Hellenic history. When we find an identical configuration in the histories of two civilizations appearing at two quite different stages and performing two quite different functions, this suggests that the common feature may mask a radical difference between the fundamental structures of the two histories.[2]

[1] This view has certainly been widely held among Egyptologists in the past. However, E. J. Baumgartel, in *The Cultures of Prehistoric Egypt*, revised edition, p. 12, maintains that 'it is *not* generally recognised that the nomes are survivals of pre-Menite states'.

[2] This radical difference is pointed out by Richard Pares in *The English Historical Review*, vol. lxxi, No. 279 (April, 1956), p. 262, by F. Borkenau in *Commentary*, May,

This impression is strengthened when we turn to a chapter in the history of China which, in the preceding volumes, I have treated provisionally as the history of a civilization separate from, and successive to, the Sinic. I have just reaffirmed my view that the configuration of Sinic history, down to and including the universal state established and maintained by the Ch'in (Ts'in) and Han dynasties, conforms closely to my Hellenic model. Moreover, the fall of the Han Empire, like the fall of the Roman Empire, was followed by a relapse into political disunity. But the emergence of the new Far Eastern Civilization—if a new civilization did emerge in China—was followed, almost as quickly as the emergence of the Egyptiac Civilization in Egypt, by the establishment of political unity. If the dawn of the Far Eastern Civilization is to be regarded as having been subsequent to the cultural interregnum following the break-up of the Han Empire at the turn of the second and third centuries of the Christian Era, then the empire in which China was united politically under the Sui and T'ang dynasties, from the close of the sixth century to the early years of the tenth, corresponds to the Old Kingdom in Egyptiac history. Thus, if there was such a thing as a separate Far Eastern Civilization that was not a mere continuation of the Sinic, the structure of this Far Eastern Civilization's history does not conform, as the structure of the preceding Sinic Civilization's history does, to my Hellenic model; it conforms to a different model presented by the political history of the Egyptiac Civilization. Moreover, the structure of the West's sister-civilization, the Eastern Orthodox Christian or Byzantine, conforms to the Egyptiac model likewise. In Eastern Orthodox Christendom the interregnum following the break-up of the Roman Empire was immediately succeeded by the establishment of political unity through a successful revival, here, of the Roman Empire—an achievement that presents a sharp contrast to the series of abortive revivals of the Roman Empire in the West from Charlemagne's attempt onwards.[1]

The second element in my Hellenic model—the disintegration of a broken-down society into an internal and an external proletariat—does occur in a considerable number of non-Hellenic instances. These have been surveyed at length in volume v, and there is no need to recapitulate this survey here. In Hellenic history this second element is closely associated with the third: the creation, by the internal proletariat, of a

1955, p. 240 ('the universal state marks the beginning, not the end, of Ancient Egypt's history'), and by D. Halévy in a French journal that I have not been able to identify, p. 59. It has been noted by P. Bagby (in *Culture and History*, p. 219) and by F. Hampl (in the *Historische Zeitschrift*, Band 173, Heft 3 (1952), p. 459) that the configuration of Egyptiac history will not conform to the Hellenic model. R. Coulborn (in *Toynbee and History*, p. 159) submits that The Old Kingdom of Egypt is clearly a universal state in the sense in which I use this term.

[1] These revivals of the Roman Empire in the West were so ineffective, and made so little mark on Western history as a whole, that K. D. Erdmann seems hardly warranted in maintaining, on the strength of them, that Western history begins with a universal state (*Archiv für Kulturgeschichte*, xxxiii. Band, Heft 2 (1951), p. 243). A slightly better case might be made for the thesis that Chinese history begins with a universal state. Yet the Chou regime, even in its first phase, was hardly more effective than the resuscitated Roman Empire in the West; it is not comparable to the Ch'in (Ts'in), Han, Sui, and T'ang regimes in point of solidity. As for the Chou's predecessors the Shang, the progress of archaeological discovery has not yet revealed either the extent or the structure of their rule. See further p. 190.

higher religion in which the inspiration comes from a foreign source. This third element is a key-part of the model, since the church in which the higher religion embodied itself in the Hellenic case served as the chrysalis out of which two new civilizations emerged. It is therefore important to reconsider whether the pattern of the history of the Christian Church is a standard one which can be detected in a number of other instances, or whether it is something exceptional.

In order to test this we must first analyse this pattern into its elements. The Christian Church arose among the proletariat of one disintegrating civilization; its inspiration came from a different civilization; it easily overcame a counter-church professedly inspired by the native traditions of the civilization in whose domain the victorious church had made its appearance; the victorious church converted the world in which it had triumphed, and also this world's barbarian invaders. It brought to birth two new civilizations which can hardly be regarded as being mere continuations of the preceding Hellenic Civilization within whose bosom Christianity had made its first appearance. It is true that the Western and Byzantine civilizations are Hellenistic, but they are distinguished from the Hellenic Civilization itself by being also Christian, and Christian from the start.

Perhaps the closest parallel to the history of Christianity at the western end of the Old World is the history of the Mahayanian version of Buddhism at the eastern end of it. The source of the Mahayana's inspiration, like the source of Christianity's, was foreign to the world in which the rising religion made its fortune. Christianity made its fortune in the Hellenic World but drew its inspiration from a Syriac source; the Mahayana made its fortune in the Sinic World but drew its inspiration from an Indian source. Again, the Mahayana made its way among the proletariat of the Sinic society, in the sense that it attracted native Chinese who were in revolt against the Confucian tradition and barbarian invaders who were suspicious of it.[1] Furthermore, the progress of the Mahayana evoked a counter-church, the Taoist Church, which was remarkably similar to the Neoplatonist Church in being constructed out of a native philosophy to combat a foreign religion and in trying to steal

---

[1] 'Buddhism commended itself to the [barbarian] rulers because it was not Chinese' (A. F. Wright: 'Buddhism and Chinese Culture: Phases of Interaction', in *Journal of Asian Studies*, vol. xvii, No. 1 (November, 1957), pp. 17–42, on p. 28; idem: *Buddhism in Chinese History* (1959), p. 57). Shih Hu, a barbarian ruler of the later Chao Dynasty, remarked in an edict that 'Buddha, being a barbarian god, is the very one we should worship' (Wright, 'Buddhism and Chinese Culture', p. 28). W. Altree points out (in *Toynbee and History*, pp. 260–1) that in China 'Buddhism received its support from emperors, scholars, and men of affairs', and on this ground he contests my description of it as being a proletarian movement. This is also contested by K. D. Erdmann (loc. cit., p. 226). Altree and Erdmann have not, however, taken the point, made by Wright (*Buddhism in Chinese History*, p. 44), that, during the three centuries of political division (*circa* A.D. 300–600), Chinese civilization developed on different lines in the South and in the North, so that Buddhism had to adapt itself in China to two evolving cultures. In the South, during this age, an aristocracy was in political control (ibid., pp. 51–52); and Buddhism did here take its social impress from its aristocratic patrons. In the North, on the other hand, Buddhism 'cut across class lines and helped to unite a divided society' (ibid., p. 59). In the North the peasantry was converted to Buddhism *en masse* (ibid., p. 58). It is also significant, however, that 'an overwhelming majority of the literate class' stayed in the North (ibid., p. 55), in spite of the adverseness of conditions for them there under barbarian rule, and maintained themselves there in sufficient numbers to be able to reassert their power as soon as the opportunity came.

this foreign religion's thunder by imitating those features of it that made it attractive.[1] These resemblances between the Mahayana and Christianity are impressive; but beyond this point the histories of the two religions do not any longer run parallel.[2]

In the Western and Byzantine worlds Christianity won a monopoly which it retained for centuries, even if it is losing it now. The Neoplatonist counter-church, as well as the four established Hellenic philosophies—Platonism, Aristotelianism, Stoicism, Epicureanism—have all been stone-dead by now for at least fourteen hundred years. Hellenism has survived only in so far as Christianity chose to incorporate it into itself. Byzantine and Western attempts at renaissances of Hellenism drawn direct from the fountain-head have been superficial and ephemeral. In so far as the Western and Byzantine societies are now ceasing to be Christian, they are still inescapably ex-Christian. Their cultural heritage is so thoroughly saturated with Christianity that it is impossible for them to disengage themselves from their Christian past (as is demonstrated, for example, by the transparentness of the Communist ideology's Judaeo-Christian origins). In Eastern Asia history has run a less revolutionary course. Here the Mahayana never succeeded, even at the height of its vigour and power,[3] in driving off the field either the

---

[1] The Taoist counter-church differed, however, from the Neoplatonist counter-church in representing a popular movement of revolt against a decadent Confucian official regime (see, for example, Wright, 'Buddhism and Chinese Culture', p. 20; *Buddhism in Chinese History*, pp. 26–30), whereas Neoplatonism was the creation of a 'highbrow' minority. This is one of the reasons why Taoism survived, while Neoplatonism went under.

[2] 'The role of Buddhism in China is not fully comparable to that of Christianity in Europe' (M. E. Cameron in *The Pacific Historical Review*, vol. viii, No. 4 (December, 1939), p. 406). The Rev. E. R. Hardy Jr. queries whether I do not 'look too eagerly for a period sometime when China was Buddhist in the same way that mediaeval Europe was Catholic' (*The Intent of Toynbee's History: A Cooperative Appraisal*).

[3] At its height, the vigour and power of the Mahayana in China was so great that, to a Western observer, it is surprising that in the end the Mahayana should have failed to win the decisive and definitive victory that Christianity did win in the Byzantine World and in the West. Buddhism interacted with the indigenous Sinic culture at all levels, among the peasantry as well as among the élite (Wright, 'Buddhism and Chinese Culture', p. 18). The Buddhist village clergy were recruited from the peasantry and remained in touch with it, and 'Buddhism became deeply interwoven with common life in the North' (ibid., p. 30). Under the Sui and T'ang regimes the domesticated elements of Buddhism were accepted (pp. 31–32), and in the T'ang Age, in spite of an archaistic revival of Confucianism, 'Buddhism remained the dominant intellectual, spiritual, and aesthetic interest of the educated' (p. 33). Metropolitan Buddhist clerics and government officials were social equals (p. 34). In the T'ang Age Buddhism was also practised by the peasantry *en masse*. 'For the peasantry, as for the gentry, Buddhism became an accepted part of individual and group life' (p. 34). Original and distinctively Chinese schools of Buddhism emerged: e.g. the 'Pure Land' school (Amidism), Ch'an (in Japanese, Zen), and T'ien-t'ai (in Japanese, Tendai) (pp. 34–36). On this evidence, Buddhism in China might have seemed to be carrying all before it, as Christianity did in the Byzantine and Western worlds.

From first to last, however, Buddhism had two serious handicaps to contend with, one political and the other intellectual. Chinese governments, even at their nadir, were jealous of possible rival authorities and were efficient enough to be able to take measures for keeping them in check. The northern governments' inclination towards Buddhism did not deter them from setting up a Buddhist clerical bureaucracy, responsible to the Crown, for keeping Buddhist institutions and property under the control of the state; and, in A.D. 446–52 and A.D. 574–8, attempts were made to impose drastic restrictions on Buddhist organizations and activities (*Buddhism in Chinese History*, pp. 60–61). These attempts ended in failure; yet the state's relation to Buddhism in the North was closer to Caesaro-papism than it was in the South (ibid., p. 62). After the reunification of China the device of setting the Buddhist hierarchy to control itself on the state's behalf was taken over by the Sui and T'ang regimes (ibid., p. 68; 'Buddhism and Chinese Culture',

Taoist counter-church or Confucianism, which was the established Sinic philosophy.[1] In China at the opening of the twentieth century Confucianism and Taoism, as well as the Mahayana, were still alive, and this was more than eighteen hundred years after the Mahayana had made its first lodgement in China, and more than a thousand years since the end of the Mahayana's partial ascendancy, which had lasted from the break-up of the United (Western) Chin (Tsin) regime early in the fourth century of the Christian Era down to the official persecution of Buddhism in A.D. 842–5.[2]

Taoism held its own against the Mahayana; Confucianism regained the upper hand over it. Confucianism had had a monopoly of being the official philosophy of the civil service of the Sinic universal state since the reign of the Prior Han Emperor Wu-ti (140 B.C.–87 B.C.). In the age of the Posterior Han Dynasty (A.D. 25–220) the Confucian-educated land-owning gentry, from which the civil service was recruited, had established its ascendancy in the Sinic society;[3] and, from that time onwards till the abandonment in A.D. 1905 of the periodical examinations in the Confucian classics for candidates for entry into the civil service, this gentry kept itself in being.[4] In the fourth, fifth, and sixth centuries, when the North was under the rule of Eurasian Nomad barbarians, the Confucian-educated indigenous Chinese gentry had an inviolate citadel in the South, which had been conquered and annexed by the Han Empire just at the time when Confucianism had been established as the official philosophy of the Sinic universal state. During the next four

---

p. 33). Under the T'ang, active persecution of Buddhism was resumed, and this time more effectively, in A.D. 842–5. Buddhism's intellectual handicap in China was even more formidable than its political one. The contrast between the structures of the Chinese and Sanskrit languages, and between the traditional styles of the two literatures, was extreme (*Buddhism in Chinese History*, p. 33). The propagators of Buddhism in China 'all had a common inclination to graft the alien on to native roots' (ibid., p. 40). In China, Sanskrit never became a 'church language'. 'Most, if not all, of the seminal thinkers and founders of schools of Chinese Buddhism knew only Chinese' (ibid., p. 76).

[1] So far from that, the indigenous ideologies 'spoiled the Egyptians'. In the encounter between them and the Mahayana, 'the Taoists stole its ritual and the Neo-Confucians its philosophy' (V. K. Ting, quoted by Cameron, loc. cit., p. 408). From the fifth century of the Christian Era onwards, popular Taoism gradually ousted popular Buddhism by copying it (*Buddhism in Chinese History*, pp. 97–98). From about A.D. 900 onwards elements of Buddhism were appropriated by the Sinic culture by being fitted into the framework of the Confucian philosophy (Wright, *Buddhism in Chinese History*, pp. 89–90; 'Buddhism and Chinese Culture', pp. 38–39). The Neo-Confucian school gleaned 'from the Confucian tradition those ideas and formulae which answered, on the authority of native philosophers, many of the questions which Buddhism had raised in men's minds' (ibid., p. 38). Wright (ibid., p. 39) quotes G. E. Sargent for the view that 'Neo-Confucianism constitutes less an autonomous system than a complex of responses to Buddhist theories.' In fact the Neo-Confucians 'proved to be in many ways the captives of the tradition they sought to replace' (*Buddhism in Chinese History*, p. 90). Wright agrees that Wang Yang-ming was truly a Buddhist in disguise; Wang's philosophy was Ch'an Buddhism in Confucian dress; but Wright comments that this Confucian disguise was all-important (ibid., pp. 91–92; 'Buddhism and Chinese Culture', p. 39).

[2] After that, Buddhism was never again regarded as being an essential adjunct of state power and 'Buddhist ideas ceased to be the common coin of intellectual life', while Taoism made inroads on popular Buddhism (Wright, 'Buddhism and Chinese Culture', p. 38).

[3] See B. Watson: *Ssu-ma Ch'ien, Grand Historian of China*, pp. 37–38; A. F. Wright: *Buddhism in Chinese History*, p. 9.

[4] 'By the Later Han, the number of students enrolled in the State University had grown to over 30,000. It was from this group that officials were appointed' (A. F. Wright: *Buddhism in Chinese History*, p. 15).

hundred years the South had been opened up and Sinified just sufficiently to provide an asylum for the traditional Chinese regime in its hour of need.[1] In the thirteenth century the Mongol barbarians conquered the whole of China, and Tongking and Upper Burma as well. But even without a southern citadel the gentry survived once again. Their close-knit network of family connexions was an invisible citadel in itself; and this, combined with a monopoly of the understanding of China's *arcana imperii*, made them indispensable and therefore invincible. The fourth-century barbarian rulers in the North tried to govern their Chinese subjects through the agency of Taoist and Buddhist administrators; the Mongols imported Muslim and Christian administrators;[2] but, sooner or later, all rulers of China before the Westernizing revolution of A.D. 1911 had to call in the Confucian-educated native Chinese gentry to make the wheels of public administration go on turning, however unsympathetic the rulers of the day may

[1] The importance, in Chinese history, of this southern citadel has been noticed in this Study already in vii. 357, footnote 1, and in ix. 655–7, 670–1, 675. In these passages I have recognized that the citadel enabled the gentry to survive and so eventually to re-emerge and recapture the administration of a reconstituted Sinic universal state. Cameron has pointed out (loc. cit., p. 409) that at the close of the Han Age the South, though now politically part of China, was culturally virgin soil, and that it was the great migration to the South under pressure of the barbarian invasions of the North in the fourth century of the Christian Era that led to the South's being culturally assimilated. As she truly observes, the existence of this city of refuge in the South made the maintenance of cultural unity possible, and this accounts for the affinity of the T'ang culture with the Han culture.

Even so, the continuity was maintained only with difficulty. Wright points out that during the years A.D. 317–589, during which China was politically divided, 'two widely different cultures developed in North and South' ('Buddhism and Chinese Culture', p. 24; *Buddhism in Chinese History*, pp. 43–44). The members of the ruling class who fled to the South 'found themselves in a rich but recently colonial area, much of it still populated by aborigines. They felt themselves exiles and behaved like émigrés; their mood was a compound of chagrin, self-pity, and deep self-doubt' ('Buddhism and Chinese Culture', pp. 24–25). 'In climate, landscape, crops, diet, and architecture', the South 'contrasted sharply with the northern plains on which their ancestors had begun to shape a distinctive Chinese civilization' (*Buddhism in Chinese History*, p. 43). The maze of waterways in the Hwai and Yangtse basins saved the southern citadel of Sinism from being overrun by the pursuing Nomad cavalry, but not from being exposed to the infiltration of the invading Indian religion. 'Many of the leading members [of the emigration] were born members of the aristocracy; they tended to move from "Confucian" basic education to an interest in neo-Taoism, and thence to Buddhism' ('Buddhism and Chinese Culture', p. 25). Neo-Taoism fitted into the South China landscape (*Buddhism in Chinese History*, p. 45). It opened the way for Buddhism by breaking the shell of Confucianism and by raising questions that could not be answered from the Taoist scriptures (ibid., p. 46). The virtuous but aristocratic and worldly hero of contemporary Indian Buddhism, Vimalakīrti, became for them the ideal hero, outshining the ideals of the Confucian gentleman and the Taoist sage (ibid., p. 52; 'Buddhism and Chinese Culture', p. 25). A new environment and a new religion worked together to produce cultural change. The emigrant society in the South made new contributions to Chinese culture: calligraphy, landscape painting, poetry, the drama, the novel, Neo-Confucianism, critical scholarship (Cameron, loc. cit., pp. 410–11). There is a Chinese saying that, 'with the southward migration, philosophy began' (ibid., p. 411). All this is like the effect on present-day Chinese civilization of the westward migration of the 'intellectuals' in A.D. 1936–45 under pressure of the invading Japanese armies.

Thus the cultural continuity which the existence of the southern citadel made possible in the fourth, fifth, and sixth centuries was a continuity shot through with change, rather than continuity pure and simple. Even so, it presents a contrast to what happened at the opposite end of the Old World after the barbarian invasions of the Roman Empire. Hellenism found no comparable citadel—for instance, not in Byzantine Anatolia, which was repeatedly overrun by Persians and Arabs and was partly repopulated by immigrant Armenians and Slavs. Consequently there was no comparable perpetuation of the Hellenic Civilization.

[2] e.g. Sayyid Ejell and the Polos.

have been towards Confucianism, and however reluctant they may have been to place themselves in the gentry's hands.[1]

Though I happen to have been born in a former province of the Roman Empire, I was born there too late to have a chance of meeting a Stoic-educated Roman civil servant in the flesh. It would already have been too late in Britain if I had been born there, not in A.D. 1889, but in A.D. 489. But, if I had been born in 1889 in China, I should have seen Confucian-educated civil servants still administering the Sinic universal state. This universal state, the traditional system of administering it, the civil service which knew how to make the system work, and the Confucian-educated gentry that was the civil service's perennial source of recruitment constituted, together, one single great integrated institution. The continuity of this institution may be held to have counted for more than even the most violent of the breaches in the continuity of other elements of civilization in China; and, on this showing, my critics will have been right in maintaining that, notwithstanding the conformity of Chinese history to my Hellenic model down to, and including, the unitary regime of the Ch'in (Ts'in) and Han dynasties, this is not enough to justify my provisional thesis that the history of civilization in China since the interregnum following the fall of the Han Empire has been the history of a new civilization,[2] in the sense in which the history of the West, since the interregnum following the fall of the Roman Empire, has been a new chapter of history that cannot be written off as being nothing but a continuation of the history of the Hellenic Civilization.

A denial of the separateness of the Western and Byzantine civiliza-

---

[1] 'The decisive factor' in the decline of Buddhism in China 'was the revival of the native tradition of Confucianism by an important segment of the Chinese élite. The Sui founder [Sui Wen-ti, originally Yang Chien] regarded Confucian teachings as arid and boring; many of the T'ang monarchs were personally Buddhists or Taoists. Yet from the time of reunification onwards the rulers adopted more and more of those measures of traditional Chinese statecraft which are usually associated with Confucianism; neither Taoism nor Buddhism had developed any such arsenal of social and political formulae. And one of the measures which [were] taken was the restoration of the examination system for the recruitment of officials. The content of the examination questions was, throughout most of the T'ang, intellectually trivial, anachronistic, and—since Confucian texts represented many stages of China's philosophical development—remarkably heterogeneous. Yet, from the beginning of the seventh century, young men were studying these texts in the hope of advancement, even though their intellectual interests might be in Buddhism or Taoism' (Wright: 'Buddhism and Chinese Culture', pp. 37–38; Cp. *Buddhism in Chinese History*, pp. 66, 86, 87).
As the same scholar puts it in another study, Sui ideology appealed to the ranking values of Buddhism and Taoism and to the residual values of endemic Confucianism (A. F. Wright: 'The Formation of Sui Ideology, 581–604', in *Chinese Thought and Institutions*, ed. by J. K. Fairbank (Chicago 1957, University of Chicago Press, pp. 71–104 and 352–63), on p. 73). Yang Chien was born in a Buddhist temple and was educated by a Buddhist monk up to the age of thirteen (ibid., p. 77). His wife, too, was a devout Buddhist (ibid., p. 78). The pair used to attend Buddhist services every night (p. 78). After his achievement of political reunification in A.D. 589, Yang Chien still relied chiefly on Buddhism (p. 93). Yet at the beginning of his reign he made use of Confucianism to consolidate his rule (p. 88), and thereby opened the door for the progressive re-establishment of a Confucian regime at Buddhism's expense. The T'ang emperors, in their turn, relied on Confucianism, though they preferred Taoism (Cameron, loc. cit., pp. 407–8).
[2] In *Toynbee and History*, p. 266, W. Altree lists, as being common to the two phases of history in China that I have labelled with the names of two different civilizations, the following major elements: 'Confucianism, the highly centralised state, the agrarian economy, the bureaucracy, the aristocracy founded on literary achievement.' Cp. E. Dyason in *The Australian Outlook*, March, 1949, p. 59, and M. S. Bates in *Christianity and Crisis*, vol. 15, No. 4 (21st March, 1955), pp. 27–30 and 32.

tions from the Hellenic Civilization would be the logical consequence of substituting a Sinic model for the Hellenic one that we are applying at the moment.[1] But an interpretation of the history of the western end of the Old World in Sinic terms will demonstrate that the Sinic model is not applicable here, any more than the Hellenic model is applicable to the history of Eastern Asia since the fall of the Han Empire. The divergence between the courses of the two streams of history from this point onwards turns on the difference between the subsequent fortunes of Christianity at the western end of the Old World and of Buddhism in Eastern Asia.

In analysing the interaction between Buddhism and the Sinic Civilization on which it impinged, Wright[2] presents the drama in four acts: a period of preparation (A.D. 65–317); a period in which the invading Indian religion became domesticated in its new Sinic environment (A.D. 317–589); a period in which it won acceptance in the Sinic Society and developed new, and specifically Chinese, schools of Buddhist thought and practice on Chinese soil (A.D. 589–*circa* A.D. 900); and a period in which it has been appropriated[3] by the Sinic Civilization (*circa* A.D. 900 to the present day).

'We find the Chinese returning again and again to the ideal of a monolithic society, economy, and polity, supported and rationalised by a thought system that is wholly consistent with itself and with the institutions it supports. The Han order approximated this ideal, and, in the Sui and the T'ang, Buddhism was more or less successfully integrated into the effort to recapture the Han ideal. Later, however, when circumstances had changed, the Sung synthesis rejected any separate and distinctive Buddhism as in conflict with the ancient holistic ideal of Chinese civilization, and appropriated only such parts of the faith as were compatible with this ideal. . . .'[4]

'Periods of disintegration and the loss of holistic and related ideals are the only periods in which Chinese have shown any responsiveness to alien ideas.'[5]

Let us apply the plot of this Sino-Buddhist drama, as Wright has presented it, to the history of the western end of the Old World, setting the dates forward by 200 years, since the Roman Empire took shape and broke up approximately that much later than the Han Empire. A period of preparation, dated A.D. 265–517, would fit well enough; and a period, dated A.D. 517–789, in which Christianity was domesticated in what had

[1] The unity of both the Byzantine and the Western Civilization with the Hellenic has, in fact, been affirmed by some scholars. E. R. Curtius, for instance, has pleaded for a study of the Hellenic and the Western civilizations as a unity, especially on the plane of literature. The field of literary study ought, Curtius maintains, to be 'from Homer to Goethe' (*Merkur*, 1. Jahrgang, Viertes Heft [Heft 4] (1947), pp. 492–3). But that would require us to ignore the Jewish vein in Western literature, and this is not less potent than the Hellenic vein. The Syriac-Hellenic culture-compost from which the Western Civilization has sprung is so closely compacted and so nicely balanced that it would be unrealistic to treat the Western Civilization or any of its four sisters as being either Hellenic or Judaic exclusively.
[2] In 'Buddhism and Chinese Culture', p. 19.
[3] Wright has chosen this term carefully, and insists on its exact meaning. 'The appropriation of Buddhism was not a process of "absorption" in the sense of swallowing up, assimilation without a trace' (*Buddhism in Chinese History*, p. 107. Cp. p. 125).
[4] Wright: ibid., pp. 123–4.   [5] Ibid., p. 124.

been the Hellenic World, would also pass muster. A period dated A.D. 789–*circa* A.D. 1100, in which Christianity was fully accepted and began to put forth new shoots, seems to fit extremely well. But what shall we say of a period, running from *circa* A.D. 1100 to the present day, in which Christianity is 'appropriated' by a resurgent Hellenic Civilization? We cannot bring this last of the four transferred Sinic formulae into any relation with the Western historical facts, even when we have made the most that can be made of the twelfth-century Western philosophical renaissance of Hellenism and the fifteenth-century Western literary, artistic, and political one. No presentation of Western history can make sense of the proposition that, in the course of the last eight and a half centuries, Christianity has been appropriated by the Hellenic Civilization on which it impinged in the days of the Roman Empire; for, whatever may have happened to Christianity during this latest age, it is certain that the Hellenic Civilization was extinct long before the beginning of the twelfth century. At the western end of the Old World the present age is a Post-Hellenic age. It is the age of two Hellenistic Christian or ex-Christian civilizations. It is evident that the Sinic model does not fit either the history of Christianity or the history of civilization at the western end of the Old World since the fall of the Roman Empire any better than the Hellenic model fits the history of Buddhism and the history of civilization in Eastern Asia since the fall of the Han Empire. In this chapter of history the two regions display two different historical configurations. In Eastern Asia continuity prevails, on the whole, over discontinuity; at the other end of the Old World it is the other way round.

This issue of continuity versus discontinuity is raised by the contrast between Christianity's triumph in the former domain of the Hellenic Civilization and Buddhism's failure to achieve the same apparently manifest destiny in Eastern Asia. The same issue is raised in regard to the history of civilization in India by a metamorphosis of indigenous Indian religion which was so revolutionary as to be comparable to the introduction of foreign religions—the Mahayana and Christianity—into China and the Hellenic World.

In the course of the last two centuries B.C. and the early centuries of the Christian Era, Indian religion underwent a transformation like the contemporary transformation of the Buddhist philosophy into the Mahayana. The religion that had been introduced into India by her Aryan invaders at some time during the latter part of the second millennium B.C. had much in common with the religion of the Aryas' kinsmen who had invaded Europe. The Aryan pantheon resembled the Hellenic: it was imagined in the likeness of a barbarian war-band. The Aryan religious ritual resembled the Roman: what mattered was correct procedure—the right form of words and the right physical gestures. The worshippers' approach to the gods was magical, or, in so far as it was rationalized, legalistic. But, before the close of the first millennium of the Christian Era, the Indian religious landscape had changed out of all recognition. The Aryan religious scriptures, while still nominally sacrosanct and authoritative, had practically been shelved in favour of what purported to be no more than a commentary but was virtually a new canon. The gods were now represented in visual form in graven images, as the Buddha and the bodhisattvas had been represented since the irruption of the Hellenic Civilization into India in 183 B.C. after the fall of the Maurya Empire. These images of the gods were eventually housed in temples; and the gods were no longer conceived of as being a troop of superhuman military adventurers. The latter-day Hindu gods, whether they are survivors of the Aryan pantheon or revenants from the Pre-Aryan world of the Indus Culture, are awe-inspiring individual figures, each representing some facet of Absolute Reality. The relation between each of them and her or his worshippers is a personal one which is highly charged with emotion. The god is a fount of grace and the worshipper is the god's devotee. It is, in fact, the relation that, in the Buddhist fold, grew up simultaneously between the devotee and his chosen bodhisattva in the course of the evolution of the Mahayana.

This was a change of religious climate in India that was of the same order of magnitude as the change produced in Eastern Asia by the arrival of the Mahayana and at the western end of the Old World by the arrival of Christianity. Was the consequent break of historical continuity in India great enough to warrant us in regarding what followed as being the history of a new civilization affiliated to, but distinct from, the antecedent Indic Civilization, as the Byzantine and Western Christian civilizations are distinct from, though affiliated to, the Hellenic Civilization? Or shall we judge that in India, as in China, the break in continuity, while comparable, as far as it went, to the break separating the Hellenic Civilization from its successors, was more than offset by the survival of elements of the antecedent culture which managed to weather the religious revolution? In the history of civilization in China continuity prevailed over discontinuity, as we have seen, owing to the survival of a social class with a potent cultural heritage: the Confucian-educated gentry which was a potential seminary for civil servants capable of rehabilitating the Sinic universal state that had originally been established by the Ch'in (Ts'in) and Han dynasties. If we apply this Chinese clue to a further examination of Indian history, we shall find that, in India as in China, historical continuity was maintained by the survival of a social class occupying a key position.

In Indian society the master activity was not the civil administration, as it was in Chinese society; it was the religious ministry. The Brahman caste was therefore the Indian counterpart of the Chinese Confucian-educated gentry; and the Brahmans managed to maintain their monopoly of the religious ministry in India in spite of the radical transformation of the spirit, as well as the practice, of Indian religion in the course of a millennium running from the beginning of the second century B.C. In view of this parallel between Indian and Chinese history at this stage, it will perhaps be prudent to suspend my provisional division of the history of India into the histories of two civilizations, one following the other. There is perhaps more to be said in favour of this division in the Indian case than there is in the Chinese. We have seen that, in

addition to the religious revolution which Indian history has in common
with Chinese history and with my Hellenic model, the political configuration of the Hellenic model—disunity eventually replaced by unity
as a result of a long series of devastating wars—recurs in Indian history
in the chapter following the religious revolution, in contrast to the
corresponding chapter of Chinese history, which does not conform to
the Hellenic pattern, but takes an Egyptiac course. All the same, the
maintenance of the Brahmans' monopoly of the religious ministry gives
Indian history a continuity,[1] throughout the period running from the
Aryan invasion to the impact of the West, which is comparable to the
continuity of Chinese history since the rise of the Confucian-educated
gentry, and which has no parallel in the history of the western end of the
Old World.

In 1930, when I was writing the first volume of this book, I believed,
on the authority of a leading Egyptologist, J. H. Breasted, that the
history of the Egyptiac Civilization afforded, in the worship of Osiris,
an example of a religious movement which closely resembled the history
of Christianity.[2] In the worship of Osiris 'we are confronted', according
to Breasted,[3] 'by a religion of the people, which made a strong appeal to
the individual believer'—in contrast to the worship of Re the sun-god of
Heliopolis, whose worship was part of the prerogative of Pharaoh and
his court. Re was believed to bestow immortality on Pharaoh and his
immediate entourage at the price of the building of pyramids. The
labour required for this was a grievous burden on the people's shoulders,
and it brought the labourers no return in the shape of immortality,
which, for Egyptians of all ranks, was the supreme goal of human
endeavours. The people gave their devotion to Osiris because he offered
the possibility of immortality for all men. The Osirian religion, as presented by Breasted, has a striking resemblance to Christianity in its
popular appeal; and the resemblance would be still closer if it were
proven that the Osirian religion was not indigenous in Egypt but was a
version of the Sumeric worship of Tammuz.

However that may be, the surviving Egyptiac literature of the age of
the Middle Empire does testify that, in the latter days of the Old
Kingdom, there had been a 'secession of the proletariat' in the sense in
which the term is used in this Study. Later evidence—for instance, the
Book of the Dead—also testifies that eventually the people did achieve
their ambition of securing a possibility of immortality for all men, and
achieved it through the worship of Osiris. Breasted's successors have,
however, now rejected Breasted's theses that the Osirian religion was
originally a specifically popular one, that there was an opposition, in the
latter days of the Old Kingdom, between the worship of Osiris and the
worship of Re, and that this religious conflict was the reflection of a

---

[1] The Rev. E. R. Hardy, Jr. queries whether I do not 'exaggerate the difference
between modern Hinduism and previous stages of Indian religion' (*The Intent of Toynbee's History: A Cooperative Appraisal*).
[2] See p. 95, footnote 1. Breasted's interpretation of this chapter of the religious
history of the Egyptiac World is expounded in *The Development of Religion and Thought
in Ancient Egypt* (London 1912, Hodder & Stoughton).
[3] Op. cit., p. 140, quoted in the present work in i. 141.

social one.[1] On this now current interpretation of Egyptiac religious history, my Hellenic model does not fit the Egyptiac facts as closely as it would fit them if Breasted's account of them still held the field.

In analysing my Hellenic model I isolated two further elements. One of these was the barbarians, with their gift for epic poetry, their taste for adopting higher religions in heretical forms, and their failure to make substantial contributions to the creation of new civilizations. The other element was renaissances. In contrast to the element in our Hellenic model represented by the role of Christianity as the chrysalis of new civilizations, barbarians and renaissances occur frequently in non-Hellenic contexts. I have surveyed their occurrences already,[2] and therefore need not repeat the operation here.

Bagby has applied his Hellenic and Western pattern of an Age of Faith followed by an Age of Reason to the histories of the other civilizations on his list. His findings[3] are that this pattern is plainly visible in early Chinese (in my terminology, 'Sinic') history and is also visible in early Indian ('Indic') history—in this case with a tendency towards over-elaboration, towards the close of the Age of Faith, which comes closer to the Western version of the pattern than to the Hellenic and Sinic versions. He finds traces of the process of rationalization in the histories of the Sumero-Akkadian, Egyptiac, Andean, and Middle American civilizations.[4]

It will now be evident that the different elements in my Hellenic model are not all of equal service as keys for elucidating uniformities in the configuration of the histories of civilizations. In the cases of four elements out of my five, and of Bagby's further element, the Hellenic pattern is reproduced both closely and frequently. For instance, the process of rationalization indisputably occurred in the histories of the Western, Sinic, Andean, and Middle American civilizations. Renaissances on the pattern of the renaissances of Hellenism in the Western and Byzantine worlds indisputably occurred in the later phases of the history of civilization in China, India, the Tigris-Euphrates basin, and Egypt, whether we interpret these later phases as being the histories of separate civilizations or whether we interpret them as being merely a

[1] This change of view among Egyptologists has been noticed already on p. 95, footnote 1. Breasted's view, as reproduced by me, is criticized by L. Thorndike in *The Journal of Modern History*, vol. vii, No. 3 (September, 1935), pp. 315–17, and by H. Frankfort in *The Birth of Civilization in the Near East*, p. 27.

[2] For barbarians, see v. 194–337 and viii. 1–87; for renaissances, see ix. 1–166.

[3] See *Culture and History*, p. 212.

[4] I agree with these findings, and the correspondences seem to be both close and numerous enough to warrant our regarding this pattern as being one of the established uniformities in the configuration of the histories of civilizations. Bagby finds the same pattern in the history of his 'Near Eastern' (i.e. Spengler's 'Magian') Civilization. He sees here an age of faith in the first five centuries of the Christian Era, marked by Early Christianity, Neoplatonism, and the phases of Judaism and of Zoroastrianism that find their respective expressions in the Talmud and the Zend. His age of reason in this case is ushered in by the epiphany of Islam, whose role he equates with Protestant Christianity's in Western history, and it comes to maturity with the Islamic World's reception of Hellenic science and philosophy. Evidently there is something to be said for this interpretation. But, if we accept it, we shall have, on the analogy of it, to distinguish an age of faith and a subsequent age of reason within the medieval age of Western history, though this, as Bagby sees it, is all one age of faith. The reception of Aristotle in the medieval West was no less, and no more, a triumph of reason than the previous reception of him in Dār-al-Islām.

continuation of the preceding phase in each case. Barbarians break out in other times of trouble besides the Hellenic and break through the frontiers of other universal states besides the Roman Empire. The political configuration of our Hellenic model recurs, as we have already reckoned, in the histories of at least nine other civilizations.[1] On the other hand, this element in our Hellenic model entirely fails, as we have seen, to fit the political history of the Egyptiac World. The configuration of Egyptiac political history is not only different; it is antithetical. In Hellenic history the universal state is the last phase; in Egyptiac history it is the first. And, when we come to the procreation of affiliated civilizations through the agency of a higher religion serving as a chrysalis, we find our Hellenic model failing to provide a key more often than it succeeds.[2] This element in the model does recur, as we have seen, in Chinese and Indian history, and perhaps in Egyptiac history too; but, in each of these other instances, the break in continuity does not seem decisive enough to entitle me to confirm my provisional interpretation of what comes after the break as being the history of a new civilization.

4. A CHINESE ALTERNATIVE MODEL FOR CIVILIZATIONS

We have now carried out our re-examination of the applicability of the Hellenic model as a key to the interpretation of the histories of other civilizations; and, as a result, the use of this model in previous volumes of this book has, I should say, vindicated itself. The Hellenic model evidently does throw considerable light on the historical structure of civilizations as a species; and the results of the re-examination indicate, it seems to me, that I have not gone astray in employing the model up to its full capacity. I have, however, I should now say, been at fault in having been content, up to this point, to operate with the Hellenic model only. Though this particular key has opened many doors, it has not proved omnicompetent. We have seen, for example, that it has not opened the door to an understanding of the structure of Egyptiac history. This and other cases in which it has proved not to fit ought to have made me aware of its limitations and to have led me, not to lose confidence in the results obtained with this key, as far as these results go, but to try other keys as well.[3] 'The paranoiac or monomaniac has to fit all phenomena to a pet idea.'[4] I do not want to cast myself for this self-defeating role. Perhaps I can avoid it if I take to heart two pieces of good advice that have been offered to me by W. Kaufmann.[5] He warns me to pay attention to evidence that appears to contradict my theories, and to test my theories, where the evidence does seem to me to bear them

---

[1] See p. 173.
[2] T. A. Sumberg questions 'whether churches are universally the link between the death and birth of related civilizations' (*Social Research*, vol. 14, No. 3 (September, 1947), pp. 267–84).
[3] This point has been taken by the Rev. E. R. Hardy Jr. 'One wonders whether a scholar starting on the same enterprise from a Chinese or Indian, or even an Islamic, perspective might not have made something quite different and equally true' (*The Intent of Toynbee's History: A Cooperative Appraisal*).
[4] A. L. Kroeber: *The Nature of Culture*, pp. 81–82.
[5] In *Toynbee and History*, p. 211. Cp. R. L. Shinn: *Christianity and the Problem of History*, p. 15.

out, by considering whether the same evidence may not also bear out alternative constructions.[1] I will also recall a maxim of Cohen's that I have quoted already in a different context.[2]

'The safeguard against bias is . . . to explore one's preconceptions, to make them explicit, to consider their alternatives, and thus to multiply the number of hypotheses available for the apprehension of historical significance.'[3]

Acting on these counsels in the present case means mounting other models besides the Hellenic-Byzantine-Western model and seeing what results we obtain by applying these, in turn, to the same body of evidence. Theoretically the Egyptiac model might be the most illuminating, since the Egyptiac Civilization is apparently the most recalcitrant of all to attempts to interpret its history in Hellenic terms. This choice, however, would have a practical drawback. The Egyptiac culture became extinct as long ago as the fourth or fifth century of the Christian Era. An observer looking at history from the Egyptiac standpoint would therefore not be in a position to take into account the fifteen or sixteen hundred years that have elapsed since then. It is true that he would have more than double that length of time to survey in looking backwards from the evening of the Egyptiac Civilization to its dawn. All the same, his historical horizon would be a restricted one by comparison with the horizon of a present-day observer's field of vision. This tells in favour of retaining a present-day standpoint; and, if we are to shift our ground from a Western present-day standpoint to some other, a Chinese present-day standpoint is perhaps the most promising for our purpose.

Let me suppose, for instance, that China, not England, had been my own birthplace in A.D. 1889. I should then have had the Confucian equivalent of an Hellenic classical education. After having prepared myself to sit for the civil service examination, I should probably have been just too late to try my fortune before the abolition of this 1,300-years-old institution in A.D. 1905. But I should already have been drilled in the classics so thoroughly that they would have governed my outlook ever since, whatever might have been my experience since the Revolution of A.D. 1911. My picture of world history would, in fact, have been determined by my picture of Chinese history, and I should have seen Chinese history through the eyes of the first oecumenical Chinese historian, Ssu-ma Ch'ien (*vivebat circa* 145 B.C.–90 B.C.) and his continuators the compilers of the successive dynastic histories.

Looking at current events and the long vista of their antecedents through these classically trained eyes, I should not have been taken by surprise when, in 1911, the unitary regime of the Ch'ing (Manchu) dynasty, under which China had been living by then for more than a quarter of a millennium, dissolved into anarchy, nor again when, in 1948–9, this bout of anarchy was brought to an end by the establishment of another unitary regime. Both these revolutionary events would have

---

[1] Cp. Sir Llewellyn Woodward's observations quoted on p. 168.
[2] See p. 60, footnote 2.
[3] M. R. Cohen: *The Meaning of Human History*, p. 80. Cp. p. 115.

conformed to the age-old pattern of Chinese history as this had been presented by Ssu-ma Ch'ien and his successors. In their view, which would consequently have been my view, Chinese history had run in a rhythmical series of alternations between bouts of unity and order and bouts of disunity and anarchy. No bout of either kind had ever come to stay; and it could be predicted with confidence that halcyon days would give way to rough weather, and that the roughest weather would give way in its turn, sooner or later, to halcyon days. These predictions could be made by induction from a canonical record that, by A.D. 1911, extended over a span of not much less than five thousand years.[1] An empirical verification of this alternating rhythm in Chinese history would, however, have seemed superfluous to a classically educated mind. The rhythm's presence here—and everywhere—was guaranteed by the fact that it was the fundamental rhythm of the Universe: the perpetual alternation of a Yin state of quiescence with a Yang burst of activity.[2] In the view of the Chinese *Weltanschauung*, the course of non-human nature and the course of human affairs are akin to each other not merely in the general sense that either realm is subject to a set of laws. Their relation to each other is, on this view, much more intimate than that. An identical set of laws governs them both and thereby gears them together.[3]

Looking at history with these Chinese eyes in the nineteen-twenties, when I was making my notes for this book, I should, of course, have taken Chinese, not Hellenic, history as my model, and I should have seen Chinese history as a series of successive realizations of the ideal of a universal state, punctuated by intermediate lapses into disunion and disorder. The phases of both kinds had varied considerably in length, so that, in the field of human history, the Yin-Yang rhythm would be cyclical without having any regular periodicity. The succession of unitary phases ran back from the Ch'ing (Manchu) regime, under which I had been born,[4] to the Ming and the Yüan (Mongol), with intervening bouts of disunion that had been relatively brief. The pre-Yüan bout of disunion had lasted for about 150 years; the preceding unitary Sung regime for 167 years; the bout of disunion before that for about half a century; the unitary T'ang regime, with its Sui overture, for more than three centuries before that; the preceding bout of disunion for about four centuries (reckoning back, beyond the collapse of the United Chin

---

[1] The canon of Chinese history established by Ssu-ma Ch'ien purported to trace the origins of Chinese Civilization back to the early centuries of the third millennium B.C. Recent archaeological research traces these origins back no farther than the thirteenth century B.C., if they are to be equated with the transition, in China, to the Bronze Age from the Neolithic Age.

[2] This point has been taken by the Rev. E. R. Hardy Jr. 'Perhaps . . . the Hindu or Buddhist view of world-cycles is a truer picture of what Indian or Chinese history feels like to the Indian or Chinese observer than our Western and Christian picture of successive stages leading to a definite end' (*The Intent of Toynbee's History: A Cooperative Appraisal*).

[3] Compare the view that became current in the Sumero-Akkadian World at least as early as the eighth century B.C. (see pp. 33–34).

[4] According to the classical Chinese doctrine, I had been born under it wherever my birth-place happened to be, since all the kingdoms of the Earth were satellites of the Middle Kingdom, even if their rulers were unwilling to acknowledge this political verity, or were blankly ignorant of it.

(Tsin), to the collapse of the Posterior Han); the unitary Han regime, with its Ch'in (Ts'in) overture, for about four centuries before that, punctuated by two sharp but short bouts of anarchy in A.D. 9-25 and 207 B.C.-2 B.C.

From the fall of the Ch'ing unitary regime in A.D. 1911 back to the establishment of the Ch'in (Ts'in) unitary regime in 221 B.C., the traditional model of Chinese history corresponds to the historical facts. But, as A. F. Wright has pointed out,[1] this model is a myth created and propagated by the Confucian litterati. They have glozed over cracks, deviations, and tensions, and have ignored radical Chinese critics of the Chinese way of life. 'The result is a self-image of the civilization which has a deceptive symmetry, a self-consistency that belongs to its myth and not to its history.'[2] According to this myth, 'the history of China' has been 'the record of men striving to realise the ideals of the sages'.[3] Simplified images tend to harden from hypotheses into articles of faith,[4] and Chinese traditionalists have cajoled themselves into giving credence to a presentation of the Pre-Han history of China which bears little resemblance to the reality.

We have noticed[5] that, from the Han Age inclusive back to the dawn of the Sinic Civilization, the configuration of Chinese history conforms to the Hellenic model. At the earliest date at which the record of Chinese history comes into clear focus—and this is no earlier than the ninth or eighth century B.C.—China makes her appearance on the scene as a politically disunited world of local states, and the political unity that she eventually attained under the Ch'in (Ts'in) and Han dynasties was the consequence of a long-drawn-out series of ever more devastating interstate wars. Throughout the age preceding the political unification of 221 B.C., China was, however, already a unity on the cultural plane; and on this plane her greatest intellectual creative work was done during the politically catastrophic period of the Contending States, before her political unity was achieved. This was the age of the founders of almost all the schools of Chinese philosophy, including Confucius himself, whose school was eventually canonized as the classical one. Confucius was a conservative. He never dreamed of an effective political unification of the Chinese World. Ch'in Shih Hwang-ti's work would have shocked him; and Han Liu P'ang's modification of it would have pleased him hardly any better. Confucius, like Plato and Aristotle, took political disunity for granted. This authentic configuration of early Chinese history—including the contemporaneity of political disunity and intellectual achievement—bears an unmistakable resemblance to the configuration of early Hellenic history, and differs entirely from the pattern of subsequent Chinese history that has been taken by Chinese scholars since the Han Age as their model for Chinese history as a whole. Consequently, this model could not be applied to early Chinese history

[1] In a paper on 'The Study of Chinese Civilization', presented to the Seminar on the Comparative Study of Civilizations at the Center for Advanced Study in the Behavioral Sciences, Stanford, California, 4th March, 1958, p. 5.
[2] Loc. cit., p. 6. Cp. *Buddhism in Chinese History*, p. 123.
[3] 'The Study of Chinese Civilization', p. 7.
[4] Ibid., **p. 35.**　　　　　　　　　　　　　　　　　　[5] On p. 173.

without doing violence to the facts; and the scholars did this violence rather than renounce their quest of self-consistency and symmetry.

Having correctly observed that the later unitary regimes were conscious and deliberate restorations of the Ch'in (Ts'in)-Han unitary regime, Chinese scholars assumed that this too must have been a restoration of some earlier regime, and accordingly they extrapolated their series of phases of unity, backwards in time, through a Chou and a Shang and a Hsia restoration of an ideal polity supposedly founded by primordial sages. These sages are perhaps gods reduced to human stature; the Hsia regime is legendary, so far as we know; the Shang and Chou regimes were realities; their historicity is attested by surviving material remains of their cultures, including such instructive contemporary documents as the Shang inscriptions on 'oracle bones'. But there is no evidence to suggest that either the Shang or the Chou regime was a polity of the same order as the Ch'in (Ts'in) and Han regimes and their subsequent avatars.[1] Our only sure evidence for conditions in China in the Shang age is that of the artefacts disinterred by modern archaeologists, and these give us no information about the political structure or the territorial extent of the Shang state. As for the Chou, when the curtain rises on the scene of Chinese history, they are no more than *rois fainéants*, like the Japanese Emperors during the seven centuries preceding the Meiji Restoration. Their political suzerainty over the contending local states was nominal. Their authority may have been greater before their disaster in 771 B.C., when a vassal prince combined with a barbarian war-band to sack their capital city. But it is unlikely that, even at the height of their power, the Chou were the rulers of an effective unitary empire comparable to the regime that was established by Ch'in Shih Hwang-ti in 221 B.C.[2] *Pace* the traditional presentation of Chinese history, the effective unification that Shih Hwang-ti achieved and that Liu P'ang salvaged must in truth have been an unprecedented achievement, as the work of Caesar and Augustus was in the Hellenic World.

The traditional presentation of Chinese history would have been impressed upon the mind of a Confucian-educated Chinese scholar born in 1889; and, if, having been born too late to sit for the last of the civil service examinations, he had made his way to one of the new American universities in China and had widened his historical horizon by adding some Western knowledge to his Chinese stock, probably he would still have applied the traditional Chinese model of the course of history in taking his bearings in his extended field of inquiry.

[1] This point has been made on p. 175, footnote 1. Bagby takes the same negative view of them (*Culture and History*, p. 219).

[2] In this point the early history of Japan perhaps comes nearer than the early history of China comes to fitting the traditional Chinese model. From the reorganization of the Japanese imperial regime in A.D. 645, on the pattern of the contemporary T'ang imperial regime in China, down to the triumph of feudalism over the imperial administration in the twelfth century, the Japanese imperial government does seem to have exercised some degree of effective power—though, no doubt, this was a wasting asset and was never anything like so effective as the Tokugawa regime and its successors have been. In copying the contemporary T'ang, the Japanese imperial government was modelling itself on a centralizing regime in contemporary China that certainly worked effectively in its earlier stages. There is no evidence that the Chou dynasty of China in its first phase had any similar model to serve it as a standard.

If he had begun by applying the traditional Chinese model to Egyptiac history, the result would have encouraged him to persevere; for the Chinese model fits the facts of Egyptiac history from beginning to end. In the Egyptiac Old Kingdom we have, at the dawn of history, a unitary regime which is neither legendary like the Hsia nor shadowy like the Chou, but is authentic and substantial. And, from that first beat of the Yin-Yang rhythm in the Old Kingdom, this rhythm marches on through the First Intermediate Period of Egyptiac history, the Middle Empire, the Second Intermediate Period, the New Empire, and a series of revivals of the New Empire in which, as in the corresponding stage of Chinese history, the empire-builders' role comes to be filled more and more frequently by foreigners—in the Egyptiac case, Libyans, Ethiopians, Assyrians, Persians, Macedonians, Romans—with indigenous dynasties putting in an appearance more and more rarely.

If our imaginary Chinese inquirer had turned his attention to the Tigris-Euphrates basin next, he would have found himself, to begin with, in a world divided politically among a number of local states, and he would not have been able to detect the expected rhythm till the rise of the dynasty of Agade; but, from that date onwards, he would have been able to trace a rhythmic alternation of political unifications and disruptions over an area that eventually expanded to embrace some of the Tigris-Euphrates basin's hinterlands. The series of unitary regimes here would run from the dynasty of Agade through the Third Dynasty of Ur, the First Dynasty of Babylon, the Assyrian Empire, the Neobabylonian Empire, the Achaemenian Empire, the Seleucid Monarchy, the Parthian Empire, the Sasanian Empire,[1] the Arab Caliphate, the Caliphate's Saljuq successor-state, the Mongol Il-Khanate, the Timurid Empire, the Safawi Empire, and finally the short-lived empire of Nadir Shah, an Afshar Turkish war-lord who was a veritable reincarnation of Naramsin or Tiglath-Pileser III. By Nadir's day the Sumerian language had been extinct for more than three thousand years and the Akkadian for nearly seventeen hundred years, and their cuneiform script had become a riddle of the Sphinx; but the military and political rhythm which the war-lords of Agade had started up had gone rolling on for more than four thousand years.

Turning from the Tigris-Euphrates basin to India, a Chinese student of the morphology of history might fail, at first glance, to detect here any trace of the Sinic pattern. In India, in contrast to the Tigris-Euphrates basin and its Iranian hinterland, the unitary political regimes are echeloned at long intervals down the corridors of time; and, when they make their appearance, they are short-lived. At first glance Indian history may look like a shapeless welter of disorder. Yet four plateaux stand out above the morass—the Maurya, the Gupta, the Mughal, and the British Raj—and these are enough to certify that the Chinese rhythm is in operation in India too, though here the rhythm labours like the engine of a car ploughing its way through a bog.

If our Chinese surveyor now switches to the western end of the Old

---

[1] The Parthian and Sasanian empires are assigned to a cycle of the history of the Tigris-Euphrates basin by R. Coulborn in *Toynbee and History*, p. 162.

World, he will find himself here in the dilemma that confronted his Chinese predecessors when they had to deal with the age of Chinese history before the unification of China by Ch'in Shih Hwang-ti. Either he must jettison a model derived from the configuration of Chinese history since the epoch-making year 221 B.C., or else he must invent a fictitious history of the pre-Augustan Hellenic World, as Chinese scholarship did invent a fictitious history of the pre-Shih Hwang-ti Sinic World, to fit a pattern to which the authentic configuration of this phase of history cannot be made to conform. A fictitious reconstruction of pre-Augustan Hellenic history on these traditional Chinese lines would have to be made of bricks without straw. The only potential materials would be the brief interlude of unity represented by Philip II of Macedon's League of Corinth, and, before that, a shadowy Minoan and a hardly more substantial Achaean thalassocracy, both of which antedate the dawn of Hellenic history. And, in this reconstruction of early Hellenic history, as in the corresponding reconstruction of early Chinese history, one would have to write off the most signal of the reconstructed civilization's creative intellectual achievements as being by-products of a bout of political disunity which was just one in a series of unfortunate lapses from the normal unitary regime. Evidently the application of the traditional Chinese model would make the same non-sense of early Hellenic history as it makes of early Chinese history.

On the other hand, the model fits well enough if, starting from the Roman Empire, the surveyor moves, not backward, but forward, in time from the year 31 B.C. and keeps his eye fixed on the Empire's central and eastern sections, which were the heart-land of this Hellenic universal state and came to be the seat of the imperial government after its location at Nicomedia by Diocletian in A.D. 284 and at Constantinople by Constantine I in A.D. 324–30. In this heart-land the Yin-Yang rhythm now promptly declares itself. The punctuations of disunity and disorder in A.D. 69 and A.D. 193–7 were repeated and intensified in an agonizing half-century of anarchy running from 235 to 285. The subsequent Diocletianic-Constantinian restoration was followed by a collapse after the imperial army's disastrous defeat by the Goths at Adrianople in 378. But this dangerous reverse, too, was quickly retrieved by a steady recovery in the course of the fifth century. A fresh collapse was brought upon the Hellenic universal state by Justinian I (*imperabat* A.D. 527–65). He overstrained it through his misguided attempt at re-expansion; and this over-exertion was followed by a fresh bout of anarchy, lasting from 602 to 717, which was at least as agonizing, and was twice as long, as the bout in the years 235–85. But in 717 the universal state was restored once more by Leo Syrus; and, after that, unity and order were maintained till 1071; were re-established in 1081; and were maintained again till 1186. The revolt of the Bulgars in that year, and the Western Christians' sack of Constantinople and partition of the East Roman Empire in 1204, precipitated a chaos that lasted for nearly two hundred years. But, in the later decades of the fourteenth century, unity was restored, yet again, by the 'Osmanlis. The new 'Caesar of Rome' (*Qaysar-i-Rum*) re-expanded the restored universal state up to the limits in South-Eastern Europe and in the Tigris-Euphrates basin that had been attained by the Emperor Trajan (*imperabat* A.D. 98–117); and this Turkish Roman Empire maintained itself for some four hundred years (A.D. 1372–1774), with punctuations of disaster and disorder at the turn of the sixteenth and seventeenth centuries and again after the failure, in 1683, of the second Ottoman siege of Vienna. The defeat of the Ottoman Empire in the Russo-Ottoman war of 1768–74 was the beginning of the end. Yet, even after that, there was a rally in the first half of the nineteenth century. In South-Eastern Europe the Ottoman Empire did not finally break up till 1878, and in South-West Asia not till 1918. The last Ottoman Qaysar-i-Rum was deposed—and the office abolished—by the Emperor's own subjects in A.D. 1922, 116 years after the renunciation of the title of Roman Emperor by the last holder of it in the West.

Here, in an epilogue to Hellenic history which has its starting-point in 31 B.C., we have a counterpart of the pattern of Chinese history since 221 B.C. which is almost as exact a replica of it as the course of Egyptiac history is from beginning to end. And in the Levant, as in China, this persistent rhythm does not peter out till a date that, in 1961, was still within living memory. The Hellenic universal state, however, had some backward outlying provinces round the shores of the western basin of the Mediterranean, including Italy and Rome itself, the semi-barbarian city that had been the universal state's political nucleus. To complete our test of the applicability of the Chinese model to the history of the western end of the Old World, we must apply it in the extreme west too; and the experiment will show that here, from A.D. 378 onwards, the Chinese model fails to fit the historical facts as signally as it fails in the Hellenic World as a whole down to 31 B.C. and in China itself down to 221 B.C.

In the West the fifth century of the Christian Era, which was an age of recovery in the central and eastern sections of the Hellenic World, was an age of disintegration that ended, in A.D. 476, in the suppression of the imperial office here and in a nominal reunification of the whole empire under the imperial government at Constantinople. This was mere camouflage for a partition of the western provinces among a number of barbarian successor-states. In the sixth century Justinian—at an excessive cost to the stamina of the universal state's heart-land—turned the Constantinopolitan Government's title into a reality in Italy, part of North-West Africa, and a smaller part of Spain. But this re-expansion of the Hellenic universal state was ephemeral; it was all undone in the course of the two hundred years following Justinian's death in 565; and the West remained disunited and derelict till the later decades of the eighth century, when the Frankish Carolingians restored the empire in the West—as, in the Levant, in the later decades of the fourteenth century, it was restored by the 'Osmanlis.

After the coronation of Charlemagne at Rome on Christmas Day, A.D. 800, the former domain of the Hellenic Civilization harboured two effective states—one centred on Gaul and the other on Anatolia—each of which claimed to be the Hellenic universal state's legitimate representative. This self-contradictory political situation would not perplex a Chinese scholar. In Chinese history it has at least two counterparts in the coexistence of the barbarian northern empire of the Wei with an indigenous southern empire (the Sung, Ch'i and Liang regimes) from A.D. 439 to A.D. 534, and again in the coexistence of the barbarian northern empire of the Kin, followed by the Mongols, with another indigenous southern empire (the Sung) from 1127 to 1279. In China on each of these occasions, the next phase was the re-establishment of unity as a result of an annexation of the south by the north. This was achieved by the Sui in A.D. 589 and by the Mongols (Yüan) in A.D. 1279. With these precedents in mind, a Chinese scholar, coming fresh to Western history, would wait expectantly for a political reunification of the entire Hellenic World in the ninth century of the Christian Era through a Carolingian conquest of the Constantinopolitan Roman Empire.[1] But in the ninth century, as in the fifth, the history of the West obstinately took an un-Chinese and un-Byzantine course.

So far from annexing Anatolia, the Carolingians lamentably failed to maintain their empire in Gaul. The West now went through another bout of political disunity and barbarian invasion; and, since the formal partition of the Carolingian Empire in 843, the reunification of most of the former western provinces of the Empire, which the Carolingians achieved but failed to maintain, has never been repeated effectively. In the West, from 888 to 962, even the title of Roman Emperor was sometimes in abeyance, and the occasional claimants to it were not in effective control of more than fragments of the whole territory. The Empire was restored again, in conformity with the Chinese pattern of history, in 962, when the Saxon Otto I was crowned Emperor at Rome, and it was once more a political reality from that date till the death of the Emperor Frederick II Hohenstaufen in 1250. But even the nominal suzerainty of this medieval Western Roman Empire was never recognized in France, which was the central and the leading country of the Western World—not to speak of Britain, which had not been incorporated in the Carolingian Roman Empire either—and, throughout the three centuries of its more or less effective existence, the nominal authority of 'the Roman Empire of the German People' was nebulous in Burgundia and was perpetually resisted, *de facto*, in Italy. Even in Germany and Lotharingia it was a wasting asset. After the death of Frederick II the Western Roman Empire was a farce. It is true that the title of Emperor was again held in a continuous succession from 1273 to 1806; but, in so far as its holders, in this phase, had any effective power, they had this in virtue of being also rulers of some local Western state, such as Luxembourg-Bohemia in the fourteenth century and the Hapsburg dominions from 1438 onwards. When the Emperor Francis II Hapsburg renounced the title on 6th August, 1806, he was not parting with any of his previous political power. The real basis of his power, which was that of a local ruler, was proclaimed in the solecism 'Hereditary

---

[1] The likenesses and differences between the sequel to the fall of the Han Empire in China and the sequel to the fall of the Roman Empire at the western end of the Old World have been discussed in this book in ix. 649–81.

Emperor of Austria'—a title that Francis II had already assumed on 10 August, 1804.

To apply the traditional Chinese model to the history of the West, we should have to take the Western wraith of the Roman Empire as being the key institution of the Western Civilization, and this would be to make nonsense of Western history, not only during the last century and a half, when even the name of the Roman Empire has been extinct on Western soil, but at least as far back as the disintegration of the Carolingian Roman Empire. The Western Roman Empire is not a key to any of the things that are characteristic or significant in Western history.

The Chinese model is equally inapplicable to the histories of the Middle American and Andean civilizations, which the Hellenic model fits so well. In the Andean World there is no evidence that there had ever been political unity before this was established by the Incas, and the Inca universal state had been in existence for only about forty years[1] by the date when it was overthrown by the Spanish *conquistadores*. In Middle America the Aztec Empire had not yet completed the political unification of its world by the date when it met the same fate at the same hands. The Spanish Viceroyalty of New Spain might perhaps be regarded as being the consummation of the Middle American universal state that the Aztecs had been building up, and the Spanish Viceroyalty of Peru as being a continuation of the Inca universal state in the Andean World. But the Spanish Empire of the Indies broke up into successor-states within three hundred years of its establishment, and there is no indication that the present regime in Latin America, in which this region is partitioned among twenty-one local republics, is an 'intermediate period' which is going to end in the re-establishment of political unity there.

Our survey of the histories of civilizations in terms of the traditional Chinese model has shown that this, like the Hellenic, fails to fit all cases. Indeed, its only perfect fit is its application to Egyptiac history, and this only on condition that we leave the 'prehistoric' age out of account. The traditional Chinese model does not fit the early history of any other civilization, not even that of civilization in China itself. Paradoxically, it can give only a negative account of the age in which its own revered patron-philosopher Confucius lived, though Confucius was a child of his age, besides being an innovator under the guise of an archaist. The traditional Chinese model has to write the Confucian Age off as part of an intermediate period between the Western Chou and the Imperial Ch'in (Ts'in). From the date of the establishment of a universal state onwards, the Chinese model does fit Hellenic and subsequent Byzantine history well, the history of the Tigris-Euphrates basin and Iran passably, the history of India barely. But it does not fit Western, Middle American, or Andean history at all. And, in a pattern that presents history as an alternation of universal states and lapses from them, and ignores both local states and diasporás, there is no place for the Jews. The Jews lost their local state, never managed (as most other peoples have never managed) to become empire-builders, but have managed

[1] See p. 373.

(unlike most other peoples) to preserve their national identity without having a state or even a national home. In world history seen through Chinese spectacles, the Jews would pass unnoticed both in the age of the Prophets and in the age of the Pharisees.

It will be seen that the shortcomings of the Chinese model are at least as great as those of the Hellenic one. What conclusion are we to draw from this? Shall we jettison both models, and dismiss the policy of operating with models as an unprofitable wild-goose-chase? It seems more reasonable to conclude that the Chinese model, like the Hellenic model, is illuminating as far as it goes, and that the two models, looked at in relation to each other, are more than twice as illuminating as each of them is by itself.

The Chinese model has one clear advantage over the Hellenic, and that is its greater generality. This makes it possible to streamline the pattern of history by getting rid of distinctions, generated by the Hellenic model, that are perhaps artificial and superfluous.

For instance, the Hellenic model—at any rate as I have constructed it—distinguishes between several kinds of universal state. There are straightforward specimens (e.g. the Roman Empire in the Hellenic World and the Ch'in-Han Empire in China); there are rehabilitations after interruptions (e.g. the Gupta Empire figures as a rehabilitation of the Maurya Empire, and the Arab Caliphate as a rehabilitation of the Achaemenian Empire); and there are renaissances, when the universal state of an antecedent civilization is conjured up again in the history of an affiliated civilization (e.g. the T'ang Empire, the Carolingian Empire, and the East Roman Empire as reconstituted by Leo Syrus figure as rehabilitations of the Ch'in-Han Empire and the Roman Empire respectively). When we substitute the Chinese for the Hellenic model, these rather tiresome distinctions disappear, and we can treat on a parity, for purposes of comparative study, all states that embrace the whole geographical domain of a civilization. This simplification of the pattern and increase in the number of the specimens of it is a gain for the cause of knowledge and understanding. Gerhard Masur has criticized my list of universal states as being arbitrary.[1] I do not agree with all the particular points that Masur makes, but, in principle, I plead guilty to his charge; and I attribute my error, not to my having used the Hellenic model, but to my having used it exclusively, without also having used the Chinese model, or some other, as a check and a possible corrective.

The Hellenic model also suggests a distinction between three different kinds of 'intermediate period': a 'time of troubles', such as that which occurred in Hellenic history between the breakdown of the Hellenic Civilization and the establishment of the Roman Empire; a lapse in the maintenance of a universal state, as exemplified in the temporary breakdowns of the Roman Empire in A.D. 69, A.D. 192–7, and A.D. 235–85; and an 'interregnum', such as that which occurred between the fall of the Roman Empire and the rise of the Western and Byzantine successors of the Hellenic Civilization. The Chinese model suggests that these

---

[1] In the *Historische Zeitschrift*, Band 177 (1954), pp. 521–2.

three kinds of relatively anarchic interlude should all be treated as so many examples of the 'intermediate period' in the alternating Yin-Yang rhythm.[1] This more general way of looking at them may give us insights into their nature; but here we must be on our guard against being led into effacing distinctions that may be significant and important. The 'time of troubles' which the Hellenic model distinguishes from other anarchic interludes in Hellenic history was not, in fact, an intermediate period between two bouts of a universal state. It was the painful period of transition to a regime of political unity from a previous regime of political disunity that had broken down. This sequence—political dis-unity, breakdown, 'time of troubles', universal state—occurs, as we have seen, in at least nine other instances, including the history of the Sinic Civilization; and even Egyptiac history will perhaps be found to conform to the Hellenic pattern if we take the pre-civilizational age of the history of Egypt into account.

5. AN HELLENO-SINIC STANDARD MODEL FOR CIVILIZATIONS

In fact, the Hellenic model is as widely applicable to the earlier phase in the histories of civilization as the Chinese model is to the later phase; and an improved model can be constructed by combining the later phase according to the Sinic model with the earlier phase according to the Hellenic.[2] This composite model for the histories of civilizations shows these societies starting as unities on the cultural plane without being united on the political plane. This regime is favourable to social and cultural progress; but its price is chronic warfare between the local states; this warfare becomes more intense and more devastating as the society grows in strength; and sooner or later it produces a social break-down which, after a long-drawn-out 'time of troubles', is belatedly retrieved by the establishment of a universal state. This universal state is subject to recurrent lapses into anarchy; but, whether these inter-mediate periods are short or long, they are apt to be surmounted by the restoration of political unity. There must be some strong force making for the maintenance and, after lapses, for the restoration of unity, when once the original achievement of unity has come to pass; for the pheno-menon of restoration occurs again and again, and this even after 'inter-mediate periods' that have been so long and so anarchic that they might have been expected to have made an irreparable break in the tradition.

This new model fits a great majority of the indisputable specimens of the species of society that we have called 'civilizations'. The Egyptiac Civilization is unique in having achieved political unity at the opening

[1] The label 'time of troubles', which I have applied to the anarchic period of Hellenic history preceding the establishment of the Hellenic universal state, is in fact taken from the traditional Russian name for a lapse in the maintenance of the Russian universal state, i.e. the Muscovite Empire, between the extinction of the House of Rurik and the accession of the Romanovs.

[2] Sinic history, by itself, offers all the necessary data for constructing the improved model. If Chinese scholars had not done violence to early Chinese history in their exces-sive zeal for symmetry and self-consistency, it would not have been necessary to resort to an Hellenic model, as we have had to do, in order to correct the traditional Chinese misrepresentation of the configuration of early Chinese history.

of its history; but, as we have observed, there was an antecedent age of
political disunity here too, if we take into account the pre-civilizational
stage of history in Egypt. The Middle American, Andean, and Hellenic
civilizations are exceptional in having experienced only a single spell of
the universal-state stage instead of the normal experience of an initial
spell followed by a series of restorations. But, in the Hellenic Civilization's case, this is true of the sequel only in the westernmost section of
its domain. Western historians are apt to be preoccupied by what
happened in these backward outlying territories, because this is the
history of their own civilization. But the sequel to the fall of the Roman
Empire in its central and eastern provinces is at least as significant; and
in this area the sequel conformed to the Chinese pattern: there was a
series of revivals of the universal state, beginning in A.D. 717 and not
coming to a final close till 1922.

The composite Helleno-Sinic model, which is evidently the standard
pattern, is explicable in human terms in all its stages. For example, when
we examine a civilization's age of growth, we shall not be surprised to
find that a period in which a society is articulated into a number of
politically separate local communities, all sharing one common culture,
should be a time of creativity and progress. The stimulus that comes
from direct personal intercourse works more powerfully in a small
community than in a large one; life in a small community that is in
active and competitive intercourse with neighbours of its own size
and kind is more stimulating still, since this is a social structure that
combines the stimulus of intimacy with the stimulus of a wider horizon.
A classic exposition of the cultural advantages of a regime of political
disunity within a unitary economic and cultural field has been given by
Hume in his essay *Of the Rise and Progress of the Arts and Sciences*.[1]
But these blessings have their price in the currency of inter-state warfare; and a point may come when the toll taken by this is greater than
any benefit that the stimuli of variety and competition can confer. If the
balance becomes decidedly adverse, the society breaks down. It might
be asked why a society does not forestall its breakdown, or at any rate
retrieve it, by promptly applying the remedy of political unification to
which it does eventually have recourse. Why do people put up with a
long-drawn-out 'time of troubles' before bringing themselves to get
rid of warfare by submitting to a universal state? The answer is that
human beings are creatures of habit, and that the regime of local
sovereignties has won such a hold on people's hearts in the age when it
was producing a balance of advantage that it takes a long experience of
its subsequent disastrous effects to induce its former beneficiaries to
abandon their allegiance to it when they have become its victims.

When once, however, a universal state has been established, it is not
surprising that this regime should win a hold on people's hearts in its
turn. The peace and order that the achievement of political unity brings
with it are appreciated by contrast with a foregoing 'time of troubles'
that had become intolerable before it was transcended; and the loss of
stimulus now seems a cheap price to pay for the inestimably precious

---

[1] This passage has been quoted in the present book in i. 473-4.

boon of being rescued from the jaws of destruction and guaranteed against a recurrence of this fearful threat so long as the universal state lasts.[1] With the passage of time, a universal state's hold over its subjects' hearts is apt to increase, unless the empire-builders have been aliens who have persistently made themselves odious.[2] It is easy to understand why a universal state, once established, should be restored again and again when it has broken down. But we still have to ask ourselves why, when once it has been established, there should be any 'intermediate periods'[3] at all, considering that normally the maintenance of the universal state is desired by at least a majority of its subjects.

In previous volumes the declines and falls of universal states have been interpreted as being the after-effects of mortal wounds that had been inflicted by society on itself during the foregoing 'times of troubles'; and this lassitude, if not exhaustion, would explain the lapse in the maintenance of a universal state; but it would not explain how a society that has lacked the vitality to maintain its universal state can subsequently summon up enough vitality to re-establish it. In seeking to account for the Yin-Yang alternating rhythm that seems normally to prevail in the history of a civilization from the date of the first establishment of its universal state, we need not rest content with the Chinese account of this rhythm as being a manifestation, in human affairs, of a fundamental cosmic rhythm that is itself inexplicable and axiomatic.[4]

---

[1] H. Frankfort has criticized my previous treatment of Egyptiac history on the ground that I have viewed it through Hellenic and Western spectacles and have consequently failed to see it as it really was (*The Birth of Civilization in the Near East*, pp. 27–31). As Frankfort sees it, 'the ideal of a marvellously integrated society had been formed long before the Pyramids were built; it was as nearly realised, when they were built, as any ideal social form can be translated into actuality; and it remained continuously before the eyes of rulers and people alike during subsequent centuries. It was an ideal which ought to thrill a Western historian by its novelty, for it falls entirely outside the experience of Greek or Roman or modern man, although it survives, in an attenuated form, in Africa. It represents a harmony between Man and the divine which is beyond our boldest dreams, since it was maintained by divine power which had taken charge of the affairs of Man in the person of Pharaoh. Society moved in unison with Nature. Justice, which was the social aspect of the cosmic order, pervaded the commonwealth' (ibid., pp. 27–31). Frankfort's thesis that the Egyptians' 'polity was not imposed but evolved from immemorial predilections' (ibid., p. 99) is not, I think, contradicted by anything that I have written in previous volumes of the present book. On the other hand, when Frankfort goes on to say that this polity 'was adhered to, without protest, for almost three thousand years', his contention here is contradicted, not just by me, but by the evidence of the surviving Egyptiac literature of the Age of the Middle Empire. This testifies that the ideology of the Old Kingdom regime, and the measures (e.g. pyramid-building) through which this ideology was put into practice, did eventually provoke a moral reaction that went to the length of political revolution in the last days of the Sixth Dynasty.

[2] This exceptional case is underlined by K. W. Erdmann in *Archiv für Kulturgeschichte*, xxxiii. Band, Heft 2 (1951), pp. 174–250, on pp. 224–5.

[3] In a previous passage (p. 55, footnote 3) it has been noticed that a comparative value judgement is implicit in the ostensibly neutral term 'intermediate periods' which has been coined by the Egyptologists but is applicable also to the bouts of disorder and disunity in Chinese and in Byzantine history. The implicit judgement that political unity, embracing the whole domain of a civilization, is the normal, proper, and desirable state of affairs may or may not be objectively justifiable; but there is no doubt that it accurately represents the feelings of populations that have had experience of a universal state or have inherited a tradition of one from their ancestors.

[4] H. A. L. Fisher has made fun of me for taking the Chinese concept of Yin and Yang seriously. 'In the great operatic performance of humanity he detects', Fisher says of me, 'the occurrence of this *Leitmotiv* of Yin and Yang. Other ears will be less sensitive to the regularity of the Chinese beat' (*The Nineteenth Century and After*, December, 1934,

The Yin-Yang rhythm does run through the histories of universal states, but there is a human explanation of it. It is an explanation in economic terms.

A universal state is a heavy charge on the economy of a civilization. It requires, for its maintenance, a well-paid professional civil service and professional defence force; and the cost of these services will rise if it is one of the laws of the history of a universal state that, with the passage of time, the administrative and military personnel is apt to become more numerous as the institutions of local self-government decay and as the pressure of the trans-frontier barbarians increases. If the universal state—and, with it, the society incapsulated in it—is to be able to meet these rising costs without being crushed by them, it must be able to draw upon a commensurately rising productivity; but, in the Age of the Civilizations up to date, the economy has been more or less static most of the time in the greater part of the *Oikoumenê*.

The deliberate application of science to technology in the West is something recent and unprecedented. Even today, when the Industrial Revolution has been in progress for some two hundred years and has spread from Britain, where it originated, to the ends of the Earth, the greater part of the human race is still in the pre-industrial stage. The last economic revolution before this was the enhancement of the productivity of agriculture through water-control, some time before the close of the fourth millennium B.C., which transformed inhospitable swamps and jungles into the cradles of the Sumero-Akkadian and Egyptiac civilizations.[1] But only a fraction of the cultivable part of the Earth's surface is capable of being made to give a comparable yield. Moreover, even in the most favourable environments, the technique of agriculture remained virtually static until the beginning of the present application of science to the improvement of crops and livestock; and this, like the present Industrial Revolution, dates back only to eighteenth-century Britain. Thus the normal economic basis of civilization, till a very recent date, has been a static agriculture at a level of productivity that in most places has been not much higher than that attained in Neolithic societies in the Pre-civilizational Age. But a civilization is a much more costly social structure than a Neolithic society is, and its costs are perhaps at their maximum when the civilization is organized politically in a universal state, and when this universal state has been in existence for some time. The inability of a pre-scientific agricultural economy to bear this economic load is evidently one of the causes of the unwished-for collapses by which so many universal states have been overtaken so many times in succession.

The importance of the part played by the economic factor in determining whether a universal state is to collapse or is to survive can be gauged by comparing the respective fortunes of the Roman Empire in its different sections. The western provinces, in which the Empire

p. 672). On this I can only comment: 'They have ears, but they hear not' (Psalm cxxxv. 17). One can, however, be alive to the prevalence of the Yin-Yang rhythm in human affairs without having to renounce all attempt to explain this.

[1] This economic revolution was made possible by an advance, not in the realm of technology, but in the realm of politics (see pp. 338–9).

collapsed in the fifth century of the Christian Era, were relatively backward economically; the central and eastern provinces, in which, in the same century, the Empire survived, were the principal seats of the Hellenic World's industry and trade; and their relative economic strength more than counterbalanced the relative unfavourableness of their strategic position. Though the centre and the east were more directly exposed than the west was to assaults from the Eurasian Nomads of the Great Western Bay of the Steppe, and from the Sasanian power in Iran and 'Iraq, the Empire managed here to hold its own; and, though it did collapse, here too, in the seventh century, it might have continued to survive in these economically stronger sections if, in the sixth century, the Emperor Justinian had not taxed their strength too severely in attempting to reconquer the derelict west. Thereafter, when, in the eighth century, the Hellenic universal state was re-established in the two rival shapes of the East Roman Empire in Anatolia and the Carolingian Roman Empire in Gaul, history repeated itself through the operation of the same economic causes. The Carolingian Empire swiftly collapsed; the East Roman Empire survived, without any further collapse, for three and a half centuries (A.D. 717–1071). The reason for this diversity of fortunes, this time once again, was that Anatolia in this age was economically capable of carrying the load of a universal state, whereas contemporary Transalpine Western Europe was not. It is significant that in the East Roman Empire, during the century immediately preceding the disaster of A.D. 1071, there had been increasing symptoms of social and economic ill-health in the Empire's heart-land, Anatolia.

These are dramatic illustrations of the survival value of economic productivity for a universal state. Yet, hitherto, the rulers of universal states have seldom been alive to this. More often they have been either indifferent to possibilities of technological advance or positively hostile to these, on the reckoning that any technological change is a menace to economic equilibrium and hence also to the social and political stability that the founders of the universal state have established with such difficulty.[1] Certainly the Roman Imperial Government did not ever realize, at any stage of its history, that technology, as exemplified in Hero of Alexandria's invention of a turbine engine, could have solved the Hellenic universal state's intertwined problems of finance and defence. And in the western provinces in the fourth century of the Christian Era, when the Empire was fighting for survival there, no attention was paid to possibilities of dealing with manpower shortage and with defence logistics by mechanization, though a set of projects for this was published in an anonymous memorandum De Rebus Bellicis.[2] In universal states at both ends of the Old World the public authorities seem normally to have confined their action to collecting the land-tax and turning the screw harder on the taxable cultivators or their landlords when agricultural production has declined or public expenses have mounted.

[1] See the story, cited in ix. 613, footnote 2, of an early Roman emperor's reaction to the news of the invention of unbreakable glass.

[2] A Roman Reformer and Inventor: De Rebus Bellicis, ed. and tr. by E. A. Thompson (Oxford 1952, Clarendon Press).

It is significant that, in China, the local state Ch'in (Ts'in), which eventually established a universal state for the first time by overthrowing the last of its competitors in 221 B.C., was also the state which, in the fourth century B.C., had distinguished itself among its competitors by systematically revolutionizing its social and economic structure with a view to increasing the population's productivity and putting the increased product at the government's disposal. But it is also significant that, when this regime was extended to the whole of China by the founder of the universal state, Ch'in Shih Hwang-ti, it provoked vehement opposition. After Shih Hwang-ti's death his regime was quickly overthrown; and both he and the 'Legist' school of philosophers, whose theories had been the inspiration of the Ch'in government's practice, were execrated in the subsequently established Chinese tradition. The school of philosophy that was officially established by the Han Emperor Wu-ti (*imperabat* 140 B.C.–87 B.C.), and that maintained its monopoly, off and on, from that time till A.D. 1911, was not the 'Legist' school, but the Confucian. And Confucianism has not been sympathetic towards non-agricultural economic enterprise, though it has understood the value of water-control for agriculture and for communications.

Wu-ti embarked on expensive military operations. He carried the southern border of the Sinic universal state to the 'natural frontier' of the south coast of China, while on the north he tried to subjugate the whole domain of the Hiongnu Nomads on the Eurasian Steppe. In order to meet his consequent heavy expenses, he revived the policy of the 'Legist' school. He put the imperial government into business and at the same time gave scope to non-agricultural private business enterprise.[1] Notwithstanding these efforts to stimulate production, Wu-ti over-taxed his empire's resources and so was perhaps responsible for the decline and fall of the Prior Han regime within the hundred years following the date of his death. But the opposite policy had no happier results. After the restoration of the universal state by the Posterior Han Dynasty, the Confucian landed gentry who staffed the imperial civil service gained the upper hand over the non-agrarian business interests.[2] And, when the universal state was thus put back on to an almost exclusively agricultural basis, it collapsed and remained in abeyance for four hundred years, save for the short interlude of the United Chin (Tsin) regime.

In China from the time of the Posterior Han dynasty (A.D. 25–220) until the enforced opening of treaty ports to Western economic enterprise in the nineteenth century, agriculture was the economic basis of the Sinic universal state, and the insufficiency of this economic foundation for this political structure was evidently one important cause of the repeated collapses of the Sinic universal state in the course of the intervening centuries. In discussing the most recent of these collapses, that of the Ch'ing (Manchu) dynasty, W. Altree notes[3] that, during its tenure of power (A.D. 1644–1911), this dynasty increased the rate of the land-tax 'twenty to thirty times'.

---

[1] See B. Watson: *Ssu-ma Ch'ien*, pp. 31–33.
[2] Ibid., pp. 37–38, and A. F. Wright: *Buddhism in Chinese History*, p. 9, cited already on p. 178, footnote 3.   [3] In *Toynbee and History*, p. 268.

'If any one reason accounts for the fall of the Ch'ing dynasty, it probably can be found in the mistaken policy of peasant exploitation that wrecked the economy of the country. This agrarian crisis was the issue of a basic contradiction in Chinese society that runs through the whole imperial history of China and far transcends in time Toynbee's Far Eastern Civilization. The Chinese administration, requiring intricate scribal techniques, depended upon scholar bureaucrats for effectiveness. These administrators were drawn from the wealthy landlord class which alone had the leisure to acquire the necessary academic preparation. Thus the government and its officials both competed through taxes or rents to preempt the basic form of wealth in the surplus production of the land. The gentry-administrator class used its strategic position in government to evade taxation by shifting it to the peasantry. Beset by the government demanding taxes and the landlords demanding rents, the peasantry was progressively impoverished, rebellion was a logical consequence, and a new regime would initiate this predatory system afresh.'[1]

The sufferings inflicted on the peasantry by exploitation were aggravated by the exploiters' technological inefficiency.

'It is almost certainly untrue that, under the old regime, [conservancy works] were maintained so effectively as to prevent recurrent disasters. Both Chinese and European scholars have investigated the history of flood and famine in China. The conclusion suggested by their work is that those catastrophes occurred over large areas at short intervals for several—perhaps many—centuries before the present one; nor should that surprise Professor Toynbee, since elsewhere he assigns the Chinese "breakdown"[2] to a fairly early date—the last quarter of the ninth century. The most significant fact, indeed, is surely the opposite of that emphasized by him. It is the failure of a great civilization, in spite—or, perhaps, because—of all its brilliant achievements in other fields, to master the problem of taming an unfriendly Nature, which the West, in some other respects so inferior to China, has in recent times largely succeeded in solving. The point is not a trifling one, since it concerns the characteristics of two important cultural types, differing sharply from each other both in their virtues and their limitations.'[3]

These two passages, taken together, go far towards explaining the successive collapses of universal states, not only in China, but in other regions where they have been erected on the same economic and social

---

[1] Altree, ibid., pp. 267–8. The cultural, social, and moral antagonism in China between the scholar-gentry and the peasantry had been mitigated by Buddhism, first in the North (see p. 176, footnote 1) and then, after political reunification, in China as a whole. Under the T'ang regime, Buddhism 'worked as a social cement, binding together all classes and races in common beliefs and activities' (A. F. Wright: *Buddhism in Chinese History*, p. 74). Under the subsequent regime, when Confucianism regained the upper hand over Buddhism by appropriating it, the neo-Confucian officials acquired a touch of the Buddhist social conscience; and, on their initiative, the Sung imperial government organized charitable work on the grand scale (ibid., pp. 92–94). But, 'in contrast to the earlier period in which Buddhism, in different forms, had formed a common bond between the two main classes of Chinese society, the modern period saw a striking cleavage between the rational ethic of the élite and the religious êthos of the peasantry' (ibid., p. 97). The Neo-Confucian litterati were contemptuous of the Buddhist and Taoist village priests (ibid., p. 103).
[2] i.e. the breakdown of the post-Sinic 'Far Eastern Civilization' (A. J. T.).
[3] R. H. Tawney in *International Affairs*, November, 1939, p. 803.

basis.[1] They explain, for instance, the collapse of the Old Kingdom of Egypt, the fifth-century collapse of the Roman Empire in its western provinces, the ninth-century collapse of the Carolingian avatar of the Roman Empire in the same region, and also the eleventh-century collapse of the Byzantine avatar of the Roman Empire in Anatolia. In all these four cases occurring at the opposite end of the Old World to China, the economic basis of the universal state was almost exclusively agricultural, and the burden on the peasantry of maintaining a universal state—a burden that is heavy even under the best regime—became intolerable when landlords armed with official authority shook off governmental control and added their private exactions to the government's demands. The technological history of the Egyptiac Civilization is significant.[2]

This economic explanation of the recurrent re-establishment and recurrent collapse of a universal state provides a key to the Chinese myth of a 'mandate of Heaven' which is received and subsequently forfeited by one imperial dynasty after another. The mandate is forfeited when the numbers and demands of the dominant minority of the day rise to figures at which the sufferings imposed on the peasantry by this excessive tax on their limited productivity come to outweigh, in their estimation, the blessings of unity and peace which the maintenance of a universal state confers. There is a subsequent mandate to a new dynasty to re-establish the universal state that has been wrecked by the late dynasty's misdemeanours because the sufferings imposed by the return of disunity and disorder are no sooner re-experienced than they re-activate the longing for the blessings attending the maintenance of a universal state. The people's nostalgia is the new empire-builders' opportunity; and these *novi homines* usually succeed, not only in re-establishing the lapsed universal state, but also in maintaining it for a further spell. This initial success of theirs is due to the very fact that they are parvenus. At the beginning of their regime they will be fewer in numbers, more modest in their personal demands, and more energetic and efficient in performing their public services than the epigoni of the preceding dynasty whom they have replaced, and also than their own

---

[1] Philip Bagby has derided my description of the T'ang Empire as being 'a vampire state' (*Toynbee and History*, p. 105). If there is anything wrong about this description, it is that I have applied it only to the T'ang Empire and not also to every occurrence of a universal state both in China and elsewhere.

[2] The Egyptiac Civilization's outstanding technological achievement was its discovery of how to quarry, transport, and dress huge blocks of masonry, and to build these into monuments of an architecture that was as accurate as it was colossal. On the other hand, this civilization lagged surprisingly in its adoption of several other technological devices that were of greater economic and social importance. The potter's wheel, for instance, was not adopted in Egypt before the age of the Third Dynasty, and then only in an inferior form (V. G. Childe: *What Happened in History*, pp. 86 and 122). Wheeled vehicles were not adopted there till the sixteenth century B.C., when the Egyptians mastered the art of chariotry in order to expel the Hyksos. From the fifth millennium B.C. till after the establishment of the Middle Empire at the close of the third, the Egyptians were content to make their metal tools of unalloyed copper (ibid., pp. 122 and 157), and these copper tools continued to be luxuries. The peasants continued, till the time of the New Empire, to use Neolithic tools for the agricultural operations that were the basis of the whole Egyptiac World's economy (ibid., pp. 123 and 157). The bronze that had been introduced no earlier than about 2000 B.C. was not superseded by iron, for general purposes, till about 650 B.C. (ibid., p. 192)—and this was three-quarters of a millennium after the discovery of the art of iron-working somewhere in Anatolia.

future epigoni, who are destined to forfeit Heaven's mandate in their turn.

It is noteworthy that this illuminating Chinese myth reappears in the work of the fourteenth-century Arabic Muslim statesman, jurist, historian, and philosopher Ibn Khaldūn. He had no knowledge of his Chinese confrères' ideas; yet, like them, he saw the pattern of history as an alternating rhythm in which the alternate periods of relative order and disorder were consequences of the successive rises and falls of a series of dynasties. In Ibn Khaldūn's view a dynasty normally brings itself to grief in the fourth generation, reckoning the founder's generation as being the first.[1] Ibn Khaldūn's myth was derived from a knowledge of the history of the Arab Caliphate and its successor-states over a period of some seven centuries ending in his own day. How is it that two different sets of historical data have given rise, independently of each other, to an identical account of how human affairs work? The answer is that there is an identical economic and social thread running through the history of China from 221 B.C. to A.D. 1911 and through the history of the Islamic World from the establishment of the Arab Caliphate in the seventh century of the Christian Era to the time in the fourteenth century when Ibn Khaldūn was writing his *Prolegomena to a History of Mankind*. This identical element is the peasant economy which has been the normal economic basis for political structures of all kinds since the beginning of the Age of the Civilizations.

The foregoing examination of the Yin-Yang alternating rhythm in the histories of universal states will now perhaps enable us to arrive at some general conclusions.

One is that the continuing recurrence of a universal state does not necessarily carry with it a continuance of the particular civilization whose vicissitudes originally brought the universal state into existence. For example, if our Chinese spectacles have not played us false in revealing to us, in the Tigris-Euphrates basin and Iran, a continuing recurrence of the same universal state from the second half of the third millennium B.C. down to the eighteenth century of the Christian Era,[2] we have here an instance of a universal state persisting through the histories of no less than four different civilizations: the Sumero-Akkadian, in which this one originated; the Syriac, which captured it from the Sumero-Akkadian Civilization while it was embodied in the Achaemenian Empire; the Hellenic Civilization, which captured it from the Syriac Civilization when the Achaemenian Empire was overthrown by Alexander and was replaced in Asia by the Seleucid Monarchy; and finally the Iranic Muslim Civilization, if we are right in assigning to this the Mongol Il-Khanate, the Timurid Empire, the Safawi Empire, and Nadir Shah's.[3] Similarly, the universal states of the two pre-Columbian

---

[1] See Ibn Khaldūn: *The Muqaddimah*, translated from the Arabic by F. Rosenthal (London 1958, Routledge and Kegan Paul, 3 vols.), vol. i, pp. 278–82 (chap. ii, section 14) and pp. 343–6 (chap. iii, section 12). The cyclic rhythm of political history and the causes of it are the central theme of the whole work.

[2] See p. 191.

[3] The accounts, given in previous volumes of this book, of the structure of Syriac history and the place of Islam in history are reconsidered in the present volume in Chapters XIII and XIV. Here there is a discussion of the cultural affinities of the

American civilizations, which were embodied originally in the Aztec Empire and in the Inca Empire respectively, were carried on, in the Spanish viceroyalties of New Spain and Peru, under the auspices of the interloping Western Christian Civilization. Similarly, again, the Roman Empire, which had started life as an Hellenic universal state, was subsequently captured, in the avatars of it in its central and eastern provinces, by two different civilizations: first the Byzantine Christian Civilization that animated the East Roman Empire, and then the Iranic Muslim Civilization to which the Ottoman Turkish rebuilders of the East Roman Empire paid allegiance. This Christian and this Islamic civilization must each be regarded as being separate from the Hellenic; for the advent of Christianity and of Islam did make a decisive break in the history of civilization not only in the West but wherever it occurred. The breach of cultural continuity here is unmistakable, even though it may not be warrantable to assume, on this analogy, that comparable breaches of continuity were made in the history of Eastern Asia by the advent of the Mahayana and in India by the emergence of post-Buddhaic Hinduism there.

In the history of civilization in India, and in its history in China as well, the institution making for continuity has not been the recurring universal state. In India this has recurred only rarely and at long intervals. In both sub-continents the thread of continuity has been provided by the persistence of a dominant social class: the Brahman caste in India and the Confucian-educated gentry in China. In China from the turn of the second and the last centuries B.C. till A.D. 1911, the repeated restorations of the universal state were made possible by the scholar-gentry's survival as a source of recruitment for the civil service. But in 1911 the 2,000-years-long innings of this class came to an end; and, when, after a 38-years-long bout of disunity and disorder, the universal state was re-established according to precedent, it resumed its sway this time under non-Confucian auspices. In China Confucianism has now been replaced by Communism, and China has been converted from her traditional indigenous civilization to an exotic one inspired by a philosophy of Jewish-Christian origin that was incubated in nineteenth-century Western Europe.[1] Yet the momentum of the Chinese universal state is not yet exhausted.

We can also see that the series of alternating collapses and restorations of a universal state is not interminable. All known universal states have had a starting-point in a revolutionary change from a previous regime of political disunity. This can be seen to be true of the Chinese universal state, if we look at early Chinese history as it actually was, and not as it has been depicted in the traditional legendary misrepresentation of it. It can also be seen to be probably true of the Egyptiac universal state, if we take into account the antecedent course of history in Egypt in its

Parthian and Sasanian empires and the Arab Caliphate, which intervened chronologically between the Seleucid Empire and the Mongol Il-Khanate.

[1] J. Madaule judges that I have underestimated the importance of the Communist revolution of 1948 in China (*Diogenes*, No. 13 (Spring, 1956), p. 43). If I have made this mistake, I take the present opportunity of correcting it. I expect that this revolution will prove to have been an epoch-making event, not only for China but for the whole World.

pre-civilizational stage. In China the universal state is still a going concern under a Communist regime. But, in most of the other regions
where a universal state has made its appearance and has passed through
the same characteristic series of collapses and restorations, it has now
come to an end. The Ottoman Roman Empire expired, as we have seen,
in 1922; the shadowy Western Roman Empire in 1806; the Spanish
Empire of the Indies in the first quarter of the nineteenth century; the
'Iraqi-Iranian universal state in 1747, if we may take the date of Nadir
Shah's death as marking its demise; the Indian universal state expired
in 1947, when the British Raj in India was replaced by three successor-
states.[1] The Egyptiac universal state expired unobtrusively in the third
century of the Christian Era, when the Roman emperors changed the
religious and constitutional basis of their dominion over Egypt. In
the time of the principate they had ruled Egypt, like the Ptolemies and the
Achaemenids before them, in the guise of Pharaohs who were sons of
Re and gods incarnate. From the reign of Aurelian onwards, they ruled,
no longer as gods in their own persons, but as vicegerents of a god who
was lord of the whole Universe. If we may take this as being the date of
the expiry of the Egyptiac universal state, this has been extinct, by now,
for nearly seventeen hundred years. No doubt it is theoretically possible
that both it and other representatives of this species of polity might
revive again. But the evidence up to date suggests that immortality is
not one of the specific properties of universal states. Though they run to
longevity, and have frequently had more than a cat's proverbial nine
lives, all but two or three of those representatives of the species that have
made their appearance hitherto are now extinct, so far as we can tell.
The only indisputably extant specimens are the Chinese and the Russian,[2]

[1] The Indian Union, Pakistan and Burma. Ceylon has derived its civilization from
India, and, in the last stage of its political history before it attained its present independence, it shared with India the experience of being under British rule. But Ceylon was not
included either in the British Indian Empire or in that empire's Mughal, Gupta, and
Maurya predecessors.

[2] In previous volumes of this book I have taken the Far Eastern Civilization in Japan
as being an offshoot of the main body, and have seen its history as following an independent course of its own. I identified the breakdown of the Far Eastern Civilization in
Japan with the victory of feudalism over the imperial regime in the twelfth century of
the Christian Era, and I found its universal state in the Tokugawa Shogunate.

P. L. Ralph has pronounced (in the *Saturday Review*, 16th October, 1954, p. 19) that
'to characterise the Tokugawa Shogunate as the "universal state" of the Japanese branch
of the Far Eastern Civilization is to push an abstraction to the point of fantasy'. The
same criticism is made by M. S. Bates (in *Christianity and Crisis*, vol. 15, No. 4 (21st
March, 1955), pp. 27–30 and 32). The equation of the Japanese Isles with the World
might indeed appear to be a geographical absurdity. Yet every *soi-disant* universal state
that has come and gone so far has fallen very far short of being literally world-wide.
The universality of a universal state has, so far, been something subjective. It has been
a state which, in the eyes of its inhabitants, has embraced the whole of the civilized
world that has been within their ken. On this test, the Hellenic, Indian, and Chinese
universal states unquestionably pass muster. The Tokugawa polity's claim to qualify
for the title is, I agree, more disputable; for, throughout the Tokugawa period, Japan
continued to live on cultural capital previously imported from China or via China:
e.g. the Chinese characters, Confucianism, Buddhism. Yet the Tokugawa regime did
succeed in stopping the importation of any fresh elements of culture from China—in
contrast to what had happened in all previous phases of the Far Eastern Civilization
in Japan, when a series of Chinese styles of art and schools of Buddhism or of indigenous
Chinese philosophy had successively been imported into Japan and been eagerly cultivated there. It was difficult to seal off a group of islands that was so close to the Continent, and equally difficult to make the population of so small a region feel themselves
to be culturally self-sufficient. Yet that was the Tokugawa regime's aim. The severity

each of which has achieved its current avatar under the auspices of Communism.

If, however, we have been right in our economic diagnosis of the cause of the recurrent collapse of those universal states that have come and gone up to date, it would seem to follow that the recent change in mankind's economic situation, thanks to the modern Western Industrial Revolution, will have brought with it a change in the prospects of a future universal state—even if this were to differ from all its predecessors in being literally world-wide. It is true that a considerable majority of the human race is still living in the insufficiently productive Pre-industrial Age. It is also true that, in the present stage of human affairs, the cost of a literally world-wide universal state would be high. For, although an all-inclusive society would be relieved of the cost of frontier defence against outer barbarians, besides being relieved of the cost of the competition in armaments between local states, this saving would be more than offset by the cost of helping the economically backward majority of mankind to approximate towards the prosperous minority's standard of living. The present disparity has, at the least, to be drastically reduced if the human race is to live together as a single family; and the cost of this will be enormous, if we aim at the goal of bringing within the reach of every family in the World the material facilities and spiritual opportunities that a Western middle-class family already enjoys.

This is, in itself, a larger economic undertaking than any that has confronted any universal state in the past; and the economic aspect of the problem is not so formidable as its social and religious aspects. Modern technology is advancing so fast, and is spreading so rapidly from its Western originators to the rest of the human race, that the increase in mankind's productivity seems likely to go to formerly unimaginable lengths. The crucial question is whether the still poverty-stricken majority of the human race will be able and willing to make a revolutionary change in its habits and outlook that has already been made by the now relatively prosperous minority. In a society in which public hygiene has been achieving sensational progressive reductions in the death-rate, a reduction in the birth-rate on a corresponding scale is required if technology's potential gift of a higher standard of living,

of the measures that it took for achieving it testifies to the regime's determination to succeed, as well as to the difficulty of the undertaking.

On reconsideration, I think it would be nearer the truth to classify the Tokugawa regime as an attempt at a universal state which failed. It was defeated from within. Japanese inquirers were secretly studying Western science, at the risk of their lives, two generations before Commodore Perry's squadron made its first appearance in Yedo Bay. M. E. Cameron makes a telling point against my previous presentation of Japanese history when she says that my 'estimate of the significance of a universal state implies that it was moribund, yet he recognises that the intelligent and efficient response of the Japanese ruling class to the challenge of Western imperialism hardly seems to be the act of a dead or dying society' (*The Far Eastern Quarterly*, vol. i, No. 2 (February, 1942), pp. 150–60). This response was, indeed, the measure of the failure of the Tokugawas' attempt to 'freeze' Japanese life.

Yet, if the Tokugawas failed in the end to make a closed world of Japan, they do seem to have succeeded in making a political unity of her. The liquidation of the Tokugawa regime did not bring with it a return of the previous disunity and disorder. The only civil war in Japan since then has been the conflict between the Meiji regime and the Satsuma insurgents in 1877; and, since the defeat of this dissident movement, the maintenance of unity seems to have been taken as a matter of course.

spiritual as well as material, is not to be swallowed up by a sensational increase in the number of mouths to be fed. Hitherto the majority of mankind has, as a matter of course, always multiplied and replenished the Earth up to the limits allowed by its food-supply at a subsistence level only just above the starvation-line. Unless this habit is abandoned, modern technology will have brought with it, for the majority, no increase in well-being, but merely an increase in miserable numbers. On the other hand, modern technology accompanied by a deliberate reduction in the birth-rate as well as in the death-rate would give an unheard-of buoyancy to a future world-state's finances. Instead of being constrained to take an intolerable toll from a poor and static peasant economy, a future world-state could afford to subsidize a revolution in the peasantry's traditional Neolithic way of life through a world-wide application of science and technology to peasant agriculture.

If this is indeed the outlook for a future world-state, that is fortunate for the human race. For the same unprecedented scientific and techno-logical progress that has opened up these prospects of higher produc-tion has already produced weapons that would turn war into genocide if they were ever to be used. And the possibility that they may be used will remain open so long as our present-day world remains divided on the political plane, as it now is, among a number of sovereign indepen-dent states. In our present situation we can no more afford than our predecessors could, in their 'times of troubles', to let this perilous political disunity continue. But we also cannot afford, in the age of atomic weapons, to let the now imperative political unification of all mankind come about, in the traditional way, through war *à outrance* ending in the destruction of all the competing powers but one. Man-kind will have to reach political unity through agreement; and, if and when this unity has once been attained, we shall not be able to afford to see the old alternating rhythm of lapses and recoveries reassert itself. For, in the Atomic Age, any lapse into disunity and disorder would be a threat to the existence of the human race. This is an unprecedently difficult problem for statesmanship. But we may take heart if it is true that the technological revolution which has presented this problem to the future architects of a world-state is also going to ease for them the econo-mic problem that has repeatedly worsted their predecessors.

6. A JEWISH ALTERNATIVE MODEL FOR CIVILIZATIONS

The comparative study of civilizations evidently stands to benefit by our new departure of setting up a second model and combining it with the first. Between them the Hellenic and the Chinese model throw light on the configuration of the histories of civilizations which could not have been obtained from either of them applied in isolation. Our new composite model seems to fit the majority of our specimens and to give us new insight into their structure. This success will encourage us to set up a third model, with a view to exploring a phenomenon which our Helleno-Sinic model does not illuminate.

When a number of mutually independent local communities have lost their former political identities through being merged in a universal state, the merger has usually been complete and lasting. Even in those exceptional cases in which the duration of the universal state has been confined to a single spell, the short-lived universal state's local successor-states have usually had no continuity with the local states out of which the universal state was originally constituted. The Teutonic and Arab principalities among which the Roman Empire's former Western provinces were carved up were not revivals of the local states, occupying the same region, that the Romans had previously conquered and annexed.[1] The Hispano-American republics among which the former Spanish Empire of the Indies was carved up in the early nineteenth century were not revivals of the local states that had been conquered and annexed by the Aztecs and by the Incas. In China, where Ch'in Shih Hwang-ti's universal state fell to pieces again only fourteen years after its establishment, the attempt to revive the former local states was abortive. Within five years the universal state had been re-established by Han Liu P'ang; and, though this second founder felt it politic to allow some local states, labelled with traditional names, to retain a limited autonomy within his unitary political framework, both their prerogatives and their territories were progressively reduced until they had been completely *gleichgeschaltet* within less than a hundred years after Liu P'ang's accession. The local states into which China broke up again politically in the subsequent successive 'intermediate periods' were new growths, though some of these, too, assumed traditional names in the hope that these might give them an aura of legitimacy. In the history of the Achaemenian Empire it was the same story. The house of the founder, Cyrus II, was patently extinct after the assassination of the Smerdis who claimed to be—and perhaps truly was —this house's last surviving representative. This dramatic event occurred only about twenty-eight years after Cyrus had first set out on his career of conquest, and it was taken as a signal for the re-establishment of the local states that Cyrus had overthrown. But all these local insurrections were overcome by Darius I in little more than twelve months; and, when, 190 years later, the Achaemenian Empire was overthrown by Alexander, only one of the successor-states into which it was subsequently carved up by Alexander's officers had any continuity with a local state that had been in existence before the Persian conquests.[2]

Thus normally the establishment of a universal state, even for no longer than a single spell, has resulted in a permanent obliteration of the identities of the local states and peoples that have been incorporated in it. A classic case is that of 'the Lost Ten Tribes'. Today the population

---

[1] The names of the Post-Roman Jutish Kingdom of Kent and Anglian Kingdom of Bernicia may have been reminiscences of the two Pre-Roman Celtic kingdoms of the Cantii and the Brigantes, but there was no continuity here in substance. There was at least a partial change in the composition of the population, and there was a total change of language.

[2] This exception was, of course, the Ptolemaic Kingdom of Egypt. In the year of insurrections, 522 B.C., Egypt had kept quiet. On the other hand, it had afterwards repeatedly shaken off the Persian yoke in the course of the fifth and fourth centuries B.C. The latest of these spells of Egyptian independence had lasted from 404 to 343/2 B.C., and had thus come to an end only ten years before the restored Persian regime in Egypt was liquidated by Alexander.

of the Kingdom of Israel, which was wiped off the map by the Assyrian Empire in 722 B.C., is represented *in situ* only by a few hundred Samaritans in the neighbourhood of Nāblus. The Israelites who were deported were completely absorbed into the population of the countries in which they were settled. Their loss of identity was not an exception; it was the rule. It has become famous only because the rule was exceptionally broken by the history of the Israelites' kinsmen, the people of Judah, after their local kingdom, in its turn, had been wiped off the map by the Neobabylonian Empire in 586 B.C. The Jews were twice uprooted from their original homeland by Nebuchadnezzar and twice by the Romans. And, before their second uprooting by the Romans in A.D. 135, they had been subjects of five empires in turn: the Neobabylonian, the Achaemenian, the Ptolemaic, the Seleucid, and the Roman. From A.D. 135 to A.D. 1948 there was no such thing as a Jewish state[1] and not even such a thing as a Jewish 'national home' in the sense of a territory that was substantially Jewish in population without being under Jewish rule. Yet, without the political framework of a state or the territorial basis of a home, the Jews have managed to preserve their separate identity, as a people, from 586 B.C.—the year that saw the obliteration of the Kingdom of Judah—down to the present day. They have preserved it as a scattered minority (diasporá) living among non-Jewish majorities in countries outside the former frontiers of the extinct Kingdom of Judah and hundreds or thousands of miles away from its historic capital, Jerusalem.

This fact is remarkable and exceptional, but it is not unique.[2] The Jews are not the only uprooted people who have achieved it. For example, it has also been achieved by the Parsees since the destruction of the Sasanian Persian Empire by the Primitive Muslim Arab conquerors;[3] by the Monophysite Christians since the Muslim Arabs' conquest of Syria, Egypt, and Armenia; and by the Nestorian Christians since the fifth century, when they found asylum in the Sasanian Empire from their Orthodox Christian persecutors in the Roman Empire. From the completion of the Ottoman conquest of the former territories of the East Roman Empire down to the revolt of the 'Osmanlis' Greek subjects in the Morea in 1821, the Greek Orthodox Christians were partially uprooted and scattered, yet managed, in diasporá, to preserve their identity as a community, Jewish-fashion. In Russian Orthodox Christendom, members of some of the dissenting Christian sects have escaped from their Orthodox persecutors by migrating to the outer fringe of the

---

[1] During this period, there were states—e.g. the Kingdom of Adiabene and the Khazar Empire—in which the royal family and some of their grandees were converts to Judaism (see the present volume, pp. 85–86). There were also oases in the Hijaz and fastnesses in Abyssinia, the Caucasus, and the Crimea in which converts to Judaism held their own, perhaps with some admixture of Jewish refugees (see ii. 257 and 402–12). But only a minority of the Jews in the World ever lived, or ever could have lived, in these holes and corners.   [2] See also pp. 483–4.

[3] 'Perhaps only the Parsees of India are comparable to the Jews of Europe in the perfect blending of their nationalism and their religion. The Parsees, too, represent a combination of extreme religious tenacity, economic specialisation, and cultural proficiency, even as the Jews, though it was not the sad lot of the Parsees to live among a people committed to a "heretical" form of their own faith' (Rabbi J. B. Agus: 'Towards a Philosophy of Jewish History', in *Judaism*, 1956, p. 42).

Russian Empire or to regions beyond the Russian frontiers. The Molo-kane have found asylum in Transcaucasia and Eastern Siberia, the Skoptsy in Rumania, the Dukhobors in Canada. In Western Christen-dom the members of the Society of Friends (the Quakers), whose earliest recruits came from rural districts in the north of England, have tended, in England at any rate, to move from their native countryside into the cities, because in an urban environment it has been easier for them to avoid a conflict with the authorities over their conscientious objection to paying tithes to the Episcopalian Established Church.[1] The migra-tion of the Quakers into the cities has also been the story of the Hugue-not refugees from France in Holland, Britain, and Germany. Another of the dissenting religious communities of Western Christendom, the Church of the Latterday Saints (the Mormons), escaped its nineteenth-century persecutors by trekking westward, beyond the advancing fron-tier of settlement in the United States, to Utah. Its missionaries have since won converts almost as far afield as the missionaries of the Baha'i faith.

These examples of a diasporá are numerous enough to make it useful to set up a model, in order to explore what the essential characteristics of a diasporá are and to what extent each of the apparent specimens of this species of community approximates to, or diverges from, the standard pattern. The Jewish diasporá evidently provides the best material for the construction. Of all the diasporás in our list it is the most famous, the most influential, and also perhaps the most unhappy, at least up to date, in its relations with the gentile majorities among whom it has been living. It has also been in existence longer than any of the others, and has been more completely divorced from the cultivation of the land in its original home. From A.D. 135 till the planting of the first Zionist Jewish agricul-tural colonies in Palestine in the eighteen-eighties, it would be approxi-mately true to say that there was no Jewish agricultural population in what had once been the territory of the Kingdom of Judah. By contrast, the Parsees are still represented in Persia, and this on the land, in the surviving Zoroastrian villages in the oases of Yazd and Kirman. And the Zoroastrian refugees who found asylum in Western India after the fall of the Sasanian Empire replanted themselves on the soil in their new home. The present prominence of the Parsees' role in the industrial and business life of the Indian sub-continent dates from no farther back than the establishment of the British Raj, which brought India within the economic, as well as the political, ambit of the modern Western World and created in India the conditions required for doing business in the modern Western way. As for the Armenian Monophysites and the Greek Orthodox Christians, they have each succeeded, as the Zoroastrians have, in holding on to the cultivation of the land in a portion of their ancestral domain.

If, on these considerations, we take the Jewish diasporá as our model for this species of community, we shall find in it the following elements. First, there is the diasporá's determination to retain its historical identity in circumstances in which most communities have resigned themselves to losing theirs. Having been deprived of its state and its home and been reduced to living as a minority—and a scattered one—abroad, the uprooted community has found new means of maintaining its cohesion and continuity under these adverse conditions. It maintains them now through the voluntary observance of an exacting religious ritual and law. The second element is the diasporá's motive for being unwilling to merge itself in the majority among whom it has come to live. It cherishes its separate identity because it believes itself to be the depository of a religious revelation of unique significance and value. A third element in the configuration of the Jewish diasporá is its recognition of the truth that it will fail to survive if it does not provide itself with an adequate economic basis. Since it has no state of its own and no national home, economic power is the only form of power within its reach; and a community must command power of some kind in order to hold its own in the world. Even economic power is difficult for a diasporá to obtain. It has lost its hold on agriculture, which has been Man's primary and staple source of livelihood since the Neolithic Age, and, in the alien countries in which it has been scattered, it has been excluded, more often than not, from public life, and even from the liberal professions, as a penalty for its refusal to adopt the religion of the local majority. A diasporá must make its fortune out of whatever economic occupations the majority leaves open to it. The least obstructed opening has usually been retail trade. But, whatever the economic opportunity has been, the diasporá has always managed to win from it the economic resources required for its survival. On the economic as well as on the spiritual plane, penalization has proved to be an unusually powerful stimulus.[1]

This model derived from the Jewish diasporá fits all the other specimens on our list more or less closely. In all these cases religion has supplied the motive for the will to preserve the scattered community's identity, while economic prowess in some non-agricultural occupation has provided the means of putting this will to survive into effect. If we now simplify the model, we shall find that the religious species of diasporá is one representative of a more comprehensive genus. Two of the most conspicuous diasporás in the present-day world are the Scottish and the Lebanese. Like the Jews, Parsees, Huguenots, and Quakers, the Lebanese and the Scots abroad are conspicuously successful in business; but the pressure that has moved them to seek their fortunes abroad has been economic, not religious or political. Neither the Lebanese nor the Scots have lost their country; both have been masters in their own house;[2] and neither have been persecuted, either at home or abroad, for clinging to their ancestral religion.[3] They have been victims, not of their fellow men, but of Nature. Their native countries

---

[1] The stimulus of penalizations has been discussed in ii. 208–59.

[2] In the case of the Lebanese, this has been true de jure as well as de facto since the establishment, in 1861, of an autonomous vilayet of the Lebanon which became the Lebanese Republic in 1920.

[3] The present world-wide Lebanese diasporá mostly dates from times subsequent to 1861, i.e. from the period in which the Lebanese people have had a state of their own. Since 1861, the one great ordeal to which they have been subjected has been the Turkish blockade during the First World War.

are poor countries, and they have been driven abroad by the difficulty of making a livelihood at home.[1]

What is common to diasporás of the religious species represented by the Jews and the secular species represented by the Scots abroad is the transformation of a social structure. In both cases we are watching a community changing the basis of the cohesion that maintains its distinctive identity. It is changing over from an originally territorial basis, on which it has been held together by having a national home and a national government of its own, to a cultural and occupational basis, on which it is held together by having common memories, beliefs, manners and customs, and skills. Both the Jews and the Scots are on this road, though the Scots have not yet travelled far from the starting-point, while the Jews have long since reached the terminus. Looked at in a wider setting that includes the alien majority among whom the diasporá has been scattered, this change through which both Jews and Scots have been passing is a change from a vertical organization of society to a horizontal one. The communities into which society is articulated are undergoing a metamorphosis from having been so many local cells to becoming so many ubiquitous strata coexisting with each other over an identical area, which, in principle, may be coextensive with the whole habitable surface of the globe.

We can follow the history of this metamorphosis. 'Civilization is deracination.'[2] The Jewish diasporá was a product, in the Fertile Crescent, of two interrelated social developments: an intensification of social intercourse and an increase in urbanization. The growing social intercourse took the peaceful forms of commercial and cultural exchanges, as well as the violent forms of war and deportation; the growing cities served as melting-pots in which the intercourse could lead to fusion. As far as we know, this process started in the Fertile Crescent earlier than anywhere else. Indeed the relative facility of physical communications between the centres of settled life in this region in the Postpluvial Age is, as will be noticed in another context,[3] one of the factors that account for the Fertile Crescent's having been the cradle of civilization. Since the fifth and fourth millennia B.C., when civilization was incubating there, the Fertile Crescent has always been precocious. Time and again something that has made its first appearance in this nurserygarden of higher culture has eventually become world-wide. And the history of the diasporá type of social organization is an instance of the Fertile Crescent's habit of giving a lead to the rest of the World.

This is where the series of 'times of troubles' and universal states has had the longest history and where the social and cultural effects have therefore been the most intense. One landmark on this road has been the extinction of local states and the deportation of their former inhabitants by the builders of the Assyrian, Neobabylonian, and Achaemenian

---

[1] This has been one of the spurs by which the Irish, too, have been driven abroad. But, unlike the Scots and the Lebanese, the Irish have been driven by political oppression as well. The Irish diasporá belongs to the same class as the diasporás listed on pp. 211–12.

[2] R. Redfield: *The Primitive World and its Transformations*, p. 49.

[3] On p. 336.

empires. Another landmark has been the reorganization, in diasporá, of the uprooted communities. This has usually started as a spontaneous movement of self-help on the part of the deportees, and has ended as an obligatory organization on which the imperial authorities have insisted for their own convenience. We can trace the evolution of these non-territorial communities backwards from its fully developed form in the Ottoman Empire to its rudiments in the Achaemenian Empire, and we can watch the official attitude changing from tacit toleration through explicit sanction to positive requirement, as the usefulness of this horizontal system of communal organization gradually becomes apparent to the administrators of universal states.

If we are right in looking upon the universal states that have already come and gone as having been the forerunners of a future world-state, the social structure for which the Jewish diasporá provides a model will have a practical, as well as an academic, interest for the living generation of mankind and our successors. 'Displaced persons' are the raw materials of a diasporá; and, since the expulsion of the United Empire Loyalists from the United States after the Revolutionary War,[1] 'displaced persons' have, unhappily, been becoming an ever larger and more important feature in the configuration of human society. It is a tragic paradox that, during the last 150 years, old-established diasporás have been uprooted and expelled—if they have had the good fortune to escape being extirpated—as a result of the ruthless application of the Western ideal of nationally homogeneous local states. This ideal is an attempt to restore the configuration of society as it was before local communities began to be mixed up and stratified in diasporás in the course of a long succession of 'times of troubles' and universal states. Such attempts to 'put back the clock' work havoc—as is illustrated by the atrocities and sufferings that accompanied the partitions of the Ottoman Empire between 1821 and 1924 and of the British Indian Empire in 1947. In the Second World War the crimes of deracination and genocide were committed on an Assyrian scale. If it were now possible for history to repeat itself, we should be today on the eve of a third world war in which our world would be unified politically by force to the accompaniment of atrocities such as we have not yet witnessed. Since, however, a third world war would be fought with atomic weapons, it looks as if the actual choices now before us were a unification of the World by consent and, alternatively, genocide on a colossal scale. So perhaps we may venture to hope that, in shrinking from genocide, mankind will save itself from further bouts of wholesale eviction and massacre.

If this hope were realized, would that mean that the transformation of local communities into world-wide diasporás would come to a halt? This seems unlikely, so long as technology continues to advance; and this is a movement that shows no sign of halting or even slowing down. The accelerating improvement in means of communication of all kinds may do more to promote the creation of diasporás by facilitating it than Assyrian war-lords were ever able to do by force. In a society that is

[1] This was an epoch-making event in modern history, as has been pointed out in iv. 165.

'annihilating distance', world-wide diasporás, rather than local national states, look like 'the wave of the future'.[1]

No doubt, in a future world society, there will still be on the map a network of social units based on locality, as there has been in all the universal states that have come and gone so far. In the administrative organization of a universal state the local states that the empire-builders have overthrown have either been retained as provinces after having been deprived of their sovereignty or have been replaced by a new network of provinces with different areas but with the same function of serving as units for local administration. There are some indispensable social services—for instance, water-supply, drains, and light and power—that are bound, by their very nature, to be organized on the basis of neighbourhood. As technology continues to advance, the optimum area for such purposes may increase in size, but, at its maximum, it will still be small compared to the total area of the Earth's habitable surface. Thus we may expect to see units based on locality survive; but we may also expect to see these come to play a progressively less important part by comparison with units whose principle of association is, not physical neighbourhood, but a community of beliefs, ideas, aspirations, interests, or activities. This has been the tendency in the social history of universal states in the past; and in the current age this tendency seems likely to be reinforced by one of the characteristic movements of our time: the present-day world-wide drift into the cities.

Urbanization is going forward today in countries of the most diverse civilization and social structure. One can watch it happening in Japan, Indonesia, 'Iraq, Australia, Mexico, Peru. All over the World the rural population is flocking into the cities, even where the cities offer the eager immigrants nothing better than a life of unemployment and penury in shanty towns. In Japan the habitable part of the country has already become one continuous city, in which a minority of the urbanized population happens still to work in fields instead of in factories; and the present aspect of Japan gives an anticipatory view of what seems likely to be the future aspect of the World as a whole. Urbanization is being promoted by two consequences of the technological revolution that are both working in this direction. The reduction of the death-rate—especially the rate of infant mortality—by preventive medicine has resulted in an increase in the rural population beyond the numbers that agriculture either requires or is capable of supporting; and 'the annihilation of distance' has removed the ancient obstacles to migration. This transformation of the World into a cosmopolis favours social organization on a non-local basis. It is a well-known feature of urban life that city-dwellers associate, not with their next-door neighbours, but with kindred spirits scattered all over the metropolitan area. In a village one must consort with one's next-door neighbour, willy-nilly. In a great city with a highly developed transportation system, one has a far wider choice of friends and companions. Now that the World is becoming one city, we may expect to see associations based on neighbourhood come to be overshadowed by others based on spiritual affinity: that is to say, by diasporás in the broadest sense of the term in which this includes ubiquitous scattered minorities that are held together by religious and other ties of all kinds that are independent of locality.

If this forecast is justified, we need our Jewish model for a diasporá, as well as our Hellenic model for the transition from local states to a universal state and our Chinese model for the alternating rhythm of a universal state's successive lapses and rallies. Each of these models is an indispensable mental tool for the comparative study of civilizations, because each of them gives us the key to one of the major configurations of human society and culture during the Age of the Civilizations up to date. And each configuration is the product of a resolution of forces. In each case Man's attempt to achieve an aim that is of major importance to him can be seen contending with the problems and the penalties that his pursuit of this particular aim brings with it. In the Hellenic model we see Man in process of civilization pursuing the possibilities of creativity that are offered by a regime of extreme local diversity and independence, until the strife which is the price of this regime reaches a pitch of intensity at which society finds itself constrained to purchase peace through unity at the cost of resigning itself to an uninspiring uniformity. In the Jewish model we see Man in the same chapter of his history clinging to some revelation, discovery, achievement, or way of life that he feels to be of supreme significance and value, and therefore exerting himself to preserve the separate identity of the 'Chosen People' that is the custodian of this pearl of great price. The 'Chosen People's' belief in its national mission gives it the spirit to maintain itself in diasporá after losing its national state and even its national home—and this in a situation in which the rest of society has resigned itself to the merger of national individualities in the oecumenical unity that is the price of peace. In the Chinese model we see *soi-disant* civilized Man exerting himself to preserve this oecumenical unity, once established, and to restore it each time that it breaks up. He restores it because he cannot bear the strife and disorder that the return of disunity brings with it. Each of these endeavours is an attempt to satisfy one of Man's fundamental requirements. But the histories of civilizations up to date do not give us any assurance that these fundamental requirements can all be fulfilled simultaneously. The extent to which Man in process of civilization succeeds in reconciling these requirements with each other gives one measure of Man's capacity for living as the social animal that he has to be if he is to survive.

7. IS IT POSSIBLE TO CONSTRUCT A MODEL FOR HIGHER RELIGIONS?

The spiritual treasure that has inspired an uprooted people to preserve its separate identity in diasporá has, so far, usually been a higher religion. The higher religions have made their epiphany in the course of the Age of the Civilizations; and, if we take them at their adherents' valuation of them, we shall find in them alternative fields of study that will be more illuminating than civilizations because, in the higher religions, we shall be studying Man's most important activity. Higher religions have, in fact, been taken as their fields by Christian and Muslim students of human affairs. But religion is at a discount in the present-day Western World; and at the beginning of this book, when I was looking for a field of study that would be more intelligible than a national state is, I took civilizations as my units without considering higher religions as a possible alternative. If it had occurred to me to take my cue from the earliest English historian, the Venerable Bede, I should have expanded my field of vision, not from England to the Western World, but from English Christians to the Church of which they are adherents and to the religion of which the Church is the social embodiment. This different approach to the study of human affairs would, no doubt, have yielded a different picture of them.[1] It is not too late to follow up the secular approach by now taking the religious one in turn. And this still open possibility raises the question whether, for a comparative study of higher religions, it is possible and necessary to set up a model—or more than one—as we have found it useful to do as an aid to our comparative study of civilizations.

In this volume[2] I have suggested two criteria for distinguishing higher religions from others. Higher religions are attempts to put individual human souls into direct communion with absolute spiritual Reality, without the mediation of either non-human nature or the human society—whichever it may be—in which the soul in search of God is a participant in consequence of Man's being a social creature. And, for this reason, the discoverers—or recipients—of a higher religion are moved to extricate it from religion's traditional social matrix and to embody it in new institutions—the Christian Church, the Buddhist Sangha, and the like—that will no longer be integral parts of the structure of some civilization but will be independent societies of a new kind. Taking these two criteria as our touchstones, we have detected[3] a distinction between two sets of religions of the 'higher' category. In one set —represented by Buddhism, Christianity, and Islam—we have three higher religions that have extricated themselves more or less completely. In the other set—represented by Judaism, Zoroastrianism, and Hinduism—we have three other higher religions that have started along this road but have halted, part way.[4] Each of these other three displays the distinctive features of a higher religion, yet at the same time each of them has continued, so far, to be an integral part of the civilization within whose bosom it has arisen. In this situation would it be legitimate—and illuminating—to construct a model out of the common essential features of Islam, Christianity, and Buddhism, and to regard this as a standard that Hinduism, Zoroastrianism, and Judaism have approached without having succeeded in attaining it completely? Before committing ourselves to this course, it may be prudent to take note of some other signifi-

---

[1] This point has been touched on already on pp. 161–2.
[2] On pp. 81–84.   [3] See pp. 85–97.
[4] The list of six higher religions with which I am operating in this volume is, of course, not exhaustive. But at any rate it is an improvement on the list of four with which I operated in vol. vii. Christopher Dawson has justly criticized me (in *Toynbee and History*, p. 134; cp. Father L. Walker, ibid., p. 342) for not having included Judaism and the Hinayana.

cant differences that divide the higher religions on our list, and to observe whether, in all the possible alternative classifications, these six religions invariably fall into the same sets.

Assuming that the distinctive purpose of a higher religion is to establish and maintain direct communion between human souls and absolute spiritual Reality, we should expect it to announce a revelation or discovery of the truth about Reality and to give instructions for acting in the light of this truth. Since a higher religion's message is addressed to individuals, we should expect this also to be delivered by individual prophets, seers, or sages—whether it is revealed progressively by a succession of heralds, or is revealed by a single unique herald once for all. Since it is a revolutionary message, we should expect its heralds to proclaim and demand a more or less radical break with traditional religious practices and beliefs. Since the soul's whole destiny is in question, we should expect each higher religion to insist that it is the sole fount of truth, means of grace, and way of salvation for all men. We should expect these features to display themselves more clearly and amply in the higher religions that have established their independence completely than in those that have not shaken themselves free from the civilizations within which they have originally made their appearance. Let us see how far these *a priori* expectations are borne out by the facts.

The most precise and relevant statement of doctrine and set of instructions to individuals is to be found in the Hinayana school of Buddhism. The other higher religions, too, have creeds, with the exception of Hinduism, and all of them have sets of instructions. But in Christianity and Islam to some extent, as well as in the three incompletely independent higher religions to a larger extent, the instructions to individuals for the conduct of their direct personal relations with Reality are encumbered with ritual and social regulations. These are a legacy from the stage at which religion is merely one element among others in a culture, and is bound up with these other elements too intimately for it to be possible, at that stage, to draw a distinction between what is religious and what is secular. Only Buddhism—and this perhaps only in its original form, before the emergence of the Mahayana—has shaken itself entirely free from this legacy of an older dispensation.

When we look into the agency by which a higher religion's message has been delivered, we find that Zoroastrianism, as well as Buddhism, Christianity, and Islam, has a unique founder. Zarathustra, Gautama, Jesus, and Muhammad are, of course, recognized to have had both forerunners and successors. But the founder's uniqueness is not impaired by this. In his followers' eyes his epiphany is the culminating event in human history; there will not be any future event of equal magnitude—at any rate, not before the winding-up of history at the end of time. The founder's epiphany divides all time and all history into two epochs. However, in the history of Buddhism, as we watch the Mahayana taking shape, we see the unique figure of the historical Buddha, Gautama, being gradually lost among a series of buddhas and a host of bodhisattvas, some of whom are now credited with greater potency, and are objects of greater devotion, than the historical founder himself. Here we see

Buddhism moving in the same direction as post-Buddhaic Hinduism, with its series of incarnations of Vishnu and its succession of sages. If we look for a founder of post-Buddhaic Hinduism, we may single out Šankara—only to find that he has not acquired the status of the unique founders of Buddhism, Zoroastrianism, Christianity, and Islam. Who would venture to maintain that Šankara is in a totally different category from, say, his successor Ramanuja or even from his remote predecessor Yajñavalkya? And, when we turn to Judaism and seek to identify a founder here, we meet with the same difficulty. Shall we find the founder of Judaism in Abraham the recipient of the Promise, or in Moses the recipient of the Law, or in Johanan ben Zakkai the father of the present-day diasporá? Indeed, shall we find him in any individual human being? Was not all Israel, collectively, the human party to the Covenant made at Mount Sinai? And is a founder of any kind, individual or collective, really the central human figure in God's dispensation as seen through Jewish eyes? Instead of being turned backwards towards a founder, are they not directed forwards towards a future fulfiller? In Judaism does not the expected Messiah overshadow the patriarchs and prophets, as, in the Mahayana, the coming buddha overshadows the historical Gautama?

In making a revolutionary breach with tradition, Gautama and Zara-thustra have been more uncompromising than Jesus or Muhammad. Jesus claimed that he was fulfilling the Scriptures, and Muhammad that he was restoring the pure religion of Abraham. Hinduism, like the English Common Law, goes still farther in asserting an unbroken continuity with the past. It innovates, not by abrogating the past, but by reinterpreting it. On the other hand, Judaism, which resembles Hinduism and Zoroastrianism in retaining a large and burdensome legacy of primitive ritual and social practice, is as uncompromising as Zoroastrianism and Buddhism in proclaiming its break with traditional polytheism.

It will be seen that the sets into which our six higher religions divide on these several different principles of classification are not always precisely the same. And, when we come to the distinction between exclusive-mindedness and embracing-mindedness, we find that, unexpectedly, this further division cuts across our original division between independence and an incomplete approximation to it. This is surprising, because the higher religions that have gone the farthest in extricating themselves might have been expected, *a priori*, to have become the most convinced of the uniqueness of their own truth and value. Yet, on the test of their degree of exclusive-mindedness, the higher religions divide on geographico-cultural lines, with the Judaic religions and Zoroastrianism on the exclusive-minded side, and the Indian religions on the other.[1]

Hinduism is all-inclusive in its own estimation. Every religion and

---

[1] This contrast is underlined by Christopher Dawson in *Toynbee and History*, p. 135. He goes on, ibid., p. 136, to express the view that Christianity's only effective rival today is Communism. He describes Communism as being a 'secular counter-religion'. It might also be described as being an heretical version of Christianity, in the sense in which Christianity itself and Islam are heretical versions of Judaism. Whatever label we may affix to it, Communism is unquestionably the offspring of Judaism and Christianity, and its characteristically Judaic exclusive-mindedness is an inheritance from its progenitors.

philosophy under the Sun is, in Hindu eyes, just one more interesting and valuable variation on Hinduism's inexhaustible theme. This is the truth about them all, as Hindus see it; and it remains the truth, however vehemently it may be denied by the blind-eyed devotees of certain fanatical sects. This is, of course, the attitude that we should expect to find Hinduism adopting; for, of all six higher religions, Hinduism is the one that has been the most frank in acknowledging its continuity with the past and the most pious in cultivating it; and one of the most prominent characteristics of religion everywhere, in the age before the higher religions made their appearance, was a spirit of live-and-let-live, which made possible the coexistence of a number of local pantheons, with a number of separate divinities in each of them. If, in the Hellenic World in the third and fourth centuries of the Christian Era, Neoplatonism had got the better of Christianity, present-day Hinduism would have met with a kindred spirit in a Neoplatonist Church at the western end of the Old World. Even the historical victor here, Christianity, has been more Hindu-minded than it admits; for it conquered Neoplatonism and its other rivals—the worships of Mithras, Isis, Cybele, and the rest—at the price of unavowedly incorporating them in itself. Islam and Judaism, too, have incorporated elements of other religions to a lesser extent. But all three Judaic religions speak with one voice in denying these failures of theirs to live up to their principles completely.

This is what we should expect of Christianity and Islam, which have made themselves wholly independent of the civilizations in which they came to birth, and have made it their mission to convert the whole of Mankind. But the repudiation of the past is surprising in Judaism, which has so far remained attached to a particular 'Chosen People' whose cultural heritage goes back to a pre-prophetic, pre-Mosaic, and pre-Abrahamic antiquity. Conversely, it is surprising to find Buddhism, which resembles Islam and Christianity in the completeness of its independence and in the universality of its mission, nevertheless behaving in practice in a Hindu way over the all-important issue of its attitude towards other religions. In Eastern Asia, which has been its major mission-field, Buddhism has not seriously attempted to wipe its rivals off the map. It has been content with coexistence, and has not shrunk from making the necessary compromises.[1] In China it has acquiesced in being fought with its own weapons. It has suffered the Taoist counter-church to purloin its organization and ritual, and the Confucian philosophy to purloin its metaphysics, in either case without acknowledgements. In Japan, Buddhism has enlisted Shinto divinities as janitors for the bodhisattvas' temples, and has agreed upon an equal division of functions and emoluments—taking for itself the monopoly of officiating

[1] The position of the Tantric Mahayana in Tibet, Mongolia, and Zungaria and of the Hinayana in Ceylon, Burma, Siam, and Cambodia is superficially different. In these countries the local form of Buddhism is not just one of several coexisting religions and philosophies, as it is in China, Vietnam, Korea, and Japan. It is *the* religion, in the sense in which, today, Christianity is *the* religion in Europe and the Americas, and Islam *the* religion in South-West Asia and North Africa. Yet, in the countries in which Buddhism has secured a local monopoly, it has bought it at the same price at which Christianity and Islam have bought theirs. It has prevailed by incorporating a great deal of the previous religion of the land.

at funerals, while leaving to Shinto the monopoly of officiating at marriages. If Buddhism had also disseminated itself in Western Asia and Europe, the Buddhist temple in a present-day English village would be rubbing shoulders with a Neoplatonist temple and a shrine of Odin or Thor, and the relations between the three non-Christian clergymen in the village would be decidedly more amicable than those between the actual Church of England parson, Methodist minister, and Roman Catholic priest.

Thus, when we try to classify the higher religions, we find ourselves confronted by an irreducible cross-division between two principles of classification that are both of major importance. On the test of the extent of the achievement of independence and universality, Buddhism, Islam, and Christianity fall into one group and Hinduism, Zoroastrianism, and Judaism into another. On the test of the degree of exclusive-mindedness, the three Judaic religions and Zoroastrianism fall into one group, as against the two Indian religions. On this evidence we can go no farther than to conclude that a tendency towards independence, universality, and exclusiveness is characteristic of the higher religions as a species. But we shall not find any particular specimen or specimens combining all three specific characteristics so markedly as to provide us with the materials for constructing a model applicable to all representatives of the class.

C

RECONSIDERATIONS OF PARTICULAR TOPICS

VII. EXPLANATIONS AND REVISIONS OF USAGES OF TERMS

I. DEFINITIONS

THERE is no need to revise my usage of the term 'definitions', since, so far, I have used it rarely, and then only, as far as I am aware, in the ordinary current meaning of it. I must, however, now explain what I believe this meaning to be, because I have been criticized, both in general and in particular, for not having defined my terms clearly in advance, before making use of them.

Christopher Hill, for example, finds that 'Mr. Toynbee eschews precise definition',[1] and Bagby pillories my work as 'an outstanding example of the difficulties and confusion into which a lack of clear definitions can lead us'.[2] A. Eban complains[3] that my use of the word 'fossil' is never defined and adds that 'it is indeed a basic weakness of his work that it evades the definition of its fundamental terms'. Since 'civilization' and 'civilizations' (singular: '*a* civilization') are key-terms of mine, I have been taken to task particularly for not defining these by critics who believe that preliminary definitions are desirable. K. W. Thompson has criticized me[4] for not defining my use of this word in the singular, and explaining how it stands to my use of the word 'society'. M. Postan considers[5] that I have used it in a great variety of senses. R. K. Merton,[6] P. Gardiner,[7] P. M. Sweezy,[8] H. Marrou,[9] W. H. McNeill,[10] and A. Hourani[11] hold that I have not defined or elucidated my use of the word in the plural. R. T. Clark holds[12] that I have given a definition that is arbitrary and incomplete. Merton and Hourani find, as Bagby does,[13] that my list of civilizations is arbitrary and that this is due to my failure to define what I mean by them. Granville Hicks

[1] *The Modern Quarterly*, Autumn, 1947, p. 295.
[2] *Culture and History*, p. 182.
[3] In *Toynbee and History*, p. 324.
[4] Ibid., p. 216. Cp. M. A. Fitzsimons in *The Intent of Toynbee's History: A Co-operative Appraisal*, and R. T. Clark in *The Nineteenth Century and After*, vol. cxxx, No. 777 (1941), p. 297. See further the present volume, pp. 274–5.
[5] In *The Sociological Review*, vol. xxviii (1936), p. 58.
[6] In *The American Journal of Sociology*, vol. xlvii, No. 2 (September, 1941), pp. 205–13.
[7] In *Time and Tide*, 30th October, 1954.
[8] In *The Nation*, 19th October, 1946.
[9] In *Esprit*, July, 1952, p. 123.
[10] In *The Intent of Toynbee's History: A Cooperative Appraisal*.
[11] In *The Dublin Review*, vol. 229, No. 470 (December, 1955), p. 380.
[12] See *The Nineteenth Century and After*, November, 1941, p. 297.
[13] In *Culture and History*, pp. 177–81.

questions[1] whether '*a* civilization' is definable, and, supposing that it is, whether it can be defined precisely enough to make it feasible to compare specimens of the class. I have also been criticized for not having defined what I mean by 'creativity',[2] by 'universal state',[3] by 'culture',[4] by 'sainthood',[5] and by 'laws of God'.[6]

However, on this issue, the critics are not unanimous. G. A. Birks, for example, defends me[7] against criticisms of me for not having defined my terms, and R. Coulborn finds[8] that I have been right in principle in not trying to define the word 'civilizations' too tightly. H. W. B. Joseph gives the reason why. Definitions of kinds, he points out,[9] cannot be demonstrated. They come from our experience of particular cases. And, since we cannot know beforehand how many more particular cases we may be going to encounter in the future, our definitions may, at any moment, become untrue to the facts if we have frozen these definitions so hard that we can no longer revise them. Here we put our finger on the weak point of definitions as instruments for acquiring knowledge and understanding of phenomena, human or non-human. Definitions are, by definition, hard-set. At least, the only definition of definitions that I can think of is that they are frozen 'models' (using the word 'models' in the sense in which it has been used in the preceding chapter). It is significant that definitions have scored their greatest successes in mathematics: for instance, in geometry. In mathematics the materials under investigation are also frozen hard, and therefore definitions, in spite of their rigidity, are effective tools for dealing with them. Mathematical entities are abstractions from phenomena; and their human makers take care to carry the process of abstraction to a degree at which the products will be incapable of committing irregularities. But phenomena, as we find them, are not equally docile. Even non-human phenomena are not amenable to complete *a priori* regimentation; human phenomena are elusively mobile. It is therefore hazardous to apply to the study of phenomena a mental instrument that has acquired its prestige through its effectiveness for the study of abstractions.

If definitions are to be used at all in the study of human affairs, they will be less hampering, and possibly more illuminating, if, instead of making them, *more mathematico*, at the beginning of our inquiry, we work them out retrospectively, as a check on the results that we have obtained by the application of ill-defined and therefore flexible 'models'. Bagby is an outstanding example of an inquirer who has pinned his faith on *a priori* definitions as being the most promising prolegomena to a comparative study of civilizations. Yet, when, in the ninth and last chapter of *Culture and History*, he sets out to give examples of similarities in the development of civilizations, he declares, to his credit,

---

[1] In *The New Leader*, 18th October, 1954.
[2] R. K. Merton in loc. cit.   [3] R. K. Merton, ibid.
[4] J. K. Feibleman in *T'ien Hsia Monthly*, vol. xi, Nos. 1 and 2 (1940), pp. 21–22.
[5] Hourani in loc. cit., p. 385.
[6] C. B. Joynt in *The Australasian Journal of Philosophy*, vol. 34, No. 3 (December, 1955), p. 196.
[7] In *Philosophy*, October, 1950, pp. 336–40.
[8] *In Toynbee and History*, p. 149, footnote 1.
[9] *An Introduction to Logic*, 2nd ed., p. 81.

that 'precise and useful definitions of basic terms can only be formulated after, not before, the facts have been carefully examined'. If he had lived to write the further volumes that he was planning, one may guess that he would have had to spend many more pages in modifying the definitions given in his prolegomena than he has spent in this preliminary volume in setting them up.

2. HISTORY

The original meaning of the Greek word *historia* was inquiry or study. The Greek adjective *polyhistor* meant an inquirer whose curiosity had led him to study a wide range of subjects. There is a vestige of this original Greek usage in the current English term 'natural history' in the sense of a study of Nature (though the realm of Nature has come, in this context, to be conventionally restricted to the province of living creatures, and this to the exclusion of Man). The Greek word, however, came to be applied particularly to the study of human affairs, and this to the exclusion of the analytical and classificatory procedure that is the human intellect's characteristic method of operation. Hence it came to mean the study of human phenomena as we see them on the move through time and space; and from this, by analogy, it has also come to mean the study of phenomena on the move, whatever their nature: e.g. the phenomena studied in astronomy, geology, and biology, which, as A. L. Kroeber has pointed out,[1] are really not scientific but historical studies.[2] Kroeber has also pointed out[3] that the true antithesis to the analytical and classificatory procedure is not the vision of human affairs as temporal events but 'the endeavour to achieve a conceptual integration of phenomena while preserving the integrity of the phenomena'. These two alternative definitions do not conflict with each other; and both bear out Kroeber's dicta[4] that science and history differ, not in their field, but in their basic approach; that the historical approach is applicable to all phenomena; and that the material of history can be used for the scientific approach as well as for the historical. Even the two basic approaches have an underlying affinity. History, as well as science, reconstructs,[5] though it does this only against the grain, and with the archaistic purpose of restoring dilapidated phenomena to their pristine integrity,[6] whereas science reconstructs with the purpose of probing its way through the phenomena to the discovery of some non-phenomenal reality behind them.

Whether we adopt the popular definition of history or Kroeber's more penetrating definition of it or both, we are led to the conclusion that the distinction between the historical approach and other approaches

---

[1] In *The Nature of Culture*, p. 80 (see Chapter II, Annex, *Ad Hominem*, pp. 604–5, in the present volume).

[2] In modern Western languages the word 'history' is used in a secondary sense to mean the subject-matter of historical study. In this objective—or would-be objective—meaning the range of the word 'history' is usually confined to human affairs.

[3] See the passages quoted on p. 14.   [4] Ibid., pp. 73 and 74.

[5] Ibid., p. 5. 'Historical determinations are in their essence subjective findings' (ibid., p. 64).

[6] The historical approach is always a reconstruction—of the phenomena themselves and of their dates and places (ibid., p. 70; cp. pp. 79 and 101).

to the study of human affairs can be maintained only in the field of epistemological theory. 'History is one of the ways of organising human knowledge';[1] but we have already taken note[2] that the method of preserving the integrity of the phenomena by arranging them in the temporal sequence in which they present themselves to us is not adequate for coping with the phenomena without also resorting to alternative ways of handling them. Since the stream of events never, in fact, presents itself in the singular, as one solitary sequence, but always in the plural, as a number of sequences occurring simultaneously side by side, we cannot cope with the phenomena without also taking a synoptic comparative view of at least two, and usually many more, simultaneous sequences; and this means bringing to bear the method of analysis and classification. Accordingly, in practice, the followers of either method have always applied the other method as well. As Kroeber sees it, history deals in phenomena, and science in process, but an interest in phenomena and an interest in process are both necessary.[3] 'If history has no end except the collection of facts for their own sake, it becomes merely an intellectual pastime, like stamp-collecting.'[4] Laws cannot be eliminated from history. Conversely, historical elements are present in all sciences.[5] Science has become historical in spirit,[6] while 'history is . . . becoming the science of social development'.[7] 'Sociology and history are two complementary parts of a single science—the science of social life.'[8] We must apply the technique of the social anthropologists to the study of the higher civilizations' constituent cultures. 'Contemporary anthropologists, like Professor Evans-Pritchard, have accepted the principle of the essentially historical character of social anthropology, and in the same way it seems reasonable that historians should begin to pay more attention to the methods and the contribution of social anthropology.'[9] 'If we throw aside . . . administrative considerations and look at the problem itself, we see that the difference between the philosopher and the historian can only be one of degree and emphasis.'[10]

Unfortunately the reaction of modern Western historians to the rise of the social sciences has, so far, been, for the most part, defensive and even hostile. This attitude of theirs has been noted in this book already in several places.[11] In the first of these passages I have criticized it, and, on reconsideration, I find myself confirmed in holding that my criticism is justified. I have, however, expressed myself there in Polybius's polemical vein, and polemical controversy is notoriously apt to defeat its own purpose by provoking opposition instead of winning assent. I will therefore now present the same criticism in the words of A. L. Kroeber, a scholar who has the art of being trenchant without being provocative.

[1] M. R. Cohen: *The Meaning of Human History*, p. 41, quoted already on p. 129, footnote 2. [2] On pp. 158–70.
[3] Kroeber, op. cit., pp. 63 and 62.
[4] Chr. Dawson: *The Dynamics of World History*, p. 19.
[5] Cohen, op. cit., p. 37. [6] Dawson, op. cit., p. 19.
[7] Ibid., p. 20. [8] Ibid.
[9] Chr. Dawson in *Toynbee and History*, p. 138.
[10] Cohen, op. cit., quoted on p. 130.
[11] e.g. in ix. 173–216, and in the present volume on pp. 13–14, 19 and 129–30.

'History does not know what to do with the flock of social sciences mill-ing around her knees. She wavers between claiming them as offspring be-cause they deal with her material, and repudiating them because they do not treat it historically. It is an attitude at once somewhat annoyed and disdainful.'[1]

In the historians' reaction to science's invasion of what they consider to be their domain,

'there has been an inclination to cling to narrative as being least easily convertible into generalisation; to hug events rather than engage with their patterns; to resign the economic aspects of history to economists rather than include them; to ignore the results of ethnography, on the external ground that they are dateless and therefore non-historical; to allow the history of the great East Asiatic civilizations to settle behind watertight bulkheads; to view any larger culture history askance; to emphasize the mechanics of documentation as evidence that history, too, was objective and scientific.'[2]

This is a fair account of the attitude that has been adopted by con-temporary Western historians—or at any rate by one school of them which, at present, probably represents the majority. We may perhaps expect to see this rigid posture gradually relax as the application of scientific method to the study of human affairs becomes more familiar, and as it continues, as, no doubt, it will, to vindicate itself by making important additions to our knowledge and understanding. In our time we are watching the merger of the old departmental 'disciplines' in a new comprehensive study of human affairs. This merger seems in-evitable, because we not only have effective means of making it, but have an imperative need to make it, in the present situation of mankind.[3] 'This great unity is the true study for the student of Man.'[4] If the historians were to persist in holding aloof, their non-co-operation would not arrest the movement towards a unification of human studies; its effect would merely be to take out of the historians' hands the job of supplying the indispensable historical component of the new comprehensive study. This would be a loss to learning, since it is obvious that nobody else could supply this component so well as the historians themselves if they chose. Kroeber believes 'the time to be near when efforts for close federation in the united sciences may well come from students of cul-ture'.[5] So long as the goal is reached, it does not matter which of the 'disciplines' has the honour and glory of having taken the initiative. What matters is that all should co-operate whole-heartedly in a common enterprise in which an important interest of mankind is at stake.

3. METAHISTORY

The word 'metahistory' needs defining because it has become current only recently. Presumably it has been coined on the analogy of Aristotle's coinage of the word 'metaphysics'. If so, it would mean a field of study

---

[1] A. L. Kroeber: *The Nature of Culture*, p. 73.   [2] Ibid., p. 74.
[3] See Chapter V.   [4] Kroeber, op. cit., p. 19, quoted already on p. 132.
[5] Ibid., pp. 10–11, quoted already on p. 132.

that comes 'after' the study of history and lies 'beyond' it (the Greek preposition 'meta' can mean both 'after' and 'beyond').

When Aristotle had completed his inquiry into physics, he found himself left with a number of unanswered questions that had arisen in the course of it. These questions were not about physics itself; they were about some hitherto nameless subject which was apparently the setting within which the inquiry into physics had been conducted. Thus the intellectual conquest of the field of physics opened up a further field of inquiry beyond it, and Aristotle labelled this 'what comes "after" or "beyond" physics' (*tà metà tà physiká*). This label might imply no more than that physics was the avenue along which Aristotle had arrived at the threshold of his new subject. It might also imply that, if one does not go on from physics (or history) to 'metaphysics' (or 'metahistory'), one will not be able to understand physics (or history) itself, or, in other words, that 'metaphysics' (or 'metahistory') is the field in which physics (or history) finds its explanation. These two implications are evidently not mutually exclusive.

Is there really a subject, analogous to Aristotle's *tà metà tà physiká*, that can properly be labelled 'what comes after history' (*tà metà tà historiká*)? If the word 'history' is defined narrowly as meaning 'the study of phenomena on the move' or 'the study of phenomena in their integrity', then the analytical and classificatory method of studying human affairs—the method applied in psychology and in the social sciences—would fall within the field of 'metahistory'. K. W. Thompson points out[1] that 'the philosophy of history', as metahistory has traditionally been called, 'has three possible meanings. It . . . may be construed as a *method* for dealing with the complexities of history or an interpretation of the *meaning* of history or a statement of the *laws* of history.' The main issue in the field of method is the question what should be the relation between the narrative method and the analytico-classificatory one—a question which has been discussed in this volume in Chapter VI and again in the present chapter under the heading of 'History'. Historical method would not usually be thought of as falling within the field of metahistory. At the same time it is impossible to take a synoptic comparative view of human affairs without taking account of regularities, recurrences, and 'laws'; 'laws', in their turn, involve meaning; and inquiries into the meaning of history certainly fall within the field of metahistory, since the meaning of a thing can be sought for only in some field outside the thing that we are trying to interpret and understand.

Metahistory, then, must mean the study of Reality in some higher dimension than that of human affairs as these present themselves to us in the phenomena and are then organized by our minds through the method of analysis and classification. This study, which arises out of the study of history, and so comes after it, must be akin to, if not identical with, metaphysics and theology.[2]

---

[1] In *Toynbee and History*, p. 201.
[2] 'The Problem of Metahistory' has been discussed by Christopher Dawson in an essay reprinted in *The Dynamics of World History*, pp. 287–93. In this essay Dawson

A classic example of a work of metahistory, in this sense, is Saint Augustine's *De Civitate Dei*. As Kohn puts it, 'What Augustine wrote was not history, as Thucydides had written it; it was a study of history.'[1] Kohn goes on to point out[2] that what I am writing in the present book is also not history, though I have written history in other works of mine. I should say myself that the present book began as an analytico-classificatory comparative study of human affairs and turned into a metahistorical inquiry *en route*. In a review of volumes i–iii[3] M. Postan has commended me for using historical information as evidence for scientific study, instead of seeking it as an end in itself.[4] Later reviewers of volumes vii–x, or of the first ten volumes as a whole, have pointed out that, in the course of the book, I have made a change in my field and in my objective.[5]

4. FACTS

In a critique of my work, P. Geyl declares his belief that 'the facts are there to be used'.[6] The same belief is mistakenly attributed to me, as well, by H. Holborn. 'To him, facts are ready-made objective elements.'[7] This belief is also implied in Geyl's and Sir Earnest Barker's criticism of my presentation of what seem to me to be facts to me. 'They are not facts; they are subjective presentations of facts.'[8] 'They are not primary and objective facts (so many stamens, so many pistils, and so on); they are secondary and subjective constructions.'[9] As Barker and Geyl see it, the authentic historian is a collector. He is like a man scrambling up a torrent bed and picking up, on his way, the boulders that he finds lying there. They therefore look askance at me, because they see in me, not a collector, but at best a manufacturer and at worst a fabricator. Even on the kindest interpretation open to them on their conception of the nature of facts, I cannot be an authentic historian. But the conception on which this criticism is based is surely a mistaken one.

Facts are not really like boulders that have been detached and shaped and deposited exclusively by the play of the forces of non-human nature. They are like flaked and chipped flints, hewn stones, bricks, or briquettes. Human action has had a hand in making them what they are, and they would not be what they are if this action had not taken

points out that 'metahistory' is not the same thing as 'universal history' (op. cit., p. 290) and that 'all historiography is pervaded by metahistorical influences' (ibid., p. 289). He then raises the question how one is to explain 'the strong reaction against metahistory which is now so common among English academic historians' (p. 289). Metahistory, Dawson notices, is even more unpopular with modern academic historians than universal history is (p. 290). Dawson cites the case of de Tocqueville as evidence that 'metahistory is not the enemy of true history but its guide and its friend, provided always that it is good metahistory' (p. 293). His conclusion is as follows: 'The experience of the great historians, such as Tocqueville and Ranke, leads me to believe that a universal metahistorical vision of this kind, partaking more of the nature of religious contemplation than of scientific generalisation, lies close to the sources of their creative power' (ibid., p. 293).

[1] H. Kohn in *Der Monat*, August, 1955, p. 464.
[2] Ibid., cited in footnote 3 to p. 130.
[3] In *The Sociological Review*, vol. xxviii (1936), p. 53.
[4] See p. 15. [5] See Chapter II, Annex, pp. 649–51.
[6] P. Geyl: *Debates with Historians*, p. 140.
[7] *The Saturday Review of Literature*, 31st May, 1947, p. 29.
[8] Geyl, op. cit., p. 141. [9] Sir Ernest Barker in *Toynbee and History*, p. 95.

place. 'The facts of history are not the brute things or events outside the mind, for they have filtered through minds before I have word of them.'[1] 'We can never catch pure facts apart from perspective.'[2] Facts are, in truth, exactly what is meant by the Latin word *facta* from which the English word is derived. They are 'things that have been made'— that is to say 'fictitious' things rather than 'factual' things—and this truth about them cannot be evaded by calling them 'data' ('gifts') instead. Gifts imply the existence of a giver, as inescapably as manufactures imply the existence of a maker. Whether we call phenomena data or call them facts, we are admitting that they have been given or have been made by somebody. We may attribute the maximum amount of credit for them to non-human nature or to God, but we shall not be able to clear ourselves of the charge that we, too, have had a hand in the transaction, and that our contribution, however small we may reckon it to have been, has nevertheless been an indispensable one. 'Facts do not "speak for themselves". Concepts do not "emerge" from the evidence.'[3] 'The process of "establishing the facts" about an event involves theory.'[4] 'The criterion of selection is not inherent in the data; it is applied by the historian.'[5] 'History is the re-enactment of the past in the mind of the historian, and even "facts" exist only there.'[6] 'All our impressions from the outer world of phenomena are, at the same time, thought, judgment, explanation.'[7] 'What we call historic facts are the results of our interpretation of certain fragmentary data or remains. Our implicitly assumed principles determine the character of our interpretation.'[8] Many of these principles are hypotheses accepted because of their relative success in explaining facts. 'They are not explained from the facts, but the facts from them.'[9] No sharp distinction can be drawn between facts and their meanings.[10] The meaning of a fact is found in one's conception of its relations to other facts.[11] 'Nature does not provide separately both facts and laws.'[12] No fact can be established or made intelligible unless it is closely related to other facts or is part of a larger system (though it is also true that no connexion between facts is purely man-made).[13] 'The so-called facts of history are cross-sections or aspects of a world in process of change.'[14] In a criticism of my work,[15] G. J. Renier asks: 'Why not just one single fact?' in place of my welter of mythology, allegory, hypothesis, and what not. The answer is: 'No hypothesis, no fact.'

Moreover, since a fact cannot come into existence without the good

---

[1] Father M. C. D'Arcy: *The Sense of History*, p. 48.
[2] M. C. Swabey: *The Judgment of History*, p. 233.
[3] Social Science Research Council's Committee on Historiography's Report (1954), p. 131.   [4] Ibid., p. 89.
[5] Ibid., p. 90.
[6] H. Holborn in *The Saturday Review of Literature*, 31st May, 1947, p. 29.
[7] J. Romein in *Toynbee and History*, p. 347.
[8] M. R. Cohen: *The Meaning of Human History*, pp. 4–5.
[9] H. W. B. Joseph: *An Introduction to Logic*, 2nd ed., p. 513.
[10] Cohen, op. cit., p. 44.   [11] Ibid.
[12] R. B. Braithwaite: *Scientific Explanation*, p. 367.
[13] Cohen, op. cit., p. 33.
[14] Ibid., p. 44.
[15] In *Toynbee and History*, p. 75.

offices of an hypothesis, the parent hypothesis cannot change without producing a corresponding change in the fact that it has engendered.

'History advances by changes in men's way of conceiving the relations of past facts to one another, as well as by changes in their view of what the facts were.'[1]

'In the framing of hypotheses . . . we are called upon to regard facts in new ways and to suggest, not simply that certain facts are connected, but how, or in accordance with what principle, they are connected. And this often involves a radical transformation in our way of looking at the facts themselves; for a fact is not such an ascertainable thing as the language we sometimes use might seem to imply. In a sense facts are stubborn; in another sense they are pliant to our thought. They are stubborn as far as we have rightly apprehended them; but what we call fact is largely a matter of inference and interpretation, performed often unconsciously and often erroneously; there is room here for a re-interpretation, in accordance with the requirements of the rest of our knowledge; and, so far as what are called facts lend themselves to this, they may fairly be called pliant.'[2]

'The familiar facts take on a new appearance in the light of new theories.[3] . . . It is possible to bind facts together by a new conception and so place them in a different light and re-interpret them, without apparently generalising.'[4]

As examples, Joseph cites the transformation of the 'facts' as a result of the substitution of the Copernican theory of the movements of the heavenly bodies for the Ptolemaic,[5] the substitution of the theory of the evolution of species for the theory of their separate simultaneous creation,[6] and the substitution by Lavoisier of the hypothetical element oxygen for the hypothetical element phlogiston.[7] In each of these celebrated instances the 'facts' changed when the theory changed because these 'facts' were changeable interpretations of unchanging phenomena.

If it is true that every fact is, as the etymology of the word implies, something that has been constructed, and if it is also true that part, at least, of the indispensable work of construction has been done by the apprehending human mind, it seems hazardous to try to classify some so-called facts as genuine on the illusory ground that they are objective, while rejecting other so-called facts as spurious on the solid ground that they are constructions of a human mind. If it is true that all facts are partly constructions of human minds, the presence or absence of this man-made element in them cannot be an effective criterion for distinguishing the spurious from the genuine.

Sir Ernest Barker's stamens and pistils are facts for him because his thinking makes them so. *A fortiori*, this is the reason why national states and national churches are also facts for him (if I interpret him right).[8] These are human institutions; and, of all the myriad kinds of phenomena within human ken, human institutions are mind-made to the

[1] Joseph, op. cit., p. 467.   [2] Ibid., p. 468.   [3] Ibid.
[4] Ibid., p. 470.   [5] Ibid., pp. 468 and 470–1.
[6] Ibid., pp. 468 and 473–5.   [7] Ibid., pp. 472–3
[8] When he writes 'I believe in the national state (and, for that matter, in the national church)', the words 'I believe' signify, no doubt, approval, not credence. But one could hardly approve of an institution without also believing in its existence.

highest degree. Institutions are networks of relations between human beings; and these relations exist solely in human minds. When they fall out of mind, they cease to exist; and their existence is already imperilled when they fall out of favour. This is a characteristic feature of institutions; it is common to institutions of all kinds: cultures, societies, churches, states, clubs, rites, war, marriage, tabus, totems, and the rest. All alike are mind-made; and, if this were valid evidence of unreality, they would have, all alike, to be written off as being hallucinations.[1]

At least two of my critics hold that one or more of the species of institutions with which I operate in this book are illusory, in contrast to others.[2] Barker, for instance, says of me:[3]

'He sees Brocken-spectres of superhuman dimensions ("civilizations", "laws", "dominant minorities", "internal proletariats", "Herodianisms" and "Zealotisms") walking along the ridges of history. May it not be better to see men like ourselves, rather than these great spectres? Of course, . . . groups too matter. . . . But . . . they must be studied in their human individuality, and in definite and visible terms—terms of territory, terms of nationality, terms of their state-systems, terms of their religious organisations. We live on Earth and not in cloudland; and we must study ourselves as we live on Earth, in terms of our earthly institutions.'

Henri Marrou makes the same point against me. A civilization, he submits, looks more like a real entity in a still-life cross-section than when we look at it on the move.[4]

'The twenty-one "objects" of which his theory seeks to give an account are nothing but abstractions treated as realities (*réifiées*); this powerful effort embraces nothing but phantoms.'[5]

These two critics of mine seem to me to be confusing reality with familiarity. I think the reason why the institutions with which I operate look to them like phantoms is simply that these do not happen to be the institutions in which these two critics themselves are accustomed to deal. Is there any sense in which 'nationality', 'state-systems', and 'religious organisations' are 'visible', in which 'civilizations', 'laws', 'minorities', and 'proletariats' are not visible except as hallucinations? All these phenomena are institutions, and the visibility of all of them alike is in the mind's, not the body's, eye. We may call this mental realm 'Earth' or we may call it 'cloudland', but it is of the same order of reality in every case. This is true also of 'territory'; for the territory that, at the present moment, is British in nationality and is occupied by the state-system of the United Kingdom has in time past been occupied by a bevy of Welsh and English successor-states of the Roman Empire; by a province of the Roman Empire before that; and, before the Roman conquest, by a bevy of Celtic principalities. If 'territory' means the geographical environment of a nationality or a state, we may here recall Spate's dicta[6] that 'this world, without Man, is not environment, is not our World', and that 'the facts of geography are the facts as they are approached.'

---

[1] This point is taken up again on pp. 270-1.
[2] This point is taken up again on pp. 288-92.   [3] In *Toynbee and History*, p. 96.
[4] *Esprit*, July, 1952, p. 124.   [5] Ibid., p. 125.   [6] Quoted on pp. 146-7.

When Barker says that groups 'are groups of actual persons, engaged in actual personal relations',[1] there is no disagreement between him and me. I should add, for my part, that these actual persons are also engaged in the far more widely ramifying and more long-lasting impersonal relations that we call 'institutions'. Persons and relations between persons are phenomena of two different orders of reality. If Barker maintains that the reality of persons is of a higher, as well as a different, order than the reality of relations between persons, I agree with him on this point too. I disagree in holding, as I do hold, that, however high or low we rate the order of reality represented by institutions, it is the same for institutions of all species.

Another critic, H. J. Morgenthau, deprecates the choice of civilizations as units of study on the ground, not that they are unreal, but that they are a kind of concept which is not easily verifiable empirically.

'It is not by accident that there has been a tendency for history to be written in terms of political or geographic units rather than of civilizations; for the former lend themselves more readily to empirical verification than do the latter.'[2]

In this context Morgenthau cites China as a case in point for his thesis. Yet surely the range of the Chinese Civilization is less difficult to verify empirically, both in time and in space, than the range of a geographical unit called 'China' or of a state or states that can be labelled 'Chinese'. The range of the Chinese Civilization can be ascertained by clear and exact criteria. Wherever and whenever we find the Chinese characters being used and the Chinese style of art being cultivated, we can affirm confidently that the Chinese Civilization is present. On the other hand, China as a geographical unit is much more elusive. The area occupied by the Chinese Civilization has varied from age to age. At the earliest date to which our records go back, its geographical domain is confined to the middle section of the basin of the Yellow River; today it extends over Manchuria, Sse-chuan, Canton, and Singapore. The configuration of Chinese political units has been still more kaleidoscopic. The changing area of the domain of the Chinese Civilization has sometimes been divided among twenty or thirty states, sometimes among half-a-dozen, sometimes among three, sometimes between two. At other times the whole area has constituted a single political entity. The Chinese Civilization seems to lend itself to verification more readily than any political or geographical unit or units associated with the Chinese name.

Cohen remarks[3] that 'a fact is simply the part of the picture on which we fix our attention'. And evidently we dilate the focus of our attention or contract it according to the particular purpose that we have in view in a particular inquiry. 'Two events which are separate for some purposes may be parts of a single event for other purposes to which the separation is irrelevant.'[4] The same point is made by Willey and Phillips.[5] The sizes of the units that are taken as objects for study are not

---

[1] *Toynbee and History*, p. 96.   [2] Ibid., p. 194.
[3] In *The Meaning of Human History*, p. 44.   [4] Ibid., p. 108.
[5] G. R. Willey and P. Phillips: 'Method and Theory in American Archaeology, II: Historical-Developmental Interpretation', in *The American Anthropologist*, New Series vol. 57, No. 4 (August, 1955), p. 724.

'right' or 'wrong' in themselves; their usefulness depends on the inquirer's angle of vision and on the purpose that he has in hand. Facts have, indeed, a gamut of different orders of magnitude which is very wide and which thus gives room for a great number of gradations, though it does have limits at either end. At the upper end the largest fact comprehensible to a human mind must fall short of total and absolute Reality; for this would include the mind itself as well as the totality of its potential objects; and it would therefore be unknowable.[1] At the opposite end of the scale the smallest fact comprehensible to a human mind will not be infinitesimally minute. But between these two limits the range of possible magnitudes is obviously enormous. I therefore think that Geyl is right in criticizing me[2] for having picked out facts of the order of magnitude of civilizations as being 'significant' and 'integral' without qualification. They are integral and significant when one is making a comparative study of civilizations; but there are, of course, other operations, on both larger and smaller scales, on which a student of human affairs can embark, and the significant and integral order of facts will be a different one in each case. Tingsten points out[3] that civilizations are not completely self-contained 'intelligible fields of study'; and I myself have implicitly admitted this in studying the contacts between different civilizations in both time and space, and finding, in these contacts, a setting for the study of the higher religions.[4]

In the passage[5] that has drawn the just-quoted criticism from Geyl I have noted that the facts of the order of magnitude of civilizations, which happen to be of special interest for me, are 'not awkwardly abundant, but awkwardly scarce'. Spate points out[6] that they are also awkwardly abundant when they are quarried on smaller scales. And Joseph observes, without qualification,[7] that 'in social studies the special difficulty is the great number of the factors involved'. I have sought relief from my own opposite difficulty by freely drawing illustrations for the configuration of the histories of civilizations from the histories of social and cultural units of smaller orders of magnitude; and I have been criticized for this procedure on the ground that it conflicts with my contention that a civilization is the minimum field of study that is intelligible for my purpose. R. H. Tawney, for instance, observes that my method

'involves detaching particular developments or episodes from their context in the life of the society to which they belong, and then using them as evidence of the general conclusion which it is desired to establish. . . . These fragments do not always look the same on the dissecting table as when they formed part of the living organism. . . . The question inevitably arises: are they really evidence? Do they illustrate what they are intended to illustrate? Are they intelligible when removed from their historical

[1] See p. 8.
[2] In *Toynbee and History*, p. 374.
[3] In *Dagens Nyheter*, 16th January, 1949.
[4] See pp. 26–27.
[5] ix. 210–11. See also the present volume, pp. 168–70.
[6] O. H. K. Spate in *Toynbee and History*, p. 290.
[7] In *An Introduction to Logic*, 2nd ed., pp. 555–6.

setting and presented without reference to the past and future of the societies in which they occur?'[1]

Geyl answers Tawney's question in the negative. He notes that I draw my data 'from national histories as if they were indisputably relevant to the history of Western Civilization';[2] and he takes my procedure in this point as demonstrating that I am 'putting forward an impossible, an impracticable, demand' in maintaining that a civilization is the smallest 'intelligible field of historical study'.[3] This procedure of mine is also noticed by W. Kaufmann,[4] T. J. G. Locher,[5] and F. Hampl;[6] and it is criticized, as involving an inconsistency, by R. Pares[7] and by M. A. Fitzsimons,[8] as well as by Geyl.

On this question of inconsistency, I myself should draw a distinction. I should agree that a part cannot properly be used to illustrate the whole of the entity to which it belongs if one is seeking to illustrate some feature of the total configuration of the whole. For instance, there is no reason to suppose that the total configuration of the history of the Western Civilization is mirrored in miniature in the configuration of the history of some particular Western people—the French, Germans, English, or whichever people one might happen to pick out. On the other hand, there are many interesting and significant features and phenomena, common to a civilization and its parts, which do not extend over the total configuration of either the whole or of any of the parts; and in such cases the use of the part to illustrate the whole is, I should say, certainly legitimate and possibly enlightening. It is so because the parts and the whole have in common the same cultural quality and the same social texture—not to speak of the common human nature that is at the bottom of all human behaviour.

5. LAWS

Laws, in the original and literal meaning of the word, are man-made rules for regulating the relations between human beings in matters in which human beings have the power to make a choice, and in which, accordingly, their course of action can be influenced by penalizing one or other of the alternatives that are open to them. Penalization can perhaps deter people from breaking a law or make them suffer for having broken it, but it cannot deprive them of their freedom to break it—or to try to break it—if they choose. Consequently the bearing of present human laws on future human action is predictable only in the sense that we can foresee how the laws will apply—and even this can be foreseen

[1] R. H. Tawney in *International Affairs*, November, 1939, pp. 801 and 804. Cp. L. Stone in *Toynbee and History*, p. 112: 'Historians argue that . . . arbitrarily selected facts torn out of their context . . . are of little help in advancing the frontier of knowledge or increasing the range of understanding.' Cp. W. Kaufmann, ibid., p. 311.
[2] P. Geyl in *Debates with Historians*, p. 147. Cp. p. 149.
[3] P. Geyl in *Toynbee and History*, pp. 71–72. Cp. ibid., pp. 46–47.
[4] In *Toynbee and History*, p. 311.
[5] In *De Gids*, May, 1948, offprint, p. 12.
[6] In the *Historische Zeitschrift*, Band 173, Heft 3, p. 462.
[7] In *The English Historical Review*, vol. lxxi, No. 279 (April, 1956), p. 264.
[8] In *The Intent of Toynbee's History: A Cooperative Appraisal*.

only so long as these laws remain unchanged. Laws are human conventions and, as such, lie within the realm in which Man's power of choice is effective. Since it is practicable to enact a law, it is also practicable to modify it or to repeal it and to replace it by a different one. 'The law of the Medes and Persians, which altereth not',[1] is unalterable, not by necessity, but by convention. 'The law of the Medes and Persians is that no decree and statute which the King establisheth may be changed.'[2]

The word 'laws' is also used analogically in the term 'laws of God', and metaphorically in the term 'laws of Nature'.

In societies in which people have an anthropomorphic vision of absolute Reality, the gods or God have been imagined as including legislation among their manifold human-like activities. The supposed 'laws of God' naturally cover the whole sphere of human legislation; and divine legislators are believed to inflict penalties on human beings who break their laws, as human legislators try to do. But the divine legislation is deemed to extend, not only over the world of men, but over the whole Universe, including the realm of non-human nature; and here it is deemed to be more effective than either divine or human law is, or can be, in the field of human affairs.

If there are such things as 'laws of God' applying to human affairs, human beings are evidently free to break these divine laws, as well as human laws, at their peril. On the other hand, the population, animate and inanimate, of the realm of non-human nature seems to differ from mankind in not possessing the power to choose, which is one of Man's characteristics.[3] And therefore the 'laws of God' applying to God's non-human subjects are laws which cannot be disobeyed because these subjects are not free to break them. In this realm the laws of God are, in fact, identical with the way in which things actually work. Here the bearing of present laws on future events is predictable, not merely in the sense that one can see that the laws will apply, but in the further sense that one can foresee what is actually going to happen in consequence of their operation, since in this realm there is nothing subject to God's laws that has power to defy them. Here again, however, prediction is possible only so long as God's laws remain unchanged—and, if human beings have power to alter or repeal man-made laws, this is, *a fortiori*, within the power of a God conceived of anthropomorphically, since He will be credited with a will that, like a human will, is free, but, unlike it, is omnipotent.

Thus the laws regulating the course of non-human nature are deemed, like human laws, to be open to change so long as they are deemed to have been enacted and to be enforced by a God who is a person in the human sense of the term. In the Western World, however, since the later decades of the seventeenth century, an increasing number of people have

---

[1] Dan. vi. 12.   [2] Dan. vi. 15.

[3] Instead of 'seems', it might be more prudent, in the present state of knowledge, to write 'has seemed to human observers till recently, since the time when an anthropomorphic view of non-human natural phenomena was replaced by an anthropomorphic view of a divine power or powers to which Nature was believed to be subject'. If physical scientists come to believe that the movements of the smallest discernible bodies are indeterminate, this will, in one point, be a return to the pre-scientific and pre-theistic anthropomorphic vision of non-human nature.

ceased to believe in God's existence, or, short of that, in His effective activity. This eclipse of God leaves the laws of Nature without a legislator; and, if there has never been anybody who has enacted them, there will not be anybody, either, with power to repeal them if he chooses. At first sight this seems to make the laws of Nature irrevocable, inexorable, and therefore predictable with assurance. And the phrase 'laws of Nature' is, indeed, popularly associated today with the notion of determinism. In the popular mind they are laws of the Medes and Persians which are unalterable, not just by convention, but by some kind of intrinsic inevitability.

This apparent absoluteness of the laws of Nature is, however, conditioned by the fact that, in so far as they are discernible, they are discerned by human minds, and are therefore, like all the mind's 'data', at least partly mind-made. As has been noted already in the first chapter of this volume,[1] all our currently accepted propositions, generalizations, and 'laws' are merely hypotheses that have not been discredited by experience so far; and all predictions, in all realms of inquiry and all fields of phenomena, are subject to the proviso *rebus sic stantibus*.[2] Moreover, the things that have to remain constant if a prediction based on an hypothesis is to be valid are at least two in number: the hypothesis itself and the mind's picture of the set of phenomena to which the hypothesis is being applied. It will be seen that laws of Nature, even when declared independent of a divine legislator, do not, after all, acquire a sovereign impersonal inevitability. They exist in human minds; and, while we may feel sure that they have worked in the past so long as we still feel sure that our picture of the relevant past phenomena is correct, we can never feel sure that they are going to continue to work in the future—though we shall, and must, for practical purposes, make a bet with ourselves that they will.

This caution with regard to the validity of predictions applies *a fortiori* in the field in which human wills have an effective power of making choices. A particular choice that is going to be made by a particular individual in a particular situation may sometimes be guessed on the strength of an observer's estimate of this individual's character; but such guesswork is notoriously apt to be refuted by the event. The outcome of an encounter between two or three or three million individuals—in a parliamentary election, for instance, or in a revolution, or in a war—is still more difficult to forecast.[3] Where no conflict of wills is involved and

---

[1] On pp. 41–45.

[2] This proviso surely governs H. W. B. Joseph's dicta that 'a statement of the way in which a cause does act is a statement of the way in which it must act' and that 'a true law is true unconditionally' (*An Introduction to Logic*, 2nd ed., p. 414).

[3] See pp. 116–17. R. Pares, in loc. cit., p. 271, holds it against me that 'he dismisses in one short paragraph the conflicts between individual human wills, which are, for most historians, the whole of history and the true explanation of this recalcitrance' (i.e. the recalcitrance of human affairs to regularity). To this criticism I have three answers. (i) In the passage to which Pares refers, ix. 334–6, I give a reference to an earlier passage, iv. 133–584, in which I discuss the conflict of wills at considerable length (350 pages). Considering that the 'one short paragraph' caught Pares' eye, he ought to have noticed this reference in it, to have followed the reference up, and to have thought again before pronouncing that I had 'dismissed' this important subject. (ii) A conflict of wills is one of the two possible outcomes of an encounter between two or more personalities, and the drama of encounters ('challenge and response') is one of my important themes all

where the number of wills in question is large, the percentages of the respective options for alternative possible choices can be predicted statistically with remarkably close approximations to accuracy.[1] It is this possibility that enables caterers of all kinds to reduce the hazard arising from ignorance of the future to proportions that make it feasible to do profitable business. Yet the evidence on which statisticians make their predictions has all to be drawn from past experience exclusively; and the subtlest mathematical refinement of the statistician's technique cannot do more for him than enable him to interpret past experience with the utmost accuracy and relevancy. In applying this quintessence of past experience to a prediction about the future, he is in the same situation as the layman; he is making a bet with himself; and he may lose his bet through some sudden change of will, temper, taste, or fashion of which the evidence of past experience has given no warning.

These are the reasons why I myself hold, and have always held, that the future course of human affairs is unpredictable—and this intrinsically, by reason of the nature of human affairs and not just because we do not know enough, or have not an accurate enough knowledge of what we do know in some fashion, or have not worked out an adequate technique for applying our knowledge to the problem of prediction. I have stated this view emphatically at an early point in this book;[2] and K. W. Thompson has testified[3] that I have maintained the proposition that history in general is unpredictable 'with unflagging steadiness'. When E. Berkovitz maintains[4] that past failures tell us nothing about the future, and that the most that I might be able to show is that my 'laws' have not been contradicted by history so far, my answer is that I have never differed from him on these points. Hourani testifies[5] that, in my work, 'there is nowhere a hint that the whole process *must* happen; on the contrary, there is every insistence that Man can always break the chains that seem to bind him, if he wills'. I do believe, like Rabbi J. B. Agus,[6] that 'those who cannot rise above history are doomed to repeat it'.[7] But, as F. Engel-Janosi[8] and W. Höpker[9] have noted, my attitude is tentative by comparison with Spengler's, and I have declared my disagreement with Spengler's determinism. Critics who assert that I believe in the possibility of prediction in the field of human affairs[10] cannot have taken

through this book. (iii) In the passage to which Pares refers, ix. 334–6, I declare my belief that the mutual frustration of wills which results from conflicts between them opens the way for the irrational and emotional forces in the human psyche to get the upper hand and to run away with the course of events. This view may be right or wrong, but, since I hold it, I attach more importance to this positive consequence, as I see it, of conflicts of wills than to these conflicts themselves, which in themselves—again as I see it—are merely negative in their effect.   [1] See ix. 220–3.

[2] In i. 300–1.   [3] In *Toynbee and History*, p. 220.
[4] In *Judaism: Fossil or Ferment?*, pp. x and xii.
[5] In *The Dublin Review*, vol. 229, No. 470 (December, 1955), p. 378.
[6] In *Judaism*, 1956, p. 3.
[7] This carries one step farther a dictum of M. R. Cohen's that those who do not study history are doomed to repeat it (*The Meaning of Human History*, p. 260).
[8] In *Wissenschaft und Weltbild*, 2. Jahrgang, Heft 4 (October, 1949), pp. 265–7.
[9] In *Zeitwende*, August, 1949.
[10] 'Can we prophesy the future from the past? Professor Toynbee, it is well known, thinks that we can' (H. Trevor-Roper in *Toynbee and History*, p. 122). According to P. Geyl (ibid., p. 365), the attainment of 'reliable conclusions about the laws of mankind's historic life, with the help of which the future might be forecast', was 'the purpose

the trouble to read what I have written on this point. Yet it is a point of capital importance, and therefore one on which a critic ought to be particularly sure of his ground before making a pronouncement.

I do believe that many students of human affairs, myself among them, have discerned genuine regularities and recurrences in the configuration of past events; but I do not believe either that these regularities were bound to occur when they did (in my belief) occur or that they are bound to recur in the future.[1] In their past occurrences I have tried to track them down with a view to seeing how often they have presented themselves and how far they have gone. I may sometimes have over-driven them in my pursuit of this inquiry, and I think this is what A. L. Guerard has in mind when he says of me[2] that 'he seems to forget, and he makes us forget, that his laws are valid only as hypotheses and approximations'. Sir Maurice Powicke is, I think, making the same point when he says[3] that I am least convincing when I succumb to the temptation to treat my 'laws' as if they were 'laws in the sense of the law of gravitation'. As he goes on to say, 'they are generalisations about human behaviour'; and human behaviour is more recalcitrant to laws than the behaviour of physical phenomena, to which the law of gravitation applies, because in human behaviour there is consciousness, will, and purpose. I myself, however, would go on to say that Powicke's 'law' of gravitation is really no more than a generalization about the behaviour of material bodies, and has as little right as generalizations about human behaviour

for which we were assured [that Toynbee's] investigation was undertaken'. Neither Geyl nor Trevor-Roper cites any passage of my work in support of his statement.

[1] I therefore contest F. Hampl's contention that I have no business *not* to be a determinist on my own theory (the *Historische Zeitschrift*, Band 173, Heft 3 (1952), p. 465), and O. H. K. Spate's contentions that the tracing of a pattern in history implies determinism and that I am accordingly a determinist, notwithstanding my disavowal of this (*The Geographical Journal*, vol. cxviii, Part 4 (December, 1952), pp. 406 and 407). H. Kuhn also maintains that I am more of a determinist than I think I am (*The Journal of Philosophy*, 28th August, 1947, p. 495), and P. Geyl that my system conflicts with my professed belief in free will (*Debates with Historians*, p. 136). According to E. F. J. Zahn, I do not succeed in saving freedom; I relapse into a new determinism (*Toynbee und das Problem der Geschichte*, pp. 22 and 26). Anyway, I do not save individual freedom, because the responses to challenges are, in my view, collective (ibid., p. 26). This is an incorrect account of what I believe. I believe that all human action is taken by individuals. I do not believe that there is such a thing as collective action. Responses to challenges are, I believe, the acts of individuals, as all human action is. K. D. Erdmann takes note that this is my view, and observes that there is a discrepancy between this view and my simile of the wheel and the wagon, according to which the successive failures of human beings are used by God to promote the progressive fulfilment of His purpose (*Archiv für Kulturgeschichte*, xxxiii. Band, Heft 2, p. 228). There is, of course, a discrepancy between a belief in the freedom of human wills and a belief in God's overriding omnipotence. This puzzle has never yet been solved and is perhaps insoluble, since it arises from an anthropomorphic vision of God which is, no doubt, a misrepresentation of Reality.

J. K. Feibleman finds in my presentation of history 'a strict determinism of the temporal order' and condemns my thesis that there is an 'unknown quantity' in encounters as an attempt 'to raise accident into a causative factor' (*T'ien Hsia Monthly*, vol. xi, Nos. 1 and 2 (1940), pp. 16 and 25). O. H. K. Spate finds that I try to bring free will and ideas, as well as chance or accident, within the framework of my 'laws' (*The Geographical Journal*, vol. cxviii, Part 4 (December, 1952), p. 409). What I do think and say is that the outcome of encounters between personalities is intrinsically unpredictable because it is, I believe, not determined in advance. A critic could call this statement of belief the formulation of a law, and then say that I am regimenting freedom; but this line of argument would, I should say, be sophistical.

[2] In *The Herald-Tribune*, 28th October, 1934.
[3] In *The Manchester Guardian*, 29th September, 1939.

have to be called a law of Nature—if, by this, we mean a regularity which is bound in principle to recur and which, unlike a human law, can never be modified or repealed. All that we know is that Newton's law of gravity has been verified by application to the phenomena up to date, subject to limiting conditions and qualifications that have since been formulated in further physical laws discovered by Einstein.[1]

Besides being criticized for having been pressed too far, my 'laws' in the field of human affairs have also met with the opposite criticism that 'they are often so loosely formed that they can be expanded or contracted at will',[2] and 'are so vague that it is hard to see what kind of empirical evidence could possibly refute them'.[3] I do not see how I can have erred in this direction as well as in the other. If I have, it is the less reprehensible error of the two, since human affairs are obviously less amenable to rigorous laws than tame planets or conditioned abstractions. Consequently, in human affairs, 'the differences will not be denied';[4] and my 'professional colleagues . . . are convinced that the differences between civilizations are more significant than their likenesses'.[5] The differences are, no doubt, more significant if one is focusing one's attention on one stream of phenomena as these present themselves, just as likenesses are more significant if one is concentrating one's effort on taking a synoptic view of a number of simultaneous streams. But it is perilous to turn a blind eye to either aspect of phenomena, since both likenesses and differences are always found coexisting in phenomena in so far as these are apprehended by human minds. Indeed, the notion of either likeness or difference is logically inconceivable without a correlative notion of its opposite, and so, too, is the notion of either necessity or freedom.[6]

[1] Apropos of the comparative study of civilizations, Bagby asks himself: 'If we cannot predict, can we call our study a science?' (*Culture and History*, p. 199). He then tentatively commits himself to a belief in the possibility of prediction in very general terms in the field of human affairs (ibid., pp. 210–11). When he comes to the question of predicting the future of the Western Civilization (ibid., p. 211), he is as cautious as I am. (He mistakenly attributes to me a belief that the dissolution of the Western Civilization is imminent—quoting vi. 312–22, especially 320. The opinion that I actually express in that passage is that the future of the Western Civilization is an open question, and that the obvious danger in which we stand is a challenge to us to save ourselves. He notices that I treat the question as an open one in ix. 406–644, and calls this a withdrawal.) H. Kuhn reports that I seem 'to set little store by' my 'attempts at prediction' (*The Journal of Philosophy*, 28th August, 1947, p. 499).

Bagby does not distinguish between prediction, made with a formula based on past experience, which has so far been vindicated by practical results, and prediction that is intrinsically valid for all time. I myself do not believe that this stricter form of prediction is possible except in the realm of pure mathematics. Prediction in the sciences dealing with non-human nature is, I should say, contingent and precarious, notwithstanding its imposing practical successes. I believe that even this laxer kind of prediction is impossible in the study of human affairs. And therefore, if it is held that a 'discipline' must be capable of making predictions of some kind in order to qualify for being called a science, I should prefer to call the disciplines dealing with human affairs by some other name: e.g. 'studies' or 'inquiries'.

A. R. Burn has made the interesting suggestion that someone should make a study of changes in the dominant êthos of a whole civilization that *cannot* be predicted statistically.

H. D. Oakeley suggests that 'the aim of historical prophecy would be to discern whether the real and inner sources of historic development are such as necessarily to operate in the future as in the past' (*Philosophy*, vol. xi, No. 42 (April, 1936), p. 186).

[2] P. Gardiner in *Time and Tide*, 30th October, 1954.
[3] S. Hook in *The Partisan Review*, June, 1948, p. 693.
[4] P. Geyl in *Toynbee and History*, p. 51.   [5] L. Stone, ibid., p. 111.
[6] H. Kuhn has the impression that, in my work, 'of the two notes, the grandly monotonous one has an authentic ring, whereas the other soaring note seems the inter-

Hourani finds[1] that, in this book, 'there is no clear explanation of why, in spite of freedom, certain recurrences can be found in history'. No explanation, he continues, is given of the Yin-Yang rhythm, to which all others can be reduced; only a poetic description 'which, as in Plato, can be hinted at in myths but not elucidated by discursive reason'. As I see it, the rhythm of conflicting and alternating order and disorder, stability and explosion, cannot be elucidated by reason because it is one of the *a priori* categories through which reason operates. I do not see how a philosopher can expect to be able to step, like Alice, through the looking-glass. But I do see that human freedom, as far as it extends, is a prize won by human consciousness, will, and purpose. 'It is only in so far as some sort of order arises as a result of individual action but without being designed by any individual that a problem is raised which demands a theoretical explanation.'[2] Where I see undesigned regularities and recurrences in the ascendant in human affairs, I look for these in the medium of the subconscious,[3] and am not surprised to find them particularly clearly pronounced in periods of social disintegration, since these, as I see them, are the periods when consciousness, will, and purpose

pretation of a well-meaning author' (*The Journal of Philosophy*, 28th August, 1947, p. 498). If the reader cares to check this impression of Kuhn's by reference to Part XI of this book which deals with 'Law and Freedom in History' (in vol. ix), he will find that my objective in trying to trace how far laws of Nature prevail in human affairs has been to find out the extent of the field in which Man has freedom. The word 'freedom' is, of course, notoriously difficult to define. It raises the same problem as the word 'new', which is discussed below under the heading 'creativity'. It is true, as Bagby says (in *Culture and History*, p. 63), that human beings 'choose what they prefer'; that 'their preference is not inexplicable or unintelligible' (ibid., pp. 63 and 65); and that it is intelligible in terms of the choosers' consistent dispositions and fundamental tendencies (ibid., p. 65). 'Always we choose in a context determined by our previous choices' (O. H. K. Spate in *Geographical Studies*, vol. iv, No. 1 (1957), p. 5). 'A choice is generally among different goods, each of which entails some evil' (F. Borkenau in *Commentary*, March, 1956, p. 242). Thus we can make reasonable guesses about the choice that somebody is going to make in a particular situation, because we can make them in the light of our knowledge of this person's experience, education, and temperament. Yet, as I believe, an exact and exhaustive knowledge of these factors in the determination of the person's choice would not enable us to turn our guesses into an infallible prediction. A human being is never completely the slave of his own past: 'a creature that moves in determinate grooves, in fact not a bus but a tram', as Mgr. Ronald Knox has put it. Even a drug-addict or an alcoholic can regain his freedom. And the majority of human beings, who have not succumbed to some compulsive habit, can surprise themselves, as well as their acquaintances, by making choices that could not have been predicted from a knowledge of their 'make-up' so far. Ninety per cent. of a person's action may be demonstrably conditioned by his past history, but never quite the whole.

Light on the problem of the nature of freedom may be hoped for from the progress of the technology of communications and the associated science of cybernetics. For instance, the invention of 'feedback' has produced what may prove to be a new concept.

'By "feedback" is meant a communications network which produces action in response to an input of information and includes the results of its own action in the new information by which it modifies its subsequent behaviour' (K. W. Deutsch in *Philosophy of Science*, vol. 18, No. 3 (July, 1951), pp. 245–6).

According to Deutsch (ibid., p. 245), 'feedback' is 'a basic pattern which minds, societies, and self-modifying communications networks have in common'.

[1] In *The Dublin Review*, vol. 229, No. 470 (December, 1955), p. 382.

[2] F. A. Hayek: *The Counter-Revolution of Science*, p. 39.

[3] Hourani has taken note of this view of mine in loc. cit., p. 389. D. B. Richardson, like Hourani, notes that on this point I am a disciple of C. G. Jung, and that I do not explore the source of regularities farther than Jung's 'collective unconscious' (*The Thomist*, vol. xx, No. 2 (April, 1957), p. 158). R. Pares holds that I attribute too much importance to the subconscious and too little to the will (*The English Historical Review*, vol. lxxi, No. 279 (April, 1956), p. 269).

are least, and the subconscious most, in the ascendant.[1] I agree with Spate[2] that the regularities and recurrences which we find—and seek—'can hardly be a matter of the free choices of men accidentally converging', and that their occurrence implies that there are 'inherent limitations to Man's free choice'.

T. J. G. Locher finds[3] a discrepancy in my thinking between a belief that, after a breakdown, disintegration is inevitable, and a belief that the future is open at all times. The second of these two opinions is the one that I hold. I do not believe in the inevitability of disintegration after a breakdown. I do believe that a survey of the histories of civilizations up to date shows that, in a number of cases in the past, disintegration has, in fact, been the sequel to a breakdown; but I do not know of any evidence that this need have happened in these cases or need recur in others, and I cannot conceive of any possible cogent proof that, when the irrational forces of the subconscious have gained the upper hand through a mutual frustration of wills, it ceases to be possible for human beings to bring their common affairs under some degree of rational control again through agreement and co-operation. Our knowledge of what has happened in the past informs us merely of one among an unknown number of future possibilities; and, by informing us of this, it gives us a chance of avoiding a repetition of this particular outcome, if we wish to avoid it and if we make the necessary effort.

If, in the past, some particular course of events has occurred a number of times and displays more or less the same pattern in all these cases, one might take this as a 'tip' for betting on what the outcome of an apparently similar current episode was going to be. But it would be rash to count on winning a bet made on the strength of such evidence from the past. Of course, if the current episode, about the outcome of which one was betting, was now already at an advanced stage, and if, up to the present point, its course displayed a pattern that was also discernible in a number of past cases in which the end of the story was known, it would be less hazardous to bet that the current story was going to have the familiar ending towards which, so far, it had been leading up. Suppose, for instance, that the civilization into which the observer himself happened to have been born had already been united politically, after a long-drawn-out 'time of troubles', as a result of a 'knock-out blow' in which all but one of the former contending local states had been wiped off the political map by one sole victorious survivor. There might then seem to be little risk in betting that the civilization in question, having reached this advanced stage of disintegration, was now on the road towards eventual dissolution, and that it was not going to be able to escape from this rut, even if it were to succeed in making one or more temporary rallies. Still, however 'safe' a bet may seem to be, there is a great gulf fixed between a bet and a certainty.

---

[1] The same view is taken by D. B. Richardson. When a civilization is in decline, 'social transactions begin to revolve abnormally . . . in exactly the same type of necessary cycles in which the animal, vegetable, and mineral worlds revolve' (*The Thomist*, vol. xx, No. 2 (April, 1957), p. 180).

[2] See *Geographical Studies*, vol. iv, No. 1 (1957), p. 3.

[3] In *De Gids*, May, 1948, offprint, p. 27.

6. EMPIRICAL

This modern Western word is derived from the Greek adjective *empeirikós*, this from the Greek substantive *empeiría*, and this in turn from another substantive: *peîra*. The Greek word *peîra* means an attempt, a try, an experiment, a test, a temptation; *empeiría* means the experience that is the fruit of experimenting; *empeirikós* means believing in the value of experience and taking account of it.

In this book I have claimed throughout that I am using an empirical method of inquiry. A number of my critics have taken note of this claim of mine, and most of these have contested it.[1] I must therefore explain what I mean by the term.

I am not claiming that I approach the historical record of human experience without preconceptions; and I entirely agree with W. H. Walsh when he says that this would be 'a claim which could certainly not be sustained'.[2] '*Some* theoretical framework and *some* working hypotheses are unavoidable',[3] because the human mind's process of

[1] For instance, A. J. P. Taylor in *Toynbee and History*, pp. 120–1; H. Trevor-Roper, ibid., p. 123; P. Geyl, ibid., p. 36 ('the pretence of an empirical investigation') and p. 44 (in his claim 'that his whole argument is based on empirical methods', Toynbee 'is deceiving himself.'); M. A. Fitzsimons in *The Intent of Toynbee's History: A Cooperative Appraisal*, and in *The Review of Politics*, October, 1957, pp. 554–5 ('the confusing profession of empiricism and scientific method and the obvious dominance of his philosophy of history'); E. E. Y. Hales in *History Today*, May, 1955, pp. 322 and 320 ('His myth of history' has no better claim than the Whig and Marxist myths have 'to be regarded as having an empirical basis. . . . He is misleading in treating his views about the births of civilizations as though they were laws, arrived at by empirical analysis'); E. F. J. Zahn in *Toynbee und das Problem der Geschichte*, p. 39 ('What Toynbee calls empiricism is in reality speculation which misuses myth'); A. Hourani in *The Dublin Review*, vol. 229, No. 470 (December, 1955), p. 388 ('The book is by no means empirical in its method'); W. H. McNeill in *The Intent of Toynbee's History: A Cooperative Appraisal* ('His "empiricism" is an empiricism which already is keenly aware of what it is seeking.' The value of his generalizations does not rest upon his empirical surveys. 'The heart of Toynbee's intellectual procedure has always been the sudden flash of insight'); T. J. G. Locher in *De Gids*, May, 1948, offprint, p. 16; C. A. Beard in *The American Historical Review*, vol. xi, No. 2 (January, 1935), p. 308; P. M. Sweezy in *The Nation*, 19th October, 1946 ('The historical uniformities which he believes he has discovered by empirical means are in reality imposed upon his materials from without'); J. A. Tormodsen and G. C. Wasberg in *Samtiden*, vol. 58, hefte 12 (1949), pp. 647–60; B. D. Wolfe in *The American Mercury*, No. 64 (1947), pp. 748–55 ('It becomes clear in volumes iv, v, and vi that his "empirical method" of studying history is only a pretence, an unconscious tribute to the secular, rational, scientific method which, at heart, he rejects' (p. 755)); H. Frankfort in *The Birth of Civilization in the Near East*, pp. 25–26 ('If he describes "the consummation of human history" as "accomplishing the transformation of Sub-man through Man into Superman" . . . we may respect his faith but can hardly accept it as the argument of "an empirical student of history"'); G. Lefèbvre in *La Revue Historique*, January–March, 1949, pp. 109–13 (what passes for empiricism in Toynbee's work is merely a means of bringing forward a new Augustinianism).
Crane Brinton, in *The Virginia Quarterly Review*, vol. 32, No. 3 (Summer, 1956), pp. 361–75, convicts me with a recommendation for mercy. My constant appeal to 'our well-tried empirical method' infuriates the matter-of-fact mind, to the point that I seem to such a mind to be deliberately hypocritical. 'This', Brinton submits, 'is surely not so. Toynbee was trained as an historian, and he is an Englishman, heir to a long tradition of philosophical empiricism. He just hasn't solved the dichotomies of this world-the other world or real-ideal or body-soul—a predicament in which he is not alone.'
On the other hand, A. L. Guerard, in *The Herald-Tribune*, 28th October, 1934, pronounces that 'there is a radical difference, in spirit and method', between Spengler and me. 'Spengler is a prophet; Toynbee is an inquirer. In his boldest attempts the British scholar remains an empiricist, a Baconian.' A. L. Kroeber, too, judges, in *The Nature of Culture*, p. 373, that my procedure is empirical in the main.
[2] *Toynbee and History*, p. 128.
[3] Social Science Research Council's Committee on Historiography's Report (1954), p. 132, quoted in this volume already on p. 43. See also footnote 11 to p. 43.

thought is analytical and classificatory.[1] If I have seemed, to so careful and discriminating a critic as Walsh, to be implying that I am approaching history without preconceptions, that must be my fault. It must mean that, in volumes i–x of this book, I have not made it clear that I agree with Walsh on this crucial point.[2] For reasons already set out in Chapter I of this volume, I disagree with Hales, when he talks of 'laws arrived at by empirical analysis'.[3] I agree with E. Berkovitz that 'laws' cannot be derived from facts,[4] and with Erdmann when he says, *ad hominem*, that my guiding ideas are not derived from the observation of history,[5] though I do not agree with Mumford that my conclusions, as well as my hypotheses, 'for all his empiricism, are inevitably as much the product of his own ideology as of the situations that he "interprets"'.[6] This point has been put in telling words by H. Baudet:[7]

'Many critics have censured Toynbee's primary vision on the theo-retical ground that it is "apriori". Certainly it is, as they say. But, "epistemologically", is not an "apriori" of this kind a basis [of mental operations] which speaks for itself because it is unavoidable? Is it not a compelling necessity?

'All vision is engendered on an "apriori", and . . . an "apriori" of this kind has its roots—as all thinking has, *au fond*—in will and passion.'

The point is driven home by K. R. Popper. He rejects

'the view that science begins with observations from which it derives its theories by some process of generalization or induction'.[8] 'I do not believe that we ever make inductive generalizations in the sense that we start from observations and try to derive our theories from them.'[9] 'Before we can collect data, our interest in *data of a certain kind* must be aroused: the problem always comes first.'[10] 'Theories are prior to observations as well as to experiments, in the sense that the latter are significant only in relation to theoretical problems.'[11]

When Trevor-Roper says that, in my work, 'the theories are not deduced from the facts',[12] the answer is that neither my theories nor any-one else's are or ever have been or ever will be generated in that way. If being 'empirical' meant this, the word would have no counterpart in reality, and had better be struck out of the dictionary.[13] On the other

---

[1] See Chapter I of this volume, *passim*.
[2] For instance, I have not made this clear to Father D'Arcy, to judge by his comment that what Geyl's criticism 'proves is that Toynbee should not have claimed to rest his case entirely on empirical methods' (M. C. D'Arcy: *The Sense of History*, p. 72).
[3] E. E. Y. Hales in *History To-day*, May, 1955.
[4] *Judaism: Fossil or Ferment?*, p. 10.
[5] *Archiv für Kulturgeschichte*, xxxiii. Band, Heft 2 (1951), p. 246.
[6] *Diogenes*, No. 13 (Spring, 1956), p. 13.
[7] In *Historie en Metahistorie*, p. 46.
[8] *The Poverty of Historicism*, p. 98. Cp. p. 121.
[9] Ibid., p. 134.
[10] Ibid., p. 121. Cp. p. 134.
[11] Ibid., p. 98.
[12] *Toynbee and History*, p. 123.
[13] 'Is it true that Toynbee's asseveration of the empirical character of his method is in fact an untruth, because his work is fundamentally aprioristic? I cannot see that these two processes are mutually exclusive.'

'The process of apriori formulation and of working the proposition out is, in the second stage of the operation, undoubtedly an empirical process of work.' It is not a valid criticism of Toynbee, or of any other author of a book *de longue haleine*, that the author foresees at the beginning what he is going to write years later (Baudet, in loc. cit., pp. 46–47).

hand, when Trevor-Roper goes on to say that my theories are not tested by the facts either, he is laying down a legitimate requirement,[1] and my claim to be using an empirical method of inquiry does stand or fall according to the verdict on this count. I agree that my claim cannot be sustained if I have not tried to test my theories and hypotheses by the facts, or if I have tried but have not done the job properly or successfully.[2] For, while it is true that theories and hypotheses can never be deduced from facts, it is also true that they can be validated only if they are confronted with relevant facts and are confirmed by them. More than that, the whole purpose of formulating a theory or an hypothesis is the heuristic one of trying to increase our knowledge and understanding by applying the theory or hypothesis to the phenomena.[3] I maintain my claim that I have tried to be empirical in this sense, which is, I believe, the correct usage of the word and does mean something that an inquirer not only can be but ought to be.

In making my claim to be empirical, I have been tacitly contrasting my approach with Dilthey's approach and with Spengler's.[4] While the plan of the present book was brewing in my mind, the first volume of Spengler's *Der Untergang des Abendlandes* was published, and, when I read it, my first impression was that, in Spengler's work, what I had been planning was already an accomplished fact. My second impression, however, was that Spengler's work suffered from being too dogmatic, in the sense that he was apt to enunciate his theories about the configuration of human affairs and to leave it at that, without putting these theories to sufficiently thorough tests on the touchstone of the phenomena.[5] Having decided to go on with my own enterprise, I was told by a distinguished philosopher, the late Lord Lindsay of Birker, that I

The points here made by Baudet answer K. D. Erdmann's contention (in *Archiv für Kulturgeschichte*, xxxiii. Band, Heft 2 (1951), p. 206) that, when I call my method 'empirical', the expression is a misapplication of the word, because 'there can be no question here of an inductive procedure'. Erdmann goes on to say, correctly, that 'the experience from which Toynbee obtains his pair of ideas is not historical but meta-historical in character'. But he is not correct in adding that 'Toynbee is a "realist" in the Schoolmen's usage of the term. Revelation, as fundamental religious experience (*Urer-fahrung*), is [for him] the criterion of truth.' I take challenge-and-response, and any other ideas of mine that come from the Bible, not as revelation, but as hypotheses to be applied to the phenomena with a view to gaining knowledge and understanding. My criterion of truth is whether the hypotheses fit the phenomena. I maintain that this is the inductive method, and that, so far from induction being incompatible with having an *a priori* hypothesis, it is impossible without having one.

Again, when W. Gurian declares that my 'fundamental concepts' are 'means of subjective classification' (*The Review of Politics*, vol. 4, No. 4, p. 511), he misses the point that this is true of everyone's 'fundamental concepts' unless and until they have been tested by being confronted with as large an array of relevant phenomena as the inquirer is able to assemble. It is a more pertinent criticism of Gurian's, supposing that it is justified, when he says (ibid.) that my fundamental concepts 'appear as very thin'.

[1] Baudet observes, in loc. cit., p. 47, that the process of proof must be kept clearly distinct from the original vision.

[2] 'Assuredly, if induction . . . were an invalid process, no process grounded on it would be valid. . . . But, though a valid process, it is a fallible one, and fallible in very different degrees' (J. S. Mill: *Philosophy of Scientific Method*, ed. by E. Nagel (New York 1950, Hafner), p. 290). [3] See pp. 22–23, 41–45, and 158–70.

[4] My wish to distinguish my approach from Spengler's has been guessed by W. H. McNeill in *The Intent of Toynbee's History: A Cooperative Appraisal*.

[5] This makes Spengler a poet, according to Holborn. 'History is the re-enactment of the past in the mind of the historian, and even "facts" exist only there. But, in contrast to poetry, they call for critical verification' (*The Saturday Review of Literature*, 31st May, 1947, p. 29).

should find in Dilthey's work the very thing that I was looking for. What I was looking for was a bridge between theory and fact. But, in Dilthey's work, I did not find even theories about the configuration of human affairs. I found nothing but epistemology. I was, and am, grateful to Dilthey for that, since the relation between theory and fact cannot be studied without taking epistemology into account. But the bridge for which I was looking was not to be found in Dilthey's work, and I had to try to build it without getting help from him.

Some critics have given me credit for making this attempt. Guerard, for instance, draws the same contrast between Spengler and me that I have drawn in my own mind.[1] Feibleman says of me[2] that 'he tries to analyse cultural structure, and, in doing so, takes the first step towards the establishment of the empirical field of human social structure as the empirical study of a science'. To try, however, is not enough. The attempt that I have made has been criticized on at least six counts. According to the critics, the examples that I have taken as test cases have been denatured by being taken out of their context.[3] Some of these examples are ruled out of order because they are taken from phenomena of a different order of magnitude from the civilizations on which I am seeking to throw light.[4] My citation of examples, relevant to whatever the point in question may be, is not exhaustive and is therefore unrepresentative and thus misleading. Alternatively, I cite so many examples that I clutter up my argument with an indigestible mass of details.[5] Whether the number of examples that I cite is too small or too great, I am guilty of selecting them to fit my theories.[6] When they will not fit,

[1] See p. 243, footnote 1.

[2] J. K. Feibleman in T'ien Hsia Monthly, vol. xi, Nos. 1 and 2 (1940), p. 171.

[3] See pp. 234–5.   [4] See p. 235.

[5] The book is criticized in this sense by A. L. Guerard (in The Herald-Tribune, 28th October, 1934), by L. Mumford (in Toynbee and History, p. 141), and by P. Sorokin (ibid., p. 178). As Mumford puts it (ibid., p. 142), 'his Study of History . . . is . . ., in its vastness, its complexity, its impenetrability, and its magnificent profusion and confusion, an image of that great overgrown megalopolis [London], stifled by its very success.'

[6] 'He selects the instances which will support his theses, or he presents them in the way that suits him. . . . Those cases he does mention can be explained or described in a different way so as to disagree no less completely with his theses' (P. Geyl in Toynbee and History, p. 45). 'Often other and quite contrary examples are readily available' (P. Bagby, ibid., p. 105). W. H. McNeill observes that a frequent procedure of mine for trying to justify my generalizations is to select for attention only those bits and pieces that fit in with my notions (The Intent of Toynbee's History: A Cooperative Appraisal). 'An apparently random citation of instances to illustrate patterns' (M. A. Fitzsimons in The Intent). 'Conclusions drawn from incomplete or partially selected evidence' (L. Stone, ibid., p. 112). My selection is arbitrary (Geyl in P. Geyl; A. J. Toynbee; P. A. Sorokin: The Pattern of the Past: Can we Determine It?, p. 85). 'Too many selected facts' (W. Gurian in The Review of Politics, vol. 4, No. 4, p. 511). T. J. G. Locher finds my procedure too selective, as well as too simple, subjective, and one-sided (De Gids, May, 1948, offprint, p. 15). H. Holborn observes that 'imagination by itself' cannot 'produce an objective selection and arrangement of facts' (The Saturday Review of Literature, 31st May, 1947, p. 29). P. Geyl finds a contradiction between my 'imaginative method and my empirical claims' (Debates with Historians, p. 154). O. H. K. Spate finds that my selectivity goes too far (The Geographical Journal, vol. cxviii, Part 4 (December, 1952), p. 409, and Toynbee and History, p. 291).

On the other hand, a number of critics point out that selection is, in itself, something inevitable.

'Any large hypothesis must go beyond immediately available data and is never completely verifiable' (Social Science Research Council's Committee on Historiography's Report (1954), p. 130). 'In history there is no possibility of making quantitative demonstrations' (Anderle's unpublished paper). While Geyl is right in saying that an a priori

I force them with Procrustean violence.[1] I have a rigid *a priori* scheme.[2] If even this Procrustean treatment cannot make awkward facts conform, I ignore them.[3] Some of these charges cancel each other out, but what is left is still formidable.

involves predetermined selection, the truth is that historical writing is always selective (H. Baudet in *Historie en Metahistorie*, p. 46). 'Any problem of interpretation involves a selective evaluation of evidence' (R. L. Shinn: *Christianity and the Problem of History*, p. 56); so 'historical method must be based on selection' (ibid., p. 7).

Ad hominem, Spate observes that 'even Toynbee's selectivity, so severely handled by Geyl, might be admitted within limits' (*Toynbee and History*, p. 290). I am content to accept Sir Llewellyn Woodward's comment that, 'for all the astonishing number of particular facts brought together, one may wonder whether Professor Toynbee (or any single man, in the present state of learning) can really be sure that his selection from the accumulated data about the past is not open to attack' (*The Spectator*, 6th July, 1934).

[1] 'Frequently his point is made at the price of a radical distortion of facts' (P. Bagby in *Toynbee and History*, p. 105). 'Dr. Toynbee *imposes* patterns on history' (Sir Ernest Barker, ibid., p. 95); and the facts rebel, like the flamingo-mallets, hedgehog-balls, and soldier-hoops in the famous game of croquet in *Alice in Wonderland* (P. Geyl, ibid., pp. 62 and 375). Facts are made to fit a Procrustean bed (L. Stone, ibid., p. 113). 'The Procrustean method of handling Chinese history' (W. Altree, ibid., pp. 266–71). 'Forcing it all into the scheme of a presumptuous construction' (Geyl, ibid., p. 373). I adapt fact to suit theory (R. H. S. Crossman in *The New Statesman*, 8th March, 1947). 'One of the dangers of "pattern history", if it may be so described, is that facts must be woven into the pattern. One of the advantages is that a good and attractive pattern prints itself upon the memory' (H. A. L. Fisher in *The Nineteenth Century and After*, December, 1934, p. 672). I impose my patterns by force (R. Pares in *The English Historical Review*, vol. lxxii, No. 279 (April, 1956), p. 262). 'His doctrine that facts are less important than the abstract system into which he herds them' (J. Bishko, in *The Richmond News Leader*, 21st October, 1954). 'Claiming to be an empiricist, he forces the facts to suit preconceived ideas' (H. Frankfort in *The Observer*, 31st January, 1954). 'He cannot resist the temptation to fit complex facts . . . into a Procrustean scheme' (Granville Hicks in *The New Leader*, 18th October, 1954, p. 23). 'He distorts some parts of it [history] by pushing it into his iron cubby-holes' (A. Nevins in *The New York World-Telegram and Sun*, 17th December, 1954). 'Sometimes Toynbee seems to force the pieces into place, whether they fit or not' (P. L. Ralph in *The Saturday Review*, 16th October, 1954, p. 19). 'The system sometimes makes a poor fit—for example, with the Arabian-Islamic' (J. A. Tormodsen and G. C. Wasberg in *Samtiden*, vol. 58, hefte 12 (1949), pp. 647–60). Other civilizations are more or less ruthlessly fitted into the Procrustean framework of the Hellenic Civilization (R. K. Merton in *The American Journal of Sociology*, vol. xlvii, No. 2 (September, 1941), pp. 205–13). J. Vogt finds that I am arbitrary in my treatment of the material and that I distort the facts (*Saeculum*, No. 2 (1951), pp. 557–74). On this point my critics are unanimous, according to Anderle (in op. cit.). The point is put genially, as well as wittily, by the Rev. E. R. Hardy Jr.: 'His scheme is in some ways Procrustean, although the bed is comfortably furnished and the pulleys work smoothly' (*The Intent of Toynbee's History*: *A Cooperative Appraisal*).

[2] 'The real rock of offence to many (including the present writer) is the somewhat rigid schematism' (O. H. K. Spate in *Toynbee and History*, p. 291). My scheme, like Ellsworth Huntington's, is too neat to be convincing (O. H. K. Spate in *The Geographical Journal*, vol. cxviii, Part 4 (December, 1952), p. 408). 'His main trouble is that he has explained too much' (A. L. Kroeber: *Style and Civilizations*, p. 121). 'It is all subordinated, and intended to contribute, to a system, a message.' Though Toynbee is obviously interested in the spectacle of the particular, 'not for one moment does it free him from the obsession of his dream' (P. Geyl in *Toynbee and History*, pp. 360–1). 'Has the [empirical] method been sacrificed to the design, or are we . . . dealing with a deeper question?' (E. Fiess, ibid., p. 380). G. Weil finds a 'contradiction between the principles on which his scheme of the development of civilization is based and his personal judgment of historical phenomena as they really are', and he criticizes my 'scheme-bound point of view' (ibid., p. 285). J. K. Feibleman reproaches me for my 'iron rigidity' (*T'ien Hsia Monthly*, vol. xi, Nos. 1 and 2 (1940), p. 23; cp. p. 20). A. Hourani judges that 'the schematism is too rigid' (*The Dublin Review*, vol. 229, No. 470 (December, 1955), p. 381). J. Vogt criticizes my schematization in *Saeculum*, No. 2 (1951), pp. 557–74. A. Nevins finds that Toynbee 'makes history too schematic' (*The New York World-Telegram and Sun*, 7th December, 1954).

[3] 'As for those items that can't be made to fit, they are quickly tossed into the huge garbage heap of discarded facts' (L. Stone in *Toynbee and History*, p. 113). I ignore exceptions to my laws (R. Pares in *The English Historical Review*, vol. lxxi, No. 279

The first of these indictments—that I have taken episodes out of their context—is evidently incompatible with the criticism that my work is superficial, and my spirit hybristic, because I attempt the impossible enterprise of trying to cover the whole history of the Age of the Civilizations.[1] It is true that I have attempted to do this; and it surely follows that my work, as a whole, is likely to have suffered less from distortion as a result of taking episodes out of their context than the work of many other present-day historians. I agree that taking things out of their context does distort them. In the first chapter of this volume I have argued that it is a grievous limitation and a radical defect of the human intellect that it is incapable of apprehending Reality as a whole, and has, perforce, to take it piecemeal at the cost of failing to see it as it truly is. When we are applying our minds to study, and not to practical action, we ought to contend against this inherent infirmity of theirs as far as is humanly possible. My own criticism of the present vogue for 'specialization' is that, so far from trying to combat and, to some extent, counteract this intellectual infirmity of ours, specialization gives way to it and thereby accentuates it. The charge of denaturing Reality by taking episodes out of their context does hit me, no doubt; but I should have thought that it hit, with rather greater force, the school of specialists which is the predominant school among present-day Western historians—a school in whose more polemical exponents' eyes I am something of a heretic, just because I have been unwilling to follow this current fashion.

The charge that I draw many of my illustrations of features in the histories of civilizations from social units of a lower order of magnitude has been noticed and discussed already[2] and therefore need not be re-examined here.

The charge that my citation of examples is not exhaustive hits not only me but everyone who has ever sought to test an hypothesis by confronting it with relevant phenomena. It hits me perhaps less hard than some of my fellow prisoners in the dock, if it is true that I have surfeited my readers with examples *ad nauseam*. But it hits every student of phenomena, human or non-human, since phenomena, of whatever kind, are innumerable. The only class of things that could conceivably have a membership that was limited by its own nature would be some class, not of phenomena, but of mathematical abstractions that had been abstracted with the express design of creating a self-evidently closed class. Even if our momentary state of knowledge enabled us to enumerate every one of the representatives of some class of phenomena that were in existence at the moment, the exhaustive enumeration would be no better, in logic, than a 'simple enumeration', as has been noticed in Chapter I.[3]

(April, 1956), p. 262). I do this although 'often other and quite contrary examples are readily available' (P. Bagby in *Toynbee and History*, p. 105, quoted above). Other critics, e.g. Anderle in his paper, hold that this criticism is unjust. Mumford says of me that 'he usually gives enough free play to the data to provide his reader with the necessary correction, and sometimes generously enlists the aid of other critical minds to correct his own bias' (*Toynbee and History*, p. 143). And he recognizes my method as being 'empirical' in the sense of 'qualifying doubtful conclusions in one place by contradictory data in another place' (*Diogenes*, No. 13 (Spring, 1956), p. 13).

[1] See p. 85, footnote 1, and Chapter II, Annex: *Ad Hominem*, p. 638, with footnote 2.   [2] On pp. 234–5.   [3] See pp. 23–24.

If the charge that my citation of examples is selective has to be dropped because it applies, not just to me, but to everyone who tries to test a theory, I am still confronted with the further charge that I make my selection of examples with an eye to fitting my theories. This charge, too, applies to everyone who tries to test a theory.[1] For my part I certainly have not consciously made selections to suit my purposes, and I doubt whether any other scholar ever has either. To do this might be a temptation to a company-promoter, politician, barrister, or member of some other practical profession in which this form of cheating, if the fraud remained undetected, might reap lucrative material rewards. But what interest could a scholar have in spending laborious man-hours in deliberately trying to diminish the knowledge and understanding that he is concerned to increase? The charge is unconvincing—whoever may be the individual against whom it has been made.[2] At the same time it is hard to rebut, because it is always possible to switch the indictment from the offender's conscious self to the subconscious underworld of his psyche. However upright his conscious self may be admitted to be, his subconscious may be a rogue that has inveigled him into cheating and into doing this bona fide, inasmuch as he has never been conscious of what he is, in fact, doing.[3] I do not know how to clear myself of a charge against my subconscious; but I do know that anyone else who was arraigned on account of alleged misdoings of his subconscious would find himself in the same plight.

The same defence holds for the charge that I force facts that will not fit. I can only reply, again, that I have never done so consciously. It is true that I start with a 'schema' in the sense of a formulated but still untested hypothesis or theory. But I plead 'not guilty' to the charge of being 'schema-bound'. Where I believe that I have found some pattern or regularity or recurrence, I have always tried to ascertain the limits of the realm in which this particular 'law' holds good—for instance, in volume ii, where I am dealing with a number of variations on the theme of challenge-and-response. So far from ignoring contradictory instances, I have always brought them up and discussed them when I have been aware of their existence. Of course, many will have escaped me, as also will many other instances that support my hypotheses instead of impugning them. In the numerous surveys made in the first ten volumes of this book, for the purpose of testing how far, if at all, my hypotheses might or might not be valid, I have always made my net as big, and its meshes as close, as I have been able. I am ready at any time to modify or abandon any of my hypotheses if I am given convincing reasons in the shape either of the citation of relevant phenomena previously unknown to me or of the reinterpretation of phenomena of which I am already

[1] 'However valid this criticism may be for Mr. Toynbee's empiricism in particular, it is unerringly true with respect to empiricism in general' (K. W. Thompson in *Toynbee and History*, p. 219).
[2] A propos of me, A. R. Burn observes: 'It would be unjust to say that he forces facts into his mould, and much more so to imply conscious lack of integrity' (*History*, February–October, 1956, p. 3). G. J. Renier thinks that 'this book cannot be a mystification' (*Toynbee and History*, p. 75).
[3] 'Though there is no deception of others, there is the nearest approach to self-deception' (Renier, ibid.).

aware.[1] In the present volume I have made a number of such revisions of my views in the light of criticisms of volumes i–x.

7. MYTH

My usage of the word myth certainly needs defining. The literal meaning of the Greek word *mythos* is 'story'. Like the word 'story' in colloquial English, the word *mythos* in Greek is used in two senses. One of these senses is the usual sense of the derivative word 'myth' in modern Western languages. But the sense in which I use the word 'myth' is that of the other usage of the word in Greek.

The distinction between the two meanings of 'myth' and the two meanings of 'story' is not the same. One kind of 'story' is fiction, the other kind is true to 'fact'. Neither kind of 'myth' is true to fact. One kind is a substitute for statements of fact where the facts are either unknown or ignored; the other kind is a story about a sphere of Reality that is of the highest significance and importance for human beings and is at the same time beyond the range of the 'factual' knowledge that human minds acquire through analytical and classificatory intellectual operations. This second kind of myth is the kind that plays so striking, and so illuminating, a part in Plato's *Dialogues*. Of all men that ever wrote in Greek, Plato has the best claim to be the father of the usage of the Greek word 'myth' in this second sense, because it was he who first consciously and deliberately used 'myth'—as many seers, in many societies, before him and after him have used poetry—to extend the range of human intuition and understanding beyond the limits of the knowledge attainable through logical processes of thought.

This Platonic meaning of the word 'myth' is the one that I have adopted; and, though I have explained this in more than one place in this book up to the present point, I fear that my usage, being not the usual one, has nevertheless caused some misunderstanding in some readers' minds, and has incidentally exposed me to criticism that may be only partly deserved.

Myth, in the sense of a fictitious substitute for the statement of facts, has been regarded in two lights, both in the Hellenic World and in its modern Western successor. It has been held to be not only innocent, but entertaining, in narrative poetry and in 'fairy-stories' told to children. It has been held—and rightly held, I too believe—to be pernicious where it has been brought in to fill a gap in our factual knowledge, and *a fortiori* where there is genuine factual knowledge on record which a mythical narrative has ousted. For instance, the Alexander Romance is so entertaining that it has been translated into a host of languages; but nobody

---

[1] 'The point is that one should recognise the fact and its difficulty, and should recognise its unavoidableness. The point is that, in and through the recognition of all this, one should strive, with a high and pure [resolve], to hold fast to "honnêteté"' (H. Baudet in *Historie en Metahistorie*, p. 46).
'One has the feeling that Toynbee, unlike Spengler, is really trying to subject his historical laws to empirical tests, and that he would have the integrity and the modesty, if given sufficient reason, to modify or abandon his laws' (W. H. Coates in *The Journal of Modern History*, vol. xxi, No. 1 (March, 1949), p. 27, quoted already on p. 46). Cp. F. Neilson in *The American Journal of Economics and Sociology*, Supplement to vol. xiv, No. 3 (April, 1955), p. 3, already cited in the Introduction to the present volume, p. 2.

would defend a self-styled historian who served up a paraphrase or résumé of this romance to his readers and told them that this was the true story. We should require the historian to base his paraphrase or résumé on Arrian's *Anabasis*, which is derived from the authentic narratives of two of Alexander's officers. Again, we should censure an historian who served up a paraphrase of the *Volsunga Saga* or the *Nibelungenlied* as a history of the fifth-century Huns or Burgundians. We should require him to base his résumé on the statements of fifth-century historical writers in Greek and Latin. As for periods of history that are not covered by any surviving contemporary or later historical records, an historian will handle mythical accounts of them, given in surviving epics or romances, with extreme caution and reserve, if he ventures to draw on these at all. For instance, he may believe, on their evidence, that there was such a person as King Atreus or King Arthur in real life, but he will be slow to accept either the deeds or the dates mythically attributed to them. He will be sceptical because, when the veracity or inveracity of myth can be tested by some scraps of historical record, the mythical story often turns out to bear little or no resemblance to the authentic one.

Here is the touchstone for criticisms of my use of myths. If critics prosecute me on the charge of using myths in substitution for statements of fact, I doubt whether they will get any convictions. For instance, when G. N. Renier objects[1] that 'what Zeus said or intended is not evidence' because 'there never was a Zeus', my answer is to ask him 'evidence for what?' If the action that I had attributed to Zeus had been military, political, economic, or any other kind of social action, I should, of course, stand convicted. But, in the passage of mine that Renier cites, 'Zeus' and 'Prometheus' are symbols for psychological forces that can be described only in symbolic language. It would be not more inept to say that 'the Oedipus complex' is not evidence because we do not know that an authentic king called Oedipus ever reigned in Thebes in the Mycenaean Age. Again, when T. J. G. Locher pronounces[2] that I have turned history into mythology, I think he means that I have made mistakes in my account of events, or have seen some pattern in events which really is not there. No doubt I have sometimes fallen into errors of both these kinds, as most historians have to some extent. But, if my interpretation of Locher's meaning is right, he has used the word 'mythology', which, for him, is evidently a term of abuse, to signify, not that I have substituted fairy-tale for fact, but that, in trying to present the facts, I have got them and their configurations wrong; and this is quite a different matter.

I use the word 'myth' in the Platonic sense and resort to myths in the same field, and for the same purpose, as Plato, if I have rightly understood his idea and intention when he does pass over to myth from reasoning.[3] Plato does this when he feels that he has reached the limit beyond which his logical thinking will not carry him,[4] and his aim is to

[1] *In Toynbee and History*, p. 75.
[2] In *De Gids*, May, 1948, offprint, p. 21.
[3] W. H. McNeill finds that I resort to myths in Plato's way (*The Intent of Toynbee's History: A Cooperative Appraisal*).
[4] E. F. J. Zahn quotes from R. Guardini: *Der Tod des Socrates* (Bern 1945, Francke),

get some inkling of Reality beyond this range.[1] The pertinent question about my use of myth is therefore whether I do or do not use it in fields where reason would still serve, and whether, if I do use it for reconnoitring the trans-rational field of Reality, my use of it here is a legitimate one. E. Fiess observes[2] that

'Toynbee arrives at his . . . theory of challenge-and-response partly through an examination of myths involving an "encounter between two superhuman personalities". . . . Yet the work never really makes clear to what extent these mythical patterns merely confirm what has been discovered by other means and to what extent they are themselves taken as evidence.'

The answer to Fiess's query does not correspond to either of his two alternatives. Myths, as I use them in this connexion and in others, are symbols of psychological phenomena.[3] Being symbols, they are models, and, being models, they are heuristic hypotheses for exploring psychological dramas both within a single human soul and in the relations between two souls or more. J. K. Feibleman does me the honour of comparing me with Vico on the point that, like him, I have 'an understanding of myths as containing the essential truths of history'.[4] He finds that my history is 'a mythological drama'.[5] If 'psychology' were substituted for 'history' in the first of these two sentences, and 'psychological' for 'mythological' in the second, Feibleman's statements would have been equally apt as regards me and, I believe, as regards Vico too. W. den Boer asks:[6] 'Why should the rhythm of civilizations correspond with the fluctuations in Man's inner life as seen by mythical speculation?' The reason is that civilizations are nothing but relations between individual persons. They are therefore effects and expressions of the workings of human nature, since human nature is to be found in human beings and nowhere else. What is distinctively human about a human being is his inner life. And the invisible world of the psyche can be explored and expressed only in the symbolic terms that we call myths when we use the word 'myth' in Plato's sense. As for mythical speculation, this is the necessary beginning, but only the beginning, of the work of exploration. Mythical models are heuristic instruments for probing psychological phenomena.

8. CREATION

Creation means the conjuring of something out of nothing. Experience tells us that this mysterious action—or happening—is always taking place everywhere, in the observer as well as in his surroundings. It is a

---

p. 41, the observation that a myth can express something that, in logic, would be self-contradictory. I have made the same observation in the passage (i. 279) cited by E. Fiess in the first of the sentences quoted below.

[1] 'This is why the expression of faith takes the form of mythology' (R. L Shinn: *Christianity and the Problem of History*, p. 18).

[2] In *Toynbee and History*, p. 380.

[3] I have said this explicitly in i. 294 and iii. 112 and 116–17.

[4] *T'ien Hsia Monthly*, vol. xi, Nos. 1 and 2 (1940), pp. 165–6.

[5] Ibid., p. 172.   [6] In *Toynbee and History*, p. 230.

fallacy to suppose that there cannot be anything really new in any process of development.[1] Novelty is evidently of the essence of Reality. 'In an intelligent operation', for instance, 'there is an advance to something new, not the old in an equivalent form'; and a human being, 'unlike a machine, is a unity, whose later states and actions are not calculable from the earlier'.[2] But, while it is certainly impossible not to have the experience of novelty, it is perhaps also impossible for human minds, constituted as they are, to have an understanding of it, since the facet of Reality that minds can grasp is the pattern of regular recurrences in it, and a new thing is, by definition, not a recurrence and is therefore not classifiable, and therefore, in turn, not intelligible.[3] This logical impasse cannot be eluded by suggesting that novelty means, not something coming out of nothing, but the rearrangement of things that are already there. For, when there is a rearrangement, the new arrangement is something coming out of nothing, even if the objects that have been rearranged are not new. F. Engel-Janosi takes issue[4] with Goethe's idea, expressed in *Faust* in the Prologue in Heaven, that God needs the Devil's help for carrying on His work of creation. He points out that this idea is not compatible with the idea of creation being the conjuring of something out of nothing. This is, no doubt, true, but, since the idea of creation *ex nihilo* is logically unintelligible, Goethe has recourse to the Platonic expedient of using a myth to transcend the contradiction between logic and experience.

F. Neilson notes[5] that I have not answered Martin Wight's challenge to me[6] to declare whether I am an evolutionist or a creationist. My present answer is that, as I see it, this antithesis is not a fundamental one. The evolutionist is a creationist inasmuch as he shares with the believer in the existence of a creator God a belief that new things, or, alternatively, new patterns of old things, are constantly making their appearance, and human minds can explain this experience only as the work of a patterning presence in the Universe. The evolutionist may conceive of this presence as being impersonal instead of personal, and he may construe the participle 'patterning' intransitively instead of transitively, but, like the authors of the Book of Genesis, he is giving a mythical account of a datum of experience that cannot be expressed in terms of logical thought. R. Coulborn tries[7] to laugh away the concept of creativity as being a freak of Bergson's when Bergson is performing, not as a philosopher, but as a poet. One may misconceive the sociology of human creativity, but that is another matter, and is discussed below under the heading 'Creative and Dominant Minorities'. But Coulborn, too, accepts the reality of creativity as a datum of experience, and he, too, offers no logical explanation of it. Daniel Halévy observes[8] that I search

[1] M. R. Cohen: *The Meaning of Human History*, p. 139.
[2] H. W. B. Joseph: *An Introduction to Logic*, 2nd ed., p. 412.
[3] See the passage from M. R. Cohen's *The Meaning of Human History*, pp. 289–90, quoted in this volume on p. 21.
[4] In *Wissenschaft und Weltbild*, 2. Jahrgang, Heft 4 (October, 1949), p. 269.
[5] In *The American Journal of Economics and Sociology*, Supplement to vol. 14, No. 3 (April, 1955), p. 15.   [6] In vii. 420, footnote 6.
[7] In *Toynbee and History*, pp. 151–2.
[8] In a review, received by me on 23rd February, 1937, of vols. i–iii of this book in a French journal that I have not been able to identify.

in history for 'the genesis of the creative acts', and, on this point, he contrasts me with Spengler, who, in his words, 'crushes history under the weight of the fatality of an inhuman order'.

K. W. Deutsch complains[1] that the creativity which I ascribe to creative minorities 'has no intrinsic details that could be described and understood'. This is inevitable, considering my belief that novelty is logically unintelligible. Deutsch is an exponent of the new science of cybernetics, which approaches the problem of epistemology through the equally new electronic technology of communications. If the idea of novelty were to be made even partially intelligible through this approach, that would be a great advance in our understanding of the nature of Reality.

J. K. Feibleman complains[2] that the loss of creativity is never explained in this book. Yet in volume iv, under the heading 'The Nemesis of Creativity', I have covered 339 pages (pages 245–584) in an attempt to explain this tragedy in human affairs. Briefly, my explanation is that creative achievement is apt—though not in the least bound—to produce self-conceit or self-complacency, and that either of these faults dries the springs of creativity up and thereby invites disaster and ruin. In terms of Chinese thought, a Yang movement of activity is apt to pass over into its opposite, a Yin state of rest. This covers the situation in which God the creator finds Himself in the Prologue in Heaven in Goethe's *Faust*; and, in Goethe's myth, God saves Himself, at Faust's expense, by deigning and daring to make His wager with Mephistopheles. This explanation is an attempt at answering merely the question 'How?', not the question 'Why?'. A genuine answer to the second of these questions would be nothing less than a reading of the riddle of Reality.

9. CHALLENGE-AND-RESPONSE

The idea of challenge-and-response, which plays a key-part in my picture of the course of human affairs, is not just a 'private interpretation' of my own. The pair of words came to me from the English poet Robert Browning. though I had forgotten that I had not coined the expression myself till I rediscovered the source of it by chance after I had published my first six volumes.[3] The idea that the words express came to me, as I have always been aware, from the Old Testament;[4] and, considering how overwhelming the influence of the Bible has been on all Western thought, including thought that has consciously been in revolt against the Bible's domination, I have no doubt that this was the source from which Browning, too, received the idea, and was also the source

---

[1] In *Philosophy of Science*, vol. 18, No. 3 (July, 1951), p. 238, quoted already on p. 37.   [2] In *T'ien Hsia Monthly*, vol. xi, Nos. 1 and 2 (1940), p. 28.
[3] See x. 231–2.
[4] In giving an account of my ideas, P. Bagby writes: 'Most prominent, perhaps, are the moral antitheses derived from mythology, poetry, and, in a few important instances, like "challenge-and-response" or "rout-rally-rout", from the ethics of the playing field—itself, of course, a schoolboy version of Late Victorian muscular Christianity' (*Toynbee and History*, p. 104). I joyfully acknowledge my debt to poetry and mythology, but the idea that I am indebted to the playing field would make my school-fellows laugh. My dislike of the playing field was well known. It is most unlikely to have been even the subconscious source of any of my notions.

from which Hegel obtained his concept of dialectic, Malthus his concept of the struggle for existence, and Darwin, through Malthus, his concept of evolution. In the Old Testament, challenge-and-response is, indeed, the master motif; and it is this motif, running through it all, that gives the Old Testament the unity that it has. The Old Testament is a collection of books of many kinds, written and rewritten by many different hands over a period running to many centuries. But all these otherwise heterogeneous books, in all their successive recensions, are dominated by the same theme. All these writers see history as a series of acts in each of which God presents a challenge to some human being individually, or collectively to the participants in some human community or society.

The idea of challenge-and-response, as it has come to me, thus originates in the Israelites' anthropomorphic vision of God as a person with whom human persons have personal encounters. K. D. Erdmann recognizes[1] that I have 'taken the idea from the Bible, myth, and poetry'. O. H. K. Spate, discussing my application of the idea to the relation between Man and his geographical environment, is right in seeing in it an anthropomorphic image, and in pointing out[2] the 'danger, shared by possibilist and determinist alike, of anthropomorphising Nature'. Stone,[3] Catlin,[4] Zahn,[5] Kuhn,[6] Borkenau,[7] and Pares[8] are wrong in asserting that my source of the idea has been the modern Western science of biology. In so far as biologists operate with the idea of challenge-and-response, they too will have obtained it from the Old Testament, as I have independently of them. My image is not biological and not physical either; it is anthropomorphic;[9] and this is explicitly and prominently stated in several passages of this book, in volumes that these critics profess to be reviewing. I have argued[10] that 'the apathetic fallacy' of trying to deal with human nature in terms of inanimate nature leads to no less confusion and error than the converse 'pathetic fallacy' of treating inanimate nature as if it were animate. I have also argued, in introducing the idea of challenge-and-response,[11] that we shall not be able to obtain insight into the genesis of a human institution—

[1] In *Archiv für Kulturgeschichte*, xxxiii. Band, Heft 2 (1951), p. 206.
[2] In *The Geographical Journal*, vol. cxviii, Part 4 (December, 1952), p. 419, quoted already in this volume on p. 37, footnote 2.
[3] In *Toynbee and History*, p. 113.   [4] Ibid., p. 169.
[5] E. F. J. Zahn points out, in *Toynbee und das Problem der Geschichte*, p. 24, that 'interaction' is a biological idea. But it is one that the biologists have obtained by 'anthropomorphising Nature'; since action, in the literal sense, can be taken only by a person who has an intellect and a will.
[6] H. Kuhn asserts, in *The Journal of Philosophy*, 28th August, 1947, that 'by origin the concept of challenge-and-response is unquestionably biological' (p. 496) and that, 'throughout these analyses, we never emerge out of the sphere of biological or quasi-biological periodicity' (ibid.).
[7] Borkenau asserts, in *Commentary*, March, 1956, p. 249, that my formula of challenge-and-response is 'fundamentally a biological notion'.
[8] R. Pares asserts, in *The English Historical Review*, vol. lxxi, No. 279 (April, 1956), p. 271, that, 'if Dr. Toynbee rejects mechanical analogies, he falls victim to the far more dangerous biological analogies'.
[9] The antithesis between personal and impersonal, and the closely related antithesis between freedom and necessity, is perhaps distinctive of Western thought and is part of its heritage from Hellenism and Judaism. 'The concepts of stimulus and response are basic in Chinese naturalism' (J. Needham: *Science and Civilization in China*, vol. ii, p. 304). But the Chinese concept of Yin and Yang is neither anthropomorphic nor deterministic.   [10] In i. 7–8.   [11] In i. 271.

civilizations—if we do not 'shut our eyes, for the moment, to the formulae of science in order to open our ears to the language of mythology'. I have cited and opposed[1] the view, held by Herbert Spencer and by Oswald Spengler,[2] that human societies are organisms.[3] I have quoted,[4] as representing my own view, a dictum of G. D. H. Cole's that society is not a mechanism, not an organism, and not a person; and I have gone on[5] to give my own definition of society as being a relation between persons.

I am astonished that these passages should have been overlooked or ignored by critics who were intending to review my work seriously. I am also astonished at C. B. Joynt's assertion[6] that I cite no cases of the operation of challenge-and-response on the spiritual plane. There cannot be any cases on any other plane, since there can be no encounter in which at least one of the parties is not human. But I have discussed many cases in which all parties concerned are human. The whole of volume ii is occupied by a discussion of the range of challenge-and-response; but Joynt need not have read the volume in order to save himself from making his mistake. He could have avoided this by simply reading the table of contents and noticing that three out of seven sections in this volume are headed respectively 'The Stimulus of Blows', 'The Stimulus of Pressures', and 'The Stimulus of Penalizations'. In the aggregate these three sections occupy 256 pages out of a total of 452 pages in the whole volume, and, out of the remaining 196 pages, 131 are also occupied by discussions of cases in which all the parties are human likewise.

Encounters taking the form of challenge-and-response are the most illuminating kind of events for a student of human affairs if he believes, as I believe, that one of the distinctive characteristics of Man is that he is partially free to make choices, and that this partial freedom is not merely apparent but is genuine.[7] Encounters are the occasions in human life on which freedom and creativity come into play and on which new things are brought into existence.[8] God reveals Himself in encounters, not in propositions;[9] and acts of creation are one of the activities in which He thus manifests Himself. A. Hourani correctly notes[10] that, as I see it, the challenger is God—that is, absolute Reality approached anthropo-

---

[1] In iii. 221.
[2] P. Bagby refrains from following Spengler on this issue (see *Culture and History*, pp. 209–10).
[3] Christopher Dawson, in *Toynbee and History*, p. 130, and A. R. Burn, in *History*, February–October, 1956, p. 2, testify that I disagree with Spengler on this point. I cannot make out whether G. Catlin, in *Toynbee and History*, p. 169, is attributing to me a belief in 'the old organic mythos, so attractive to the public'.
[4] In iii. 22.   [5] In iii. 223–30.
[6] In *The Australasian Journal of Philosophy*, vol. 34, No. 3 (December, 1956), p. 197.
[7] I agree entirely, and heartily, with J. Maritain's account of human freedom in his book *On the Philosophy of History*. 'One of the deepest trends of human history is . . . to escape more and more from fate' (p. 22). Some changes may be inevitable; yet there will be a choice between alternative ways of making them (pp. 20 and 22). And the difference in the consequences of these alternative choices between different ways of making an inevitable change may matter more to the human beings concerned than the inevitable change itself (p. 27).
[8] Maritain holds that the recognition of both Man's freedom and God's existence is the necessary basis for a genuine philosophy of history (op. cit., pp. 26–27).
[9] R. L. Shinn: *Christianity and the Problem of History*, pp. 17–18.
[10] In *The Dublin Review*, vol. 229, No. 470 (December, 1955), pp. 390–1.

morphically—even when the challenge comes ostensibly from Man or Nature.[1] When a challenge has been delivered, then, 'however scientifically exact the identity between two or more situations may be, we shall not expect the respective outcomes of these situations to conform with one another. . . . Even if we were exactly acquainted with all the racial, environmental, or other data that are capable of being formulated scientifically, we should not be able to predict the outcome of the interaction between the forces which these data represent.'[2] We should be unable because, on this plane of action, the 'forces' are persons. 'To say that the same thing acting on the same thing under the same conditions may yet produce a different effect is to say that a thing need not be what it is';[3] and to say this about a thing is to say that this thing is a person, human or divine. Not needing to be what one is is a good definition of a personality's freedom. It follows that the response to a challenge is not the effect of a cause; for to say that a cause need not act uniformly is to deny causal connexions altogether.[4]

I believe that the outcome of a response to a challenge is not causally predetermined, is not necessarily uniform in all cases, and is therefore intrinsically unpredictable. But this is difficult to demonstrate empirically by applying to the phenomena the hypothesis that responses have varied in encounters in which the challenge and the circumstances have not. In previous volumes I have tried to demonstrate this by citing instances in which different responses to an apparently identical challenge have been made, in apparently identical circumstances, by different representatives of the same class of individual, community, or society. But, in contrast to mathematical abstractions, human phenomena are so complex and so mobile that it is always possible to represent that either the challengers or the respondents or the circumstances or all three elements were not, after all, exactly identical,[5] and then to argue that the success of one response and the failure of another have been due precisely to these differences.[6] Joseph points out[7] that, if it is contended that no two things ever are the same, this commits one to the proposition that no one thing is the same for two successive moments. But a believer in the reality of human freedom of choice is debarred from using this conclusion as a *reductio ad absurdum* of a critic's argument. So this argument opens the way for a denial of freedom and an assertion that the different outcomes of the encounter in different cases have been the necessary effect of causes that could be seen to operate inevitably and uniformly if only we could isolate exactly identical elements for the purpose of our test. Since, however, the critic has implicitly denied the

[1] This truth is acknowledged in the Lord's Prayer, where the plea 'Do not subject us to ordeals (*peirasmón*)' is addressed to God, not to Satan.   [2] i. 300.
[3] H. W. B. Joseph: *An Introduction to Logic*, 2nd ed., p. 408.
[4] Ibid., pp. 406–7.
[5] 'The differences will not be denied. . . . And the exceptions!' (P. Geyl in *Toynbee and History*, p. 51).
[6] This line of argument has been pursued most effectively by O. H. K. Spate in his critiques of my attempt to demonstrate the unpredictability of the outcome in cases of challenge-and-response in which the challenge is presented by—or through—Man's geographical environment (see pp. 146–7 and 314–27 of the present volume). The same argument could be applied equally well in other fields—as, in fact, it has been by Geyl.
[7] *An Introduction to Logic*, 2nd ed., p. 408.

possibility of this in the realm of human affairs, he, too, lacks the means of clinching his counter-argument; and the result of the debate between the determinist and the believer in the reality of freedom is bound to be inconclusive. It seems impossible to devise a test that will be objective in the sense of answering the question at issue in terms that are recognized as cogent by both parties. Either party is then likely to hold to his own view of the nature of Reality; and, on either side, this will be an act of faith. Here, once again, we are confronted with the relativity of an inquirer's picture of human affairs to his own fundamental beliefs about the nature of Reality, and, in this crucial case, the gulf that relativity has set between mind and mind appears to be unbridgeable.

The concept of challenge-and-response, as presented by me, has been criticized on several grounds. Encounters are fictitious, since the distinction between the alleged parties to them is artificial.[1] The concept is unanalysed, undefined, and vague.[2] It is a simplification, a truism, or a tautology.[3] The argument implied in it is a circular one.[4] It is incompatible with other hypotheses of mine.[5]

The first of these criticisms is discussed in this volume[6] apropos of the case in which the challenge is presented to Man through his geographical environment, and I give my answer to it in that context. I admit that the distinction between the giver and the receiver of a challenge is a mental misrepresentation of Reality. This is true not only when the challenge comes through Man's non-human environment and not only when a mind is thinking in terms of challenge-and-response. All thought is a misrepresentation of Reality inasmuch as it mentally divides what, for all we know, is an indivisible whole. But, without this distorting mental division of Reality, there would be no thought at all. This inherent imperfection of Man's intellectual powers has been noted in the first chapter of this volume. In earlier volumes I have implicitly submitted to intellectual necessity by taking the phenomenon of encounters at its face value and inquiring into the operation of challenge-and-response in terms of encounters between God and a human being, between human beings and their non-human environment, between one human being and another, and between different elements within a single human psyche.[7] I admit that I have misrepresented Reality in drawing my distinctions between creator and creature, environment and Man, soul and soul, psychic element and psychic element. But the price of restoring to

---

[1] E. F. J. Zahn: *Toynbee und das Problem der Geschichte*, pp. 25 and 32.

[2] P. Geyl in *Toynbee and History*, p. 5; K. W. Thompson, ibid., p. 217; M. Postan in *The Sociological Review*, vol. xxviii (1936), p. 6; H. Frankfort in *The Observer*, 31st January, 1954; S. Hook in *The Partisan Review*, June, 1948, p. 692; Zahn, op. cit., p. 27; T. J. G. Locher in *De Gids*, May, 1948, offprint, p. 13; R. K. Merton in *The American Journal of Sociology*, vol. xlvii, No. 2 (September, 1941), pp. 205-13.

[3] P. Geyl in *Toynbee and History*, p. 49; K. W. Thompson, ibid. (formulating the objections of scientific historians); H. Werner in *Deutsche Vierteljahrsschrift für Literaturwissenschaft und Geistesgeschichte*, 29. Jahrgang, xxix. Band (1955), p. 529; P. Gardiner in *Time and Tide*, 30th October, 1954, p. 1456; M. C. Swabey in *The Judgment of History*, pp. 11-12.

[4] R. H. S. Crossman in *The New Statesman*, 8th March, 1947; Werner in loc. cit., p. 539; Postan in loc. cit., pp. 54-55 and 59; Merton, ibid.; T. R. Fyvel in *The Tribune*, 21st March , 1947; F. Borkenau in *Commentary*, March, 1956, p. 242.

[5] H. S. Warwick in *The Louisville Courier-Journal*, 14th November, 1954.

[6] On pp. 148 and 314-27.

[7] In, for example, i. 271-338; ii. *passim*; iii. 1-217; v. 35-568; vi. 1-175.

Reality its true undifferentiated unity is to renounce the possibility of thinking about it;[1] and, even at this price, it is impossible to deprive Reality of the vein of freedom that runs through it and that manifests itself in the play of challenge-and-response. Spate argues:[2]

> 'This unpredictable reaction we may grant; but then this unknowable human positive is not positive, but only potentially so, until it is matched with the environmental change, and we are back where we started.'

We are back in an integral and therefore incomprehensible Reality, but not back where we started; for, in analysing Reality into an observer and an observed encounter between two parties, we have put our finger on the vein of freedom in Reality, and a reintegration of Reality does not get rid of this discovery about its nature; it merely inhibits us from locating and defining the circumstances in which Reality's freedom comes into action; and this inhibition is an unnecessary restraint upon the advancement of knowledge and understanding.

The criticisms of my concept of challenge-and-response as being unanalysed, undefined, and vague are, in effect, demands (so it seems to me) that I should translate my non-deterministic reading of the movement of human affairs into a deterministic one. This cannot be done, since, in this antithesis between 'non-deterministic' and 'deterministic', the two terms are mutually exclusive—at any rate in my native Western way of thinking, though in the Chinese way this antithesis is, perhaps, transcended or eluded. Moreover, I would not turn my non-deterministic view into a deterministic one, even if this were in my power, since I believe that a partial freedom to choose is an essential and distinctive characteristic of human nature. When Thompson reminds me[3] that 'the question that both spiritual and scientific interpretations of history have consistently asked has been, What is the true mechanism of history?', my answer is: 'There is no such thing. Human actions are not the mechanical effects of causes; they are purposive executions of decisions between alternative possible choices.' When Frankfort takes note[4] that I do not explain 'the one fact which requires elucidation above all—that challenging conditions [have] worked as stimuli in certain cases and not in others'—my answer to this is that, when the cases that have fallen out differently have been truly comparable, the only possibility of elucidation lies in accepting, as correct, the hypothesis that human affairs are at least partly non-determined.

Hook declares[5] that,

> 'unless we can define what constitutes a successful response, unless we can say in advance what kind of unsuccessful response to what kind of problem spells disaster for a culture, unless we can formulate a hypothesis

---

[1] I cannot follow M. Postan's reasoning when he says that the notion of challenge-and-response 'might have enabled Professor Toynbee to proceed much further than the biologists and the sociologists have so far done in abolishing the artificial abstraction of the object from the environment' (*The Sociological Review*, vol. xxviii (1936), p. 60). Surely Spate is right in holding that a distinction between two parties is inherent in the notion of an encounter. I do not agree with either Spate or Postan in holding that this distinction can be dropped without stopping thinking.

[2] In *The Geographical Journal*, vol. cxviii, Part 4 (December, 1952), p. 413.

[3] In loc. cit.   [4] In loc. cit.   [5] In loc. cit.

concerning the determinate conditions under which a creative response will or will not be made, we have hardly made a beginning towards a scientific study of the rise, growth, and decline of cultures.'

My answer is that I have given a definition of what constitutes a successful response in my view.[1] It is one that, in addition to merely surmounting the current challenge, surmounts it in a way that evokes a new challenge and thus keeps life on the move. In surveying the recorded past we can find instances in which this has happened; but we can never say in advance what the outcome of a challenge is going to be; and, if scientific knowledge and understanding is properly defined as being of a kind that makes prediction possible, then we have to acknowledge that there never has been, and never can be, such a thing as a scientific study of human affairs.

Postan, in his critique of my work, writes[2] that,

'had he responded to the challenge of his own terminology, he would have tried to bring out the factors that make a challenge challenging. He would have given us the analysis of societies challenged, and would have tried to find by what social arrangements, by what changes in their material and spiritual equipment, some societies were made to feel a certain phenomenon as a moderate challenge, while others were either not challenged by it at all, or challenged only too severely. He would also have classified responses as well as challenges, and would have analysed the mechanism [*sic*] of response. Why did the Assyrians fail to respond to the Scythian challenge while the Medians succeeded? Why was the English response to the Scandinavian challenge different from that of the Irish? Why did the Zoroastrian and the Jewish societies fail while the Mohammedans succeeded in meeting the Hellenic challenge? How does the capacity for experiencing a challenge differ from the ability to respond to it successfully? Do the same social factors which determine the degree of the challenge also determine the quality of the response?'

I agree, of course, with the general point made by Postan in this passage. The sociologist's microscope is an invaluable instrument for the study of human affairs, and the use of it would give me a chance of pushing my inquiries farther than I have pushed them yet. I have, as a matter of fact, discussed—for instance, apropos of the primeval forest in the basin of the River Po and in Eastern North America[3]—the question why this presented an overwhelming challenge to a society with a certain organization and equipment, and a stimulating challenge to another society whose organization and equipment were different. A further use of this instrument would perhaps give me the means of meeting a challenge presented to me by Spate and Geyl. It would enable me to identify and dismiss those cases in which a difference in the responses to an identical challenge was due to a difference in the organization, equipment, and circumstances of the parties subjected to this common ordeal. I might then perhaps be able to confront Spate and Geyl with instances in which they would agree that two or more parties, confronted with an identical challenge, had been strictly uniform with each

[1] This definition will be found in iii. 119.
[2] In loc. cit.   [3] See ii. 275–8 and the present volume, pp. 147–8.

other, and therefore properly comparable in all relevant points, and yet had responded differently. But we should then, I believe, still be left in the presence of differences in the response that would be explicable only on the hypothesis that, when there is an encounter between persons, a genuine freedom, inherent in the nature of Reality, comes into action. Postan's and Thompson's word 'mechanism', used apropos of responses to challenges, is, I should say, an inappropriate and misleading metaphor taken from the working of Reality on the inanimate level.

Challenge-and-response is a pattern in human life. It is a pattern with a texture of freedom, not of necessity; but, like other observable patterns, it is unlikely to be all-prevailing and ubiquitous. I have therefore spent volume ii of this book on trying to ascertain the range within which this particular pattern asserts itself. The question in my mind was whether or not every challenge in all circumstances evokes differing responses from different parties when these parties are uniform, and therefore comparable, in all relevant points. In putting my question to the phenomena of human history, over as wide a field as I could, I came to the conclusion that, at one end of the scale, there were some challenges that had been met so easily by all the parties confronted by them in some particular episode that they gave them no stimulus. At the other end of the scale I found that there were some challenges that had been so severe for all parties that all alike had been defeated by them. In between these two extremes there was a range of challenges which had been met successfully by some parties but not by others, in circumstances in which this difference between the responses could not be accounted for, as far as I could see, by any relevant difference between the parties whose respective responses had been successful and unsuccessful.

This conclusion is neither unexpected nor exciting,[1] but it is not a truism; for we have no warrant, *a priori*, for assuming that a pattern's range is limited; and therefore to ascertain that some particular pattern's range does have limits is always worth while. In me, at any rate, any attempt to do this is a merit, considering that I have been accused of pushing my ideas to extremes in some cases. I do not agree with Werner[2] that challenge-and-response are terms without content. As I see it, they have a content that is an important one. It consists in the establishment of the reality of freedom and the identification of one field in which freedom can be seen at work. Nor do I agree with Geyl[3] that it is 'essential to define what is too much and what too little', and 'to stipulate where the golden mean lies'. I do agree with him that my 'law' has nothing to say about this. It could not have anything to say about it without substituting determinism for the belief in the reality of freedom which is the essence of the notion of challenge-and-response. The notion would be tautologous only if challenge-and-response were presented as being a species of cause-and-effect; and, if I have ever fallen into this misrepresentation of my own idea, I have thereby exposed myself—but not the idea—to Geyl's and Werner's criticisms.

[1] 'Robbed of Toynbee's profuse wealth of illustrations, this sounds painfully like common sense' (A. L. Guerard in *The Herald-Tribune*, 28th October, 1934).
[2] In loc. cit. [3] In loc. cit.

K. D. Erdmann judges[1] that I have tried to retranslate my idea into scientific terms; and, in the act, have fallen into a tautology—the golden mean—which throws no true light on historical causation. But he goes on to say that this scientific failure does not empty the idea of challenge-and-response of significance, so long as the critic remembers that the origin of the idea is non-empirical.

'Does the pair of concepts "challenge-and-response" lose its importance on this account? To my mind the opposite is the truth. Let us not forget how Toynbee has obtained the concept. He has taken it from the Bible, myth, and poetry, and not from historical observation.'

I myself would add that I have tried to apply it to observed historical phenomena, and that I believe that my survey has brought to light empirical evidence for the view that there is an element of freedom in human life.

The criticism of my argument as being a circular one has been expressed most clearly, perhaps, by Werner.[2]

'A challenge is that which has the capacity to evoke a civilization, and a civilization is that which follows a challenge.'

This account of my exposition would be correct if it were my thesis that the responses to challenges have invariably been successful; but my actual thesis is that the responses of comparable parties to an identical challenge have varied: they have been successes in some cases only, and have been failures in others; and there have also been challenges that have been met successfully by nobody and others that have been met successfully by everybody. Thus Werner's attempt to formulate my thesis gets it wrong in every particular. If other criticisms of my argument, as being circular, are based on a similar misunderstanding, they are no more to the point than Werner's criticism is. Postan, at any rate, appears to be in Werner's company when he says[3] that

'a complete and impartial list of Professor Toynbee's "successes" would be merely a list of events and situations which happen to have made sufficient splash to receive large notices in history books.'

This cannot be true, considering that the events and situations that have made a splash have been signal failures as often as signal successes. If my findings are to be judged by the conventional presentation of history caricatured in *1066 and All That*, Postan will have to make a complete and impartial list, not only of my 'successes', but also of my 'failures'. If this list of both the two alternative possible kinds of response turns out to coincide with the list that is commonly accepted, this will surely be presumptive evidence in favour of mine.

Warwick[4] argues that my concept of challenge-and-response, with its implication that freedom is a reality, applies to my account of the geneses of first-generation civilizations only. When I come to discuss the geneses of later civilizations, which are affiliated, in my view, to earlier civiliza-

[1] In *Archiv für Kulturgeschichte*, xxxiii. Band, Heft 2 (1951), p. 206.
[2] In loc. cit.　　　　　　　　[3] In loc. cit.　　　　　　　　[4] In loc. cit.

tions, I hold that the link has been provided by a higher religion which has served the nascent new civilization as a chrysalis; and Warwick maintains that 'the chrysalis metaphor is fatal to challenge-and-response', because 'an insect's pupal stage is one of suspended animation'.

My answer to this point is that, in an insect's career, the pupal state is followed by a bursting of the chrysalis, and that this, like the breaking of the egg-shell by a chick and like the birth of a mammal, is a manifest challenge, considering that it is an exposure of a previously sheltered creature to the buffets of an inclement world. But I would also remind Warwick that, in my presentation of the sequence of events when a disintegrating civilization is succeeded by a new one, the chrysalis from which the new creature eventually emerges is, itself, the result of a previous successful response to a previous challenge. In my picture the 'chrysalis' is the product of a 'higher religion'; this 'higher religion' is the product of an 'internal proletariat'; and this 'internal proletariat' has brought itself into existence by an act of secession from a 'dominant minority'. This act of secession has been a successful response to a challenge in the shape of a sinister change in the ruling minority's character. It has become a 'dominant minority', continuing to impose itself by sheer force, after having originally been a 'creative minority', leading the majority of the members of the society in virtue of its attractiveness. I have already noted[1] that I may have exaggerated the antithesis between the characters of the ruling minority in the earlier and in the later chapter of its history, and I recur to this again.[2] But I still maintain that, in the histories of civilizations that have broken down and disintegrated, there has been a change, of the kind that I have diagnosed, in the ruling minority's ethos; and I also still maintain that this change on the minority's part has been a challenge, and a severe one, to the majority.

10. WITHDRAWAL-AND-RETURN

I have suggested that one of the agencies of social change has been the withdrawal of an individual or a group from its social milieu, followed by a period of aloofness, during which the temporarily retiring group or individual incubates something new. As I see it, this period of withdrawal is eventually followed by a third stage, in which the party in question re-enters the society from which it has retired, but re-enters it in a new role, acquired during its temporary absence. In this new role it sometimes makes a greater impression than it had ever made in its original role, and this gives it a chance of converting the other members of the society to its own new ideas and ideals. I saw in this spiritual voyage of withdrawal-and-return one of the ways in which the recipient of a challenge has responded to it, and responded successfully. I suggested that a series of withdrawals and returns had played an important part in the growths of civilizations, and I cited[3] a number of instances, some drawn from the lives of individuals, and some from the histories of groups. I also saw withdrawal-and-return as one particular form of a

---

[1] On pp. 149–50.   [2] On pp. 305–6.   [3] In iii. 248–377.

more general pattern, in which—with or without an intervening with-drawal—a party to an encounter who has been worsted on one plane of activity makes a successful *riposte* by reacting on another plane on which the other party is not prepared for action.[1]

The notion of withdrawal-and-return has been perhaps more sharply criticized than any other idea of mine,[2] and, on reconsideration, I am inclined to think that I have put more weight on it than it will bear. I would agree that it has not been a universal feature of responses to challenges. In whatever field one looks—for instance, the fields of re-ligion, human studies, and politics—one will find that, while withdrawal-and-return has been one way of responding to a challenge, in every field there have also been other ways.[3]

In the fields of religion and of human studies withdrawal-and-return has, I still believe, been the course followed by some of the greatest and most influential figures.[4] In the religious field, Paul withdrew after re-ceiving the challenge of his vision on the road, and returned as a Christian apostle instead of a Jewish persecutor. Saint Ignatius Loyala withdrew after receiving his wound, and returned as a spiritual soldier instead of a military one. The Buddha withdrew after His experiences of the ills of life, and returned as a preacher instead of a prince. More pro-saically, Confucius withdrew after failing to obtain permanent employ-ment as a civil servant, and returned as a teacher of ethics instead of a would-be administrator of public business. Jesus withdrew into the wilderness after His experience at His baptism, and returned as a preacher and healer instead of a carpenter. Saint Benedict and Saint Gregory the Great received challenges of an inward spiritual kind, not signalized by any dramatic outward event, but their lives, too, followed the same pattern. Benedict withdrew as the child of well-to-do middle-class parents and returned as the founder and abbot of a monastic com-munity. Gregory withdrew as a senior civil servant and returned as a

---

[1] See viii. 466–76.

[2] For instance, by Geyl in *Toynbee and History*, pp. 49–50; by K. W. Thompson, ibid., pp. 216–17; by W. Kaufmann, ibid., p. 311; by R. Coulborn in *Phylon*, 1940, offprint, p. 5; by R. H. S. Crossman in *The New Statesman*, 8th March, 1947; by W. Gurian in *The Review of Politics*, vol. 4, No. 4 (October, 1942), p. 512; by A. H. Hanson in *Science and Society*, No. 13 (1949), pp. 118–35. Crossman calls my presentation of the idea a pastiche. Hanson calls the idea itself 'mystic nonsense'. On the other hand, A. L. Guerard finds my treatment of withdrawal-and-return the most interesting thing in vols. i–iii of this book (*The Herald-Tribune*, 28th October, 1934).

[3] J. K. Feibleman comments: 'Is withdrawal from worldly affairs to a state of con-templation which constitutes a preparation for return with "new powers" to interference in those affairs a necessary pattern for the creative leader? It would hardly appear so. Napoleon and Abraham Lincoln are examples of men whose leadership, so far as it lay within their decision to control their own destiny, was unremitting, and there are many others who could be named. It may not always be necessary to withdraw; and, further, withdrawal may be fatal if there is no return' (*T'ien Hsia Monthly*, vol. xi, Nos. 1 and 2 (1940), p. 27).

[4] In H. Holborn's view, the concept of withdrawal-and-return 'is fairly well appli-cable to a long series of prophets and religious leaders. With regard to intellectual and political leaders it is of more questionable value' (*The Saturday Review of Literature*, 31st May, 1947, p. 12). K. D. Erdmann likewise judges that the concept ceases to work when the creative personalities to which it is applied are people whose field of action has been not religious but mundane (*Archiv für Kulturgeschichte*, xxxiii. Band, Heft 2 (1951), p. 211). H. Frankfort finds that my illustrations of withdrawal-and-return 'rob it, not only of the obvious, but of all definite, meaning' (*The Birth of Civilization in the Near East*, pp. 28–29. Cp. p. 24, footnote 1).

papal envoy and then as a pope. In the field of the study of human affairs Thucydides, Xenophon, Josephus, Ollivier,[1] Machiavelli, Polybius, Clarendon, and Ibn Khaldun were all men of action—statesmen or soldiers or both—who were put out of action permanently or temporarily by being disgraced or cashiered or exiled or deported, and who then returned as observers in the field in which they had previously been actors. Dante was one of this company. Exiled for life from Florence, he returned as a poet instead of a citizen.

Most of these examples are so eminent that, in these two lines at any rate, it looks as if withdrawal-and-return was really one kind—and an important kind—of prelude to outbursts of creativity. Yet in both these fields one could find other eminent representatives whose creative activities were not inaugurated by any conspicuous break in their lives. Conversely, in the field of politics, one can find striking instances of withdrawal-and-return. Muhammad, for instance, withdrew from Mecca as an unsuccessful prophet and returned as a triumphant statesman. But I admit the criticism that in politics this pattern of career has not been particularly outstanding. Thus, on reconsideration, I find myself still holding that withdrawal on one plane, followed by return on another plane, is one of the patterns that individual lives may take, but I no longer think it as important or as pervasive a pattern as I once thought it.

I also still believe that this pattern has displayed itself in the histories of peoples, as well as in the lives of individuals. Athens, for instance, played an important part in the life of the Hellenic World in the Dark Age of Hellenic history (*circa* 1125–725 B.C.). She served as a base of operations for the Greek colonization of Ionia, and her geometric pottery dominated the Hellenic market. Thereafter, in the ensuing age of Greek colonization in the western basin of the Mediterranean, Athens lapsed into comparative isolation and obscurity. After that, again, there was a third act, opening in the sixth century, in which Athens once more came to the front in politics, war, literature, and all the visual arts, including architecture and sculpture as well as pottery. And, in this age following the temporary withdrawal, she shone as she had never shone before. English history, too, displays the same pattern (I still maintain, in spite of Geyl's trenchant criticisms). From the Norman conquest to her eventual defeat in the last bout of the Hundred Years War, the rulers of England were bent on winning and holding a Continental European empire. After their discomfiture by Joan of Arc they renounced their continental ambitions and turned their energies to overseas enterprise; and this was the creative age of English history in literature and politics. After the Revolution of 1688 England re-entered the Continental European arena from which she had been evicted more than two hundred years back; but she returned in a new role. The English had not forgotten the lesson of their repeated loss of a continental empire—first in 1202–4 and then again in 1449–51. This had implanted in English minds a lasting inhibition against further attempts to acquire continental

---

[1] I have been criticized by Geyl, in loc. cit., and by Guerard in *The Herald-Tribune*, 28th October, 1934, for including this relatively minor figure in my list. Yet a minor figure may be a significant instance.

territory. England now resumed her participation in European affairs, but no longer as an aspirant to a continental empire of her own; she returned as the protagonist in the opposition to successive attempts, by continental powers, to acquire empires on continental soil that might be a menace to England's security. Geyl's criticisms[1] of my account of English history[2] are telling, besides being witty. They prove me wrong on a number of incidental points, but, as far as I can see, they leave my thesis still standing. With Geyl's aid to help me steer clear of some pitfalls into which I have stumbled at my first attempt, I believe I could produce a revised version of my thesis that would be acceptable to Geyl himself.

11. PROGRESS

The Latin word *progressus* means literally an advance in whatever the direction may be. But it is also used metaphorically, and this metaphorical usage is the one that usually attaches to the transliterations or translations of the word in modern Western languages. In this metaphorical meaning the idea of progress is subjective in two senses. In the first place it implies a judgement of value in the mind of anyone who applies the idea to a series of phenomena. In declaring that the change between an earlier phase of something and a later phase of it is a case of progress, he is judging that the later phase is better than the earlier one from his point of view in that particular context. In the second place the idea of progress is relative to the kind of phenomena with which one happens to be concerned at the moment. Since the kinds of phenomena are infinite for practical human purposes, and since few movements, either physical or spiritual, are known to have gone forward in the same direction without stopping, veering, or backsliding sooner or later, the use of the word 'progress' in the absolute is meaningless.[3] There have been bouts of progress in an almost infinite number of different fields; but progress in certain fields has often been accompanied by retrogression in other fields. Progress in the art of war, for instance, has sometimes been accompanied by retrogression in the spiritual sphere; retrogression in civilization has sometimes been accompanied by progress in religion.

For these reasons, I do not dispute W. Altree's judgement[4] that

'Toynbee's depreciation of the material aspects of civilization and his mystical orientation deprive him of any set of objective criteria for the measurement of the progress of civilizations,'

and that this Study is 'a normative system based on a very private interpretation of human destiny'. But, in accepting Altree's verdict, I generalize it and apply it to him and to everyone else, as well as to myself. On Altree's showing, Altree's own valuation of the material aspects of civilization and his own orientation in regard to religion, whatever this may be, deprive him, too, of objective criteria for measuring progress;

---

[1] In *Toynbee and History*, pp. 53–55.   [2] In iii. 350–63.
[3] Here I disagree with F. S. Marvin, who criticizes me for not believing that there has been progress in an absolute sense (*The Hibbert Journal*, July, 1935, pp. 624–5).
[4] In *Toynbee and History*, p. 271.

and his or anyone else's interpretation of human destiny, if made in terms of progress, is bound, like mine, to be 'very private'. I am sceptical of Altree's apparent belief that 'a set of objective criteria for the measurement of the progress of civilizations' is obtainable. In my belief, every judgement of progress, in whatever field, is subjective intrinsically and incurably. C. Trinkaus[1] and F. S. Marvin[2] are right when they report that my theory implies a disbelief in progress, if they mean progress in the absolute. I do not disbelieve in the experience of progress in an immense number of different fields, in discontinuous bursts, each of limited duration and limited achievement. But this experience is, as I see it, determined by the particular criterion that one happens to be applying. If one looks for progress in human affairs in terms of technology, in terms of sociality, and in terms of spirituality, one will obtain a different chart of human history in each case. Therefore, when Trinkaus declares[3] that history is progress or nothing, my answer is that it is neither. It is a kaleidoscopic panorama in which the patterns and colours change with each change in the viewer's focus of interest.

As Altree points out in the passage quoted above, I have (as he and everyone else has) a set of values that are personal—though the person in question may share them with a greater or a lesser number of his fellow human beings. My own set of values has led me to see progress in terms of progressive 'etherialisation',[4] progressive power of self-determination,[5] and progressive accessibility of means of grace.[6] A. L. Kroeber rightly calls 'etherialisation' an 'unfortunate' word.[7] It is unfortunate because it is a word of my own coinage, and is therefore unfamiliar and obscure. Kroeber has defined it for me, neatly as well as accurately, as meaning 'simplification with increased efficiency'. Each of my three criteria of progress has been disputed by inquirers whose own criteria are different. Mumford finds my valuation in terms of 'etherialisation' one-sided.[8] 'In a healthy society', he maintains, 'the two processes of etherialisation and materialisation are—if my interpretation holds—in continuous interplay.'[9] He also disputes[10] my measurement of growth in terms of 'a progressive and cumulative self-articulation', a transfer of the field of action from the outer to the inner world, and the displacement of quantitative criteria of success by qualitative criteria. G. Masur calls my doctrine of progressive self-determination 'the most arbitrary and unsatisfactory part' of my whole undertaking.[11] Criticisms of my third criterion—a progressive increase in the means of grace— have, I should guess, been still more vehement and more frequent. Such differences between different inquirers' criteria of progress have arisen whenever and wherever the idea of progress has been current. They are one of the most striking evidences of the truth that a human being's judgements are relative to his personal outlook.

If I am right in holding that the criteria of progress are, by their very

---

[1] In *Science and Society*, vol. xii, No. 1 (1948), p. 223.
[2] In *The Hibbert Journal*, July, 1935, pp. 624–5.   [3] In loc. cit.
[4] See iii. 174–92.   [5] See iii. 192–217.
[6] See vii. 562–8.   [7] *The Nature of Culture*, pp. 373–4.
[8] See *Diogenes*, No. 13 (Spring, 1956), pp. 19–20.   [9] Ibid., p. 20.
[10] Ibid., p. 19.   [11] The *Historische Zeitschrift*, Band 177 (1954), pp. 521–2.

nature, subjective, is it possible to arrive at an objective description of the process through which a bout of progress is achieved, irrespective of the standard that is being applied and of the field that is under consideration? This question has been raised, apropos of my work, by P. A. Sorokin.

'Toynbee's theory [he writes][1] is not so much a theory of civilizational change as much as an evaluative theory of civilizational progress or regress. This clearly comes out in his formulae of "growth" and "disintegration". They are evaluative formulae of progress and regress but not the formulae of change.'

The two labels here cited by Sorokin are evaluative, I agree. They imply that one process of change in a network of relations of the species called civilization makes this network do better service for the human beings participating in it, and that another process of change in the same network has the contrary effect in terms of human interests. But the evaluative labels for processes are not the same thing as the processes themselves. In volume iii of this book[2] I have tried to analyse in psychological and social terms the process that, in 'evaluative' terms, I have appraised as growth or progress. I have seen it as a series of acts of the drama of challenge-and-response in which each act results in a successful response to the challenge with which this act has opened, while each of these successful responses results in the presentation of a new challenge which produces a further act. On this view, the rhythm of progress or growth is a repeated overbalance that gives the challenged party a continuing momentum; and this momentum carries him along from one act of challenge-and-response to another. There is no reason why the series of acts, thus generated, should ever come to an end. There is no predetermined or fated limit to the number of the acts, and no fixed maximum time-span within which the drama must play itself out. There may be no known instance of a bout of progress that did not come to an end sooner or later. But the failure of a particular past bout of progress to perpetuate itself will not have been inevitable. It will have been a consequence of 'the nemesis of creativity'; and a successful creator is never fated, though always tempted, to allow this nemesis to overtake him.

12. INSTITUTIONS

Institutions, as I understand them, are relations between persons that have been systematized in a more or less formal pattern. Being relations between persons, institutions are not mechanized relations, if I am right in holding that, in encounters between persons, the play is not the mechanical play of cause-and-effect but the free play of challenge-and-response.[3] For the same reason, institutions are not organic relations.[4] A person is an organism, but a relation between persons is not. This last-mentioned fact about the nature of institutions means that, unlike organisms, they have no fixed and fated time-span, either maximum or

---

[1] In *Toynbee and History*, p. 182. Cp. p. 188.
[2] iii. 112-27, especially 119-20.   [3] See pp. 255-7.   [4] See ibid.

minimum. Since an institution is the product of a consensus of human wills, it can be dissolved by a consensus at any moment, however soon, after it has been created. On the other hand, there is no reason in principle why any institution, once established, should not last for an indefinite time to come—in fact, as long as mankind itself.[1] Institutions have no maximum time-span because the human participants in a systematic relation, or set of relations, may change, and change entirely and repeatedly, without this bringing the institution to an end. *Le roi est mort, vive le roi!* The office survives the death of each of its successive human occupants.[2] Again, there is no fixed number, either minimum or maximum, for the participants in an institution. At one extreme they may run to hundreds of millions. The missionary religions, which are the largest and most enduring institutions that have made an appearance so far, have had, as one of their objectives, the permanent conversion of the whole human race; and today we can foresee the possibility that the whole of mankind may come to form a single society, and perhaps even a single political community. At the other extreme the participants in an institution may form a narrower circle than that of each participant's personal acquaintances.

The existence of an institutional relation between two or more human beings does not preclude the existence of a personal relation between them as well.[3] On the other hand, the absence of a personal relation does not preclude the existence of an institutional relation. This, being a systematic kind of relation, can subsist between people who have not ever met and are not likely ever to meet each other. Indeed, it can subsist between non-contemporaries. At this moment, for example, a

---

[1] This conclusion of mine strikes W. Höpker as being an extreme one (*Zeitwende*, August, 1949, p. 136).

[2] G. A. Birks and P. Bagby are stating what is my belief, too, when Birks says that a society (which is one species of institution) differs from an organism in not having any definite birth or death (*Philosophy*, October, 1950, pp. 336–40) and when Bagby says that civilizations (which are one species of society) 'do not die at all' (*Toynbee and History*, p. 106; cp. *Culture and History*, p. 116). When Bagby goes on to say (*Toynbee and History*, loc. cit.) that I have 'not it seems, done away with every vestige of the organic analogy', my answer is that I have done away with every vestige of it in my thinking, but that, in writing about civilizations and other institutions, I have not managed to get rid of every vestige of anthropomorphic language. To do that would be the ideal, but the poverty of the vocabulary at our disposal makes this difficult to achieve. This unavoidable use of anthropomorphic language is, no doubt, insidious. Birks (ibid.) finds that, as a result of using such terms as 'rise and fall' and 'growth and decline', I slip into thinking of societies as organisms subconsciously.

[3] A good illustration of this is the institution of marriage (irrespective of whether the prevailing marriage system happens to be polyandrous, polygynous, or monogamous). In one aspect, marriage, under whatever system, is a pre-eminently personal relation; indeed, there could not be such a thing as marriage without this; and, so long as the relation between married people is harmonious, no other aspect of marriage except its personal aspect arises either for the married people themselves or for any other participants in the same society. On the other hand, if a marriage goes wrong enough to lead one or other party to go to law about it, it immediately becomes evident that this is an institution in which all participants in the society feel a concern and, through the law, assert it. A marriage cannot be dissolved without the law's sanction. Nor can it be contracted without being 'solemnized' in either a religious or a civil ceremony, the effects of which are binding on the parties. The parties can neither become nor cease to be man and wife just by their own private common consent. Society, acting through the law, insists that, besides being a private affair, a marriage is a public one. Even if the marriage has been duly solemnized and is harmonious, the law may intervene if some third party alleges that the marriage is, after all, unlawful in terms of the legislation, civil or ecclesiastical, that is in force at the particular time and place.

Buddhist, a Christian, or a Muslim is linked by an effective institutional relation, not only with his living co-religionists in the antipodes, but with his dead co-religionists in every generation right back to the founder of his faith. This capacity of institutions for linking human beings with each other by an impersonal bond, without the support of any personal relation between them, is the reason why mankind has found institutions indispensable. Man is not merely a social animal; he is one that could not survive if his society had to be confined to the inevitably narrow circle of living human beings who are in personal relations with each other. The simplest and most rudimentary society has to extend farther than that in both space and time, and it cannot extend beyond the range of personal acquaintance except by availing itself of institutions.[1]

It is true, at the same time, that impersonal institutional relations are morally, and therefore socially, a poor second-best by comparison with personal relations. If the parties to a marriage ever come to deal with each other only in terms of legal or customary rights and duties, without being animated by any mutual love, the marriage may still be legally valid but it will be spiritually dead. It is also unfortunately true that most people usually behave more callously and less responsibly as committee men, citizens, or churchmen than they behave as human beings in personal relations with their neighbours. Next to the innate self-centredness that afflicts human beings like other living organisms, the relatively low level of feeling and conduct in institutional relations, as contrasted with personal relations, is perhaps the second most potent cause of mankind's miserable failure in the field of human relations, in contrast to its brilliant success in the fields of science and technology, in which Man has the relatively easy task of dealing with non-human nature.[2] For this reason I have labelled institutions 'slums'; and, on reconsideration, I do not see any reason to withdraw the word, though I am ready to consider substitutes for it, to meet the protest that my word has drawn from Sir Ernest Barker.[3]

Whatever may be one's judgement on the moral standing of institutions by comparison with human beings, it must be agreed that institutions, as well as human beings, are realities.[4] They are, of course,

[1] R. Redfield holds that, till the rise of civilization, communities were so small that all the participants in a community knew each other personally (*The Primitive World and its Transformations*, p. 7). But they did not, and could not, know their ancestors personally, and the bond between the living and the dead has been stronger in pre-civilizational societies than in the civilizations.

[2] In this field, too, of course, Man cannot get far without co-operation; and this means that human relations are the crucial factor in everything whatsoever that Man does.

[3] In *Toynbee and History*, p. 96. On this, see further Chapter II, Annex, pp. 636–8.

[4] This point has been made already on pp. 231–4. I cannot follow C. Trinkaus' reasoning in *Science and Society*, vol. xii, No. 1 (1948), pp. 218–39. Commenting on my definition of society as being the common ground of the respective fields of action of a number of human beings, Trinkaus declares that 'this notion . . . abandons his conception of society as objectively existing and leads back to what is a more elaborate atomic conception. . . . Society disappears as an active structure and becomes the mere resultant of the socially undetermined individual actions emanating from each point on the plane.' Here Trinkaus seems to be maintaining that society cannot have an objective existence if it is not 'an active structure'. On this line of reasoning, inanimate nature would not have an objective existence. Trinkaus goes on to say that, as a result of my conception of society as being a network of relations between individuals, I completely ignore society's influence on, and importance for, the individual and am therefore not in a position to do

realities of a different order.[1] They are the products of continual encounters between the feelings, thoughts, and wills of a number of persons, and they cease to exist if there is no one who is any longer wanting to maintain them or is any longer having any feelings or thoughts about them.[2] But the fact that they exist in a psychic, not a physical, medium does not make them unreal. All that is distinctively human about a human being exists in a psychic medium likewise; and institutions prove their potency by dealing death and misery or life and happiness to myriads of human beings. Thus institutions, too, are realities, though not of the same kind as the human beings who create and maintain them. There is, however, no difference in either the kind or the degree of the reality of any one species of institution as contrasted with any other species. All institutions are on the same plane of reality in consequence of their all being psychic relations between human beings. This is the common nature of all of them: totems, tabus, marriage, war, rites, cultures, languages, nationalities, communities, states, societies, civilizations, higher religions, and so on.

Even an institution that has only a small number of participants and a relatively simple structure is the product of innumerable encounters between the human beings concerned; and the consequent problem of quantity in the study of human affairs has baffled human intellects so far. This is a point of capital importance; but it need not be discussed further here, since it has been examined in Chapter IV.[3]

13. SOCIETY

Society is the total network of relations between human beings.[4] The components of society are thus not human beings but relations between them. In a social structure 'individuals are merely the foci in the network of relationships'.[5] The famous frontispiece of Hobbes' *Leviathan*, displaying society as a gigantic human figure composed of a multitude of life-sized human figures, is an anthropomorphic misrepresentation of reality;[6] and so is the practice[7] of speaking of human beings as 'members'[8]

justice to society's historical importance. This, again, seems to me to be a non-sequitur. A thing—inanimate nature, for example—can have an influence on, and importance for, human beings without having the 'active structure' that a human being has. Nature does not cease to be important for human beings if and when they grow out of taking an animistic or an anthropomorphic view of her. For the word 'nature' substitute the word 'society', and Trinkaus's argument evaporates, so it seems to me.

[1] See pp. 115–16 and 128. Bagby, in *Culture and History*, pp. 127–8, rightly combats the view 'that only individual actions are real and that the common or regular aspect of these actions is somehow tenuous, elusive, a construction of the human mind, and therefore unreal'. He points out that individual human beings and their actions, as well as 'regularities' in the behaviour of groups, are abstractions, though they are abstractions on different levels.

[2] F. A. Hayek points out that institutions, 'though in a sense man-made, i.e. entirely the result of human actions, . . . may yet not be designed, not be the intended product of these actions' (*The Counter-Revolution of Science*, p. 83).   [3] On pp. 103–35.

[4] See p. 81.   [5] F. A. Hayek: *The Counter-Revolution of Science*, p. 34.

[6] P. Bagby has made the same mistake. In *Culture and History*, p.84, he defines society as being 'a number of people' and endorses the statement 'a society is composed of people', which he quotes from M. J. Herkovits: *Man and His Works* (New York 1948, Knopf), p. 29.

[7] Presumably derived from the simile in the New Testament in which the adherents of the Christian Church are spoken of as members of the body of Christ (e.g. 1 Cor. vi. 15; Eph. v. 30).

[8] i.e. limbs, according to the literal meaning of the Latin word *membra*.

of society or of one or other of its component institutions (e.g. a club, a church, a class, a family, a 'corporation'). A visible and palpable collection of people is not a society; it is a crowd. A crowd, unlike a society, can be assembled, dispersed, photographed, or massacred. Of course, the human beings composing a crowd may also be in social relations with each other. They may all be voters in the same electorate, or soldiers in the same army. But the army or the electorate, unlike a crowd of the human participants in the institution, is itself impalpable and invisible. An army cannot be massacred; the corpses on a battlefield are those of men of flesh and blood who have been brought to the shambles by the incorporeal social bond of military service.

14. CULTURE

I have already[1] adopted P. Bagby's definition of culture as being 'regularities in the behaviour, internal and external, of the members of a society, excluding those regularities which are clearly hereditary in origin'. Bagby adds[2] that, in virtue of being 'the patterned or repetitive element in history', 'culture is history's intelligible aspect'. A. L. Kroeber proposes[3] a definition in four points, of which the first three agree with Bagby's definition. According to Kroeber, culture is transmitted by the inter-conditioning of zygotes;[4] it is suprapersonal and anonymous; and it falls into patterns or regularities of form, style, and significance. Kroeber's fourth point is that culture embodies values; and this is a thesis that Bagby rejects. 'Culture', Bagby maintains,[5] 'includes modes of thinking and feeling and modes of behaviour, but not any of the invisible entities, whatever they may be, which determine these modes.' The entities to which he is here referring are 'beliefs, values, and so forth'.[6] If one of the included modes of feeling is value-judgements, as Bagby's words seem to imply, the exclusion of the values that are asserted in such judgements seems to introduce an unnecessary complication. Moreover, Bagby finds, at a later point in his inquiry,[7] that 'it is ideas and values . . . which provide the basis for differentiation between cultures'.[8] Bagby's argument here is, for me, too fine-drawn to carry conviction. It does not seem to me to refute Kroeber's downright statement that culture embodies values. So I prefer, *pace* Bagby, to add this to Bagby's definition in working out my own.[9]

---

[1] On pp. 76–77. The reference is to *Culture and History*, pp. 84 and 95.
[2] In op. cit., p. 124.   [3] In *The Nature of Culture*, p. 104.
[4] I take this to mean: by the influence on each other of human beings who are in social relations with each other, in contrast to biological transmission through the physical process of reproduction.   [5] In *Culture and History*, p. 80.
[6] Ibid., p. 78.   [7] Ibid., p. 109.
[8] Cultures in the plural mean the different historical exemplifications of the general idea of culture. See p. 282, footnote 2.
[9] In previous volumes (e.g. iii. 151–2, v. 199–201, viii. 495–521) I have used the word 'culture' in two different senses: (i) the comprehensive sense in which it is used by Kroeber and Bagby, in the passages cited here, and, in general, by cultural anthropologists; (ii) in an exclusive sense, in which the word has been current in contemporary English since the time of Matthew Arnold. In this narrower usage, 'culture' means spiritual, in contrast to material, activities and interests, or, in more precise terms, religion, philosophy, science, literature, and the visual arts in contrast to politics and economics (A. L. Kroeber observes, in *The Nature of Culture*, p. 155, that 'the cultural

Kroeber insists[1] that culture is a reality that cannot be explained in terms of anything but itself, and that what is cultural must be distinguished from what is social.[2] He points out[3] that the social insects (ants, termites, and the rest) possess society but not culture; and this is, of course, true if one accepts Bagby's definition of culture, which excludes from it regularities that are hereditary, and also accepts the first point in Kroeber's definition, according to which the means by which culture is transmitted is education in the broad sense of the word. On the other hand, 'culture can exist only when a society exists; and, conversely, every *human* society is accompanied by a culture'.[4] Thus, while it is true that the ideas of culture and society refer to realities of two different orders that ought not to be confused with each other, it is also true that, when we come to study the 'cultures' and 'societies' that have been the historical exemplifications of these two general ideas, it proves impossible, in practice, to study either apart from the other. 'The subject matter of anthropology is both society and culture', and the two things are, in fact, inseparable.[5]

15. CIVILIZATION

This is a hybrid modern Western word, compounded of a Latin adjectival stem, a French verbal affix, and a Latin abstract substantival suffix indicating, not a static condition, but a process that is still going on. Interpreted literally, the word ought to mean an attempt to attain the kind of culture that had been attained by citizens of a Graeco-Roman (in my terminology, Hellenic) city-state. The word 'civilization', in its literal meaning, would, in fact, accurately describe the process of Hellenization that played so important a part in the history of the Hellenic Society and of that society's relations with its non-Hellenic neighbours. This was the process to which the rural population of, for example, Pontic Cappadocia was subjected—or a privilege to which it was admitted—by Pompey when, after his annexation of this kingdom to the dominions of Rome, he attached the rural districts to one or other of the rare local Hellenic cities.

Actually, the word was never introduced into the Latin language. It is a modern French coinage, and Dr. Johnson refused to include the English counterpart of it in his dictionary of the English language.[6] Since then, this pseudo-Latin word, or some equivalent for it, has become current in all modern languages in the meaning of a particular kind or phase of culture that has been in existence during a particular

portion of culture' has religion, philosophy, and art as its core). This use of the word culture to include everything in human life that is both non-political and non-economic is inexact, and the exclusion of politics and economics is confusing, because these are not excluded in the anthropologists' usage of the word 'culture'. I therefore propose to stop using the word in my previous way, and to refer to religion, philosophy, science, literature, and the visual arts each under its own proper name, without bundling them together.   [1] In op. cit., p. 113. Cp. Bagby, op. cit., pp. 90–91.

[2] Kroeber, op. cit., p. 118. Cp. Bagby, op. cit., pp. 92–94 and 115.

[3] Kroeber, op. cit., pp. 22 and 52.   [4] Kroeber, op. cit., p. 118. Cp. p. 162.

[5] G. R. Willey and P. Phillips: *Method and Theory in American Archaeology* (1958), pp. 2–3.   [6] M. R. Cohen: *The Meaning of Human History*, p. 230.

age. In the present stage of knowledge the Age of Civilization appears to have begun approximately five thousand years ago. But these words were written in January 1959; and, at this time, the progress of archaeology was so rapid that the figure might have to be raised—and this, perhaps, drastically—before the end of the calendar year. Another season's excavations in the tell at Jericho, for example, might set back the date of the beginnings of the Age of Civilization by several millennia.

When one has described civilization as being a kind or a phase of culture, and when one has discussed the date at which it made its first appearance, one has perhaps implied that one has already arrived at a definition of what civilization is. I myself have been criticized for having operated with the idea without having defined my usage of the word explicitly.[1] I did raise, in volume i[2] of this book, the question whether one could identify the features in which the difference between civilization and the pre-civilizational stage or stages of culture resides,[3] and I concluded that the difference did not consist in the presence or absence of institutions or of the division of labour or of the practice of social imitation (mimesis). These features, I found, were common to the culture of human society in all phases. I put my finger on the point that, in the present-day life of surviving pre-civilizational societies, mimesis is directed towards the ancestors, whereas, in the present-day life of societies now in process of civilization, it is directed towards creative personalities who are leaders on the road towards a goal in the future.[4] I admitted that this observable present-day difference did not provide the definition for which I was in search.[5] Though stationary now, the surviving pre-civilizational societies must have been on the move once,[6]

---

[1] See, for instance, R. T. Clark in *The Nineteenth Century and After*, vol. cxxx, No. 777 (1941), p. 297; and the references to a number of criticisms on this account in Anderle's unpublished paper. See also the present volume, pp. 223–4.

[2] On pp. 188–204.

[3] R. Coulborn (in *Toynbee and History*, p. 149, footnote 1) notes that K. W. Thompson (in *Ethics*, No. lxv (1955), p. 299) 'complains that Toynbee never defines his concept of civilization "by more than a few illustrations"'. Coulborn comments: 'I feel that Toynbee's looseness is right in principle. There are many conflicting uses of the term, and, rather than a formal definition, I find it practical to offer a historical one, namely that civilized societies are those societies, of magnitude far greater than earlier primitive societies and surviving primitive societies, which arose, by reason of special climatic conditions, at the end of the Quaternary Ice Age . . . and all those societies which have been derived from them. This kind of definition suits Toynbee's use and could be said to be implied by it.'

[4] This point has since been made, with much greater knowledge and authority, by R. Redfield in *The Primitive World and its Transformations*. 'The preacher of conversion and the preacher of moral regeneration are creatures of civilization' (p. 55). 'In the folk societies men do not seek to make over their own natures' (p. 112). Man makes himself (to use Childe's phrase) in two senses: (i) in primitive life unintentionally and unconsciously, (ii) in civilization intentionally and consciously (p. 113). 'Civilization is the cultivation of our ultimate purposes' (p. 119). Primitive people see life as being static; they expect the immediate future to be like the immediate past (p. 120). Primitive education is conservative (pp. 120–1). By contrast, Redfield endorses Margaret Mead's observation (in *The American Journal of Sociology*, vol. xviii (1943), p. 9) that 'modern education includes a heavy emphasis upon the function of education to create discontinuities', and that, in this phase of culture, 'education becomes a mechanism of change'. In short, civilization, as Redfield sees it, 'is breakdown of old ways' (p. 136). A present-day inquirer can catch this process at work in his own world in his own generation if he visits any village in India in which the community development project is in operation.

[5] Here I anticipated one of G. Lefèbvre's criticisms in *La Revue Historique*, January–March, 1949, pp. 109–13.

[6] Here I anticipated another of Lefèbvre's criticisms in loc. cit.

while, on the other hand, there was no warrant for assuming that the surviving civilizations would always continue to be on the move. Indeed, some of them had already lapsed into stationariness, like the survivors of the societies of the pre-civilizational kind. At this point I broke off my search for a definition of the idea of civilization in the singular, and set myself, instead, to study the rhythm of the histories of civilizations in the plural. This inquiry has occupied most of the rest of the first ten volumes of this book. I believe that this was the more promising procedure. To propound a definition before one has surveyed the phenomena to which it applies is to expose oneself to the risk of seeing one's preliminary labour lost. It is now time for me to try to respond to my critics' challenge. But first I will report some definitions of civilization that have been offered by other inquirers.

A. H. Hanson, for example, brings up[1] a number of changes that, in his view, have been decisive factors in the metamorphosis of a pre-civilizational culture into a civilization. He mentions the discovery of new techniques, the introduction of the division of labour,[2] the emergence of economic inequality, the division of society into classes, the opposition between these new phenomena and the structure of the primitive tribe, and the emergence of the state as a means of transcending this opposition. R. J. Braidwood proposes[3] a combination of eight criteria: fully efficient food production, urbanization, a formally organized political state or states, formal laws (implying a new sense of moral order), formal public projects and works, social classes and hierarchies, literacy, and monumentality in art. Bagby reviews several proposed criteria for classifying a culture as being a civilization, and rejects magnitude of population, complexity, in the sense of far-going division of labour, and literacy. He rightly argues that the first two criteria out of these three demand the drawing of lines that would be arbitrary. In discussing the proposed criterion of literacy, he points out that at least one culture that is usually recognized as being a civilization, namely the Andean, was non-literate, whereas there are some living societies that possess scripts but are in other respects pre-civilizational. Moreover, the Incas did have, in the quipu, a method of keeping records in a non-literary form.[4]

It may be added that at least one literate society, the Western, made an extensive use of a similar non-literary method of keeping records in the shape of the tallies used in the Exchequer in the medieval chapter of the administrative history of the Kingdom of England; and also that many pre-civilizational societies, and some of those in process of civilization, have done without any system of physical mnemonics—written, painted, or inscribed characters, knotted cords, notched sticks, or what not—and have relied on the human memory. When the use of the

---

[1] In *Science and Society*, No. 13 (1949), pp. 118–35.
[2] Hanson asserts that I have not even mentioned, let alone described, any of the things that he mentions in this passage. Actually, I have spent two pages (i. 189–91) on discussing whether the division of labour provides a criterion for distinguishing between civilizations and pre-civilizational societies, and have come to the conclusion (for the reason here recalled) that it does not.
[3] In *The Near East and the Foundations of Civilization*, p. 2.
[4] P. Bagby, op. cit., p. 184.

memory is not made superfluous by visual mnemonic devices, it is capable of feats that seem extraordinary to people who have become accustomed to rely on visual forms of records. The extensive scriptures of Hinduism have been preserved and transmitted for centuries by memorization, as well as the long genealogies of Arab and Polynesian clans; and in the Islamic World a *ḥāfiẓ*—meaning a man who knows the Qur'ān by heart[1]—is still a familiar figure. In once non-literate societies that have eventually acquired a script, there has often been a significant reluctance to use this for recording anything but prosaic business documents. Law and poetry, secular as well as religious, have sometimes been handed down orally long after the means of committing this lore to writing have been at the disposal of the lore's traditional guardians.

Bagby proposes[2] that we should take our cue from the etymology of the word 'civilization' and should define civilization as 'the kind of culture found in cities'. And he proposes to define 'cities' as being 'agglomerations of dwellings many (or, to be more precise, a majority) of whose inhabitants are not engaged in producing food'. Lewis Mumford, whose most brilliant work has been his study of the relation between the development of civilization and the development of urban life, has accused me,[3] perhaps justly, of ignoring the role that cities have played in history. In attaching importance to their role, Bagby is, I feel sure, on the right scent. One effect of the change from rural to urban life will have been to break 'the cake of custom'.[4] Even a city such as Jericho at its earliest hitherto disinterred level—a city that, by present-day standards, was tiny—will have had a revolutionary effect on the lives and outlook of the people who left their previous homes and occupations in the countryside in order to settle there. The migration involved may have been one of no more than a few hours' or a few minutes' walk. Yet it will have detached the people who ventured to make it from an age-old social and cultural setting; it will have thrown them together with migrants from other villages and tribes; and it will have required them to master new, non-agricultural, ways of earning their living. This process of deracination will have facilitated the psychological and social revolution which, if a suggestion of mine is right, marks the transition, *de facto*, to civilization from the pre-civilizational phase of culture. It will have provided the conditions under which the majority of the participants in the changing society reoriented their mimesis away from the ancestors towards living leaders pointing towards new goals in the future.

Bagby points out[5] that, while agricultural communities are a necessary part of every civilization, 'their character is substantially altered by the fact that they have become culturally dependent on cities'.[6] Today

---

[1] The Qur'ān is longer than the Bible.   [2] Ibid., pp. 162–3.
[3] In *Diogenes*, No. 13 (Spring, 1956), p. 16.
[4] See i. 192, footnote 1.   [5] Op. cit., p. 163.
[6] The same point has been made in more circumstantial terms by R. Redfield in *The Primitive World and its Transformations*. 'There were no peasants before the first cities. And those surviving primitive peoples who do not live in terms of the city are not peasants' (p. 31). The peasantry is linked to the cities by money transactions (pp. 31–33). 'The peasant knows himself as part of a moral world in which the city man is also included' (p. 38).

we are fast approaching a state of affairs in which the food-producers will have shrunk in numbers to being only a minority—and this a small one—of the World's population, and in which they too will be urban in spirit. But even the earliest and the smallest cities must have exerted a potent transforming influence on an agricultural population that, in their day, was still in an overwhelming numerical majority. H. Frankfort notes[1] that, in the Sumeric and Hellenic worlds, and in the Western World, too, until a recent date, the present-day Western contrast between town and country was non-existent, and that the townsmen worked in the fields—at least at harvest-time—as well as at their urban crafts.[2] But this does not invalidate Bagby's point; and Frankfort himself points out[3] that, in the cities of Sumer and Akkad, as in those of the Hellenic World and the medieval West (above all, in medieval Italy), 'the physical existence of the city is but an outward sign of close communal affinities which dominate the life of every dweller within the walls. The city sets its citizens apart from the other inhabitants of the land. It determines their relations with the outside world. It produces an intensified self-consciousness in its burghers.'

Bagby's definition thus comes near to hitting the mark. Yet it will not quite serve. Nor will V. G. Childe's coinage of the phrase 'the Urban Revolution' (on the analogy of 'the Industrial Revolution') as a synonym for the emergence of the species of culture known as 'civilization'.[4] There have been city-less societies that have nevertheless been in process of civilization. In the Mayan province of the Middle American World, for instance, the imposing conglomerations of temples and other public buildings are held by at least one—and this perhaps the predominant—school of present-day archaeologists to have been ceremonial centres only, with no permanent inhabitants except a small number of priests and rulers and their immediate attendants. It is still more to the point that 'in Egypt the great change did not lead to a concentration of social activity in urban centres. It is true that there were cities in Egypt; but, with the single exception of the capital, these were no more than market towns for the countryside.'[5] Nomadic culture, again, would be a case of civilization without cities, if I am right in reckoning this among the civilizations—though it is true, I believe, that, on the economic plane, there has always been a symbiosis between the Nomadic societies and one or other of the sedentary societies that have possessed both cities and agriculture. Both these instances of city-less civilizations are perhaps controversial. Nevertheless, they suggest that the definition of civilization as being 'the kind of culture found in cities' is not quite exact. Bagby is, no doubt, right, as far as he goes, in

---

[1] In *The Rise of Civilization in the Near East*, pp. 57–58.
[2] In Southern Italy and Sicily in 1959, there were still large agglomerations of dwellings most of whose inhabitants were engaged in producing food—in many cases from fields that, according to a motorized Westerner's standards of walking, were fantastically distant from the place where the people who cultivated them passed the night. These pseudo-cities were agricultural counterparts of the 'dormitory towns' that surrounded the contemporary Western hives of business and industry.
[3] In op. cit., p. 51.
[4] See H. Frankfort's criticism of Childe's phrase in op. cit., pp. 57–58 and p. 57, footnote 2.   [5] Frankfort, op. cit., p. 83.

his observation[1] that it is 'freedom from the need of directly producing their own food which presumably enables the inhabitants of cities to devote all their time to specialization, and so to complicate their culture'. But we have, I believe, to go farther, and to equate civilization with a state of society in which there is a minority of the population, however small, that is free from the task, not merely of producing food, but of engaging in any other of the economic activities—e.g. industry and trade—that have to be carried on to keep the life of the society going on the material plane at the civilizational level.

'So important . . . is surplus and its effects on society that a striking convergence may be found between the peaks of civilization and peaks of economic well-being. . . . Without surplus, members of a society have no time for contemplation, experimentation, or the exchange of ideas—the very well-springs of change—and tend to remain in a static condition.'[2]

These non-economic specialists—professional soldiers, administrators, and perhaps, above all, priests—have certainly been city-dwellers in the cases of most of the civilizations known to us.[3] But the Maya priesthood, with its advanced astronomical knowledge and its complicated calendrical technique, may have been an instance of a body of non-economic specialists in a non-urban social milieu. On this view, civilization would have originated in the emergence, not of cities, but of economic inequality and the division of society into classes—two of the factors in Hanson's list.

If this is the correct diagnosis, it is a tragic one; for it means that civilization will have originated in social injustice, and that, as far as we know, it could not have come into existence in any other way. Social injustice has been one of the two specific diseases of civilization since the earliest date to which our surviving records of it go back. Its other specific disease has been war. In our own day, civilization has reached a crisis as a result of the unprecedented advance of technology in the Western World in recent times. Used for constructive purposes, technology has now, for the first time since civilization began, opened up a prospect of our being able soon to provide the whole of mankind with the amenities of civilization, which, hitherto, have been the monopoly of a small minority. Used for destructive purposes, it has now also opened up the unprecedented prospect of our being able soon to wipe mankind, and perhaps all other extant forms of life, off the face of the Earth. This pair of alternative prospects suggests that civilization has now arrived at a fateful parting of the ways. If we are not now to let civilization become an instrument in our hands for its own destruction —and perhaps for our destruction too—we shall have to abolish the institution of war and to achieve a radical reform of social injustice. And either of these tasks, by itself, would be a gigantic one.

[1] Op. cit., p. 162.
[2] Social Science Research Council's Committee on Historiography's Report (1954), p. 115.
[3] Redfield, in *The Primitive World and its Transformations*, equates civilization with the rise of cities (p. ix) on the ground that it was in the cities that 'the administrative élite', 'the literate priest', and 'the specialized artisan' made their first appearance (p. 30).

Mankind's present situation raises the question what the goal of civilization is, and the further question whether or not civilization can be reformed and salvaged by drawing solely on the resources of this particular species of culture. On the first of these questions, I agree with H. Frankfort[1] in rejecting the view that 'such changes as an increase in food-production or technological advances (both, truly enough, coincidental with the rise of civilization) . . . explain how civilization became possible'. A. N. Whitehead surely hits the truth in a passage,[2] quoted by Frankfort in this context, in which he declares that

'in each age of the World distinguished by high activity, there will be found at its culmination, and among the agencies leading to that culmination, some profound cosmological outlook, implicitly accepted, impressing its own type on the current springs of action.'

Christopher Dawson is making the same point when he says that 'behind every civilization there is a vision'.[3] On this view, to which I adhere, the presence in a society of a minority liberated from economic activities is an identification-mark of civilization rather than a definition of it. Following Whitehead's lead, I should define civilization in spiritual terms. Perhaps it might be defined as an endeavour to create a state of society in which the whole of mankind will be able to live together in harmony, as members of a single all-inclusive family. This is, I believe, the goal at which all civilizations so far known have been aiming unconsciously, if not consciously.

The second question—whether civilization can save itself solely out of its own resources—is a controversial one; and, on this issue, my considered answer is in the negative. I believe that civilization can be saved only by drawing on the resources of the higher religions as well as on those of civilization itself. I believe that human beings *can* save civilization by thus rising above it, but I do not believe that, if they do turn again for help to the higher religions, this is bound to secure a future for civilization or for religion or for the human race. I believe that, now and always, the future is open for human beings, and that it lies at least partly in our own hands to make of it what we choose.

Hourani is right in finding[4] that, in the first six volumes of this book, there are two different answers to the question: What is the goal of human endeavours? 'On the one hand, "civilization" is seen as ultimate.' On the other hand, 'all growth in civilization is equated with progress towards sainthood'. The second of these two answers of mine is, in effect, the declaration of a belief that the goal of human endeavours, which is being aimed at in the particular endeavour that we call 'civilization', is something beyond and above civilization itself. This second answer is my considered answer, and further consideration has not led me to change it.

[1] In *The Rise of Civilization in the Near East*, pp. 7–8.
[2] A. N. Whitehead: *Adventures in Ideas* (Cambridge 1933, University Press), pp. 13 and 14.
[3] *The Dynamics of World History*, p. 41.
[4] In *The Dublin Review*, vol. 229, No. 470 (December, 1955), pp. 384–5.

16. SOCIETIES

I use the words 'societies' in the plural and 'a society' in the singular to mean particular historical exemplifications of the abstract idea 'society' which has been examined above. The relation of 'societies' or 'a society' to 'society' is the relation of one or more representatives of a class of phenomena to the class that it represents.

Since I use the word society to mean the total network of relations between human beings, I use the words 'societies' and 'a society' to denote particular networks that can be analysed as being combinations of a number of institutions that are their components, but which cannot be identified as being, themselves, components of any more comprehensive network. If one defines societies in these terms, one finds that there are several kinds of them. In other words, one finds that the genus 'society' consists of several species. There are, for instance, pre-civilizational societies, societies in process of civilization, and societies that are embodiments of higher religions. The pre-civilizational societies, again, fall into a number of different sub-classes: Lower Palaeolithic, Upper Palaeolithic, Mesolithic, Neolithic, Chalcolithic. The last three of these sub-classes, or at any rate the last two, have more in common with civilizations than they have with their Palaeolithic predecessors.

Societies of all these different species of the genus have in common the generic characteristic that they are not identifiable as being components of any network of relations between human beings that is more comprehensive than these societies themselves. It is true that some of the higher religions are professed by participants in two or more civilizations of the third generation. But this does not mean that these civilizations are parts of those churches. We have seen[1] that the appearance of the higher religions on the scene has brought with it a fission of the previous unity of culture in the form of a separation between 'church' and 'state'. In consequence, since that time there have been in existence, side by side, societies of two species—higher religions and civilizations—consisting of networks of relations that are specifically different in nature and pattern; and the networks of either kind are not components of other networks, either of the second kind or of any different kind.

Though, according to my definition, societies are systems of relations that are not components of other societies, they are not, in my view, Leibnizian monads. All societies exert a constant reciprocal influence on each other. The extant representatives of the species are being influenced, in different degrees, not only by all their surviving contemporaries but also by the legacies of all societies that have come and gone up to date.

Every social network is the carrier of a culture, and it is impossible in practice to study a society and its culture apart from each other.

17. COMMUNITIES

I use the words 'communities' in the plural and 'a community' in the singular to mean a network of relations which—in contrast to the networks that I call 'societies'—*are* components of some more comprehen-

[1] On pp. 76–85.

sive network in the shape of a society. A community is like a society in being a combination of a number of component institutions, but a community's set of institutions will not be identical with its society's set. If it were, it would not be possible to distinguish the community as being a recognizable sub-network within the society. Participants in a community may have a distinctive religion, language, state, or other institution that is not shared with them by other participants in the same society. For example, the English people are a community within the Western Society; but other Westerners are not natives of the Kingdom of England, do not have the English Episcopalian Church as the established church in their respective states, and do not speak the cis-Tweed cis-marine dialects of English. Conversely, a society may have distinctive institutions that are not contained in the network of any of its component communities. In the Hellenic World, for example, the Olympian pantheon, the Homeric epic, the Delphic oracle, and the four Panhellenic festivals were institutions that meant much to every Hellene, but he partook in them in virtue of being a participant in the Hellenic Society. They were not the institutions of any particular Hellenic city-state, and a Hellene could not partake in them if he chose —or was constrained—to confine his activities within the bounds of his own community. At a certain stage of Hellenic history Lacedaemonian men (not women) were debarred, by a standing order of the Lacedaemonian Government, from competing at the Panhellenic festivals. In imposing this prohibition on its citizens, this government was deliberately seeking to cut off their relations with non-Lacedaemonian Hellenes and, whether consciously or not, was turning Lacedaemon into a separate society, outside the Hellenic pale.

Communities and societies are not distinguished from each other by being networks of relations of different kinds. For instance, it would not be true to say that the relations constituting a community are political, and those constituting a society non-political. This point can be illustrated from the history of the Hellenic World. Before the establishment of an Hellenic world-state by the Romans, the communities within the Hellenic Society were sovereign city-states, confederacies, and kingdoms (i.e. political entities of various types), while the institutions in which the Hellenic Society itself was embodied were non-political (some of them religious, some literary, some athletic). On the other hand, after the establishment of the world-state, the situation was reversed. The Hellenic Society, as such, now had a political embodiment in the shape of the Roman Empire, while the distinctive institutions of the Hellenic Society's component local communities were now non-political (e.g. cults, shrines, dialects). Moreover, at this stage of Hellenic history, the most characteristic and significant communities in the Hellenic World were so far from being even the ghosts of once sovereign independent states that they had no piece of territory of their own in which the participants in them were in a local majority. They were religious denominations—the Jewish, Christian, Mithraic, Isiac, and others—whose adherents were scattered over the Hellenic World and were everywhere locally in a minority.

Some word is needed to denote what I mean by 'communities'. But I confess that my definition of both 'communities' and 'societies' is arbitrary. Every definition of them is and must be. The popular usage of both words is vague, yet at the same time it is almost impossible to avoid conscripting and regimenting both words for use as more precise instruments if one is trying to make a systematic study of human affairs. In most usages, popular or technical, the word 'societies' seems to stand for larger and looser networks, and 'communities' to stand for smaller and tighter networks. K. W. Deutsch, for instance, who is thinking in terms of the technology of man-made communications-networks and of the associated science of cybernetics, defines a society, for his purpose, as 'a group of persons who "have learnt to work together"', and a community as 'a group of persons united by their ability to exchange information'.[1]

18. CIVILIZATIONS

I use the word 'civilizations' in the plural and 'a civilization' in the singular to mean particular historical exemplifications of the abstract idea 'civilization' which has been examined above. The relation of 'civilizations' or 'a civilization' to 'civilization' is the relation of one or more representatives of a class of phenomena to the class that it represents. The class represented by civilizations is one species of the genus 'culture'.[2] Every civilization is carried on the network of a society, and it is impossible in practice to study a civilization and its society apart from each other.

Before examining criticisms of my definitions of what I mean by a civilization, we must consider the thesis, put forward by several of my critics, that there is not, and never has been, more than one single representative of this class of culture and society. An uncompromising declaration of the unity of civilization, not merely as an abstract concept but also as a concrete phenomenon, has been made by a Communist critic, B. Bykhovsky.[3]

'Professor Toynbee's philosophy of history . . . discountenances the idea of an integral world history. As against the unity and historical continuity of civilization, Toynbee sets up a scheme of numerous segregated civilizations, each of which bears throughout the whole cycle of its development the impress of specific and immutable characteristics. From this viewpoint the integral and natural process of development of universal history breaks down into separate and discrete parts, and historical science becomes the comparative history of different and distinct civilizations.'

---

[1] *Philosophy of Science*, vol. 18, No. 3 (July, 1951), p. 243. It will be noticed that Deutsch, like Hobbes and Bagby, thinks of societies and communities as being composed of persons, not of relations between persons. On this rather crucial point, they all go wrong, I believe.

[2] G. R. Willey and P. Phillips use the word 'cultures' to describe the maximum units, according to their system of classification, up to the New-World Formative stage inclusive, and reserve the word 'civilizations' for the maximum units in their Classic and Postclassic stages (*Method and Theory in American Archaeology* (1958), p. 48).

[3] In *New Times*, 12th November, 1947, p. 27.

The same point has been made, with greater discrimination, by a liberal critic, F. S. Marvin.[1]

'There is a unity in civilization as well as different types of civilization; and, from the point of view of both philosophy and religion, it is still more important to seek the unifying than the distinctive features.'

In this context, Marvin notes that

'much in this whole discussion is purely verbal. We may speak of as many distinctive civilizations as we please, so long as we make clear what our dividing canons are and so long as they can be consistently maintained.'

The notions of 'distinctiveness' and 'unity' are, indeed, relative in their application to human affairs. Every human being now alive has links, however tenuous, not only with every one of his contemporaries but also with every other human being that has ever lived. In this sense human history is one single seamless web, and any dissection of it is an arbitrary misrepresentation of Reality. The unity and continuity of civilization as a concrete historical phenomenon are most apparent on the technological and scientific planes.[2] Yet, even on these planes, there has never, as far as our knowledge reaches back, been a simultaneous advance of the whole human race all over the World. Both the two great technological and economic revolutions up to date have been made by a small minority of the human race in a particular limited area. The Neolithic Revolution was made on the outer rim of 'the Fertile Crescent' in South-West Asia; the Industrial Revolution was made in Great Britain. The achievements of these two revolutions have been spreading from their places of origin to other parts of the World; but even the Neolithic Revolution has not yet reached the whole human race. There are still some food-gathering communities extant today, some ten or twelve thousand years later than the date of the earliest of the Neolithic strata so far unearthed at Jericho.

Moreover, even if we hold, as Marvin holds,[3] that, in human affairs, the identities are more fundamental than the differences, it is, as he judiciously concedes, 'always instructive to discover, and to attempt to explain, differences'. The question is really a practical one. Does the study of the phenomenon of civilization in its unitary aspect throw more light on this phenomenon than the study of it in its multiple aspect? In practice we are compelled, as we have already found,[4] by the multiplicity of the manifestations of a theoretically unitary phenomenon to break it up mentally into a number of simultaneous and parallel streams of events, and to reunify these by resorting to the comparative method of study that Bykhovsky deprecates. For heuristic purposes, at any rate, we have to think in terms of 'civilizations' in the plural; but, if we do use 'civilizations' as an indispensable piece of intellectual apparatus, this imposes on us, as Marvin points out, an obligation to give a tenable definition or definitions of what we mean by 'a civilization'.

---

[1] In *The Hibbert Journal*, July, 1935, p. 623.
[2] This point is made by K. D. Erdmann in *Archiv für Kulturgeschichte*, xxxiii. Band, Heft 2 (1951), p. 240.   [3] See loc. cit.   [4] See pp. 163–8.

Some critics have asserted, mistakenly, that I have not tried to define what I mean by a civilization.[1] Granville Hicks raises the question whether a civilization can be defined with enough precision to make the concept useful.[2] Other critics[3] have noted that, in previous volumes of this book, I have given several definitions of what I mean by a civilization. I have defined it as being 'an intelligible field of study'; as being the common ground between the respective individual fields of action of a number of different people; and as being a representative of a particular species of society. So far as I can see, these definitions are compatible with each other, and something essential would be missing if any of them were left out.

The first of these definitions is, of course, put in subjective terms. Its approach to the definition of a civilization is epistemological. The other two definitions are objective. They are attempts to describe the reality that the inquirer's mind believes (and believes correctly, in my view) that it has apprehended in the phenomena. Ideally, any definition that we make of anything whatsoever ought to be made in this dual form, considering that the duality of subject and object, and the problem of what the true relation between them is, are inherent in all thinking. Anyway, it cannot be wrong to do this; and one would surely be remiss if one did not do it when one is trying to define something that is a key idea in one's particular field of study, as the idea of 'a civilization' is in my study of history.

M. Watnick finds[4] that my definition of a civilization as being 'an intelligible field of study' is 'completely lacking in operational utility', because I do not say when a field is intelligible and what makes it so. He calls this definition 'a jejune and unenlightening tautology'. A society, as he interprets my train of thought, becomes an intelligible field in virtue of being a society. O. Handlin, too, finds this definition 'circular and tautological'.[5] These criticisms might perhaps have hit the mark if I had propounded this definition of mine *in vacuo*. Actually, I arrived at it[6] by way of an inquiry in terms that were concrete and also, I think, practical.

I started—reasonably, I should say—by looking at 'what is the usual field of vision of contemporary Western historians'. I found this—correctly, I should say—to be 'some national state'. I then asked myself whether a national state was an intelligible field of study in isolation. As a test case I took Great Britain, on the ground that this national state, if any, ought to be an intelligible field in isolation in virtue of its insularity, and that, if Great Britain proved not to meet the test, it would seem unlikely that any other national state would meet it. Running through the principal chapters of Great Britain's, and her principal constituent, England's, history, I found that none of these episodes

[1] e.g. Chr. Hill in *The Modern Quarterly*, Autumn, 1947, p. 293; M. A. Fitzsimons in *The Review of Politics*, October, 1957, pp. 544–53.

[2] *The New Leader*, 18th October, 1954, p. 22.

[3] e.g. R. T. Clark in *The Nineteenth Century and After*, vol. cxxx, No. 777 (1941), p. 297; L. Mumford in *Diogenes*, No. 13 (Spring, 1956), p. 14; P. A. Sorokin in *Toynbee and History*, pp. 179–80.

[4] In *The Antioch Review*, No. 7 (Winter, 1947–8), pp. 587–602.

[5] *The Partisan Review*, July–August, 1947, pp. 371–9.   [6] In i. 17–50.

were intelligible if one tried to limit one's historical horizon to the shores of this island. At the same time, in expanding my field of vision outwards in space and backwards in time, I found myself, in both dimensions, eventually reaching limits beyond which, on the criterion of intelligibility, this expansion of the field began to bring in diminishing returns. This line gave me the boundary of the field of vision within which the intelligibility of the history of one national state, Great Britain, was at its maximum. I found that this spatio-temporal field included the histories of all the present-day Roman Catholic and Protestant Christian nations back to the origins of the Christian Church among the 'internal proletariat' of a society that, at the time when Christianity made its first appearance, was embodied politically in the Roman Empire. Looking next for the origins of this proletariat, I traced these back, provisionally, as far as the Hannibalic War. Looking for a name for this field of study within which the study of the history of Great Britain seemed to be at its maximum of intelligibility, I found that the most informing label for it would be 'Western Christendom' or simply 'the West' when one came to consider the latest chapter in its history. While including the Catholic and Protestant—or ex-Catholic and ex-Protestant—nations, it did not include the Eastern Orthodox Christians or the Muslims or any other societies to the east of these. Within this line, the network of relations was so closely knit that the histories of Great Britain, France, the United States, and the other Western Christian or ex-Christian national states were intelligible if studied synoptically but not intelligible if one tried to study each of them in isolation. Outside the same line, Eastern Orthodox Christian history and Islamic history had followed different courses. This pointed to the likelihood that there were at least two living societies of the same species as the Western Society, as well as at least one no longer extant society— namely the Graeco-Roman or Hellenic, among whose proletariat Christianity had made its first appearance.

On reconsideration, I still do not think that this intellectual operation of mine was an argument in a circle, or that it was not of any use for the purpose of increasing one's understanding of history. As an 'heuristic' reconnaissance, I think it was both legitimate and rewarding. It led to the identification of a unit of study—societies of this species that I call civilizations—which, in my belief, is a more practical tool for the study of human affairs during the last five thousand years than national states of the Western type seem to me to be. While I was growing up, a firm of British publishers, Fisher Unwin, was bringing out a series of volumes under the general title of 'the Story of the Nations'. Many of these volumes were excellent pieces of work. Several of them had, incidentally, a great and lasting influence on me, in helping me to enlarge my historical outlook. All the same, I think that 'the Story of the Civilizations' would have been a better series for Fisher Unwin's purpose of giving a comprehensive account of the latest phase of the history of mankind.

This is my case for holding that civilizations are 'intelligible fields of study'. But, as my way of arriving at this conclusion shows, the word 'intelligible' has, for me, a connotation of relativity. A civilization is an intelligible field by comparison with its component communities—nations, city-states, millets, castes, or whatever else these components may happen to be in different instances. In general, a larger unit of study is likely to be more intelligible than a smaller one, considering that nothing can be completely intelligible short of the sum total of Reality. This, however, cannot be intelligible either, because things are intelligible only to minds, and, *ex hypothesi*, there would be no mind, outside the sum total of Reality, to be the subject of this object. Accordingly, as I have noted in this volume from the first chapter onwards, the intelligibility of phenomena, on whatever scale, can never be more than partial and imperfect.

This, again, indicates, from another angle, that a civilization is 'an intelligible field of study' in a relative sense only. In my process of identifying the Western Civilization, I was already finding that this was no completely self-contained Leibnizian monad. In the course of the reconnaissance in which I hit on it, I also hit on two other contemporary units of the same species—the Eastern Orthodox Christian and the Islamic—and on one extinct unit, the Hellenic. It was true that the network of external relations linking the civilizations with each other had proved to be significantly more tenuous than the network of internal relations between the participants in any one of them. Yet the proletariat among whom Christianity had made its appearance had been recruited from participants in more civilizations than one, and this indicated that trans-civilizational relations must be important. Thus, from the outset, I was committed to something more than a comparative study of the histories of civilizations regarded as so many separate representatives of their species. I had also to study the encounters, in the two dimensions of time and space, between human beings who were participants in different civilizations. And I had to study the higher religions as a distinct species of society. For Christianity was an example of a higher religion that had broken out of the framework of one society, the Hellenic, and had broken down the barriers between this society and others, both contemporary with it and subsequent to it. These topics were set out in the plan of the book, printed at the beginnings of volumes i, iv, and vii, and they have all been dealt with—though, of course, not exhaustively and not adequately—in volumes i–x.[1]

---

[1] I therefore think that I do not deserve Lynn Thorndike's comment that it does not 'seem quite consistent for such a doughty defender of internationalism so to segregate civilizations in separate compartments and almost deny the possibility of any such thing as intercivilization' (*The Journal of Modern History*, vol. vii, No. 3 (September, 1935), pp. 315–17). Studies of 'intercivilization' occupy the whole of volume viii and a large part of vol. ix. It is true that Thorndike was reviewing vols. i–iii at a date when only these three had yet been published. Yet he might have looked at the plan on p. vi of vol. i before committing himself to his anticipatory judgement.

In his review of the same first batch of three volumes in *The Hibbert Journal*, July, 1935, pp. 622–5, F. S. Marvin has, I should say, better warrant when he criticizes me for denying the unity of civilization in treating it as a species represented by a number of different specimens. This is, of course, one of the things that I do, and, *pace* Marvin, I still believe that I am right in doing it. But I should agree that I should have been wrong if I had limited my study to this, and had treated the separateness of the different civilizations as if it were, not relative, but absolute.

K. D. Erdmann in *Archiv für Kulturgeschichte*, xxxiii. Band, Heft 2 (1951), pp. 174–

So much for my subjective definition of what a civilization is. As for my two objective definitions of this, they seem to me to be not only compatible but complementary. The common ground between a number of different people's individual fields of action is an alternative phrase for describing what, in this chapter, I have called a network of relations between a number of human beings.[1] I have already made the point that relations between people, as well as the people who have these relations with each other, are realities, though people and relations are not realities of the same order. And a reality means something that is apprehended by human minds as being a reality, and is therefore apprehended by them as being a representative of a class—the only mode in which human minds can apprehend anything. The class here in question is a species of the genus society, which I have defined[2] as being the total network of relations between human beings. A specimen of this species will be a particular network that is not a component of any other network. A network of relations, being a phenomenon in the time-dimension as well as in the space-dimension, will have phases. The civilizations whose histories are on record up to date are objective realities that have all had geneses; most of them have also grown, over various periods of time, to various extents; some of them have had breakdowns; and some of them have then gone through a process of disintegration ending in dissolution.

In crediting civilizations with histories in a pattern of phases, I am not personifying them or conceiving of them in anthropomorphic terms.[3] A non-human intelligible field of study—for instance, a crystal —can also be an objective reality that changes in a regular pattern of phases. But it is, of course, true that any concept of an entity, human or non-human, that appears to some particular mind to be a real, as well as an intelligible, field of study may be an hallucination or illusion of that particular mind. Our concepts are no more than working theories or hypotheses so long as we have not tested them adequately by applying them to the phenomena and ascertaining whether they do or do not fit.[4] Till we feel sure that they have satisfied this test, we have no warrant for assuming that there are objective realities corresponding to them.

250, and C. Trinkaus in *Science and Society*, vol. xii, No. 1 (1948), pp. 218–39, criticize me, in particular, for exaggerating the degree of the separateness of the Western Civilization from the Hellenic. I may perhaps have underestimated the closeness of the network of relations between them, but I have not ignored it. As early in this Study as i. 44 I coined the phrase apparentation-and-affiliation to describe the relation in which these two civilizations, and several other pairs, seemed to me to stand to each other. On reconsideration, I find myself still holding that the Western, Orthodox Christian, and Islamic civilizations are distinct representatives of the species and not just later phases of the older civilizations to which, in my view, they are 'affiliated'. On the other hand, I am convinced by Erdmann's and Trinkaus' thesis of continuity in the cases of the history of civilization in the Tigris-Euphrates basin, India, and China; and accordingly I have struck my supposed Babylonic, Hindu, and Far Eastern (main body) civilizations out of my list. My Mexic and Yucatec civilizations, too, have been abolished by the progress of archaeological discovery. For these changes in my list of civilizations, see further pp. 549–51.

[1] H. Werner, however, finds that I have no insight into what it is that holds a civilization together internally (*Deutsche Vierteljahrsschrift für Literaturwissenschaft und Geistesgeschichte*, 29. Jahrgang, xxix. Band (1935), p. 543).

[2] On p. 271.

[3] See p. 45, with footnote 3.

[4] See pp. 42–45.

Does my concept 'civilizations', as I have defined it, have realities corresponding to it or not?

This has been denied by P. A. Sorokin in a critique of the first six volumes of this book. Toynbee assumes, Sorokin writes,[1] that his 'civilizations' are 'a real system and not mere congeries or conglomerations of various cultural (or civilizational) phenomena and objects adjacent in space or time but devoid of any causal or meaningful ties'. This account of my view, which Sorokin supports by a quotation and by further references, is correct except in one important point. I believe, and have repeatedly declared my belief, that the ties between the different relational strands in the network of a civilization are 'meaningful', but I do not believe that they are causal, because I believe that human relations take the form of free responses to challenges, not the form of inevitable effects of causes. Subject to this vital reservation,[2] I acknowledge that the rest of Sorokin's account of my assumption is correct. Sorokin then asks whether this assumption is valid, and answers his question emphatically in the negative.

'His "civilizations" are not united systems but mere conglomerations of various civilizational objects and phenomena (congeries of systems and singular cultural traits) united only by spatial adjacency but not by causal or meaningful bonds. For this reason, they are not real "species of society";[3] therefore they can hardly be treated as unities and can hardly have any uniformities in their genesis, growth, and decline. These concepts cannot even be applied to the congeries, because congeries do not and cannot grow or decline. Like the components of a dumping place, they can only be re-arranged, added to, or subtracted from. . . . The total civilization of even the smallest possible civilizational area—that of a single individual—is but a coexistence of several and different systems and congeries unrelated with one another in any way except spatial adjacency in a biological organism.'[4] 'The Spenglerian-Toynbee ascription of some specific perennial tendency to this or that civilization, regardless of the period of its history, is misleading and inaccurate.'[5]

As far as I can make out from these passages, Sorokin does not, after all, differ from me in principle, since he seems to hold that there are some genuine congeries of 'systems', as well as congeries of single cultural traits. What he is disputing so vigorously is the reality of systems of relations of a particular species—the species that I call civilizations and in whose reality I believe. This dispute is not just a duel between Sorokin and me. Sorokin frankly acknowledges[6] that my

---

[1] In *Toynbee and History*, p. 180.

[2] Sorokin's mistaken impression that I think of the interconnexions between the different elements in a civilization as being causal has led him (ibid., pp. 180-1) to suppose that I myself have refuted my own belief that civilizations are systems by demonstrating that two of the components of a civilization, technique and economy, 'are causally unrelated to the rest of the "whole"'. Sorokin would indeed have caught me out here if I were a determinist who held that the system in a civilization was a system of causes and effects. My actual belief is that it is a system of challenges and responses and that it is therefore one in which there is some free play and some possibility of change.

[3] Sorokin means, I think, 'not specimens of a real species of society'. A particular civilization cannot, itself, be a species.

[4] Sorokin in loc. cit., pp. 180-1. Cp. p. 182.

[5] Ibid., p. 186.   [6] Ibid., p. 180.

position is that of the 'so-called "functional anthropologists"'. A belief that the concept of a culture corresponds to a significant and important reality seems, in fact, to be prevalent among present-day anthropologists. 'A civilization' is a representative of one species of culture; and most modern Western historians who deal with the history of Man in process of civilization seem to take the reality of at least some civilizations for granted:[1] for instance, their own Western Civilization and the Graeco-Roman (in my terminology, 'Hellenic') Civilization at any rate. Indeed, most Westerners today are up in arms for the defence of 'the values of Western Civilization' against threats from a traditional enemy, 'Oriental despotism', and a new enemy, 'Communism', to which the Western Civilization is exposed in their opinion. This militant expression of what is certainly a genuine anxiety surely implies a belief that the Western Civilization is a reality, and that there are alternative realities of the same order which are presumably real since they are felt to be menacing.

Of course, even if the validity of an hypothesis has been verified, up to the hilt, by the test of a thorough application of it to the phenomena, it is improbable that its validity will not be subject to any limitations. Kroeber notes,[2] with characteristic good sense, that 'a culture is always, so far as we can judge, highly composite in the origin of its constituent materials'. He compares cultures to ecological aggregates.[3] And he points out[4] that, while cultures tend towards integration, they never achieve total integration, and that 'there is almost nothing in culture to correspond to . . . organic repetitiveness'. Albright, too, suggests[5] that 'a culture represents an empirico-adaptive system' and that 'inner bonds are, in general, quite secondary'. But this recognition that the interdependence of the different elements in a culture is not absolute and unqualified is a decidedly different position from Sorokin's uncompromising denial of any interdependence between them whatsoever (a denial that is compromised, nevertheless, by his admission that some of the components of the 'congeries' are 'systems').

If Sorokin's thesis were right, it would prove that not only civilizations, but all institutions of all kinds, were figments of other people's imaginations that had nothing corresponding to them in reality. This would follow because the reality of institutions, if they are real, is of one and the same order.[6] They exist in the psychic medium of human thoughts and feelings and wills. I can see no rational basis for the apparently rather common assumption that institutions which have an

---

[1] In his unpublished paper, Anderle comments as follows on Sorokin's thesis that civilizations are not real unities. 'It is obviously a very arbitrary, controversial, and, above all, unproven, assertion; and to prove it in its negative form would be extremely difficult. Sorokin's dumping-place theory is also not likely to win the approval of historians—at any rate, those of them who study whole cultures and their total aspects and who therefore presumably cannot refuse to take account of the overwhelming impression of compactness (*Geschlossenheit*), inner cohesion (*Zusammenhanges*), and consequentiality (*Folgerichtigkeit*) which even the layman receives when he strolls through the galleries of the Egyptian, Chinese, and Graeco-Roman departments of a museum.'
[2] In *The Nature of Culture*, p. 93.
[3] Ibid.   [4] Op. cit., p. 131. Cp. p. 148.
[5] In *From the Stone Age to Christianity*, 2nd ed., p. 125. Cp. p. 104.
[6] This point has been made already on pp. 232–3.

administrative structure are realities but that those which do not have this feature are hallucinations. This assumption is made by, for instance, K. D. Erdmann.[1] The true units of history, he maintains, are not civilizations, but states, because states, he holds, are 'the units in which an operative will crystallizes itself in institutional form'. H. J. Morgenthau likewise maintains[2] that political and geographical units 'lend themselves more readily to empirical verification' than civilizations do, and therefore, as he sees it, 'it is not by accident that there has been a tendency for history to be written in terms of political and geographical units rather than of civilizations'. The same assumption seems to be made by Sir Ernest Barker when he labels civilizations 'Brocken-spectres', while describing state-systems and religious organizations as being 'definite and visible'.[3]

Is not Barker here falling into the mistake—which he attributes to me on the next page—of confusing metaphors with arguments? Was the Kingdom of Prussia or the Christian Church, for instance, really ever 'visible' or 'definite' in any sense in which these terms are not equally true of the Western Civilization or of Hellenism? Surely neither Prussia nor the Church has ever been visible at any time. Prussia has been consistently invisible. Obviously it is invisible at the present time, when there is no longer a Prussian state to be displayed in symbolic lines and colours on a map; obviously, too, it was invisible in the year A.D. 1, when no such state had yet been dreamed of; but it was also invisible during the reign of King Frederick the Great and during the chancellorship of Prince Bismarck. The Prussian state was more potent in Frederick's and Bismarck's generations than in others, but its potency was exercised in the invisible realm of psychic relations between the thoughts, feelings, and actions of human beings. The human beings labelled 'King' and 'Chancellor' were visible, certainly; but, notwithstanding Louis XIV's famous dictum, a ruler—even as absolute a one as any human being can be—can never be an incarnation of a state; his title does no more than make him a symbol, and his personality, however commanding, can make him no more than the most prominent, and perhaps the most effective, among a vast number of persons whose relations with each other weave the pattern called, say, the Kingdom of Prussia. We can see the King, the Chancellor, the civil servants at their desks in government offices, the soldiers in uniform on parade-grounds or on battlefields; we can see the flags displaying, in conventional colours, the heraldic device that is the Kingdom's emblem; we can see the posts and barriers, delimiting the frontiers, also painted in the Kingdom's conventional colours. But the one thing that we can never see is the Kingdom itself. The same is true of the Church. We can never see the Church itself; we can see only its places of worship, its altars, crosses, and monstrances, its clerics in their vestments. We can, of course, feel its influence. The influence of a higher religion is more potent than that of any state has ever been, but a church's influence, like a state's, is exer-

---

[1] In *Archiv für Kulturgeschichte*, xxxiii. Band, Heft 2 (1951), p. 244.
[2] In *Toynbee and History*, p. 194, quoted already on p. 233. G. Catlin, ibid., p. 169, suggests that cultures are entities of a different order from both governments and human beings. I do not dispute this.   [3] *Toynbee and History*, p. 96.

cised in the invisible realm of psychic relations. It, too, is a network of relations between human beings.

And what about the British and the American Constitution, which are respectively key-parts of the state-systems of the United Kingdom and the United States? The British Constitution is invisible by definition, since it has been left unwritten. But has the American Constitution really been made visible in the celebrated document that has been duly drafted, agreed, enacted, and promulgated? Are we seeing the Constitution of the United States when we read in print the words of a text bearing that title? No, this 'written' constitution is no more visible than the 'unwritten' one or than the United States of North America themselves or than the United Kingdom of Great Britain and Northern Ireland. A constitution is not a series of ink marks on paper. These visible marks are merely a mnemonic device for recording an agreement between a number of human beings about the terms on which they are going to regulate their political relations with each other. The agreement, its terms, and the relations between people through which these terms are put into effect are invisible, all alike.

Civilizations are invisible, just as constitutions, states, and churches are, and this for just the same reasons. But civilizations, too, have manifestations that are visible, like the Prussian state's gold-crowned eagles and spiked helmets, and like the Christian Church's crosses and surplices. Set side by side an Egyptiac, an Hellenic, and a pre-Renaissance[1] Western statue. It will be impossible to mistake which of these is the product of which school of sculptors. The distinctiveness of each of the three artistic styles is not only visible; it is definite—more definite than any of the visible products or emblems of any church or state. By exploring the range, in space and time, of a civilization's distinctive artistic style, one can ascertain the spatial and temporal bounds of the civilization that this style expresses. As Kroeber points out,[2] an artistic style is a sensitive indicator of historical connexions. Within the ambit of any one civilization the various styles 'tend towards a certain consistency among themselves',[3] and 'styles are the very incarnation of the dynamic forms taken by the history of civilization'.[4] Our ability, Kroeber adds, to locate an unassigned work of art to its place in a style sequence implies that the development of a style follows a one-way course. 'A style is a strand in a culture. . . . It is also a selective way. . . . Where compulsion or physical or physiological necessity reign, there is no room for style.' In being selective, a style, as well as a state, is an expression of will.[5] Bagby, too, observes[6] that 'the art-historians have shown that the styles of works of art are not absolutely indefinable', and that 'something of the same kind is done by the anthropologist and the culture historian. He, too, feels a common

---

[1] The Western statue must be pre-Renaissance if it is to be characteristic and distinctive. It must antedate the Western reception, at 'the' Renaissance, of the Hellenic style of visual art. [2] In *Style and Civilizations*, pp. 2–3 and 155–6.
[3] *The Nature of Culture*, p. 402.
[4] Ibid., p. 403. Cp. Anderle, in the passage quoted on p. 289, footnote 1.
[5] *Style and Civilizations*, p. 150. This is the answer to Erdmann's contention, cited on p. 290, that states are the only kind of institution in which the human will finds expression. [6] In *Culture and History*, p. 108.

flavour in the diverse features of a culture or a period; he too tries to point out the observable qualities which give rise to this feeling.'[1] Frankfort points out[2] that 'we recognise . . . the character of a civilization . . . in a certain coherence among its various manifestations, a certain consistency in its orientation, a certain cultural "style" which shapes its political and its judicial institutions, its art as well as its literature, its religion as well as its morals.' He illustrates his point by a masterly characterization[3] of the Sumero-Akkadian and Egyptiac civilizations, in which he brings out the fundamental features of each and the differences in their respective ways of pursuing the common endeavour of civilization.

The visible works of art that reveal so much about their civilization are merely expressions of it. They are not the civilization itself. That remains invisible, like a church or a state. When the anthropologist or the cultural historian tries to analyse the observable qualities that have been his clues to the diagnosis of a culture, he analyses them, as Bagby notices,[4] in terms of ideas and values. Invisibility is, indeed, a common characteristic of all forces that are potent in human affairs. Even in the realm of non-human nature, over which Man has now established his mastery, invisible microbes and protons are more potent than visible lions and flashes of lightning. In the spiritual realm, where Man is not master, he has to cope with an invisible network of relations between elements in his own psyche, and with another invisible network of relations between himself and his fellow human beings. And the most potent of the forces that move human souls is the spirit that blows like the incalculable wind whose passage is audible but invisible.[5]

19. 'FOSSILS'

In the process of identifying systems of human relations of the kind that I have called 'civilizations', I found that the specimens of the species were not all of the same generation and not all even partially contemporaneous. For instance, the still extant Western Civilization has, in its historical background, an extinct civilization, the Hellenic, to which the Western Civilization is related in a way that I have called 'affiliation'. I went on to identify other civilizations that are now extinct, as the Hellenic is. I identified some of these by the procedure by which I had identified the Hellenic. I delved back into the origins of some extant civilization till I struck (so I believed) an earlier civilization, distinct from the extant one, though this was obviously affiliated to it. In two cases, however, I identified an extinct civilization by a different clue in the present-day world. Instead of ascertaining the former existence of an extinct civilization through the present existence of an extant civilization, I ascertained it, in a more direct way, through the present existence of what appeared to me to be extant relics of a civilization that, but for these, was extinct. 'One set' of extant communities—'including the Monophysite Christians of Armenia, Mesopotamia,

---

[1] *Culture and History*, pp. 108–9.
[2] In *The Rise of Civilization in the Near East*, p. 16.   [3] Ibid., pp. 49–50.
[4] In *Culture and History*, p. 109.   [5] John iii. 8.

Egypt, and Abyssinia and the Nestorian Christians of Kurdistan and Malabar, as well as the Jews and the Parsees'[1]—seemed to me to be relics of an otherwise extinct Syriac Civilization. 'A second set—including the Lamaistic Mahayanian Buddhists of Tibet and Mongolia and the Hinayanian Buddhists of Ceylon, Burma and Siam,[2] as well as the Jains in India'[3]—seemed to me to be relics of an otherwise extinct Indic Civilization. I may or may not have been right in my identifications of the civilizations represented by these two sets of extant communities, but I do not think I was wrong in diagnosing these communities as being relics of something that is otherwise no longer in existence today. If the societies represented by these extant communities are not extinct civilizations, they are at any rate extinct phases of civilizations that are still extant in later forms.[4]

These extant communities that I have labelled 'fossils' interested me for the reaon that literal fossils interest palaeontologists. They seemed to me to be clues to something in the past which I was eager to rediscover and reconstruct. I seized on as many of them as I could find, and used them for tracking down civilizations, or phases in the histories of civilizations, which did not seem to have any other representatives than these in the present-day world. The fact that my 'fossils' were not just isolated phenomena but presented themselves in sets and sub-sets seemed to me to enhance their value as evidence. In one set the Jews and the Parsees seemed to me to be relics of the Syriac Civilization as it had been developing before this development was interrupted by the intrusion of Hellenism on the Syriac World; the Nestorian and Monophysite Christians seemed to be relics of the same Syriac Civilization as it was when it was reacting against the Hellenic Civilization's ascendancy. The Hellenic Civilization intruded on India too, and the second set of 'fossils' seemed to fall into two sub-sets, like the first. The Jains and the Hinayanian Buddhists seemed to be relics of civilization in India as this had been developing before the intrusion of Hellenism. The Lamaistic Mahayanian Buddhists seemed to be relics of civilization in India as it was when it was reacting against Hellenism's ascendancy there.[5]

One Jewish critic of my work, E. Berkovitz, has noted that, in my view of history, 'fossils' are apt to come in clusters.

'One of the charms of the *Study* is that it prevents Jews, as well as Judaism, from falling into the sin of vain conceit by imagining that there

---

[1] i. 35. Cp. i. 51 and i. 90–92. I noted that the former Nestorians of Malabar had now become Monophysites.

[2] Cambodia ought to have been included in the list of countries in which the Hinayana is now practised. [3] i. 35.

[4] As a result of the reconsiderations set out in the present volume, I now think that there is more continuity than discontinuity in the history of civilization in India since after the disappearance of the Indus Culture there, and that it is therefore truer to reality to treat this as the history of one single civilization, instead of treating it as the history of an 'Indic' Civilization followed by an affiliated 'Hindu' Civilization. On the other hand, I find myself confirmed in my previous view that there is a break of historical continuity between the now extinct Syriac Civilization and the still extant Islamic Civilization. Most of my critics seem to hold that this break is still greater than I judge it to be.

[5] This is a recapitulation of what has been set out more fully in i. 90–92.

could be anything unique about either of them. In good and bad fortune, in their greatness as well as in their fall, they have for their yoke-fellows of destiny the Parsees and Zoroastrianism.'[1]

This is a correct account of my view. I do see the Jews and the Parsees as a pair of peoples who have had an identical experience and have reacted to it in an identical way. And I do see Judaism and Zoroastrianism as a pair of religions that are like each other in each being Janus-faced.[2] One face is turned outwards towards the whole of mankind, for whom the religion has a message of universal significance and value. The other face is turned inwards towards the nation among whom this potentially universal religion originated. Paradoxically—so it seems to an observer from outside—the potentially universal religion has been turned by its original discoverers or recipients into an instrument for keeping alive their distinctive national consciousness as a peculiar people who deliberately hold themselves apart from the rest of mankind, though this costs them a constant effort of will and also exposes them to a constant threat of being severely penalized on this account.[3] Having lost not only their historic national state but also their historic national home, and finding themselves scattered abroad as a minority in an alien world, both the Parsees and the Jews have devised an alternative kind of social cement for holding their community together in these unusually difficult circumstances. They have elaborated the traditional rites and tightened up the traditional rules of their ancestral religions to a degree that has made these religions into effective instruments for accomplishing their adherents' secular social purpose.[4] But the consequent host of

---

[1] E. Berkovitz: *Judaism: Fossil or Ferment?*, footnote 31 on p. 149. See also Rabbi J. B. Agus in *Judaism*, vol. 4,, No. 4 (Fall, 1955), p. 320.

[2] This characteristic, which Hinduism shares with Zoroastrianism and Judaism to some extent, has been noticed on pp. 85–88.

[3] I agree with E. Berkovitz that, in this sense, 'exile has been the highest form of activism' (op. cit., p. 123), and with M. Samuel that 'the endurance of the Jewish people is a continuous exertion of the will in the face of adversity' (*The Professor and the Fossil*, p. 182). As Berkovitz finely expresses it: 'While the others persecuted, the Jews chose' (op. cit., loc. cit.).

[4] Their effectiveness for this purpose is graphically illustrated by Samuel in op. cit., pp. 177–8. As he puts it, 'these practices kept the people alerted, as it were, for the restoration and for a resumption of life in Palestine'. In other words, it fortified their tribal consciousness, as exiles who had once had a state of their own in a country of their own, as against their universal consciousness as worshippers of a God who is absolute spiritual Reality and whose worshippers can therefore worship Him equally well, wherever they may find themselves—being, as they are, representatives of a church that, in God's eyes, must embrace all mankind. Rabbi Agus notes, in *Judaism*, 1956, p. 10, that, according to Achad Ha'am, 'the cumbersome rites of Judaism constituted the "exilic garments" for the bruised body of the national soul'.
R. Travers Herford, too, notes that 'the *halachah* served as the chief bond to hold the Jewish community together when every other bond of national life was broken and Jews were scattered wide over the face of the Earth' (*The Pharisees*, p. 106). 'It acted . . . also as an external protective covering, within which the spirit of Judaism could maintain its strength and vitality' (ibid., p. 237). 'Wherever a Jew lived in the same locality with gentiles, his observance of the *halachah* would at once draw attention to him. The gentile would notice that the Jew did many special acts as a religious duty, that he made a point of doing many things, in themselves apparently trivial, in a particular way, and that he refrained from doing other things which to the gentile seemed harmless or indifferent' (ibid., p. 77). Herford, being both a gentile and a life-long student of the Rabbinical Jewish literature, warns his fellow gentiles that the *halachah*, besides being the most conspicuous factor in Pharisaism to the outsider, is also one 'whose inner meaning is usually hidden from him' (ibid., p. 107). 'The essence of the *halachah* was the doing of an action exactly in the appointed way because that was what God com-

meticulous observances seems, to an outside observer, not only to be irrational and spiritually unprofitable in itself; it seems also to be a strangely incongruous accompaniment of the spiritual insight or revelation that has been attained in these religions and that, in an outsider's eyes, is their essence.

These seem to me to be cogent reasons for coupling the Parsees and Zoroastrianism with the Jews and Judaism. Yet the ironical language in which my practice is reported by the Jewish critic whom I have quoted shows that my bracketing of these two peoples and two religions is distasteful to him.[1] At the same time, both Berkovitz and other Jewish critics have attacked me for my use of the word 'fossil' as if I had applied it to the Jews alone, and had applied it to them as a term of abuse, or at least of depreciation. This would have been a left-handed way of recognizing the validity of the Jewish claim that the Jewish people and Jewish religion are unique. Actually, I have invariably thought and written of them as being representatives of a class, and have thereby also incurred their displeasure—though the class of communities that I have labelled 'fossils' is one whose characteristic tenacity I admire, in spite of my opposition to the nationalism to which this specific virtue of theirs is dedicated.

Since my use of the word 'fossil' has been so hotly attacked by Jewish critics, I have asked myself the questions: Is the word offensive? And does it accurately convey what I mean by it?

The criticisms of my use of it that have come to my notice have all come from Jews. I know of no Parsee, Nestorian, Monophysite, Jain, Hinayanian Buddhist, or Tantric Mahayanian Buddhist objectors to it. I can only declare—and I do this with complete sincerity—that, when I coined the word, I neither intended it to be offensive nor foresaw that anyone would take it as being so.[2] The question whether the word conveys my meaning is, in my opinion, the more important of the two.

Berkovitz has saved me work by giving a clear and accurate statement of what my meaning is; and, though he gives it apropos of the Jews alone, it applies equally to all the other 'fossils' on my list. I mean, he correctly writes,[3] 'that Jewry does not really *belong* to the West, or to the other dominant civilizations of the East, though it once did belong to a civilization of a category similar to the now "living" ones; there is therefore something "abnormal" about Jewry'.[4] Berkovitz goes on to

manded. . . . The question did not arise for the Pharisee whether the prescribed action in a given case was trivial or important. . . . The action by itself, without the conscious intention of serving God by the doing of it, was worthless' (ibid., pp. 76–77).

Thus the spiritual power of a sublime conception of, and attitude towards, absolute Reality was harnessed to the devoted performance of hereditary tribal observances in which ethical commandments were yoked incongruously—as it looks to an outsider—with regulations that had been retained and embroidered after they had become purposeless and meaningless in themselves.

[1] I myself should be gratified, as an Englishman from the Danelaw, to find myself bracketed with representatives of any of the historic communities that I have labelled 'fossils'.

[2] I now recognize, however, that it must seem offensive, since Rabbi Agus finds the phrase 'distressing' (*Judaism*, vol. 4, No. 4 (Fall, 1955), p. 320), and no critic could be more temperate and objective-minded than he is.   [3] In op. cit., pp. 83–84.

[4] Rabbi J. B. Agus observes (in *Judaism*, 1956, p. 10) that Jewish history in its diasporá phase was 'abnormal' in the eyes of Jews, too, of the nationalist school. As they

say[1] that I regard Judaism, as well as Jewry, as being a fossil. I describe Judaism sometimes, he says, as being a fossil of the Syriac Civilization, and sometimes as being a fossil of Syriac religion. He comments:[2]

'A fossilised community is not the same as a fossilised religion; nor is it understandable how Judaism may be, at the same time, a fossil of a civilization as well as a religion.'

I do hold that Judaism, as well as Jewry, is a fossil both of the Syriac Civilization and of Syriac religion. The ambiguity which has been remarked by Berkovitz has also been remarked by Rabbi J. B. Agus in an unpolemical and constructive critique of my work. Commenting on my view of Jewry as being a fossil, Rabbi Agus observes:

'His judgment derives from an ambiguity in the use of the term Judaism. At times he equates Judaism with the ethnic culture of Jewry; at other times he thinks of the Jewish faith as a separable pattern of ideas, which is included more or less in our modern Western culture. The elements of nationality—language, political organisation, common sovereignty, sense of ethnic kinship—he regards as a fossilised part of the larger whole of the ancient Syriac Civilization. The faith of Judaism is embraced for him within the general context of Christianity. . . . More recently, he has begun to speak of Judaism as one of the great religions of mankind. But the ambiguity of his original judgment persists—largely because he does not always bear in mind his own distinction between Judaism as a "higher religion" and the outer, civilizational elements of Jewish life.'[3]

This is an accurate, as well as scrupulously fair-minded, résumé of my ideas.[4] I agree that there is an ambiguity. As I see it, however, this lies, not in my judgement of Jewry and Judaism, but in the nature of Jewry and Judaism themselves. My judgement reflects, I believe, not a confusion in my mind, but my recognition of an ambiguity that has been characteristic of the attitude of the Jews since the Exile.

The different points in my position are not incompatible with each other, as far as I can see. There is surely no reason why a religion, as well as a community, should not be a survival of something that is otherwise extinct, and no reason either why Judaism should not be a survival both of the otherwise extinct Syriac Civilization and of this civilization's otherwise extinct religion. In the age before the Syriac Society was

---

saw it, in this phase 'the Jews were an "abnormal" nation preserving its identity and cherishing its institutions under the protective covering of a religious faith'. He also observes (in *The National Jewish Monthly*, November, 1956, p. 41) that Jewish historians of the Idealistic or Classical Reform School thought of the Jews as being what I have called 'fossils', 'though the terms they employed were free of the derogatory connotations' of this word. 'The historians Yost and Geiger believed that Jewish national life ended with the destruction of Jerusalem. Thereafter, only a religious community continued to live, within a shell, as it were, composed of petrified forms of communal institutions and customs.'   [1] In op. cit., p. 84.

[2] Ibid., p. 84.   [3] *Judaism*, vol. 4, No. 4 (Fall, 1955), p. 321.
[4] In a review of Samuel's book in *The National Jewish Monthly*, November, 1956, Rabbi Agus notes that he had 'pointed out, more than a year ago, the several errors that are contained in the phrase "fossil of Syriac Civilization", but without attributing to Toynbee either malevolence or confusion. In acknowledging this critique, Professor Toynbee stated that he was preparing to re-evaluate his findings.' I have now done this in the present volume, pp. 85–88, the present passage, and Chapters XIII and XV.

uprooted by Assyrian and Babylonian militarism and was subsequently
penetrated by the radiation of Hellenism, it was still in the stage—
characteristic of societies of all kinds and all dates before the rise of the
higher religions—in which religion is an integral part of culture and is
intimately associated with the non-religious elements in it. At this stage
the gods of the Syriac World—Melkart of Tyre, Rimmon of Damascus,
Yahweh of Israel, Judah, and Edom, Dagon of Gaza, Milcom of
Ammon, Chemosh of Moab, and the rest—were none of them identified
by their respective worshippers with an absolute spiritual Reality beyond
the phenomenal universe. They were each identified with some local
Syriac community, and indeed identified with every aspect of that
community's life in an age in which a distinction had not yet been
drawn between what was religious or sacred and what was secular or
profane.[1] In this volume it has been noticed[2] that, down to this day,
Judaism has never ceased to be a religion of this antique kind—never
ceased, that is to say, to be the tribal worship of a particular single community, and never ceased to be an integral part of this community's
particular culture—notwithstanding the fact that, since the deportation
of the notables of the Kingdom of Judah to Babylon, Judaism has come
to be also a universal religion which identifies Yahweh with absolute
spiritual Reality and which therefore has a meaning and a message for
all mankind. Thus Post-Exilic Judaism is a fossil both of the Syriac
Civilization and of the religion that was an integral part of that civilization in the Pre-Exilic Age, besides being a 'higher religion' with a
message for all men. This duality of Judaism may seem paradoxical, but
it is a paradox which is an historical fact.

I have still to ask myself whether the word 'fossil', when applied
either to a religion or to a community, is an apt word for conveying
what I mean by it. In the two cases of the Jewish community and Judaism
and the Parsee community and Zoroastrianism, the word 'fossil'
evidently does provide an apt metaphor for conveying the two important facts that the religious observances of the two communities have
become ossified and that these ossified observances have served as an
effective social cement. They have enabled the participants in each of
these two communities to keep their communities in existence, and this
for many centuries running, without having a state of their own or even
a country in which they were at home and in a majority. Most communities that have been exposed to these adverse conditions have failed
to preserve their identities.[3] The ossification of Jewish and Parsee

---

[1] 'All law in ancient pre-Mosaic Israel, as among all the Semites, was originally based
on tribal custom. . . . A great deal of what was contained in the Hebrew Law during all
periods of Israelite history had its source in the earliest ages. Moreover, as is well known,
tribal custom was inseparable from religious custom because the tribe was under the
special protection of its god, who was looked upon as directing the life of his worshippers
in every sphere' (W. O. E. Oesterley: *The Jews and Judaism during the Greek Period*
(London 1941, S.P.C.K.), p. 56).   [2] On pp. 85–88 and 294–5.
[3] M. Samuel declares that there is only one people—the Jews—whom Time has
never yet succeeded in selling to Oblivion (*The Professor and the Fossil*, p. 163). If he
had said 'there are only one or two peoples' he would have been nearer to the truth;
for, as Berkovitz notes that I note, the Jews 'have as their yoke-fellows of destiny the
Parsees'. In Chinese eyes, no doubt, both Parsees and Jews are rather late competitors
who have hardly yet had time to begin to show their mettle.

religious observances is at least one important factor that has enabled these two communities to make themselves exceptions to the usual rule. 'Fossilization' is surely an informative word for describing this social expedient.

Does the concept of 'fossilization' apply equally well to the other 'fossils' on my list? It seems to apply to those that, like the Parsees and the Jews, are 'dispersed abroad' among alien populations. The observances of Nestorian and Monophysite Christianity, for instance, seem already to be in process of becoming a social cement as tough as Zoroastrianism and Judaism. If the Nestorian and Monophysite 'diasporás' were to manage to survive as long as the Parsees and Jews have survived up to date, a comparable degree of ossification in their religious institutions would probably be the price that they would have to pay. On the other hand the word 'fossil' is less apt as a label for the Hinayanian and the Tantric Mahayanian Buddhists. It is true that these Buddhist communities outside India represent a phase of Indian civilization that is otherwise extinct. But, unlike the Monophysites, Nestorians, Parsees, and Jews, the Tibetans, Mongols, Sinhalese, Burmans, Siamese, and Cambodians are not 'diasporás'. They are all geographically more or less compact peoples with countries and governments of their own. In Tibet, before the recent Chinese reoccupation and the abortive insurrection against it in 1959, the government was actually in the hands of the local Tantric Mahayanian Buddhist monks; in the South-East Asian countries Hinayanian Buddhism is the established religion. In Tibet and Mongolia religious observances have become ossified; but in the Hinayanian Buddhist countries some of the monks, at any rate, are still genuinely practising the strenuous spiritual exercises prescribed in the Hinayana as the way of release from desire, from feeling, and from selfhood; and this form of practical religion or philosophy is, of course, the extreme antithesis of 'fossilization'.[1] On the whole, it seems more enlightening to think of both the present-day Hinayanian Buddhist communities in South-East Asia and the present-day Tantric Mahayanian Buddhist communities in Central Asia as being, not fossils of the civilization of India in one or other of its past phases, but satellites of it that have developed distinctive characteristics of their own.[2]

One misfit, in my use of the word 'fossil', which applies to all the specimens in my list, is the implication that the life has gone out of them. A literal fossil is dead *ex hypothesi*; it is a dead relic of a once living organism. The communities and religions that I have labelled 'fossils' are also not alive; only organisms can be that. But they are going concerns, consisting of networks of relations between a number of living

---

[1] No doubt, there is also spiritual life in other 'fossils' on my list. For example, Rabbi J. B. Agus observes that 'the atrophy of the outer civilizational elements in Jewish life, giving the appearance of fossilisation to an outside observer, was itself due to the intense moralistic and pietistic standards of value that prevailed within it' (*Judaism*, vol. 4, No. 4 (Fall, 1955), p. 322). Berkovitz makes the sweeping claim that 'the vitality of a higher religion is of the spirit; it can never become fossilised' (*Judaism: Fossil or Ferment?*, p. 88). Unhappily, this dictum is contradicted by history, which is full of records of the spirit being killed by the letter. Rabbi Agus notes that 'the spectre of slow stagnation and even fossilisation is always present in Jewish life as a warning and as a challenge'—since the dogmatic assertion of the will of God puts a stop to all inquiry (*Judaism*, 1956, p. 37).   [2] See pp. 552–3, and the table facing p. 558.

people.[1] I am conscious that any metaphor taken from organic life is inadequate for conveying the nature of a social phenomenon, but at least it would make a better fit if I called these communities that have survived from some extinct phase of social life by the name of some antediluvian living organism. The word 'Coelacanthus', for instance, would not be open to the objection of implying, as the word 'fossil' implies, that the object designated by it no longer has any life in it. I should have no objection to substituting 'coelacanthus' for 'fossil' in my terminology. What I want is the aptest possible short title for a definition which, if written out, will run, as Berkovitz's succinct version of it shows, to far too many words for anyone to repeat each time that he needs to employ the concept.

Like organisms that, in the struggle for survival, have contrived to encase themselves in natural armour, the communities in diasporá, within their protective integument of ossified religious observances, have, of course, an active internal life of their own. Like all communities and societies, they are networks of relations between people, and the fossilization of people's institutions does not make fossils of the human beings whose institutions these are.[2] Berkovitz asks:[3] 'How can human beings . . . be fossils?' As far as I know, they cannot be, though it is obvious that their institutions can. It is one of the characteristic virtues of human beings whose communities are scattered minorities that they have, on the average, a higher standard of mutual aid and mutual loyalty than people whose communities are in less precarious circumstances. They may also be active on the plane of the individual's inner spiritual life, as well as on the social plane.

Moreover, their own separate communal life is not the only network of social relations in which the representatives of a diasporá are engaged. Since they are scattered among alien populations, and since, like other human beings, they have to earn their living, they could not survive if they did not do business with representatives of the majorities in whose midst they live. Since, moreover, they have frequently been penalized by being prohibited, or anyway prevented, from engaging in certain staple occupations (e.g. agriculture and public administration), they have been stimulated to acquire greater skill than their neighbours in such professions as have been left open to them[4]—for instance, retail trade, with the opportunities that this has given to an outstandingly able few to become financiers on the grand scale. Thus, in certain fields of social activity, the representatives of 'fossil' diasporás are, and always have been, full participants in the life of the alien societies in whose midst they have been living. Nor have they confined this participation to the economic plane when they have been permitted by the alien

[1] M. Samuel is mistaken in thinking that I mean that the Jewish people 'is completely dead as a spiritually functioning entity' (*The Professor and the Fossil*, p. 20). But I think his mistake may be partly due to the inadequacy of the word 'fossil'—which does mean something dead—for expressing my exact meaning.
[2] On this point M. Samuel has caught my meaning correctly. 'He is not referring', he says, 'to individual Jews. . . . He is referring to the corporate personality' (*The Professor and the Fossil*, p. 20). [3] In op. cit., p. 84.
[4] M. Samuel justifiably credits the Jews with 'a continuous exertion . . . of creative ingenuity in the midst of change' (*The Professor and the Fossil*, p. 182).

majority to take part in this majority's life on other planes as well. The abrogation of previous legal or customary prohibitions is what, in the recent history of Jewry in the West, has been called 'emancipation'. The Jews in the West have been 'emancipated' in this sense since Napoleon's time, the Parsees in India since the contemporary establishment there of the now defunct British Raj. Since the opening of these doors, very many Jews in the West and many Parsees in India have taken not only active but eminent parts in Western and Indian cultural and political activities of many kinds.[1]

I have now admitted that the word 'fossil' describes only partially and inadequately what I mean by it. But it does express important parts of my meaning, and I still have not found an apter word to replace it. If some Jewish, Parsee, Armenian, or Assyrian reader of this book can supply me with a word that does fit better the social, cultural, and religious phenomena for which I need a label, I will adopt his golden word with alacrity.

20. BREAKDOWNS

In ordinary usage the English word 'breakdown' is employed in two different spheres: the world of man-made machinery and the world of Man himself; and, in the human sphere, it is employed in two different provinces: the life of an individual human being and the network of relations between a number of people. We speak of the breakdown of a motor-car, a railway-engine, or a generator in a power-station; the breakdown of a human being's physical or mental health or of his will-power; and the breakdown of some standing arrangement of relations between human beings: a system of government or of communications; an organization for the distribution of milk or of newspapers. This last-mentioned sense is the one in which I use the word breakdown in this Study. I use it specifically to mean the breakdown of a network of human relations of the kind that we call a society in process of civilization, and also to mean the accompanying breakdown of the pattern of ideas and values and consequent behaviour that is carried on a social network and is known as a culture.[2]

---

[1] Rabbi Agus, in *Judaism*, 1956, pp. 320-1, points out that in pre-emancipation days already there was a 'dynamic impulse' in Jewish spiritual and intellectual life and that, though the main expressions of this occurred within the interior life of Jewry, they were answers to the challenge of the contemporary climate of ideas and sentiments in the encompassing Islamic and Christian worlds. In Jewish history there has been a tension between a process of 'fossilization' and a process of spiritualization. On this, see the passages quoted on p. 514 from works of Rabbi Agus's, and also his comments printed in the annexes to the present chapter and to Chapters XIII and XV.

[2] On pp. 156-7 I have already discussed criticisms of my practice of dating a breakdown by some precisely datable event, such as the outbreak of a war, that I have taken as a symbol of it. An event may, of course, aptly symbolize a social breakdown without being more than a symptom of a more gradual change beneath the surface. I agree with Coulborn (in *Toynbee and History*, p. 151) that wars, for example, are symptoms of social breakdown rather than causes of it. But I would add that they have often been potent agencies in carrying a broken-down society along the road to disintegration.

Though I do not think of the breakdown of a civilization as being an instantaneous occurrence, I also do not use the word to include the long-drawn-out process of disintegration which has often, and perhaps usually, followed when a civilization has broken down. P. Geyl notes that, in my usage, 'breakdown' means only the beginning of the

The breakdowns of institutions—particularly those that are as comprehensive as societies and cultures are—can inflict loss and suffering on individual human beings in vast numbers and to an extreme degree; but these human beings do not have to break down themselves because one of their institutions—however important a one—has miscarried. Except in so far as the number of physical and mental breakdowns of individuals per thousand is reduced by progress in medical science, or the number of moral breakdowns by increase in accessible means of spiritual grace, there is no evidence, so far as I know, that the rate of individual breakdowns varies in accordance with differences in the population's social circumstances. We must presume that, on the average, approximately the same number of people per thousand retain, in all social circumstances, their normal human faculties, including normal moral stamina and normal creative power. These two faculties are the fundamental endowment of human nature. They are the ultimate source of all human achievement. So, as long as normal human beings survive in conditions in which they can still propagate their kind and pass on a social and cultural heritage of some sort to posterity, the cause of mankind is not lost and the door opening into the future still stands open. K. D. Erdmann is right in saying[1] that, in my eyes, history is the tragedy of civilization. But I must add that, in my eyes, the tragedy of civilization is not necessarily a tragedy for the human race.

Thus the breakdown of an institution, however comprehensive and however valuable that institution may have been, means no more than that the human race, or some portion of it, has shot one of its bolts. It will still have others in its quiver. At a cost—which may, of course, be a very high one—a broken-down institution can be replaced eventually by another one. Moreover, when a social disaster occurs, the account will not necessarily show no profit to be set against the loss. One of the truths about human nature is *pathei mathos*.[2] Human beings are capable of learning through suffering, and in this hard way they have often learnt lessons that they have been unable or unwilling to learn at less cost to themselves. The suffering that the breakdown of a civilization brings upon people inevitably, whatever may be the eventual outcome

end (*Debates with Historians*, p. 136). O. H. K. Spate objects (in *Toynbee and History*, p. 293) to 'the use of the word "breakdown" for the initial false step which sets a civilization *on the road* to breaking down'. I myself should say here: 'on the road, via disintegration, to dissolution'. I believe that my usage of the word 'breakdown', not Spate's, is the usual one. In ordinary parlance, a 'breakdown' is something that has a sequel. It is the beginning of a drama, not the whole play, and certainly not the denouement to the exclusion of its antecedents.

F. Creedy has suggested, in an unpublished letter to me, that I should substitute for the word 'breakdown' some non-committal phrase such as 'cessation of growth on the old lines' or 'change of form'. This might shield me from criticism, but it would not convey my meaning—which is that there has been a real breakdown of something: viz. a civilization. John Strachey has suggested, in an unpublished letter, that I should substitute the word 'crisis'. This word has the merit of implying that what has gone wrong is not necessarily irretrievable. If irretrievability is part of the connotation of the word 'breakdown', the word 'crisis' would be preferable from my point of view. I do not believe that any of the recorded breakdowns of civilizations have been irretrievable, though I can think of a number that have not, in fact, been subsequently retrieved.

[1] In *Archiv für Kulturgeschichte*, xxxiii. Band, Heft 2 (1951), p. 190.
[2] Aeschylus: *Agamemnon*, ll. 177-8 (see pp. 580-1, 609, 617). P. Sorokin maintains that this is 'a one-sided pseudo law' and that it 'does not stand an elementary empirical test' (*Toynbee and History*, p. 189).

of the calamity, is thus a challenge to human souls. The challenge may not evoke any creative response, and then the result of the calamity will be uncompensated suffering, loss, and setback. But, as a matter of historical fact, some of the breakdowns of civilizations whose histories are known to us have evoked mighty creative responses in the forms of philosophies, higher religions, and universal states[1]—these last being political expressions of a social rally that are also, as the higher religions are, symbols of the ideal unity of mankind and auguries of a future practical achievement of this unity once for all on a literally world-wide scale.[2]

[1] Hourani rightly interprets me as holding that, when a civilization is disintegrating, the conflict between a dominant minority and an internal and an external proletariat 'is not the whole story; for, at the moment when the three classes by the violence of their conflict are destroying both themselves and the civilization as a whole, all three of them explode in acts of creation which light up the dying world' (*The Dublin Review*, vol. 229, No. 470 (December, 1955), p. 379). R. Coulborn notes that it is in times of social decline that great men seem to stand out from the mass (*Phylon*, 1940, offprint, p. 36).

[2] These creative responses to breakdowns have been a stumbling-block for several critics. For instance, O. H. K. Spate quotes a note of Somervell's on my usage of the word 'breakdown' in which Somervell points out that, 'when the term is used in this sense, some of the most fruitful, illuminating, and celebrated achievements in the history of a civilization may come after the breakdown and, indeed, in consequence of it'. Spate's comment is that I am using the word 'breakdown' with a 'Humpty-Dumptyish licence'. O. Handlin is equally caustic in *The Partisan Review*, July–August, 1947. 'The disintegration of a civilization is', he writes, 'very sad from the point of view of the creative minority. Yet we also learn that the process of decay is often marked by a rapid expansion of productive techniques, by a flourishing of the arts, and by the development of science, philosophy, and religion. To some readers and, no doubt, to many people who participate in the process, this turn of events seems almost desirable. If such is decay and such is growth, then it is clear that decay and growth have meaning only in terms of the artificial devices of the author's system. Since these processes have no relevance to the historical fate of human beings, the system itself can hardly contribute to an understanding of what happened to the real lives of the people of the past.' C. Trinkaus makes a similar comment in *Science and Society*, vol. xii, No. 1 (1948), p. 226. Toynbee, he says, equates growth with stability and disintegration with 'that dynamic phase where the most enormous leaps forward in human history are taking place'. Handlin's account of my position is, of course, a caricature. I have never suggested that the geneses, growths, breakdowns, and disintegrations of civilizations have had 'no relevance to the historical fate of human beings'. I believe that they have had a profound effect on the fate, not just of 'creative minorities', but of all the participants in the civilizations that have passed through these phases. Subject to these important reservations, I agree that his and Spate's and Trinkaus's strictures would have been to the point if I had been discussing 'breakdowns' in some absolute sense of the word. Actually, of course, there can only be breakdowns of something or other. In this book I am concerned with breakdowns of civilizations. And there is no reason whatever why these should not be followed by creative achievements. Indeed, it would be strange if this were not the sequel, if I am right, *pace* Sorokin, in believing that *pathei mathos* is one of the fundamental truths about human nature.

In an unpublished letter John Strachey has noted that, in my view, the miscarriages of civilizations, which have brought so much suffering on the human beings who have been their perpetrators and their victims, have in some cases been more fruitful for mankind than these civilizations' previous halcyon days. But, no doubt, L. Mumford (in *Diogenes*, No. 13 (Spring, 1956), p. 28) and G. Masur (in the *Historische Zeitschrift*, Band 177 (1954), pp. 521–2) may be right in judging that I exaggerate the relative importance and value of the role of the disintegrations of civilizations in human history. However, Frankfort, too, may be right in holding that 'a preoccupation with decay, such as underlies Toynbee's work, need not in itself vitiate study of the birth of civilization' (*The Birth of Civilization in the Near East*, p. 23).

Some comments of Feibleman's are telling, as well as witty. In my view, he says, 'the failure of human culture is the salvation of mankind' (*T'ien Hsia Monthly*, vol. xi, Nos. 1 and 2 (1940), p. 22). 'It is in ... civilization's decline that all the good things for which civilization deserves its name take their start' (ibid., p. 140). 'There is really nothing that a civilization can do that will please Toynbee except to collapse and then, after having given birth to a universal church, to get out of the way!' (ibid., p. 144). I cannot re-read this without bursting out laughing and crying 'touché'. I have not, after all,

Consequently, the sequel to the breakdown of a civilization has usually had two sides to it. On the one hand the breakdown of any institution must bring with it, for the people involved in it, a loss, to some degree, of rational and purposeful control over their own collective destiny. This must be so, because rational and purposeful control of common affairs requires effective arrangements for co-operation, and such arrangements require a systematic organization of relations. An emergency in which an established pattern of relations goes wrong will inflict loss and suffering on all concerned; it will block some previous opportunities, and will deprive some people of an initiative that was formerly in their hands. At the same time, the same emergency may transfer the initiative to other hands that did not previously hold it, and it may open up new opportunities that will not be the same as those that have been blocked, yet may be not less valuable.[1]

The loss of rational and purposeful control over common affairs arises from the mutual frustration of conflicting wills. The effect of this is to shift the ever oscillating psychic frontier between the realm of the reason and will and the realm of the irrational and emotional underworld of the psyche, and to shift it, in this event, in the subconscious psychic underworld's favour. In contrast to the psyche's conscious surface, its underworld is subject to 'laws of Nature' of the kind that govern non-human fauna and flora and inanimate matter. Accordingly, when the psychic frontier shifts markedly in the subconscious underworld's favour, as it does when any important institution breaks down, one of the symptoms in which this shift reveals itself is a marked increase in the vein of regularity in the course of social and cultural history. This is the explanation, as I see it, of a difference that I believe that I have observed between the patterns in the history of a broken-down civilization before its breakdown and the patterns in it after the disaster has occurred. Institutions, unlike organisms, have no inherent predetermined maximum duration.[2] There is no reason, in principle, why an institution, once established, should not last as long as the human race. But in fact we know of no institution that has not broken down sooner or later; and the histories of institutions seem to display more conspicuous regularities after a breakdown than before it. If this observation is correct, the change observed is explicable as a consequence of a recession of the realm of reason and will and an extension of the realm of the subconscious—bringing with it, as this does, an extension of the realm of 'laws of Nature'.

In previous volumes of this book I took the history of the Hellenic Civilization and its relation to the subsequent Western Civilization as my 'model' for the histories of other representatives of the same species of society. In Hellenic history I analysed the post-breakdown phase of it as falling into three periods: a 'time of troubles' lasting for approxi-

---

succeeded in jumping clear of a standpoint that I have inherited from my ancestral religion.

[1] C. Trinkaus asks why the secession of the proletariat should not be regarded as being a movement of liberation and progress and integration (*Science and Society*, vol. xii, No. 1 (1948), p. 237). Why not, indeed?

[2] See p. 269.

mately four hundred years; a 'universal state' lasting for approximately another four hundred years; and an 'interregnum' lasting for approximately three hundred years, between the dissolution of the Hellenic Civilization in the western provinces of the Roman Empire and the emergence, in the same region, of a Western Christian Civilization— a society of the same species as its Hellenic predecessor, to which it is affiliated. Applying this model to the histories of other civilizations, I found the Hellenic-Western chronological pattern recurring clearly enough and often enough—so it seemed to me—to make me think of it as a specific pattern in the histories of civilizations in general. Now that I have replaced my former Hellenic-Western model by an Helleno-Sinic model,[1] I have, of course, to reconsider the chronological pattern that I derived originally from an analysis of my former Hellenic-Western model.

As far as I can see, an approximately four-hundred-years-long 'time of troubles' still stands as the usual immediate sequel to a breakdown.[2] On the other hand, I feel less certain now about my supposed four-hundred-years' span for the duration of universal states. The Ch'in-Han first bout of the universal state in China did have this duration, like the Roman Empire in the West. But the Roman Empire itself lasted about two hundred years longer in its more important central and eastern provinces than it lasted in its outlying western provinces; and, in re-examining my list of universal states, I find too many exceptions to my supposed normal span of four hundred years to allow this supposed norm to stand. As for the three-hundred-years-long interregnum between the dissolution of the Hellenic civilization in the west and the emergence of Western Christendom there, the application of a Chinese or a Helleno-Sinic model suggests that the course taken by events in the West was not the most usual one.[3] Usually the end of the first bout of a universal state has been followed, not by the dissolution of the civilization politically embodied in it and by a consequent inter-civilizational interregnum, but by a less violent social and cultural break. The usual sequel has been a bout of anarchy followed by a revival of the previous universal state. This is the pattern, not only of Chinese history after the fall of the Ch'in-Han Empire, but also of Eastern Orthodox Christian history after the fall of the Roman Empire in its central and eastern provinces. Other instances of this pattern have been noticed in this volume in the passage just cited. This pattern is strongly pronounced and is also frequent in its occurrence. At the same time, there does not seem to be any correspondingly exact chronological regularity. The lengths of the alternating bouts of anarchy and oecumenical order seem to vary.

The results of my reconsiderations in this field may be summed up as follows. It still seems to me that there is a common pattern in the post-breakdown phases of the histories of those civilizations that have broken

---

[1] See pp. 197–204.
[2] This four-hundred-years-long 'time of troubles' has sometimes been punctuated by a first attempt at a universal state. In the Hellenic 'time of troubles' this role was played by Alexander's abortive empire; in the Sumeric 'time of troubles' it was played by the less ephemeral empire of the dynasty of Agade.　　　[3] See pp. 186–97.

down up to date; and I also still think that the first stock episode after the breakdown in this recurring pattern of events—namely the bout of anarchy that I have called a 'time of troubles'—has had an approximately uniform duration as well as an approximately uniform plot. But I no longer think that this uniformity of duration extends to the subsequent episodes in the common pattern of disintegration as this has now been revised in the light of my replacement of my former Hellenic-Western model by a new Helleno-Sinic one.

Thus I have retained my previous belief that the sequel to the breakdowns of civilizations follows a standard pattern, but I have abandoned my previous belief that it also has a standard time-span. I have never believed that there is either a standard pattern or a standard time-span for the history of a civilization that has not yet broken down. I have never believed, either, that every civilization is predestined to break down. Consequently I have never believed that there is a uniform maximum time-span for the duration of all societies of the species 'civilizations', as there is for all specimens of any species of living organism. On this issue I always have differed, and still do differ, *in toto*, from that great man of genius Oswald Spengler. I am surprised to find Philip Bagby following Spengler to the length of suggesting[1] that 'we may say, with a fair degree of certainty, that the whole process of development from the beginnings of a civilization to the beginnings of a "universal state" . . . takes between a thousand and fifteen hundred years', and even looking forward to being able eventually to pin the standard duration of this period down to something 'between 1100 and 1300 years'. I do not find Bagby's arguments in favour of this unqualified chronological determinism convincing. The calculations by which he arrives at this result are, it seems to me, of the 'Procrustean' kind of which I, too, have been accused.

21. CREATIVE AND DOMINANT MINORITIES

By a creative minority I mean a ruling minority in which the creative faculty in human nature finds opportunities for expressing itself in effective action for the benefit of all participants in the society. I do not believe that, in a creative minority, there is a higher percentage of creative individuals, endowed with a larger fund of creativity on the average, than there is in any other section of the population. What distinguishes a creative minority, and wins goodwill towards it among participants in society outside the creative minority's ranks, is that it is a ruling minority in which the creative faculty has free play and in which it is exercised in the public interest.

By a dominant minority I mean a ruling minority that rules less by attraction and more by force. As I see it, this change in emphasis—from ruling mainly by attraction to ruling mainly by force—occurs when a creative minority, in my sense of the term, loses its opportunities for creative action. It may forfeit these by its own fault, by falling into one of the snares by which the path of creativity is beset. It may be tempted

1 In *Culture and History*, p. 221.

by success either into losing its head or into resting on its oars. Alternatively, a creative minority may be deprived of its opportunities for creative action by changes in social and cultural circumstances for which the representatives of the minority have had little or no moral responsibility. In whichever of these ways the minority may have lost its opportunities for creative action, it will arouse resentment, opposition, and resistance among the rest of the population if it tries to cling to power by force after having ceased to perform for society as a whole the services that previously made its rule acceptable.

On reconsideration, I think that, in previous volumes, I have painted the contrast between the 'creative' and the 'dominant' phase in the rule of a minority in too strong colours. I have painted it white in its 'creative' phase and black in its 'dominant' phase, whereas the true colours are a lighter and a darker shade of grey. Perhaps I also drew too sharp a dividing line between a ruling minority of either kind and the rest of the population. I have discussed these points earlier in this volume,[1] and therefore need not go into them further here.

22. THE PROLETARIAT

I defined my usage of this word at an early point in this Study.[2] I meant, and mean, by it 'any social element or group which in some way is "in" but not "of" any given society at any given stage of such society's history'. I have, I believe, kept to this usage consistently. It is based on the literal sense of the Latin word *proletarii*, and it coincides with the usage of this word in the terminology of Roman constitutional law. On the other hand, it does not coincide with the celebrated Marxian modern usage. In this Marxian usage 'the proletariat' means a labouring population employing a technique called 'machine industry' under a regime called 'capitalism'. People working under these conditions may, of course, be proletarians in my sense too. Many, indeed perhaps most, of them were that in Marx's and Engels' generation. Today probably a majority of the World's industrial workers have ceased to be proletarians in my sense through having acquired a stake in society. In 1961 this would, I should guess, be the situation in most parts of the Soviet Union, as well as in most, though not in all, Western countries. On the other hand, the proletariat in my sense includes people of many kinds who are not proletarians in the Marxian sense. It includes anyone who is penalized in any respect—economically, politically, or socially. A person's material standard of living is not the criterion. A pauper freeman—e.g. an Egyptian peasant—is a proletarian, but so too is a Roman magnate's confidential slave who has been permitted by his master to accumulate a large *peculium*; for the well-to-do slave is penalized by being kept in a sub-human juridical status. But a millionaire can still be proletarian, even if he is a freeman: for instance, a New Yorker Jewish millionaire who is a citizen of the United States but whose candidature for election to membership in a club has been rejected because he is a Jew and not because there is anything personally objectionable about

[1] On pp. 124–7 and 148–50.   [2] In i. 41, footnote 3.

him. The term, as I use it, includes all 'displaced persons' (refugees, exiles, and deportees), however highly gifted and distinguished; all mercenary soldiers, however highly paid and however formidable, from Cyrus the Younger's ten thousand Greeks to the French Crown's Swiss Guard; all subject peoples (e.g. the Bantu in South Africa and Kenya); all insurgents (e.g. those that, at the time when I was writing these words, were under arms in Cyprus and in Algeria), so long as they have not yet turned the tables on the powers that be, as the Coelesyrian Jewish insurgents against the Seleucid monarchy did in the second century B.C.; and all barbarians beyond the pale, such as the Pathan tribesmen in the unadministered areas of Western Pakistan used to be before the Pakistan Government began to convert them, by methods of civilization, into voluntary citizens of the country.

23. HIGHER RELIGIONS

By higher religions I mean religions designed to bring human beings into direct communion with absolute spiritual Reality as individuals, in contrast to earlier forms of religion that have brought them only into indirect communion with It through the medium of the particular society in which they have happened to be participants.[1] Religion, in these earlier forms, is an integral part of the culture of some particular society. On the other hand the higher religions have broken—some partially, some completely—out of the configuration of the particular cultures in which they originated. They have become separate systems of specifically religious culture, in a state of tension with the systems of secular culture with which they have parted company. The advent of a higher religion thus brings with it the distinction—previously unknown —between 'religious' and 'secular', 'spiritual' and 'temporal', 'sacred' and 'profane'.

A religion cannot be extricated from the non-religious elements in culture without being divorced from the society that carries these non-religious elements on its network of relations between people. But no form of culture, secular or religious, can subsist without a social setting; and therefore the adherents of a higher religion cannot assert its independence of secular culture without at the same time incorporating it in an independent society. Every higher religion is carried on a network of social relations of its own.[2] This is a specific form of society, distinct from both civilizations and pre-civilizational societies. A name is needed for a society of this religious species, and it would be convenient if we could label it 'a church'. I have sometimes used the word 'church' in this wide sense; but this usage has been contested by several of my critics, and they are, I think, right. The word 'church' implies a unified ecclesiastical government, and this is possessed by perhaps no more than two of the extant higher religions: the Tantric Mahayana and the Roman Catholic denomination of Christianity. The Christian churches of the Eastern Orthodox and the Western Protestant Episcopalian

[1] A fuller definition has already been given on pp. 83–84.
[2] See p. 84.

denomination are respectively in communion with each other without having any common organs of ecclesiastical government. The ecclesiastical organization of most other extant higher religions is still less formal and more loose.

24. UNIVERSAL STATES[1]

A state may be defined as a non-voluntary system of impersonal relations that is maintained partly by force exercised by a governing minority and partly by the consent, or at least the acquiescence, of this governing minority's subjects.[2] I cannot think of any state in which either of these bases of state authority has been completely lacking, and there are countless historical examples of states being wrecked either by the government's failing to muster the minimum necessary amount of force or by their subjects' ceasing to have the minimum necessary feeling of obligation to obey the powers that be.

If a state may be defined in these terms, it is obvious that, up to date, there has never been a universal state in the literal sense of one whose government has exercised effective authority over the whole living generation of mankind in all the habitable lands and navigable seas and air levels of this planet.[3] At the same time it is also obvious that in our day, for the first time in history, human beings have it in their power to establish a world government. The less than world-wide empires of the past have mostly been established by military conquest; and the invention of atomic weapons has made it practicable now for some single local state to conquer and hold down the whole world. It is true that the cost, in terms of spiritual as well as material devastation, of conquering the World in an atomic war looks as if it would be prohibitively high; and this consideration is already acting as a perceptible deterrent to any impulses to try to impose political unity by the traditional military method. Military conquest, however, has never been the exclusive means by which empires have been established, and it may be doubted whether any of them could have been established by force alone, without the support of other agencies. The use of military force on a large scale would not be possible without the previous establishment of a well-developed system of communications, mental as well as physical; and the development of any such system has many effects besides that of enabling staff officers to solve their logistical problems. Long before it has reached the point at which it is of practical military

---

[1] This subject has been touched upon already on pp. 186–204.

[2] It is not easy to draft a definition of the state that distinguishes it from another ancient institution: slavery. The distinction would be drawn if one could say that slavery is 'a non-voluntary system of personal relations resting wholly upon force'. But slavery, too, can be a system of impersonal relations when it takes the form of labour on plantations or in factories or the form of public penal servitude; and, on the other hand, when slavery is domestic, it may be maintained partly, or even mainly, by consent on the slave's part. In the Roman and the Islamic versions of the institution there was not much difference in practice between the relations of the head of a family with his slaves and his relations with his children.

[3] This is, perhaps, what G. Masur has in mind when he dismisses my concept of 'universal states' as being illogical (the *Historische Zeitschrift*, Band 177 (1954), pp. 521–2).

value, it will have gone far towards producing a consensus of feelings, minds, and wills by making people familiar with each other across the traditional barriers between different societies and different cultures. Without some such consensus on the part of its potential subjects, a state, even on the smallest scale, could never be established and certainly could not be maintained.

The particular point of consensus that has made the establishment and maintenance of relatively large empires psychologically possible has been a recognition, however reluctant, that a continuance of war, revolution, and anarchy in a crescendo movement is a greater evil than the forfeiture of cherished peculiarities such as national states, religions, languages, and other national manners and customs. In our world in our time we can see this recognition gaining ground, and this time over a literally world-wide field. It is true that non-Western subject peoples are asserting claims to national independence as against the less than world-wide Western colonial empires that, between them, have been ruling over so large a part of the human race in recent times. But these revolts of the previously subject majority against Western rule are being made in the name of Western political and moral principles, and the formerly subject non-Western peoples that have already achieved national independence are all using their newly won power of self-determination to Westernize their social structures and their cultural configurations of their own accord. In doing this, they are laying the foundations for a single world-wide society and for a uniform world-wide culture that will take its first shape within a Western-made framework—though, no doubt, it will become less specifically Western in complexion as all the cultural heritages of all the extant societies come to be the common possession of the whole of mankind. This progressive cultural and social unification of the whole human family is bound to find some expression on the political plane. The political expression need not necessarily take the form of a central government of the kind that has been established in the past as the result of less than world-wide wars of conquest. The most likely nucleus of a future political world order is perhaps a central authority exercising an effective world-wide control over the use of atomic energy and thereby making it impossible for any of the atomically armed local states to attack and conquer the rest.

The present movement of world affairs makes the study of past empires a matter of practical as well as theoretical interest for us in our generation. The empires that have most significance as pointers to the possible destiny of mankind are not those established by local states within the body social of some single civilization, such as the recent colonial empires of Britain, France, the Netherlands, Portugal, Spain, and other modern Western local states, or the similar empires carved out of the carcass of the Achaemenian Empire by the successors of Alexander the Great. They are those that, like the Roman Empire in the Hellenic World or the Maurya Empire in India or the Ch'in-Han Empire in China, have given political unity to the whole, or almost the whole, of the domain of an entire civilization at a stage when this civilization has been brought within sight of dissolution by a series of wars and revolutions on a progressively increasing scale of spiritual and material destructiveness.

None of these empires, up to date, has been a 'universal state' in the literal sense, and John Strachey has suggested[1] that 'single state' would be a more informative label for them. The word 'single' would, indeed, convey the important historical fact that the means by which peace and order have been established has been the replacement of a number of warring local states by one state embracing all their former territories and populations. The word 'universal' does, however, convey the further important historical fact that these states have actually been world-wide—not objectively, but in the significant subjective sense that they have looked and felt world-wide to the people living under their regime. It is, of course, one of the radical infirmities of human nature that each of us is under constant temptation to equate himself and his society and his culture with the Universe. He will be particularly prone to fall into this illusion when the society in which he is a participant happens, as it does in these cases, to be the carrier of a civilization, since, until the advent of the higher religions, civilizations were the finest, as well as the most widely extended, configurations of culture that mankind had achieved so far. The Ch'in-Han, Maurya, and Roman empires, and all the other known representatives of the same kind of state, did seem, to a majority of their respective subjects, to embrace all peoples in the World that were of any account. The Hellenes thought of the Roman Empire as being 'the entire inhabited world' (*hê oikoumenê*); the Chinese thought of the Ch'in-Han Empire and its successive avatars as being 'all that is under Heaven' (*T'ien Hsia*), or, short of that, as being 'the middle kingdom', surrounded by a superfluous fringe of barbarians and hardly less barbarous exponents of civilizations other than the Chinese.[2]

Most 'universal states', in my sense of the term, have, in fact, been heralds of a potential world-state. Besides being 'single states' from the standpoint of participants in the particular civilization whose domain has been united politically by one of the states of this kind, most of them have included portions of the domain of one or more other civilizations, and also portions of their own society's barbarian hinterlands. Moreover, in the course of time, their originally heterogeneous subjects have tended to acquire a sense of solidarity with each other as children of a common human family whose unity has been symbolized for them politically in the world-state in which they have had the good fortune to have been living. From our point of view in our day, the historic 'universal states' may be seen, in retrospect, as having been so many preparatory exercises for the eventual establishment of a literal universal state which, though still unachieved, is now, at last, no longer below our horizon.

K. D. Erdmann[3] correctly observes that my concept of a 'universal

---

[1] In an unpublished letter.
[2] The case of Japan under the Tokugawa regime has been discussed on p. 207, footnote 2.
[3] In *Archiv für Kulturgeschichte*, xxxiii. Band, Heft 2 (1951), pp. 224–5.

state' was originally derived from an Hellenic model, and he contends that this model—i.e. a 'universal state' on the pattern of the Roman Empire—is not applicable to empires imposed by conquerors who, in their culture, have been aliens from the standpoint of the society to which they have given political unity. Presumably Erdmann has in mind such 'universal states' on my list as the Mongol and Manchu empires in China, the Mughal and British empires in India, the Spanish Empire in Mexico and Peru, and the Ottoman Empire in Orthodox Christendom (apart from Russia), and is contrasting these with the Muscovite Empire in Russia, the Aztec and Inca empires in pre-Columbian America, the Maurya and Gupta empires in India, and the Ch'in-Han, T'ang-Sung, and Ming empires in China, as well as the Roman Empire in the Hellenic World.

No doubt it is true that the resistance always aroused by empire-builders is intensified when, in addition to being enemies of a traditional parochialism, they also present themselves as aliens who do not appreciate or even understand the traditional common culture of the communities that they are subjugating. But the last column in my table of universal states,[1] in which I have noted the provenance of their respective founders, continuators, and restorers, brings out the truth that the founders have been 'metropolitans', from the heart of the world to which they have given political unity, still less frequently than they have been 'aliens' in the sense of representatives of some other civilization. Usually they have been either barbarians, from just outside the pale of the society that they have united politically, or else 'marchmen', from just inside it. The Romans, for instance, were marchmen of the Hellenic World, and so were the Illyrians, who re-established the Roman Empire after its first collapse. The Ch'in were marchmen of the Sinic World; the successive Theban founders of the Egyptiac Middle Empire and New Empire were marchmen of the Egyptiac World; the Incas were marchmen of the Andean World; the Akkadian founders and the Babylonian Amorite restorers of the Empire of Sumer and Akkad were marchmen of the Sumero-Akkadian World, and so were the Chaldaeans who restored this empire again, some eleven hundred years after the time of Hammurabi.

The second founders of the Empire of Sumer and Akkad were 'metropolitans', and so were the Maurya founders and the Gupta restorers of a universal state in India. The Mauryas and the Guptas both came from Magadha; Ur-Nammu came from Ur. But 'metropolitan' founders of universal states have been rare exceptions, and it is not difficult to see the reason for this. Communities in the heart of a society's domain are likely to have played prominent parts in its history since an early date, and later generations of their human representatives are therefore likely to have accumulated arresting memories of the community's past glories as a parochial state. Such memories are an incubus; and people who are haunted by them are thereby inhibited from casting themselves for a new role that will enable them to cope with a new situation. The people who find no difficulty in adapting

[1] Printed in vi. 327 and in vii. 769.

themselves to a new situation are those who have no anachronistic memories to paralyse them. In view of this it is not surprising that the Hellenic universal state should have been founded, not by the Spartans or by the Athenians, but by the Romans, and the Sinic universal state not by Ch'i but by Ch'in. On the contrary, it is surprising that the second founder of the Empire of Sumer and Akkad should have come from Ur and not from Asshur, and that the non-alien founders and restorers of a universal state in India should have come from Bihar and not from the Panjab.

Marchmen are not aliens, but they are the nearest thing to being this that it is possible to be for any individual or community within a civilization's pale. Accordingly, marchmen empire-builders draw on themselves, from their metropolitan subjects, a large measure of the odium that is incurred by empire-builders who are complete outsiders. After the Romans had established an unchallengeable ascendancy over the rest of the Hellenic World in the course of the years 218–168 B.C., it took the Hellenic public more than a quarter of a millennium to reconcile itself to Roman rule, and nearly a hundred years more passed before an Hellenic man of letters with a Graeco-Roman name, Publius Aelius Aristeides, saluted the Roman Empire, in his classic encomium *In Romam*, as the beneficent universal state that had providentially saved the Hellenic World when it had been on the verge of self-destruction. As for the Ch'in regime in China, it made itself so odious that it survived for only fourteen years after its redoubtable founder had overthrown the last of the other independent states of the Sinic World, and for only three years after the founder's death. And, though, by that time, a universal state had become such an imperious necessity for the Sinic Civilization that it had immediately to be rehabilitated, it is significant that it was deliberately reconstituted on ostensibly different lines, and that the founder of this new and far longer-lived Han regime was a peasant from the interior.

The Persians, again, made their entry into civilization as marchmen of the Sumero-Akkadian World and as proselytes to its civilization; yet this civilization's contemporary representatives the Babylonians revolted against the Achaemenian 'Realm of the Lands' again and again; were finally crushed without ever being reconciled; and eventually welcomed Alexander the Great as a liberator. The Egyptians, for whom the Persians were outright aliens, did not react against them more vigorously than the Babylonians did. The Romans, too, were outright aliens for the Egyptians, Jews, Syrians, and other non-Hellenic peoples south-east of Taurus who had been forcibly incorporated in the Hellenic World by Alexander and had afterwards been forcibly prevented by Alexander's Roman successors from breaking away from it. When they did at last succeed, in the course of the fifth, sixth, and seventh centuries of the Christian Era, in shaking off Roman rule, their long-repressed resentment burst out as furiously as the Eastern Orthodox Christian peoples' resentment against Ottoman rule when they succeeded in shaking this off in the nineteenth and twentieth centuries.[1]

---

[1] In both these cases the successful insurgent movements found their inspiration in

In the light of this analysis, Erdmann's distinction between universal states of indigenous origin and those of alien origin turns out, I should say, not to have the significance that Erdmann attaches to it. All universal states have provoked both resentment and gratitude in different quantities at different stages; and, though the differences between their respective experiences in this matter have been great, they have been not more than differences of degree. The criterion by which universal states should be appraised and classified is not the provenance of their founders; it is the service that they have performed for their subjects.

25. UNIVERSAL CHURCHES

Like the historic 'universal states', the historic 'universal churches' have been universal, so far, not in the literal meaning of the word, but in the belief and expectation of their adherents. They have been the institutional vehicles of missionary religions whose exponents have set out to convert the whole of mankind. The vigour and success of their missionary work has been proportionate to the degree in which their adherents have succeeded in changing over from a traditional national outlook to a revolutionary oecumenical one.[1]

A generic application of the word 'church' is convenient, but is perhaps misleading, for the reasons that have been suggested already.[2]

26. SCEPTICISM

I have already defined my usage of this word in this volume.[3] I mean by it, not disbelief in the human intellect's capacity to apprehend Reality, but disbelief in the existence of any alleged element in Reality, or aspect of it, that cannot be apprehended by reasoning. In this usage 'scepticism' is a synonym for 'rationalism', which brings out 'rationalism's negative side.

27. RATIONALISM

I have already defined my usage of this word, too, in this volume.[4] I mean by it a belief in the human intellect's capacity to apprehend Reality, coupled with a disbelief in the validity of any alleged knowledge that has not been, and could not have been, acquired in the first place, and subsequently verified, by reasoning.

28. AGNOSTICISM

I have already defined my usage of this word, too, in this volume.[5] I mean by it a recognition and acknowledgement of ignorance about

new ideologies. The Greeks and Serbs revolted from the Ottoman Empire and against Islam in the name of modern Western nationalism; the Egyptians and Syrians revolted against the Roman Empire and against the 'Melchite' ('Imperialist') version of Christianity in the successive names of Nestorian Christianity, Monophysite Christianity, and Islam.   [1] See pp. 84 and 85–88.   [2] On pp. 307–8.
[3] On p. 69, footnote 1.   [4] On p. 72, footnote 3.
[5] On p. 98, footnote 2.

Reality, not in so far as the human intellect is able to apprehend Reality by reasoning, but about Reality beyond the limits of the human intellect's reach through the operations of which it is capable. In regard to this unknown possible sphere, or dimension, of Reality, rationalism, as I have defined rationalism, is dogmatically sceptical. The rationalist's stand is accurately described, in caricature, in words that are put into Benjamin Jowett's mouth in a celebrated rhyme: 'What I don't know is not knowledge.' The agnostic agrees with the rationalist in holding that what I do know *is* knowledge, but holds, in opposition to the rationalist, that what I do not and cannot 'know'—in the sense of 'apprehend by reasoning'—may, nevertheless, be real, and, what is more, may be the essence of Reality and the hidden key to the full understanding of those fragments of it that the human reason can grasp. While agreeing with the rationalist that we cannot know the unknowable, the agnostic does not think that our knowledge, so far as this extends, warrants a denial of the possibility that human beings may receive genuine intimations of the unknowable through non-intellectual channels—for instance, those channels, whatever they may be, that are the founts of poetry and of prophetic vision. The agnostic recognizes that the genuineness of such intimations cannot be 'proved' by reasoning; but, for this very reason, he holds, as against the dogmatic rationalist, that it also cannot be 'disproved' by reasoning. I have called the agnostic in my sense of the word a 'trans-rationalist', because he goes with the rationalist all the way that the rationalist goes, but does not believe that the limits of the human reason's reach are necessarily the limits of the human soul's possibilities of understanding. A more familiar synonym for 'agnostic' in my sense would be 'Platonist'.

VIII. THE RELATION BETWEEN MAN AND HIS ENVIRONMENT

IN a previous chapter[1] I have taken note of criticisms of my practice (one not peculiar to me) of treating Man and his environment as two distinct entities. I have agreed that, in reality, they constitute one indivisible whole, and that it is a misrepresentation of Reality to draw the distinction between them. But, while admitting this, I have made the proviso that we must continue to distinguish them from each other if we are to continue to study the monolithic reality that is analysed, for 'operational' purposes, into these two components. 'It is only in the interaction of Man and his environment that the basic elements of history can be found.'[2] At the same time I have taken Spate's point that 'the facts of geography are the facts as they are approached'.[3] The term

[1] Chapter VI, pp. 146–8.
[2] M. R. Cohen: *The Meaning of Human History*, p. 171.
[3] O. H. K. Spate in *The Geographical Journal*, vol. cxviii, Part 4 (December, 1952), p. 419, quoted on p. 147.

environment refers always to a body of facts relative to a particular focus or perspective.'[1]

An objectively identical geographical 'set-up' will offer a promising environment to one group of human beings, whose social structure and cultural configuration put it within their power to turn this particular geographical 'set-up' to account, while it will offer only a bleak and niggardly environment, or no environment at all, to other groups with other organizations and equipments. These other groups may be at opposite extremes of the social and cultural scale from each other. They may be either too poorly equipped or too demanding in their expectations to make anything of what might be a golden opportunity for some third party. For instance, both a New York business man and a Palaeolithic hunter or food-gatherer would be in danger of starving if marooned on a derelict Javanese paddyfield. Neither of them would be able to make anything of what had been a cornucopia for a rice-cultivating Javanese peasant. Though one cannot in practice treat Man's environment as being indistinguishable from Man himself, one can and must regard the potentialities of a geographical 'set-up' as being relative to a particular human group's capacity for making something of them.[2]

This point has been made by Spate apropos of Man's relation to non-human nature; but it is equally pertinent to Man's relation to his fellow human beings. A human being's environment can be analysed into two sectors, the geographical and the social. This analysis, like all analyses, may be misleading. 'The environment of every human being and the context of every human action contains human and non-human elements inextricably intertwined.'[3] Yet the distinction is also perhaps useful and certainly necessary. In any case it is true of the social, no less than of the geographical, sector of Man's environment that the facts 'are the facts as they are approached'. An objectively identical social 'set-up' will offer a promising environment to one individual,[4] or to one group or class of people, while others will be able to make little or nothing of it. The potentialities will be relative to the character, ability, social and cultural heritage, education (in the broadest sense), and personal experience of each individual who finds himself in this situation.

If we accept this point, it raises a question. Suppose that we had an exhaustive knowledge of both the geographical or social 'set-up' and the person or people encountering it: a knowledge, that is to say, which covered everything in each of the two parties that was relevant to the encounter between them: Should we then be able to predict the outcome of this encounter? I myself do not believe that we should. I believe that necessity, in the sense of a predetermined and therefore potentially predictable nexus of cause and effect, is not all-pervasive in the structure of Reality. I believe that Reality has in it a vein of something genuinely unpredetermined and therefore intrinsically unpredictable.

---

[1] Cohen, op. cit., p. 171.
[2] This has been observed not only by Spate but also by M. R. Cohen, op. cit., pp. 160–3.
[3] Cohen, op. cit., p. 171.
[4] 'A single human being is the ultimate "environed unit"' (H. and M. Sprout: *Man-Milieu Relationship Hypothesis in the Context of International Politics*, p. 18).

At the inanimate level this can perhaps be described only negatively as a vein of indeterminacy. At the human level, in beings endowed with a measure of consciousness, reasoning power, and will, the same vein displays itself as freedom of choice. This freedom is not, of course, absolute. It is limited by the pressure of external forces, non-human and human, that are not under the control of the human party to the encounter. It is also limited by the spiritual history, up to date, of the person to whom the choice is offered. As Bagby points out, in the train of many previous students of ethics, human freedom is not non-determination; it is self-determination.[1] 'We choose what we prefer; it is meaningless to say that we can choose what we do not prefer.'[2] Indeed, if we could, it is difficult to see what would distinguish human choice from the sheer senseless haphazard indeterminacy that is the form apparently taken by non-necessity when this displays itself in inanimate nature. Thus human freedom is in any case limited. But its apparent play, within these limits, raises the question whether it is genuine as far as it goes or whether it is altogether illusory.

I myself believe that it is genuine within its apparent limits. I also believe that the occasions on which it comes into play are laid bare by the 'heuristic' intellectual operation of mentally dissecting an indivisible reality into two entities, 'Man' and 'environment', that have encounters with each other. In laying bare these occasions of freedom, this particular mental dichotomy does, I believe, bring to light a genuine—and, if genuine, evidently most important—feature in the nature of Reality. Choice means the creation of something new.[3] In the first volume of this book I illustrated the ideas of novelty, creation, and choice from mythology,[4] and I declared my conviction that, on these points, mythology is illuminating.[5] In thus avowing myself to be a believer in an at least partial freedom of human wills, I was, of course, taking sides in an ancient but so far undecided philosophical controversy.

In another chapter of the same volume[6] I tried to prove my case. I tried to demonstrate, by examples, that the challenge of an identical 'set-up' did not invariably evoke an identical response from identically endowed and equipped human beings to whom this 'set-up' offered a potential environment. If this attempted demonstration of mine had held water, it would, I should say, have proved that, in an encounter, something comes into play that is not present in the previous 'make-up' of either party to the encounter, and that this intervention of something new is the decisive factor in determining the outcome. I am still convinced that this is the truth, but I have also been convinced, partly by new archaeological evidence, and partly by criticisms from Spate,[7] that I have not succeeded in giving a cogent demonstration of the validity of my tenet.

For example, I tried to demonstrate[8] that the particular potential

---

[1] *Culture and History*, p. 63.   [2] Ibid., p. 65.
[3] The concept of 'creation', which involves the meaning of the word 'new', has been discussed on pp. 252–4.   [4] i. 271–99.
[5] i. 299–302.   [6] i. 249–71.
[7] In *Toynbee and History*, pp. 287–304, and in *The Geographical Journal*, vol. cxviii, Part 4 (December, 1952), pp. 406–28.   [8] In i. 256–8.

environment offered by the Nile in Egypt was not the positive factor to which the genesis of the Egyptiac Civilization was due. I argued this by citing what I then believed to be evidence that there were other river valleys, offering potential environments similar to that offered by the lower Nile valley, in which no civilization had ever come to birth, though some of them had eventually been turned to account by pioneers of civilizations that had come to birth elsewhere. I observed that the lower valley of the Tigris and Euphrates did offer a similar potential environment; that here an independent civilization, similar to and more or less coeval with the Egyptiac, had come to birth; and that this was evidence, so far as it went, in favour of the thesis that civilizations are products of geographical 'set-ups'. But, taking a cue from Eduard Meyer,[1] I went on to say that no independent civilization had come to birth in the Jordan valley, in the lower Mississippi valley and delta, or in the valleys of the Colorado and the Rio Grande. Apropos of the Jordan valley, I quoted Meyer's statement that

'the Jordan valley between Betše'an and Pella, the Ghor, a broad deep rift between mountain walls, with a glowing hot climate, lay completely desolate [in the sixteenth century B.C.] and has remained as good as uninhabited to-day'.

I then quoted Meyer's judgement that

'much light is thrown on national character (*Volkscharakter*)[2] by the fact that here the attempt has never been made—as it has been made under the substantially similar conditions in the Nile valley—to take advantage of the soil and to render it productive by systematic irrigation. It is only when we draw this comparison that we become fully able to appreciate the energy with which the Egyptians have made their country the most productive agricultural country in the World for thousands of years on end.'

On reconsideration, I do not think I am to blame for having accepted Eduard Meyer's statement and judgement at the time. I was writing my first volume in 1930, two years after the publication of the volume of Meyer's book from which I was quoting, sixteen years before the publication of Nelson Glueck's *The River Jordan*, and twenty-two years before the beginning of Miss Kenyon's work at Jericho. The point that Meyer was making, as I interpret the passage, was that, notwithstanding the formidable heat in a rift valley far below sea-level, it is likely that the prehistoric ancestors of the historical Egyptians would have made of the Jordan valley something like what they did make of the lower Nile valley if the bluffs on which they had settled had happened to be those overlooking the Ghor and not those overlooking the section of the Nile valley that their historical labours eventually transformed into Upper Egypt. Here Meyer was showing an

[1] In *Geschichte des Altertums*, vol. ii (1), 2nd ed. (Stuttgart and Berlin 1928, Cotta), p. 96, and in vol. i (1) 4th ed. (Stuttgart and Berlin 1921, Cotta), p. 65.
[2] As I mentioned in quoting Meyer in the first volume of this book, I myself would attribute the successful human response to the challenge of the lower Nile valley, not to a hypothetical fixed 'national character', but to a particular human effort to cope with a particular emergency.

intuition which was not put off the scent by his (to my mind, unwarrantable and mistaken) postulate of a fixed Egyptian national character. He was showing surprise that the Jordan valley should not (as he believed) have been turned to account by human enterprise, in spite of its daunting climate. Accepting the contrast, as Meyer had stated it, between the respective histories of the Jordan valley and the Nile valley, I interpreted this as indicating that the outcome of an encounter between human enterprise and a difficult geographical environment has, in at least one pair of instances, been non-uniform, and that it is therefore intrinsically unpredictable. In the light of the state of knowledge at the time, I do not think that either Meyer's statement, or my reading of its significance, was unreasonable.

Meyer, however, has been taken to task by a great scholar of my generation, W. F. Albright, in a book published in 1949,[1] at a date when Glueck had carried out his explorations and had published the results.

'In 1928 [Albright writes], the greatest ancient historian of modern times, Eduard Meyer, wrote, two years after visiting the Jordan valley for the first time in his life—unfortunately in the early autumn—that the Jordan valley south of Beth-shan and Pella was absolutely barren, "burning hot between its mountain walls", and that no attempt had ever been made in pre-Roman times to make the soil productive by systematic irrigation! No one who reads Nelson Glueck's vivid account of the very same district . . . can fail to see how completely archaeological research has disproved this off-hand impression of the great historian.'[2]

This criticism of Meyer's dictum has been justified, more sensationally than Albright could have foreseen when he wrote and published it, by Miss Kenyon's subsequent discoveries at Jericho. So far from having been left undeveloped till the sixteenth century B.C. or till the Roman Age, the Jordan valley has been occupied and cultivated by irrigation for at least twice as long, up to date, as either the lower Nile valley or the lower valley of the Tigris and Euphrates. Miss Kenyon finds[3] that the beginnings of Jericho must have been not much later than the end of the pleistocene period—that is to say, not much later than 10,000 B.C. The Jordan valley has been cultivated, on and off, from that day to this, and the interruptions are attributed, by both Miss Kenyon and Dr. Albright, not to oscillations in the local climate, but to barbarian invasions from the eastern desert. In other words, the history of the Jordan valley, like the history of the Tigris–Euphrates valley, tells against, not for, my hypothesis that encounters between comparable parties under comparable conditions have not always had similar outcomes.

Spate has taken issue with me over this question of the significance of the Jordan valley's history, but here he, too, has gone astray—and this with less excuse, I should say, than I or Eduard Meyer had, since Spate published his two critiques of my work in 1952 and 1953 when both Glueck's and Albright's books were already accessible to him, and

---

[1] *The Archaeology of Palestine* (Harmondsworth 1949, Penguin).
[2] Albright, op. cit., pp. 251–2.   [3] K. Kenyon: *Digging up Jericho*, p. 75.

when the main findings of the excavations at Jericho were already public knowledge thanks to progress reports in the press. Yet Spate in 1952 and 1953 accepted Meyer's statement as correct, as I had accepted it in 1930–4. He, too, assumed that the Jordan valley had never been irrigated, and found the explanation of this in the climate of the Ghor and in the physiography of the Jordan valley, which he contrasts with the situation in Egypt.

'The Jordan . . . has only 1 per cent of the annual discharge of the Nile, with nothing comparable to the Nile flood regime, while its valley is far less well endowed than that of the Nile as regards both terrain (much of which is dissected) and soils. Many of these are coarse and porous and lie on terraces well out of reach of irrigation; to say nothing of the stimulating climate of a walled-in valley 1000 feet below sea-level. All Palestine has about 1000 cubic metres of water per inhabitant (about 1½ millions), against 5000 cubic metres of Nile water for each of Egypt's 17 million people.[1] The further comparisons with the Nile overlook the structure of its valley, in which coarser sediments are trapped in the upper basins, but not the fine basaltic silts brought by the Blue Nile. . . . The uniqueness of the Nile flood region and the Etesian winds, so important to the navigation which held together the Egyptian Civilization, are not so much as mentioned: perhaps for good reason; for, once the Nile is recognised as unique, one of Toynbee's main arguments against environmentalism falls to pieces forthwith.'[2] 'Even the Euphrates-Tigris environment is only generically, not specifically, akin to the Nilotic.'[3]

In these passages Spate shoots wide of the mark in one case and overplays his hand in another.

His ironical quip about 'the stimulating climate of a walled-in valley 1000 feet below sea-level' invites the crushing retort that, during the first 6,000 of the last 12,000 years, Jericho was, so far as we yet know, the only place in the World where a state of culture that might be called civilization was already a going concern. His facts and figures are beside the point. He has overlooked the obvious consideration that, after the Ghassulian period, i.e. since about 3500 B.C.,

'settlements in the Jordan valley were nearly always established at the entrances of the valleys, near perennial streams and springs which are still sources of water.'[4]

The cultivation of a piece of the Jordan valley by irrigation from the spring at Jericho antedates the cultivation of another piece of it at Ghassul by some five or six thousand years. The water that irrigated the fields round Ghassul may have been drawn from the Jordan, which flows between flat banks for those last few miles above its debouchure into the Dead Sea, but it may also have been drawn from a lateral stream that flowed out farther into the Jordan valley in the first half of the fourth millennium B.C. than at any time since. The abandonment of Ghassul may have been due to increasing difficulties in drawing the

[1] 'E. C. Willatts: "Some Geographical Factors in the Palestine Problem", in *The Geographical Journal*, vol. cviii (1947), pp. 145–79; reference at p. 166.'
[2] *The Geographical Journal*, vol. cit., p. 410.
[3] *Toynbee and History*, p. 299.   [4] Albright, op. cit., p. 69.

water, whatever its source, or it may have been due to a barbarian invasion.[1] In any case, archaeological exploration has now made it clear that the water with which the Jordan valley has been irrigated, on and off, for the last twelve thousand years has seldom, if ever, been drawn from the Jordan River. I took this point myself when, in July 1957, I had an opportunity of crossing the Jordan valley several times at different places, and visiting Jericho among other sites on its floor. By that date I could already have learnt the facts, as Spate could have learnt them in 1952, from authoritative accounts of them in accessible publications. Geographers, as well as historians, are fallible; and Spate's failure to keep his knowledge of the Jordan valley's history up to date would have been venial if the tone of his criticism had not been supercilious.

Again, Spate's assertion[2] that the geographical 'set-up' in the Nile valley is 'unique' seems to be unwarrantably sweeping. V. G. Childe points out[3] that the lower Tigris–Euphrates valley, too, was 'periodically inundated by floods', though he also notes[4] that these were not so regular or so well-timed for agricultural operations as the annual inundation of the Nile was, and that 'only the wide marshy delta offered the challenge and reward that had evoked the artificial environment of Sumerian cities. . . . South of Cairo the narrow valley through the barren desert plateaux has analogies, real but remote, with Sumer.' If the picture here drawn by Childe is correct, Egypt and Sumer, in their respective states of nature, had too much in common with each other to warrant our considering either of them to have been unique. Moreover, if Spate were right in claiming uniqueness for Egypt, we should have to conclude that what is unique about the Nile valley is what determined the birth of a civilization there, and consequently that the British school of diffusionists were right in holding that the genesis of civilization in Egypt was a unique event and that all the civilization that there has ever been, either in the Old World or in the New World, has been propagated by prospectors fanning out from an original base of operations in the unique Egyptian cradle of civilization.[5] By the years 1952–3, when Spate was writing the two papers from which I have been quoting, the progress of archaeological discovery was already pointing in other directions. It was proving that, in the Jericho oasis in the Jordan valley, civilization is twice as old as it is anywhere else in the World, not excluding the lower valleys of the Nile and the Tigris–Euphrates. And it was also showing that in the lower Nile valley, when the local Neolithic culture did at last blossom into civilization, it did so under a stimulus from an already achieved civilization in the lower Tigris–Euphrates valley. Thus, if it were true that the geographical 'set-up' in the lower Nile valley offered a 'unique' opportunity for transforming it into an environment for a civilization, this would have to be reconciled with the fact that the human occupants of other, in themselves less favourable, geographical 'set-ups' were the first in the race.[6]

---

[1] Albright, op. cit., loc. cit.
[2] In *Toynbee and History*, p. 300, as well as in *The Geographical Journal*, loc. cit.
[3] In *What Happened in History*, p. 89.   [4] Ibid., p. 113.
[5] A critique of this theory will be found in this book ‚i. 221–3.
[6] Spate himself, in the passages quoted above, has pointed out the advantages offered

However, my concern with Spate is, not to return his fire, but to follow out the second thoughts into which I have been stung by the stimulating shot with which he has peppered me. He has given me food for thought; for, though his criticism of my reading of the Jordan valley's history misses fire, he has made effective criticisms of my attempt[1] to reconstruct the state of the lower Nile valley as it was before Man cleared, drained, and cultivated it, on the analogy of the present state of the upper basin of the White Nile along the Bahr-al-Jabal and the Bahr-az-Zaraf.

'There is obviously a good deal in this, but is the emphasis on the severity of the challenge, one of Toynbee's leading motifs, really valid? Assuming that the ecological reconstruction is correct, the comparison of the valley bottom in Egypt with the swamps of the Bahr-el-Ghazal leaves out of the reckoning the all-important difference in scale between a strip of marsh 10 or 15 miles wide, which can actually be overlooked from the firm ground on either side (ground which provided settlement-sites with tool- and building-stone), and on the other hand vast swamps ten times as wide and with no compensating advantages. There is an obvious difference in tractability, not to mention the point already made about the river navigation, and later the accessibility of copper and other minerals lacking in the Sudan.'[2]

Spate also draws a telling contrast between the geographical 'set-up' in the Nile basin on the one hand and in the Colorado and Rio Grande basins on the other, in opposition to Eduard Meyer's thesis, adopted by me, that 'the great river valleys of America . . . could just as well have become centres of the development of higher civilization as the valleys of the Nile, Euphrates, and Hwangho'.

'Hardly any of the basin of the 1750 miles long Colorado has over 20 inches of rain; contrast this with the 40–80 inches of the Blue and White Nile catchments in Abyssinia and Uganda. The topography of the Nile and the Colorado basins is different in the extreme; the Colorado is much more broken, but there is nothing like the staggered series of tributaries above Khartoum, with the Blue Nile ponding back the White and prolonging the period of high water. The vegetation cover of the more humid parts of the Nile basin, and its lakes and marshes, are far more efficient regulators of run-off than the vegetation of the Colorado. In the Nile basin rainfall is either almost non-existent or falls fairly steadily in well-defined seasons; in the Colorado as a whole there is more rain than on the lower Nile, but much of it falls in irregular violent downpours, and erosion is intense. The Rio Grande approximates more nearly to the Colorado than to the Nile, though it is not a very close approximation. Neither the Colorado (obviously) nor the

by Upper Egypt as a site for the establishment of a civilization: an abundant water supply; a navigable river with a prevailing up-stream wind; a manageably limited area of potentially cultivable land to reclaim; a rocky rim, affording sites for habitation above flood-level and stone for making tools. Of these advantages, the Jordan valley offered the last two only; the lower Tigris–Euphrates basin the first only. The lower Tigris–Euphrates basin was so distant from sources of stone and metal that the pioneers on this vast expanse of alluvium were reduced to making their tools out of ultra-hard-baked clay in an age when the older seats of culture to the north were already using metal tools (R. J. Braidwood: *The Near East and the Foundations of Civilization*, p. 33). Yet Jericho, in the Jordan valley, won the race for civilization; Sumer came in second; Egypt came in only third.

[1] In i. 311–15.
[2] *The Geographical Journal*, vol. cit., p. 412. Cp. *Toynbee and History*, pp. 298 and 300–1.

Rio Grande offers anything like the potentialities for navigation which are found on the Nile, with its peculiar advantage of the Etesian winds blowing upstream; and the role of the river as a highway (which Toynbee does not so much as mention)[1] was only second to its value for irrigation in the development of Egyptian civilization.

'In both the Colorado and the Rio Grande there are doubtless some broad and general analogies to the Nile; but they are far from "offering the environmental conditions" of Egypt, and the differences are very significant from the cultural point of view. The most fundamental are that the Nile has a unique advantage in its flood-regime, and that in its Nile basin "the coarse stuff is caught in the sunken fault-block depressions into which the Upper Nile flows" (the fine and fertile basaltic silt of the Blue Nile passes on), while "the Tigris and the Colorado, fresh from the canyon, are ditch-chokers".'[2]

Thus Spate's pair of papers raises for me the question: Where have I gone wrong? In choosing river valleys as my field for investigation, did I make a good choice, and is the reason why the result has been unsatisfying, nevertheless, because, as Spate has shown, 'the essential step of detailed verification of hypothesis against fact has been sketchy'?[3] Or has my error lain in not taking account of all the elements in this 'set-up' and of their relations with each other? Or did I make a bad choice, in the sense that I chose a 'set-up' that was highly complex, when I could have found a simpler one, in which it might have been less difficult to make sure that one had isolated all the relevant elements and had taken adequate account of all of them in their mutual relations? Did I also make a bad choice in choosing a field in which we do not know enough about the several human parties to the encounter in the several different instances to be able to tell whether or not they were truly comparable in endowment and equipment at the time when their respective encounters with a river valley took place? Or is demonstration by this comparative method inherently impossible because, when one is dealing in terms of human beings and of geography, it is never possible to be sure that, in reconstructing the parties to the encounter in a number of different cases, one has really isolated properly comparable examples on either side?

I plead guilty to the charge of not having carried out a detailed verification on the lines that Spate indicates, and also to the charge that in any given case I have taken into consideration only one or two of the factors in the physical setting, and that 'the idea of the environment as an indivisible complex of all these factors . . . hardly ever appears'.[4] I leave it as an open question whether, if my investigation had not been inadequate, as it has been, in these two ways, my choice of river valleys for my field would have been a specially good or bad one. The fourth question is the fundamental one, and I will approach it by applying the same train of reasoning in two other fields, in order to counteract

---

[1] It is mentioned in vol. vii, p. 81, footnote 1.—A. J. T.

[2] *Toynbee and History*, pp. 299–300, quoting J. Russell Smith and M. Ogden Phillips: *North America* (New York 1942, Harcourt Brace), p. 599, footnote 16.

[3] *The Geographical Journal*, vol. cit., p. 410. Like a boomerang this criticism hits the critic as well as his target in their encounter over the Jordan valley.

[4] Ibid., vol. cit., p. 412.

the chance that the field of river valleys may have been an unusually complex one. Let us see how we fare if we apply the same method of reasoning to the opening up of the western basin of the Mediterranean in the last millennium B.C. and to the Western Industrial Revolution in the late eighteenth and early nineteenth centuries of the Christian Era.

In each of these two fields we have the advantage of dealing with a single 'set-up'—a geographical one in the first field and a socio-economic one in the second—which confronted all the human competitors alike and in which all of them alike were free to try their fortunes. Obviously this is, in itself, a simpler situation than that of the river valleys. In these the several competitors were confronted with different river valleys which were deemed by Eduard Meyer and by me to be uniform in all points relevant to their human occupants' encounters with them, but which, as Spate has shown, may have differed from each other in points that made all the difference to the circumstances of the encounter in each case. In the opening-up of the Western Mediterranean and in the making of the Industrial Revolution some of the human competitors were conspicuously more successful than others. If it were to be ascertained that the successful and unsuccessful competitors all had the same endowment and equipment for meeting what, in these two fields, really was an identical challenge, then it would have been demonstrated that, with uniformly identical conditions on both sides, the result of the encounter was different in different instances: in other words, that the relation between the factors in the encounter and the outcome of the encounter was not a relation of cause and effect.

In the opening up of the Western Mediterranean the Canaanite and the Hellenic competitors (leaving the enigmatic Etruscans out of account) were like each other in being people with a maritime tradition who were organized politically in city-states. Why, then, were some active, and others inactive, in the West Mediterranean maritime enterprise? The Phoenicians embarked on it, but not their neighbours the Philistines farther down the coast of Canaan, though the Philistines had been one of the 'Sea Peoples' who had made the Völkerwanderung in the early years of the twelfth century B.C. The Achaeans took part, but not the Eleans; the Locrians, Chalcidians, and Eretrians, but not the Boeotians; the Megarians, but not the Athenians; the Corinthians, but not the Argives; the Phocaeans, but not the Erythraeans; the Milesians, but not the Ephesians. We cannot explain why some of these communities did and others did not take part in the overseas enterprise by the hypothesis that those who abstained were relatively rich, and those who participated were relatively poor, in agricultural resources at home. This hypothesis will not fit the facts. It is true that the enterprising Phoenicians, Achaeans, Locrians, Corinthians, Phocaeans, and Milesians had comparatively small agricultural resources, and also true that the unenterprising Philistines, Boeotians, Argives, and Ephesians had comparatively large agricultural resources. But so had the enterprising Chalcidians and Eretrians (they kept on fighting each other for the rich Lelantine Plain in their homeland Euboea); and the Megarians, too, were not badly off for good agricultural land at home. On the other hand, the

Athenians, who were conspicuously unenterprising in this period of Hellenic history, though ultra-enterprising both before and after, were also conspicuously badly off, in all periods, for good agricultural land at home. In short, in the Hellenic case, at any rate, the enterprising group and the unenterprising group each included both agriculturally poor and agriculturally rich communities. Each of these groups, therefore, may be taken as being a fair sample of its society in that age. And, if this is granted, then we do seem to have, here, a case in which an identical challenge did evoke non-identical responses from different sets of recipients of the challenge who, at any rate on the average, had an identical social and cultural 'make-up'.

The same train of reasoning may be applied in the field of the modern Western Industrial Revolution. Eighteenth-century Western Europe was inhabited by a number of peoples with approximately the same endowment and the same equipment, cultural and technological. The intercourse between them at the time was active and intense, so that the achievements of any one of them could be adopted rapidly by any of the rest. Why, then, was the Industrial Revolution made in Britain, not in France, and in Belgium, not in Holland? And why was Germany, with the Ruhrgebiet and Upper Silesia in her pocket, so slow in pulling them out and turning their industrial potentialities to account? If we have made sure that the late-eighteenth-century West European peoples are truly comparable in all points that are relevant to the making of the Industrial Revolution or to the failure to make it, then we seem, here, to have another field in which uniform antecedents have been followed by diverse consequences.

But can we guarantee in this case that the endowments and equipments of the human parties were truly identical for the purpose of our particular comparison of them? I myself have cited[1] the well-known fact that 'in the eighteenth century, after the union of England and Scotland in A.D. 1707, Great Britain was the largest single free-trade area in the World', and have made, in my turn, the well-worn point that 'undoubtedly this was one of the principal reasons why Great Britain forged ahead of all her neighbours in her economic development before the eighteenth century was over'. In fact, closer inspection shows that, after all, the France of the *ancien régime* was not on a par with Great Britain in a matter that goes at least some way towards explaining why Great Britain, not France, was the European country in which the Industrial Revolution was made.

If we apply the moral of this conclusion to the geographical field of investigation, it justifies Spate's observation[2] that, in order to carry out my test under conditions in which its results would have validity, 'it would be essential to construct a model (in the economists' sense) in which all variables except physical setting are reduced to uniformities, and moreover the variations in the physical setting are themselves merely and strictly repetitive'. Spate and, indeed, any other critic will always be able to show that this requirement has not been met by me or, indeed, by any other inquirer.

[1] In iv. 170.   [2] In *The Geographical Journal*, vol. cit., p. 411.

Spate has, so it seems to me, done more than show that one particular believer in the genuineness of freedom has failed to prove his case. He has shown, I should say, that this case is intrinsically unprovable, and, if he has indeed shown this, he has also shown that, for the same reason, the determinist's case, too, is intrinsically unprovable.[1]

Spate's logical weapon is a penetrating and far-ranging one. It is a reminder that, when we are reasoning in terms, not of abstractions, but of phenomena, we are never in a position to guarantee that we have succeeded in insulating the relevant points, all of these, and nothing but these, and are consequently never in a position to guarantee that the entities which we are bringing into comparison are properly comparable for the purpose of our investigation. When the phenomenon with which we are concerned is an encounter, our difficulties are doubled, because here there are two sets of entities within each of which a uniformity, in all points relevant to the encounter, has to be guaranteed, as between the several examples in each set, if our reasoning is to hold good. On the one side we must be able to guarantee that the human individuals, communities, or societies that receive, and respond to, a challenge have identical endowments and equipments for dealing with the 'set-up' that offers itself as a potential environment for them. On the other side we must be able to guarantee that this 'set-up' offers itself in an identical form in each case. However far we may succeed in going in our search for sets of identical examples on either side, we shall never be

[1] In these two papers about my work Spate does not disclose where he himself stands in the controversy. He is critical of 'possibilism', which is, if I understand right, the doctrine of a school of geographers who hold that Man has a considerable latitude of choice in responding to the challenge of a geographical 'set-up'. As H. and M. Sprout put it, possibilists believe that the environment contains both opportunities and limitations—neither of them more than potential till Man takes action (op. cit., p. 40). 'Calculation of what is possible is not to be compared with prediction of what will be attempted' (ibid., p. 44). 'Possibilism does not provide any approach whatever to explanation or to prediction of motivation, choice, and decision' (ibid., p. 48). At the same time, it evidently does allow room for some measure of free play of human wills. In Spate's view 'it does not seem certain that "possibilism", as often understood (or misunderstood), is the automatic alternative to a rigorous environmentalism. There may be a middle term, which one might call "probabilism"' (*The Geographical Journal*, vol. cit., p. 419). Quoting Febvre's dictum that 'there are no necessities but everywhere possibilities', Spate comments that Febvre ought to have added: 'of which some are more possible than others' (ibid., p. 420). He finds that 'the emphasis on human initiative, though correct in itself, has sometimes been' allowed to go too far in practice, and that this leads to vagueness of thinking which is as deplorable as the narrowness induced by rigorous environmentalism (ibid., p. 420). He commits himself to concluding that 'we may find ourselves left with a considerable residue of determinism' (ibid., p. 423). The Sprouts concede (in op. cit., p. 31) that strict environmental determinism may explain some small part of human behaviour. P. Bagby (in *Culture and History*, p. 147) makes the point that the environment 'cannot be a fully determining factor, as some authors, notably Montesquieu and Buckle, have supposed. After all, Nature simply lies there passively. It is up to the human beings to decide whether, and in what way, they are going to use it.'

Spate recognizes that 'the problems of chance or free will or necessity must be faced in some fashion', because a geographer's 'attitude on this most fundamental general problem can hardly fail to have its effect upon his thinking on the more restricted question of geographical determinism versus possibilism' (ibid., p. 408). But he adds that, 'though these matters are not so irrelevant as may seem', it would be 'folly' on his part to proceed into them very far. 'It is not the function of the geographer to write philosophy' (ibid., p. 408). A philosopher might ask how, if one steered clear of philosophy, one would be able to inquire into human affairs at all, in either their geographical aspect or any other. Spate does go rather farther into the philosophical issue in a later paper with the title 'How Determined is Possibilism?' (*Geographical Studies*, vol. iv, No. 1 (1957), pp. 1–10). Here he looks for a *modus vivendi* between determinism and possibilism, inclining more towards determinism, but this not so far as to commit himself to it.

326 RECONSIDERATIONS OF PARTICULAR TOPICS

able to prove that there is not some non-identical feature that we have overlooked, and that this non-identical feature is not the decisive factor that accounts for the different outcomes in different cases of what has looked to us like an identical situation but may not have been this in truth. This point is made very clearly in the following passage of an unpublished letter written to me by Gilbert Murray on 8th April, 1932, after he had read volume i of this book in typescript.

'In all this argument to show that similar conditions do not produce similar results, I kept feeling that the reasoning did not convince because you never had *all* the conditions nor exactly similar conditions. E.g., conditions on the Jordan and the Nile may have been generally similar, but no-one would say that the human result in civilization must be exactly proportionate to the geographical data. You speak of the "total environment", but I did not feel as if I had ever been given the total environment.'

This comment anticipates Spate's, quoted above,[1] and, if I had been moved by it, as I ought to have been, to do some further thinking before publication, perhaps I might not have offered so vulnerable a target, twenty years later, for Spate's shot-gun.

Thus the believer in free will can never demonstrate, to a determinist's satisfaction, that he is presenting water-tight evidence of an identical situation having a different outcome in different cases. Conversely, the determinist can never demonstrate, to the satisfaction of the believer in free will, that an identical situation invariably has the same outcome in different cases. His non-determinist opponent can block his attempted demonstration that the same cause invariably produces the same effect by either admitting, for the sake of the argument, the sameness of the effect and challenging the determinist to guarantee the sameness of the cause in the cases that he cites, or, conversely, the believer in free will can admit the sameness of the cause and contest the sameness of the effects in the different cases cited. Whichever tactics the believer in free will adopts, the determinist will never be able to demonstrate that the same cause invariably produces the same effect—unless, of course, he takes refuge in defining the words 'cause' and 'effect' to mean phenomena that are invariably linked together.

This is another way of saying that, to demonstrate any proposition conclusively, one must transfer it from the field of phenomena to the field of mathematics. Mathematical entities are abstractions so drawn as to be self-evidently identical with or different from each other. In mathematics, therefore, it is possible to make demonstrations that an opponent will be bound to recognize as being valid. But the possibility of conclusive demonstration dwindles if we retrace our course from the world of mathematics towards the world of phenomena. In physics, perhaps, conclusive demonstration may be nearly attainable. In chemistry it will be less nearly within reach; in physiology, biology, botany, and zoology less so again; and least of all in the study of human affairs. 'One has to expect a certain degree of inconclusiveness in any exploration of complex states of human affairs.'[2] In this field, which is the one

---

[1] On p. 322.　　　　　　　　　　　[2] H. and M. Sprout in op. cit., p. 83.

that has the greatest practical importance for us human beings, perhaps the nearest approach to certain knowledge that is possible for us is an interim report in terms of percentages yielded by the retrospective analysis of statistical records.

Judged by a mathematician's standards, this level of knowledge might seem so low as to make the study of human affairs a futile pursuit. Yet, in practical life, statistical knowledge enables business men to make predictions that come near enough to the mark to allow of profits being made on the strength of them.[1] And, when our study is for the sake of gaining profits that are, not monetary, but intellectual, our understanding of what lies behind and beyond the phenomena may be valuably increased by conclusions that get no farther than being probable, or even than being no more than possible, approximations to the truth. Such inexact results might move a mathematician to throw up his profession in disgust. They will move a student of human affairs to pursue his with zest. Meanwhile, the respective believers in the genuineness of freedom in human affairs and in the illusoriness of the appearance of it must be content to go on waging an indecisive warfare with each other. A decision that neither party can contest is not to be expected in this arena unless and until the progress of human understanding on some different level—perhaps the psychological—enables us to see this pair of so far unreconciled standpoints in the light of a new concept that transcends them both.

IX. THE TRANSITIONAL SOCIETIES

IN an earlier chapter[2] I have already noticed, in passing, that the distinction between 'primitive societies' and 'civilizations', which I have drawn in the first volume of this book, is too sharp, because it is too simple. As I then saw it, human history, so far, can be analysed into a sequence of two enterprises—the first already achieved, the second now in course of being attempted, with no certainty that it, in turn, is going to succeed. On this view the already accomplished enterprise is the transformation of Sub-Man into Man; the enterprise on which Man is now engaged is the raising of human life from its primitive level to a higher one which is the goal of the endeavour that we call 'civilization'.[3] The nature of this goal, and the kind of change in human life, as hitherto experienced, that is practicable and desirable, are reconsidered in Chapter XIX of this volume. In the present chapter I want to reconsider my previous, too simple, account of the circumstances in which civilization first got on the move.

---

[1] See ix. 220–3.　　　　　　　　　　　　　　　[2] On pp. 150–3.

[3] See i. 191–6. This classification of human societies into two classes only—'primitive societies' and 'civilizations'—is justly criticized by Chr. Dawson in *Toynbee and History*, pp. 137–9. O. Höver criticizes me, also justly, in an unpublished paper for my failure to appreciate sufficiently the importance of the Neolithic revolution. See also eundem: 'Buchführung und Bilanz der Weltgeschichte: zu A. Toynbees Deutung des Frühzeitlichen Menschengeschens', in *Zeitschrift für Religions- und Geistesgeschichte*, Jahrgang 2, Heft 3 (1949/50), pp. 247–59.

I saw the rise of civilization as a consequence of one of the responses made by Upper Palaeolithic Man, in the region that is now the arid zone of the Old World in the northern hemisphere, to the challenge presented to him there by the recession of the latest in a succession of glacial-pluvial ages.[1] The changes in the flora and fauna of the north-western quarter of the Old World that followed in the train of this change of climate did indeed threaten the human inhabitants of this quarter with starvation and extinction through the loss of their previous means of livelihood. The geographical range of the challenge was even wider than I had originally realized. The recession of the ice not only turned what had been the savannahs of North Africa and South-West and Central Asia into steppes and deserts; it turned what had been the tundras of Northern Europe, at the foot of the ice-cap, into forests; and both these changes killed out or drove out the game that had pro-vided food for the Upper Palaeolithic inhabitants of these two regions. In Northern Europe that once mighty hunter, Magdalenian Man, apparently failed to survive the disappearance of his big game. During the latest glaciation the game had been so abundant, and his skill in dispatching it so great, that he had acquired a surplus of food and energy which gave him the opportunity to leave behind him a memorial in the shape of his wonderful paintings on the walls of caves. But the high degree of specialization that had rewarded him with a temporary pros-perity was his undoing when his environment played him false. He did not succeed in adapting himself, and consequently died out, or at any rate dwindled to a remnant living on in misery.[2] Magdalenian Man's humbler contemporaries to the south and south-east partly died out and partly decamped still farther southwards, in step with the southward drift of the savannahs at the expense of the tropical forest. But some of them stood their ground and made history.[3]

In giving this account of the response made by the Upper Palaeolithic inhabitants of the former savannahs to the challenge of desiccation, and in suggesting that civilization had been an outcome of this response, I was not wrong.[4] But I did go wrong in carrying history from the Upper Palaeolithic hunter's way of life to civilization at one bound. Actually, this immense revolution was achieved, not at one bound, but in two great steps. In my previous account of the transition from the higher hunting and food-gathering culture to civilization, I telescoped two stages into one. Palaeolithic hunters and food-gatherers did not, as I

---

[1] i. 302–21.

[2] See V. G. Childe: *Man Makes Himself*, p. 73; *What Happened in History*, pp. 41–43. On the Great Plains of North America a change of climate seems likewise to have been followed by the extinction of the big game that had been hunted by Early Lithic (corre-sponding to Old-World Palaeolithic) Man. Here, however, the hunting economy (now based on the bison) continued until the pre-Columbian population was supplanted by settlers of European origin in the nineteenth century of the Christian Era (G. R. Willey and P. Phillips: *Method and Theory in American Archaeology* (1958), pp. 86–88 and 107).

[3] In the Americas, too, there were people who made history by advancing from hunting through mainly depending on food-gathering to partly depending on agricul-ture; and here, similarly, these people seem to have been relatively backward representa-tives of the Archaic (i.e. Postlithic and Preformative) stage of culture (Willey and Phillips, op. cit. (1958), pp. 107, 127–8, 145, and 201).

[4] See V. G. Childe: *Man Makes Himself*, p. 86; H. Frankfort: *The Rise of Civiliza-tion in the Near East*, pp. 33–34.

had pictured them,[1] plunge straight into the jungle-swamps of the lower Nile valley and the lower basin of the Tigris and Euphrates and convert these into fertile fields by hydraulic engineering on the grand scale. The challenge presented by the jungle-swamp to a pre-agricultural society would have been altogether too severe to allow of these potential granaries being used as experimental stations for the discovery of the art of agriculture.[2] The stations in which the hunters pioneered in this new act were not the formidable jungle-choked river valleys; they were other green patches, of more tractable kinds, that also held out against the onset of desiccation: for instance, oases watered by springs, and the flood-plains of fertile soil deposited by lesser streams at the foot of their parent mountains before they ran out into the spreading sands.

Famous examples of these two types of geographical 'set-ups' that could be, and were, converted into nursery gardens are the oasis of Jericho and the ghutah of Damascus watered by the rivers Abarna (Barada) and Pharpar (Nahr al-Awaj). Early cultivators did also settle in, or on the brows of, the side valleys, not only of the Jordan valley, but of the lowest section of the Nile valley that later generations eventually transformed into Upper Egypt. But the oases and flood-plains in which agriculture was invented seem to have been those on the outer rim of 'the Fertile Crescent' of South-West Asia and farther east in what are now Iran and Türkmenistan (Transcaspia). This region, unlike both the heart of 'the Fertile Crescent' and the valley of Upper Egypt, was a rainfall zone. It is so still.[3] But Iran was better watered in the Post-glacial Age than it is today, and its flood-plains and oases are thought to have been the training ground of the agriculturists who eventually reclaimed the lower basin of the Tigris and Euphrates[4]—a larger and proportionately more difficult task than the later reclamation of the Nile swamps in the narrow valley of Upper Egypt.[5] As for the provenance

---

[1] In i. 305–6.

[2] 'For the understanding of the genesis of civilization in the Near East, nothing is more important than a knowledge of the vigorous and progressive Neolithic cultures of the fifth and fourth millennia B.C. However great the credit due to the Sumerians for their response to the challenge of the untamed Mesopotamian landscape, it would have been impossible without the prior achievements of what Gordon Childe has called "the Neolithic Revolution". In this connexion it is significant that there is no case on record of what we may perhaps call truly primitive societies, that is pure "food-gatherers", being successfully brought within the orbit of a civilization, whereas so-called primitive peoples who have passed through the agricultural revolution often have so been, even if often as hewers of wood and drawers of water under civilized oppression. Food-gatherers find the strain of such forcible integration into an alien society too great, and die out, like the West Indian islanders and most of the North American Indians, while African slaves are successfully—from the invaders' point of view—introduced to replace them. The Maori have been integrated into a civilized society, but not the Australian Blacks, while the Tasmanians have been totally destroyed. The Bantu multiply throughout South Africa; the Bushmen survive precariously in the Kalahari' (A. R. Burn in *History*, February–October, 1956, pp. 7–8).

[3] R. J. Braidwood: *The Near East and the Foundations of Civilization*, p. 11. See also ibid., p. 12, the instructive map: 'Fig. 4: Physiographical and rainfall map of Nuclear Western Asia, with the major sites of occurrence of terminal food-gathering and of earliest food-producing (pre-Late Hassuna phase) antiquity.'

[4] See H. Frankfort: *The Rise of Civilization in the Near East*, p. 44.

[5] See W. F. Albright: *From the Stone Age to Christianity*, 2nd ed., p. 146. Frankfort notes, in op. cit., p. 45, that the reclamation of what became the land of Sumer was comparable, in scale and in difficulty, to the reclamation, not of Upper Egypt, but of the Nile Delta. On the evidence of landscapes portrayed on reliefs in Egyptian tombs dating

of the people who eventually did for Upper Egypt what had, by then, already been done for Sumer, they seem not to have been descended—anyway, not directly—from previous occupants of the bluffs, overhanging the Nile valley in Upper Egypt, where we find these earliest local agriculturists first installed. Though the Lower Palaeolithic culture is well represented by remains found on these bluffs, the Upper Palaeolithic and Mesolithic cultures are not, so that there is a signal break of continuity between the latest Palaeolithic remains here and the earliest of those left by an agricultural population.[1]

'The early stages of the culture which develops into the civilization of dynastic Egypt is [sic] . . . not in the line of evolution of the Mesolithic or Upper Palaeolithic of the Nile valley, but is fundamentally different from it, as well as from the Capsian of North Africa and the Natufian of Palestine.'[2]

The earliest local pre-dynastic cultures are post-Sebilian[3]—i.e. they date from an age in which the physiography, though not yet the flora and fauna, of Upper Egypt was already approximately what it has been during the present Age of Civilization.

'This . . . does away with the story of hordes roaming through North Africa and eventually settling in the Nile valley because desiccation had made life impossible there.'[4]

The predynastic agricultural age on the fringes of what was to become Egypt began only a few centuries before 4000 B.C., and it began in a period, not of increasing aridity, but of increasing humidity,[5] which made the bluffs above the Nile valley cultivable while making the jungle-choked valley bottom more forbidding, for the time, than ever. 'Not before Nakāda II [alias Gerzean] did the first settlers venture down into the valley itself.'[6] All the same, the revolutionary progress of archaeological discovery in, and on the fringe of, Egypt has not done away with the story of hordes roaming through North Africa and South-West and Central Asia which eventually settled somewhere and responded to the challenge of desiccation by making the economic transition from food-gathering to agriculture and from hunting to the domestication of animals. Though the scene of this revolution in human history proves not to have been the north-east corner of Africa, the revolution did take place; and it happened in Asia, as is indicated by the amazing discoveries at Jericho, as well as by the now apparently proven priority of Sumer over Egypt as the seat of an irrigational civilization on the grand scale. Baumgartel points out[7] that the Badarians, who were the earliest of the

---

from the Age of the Old Kingdom, E. J. Baumgartel holds, in *The Cultures of Prehistoric Egypt*, p. 3, that the Delta was then still largely unreclaimed.

[1] Baumgartel, op. cit., p. 18.   [2] Ibid., p. 19.
[3] Ibid.   [4] Ibid.
[5] Ibid. In the course of the present Post-glacial or Inter-glacial Age up to date, there have been a number of minor oscillations of climate which are perhaps of the same nature, though not on the same scale, as the previous series of glacial-pluvial peaks and troughs. There seems to have been 'some increase in moisture at the end of the Pleistocene' (Braidwood, op. cit., p. 11).
[6] Baumgartel, op. cit., p. 3. Cp. p. 28.   [7] Ibid., pp. 23-24.

pre-dynastic agricultural societies on the fringe of Upper Egypt, possessed domesticated cattle, sheep, and goats; that sheep and goats are not indigenous in Africa;[1] and that the pre-dynastic Egyptians' sheep seem to have been of South-West Asian breeds. My error in volume i lay in presenting the transition from the Upper Palaeolithic culture to river-valley irrigational civilization as having taken place at one bound, and in taking the eventual reclamation of Egypt as my principal illustration for my thesis. What Egypt does illustrate is the transition to river-valley irrigational civilization from a culture, of apparently Asian origin, based economically on the cultivation of small flood-plains and oases.

The type or phase of culture that was transitional between the Upper Palaeolithic and the civilizations of the first generation which arose in the Lower Tigris-Euphrates valley and the lower Nile valley *circa* 3000 B.C. is commonly known as Neolithic, in allusion to its characteristic tool, the ground-stone axe, which was much more potent than even the finest of Upper Palaeolithic Man's chipped or flaked flints. The practice of labelling phases of culture by technological inventions that are characteristic, or at least symbolic, of their specific genius has the advantage of being applicable to all manifestations of human culture at all times and places. Technology is perhaps the one product of human activity in which there has been continuous progress,[2] and it has also been a province in which the network of human relations has always embraced the whole human race; for, though every technological invention must have been made at some particular place at some particular moment, a type of tool or a process of work, once invented, has been apt to spread, in course of time, to the ends of the Earth, so that, by the present day, most societies in the World, however isolated or backward, have progressed technologically and economically at least as far as the pre-civilizational agricultural phase, though they may have entered it as much as ten or twelve thousand years later than the pioneer inventors of it. The ground-stone axe was, indeed, a key tool of the Neolithic culture, since it enabled its possessors to master the trees that were invading post-glacial Northern Europe and were only slowly receding from post-glacial Afrasia.[3] But it is not a quite accurate hall-mark of the Neolithic culture. For instance, it was not possessed by the Palestinian Natūfians, who were early semi-agriculturists, while, on the other hand, it had been acquired by the North Europeans in advance of their acquisition of the art of agriculture.[4] Moreover, the purpose of cutting down the scrub in an Afrasian oasis, or the trees in a northern forest, was not just to use the timber for making tools or utensils; it was to clear the ground for cultivation.

'The outstanding new feature of the Neolithic Age is agriculture',[5] and it is still the key activity of this culture in the places where it survives. The earliest known Neolithic societies in South-West Asia

[1] Cp. V. G. Childe: *Man Makes Himself*, p. 86.
[2] See, for instance, A. L. Kroeber: *Style and Civilizations*, pp. 62–64.
[3] Childe: *Man Makes Himself*, p. 99; *What Happened in History*, p. 44.
[4] *Man Makes Himself*, p. 100; *What Happened in History*, p. 50.
[5] H. Frankfort: *The Rise of Civilization in the Near East*, p. 35.

and in the countries round the Mediterranean Sea possessed domestic animals besides cultivating domestic plants.[1] But elsewhere there are, even today, some Neolithic agricultural societies without domestic animals;[2] and it is easier to imagine how, in an age of increasing desiccation, wild animals could have been domesticated by human beings who were already cultivators of crops than it is to see how this marvellous feat could have been achieved by people who were still hunters.[3] As for the two arts of pottery and spinning and weaving, which are characteristic of the full-blown Neolithic culture in the New World[4] as well as in the Old World, neither of them is coeval with agriculture. There is a pre-pottery agricultural stage at Jericho, for instance, and likewise in Peru as Huaca Prieta, at the mouth of the Chicama valley.[5] Agriculture and, to an almost equal degree, the keeping of domestic animals, which was the normal concomitant of agriculture in the region where the agriculture of the Old World originated, are the essence of the Neolithic culture and are its greatest enduring legacy to cultures of subsequent phases that are 'higher' in the sense of having been built up on Neolithic foundations, whether or not they are higher in terms of spiritual achievement and value.

By achieving the agricultural-pastoral revolution,[6] human beings made themselves into active partners of Nature instead of continuing to be parasites on her like their human predecessors and like all other kinds of living creatures except some of the social insects.[7] Both vegetable and animal husbandry are fruits of foresight, forethought, perseverance, and self-control, and require an unfailing practice of these virtues to keep them going.[8] Husbandmen have to take thought, not only for the morrow, but for next year; and, however hungry they may be, they must not eat the seed-corn or slaughter the cows, ewes, and she-goats that yield them milk, besides replenishing their herds and flocks. The reward of husbandry is the production of a food supply that can maintain a denser population in greater security than hunting and food-gathering can. But to describe this revolution solely in technological and economic terms would be to give an inadequate account of it. In an earlier chapter we have noted[9] that, before the epiphany of higher religion led to the extrication of the religious from the secular side of life, all social and cultural activities were religious activities as well. Husbandry, both vegetable and animal, certainly had a religious, as well

---

[1] *Man Makes Himself*, p. 85; *What Happened in History*, p. 49.
[2] *Man Makes Himself*, p. 75.　　　　　　　　　　　　　　　　　[3] Ibid., p. 87.
[4] The Formative stage of culture in the Americas, as defined by Willey and Phillips: *Method and Theory in American Archaeology* (1958), seems to correspond approximately (at any rate in its earlier phases) to the stage labelled 'Neolithic' by students of Old-World history. According to Braidwood, op. cit., p. 3, Middle American Later Formative (beginning *circa* 500 B.C.) corresponds to the Protoliterate stage of culture in the lower Tigris–Euphrates basin (beginning *circa* 3500 B.C.).
[5] J. A. Mason: *The Ancient Civilizations of Peru*, p. 31.
[6] R. Redfield prefers to use the word 'transformation'. He points out that the word 'revolution' has associations, in present-day minds, with famous and controversial events in Western history—e.g. 'the Industrial Revolution'. The use of the word 'revolution' is therefore likely to import something alien and irrelevant into our picture of the changes brought about by the invention of agriculture (*The Primitive World and its Transformations*, pp. ix–x).　　　　　　[7] *What Happened in History*, p. 48.
[8] *Man Makes Himself*, p. 93.　　　　　　　　　　　　　[9] On pp. 78–79.

as an economic, aspect to begin with; and the agricultural-pastoral revolution might never have been achieved if it had not been a religious revolution in one of its aspects.

'The period when the food-producing economy became established was one of climatic crises adversely affecting precisely that zone of arid sub-tropical countries where the earliest farmers appear and where the wild ancestors of cultivated cereals and domestic animals actually lived.'[1]

These farmers were not descended from the magnificent Magdalenian hunters who had flourished at the foot of the ice-cap, but from the less successful, because less specialized, Upper Palaeolithic hunters on the Afrasian savannahs.[2] 'Nowhere has a series of continuous remains covering the transition been recognised.'[3] The Natūfian Palestinians used sickles set with flint teeth, but this proves merely that they reaped, not that they sowed. They may have been reapers of grass that grew wild,[4] and, whether or not they were still food-gatherers, they were certainly still hunters,[5] and their cereals, even if cultivated, may have been no more than a supplementary and subsidiary part of their food supply. Food-gatherers may not only reap; they may also practise artificial irrigation. Frankfort[6] cites a case of this from the Great Basin of Western North America. Conversely, cultivators of crops may take advantage of the natural irrigation of the flood-plains of small streams— a source of water-supply that confers the additional benefit of renewing the fertility of the soil. At Tepe Sialk—a tiny oasis, watered by a spring, on the western edge of the Central Desert of Iran, near Kashan— hunting continued to be an important economic activity when the local people were already cultivating the soil by irrigation, maintaining domestic animals, and practising the arts of spinning and weaving and pottery.[7] In the Fayyum and at Merimde, on the western brow of the Nile Delta, the earliest state of affairs in the Neolithic Age seems to have been like that at Tepe Sialk; agriculture, there too, was still subsidiary.[8] Yet, once introduced, it everywhere grew steadily in relative importance,[9] and this without depending on irrigation.

Though artificial irrigation was the key to the eventual reclamation and cultivation of the great river valleys and basins of Afrasia, it seems likely that the Neolithic inventors of farming in Afrasia depended on a natural supply of water from floods or springs or rains or combinations

---

[1] *Man Makes Himself*, p. 86.   [2] *What Happened in History*, p. 48.
[3] Frankfort, op. cit., pp. 34–35.   [4] Ibid., p. 35.
[5] *What Happened in History*, p. 48.   [6] In op. cit., p. 36.
[7] *What Happened in History*, p. 52.   [8] Ibid., p. 53.
[9] In the Americas, too, there is archaeological evidence for a stage in which agriculture was known and practised without yet having become the staple means of subsistence. Willey and Phillips report (*Method and Theory in American Archaeology* (1958), p. 145) that, on second thoughts, 'we found that agriculture *per se* was not the explosive stimulus to cultural development that we had supposed it to be. The early evidences of plant domestication seem to be associated with cultures that we should be inclined to think of as "lower" Archaic if we had such a division.' They note (ibid., p. 135) that these cultures were equalled or surpassed in well-being and in stability by others that still depended wholly on hunting, fishing, or food-gathering. At the same time they also note that no wholly non-agricultural American culture proved capable of advancing to the Classic stage of civilization (ibid., pp. 144–5 and 203).

of these different natural sources.[1] Certainly the Neolithic agriculture that was propagated, from its original seed-bed in the Afrasian oases, to Europe and North-West Africa in one direction and to North-West China in another did depend on rainfall and therefore had to be constantly moving on from old fields to new fields.[2] It went on moving, and therefore also spreading, till its practitioners discovered how to restore the fertility of the soil by manuring it with cattle dung and by letting it lie fallow for alternating periods. This was a more efficient alternative to the primitive practice of fertilizing a patch of cleared woodland with the ash obtained by burning the felled trees, and then leaving that season's field untouched till it had become covered by a second growth that could be felled and burnt in its turn.[3] Yet even this 'slash-and-burn', 'reap-and-run' kind of agriculture was effective enough to become a staple source of food-supply. The Danubian Neolithic pioneers of agriculture in Europe in the fourth and third millennia B.C., who discovered and exploited the patches of loess soil among the European forests, already depended on agriculture exclusively.[4]

How early in the present Post-glacial or Inter-glacial Age was agriculture started? The length of our vista of agriculture's past history has been doubled by the discoveries at Jericho since the end of the Second World War. Before that, other South-West Asian Neolithic sites seemed ancient. At Tepe Sialk seventeen layers of deposit, to a total height of ninety-one feet, had been laid down by 3000 B.C.[5] At Tepe Gawra, near Mosul, the pre-civilizational deposit was 104 feet thick in twenty-six layers.[6] At Ras ash-Shamrah it was forty feet thick.[7] K. Kenyon,[8] on the strength of carbon-14 tests, dates the pre-pottery stage at Jarmo, in North-Eastern 'Iraq, circa 4750 B.C.[9] Braidwood, publishing in 1952 before Miss Kenyon's excavations at Jericho, considered Jarmo to be the earliest of the fully Neolithic village sites.[10] He distinguishes five groups of these: Tepe Sialk in North Central Iran; Hassuna in Northern 'Iraq; 'Amuq, Saqja Gözü and Mersina in Northern Syria and Cilicia; Jericho XVII–IX; Fayyum A and Merimde.[11] He dates Hassuna circa 4400 B.C.;[12] Fayyum A 4145 B.C.±250 years (by a carbon-14 test);[13] and the pre-Neolithic Natūfian stage of culture in Palestine circa 6000 B.C.[14] Frankfort[15] dates Tepe Sialk and also Hassuna in Northern 'Iraq as early as circa 5000 B.C., and the Palestinian Natūfians about a thousand years earlier than that (thus agreeing, as regards the date of the Natūfian culture, with Braidwood). But these and all other Neolithic and immediately pre-Neolithic sites so far discovered and explored are of relatively recent origin compared with Jericho.

---

[1] See Frankfort, op. cit., pp. 37–38.   [2] See *Man Makes Himself*, p. 96.
[3] See ibid., pp. 80–84 and 96.
[4] *What Happened in History*, p. 54.
[5] Ibid., pp. 51 and 52.
[6] Ibid., p. 51.   [7] Ibid., pp. 51–52.
[8] *Digging up Jericho*, pp. 52 and 90.
[9] According to Braidwood, op. cit., p. 31, the earliest carbon-14 dates from Jarmo are 4758 B.C.±300 years (obtained from shell); 4743±360 and 4654±340 years (obtained from charcoal).   [10] Op. cit., p. 26.   [11] Op. cit., p. 14.
[12] Op. cit., p. 31.   [13] Op. cit., p. 14.
[14] Op. cit., p. 14.   [15] In op. cit., p. 35.

The third level at Jericho corresponds to the first level at most other Afrasian sites,[1] and the first level at Jericho is 3,000 years older.[2] The end of the pre-pottery age at Jericho is dated *circa* 5000 B.C.[3] The aggregate height of the layers deposited on the *tell* by this date is already forty-five feet,[4] and it may prove not to have been the first stage.[5] The origins of Jericho must be not much later than the end of the Pleistocene (that is, the end of the Palaeolithic) Age, *circa* 10000 B.C.[6] The pre-pottery Neolithic settlement at Jericho may have been larger than the subsequent Bronze-Age town.[7] Its area was at least eight acres, and, on the basis of present-day local density of urban settlement, this area would imply a population of about three thousand.[8] This settlement had a massive defensive wall of large undressed stones.[9] A still earlier, and also still finer, wall was found below the one first discovered.[10] A ditch, nine metres wide and three deep, has been cut out of the solid rock.[11] There is a tower, nine metres in diameter, with a staircase inside.[12] This tower has two outer skins, and there is a still earlier wall in its core.[13] The system of defences of which the tower is part belongs to the earliest phase so far discovered.[14]

When one stands on the brow of Miss Kenyon's great trench, as I did on 24th July, 1957, and gazes at that magnificently built tower at the bottom, one has the extraordinary sensation of reading the history of civilization, at one glance, back to a date which may be as far removed from the date of the beginning of civilization elsewhere *circa* 3000 B.C. as the year 3000 B.C. is from our own day. Who can deny that there was such a thing as civilization at Jericho at the time when the tower was built, if I have been right in defining civilization as a state of society in which there is a minority that is free from the task of keeping life going from day to day, and that therefore has leisure to think and plan and direct the work of the community as a whole?[15] Without the presence and activity of such a minority, the execution of those arduous and skilful public works is inconceivable. Therefore something that we are bound to call civilization existed about twice as long ago at Jericho as anywhere else that we know of. Yet Miss Kenyon holds[16] that 'Jericho cannot have been unique'. And indeed the sequel, at Jericho itself, to the pre-pottery stage shows that there must have been at least one contemporary civilization that was not only independent but was, in at least one technological respect, farther advanced. The earliest users of pottery at Jericho came from outside, ousted the pre-pottery population, and brought in the art of pottery with them ready-made.[17] There was a complete break in the history of Jericho at this stage.[18] Pre-pottery urban Jericho has no heirs. It was the later and cruder Neolithic cultures of Afrasia that developed, without a break, into the historic civilizations that arose in the great Afrasian river valleys *circa* 3000 B.C.[19]

The Afrasian inventors of agriculture turned their energies to two

[1] Kenyon, op. cit., pp. 51–52. [2] Ibid., p. 91. [3] Ibid., p. 52.
[4] Ibid., p. 73. [5] Ibid., p. 51. [6] Ibid., p. 75. [7] Ibid., p. 65.
[8] Ibid., p. 65. [9] Ibid., p. 66. [10] Ibid., p. 67. [11] Ibid., p. 68.
[12] Ibid., p. 68. [13] Ibid., p. 69. [14] Ibid., p. 72. [15] See p. 278.
[16] Op. cit., p. 75. [17] Ibid., pp. 75, 79, 81, 82–83.
[18] Ibid., pp. 81–82. [19] Ibid., p. 92.

different purposes, with two different consequences. Some of them, as we have seen, moved out as pioneers and won new lands for agriculture without being stimulated to improve upon the Neolithic cultivators' basic technological equipment: the ground-stone axe, the flint-toothed sickle,[1] domestic animals, the arts of spinning and weaving and pottery, and the primitive agricultural technique of 'slash-and-burn', which compelled people who depended on it for their livelihood to be continually moving on. With this equipment the great continental hinterlands of the Afrasian 'Nuclear Old World' were won for agriculture as far afield as North-West Africa and Europe and North-West China[2] in the course of the fourth and third millennia B.C.[3] Other Afrasian agriculturists were content to stay at home, and therefore could not remain content to make no improvements on their primitive equipment. In the Afrasian oases the fourth millennium B.C. was rich in inventions:[4] the working of copper, the making of bronze, the inventions of animal traction, and of wheels, bricks, and seals.[5] Copper was already known to the Badarians, who were the earliest agriculturists in Upper Egypt;[6] and E. J. Baumgartel goes so far as to say that 'we do not know of any period in pre-dynastic Egypt (apart from Palaeolithic times) when metal was certainly absent'.[7] Inventiveness was stimulated by intercourse between local cultures with different ways of doing things, and here desiccation proved a help to Afrasian man, besides being a challenge to him. 'Only in the arid zone round the Mediterranean and east thereof was intercourse at all rapid and extensive.'[8] Even so, the wheel, which

---

[1] This Natūfian tool turns up in pre-pottery Jericho (K. Kenyon: *Digging up Jericho*, pp. 56–57). It is also found at Tepe Sialk and at Hassuna; and the flint teeth, though not complete blades, have been found in Southern Russia and the Danube basin, in Anatolia, in North-West Africa, and at Almeria on the south-east coast of Spain (H. Frankfort: *The Birth of Civilization in the Near East*, pp. 35–36).

[2] It is easy to see how agriculturists from the oases of Iran and Transcaspia could have drifted north-eastwards across Asia to North-Western China—especially in an age before the rise of the pastoral Nomads had begun to make the steppes dangerous for anyone else. But by what route did other agriculturists spread from Afrasia into Europe? Anatolia is the obvious bridge, and the Dardanelles and Bosphorus have never been serious obstacles to migration. But according to Seton Lloyd, *Early Anatolia*, p. 53, Anatolia was uninhabited at the time of the Neolithic Revolution in the adjoining 'Fertile Crescent'; it remained a *terra incognita* until almost the end of the Chalcolithic Age in 'the Fertile Crescent' (p. 58; cp. p. 74); there was an unsurmounted barrier along the 2,000-feet contour-line along the southern slopes of the Taurus (p. 59); the earliest Chalcolithic culture in Anatolia, at the close of 'the Fertile Crescent's' Chalcolithic Age, is uniform all over the peninsula, including the west face (pp. 60–61); and Lloyd suggests that Anatolia may have been first populated, not from 'the Fertile Crescent', but from the Danube basin (p. 61). This indicates that the Danubian pioneers of agriculture in Europe must have come from Afrasia by a route running north of the Black Sea; and indeed the Kuban valley is known to have been a relatively early seat of an agricultural culture. The route by which agriculture reached North-West Africa and, from there, the Atlantic coast of Europe is an even greater puzzle, if E. J. Baumgartel is right in her contention that the Nile Delta remained an unreclaimed swamp until the Age of the Old Kingdom. This would rule out a route from or via Palestine along the north coast of Africa. In, say, the fourth millennium B.C., was what is now the Libyan Desert still hospitable enough to allow primitive cultivators to snatch a living from it while drifting across it from Upper Egypt or Nubia towards the Atlas?

[3] *What Happened in History*, p. 57; *Man Makes Himself*, p. 96. See also Braidwood, op. cit., p. 22, 'Fig. 11: the spread of the food-producing economy out of the Nuclear Near East, from an assumed beginning at *circa* 6000 B.C., suggested by means of isochronic lines.'   [4] *What Happened in History*, p. 69.

[5] Ibid., p. 75. Cp. *Man Makes Himself*, pp. 118 and 257.

[6] E. J. Baumgartel: *The Cultures of Prehistoric Egypt*, p. 22.

[7] Ibid., p. 14.   [8] *Man Makes Himself*, p. 98.

had been invented in Sumer about 3500 B.C., and had been applied
there to traction as well as to pottery-making, was not applied to traction in Egypt till about 1650 B.C.[1]

Primitive agriculture had produced no surplus of food and therefore
no reserves for maintaining specialists.[2] The only division of labour had
been between men and women, and each local community had been
self-sufficient.[3] The new arts that arose in the Afrasian oases during the
fourth millennium B.C. required male specialists,[4] and this indicates
that a certain surplus must by then have been accruing.[5] Metallurgy
is a full-time occupation;[6] 'metallurgical lore is the first approximation
to international science';[7] and metallurgy destroys Neolithic self-
sufficiency[8]—requiring, as it does, not only smiths, but miners, smelters,
and carriers. 'Potters who use the wheel are normally male specialists.'[9]
'By relieving women of a lot of heavy but essential tasks in the way of
hoeing, carrying burdens, and making pots', these new male avocations
—metallurgy, casting, ploughing, and making pottery on the wheel—
'cut away the economic foundations of mother-right'.[10] The fourth-
millennium masculine inventions—metallurgy, the wheel, the ox-cart,
the pack-ass, the sailing-ship—provided the technological foundations
for a new economic organization which could undertake a task that
Afrasian man had not yet attempted: the reclamation, for agriculture,
of the jungle-swamps in the great Afrasian river basins and valleys.[11]
The Afrasian oasis-cultivator had already mastered the art of water-
control on the small scale.[12] 'The economic organisation and social
framework were alone deficient',[13] but they were indispensable, since
without them there could be no public works,[14] and without these the
fourth-millennium technological inventions would not have enabled
Afrasian man to achieve his great new enterprise.

No doubt every technological revolution is also a social one in the
sense that technological changes are both consequences and causes of
social changes. R. J. Braidwood points out[15] that the nature of the surviving evidence for pre-civilizational culture yields a picture in which
technology looms too large. But, in contrast to the Neolithic revolution,
which had been a technological one first and foremost, the civilizational
revolution was a social and cultural one in its essence. The technological
stages of history—food-gathering, food-production, industrialism—do

[1] Ibid., p. 140. It was used in Egypt for pottery-making from the time of the Third
Dynasty onwards (*What Happened in History*, p. 86).
[2] *What Happened in History*, p. 68.   [3] *Man Makes Himself*, p. 94.
[4] Even in the technologically simpler Andean World, the transition from the Formative to the Classic stage of culture was accompanied, in the Moché valley, by a specialization of professions and classes (Bennett and Bird: *Andean Culture History*, p. 6; Bennett
in *A Reappraisal of Peruvian Archaeology*, p. 6).
[5] An increase in the amount and variety of food is also attested directly by an increase
in average human stature between the Mesolithic and the Chalcolithic Age (W. F.
Albright: *From the Stone Age to Christianity*, 2nd ed., p. 145).
[6] *What Happened in History*, p. 77.   [7] Ibid., p. 78.
[8] Ibid., p. 79.   [9] Ibid., p. 85.   [10] Ibid., p. 86.
[11] Ibid., p. 89.
[12] 'Chalcolithic culture may . . . be justly called "irrigation culture"' (W. F. Albright:
From the Stone Age to Christianity, 2nd ed., p. 144. Cp. p. 137).
[13] *What Happened in History*, p. 75.   [14] Braidwood, op. cit., p. 16.
[15] In op. cit., p. 8.

not correspond to its cultural stages.[1] The Neolithic technological revolution, in which food-production supplanted food-gathering, was a technological change of the same order of magnitude and momentousness as the modern Western Industrial Revolution in which muscle-power was replaced by harnessed inanimate power as Man's material means of manufacture and locomotion.[2] There was no comparable technological change during the intervening age. 'The technological and economic differences between civilization and the pre-civilizational phases of food-production were differences of degree.'[3] On the other hand, this intervening age saw, in the emergence first of civilization and then of higher religion, the two greatest single cultural changes in human history so far. The civilizational stage of culture could not have been achieved if it had not been preceded by the invention of food-production and the other concomitant and subsequent technological advances that have been noticed just above. But the emergence of civilization was, in itself, an event on a non-technological plane. It was brought about by developments on the spiritual plane.[4] So far from being caused, or accompanied, by any fresh technological advance, it was soon followed by an arrest of the movement of technological advance that had been set going in the Neolithic technological revolution.[5] Conversely, the Neolithic technological revolution had cost a spiritual price. It had been accompanied by an arrest of the movement of spiritual advance that had been set going in the technologically more backward Upper Palaeolithic Age. 'The hunter's wide-ranging life had freed Man's spirit; agriculture made it a prisoner of the clod.'[6]

'All through the Near East the best sites were reclaimed with toil.'[7] The undertaking required the production, collection, and storing of a large food-surplus to feed a great labour-force diverted from food-production to large-scale public works bringing in no immediate return in the form of foodstuffs. This labour-force had to be raised, controlled, and directed. Neither task would have been possible without a governing minority possessed of both immense ability and immense authority;[8] for the task was heart-breaking as well as back-breaking, and the scale of it was so vast that the ordinary labourer can hardly have foreseen in imagination the fruits of his efforts.[9] He must have worked in faith or under coercion or, more probably, have been driven by both these forces simultaneously. It is significant that, in both Sumer and Egypt at the dawn of history, the reclaimed land is the property of a god,[10] and

---

[1] Braidwood, op. cit., p. 5.
[2] F. Borkenau in *Merkur*, 3. Jahrgang, 7. Heft (July, 1949), p. 629.
[3] Braidwood, op. cit., p. 42.   [4] Braidwood, op. cit., pp. 5–6 and 42.
[5] Borkenau, op. cit., p. 631. It is noteworthy that, in Peru likewise, technological progress was characteristic of the Formative Age (Bennett in *A Reappraisal of Peruvian Archaeology*, p. 6), and that the subsequent Classic Age 'was an era of realisation in terms of techniques already known' (R. G. Willey, op. cit., p. 12).
[6] Borkenau, op. cit., p. 630.   [7] *Man Makes Himself*, p. 122.
[8] In the Andean World likewise, the transition from the Formative Age to the Classic Age, in which the valley bottoms in coastal Peru were mastered and irrigated, was accompanied by a shift of interest from technology to the social and political enterprise of manipulating manpower (Bennett and Bird: *Andean Culture History*, pp. 181–2; Bennett in *A Reappraisal of Peruvian Archaeology*, p. 6).
[9] See *Man Makes Himself*, pp. 120–2.
[10] In Egypt the whole land was owned by a single god incarnate, Pharaoh. In Sumer

that this god is represented by effective economic and political institutions managed by a ruling minority.

'Conditions of life in a river valley or other oasis place in the hands of society an exceptional power for coercing its members; the community can refuse a recalcitrant access to water and can close the channels that irrigate his fields. . . . The social solidarity needed by irrigators can thus be imposed owing to the very circumstances that demand it.'[1]

It was this disciplined corporate effort, with a religious faith as its inspiration and with the necessary political authority and technological equipment at its command, that reclaimed the Afrasian river basins and valleys for agriculture. 'Unless a markedly different rainfall and weather pattern could be postulated for four or five thousand B.C., which we doubt, extensive life in alluvial Mesopotamia would have been literally impossible without irrigation.'[2] 'The alluvial valleys of the great rivers offered a more exacting environment, but also greater material rewards for its exploitation. In them, Copper-Age villages turned into Bronze-Age cities.'[3] 'The food-producing revolution was perhaps the turning-point in the human career, but it was through the urban revolution that the consequences of the turn were realised.'[4] The biggest and most difficult of the primary feats of civilization—the creation of the land of Sumer out of the marshes of the lower Tigris-Euphrates basin—was also the earliest. Sumer was about the size of Denmark, and by about 2500 B.C. the yield from the crops grown on these ex-marshes was eighty-six-fold.[5] The limited enterprise of creating Upper Egypt out of the Lower Nile valley seems to have been achieved later—possibly to some extent under the stimulus of what the Sumerians had already accomplished.[6] The reclamation of the Nile Delta—a task on the scale of the creation of Sumer—may have been completed only in the Age of the Egyptian Old Kingdom. If so, it will have been little earlier than the reclamation of the Indus valley.[7] The reclamation of the marshlands in the basins of the East Asian rivers seems to have come decidedly later.[8]

Thus the reclamation of the river valleys of Afrasia for agriculture was in truth a response to the challenge of the progressive desiccation of Afrasia in the present Post-glacial or Inter-glacial Age. The cultivation of the minor oases, which had been the first response to this challenge, had turned out not to be enough in itself to make Afrasia permanently habitable by Man under post-pluvial conditions. In the end he was confronted with a choice between emigrating, as was done by the pioneers who carried agriculture from Afrasia to the ends of the Old World, and reclaiming the Afrasian swamps, as was done eventually

it was parcelled out among the territories of a number of independent city-states, and each of these city-state territories contained the estates of several gods. These Sumerian gods were not incarnate.   [1] *Man Makes Himself*, p. 123.
   [2] Braidwood, op. cit., p. 37. Cp. p. 39 and also p. 35: 'Fig. 25: Physiographical and rainfall map of Nuclear Western Asia, with major sites of occurrence of Ubaid phase antiquities or of materials judged to be contemporary with the Ubaid phase.' This was the phase in which the alluvium of the lower Tigris–Euphrates basin was occupied by Man (ibid., p. 36).   [3] *What Happened in History*, p. 59.
   [4] R. Redfield: *The Primitive World and its Transformations*, p. 6.
   [5] *What Happened in History*, pp. 89–90.   [6] See pp. 345–8.
   [7] See p. 348.   [8] See pp. 348–54.

by the makers of the earliest Old-World civilizations. The reclamation of the swamps was a permanent solution, because the new fields thus brought under cultivation were irrigated perennially by rivers whose sources rose outside the arid zone, and whose waters continually refertilized the soil with silt drawn by erosion from a virtually inexhaustible supply. In the reclaimed river valleys Man could be sure of making a livelihood so long as he continued to do organized and disciplined hard labour. Desiccation was the challenge; the lands of Sumer and Egypt were the response. But this bare statement would be a misleading simplification of the story. It does not become intelligible until we have also taken account of the primitive agricultural societies that made the transition to the earliest of the civilizations from the latest of the Upper Palaeolithic food-gathering and hunting societies. Even higher Primitive Man lacked the technology, as well as the organization, for coping with the jungle-swamps. Man had to put himself through a transitional apprenticeship before he could venture on the enterprise of civilization.

The intervention of this transitional stage between the primitive level of culture and the higher level that we call 'civilization' is not peculiar to the Old World; we find the same phenomenon in the history of the Americas. In the present chapter all that we need to do is to take note of this significant fact, leaving over, for the next chapter, the discussion of the question whether there was or was not any diffusion of culture, or of elements of it, from the Old World to the Americas at the transitional stage or at some later one.

In 1917 a distinguished student of Middle American archaeology, H. T. Spinden, threw out the idea that the Neolithic stage of Old-World culture had a counterpart in America in an 'Archaic' culture there which had originated in Middle America and had spread thence, as we now know that the Neolithic culture spread from Afrasia. This 'Archaic' American culture constituted a 'platform' on which the subsequent civilizations of Middle America and Peru reared themselves.[1] Willey testified in 1955[2] that this idea of an archaic cultural sub-stratum still stood, and that 'significant portions of this constant were diffused widely beyond the geographical boundaries of the later civilizations'. In some regions, e.g. Chile and Brazil, the 'Archaic' culture—in Willey's and Phillips's transference of Spinden's term to denote a transitional stage immediately preceding Spinden's 'Archaic'—seems actually to have been the earliest of any. At any rate, in these two regions there are no surviving traces of the 'Early Lithic' that corresponds in the Americas to the Palaeolithic stage of culture in the Old World.[3]

In terms of the classification of stages of culture in the Americas

---

[1] G. R. Willey: 'The Inter-related Rise of the Native Cultures of Middle and South America', in *The Seventy-Fifth Anniversary Volume of the Anthropological Society of Washington*, pp. 28–45. The reference here is to p. 29.

[2] G. R. Willey: 'The Prehistoric Civilizations of Nuclear America', in *The American Anthropologist*, vol. 57, No. 3, Part 1 (June, 1955), pp. 571–93. The reference here is to p. 572.

[3] G. R. Willey and P. Phillips: 'Method and Theory in American Archaeology, II', in *The American Anthropologist*, vol. 57, No. 4 (August, 1955), pp. 723–819. The reference here is to p. 753. Cp. eosdem, 1958, p. 141.

proposed by Willey and Phillips in 1955, Spinden's 'Archaic' stage was represented approximately by the later phase of their 'Preformative' stage together with their 'Formative' stage. In terms of the revised classification proposed by them in 1958, it corresponds to their Formative stage.[1] In both of their classifications the term 'Archaic' is used to describe, not Spinden's 'Archaic' stage, but an earlier stage immediately preceding it and making the transition to it from Willey's and Phillips's 'Lithic' stage; the 'Archaic' stage of culture in the Americas, in Willey's and Phillips' usage of the term, would thus appear to correspond to the Mesolithic stage in the Old World. It is characterized by the grinding and polishing of stone tools, in addition to the use of the processes of percussion and pressure flaking.[2] In the 'Archaic' culture in this usage of the term, tools made of bone and horn and ivory were also important.[3] Fishing and shell-hunting had made sedentary life possible,[4] and in the Americas in this stage, as in the Old World at the corresponding stage, food-gathering and hunting continued to be staple occupations after agriculture had emerged.[5] Agriculture brought with it no new implements; it used those that had been used already in a gathering economy.[6] On the Pacific slope of Peru the earliest cultivators lived on the edges of the valleys,[7] as in the lower Nile valley they lived on the bluffs and in the lateral ravines. The Peruvian Pacific-slope rivers are, of course, puny compared to the Nile; but the jungle-swamps with which their valleys, too, were choked in their original state of nature proved a formidable obstacle here also.[8] The draining and irrigation of the valleys themselves, as distinct from their margins, was an achievement, here too, of the subsequent Age of Civilization.[9] The emergence of agriculture, combined with stable settlement, technological specialization, and some degree of ceremonialism, are characteristic of the 'Preformative' stage,[10] or, in terms of Willey's and Phillips' revised classification, of the transition to the 'Formative' from the 'Archaic'. At this transitional stage there was no functional relationship between agriculture and pottery,[11] and in the Americas, as in the Old World, there was a pre-pottery stage of agricultural culture. But some cultures of the 'Archaic' type (in Willey's and Phillips's usage of the term 'Archaic') had already acquired the art of pottery-making.[12] It was acquired by the 'Preformative' culture at Huaca Prieta, in Northern Peru, before its close,[13] though, in its stone-work, this culture was still primitive: it was ignorant of both grinding and pressure-flaking.[14] The 'Preformative' (in

---

[1] Willey and Phillips, 1958, p. 105, footnote 8.
[2] Willey and Phillips, 1955, p. 740.   [3] Ibid., p. 741.
[4] Ibid.   [5] Ibid., p. 755.   [6] Ibid., p. 756.
[7] See G. H. S. Bushnell: *Peru*, p. 42; Bennett and Bird: *Andean Cultural History*, p. 125.
[8] In the Chicama valley, for instance, in the Pre-agricultural Age, 'the river probably meandered back and forth more freely than at present, forming lagoons and swamps and supported a dense undergrowth' (Bennett and Bird, op. cit., p. 118).
[9] Irrigation in coastal Peru was achieved first in the narrow upper valleys of the rivers (ibid., p. 142). Eventually the flatter and broader lower valleys were mastered and became the centres of population (ibid., p. 157).
[10] Willey and Phillips, 1955, p. 755.
[11] Ibid., p. 756.   [12] Ibid., p. 741.
[13] Willey: 'The Prehistoric Civilizations of Nuclear America', p. 577.
[14] J. A. Mason: *The Ancient Civilizations of Peru*, pp. 31 and 33.

the revised terminology, 'Late Archaic') culture developed into the 'Formative' gradually, not suddenly.[1]

The picture of American facts and events, given in the preceding paragraph on the authority of Willey and Phillips, was still maintained by them, as far as I know, at the time of writing in 1959. But, as has been noted, Willey and Phillips had revised their terminology between 1955 and 1958; and, already by 1955, they had, as has also been noted, changed the usage of the word 'Archaic' that had been brought into currency by Spinden in 1917. Since these successive changes in the usage of terms are both confusing and important, it may be as well to recapitulate them. In 1955 Willey and Phillips were already using 'Archaic' as a label for a stage between their 'Preformative' and their 'Early Lithic', instead of using it, in accordance with Spinden's usage, to cover the two stages labelled by them 'Late Preformative' and 'Formative'. In 1958 they eliminated their previous 'Preformative' stage and distributed its phases between 'Formative' and 'Archaic'; and, in their present classification, Spinden's 'Archaic' is represented, not by their 'Archaic', but by their 'Formative'.[2] Their language in passages quoted from the joint study that they published in 1955 must be revised accordingly to bring it up to date. Their 1958 classification articulates Spinden's 'Archaic' platform into two tiers: an 'Archaic' tier with a 'Formative' tier above it, and with the two classic pre-Columbian civilizations of the Americas springing from this upper tier.

'Cultures of the Formative stage occupy a geographically central position in the Western Hemisphere. They are found throughout much of Middle America and most of Andean South America.[3] From these areas they extend northward, with some lacunae, into the south-western and eastern United States, and in South America they run down the Cordillera to central Chile and eastward along the Amazon and Orinocan drainages of the lowlands.'[4]

A culture of the Formative level has been identified at the mouth of the Amazon.[5]

This change of labels is less important, in itself, than one of the reasons for it. In their revised version of their study, Willey and Phillips classify less than before by material traits (e.g. types of tool and kinds of technique) and more by ways of life. They now equate their 'Formative' stage with village life and their 'Classic' stage with urban life. They still hold[6] that the change from hunting and food-gathering to agriculture is more profound and significant than any other at any point in the whole

---

[1] Willey and Phillips, op. cit., 1955, pp. 755 and 765; Willey: 'The Prehistoric Civilizations of Nuclear America', pp. 577-8.

[2] G. R. Willey and P. Phillips: *Method and Theory in American Archaeology*, 1958, p. 105, footnote 8. 'Archaic', as defined by these two authorities in 1958, is 'the stage of migratory hunting and gathering cultures continuing into environmental conditions approximating those of the present' (ibid., p. 107). In the Archaic stage 'there is no important shift in economic and social patterns from the previous Lithic stages' (ibid., p. 106). 'Archaic', as thus redefined, seems to correspond to the 'Mesolithic', not to the 'Neolithic', of Old-World archaeology.

[3] And also, of course, in the region between, though this is not mentioned in the present passage (A. J. T.). [4] Willey and Phillips, 1958, pp. 146-7.

[5] Ibid., p. 180. [6] Ibid., p. 72.

series of Pre-Columbian American stages of culture. But they now also hold[1] that 'the settlement patterns, etc.—not the agriculture—are the effective criteria for classification'. They declare[2] that they 'are not retreating from the position that agriculture was the principal *formative* agent in the development of "Formative" cultures, but only from a rigidity that makes it the indispensable agent'.

'Therefore, we now define the New-World "Formative" by the presence of agriculture or any other subsistence economy of comparable effectiveness, and by the successful integration of such an economy into well-established, sedentary village life.'[3]

In taking up this position, Willey and Phillips have Redfield's support. He has noted[4] that 'a sedentary life is possible to a people who know nothing of agriculture or animal husbandry'.

Whatever criteria may be the most illuminating for defining the 'Formative' stage of culture in the Americas, it looks as if this stage of Pre-Columbian American history, as now defined, corresponds structurally to what happened in the Old World, in the Afrasian oases, in the course of the fifth and fourth millennia B.C. In the Americas there was nothing at this stage to compare with the enormous technological advances that were achieved in the Old World on the eve of the genesis of the earliest Old-World civilizations. Nevertheless, it is evident that in the Americas, as in the Old World, the dawn of civilization was separated culturally, as well as chronologically, from the end of the Palaeolithic Age by a transitional series of cultures. This series straddles the 'Archaic' and the 'Formative' stages in terms of Willey's and Phillips's most recent classification. The corresponding stages in Old-World terminology would be the 'Mesolithic', 'Neolithic', and 'Chalcolithic'.

X. ORIGINALITY VERSUS MIMESIS

I. STIMULUS DIFFUSION

I HAVE noted already in this volume[5] that, in previous parts of this work, I have tended to over-simplify, and hence to exaggerate, the contrast between original creation and 'mimesis', meaning the reception and adoption of elements of culture that have been created elsewhere and have reached the recipients by a process of diffusion. In 1930, when I was writing volume i, the British Diffusionists, led by W. H. Perry and G. Elliott Smith, had just published their rather provocative works.[6] Like many other students of human affairs, I reacted strongly against them.[7] In the perspective given by a further thirty years of discovery and discussion, the general verdict now does seem to be that they pushed their claims on behalf of the role of diffusion to excessive lengths; and their particular theory that Egypt was the centre from which civilization

[1] Ibid., p. 145. [2] Ibid., p. 146. Cp. p. 202. [3] Ibid., p. 146.
[4] R. Redfield: *The Primitive World and Its Transformations*, p. 5.
[5] On pp. 145–8. [6] See the references in i. 425, footnote i.
[7] See i. 221–3 and 425–40.

was diffused all over the World has now been refuted by the apparently well-established discovery that civilization in Egypt itself was a product of 'stimulus diffusion' from Sumer. Thus my negative reaction to the British Diffusionists' theory was not mistaken. But the effect on me at the time was certainly to make me 'lean over backwards' in emphasizing the part played by original creation and therefore to under-estimate the role of diffusion and mimesis. I afterwards corrected this original bias to some extent in volume viii, in which I have dealt with two types of contact between societies that are each other's contemporaries: the contact between a civilization and the barbarians beyond its frontiers (Part VIII) and the contact between one civilization and another (Part IX). Nevertheless, I still need to reconsider the whole question in the light of the new knowledge and new ideas that the last thirty years have brought with them.

Neither the concept of originality nor the concept of mimesis can ever be dispensed with in the study of human affairs. Creation and innovation are realities, even if we cannot give a logical account of what we mean by these terms.[1] If they were not realities, no changes could ever have occurred. And, if creation and innovation are realities, every act of creation and innovation must have been achieved by some agent at some particular point of space-time. On the other hand, if diffusion and mimesis were not realities too, this again would make human history inexplicable. If the only possible form of human action were original creation, a human being's whole energies would have to be taken up, from birth to death, in willing each pulsation of his heart and each inflation of his lungs. So far from this being characteristic of human nature, one of its distinctively human features is its capacity for learning and for translating what it learns into habits organized in those patterns of relations between people that we call 'institutions'. Besides the psycho-physical heritage that Man, like all other living creatures, transmits to his offspring automatically and involuntarily, he transmits a cultural heritage by the social process of teaching and learning; and it is this second capacity that makes and keeps Man human. G. R. Willey is therefore surely right in saying that 'diffusion and independent invention are, after all, polar abstractions concerning complex human events, and the two processes work in concert'.[2] Meanwhile, A. L. Kroeber has transformed our whole approach to the question by showing that an antithesis between two terms—originality and mimesis—does not cover all the phenomena. There is at least one more alternative, which Kroeber calls 'stimulus diffusion'.[3]

'Stimulus diffusion might be defined as new pattern growth initiated by precedent in a foreign culture. . . . A goal or objective was set by something previously existing in another culture; the originality was limited to achieving the mechanisms by which this goal could be attained.'[4]

[1] See pp. 252–4.
[2] *The Seventy-fifth Anniversary Volume of the Anthropological Society of Washington* (1955), p. 29.
[3] See A. L. Kroeber: 'Stimulus Diffusion', in *The American Anthropologist*, New Series, vol. 42, No. 1 (January–March, 1940), republished in *The Nature of Culture*, pp. 344–57. [4] Kroeber, *The A.A.* num. cit., pp. 20 and 2; *The N. of C.*, pp. 357 and 345.

Kroeber demonstrates his case by bringing forward illustrations from the most diverse fields of human activity. Since then his new concept has been employed to account for the genesis of the Egyptiac Civilization as a creative response to a stimulus received from the Sumeric Civilization. If this explanation of the origins of the Egyptiac Civilization had come from the Assyriologists, it might perhaps have been dismissed as being just an amusing example of academic imperialism. But it has been put forward by the Egyptologists themselves, and therefore has presumably found favour on its merits. One of its merits is its possible applicability to other cases. In the Egyptiac case it is supported by definite archaeological evidence; but, even without the support of this, it might also throw light on the origins of civilization in the Indus basin and in China. A stimulus from the Sumeric World may have struck the spark here too. Similarly, in the Americas, the Andean Civilization may have arisen through stimulus diffusion from Middle America. Kroeber's fruitful idea may even eventually help to solve the hotly debated problem of the extent and influence of the Pre-Columbian cultural relations between the Americas and the Old World.

Kroeber himself draws one conclusion that is of great importance. 'Independent origins are not necessarily proved because we are unable to prove specific connexion by specific historical documents.'[1] The hypothesis of the common psychic structure of mankind—the so-called uniformity of human nature—is no explanation of specific cultural manifestations.[2] Where strikingly similar cultural manifestations recur, and specially where a number of them recur in association, the presumption is that there is an historical link between the several cases: that is to say, that one case only is original and that the rest are derivative. Since it would be difficult to produce evidence that would rule out this possibility, the independent origin of similar cultural and social phenomena is difficult to establish conclusively, even in cases where all the positive evidence hitherto brought forward in support of the hypothesis of diffusion has proved unconvincing.

2. THE GENESIS OF THE EGYPTIAC CIVILIZATION

The style of the Egyptiac Civilization was unquestionably distinctive, and this in all facets of cultural and social life: art, architecture, writing, religion, government. Yet there is convincing evidence that this distinctive style took shape suddenly[3] under a stimulus from an alien style, the Sumerian, which was equally distinctive and which had taken shape, not suddenly, but gradually, in a series of stages of which the record has now been recovered by the progress of archaeological discovery in 'Iraq. The period during which the Egyptiac Society was open to Sumeric influences was short, but it was crucial. It not only saw the formation of the distinctive Egyptiac cultural style, a style that was to maintain itself for more than three thousand years; it also saw the

[1] 'Stimulus Diffusion', p. 16. Cp. W. Koppers' 'Der Historische Gedanke in Ethnologie und Prähistorie', in *Kultur und Sprache*, pp. 15 and 23–24.
[2] A. L. Kroeber: *The Nature of Culture*, pp. 60–61. Cp. pp. 58 and 390–1.
[3] Frankfort: *The Birth of Civilization in the Near East*, p. 50.

reclamation of the lower Nile valley for agriculture,[1] and the political unification of this reclaimed land of Upper Egypt with the still mostly unreclaimed Delta in a united kingdom. The opening of Egyptian hearts and minds to Sumeric influences began only towards the end of the latest pre-dynastic period, the so-called 'Nakāda II' or 'Gerzean'; and this state of receptivity came to an end soon after the establishment of the First Dynasty. In the meantime this exceptionally receptive mood had made history.

Fields in which Sumerian influence made itself felt in Egypt during this formative age were the practice of sealing with engraved cylinders, a recessed style of brick building, a Sumerian build of ship, a number of artistic motifs—for instance, symmetrical patterns of fantastic animals —and the art of writing.[2] The build of ship, taken together with the probability that the Nile Delta remained an impassable swamp until far on in the Age of the Old Kingdom, is the most significant pointer to the route by which these Sumeric influences may have reached Upper Egypt. 'In Egypt, signs of contact with Sumer almost cease after Narmer's reign; and, since contact with Syria increased rather than diminished during the First Dynasty, it seems unlikely that the Mesopotamian influences reached Egypt from the North'[3]—though it is true that it is no far cry from Byblos, on the Phoenician coast, with which Egypt was trading from the time of the Old Kingdom onwards, to Brak, on the River Khabur in Mesopotamia,[4] where a Sumeric temple had been founded in the Protoliterate Age of Sumeric history. Frankfort conjectures[5] that the place where the Egyptians encountered the Sumeric Civilization may have been a common source of frankincense somewhere in South Arabia.

Whatever the route, the reality of the contact seems to be indubitable. 'The strongest evidence . . . is supplied by three cylinder seals shown by their very material and by their designs to have been made in Mesopotamia during the second half of the Protoliterate period, but found in Egypt.'[6] 'In view of [the] great variety of detailed resemblances, there can be no reasonable doubt that the earliest monumental brick architecture of Egypt was inspired by that of Mesopotamia, where it had a long previous history.'[7] But the most remarkable evidence is in the field of writing. In Sumer the gradual evolution of the Sumeric script can be traced from its very beginnings,[8] and 'it has been customary to postulate prehistoric antecedents for the Egyptian script, but this hypothesis has nothing in its favour'.[9]

---

[1] Frankfort: *The Birth of Civilization in the Near East*, p. 43. 'The Nile valley north of Asyut itself was not inhabited prior to Nakāda II' (E. J. Baumgartel: *The Cultures of Prehistoric Egypt*, p. 25). The Nakāda II people were the first to drain and irrigate Upper Egypt (ibid., p. 46).

[2] See the Appendix on 'The Influence of Mesopotamia on Egypt towards the end of the Fourth Millennium B.C.' in H. Frankfort: *The Birth of Civilization in the Near East*, pp. 100–11, especially the table on p. 109.   [3] Ibid., p. 110.

[4] This word 'Mesopotamia' is used here in its strict meaning, to denote the country between the middle courses of the Tigris and Euphrates north-west of, and exclusive of, Babylonia. Frankfort uses the word to denote 'Iraq minus 'Iraqi Kurdistan but with the addition of the territory, east of Euphrates, that is included in the present state of Syria.   [5] Op. cit., pp. 110–11.

[6] Ibid., p. 101.   [7] Ibid., p. 105.

[8] Ibid., pp. 55–56. Cp. Baumgartel, op. cit., p. 48.   [9] Frankfort, op. cit., p. 106.

'In the annals of the kingdom (which happen to survive in a version of
the Fifth Dynasty), events are recorded only from the First Dynasty onwards, a fact suggesting that no records of earlier times existed. . . . But
the writing which appeared without antecedents at the beginning of the
First Dynasty was by no means primitive. It has, in fact, a complex
structure. It includes three different classes of signs: ideograms, phonetic
signs, and determinatives. This is precisely the same state of complexity
that had been reached in Mesopotamia at an advanced stage of the Protoliterate period. There, however, a more primitive stage is known in the
earliest tablets, which used only ideograms.'[1]

Frankfort reasonably concludes that the Egyptiac script cannot have
been invented without knowledge of the Sumeric, but he hastens to
add[2] that 'the Egyptians did not copy the Mesopotamian system
slavishly; they were merely stimulated to develop a script of their own,
once the notion that language could be rendered graphically had been
conveyed'.

Baumgartel, too, points out[3] that

'only at the end of Nakāda II [the Gerzean period], shortly before the rise
of the dynasties, do we find writing established in Egypt also [i.e. as well as
in Sumer]. The system employed is too similar to that of the Sumerian
script to make an independent origin likely, yet the repertory of signs is
derived entirely from the surroundings of the Nakāda II people. There is
no evidence of a gradual development of script in Egypt, as there is in
Mesopotamia. The system appears from the first ready-made, much the
same as it was throughout Egyptian history.'

Baumgartel holds[4] that 'certain hieroglyphs originally had Semitic
values, to which were later added the commonly used names of the
objects represented'. 'It follows', she concludes, 'that the Nakāda II
people spoke a Semitic language different from that of the Nakāda I
people', whose language, in her opinion, was Hamitic. As she sees it,[5]
the Nakāda II people were Asiatic invaders who brought in with them
painted pottery[6] and a blade technique of stone-working in place of their
local predecessors' bifacial technique.[7] She points out that in Sumer the
blade technique was the predominant one.[8] Frankfort is more guarded
in his judgement.

'It would [he sums up][9] be an error to see the birth of Egyptian civilization as a consequence of contact with Mesopotamia. The signs of change
accumulating towards the end of the Predynastic Age are too numerous,
and the outcome of the change is too emphatically Egyptian, in its general
character and its particulars, to allow us to speak of derivation or dependence. . . . We observe that Egypt, in a period of intensified creativity,
became acquainted with the achievements of Mesopotamia; that it was
stimulated; and that it adapted to its own rapid development such

---

[1] Ibid., p. 106. [2] Ibid., p. 107. [3] In op. cit., p. 48.
[4] Ibid., p. 48. [5] Ibid., pp. 38–39 and 50.
[6] According to Baumgartel, op. cit., pp. 29 and 53, all painted pottery, anywhere in the
Old World, originated in Asia.
[7] Ibid., pp. 38–39. Frankfort, in op. cit., pp. 42–43, suggests, more cautiously, that,
while the Gerzean culture included Asian elements, it was still predominantly African.
[8] Baumgartel, op. cit., p. 39. [9] In op. cit., p. 110.

elements as seemed compatible with its efforts. It mostly transformed what it borrowed and after a time rejected even these modified derivations.'

It will be seen that the role of Sumeric influence in the genesis of the Egyptiac Civilization, as described by Frankfort in this passage, is a classic illustration of Kroeber's concept of 'stimulus diffusion'.

3. THE GENESIS OF THE INDUS CULTURE

The archaeological record of the Indus Culture that has been recovered in our time gives the impression that this civilization, like the Egyptiac, made a sudden appearance in the river valley in which it found a home for itself. It does not seem to have developed out of the Neolithic and Chalcolithic cultures in the adjacent highlands of Eastern Iran. It would seem to have entered the Indus valley from elsewhere, with its script and its advanced technique of brick architecture ready-made. On the analogy of what we now know about the genesis of the Egyptiac Civilization, one obvious hypothesis for explaining the genesis of the Indus Culture is that it, too, was brought to a head by the influence of the Sumeric Civilization on some people who, like the 'Gerzean' (*alias* Nakāda II) invaders of Upper Egypt, were within Sumer's cultural range, and who, in response to this stimulus, created an independent civilization of their own in a new country that they brought into existence by reclaiming a hitherto virgin tract of jungle-swamp. In the case of the Indus Culture, however, we lack the archaeological evidence which substantiates the parallel hypothesis in the Egyptiac case. Above all, the Indus script still remains undeciphered, so that we do not yet know, as we do know about the Egyptiac script, how it compares in point of structure with the Sumeric script. We do know that, after the establishment of the Indus Culture in the Indus basin about half-way through the third millennium B.C., there was commercial contact between it and the Sumeric World. Seals inscribed in the Indus script have been found in 'Iraq on Sumeric sites. This archaeological evidence for subsequent intercourse does not, however, throw light on the question whether the Sumeric Civilization exerted any stimulus on the Indus Culture in its formative stage. Still less does it throw light on the question of the region in Afrasia from which the founders of the Indus Culture originally came.

4. THE GENESIS OF CIVILIZATION IN CHINA

Today China, like the Indus valley, 'Iraq, and Egypt, is an agricultural country in which the bulk of the produce comes from drained and irrigated land that has been reclaimed from the primaeval swamps of great river valleys, and in which the greater part of the population works and lives on these reclaimed fields. Present-day China is, in economic terms, virtually identical with the lower basin of the Yellow River, the basin of the Hwai River, the lower basin of the Yangtse, together with its upper basin in Szechwan, and the basins of the East and West rivers, opening on to the south-west coast. In the first volume of this book I assumed that, in China, history had followed the same course as in the other three regions, above-mentioned, in which the present-day basis of economic life is, as in present-day China, a system of agriculture based on water-control. I assumed that in China, as in these three other regions, the reclamation of the river-valley swamps had been the economic aspect of the local genesis of civilization. I had thought of civilization as being a state of society in which there is a ruling minority that is exempt from the common tasks of food-production and technology, on which the majority of the human race have hitherto had to spend all their working time in order to keep life going. I had supposed that in China, as elsewhere, this leisured class, which is the distinctive index of civilization,[1] had been coeval with the reclamation of the swamps. These had been reclaimed under its direction, and at the same time this achievement had brought with it the surplus of food production which had made it possible for society to support a governing class that did not have to take its share in mankind's daily work.

This picture of the genesis of civilization in China was not my private fancy. It was the established doctrine of the official Chinese account of Chinese history that began to take shape in the time of Confucius (*vivebat circa* 551–479 B.C.) and that finally crystallized in the hands of the father of Chinese history, Ssu-ma Ch'ien (*vivebat circa* 149–90 B.C.). In this tradition the reclamation of the swamps in the river basins of China was attributed to a legendary culture-hero, Yü the Great. Yü was eventually taken to have been a human being who had founded the pre-Shang Hsia dynasty. The historicity of this dynasty has not been confirmed, up to date, as the historicity of the Shang dynasty has been, by the progress of archaeological discovery. In making Yü the founder of the Hsia dynasty, the authors of the official legend were intending to imply that he was the creator of civilization in China. The official legend, after maintaining itself for not much less than two thousand years, has now been exploded, partly by archaeological discovery and partly by a critical examination of the earliest surviving Chinese literature. It appears that, in the early Chou period, Yü was held to be, not a human being, but a god, who had made the earth rise above the surface of the water.[2] The Chinese official legend has now been recognized to be unhistorical. Yet the idea that the reclamation of the swamps and the beginning of civilization in China were coeval, and were, in fact, simply two facets of a single event, was retained by as great and as recent a modern Western Sinologist as H. Maspéro. It was on Maspéro's authority[3] that I equated the genesis of civilization in China with a response to a particular physiographical challenge— the challenge of the swamps—that admittedly accounts for the genesis of civilization in the Indus valley, Sumer, and Egypt.

Meanwhile, within the last thirty years, the traditional picture of the

[1] See p. 278.
[2] J. Needham, in a letter to me of 26th October, 1958.
[3] See H. Maspéro: *La Chine Antique* (Paris 1927, Boccard), pp. 20–26, quoted in this book in i. 318–20.

genesis of civilization in China, which Maspéro rationalized, has come under fire. It has been suggested that the reclamation of the river-valley swamps, which is the dominant factor in China's present-day economic configuration, did not come at the beginning of the history of civilization in China but has been a gradual achievement and a comparatively late one. It is now suggested that the origins of civilization in China, on their technological and economic side, are more like its origins in Europe than like its origins in the valleys of the Indus, the Tigris-Euphrates, and the Nile.

P. M. Roxby[1] has put forward the thesis that

'the essential geographical element in the rise of early Chinese civilization would seem to have been the existence of an almost continuous west–east belt of relatively forest-free and fertile loess soil, initially favourable, in spite of some handicaps, which admittedly may have acted as a spur, to agricultural development, and also open on its continental side to the entry of fresh cultural stimulus from Western Asia.'[2]

The primary loess of the western highlands has to be distinguished from the redeposited and reassorted loess of the eastern plains.[3] The loess is thick in Kansu, round Lanchow, and westward along the Kansu corridor.[4] North-westward it stops at what is now the line of the Great Wall,[5] and there is also no loess south of the Tsin-ling Range; but the redeposited loess does extend south-eastward into southern Honan and eastward as far as Kai-fêng.[6] There are, indeed, two belts of redeposited loess between the western and the Shantung highlands.[7] The more northern part of the Eastern Plain, corresponding to the modern province of Hopeh, was originally occupied by rivers and swamps.[8] 'But the central portion of the Great Plain, lying between this Hopeh basin in the north and the swamps of the lower Hwai in the south, is much higher. It has been the scene of maximum sedimentation by the Yellow River where it emerges from the Tung-Kwan gorge.'[9] Roxby labels this comparatively high ground 'the Honan Water-Parting'. It closely coincides with the more northerly of the two bands of redeposited loess that extend across the Eastern Plain.[10] Following V. K. Ting,[11] Roxby notes[12] that the loess is essentially a valley-filling deposit and is not sufficiently hard to obstruct drainage, so that in the loess belt there cannot have been swamps of the kind that filled the alluvial plains. Ting maintains that the loess area has always been a semi-steppe and that there has never been any forestation there; and Roxby, too, holds[13] that, in Northern China, there was almost certainly no post-glacial pine-forest phase of the kind that impeded agriculture in Europe.

'All this applies, of course, primarily to the loessial plateaux of the west, but in large measure also to the Honan Water-Parting extending east-

[1] In 'The Terrain of Early Chinese Civilization', in *Geography*, the quarterly journal of the Geographical Association, vol. 23 (Manchester, 1938), pp. 225–36. Cp. eundem: 'The Major Regions of China', ibid., pp. 9–14.   [2] Ibid., p. 236.
[3] Ibid., p. 226.   [4] Ibid., p. 227.   [5] Ibid.
[6] Ibid.   [7] Ibid.   [8] Ibid.
[9] Ibid., pp. 227–8.   [10] Ibid., p. 228.
[11] In *The Chinese Social and Political Science Review*, vol. 15 (1931), pp. 265–90.
[12] In *Geography*, vol. 23, p. 228.   [13] Ibid., p. 231.

wards towards the foothills of the Shantung highlands and particularly to the higher western margins of the Plain and the headwaters of the Hwai. This extension is postulated in the important generalisation of Dr. Ting that "this continuous semi-steppe stretching from the sea to Turkestan, free from both forest and marsh and favourable to agriculture and to wheeled vehicles, made early settlement and continuous diffusion of culture possible".'[1]

The waist of the plain, between the Shansi and Shantung highlands, mostly consists of calcareous alluvium, alluvioloess, with only small patches of saline alluvium.[2]

'It is an unleached soil of great fertility, and both the re-sorting process of the wind and human agency can expose new surfaces, producing much the same effects as the renewal of the soil by the Nile floods. The loess in all its direct and indirect effects must be reckoned as a positive factor of the greatest importance in the environment of the Yellow River basin. In contrast, the non-lime-accumulating soils and the semi-tropical climate of the Yangtse basin were essentially favourable to marsh and forest. That must indeed have been real jungle, as all the references to it in the Tribute of Yü, and the name Ch'u (meaning jungle-land) of the first important Chinese or semi-Chinese principality which developed in it, suggest. The Yangtse region was very far from being "gracious" to the early cultivators. It required many centuries of human effort before it became the fertile region which it is to-day.'[3]

The non-calcareous alluvium and rice paddy-fields of the middle and lower Hwai valley and the saline alluvium soils of the coastal regions north and south of Shantung likewise 'indicate areas of former swamp, and much of the saline alluvium has only recently been reclaimed and put under cultivation'.[4]

By what stages, then, did the Chinese World's agricultural centre of gravity shift from the loess lands, where rainfall agriculture could be practised without any preliminary task of clearing forests or draining swamps, to the former swamp-lands in the river valleys which have been reclaimed at some date between the dawn of Chinese history and the modern age? J. Needham suggests[5] that the establishment of water-control in China began in the Chou Age, and that the most important features were probably not the reclamation of swamp-land by drainage but rather the impounding of run-off water from hill valleys in tanks,[6] the digging of navigation canals, and the building of dykes along the great rivers. Perhaps the earliest record is a reference to the irrigation of rice-fields in a song in the *Shih Ching* which may date from the eighth century B.C. The first dykes along the lower course of the Yellow River seem to have been built during the first half of the seventh century B.C. by Duke Hwan of Ch'i. The earliest known irrigation tank, the Anfêng

[1] Ibid., p. 228.   [2] Ibid., p. 229.
[3] Ibid.   [4] Ibid.
[5] In a letter to me of 26th October, 1958.
[6] Needham mentions the analogy of the tanks in Ceylon. Perhaps both these and the similar works in China were ultimately inspired by the small-scale irrigation works in the Afrasian oases in the age before the reclamation of Sumer, Egypt, and the Indus valley.

T'ang in the present-day province of Anhui, which eventually watered six million acres of land, is said to have been constructed in the sixth century B.C. by the government of the state of Ch'u. The Hung Kou (Canal of the Wild Geese), linking the Yellow River, at a point near Kai-fêng, with the Pien River, may have been dug about 500 B.C. In 483 B.C. King Fu Ch'ai of Wu dug the Han Kou canal to link the Hwai River with the Yangtse. In the fourth century B.C. the Chang River was diverted to flow into the Wei River instead of flowing into the Yellow River. In the third century B.C. in Szechwan an artificial arm of the River Min was carried through a cutting in a mountain-side to irrigate a great area in the Ch'êngtu plain. These notices, which I owe to Dr. Needham's kindness, indicate that in China the establishment of water-control was a gradual process, as it may have been in Sumer and in the Nile Delta, in contrast to its apparently sudden establishment in Upper Egypt and perhaps also in the Indus valley. This is the physiographical background to the genesis of civilization in China.

China has yielded relics of the late Neolithic stage of culture, but none of the middle or the early stage.[1] The oldest Neolithic culture in China is the Painted Pottery Culture. It extended as far east as Honan, and has been labelled with the name of a site at Yang Shao in that province; but it seems to have started earlier and lasted longer in Kansu, and its affinities are with Neolithic cultures in Transcaspia (at Anau), in South-West Asia, and in the Danube basin.[2] This Yang Shao culture never occupied Shantung,[3] and, in its lodgements in the Eastern Plain, it succumbed to a later and more advanced Neolithic culture, the Black Pottery Culture,[4] using the potter's wheel, which is labelled with the name of a site at Ch'eng Tzŭ Yui, east of Tsinan.[5] The sequence of archaeological strata is: Yang Shao Painted Pottery Neolithic Culture, Ch'eng Tzŭ Yui (alias Lungshan) Black Pottery Neolithic Culture, Shang Bronze Age Culture.[6] At each stage the range of domestic animals increased. The Painted Pottery people had only pigs, dogs, and cattle; the Black Pottery people had also sheep and horses. The Shang had also buffaloes and goats. The Shang had two breeds of pig, and they hunted many kinds of game (they were passionate hunters, in contrast to their Neolithic predecessors of both phases).[7] The Black Pottery Culture site at Ch'eng Tzŭ Yui was a rectangular walled city, measuring 450 by 390 metres,[8] with walls of pounded earth.[9] This latest Neolithic culture in China had in common with the succeeding Bronze-Age Shang Culture these pounded earth walls, tripods of the 'li' shape, horses, cattle, white pottery made of porcelain clay, and divination bones

[1] H. G. Creel: The Birth of China, p. 42.
[2] Roxby in loc. cit., p. 232; Li Chi: The Beginnings of Chinese Civilization, p. 12; Creel, op. cit., p. 45. [3] Li Chi, op. cit., p. 13.
[4] Roxby, loc. cit., pp. 230–1 and 232.
[5] Creel, op. cit., p. 48; idem: Studies in Early Chinese Cultures, First Series, p. 176; Roxby, loc. cit., p. 231.
[6] Li Chi, op. cit., p. 14.
[7] Ibid., pp. 22–23 and 23–25. Roxby, loc. cit., p. 231, says that cattle, as well as horses and sheep, make their first appearance in China in the Black Pottery Age. See also Creel: Studies, pp. 182–3 and 189, and The Birth of China, p. 49.
[8] Creel: Studies, p. 176.
[9] Ibid., pp. 177–82; The Birth of China, p. 48; Roxby, op. cit., p. 231.

(though, in the Black Pottery Age, these were not inscribed).[1] The Shang pottery technique was a continuation of the Black Pottery technique; the Black Pottery Culture 'li'-shaped tripods set the pattern for the subsequent Shang bronze sacrificial vessels; and Creel sees in the Black Pottery Culture the link between the Neolithic Age and the Bronze Age in China.[2] Moreover, the area occupied by the Shang Culture, before the removal of the capital to Anyang *circa* 1384 B.C., seems to have coincided with the area previously occupied by the Black Pottery Culture—unlike the course of events in Afrasia, where the passage from Neolithic-Chalcolithic cultures to Bronze Age civilizations was accompanied by a change of location from the oases to the river valleys. On the other hand, Li Chi lays stress[3] on the discontinuity between the Black Pottery Culture and the Shang Culture. He names[4] six features of the Shang Culture that were innovations: a new development of the pottery industry; the use of bronze for casting tools, weapons, and sacrificial vessels; the possession of a highly developed system of writing; chamber burials and human sacrifices; the use of chariots; and advanced stone carvings.

In the Shang script and the Shang bronze technique we are confronted with the same puzzle as at the geneses of the Egyptiac Civilization and the Indus Culture. These achievements burst upon us full-blown. Each of them must have had a long back-history.[5] The Shang style, like the Egyptiac and Indus styles, is quite distinctive; yet, in the light of what we know about the genesis of the Egyptiac Civilization, we can guess that the Shang Culture may have come to birth under the stimulus of some older culture whose influence we cannot detect because it inspired the fathers of the Shang Culture, not to imitate it, but to make something original of their own. 'Certainly the superlative technique of Shang bronze-casting must have represented the end point of a course of evolution, from the first discovery of the process, requiring many centuries, if not millennia.'[6] The tin content of Shang bronze amounts to 17 per cent.[7] As for the script, it was not crude or primitive.[8] No traces of primitive Chinese writing have been recovered up to date.[9] 'Every important principle of the formation of modern Chinese characters was already in use.'[10] It is now possible to read most of the characters in any oracle-bone inscription, and to date a large proportion of them with a margin of error of only a few decades.[11] Great progress was made during the 300 years during which we can follow the development of the script on the Shang oracle bones.[12] Conventionalized ideograms predominate; and, though some characters are borrowed for phonetic use, the Chinese scribes, like their Sumeric and Egyptiac predecessors, held back from going over to a completely phonetic system of writing.[13]

How are we to account for the genesis of civilization in China in the form of the Shang Culture? Was it an independent local development

---

[1] Creel: *The Birth of China*, p. 50. Cp. *Studies*, p. 191.
[2] *The Birth of China*, p. 50; *Studies*, pp. 190–1.   [3] In op. cit., p. 15.
[4] Ibid.   [5] Li Chi, op. cit., pp. 16–17; Roxby, loc. cit., p. 230.
[6] Creel: *Studies*, p. 225.   [7] C. S. Coon: *The History of Man*, p. 330.
[8] Creel: *The Birth of China*, p. 159.   [9] Creel: *Studies*, p. 34.
[10] Creel: *The Birth of China*, p. 160.   [11] Creel: *Studies*, p. 16.
[12] Ibid., p. 39.   [13] Creel: *The Birth of China*, p. 159; *Studies*, p. 39.

out of the Neolithic Black Pottery Culture, which was, itself, apparently, less dependent on western influences than the older Neolithic Painted Pottery Culture? Braidwood considers[1] it to be non-proven that civilization in Eastern Asia is an independent development. Then was the Shang Culture imported, ready-made, by invaders from abroad? If it was, was it brought in from the west or from the south, or partly from each of these two quarters? Or was it a local creation under inspiration from outside? These several possible explanations are not mutually exclusive, and perhaps the truth is to be found in a combination of them.

Rice seems to have been cultivated in Northern Honan as early as the Painted Pottery phase of the Neolithic Age, though at this stage without being accompanied by the buffalo.[2] Rice cultivation implies irrigation. It also implies an origin in the south.[3] According to Coon,[4] there is a consensus among botanists that rice, both wet and dry, was first cultivated somewhere in the tropical monsoon forests, and he raises the question whether the invention of agriculture in South China and South-East Asia may not have been independent of its invention in Afrasia.[5] Rice, as well as wheat and millet, was cultivated by the Shang people in the Anyang period.[6] They also had the water buffalo, though it was less common than ordinary cattle.[7] The additional breed of pig possessed by the Shang people, *sus vittatus*, was also of southern origin, in contrast to the original Chinese pig, which came from the north.[8] The Shang people's cowrie shells and pottery must also have come from the south.[9] Moreover, the nearest sources of tin for Shang bronze, with its high tin content, were in Yunnan and Malaya.[10]

It thus looks as if elements of culture had seeped into the birth-place of the Neolithic and Bronze-Age cultures of China, on the Honan Water-Parting, from the south as well as from the west, and this from the beginning of the local Neolithic Age, some time in the third millennium B.C. This southern source of culture in Northern China is mysterious in the present state of our knowledge. It is easy to see how cultural influences originating in Afrasia could have reached China from the north-west. But, to the south and south-west, the nearest centre of civilization to North China was the Indus valley, and the obstacles to the radiation of culture from there to China by an all-tropical route, south of the Tibetan plateau, were enormous. South-East Asia was one of the latest parts of the Old World to be brought within the *Oikoumenê*. The civilizations of India and China did not make contact in that quarter till the second century of the Christian Era, about 250 years later than the date of their earliest meeting via the steppes and oases of Central Asia. The southern provenance of important elements in the civilization of China seems to be unquestionable, but it presents us with a baffling problem.

[1] R. J. Braidwood: *The Near East and the Foundations of Civilization*, pp. 2–3.
[2] Li Chi, op. cit., p. 35; Creel: *Studies*, p. 175.
[3] Creel: *The Birth of China*, p. 51.
[4] Op. cit., p. 333.   [5] Ibid., pp. 149 and 320.
[6] Roxby, loc. cit., p. 234.
[7] Creel: *The Birth of China*, p. 80; *Studies*, p. 251.
[8] Creel: *The Birth of China*, p. 78; Coon, op. cit., p. 331.
[9] Coon, ibid.   [10] Coon, op. cit., p. 330.

5. THE GENESIS OF THE ANDEAN CIVILIZATION

The style of the Andean Civilization—if we use the word 'style' in the broadest sense to cover cultural activities of all kinds—is as distinctive as the style of the Egyptiac Civilization. Yet in this case, as in that, the archaeological evidence suggests that this distinctive civilization came to birth under the stimulus of a different, and equally distinctive, civilization with whose domain it was not immediately contiguous, though the domains of both civilizations were contained in one geographically continuous *Oikoumenê* in which the intervening regions were at a transitional stage of culture. In the Americas the civilization that played the role of the Sumeric civilization in the Old World was the Middle American Civilization, and the transitional culture that was the Middle American and Andean civilizations' common platform—from which they rose like two peaks[1]—was the one that Spinden labelled 'Archaic' and that Willey and Phillips now label 'Formative'.

The evidence linking Middle America and Peru is in the sphere of culture contact, not of style;[2] and 'the story is obviously not one of diffusion alone'.[3]

'In style and patterning the arts and institutions of the two areas are quite distinct. This distinctiveness is more pronounced in the Classic and Postclassic cultures than in those of the Formative. There is little question but what styles and patterns resulted from local creativeness and inventiveness in each area and within smaller regions of each area.'[4]

There is no good evidence of diffusion between Middle America and Peru before about 1000 B.C.;[5] but it does seem to have occurred during the last millennium B.C.[6] During this period the main movement seems to have been from north to south, considering that the Formative cultures arose earlier in Middle America than in Peru[7] and that the development of culture at the southern end of the Pacific coast of Peru lagged several centuries behind its development at the northern end.[8] The most convincing single proof of Middle America's priority is to be found in the history of the diffusion of maize, which eventually became the staple crop of all agricultural societies in America living in climatic and physiographical conditions that allowed of maize being cultivated. It may be true that pre-maize root-crop horticulture was

[1] A. L. Kroeber, quoted by G. R. Willey in 'The Intermediate Area of Nuclear America: Its Prehistoric Relationships to Middle America and Peru', a paper read to the Thirty-Third International Congress of Americanists, held at San José, Costa Rica, in July, 1958: *Actas del XXXIII Congresso Internacional de Americanistas*, vol. i (San José, Costa Rica, 1959), pp. 184–94.
[2] G. R. Willey: 'The Prehistoric Civilizations of Nuclear America', in *The American Anthropologist*, vol. 57, No. 3, Part 1 (June, 1955), pp. 571–93. The present reference is to p. 580.   [3] Ibid., p. 588.   [4] Ibid., p. 589.   [5] Ibid., p. 581.
[6] G. R. Willey: 'Estimated Correlations and Dating of South and Central American Culture Sequences', in *American Antiquity*, vol. 23, No. 4 (April, 1958), pp. 353–78. The present reference is to p. 358.
[7] Willey: 'The Intermediate Area', p. 7. According to Willey and Phillips, 1958, the carbon-14 test has given 1359±250 B.C. as the date for the Early Zacatanco culture in the valley of Mexico, and 714±200 B.C. for the coastal Chavín culture in North-Western Peru.   [8] Willey: 'Estimated Correlations', p. 356.

invented in Peru, at the north-western end of the Peruvian coast;[1] but 'sedentary agriculture-based village life and well-developed ceramics have been dated back to 1500 B.C. in Middle America ... and cultivated maize is considerably earlier than this'.[2] Willey and Phillips raise the question: 'Was the challenge of unfavourable environment a significant factor in the development of early maize culture? The earliest known Preformative[3] developments are in semi-arid regions.'[4] According to J. A. Mason, the carbon-14 test dates maize found in Bat Cave, New Mexico, to as early as 3650 B.C., with a margin of error of ±290 years. And maize pollen found in the valley of Mexico, 200 feet below the surface, must be at least 60,000 years old.[5] The domestication of maize was taking place in San Agostin, in West Central New Mexico, by about 3000 B.C.[6] It was being cultivated in Middle America by 2500 B.C.[7] But maize does not appear in Peru—not even in Northern Peru—till after the end of the Huaca Prieta Age, that is to say till after about 1250 B.C.[8] In Northern Peru in the Virú valley the carbon-14 test indicates that plain pottery came in about 1200 B.C. and maize perhaps not till about 848 B.C.[9] or perhaps even not till about 715 B.C., which appears to be the carbon-14-test mean date for the Cupisnique phase of North Peruvian coastal culture.[10]

Maize cultivation and the art of pottery are not the only elements of culture that appear to have been diffused from Middle America to the Andean World during the last millennium B.C. The idea of the platform mound seems to have been diffused in this direction between 1000 and 500 B.C.[11] Rocker-stamped decoration of pottery appears in Mexico *circa* 1000–500 B.C. and in North-West Peru *circa* 700 B.C.[12] Rocker-stamped decoration and the platform mound and maize appear in North-West Peru simultaneously.[13] The diffusion of 'resist-dye' painting is another example.[14] In general, during the last millennium B.C., there seems to have

1 Willey: 'Estimated Correlations', p. 372; 'The Intermediate Area', p. 7. According to J. A. Mason: *The Ancient Civilizations of Peru*, p. 30, more than a hundred food plants were cultivated in the Americas and more than thirty of these in Peru. Cp. G. H. S. Bushnell: *Peru*, p. 36. A list of pre-Columbian domesticated plants in the Andean highlands is given by W. C. Bennett and J. R. Bird in *Andean Culture History*, pp. 30–31. These two authorities claim, ibid., p. 29, that the cultivation of the potato, coca, quinoa, and oca originated in the Andean area.

2 Willey: 'The Intermediate Area', p. 7. Cp. G. H. S. Bushnell: *Peru*, p. 41.

3 i.e. late Archaic in terms of Willey's and Phillips' revised classification (A. J. T.).

4 'Method and Theory in American Archaeology, II' (1955), p. 792.

5 J. A. Mason: *The Ancient Civilizations of Peru*, p. 30. Willey, however, gives the carbon-14 date of the maize in Bat Cave as *circa* 2500 B.C. ('The Interrelated Rise of the Native Cultures of Middle and South America', p. 33).

6 Willey and Phillips, 'Method and Theory in American Archaeology, II' (1955), pp. 756–7. C. S. Coon, *The History of Man*, p. 353, gives the date as 5000 B.C.

7 Willey: 'The Prehistoric Civilizations of Nuclear America', p. 581.

8 Mason, op. cit., pp. 31 and 35. Cp. W. C. Bennett and J. R. Bird: *Andean Culture History*, p. 126.

9 G. R. Willey: *Prehistoric Settlement Patterns in the Virú Valley, Peru*, p. 34.

10 Willey: 'The Prehistoric Civilizations of Nuclear America', p. 581. On p. 577, ibid., Willey dates the beginning of the Cupisnique phase *circa* 1000 B.C. Bushnell, *Peru*, p. 41, places the arrival of maize in Peru about 1000 B.C. Willey dates it *circa* 700 B.C. in 'The Interrelated Rise of the Native Cultures of Middle and South America', p. 33.

11 Willey: 'The Prehistoric Civilizations of Nuclear America', p. 583; idem: 'The Interrelated Rise of the Native Cultures of Middle and South America', pp. 36–37.

12 Willey: 'The Interrelated Rise of the Native Cultures of Middle and South America', pp. 34–36.   13 Ibid., p. 44.

14 Willey: 'The Prehistoric Civilizations of Nuclear America', pp. 583–4.

been a diffusion of the Middle American Formative stage culture of Tlatilco, on the Mexican plateau near the present-day Mexico City, to Chavín, in the north-western highlands of the Andean World,[1] as well as to the north-west coast of Peru in the Cupisnique (Coastal Chavín) phase of culture there. There are geographical links between Tlatilco and Chavín in Honduras at Playa de los Muertos in the Ulua Valley and on the Babahoyo River in coastal Ecuador.[2] Among the features shared with the Tlatilco culture by the Chavín and Cupisnique cultures, Willey mentions[3] (in addition to the rocker-stamped decoration) incised colour zones in pottery decoration, stirrup-spouted vessels, pottery stamps, whistling jars, the jaguar motif, and a concept of dualism. On the other hand, there is no parallel in the Tlatilco culture to the massive buildings at Chavín, and none in the Chavín culture to the Tlatilco culture's pottery figurines.[4]

The technique of making figurines in moulds seems to have spread from the Teotihuacán Classic culture of Middle America to the Andean World early in the first millennium of the Christian Era.[5] Willey conjectures[6] that the mould technique may have travelled by sea from Middle America to Ecuador. And it seems certain that a sea-passage, based on ports on the north-west coast of Ecuador, was at least one of the routes by which metallurgy was diffused to Middle America from the Andean World.[7]

6. WHAT WERE THE EXTENT AND THE IMPORTANCE OF THE PRE-COLUMBIAN CULTURAL RELATIONS BETWEEN THE OLD WORLD AND THE AMERICAS?

It seems certain that the first human occupants of the Americas came, like their successors, from the Old World, and that this happened at what is a relatively late date in the time-scale of Old-World human history. In the Americas no trace has been found of anthropoid apes, and none of any kinds of hominid other than *homo sapiens*.[8] The predominant type of

[1] G. H. S. Bushnell: *Peru*, pp. 52–53.   [2] Ibid., p. 53.
[3] In 'The Interrelated Rise of the Native Cultures of Middle and South America' p. 35; and in 'The Prehistoric Civilizations of Nuclear America', p. 581.
[4] Bushnell, op. cit., p. 53.   [5] Willey: 'The Intermediate Area', p. 9.
[6] In 'The Prehistoric Civilizations of Nuclear America', pp. 583–4.
[7] Willey, op. cit., p. 584. According to Willey, 'The Interrelated Rise of the Native Cultures of Middle and South America', p. 41, 'American metallurgical techniques were first developed in South America.' Gold work is found in North-West Peru (in the Lambayeque valley) as early as the Coastal Chavín horizon, copper work in the Gallinazo period, i.e. the transition from the Formative to the Classic. Metal was first used for weapons and tools in North-West Peru in the Mochica period (ibid., p. 41). Bronze was invented in the south-east highlands of the Andean World in the classic Tiahuanaco period, and was eventually diffused to Ecuador by the Incas (ibid., p. 42). Copper tools had been in use in Ecuador as early as the Mochica period of North-West Peru (ibid., p. 42). On the other hand, in the Maya cultural province of Middle America metal objects were not in circulation before the Late Classic period, *circa* A.D. 900–1000, and then only as foreign imports (ibid., p. 42). Copper tools seem to have come to the south-west coast of Mexico in the Late Postclassic period direct by sea from Ecuador, and Ecuadorian mariners seem to have been the middlemen between the Andean World and Middle America (ibid., pp. 42–43). According to Willey, 'The Prehistoric Civilizations of Nuclear America', p. 584, metallurgy arrived in Middle America from the Andean World within the last five centuries before the Spanish conquest; according to C. S. Coon, *The History of Man*, pp. 345–6, it arrived only within the last three centuries before that date.   [8] J. A. Mason: *The Ancient Civilizations of Peru*, p. 20.

pre-Columbian *homo sapiens* in the Americas is Proto-Mongoloid, but the oldest skulls found in the Americas are dolichocephalic, of an Australoid-Melanesoid type.[1] These various pre-Columbian representatives of *homo sapiens* entered the Americas via Alaska, during the latest (so far) of the glaciations. In that age, sea-level may have been 300 feet lower than it is now. The present Behring Straits will have been an isthmus. And the geological evidence indicates that this isthmus and the Mackenzie River basin were unglaciated at the time.[2] 'Early migration southward from Alaska was mainly in the intermontane and High Plains "corridors" on either side of the Rocky Mountains.'[3] Along the Pacific coast of North America remains dating back to the 'Lithic' Age are relatively rare.[4] They are also rare in Peru and Bolivia.[5] In South America 'Lithic' remains are concentrated in temperate and arid areas— perhaps because these provided better hunting.[6] The earliest human entrants into the Americas from the Old World brought their Old-World Palaeolithic tools with them. The carbon-14 test gives an antiquity of 9,000 years to a pair of sandals found in a cave in Oregon, and an antiquity of 8,639 years for the human occupation of a cave near the southern tip of South America.[7] On the High Plains of central and southern North America the date of 'Early Lithic' (i.e. late Pleistocene and early Post-Pleistocene) remains is *circa* 8000–4000 B.C.[8] 'Early Lithic' remains astride the Straits of Magellan are dated, by the carbon-14 test, 6688 B.C., with a margin of error of ±450 years.[9] Willey and Phillips date the Lithic Age in the Americas *circa* 20000–5000 B.C.[10] 'By 5000 B.C. or before, Man had found his way over most of the New World.'[11] In fact, as C. S. Coon puts it,[12] a single migration across the Behring Straits in the Fourth Glacial Age suffices to explain the human occupation of all the Americas except the Eskimo region by about 5000 B.C.

This first chapter of the history of Man in the Americas is not controversial. The controversies arise over the question of later contacts, and the related question whether such contacts, if they occurred, were made by sea across the breadth of the Pacific Ocean and whether, if so, the traffic was one-way or was reciprocal.

Braidwood holds[13] that civilization has arisen independently in two places: the Tigris–Euphrates basin and the New World. Kroeber, too, judges[14] that,

'all in all' the Americas' 'culture has evidently both developed and crystallised independently of that of the [Old-World] *Oikoumenê*. The New World possesses its own heartland of civilization, stretching from Central

[1] J. A. Mason: *The Ancient Civilizations of Peru*, pp. 25–27.   [2] Ibid., p. 25.
[3] Willey and Phillips: *Method and Theory in American Archaeology* (1958), p. 96.
[4] Ibid., p. 96.   [5] Ibid., p. 102.   [6] Ibid., p. 103.
[7] Mason, op. cit., p. 21. Willey, however, dates the earliest human occupation of South America as late as 7500–5000 B.C. in 'The Interrelated Rise of the Native Cultures of Middle and South America', p. 43.
[8] Willey and Phillips: 'Method and Theory in American Archaeology, II' (1955), p. 731.   [9] Ibid., pp. 737–8.
[10] Willey and Phillips (1958), p. 201.
[11] Ibid.   [12] In *The History of Man*, p. 352.
[13] R. J. Braidwood: *The Near East and the Foundations of Civilization*, p. 1.
[14] In *The Nature of Culture*, p. 394.

Mexico to somewhat beyond Peru. The axis of this cultural Nuclear America is oriented without reference to that of the ancient *Oikoumenê*. It is both well separated from it and pointed in a different direction.'

In Kroeber's view[1] the histories of the Old-World civilizations and the New-World civilizations 'are not, as far as we can see, parts of a single plot. Resemblances are either analogies instead of homologies; or, where they are the latter, they are also *disjecta membra*.' Willey, too, holds[2] that Nuclear America, to the best of our knowledge, 'stands clearly apart and essentially independent from the comparable culture core of the Old World'. Nuclear America and the Old-World *Oikoumenê* are parallel cultural structures. 'Within each, diverse civilizations (or styles) have sprung up as unique re-workings of a common cultural content held within the *Oikoumenê*.'[3] As Kroeber sees it,[4] the independence of the Pre-Columbian American civilizations is made probable by the absence, in them, of iron, wheels, ploughs, the usual grains and domestic animals, stringed instruments, ordeals, and proverbs. In plough-agriculture Kroeber sees[5] a specific cultural pattern, which is unlikely to have been invented more than once. He does not feel the same about agriculture itself, and he points out that the pattern of agriculture in the Americas and in the Old World is not the same. Kroeber's view on this point is shared by J. A. Mason. More than a hundred food plants, Mason notes,[6] were cultivated in the Americas, and,

'of these, only very few, such as gourds, cotton, sweet potatoes, possibly plantains, peanuts, and coconuts, have close enough relatives in the Old World to suggest importation (and the sweet potato almost certainly was of American origin); the great majority have no foreign congeners, but rather close wild relatives in America.'

That bronze should have been invented twice over—once in Sumer and then independently in the Andean highlands—is surprising, if true. Kroeber submits[7] that, all the same, it seems probable that bronze was invented independently in the New World when one takes into consideration all the associated data, such as the shapes and uses of the objects made of it. He notes[8] that the Sumerians and the Chinese used their bronze for making swords and ritual vessels and that the Andeans did not.

Neither Kroeber nor Willey seeks to deny that there was some diffusion of elements of culture from the Old World to the Americas in the Post-Palaeolithic Age. Willey states his position as follows:[9]

'I am unconvinced of the linkages of style, in art and architecture, which have been advanced (Heine-Geldern and Eckholm 1951; Eckholm 1953). On the other hand, certain technical inventions, modes, or complex features do argue for pre-Columbian contact.'

---

[1] Ibid.   [2] 'The Prehistoric Civilizations of Nuclear America', p. 571.
[3] Ibid.   [4] In op. cit., p. 60.
[5] Ibid., p. 91.
[6] In *The Ancient Civilizations of Peru*, p. 30.
[7] Ibid., p. 60.   [8] Ibid., p. 91.
[9] In 'The Prehistoric Civilizations of Nuclear America', p. 585.

'The Early Lithic and Archaic reflect a general situation of marginal dependence on the Old World.'[1] Willey and Phillips consider[2] the possibility that the 'Archaic' culture of the Americas may have been derived from Northern Eurasia. The culture of the north-west coast of North America appears to be 'Archaic' in all its phases;[3] and here 'Asiatic and possibly Oceanic influences played a more decisive role than those from more southerly parts of the North American continent'.[4] Kroeber notes[5] that northern North America has received by import from Asia a number of non-mutually related items: e.g. the composite bow, slat-armour, conical tents, scapulomancy, bear rituals, the shamanistic tambourine drum, the magic flight story, and so on. But, in his view,[6] this indicates that North America was *not* a passage-way for historic continuity between the Old-World *Oikoumenê* and Nuclear America. North America has *not* played the transmissional role that has been played by Turkestan. The same point is made in another form by Willey and Phillips.[7] As they put it, the fact of diffusion 'does not deny that the cultures of human societies are integrated functioning wholes rather than random assemblages of elements, but it does negate the theory that such cultures, or institutions within cultures, are necessarily transmitted as integrated wholes'.

Willey and Phillips also insist[8] that the independence of the pre-Columbian American civilizations increased *pari passu* with their development.

'With the Preformative[9] . . . we begin to reckon with elements that have no specific Old-World parallels. . . . Asiatic influences may have continued to filter through from the North, or directly across the Pacific, but these influences were never again paramount except on the periphery of the North American continent. Leaving aside the important but unresolved question of whether or not trans-Pacific influences were significant forces in the rise of American agricultural civilizations,[10] there can be no doubt that the Nuclear American centers (Middle America to Peru) were culturally dominant in the later stages of New World development.'

These general considerations, put forward by Kroeber, Willey, and Phillips, seem decisive. They hold good in the face of evidence that particular elements of culture were diffused from the Old World to the Americas and also, in a much smaller number of instances, in the opposite direction. The evidence cited for these cultural contacts and interchanges looks as if it were very uneven in value. There are sweeping dogmatic assertions that can be discounted, but there are also well-attested facts that cannot be explained away, and some of these are enigmas in our present state of knowledge. The difficulty of the problem

[1] Willey and Phillips: 'Method and Theory in American Archaeology, II' (1955), p. 794.　　[2] Ibid., p. 744.　　[3] Ibid., pp. 750–1.　　[4] Ibid., p. 751.
[5] In *The Nature of Culture*, p. 394.　　[6] Ibid.
[7] 'Method and Theory in American Archaeology, II' (1955), pp. 729–30.
[8] Ibid., p. 794.
[9] i.e. Late Archaic and Early Formative, in Willey's and Phillips's own revised terminology (A. J. T.).
[10] Willey is sceptical about the possibility of identical culture traits having been introduced separately into Middle America and into Peru by diffusion across the Pacific ('The Prehistoric Civilizations of Nuclear America', p. 586).

has been accentuated by the results of the application of the carbon-14 test in the field of Pre-Columbian American archaeology. This has consistently set back the dates of the earlier phases of Pre-Columbian American history as compared with the previous datings obtained by dead-reckoning on the basis of estimates of the time required for the depositing of such-and-such a thickness of stratum of human refuse. The results of the carbon-14 test may be surprising, and they are subject to many possibilities of error, so that they have to be accepted with some reserve unless and until we obtain a large enough number of them to be able to arrive at a statistical average. On the other hand, datings based on a supposed correlation between thickness of deposit and passage of time are incurably subjective.

When we have reduced the alleged correspondences between particular Old-World and New-World culture elements to a minimum, what remains is still impressive.

The greatest puzzle of all is presented by the history of cotton. The earliest known Old-World cotton fabrics come, it is said,[1] from Mohenjo-daro. According to Kroeber,[2] cotton originated in India and spread from there till, in the end, it largely replaced wool in 'Iraq, linen in Egypt and Europe, hemp in China and Japan. 'Its abundant growth and use in Peru precedes that in either China or the West.'

'It has been established that the cultivated New-World cottons resulted from the hybridisation of Old-World cotton and a wild American cotton plant,[3] probably gossypium raimondii of Peru.'[4]

And it is the unanimous conclusion of botanists 'that Old-World cotton could have been introduced into America only by human agency'.[5]

'Aboriginal American cultivated cotton has recently been indicated to the satisfaction of botanists to be a hybrid between Asiatic cultivated and American wild cotton. Cotton was present in the lowest agricultural, pre-ceramic horizons of coastal Peru. Carriage by human hands across the Pacific at this early period would appear to be the only explanation.'[6]

The carbon-14 test has now set back the date of this pre-maize and pre-pottery, but not pre-cotton, stage of culture in Peru to 2550–1250 B.C.[7] According to R. Heine-Geldern,[8] J. R. Bird found crude cotton textiles at the pre-ceramic site of Huaca Prieta, in North-West Peru, which he dates *circa* 2575–2370 B.C. by the carbon-14 test. In fact, by 2500 B.C. cotton was being cultivated in both the Indus valley and Peru.[9]

At Huaca Prieta at this period a species of gourd was being cultivated that was practically identical with one cultivated in Polynesia.[10] According to Coon,[11] gourds were originally domesticated in Africa or India.

---

[1] R. Heine-Geldern: 'Some Problems of Migration in the Pacific', in *Kultur und Sprache* (Vienna 1952, Herold), p. 346.   [2] *The Nature of Culture*, p. 388.
[3] According to Coon: *The History of Man*, p. 255, cultivated American cotton has thirteen large chromosomes, like wild American cotton, and also thirteen small chromosomes, like both wild and cultivated Indian cotton.
[4] Heine-Geldern, ibid., p. 346.   [5] Heine-Geldern, ibid.
[6] Mason, op. cit., p. 24; cp. p. 32. See also G. H. S. Bushnell: *Peru*, p. 26.
[7] Mason, op. cit., p. 31.   [8] In loc. cit., pp. 346–7.
[9] Coon: *The History of Man*, pp. 304–5.
[10] Mason, op. cit., pp. 32–33.   [11] In op. cit., p. 354.

Coon concludes[1] that, if cotton and gourds were brought to America by human agency, this must have been the work of Neolithic navigators. This is as much as to say that the evidence forces upon us a *reductio ad absurdum*. But so incredible a conclusion is surely not necessary. If there is a possibility that the archaeologically well attested influence of the Sumeric Civilization on the late predynastic culture of Upper Egypt towards the end of the fourth millennium B.C. was diffused by sea via the Indian Ocean, it is perhaps just conceivable that Sumerian or Indian navigators may have found their way across the Pacific (no doubt unintentionally and accidentally) 500 or 1,000 years later. In any case the carriers cannot have been the Micronesians or the Polynesians. The carbon-14 test dates the first human occupation of Western Micronesia between 1727 and 1327 B.C., the occupation of the Marianas *circa* 1500 B.C., and the occupation of Hawaii *circa* A.D. 825–1125.[2] Yet

'While it is certain that the Polynesians did not carry the cultivated cotton plant from the Old World to America, it is equally certain that it was American cultivated cotton which subsequently was introduced into the Polynesian islands.'[3]

The sweet potato also seems to have come to Polynesia from America before the arrival of European mariners in the Pacific. It was found already being cultivated in Polynesia by the eighteenth-century European explorers.[4] It was found in Easter Island, Hawaii, and New Zealand,[5] and in both Easter Island and New Zealand there were a great number of varieties. The name by which it is known in Polynesia also points to a South American origin. In the Quechua language of the Andean World the sweet potato is called *kumar, komal, kumal*. It is called *kumara* in New Zealand, Raratonga, the Tuomotos, Mangareva, Easter Island; *umara* or *umaa* in Tahiti; *kumala* in Tonga; *'umala* in Samoa; *uala* or *uwala* in Hawaii; *kumaa* in the Marquesas; *ku'a'ra* in Mangaia.[6] The question whether the mariners who brought the sweet potato and cotton from America to Polynesia were Americans or Polynesians is one that is notoriously still in dispute. Hornell stresses the efficiency that had been attained in the technique of shipbuilding in both Polynesia and South America before the advent of the Europeans. In Polynesia 'double canoes of large carrying capacity were possessed by the people of every principal island group'.[7] In A.D. 1526 Pizarro's pilot Bartolomeo Ruiz captured, *en route* between the Isthmus of Panamá and Peru, a thirty-ton balsa raft with bipod masts (like Burman and Indonesian boats), cotton sails, and hennequen rigging.[8] Mason holds[9] that the

[1] In op. cit., p. 59.
[2] A. Sharp: *Ancient Voyagers in the Pacific*, pp. 84 and 100.
[3] Heine-Geldern, ibid., p. 347.
[4] R. B. Dixon: 'The Problem of the Sweet Potato in Polynesia', in *The American Anthropologist*, New Series, vol. 34, No. 1 (January–March, 1932), p. 40. Cp. J. Hornell: 'Was there pre-Columbian Contact between the People of Oceania and South America?' in *The Journal of the Polynesian Society*, vol. 54 (Wellington, N.Z., 1945), pp. 186–7.
[5] Dixon in loc. cit., p. 44; Coon, op. cit., p. 357.
[6] Hornell, ibid., p. 175. Cp. Mason, op. cit., p. 23; A. Sharp: *Ancient Voyagers in the Pacific*, p. 87.
[7] Hornell in loc. cit., p. 169.
[8] Ibid., p. 179.
[9] In op. cit., p. 21.

elements of culture shared by the American societies with Polynesia, Melanesia, and South-East Asia are too many, and the correspondences too close, to be dismissed as being accidental coincidences. At the same time he points out that 'Polynesians did not reach Easter Island before the fourteenth century A.D.', and that there is no evidence that they had any predecessors who were their equals in navigational skill.[1] He also notes that there is no trace of any infusion of Polynesian blood in the Pre-Columbian population of the Americas.[2] Indeed, as we have seen, chronology rules out the possibility that the Polynesians can have played any appreciable part in conveying elements of Old-World culture to the Americas, even if we accept Hornell's thesis[3] that the Polynesians made systematic long-distance voyages of exploration. But account should also be taken of A. Sharp's thesis that there were no deliberate voyages, even between Eastern and Western Polynesia;[4] that 'all these separate worlds were settled by one-way voyages of isolated canoes';[5] and that 'no accounts of deliberate two-way contact have been found'.[6]

A number of miscellaneous culture elements common to the Old World and the Americas have been noticed. H. G. Creel, for instance, notices that a particular make of stone knife, which is characteristic of the Shang Culture in China, as well as the composite bow and the sleeved coat, has a circum-polar diffusion, and that the knife is found in the New World as far afield as South America.[7] He draws attention to the affinity between the art of the Shang and that of the Pre-Columbian peoples along the north-west coast of North America.[8] In particular he mentions the motif of bisected animals, joined only at the nose.[9] Willey notes that the rocker-stamped decoration, which was eventually diffused to Peru from Mexico,[10] had previously been diffused to Mexico from North-East Asia.[11] Mason notes[12] that 'on the coast of Chile characteristic stone implements have been found that must have come from Easter Island'. The pan-pipes in use in early China and in Peru are identical in detail.[13] The chewing of betel nut in Malaya, Indonesia, and the Pacific has its counterpart in the chewing of coca in the Andean World, and in both cases the drug is chewed with an admixture of lime.[14] Bark cloth and feather mosaics were manufactured on both sides of the Pacific by identical processes.[15] Weaving was done by the same processes, including methods of keeping part of the fabric untouched by the dye (the 'resist-dye' process).[15] Heine-Geldern's list[16] of culture elements common to the Old World and the Americas includes the *cire perdue* process of casting metal; the use of tin; the colouring of gold by chemical processes; methods of weaving; tie-dyeing (i.e. 'resist-dyeing'); batik;

[1] Ibid., p. 23.   [2] Ibid., p. 25.   [3] In op. cit., p. 168.
[4] A. Sharp: *Ancient Voyagers in the Pacific*, p. 12.
[5] Ibid., p. 30.   [6] Ibid., p. 78.
[7] Creel: *Studies*, pp. 173–4 and 246–7; *The Birth of China*, p. 97.
[8] *Studies*, p. 249.   [9] *Studies*, p. 248.   [10] See p. 356.
[11] G. R. Willey: 'The Interrelated Rise of the Native Cultures of Middle and South America', p. 35; idem: 'The Prehistoric Civilizations of Nuclear America', p. 585.
[12] In op. cit., pp. 24–25.   [13] Ibid., pp. 24–25 and 231.
[14] Ibid., pp. 24–25 and 142.
[15] Ibid., pp. 24–25.
[16] In *Diogenes*, No. 13 (Spring, 1956), pp. 91–92.

the parasol as an emblem of royalty; the ball-game;[1] the symbolization of the points of the compass by colours—and these the same colours on both sides of the Pacific. Another list of Heine-Geldern's[2] is longer.

'To mention only a few out of many items of Asiatic cultural elements we find in Peru: Highly characteristic art motifs of the Late Chou period of China in the Chavín culture; an Asiatic form of the loom; gauze weaving and other Asiatic weaving techniques; the lost-wax (cire perdue) process of metal-casting; cormorant fishing; metal mirrors; star-shaped clubs (found also in Eastern Asia); the use of the throne, the litter, and the umbrella as insignia of rank and royalty, the umbrella being of a very unusual type, known only from Peru and from China, where it appears already in the second century A.D.'

So long as Heine-Geldern is dealing in terms of particular elements of culture, he is on uncontroversial ground in so far as he can bring forward convincing evidence that the elements that he pronounces to be identical really are so. Mason and Willey and Kroeber agree that a number of elements were diffused from the Old World to the Americas, and a smaller number in the opposite direction. Such facts, when demonstrated, have to be accepted, even though the dates and circumstances and agencies of the transmission remain obscure. But Heine-Geldern plunges into deeper waters when he suggests that the whole configuration of an Old-World culture made its way into the Americas complete. In another context[3] he maintains that the motifs of Andean sculpture of the Chavín horizon echo those of the Chinese sculpture of the eighth century B.C., and that the motifs of the Andean Salinar culture echo those of the Chinese culture of the seventh and sixth centuries B.C.[4] He holds that the influence of the subsequent Dong-son culture of North-Eastern Indochina was still more potent in the Americas from Panamá to Northern Chile and North-Western Argentina—especially in metallurgical designs and processes.[5] As for the Tajín culture of Eastern Mexico, he writes[5] that 'one would be justified in speaking of a local variant of the Chinese art of the seventh to the fourth centuries B.C.'. He suggests[6] that the Hindu-Buddhist culture of South-East Asia influenced the architecture, art, symbols, cosmological ideas, institutions, insignia, and games of Middle America—especially in its Olméca and Maya cultural provinces—in the seventh to tenth centuries A.D. And he concludes[7] that

'the processes involved in the formation of the Meso-American and Andean civilizations can be compared to those which resulted in the Hinduisation of South-East Asia'.

This daring parallel surely refutes itself. The Indian origin of the culture that was diffused over South-East Asia in and after the early centuries of the Christian Era is attested, not only by styles of art and architecture and by forms of social organization and government, but by

---

[1] Also mentioned by Willey in 'The Interrelated Rise of the Native Cultures of Middle and South America', pp. 29–31.   [2] In Kultur und Sprache, p. 346.
[3] Diogenes, No. 13 (Spring, 1956).   [4] Loc. cit., p. 93.
[5] Ibid., p. 93.   [6] Ibid., p. 94.   [7] Ibid., p. 96.

the introduction of Indian scripts and Indian literary languages; and this latter evidence would remain uncontrovertible, even if it were to be argued that the attribution of the new styles of South-East Asian art to an Indian origin is, by its very nature, subjective and therefore disputable.

During the span of perhaps ten or twelve thousand years that intervened between the arrival of Palaeolithic Man in the Americas via Alaska and the eventual arrival of Modern Western Man there via the Atlantic, there is evidence that particular elements of culture made their way, by whatever routes, to the Americas from the Old World. But the thesis that the same transit was made by complete configurations of culture seems to go far beyond the attested facts. If this finding is the right one, the pre-Columbian civilizations of the Americas must be regarded as having been original creations of the descendants of those representatives of *homo sapiens* who had entered the Americas from the Old World in the last phase of the Palaeolithic Age. 'Almost every element of culture in the New World can be explained on the basis of a purely local growth.'[1]

XI. THE CONFIGURATION OF MIDDLE AMERICAN AND ANDEAN HISTORY

PRE-COLUMBIAN American archaeology has made enormous advances since the years 1927–33, when I was planning the first ten volumes of this book and writing the first three. But the effect on the pictures of Andean history and of Middle American history has not been the same. The general configuration of Andean history remains much what it was, in spite of the filling in of details and the lengthening of the chronological vista.[2] On the other hand the general configuration of Middle American history has been transformed out of all recognition.

In the late nineteen-twenties the picture of Middle American history was dominated by the Maya Classic Civilization in the tropical lowlands of Northern Guatemala and in the Mexican territories adjoining it on the north-west (as, in the same years, the picture of Pre-Hellenic Aegean history was dominated by the Minoan Civilization of Crete). The Olméca cultural province of Middle America, in the tropical lowlands along the Atlantic coast of Mexico south of Vera Cruz, was still quite out of the picture, though subsequent archaeological discoveries here have led one school of archaeologists to see in the Olméca province the

---

[1] C. S. Coon: *The History of Man*, p. 351.
[2] The vista of both Andean and Middle American history has been lengthened partly by new discoveries, and partly by the redating of already known artefacts by the carbon-14 test. This test seems, more or less consistently, to give dates that are earlier than those previously guessed, by dead reckoning backwards from the advent of the Spaniards, on the basis of estimates of the time that would have been taken to lay down such and such a thickness of débris. This conversion of strata into time-spans is, of course, highly conjectural. On the other hand, the carbon-14 test's margin of error is also high, unless and until a great enough number of tests have been made to produce a statistical average.

birthplace of the whole Middle American Civilization.[1] Again, the cultural province on the plateau, including the Valley of Mexico, and the cultural province in Yucatan, did not, in the nineteen-twenties, enter into the picture until after the mysterious abandonment of the Classic Maya sites. Archaeologists accepted the tradition presented in the Yucatec Mayan codices and in the information gathered by the earliest Spanish inquirers. And this tradition was that the Mayan civilization in Yucatan was started there by migrants from the already abandoned Classic sites to the south and south-west. As for the plateau, history here began, in the nineteen-twenties, with the arrival of the Toltecs from the north. The civilization of the Classic stage and age at Teotihuacán was still below the archaeological horizon, though the pyramids of the Sun and Moon had been towering into the sky ever since the days of their Classic builders.

Using, as I did, an Hellenic model to interpret the histories of non-Hellenic civilizations, I concluded, from the picture presented by the archaeologists at the time, that in Middle America there had been two generations of civilizations. The first generation had been represented by the Maya Classic Civilization of the tropical lowlands; and, when this had mysteriously come to an end, it had been followed by two new civilizations that were affiliated to it in the sense in which the Western and Byzantine civilizations were affiliated to the Hellenic. One of these two affiliated civilizations of the second generation in Middle America was that of the Postclassic Maya, followed by Toltec, immigrants into Yucatan; the other was that of the Toltecs and their Aztec successors on the plateau.

Thirty years' progress in Middle American archaeology has effaced the picture on which this construction of mine was based. The Middle American World now appears as a geographical unity with much the same area from beginning to end. The tropical lowland Maya region, in which the Maya Classic Civilization rose and fell, turns out to be only one Middle American cultural province out of five; and the conquest of the tropical forest here for civilization turns out to be a relatively late event in the long course of Middle American history. The Middle American Civilization had almost as old a footing in Yucatan as in the forested lowlands farther south, and perhaps an older footing on the highlands of Southern Guatemala, on the Mexican plateau, and in the 'Olméca' cultural province in the tropical lowlands round Vera Cruz.[2]

In the light of this new knowledge I now have to abandon my previous construction of three distinct civilizations in the Middle American cultural area, and to think in terms of a single civilization here, as in the Andean World.

One general effect of the progress of archaeological discovery in both these Pre-Columbian American worlds has, indeed, been to bring out points of resemblance between the cultural configurations and the histories of their respective civilizations, and at the same time to bring

[1] G. R. Willey and P. Phillips suggest, with greater caution, that the Middle American Classic Civilization may have started slightly earlier in the Olméca cultural province than elsewhere (*Method and Theory in American Archaeology* (1958), p. 185).
[2] See G. R. Willey: 'The Interrelated Rise of the Native Cultures of Middle and South America', p. 39.

out points of difference between their respective styles. Though there is, as we have seen,[1] good archaeological evidence for the diffusion of elements of culture from Middle America to North-West Peru at a time when the Andean World was still in the late 'Archaic' (ex-'Preformative') stage of culture, the style of each of the two civilizations is quite distinctive and the most striking likenesses between them are in their total cultural configuration.[2] Moreover, though the diffusion of culture elements between these two worlds occurred at least twice—first during the late 'Archaic' (ex-'Preformative') stage of Andean history and again during the last few centuries before the Spanish conquest—the two worlds were not, and never became, geographically contiguous with each other. From first to last they were separated by a region in South-Eastern Central America and North-Western South America, extending from the present-day Honduras and Salvador to the present-day Colombia and highland Ecuador, which kept in step with them only as far as the 'Formative' stage[3] of culture and fell out of the running when Middle America and the Andean World each went on to rise to the Classic level.[4] This makes the similarities between the configurations of the two Pre-Columbian American civilizations all the more remarkable. These similarities are both geographical and historical.

Geographically, each of these two worlds consisted of a number of distinct cultural provinces, in each of which a common civilization was given a particular local colour.[5] In either world these different provinces were always in communication with each other. In general the more

[1] On pp. 355–7.

[2] Willey: 'The Prehistoric Civilizations of Nuclear America', p. 586.

[3] See Willey: 'The Interrelated Rise of the Native Cultures of Middle and South America', p. 28; eundem: 'The Intermediate Area of Nuclear America', p. 11; Willey and Phillips: 'Method and Theory in American Archaeology, II' (1955), p. 778; eosdem, 1958, pp. 171–4. Honduras and Salvador never rose to the Classic level. Nicaragua and Costa Rica, too, did not rise above Formative, though their relations with Middle America were with Middle American late Classic and Postclassic. The cultures of Panamá never rose above Formative, though they were late. Nor did the cultures of the Colombian and Ecuadorian highlands. Even in the southernmost of the ten intermont basins of highland Ecuador, civilization was not very old (W. C. Bennett and J. R. Bird: *Andean Culture History*, p. 84). In both Ecuador and Colombia, Pre-Inca culture was pluralistic and was quite distinct from the culture of the central Andean region (ibid., p. 86). 'Ecuador has little stone-carving (except in Manabi), a weak development of architecture and little use of stone buildings, only slight development of terracing and irrigation systems, and little use of the llama. Lacking are highly concentrated populations, large ceremonial centers (except possibly on the coast), cities, and wide political integration' (D. Collier, in W. C. Bennett [ed.]: *A Reappraisal of Peruvian Archaeology*, pp. 85–86). The relative cultural backwardness of even the southern end of highland Ecuador is not surprising, considering the formidableness of the physical barrier separating the Ecuadorian highlands from the cradle of the Andean Civilization in Peru. Cajamarca in Peru is insulated from Loja in Ecuador by 400 kilometres of rough, forest-covered mountains (W. C. Bennett in op. cit., p. 3). Moreover, in the Northern Andes, including the North Peruvian highlands, there is a double rainy season. This enables a rain-forest to occupy the zone between the 10,000-feet contour line and the snow-line; and this excludes llamas and alpacas (ibid., p. 3; W. C. Bennett and J. R. Bird: *Andean Culture History*, p. 4). On the other hand, the Ecuadorian coast did rise to the Classic and Postclassic levels. At Manta, for instance, there was a true Postclassic urban centre (Willey and Phillips: 'Method and Theory in American Archaeology, II' (1955), pp. 772–4; eosdem, 1958, p. 175). Willey and Phillips (1955, pp. 775 and 788) raise the question whether the Ecuadorian coast may perhaps have risen, at one move, from Formative to Postclassic as a result of trading with Postclassic coastal Peru.

[4] 'The Classic stage in the New World is limited to Middle America and the central Andes' (Willey and Phillips, 1958, p. 183).

[5] Willey and Phillips: 'Method and Theory in American Archaeology, II' (1955), p. 780.

active the communication between the provinces the higher rose the level of the civilization as a whole. In the Middle American World there were five provinces: the Olméca region along the Atlantic coast south of Vera Cruz; the Valley of Mexico; Oaxáca; the Guatemalan highlands; and the tropical lowlands (Petén, the Usumacinta River valley, and the Motagua River valley in Guatemala).[1] In Peru there were only two major provinces: the lowlands along the Pacific coast and the highlands overhanging them.[2] But within each of these there were sharply defined subdivisions. In the coastal lowlands in the earlier stages of Andean history almost every river valley, however small—and, in all, there are about twenty-five of these[3]—developed the common civilization on distinctive lines of its own. The stretches of desert between the ribbons of green were barriers to intercourse that were not easily or quickly overcome. In the highlands there were six subdivisions: the Cajamarca basin; the Callejón de Huaylas; a portion of the Montaro River valley; the Cuzco basin; the plateau north-west of Lake Titicaca, in what is now Peru; and the plateau south-east of the lake, in what is now Bolivia.[4]

'Two fundamental forces were at work in [the] Classic cultures [of Middle America]. Intercommunication existed among them and was an important factor in their growth. They profited from being a part of a larger community of ideas than did the various cultures of the Middle American Formative. . . . The intertwining of the many varied [regional] strands produced the Classic.[5] . . . Regionalism persisted, but it was a regionalism in which the various Classic cultures had assimilated sufficient from each other so that all drew upon a common fund of great depth and richness. . . . Yet this intercommunication and interchange were by no means all-embracing. Technologies, elements, things—these were exchanged, but complete idea systems remained regionalised.'[6]

There was inter-regional interaction in Peru as well.[7] In fact, in both worlds there was a combination of active inter-regional trade with regional ethnocentrism.[8] In Peru, horizon styles—i.e. styles transcending the provincial and sub-divisional boundaries—are much more frequent than they are in Middle America.[9] The count of them in Peru runs to five[10] or six.[11]

[1] Willey and Phillips: 'Method and Theory in American Archaeology, II' (1955), p. 779; iidem, 1958, p. 184.
[2] Willey: 'The Prehistoric Civilizations of Nuclear America', p. 577.
[3] W. C. Bennett and J. R. Bird: Andean Culture History, p. 96.
[4] Ibid., pp. 97–99; Bennett in A Reappraisal of Peruvian Archaeology, pp. 4–5; G. H. S. Bushnell: Peru, p. 14. The eastern cordillera of Bolivia did not come within the Peruvian cultural area (Andean Culture History, p. 99; A Reappraisal of Peruvian Archaeology, p. 4).
[5] 'Individually, these strands would have supported nothing of greater moment than a culture like the Mississippian of the eastern United States, with its temple mounds, or the Coclé culture of Panamá, with its fine pottery and metal craft. Together, they emerge as Middle American Civilization' (Willey and Phillips, 1958, p. 151). The failure of the Formative-stage cultures of the south-western United States to rise to the Classic level, notwithstanding the early date of the maize found in Bat Cave, is perhaps to be explained by the lack, here, of the stimulus of intercourse between different local cultural provinces (ibid., p. 155).
[6] Willey and Phillips: 'Method and Theory in American Archaeology, II' (1955), p. 780; see also p. 767. Cp. eosdem, 1958, pp. 151 and 187.
[7] Iidem, 1955, p. 775.   [8] Ibid., p. 779.
[9] Willey: 'The Prehistoric Civilizations of Nuclear America', p. 577.
[10] Willey in A Reappraisal of Peruvian Archaeology, p. 9.
[11] Bennett and Bird: Andean Culture History, pp. 108–10.

'The two configurations of culture-growth are not only similar but synchronous'—and this over a period of 2,000 years.[1]

'The carbon-14 dates tend to make the full flowering of Meso-American and Andean cultures in general coeval, the [Meso-American] Early Classic contemporaneous with Nazca "A", and the Late Classic with Nazca "B", Mochica, and Classic Tiahuanaco.'[2]

Coon notes[3] that the American civilizations resemble those Old-World civilizations that grew up gradually (e.g. the Sumeric Civilization), not those that were transformed by sudden impacts from outside (e.g. the Egyptiac Civilization). This makes it difficult to delimit the phases of the two Pre-Columbian American civilizations precisely; but most archaeologists now seem to find in both worlds an identical series of four phases: Archaic (ex-'Pre-Formative'); Formative; Classic; and Postclassic.[4]

In the Formative period there is, as we have seen, linkage, as well as synchronicity, between Middle America and Peru.[5] 'The Peruvian Formative has a closer configurational resemblance to the Middle American Late Formative.'[6] In Middle America the Formative begins in the second millennium B.C., and in Peru soon after.[7] The Chavín horizon in the Andean World was contemporary with the Olméca horizon in Middle America and is to some extent parallel with it. Both horizons were expansive.[8] The feline motif appears in the artistic expression of Olméca as well as Chavín religion.[9] The Formative styles of Middle America and Peru were more like each other, besides being each internally more homogeneous, than the subsequent Classic styles.[10]

'The subsequent Classic civilizations of Middle America—Lowland and Highland Maya, Monte Albán, Tajín, Teotihuacán—all drew upon this Formative period art and intellectual achievement. It is as though, from Late Formative times forward, Middle American societies were participating not only in common technical traditions but in an ideational heritage.'[11]

In the Peruvian Classic, on the other hand, regional differences crystallized into what amounted to distinctive civilizations.[12]

1 Willey: 'The Prehistoric Civilizations of Nuclear America', p. 588.
2 R. Wauchope: 'Implications of Radiocarbon Dates from Middle and South America', in Publication No. 18 (1954), p. 25, of the Middle American Research Institute of Tulane University, New Orleans.
3 In The History of Man, p. 353.
4 See Willey: 'The Prehistoric Civilizations of Nuclear America', pp. 573 and 577.
5 Willey: 'The Intermediate Area of Nuclear America', p. 2.
6 Willey: 'The Prehistoric Civilizations of Nuclear America', p. 586.
7 Willey and Phillips: 'Method and Theory in American Archaeology, II' (1955), p. 765. Cp. eosdem, 1958, p. 147. Here, on the basis of carbon-14 tests, more precise dates are given: 1359±250 B.C. for Middle American Formative, 714±200 B.C. for Peruvian.
8 Willey: 'The Prehistoric Civilizations of Nuclear America', p. 586; idem: 'The Intermediate Area of Nuclear America', p. 10.
9 Wauchope, loc. cit., p. 32.
10 Willey and Phillips: 'Method and Theory in American Archaeology, II' (1955), p. 788.
11 Willey: 'The Intermediate Area of Nuclear America', p. 10.
12 Willey and Phillips: 'Method and Theory in American Archaeology, II' (1955), p. 782.

The Classic is easy to identify and even to date,[1] but it is difficult to define. Its criteria are qualitative and relative: aesthetic excellence, religious climax, general florescence,[2] and differentiation between the cultures of the different provinces of each of the two worlds.[3] The Middle American and Peruvian Classic cultures were approximately contemporary.[4] But in the Classic Age the two civilizations diverged,[5] to reconverge in the Postclassic.[6] In the Classic period the differences were, indeed, sharp. Metallurgy was by then already common in the Andean World but was still rare in Middle America. There was already irrigation in coastal Peru, but not yet in Middle America. There was already organized warfare and conquest in North-West Peru,[7] but not yet in Middle America. On the other hand, in the Andean World there was no calendar and no system of writing.[8]

The Classic Age ended in catastrophe, apparently in most cases in the form of war, though war does not seem to account for the abandonment of the lowland Maya Classic sites that had been won with such labour from the tropical forest.[9]

[1] On the north-west coast of Peru, Formative turns into Classic during the Gallinazo period. Gallinazo III may rank as being Classic (Willey and Phillips, 1958, p. 177). Carbon-14 tests have pushed the beginning of Peruvian Classic back towards the beginning of the Christian Era and have made it approximately contemporary with the beginning of Middle American Classic (ibid., p. 189). This begins *circa* A.D. 300, or 260 years earlier according to Spinden's chronology. The carbon-14 tests support Spinden's system (ibid., pp. 184-5).

[2] Willey and Phillips: 'Method and Theory in American Archaeology, II' (1955), p. 778.

[3] Willey and Phillips, 1958, p. 191. These two authorities also observe (ibid., p. 182) that 'the Classic stage in native New World cultures marks the beginning of urbanism', and that this 'overrides in importance' the criteria listed by them in 1955. There is material evidence for urbanism at Teotihuacán in its Classic Age and in coastal North-West Peru in the Gallinazo III period. But they admit that 'in other cases . . . of which the Classic Maya of the Petén lowlands is a prime example, urban dwelling clusters are either lacking or undiscovered'. And the case of the Maya Classic Civilization compels them (ibid., p. 183, footnote 2) to emphasize 'the functional, rather than the purely formal, definition of urbanism. . . . The crucial factor', they here suggest, 'is the number of people who could be drawn upon and organised in the interests of the society and the culture. Maya society undoubtedly drew upon and coordinated the energies of a great many people.' The words 'Maya society' in this context presumably mean a directing minority of the participants in the society. This minority will have had the leisure to direct because it will have been exempt from spending its time and energy on day-to-day economic tasks. This brings us back to my suggestion, on p. 278, that the presence of a leisured minority is a more accurate and illuminating criterion of civilization than urbanism is.

[4] Willey and Phillips: 'Method and Theory in American Archaeology, II' (1955), p. 782.

[5] The Middle American and Andean civilizations were more different from each other in the Classic Age than either before or after (Willey and Phillips, 1958, p. 192).

[6] Willey and Phillips: 'Method and Theory in American Archaeology, II' (1955), pp. 783-4.

[7] 'Mochica representative art is a testimonial to warfare' (Willey: 'The Prehistoric Civilizations of Nuclear America', p. 579). 'Militarism seems to have been a force in old Peruvian society from an early time. In this . . . Peru differs from Middle America' (Willey and Phillips, 1958, p. 196).

[8] Willey: 'The Prehistoric Civilizations of Nuclear America', p. 587; Willey and Phillips: 'Method and Theory in American Archaeology, II' (1955), p. 783.

[9] There is still no agreement about the answer to this baffling question.

Some scholars have sought to account for the abandonment of the ceremonial centres by the hypothesis of a loss of faith, among the peasantry, in the efficacy of the priests' burdensome prescriptions for bringing rain to make the crops grow. This hypothesis is advocated by, for example, S. F. de Borhegyi, 'The Development of Folk and Complex Cultures in the Southern Maya Area', in *American Antiquity*, vol. xxi, No. 4, pp. 343-56. De Borhegyi maintains (ibid., pp. 343-4) that there is archaeological evidence for the

'The carbon-14 dating of previous periods and the known dates of the proto-historic horizon tend to indicate that socio-political upheavals followed the full flowering of high culture in both Middle and South America at about the same time.'[1]

In Middle America one of the most striking pieces of evidence for this is the apparently violent destruction of Classic Teotihuacán. In the Andean World the corresponding symptom is the sudden, and apparently violent and catastrophic, expansion of the Tiahuanáco horizon from the south-easternmost subdivision of the highland province over most, though not the whole, of the rest of the Andean World[2]—perhaps via a secondary centre of diffusion at Huari (Wari) in the Mantaro River basin, in the highlands farther north-westwards.[3] The Tiahuanacoid is comparable to the previous Chavinoid and to the later Inca horizon. Yet 'the Tiahuanáco influence, while strong, was not an engulfing or permanent one'.[4] In the highlands the Tiahuanáco style had less influence in the almost adjacent Cuzco district than anywhere else in Peru.[5] Along the coast the Huari-Tiahuanáco influence swamped the South-East (the Nazca sub-division),[6] but north-westward it spread as far as Chicama only, not to Lambayeque, and it was soon thrown off by Moche.[7]

The salient features of the Postclassic Age in both worlds were militarization, secularization, urbanism,[8] standardization, and mass produc-

existence of a folk culture in this region, side by side with a sophisticated one, for more than two thousand years. After the Early Formative, he holds (p. 352), each folk society 'existed in a symbiotic relationship with the more complex urban component'. But, at the end of the Late Classic period in this region, folk-cult objects reassert themselves (p. 350). 'Recent evidence points towards the possibility of a revolt of the food-producing classes against the exploitative abuses of the theocrats' (p. 350). De Borhegyi suggests that there was a chain-reaction of revolt which spread all through the Maya region and took a violent form in the north-west, at Bonampak and at Piedras Negras (p. 350).

On the strength of archaeological evidence from the opposite side of the Maya region in southern Belice (British Honduras), this hypothesis is rejected by G. R. Willey: 'The Structure of Ancient Maya Society', in *The American Anthropologist*, New Series, vol. 58, No. 5 (October, 1956), pp. 777–82. Willey here raises the question: How deep was the gulf between the peasantry and the élite in the Maya culture? In this connexion he notes that, in Southern Belice, one finds clusters of house-mounds with small pyramid bases among them. This suggests, to his mind, that the culture was not confined to the great ceremonial centres. Luxury pottery, known from the ceremonial centres, is also found in the refuse in these house-clusters. 'All these British Honduran discoveries add up, I think, to a conception of a Maya peasant class that was reasonably prosperous and participating in a cultural tradition not markedly apart from the inhabitants of the great religious centers.' Moreover, in the Belice Valley in the Postclassic age the peasantry disappeared simultaneously with the great ceremonial centres. This archaeological evidence impugns, in Willey's view, the theory that the fall of the Maya Classic Civilization was due to an internal revolt.

P. Armillas holds 'that the movements of people were the result and not the cause of the crisis. The disintegration was from within, and the internal factor causing the decline was probably an economic crisis' (*A Reappraisal of Peruvian Archaeology*, p. 108). Thus there is still no generally accepted explanation of the mystery.

[1] Wauchope, in loc. cit., p. 27.
[2] J. A. Mason: *The Ancient Civilizations of Peru*, pp. 88–89; G. H. S. Bushnell: *Peru*, p. 92.
[3] Mason, op. cit., p. 93; Bushnell, op. cit., p. 94; Bennett and Bird: *Andean Culture History*, p. 194.
[4] Mason, op. cit., p. 89.
[5] Mason, ibid., p. 92; Bushnell, ibid., p. 102; Bennett and Bird, op. cit., p. 200.
[6] Mason, op. cit., p. 94; Bushnell, op. cit., p. 94.
[7] Mason, op. cit., p. 94; Bushnell, op. cit., p. 99.
[8] Willey and Phillips, 1955, p. 784. Willey in *A Reappraisal of Peruvian Archaeology*, pp. 13–14.

tion.[1] Postclassic militarism developed more abruptly in Middle America than in Peru.[2] In Peru it was intensified in this age, but there it had already been asserting itself, not merely since the Classic,[3] but since the Late Formative.[4] In the Postclassic age the imposition of ways of life by military conquest was a common phenomenon.[5] There were 'widespread movements of peoples and idea systems throughout each of the two major areas'.[6] Successive waves of 'Chichimec' barbarians from the north descended on Middle America. The Toltec wave penetrated not only eastwards into Yucatan but also southwards into the Guatemalan highlands.[7] The following Aztec wave was flooding still more widely when it was suddenly broken by the Spanish conquest. In the Andean World there is no evidence that the wave of violent disturbance represented by the spread of the Tiahuanáco horizon took the form of military conquest resulting in the establishment of an empire.[8] On the other hand the subsequent Inca horizon is known, from historical records, to be the archaeological imprint of an Andean universal state that was established by force of arms. In both worlds in the Postclassic Age the tendency towards standardization and mass-production was accompanied by a decline in the level of art.[9]

'The native city of the New-World Postclassic had large population aggregates, was the economic (and probably social, political, and religious) hub for outlying populations, maintained complex and diverse divisions of labor among its citizens, and was a sort of politico-religious power.'[10]

In Peru the Postclassic cities, unlike the Classic, had a planned layout, especially those along the north-west coast.[11] In Postclassic Middle America there were two series of cities: in the first series, Tula on the plateau and Chichén Itzá in Yucatan; in the second series, Tenochtitlan in the Valley of Mexico, Mitla in the Oaxáca cultural province, Tzintzuntzan in Tarasco, west of the Valley of Mexico, Totonacan Cempoala in Vera Cruz, Mayapan in Yucatan.[12] Tenochtitlan had 60,000 inhabitants. These received their supplies by water transport, and part of their food was grown on floating gardens.[13] Neither Mayapan nor Chichén

---

[1] Willey and Phillips, 1958, p. 193.

[2] Willey: 'The Prehistoric Civilizations of Nuclear America', p. 587. 'It is not likely that the replacement of the priest-controlled society by the war-state was marked by an actual schism. The pyramid and temple centre, symbols of authority in the old system, were retained, enlarged, and glorified. The transfer from sacred to secular was probably accomplished by a gradual shifting in the nature of the powers exercised by public leaders' (Willey in *A Reappraisal of Peruvian Archaeology*, p. 12).

[3] In the Classic Age in Peru, not only Moche but all Andean communities except Nazca had turned militarist (Bennett and Bird: *Andean Culture History*, pp. 179 and 182).

[4] Willey and Phillips: 'Method and Theory in American Archaeology, II' (1955), pp. 786–7.   [5] Ibid., p. 788. Iidem, 1958, p. 199.
[6] Willey and Phillips, 1955, p. 784.

[7] See S. F. de Borhegyi: 'The Development of Full and Complex Cultures in the Southern Maya Area', pp. 350–1.

[8] On this point see Mason, op. cit., pp. 88–89.

[9] Willey and Phillips, 1955, p. 784. Cp. Bennett and Bird: *Andean Culture History*, p. 208; Bennett [ed.]: *A Reappraisal of Peruvian Archaeology*, p. 14.
[10] Ibid., p. 785.   [11] Ibid., pp. 785–6; iidem, 1958, p. 195.
[12] Iidem, 1955, p. 784; 1958, pp. 196–7.
[13] Iidem, 1955, p. 787; 1958, p. 197.

Itzá could compare with Tenochtitlan, and 'we can conclude that urban-isation was decidedly less successful in the Maya lowlands than in the Valley of Mexico'.[1]

In coastal Peru, at any rate, the advances in technology during the Formative and Classic periods that made it possible to irrigate and culti-vate entire valleys, instead of just their fringes,[2] were accompanied by increases in population, concentrations of political power, and an ex-acerbation of warfare and class-divisions. 'Gallinazo is the first Virú period at which we can say, for certain, that there was both large-scale irrigation and extensive wall construction.'[3] And irrigation implies political unification of the valley from at least as early as Late Gallinazo.[4] In the Virú Valley in the Classic period (labelled in this valley 'Late Gallinazo') there were settlements all over the valley; 'both the castillos and the big pyramids represent millions of man-hours of labor'; and the irrigated area was 40 per cent. as large again as it is at the present day.[5] In the Andean World there was a sharp increase in the size of the states, and consequent diminution in their number, during the second phase of the Postclassic period, which occupied the last four and a half centuries, according to the carbon-14 dating, or the last one and a half, according to the shorter reckoning,[6] before the political unification of the whole Andean World in the Inca universal state. In this age the whole series of valleys from the north-western to the south-eastern end of the Peruvian coast was divided politically between no more than four states, with formidable fortresses guarding their frontiers. The Chimú Empire, with its capital at Chanchán, laid out on a rectangular plan covering eight, or even eleven, square miles, ruled from the Lambayeque Valley to the Casma Valley. The Cuismancu Empire, with its capital at Cajamarquilla, held the Chancay, Lurín, and Rimac valleys; south-east of this lay the relatively small Chuquimancu state. The south-easternmost of the four coastal states was the Chincha Empire, which held the Chincha, Pisco, Ica, and Nazca valleys.[7] If we translate Andean history into terms of Hellenic history and equate the Inca Empire with the Roman Empire, the Pre-Inca regional empires along the coast will correspond to the empires established by Alexander's successors which were eventually extinguished by Roman conquest. The Incas may have borrowed much of their imperial organization and institutions from Chimú,[8] as the Romans certainly did borrow much of theirs from the Post-Alexandrine Hellenic monarchies.

The Inca conquest of the Andean World was sudden and rapid. According to the chronology now in favour, it was accomplished be-tween the years 1438 and 1493, and within the last thirty of those years (1463–93) the area of the Inca Empire was increased by 1,000 per cent.[9] Thus the Andean universal state had been in existence for only about forty years by the time of its sudden overthrow by the Spaniards. Yet it

---

[1] Iidem, 1958, p. 199.   [2] See p. 341, footnotes 7, 8, 9.
[3] G. R. Willey: 'Prehistoric Settlement Patterns in the Virú Valley, Peru', p. 362.
[4] Ibid., p. 381.   [5] Ibid., p. 393.   [6] Mason, op. cit., p. 96.
[7] See J. A. Mason: *The Ancient Civilizations of Peru*, pp. 96–102; G. H. S. Bushnell: *Peru*, pp. 103–11; Bennett and Bird: *Andean Culture History*, p. 203.
[8] Bushnell, op. cit., p. 106.
[9] Mason, op. cit., pp. 116–22. Cp. Bushnell, op. cit., pp. 116–18.

left an impress on the Andean World which even the Spaniards could not efface. The Inca Empire had its counterpart in Middle America in the universal state that the Aztecs were in process of establishing when the arrival of the Spaniards cut this short. At the time of the Spaniards' arrival in Middle America, not only the little state of Tlaxcála, to the east of Tenochtitlan, but the great state of Tarasco, to the west of it, was still holding out. The Aztecs were more atrocious than the Incas, and the resistance to their empire-building was correspondingly more stubborn. Moreover, even as far as they had gone in building their empire up, they had established nothing like the Inca Imperial Government's centralized control over economic and social life. In Middle America under the Aztec regime, the artisans and merchants were still largely independent forces in society.[1]

Nevertheless, the general resemblance between the configurations of Middle American and Andean history is striking. And there is also a notable resemblance between the histories of these two pre-Columbian American civilizations and those of a number of civilizations in the Old World. Down to the point where the histories of Middle America and the Andean World are cut short by the Spanish conquest, their pattern is recognizably similar to the patterns of Sumeric, Hellenic, and Sinic history. The pre-Columbian American pattern resembles the Sumeric pattern, in particular, in the gradual rise of civilization out of a pre-civilizational stage of culture.[2] It resembles both this and the Hellenic and Sinic patterns in the subsequent accentuation of militarism and the consequent eventual unification of society through the overthrow of all the warring states except one by the military might of this sole survivor. In the Andean World this denouement had been reached before the arrival of the Spaniards; in the Middle American World it was within sight.

This resemblance between configurations of history in the Americas and in the Old World is of great significance for the study of human affairs, because the Old-World and the New-World series of events unquestionably occurred quite independently of each other. The resemblance therefore suggests that there must be something in human nature —or at any rate in human circumstances—which has made events take these parallel courses in the Age of the Civilizations. J. A. Mason maintains[3] that, 'with only minor deviations, practically all of the great ancient civilizations of the World developed along more or less the same lines'. As he sees it, the drama has been a tragedy in three acts. The first act sees the economic revolution in which agriculture supersedes food-gathering and hunting, and this produces a 'golden age'. In the second act the pressure of increasing population produces conflicts. In the third act the contending states are united by military force. If this has indeed been the plot of the play up to date, can we liberate ourselves from it? Man's recent technological progress has no precedent; yet, by itself, it

---

[1] Willey: 'The Prehistoric Civilizations of Nuclear America', p. 587.
[2] The Hellenic Civilization had a previous one, the Minoan-Helladic-Mycenaean, in its historical background. Similarly the Sinic Civilization of the Chou period and after had in its historical background the civilization of the Shang period.
[3] In op. cit., p. 14. Cp. p. 96.

will not suffice to solve the problem of civilization. Unprecedently potent technology may be misused for waging unprecedently destructive warfare; or, if it is used for increasing the production of the necessities of life, the additional product may be swallowed up by an unplanned and aimless increase in population, without any rise in the average standard of living, either material or spiritual. Thus now, as always, the spiritual virtues of imagination, wisdom, self-control, and, above all, good intent, are the keys to mankind's destiny.

XII. ROME'S PLACE IN HISTORY

AS I see the history of Rome, it is part of the history of what I call 'the Hellenic Civilization', and it is intelligible only in this historical setting. One cannot understand the history of Rome without taking into account the history of the Hellenic World before as well as after Rome began to play her part in it. One can imagine Hellenic history without Rome. Some other Hellenic or Hellenized state might have performed for the Hellenic Society the function that Rome eventually did perform for it. Sparta, Athens, Olynthus, Macedon, Syracuse were all in the running, at different stages of Hellenic history, for being the state that was going to unite the Hellenic World politically. But Roman history without the Hellenic Society and Civilization is not imaginable. There was never any such thing as a self-contained Roman society and civilization, and to try to divorce Rome from Hellenism and to treat Rome as an independent historical entity would make nonsense of Roman history by placing it in an historical vacuum. J. F. Leddy has interpreted my view correctly in saying[1] that

'What is all-important to Toynbee in the history of Rome is her Hellenization, and he seems to think of this cultural conquest almost as the filling of a vacuum. Throughout *A Study of History* we see Rome only in the shadow of Greece, only as the protector of the Greek legacy, always in a Greek context, and (in his technical sense) as the "universal state" briefly sustaining Hellenic Civilization before its final and inevitable collapse.'

The same point is being made by Fyvel when he says[2] of me that 'he telescopes Greece and Rome into a single Hellenic Society in which all Roman history masks mere disintegration'.

I accept Leddy's interpretation subject to the substitution of the words 'Hellas' or 'Hellenic World' for 'Greece' and the word 'Hellenic' for 'Greek'. In the English language the word 'Greece' suggests a geographical area, more or less conterminous with the present-day Kingdom of Greece, which was never more than part, and originally not the most important part, of the Hellenic World. The most important part of the original Hellas was the west coast of present-day Turkey, and the Hellenic World expanded in the course of its history till, at the

[1] In *The Phoenix*, vol. 11 (1957), No. 4, p. 144.
[2] T. R. Fyvel in *The Tribune*, 21st March, 1947, p. 20.

time of the establishment of the Augustan Peace in 31 B.C., it extended from Alexandria-on-Nile eastward to Central Asia and the Panjab and westward to the Atlantic coasts of North Africa and Europe. The word 'Greek', too, is a misnomer, because in English it suggests the Greek language, and the domains of the Greek language and of the Hellenic Civilization were never conterminous. From the beginning the Hellenic Society included non-Greek-speaking peoples: for instance, the Luvian-speaking Carians and Lycians; and, as it expanded, it converted many more: for instance, the Lydians, Messapians, Apulians, Etruscans, and, most notable converts of all, the Latin-speaking Romans. On the other hand, in Northern Continental European Greece, north and west of a line joining Thermopylae to Delphi, there were Greek-speaking semi-barbarians and barbarians, some of whom were not Hellenized till a late date in Hellenic history. The Greek-speaking Agrianes and Den-theletae round the head-waters of the Rivers Strymon (Struma) and Oescus (Isker) were not brought within the pale till the kingdom of the Thracian Odrysae was annexed to the Roman Empire by the Emperor Claudius and was then deliberately Hellenized by him and his successors. Subject, however, to this verbal *caveat*, I accept the passage that I have quoted from Leddy's paper as being an accurate statement of my point of view.

This point of view has been vigorously criticized, not only by Leddy, but by other critics as well. J. Vogt, for instance, maintains[1] that it is inadmissible to treat the Roman Age as an appendage to the Hellenistic Age, as if the Roman Age's destiny were determined in advance. In Roman history, he holds, a new force made itself felt. This gave the Roman way of life a distinctive character of its own, and that puts the Roman way, in its own fashion, on a level with the Hellenic way. Rome, according to Vogt, created a new and more profound ideal of human personality. W. den Boer maintains[2] that,

'though, in the words of Horace, the vanquished triumphed over the victor, the interpretation which considers the history of Italy and Latium to be bound up with Greece even before this victory is alien to historical reality.'

H. Baudet judges[3] that I under-estimate Rome, perhaps partly because, for me, Rome is a symbol of unacceptable materialism. H. Marrou suggests[4] that I am too Athenian-minded to appreciate the Roman Empire at its proper value. H. Holborn makes the same point.[5]

'The Roman Empire receives no praise. . . . Rome's capacity to create law and unity in a chaotic world was her own genius, and it seems arbitrary to disregard her contribution and see in her history a senescent continuation of Hellenic life.'

Leddy, too, takes me to task[6] for describing the age extending from the

[1] In *Saeculum*, No. 2 (1951), pp. 557–74.　　[2] In *Toynbee and History*, p. 236.
[3] In *Historie en Metahistorie*, p. 57.　　[4] In *Esprit*, July, 1952, pp. 120–1.
[5] In *The Saturday Review of Literature*, 31st May, 1947, p. 12.
[6] In loc. cit., pp. 146–7.

reign of the Emperor Nerva to the reign of the Emperor Marcus Aurelius inclusive as being 'the Indian Summer' of Hellenic history. He
considers that I am denigrating that age in giving it this label. W.
Gurian finds me inconsistent[1] in bracketing Greeks and Romans together when I
draw a distinction between the Irish society of the Post-Graeco-Roman
Age and the contemporary Latin West. D. M. Robinson concedes that
Rome owed much to Greece; that the changes in Roman society after
the Hannibalic War 'resulted from foreign conquests and the economic
consequences of imperial expansion'. Italy was not 'a separate and
independent entity'. 'Rome and Italy became a part of the Mediterranean economic system.' Yet Robinson, too, protests, in opposition
to my treatment of Rome, that 'the Romans were an original people
with a capacity for world government and with powers of organisation
and unification rarely excelled in all history'.[2]

What are the Roman achievements that have moved some scholars,
at any rate in the Western World, to insist that Rome ought to be
treated as a separate historical entity in its own right, rather than as an
element, however important, in the history of the Hellenic Civilization?
There are two achievements on which, above all, this claim on Rome's
behalf is based. One of these is Roman law; the other is Rome's political
feat of eventually uniting, in a single 'universal state', the whole of the
Hellenic World west of 'Iraq and Iran. The second of these two achievements was, I should say, the key to the first. When once Rome had won
for herself the role of being the Hellenic World's unifying state, Roman
law was bound to become the oecumenical law of the Hellenic Society,
and was consequently bound to undergo something like the evolution
and transformation that made it what it eventually came to be. On the
other hand, if the Hellenic World had been united politically by some
other state, and if Rome had remained the small, obscure, and backward state that she originally was, on the Hellenic World's outer fringe,
there is no reason to suppose that Roman law would ever have got far
beyond a primitive and rudimentary stage before being replaced—as
eventually it would have been in these political circumstances. It
would have been replaced by the oecumenical law of the other state—
whichever it might have been—by which the Hellenic World's political
unity would have been achieved if history had taken this non-Roman
course.[3]

---

[1] *The Review of Politics*, vol. 4, No. 4 (October, 1942), p. 513.
[2] *The Intent of Toynbee's History: A Cooperative Appraisal.*
[3] This is indicated by what happened when Roman Law did come into contact with
more advanced legal systems: for instance, with Egyptian and Greek law in Egypt.
By the beginning of the second century B.C., Egyptian and Greek private law in Egypt
had become assimilated to each other. Both these systems had carried juridical individualism to a high point. Of the two, the Egyptian was the more advanced, especially in
the status that it gave to women. But, 'notwithstanding fairly strongly pronounced
formal differences, the Egyptian and the Greek juridical modes are not differentiated by
incompatibilities of the same gravity as those which, for several centuries, prevented a
Hellenised Egypt from "receiving" from the Romans a law that was more archaic than
hers' (C. Préaux: *L'Économie Royale des Lagides* (Brussels, 1939, Fondation Égypto-
logique Reine Elisabeth), p. 23).
This is significant, considering that, in Egypt, Roman Law had the advantage of being
the legal system of the ruling power, and also that, by the date of the annexation of Egypt,
Roman Law had already been in process of Hellenization for more than a hundred years.

Considerable elements of an original barbaric parochial Roman law did, even as it was, survive Rome's reception of Hellenism and simultaneous establishment of her political supremacy over the Hellenic World, and these intractable relics of barbarism were not trivial; they were concerned with some of the most important and fundamental relations between one human being and another. The most notorious of them is the tyrannical power that Roman law left in the hands of the father of a family—a power which placed the free male members of his household at his mercy, as well as the women and the slaves. A remnant of this original barbaric *patria potestas* survived the seven centuries of progressive modernization and humanization which Roman law underwent from the second century B.C. onwards until its eventual codification in the reign of the Emperor Justinian. This is remarkable, considering that, since the miscarriage of the city-state regime in the Hellenic World in and after the Great Atheno-Peloponnesian War that had broken out in 431 B.C., the moral climate of the Hellenic Civilization had become increasingly favourable to the rights of individuals, and of women in particular, and that the status of women had been still further improved in the Hellenic World by the spread of Judaism and the subsequent far wider spread of Christianity. Other primitive survivals were the antique Roman forms of procedure for marriage and for sale and purchase—though, in these fields, less clumsy and more practical alternative procedures had been introduced in the course of time.

On the whole, Roman law was successfully developed into a modern oecumenical law, adapted to the needs of the Hellenic World, by the interpretative work of Roman jurists over a period of about four hundred years, running from the second century B.C. to the third century of the Christian Era. The jurists who initiated this great work of transformation were, of course, native Romans who had imbibed a tincture of Hellenic culture. But, as Roman rule spread more widely over the Hellenic World, and as this was followed by the progressive grant of Roman citizenship to Rome's allies and subjects, the development of Roman law became more and more a common Hellenic enterprise, in which Roman citizens from all quarters of the Hellenic World played an increasingly active part. The school of Roman law at Bayrūt (Bêrŷtus) came more and more to the fore, and its professors played a dominant part in the Justinianean codification. An authentic Roman colony of Latin-speaking Italians had been founded at Bayrūt by Augustus not long after the year 20 B.C.[1] This had been a Latin-speaking bridgehead in a Levant in which Greek was the oecumenical language of administration and culture for nearly a thousand years, running from the generation of Alexander the Great to the seventh century A.D., when the Arabs overran the provinces of the Roman Empire south-east of Taurus. The Bayrūt school of Roman law was thus in a particularly favourable position for carrying on the work of transforming Roman law by 'receiving' into it Hellenic legal principles—and philosophical principles too.

[1] See A. H. M. Jones: *The Cities of the Eastern Roman Provinces* (Oxford 1937, Clarendon Press), p. 272.

In a criticism of my point of view, Leddy writes[1] that Toynbee

'glances at the celebrated Roman jurists, calls them Stoics, and, having thus thrown them back under a Greek classification, is absolved from any necessity of seeking to account for their unique contribution to civilization.'

This criticism misses its mark; for I agree with Leddy regarding the Roman jurists' contribution to civilization as having been unique, and I do seek to account for it by seeing in it a common achievement of the whole Hellenic World after this had been united politically under Roman rule. But I disagree with Leddy—and with Maine, whose *Ancient Law* he cites[2] in support of his view—when they maintain that this 'unique contribution to civilization' was the work of the original native Romans, to the exclusion of other Hellenic or Hellenized populations that were brought within the Roman polity through the Romans' feat of turning their polity into an Hellenic universal state. In the passage here quoted by Leddy, Maine maintains that

'neither the Greeks nor any society thinking and speaking in their language ever showed the smallest capacity for producing a philosophy of law. Legal science is a Roman creation.'[3]

My comment on this thesis of Maine's would be that the Romans who created legal science were, many of them, also Greeks and Syrians too, and that, in the later stages of the Bayrūt Law School's history, during which its influence was at its zenith, the Roman jurists there were speaking Greek and thinking in Greek, as is testified by their surviving works of this date. I should go on to contend that the same great work of producing a scientific and philosophical system of law would inevitably have been carried out in any case, and this by the same cooperation among jurists from all quarters of the Hellenic World, if the state that gave the Hellenic World its political unity had been, not Rome, but some other.

Let us suppose that the partial political unification of the Hellenic World that was achieved by Athens in the fifth century B.C. had lasted, not for a bare half-century, but for a length of time of the order of magnitude of the actual duration of the Roman Empire. And let us suppose that Athens had succeeded, as Rome eventually did succeed, in extending the process of political unification round all the shores of the Mediterranean. Is it credible that, if Athenian, instead of Roman, law had been given this uniquely favourable political opportunity, Athenian law would not have become the scientific and philosophical system that Roman law actually became as a result of Rome's historical political achievement? Even during the forty-eight years between the common Hellenic victory over Xerxes in 480–479 B.C. and the outbreak of the Great Atheno-Peloponnesian War in 431 B.C. Athenian law made some progress towards becoming the oecumenical law of all the maritime states round the shores of the Aegean that were under Athenian

[1] In loc. cit., pp. 149–50.   [2] Ibid., p. 150, footnote 24.
[3] Leddy quotes this passage from p. 375 of a revised edition of Sir Henry Maine's *Ancient Law* (London 1930, John Murray).

domination during that brief period. In the fifth-century Hellenic World there was already a crying need for an oecumenical law, in the province of commercial law at any rate. As Athens came more and more to be the commercial centre of the Aegean, she also came more and more to be the place where commercial contracts were made and where litigation arising out of them was conducted. The benefit of doing business under a common law at least partly offset the hardship, for non-Athenian litigants, of having to go to Athens for the trial of their cases; and their resentment might not have been great if the Athenians had dealt fairly with them. The normal principle informing Hellenic international treaties for the legal settlement of disputes between citizens of different states was that a case should be tried in the court of the defendant. Considering the progressive increase in the concentration of business in Athens, this principle, scrupulously applied, would have tended also to bring an increasing volume of international commercial litigation to the Athenian courts.

The Athenians, however, were not content to play fair. They misused their political power to bring to Athens litigation—including criminal as well as civil cases—that, according to the treaties, ought to have come before the courts of other states. They did this partly in order to provide work, and consequently pay, for Athenian jurymen, and partly—which was still worse—in order to favour their political supporters and penalize their political opponents in the states that were subject to them. This was a grievance indeed. It was one of the causes of the overthrow of the Athenian Empire into which the Athenians had perverted the Delian League. In throwing away her opportunity to become the political unifier of the Hellenic World, Athens forfeited her opportunity to develop Athenian law into an oecumenical Hellenic law. Her political failure explains why her law did not have a Roman success. Conversely, if Athens had achieved the political success that Rome did achieve, it seems most improbable that, in these political circumstances, Athenian law would not have become the scientific and philosophical system that Roman law did become in the course that history actually took.

The key to Rome's legal achievement is, in fact, her political achievement. Was this a unique product of a distinctively Roman genius for political construction? The answer to this question will be decisive for or against the claim, put forward by some Western scholars on Rome's behalf, that she is entitled to be treated as a cultural and historical entity in her own right, independent of the Hellenic World.

What were the causes of Rome's political success? There are five that are conspicuous.

In the first place, Rome was fortunate in her geographical location. She herself was a city-state in a world of city-states. She possessed the political cohesion and vitality that a city-state constitution gave to a community. But in her immediate hinterland in the highlands of Central Italy there was a world of communities that were still in the pre-city-state stage of political development. Their people had not yet acquired the political self-consciousness and the political memories that made the citizens of city-states reluctant voluntarily to renounce their sovereign independence. Rome found it as difficult as Sparta and Athens found it to reduce ancient and famous city-states to a position of subordination to her, however mild the terms. Capua, Tarentum, and Syracuse, for example, all kicked against the pricks and were finally subdued only by extreme measures of coercion. By contrast, the highlanders could still be induced to merge themselves, without much recalcitrance, in a more advanced polity representing a higher level of culture. Rome took full advantage of this opportunity, at her doors, of bringing proselytes into her commonwealth. But even these backwoodsmen would not have been willing proselytes if Rome had not shown political generosity.

The second cause of Rome's political success was that she was politically generous to peoples that became her allies on the basis of their accepting her political paramountcy. Unlike Athens, she did not exact tribute from them. Like Sparta in her treatment of her satellites (*perioeci*) and her Peloponnesian allies—at least down to the time when the Spartans were demoralized by their dearly bought victory in the Great Atheno-Peloponnesian War of 431–404 B.C.—Rome demanded of her allies no more than that they should follow her lead in foreign policy and should send contingents of troops to reinforce her armies when she went to war.

The third cause of Rome's success was her generosity in granting Roman citizenship to her allies and her subjects. She was conspicuously generous in doing this during the century (*circa* 340[1]–241 B.C.) that saw the political unification of Italy under Roman supremacy and the expulsion of the Carthaginians from Sicily in the First Romano-Carthaginian War.[2] There were two different sets of conditions on which the grant of Roman citizenship was made. The less favourable terms of admission imposed all the duties of Roman citizenship without simultaneously granting the right to vote or the right to stand for election. The more favourable terms gave the rights, as well as imposing the duties. But communities that had originally been given the citizenship on the less favourable terms were eventually given the full franchise sooner or later. Generosity in the matter of enfranchisement was, indeed, the long-term tendency of Roman policy, and it eventually reached its logical conclusion in the *Constitutio Antoniniana* of A.D. 212. This ordinance enfranchised all but a small residual minority of the still unenfranchised inhabitants of the Roman Empire; and at that date the Empire included the whole contemporary Hellenic World west of 'Iraq and Iran and embraced the whole circuit of the Mediterranean.

This generous policy did not prevail, however, without halts and pauses during which the contrary policy of treating Roman citizenship as a privilege, and jealously confining it to the existing citizen body, temporarily gained the upper hand. The narrow-hearted attitude was the normal one in Hellenic city-states that had acquired an ascendancy over their neighbours. At Athens, for instance, in the heyday of the fifth-century Athenian Empire, a law was passed in 451 B.C. confining

---

[1] Or 336, if the dictatorships occupying 333, 324, 309, and 301 B.C. are fictitious.
[2] This Roman policy was cited by King Philip V of Macedon as an example in his two letters to the Larisaeans (texts in W. Dittenberger: *Sylloge Inscriptionum Graecarum*, 2nd ed. (Leipzig 1898–1901, Hirzel, 3 vols.), Nos. 238–9, in vol. i, pp. 381–4; 3rd ed. (1915–1923, reprinting in 1959, 4 vols.), p. 543).

Athenian citizenship to persons who could prove that both their parents possessed it; and, on the strength of this law, an investigation was made in 445 B.C. and was followed by a drastic purge which was carried out very harshly. At Rome this narrow-hearted spirit prevailed during the 160 years running from the close of the First Romano-Carthaginian War till the year 80 B.C., when a majority of Rome's allies in Central and Southern Italy took the extreme measure of seceding from the Roman alliance, going to war with Rome, and setting up a counter-confederacy of their own. This political catastrophe brought the Roman Commonwealth into imminent danger of destruction, and the Roman Government capitulated. It now offered the Roman citizenship to all allied states in Italy that had not taken up arms or were willing, if they had, to lay them down. But this concession, having been extorted by extreme military pressure, was made against the grain and on pettyminded terms. There seems to have been an attempt to neutralize the newly enfranchised citizens' votes by enrolling them either in only eight of the thirty-five constituencies among which the pre-war Roman voters were already distributed, or else only in ten new constituencies that were to be created to contain the new citizens. Moreover, the Italian communities north of the River Po were fobbed off with the status of Latin city-states—the highest category of allied communities, but a poor consolation prize for a continued refusal to give the Transpadanes the status of Roman citizens.

The generous attitude that had been prevalent down to 241 B.C., and that had made Rome's political fortune, did not prevail again till Caesar made himself master of the Roman state. Caesar not only enfranchised the Italians beyond the River Po but started giving Roman citizenship to Roman subjects outside Italy. Augustus followed this course more slowly and cautiously than his adoptive father; but Caesar had given Roman policy in the matter of the Roman franchise a decisive turn in the direction of renewed generosity. From Caesar's time onwards it was certain that the general enfranchisement, eventually conferred by the *Constitutio Antoniniana* of A.D. 212, was going to come sooner or later. Thus in spite of the disastrous delays during the last two centuries of the Roman republican regime—centuries that were an age of agony for the Hellenic World—the generous policy inaugurated in the century ending in 241 B.C. did prevail in the long run.

The fourth cause of Rome's political success was her adoption of the liberal institution of dual citizenship. When she gave Roman citizenship to foreign communities either on the less or on the more favourable of the two alternative sets of conditions, she did not dissolve their previous political institutions and simply merge them in the Roman body politic. She allowed an incorporated foreign state to retain its former local political organization, no longer, of course, in the form of a sovereign independent state, but in the form of a self-governing municipality of Roman citizens, still managing their own local affairs through locally elected magistrates of their own. These municipal Roman citizens were thus, in effect, citizens of two city-states: their own local city-state and the oecumenical city-state Rome. This liberal dispensation gave them the best of two worlds: they were now citizens of a local state and of a world-state as well. As Rome extended her rule over the Hellenic World and followed this up by eventually, though at some stages tardily, giving Roman citizenship to her allies and subjects, dual citizenship became the standard form of political status in the Roman Commonwealth.[1]

The fifth cause was Rome's policy of planting colonies in the new territories that she brought under her control.[2] These colonies were of two kinds. There were colonies with the status of the Latin city-states allied to Rome—the highest category of Rome's Italian allies. There were also colonies of Roman citizens. Originally the Latin colonies were much more important than the Roman colonies. The Latin colonies served both as fortresses for maintaining Rome's hold on her other allies and as outlets for agricultural settlement. The colonists were recruited from the Roman citizen body, as well as from among the citizens of the existing Latin city-states. Roman citizens who enrolled themselves in a Latin colony lost their Roman citizenship, for the Latin colonies were juridically sovereign independent city-states bound to Rome by a perpetual alliance on the usual terms. The colonies of Roman citizens were originally small settlements of coastguards, but they were each organized as a miniature city-state within the Roman city-state, and they thus enjoyed the privilege of possessing 'dual citizenship', like the formerly foreign communities that were granted the Roman franchise.

As the value of Roman citizenship increased, Roman citizens became more and more reluctant to forfeit their status, even in exchange for obtaining a large allotment of land in a Latin colony. Accordingly, when, after the Hannibalic War, Rome resumed her interrupted enterprise of subduing and colonizing the basin of the River Po, the Roman Government soon found itself constrained to give the status of Roman colonies to new foundations between the Appennines and the south bank of the Po in order to attract Roman citizens to these new foundations in sufficient numbers.

Rome's political success is adequately accounted for by these five causes. We have now to ask ourselves whether there was or was not something uniquely Roman and specifically un-Hellenic about Rome's situation and policy.

Rome was certainly un-Athenian in her generosity towards her allies. Athens' constant and incorrigible narrow-heartedness had quickly put her out of the running in the competition for becoming the Hellenic World's unifying state. On the other hand, Rome's early generosity towards her allies had, as has already been noted, an Hellenic precedent in Sparta's early generosity towards her allies and satellites. At the same time Rome refrained from making the capital blunder—a moral

[1] This constitutional arrangement, under which a citizen of Rome itself and a citizen of a Roman municipality each enjoyed equal civic rights, at least of the passive kind, in the other's city-state, was called *isopoliteia* (equality of civic rights) in Greek. Vogt, op. cit., points out how important this institution was in the building of the Roman Empire. I agree, and have never dissented.

[2] The Romans' activity in founding colonies, as well as their generosity in granting Roman citizenship to aliens, was cited by King Philip V of Macedon as an example in his two letters to the Larisaeans (see p. 381, footnote 1).

aberration as well as a political folly—through which Sparta had thrown away her chance of becoming the political unifier of the Hellenic World. When the Spartans conquered the lower Eurotas basin and subsequently went on to conquer Messenia, they reduced their fellow Hellenes in these territories to serfdom, and, in consequence, had to spend the greater part of their energy, ever afterwards, on holding them down. Thereafter they could never conduct diplomacy or war beyond the borders of their home territory without having to look back, all the time, over their shoulders for fear that their helots might seize the opportunity to make another of their repeated revolts. Let us suppose that, instead of reducing the South Laconians and Messenians to serfdom, the Spartans had granted them the status of satellites (*perioeci*), retaining self-governing city-states of their own, that the Spartans did give to the highlanders on either side of the Eurotas Valley. In that event Sparta might have given political unity to at least the whole of Continental European Greece with the consent and good will of her neighbours. She did in fact succeed—even with the incubus of her helot population weighing upon her—in unifying the greater part of the Peloponnese politically with the consent and good will of her satellites inside Laconia and of her Peloponnesian allies beyond Laconia's frontiers. If she had treated the South Laconians and Messenians as generously as she treated her *perioeci* in the Eurotas basin, she might have achieved union on the larger scale before the Achaemenian Empire appeared above the Hellenic World's horizon mid-way through the sixth century B.C. In that event the Hellenic World would have been spared the fatal division of leadership between Sparta and Athens. If the constant menace of the helots at home had not so severely limited Sparta's capacity for effective action abroad, Athens would, no doubt, have been brought back into the Spartan Confederacy in 508 B.C. and would not have been in a position to organize a separate and rival confederacy of her own in 478 B.C.

Rome distinguished herself by resisting the temptation to reduce conquered or reconquered peoples to serfdom, even when they had given her serious provocation. The Hannibalic War was the emergency in which Rome's political self-restraint was put to the severest test. In this war on Italian soil, in which Rome was fighting for her existence, a number of South Italian communities seceded from the Roman Commonwealth and took up arms against Rome on Hannibal's side. After Hannibal's eventual evacuation of Italy the Romans punished some of these secessionist communities by sweeping confiscations of land at their expense; and Rome did then reduce one of them—the southern Bruttians in the toe of Italy—to the status of *dediticii* (enemies who had surrendered at discretion), which was perhaps comparable to the status of Sparta's helots. On the other hand, the Romans showed decided restraint in their treatment of Capua after they had reconquered her.

At the time of the Hannibalic War, Capua was, next to Rome herself, the most important city in all Italy, with the possible exception of Tarentum. Moreover, Capua's territory was one of the most productive regions of the peninsula. Her secession was thus a material blow of the first magnitude for Rome, and it was also a moral blow of comparable severity. For 122 years[1] before Capua's secession in 216 B.C. after the Battle of Cannae, the Capuans had been Roman citizens, albeit in the less favourable of the two categories. Thus from the Roman point of view Capua's secession was a more heinous offence than the breach of treaty of which Rome's seceding South Italian allies were guilty. It was treason committed against Rome by Roman citizens. After the capitulation of Capua in 211 B.C. there were executions of leading secessionists, and others were permanently deported to places north-west of the River Tiber. Capua was deprived of her municipal constitution and reduced juridically to the status of a village. Her territory was confiscated by the Roman state, and the agricultural population had, thenceforth, to cultivate their land as tenants of the Roman Government. Municipal self-government and property rights were restored to the Capuans only in 59 B.C., by an agrarian law carried through in that year by Caesar. But in the meanwhile the native agricultural population does not seem to have been either evicted from its land or deprived of the second-class Roman citizenship that had been its status before secession. The treatment of Capua was mild according to the standards of the time, and was to that degree to Rome's credit.

Thus Rome refrained, even under provocation, from creating helots, whereas Sparta never learnt the lesson that the wrong which she had done to her helots was the cause of her perennial weakness. Under the stress of the Great Atheno-Peloponnesian War and the subsequent military commitments in which her eventual victory in that war involved her, Sparta did emancipate a few thousand helots in return for their doing military service as heavy-armed infantry. But these 'new nationals' (*neodâmôdeis*), as they were called, were not given the Spartan citizenship, and they were got rid of as quickly as possible—partly by foul means, so it was said. In the matter of Spartan citizenship the revolutionary King Cleomenes III (*regnabat* 237–222 B.C.) did show a Roman generosity towards Sparta's satellites (*perioeci*). He swamped the existing Spartiate citizen body, whose numbers had dwindled to about seven hundred, by granting the Spartan citizenship to *perioeci* in sufficient numbers to give Sparta 4,000 citizens of military age in the heavy-armed infantry class; and these new Spartan citizens received allotments of land on the territory of Sparta herself. But even Cleomenes III never thought of emancipating and enfranchizing the helots who still remained in the lower Eurotas Valley, 140 years after Messenia had recovered her independence.

Thus the Romans did show greater statesmanship in building up their commonwealth than either the Athenians or the Spartans. But did they show greater statesmanship than the Olynthians? The Olynthians were fifty or sixty years ahead of the Romans in starting to build, in northern Continental European Greece, a commonwealth[2] of the kind that Rome began to build in Central Italy in and after the years 340–338 B.C.[3] Olynthus enjoyed the geographical advantage, enjoyed by Rome, of being a city-state that had in her immediate hinterland a number of

[1] Or possibly 118 years.   [2] See iii. 477–89.   [3] Or 336–334 B.C.

communities that were still in the pre-city-state stage of development and were therefore amenable, if generously treated, to being assimilated by a city-state community with a more effective political organization and a higher culture than theirs. *Circa* 385–383 B.C. the Olynthians, like the Romans in 340–338 (or 336–334) B.C., embarked on an ambitious forward policy. They incorporated in their own state large adjoining tracts of the Kingdom of Macedon, which had fallen into anarchy after the death of King Archelaus in 399 B.C., and at the same time they forced a number of the neighbouring colonial Hellenic city-states along the north coast of the Aegean to become their allies.

The Olynthians' power to take advantage of this opportunity was the outcome of their having adopted, perhaps as early as 432 B.C., the institution of 'dual citizenship', which was subsequently adopted by Rome and which had made its first known appearance in the Hellenic World in the federal constitution devised by the Boeotians after the liberation, in 447 B.C., of the Boeotian city-states that had been temporarily under Athenian rule. Olynthus was no ordinary city-state. She had been created by the Chalcidian colonial city-states along the adjacent coast as a new common Chalcidian body politic of which every Chalcidian became a citizen, while continuing to be a citizen of his own local Chalcidian city-state—Torone or Methone or whichever other one it might happen to be. The closeness of the parallel between the building of the Olynthian Commonwealth *circa* 385–383 and the building of the Roman Commonwealth after the Romano-Latin War is remarkable. There is no evidence to show whether Rome re-invented the institution of 'dual citizenship' independently or whether she borrowed the idea from the Chalcidians or from the Boeotians or from both. The relevant point is that in the Olynthian commonwealth this institution was already in operation, and was already producing striking constructive political effects, more than forty years before Rome started on her own common-wealth-building career in Central Italy. It is also noteworthy that, as near to Rome as Sicily, and this in the years 342–336 B.C., the Corinthian statesman Timoleon was successfully persuading the Sicel and Siceliot Greek city-states to receive and enfranchise large numbers of immigrants from Greece and Italy, as well as from other parts of Sicily, and apparently also to make reciprocal grants of civic rights in one state to the citizens of another (e.g. as between Syracuse and Agyrium).[1]

Fortunately for Rome, Central Italy lay on the outer edge of the Hellenic World. The nearest Greek states, Syracuse and Tarentum, could not intervene to checkmate Rome's ambitious designs, and the expeditionary forces from Continental European Greece that came to the rescue of Hellenism in Sicily and Magna Graecia in 344 and 342 and 333 and 303 B.C.[2] found it as much as they could do to give a temporary check to Carthaginian and Oscan assaults. Central Italy was beyond their horizon; and when, in 280–274 B.C., Pyrrhus did attempt, with stronger forces, to achieve the more ambitious double feat of expelling the Carthaginians from Sicily and breaking the Roman

---

[1] See N. G. L. Hammond: *A History of Greece to 322 B.C.* (Oxford 1959, Clarendon Press), p. 579.   [2] See iv. 589.

Commonwealth, it was too late. Rome alone, without her ally Carthage, was far more than a match for Molossia. Unfortunately for the Chalcidians, their field of operations lay much nearer to the heart of the Hellenic World, and they embarked on their commonwealth-building enterprise at a time when Sparta was a great enough power to be able to strike effectively as far afield as northern Continental European Greece. In 382–379 B.C. a Lacedaemonian expeditionary force brought Olynthus to her knees and broke her commonwealth up.

This opened the way for Philip of Macedon. It gave him the chance of constructing a great power in Northern Greece based not on city-state institutions but on monarchy; and the decisive step in Philip's career was his destruction of Olynthus in 348–347 B.C. In thus unintentionally opening the way for Macedon, Sparta had opened it eventually for Rome. For the Macedonians did not prove equals of either the Olynthians or the Romans in political common sense. Under Alexander's romantic leadership, they exhausted themselves in the *tour de force* of overrunning the whole of the Achaemenian Empire and thereby opening up for Hellenism a far larger *Lebensraum* than could be incorporated in the Hellenic World permanently. Through this impolitic diversion of their energies the Macedonians deprived themselves of the power to complete and consolidate Philip's work. They lost their chance of building, in Continental European Greece and its hinterland, a commonwealth that, in spite of the weakness of its monarchical basis, might have come to be not much less strongly knit than the one that, by Alexander's time, the Romans were already building in Italy.

As for the colonies founded by Rome as a device for maintaining her hold on foreign territories that she had brought under her control, there was nothing uniquely Roman about these. During the same period of Hellenic history this institution was being used, for the same purpose, by Alexander the Great, and, after him, by the governments of most of the Macedonian or Greek successor-states of the Achaemenian Empire. In these Hellenic foundations in the East there was the same distinction as in the Roman foundations in Italy between two categories of colonies. There were military cantonments of Macedonian soldiers and their descendants, corresponding to Rome's colonies of Roman citizens; and there were full-fledged colonial city-states, juridically sovereign and independent, but actually bound to the founding monarchy by permanent ties like those which bound Rome's Latin colonies to Rome. There is no evidence to show whether Rome's policy of founding colonies was inspired by these Hellenic examples or whether it was devised by the Romans independently. The relevant point is that, in founding colonies, the Romans were doing something that was the general practice of contemporary Hellenic states.

Of all the Macedonian successor-states of the Achaemenian Empire, the Seleucid Monarchy in South-West Asia was the most active in founding colonies on the grand scale. If the power of the Monarchy had not been broken as a result of King Antiochus III's impolitic decision to go to war with Rome, the Seleucid Monarchy might eventually have grown into what the Roman Empire eventually became: a confederation of autonomous city-states held together by an oecumenical govern-ment.[1] The loyalty of the Seleucid city-states to the Monarchy was demonstrated more than once when the Monarchy temporarily re-covered parts of its dominions that had been overrun by the Parthians. This loyalty was the more remarkable considering that the Parthians were careful to give considerate treatment to colonial Hellenic city-states that came under their rule. They left them in full possession of their municipal autonomy.

From the military point of view the Seleucid Monarchy was proved, by the disastrous results of its collision with Rome in 192–190 B.C., to be a giant with feet of clay. From the political point of view, on the other hand, the Monarchy was a serious candidate for the role of being a unifying state. Let us suppose that Antiochus III had accepted the Roman suggestion that Rome might abandon her support of the city-states on the west coast of Anatolia which were refusing to accept Antiochus' suzerainty, if Antiochus would abandon his claim to the recovery of former Seleucid possessions on the European side of the Dardanelles.[2] If Antiochus III had had the wisdom to close with this tentative Roman offer, the Seleucid Monarchy might have survived, and the Asiatic domain of Hellenism, from the east shore of the Aegean as far east as the Caspian Gates, might have been consolidated politically under Seleucid auspices.

What conclusion are we to draw from this comparison between Rome's political achievement and the attempts made by the Seleucid Monarchy, Macedon, Olynthus, Syracuse, Sparta, and Athens to give the Hellenic World political unity? Of course these other attempts were unsuccessful, whereas Rome's enterprise was a success. Yet, when we compare the enterprises, the points in common—such points as geographical opportunity, generous statesmanship, and constructive institutions (above all, 'dual citizenship' and colonies)—are surely too numerous and too important to permit the thesis that Rome's political genius was something uniquely her own. Her opportunity, her genero-sity, her institutions of 'dual citizenship' and colonies, which, between them, account for her success, were not hers exclusively. All were common to Rome and at least one other of the competitors for the prize of being the political unifier of the Hellenic World. Olynthus would surely have anticipated Rome in performing this feat if her career had not been cut short at an early stage by the intervention of Sparta. Con-versely, Rome's career would surely have been cut short, too, whatever Livy may say,[3] if Alexander of Macedon had chosen to join forces with his kinsman Alexander of Epirus for an invasion of Italy instead of Asia, or if, after having overrun the Achaemenian Empire, he had lived

---

[1] Vogt, in loc. cit., challenges my comparison between the respective constitutional structures of the Seleucid Monarchy and the Roman Commonwealth on the ground that, in the Monarchy, the local city-states were not linked to the central government by the institution of *isopoliteia* (i.e. dual citizenship), as they were in the Commonwealth. This goes without saying, considering that the central power in the Seleucid Empire was not a city-state but a crown. The Seleucid crown did, however, provide an effective bond, as Vogt himself concedes.

[2] For this proposal, see Livy, Book XXXIV, chap. 58.

[3] See Livy, Book IX, chaps. 17–19.

to spend the resources that he had acquired in the East for a subsequent attack upon the West. In this perspective Rome presents herself, not as an historical force outside the Hellenic Society and on a par with it, but as the eventually successful competitor among a number of states that each, in turn, made the attempt to give the Hellenic World political unity.

If this is, as I believe it is, the true historical setting of Rome, of Roman law, and of the Roman political achievement, why are so many Western historians apparently bent on awarding to Rome an even greater historical role than is hers in the picture that I have drawn? I suspect that the motive behind this Western insistence on magnifying Rome's place in history is a covert Western chauvinism. If the West is to be credited with a major role in history, Rome must be credited with a major role too. Rome gave the West its first lessons in civilization, laid the foundations in the West for the building of a new and distinctively Western civilization there, and left a permanent Roman imprint on what was otherwise a new creation. Roman law still inspires awe in Western minds because most modern Western systems of law except the English common law are deeply indebted to it. Even the Scottish common law has a tincture of Roman law in it. Napoleon's jurists would hardly have been able to elicit the Napoleonic Code out of medieval French customary law if the resources of Roman law had not been at their disposal. In Roman-Dutch law Roman law itself is still a living force in the present-day Western World. Again, Latin is the liturgical language of the Roman Catholic Church, to which one half of modern Western Christendom adheres. The Roman Church's official text of the Christian Bible is the Vulgate Latin version.

When, however, these legal and literary contributions of Rome to the present-day Western Civilization are analysed, they prove to be Hellenic contributions in Latin dress. If Rome had not herself previously received Hellenism, she would have had little or nothing to pass on to the Western barbarians. She was an intermediary transmitter of Hellenism in a Latin dress. The West European barbarians might have had a better start in civilization if they had received Hellenism in its original Greek dress from one of the colonial Hellenic outposts in the Western Mediterranean: Massilia or Cumae or Tarentum or Syracuse. But the historical fact is that they received it at second hand through the agency of Rome, and the agent has eclipsed the principal in the historical vista seen by the West European barbarians' descendants. Rome's transmission of the Hellenic heritage to their forebears in Latin dress looms larger in their eyes than Rome's previous acquisition of this heritage from the heart of Hellas.

The Hellenic colonial outposts—Syracuse, Tarentum, Cumae, Massilia—were not powerful enough to radiate their cultural influence deep into Western Europe. The Canaanite colonial outposts—Utica and Carthage and Gades—were no more effective. The incorporation of Western Europe in the *Oikoumenê* was accomplished by Rome during the three hundred years running from the first Roman campaigns in Spain during the Second Romano-Punic War to Agricola's campaigns in

North Britain in A.D. 78–85. This pacification and rudimentary education of Western Europe was, no doubt, a considerable achievement, in whatever historical perspective it is viewed. It is, inevitably, an achievement of capital importance from a standpoint which sees the culmination of all previous history in the present-day Western World;[1] for this Roman enterprise was the means by which the West was first brought within the field of any civilization. Yet these Roman activities in the West had little effect, and consequently made little impression, on the heart of the Hellenic World. Hellenes in the heart-land hardly noticed this enormous westward expansion of their world by Roman hands, and they were also little affected, and therefore hardly aware, when, in the fifth century of the Christian Era, this semi-civilized western fringe of the latter-day Hellenic World relapsed into the barbarism from which it had only recently and only partially been extricated. The loss of Sicily, Italy, and the North-West African region round Carthage that is now Tunisia did, no doubt, give a shock to the public in Alexandria, Antioch, and Ephesus, as well as to the Imperial Government at Constantinople. The recession of civilization farther to the west can have made little difference to anyone living east of the Syrtes and the Adriatic.

The perspective in which Rome has appeared to Greek-speaking Hellenes and Orientals and their successors since the last thirty years of the third century B.C., when Rome first began to make her power felt east of the Adriatic, is piquantly different from the perspective in which Rome appears to a modern Western historian; and this difference of outlook is an historical consequence of a differential Roman policy.

Towards the west the Romans insisted on making their native Latin language the linguistic and literary medium for the transmission of the Hellenic culture that they themselves had drawn from a Greek fountain-head. They deliberately overlaid with Latin the Etruscan language north-west of the Tiber, the Canaanite language in North-West Africa, and the Greek language in its surviving bridgeheads along the coasts of Southern Italy. But, in revenge, the Greek language half captured Rome itself from the second century B.C. to the third century of the Christian Era; and, with the one exception of Southern Italy, the Romans never deliberately attempted to dislodge the Greek language in favour of Latin in any country in which Greek had already established itself as the people's mother-tongue, or even merely as a *lingua franca* for purposes of public administration and private business. Even the island of Sicily, wedged in between an already Latinised Italy and a progressively Latinized North-West Africa, remained, through seven centuries of Roman rule, the Greek-speaking country that the native interior as well as the Hellenic colonial fringe along the coasts had come to be before

[1] This point is made, from this standpoint, by Vogt in loc. cit. and by F. H. Underhill in *The Canadian Historical Review*, vol. xxxii, No. 3 (September, 1951), pp. 201–19. Vogt suggests that the point has been overlooked by me. It could hardly be overlooked by anyone who has had a Western education, since Rome's role as the layer of the foundations for the subsequent Western Civilization is the first and last thing about Rome that is impressed upon the mind of a Western school-child. I agree, of course, that the West owes this debt to Rome, and I have not overlooked the point. It has, however, no relevance to the question of what Rome's relation to the Hellenic Civilization was.

the date of the Roman conquest. In all regions, east of the Adriatic and the Syrtes, in which the Greek language had already established itself, the Roman Government accepted Greek, as a matter of course, as the administrative language of the world-state. In the Aegean and Levantine heartland of the Hellenic World, Greek, under the Roman regime, was officially on a par with Latin, and in practice it continued here to enjoy the almost exclusive currency for administrative and business purposes that it had previously enjoyed in the states founded by the successors of Alexander. When Thrace, which Alexander's successors had failed to hold and Hellenize, was eventually converted into a Roman province, the Roman Imperial Government chose Greek, not Latin, to be the linguistic medium for the tardy Hellenization of this obstinate outpost of barbarism. The only region, east of the Adriatic, in which Latin was allowed to propagate itself was the Balkan Peninsula beyond the northern borders of Thrace and Macedon; and this region—close to the heart of Hellas though it was—was still culturally virgin soil at the date of its annexation by the Emperor Augustus.

In spite of the liberality of Rome's linguistic policy the Greek-speaking intelligentsia was not reconciled to Roman rule till the age of enlightened Roman government extending from the reign of Nerva to the reign of Marcus Aurelius. And they did not begin to feel themselves to be Romans till after the world-wide grant of Roman citizenship in A.D. 212. East of the Adriatic the Latin language attained its maximum currency in and after the revolutionary convulsions in the third century of the Christian Era, when the Roman Empire and the Hellenic Civilization were rescued from the jaws of destruction by Illyrian soldiers whose passport to civilization was the Latin language and who knew no Greek, unlike the cultivated Roman aristocrats whom they had superseded. In the fourth and fifth centuries of the Christian Era Latin was temporarily cultivated in the Levant for literary as well as for administrative use. It was used by the fourth-century Antiochene historian Ammianus Marcellinus, and by the fifth-century Alexandrian poet Claudius Claudianus. But after the loss, in the fifth century, of all the Latin-speaking provinces of the Empire except those in the Balkan Peninsula, the use of Latin east of the Adriatic soon evaporated even at Constantinople, with its imperial administrative bureaux and its Balkan Latin-speaking hinterland. The Emperor Justinian came from a district in Latin-speaking Dardania round the head-waters of the River Axius (Vardar); and he used the Latin language for his codification of Roman law. But even Justinian promulgated his own subsequent supplementary laws in Greek, in order to make them intelligible to the majority of his subjects; and Latin had almost ceased to be current in Constantinople before the end of the sixth century.

The Greek-speaking Hellenes had no sooner accepted Rome than they absorbed her. After the conversion of the majority of the population of the world-state to Christianity, the famous and ancient word 'Hellene' inevitably changed its connotation. Previously it had meant someone inside the pale of the only true civilization, in contrast to a barbarian. Now it came to mean someone outside the pale of the only true religion, in contrast to a Christian. Since Greek-speaking Christians could no longer call themselves Hellenes, they took to calling themselves Romans instead. The name 'Roman' was unobjectionable, because it had not acquired the religious associations of the name 'Hellene'. In the authentic popular form of the Modern Greek language, 'Roman' (*Romaîos*, pronounced *Romyós*) still means today a Greek-speaking Eastern Orthodox Christian, while 'the Roman language' (*Romaïká*) means Modern Greek. In Italy today there is a province called Romagna, but the district that bears this name is not the country round the city of Rome: it is the country round the city of Ravenna, where the Greek-speaking Romans of Constantinople and Anatolia held a bridge-head for the Roman Empire against the Lombard invaders of Italy from A.D. 568 to A.D. 750.

The Muslims have taken their cue from the Greek-speaking Orthodox Christians. In the languages of the Islamic World 'Rum' means the Greek-speaking remnant of the Roman Empire that maintained itself after the Latin, Syriac, Coptic, and Armenian-speaking provinces had been lopped off by German and Arab barbarian invaders. Alexander the Great is known, in these languages, as a 'Rumi' by anticipation, or perhaps rather because, in Islamic, as in Modern Greek, eyes, 'Roman' just means 'Greek'. As the successor of the Greek-speaking Roman emperors at Constantinople, the Ottoman Padishah was styled 'the Qaysar-i-Rum' (the Caesar of Rome);[1] and 'millet-i-rum' (the Roman nation) was the official name of the autonomous Eastern Orthodox Christian community within the Ottoman Empire.

Thus conquered Greece did indeed take her ferocious Roman conqueror captive. She annexed him in the most complete way possible by identifying him outright with herself. The outstanding event in Rome's history is Rome's absorption by Hellenism, not the Hellenization of barbarian Western Europe by Rome through a Latin medium; and this is the perspective in which Rome's history ought to be viewed and interpreted. Rome's Hellenic destiny is portended in one of the earliest historical notices of her existence. A pupil of Plato's and Aristotle's, Heracleides Ponticus, reports, in a passage cited by Plutarch,[2] that 'an Hellenic city called Rome', which lay 'somewhere in the direction of the Atlantic', has been captured, according to rumour, by a horde of Hyperboreans. This vague report is a faint echo of the historical capture of Rome by a Gallic war-band *circa* 390–383 B.C.; but, in contrast to his general lack of precision, the Hellenic scholar has got one point clear and correct. In calling Rome 'an Hellenic city' he is telling the fundamental truth about her.

---

[1] See p. 192.
[2] Plutarch's *Life of Camillus*, chap. 22, quoted in v. 212, footnote 3.

XIII. THE CONFIGURATION OF SYRIAC
HISTORY

I. THE PROBLEM

THE word 'Syriac' is commonly used as a label for a language, an alphabet, and a literature written in these. The Syriac language and alphabet are late phases of the Aramaic, and both developed out of the local Aramaic dialect and script of North-Western Mesopotamia (Osrhoene).[1] On the other hand, the Syriac literature is a new departure[2] in as much as it shows few traces of its pre-Hellenic Aramaic past, while it has a partially Hellenic cultural background. Most of it is Christian, and this includes translations from the Greek Christian Fathers, as well as original works. Much of the rest consists of translations of Greek works of philosophy and science written in the Hellenic Age.

In this book the word 'Syriac' has been borrowed to serve the different purpose of labelling a civilization, approximately contemporary with the Hellenic, that originated in Syria.[3] Some distinctive word is required, and the word 'Syrian' has a primarily geographical connotation and is therefore applicable to Syria at any period of Syria's history, from the time when the Earth's surface first arrived at its present configuration down to the present day.

The Syria that was the original home of the 'Syriac' civilization is Syria in the broadest usage of the word: that is to say, the whole region between the domain of the Egyptiac Civilization on the south-west and the domain of the Sumero-Akkadian Civilization on the south-east. *Vis-à-vis* Egypt the boundary is clearly marked by a stretch of desert, about a hundred miles broad, that insulates Rafa (Raphia), the south-westernmost habitable point in Greater Syria, from Pelusium, the former fortress covering the north-easternmost corner of the Nile Delta. *Vis-à-vis* the Sumero-Akkadian World the boundary is vaguer; but Syria's extreme limits in this direction can be defined as anyway excluding the alluvial country in the lower basin of the rivers Tigris and Euphrates, and also the fertile rain-watered lands of Assyria, between the Tigris, in the latitude of the city of Mosul, and the south-western rim of the Iranian plateau in this quarter. On the north the boundary of Greater Syria is well defined by the southern rim of the Armenian-Anatolian plateau, which is continuous with the south-eastern rim of the Anatolian plateau. The upper basin of the River Tigris, as well as Commagêné and Eastern (Lowland) Cilicia, would fall within the limits of Syria as thus defined. On the south, on the other hand, the boundary is indefinite. Here Syria melts into Arabia. The plateau of Gilead, in Transjordan, extends southward and south-eastward without a break, through Ammon, Moab, Midian, the Ḥijāz, Asīr, and the Yaman almost to within sight of Aden. The Syriac Civilization that, as I see it, took shape in Greater Syria during the second half of the second millennium

---

[1] See pp. 442–3.
[2] See W. F. Albright: *The Archaeology of Palestine*, pp. 202–3.
[3] See i. 82, footnote 2.

B.C. subsequently spread all the way down this long south-eastward extension of Syria. This happened soon after the beginning of the last millennium B.C.,[1] to judge by recent estimates of the dates of the earliest inscriptions written in the South Arabian version of the Alphabet.[2] It will be seen that the Syria which was the original home of the 'Syriac' Civilization is approximately coincident with the combined areas of the present states of Syria,[3] Lebanon, Jordan, and Israel, together with a strip of Southern Turkey, from Mersina eastwards to the upper basin of the Tigris, and with a southern hinterland in Western Arabia.

Some scholars do not admit that there was any unity in the civilization in Syria which was contemporary with the Hellenic Civilization in the Aegean area. This question is discussed at a later point in the present chapter.[4] On the other hand, no scholar would deny that Syria in this age was the seat and source of civilizing enterprises and achievements which—whether unitary or multiple—were in any case fruitful and potent. For example, it is impossible to trace the course of Hellenic history without recognizing both the potency and the fatefulness, at almost every stage, of influences that played upon the Hellenic World from Syrian sources. In, if not before, the eighth century the Hellenes adopted from Syria the Phoenician invention of the Alphabet, including not only the shapes but the names of the Phoenician letters. From the eighth century onwards they entered into competition with the Phoenicians for the domination of the western basin of the Mediterranean, and this competition went on for more than 500 years, until the issue was finally decided in favour of Hellenism as a result of Rome's victories in the First and the Second Romano-Carthaginian War. In the seventh century Hellenic art drew inspiration from an 'Oriental' style that the Phoenicians transmitted to Hellas.

The most fateful single event in all Hellenic history was the ideological and religious collision, in Coele Syria in the second century B.C., between Hellenism and Judaism. The Jewish anti-Hellenic resistance movement in Judaea proved strong enough to overcome the attempt of the Judaean Jewish Hellenists, backed by the military and political power of the Seleucid Monarchy, to convert Judaea to Hellenism from its native Jewish tradition; and the encounter was fateful because the story did not end in Hellenism's second-century cultural and political defeat. The political defeat was ephemeral; for the Judaean Jewish state which won its independence from the Seleucid Government first in 142–141 and finally in 129 B.C. became subject to Rome in 63 B.C., and

---

[1] It was, no doubt, a consequence of the domestication of the Arabian camel, which W. F. Albright, in *Archaeology and the Religion of Israel*, 4th ed., p. 227, dates between the sixteenth and the twelfth century B.C. on the authority of R. Walz in the *Zeitschrift der Deutschen Morgenländischen Gesellschaft*, vol. 101 (1951), pp. 29–51. See also Albright: *From the Stone Age to Christianity*, 2nd ed., pp. 165–6. The intercourse between the heart of the Syriac World and South Arabia was intensified when a sea-route from the head of the Gulf of 'Aqabah through the Red Sea to the Indian Ocean was opened—or re-opened—in the tenth century B.C. by joint Phoenician and Judahite enterprise.

[2] See W. F. Albright: *Archaeology and the Religion of Israel*, 4th ed., pp. 56–57 and 225. In Qatabān the earliest rock inscriptions may be dated about 1000 B.C., though the earliest monumental inscriptions are thought to date only from the eighth century B.C.   [3] Now a component of the United Arab Republic.

[4] On pp. 411–30.

Jewish political nationalism in Palestine was eventually crushed—and this decisively—in the Romano-Jewish wars of A.D. 66–70 and A.D. 132–5. But conquered Judaea took its Hellenic conquerors captive on the religious plane. The Hellenic World was eventually converted to a religion of Jewish origin that was, and remained, essentially Judaic in its inspiration and its principles, notwithstanding its compromises with Hellenism in the fields of theology and visual art. And this conversion of the Hellenic World to Christianity was the end of the Hellenic Civilization. As a result of the conversion, Hellenism lost its identity.

2. RESULTS OF USING THE HELLENIC MODEL AS A KEY TO THE SOLUTION OF THE SYRIAC PROBLEM

What was the configuration of the history of this Syriac Civilization which, whether unitary or multiple, unquestionably had a fateful influence on the course of Hellenic history? In seeking to trace this I used the same Hellenic model[1] as in my attempts to identify other civilizations. In the early chapters of the story the courses of Syriac and Hellenic history seemed to me to run parallel, at least on the political plane. In the background of both histories there was an identical Völkerwanderung—the huge upheaval that racked the whole of the Levant during the fourteenth, thirteenth, and twelfth centuries B.C. After the dust raised by the feet of the migrants and conquerors had settled, the political configuration of the emergent civilizations in the Syriac and Hellenic worlds was similar. At this stage, when the history of both worlds begins to become clearer, we find them both divided up politically among a host of petty states. These states were constantly going to war with each other, yet their peoples displayed some consciousness of having a common culture, and, at moments of extreme peril from powerful foreign aggressors, they temporarily put their local quarrels aside and made common cause to defend their threatened independence. The Mesopotamian Aramaeans, who had pressed Assyria hard in the eleventh and tenth centuries B.C., were conquered and annexed by Assyria between 932 and 859 B.C.;[2] and in 858–856 B.C. Assyria conquered and annexed the state of Bit Adini, which commanded the crossings of the Euphrates at its westward elbow, after defeating a coalition of North Syrian states that had attempted to save Bit Adini from its fate.[3] But in 853 B.C. the Assyrians' first serious attempt to conquer Syria west of the Euphrates[4] was foiled by the united forces of a coalition of Syrian states, ranging from Qu'e in the north-west to Ammon in the south-east, in which King Ahab of Israel served under the high command of his perennial rival and enemy the King of Damascus. This is a striking Syriac parallel to the Hellenic feat of foiling the Achaemenian Persian Empire's attempt to conquer Continental European Greece in 480–479 B.C., when the Athenians served under the high command of Sparta.[5]

[1] See i. 73. [2] See A. Dupont-Sommer: Les Araméens, pp. 31–32.
[3] See ibid., p. 35.
[4] Tiglath-Pileser I's march to the sea circa 1060 B.C. had been no more than a raid.
[5] The Assyrians were more persistent than the Persians in returning to the charge. Shalmaneser III crossed the Euphrates again in 849, 848, and 845, but each time he

After that, however, the two histories took different courses. The Hellenes were never conquered by an alien power (Macedon and Rome were already more or less Hellenized before they imposed their political domination on other Hellenic states). The plane on which the Hellenic Civilization was eventually conquered and dissolved was the religious plane, not the political or the military. On the other hand the states of the Syriac World all lost their political independence to alien powers in and after the eighth century B.C., when Assyria resumed her career of aggression with greater driving force than she had ever shown before. By the time of Assyria's fall in 612 B.C. the only states in the Syriac World that had not been liquidated were Arvad (Aradus), Byblos, Tyre, Ekron, Ashdod, Ascalon, Gaza, and Judah; these had escaped only by abject submission; and in the sixth century B.C. these, too, were swept off the board by one of the Assyrian Empire's successor-states, the Neobabylonian Empire. This empire, in turn, including its subject peoples, was conquered and annexed in 538 B.C. by the Achaemenian Persian Empire. The colonial extension of the Syriac World in the western basin of the Mediterranean was the only part of it that remained politically independent after the sixth century B.C. Independence was preserved here by the sixth-century political unification of all the colonial Phoenician city-states under the hegemony of Carthage. The establishment of the Carthaginian Empire saved this colonial Canaan from being submerged under the tide of Hellenic colonial expansion. The Carthaginian Empire was a great power in the Mediterranean for three hundred years. But it, too, eventually succumbed to Rome, and in 146 B.C. Carthage itself was erased much more thoroughly than Judah had been in 587 or 586 B.C.

What is one to make of the history of the Syriac Civilization after the disappearance of the states that had originally represented it on the political plane? The loss of political independence was certainly not the end of the story.

Judah, which was one of the original states of the Syriac World, and which lost its independence in 587/6 B.C., is still represented in the present-day world by a living community, the Jewish diasporá. The deportees from the extinguished Kingdom of Judah quickly discovered, in their Babylonian exile, how to keep their community in existence, not only without possessing a state of their own, but even without having a country in which they were in a local majority. The Jewish diasporá has maintained itself from that day to this. In the course of 2,500 years it has spread from Babylonia and Egypt, first over the Hellenic World, and then over the still wider areas of the Christian and Islamic worlds. And its fortunes have not been dependent on those of its country of origin. Twice, so far, in the course of subsequent history, the Jewish diasporá has re-established a Jewish community in Palestine: first in the Age of the Achaemenian Empire and then again in our own day. But the Jewish diasporá lived on when the Neo-Judaean Jewish community, founded

---

seems to have been foiled again by the same coalition of Syrian states. In 841 and 834 he attacked the Kingdom of Damascus, but he failed to capture the capital and to destroy the Kingdom's military power (see A. Dupont-Sommer, op. cit., pp. 37–39).

under the aegis of the Achaemenian regime, lost its independence to Rome in 63 B.C. after having won it from the Seleucid Monarchy in 142–1 and 129 B.C.; and it lived on again when the Judaean Jewry was crushed in its hopeless trials of strength with Rome in A.D. 66–70 and A.D. 132–5.

The survival of the Jews and Judaism is such a signal example of the continuance of the Syriac Civilization after the loss of political independence that it is apt to eclipse other examples that are hardly less remarkable. In North-West Africa, for instance, the Canaanite language, religion, and culture survived the destruction of Carthage and continued to spread ever more widely among the native Berber population in an advancing wave with which the pursuing wave of Latinization never succeeded in catching up. Indeed, the Canaanite language—better known today as 'Hebrew'[1]—may have held out longer than Latin did against the Arabic language that eventually replaced both Latin and Canaanite in North-West Africa after the Muslim Arab conquest.[2] Yet a thousand years before Canaanite became extinct in North-West Africa it had yielded in its Asiatic homeland to another of the languages of the Syriac World, Aramaic.[3]

The fortunes of the Aramaic language and alphabet were made by the Assyrian conquest that wiped the Aramaic-speaking peoples' as well as

[1] We think of the Canaanite language as being 'Hebrew' because by far the largest, most important, and most famous body of literature, written in it, that we possess is the collection of scriptures composed and preserved by the peoples of Israel and Judah and their heirs the Jews; and the Israelites were one of a group of Hebrew peoples from the North Arabian steppe who had gained a foothold in South-East Syria in the thirteenth century B.C. (other Hebrew peoples were the Edomites, Kenites, Moabites, and Ammonites).

However, to call the Canaanite language 'Hebrew' is really misleading, since it is improbable that the Hebrews were already Canaanite-speaking when they first occupied those parts of Canaan in which we find them subsequently settled. The Canaanite language had been current in Canaan for something like two thousand years before the Hebrews' arrival (see W. F. Albright: *Archaeology and the Religion of Israel*, 4th ed., p. 69); and it therefore seems probable that the Hebrews learnt to speak Canaanite from the native population whom they conquered and with whom they subsequently coalesced. The Hebrews themselves were part of a wave of Nomad or semi-Nomad invaders which broke upon all the steppe-coasts of the Fertile Crescent during the centuries round about the turn of the second and the last millennium B.C. The wave broke in an arc, with the Hebrews on the south-west wing, the Chaldaeans on the south-east wing, and the Aramaeans in the centre. The Aramaeans penetrated farthest, and would appear to have been the most numerous people in the whole of this Völkerwanderung. We may conjecture that the Aramaic language, which the Aramaeans themselves retained after their settlement, was the original language of the Hebrews too (A. Dupont-Sommer: *Les Araméens*, pp. 81–82). According to the Israelite tradition, the Hebrew Patriarchs were kinsfolk of the Aramaeans and married Aramaean wives (ibid., pp. 15–16), and Jacob himself is called an Aramaean outright in the commemorative formula in Deut. xxvi. 5.

The nomenclature of the political map of post-Völkerwanderung Syria suggests that, at the time of the incoming Hebrew and Aramaic tribes' settlement, they were conscious of their unity. The Aramaean state astride the Amanus called Sam'āl, meaning 'the left-hand', i.e. 'the North', has its 'opposite number' in the Israelite tribe called Ben-Yamin, meaning 'the right-hand', i.e. 'the South'. It looks as if all the tribes that had broken out of the desert into Syria between the north end of the Dead Sea and the south face of the Taurus had originally constituted a single confederacy (see S. A. Cook in *The Cambridge Ancient History*, vol. iii (1925), p. 425). Sam'āl's proper name was Ya'udi, which sounds as if it were the same word as 'Judah' (see p. 421).

If this is the truth, then the Jews were reverting, without knowing it, to the original language of their forefathers when they took to speaking Aramaic instead of Canaanite, as they did in the course of the Achaemenian Age.

[2] See iii. 138, footnote 3.
[3] See i. 80–81; v. 499–500; and vi. 70, footnote 3.

the Canaanite-speaking peoples' states off the political map. In the next chapter of the story 'Aramaean merchants were replacing Phoenician traders, and a new Aramaic culture, composed of Canaanite and Neo-Assyrian with the latter dominant, was spreading rapidly over the West, strongly supported by Assyrian military power.'[1] The conquered Aramaeans' language and alphabet steadily gained ground on the conquering Assyrians' and Babylonians' Akkadian language and clumsy cuneiform script, till, by the first century of the Christian Era, these became extinct. Aramaic eventually became the vernacular language of the whole of the Fertile Crescent, including Palestine[2] and Phoenicia. In the fifth century B.C. Aramaic was spoken and written by the Jewish military colony at Elephantinê, on the Ethiopian frontier of Egypt.

As a *lingua franca* for international commerce, diplomacy, and public administration, Aramaic had a still wider currency in a standardized form comparable to the Attic Greek *koinê* which served the same purpose in the same area in the Post-Alexandrine Age. Before the end of the eighth century B.C. this Aramaic *koinê* had been substituted for the local dialect in the official inscriptions of the North-West Syrian state of Ya'udi (Sam'āl).[3] An international language written in a simple script was a convenient instrument for the administration of a multi-national empire. A fresco dating from the Assyrian Age (ninth or eighth century B.C.) at Til-Barsip, the former capital of the Aramaean state of Bit Adini, astride the elbow of the Euphrates, shows a pair of secretaries standing side by side and taking notes, one on a clay tablet (i.e. in cuneiform) and the other on a sheet of papyrus or parchment (i.e. in the Aramaic alphabet).[4] Towards the end of the eighth century B.C. an Assyrian high official, the rabshakeh, and the official representatives of the state of Judah could have communicated with each other in Aramaic, if the rabshakeh had not preferred to make his speech in Canaanite, in order to appeal, over the officials' heads, to the people—who, at this date, had not yet acquired the Aramaic language.[5] An ostrakon found at Asshur, dating from about 650 B.C., is inscribed with a letter, written in the Aramaic *koinê* with a few Akkadianisms, from one Assyrian official to another. There are bilingual inscriptions in Aramaic and Akkadian dating from the reigns of the Assyrian Kings Shalmaneser V, Sargon, and Sennacherib (727–681 B.C.) and also from the time of the Neo-babylonian Empire.[6] Before the end of the seventh century B.C. Aramaic had supplanted Akkadian for serving as the diplomatic language of South-West Asia and Egypt—a role which had been the Akkadian language's for at least a thousand years. Aramaic is the language of a letter, written about 605 B.C. by a Phoenician King Adon to the King of Egypt, asking for help against the Babylonians.[7] The Achaemenian

---

[1] W. F. Albright: *Archaeology and the Religion of Israel*, 4th ed., p. 161.

[2] In Judah, Canaanite was not replaced by Aramaic as the local vernacular language until after the liquidation of the Kingdom in 587/6 B.C. The Lachish ostraka, which were written in the autumn of 589 B.C. (see W. F. Albright, op. cit., p. 41), are all in Canaanite (Dupont-Sommer, op. cit., p. 88). At Samaria, Aramaic was replacing Canaanite in the Achaemenian Age, on the evidence of Aramaic inscriptions on jars dating from this period (ibid., p. 92). [3] Dupont-Sommer, op. cit., p. 82.

[4] Ibid., p. 84. [5] 2 Kings xviii. 26–28.

[6] Dupont-Sommer, op. cit., pp. 86 and 89. [7] Ibid., p. 89.

Imperial Government gave the Aramaic *koinê* the status of an official language in all provinces of the Empire west of Iran, at any rate.[1] In Egypt, Persian officials used Aramaic in their correspondence both with Egyptians and with each other;[2] and Aramaic texts, dating from the Achaemenian Age, have been found all over the country.[3] In the same age Aramaic appears in inscriptions and in coin-legends in Anatolia.[4] It is still more significant that about five hundred documents written in Aramaic have been found at Persepolis.[4] These conquests made by the Aramaic language were far outranged by those made by the Aramaic alphabet as an instrument for conveying non-Aramaic languages of many different families. The Aramaic alphabet spread eastwards across Iran to the Panjab, and also, via Central Asia, to the northern marches of China. At the present day it is used for writing the Mongol and Manchu languages.[5]

This genius for not merely surviving, but actually prospering and expanding, after the loss of political independence is thus not something that is peculiar to the Jews and Judaism. All the other states of the Syriac World shared the political fate that overtook Judah in 587/6 B.C.; and other disinherited Syriac peoples, besides the Jews, responded to this challenge triumphantly. There were, of course, some—notably the deportees from the Kingdom of Israel—who succumbed to adversity and lost their identity. Yet even the Israelites are still represented today by a few hundred Samaritans in the neighbourhood of Nablūs in the former hill country of Ephraim. And on the whole, taking the Aramaeans and the colonial Phoenicians into account, as well as the Jews, we may conclude that the capacity for living and growing in diasporá was a distinctive common characteristic of the peoples that were partakers in the civilization or civilizations of the Syriac World in and after the last millennium B.C. If we accept this conclusion, it raises a difficult historical question. Except for the Jews and the Samaritans, all the peoples of the original Syriac World are now extinct. No others survive, even in diasporá, today. How long, then, did the rest outlive the loss of their political independence? And when did the Syriac Civilization as a whole lose its identity?

In searching for answers to these questions in earlier volumes of this book, I applied my Hellenic model,[6] as I had applied it in trying to elucidate the early chapters of Syriac history in which the states of the Syriac World had not yet lost their independence. The configuration of the last phase of Hellenic history is clear. The warring local states of the Hellenic World were eventually united politically in a universal state. Within this unitary political framework, a higher religion, embodied in a universal church, had eventually converted to itself the whole population of the Hellenic World before the universal state collapsed and fell a prey to barbarian invaders from beyond its frontiers. Could one put one's finger on any parallel configuration which might give one the clue

[1] Ibid., pp. 89–90.   [2] Ibid., pp. 90–91.
[3] Ibid., p. 94.   [4] Ibid., p. 91.
[5] The histories of the Aramaic language and the Aramaic alphabet have been taken, in i. 79–82, as clues to the expansion and the duration of the Syriac Civilization.
[6] See i. 73.

for identifying the last phase of Syriac history? In other words, could one find, associated with each other in what had been the Syriac World, any counterparts of the Roman Empire, Christianity, and the barbarians who eventually overran the Roman Empire's former territory?

Christianity has a conspicuous counterpart in Islam. Both religions were derived from Judaism, and both parted company with Judaism in order to preach Judaic monotheism to the non-Jewish world. Islam developed and spread within the framework of the Caliphate under the Umayyad and 'Abbasid regimes; so, in this point at least, the Caliphate might be taken to be a counterpart of the Roman Empire.[1] Moreover, the Caliphate, like the Roman Empire, fell a prey to barbarian invaders in the end. The German, Sarmatian, Hun, Slav, Berber, and Arab invaders of the former domain of the Roman Empire have obvious counterparts in the Turkish, Mongol, Arab, Berber, and Frankish invaders of the former domain of the Caliphate.[2] If one provisionally took the post-'Abbasid Völkerwanderung, the Caliphate, and Islam, as being symptoms of the last phase of Syriac history, could one then trace Syriac history back from this point to the time at which the local states of the early Syriac World had lost their independence?[3] If this were to prove possible, the application of the Hellenic model would have enabled one to identify the whole course of Syriac history.

When, however, one recalled the immediate antecedents of the Caliphate, it was obvious that they were quite different from those of the Roman Empire. The Roman Empire had united the Hellenic World politically by suppressing its warring local states; but the warring local states of the Syriac World had not been suppressed by the Caliphate. They had been suppressed by the Assyrian and Neobabylonian empires, twelve or thirteen hundred years before the Caliphate had come into existence. The Caliphate had established itself not, like the Roman Empire, by suppressing a considerable number of relatively small states, but by conquering the whole of one great state, the Sasanian Persian Empire, and the best part of another, the Roman Empire. So, in the immediate antecedents of the Roman Empire and of the Caliphate, there was no correspondence at all between Hellenic history and the history of the civilization to which Islam, the Caliphate, and the post-'Abbasid Völkerwanderung were to be attributed.

At this point I recollected that it was, after all, improbable that the course of Syriac history had run parallel to the course of Hellenic history from beginning to end, considering that the Syriac World had had an

---

[1] K. D. Erdmann remarks (in *Archiv für Kulturgeschichte*, xxxiii. Band, Heft 2 (1951), p. 243) that Islam begins with a universal state as well as with a religion. This is true, but it is also true of Christianity, as was noticed by a series of Christian apologists and theologians who were writing under the Roman imperial regime. The Roman Empire was already serving, unconsciously and unintentionally, in its Pre-Constantinian Age as a political framework for the propagation of Christianity. We must agree with the Christian writers of that age in recognizing this as being a matter of historical fact, even if we do not share their belief that the establishment of the Roman Empire in the generation of Augustus was ordained by God's providence for the Christian Church's benefit.

[2] See i. 72.

[3] I have been criticized for thus arguing backwards from the Caliphate by F. Hampl in the *Historische Zeitschrift*, Band 173, Heft 3 (1952), p. 461.

experience which the Hellenic World had been spared. The Syriac World had been overrun by Hellenic invaders in the generation of Alexander the Great, and this forcible Hellenic intrusion upon it had lasted in Syria itself for nearly a thousand years. The intruders had not been completely expelled till Alexander's sweeping conquests in the fourth century B.C. had been finally annulled, in the seventh century of the Christian Era, by the sweeping counter-conquests of the Muslim Arabs.[1] Perhaps it was conceivable that, during this millennium of alien domination, the Syriac Civilization had kept itself alive underground, till at last it had emerged again on the religious plane in Islam and on the political plane in the Caliphate. If so, perhaps the Caliphate might be regarded as being a resumption of the Achaemenian Empire—a universal state in which the Syriac World had been united politically before Alexander's assault had overthrown it.[2] The Achaemenian Empire, unlike the Caliphate, did stand in an historical relation to the warring local states of the early Syriac World that was comparable to the Roman Empire's historical relation to the warring local states of the Hellenic World. The Achaemenian Empire had given the Syriac World, at last, the unity and peace that the Assyrian and Neobabylonian empires had failed to establish. So perhaps, after all, the course of Syriac history down to the beginning of the Hellenic intrusion on the Syriac World and the consequent break-up of the Achaemenian Empire in the fourth century B.C. did run parallel to the course of Hellenic history down to, say, the temporary break-up of the Roman Empire in the third century of the Christian Era, and then eventually ran parallel to it again from the date of the final liquidation of the Hellenic intrusion onwards. On this analysis the Caliphate would be the belated counterpart, in Syriac history, of the Diocletianic and Constantinian Roman Empire in Hellenic history.

This reading of Syriac history seemed to be supported by the configuration of Indian history and also by a series of events in the Syriac World itself during the age of the Hellenic Civilization's intrusion on it.

The eastward expansion of the Hellenic World initiated by Alexander did not hit the Syriac World alone; it also hit India; for, though Alexander's own raid into India had no lasting effects, it was followed up, *circa* 183 B.C., by a more effective intrusion based on an Hellenic state that had established itself in the Oxus-Jaxartes Basin. This Bactrian Greek intrusion brought the Panjab, at least, and possibly a wider area in North-West India, under an Hellenic rule that lasted for about two hundred years, and the end of this Hellenic political regime in India was not the end of Hellenic cultural influence there. The Bactrian Greek wave of invasion was followed by a Eurasian Nomad wave— Sakas and Partho-Sakas and Kushans—which lasted longer and penetrated deeper into the Indian sub-continent. Though these Nomad invaders of India were Iranians, not Greeks, they were nevertheless Philhellenes. In occupying the Greeks' former domain in Bactria and India, they had encountered Hellenism and had been attracted by it;

[1] This chapter of Hellenic history has been discussed in i. 73–76.
[2] This interpretation of the Caliphate has been suggested in i. 76–78.

and, in the Kushan Age (first to third century of the Christian Era) this original influence of local Hellenism upon them was reinforced by maritime intercourse between the Kushan Empire in India and the Roman Empire via Alexandria. Hellenism was, in fact, protected and fostered in India by the Kushans in somewhat the same way as it was by the Romans in the Levant. In India the Hellenic intrusion lasted for about five hundred years. It was finally liquidated here in the fourth century of the Christian Era by the establishment of an Indian universal state, the Gupta Empire, and the Gupta Empire might be regarded as being a resumption of an earlier Indian universal state, the Maurya Empire, whose collapse had opened the way for the Greek Prince of Bactria, Demetrius, to invade India *circa* 183 B.C.[1]

The configuration of Indian history in this chapter, in which an Hellenic intrusion is both preceded and followed by a universal state, is evidently the same as the configuration of a chapter of history in South-West Asia and Egypt in which an Hellenic intrusion is likewise both preceded and followed by a universal state. This Indian parallel is illuminating for the interpretation of Syriac history. It has not ever been suggested, as far as I know, by any student of Indian history that the continuity of this was broken by the Hellenic intrusion, and that the period of Indian history following the intrusion is to be regarded as being the story of a different civilization from the one that was current in India during the period preceding the intrusion. Most students of Indian civilization seem to hold that this has been continuous from at least as early as the time of the arrival of the Aryas in India down to the present day. Some of them have been critical of my division of Indian history since the disappearance of the Indus Culture into the histories of two civilizations that I have distinguished from each other.[2] But the event in the history of India which seemed to me to mark a break in its social and cultural continuity was not the intrusion of Hellenism into India; it was the victory of the Post-Buddhaic form of Hinduism over Buddhism in India during and after the Gupta Age, together with the contemporary Völkerwanderung of the Hun and Gurjara barbarians from Central Asia. In my interpretation of the Hellenic intrusion into India I never thought of dissenting from what may perhaps be called the orthodox view that the Pre-Hellenic Maurya period of Indian history and the Post-Hellenic Gupta period are chapters in the history of one and the same civilization.

If, however, this is the agreed verdict in the case of the Hellenic episode in India, it seems inconsistent to pronounce a contrary verdict in the case of the Hellenic episode in the Syriac World. If the Hellenic incursion is held not to have made a caesura in Indian history, it seems illogical to hold that it made one in Syriac history nevertheless. It is true that in India the Hellenic intrusion lasted for only about half the time-span of its duration in South-West Asia and Egypt. It is also true that India is a more clearly pronounced and clearly demarcated geographical entity than Syria—and, *a fortiori*, than the Syriac World after its states

---

[1] This chapter of Indian history has been discussed in i. 85–86.
[2] See p. 169, footnote 5.

had disappeared from the political map and after its culture had simultaneously begun to spread. But these are differences of degree only, not differences of kind that might be expected to give different turns to the course of history. Accordingly, the consensus in favour of continuity in the Indian case does call in question the validity of a dissenting verdict in the Syriac case.

Moreover, the case for the continuity of history in South-West Asia and Egypt from the Pre-Hellenic to the Post-Hellenic chapter of the story does not rest solely on an analogy from the less obscure course of history in India. There is internal evidence for it as well.

When we look back to the antecedents of the seventh-century eruption of Islam, which completed the expulsion of Hellenism from countries south-east of Taurus, we can see that the Islamic reaction against Hellenism was the last and most successful one in a series that had punctuated the whole period of Hellenic ascendancy in this area. Though the Islamic reaction operated on the military and political as well as on the religious plane, it is manifest that it had precursors in the non-military Monophysite and Nestorian Christian reactions against the 'Melchīte' Christian Church, the Greek language, and the Roman imperial regime. Measured in terms of relative effectiveness, this series of reactions is a *crescendo* movement; and, each time, the dominant Catholic Christian Roman regime found it more difficult to cope with the mounting opposition to it. When the Nestorians challenged its authority, it succeeded in expelling them from its dominions and forcing them to take asylum in the Sasanian Empire. When the Monophysites challenged its authority, it found them too numerous and too solidly united for it to be possible to expel them or even to prevent them from setting up a dissident ecclesiastical organization underground, but it was still able to maintain its own military and political control over the provinces in which the Monophysites were in a majority. When the Muslim Arabs attacked the Roman Empire, the imperial government was worsted. It soon had to give up the struggle to hold its Monophysite provinces.[1]

Moreover, this series of three reactions on an ascending scale of vigour was not an isolated episode. It was only the tail-end of a longer series stretching back in time to within less than a hundred years of the date of the conquest of South-West Asia and Egypt by Alexander the Great. The first of these anti-Hellenic moves in the conquered countries was the occupation of the Seleucid Monarchy's province of Parthia by a Eurasian Nomadic horde, the Parni, not much later than half way through the third century B.C. Before the end of the same century the Ptolemaic Monarchy began to lose control over its Egyptian subjects. In the second decade of the last century B.C., when King Tigranes of Armenia occupied the Seleucid Monarchy's capital, Antioch, and when King Mithradates of Pontic Cappadocia pushed his way as far into Continental European Greece as the Achaemenian Emperor Xerxes had penetrated in 480–479 B.C., it looked for a moment as if the whole of Alexander's achievement was on the point of being undone. At this

---

1 This *crescendo* movement has been noticed in ii. 286–8.

critical moment the Hellenic ascendancy in the Levant was given a new lease of life by the Romans,[1] who played here the part that the Kushans played, about a hundred years later, in India. The power of Rome was much greater than that of the Macedonian successor-states of the Achaemenian Empire into whose shoes Rome stepped; and, after Rome had ousted Tigranes and Mithradates, no opposition in the Levant was a match for her till, 500 years later, in the fifth century of the Christian Era, the struggle here was transferred to the religious plane. Yet Rome did not go unchallenged in the Levant during these five centuries of her overwhelming supremacy there. The Palestinian Jews, who had shaken off the Seleucid Monarchy's control in the second century B.C. and had then lost their independence to Rome in 63 B.C., dared to measure their strength against Rome, though this with disastrous consequences for themselves, in A.D. 66–70 and again in A.D. 132–5. And, from the third century of the Christian Era onwards, Rome's hold on the portion of Alexander's conquests that she had salvaged for Hellenism was challenged repeatedly during the next four hundred years, though this without any ultimate success, by the sluggish Parthian Empire's dynamic Sasanid Persian successors.[2]

Thus the Hellenic ascendancy in South-West Asia and Egypt met with constant opposition throughout all but the first ninety years of its millennium. Opposition implies the existence of an opponent; and, since the opposition to Hellenism extended, at one time or another, over most of the area over which the Syriac Civilization had previously expanded, this opposition is presumptive evidence that the Syriac Society was still in existence throughout this period.

On the strength of these indications that the Syriac Civilization had survived the Hellenic intrusion, long-drawn-out though this had been, I analysed the structure of Syriac history in terms of my Hellenic model, though with an allowance for the difference in the course of Syriac history that the Hellenic intrusion had made. Looking back to the earlier chapters of the story, I found the beginning of a Syriac 'time of troubles' in the intensification of the fratricidal warfare between the local states of the Syriac World after the break-up, at Solomon's death, of the South Syrian Empire that David had built. Even after Assyria had cast her shadow over the Syrian states west of the Euphrates, these continued to fight each other during the ever-shortening intervals between the successive Assyrian attacks; and, by weakening each other in this way, they facilitated the Assyrian and subsequent Babylonian conquest of them all. I found the end of the Syriac Civilization's 'time of troubles' in the establishment of the Achaemenian Empire. This, as I saw it, served the Syriac World as its universal state. And I saw a resumption of this universal state in the Caliphate. The Achaemenian Empire had been overthrown by Alexander before it had had time to complete the social and cultural unification of its people and to enable a higher religion to make headway in converting them. If the Achaemenian

---

[1] See i. 75–76.
[2] The Jewish and Sasanian Persian challenges to Rome have been noticed in ii. 285–6.

Empire had been allowed to reach the term of its natural expectation of life, either Zoroastrianism or Judaism might perhaps have played the part that was played later by Christianity and Islam. But, after the establishment of the Hellenic ascendancy over South-West Asia, Judaism and Zoroastrianism were diverted to serving as militant anti-Hellenic movements. Thus Alexander's conquest had overtaken the Achaemenian Empire before its historical task had been accomplished. And, after the expulsion of Hellenism from Syria and Egypt by the Arabs and the reunion of most of the dominions of the Achaemenian Empire in the Caliphate, this avatar of the Achaemenian Empire had (so it looked to me) taken up and completed the Achaemenian Empire's uncompleted work. The re-established Syriac universal state had provided a political framework for the development and spread of a Syriac universal church in the shape of Islam. The subsequent decline of the Caliphate had been followed by a Völkerwanderung.

3. REASONS FOR RECONSIDERING THESE RESULTS

One obvious weak point in this analysis of the configuration of Syriac history is the implicit assumption that it must have had the same pattern as the configuration of Hellenic history, except for the difference arising from the Hellenic intrusion on the Syriac World. On reconsideration, I do not think that I was at fault in applying the Hellenic model as an instrument for trying to elucidate the structure of Syriac history. I do think, however, that I ought to have drawn a distinction, which I did not draw, between the use of a model for the purpose of exploration and the assumption—which is undemonstrable and therefore arbitrary—that the structure of the history of one civilization will prove to be reproduced in the structure of the history of another civilization. A recognition of this weakness in my construction of Syriac history counsels me now to take very serious account of the criticisms that this construction of mine has evoked.[1] Many of these criticisms have been vigorous, and some of them have been telling. In the light of them, I must reconsider the whole of my construction of Syriac history, point by point.

This renewed inquiry can be handled most conveniently by breaking it up into the following questions: What was the historical background to the distinctive civilization or civilizations that emerged in Syria at some date during the last few centuries of the second millennium B.C.? Was this new cultural configuration a single civilization or was it a cluster of two civilizations or perhaps more? What was the extent of the Syriac Society's expansion on the cultural plane after its loss of independence on the political plane; and, in particular, what was the history of the relations, at this stage, between Syriac and Iranian culture

---

[1] These criticisms have been summarized by O. Anderle in an unpublished paper. One point that has been criticized particularly vigorously is my treatment of the Arab Caliphate as being a reintegration or resumption of the Achaemenian Empire. See, for instance, W. H. McNeill in *The Intent of Toynbee's History: A Cooperative Appraisal*; G. E. von Grunebaum, ibid., the Rev. E. R. Hardy Jr., ibid.

and religion? After the Syriac Society's loss of its political independence, how far down through the ensuing centuries can we trace its continuing history on non-political planes of activity, considering that no representatives of original Syriac communities except the Jews and the Samaritans have survived right down to the present day? What are we to say to Spengler's hypothesis that, at about the beginning of the Christian Era, a new civilization—the 'Magian' Civilization, as he calls it—arose and made headway in South-West Asia and Egypt under an Hellenic camouflage that made it invisible? Is this hypothesis illuminating or is it an hallucination? If it has to be discarded, what were the real results of the Syriac Society's encounter with the Hellenic Society? How are Christianity and Islam related to the Syriac Civilization?[1] How are the present-day Christian and Islamic civilizations related to the Syriac Civilization?

4. THE HISTORICAL BACKGROUND TO THE HISTORY OF SYRIA IN THE LAST MILLENNIUM B.C.

The civilization (whether unitary or multiple) that we find in Syria in the last millennium B.C. was not only contemporary with the Hellenic Civilization; it also displays some striking resemblances to it. In contrast to the irrigational civilizations in the lower Tigris-Euphrates basin, the lower valley and the delta of the Nile, and the Indus basin, the Syriac World resembled the Hellenic World in depending on rain for the watering of its rare fields and in eking out its scanty agricultural resources by long-distance maritime enterprise. (Even the landlocked highland canton of Judah took the Phoenicians into partnership for opening up sea-borne trade with countries on the Indian Ocean as soon as Judah had acquired a south-sea port at Elath at the head of the Gulf of ʿAqabah.) The Syriac World in this age also resembled the Hellenic World in its political configuration. It too presents itself, when the curtain rises on its history, as a mosaic of small sovereign independent states. These Syriac statelets, like their Hellenic counterparts, were perennially at war with each other; and, though they occasionally made common cause against formidable aggressors from outside, they too were eventually extinguished, as the Hellenic statelets were, by empire-builders on the grand scale.

Was the relation between the Syriac and Hellenic civilizations even closer than this? Was it a relation, not only of resemblance, but of affinity? In previous volumes of this book,[2] I suggested that the Syriac Civilization might prove to be the Hellenic Civilization's 'sister', in the sense of being affiliated, as the Hellenic Civilization was, to the antecedent Minoan-Helladic-Mycenaean Civilization in the Aegean area. Indisputably the Minoan-Helladic-Mycenaean Civilization was one of the Syriac Civilization's sources. From at least half-way through the second millennium B.C. onwards, until the Mycenaean Civilization

---

[1] A. L. Kroeber finds my previous account of the relation of Islam to the Syriac Civilization ambiguous (*The Nature of Culture*, p. 376).
[2] In i. 102–3; ii. 386.

foundered, Minoan-Helladic-Mycenaean cultural influences had been playing on the coast of Syria with increasing intensity; and, after that, the Völkerwanderung of the 'Sea Peoples', which had been set in motion soon after the beginning of the twelfth century B.C. by the Mycenaean Civilization's last convulsions, had deposited two peoples from the Aegean or from its hinterlands, the Zakkaru (Teucrians) and the Philistines, along the southernmost stretch of the Syrian coast, from the south side of Mount Carmel to the north-east frontier of Egypt. These historical facts are impressive, and, when I was writing volume i of this book, I was also impressed by Sir Arthur Evans' conjecture that the linear Minoan scripts might turn out to be parents of the Phoenician alphabet.[1] At that time the Minoan, like the Mayan, Civilization stood at the zenith of its prestige, and it was easy to fall into the mistake of attributing to it a greater role in history than is attributed to it today in the light of the additional knowledge gained through the continuing progress of archaeological discovery. On reconsideration, I now think that I over-estimated the importance of the Minoan-Helladic-Mycenaean contribution to the civilization or civilizations that arose in Syria towards the end of the second millennium B.C.[2]

For example, Evans' conjecture about the origin of the Phoenician Alphabet has now been put out of court by Ventris' decipherment of the Minoan 'Linear B' script. This script turns out to be, after all, not alphabetic, but syllabic, and this discovery creates the assumption that 'Linear A', and the antecedent Minoan pictographic scripts, would prove to be syllabic too, if we were to succeed in deciphering these in turn. Meanwhile, scholars seem to be inclining towards the view that the script of the enigmatic Sinai inscriptions, whose date is at least as early as 1500 B.C., is alphabetic, and that it is also an early form of the historic Phoenician alphabet.[3] Moreover, the Phoenicians at Ugarit, towards the north end of the Syrian coast, were writing, during the early years of the fourteenth century B.C.,[4] in an alphabet in which Sumero-Akkadian cuneiform characters were used to represent the letters. These clumsy notations of the letters of the Alphabet were afterwards driven out of currency by the simpler set of Phoenician letters, perhaps derived from the Sinaitic, that is the ancestor of all alphabets current today. It seems evident that the analysis of the sounds of human speech into their primary elements, which is the principle of an alphabetic script, was an original invention of the Canaanites', and that they were experimenting in the use of at least two different sets of characters

[1] See i. 102, footnote 3; ii. 50; ii. 386, footnote 2.
[2] I have been criticized on this ground by R. Coulborn in *Toynbee and History*, p. 160; by M. Samuel: *The Professor and the Fossil*, pp. 56–64; and by A. R. Burn in *History*, February–October, 1956, p. 7.
[3] According to W. F. Albright in *The Archaeology of Palestine* (1949), p. 188, the Sinaitic inscriptions 'prove to date from *circa* 1500 B.C., and to be written in a good Canaanite dialect'; and three short inscriptions, written in a Pre-Sinaitic alphabetic script and dating perhaps from 1800–1500 B.C., have turned up at Gezer, Shechem, and Lachish (ibid., pp. 189–190). In *Archaeology and the Religion of Israel*, 4th ed. (1956), p. 40, Albright maintains his opinion that the Sinaitic script is alphabetic and dates the Sinai inscriptions 1800–1500 B.C.
[4] According to Albright, *The Archaeology of Palestine*, p. 187, all datable texts found at Ugarit date from the first third of the fourteenth century B.C. Cp. eundem, *Archaeology and the Religion of Israel*, 4th ed., p. 38.

for conveying the Alphabet during the second half of the second millennium B.C. There is no evidence to suggest that the Minoan scripts contributed in any way to this Canaanite achievement. Indeed, their syllabic structure is good evidence that they had nothing to do with it.

The Minoan-Helladic-Mycenaean Civilization did play upon Syria during the latter half of the second millennium B.C.[1] But its influence on Syria was slight compared with the Egyptiac Civilization's, and slighter still compared with the Sumero-Akkadian Civilization's. In Palestine, Mesopotamian [i.e. Sumerian] influence is manifest in the Esdraelon culture, which is dated in the last quarter of the fourth millennium B.C.[2] 'The influence of Mesopotamia [i.e. Sumer and Akkad and Assyria] on Canaan was practically continuous during the last 3,000 years B.C.'[3] In Palestine, Middle Bronze Age I (twenty-first to nineteenth centuries B.C.) saw a 'diffusion of the Syro-Mesopotamian culture of the period immediately preceding the Third Dynasty of Ur (circa 2070–1960 B.C.)'.[4] In Palestine in the Late Bronze Age (fourteenth and thirteenth centuries B.C.), among the five scripts then in use there side by side,[5] the Akkadian cuneiform was the script in common use, and the language that was written in cuneiform in Syria, as in Babylonia and Assyria, was also Akkadian,[6] not Canaanite-Amorite.[7] The Sumero-Akkadian Civilization was more potent in Syria than the Egyptiac Civilization was.[8] For instance, Canaanite religion had much closer ties with Sumero-Akkadian religion than it had with Egyptiac.[9] This is remarkable, considering that Egypt was closer to Syria than Akkad was geographically, and also considering that Syria was under Egyptian military and political control more frequently, and for longer periods at a time,[10] than she

---

[1] Late Mycenaean pottery was imported into Palestine circa 1400–1200 B.C. (Albright, *The Archaeology of Palestine*, p. 99).
[2] Albright: *From the Stone Age to Christianity*, 2nd ed., p. 144.
[3] Albright: *Archaeology and the Religion of Israel*, 4th ed., p. 44.
[4] Albright: *The Archaeology of Palestine*, p. 80.
[5] Ibid., p. 101.   [6] Ibid., pp. 102–3.
[7] Except for glosses in Canaanite on some of the Amarna documents (W. O. E. Oesterley and T. H. Robinson: *A History of Israel*, vol. i, p. 39).
[8] Oesterley and Robinson, op. cit., vol. i, pp. 40–1.
[9] Albright: *Archaeology and the Religion of Israel*, 4th ed., p. 44.
[10] An Egyptian Empire was established in Western Palestine, Phoenicia, the Baqā', and the oasis of Damascus by the Pharaohs of the Twelfth Dynasty (circa 1991–1786 B.C.). This empire did not outlive the Twelfth Dynasty itself; but these parts of Syria were dominated by the material culture of the Egyptiac Civilization throughout the Syro-Palestinian Middle Bronze Age IIA (i.e. the nineteenth and eighteenth centuries B.C.) (Albright: *The Archaeology of Palestine*, p. 85); and there was a brief restoration of Egyptian political authority there circa 1750 B.C. (ibid., p. 85). As far afield as Ugarit, on the northern stretch of the Syrian coast, and Qatna, in the middle reach of the Orontes Valley, there are traces of Egyptiac influence as far back as the nineteenth century B.C. (ibid., p. 85).
The Egyptian dominion in Syria in the Age of the New Empire of Egypt extended farther and lasted longer. Both Thothmes I and Thothmes III carried Egyptian arms up to the west bank of the Euphrates at the river's westward elbow. And, though the northern half of this dominion was lost to Egypt for ever in the time of Ikhnaton (regnabat circa 1380–1362 B.C.), his successors succeeded in recovering territory in South Syria that was approximately coextensive with the Twelfth Dynasty's Syrian Empire. Even after the 'Sea Peoples' had migrated, in force, through Syria as far as the north-east corner of the Nile Delta in the early twelfth century B.C., the Egyptians managed to retain, or subsequently reoccupy, some of their South Syrian fortresses. If T. H. Robinson is right in thinking that an Egyptian garrison held Bethshean till the Philistines occupied this fortress circa 1050 B.C. (see Oesterley and Robinson: *A History of Israel*, vol. i, p. 133), the New Empire of Egypt's military and political hold on parts of Syria

was ever under the control of any power to the east of her until, towards the end of the tenth century B.C., Assyria started on a course of westward expansion which, in spite of intermissions and set-backs, eventually brought almost all Syria under her rule. Yet the Egyptiac Civilization's influence on Syria was second only to the Sumero-Akkadian's, and it was probably the older of the two. Intercourse between Egypt and Byblos seems to have begun soon after the establishment of the Egyptian United Kingdom;[1] and the Egyptian culture that made such a conspicuous impression on Byblos itself must have penetrated from this bridgehead into the interior.[2] Anyway, Egyptiac, as well as Sumero-Akkadian, cultural influence in Syria was much greater than Minoan-Helladic-Mycenaean.

Nor did the settlement of the Philistines and Teucrians in the Plain of Sharon in the early twelfth century B.C. make the Minoan-Helladic-Mycenaean contribution to civilization in Syria the preponderant one. The migration of the 'Sea Peoples' was only one incident in the thirteenth-century and twelfth-century Völkerwanderung in the Levant. In falling upon and overthrowing the Khatti Empire on their way, the 'Sea Peoples' themselves had set in motion a southward migration of Hittite refugees. These reinforced, and perhaps extended, the Hittite settlements that had been planted in Northern Syria previously. At any rate, Hamath, as well as Carchemish, was a Hittite state in the Post-Völkerwanderung Age. But both the Hittite and the Philistine settlements in Syria were surpassed in extent by previous Hebrew and Aramaean settlements.[3] The Hebrews occupied Transjordan (Moab,

lasted about 420 years, reckoning back to Thothmes III's first Syrian campaign, or perhaps as much as about 475 years, reckoning back to Thothmes I's. Albright does not retain the Egyptian garrison in Bethshean beyond the twelfth century B.C. (*The Archaeology of Palestine*, p. 40).

[1] The last king of the Second Dynasty of Egypt is known to have sent offerings to Byblos (Albright: *From the Stone Age to Christianity*, 2nd ed., p. 158).

[2] Egyptian artefacts dating from the time of the Old Kingdom have been found at Ai (ibid., pp. 158 and 163).

[3] The question of the date, or dates, of the Israelite settlements in Palestine is now no longer complicated by Garstang's belief that, in his excavations at Jericho in 1930–6, he had identified the walls that fell for Joshua's benefit. These particular walls have proved to date, not from the late, but from the early, Bronze Age, and the latest (i.e. topmost) Bronze Age strata have been carried away by erosion. 'The excavation of Jericho, therefore, has thrown no light on the walls of Jericho of which the destruction is so vividly described in the Book of Joshua' (K. Kenyon: *Digging up Jericho*, p. 262).

H. H. Rowley holds that the accounts of the invasion of Palestine from the adjoining desert in the 'Amarnah archives and in the Book of Joshua refer to two different sets of events (*From Joseph to Joshua*, pp. 38–45). He thinks that in the Pharaoh Ikhnaton's time (*imperabat circa* 1380–1362 B.C.) the Ḥabiru succeeded in occupying the hill countries of Galilee and Judah, but failed to occupy the hill country of Ephraim (ibid., pp. 110–12 and 164). The 'Aseru (i.e. the Israelite tribe Asher) are mentioned as being already settled in Palestine in the time of the Pharaohs Seti I and Ramses II (ibid., pp. 3, 109, and 113). The archaeological evidence suggests that there was an occupation of the hill country of Ephraim in the second half of the thirteenth century B.C., and this may be identified with the conquest traditionally ascribed to Moses' successor Joshua. There is strong evidence for a break in the continuity of history in Palestine in the thirteenth century (ibid., pp. 23 and 109). There is a consensus among the archaeologists that Bethel fell in the thirteenth century B.C. (ibid., p. 19), and that Lachish fell at some date during the second half of that century (ibid., pp. 17–18). The fall of Tell Beit Mirsim, which may be the Biblical Debir, seems to have been more or less contemporaneous with the fall of Lachish (ibid., p. 18). W. F. Albright dates the fall of Lachish *circa* 1220 B.C. or a little later, and the fall of Bethel before the fall of Lachish, in *From the Stone Age to Christianity*, 2nd ed., p. 278. The Pharaoh Merneptah claims to have destroyed Israel, among his other achievements in his military expedition to Palestine and Syria. This

Ammon, Gilead), the Negeb (Edom), and, west of Jordan, the hill country of Ephraim and the hill country of Galilee (Naphthali, Zebulon, Asher). The Aramaeans occupied the Hawran and the Damascus oasis (later known as Aram *par excellence*), the Baqāʿ (Sobah), the Aleppo district (Bit Agushi and Bit Adini), and even the district round the present-day Zenjirli, astride the Northern Amanus (Yaʾudi, *alias* Samʾāl, meaning 'the left-hand', i.e. 'the North').[1] There was another northerly Aramaean state called Musri (meaning 'the border')[2] whose exact location is, so far, unknown. The important Aramaean state called Bit Adini bestrode the elbow of the Euphrates; and other Aramaean peoples occupied the whole of Transeuphratean Syria, up to the north-western borders of Babylonia and the western borders of Assyria. Eastwards they crossed the Tigris, between Assyria and Babylonia, and occupied the steppes north-east of Babylonia up to the foot of the Iranian plateau. North-eastwards they pushed their way into the upper basin of the Tigris (Bit Zamani).

In the course of the last millennium B.C. these Aramaean settlers in Syria, as we have seen,[3] slowly but surely imposed their language on the Hittite and Philistine settlers, and also on the native Canaanites and on the Aramaeans' own Hebrew kinsmen, who had taken to speaking Canaanite after their settlement in the south-east of the Syriac World.[4]

It will be seen that the cultural heritage of the civilization or civilizations in Syria with which the Hellenic Civilization was contemporary was both richer and older than the Hellenic Civilization's was. Hellenism had little behind it beyond the Minoan-Helladic-Mycenaean Civilization, and the loss of the Minoan art of writing shows how great the breach of cultural continuity in the Aegean was at the time of the Post-Minoan Völkerwanderung. Contemporary civilization in Syria was the heir of four older civilizations: the Sumero-Akkadian, the Egyptiac, the Minoan-Helladic-Mycenaean, and the Hittite. Civilization had reached a peak in Palestine in the third millennium B.C.[5] At Jericho civilization was about twice as old as at any other hitherto explored site in the World. Perhaps we ought not to count the pre-pottery Neolithic culture of Jericho as being part of later Syria's cultural heritage, since there seems to have been a complete break, even at Jericho itself, between this culture and its successors. Even so, the antiquity of civilization in Syria is comparable to its antiquity in Sumer and Egypt.

It was not, however, till the later centuries of the second millennium B.C. that civilization in Syria became something distinctively Syriac. After the extinction of the pre-pottery Neolithic culture at Jericho, the Alphabet is the first original invention in Syria on which one can put

---

expedition—which Albright dates *circa* 1219 B.C. (op. cit., p. 255)—was presumably an abortive retaliation for the recently accomplished Israelite occupation of the hill country of Ephraim.

On this evidence, the second Hebrew invasion of Palestine was the main one, and it took place about forty or fifty years before the Philistine and Teucrian occupation of the coast south of Mount Carmel.   [1] See p. 397, footnote 1.

[2] See S. A. Cook in *The Cambridge Ancient History*, vol. iii (1925), p. 425.

[3] See p. 397, footnote 1, and pp. 397-9.   [4] See p. 397, footnote 1, above.

[5] K. Kenyon: *Digging up Jericho*, p. 101.

one's finger; and, in the field of art, Syria never achieved originality[1]—though, even so, the syncretism of Babylonic and Egyptiac art which the Phoenicians introduced into the Hellenic World in the seventh century B.C. had an enormous influence there. Syria's difficulty in achieving cultural originality is perhaps partly accounted for by the very wealth of the cultural gifts that she had been receiving from all quarters since the third millennium B.C.;[2] and, conversely, the eventual rise of a distinctive Syriac civilization or civilizations during the last half of the second millennium B.C. is no doubt partly accounted for by the relaxation, in that age, of the previous pressure on Syria from her two most potent neighbours.[3]

The Sumero-Akkadian World fell into adversity when, in the eighteenth or seventeenth century B.C., the First Dynasty of Babylon decayed after the death of Hammurabi. Babylonia was then occupied by the Kassite barbarians from the Zagros highlands, while Assyria was encircled by the Mitanni barbarians from the Eurasian steppe; and, after a brief recovery in and after the fourteenth century B.C., Assyria was driven to the wall again by the thirteenth-century and twelfth-century Völkerwanderung. The Aramaeans now pressed upon her from the south-west, the Phrygians from the north-west, the Iranians from the east. It was not till towards the end of the tenth century that Assyria was able to start the counter-offensive that made her the mistress of the whole of the Fertile Crescent in the course of the next 200 years. As for Egypt, she was exhausted by her hundred years' war with the Hittites, and the last straw was the supreme effort that she made when the 'Sea Peoples' reached the Delta in 1188 B.C. She just succeeded in repulsing them, but she herself was left prostrate. Later Egyptian incursions into Syria in the tenth century and again in the seventh century B.C. were ineffectual. Thus from 1188 to 932 B.C. there was no great power within range of Syria.[4] This unprecedented relief from external pressure explains why a distinctive Syriac culture was able to flower in this age. The respite was only about two hundred and fifty years long, but Syria took advantage of it to make a permanent mark on mankind's history.

5. WAS THERE ONE ONLY, OR MORE THAN ONE, CIVILIZATION IN SYRIA IN THE LAST MILLENNIUM B.C.?

No one disputes that in Syria, during and on the eve of the last millennium B.C., things were achieved that are evidence of the presence of high civilization there at the time, and are, indeed, among the greatest of mankind's achievements up to date since civilization began. The

[1] F. Hampl, among others, has made this point (see the *Historische Zeitschrift*, Band 173, Heft 3 (1952), p. 452). Albright notes that the Samaria ivories of the ninth and eighth centuries B.C. are entirely Egyptiac in their style (*The Archaeology of Palestine*, p. 137).
[2] The failure of Syria to create a distinctive civilization of her own in the Hyksos Age has been discussed in ii. 388–91.
[3] This point has been made already in ii. 387–8.
[4] See W. O. E. Oesterley and T. H. Robinson: *A History of Israel*, vol. i, pp. 141–2 and 174–5.

Phoenician alphabet invented by the native Canaanite people of Syria before the arrival of the new-comers in the thirteenth and twelfth centuries B.C. is the ancestor of all the systems of writing that are in use in the World today outside the domain of the Chinese characters in Eastern Asia. The contemporary domestication of the Arabian camel gave Man the mastery of the steppes and deserts, not only in the southern hinterland of the Fertile Crescent, but eventually in North Africa as well. The exploration of the western basin of the Mediterranean by the Phoenicians in and after the tenth century B.C.[1] was crowned by the discovery of the Atlantic and thus led eventually to the discovery of the Americas by Transatlantic voyagers from the Old World. The revolutionary change in the conception of the nature of Yahweh, the god of Israel and Judah, which was started in these two countries in the eighth century B.C. by prophets of a new kind, was a first step towards Post-Exilic Jewish monotheism and hence towards Christian and Islamic monotheism as well.

Are these achievements in Syria in this age to be attributed to a single civilization or to more than one? They are heterogeneous, in the sense that they are achievements in different fields of activity. But this is also true of the great achievements of the contemporary Hellenic Civilization; and no one would think of denying the unity of the Hellenic Civilization on this account. Nor indeed is this the reason why the unity of the Syriac Civilization has been contested. The reason is an unwillingness to admit that Judaism and its antecedents, as far back as these can be traced in the histories of Judah and Israel, is a part of some larger whole and is therefore not something quite distinct, separate, and unique. It is the Canaanite-speaking peoples of Judah and Israel, not the non-Semitic-speaking Philistines and Hittites, whom scholars of this school refuse to associate with the Canaanite Phoenicians. This position is put clearly by A. R. Burn:

'It is open to argument whether *a* distinctive "Syriac" Civilization, as opposed to several different civilizations of much interest and originality, ever existed. There is as much difference between the cultures of the Phoenicians and Hebrews, in spite of their kinship in blood and language, as between either of them and that of the Hittites. . . . The history of the Hebrews *alone* comes nearer to being "an intelligible field of study" than that of Syria at large; and, if we seek a larger field, there is no stopping-place short of the limits of the history of civilization in South-Western Asia from the Neolithic Age onwards.'[2]

Burn is not alone in taking this view.[3] Yet the thesis is suspect because

---

[1] Albright notes that the Phoenicians acquired their overseas realm suddenly, after the Philistines had been crushed by David's victories over them in 990–980 B.C. (*The Archaeology of Palestine*, p. 122). The Phoenician ivories found in Spain at Carmona, and the oldest painted pottery from the Tanit cemetery at Carthage, are of the archaeological period 'Megiddo V', *circa* 1050–975 B.C. A ninth-century Phoenician inscription has been found at Nora in Sardinia, and a ninth-century Phoenician tomb in Cyprus (ibid., pp. 122–3). Cp. *Archaeology and the Religion of Israel*, 4th ed., pp. 131–2.

[2] *History*, February–October, 1956, p. 6.

[3] M. Samuel, for instance, maintains that the Israelites were not participants in a Syriac Civilization (*The Professor and the Fossil*, pp. 68–70); Rabbi J. B. Agus that it makes 'little sense to speak of Jewry as part of the Syriac Civilization' (*Judaism*, vol. 4,

it has not been arrived at exclusively by a disinterested and detached appraisal of the historical evidence. It is at least partly a corollary of the Jewish and Christian religious conviction that the Israelites' god Yahweh is the One True God and that the Israelites and their heirs the Jews are—or were—His 'Chosen People'.[1] Scholars with a Jewish or Christian background who do not hold this conviction may still remain under the influence of the interpretation of history to which their ancestral religious outlook has given rise. They may find it difficult to break away from the habit of reading back into the age of Moses, or even of Abraham, conceptions of the nature of the Israelites' god and of the status of the Israelites themselves which did not begin to take shape before the eighth century B.C., and did not reach their final shape till they had passed through many stages of gradual evolution, according to the picture presented by a critical sifting of the historical evidence.

In truth, of course, a thing need not always have been what it has eventually become. Indeed, it is impossible that anything within human experience should have had an unchanging identity since an infinitely long time ago, if it is true that this planet and everything on it and all the rest of the cosmos within an astronomer's ken is a metamorphosis of some primaeval nebula. The concept of unchangingness is chimerical; but it is attractive to human minds for two reasons. One reason is that change—i.e. the emergence of something new—cannot be expressed in logical terms and is therefore intellectually incomprehensible,[2] however forcibly its reality may be attested by experience. The other reason for the widespread unwillingness to acknowledge the reality of change is the notion that one is being disrespectful to what is worthy of respect if one admits that it can have emerged, in the course of time, out of something inferior to itself. This notion is surely the exact opposite of the truth; for in truth nothing is so remarkable or sublime as the fact of rising, or raising oneself, from a lower level to a higher one; and therefore the recognition that some thing or person has achieved this feat, so far from being insulting, is the greatest honour that one can pay to him or it.

If this is the truth, it is neither blasphemous towards the Jewish-Christian-Muslim One True God (if one believes in His reality) nor derogatory to the prophets of Israel and Judah and their Jewish, Christian, and Muslim successors to hold that the present Judaic conception of God—whether revealed by God or discovered by Man progressively—is so much higher than the picture of Yahweh presented in the earliest strata of the Israelitish scriptures that we should hardly guess that there was any connexion between the two pictures if we were

No. 4 (Fall, 1955), p. 320), and that, indeed, there was no such thing as a Syriac Civilization, though the progress of archaeology is bringing to light the Canaanite background of the origins of Israelite culture (*The National Jewish Monthly*, November, 1956, pp. 41–42); K. D. Erdmann that Jewish history cannot be expressed in terms of Syriac (*Archiv für Kulturgeschichte*, xxxiii. Band, Heft 2 (1951), p. 244); J. L. Talmon that a wider Syriac context is hardly relevant to Jewish history (*Commentary*, July, 1957, p. 7); F. Hampl that I ought to have discriminated between the monotheistic Israelites and their polytheistic neighbours (the *Historische Zeitschrift*, Band 173, Heft 3 (1952), p. 452).

[1] The official Christian belief is that the Jews forfeited this privilege through their refusal to recognize Jesus as being the Messiah and the Son of God, and that the role then passed to the Christian Church.   [2] See pp. 252–4.

not informed, by a continuous chain of historical evidence, that the later picture has, in fact, grown out of the earlier one.[1] As for the distinctiveness of Judaism, this has been manifest since the conversion of the western end of the Old World to Christianity and Islam; for, since then, Judaism has been the only other religion of any account that has survived to the west of India; but a recognition of the fact that Judaism had become a distinctive religion by this date does not commit one to having to believe, in consequence, that the religion of Israel must have been distinctive in the ninth or in the thirteenth century B.C. Similarly, we may recognize that the Jewish people has distinguished itself by having contrived to survive in diasporá for 2,500 years, up to date, after having lost its state and country in Palestine in the sixth century B.C.; but this, again, does not commit us to having to believe that Judah was already peculiar when she was in existence as a statelet rubbing shoulders with Edom, Moab, Ammon, Israel, and the five Philistine city-states. Nor does it commit us to having to believe that the Jewish diasporá is as peculiar today as it may have been at an earlier stage of its already long history. The Jewish diasporá may have been the earliest community to discover how to maintain itself in existence after having been uprooted; but in the meantime this pioneer achievement has proved to be 'the wave of the future'.[2]

In this historical perspective the peculiarity of the Post-Exilic Jewish diasporá, like the distinctiveness of Post-Exilic Judaism, looks as if it were no more than a passing phase. Distinctiveness was not an original characteristic of either the people or its religion; for their present distinctiveness can be seen to have originated in particular social and religious innovations that are of relatively recent date; and it is not a permanently acquired characteristic; for the monotheism that is the essence of Judaism has already become the religion of half the World in its Christian and Islamic versions, while the social structure that is characteristic of the Jewish diasporá seems to be now on the way to becoming the standard pattern for all mankind.

The Jews themselves have never maintained that the division between gentiles and Jews, and the corresponding gulf between the worship of false gods and the worship of the One True God, goes back to the beginning of time. They do not trace this dichotomy of mankind and its religion back to Adam, or even to Noah, but only to Abraham; and they do not date earlier than the time of Moses the covenant between Yahweh and Israel in which Yahweh is believed to have chosen Israel to be his people, and Israel to have adopted Yahweh to be its god.[3] Yahweh is tacitly identified with the god of the Israelites' forefathers, Abraham, Isaac, and Jacob.[4] Yet, according to the account given by

---

[1] See pp. 488–96. [2] See pp. 209–17 and 484.

[3] For all that we know, the god of the Covenant may originally have been, not Yahweh, but a pre-Hebrew 'Baal Berith' at Shechem (see p. 420, footnote 3, and pp. 489–90), where, according to the Book of Joshua, chap. xxiv, the Israelites pledged themselves to their god after the completion of their conquest of Canaan (see H. H. Rowley: *From Joseph to Joshua*, pp. 125–9, for a full discussion of this).

[4] Can the Hebrew Patriarchs' god be identified? T. H. Robinson points out that both Ur and Harran were seats of the worship of the Sumero-Akkadian moon-god whom the Akkadians called Sin, and he conjectures that this god's name may be contained in the

two of the three oldest main sources of the Pentateuch,[1] even in the assiduously revised form in which we now have it, the Israelites did not know Yahweh's name before he revealed himself to Moses and commissioned Moses to be his messenger to them.[2]

Down to this point the traditional Jewish account of the relations between Yahweh and Israel and between the Israelites and the rest of mankind represents these as having developed progressively. The anonymous god who has called Abraham reveals his name to Abraham's descendants at Sinai. The children of Israel, who at Sinai become Yahweh's 'Chosen People', are kinsmen, through Isaac, of the children of Esau; through Abraham, of the children of Ishmael; and, through Terah, of the children of Lot. Through Noah's son Shem ('the name') they are kinsmen of all the other Hebrew and Aramaean peoples who erupted out of Arabia into the Fertile Crescent in the Völkerwanderung of the thirteenth and twelfth centuries B.C. On the other hand, it is the official Jewish view that the whole of the Pentateuch, and this in the form in which we now have it, was revealed by Yahweh at Sinai to Moses, together with an accompanying revelation that was not committed to writing but was transmitted orally.[3] It is also the official view that this Mosaic revelation was, and is, definitive.[4] The rest of the Torah (Yahweh's teaching, known by Christians as 'the Old Testament') is officially held to be, not only consistent with the Pentateuch, but also demonstrably implicit in it, when the two bodies of scripture are interpreted in the light of the traditional unwritten revelation. The

name of Mount Sinai (W. O. E. Oesterley and T. H. Robinson: *A History of Israel*, vol. i, p. 90). This conjecture is rejected by W. F. Albright (*From the Stone Age to Christianity*, 2nd ed., p. 263).

[1] E and P as opposed to J (Oesterley and Robinson, op. cit., vol. i, p. 83).

[2] Robinson suggests (ibid., p. 82) that the god who spoke to Moses from the burning bush was the god of the priest in Midian whose daughter Moses had married. He suggests that Yahweh was a Midianite or Kenite god (ibid., p. 88). Yahweh was a fire-god, and the Kenites were smiths (ibid., p. 92). This is also H. H. Rowley's view (see *From Joseph to Joshua*, pp. 149–56). Rowley points out (ibid., p. 152) that Jethro and Moses' brother-in-law Hobab are both called Midianites as well as Kenites.

Albright finds Egyptian elements in Yahweh-worship. He suggests that the word 'Yahweh' itself may originally have been the first word in a formula meaning 'He causes to be what comes into existence'; and he points out that this formula occurs in Egyptian religious texts of the second millennium B.C., e.g. a hymn to Amun (*From the Stone Age to Christianity*, 2nd ed., p. 261). He also points out (ibid., p. 270) that 'sbâyet', the Egyptian name for Ikhnaton's monotheistic doctrine, has the same meaning, i.e. 'teaching', as the Hebrew word 'torah'.

Believing, as he does, that Moses was a monotheist in the full sense of the word (see, for instance, his *Archaeology and the Religion of Israel*, 4th ed., p. 96), Albright conjectures that he may have derived from Egyptiac sources the concepts that Yahweh was the sole creator, the sole god in the Universe, and the master of the whole of it (ibid., p. 270). It is credible that Ikhnaton's monotheism might have influenced the Kenite and Midianite barbarians on or just beyond the south-eastern fringe of the Egyptian New Empire's dominions in Syria. It is also credible that a new religion which, in Egypt, had been invented and imposed by a sovereign, and which did not, there, outlast its author's lifetime, should have survived, outside Egypt, among non-Egyptian voluntary converts. The Druz religion, invented by the Fatimid Caliph of Egypt, Hākim bi 'amr'illāh (*imperabat* A.D. 996–1020), survives today in Syria and the Lebanon, more than nine hundred years after its death in Egypt, where it died with Hākim himself. If the Yahweh-worship that Moses found in vogue among the Kenites and Midianites was an echo of Atonism, and if Moses himself was born and brought up in Egypt, he might have been predisposed in this originally Egyptian religion's favour by some echo of it that might have come to his ears in Egypt when he was a child.

All this, however, is sheer conjecture.

[3] See pp. 506 and 508.   [4] See p. 506.

rules of conduct implicitly prescribed in the Torah have been elicited in the *halachoth* (formulations that have been approved by a consensus of the recognized rabbinical authorities);[1] the *halachoth* have been codified in the Mishnah; and the Mishnah has been expounded in the Gemara.[2] The Talmud (i.e. the Mishnah plus the Gemara) and the Torah constitute a monolithic unity. The core of the monolith and the principle of its unity is to be found in the Pentateuch.

Thus the official Jewish view is that the Jewish religion and the Jewish people have been what they now are ever since the time of Moses. But this thesis is incompatible with known historical facts, many of them attested by the internal evidence of the Jewish scriptures themselves. Moses may be an historical character;[3] but, even if he is not legendary, his alleged literary work is. A critical analysis of the Pentateuch shows that it is a composite work; that each of the books in which it is now arranged has been spliced together out of pieces of older written documents; and that these sources are not older than the ninth century B.C., or the tenth century at the earliest.[4]

Moses is not mentioned in connexion with the Torah by the eighth-century prophets of Israel and Judah. They used the word 'torah' as a name for their own utterances.[5] The first authority to ascribe the authorship of the Torah to Moses was Ezra,[6] who went on his mission from Babylonia to Judaea in either 458 or 397 B.C.[7] The canon of the Torah was probably not fixed and closed till after the Romano-Jewish war of A.D. 66–70.[8] The composition of the whole corpus of authoritative Jewish religious literature, from the earliest strata of the Torah to the final form of the Babylonian Talmud, was a long-drawn-out process. Its time-span may be not less than fourteen hundred years (*circa* 925 B.C.–A.D. 475).

It would be surprising if, in the course of this long period, there had been no changes in the religious conceptions, outlook, and beliefs of the Israelites and their Jewish heirs. In truth, there were great and continuous changes from the days of the eighth-century prophets onwards; the changes introduced by the Pre-Exilic prophets themselves were both revolutionary and creative; the subsequent changes associated with

---

[1] See pp. 508–9.   [2] See pp. 480, 488, and 508.
[3] One piece of presumptive evidence for the historicity of Moses is his name. This looks like the second half of an Egyptian compound theophoric name of the type Ahmose, Tutmose, Ramose, Graecised as Ramesses or Ramses (see W. O. E. Oesterley and T. H. Robinson: *A History of Israel*, vol. i, p. 81). The Israelites would hardly have given an Egyptian name to their national hero if he was not an authentic historical figure by whom this name had actually been borne. On the other hand, if their historical leader did bear an Egyptian compound theophoric name, they might well have docked the name, retrospectively, of its first element, since this would have been the name of some Egyptian god. Robinson (in loc. cit., p. 81, footnote 4) conjectures that the story of the preservation of the infant Moses' life may have been transferred to the Israelite national hero from the Egyptian national hero Ahmose. In the original Egyptian version of the story the wicked Pharaoh would have been a Hyksos king, not one of the Hyksos' native Egyptian xenophobe successors.

Albright points out that, in the House of Aaron, Egyptian personal names were in use for at least two hundred years after Moses' probable date: e.g. the names of Eli's two sons, Hophni and Pinehas. Pinehas means Pi-nehase: 'the Nubian' (*From the Stone Age to Christianity*, 2nd ed., pp. 254 and 282.)   [4] See p. 506.
[5] G. F. Moore: *Judaism in the First Centuries of the Christian Era*, vol. i, p. 263.
[6] R. Travers Herford: *The Pharisees*, p. 55.   [7] See p. 484, footnote 2.
[8] See p. 480.

the names of Ezekiel, Ezra, and the Pharisees, if not equally creative, were equally revolutionary (e.g. the Pharisees' postulate that, besides the written revelation to Moses, there must have been an oral one represented by traditions still alive in their day). These changes were the product of spiritual travail that was a response to shattering experiences: the eighth-century social revolution and Assyrian conquest; the sixth-century deportation to Babylonia; the second-century collision with Hellenism; and the two disastrous wars with the Romans in A.D. 66–70 and A.D. 132–5. Judaism and the Jewish people, as we know them now, are products of these experiences in and after the eighth century B.C. The official Jewish thesis that they have been what they now are since a Mosaic Age, before the Israelites' settlement in Palestine in the thirteenth century B.C., is not only irreconcilable with the historical evidence; it makes the course of Israelite and Jewish history since that date unintelligible. Accordingly, we must put this official Jewish thesis out of our minds in considering the question whether the civilization that emerged in Syria after the dust of this Völkerwanderung had settled was multiple or unitary.

There are at least three cogent pieces of evidence which indicate that, whatever may have happened in Syria to the Aramaeans, Philistines, and Hittites after their settlement in Syria at this time, the Israelites, at any rate, mixed with the older inhabitants of the country that they occupied. In the first place the Israelites went over from a nomadic or semi-nomadic way of life to agriculture; and, since agriculture was (and, even now, to some extent still is) a religious activity as well as an economic one, they adopted the indigenous agricultural religious rites and festivals. Since the earliest times after the Israelites' settlement to which their own historical records go back, we find this Canaanite religious practice associated with the worship of the god Yahweh[1] which, according to their tradition, they brought in with them. In the second place the Israelites took to speaking the indigenous Canaanite language,[2] and this so rapidly that, perhaps before the end of the tenth century B.C., they were already writing magnificent literary works in the borrowed language that, in virtue of these monuments of it, we call 'Hebrew'. This swift and thorough change of language indicates that the settlers and the early generations of their descendants must have made a frequent practice of marrying Canaanite women. In the third place the Israelites acquired the physiognomy that is now associated with Jews in Western minds, though it is at least as characteristic of present-day Armenians and Anatolian Turks, and also of the Assyrians in the first half of the last millennium B.C. as these have portrayed themselves on bas reliefs and in statues. Neither the Assyrians nor the Jews' forefathers, the people of Judah, can have brought this physiognomy with them from their original home in Arabia; for the characteristic physiognomy of the present-day Semitic-speaking inhabitants of Arabia is not 'Jewish' but Mediterranean. The people of Judah must have acquired the 'Jewish' physiognomy in Palestine, after their settlement there; and this acquisition

[1] See Oesterley and Robinson: *A History of Israel*, vol. i, pp. 167-8.
[2] See p. 397, footnote 1.

of an exotic physiognomy is another indication of inter-marriage with older elements in the population that had come in, not from Arabia, but from what is now Eastern Turkey.[1] We know of two waves of immigration that had entered Syria from the north before the Israelites' arrival there: a Hurrian wave in the eighteenth or seventeenth century B.C.[2] and a Hittite wave in the fourteenth century. The Hurrian wave was evidently a big one,[3] and the subsequent Hittite wave was reinforced, soon after the Israelites' arrival, by Hittite refugees driven out of Anatolia by the 'Sea Peoples' who had overthrown the Khatti Empire and by the Phrygians who had flooded into Anatolia in the Sea Peoples' wake. A memory of the Israelite settlers' racial fusion, in Palestine, with Amorites[4] and Hittites is preserved in Ezekiel's taunt: 'the Amorite was thy father, and thy mother was a Hittite'.[5]

Let us now try to look, without Jewish-Christian prepossessions, at the course of history in Syria from the time of the Völkerwanderung of the Aramaeans and Hebrews and Philistines[6] down to the later decades of the eighth century B.C., when the majority of the Syrian states west of Euphrates were extinguished, as those east of the river had been in the ninth century, by the Assyrians. We shall find that the plot of the historical drama during this period is the same in Syria as in the contemporary Hellenic World. In a world in which society has been broken up, and civilization set back, by the impact of the Völkerwanderung, a new social unity and a new civilization emerge. The main source of both is the remnant of a previous society that has survived the devastating experience of being invaded and overrun and has salvaged enough of its cultural heritage to provide the nucleus for the creation of a new culture which is the common achievement and possession of all elements, old and new, in the population.

Albright points out that there was a major break in the continuity of Canaanite history in the thirteenth and twelfth centuries B.C. Within a span of only fifty years (? *circa* 1230–1180 B.C.), the Canaanites lost over nine-tenths of their former territory to the Aramaeans, Hebrews,

---

[1] See W. O. E. Oesterley and T. H. Robinson: *A History of Israel*, vol. i, pp. 41 and 46.

[2] For the Hurrians, see, among others, W. F. Albright: *The Archaeology of Palestine*, pp. 183–4. The Hurrians are the Biblical 'Horites'. This name has been preserved correctly in the Septuagint Greek text, but has been corrupted to 'Hivites' in the canonical Hebrew text, owing to the similarity of the letters R and W in the 'square' form of the Aramaic alphabet which the Jews eventually adopted for the writing of Hebrew (i.e. Canaanite).

[3] In records dating from the period *circa* 2000–1750 B.C. all personal names in Syria south of Carchemish are exclusively Canaanite or Amorite. When, after a break corresponding to the Hyksos Age, the records begin again in the time of the New Empire of Egypt, there are Indo-European and Hurrian personal names, too, in this region. 'There must have been a great barbarian irruption from the north-east into the Fertile Crescent in the course of the eighteenth century B.C.' (W. F. Albright: *From the Stone Age to Christianity*, 2nd ed., p. 205). At Megiddo brachycephalic people replaced dolicocephalic people at the same date (ibid., p. 206).

[4] The Amorites were the last arrivals in the Fertile Crescent from Arabia before the Aramaeans, Hebrews, and Chaldaeans. They appear to have come in before the end of the third millennium B.C. (Albright: *From the Stone Age to Christianity*, 2nd ed., pp. 151–2 and 164), whereas the Canaanites had been in Syria since the early centuries of the third millennium B.C. at least (ibid., p. 163). But the Amorites spoke, or learnt from the Canaanites to speak, a language that was virtually identical with Canaanite; and, by the time of the Hebrew-Aramaean invasion of Syria, Canaanites and Amorites must have become indistinguishable.   [5] Ez. xvi. 3, repeated in 45.   [6] See pp. 409–10.

and Philistines.[1] There was a sharp decline in material culture;[2] and the Canaanite language did not come out unscathed. The case-endings, which are intact in the Ugaritic literature of the fourteenth century B.C., were being lost in the thirteenth and twelfth centuries, on the evidence of Phoenician inscriptions of that age. The language is without case-endings in the earliest monuments of Israelitish literature.[3] The effects of the inroads of new-comers into Syria were thus disruptive. But they were not more disruptive than the effects of the contemporary upheaval in the Aegean World. Here, too, the previous population—in this case, the Greek-speaking participants in the Mycenaean Civilization—was dispossessed and uprooted on the grand scale. Luvian-speaking Carians —jetsam from the same shattered Hittite World as the Hittite refugees in Syria—broke their way into the Aegean basin from the north-east. A far larger wave of North-West-Greek-speaking barbarians washed across Continental European Greece and on overseas as far as Crete and Rhodes. On the European mainland, the descendants of the earlier Greek-speaking stratum preserved their independence in only a few pockets of territory: Arcadian-speakers in the central highlands of the Peloponnese and in Triphylia; Aeolic-speakers in Boeotia and Thessaly; Ionic-speakers in Attica. It was no consolation for them that the barbarian invaders from the north-west spoke a dialect of their own Greek tongue, any more than it was a consolation for their Canaanite companions in misfortune that the Hebrew and the Aramaean barbarian invaders of Syria spoke a language that, like Canaanite, was Semitic. Yet, in Syria and in the Aegean alike, society recovered from the shock and a new civilization eventually blossomed.

Albright holds[4] that the unsubmerged minority of the Canaanites was already rallying in the twelfth century B.C. Still more important, possibly, was the influence of a Canaanite majority that had been subjugated but had not been exterminated. The genocide committed by the new-comers may not have been extensive.[5] The Israelites, for instance,

[1] W. F. Albright: *Archaeology and the Religion of Israel*, 4th ed., pp. 68–69. Presumably Albright is here counting as Canaanites the Amorites who at this date were established in those north-eastern districts of Syria that were now occupied by the Aramaeans.   [2] Albright: *The Archaeology of Palestine*, p. 119.
[3] W. F. Albright: *Archaeology and the Religion of Israel*, 4th ed., p. 181.
[4] Op. cit., 4th ed., p. 69.
[5] Albright brings forward archaeological evidence to this effect—some of it discovered by himself—which is cited in the next paragraph of the present chapter. Yet his inflexible will to believe that the Israelites were pure monotheists from the time of Moses onwards has moved him to fly in the face of his own evidence and to paint the thirteenth-century B.C. Israelite invaders of Palestine blacker than they deserve on his own showing. In *From the Stone Age to Christianity*, 2nd ed., p. 281, he has written: 'It was fortunate for the future of monotheism that the Israelites of the Conquest were a wild folk, endowed with primitive energy and ruthless will to exist, since the resulting decimation of the Canaanites prevented the complete fusion of the two kindred folk which would almost inevitably have depressed Yahwistic standards to a point where recovery was impossible. Thus the Canaanites, with their orgiastic nature-worship, their cult of fertility in the form of serpent symbols and sensuous nudity, and their gross mythology, were replaced by Israel, with its pastoral simplicity and purity of life, its lofty monotheism, and its severe code of ethics.' This passage invites several obvious comments. First: monotheism may be worth a mass, but it is certainly not worth a massacre. 'By their fruits ye shall know them' is as true of ideologies as it is of human beings. Second: the primitive Israelite code of ethics was not severe enough to restrain the Israelites from seizing by force a country that did not belong to them and decimating its inhabitants in order to make room for themselves. Third: the religion that led from the Stone

settled west of Jordan, largely in territory—the hill country of Ephraim
—that had previously been only thinly occupied. The recent invention
of waterproof plaster lining for cisterns enabled them to settle wherever
there was rainfall, whereas, before this invention, settlements had
necessarily been confined to the neighbourhood of springs and rivers.[1]

Thus the now dominant Hebrews came to live side by side with the
conquered Canaanites. The two peoples were intermingled geographically at close quarters; and this favoured both racial and cultural fusion.
'Progress was made through a gradual assimilation, not through military conquest.'[2] Canaanite cities came to be incorporated in Israelite
tribes. Shechem,[3] Hepher, Tirzah, Zaphron, and the four towns of the
Gibeonite confederacy are examples.[4] At the time of the war, com-
memorated in the Song of Deborah, between a muster of Israelite tribes
and a league of Canaanite city-states in the plain of Jezreel, this stretch
of fertile agricultural land had not yet lost its independence; and the
contemporary Israelite poem, which celebrates Israel's victory and the
Canaanite leader Sisera's death, does not claim that, as a result of this
victory, the plain fell into the Israelites' hands. The Philistines held it for
a time in the eleventh century B.C. Yet, by the date of Israel's secession
from Judah in 936 B.C., this former enclave of Canaanite territory was,
apparently, already incorporated in Israel, and one of the capitals of the
new kingdom, Jezreel, was situated there.

The latest and most momentous instance of the incorporation of a
Canaanite city in a Hebrew state was the annexation of the Jebusite
city-state of Jerusalem to the Kingdom of Judah by David at some date
early in the tenth century B.C. David not only made this Canaanite city
the political capital of a Hebrew state whose frontiers he eventually
carried southward to the head of the Gulf of 'Aqabah and northward to
the Baqā' and the oasis of Damascus. He also made it the central shrine
for the worship of Yahweh in his dominions. He gave this privileged
status to Jerusalem deliberately,[5] just because it was a piece of Canaanite
neutral ground between Judah and Israel.[6] 'On the distaff side the
House of David was . . . shot through with pagan elements.'[7] In

Age to Christianity was not the pastoral religion of Israel; it was the agricultural religion
of Canaan. It was a Canaanite vegetation-god who sacrificed himself for his people in
order that they might draw life from eating his flesh and drinking his blood. The
Ugaritic Baal and the Byblian Adonis, not the Israelite Yahweh, were the historic
models for the Galilaean Jesus Christ. This side of the Canaanite agricultural religion
has to be taken into consideration as well as the figurines of the naked fertility goddess,
which are found in sites that are indubitably Israelite (Albright: *From the Stone Age to
Christianity*, 2nd ed., p. 311).

The passage here criticised reveals the strength of ancestral religious prejudice. The
writer of it is not only a particularly eminent scholar; he is also a singularly open-
minded man on all points but this.

[1] *The Archaeology of Palestine*, p. 113; *From the Stone Age to Christianity*, 2nd ed.,
p. 279.   [2] Oesterley and Robinson: *A History of Israel*, vol. i, p. 138.

[3] The Shechemite Canaanites called themselves Beni Hamar ('Sons of the Ass': see
Albright: *From the Stone Age to Christianity*, 2nd ed., p. 279; *Archaeology and the Religion
of Israel*, 4th ed., p. 113) and their god was Baal Berith ('the Lord of the Covenant':
see the present chapter, p. 414, footnote 3, and pp. 489–90).

[4] *Archaeology and the Religion of Israel*, 4th ed., p. 102; *From the Stone Age to
Christianity*, 2nd ed., p. 279.

[5] Albright: *Archaeology and the Religion of Israel*, 4th ed., p. 138.

[6] Oesterley and Robinson, op. cit., vol. i, p. 217.

[7] Albright, op. cit., 4th ed., p. 158.

936 B.C. the House of David lost all its northern dominions to within a few miles' distance of Jerusalem itself. But Jerusalem remained the religious as well as the political capital of Judah for 350 years after that; and, though it was not till 621 B.C. that Jerusalem was given the privilege of being the only place in Judah where the public worship of Yahweh could thenceforth be performed legitimately, the native Jebusites and their ancestral religion must have been having a profound influence on the worship of Yahweh, not only at Jerusalem, but throughout Judah, ever since David's day. The sacrificial ritual described and prescribed in the Priestly Code has Canaanite counterparts in archaeological evidence dating from the thirteenth century B.C. in Syria and from the fourth century B.C. at Carthage.[1] The process of intermingling and fusion followed the same course farther north. The north-western Aramaean state Ya'udi (Sam'āl) was an enclave established in the heart of the Syrian Hittites' domain. The Aramaeans also supplanted the Hittites at Hamath shortly before 1000 B.C. But, in both Ya'udi and at Hamath, the Hittite culture survived the Aramaean occupation.[2]

Ya'udi and Judah look like variants of the same tribal name.[3] If they are, this tribe will have been split into two splinters in the course of the Aramaean-Hebrew Völkerwanderung, and these fragments will then have been pushed into opposite corners of the territory occupied by the incomers west of Euphrates. Presumably the Judah-splinter entered Cis-Jordanian Syria from the south, while the Ya'udi-splinter entered it from the west, on the northernmost wing of a group of tribes whose southernmost wing was Benjamin,[4] from whom Judah was insulated by the Canaanite stronghold Jerusalem until its capture by David in the tenth century B.C. If this explanation of the resemblance between the two names Ya'udi and Judah is correct, it tells against Robinson's conjecture[5] that Judah was a Canaanite people that was eventually admitted to membership of the Israelite amphictyony after having been converted to the worship of Yahweh by Kenite and Kenizzite Yahweh-worshippers who had seeped into Judah from the south. H. H. Rowley's view[6] that Judah was an originally Hebrew people that had fused with a previous Canaanite population seems more credible in the light of the existence, at the opposite end of Cis-Euphratean Syria, of an Aramaic-speaking Ya'udi that is proved by archaeological evidence to have fused with the local Hittite population there.

Rowley and Robinson both hold that the fusion between native Canaanite elements and immigrant elements in Judah, and the subsequent association of Judah with Israel, were promoted by the pressure of the Philistines in the eleventh century. And threats from common enemies seem to have been a major factor in producing fusion in other cases too. 'The Book of Judges makes it clear that it was not by defeating

[1] Albright: *From the Stone Age to Christianity*, 2nd ed., p. 294.
[2] A. Dupont-Sommer: *Les Araméens*, pp. 24–25.
[3] See p. 397, footnote 1.   [4] Ibid.
[5] In Oesterley and Robinson: *A History of Israel*, vol. i, pp. 49, footnote 1, 60, footnote 1, 100, 112, 119, 120, 134–5, 169–70.
[6] See *From Joseph to Joshua*, p. 5, footnote 3. Rowley agrees (ibid., pp. 153–4) with Robinson in thinking that Judah and the rest of the southern group of Hebrew tribes had been converted to Yahweh-worship gradually by the Kenites.

the Canaanites, but by defending them, that Israel obtained a dominant position in Palestine.[1] The common enemy in this chapter of history was the Nomad peoples who were now trying to force their way into Palestine at the Israelites' heels. In the period following the end of the Hebrew-Aramaean Völkerwanderung the Israelites were in danger of suffering the fate of being invaded and overrun that they had inflicted on the Canaanites[2]—the more so because the domestication of the camel had given the Israelites' successors on the North Arabian steppe a new weapon that the Israelites themselves had never possessed. The Israelites, before becoming peasants, had been mere ass-nomads without prestige.[3] The first recorded eruption of camel-nomads out of the desert into the sown is a Midianite raid on Palestine in the early eleventh century B.C.[4] In the next chapter of history in Syria the pressure from the Philistines, that fused Judah into a unity and pushed her into association with Israel, led her war-lord David[5] to make an alliance with Tyre.[6] In the ninth century the pressure from the Assyrians moved Tyre and the Kingdom of Israel to make a similar alliance and to cement it by a royal marriage (Ahab and Jezebel).[7] The extensive, though ephemeral, coalitions of Syrian states against Assyria have been noticed already.[8]

In these conducive circumstances the intercourse between the different local peoples in Syria became both more intensive and more intimate in all the main fields of social and cultural activity. The local princes and their professional officials and officers might go to war with each other besides fighting side by side against common enemies; but all the time they were evidently on familiar terms with each other, and this familiarity was not confined to the diplomatic level. Before David made his political treaty with Tyre, the north-western Israelite tribes in the highlands of Galilee may already have been finding an economic outlet in Phoenicia. The Song of Deborah chides Dan for staying on board ship and Asher for sitting on the sea-shore instead of responding to the call to arms against Sisera.[9] Solomon and Hiram went into partnership in maritime ventures in the Indian Ocean.[10] In ninth-century treaties between the states of Damascus and Israel it was stipulated by the state which momentarily had the upper hand that the weaker contracting party should assign a quarter in its capital city to the stronger party's merchants.[11] Solomon's temple at Jerusalem and the works of art with which it was adorned were made for him by Phoeni-

---

[1] Oesterley and Robinson: *A History of Israel*, vol. i, p. 140.

[2] There is archaeological evidence that Bethel was destroyed four times between 1200 and 1000 B.C. (Albright: *From the Stone Age to Christianity*, 2nd ed., p. 287).

[3] W. F. Albright: *Archaeology and the Religion of Israel*, 4th ed., pp. 96–97 and 101; *From the Stone Age to Christianity*, 2nd ed., pp. 65–66.

[4] *Archaeology and the Religion of Israel*, 4th ed., p. 132, following Judges vi-vii. Cp. *From the Stone Age to Christianity*, 2nd ed., p. 287. See also the present chapter, p. 394, footnote 1, and p. 412.

[5] 'David' is said to mean 'war-lord', and not to be a proper name.

[6] Oesterley and Robinson, op. cit., vol. i, p. 222.

[7] Ibid., p. 290.   [8] e.g. on p. 395.

[9] Judges v. 17. The difficulties with which this passage bristles are discussed by Rowley in op. cit., pp. 81–84.   [10] See p. 394, footnote 1.

[11] 1 Kings xx. 34, as interpreted by Oesterley and Robinson, op. cit., vol. i, pp. 292, 294, 313, and by A. Dupont-Sommer: *Les Araméens*, pp. 34–35.

cian craftsmen lent by Hiram.[1] And 'Israelite art, from the ninth to the early sixth century B.C., reflects a stage of Phoenician art during which the latter was diffused throughout the Mediterranean, transforming Greek art completely.'[2]

We can follow the process of fusion in the field of language and literature too. The Hebrews (including the Moabites) adopted not only the Canaanite language but also the Phoenician alphabet for writing it. The Aramaeans kept their own language; but they too borrowed the Phoenician alphabet and adapted it to Aramaic by using four of the Phoenician consonants to stand for vowels as well.[3] The discovery of the Ugarit texts shows that the Biblical Psalms, whatever their date, are indebted to a Phoenician hymnology that had a long tradition behind it.[4] The Phoenicians also seem likely to have been the intermediaries through whom some of the Egyptian proverbs of Amenemope found their way into the Biblical Book of Proverbs almost verbatim.[5] And the Canaanite origin of chapters viii–ix of the Book of Proverbs, on the theme of Wisdom, is attested by echoes here of themes in the Phoenician literature disinterred at Ugarit.[6] The Sumero-Akkadian story of the creation of the World must have found its way to Palestine long before the Israelites' advent there, and must have been learnt by them from the Canaanites on whom they imposed themselves.[7] Canaanite elements have not been detected in the eighth-century B.C. prophetic literature of Israel and Judah. But they reappear thereafter.[8] 'There is a veritable flood of allusions to Canaanite (Phoenician) literature in Hebrew works composed between the seventh and the third century B.C.'[9]: e.g. in Job, Deutero-Isaiah, Proverbs, Ezekiel, Habakkuk, the Song of Songs, Ecclesiastes, Jubilees, and part of Daniel. Albright sees in this a consequence of a Phoenician literary renaissance associated with the name of Sanchuniathon—a Phoenician historian whose date, in Albright's belief, is either the seventh or the sixth century B.C.[10]

Robinson holds[11] that the Israelites also acquired the 'Mosaic' Law from the same source at the same stage in their history.

'Not only are many of the laws designed for an agricultural and commercial community, and none of them confined to a nomad tribe, but they

---

[1] According to Albright, the architecture and furniture of Solomon's temple were Canaanite. The word used for it—hêkhal—is a Canaanite word that had been borrowed from the Sumerians *circa* 2500 B.C. (*From the Stone Age to Christianity*, 2nd ed., p. 294). Both the Israelites and the Greeks derived their style of temple-building from Syria, as has been demonstrated by the excavation of a ninth-century B.C. temple at Tell Taynât in Northern Syria (*Archaeology and the Religion of Israel*, 4th ed., p. 143). Solomon's temple and its appurtenances presented an elaborate cosmic symbolism of ultimately Sumerian origin (ibid., p. 154).

[2] Albright, op. cit., 4th ed., p. 15. [3] Dupont-Sommer, op. cit., p. 81.

[4] Albright: *Archaeology and the Religion of Israel*, 4th ed., p. 15.

[5] Ibid.; cp. p. 191, footnote 70.

[6] Albright: *From the Stone Age to Christianity*, 2nd ed., pp. 367–8. There are also parallels in (i) the Aramaic proverbs of Akhiqar, dating from the sixth century B.C.; (ii) the Book of Enoch xlii. 1–2, dating from the second century B.C.; (iii) Ben Sira xxiv. 3–4; (iv) the Wisdom of Solomon vii. 25; (v) Philo (Albright, ibid., pp. 368–9).

[7] Oesterley and Robinson, op. cit., vol. i, p. 34.

[8] Albright: *Archaeology and the Religion of Israel*, 4th ed., p. 128.

[9] Albright: *From the Stone Age to Christianity*, 2nd ed., p. 318; cp. p. 374.

[10] Ibid., p. 17, with note 57.

[11] Oesterley and Robinson, op. cit., vol. i, pp. 34, 95, 327–9.

closely resemble that type of code which we know to have been generally current in Western Asia. Four forms are known: a fragmentary Sumerian code, that of Hammurabi, proper to Babylonia, an Assyrian code, and a Hittite code.[1] . . . A comparison of these with the Israelite code shows that they cannot be independent of each other.[2] . . . [But] none of them is directly derived from one of the others.[3] . . . As compared with the other codes, those of Israel were closely adapted to an agricultural community rather than to a commercial people.'[4]

This brings us to the crucial and controversial question whether the religion of Israel and Judah, in the age between the immigrant peoples' settlement on the land as cultivators and the rise of the revolutionary prophets about half-way through the eighth century B.C., differed in any significant way from the religion of the other contemporary communities in Syria. If a pilgrim from Ya'udi or Hamath or Damascus had visited a tenth-century or ninth-century rural shrine in Israel, or, *a fortiori*, the temple at Jerusalem that had been built and furnished for Solomon by Tyrian artificers, would he have been conscious of any striking contrast with the shrines of his own country? The accounts, in the Second Book of Kings, of the successive purges of Solomon's Temple by Hezekiah[5] in 705 B.C. and by Josiah[6] in 621 B.C. show that, down to Hezekiah's time, the brazen serpent Nehushtan had held its own in the sanctuary of Jerusalem side by side with Yahweh's ark, and that in Josiah's time Yahweh shared the temple with the god Baal, the goddess Asherah (whose symbol Hezekiah was said to have cut down), and the heavenly bodies—in particular the Sun, to whom chariots and horses were dedicated there as votive offerings. In 621 B.C. the temple at Jerusalem also housed consecrated prostitutes, male as well as female;[7] and in the valley of Hinnom, below Jerusalem on the city's south side, was a 'tophet' where children were sacrificed by being burnt alive[8]—a cult to which the Carthaginians, too, were addicted.

Ritual prostitution was an agricultural fertility rite which was common to Syria and the Sumero-Akkadian World; and it may have come to Syria from there. Human sacrifice was an atrocity of Syria's own.[9] If it had ever been practised in Sumer and Akkad or in Egypt, it was extinct there in historical times. The Assyrians were innocent of it. The slaughter and torture of which they were guilty had no religious sanction or excuse. In the Syriac World, both at home and overseas, human sacrifice was practised as a last resort in a public crisis. In the ninth century B.C. King Mesha of Moab sacrificed his eldest son on the wall of his capital city when the combined forces of Israel, Judah, and Edom were at the gates.[10] In similar circumstances King Ahaz of Judah 'caused his son to pass through the fire'[11] when Jerusalem was being besieged by the combined forces of Damascus and Israel in the eighth century. King Manasseh of Judah—Hezekiah's son and Josiah's

---

[1] p. 95.   [2] p. 127.   [3] p. 128.   [4] p. 128.
[5] 2 Kings xviii. 4.   [6] 2 Kings xxiii. 4–7 and 11.
[7] 2 Kings xxiii. 7.   [8] 2 Kings xxiii. 10.
[9] For this rite see Oesterley and Robinson, op. cit., vol. i, p. 375, and Albright: *Archaeology and the Religion of Israel*, 4th ed., pp. 162–3. There is, however, no mention of it in any of the Ugaritic texts so far discovered (ibid., p. 92). Did it come in with the Völkerwanderung?   [10] 2 Kings iii. 27.   [11] 2 Kings xvi. 3.

grandfather—'made his son to pass through the fire'[1] without, as far as we know, having Mesha's and Ahaz's occasion for performing the rite.[2]

The Torah as we have it today has been edited and re-edited to make it conform with successive phases through which religion passed in Judah and in the subsequent Jewish diasporá in and after the eighth century B.C. Hence the recorded identification of Yahweh with other gods, and association of other gods with him, are represented in retrospect as having been lapses from a previous strict Mosaic monotheism, while purges such as Hezekiah's and Josiah's are represented as having been reformations. Considering that syncretism and polytheism seem to have been the normal practice in Israel and Judah, as well as in other Syriac communities, in this age, it might be nearer to the historical truth to think of Hezekiah and Josiah as having been iconoclastic innovators, and of Manasseh and Amon as having been pious conservatives. At any rate, this is how these posthumously anathematized religious reactionaries must have appeared to themselves; and they had history on their side. Among the theophoric names given to members of Saul's and David's families, there were names compounded with 'Baal' as well as names compounded with Yahweh.[3] On the other hand, 'Yahweh', not 'Baal', was the god-compound in the names of all the three children of Ahab,[4] the King of Israel who tolerated his Tyrian wife's propagation in his kingdom of the cult of her own national god. Ahab evidently did not agree with Elijah that, in showing this tolerance to Melkart, he was being disloyal to Yahweh. Of the personal names inscribed on *ostraka* found at Samaria and dating from the years 778–770 B.C., the ratio of personal names compounded with 'Yahweh' to those compounded with 'Baal' is 11:7.[5] Conversely, names compounded with 'Yahweh' appear in kingdoms in which Yahweh was not the national god. An Azriyahu king of Ya'udi, who figures in the Assyrian records in the years 740–738 B.C., is an Azariah, but his kingdom is not Judah but Sam'āl.[6] A king of Hamath who was flayed alive by Sargon in 720 B.C. bore the name of Yahu-bi'di (alias Ilu-bi'di).[7] Azriyahu's contemporary and neighbour, King Bar-Ga'yah of Katka, may also have borne the mark of Yahweh in the second half of his name.[8] Already in the tenth century B.C. the son of David's friend King To'i of Hamath had borne the name Joram.[9]

At this stage of religious development it was natural that the peoples of Syria, including those that were Yahweh-worshippers, should each tolerate and even welcome the association of its neighbour's gods with its own national god, so long as the national god's primacy on his own

[1] 2 Kings xxi. 6.
[2] A striking conspectus of the points in common between the Israelites' religion and that of their neighbours before the prophetic revolution in the eighth century B.C. is given by S. A. Cook in *The Cambridge Ancient History*, vol. iii (1925), pp. 426–32.
[3] Oesterley and Robinson, op. cit., vol. i, p. 193, footnote 1.
[4] Ibid., p. 323.
[5] Albright: *Archaeology and the Religion of Israel*, 4th ed., p. 160.
[6] Dupont-Sommer, op. cit., pp. 61 and 115; Oesterley and Robinson, op. cit., vol. i, p. 374.
[7] Dupont-Sommer, op. cit., pp. 68–69 and 115; Oesterley and Robinson, op. cit., vol. i, p. 380, footnote 1.
[8] Dupont-Sommer, op. cit., p. 115.   [9] Ibid.

ground was not challenged. Subject to this, it was felt to be prudent to conciliate the neighbours' gods, since all agreed in believing, not merely in the existence of each local god, but in the potency of each of them in his own national domain. The Yahweh-worshipping besiegers of Qir-Hareseth evidently believed in the potency of Chemosh within the frontiers of Moab; for Mesha's counter-move of conjuring Chemosh by the sacrifice of his eldest son caused them to beat a hasty retreat in the belief that Mesha's action had been efficacious in calling down on them Chemosh's wrath.[1] This is surely the light in which we have to interpret Elijah's opposition in Israel to the Tyrian queen Jezebel's attempt to impose her national god Melkart on her husband's Yahweh-worshipping subjects, and the subsequent revolution in which Jehu stamped out the Tyrian cult by ruthless massacres. Seen in retrospect through Jewish eyes, this counter-movement was interpreted as a return to a temporarily compromised Mosaic monotheism. Probably it would be nearer the truth to see in it an outbreak of national chauvinism of the kind that, at Athens in 399 B.C., inspired the prosecution of Socrates on a charge of addiction to new gods, and that repeatedly inspired the Roman Government to purge Rome and her territory of foreign cults. If an Israelite queen, married to a Tyrian king, had tried to impose the cult of Yahweh on her husband's Melkart-worshipping subjects, we may guess that she would have roused a Tyrian Elijah and a Tyrian Jehu to action.

Moreover, the issue that was fought out in Israel on this historic occasion was not simply one between Yahweh and Melkart; it was also an issue between Yahweh and Yahweh. The Yahweh of Jezreel might perhaps have co-existed amicably with Melkart; for this Yahweh, like Melkart, was the god of an agricultural and urban people. He and Melkart alike were defeated by a Yahweh from Israel's still semi-nomad desert fringe, which was the homeland of both Elijah and Jonadab. The struggle between the contending gods was an expression of the semi-nomad Gileadites' revolt against the process of settlement on the land and in the cities that had been transforming Israel west of Jordan at an accelerating pace.[2] The Gileadite form of Yahweh-worship that now temporarily triumphed was provincial, fanatical, and archaistic; but there is no evidence that it was monotheistic in the eventual Jewish sense of the word.

In Jewish and Christian minds today prophets are associated particularly with Israel and Judah, but this is not warranted by the evidence. In the history of Israel prophets make their first recorded appearance about half-way through the eleventh century B.C. as bands of devotees falling into infectious ecstasies. Saul caught the infection from a band with which he fell in on the first day of his political career,[3] and he remained prone to prophetic fits for the rest of his life; but the phenomenon was not just a local one. At about the same date an Egyptian envoy,

[1] 2 Kings iii. 27.
[2] See W. O. E. Oesterley and T. H. Robinson: *A History of Israel*, vol. i, pp. 303–4 and 345–6. Compare the tension between the nomad and the peasant element in present-day Jordan.
[3] 1 Sam. x. 10–13.

Wen Amon, came across the same phenomenon at Byblos.[1] Anatolia may have been the source from which Syria acquired the institution of congregational ecstatic prophesying.[2] At any rate, in Anatolia this institution has a long history. In the Hellenic Age it is represented there by the bands of 'galli' who were devotees of the goddess Cybele; in the Christian Age by the Montanists; in the Islamic Age by the Mevlevi dervishes, who carried on this ancient Anatolian tradition on its native ground till A.D. 1925, when the Islamic religious orders were suppressed in Turkey.[3]

In Syria in the ninth century B.C. we find ecstatic prophets still operating in bands—by this date more or less under royal control. Ahab has his band of prophets of Yahweh;[4] Jezebel has her band of prophets of Baal. But at this stage individual prophets stand out from the mass—for instance, Micaiah, Elijah, and Elisha in Israel—and these engage in politics as independent and redoubtable powers. Was this second phase in the evolution of the prophet confined to Israel? We do not hear, in the Israelite scriptures, of individual prophets who were Tyrians or Damascenes. But the *argumentum ex silentio* is hazardous where one party has monopolized the telling of the story. It is more prudent to suspend judgement in the expectation that the Israelite scriptural monopoly may one day be broken, in this chapter too, by the progress of archaeological discovery. The Israelite scriptures themselves testify that Elisha, at any rate, did not confine his activities to his own country. According to this testimony,[5] Elisha engineered a political revolution in Damascus before engineering one in Israel. The usurper Hazael as well as the usurper Jehu is said to have committed his act of high treason at Elisha's instigation. In the next phase, too, the prophets played their parts on an international stage. When Amos of Tekoa made his pronunciamiento *circa* 760 B.C., he made it in Israel,[6] which was a bigger forum than his native Judah.

Prophets, as well as courtiers, craftsmen, and traders, felt themselves at home in any of the statelets among which the Syrian World was divided politically.

'Except for the Philistines, all the tribes and princedoms involved recognised a certain kinship one with another, though only two had the uniting bond of a common worship. Damascus, Israel, Judah, Ammon, Moab, and Edom all belonged to much the same racial group, and the traditions preserved in Israel . . . asserted a common ancestry for all.'[7]

On the eve of the Assyrian conquest of Syria west of Euphrates, King Bar-Ga'yah of Katka made an anti-Assyrian treaty with 'all Aram'. This phrase

'denotes the Aramaean states collectively. Notwithstanding the looseness

[1] Oesterley and Robinson, op. cit., vol. i, p. 179, footnote 1. Cp. Albright: *Archaeology and the Religion of Israel*, 4th ed., p. 120; *From the Stone Age to Christianity*, 2nd ed., p. 304.
[2] Albright conjectures that the prophetic movement in Palestine and the Bacchic movement in the Hellenic World may have had a common origin (*From the Stone Age to Christianity*, 2nd ed., pp. 304–5). Anatolia seems the most likely common source.
[3] As a result of three decrees dated 2nd September, 1925.
[4] 1 Kings xxii. 6.   [5] 2 Kings viii. 7–ix. 37.
[6] Oesterley and Robinson, op. cit., vol. i, p. 370, footnote 1.
[7] Ibid., p. 266. The worship of Yahweh was common to three of these communities not two only. Yahweh was the god of Edom as well as of Judah and Israel.

of the links between them and notwithstanding their mutual conflicts, these states retained a certain consciousness of their community, both racial and political. In grave circumstances they instinctively came together to present a common front.'[1]

Thus in the Syriac World during its five centuries of political independence the prevailing social and cultural tendency was already the movement towards fusion that subsequently went with a run after the local political barriers to it had been swept away by the Assyrians. The subsequent process of standardization, in which the most impressive single development was the triumphal progress of the Aramaic *koinê*, had already been foreshadowed in the tendency of the preceding age, and it merely carried this tendency towards its logical conclusion.

The deportees from the Kingdom of Israel went the whole way. In exile they lost their distinctive communal identity completely and once for all. So too, we may guess, did those Judahite refugees in Egypt who saw in the liquidation of the Kingdom of Judah by Nebuchadnezzar a retribution for their neglect, not of Yahweh, but of the Queen of Heaven. They sharply rejected Jeremiah's thesis that their apostasy from Yahweh had been the cause of Judah's national disaster, and they were unmoved by the prophet's threat that, if they remained obdurate, another stroke of Yahweh's vengeance would overtake them in their Egyptian asylum. The lesson that these Judahites had learnt from the disaster was to beware of ever neglecting the Queen of Heaven again.[2] In this case we have no information about the sequel; but the Aramaic documents, dating from the fifth century B.C., which give us a glimpse of the life and outlook of a Judaeo-Aramaean military colony at Elephantinê in Upper Egypt under the Achaemenian regime, enable us to catch another expatriated Syriac community at a point part way along the road that the deportees from Israel undoubtedly travelled to the end. This colonial Jewish community followed Solomon, Ahab, Athaliah, and Manasseh in feeling it no disloyalty to Yahweh to associate other gods with him. Out of a fund of 628 (or 626) shekels collected by the colonists in 419 B.C., 246 shekels were allocated to Yahweh, 140 to Eshem Bethel, and 240 to 'Anath Bethel.[3] Here we see a new cult arising within Yahweh's own domain. Archaeological investigation has shown that the sanctuary at Bethel was prosperous in the sixth century B.C.; and, though it was burned down towards the end of the Neobabylonian period,[4] the cult, which found a secondary focus in Babylonia, attained its maximum diffusion in the fifth century B.C.[5] Theophoric names containing 'Bethel' as one of their components begin to appear about 600 B.C.[6] They are

---

[1] Dupont-Sommer, op. cit., p. 58.

[2] Jer. xliv. The refugees' truculent reaction to Jeremiah's expostulations is reported in Jeremiah's own account of the affair. 'As for the word that thou hast spoken unto us in the name of the Lord, we will not hearken unto thee; but we will certainly do whatsoever thing goeth forth out of our own mouth, to burn incense unto the Queen of Heaven and to pour out drink offerings unto her, as we have done—we and our fathers, our kings and our princes—in the cities of Judah and in the streets of Jerusalem. For then had we plenty of victuals, and were well and saw no evil. But since we left off to burn incense to the Queen of Heaven and to pour out drink offerings unto her, we have wanted all things and have been consumed by the sword and by the famine' (Jer. xliv. 16–18).

[3] Albright: *Archaeology and the Religion of Israel*, 4th ed., pp. 168–9.

[4] Ibid., p. 172.   [5] Ibid., p. 171.   [6] Ibid., p. 170.

all either Aramaic or Neobabylonian, and none are earlier than the reign of Nebuchadnezzar.[1]

In the former territory of Judah the peasantry, whom Nebuchadnezzar had not uprooted, started on the same road, and their drift towards fusion was not reversed by the return of a batch of exiles immediately after the fall of the Neobabylonian Empire. It needed the subsequent missions of Nehemiah and Ezra, backed by the Achaemenian Imperial Government's authority, to make them ruefully conform to the new ideals of monotheism and nationalism that had been conceived in adversity by the diasporá in Babylonia. An effective agency of religious fusion between the un-uprooted Judaeans and their Palestinian neighbours had been intermarriage. The foreign wives were carriers of their ancestral religions. The Babylonian Jewish innovators closed this avenue to fusion by insisting on the dissolution of mixed marriages and prohibiting them for the future. This was a high price to pay for satisfying the requirements of a new-fangled orthodoxy; and the Judaean peasantry's reluctant submission did not save these authentic heirs of the defunct Kingdom of Judah from being written off by the Babylonian Jewish puritans as 'the people of the land' ('am ha-aretz)—a label which carried the contemptuous connotation of the English word 'natives'.[2]

The revolutionary social and religious ideals that the Babylonian Jewish diasporá thus imposed on Judaea were partly the product of an unusual response that this particular uprooted community had made to the experience of deportation. Other deported Syriac communities had bowed to fate and had reconciled themselves to being assimilated. The Jewish diasporá had been peculiar in determining to maintain its distinctive communal identity in circumstances in which most of its fellow deportees had felt assimilation to be inevitable. This exceptional Jewish reaction is partly accounted for by the exceptional history of Judah in the preceding age of Assyrian and Neobabylonian militarism. The states of Damascus and Israel had been wiped off the map, and the social structure of their people had been broken up, within thirty or forty years of the first appearance of prophets of a new kind, whose first representative had been Amos. The state of Judah had survived for nearly a hundred and fifty years longer, and a succession of great prophets had arisen within her borders before she, in her turn, was *gleichgeschaltet*.

The prophets of this third kind were politicians, like Elijah and Elisha. Unlike these predecessors of theirs, they were also social reformers. But their distinctive and revolutionary new departure was their new vision of the nature and the potency of Judah's national god Yahweh. They started a spiritual and intellectual revolution which was to end in a conception of this national god of Judah and Israel as being also the only true god in the Universe,[3] and as being righteous and loving, not capricious and violent-tempered.[4] While the prophets of Amos' line

[1] Albright: *Archaeology and the Religion of Israel*, 4th ed., p. 168.
[2] See further pp. 501-3.
[3] Albright holds (*From the Stone Age to Christianity*, 2nd ed., p. 327) that Amos, Hosea, Isaiah, and Jeremiah were monotheists already as fully as the post-Exilic Deutero-Isaiah. This view is almost required by Albright's belief that Moses, too, was a monotheist in the strict sense of the word.   [4] See further pp. 488-96.

lived and while the Kingdom of Judah lasted, these prophets' words—political, ethical, and religious—mostly fell on deaf ears. But, unlike their predecessors, they put their oracles in writing; and the written word made its effect posthumously. The sixth-century Jewish deportees to Babylonia had to leave behind them the ruins of the temple at Jerusalem, as well as their houses and fields. Their chief portable treasure was their books, and these, including the books of the Prophets, fructified in exile.[1]

Thus, from the time of the loss of political independence onwards, the Syriac Civilization did divide into two streams. There was a stream heading towards nationalism and monotheism, and a stream heading towards social and cultural fusion and religious syncretism. Both streams flowed from a common fount. Their common source was the unitary culture which had developed in Syria during the preceding five centuries. In the subsequent Achaemenian Age the stream represented by the Jewish diasporá was a mere trickle, while the stream represented by the Aramaic *koinê* was a flood. Yet at the present day the only surviving representatives of the Syriac Civilization of the first half of the last millennium B.C. are the Jews and the Samaritans.[2] This historical fact confronts us with the questions: How widely did the flood of the cosmopolitan Syriac Civilization spread, and when and why did it lose itself in the sands?

6. THE EXTENT OF THE SYRIAC SOCIETY'S CULTURAL EXPANSION AFTER THE LOSS OF POLITICAL INDEPENDENCE

In a previous section of this chapter[3] we have noticed that, after the states of the Syriac World had been overthrown, and their territories annexed, by the Assyrian and Neobabylonian empires, the Aramaic language and alphabet rapidly gained ground at the expense of cunei-

[1] See further pp. 496–9.
[2] The present-day Samaritans have more in common with the present-day Jews than just the common feat of surviving. They too preserve and revere the Torah; they too believe that Yahweh is the One True God; they too hold that the public cult of this One God ought to be carried on in one place only (see G. F. Moore: *Judaism in the First Centuries of the Christian Era*, vol. i, pp. 24–25). The issue that has kept Samaritans and Jews apart for more than two thousand years is over the question of what place should have the privilege of possessing this liturgical monopoly. The Samaritans contend for Mount Gerizim, on the strength of chap. xxiv of the Book of Joshua, the Jews for Jerusalem, on the strength of David's having brought the Ark there and Solomon's having built the Temple there and Josiah's having suppressed the worship of Yahweh at all other sanctuaries within his political jurisdiction.

These are indisputable facts, and the Jewish account of the Samaritans in 2 Kings xvii. 24–41 can neither be reconciled with them nor be maintained in the teeth of them.

According to this story the Samaritans are descended, not from the population of Israel, but from a mixed multitude of settlers whom the Assyrians planted in the previous population's place. It is no doubt likely that the Assyrians did bring in non-Israelite colonists; but it is also likely that in Israel, as in Judah, a portion, at least, of the previous population was left undisturbed. According to the Jewish story, again, the immigrants began by worshipping their own ancestral gods only; took to worshipping Yahweh as well when they were plagued by lions; but worshipped him side by side with ancestral gods, whom they were unwilling to abandon.

This picture of the second phase of Samaritan religion is not unlike the picture of Jewish religion in fifth-century Elephantinê which the Aramaic papyri, discovered there, have revealed to us. But, if the religion of the Samaritans ever did pass through this phase of syncretism, it has since been purged of it as thoroughly as Judaism has been. The present-day religion of the Samaritans, like present-day Judaism, is strictly monotheistic.   [3] On pp. 397–9.

form and Akkadian. The cuneiform script had fallen completely out of use before the end of the first century of the Christian Era, and, long before that, the Akkadian language conveyed in it must have passed out of ordinary currency and have lingered on only as a learned language mastered by a few specialists. In fact the Syriac Civilization had absorbed and supplanted the 3,000-years-old civilization of Sumer and Akkad and Babylon and Assyria.

This was an impressive feat of cultural assimilation; but there are several obvious factors that, between them, go some way towards accounting for it. Aramaic-speaking peoples had encircled Babylonia as long ago as the time of the Völkerwandering at the turn of the second and the last millennium B.C. The Aramaeans themselves, as we have noticed,[1] had pushed their way into the steppe-country, north-east of Babylonia, between the River Tigris and the Iranian plateau; their Chaldaean kinsmen had established themselves on Babylonia's southern fringe.[2] And this Aramaic-speaking population in the Sumero-Akkadian World was reinforced, from the ninth century B.C. onwards, by Assyrian conquests and deportations of Aramaean peoples. Moreover, the Akkadian language, which had driven Sumerian out of ordinary currency, even in Sumer itself, before the age of Hammurabi, was a language of the same Semitic family as Aramaic, so that it was comparatively easy for Akkadian-speakers to acquire a sister Semitic dialect. As for the Aramaic alphabet, it was attractive because of its enormous superiority over cuneiform in both simplicity and clarity.

These propitious circumstances go far towards explaining the Syriac Civilization's success in swamping and assimilating the Sumero-Akkadian Civilization. Its feat of drawing the Iranian peoples, too, into its sphere of influence is more remarkable. The Iranian languages—belonging, as they do, not to the Semitic, but to the Indo-European family—were no more akin to Aramaic than the Sumerian language was. The Iranian plateau and the Oxus-Jaxartes basin, which were the homelands of the non-Nomadic Iranian peoples, were more remote geographically from the heart of the Syriac World than Babylonia and Assyria were. Moreover, Babylonia and Assyria lay between Iran and Syria; and therefore the Sumero-Akkadian Civilization of these countries was the first civilization with which the Iranians came into contact while they were still impressionable semi-barbarians. Both the geographical proximity of the Sumero-Akkadian Society and the prestige that it had acquired in virtue of its antiquity gave it a unique opportunity for converting the Iranians and so perhaps saving itself, through this eastern reinforcement, from succumbing to the Syriac Civilization that was expanding at its expense from the west. The Sumero-Akkadian Civilization did impress and influence the Iranians at their first contact with it. But they afterwards transferred their cultural allegiance to the more vital and more convenient Syriac Civilization in its Post-Assyrian Aramaic dress; and this change in the Iranians' cultural orientation expanded the

[1] On p. 410.
[2] This point is noticed by W. F. Albright in *From the Stone Age to Christianity*, 2nd ed., p. 340.

Syriac Civilization's cultural domain eastwards as far as Western India and Central Asia.

In geographical terms the Achaemenian Persian Empire was, as we have now noted,[1] one representative of a long series of universal states, beginning with the empire of the dynasty of Agade (*circa* 2360–2180 B.C.), that were based on the alluvial basin of the lower Tigris and Euphrates. In terms both of economics and of communications the Achaemenian Empire was the heir of the Neobabylonian Empire rather than of the Median Empire. Though it dwarfed the Neobabylonian Empire in its total area, Babylonia was its main source of supply, and was also the centre from which all its roads radiated. The founders of the Achaemenian Empire were naturally conscious of having entered into the Sumero-Akkadian Civilization's political heritage; and their first impulse was to adopt the Sumero-Akkadian culture as well.

For instance, their first experiment in providing their own language with a script took the same form as the experiment made in the Phoenician city of Ugarit eight or nine hundred years earlier. Though the Achaemenidae did not adopt the clumsy Sumerian system of writing (a system in which some characters were used ideographically and others phonetically side by side), they did use selected cuneiform characters to stand for a purely phonetic, and all but alphabetic, syllabary for conveying the West Iranian (Medo-Persian) language; and their first intention seems to have been to give parity of official status to three languages, all conveyed in cuneiform characters used in different ways. These original three official languages of the Achaemenian Empire were Medo-Persian (the language of the pair of ruling peoples), Elamite (the language of the chief imperial capital, Susa), and Akkadian (the language of Babylonia, the Empire's geographical and economic heart). Darius I's trilingual inscription on the cliff-face at Behistan is the chief monument of this linguistic policy. Another striking piece of evidence for it is the collection of archives, written on clay tablets in the cuneiform script and mostly in the Elamite language, that has been disinterred at Persepolis —the Persians' national capital in their own home territory. Yet the Medo-Persian syllabary conveyed in cuneiform characters never caught on; it seems to have been passing out of use even before the Achaemenian Empire was overthrown by Alexander, and it certainly did not survive that catastrophe. Soon after, if not simultaneously with, the official adoption of the three languages written in cuneiform, the Achaemenian authorities gave official currency, as we have seen, to the Aramaic *koinê* written alphabetically on papyrus or on parchment. Apparently Aramaic was given this status not only in the Semitic-speaking provinces of the Empire, but in all its dominions, including Anatolia and Egypt on the west and Iran, the Oxus–Jaxartes basin, and the Panjab on the east. With this official backing, the handy Aramaic language and alphabet inevitably prevailed over the three official languages conveyed in the cumbrous cuneiform script. In thus prevailing, the Aramaic language and alphabet also served as spear-heads which opened the way for the Syriac culture to win the allegiance of the Iranian-speaking peoples.

[1] On p. 191.

This process of cultural assimilation can be followed in the history of the Aramaic language and alphabet on Iranian ground. After the break that the Hellenic conquest made in Iranian cultural history, we find the Iranian languages being written in variants of the Aramaic alphabet with an infusion of Aramaic words that are thought to have been read, not phonetically, but as ideograms standing for Iranian words of the same meaning, so that the whole text, including this minority of Aramaic words in it, would have been read uniformly as Iranian. This system of writing seems peculiar, and it seems still more peculiar that there should be at least three variants of it, each of which made up its own set of Aramaic ideograms differently from, and therefore independently of, each of the others. There is a northern Pehlevi (i.e. 'Parthian'), which must have been the official script and language of the Parthian Empire; a southern Pehlevi, which must have been developed in Fars, the Persian imperial people's homeland, when this secluded highland country shook itself free from Seleucid Macedonian rule; and a Sogdian, which was the local form taken by the same peculiar system in the Oxus–Jaxartes basin, where it developed on its own lines after this region had been insulated politically and culturally from the Iranian plateau as a result of the Eurasian Nomad Völkerwandering in the second century B.C. A bilingual inscription of the Sasanian Emperor Narse (*imperabat* A.D. 293–302), in which the same text is given in the northern as well as in the southern Pehlevi, has been found at Paikuli on the Great North-East Road, a short distance north of Qasr-i-Shirin.[1]

How are we to explain these at first sight strange phenomena? Dupont-Sommer seems to have found the key. The Aramaic words used as ideograms in texts written in the Aramaic alphabet in these three Iranian languages are survivals—the only Post-Achaemenian survivals—of the Aramaic *koinê* that had become the prevailing official language of the Achaemenian Empire before its overthrow.[2] Dupont-Sommer suggests[3] that, under the Achaemenian regime, Iranian-speaking imperial officials used to dictate—each in his own Iranian dialect—to bilingual secretaries, who translated the Iranian words instantaneously into Aramaic and wrote them down in the Aramaic language and alphabet. It was not difficult to discover that this convenient alphabet would serve equally well for taking down the original Iranian words, without these having to be translated into the Aramaic language *en route*. This simplification of the secretary's task would naturally become the ordinary practice in a state in which not only the administrators but the population that they were administering spoke one and the same Iranian language and no other. This was never the situation in the multi-lingual Achaemenian Empire; but it was the situation in the independent principality of Fars in and after the third century B.C., and likewise in the contemporary Parthian Empire before it conquered Babylonia and transferred its headquarters to Ctesiphon. This hypothesis of Dupont-Sommer's does give a satisfactory explanation of the origin of the Pehlevi

[1] See A. Christensen: *L'Iran sous les Sassanides* (Copenhagen 1936, Levin and Munks-gaard), pp. 46–47, and A. Dupont-Sommer: *Les Araméens*, p. 96.
[2] Dupont-Sommer, op. cit., pp. 95 and 97–98.   [3] Ibid., p. 97.

and Sogdian scripts in which Iranian languages are written phonetically in variants of the Aramaic alphabet, with an admixture of Aramaic
words apparently used as ideograms for Iranian words. On this interpretation these Aramaic ideograms are survivals of an original procedure
in which the whole document would have been recorded in the Aramaic
koinê.

Without prejudice to the question of the relation of Islam to the
Syriac Civilization, we can follow into the Islamic Age the further progress of the cultural tendency revealed in the method of writing Sogdian
and Pehlevi. Except for the ideograms in the Aramaic *koinê* that survived
in the writing of these Post-Achaemenian languages, the Aramaic *koinê*
did not outlast the fall of the Achaemenian Empire. Its role was taken
over by the Attic Greek *koinê* in the Achaemenian Empire's Hellenic
successor-states; and, after the whole of Iran and Babylonia had been
liberated from Hellenic rule in the second century B.C., South-West
Asia and Egypt had no *lingua franca* with the range either of the Aramaic
or of the Attic *koinê* before that date, until Arabic came to perform the
old function on the old scale after the reunion of most of the Achaemenian
Empire's former dominions in the Caliphate. Arabic, like Aramaic, is
a Semitic language, and the Arabic alphabet, like the 'square' alphabet
now used for writing Hebrew, is a variety of the Aramaic alphabet. The
overthrow of the Sasanian Persian Empire by the Muslim Arabs made
another break in Iranian cultural history, comparable in magnitude to
the break that had been made by the overthrow of the Achaemenian
Empire by Alexander. Thereafter the New Persian (i.e. Islamic Persian)
language came to be written, as might be expected, in the Arabic form
of the Aramaic alphabet in place of the forms used for conveying Pehlevi
and Sogdian; and, with the Pehlevi and Sogdian alphabets, the Aramaic
ideograms dropped out. But this did not mean the end of Semitic influence on the Iranian vocabulary. So far from that, the Arabic alphabet
and Islam, between them, imported into New Persian a vast vocabulary
of Arabic words; and these, unlike the Aramaic words in Pehlevi and
Sogdian, are not used as ideograms for Iranian words. They are pronounced in New Persian as they are written, like the French, Latin, and
Greek words in Modern English.[1] Like these, they have half swamped
the native vocabulary, and all the patriotic endeavours of the New
Persian purists, from Firdawsi onwards, have not availed to purge this
Iranian language of its Arabic alloy.

If the history of the Pehlevi and Sogdian scripts may be taken as an
indication of the expansion of the Syriac Civilization's influence over
the Iranian World, we may next inquire whether this movement, which
we have now observed in the field of language, can also be detected in
other fields—for instance, in the field of religion.

Was the religion founded by Zarathustra an entirely indigenous creation of the Iranian World's, or was Zarathustra inspired, at least in part,
by some stimulus from outside his own semi-barbarian cultural milieu?
The question arises because Zarathustra's conception of God and Man

---

[1] If Modern English were written on the Pehlevi system, the word written 'commence'
would be read as 'begin', and the word written 'serviette' would be read as 'napkin'.

and of Good and Evil, as revealed in the Gathas, are so lofty, and also so abstract, that it is not easy to believe that he could have arrived at them, unprompted by inspiration from abroad, in the otherwise rustic and unsophisticated social and cultural milieu that the Gathas also reveal to us as being Zarathustra's environment. Moreover, Zarathustra's message, like Muhammad's, seems to have been revolutionary. He rejected, deposed, and renounced his people's traditional pantheon, and substituted for it a One True God who is righteous and loving. Whether we classify the Zoroastrianism of the Gathas as being monotheistic or as being dualistic, it is certainly not either polytheistic or parochial. Whether Ahuramazda and his adversary Angramainyush are to be regarded as being equals in power or not, the power of each is universal in its range, and Angramainyush, as well as Ahuramazda, is a being of a different order from the former gods whom Zarathustra degraded to the rank of demons. Can this revolutionary universalism, and this ethical interpretation of the nature of absolute Reality, be credited exclusively to Zarathustra's native genius, or is it reasonable to guess that influences from abroad may have played a part in the formation of his ideas and ideals?

If Zarathustra is indebted in some measure to foreign religious influences, these must have come, not from India, but from the Fertile Crescent. His revolution carried Iranian religion in an anti-Indian direction. He turned his back on the traditional Irano-Aryan pantheon. He saw the godhead as being singular, not plural, and as being righteous, not as being the morally indifferent source of Evil as well as Good. This was the conception of the godhead towards which the prophets of Israel and Judah had begun to move in the eighth century (though, unlike Zarathustra, they did not face the problem of the incompatibility between divine goodness and divine omnipotence). After the liquidation of Israel, the prophets of Judah and their Post-Exilic Jewish successors carried the movement farther till, about half-way through the sixth century, on the eve of the establishment of the Achaemenian Empire, Deutero-Isaiah attained a vision of Yahweh not only as being righteous and loving, but also as being the One True God of the Universe. In Deutero-Isaiah's eyes all other gods were not simply inferior; they were non-existent, and the belief in their reality and their efficacy was a delusion. Is it possible, and, if so, is it probable, that Zarathustra was inspired, if only indirectly, by this progressive revolution in the concept of the godhead in one of the uprooted communities of the Syriac World?

The answer to this question partly depends on the answer that we give to another. What were Zarathustra's place and date? Henning has argued convincingly in favour of accepting the Zoroastrian tradition that Zarathustra's ministry had begun 258 years before the coming of Alexander.[1] If the second of these two events is equated with the death of the last Darius in 330 B.C., we have 588 B.C. as the traditional date of the beginning of Zarathustra's ministry—whether this event is to be equated with the date of his receiving his first revelation at the age of thirty, or with the date of his first success at the age of forty, or with the date of his

[1] W. B. Henning: *Zoroaster*, p. 38.

conversion of King Vištāspa at the age of forty-two. The years in which Zarathustra's creative ideas were germinating would thus be either just before or just after 600 B.C.[1] This dating would rule out the identification of the Vištāspa who was Zarathustra's royal convert with the one who was the father of the Achaemenian Emperor Darius I. Henning points out[2] that the fathers of the two Vištāspas had different names, and that they came from different families. He suggests that Zarathustra's Vištāspa, who is traditionally represented as having had no successors,[3] was the last prince of a Khwarizmian empire that coexisted with the Median Empire and embraced the Iranian plateau north-east of the Caspian Gates (the present-day Khorasan), as well as the Oxus–Jaxartes basin.[4] Henning conjectures[5] that this Khwarizmian empire was conquered and annexed by Cyrus after he had liquidated the Median, Lydian, and Neobabylonian empires.

Henning's dating of Zarathustra's ministry and his location of its field are compatible with a conjecture of mine that I threw out tentatively in my first attempt to identify the Syriac Civilization and to ascertain the Iranian World's relation to it. I suggested[6] that Zarathustra might have been influenced by the Israelite deportees who, according to Jewish tradition,[7] were planted by the Assyrians in 'the cities of the Medes' after the capture of Samaria and liquidation of the Kingdom of Israel in 722 B.C. These deportees from the west would probably have been planted on the Assyrian Empire's eastern frontier; and, up the Great North-East Road, the Assyrian outposts may have been pushed forward, at their farthest, as far as Hamadan.

On Henning's dating of Zarathustra, the influence of these expatriated Israelites would have had more than a century—reckoning from the time

---

[1] Henning, *Zoroaster*, p. 41.   [2] Ibid., p. 24.   [3] Ibid., p. 43.

[4] This suggestion is based on Herodotus's statement (Book III, chap. 117) that the Achaemenian Imperial Government had inherited from the Khwarizmians an engineering system that controlled the distribution of the waters of the River Aces to the Khwarizmians themselves, and also to the Hyrcanians, Parthians, Sarangians, and Thamanaeans (i.e. Arachosians). Henning identifies the Aces with the Heri Rud, and thinks that this list of five nations, formerly under the rule of one of their number, the Khwarizmians, informs us of the existence and extent of a Khwarizmian Empire, contemporary with the Median Empire, which eventually suffered the same fate of being annexed by the Achaemenian empire-builder Cyrus to his universal state (Henning, op. cit., pp. 42–43). This pre-Cyran Greater Khwarizm would be the Khwarizm that is identified, both in the Avesta and in the later Zoroastrian tradition, with the region called Airyanam Vaējo in which Zarathustra and his convert King Vištāspa lived according to the Avesta. (The 'Ariana' of the Post-Alexandrine Hellenic geographers includes approximately the same area.)

Henning points out (ibid., p. 43) that in the Avesta 'we find references to such regions as Seistan, Arachosia, the Hindu Kush, Bactria, Sogdiana, Marv, Herat, Hyrcania; but the very name of Media is not mentioned in the whole of it (nor, incidentally, is the name of Persia or the Persians mentioned). Only Raghā, the north-easternmost town of Media, the first town entered by a traveller from the east, occurs in two particularly late passages. Moreover, one can say confidently that any unbiased reading of the Gathas always has given, and always will give, the impression that their author was untouched by urban civilization.'

The picture of Zarathustra's world that the Gathas do give is one of a predominantly pastoral society—but this a sedentary one that found itself at close quarters with the different pastoral society of the Eurasian Nomads and was bitterly hostile to it. This picture corresponds to what we should expect in the settled districts of Ariana in the age of the Nomadic Völkerwanderung of the eighth and seventh centuries B.C.

[5] Henning, op. cit., p. 43.

[6] In i. 81, footnote 1.   [7] 2 Kings xvii. 6 and xviii. 11.

of their arrival in Media to the time of Zarathustra's inspiration—to seep into the Iranian countries on the far side of the Caspian Gates; so my conjecture is chronologically possible. Its weak point is the doubt whether the religion that the Israelite deportees brought away with them when the prophetic movement in Israel and Judah was still in its early days would have been exalted enough to have been the inspiration of Zarathustra's sublime conception of the nature of the godhead. Moreover, we have to reckon with the possibility that, after 120 years in exile, the Israelites marooned in Media may have been on a lower level of religious enlightenment in 600 B.C. than their level in 722 B.C. We know that they eventually lost their communal identity, and, in the process of becoming assimilated to the population among whom they had been settled, they presumably relapsed into polytheism sooner or later. It is conceivable that, by 600 B.C., their religion had come to be not unlike that of the Judaeo-Aramaean colony at Elephantinê in the fifth century B.C., and there would have been no inspiration for Zarathustra in that.

There would, of course, have been inspiration for him in the religion of Israel and Judah in the form that this eventually took among the Judahite deportees in Babylonia. But, if we look in this alternative direction for a possible source of Zarathustra's inspiration, we run into a chronological difficulty. In the history of the evolution of the Jewish religion we have to come down to Deutero-Isaiah in order to find a Jewish prophet whose vision of the nature of God can compare with Zarathustra's. But Deutero-Isaiah must have been only at the beginning of his mission by the time when Zarathustra was nearing the end of his. If there is any internal evidence in the literary remains of either prophet for the transmission of ideas between one and the other, it points to Deutero-Isaiah's having been influenced by Zarathustra and not the other way round.[1] Moreover, even if we hold that Deutero-Isaiah worked in Babylonia and not in Judaea,[2] the distance from Babylon to the far side of the Caspian Gates is much greater than the distance from Hamadan—even allowing for the improvement in both the speed and the security of communications that must have resulted from the political union of Babylonia, Media, and the North-East Iranian countries under an all-embracing *Pax Achaemenia*.

These considerations do not, I think, tell conclusively against the possibility that Zarathustra may have been inspired by the prophetic movement in Israel through contact with descendants of Israelite deportees. In the case of the Judahite deportees, whose spiritual history after their expatriation is recorded in surviving books of theirs, we know that the challenge of being uprooted evoked a spiritual response that was immediate, powerful, and far-going. For all that we know, the Israelite deportees' undocumented response to the same challenge 150 years earlier may have been comparable to the well-known subsequent response

[1] C. F. Whitley: *The Exilic Age*, pp. 144–5, quoting Isaiah xlv. 6–7. Whitley takes this passage as a reference to the dualistic element in Zarathustra's theology and an insistence on the omnipotence of Yahweh at the cost of recognizing in him the creator of Evil as well as of Good.

[2] Considerations in favour of Babylonia's having been his mission-field are set out by Whitley, ibid., pp. 126–7.

of their Judahite kinsmen and co-religionists. This possibility is not incompatible with the known historical fact that the Israelite, unlike the Judahite, deportees eventually failed to preserve their communal identity, and therefore failed to hand down to posterity any Exilic Israelite literature, if there was any. Even if there was none, there may have been Israelite deportees in the first few generations after the Exile whose reaction to the ordeal of expatriation resembled Deutero-Isaiah's rather than the Elephantinians'. And, if there were any such forgotten Israelite men of vision marooned on the Median frontier of the Assyrian Empire in the seventh century B.C., it was certainly possible for Zarathustra to be influenced by them directly or indirectly. In our present ignorance of the Israelite deportees' history we cannot rule out this possibility, any more than we can convert it into a certainty. The question remains an open one, and therefore I neither press nor renounce my conjecture that this transmission of influence may have taken place.

I do, however, accept A. R. Burn's criticism that, in previous volumes, I have not made enough allowance for the originality of the Iranian culture in general and of Zoroastrianism in particular,[1] and I therefore also keep an open mind towards an alternative suggestion that I made in the same place.[2] The similarity between Zarathustra's vision and Deutero-Isaiah's can also be explained, not as a result of stimulus diffusion in either direction, but as a result of independent similar reactions to similar experiences. Unlike Syria, and like the Hellenic World, the North-East Iranian countries had lain beyond the range of Assyrian militarism. On the other hand they had had a double measure of tribulation from the Eurasian Nomad Völkerwandering of the eighth and seventh centuries B.C., which had rolled across the Oxus-Jaxartes basin on its way to India as well as on its way to South-West Asia.

One thing that does seem quite certain is that the respective lines of development of Judaism and Zoroastrianism converged, and that this convergence was eventually followed by contact. I accept R. Coulborn's criticism[3] that there is no evidence for contact earlier than the Achaemenian Age. Indeed, 'there is no clear evidence of Iranian influence on Judaism before the second century B.C.',[4] some two hundred years after the Achaemenian Empire's fall. By that time Judaism had borrowed from Zoroastrianism some beliefs on the fringe of religion—for instance, in the field of angelology and demonology,[5] including the figure of the Son of Man, whom Albright identifies[6] with the Iranian Gayomart. Eventually Judaism and Zoroastrianism came also to share such crucial doctrines as those of immortality, the Last Judgement,[7] and God's operation through the Holy Spirit. It may be debated whether either religion borrowed these doctrines from the other and, if there was borrowing, which of the two borrowed from which. But it can hardly be disputed that Zoroastrianism and Judaism had become assimilated to

[1] See History, February–October, 1956, p. 7.
[2] i. 81, footnote 1.　　　　　　　　　　[3] In Toynbee and History, p. 160.
[4] Albright: From the Stone Age to Christianity, 2nd ed., p. 360.
[5] Ibid., pp. 362–3; W. O. E. Oesterley: The Jews and Judaism during the Greek Period, pp. 270–87.　　　　　[6] Albright, op. cit., p. 378; Oesterley, op. cit., p. 89.
[7] Albright holds (ibid., p. 363) that the picture of the Last Judgement in the Book of Enoch is Iranian, but not the picture of it in the Book of Daniel.

each other long before the third century of the Christian Era, when the 'Iraqi Iranian prophet Mani created a synthetic religion of his own out of elements drawn from Zoroastrianism direct and drawn from Judaism through the medium of its daughter religion Christianity.[1] By Mani's time the Syriac and Iranian worlds had coalesced on the plane of religion as well as on the plane of language and script; and at the present day the Jewish diasporá in the Christian and Islamic worlds and the Zoroastrian diasporá in India are manifestly two specimens of an identical species of non-territorial community that has learnt how to preserve its identity in an alien social and cultural environment by strictly observing a distinctive religious law.

7. THE DURATION OF THE SYRIAC SOCIETY'S CULTURAL CONTINUITY AFTER ITS LOSS OF POLITICAL INDEPENDENCE

In the present-day Jewish and Zoroastrian communities the Syriac Civilization of the age before the Assyrian conquest has living representatives who are linked with it—and linked consciously—by an unbroken chain of tradition which these two communities have deliberately maintained in a continuous effort to preserve their communal identities. On the other hand, all other Syriac communities except this minority have lost their identities at some date between the Assyrian conquest and the present day. The classic case of this is the disappearance of those Israelite kinsmen of the Samaritans whom the Assyrians deported. At what point in history are we to place the disappearance of the Syriac Society in general, apart from the Samaritans and the Jews?

Our answer to this question will depend on our conception of the nature of civilization. Do we see it, with Spengler's eyes, as being an unconscious physical life-process? Or do we see it, with Collingwood's eyes, as being a spiritual movement of ideas?[2] Evidently Collingwood's conception is more strict and more exacting than Spengler's is. My own conception, originally put forward in volume iii of this book[3] and reaffirmed in the present volume,[4] is that a culture is carried by a society, and that a society is the common ground between the individual fields of action of a number of human beings. Human nature is, no doubt, partly subconscious, instinctive, and automatic, but the distinctive mark of being human is to will and to plan, and to do this consciously. My position is thus nearer to Collingwood's than it is to Spengler's, and one of my critics[5] has shrewdly questioned whether my general definition of the nature of human society does not rule out my particular reading of the history of the Syriac Society. In the previous

---

[1] Another 'Iraqi synthetic religion, Mandaeanism, has proved to have arisen under Manichaean influence, now that the Coptic corpus of Manichaean scriptures has been discovered (Albright: *From the Stone Age to Christianity*, 2nd ed., p. 366). Albright conjectures (ibid., p. 366) that Mandaeanism originated in Southern 'Iraq in the fifth century of the Christian Era. 'The Mandaeans inherited the debris of Canaanite and Aramaean mythology on the one hand and of Babylonian mythology and folklore on the other.'

[2] The antithesis between these two conceptions is pointed out by Chr. Dawson in *The Dynamics of World History*, p. 387.

[3] iii. 230.　　　　　　　　　　　　　　　　　　[4] On pp. 272–3.

[5] K. D. Erdmann in *Archiv für Kulturgeschichte*, xxxiii. Band, Heft 2 (1951), p. 243.

volumes of this book, I have suggested that the Syriac Society remained in being until the decline and fall of the 'Abbasid Caliphate, and that it dissolved in the course of the Post-'Abbasid Völkerwanderung (*circa* A.D. 975–1275). Erdmann raises the question whether there was any common ground between the fields of action of the adherents of Islam, even in the first phase of Islamic history, and the participants in the Syriac Society in the Achaemenian and the Pre-Achaemenian Age. Of course, neither Erdmann nor anyone else would deny that the Muslims are, and always have been, conscious of Islam's continuity with Judaism. But the Jews and their predecessors the people of Judah and Israel are only a fraction of the original Syriac World. Are the Muslims also conscious of being heirs of the non-Jewish majority of the Syriac Society in, let us say, the Achaemenian Age? I agree with Erdmann that, when the question is put in these terms, the answer to it is in the negative.

I also agree with him in his general contention that 'common ground', in the sense in which I have used this phrase in my definition of what a society is, implies, in the time-dimension, not merely historical continuity but a consciousness of it[1] and a desire and endeavour to preserve and hand on the cultural tradition that one is conscious of having inherited. The Pharisees were consciously trying to carry out the commandments of the Torah; the Neoplatonists to be true to Plato's philosophy; the Egyptians of the Post-Assyrian Age of Egyptiac history to follow in the footsteps of their predecessors (they singled out as their chief examplars the particularly impressive, but also particularly ancient, worthies of the Age of the Old Kingdom).[2] The maintenance of a tradition is not, of course, the same thing as the integral conservation of a past state of society and culture. It cannot be, since change is of the essence of life. If Plotinus and Plato could have met, Plotinus would not have known what to make of his revered master, any more than Plato would have known what to make of his devout disciple. All the same, the continuity of the history of the Hellenic Civilization between Plato's day and Plotinus's is indisputable. Plotinus was not merely aware that Plato had existed; he was a diligent reader of Plato's works and a keen student and practitioner of his philosophy as he interpreted it. The probability that Plotinus's interpretation would have seemed quaint to Plato if Plato could have been cognisant of it does not mean that there had been any break in the golden chain of the Platonic tradition.

This recognizable continuity in the traditions of the Hellenic and the Egyptiac societies gives us a standard for testing how long the Syriac Society (apart from the invincible Jews and Samaritans) succeeded in maintaining the continuity of its tradition unbroken.

Did it maintain it throughout the millennium of the Hellenic Society's intrusion on South-West Asia and Egypt? We should have no difficulty

---

[1] G. R. Willey and P. Phillips, approaching the same question in regard to the Pre-Columbian civilizations of the Americas, suggest that 'a consciousness of a larger social order is . . . a feature of civilization' (*Method and Theory in American Archaeology* (1958), p. 56).

[2] On the archaism of the Saïte Age of Egyptiac history, see, for example, W. F. Albright: *From the Stone Age to Christianity*, 2nd ed., p. 316.

in answering this question if the civilization whose continuity we were trying to test were not the Syriac but the Egyptiac. The participants in the Egyptiac Civilization consciously and deliberately kept up the Egyptiac tradition till they were converted to Christianity. This happened between the third and the sixth century of the Christian Era—the fourth century being the critical one in which, in Egypt, Christianity achieved a decisive predominance. Thus the Egyptiac Civilization went into dissolution at the same time as the Hellenic, and it succumbed to the same solvent. Down to the time when these two civilizations simultaneously disappeared, one of the expressions of an Egyptiac cultural consciousness was the negative one of unremitting opposition and resistance to the Hellenic ascendancy that had been inaugurated, more than three hundred years before the establishment of the Ptolemaic regime, by the seventh-century Saïte Pharaoh Psammetichus I's hazardous policy of hiring Carian and Ionian mercenaries; and it is noteworthy that this Egyptiac Hellenophobia outlived the Egyptiac Civilization itself.

The conversion of the Egyptians to Christianity brought with it a revolutionary break with their cultural past. Besides substituting the Christian Trinity, angels, saints, and martyrs for the Egyptiac pantheon, the Egyptians also now substituted an alphabet, modelled on the Greek alphabet, for all forms of the traditional Egyptiac script, and thereby obliterated even their memory of their Pre-Christian past. Their inveterate Hellenophobia was the only relic of the past that survived this great cultural revolution; and it now found for itself a new expression in Christian terms. The descendants of the Egyptians who had combated the Hellenes in the names of Amun-Re and Apis now combated those Hellenes' 'Melchite' ('Imperialist') Christian successors in the cause of a Monophysite doctrine of the relation between the divine and human natures in Christ.

The fifth-century and sixth-century Coptic-speaking Monophysites in Egypt were hand in glove with their Syriac-speaking Monophysite contemporaries in Syria. In Syria, as in Egypt, the anti-Melchite feeling that expressed itself in these theological terms in these centuries was the conscious expression of a regional tradition. In Egypt, as we have seen, this Christian regional tradition was a recently established one, and it was dissevered from the pre-Christian Egyptiac tradition by a revolutionary break in cultural continuity. Was it the same story in Syria? Or can the opposition to the Melchite ascendancy be traced back, in Syria, without a break in continuity of consciousness, to the beginning of the Graeco-Roman domination? In other words, can the distinctive Syriac consciousness expressed in Monophysitism be traced back continuously to the age when the Aramaic *koinê* was the *lingua franca* of the Achaemenian Empire? We may assume that the users of the Aramaic *koinê*, so long as it remained in use, were conscious, in virtue of their using it, that they were partakers in a common culture—as the use of the subsequent Attic Greek *koinê* gave its users a sense of being partakers in a common Hellenism. Do this Aramaic linguistic consciousness and the Monophysite religious consciousness, between them, span the chronological gulf between the fourth century B.C. and the fifth century of the

Christian Era? Or is there a break in the continuity of history in the Syriac World between these two dates? The evidence suggests that there is a break, and that in the history of Syria the chronological interval between the old civilization and Monophysite Christianity is considerably longer than the corresponding interval in the history of Egypt.

The Aramaic *koinê* was hard hit by Alexander's destruction of the Achaemenian Empire. It not only lost its privileged status of being an official *lingua franca*; it was deliberately replaced, in this role, by the Attic Greek *koinê* in the Achaemenian Empire's Hellenic successor-states;[1] and, during the Seleucid regime in South-West Asia, Aramaic was under eclipse. Few Aramaic inscriptions dating from this period have been found except in Transjordan and Arabia,[2] and no Aramaic literary works are extant that date from the time between the third or second century B.C. and the second or third century of the Christian Era.[3] During this dark age the Aramaic language was contaminated by the intrusion of Hellenisms,[4] and the standard language and alphabet of the Aramaic *koinê* broke up into different local varieties.[5] The two dialects that remained the closest to the Aramaic *koinê* were the Nabataean and the Palmyrene; but Nabataean Aramaic was contaminated with Arabisms, and Palmyrene Aramaic with the Eastern Aramaic dialect of the region on the farther side of the River Euphrates.[6] The continuing advance of the Aramaic language in Palestine at the expense of Canaanite, even in this age of adversity, is attested by the fact that about half the Book of Daniel is in Aramaic,[7] and this book is thought to have been published in 164 B.C.; but the Biblical Aramaic is already a local dialect.

The chief literary monuments of Palestinian Aramaic are the Samaritan translation of the Pentateuch and the Jerusalem Talmud[8] (including the Mishnah). The future lay with the Eastern Aramaic dialect of Mesopotamia and Babylonia; and this stemmed, not from the *koinê*, but from dialects, current east of the Euphrates, which had not been used for literary purposes in the Assyrian and Achaemenian Age.[9] The chief literary monuments of Eastern Aramaic—all dating from after the beginning of the Christian Era—are the Babylonian Talmud, the scriptures of the Mandaean religion, and the Christian literature in the dialect of Urfa (better known by its Macedonian name 'Edessa') in North-Western Mesopotamia.[10] This Osrhoenian dialect is known as

---

[1] The Attic Greek *koinê*, together with other elements of Hellenism, naturally made its most rapid conquests on Syriac ground in the Phoenician and Philistine maritime cities along the Mediterranean coast, since these were within easier reach of the Hellenic World than the interior was. The early Hellenization of the Phoenician cities, in particular, did much to break the continuity of the Canaanite Syriac tradition in its homeland. The Phoenician states had recovered, under the Achaemenian regime, something of what they had lost in the preceding Assyrian and Neobabylonian Age. The Achaemenian Government had not only granted them autonomy, but had bestowed on them miniature local empires of their own—of course, under Achaemenian suzerainty. After the overthrow of the Achaemenian Empire the Phoenician city-states retained these privileges under the subsequent Ptolemaic and Seleucid regimes, and they even recovered complete independence during the brief interval (*circa* 129 B.C.–63 B.C.) between the break-up of the Seleucid Empire and its replacement by Roman rule. But, in the Post-Alexandrine Age, they soon became virtually part of the Hellenic World.
[2] W. F. Albright: *The Archaeology of Palestine*, p. 208.
[3] Ibid., pp. 201–2.   [4] A. Dupont-Sommer: *Les Araméens*, p. 98.
[5] Ibid., p. 98.   [6] Ibid., p. 100.   [7] Ibid., p. 99.
[8] Ibid., p. 99.   [9] Ibid., pp. 101–2.   [10] Ibid., pp. 100–1.

'Syriac' *par excellence*, and it won the standing of an unofficial *koinê* for Aramaic-speaking Christians of all sects; but both the language itself and the literature written in it are rather remote from the *koinê* of the Achaemenian Age and from the literary monuments of that.

Each of these dialects that thus asserted themselves against the former *koinê* developed its own variation on the *koinê*'s standard alphabet. Separate Syriac, Mandaean, Palmyrene, Nabataean, Jewish, and Samaritan alphabets established themselves. The Jewish variation on the original Aramaic alphabet is the one that is now familiar under the name of 'Square Hebrew'.[1]

We must conclude that the conscious continuity of the Syriac Civilization did not long survive the fall of the Achaemenian Empire[2]—always excepting the still unbroken tradition of the Jews and the Samaritans.

8. SPENGLER'S HYPOTHETICAL 'MAGIAN CIVILIZATION'

In previous sections of this chapter we have taken note of the dissolution of no less than four civilizations. We have seen that, except for a lingering survival here and there,[3] the Sumero-Akkadian Civilization had disappeared by about A.D. 100, the Egyptiac and Hellenic civilizations by about A.D. 400,[4] and the Syriac Civilization, as we have now found, as early as the third or second century B.C. These are portentous historical events—particularly the disappearance of the Sumero-Akkadian and Egyptiac civilizations after they had each succeeded in maintaining their identity for more than three thousand years. Within the relatively short span of some five centuries, round about the beginning of the Christian Era, we find ourselves deprived of four of the principal landmarks on our chart of history. The Sumero-Akkadian and Egyptiac civilizations have been with us since the dawn of civilization itself, the Hellenic and Syriac civilizations since the later centuries of the second millennium B.C. Their departure leaves what looks, at least at first sight, like 'a perfect and absolute blank' on the chart in the space that should be occupied by the history of the heart of the *Oikoumenê* in its ensuing chapter. It is true that, farther east, we can continue to follow the threads of history continuously in India and in Eastern Asia. Farther west, again, we obtain a new landmark when the Western Civilization, which

---

[1] A. Dupont-Sommer: *Les Araméens*, p. 99.

[2] H. Werner has made the point that I have not succeeded in demonstrating that there was any *inner* connexion between the Achaemenian Empire and the Caliphate (*Deutsche Vierteljahrsschrift für Literaturwissenschaft und Geistesgeschichte*, 29. Jahrgang, xxix. Band (1955), p. 543).

[3] e.g. the Sumero-Akkadian Civilization survived in the Aramaic-speaking community at Harran, on the River Balikh, which was still worshipping the gods of the Sumero-Akkadian pantheon in the ninth century of the Christian Era, though it was within a stone's throw of the Syriac Christian metropolis Urfa (see viii. 408, footnote 5). Harran had been an early north-western outpost of the Sumeric Civilization and a seat—only second in prestige to Ur itself—of the worship of the Sumeric moon-god Nanna (Nannar) under his Akkadian name Sin.

[4] The Hellenic Civilization, too, survived here and there until the ninth century of the Christian Era. In A.D. 800 the Olympian gods were still being worshipped in the Mani (the Taenarum peninsula of the Peloponnese); and Chersonesus Taurica in the Crimea (on the site afterwards occupied by the Russian fortress of Sebastopol) was still an independent Greek city-state, though, by this date, a Christian one.

is still alive today, looms up above the historian's horizon. But Spengler, and Bagby following him, date the emergence of a distinctive Western Civilization no earlier than the eleventh century of the Christian Era; and, even if one dates it, as I do, before the end of the seventh century, there is still an interregnum of about three hundred years between the disappearance of the Hellenic Civilization and the emergence of the Western Civilization, and one of not less than about seven hundred years, on the shortest count, if we reckon back from the emergence of the Western Civilization to the submergence of the Syriac Civilization in the third or second century B.C.

What, then, is the configuration of history during this intervening period in the vast region extending from the western borders of India to the Pillars of Hercules? This region includes the heart of the *Oikou-menê* and the cradle of civilization in the Fertile Crescent, as well as the *Oikoumenê*'s westward extensions; and the period during which the configuration of its history is enigmatic is the crucial one that saw the epiphany first of Christianity and then of Islam, followed in either case by the conversion of a large part of the human race to the new religion. Evidently this period in the history of this portion of the *Oikoumenê* cannot in truth be void and without form. If one is trying to make a comprehensive study of human affairs, one cannot resign oneself to leaving this vast and vital tract of one's chart unmapped. How, then, ought the apparently blank space to be filled?

Spengler proposes to fill it by a characteristically original and auda-cious operation. He posits the presence here of an independent civi-lization with a distinctive character of its own which he indicates by labelling this hypothetical civilization the 'Magian' one.[1] He suggests, persuasively, that this civilization's existence had remained unrecognized until he dragged it up into the light, because it made its first appearance in disguise and has led a subterranean existence since then. It has not ever quite avowed its identity, and consequently has not ever been acknowledged to be a separate, independent, and distinctive civilization in its own right.

The 'Magian Civilization' comes on to the stage of history as a 'pseudo-morphosis' (a concept that is one of the most brilliant of Spengler's in-numerable flashes of insight).[2] After Alexander had forcibly imposed the Hellenic Civilization's ascendancy on Egypt and South-West Asia, social and cultural activities in this region assumed an Hellenic form for the next thousand years. But Spengler finds that this imported Hellen-ism never penetrated more than skin-deep. From first to last, he main-tains, it was a deceptive veneer, and the underlying reality, masked by it, was the genesis and growth of a new civilization. The progress of this can be traced, he suggests, in the history of the progressive Oriental reactions against Hellenism, not just on the military and political plane but, more significantly, on the cultural plane—above all, in the field of religion taken in the broadest sense of the word. Following the scent that

---

[1] See O. Spengler: *Der Untergang des Abendlandes*, vol. ii, chap. 3: *A*. 'Historische Pseudomorphosen'; *B*. 'Die Magische Seele'.
[2] See further the Annex to Chapter XVIII on pp. 670–4.

Spengler has signalled to us, we may perhaps find the first germ of the Magian Civilization sprouting within Alexander's lifetime—if we can detect this in the foundation of the Stoic school of *soi disant* Hellenic philosophy by the Phoenician Zeno of Citium (*vivebat circa* 335/3–261 B.C.).[1] At any rate, Zeno's Syrian successor, Poseidonius of Apamea (*vivebat circa* 135 B.C.–51 B.C.), is at least a percursor of the Magian style of culture as Spengler portrays it. This new civilization eventually flowers, according to Spengler, in Christianity and Islam; but it also embraces Judaism and Zoroastrianism; in Spengler's view they have been swept into the Magian Civilization's net, though they have been in existence since, at latest, the sixth century B.C., and one of the two, Judaism, has antecedents in Judah and Israel that can be traced back to the latter part of the second millennium B.C. The Magian Civilization is, in fact, capacious. It can be made to hold all religions and all peoples in the *Oikoumenê*, west of the Hindu World, since the beginning of the Christian Era at the latest. The one exception is the Western Civilization. This cannot be retained within Magian meshes, and therefore it has to be allowed its independence.[2]

In this reading of history, Spengler has put his finger on some unquestionable and important historical truths. It is true that there was a series of Oriental reactions against the Hellenic ascendancy, and that these culminated in the conversion of the Hellenic World to Christianity and in the subsequent conversion of about half the Christian World to Islam. It is also true that Christianity, as well as the other Oriental religions that competed with it in the Hellenic mission-field, commended itself to the Hellenes by presenting itself to them in Hellenic dress, though the living body which this tactful and attractive dress concealed was so alien to Hellenism that conversion to Christianity spelled the dissolution of the Hellenic Civilization. Finally, it is true, as we have seen in the preceding section of this chapter, that something new did arise in South-West Asia soon after the beginning of the Christian Era. The eastern dialect of the Aramaic language became a literary vehicle for three South-West Asian religions: Judaism (in its Babylonian wing), Christianity, and Mandaeanism. We may add that the Pehlevi alphabet was the script in which the Zoroastrian scriptures (the Avesta) were eventually committed to writing, and that the Pehlevi language was used for the writing of the commentaries that were the Zoroastrian equivalent of the Jewish Talmud. Zoroastrianism, which seems to have arisen in the Iranian-speaking countries north-east of the Caspian Gates,[3] found a second home in North-West Iran. From about the beginning of the Christian Era onwards the Arsacid Parthian emperors seem to have

---

[1] W. F. Albright points out that two of Zeno's disciples, including his successor, Chrysippus, were Cilicians. Chrysippus's fellow Cilician, Antipater, came from Tarsus, which was afterwards to produce Saint Paul. Another of Zeno's disciples, Diogenes, was a Babylonian (*From the Stone Age to Christianity*, 2nd ed., p. 339). In the second century B.C. the Epicurean philosopher Philodemus came from Gadara or, more probably, from Gezer, and the Platonic philosopher Antiochus from Ascalon. The Epicurean philosopher Zeno came from Sidon (ibid., p. 344). The Platonic philosopher Cleitomachus-Hasdrubal, the disciple and successor of Carneades, was a Carthaginian who came to Athens in the fortieth year of his age.

[2] See pp. 89–90 and 92–93.   [3] See p. 436, footnote 4.

been more or less devout Zoroastrians; and, after the overthrow of the Arsacids by the Sasanids in the third decade of the third century of the Christian Era, Zoroastrianism became the established religion of the Sasanian Persian Empire until this, in its turn, was overthrown in the seventh century by the Muslim Arabs.

Do these symptoms of new life in the regions under Hellenic ascendancy bear out Spengler's hypothesis? An objection brought forward by Christopher Dawson is, surely, unanswerable. In discussing whether Spengler's construction of a 'Magian Civilization' can stand up to criticism, Dawson observes that

'certainly the new elements in later Hellenistic civilization may be explained as due to Oriental influences, but these influences come, not from the budding energies of a new people, but from older peoples whose cultural development was even older than that of the Hellenes.'[1]

As Dawson sees it,[2] and in this he is surely right,

'the Gospels and Primitive Christianity belong rather to the last stage of the Judaeo-Aramaean culture[3]—a culture which had expressed its "heroic" phase a thousand years earlier in the sagas of Sampson, of Deborah, of Gideon, and the like.'

The Zoroastrianism of the Christian Era likewise has antecedents that can be traced back, as we have seen, at least as far as the beginning of the sixth century B.C. In fact, all the main elements from which Spengler has compounded his 'Magian Civilization' have a continuity with the Syriac and Iranian civilizations which is not only recognizable by the historian but—what is still more to the point—is, and always has been, recognized by the communities that are assigned to the 'Magian Civilization' on Spengler's hypothesis.

Thus, whatever label we give to the civilization of which the Jews and the Zoroastrians are representatives, it cannot have been one that was non-existent before the beginning of the Christian Era. And, since the Zoroastrians, the Jews, and the adherents of religions derived from Judaism are the principal participants in the 'Magian Civilization' in Spengler's picture of it, we must conclude that there never was such a thing. We are therefore still left with the problem of filling the apparent blank in the chart of history which Spengler has sought to fill by an hypothesis that is brilliant but untenable.

9. A SYRIAC-HELLENIC CULTURE-COMPOST

The apparent blank in the chart must be an illusion. It must conceal some positive historical reality. If this reality is not a new independent and distinctive civilization, it must be some socio-cultural phenomenon of some other kind. Can we now identify this? Dawson has, I think, found the clue[4] in observing that the distinctive feature of the last stage

---

[1] *The Dynamics of World History*, p. 382.   [2] Ibid.
[3] Dawson's 'Judaeo-Aramaean culture' would seem to be more or less equivalent to my 'Syriac Civilization' (A. J. T.).
[4] In *The Dynamics of World History*, p. 385.

of culture is not decay but syncretism. Perhaps one may modify Dawson's dictum by putting it that 'decay' and 'syncretism'—or, in Borkenau's terms, 'decay' and 'creation'[1]—are two aspects of one process. The process is the mysterious one that we call change. Its nature eludes logical formulation, as we have seen.[2] But at least this much is clear: there can be no new crop without a fertile soil to nourish it; and the best fertilizer for fostering new life is the dead and decaying refuse bequeathed by an old crop.

> Cedit enim rerum novitate extrusa vetustas
> semper, et ex aliis aliud reparare necessest. . . .
> materies opus est ut crescant postera saecla. . . .
> sic alid ex alio nunquam desistet oriri.[3]

In and immediately around the Fertile Crescent, civilizations have jostled each other at exceptionally close quarters, and their remains have therefore lain thick on the ground. Here, therefore, we may expect to find the cumulative deposits of culture piling up to an exceptional thickness. This will be comparable to the literal thickness of the pile of strata, deposited by the debris of successive occupations, that has built itself up, in the course of ages, into an artificial miniature mountain such as is the *tell* at Jericho or the *tell* at Ur. We may also expect to find that the culture-deposits are not homogeneous, but have the consistency of a compost in which the decaying remains of more than one culture have mixed and blended. On the analogy of the physical phenomena of the vegetation-cycle, we may expect, in the third place, to find that a culture-compost, compounded of the remains of several cultures, is a richer fertilizer than the remains of a single culture, and that a proportionate vitality and luxuriance is exhibited by a crop that has sprung from this exceptionally nourishing soil.[4] In the chapter of history that we are now trying to elucidate the salient event is the contemporaneous decay of no less than four civilizations. The culture-compost deposited by them in the process must have been particularly thick and rich. Perhaps here we have the historical substance that really fills our history-book's apparently blank pages.

Of the four civilizations that decomposed in the course of about five centuries running from the second century B.C. to the fourth century of the Christian Era, the Syriac and the Hellenic manifestly played a more active part than the Sumero-Akkadian and the Egyptiac. The huge dead trunks of these two ancient and gigantic trees provided, between them, a prodigious quantity of potentially fertile decaying organic matter. But

[1] 'It is only when petrifaction has been followed by collapse that the creative process of recasting begins' (F. Borkenau in *Merkur*, July, 1949, p. 635).

[2] On pp. 252–4.

[3] Lucretius: *De Rerum Natura*, Book III, ll. 964–5, 967, 970. 'Something old is always giving way; it is always being pushed aside by something new. Everything has to be built up out of something else. . . . Nature needs matter to enable future generations to grow. . . . This process by which one thing arises out of another will never cease.'

[4] In this context richness and vitality have to be measured by spiritual standards. Christopher Dawson makes the point that 'the fate of a civilization is not determined solely, or even predominantly, by political and economic causes. The age of the decline of the Roman Empire was also an age of spiritual rebirth, which prepared the way, not only for the coming of mediaeval [Western] Christendom, but also for the civilizations of Byzantium and Islam' (*The Dynamics of World History*, p. 408).

the conversion of dead matter into a fertilizer requires the action of solvents, and this was evidently the particular contribution of the Syriac and Hellenic civilizations to the total result. Each of them was a potent solvent by itself, as their individual catalytic feats testify. In combination, their potency was more than doubled; and they entered into a more and more intimate combination with each other in the course of their histories. Indeed, in each of the two histories, this tendency towards syncretism seldom faltered, and it persistently increased in intensity.

One of the Syriac Society's feats has been noticed already in this chapter. Before it succumbed, in its turn, to the solvent action of the Hellenic Civilization, the Syriac Civilization had gone so far towards dissolving the Sumero-Akkadian Civilization that the process went on to its conclusion even after the participants in the Syriac Civilization had lost consciousness of their society's distinctive cultural identity. It is easy to see that, when a culture has gone this far along the road towards disintegration, its potency as a solvent may be greater than in the earlier stage of its history in which its own fabric was still more or less intact.[1] However, this was not the first time that the Syriac Civilization had taken a conqueror captive.

Before its forcible incorporation in the Sumero-Akkadian World as a result of Assyrian and Neobabylonian annexations and deportations in and after the eighth century B.C., the Syriac Society had been similarly incorporated in the New Empire of Egypt in the second half of the second millennium B.C. At that time the Syriac Civilization was only in its formative stage; yet even at this early stage the Syriac culture made an impression on the Egyptiac culture, though this had a harder grain than the Sumero-Akkadian culture had. In this period of Egypt's political domination over Syria the Egyptians not only adopted Canaanite musical instruments[2] (and presumably the style of music that was played on them). They received numerous Canaanite words (including the Canaanite names of the borrowed musical instruments) into their vocabulary. More significant still, they received into their pantheon a number of Canaanite goddesses and gods: e.g. Ashtart (Astarte), 'Anath, Hauron, Rashap.[3] This penetration of the Egyptiac culture by elements of the Syriac culture was remarkable in a period of Egyptiac history in which the conscious attitude of the Egyptians was a chauvinistic reaction against Asian influences that were associated in Egyptian minds with the bitter memories of the Hyksos conquest and domination of Egypt.

The foothold in the Egyptiac World that was gained, nevertheless, by Canaanite influences in the Age of the New Empire was the first stage in the dissolution of the Egyptiac culture by exotic solvents, though it needed the reinforcement of the Syriac solvent by the Hellenic one to overcome the Egyptiac Civilization's immense capacity for self-conservation, and the process was not completed till the Egyptians eventually adopted the Christian religion and the Coptic version of the Greek

---

[1] See viii. 501–8.
[2] W. F. Albright: *Archaeology and the Religion of Israel*, 4th ed., p. 14.
[3] W. F. Albright: *From the Stone Age to Christianity*, 2nd ed., pp. 12 and 112.

alphabet. The task of dissolving the monolithic Egyptiac Civilization required, in fact, the combined action of the Syriac Civilization, the Hellenic Civilization, and a higher religion, rooted in a Syriac-Hellenic culture-compost, that was a more powerful solvent than either the Syriac or the Hellenic Civilization operating separately.

The reciprocal influence and counter-influence of the Syriac and Hellenic civilizations on each other was also exerted over a long period of time, and, as time went on, ever more intensively. The eventual effect was to decompose each of the two, and to compound their tissues into a new fabric, which, though composite, was so closely compacted that its original components came to be almost indistinguishable. At least as early as the eighth century B.C. the Syriac Civilization produced a permanent effect on the Hellenic by giving it the Phoenician alphabet. In the seventh century it gave it a Phoenician style of art which was itself an amalgam of the Egyptiac and Akkadian styles. In the fourth century it gave it a Phoenician code of ethics and system of cosmology: the Stoic philosophy, whose founder, Zeno, was a citizen of the Cypriot Phoenician city-state Citium. The cultural intercourse between the Syriac and Hellenic worlds was reciprocal, and Hellenism was radiating into Syria long before the time of Alexander the Great.[1] By the fifth century B.C. Syria was importing Hellenic pottery and other Hellenic wares and works of art, and was also adopting the Attic standard of coinage. 'By the middle of the fourth century Greek coins were being imitated by the Persian satraps and local rulers of Cilicia, Syria, and Palestine'[2] (including the priest-presidents of the autonomous Jewish state in Judaea). Even at the opposite extremity of the Syriac World from its Phoenician façade facing the Hellenic World, 'the South Arabians then fashioned crude imitations of Attic coins'.[3] The potency of this previous radiation of Hellenic culture into the Syriac World goes far towards explaining the rapidity with which the Syriac World succumbed to Hellenism after Alexander's military conquest of the Achaemenian dominions in South-West Asia and Egypt. The eventual result, however, was the decomposition of Hellenism as well.

The Syriac Civilization did not achieve this posthumous revenge by assaulting Hellenism single-handed. It was, indeed, no longer in a position to mount a counter-offensive, since by this time it was no longer in being. Anyway, a single-handed assault on Hellenism by an alien culture would have courted a repulse at any time from the fifth century B.C. onwards. From that time on, the Hellenes were so strongly convinced of the superiority of their own civilization over all others that they were no longer in the mood, as they had been in earlier days, to accept gifts from an alien culture that presented itself as such. In the Post-Alexandrine Age the alien cultural agencies that eventually brought Hellenism down found that they could not stalk their quarry with any hope of success unless they disguised themselves in Hellenic dress. Stoicism, for example, presented in terms of Hellenic philosophy a *Weltenschauung* that was akin to that of the prophets of Israel and Judah. But this self-transformation

---

[1] See Albright: *From the Stone Age to Christianity*, 2nd ed., pp. 337–8.
[2] Ibid., p. 338.   [3] Ibid.

was no mere sly and superficial masquerade; it was a genuine metamorphosis; and the decomposition of Hellenism was achieved by
an instrumentality that was, itself, already semi-Hellenic. When the
Hellenic Civilization that had decomposed the Syriac Civilization was
hoist with its own petard, there was an Hellenic as well as a Syriac ingredient in the lethal charge of gunpowder. The final dissolution of
Hellenism was the work of Christianity; and it is significant that, of all
the non-Hellenic religions that competed for the conversion of Hellenic
souls in the age of the Hellenic universal state, Christianity went the
farthest in Hellenizing itself. Besides presenting itself visually in the
established forms of Hellenic art, Christianity, like its forerunner
Stoicism, expressed itself intellectually in terms of Hellenic philosophy.
More than that, its crucial departure from its parent religion, Judaism—
namely, the belief that Jesus was the Son of God and was, in fact, one of
the three persons in a triune godhead—was, from the standpoint of
Jewish monotheism, a shocking concession to two Hellenic religious
aberrations: man-worship and polytheism.

It is also significant that Islam, which was a conscious and deliberate
reaction against Christianity's Hellenizing departure from Jewish monotheism, did not revert to Judaism's strictly un-Hellenic tradition. When
Islam was confronted with the need to equip itself with a systematic
theology, it worked this out on the pattern of Christian theology;[1] and
the Islamic theologians found, as their Christian predecessors had
found, that they needed to draw upon Hellenic philosophy for their
theological purpose and that they could not do this effectively without
going back to the Hellenic fountain-head. From the ninth century of the
Christian Era onwards the works of the Hellenic philosophers and
scientists themselves became part of the recognized, and even obligatory,
apparatus of Islamic culture,[2] as they had become part of the apparatus

[1] This work was done for Islam by converts from Christianity and Zoroastrianism.
See pp. 467, 471, and 671, footnote 1.
[2] Any selection of references to the extensive literature on this subject is inevitably
arbitrary. Among many other works, see D. S. Margoliouth: *The Early Development
of Mohammedanism* (London 1914, Willians & Norgate); J. W. Sweetman: *Islam and
Christian Theology* (London, Lutterworth Press: Part I, vol. i, 1945; Part I, vol. ii, 1947;
Part II, vol. i, 1955); De Lacy O'Leary: *How Greek Science Passed to the Arabs* (London
1948, Routledge & Kegan Paul); A. J. Wensinck: *La Pensée de Ghazzālī* (Paris 1940,
Adrien-Maisonneuve); W. Montgomery Watt: *The Faith and Practice of Al-Ghasālī*
(London 1953, Allen & Unwin); A. J. Arberry: *Avicenna on Theology* (London
1951, John Murray); L. Gardet and M.-M. Anawati: *Introduction à la Théologie
Musulmane* (Paris 1948, Vrin), pp. 220–4 ('Intégration de l'Hellénisme').
This last-mentioned work brings out the conditions and the limitations of Islam's
reception of Hellenism.
'C'est avant tout à titre d'arme défensive . . . que le kalâm demandera à l'apport
hellénistique certaines lignes au moins de son armature intellectuelle' (p. 222). 'Né
d'une réflexion plus poussée des docteurs musulmans sur les sciences religieuses qu'il
s'agissait de défendre, c'est grâce à l'influence de la philosophie grecque venue du
dehors que le kalâm put cependant se constituer: tout à la fois en luttant contre elle et en
lui empruntant . . . la méthode argumentative qui lui manquait' (p. 224).
The authors point out, ibid., that the relation of Christian theology to Hellenism was
more positive and more intimate; yet its relation, too, was partly defensive.
'In marking the distinction of its doctrine from the rationalisations by which it felt the
faith was threatened, the Church was forced, in order that the distinction should be
apparent, to define its dogma in the same kind of language as that in which the heresies
themselves were framed; it was forced, that is, to use the language of philosophy, to
adapt for its own use expressions and phrases which belonged precisely to that world of

of Christian culture since the fourth century. Dawson is right in pointing out[1] that Islam and Christianity both have roots in a composite Helleno-Judaic soil.

The compositeness of the soil in which Islam and Christianity both germinated is one key to the explanation of the fission of Judaic religion into three separate and rival sects. Why did Christianity break away from Judaism in the first instance? And why, when Islam, in its turn, had broken away from Christianity in the direction of Judaism, did Islam not revert to Judaism? Why did it set itself up as a separate sect that was not Christian but was not Jewish either? Part, at least, of the explanation[2] of this unhappy course of Judaic religious history is to be found in a residual incompatibility between the Syriac and the Hellenic element in the Syriac-Hellenic culture-compost that had been compounded in the course of the five centuries ending with the fourth century of the Christian Era. The coalescence of the two elements had been nearly complete but not quite; and the resulting cultural amalgam had been acceptable to nearly, but not quite, all the peoples in the section of the *Oikoumenê* between India and the Atlantic. Thus the psychological harmony produced by this all but completely successful feat of cultural fusion had been subject to strains, and these strains partly account for the subsequent religious schisms.[3]

Why did not Judaism, which was the first of the three Judaic religions, seize the opportunity for becoming the missionary religion, addressing itself to all mankind, that its two daughter religions, Christianity and Islam, have each since become? Why did it leave this great field free for these upstart travesties of itself, when it might have occupied the field in advance? Judaism did take a step in this direction. The Aramaic-speaking Galilaean-Jewish religious teacher Jesus had a Greek-speaking Alexandrian Jewish contemporary, Philo, who was even more at home in the world of Hellenic thought than he was in the world of Jewish religious faith. Philo devoted his intellectual powers to working out a concordance between the Torah and Hellenic philosophy. Perhaps he may have looked forward to accomplishing what Paul eventually achieved: the creation of a church, open to all mankind, through an unlimited increase in the number of the non-Jewish adherents of Judaism—marginal 'God-fearers' as well as thorough-going proselytes—who had already gathered round the Jewish communities dispersed through the Hellenic World. As it turned out, Philo proved to have worked, not for Jewry or for Judaism, but for a nascent Christian Church. Gentile Christianity, not

concepts against whose dominance it was most anxious to protect its own doctrine' (P. Sherrard: *The Greek East and the Latin West* (London 1959, Oxford University Press), pp. 57–58). [1] In *The Dynamics of World History*, pp. 385–6.
[2] The secessions of Christianity and Islam from Judaism are also partly explicable as reactions to Jewish nationalism (see pp. 85–88 and 511–17).
[3] With this qualification we can perhaps accept Father G. F. Klenk's dictum (in *Stimmen der Zeit*, No. 145 (1949–50), pp. 376–84) that it would be an error, at least in the field of religion, to talk of a fundamental opposition between Hellenism and the Syriac way of life. An opposition of this kind between East and West did not declare itself, Father Klenk maintains, till much later, when it made its appearance in the form of the schism between the Eastern Orthodox and the Western Christian Church. My comment would be that this opposition had already declared itself, long before that, in the previous schisms between Judaism, Christianity, and Islam.

Rabbinical Judaism, was Philo's heir. Without having to answer the question whether the Palestinian Pharisees could have been won over to Philonism in any circumstances, we can say for certain that any such possibility vanished for ever after the disastrous military collision between Palestinian Judaism and Hellenism in the Romano-Jewish War of A.D. 66–70. After Jewry had suffered that crushing material disaster, it turned inwards on itself; and the Hellenizing Jews of the diasporá, as well as their gentile proselytes and outer fringe, had to choose between the two extremes of abandoning Judaism for gentile Christianity and embracing a now deliberately anti-Hellenic Palestinian Pharisaism. The only Jews who survived in diasporá were those who made the second of these two choices, and their choice carried the Aramaic and Hebrew (i.e. Canaanite) languages and alphabets all over the Greek-speaking and Latin-speaking world. Thus at this critical point in history the Jews shook the Syriac-Hellenic culture-compost from off their feet and made up their minds to live thenceforward as exclusively Syriac dissenters in a Syriac-Hellenic cultural environment.

A parallel decision had been taken, long since, by the Iranians. The destruction of the Achaemenian Empire by Alexander had been, for them, as great a material disaster as the destruction of Jerusalem in A.D. 70 was for the Jews, and they had already reacted to this as the Jews reacted to that. Alexander had seen through the Hellenic prejudice against Iranians when he had met these in personal intercourse, and he had dreamed of an Helleno-Iranian partnership, on a footing of equality, for the government of the *Oikoumenê*. Alexander's attempts to translate this generous dream into a reality fell flat—except in Zarathustra's country, where the Iranian natives and Hellenic settlers in the Bactrian successor-state of the Achaemenian Empire did, apparently, fraternize, perhaps because both alike were threatened by a common danger from the adjacent Eurasian Nomads.[1] Except in Bactria, the Iranians, like the Jews, rejected the Syriac-Hellenic cultural syncretism that most of the *Oikoumenê* west of India was finding acceptable in the Post-Alexandrine Age.[2]

[1] A common interest in parrying this same threat induced the Iranian natives and the Arab settlers in Khurāsān to fraternize in the eighth century of the Christian Era (see ii. 141, footnote 3).

[2] The cause of this failure of Alexander's policy of political reconciliation and cultural fusion to capture the imagination and allegiance of the Iranian peoples on the plateau was not solely an attitude of resentment and hostility on the Iranian side. The failure was due also, in large part, to the repudiation, or at least neglect, of Alexander's policy by the Macedonian war-lords who emerged as the survivors from the forty-years-long struggle for existence for the possession of Alexander's heritage. It is true that the Seleucidae, who acquired the Iranian provinces, were the least illiberal of Alexander's successors in their treatment of the alien peoples under their rule. Seleucus I Nicator, for instance, was singular in remaining faithful to his Iranian wife Apame when, after Alexander's death, other Macedonian grandees repudiated the Iranian wives whom Alexander had wished upon them in 324 B.C. in his pursuit of his policy of a union of hearts. Yet the Seleucid Monarchy was based on an ascendancy of the Macedonian military settlements (*katoikiai*) and non-Macedonian Greek colonial city-states, which the Seleucidae sowed thick throughout their dominions, over the vast non-Hellenic majority of the population.

The Post-Alexandrine chapter of history in Iran might perhaps have taken a different turn if Alexander's eventual successors there had been animated by the spirit of Peucestas, who was appointed satrap of Persis (Fars) by Alexander in 324 B.C. and held this position till 316 B.C. Alexander chose Peucestas for this delicate mission of governing

This synthetic culture prevailed, in the course of that age, from the south-west foot of the Iranian plateau westwards to the Atlantic, save for one pocket of dissident Jews in Babylonia and another in Palestine which after the second Romano-Jewish War (*debellatum* A.D. 132–5), was reduced to a remnant in Galilee. When the cultural unification of the *Oikoumenê*, west of Iran, had found religious expression and institutional form in a common Christianity in which the Syriac and the Hellenic element were nicely balanced, it must have looked to contemporaries as if the unity, established on this basis, had a long future ahead of it. However, even a common adherence to Christianity did not avail to relax completely the tension between the descendants of the people whom Alexander had forcibly annexed to the Hellenic World and the descendants of these people's Greek, and subsequently also Roman, rulers.[1] This residual tension declared itself, as we have seen, in the successive schisms between the Graeco-Roman ('Melchite') Church and the Nestorians, and between the same officially established church and the Monophysites. These resistance movements within the Christian Church were a continuation, on the theological and linguistic planes, of a struggle that had been waged in previous centuries by force of arms. The military resistance was resumed, and was carried this time to a successful conclusion, by the Muslim Arabs. The Arab conquest was eventually followed by the conversion to Islam of the majority of the population of the Caliphate, except for a remnant of Jews, Zoroastrians, and Christians who succeeded in still maintaining their communal identity in diasporá.

This left the *Oikoumenê*, west of India, partitioned between Dar-al-Islam and Christendom, but this fission did not have the effect of reproducing what had been the state of affairs during the early centuries of the last millennium B.C., when the Syriac and Hellenic civilizations had coexisted as two separate and distinct cultures. It was impossible to undo the effects of the fusion between them which had begun as far back as the eighth century B.C. and which had reached its climax, after each of them had lost its identity, in the union of their two former domains in the oecumenical Christendom of the fourth to the seventh century of the Christian Era. Islam and the half of Christendom that survived its inroads might seem irreconcilable to their respective adherents; yet both were products of a combination of two identical elements—a Syriac element and an Hellenic one—and neither Christianity nor Islam could

the home-land of the deposed Persian imperial people because Peucestas had already shown a liking for them and for their way of life. He had taken the trouble to learn the West Iranian language, and he had no inhibition against wearing Persian dress. Peucestas's Persophilism did, in fact, win for him the loyalty, and even affection, of his Persian subjects, and at least one Farsi notable protested when Peucestas was deprived of the governorship of Persis by Antigonus. In consulting his own personal interests at the expense of the interests of Macedon and Hellas, Antigonus made history. Persis was one of the first Iranian countries to shake off Macedonian rule; and, in the third century of the Christian Era, it did again what it had done in the sixth century B.C. For the second time it gave birth to a Persian Empire.

[1] Roman rule was never successfully established over 'Iraq (Babylonia). The Emperor Trajan's momentary success and swiftly following failure demonstrated that a permanent incorporation of Babylonia in the Roman Empire was beyond Rome's power. On the other hand, Christianity had become the predominant religion in 'Iraq before the date of the Muslim Arab conquest in the seventh century of the Christian Era.

—or can—purge itself of either element without committing suicide. The Syriac and the Hellenic element are both ineradicable, not only in Christianity and Islam themselves, but also in the Christian and Islamic civilizations for which they have respectively served as chrysalises.

10. THE SYRIAC-HELLENIC CULTURE-COMPOST'S HARVEST

What has been the sequel to the Syriac and Hellenic civilizations' decomposition and amalgamation? This question does not arise if one follows Spengler in seeing the culture of the *Oikoumenê*, west of India, in the first millennium of the Christian Era as being a separate and distinctive civilization. As we have noted in another chapter,[1] civilizations are not organisms, and one of the differences between a civilization and an organism is that a civilization has no fixed maximum life-span. There is no reason why a civilization should not remain in existence for more than three thousand years. We know of two in the Old World, the Sumero-Akkadian and the Egyptiac, which did each remain in existence for more than three thousand years. Accordingly, if we accepted Spengler's hypothesis, we could imagine his hypothetical 'Magian Civilization' surviving, as a going concern, down to the present day, and we could use it, as he and Bagby do, as a hold-all.[2] We could stow away in it every cultural phenomenon at the west end of the Old World, since the beginning of the Christian Era, which we do not see how to dispose of otherwise. If, however, we think of the Syriac-Hellenic syncretism, not as being a new civilization, but as being a culture-compost compounded from intermingled fibres of two old civilizations as a result of their decomposition, then we do have to ask ourselves: What happened after that? This question now forces itself upon us because a compost—whether vegetational or cultural—is inevitably a transitory state of things. A compost is created by a combination of decaying remnants of last year's crop; it is exhausted in the process of giving sustenance to this year's crop. Therefore, if we find that there has been a compost, we have to expect that it will have produced a harvest. What, then, has been the Syriac-Hellenic cultural syncretism's harvest? The answer is: two missionary religions and several civilizations which these two religions have incidentally mothered.

Christianity and Islam are manifestly two specimens of one and the same species. Both have sprung from the same syncretism of the debris of two extinct civilizations. Both address themselves to all mankind and aim at nothing short of the conversion of the whole World. Both established themselves first within the framework of a universal state, progressively converted this state's population, and survived its fall, to go on spreading, far and wide, into regions beyond the fallen state's horizon. As far as I can see, this parallelism in the histories of Christianity and Islam is indisputable; and, if it is, I did not go astray in pointing it out in previous volumes. But I was, I now think, mistaken in associating Christianity more closely than Islam with the antecedent Hellenic Civilization and in associating Islam more closely than Christianity with

[1] Chapter VII, section 12, pp. 268–9.   [2] See pp. 89–90.

the antecedent Syriac Civilization. Both religions have both Syriac and Hellenic antecedents; and in both religions both these elements are of capital importance. It is therefore an error to think of Christianity and the Christian and Post-Christian civilizations as stemming primarily from the Hellenic Civilization, and to think of Islam and the Islamic Civilization as stemming primarily from the Syriac Civilization. Islam, Christianity, and the several civilizations that these two religions have mothered, are all products, direct or indirect, of an identical compost consisting of both Syriac and Hellenic elements.

My error on this point led me into another. As a result of deriving Islam from the Syriac Civilization exclusively, I thought of the Caliphate, within which Islam developed in its formative stage, as being a Syriac institution—a Syriac universal state—on the analogy of the Hellenic universal state embodied in the Roman Empire. The Roman Empire certainly played the same part in the early history of Christianity that the Caliphate played in the early history of Islam;[1] and the Roman Empire was, as I saw it and still see it, an Hellenic institution: the Hellenic universal state. But it does not follow that the Caliphate played an analogous part in Syriac history, just because it did play an analogous part in the history of Islam. I still think that I was right in connecting the Caliphate with the Achaemenian Empire, and in seeing the Caliphate as a resumption of this earlier polity. Their areas were approximately coincident, and each of them found its centre of gravity in 'Iraq (Babylonia), though the empire-builders who founded each of these two polities came from elsewhere (from Iran in the earlier case and from Arabia in the later one). But I now hold that the Achaemenian Empire and the Caliphate are, not two phases of a Syriac universal state, but two representatives of a long series of empires based on the agricultural productivity of the alluvial soil of the lower basin of the Tigris and Euphrates.

This series begins, as I now see it, with the Empire of Agade (*circa* 2360–2180 B.C.) and ends, perhaps, with the Safawi Empire (sixteenth and seventeenth centuries of the Christian Era), which failed in the end to hold 'Iraq against the 'Osmanli successors of the Roman Empire, or with the ephemeral eighteenth-century empire of Nadir Shah—the Afshar war-lord who succeeded in momentarily reuniting 'Iraq with Iran.[2] The Seleucid, Parthian, and Sasanian empires, which were all likewise based on 'Iraq, are other links in the chain. These three last-mentioned empires cover continuously the whole chronological interval between the destruction of the Achaemenian Empire and the establishment of the Caliphate. The recognition of these connecting links makes my association of the Caliphate with the Achaemenian Empire more convincing; but in doing that it refutes my hypothesis that the Achaemenian Empire and the Caliphate were products of the Syriac Civilization—in fact, successive embodiments of a Syriac universal state. The series of empires based on 'Iraq can be interpreted, more convincingly, as being products of the Sumero-Akkadian Civilization. This interpretation of them is self-evident down to the date of the extinction of the

---

Sumero-Akkadian Civilization in the later days of the Parthian Empire; but it is also reasonable to suppose that an institution may have a momentum that carries it on after the civilization that generated it has passed out of existence. This is still easier to imagine if the institution in question has, as it has in this case, an enduring[1] geographical, as well as an ephemeral cultural, basis. And this would explain the continuing recurrence of empires based on 'Iraq down to the seventeenth century of the Christian Era.

In assigning the Achaemenian Empire to the Sumero-Akkadian Civilization and seeing in the Caliphate one of the Sumero-Akkadian Civilization's posthumous political products, one is, of course, implying that the Syriac Civilization did not ever produce a universal state of its own. This is, after all, what we should expect *a priori*, considering the comparative earliness of the stage in Syriac history at which the local states of the Syriac World lost their independence and were liquidated. After that, the Syriac Society had to live as a hermit crab within political frameworks that were not of its own making. Its success in maintaining its cultural identity under these adverse political conditions is one of the most remarkable of the Syriac Civilization's many remarkable feats. The uprooted and scattered speakers of the Aramaic *koinê* lived to see the Persian builders of the Achaemenian Empire prefer the Aramaic *koinê* to both Medo-Persian and Akkadian for use as an imperial *lingua franca*; and this oecumenical Aramaic language and alphabet had drawn the Iranian peoples into the Syriac Civilization's field before this civilization lost its identity except for the survival of the Samaritans and the Jews. The Jews and the Samaritans have outdone all other Syriac communities in managing to survive, as distinct communities, right down to the present day.[2]

The interpretation of history that has been given in this chapter up to this point maintains the historical connexion between the Syriac and Hellenic civilizations on the one hand, and the Christian and Muslim religions on the other, that I have assumed in volume i of this book. But the configuration of this passage of history that emerges from my present reconsideration of it is materially different. In my revised picture, Christianity and Islam are each derived from both the Syriac and the Hellenic Civilization, but neither religion is derived from either of these two civilizations direct. The immediate origin of both lies in a compost compounded of elements of the two civilizations after the civilizations themselves had both decomposed.

We have still to consider the affiliations and the status of the civilizations now in existence in that part of the *Oikoumenê* that lies to the west of the Hindu World. This question need not arise for anyone who is convinced of the reality of Spengler's hypothetical 'Magian Civilization'. He might simply take it for granted that this civilization is still a

---

[1] 'Enduring', not 'permanent', since the agricultural potential of 'Iraq, like that of Egypt, is a creation of human imagination, enterprise, organization, and industry; and, having been wrung from Nature by Man's efforts, it can revert to its original state of Nature if these efforts relax (see i. 315–18; ii. 42–43).

[2] A Jewish model for civilizations, in which the key institution is a diasporá, not a universal state, has been sketched on pp. 209–17.

going concern today and that what we think of as the Christian and Islamic worlds are really just two provinces of the 'Magian Civilization's' present-day domain. However, Spengler himself, and Bagby following him, shy away, as we have seen,[1] from labelling the civilization now existing in the West as a phase of the 'Magian Civilization' (or the 'Near Eastern Civilization', as Bagby has re-labelled it). Such a dismissal of the Western Civilization, and denial of its title to be regarded as being a separate and distinctive civilization in its own right, would fly too flatly in the face of manifest and intractable facts. The civilization that is in existence today in the West has distinctive characteristics of its own which are as definite as those of, say, the Hellenic Civilization or the Egyptiac or the Sumero-Akkadian or the Indian or the Chinese. The reality of each of these five specimens, at any rate, is indisputable, even if the status of others—the 'Magian' and the 'Syriac' among them—may be in doubt. To deny the reality of the Western Civilization would impugn the reality of all civilizations, and would thus be tantamount to denying the existence of the species itself. Students of history may discuss the date at which the distinctive lineaments of the Western Civilization first become discernible. Can we trace this civilization's distinctive identity back to the seventh century of the Christian Era or only to the eleventh century or the fifteenth or the seventeenth or the eighteenth? However late we may place the date of a distinctive Western Civilization's emergence, we shall be admitting that there is a Western Civilization today. The truth is that, today, this civilization not only exists but overshadows the rest of the World.

Spengler and Bagby have admitted the Western Civilization's reality and distinctiveness, but they have not realized that, in making this admission, they have implicitly acknowledged the existence, not just of the Western Civilization itself, but of a number of others as well which they leave unrecognized, packed away in the 'Magian' or 'Near Eastern' Civilization's capacious hold-all. The recognition of these other civilizations follows automatically from a recognition of the Western Civilization, because these other civilizations have the same title to be recognized that the Western Civilization has.

The Western Civilization has a Christian origin. The Christian religion has mothered it; and the Christian Church has served as the chrysalis from which it has emerged. But it is not the only civilization that stands in this relation to Christianity. The ecclesiastical chrysalis of the Western Civilization has been the Roman See, but the Roman Patriarchate is one of five. Rome has not ever succeeded in winning more than a temporary and local acceptance of her claim to supremacy over the entire Christian Church. This claim is rejected today by all the four Eastern Orthodox patriarchates—Constantinople, Antioch, Alexandria, and Jerusalem—and by the autocephalous Eastern Orthodox churches that are in communion with them. Moreover, the Eastern Orthodox Church's possession of two of its patriarchates is disputed by other Christian churches. There is a Coptic Monophysite, as well as an Orthodox, Patriarchate of Alexandria. There is both a Jacobite Monophysite

[1] On pp. 92–93.

and a Nestorian Dyophosite, as well as an Orthodox, Patriarchate of Antioch. This fission of the Christian Church has produced a plurality of Christendoms and Christian civilizations; and the Western Civilization is only one among them.

The West has been fond of imagining that it is the only civilization in Christendom. It has arrived at this picture of itself by ignoring the Nestorian and Monophysite Christendoms and by thinking of Eastern Orthodox Christendom as having been first subordinate to the West and then superfluous to it. Medieval Westerners wrote off the Eastern Orthodox Christians as being rebellious ecclesiastical subjects of the Roman See. Modern Western historians have followed this Western tradition. They have interpreted the history of the Eastern Orthodox Christian Byzantine (alias East Roman) Empire in Western terms. They have seen it as a temporary carapace which served to shield the Western World's eastern flank from Muslim assaults in the Western Civilization's early days, when it might have succumbed altogether to these attacks if it had been exposed to them at short range, as it did succumb in the Iberian Peninsula to a Muslim attack delivered at very long range from the Muslim Arabs' base. When the Byzantine carapace had served its purpose of allowing the Western Civilization time to grow strong enough to defend itself, it crumpled up, worsted at last by the blows that the Muslims had been raining on it all this time. The Western view about this is much the same today as it was in the fourteenth and fifteenth centuries. Sentimentally the East Roman Empire's fall was regrettable; practically, it did not now matter.

The Western reading of Eastern Orthodox history is, of course, belied by the historical facts. The Greek Christian Roman Empire fell to rise again in the shape of a Turkish Muslim Roman Empire; and the Eastern Orthodox Christian peoples' loss of their political independence did not bring either their existence or their civilization to an end. Moreover, one Eastern Orthodox country, Russia, never did lose its independence, and today Russia is challenging the West's ascendancy over the rest of the World. The West's attempt to read the history of this sister Christian civilization in Western terms, and to treat it as subordinate to the West, is, in fact, preposterous. Its preposterousness can be measured by a Westerner if he reminds himself of Eastern Orthodox Christendom's treatment of the Westerner's own civilization. In Eastern Orthodox Christian eyes the Western peoples have been semi-barbarian schismatics living in the penumbra of civilization. To an Orthodox theologian's mind the difference between Catholic and Protestant Western schismatic Christians is obscure, and anyway it is not significant, since they agree in holding the same aberrant Western doctrine about the Procession of the Holy Spirit. This Byzantine caricature of the West is no more preposterous than the Western caricature of Byzantine civilization and history.

The story of Christendom has repeated itself in Dar-al-Islam. Here, too, there have been, and are, more Islamic civilizations than one, and the cultural consequences of the break-up of the Caliphate are comparable to those of the break-up of the Roman Empire.[1] The subsequent

---

[1] The configuration of Islamic history has been dealt with in some detail in i. 67–72

division between an Eastern Orthodox Christian Civilization and a Western Christian Civilization, with Greek and Latin as their respective classical languages, has had its counterpart in a division between a distinctively Arabic Muslim Civilization and a distinctively Iranic Muslim Civilization whose classical language is, not Arabic, but New Persian. The fission of Dar-al-Islam into the domains of two distinct Islamic civilizations was confined to the linguistic and cultural plane. Unlike the corresponding fission in Christendom, it was not accompanied by an ecclesiastical schism over points of jurisdiction and of doctrine. But, when we have recognized the titles of each of the two Christian civilizations, it would be inconsistent to refuse to recognize that there have also been two distinct Islamic civilizations.[1]

At the beginning of the sixteenth century of the Christian Era the religious, as well as the cultural, configuration of the Islamic World underwent a revolutionary transformation. There was then a sudden and surprising revival of the military and political power of the Shi'ah, which had been dormant during the previous four or five hundred years. A Shi'i empire-builder, Isma'il Shah Safawi, now rapidly made himself master of Iran and 'Iraq, imposed his own ancestral variety of the Shi'ah on his subjects, and thereby split the Iranic Muslim World into mutually hostile fragments. Since then, the main division in the Islamic World has not been one between two cultures differentiated by their cultivation of two different classical languages. It has been a division between two incompatible views on a jurisdictional question that had split the Islamic World during the first four centuries of Islamic history. Today there are still two Islamic civilizations, as there were during the five centuries ending *circa* A.D. 1500; but they are no longer an Arabic and an Iranic one; they are a Sunni and a Shi'i one. Of these two, the Shi'i is relatively parochial. Today it is more or less confined to Iran, the north-western corner of Afghanistan, the Lebanon, and the Yaman, with a diasporá in Pakistan and India, and the Yamani Shi'is are not of the same sect as the Lebanese and the Iranian. The recrudescence of the Shi'ah in the heart of the Islamic World, followed by the pressure of the West in more recent times, has had the effect of drawing all the Sunnis together. Their sense of doctrinal unity has proved stronger than their linguistic and cultural differentiation. In the light of this, it might be nearest to the truth to say that today there is a unitary Islamic civilization based on the Sunnah, and to think of the Shi'i enclaves in present-day Islam as being no more than islands of dissent.

Even so, we are left with three civilizations—the Islamic, the Byzantine, and the Western—in the *Oikoumenê* west of the Hindu World; and we have still to consider the diasporás that survive in these three civilizations' domains.

The Jewish diasporá and the tiny remnant of the Samaritans in

and 347–402. I still hold the views there propounded. See further Chap. XIV of the present volume, pp. 461–76.

[1] In G. E. von Grunebaum's eyes, this conclusion 'is a lapse from historical perceptiveness induced by the temptations of a self-devouring system'. But he concedes that it is legitimate, and even convenient, to distinguish an Iranic and an Arabic 'segment' of the Islamic World as 'interacting groups within one and the same continuum' (*The Intent of Toynbee's History: A Cooperative Appraisal*).

Palestine, round Nablūs, are clearly survivals of the Syriac Civilization. The Jews and the Samaritans refused to allow themselves to be swallowed up in the Syriac-Hellenic cultural amalgam. They have preserved their identity, without a break, since the age of Syriac history before the political extinction of Israel, Judah, and the other independent states of the Syriac World. The Zoroastrian diasporá has likewise preserved its identity by refusing to be drawn into the Syriac-Hellenic syncretism. We shall reckon the Parsee community as being a third living representative of the Syriac Civilization if we consider that the convergence of the Syriac and the Iranian culture and their reciprocal influence on each other, in and after the Achaemenian Age, went to the length of cultural fusion. Otherwise, we must regard the Parsees as being living representatives of a separate civilization, which we shall have to label the 'Pre-Islamic Iranian'.

How are we to classify the surviving Nestorian and Monophysite Christian diasporás, and the two Monophysite Christian nations—the Armenians and the Amharas—that still possess national states of their own: the Republic of Erivan and the Empire of Ethiopia? When we have conceded that there are a Byzantine and a Western Christian Civilization, we can hardly refuse to give an equal status to the Monophysite and Nestorian quarters of Christendom. In the twelfth and thirteenth centuries of the Christian Era, Nestorian Christendom was sprinkled across the breadth of Asia from the Euphrates to the Yellow River, and Monophysite Christendom still extends from the Caucasus to the headwaters of the Blue Nile, with a solid link at each end of the chain, though the intermediate links in Syria and Egypt have now worn thin and the former link in Nubia has quite rusted away. These two quarters of Christendom have each played an important part in history; and an historian who ignores or depreciates them does this at the risk of falsifying his picture of both past and present. If we choose, we may classify them as 'abortive civilizations'[1] on the ground that they failed to fulfil the role for which their adherents had cast them, and therefore forfeited this role to the younger Islamic Civilization. Yet 'abortive', as well as effective, civilizations are specimens of the species; and, as such, they have to be taken into account.

If the foregoing survey is correct, an impressive crop of higher religions and civilizations has sprung from the culture-compost deposited by the decomposition and amalgamation of the Syriac and Hellenic civilizations. The higher religions in this cultural harvest are Christianity and Islam; the civilizations are those of the four Christendoms, together with an Islamic Civilization that first divided into two and then re-coalesced except for a Shi'i minority.[2]

---

[1] For my use of this term, see ii. 322–94 and 424–52, and the present volume, Chapter XVIII, p. 554.
[2] This picture of the configuration of the histories of civilizations in the Old World, west of India, since the last millennium B.C., seems to me to fit the complicated facts rather better than Spengler's picture fits them. But Spengler's attempt to solve the problem has found able supporters. Bagby swallows it whole, as has been noted, and Borkenau finds it at any rate more convincing than mine. Borkenau inclines to Spengler's and Bagby's view that a single civilization only, and not a litter of civilizations, has been generated by the coalescence of the Hellenic Civilization and the Syriac. 'One

These second thoughts on the configuration of the Syriac Civilization have inevitably run to some length because the subject of the inquiry is a complicated and a difficult one. We are dealing here with the history of the heart of the *Oikoumenê* in its most critical, and also most creative, phase. It will be seen that I have revised my original picture considerably. I shall not be surprised if my second picture is criticized as vigorously as my first has been; but I hope that, in any case, the reconsideration of the whole question in this chapter may at least help to elucidate a passage of history which is as important as it is enigmatic.

XIV. ISLAM'S PLACE IN HISTORY

ISLAM's epiphany was dramatic by comparison with Christianity's and Buddhism's. Jesus's life and death passed unnoticed at the time, except among the obscure and tiny band of His Galilaean Jewish disciples. Our information about His ministry comes exclusively from the scriptures of the Christian Church. We should know next to nothing about it if our only sources were the Hellenic literature in Greek and Latin and the Jewish literature in Aramaic of the first century of the Christian Era. Siddhārtha Gautama's ministry, likewise, is known only from the Pali scriptures of the Hinayana, though, according to these records, Gautama, unlike Jesus, was something of a public figure in His own lifetime. He was a king's son; and, after He had renounced His worldly heritage, He still consorted with kings during His ministry. Yet Buddhism did not make a political impact on the World on a grand scale till about two hundred years, and Christianity not till about three hundred years, after the founder's day, when their respective political fortunes were made by the conversions of Açoka and Constantine. On the other hand, Islam made a comparable impact during the founder's own lifetime, and its political fortunes were made by the founder himself.

Muhammad yielded, in the thirteenth year of his ministry, to the temptation which, according to the Gospels, was resisted by Jesus at the beginning of His. For twelve years Muhammad had been a sincere and intrepid but utterly unsuccessful prophet.[1] He had won only a tiny band

might conclude', he writes, 'that Alexander's conquests and the ensuing Hellenisation of the Middle East masked the death of this [i.e. the Syriac] Civilization and the emergence of a new affiliated civilization from the fusion of the East and Hellas' (F. Borkenau in *Commentary*, March, 1956, p. 247). Borkenau holds that Spengler is right, as against me, in assigning to this single Magian Civilization all those communities that have lost their territorial bases but have nevertheless preserved their distinctive communal identities in the form of millets (ibid.).

   [1] Philip Bagby has derided me (in *Toynbee and History*, p. 105) for stating this notorious fact in previous volumes of this book (e.g. iii. 467; v. 128 and 676), as if I had made a ludicrous gaffe. The statement is, of course, a commonplace. It will be found in every serious account of Muhammad's career. Muhammad was, in the end, a conspicuously successful man, but he succeeded, not as a prophet, but as a statesman. Islam, too, was, in the end, a conspicuously successful religion, but its spiritual fortune was made by the converted descendants of Christians and Zoroastrians who had become political subjects of the militant Islamic state. These equally notorious facts are also mentioned by me in the contexts cited in the present footnote. In order to understand the character and career of Muhammad and the history of the religion that he founded, we have to distinguish (i) between Muhammad's success as a statesman and his failure as a prophet, and (ii) between the immediate success of his Islamic state and the eventual success of Islam itself as a universal religion.

of converts; most of these had had eventually to take asylum in Abyssinia; and Muhammad himself was in daily danger of meeting Jesus's fate. After his acceptance of the invitation from the people of Yathrib (subsequently known as Medina)[1] to become the head of their state, Muhammad proved to be not only a prophet but also a political genius. Before his death he had compelled the commercial oligarchy of his native city-state Mecca to capitulate to him, and had shown his statesmanship—and also the generosity of his character—in the moderateness of the terms with which he had contented himself. In addition he had extended his rule from the city-state of Yathrib over a large part of the Arabian Peninsula besides Mecca, and his troops had made a probing raid on the Roman Empire's dominions in Transjordan. This piece of audacity had met with prompt chastisement, but it was premonitory of the sweeping conquests that were to be made by Muhammad's immediate political successors. Within less than twenty years of his death they had conquered the whole of the Sasanian Persian Empire and the best part of the Roman Empire: that is to say, Syria, in the broadest sense of the word, and also Egypt.

These dramatically rapid military and political successes of early Islam have given some Western students of history the impression that the epiphany of Islam made an unusually sharp break in the history of the Old-World *Oikoumenê* and that it had no antecedents and no precedents. Christopher Dawson's dictum[2] that history 'allows the whole world situation to be suddenly transformed by the action of a single individual like Muhammad or Alexander' has already been quoted in this volume.[3] A. L. Kroeber has expressed the same view. 'Islam', he says,[4] 'had no infancy and no real growth, but sprang up, Minerva-like, fullblown with the life of one man.'

If this were the truth, Islam's lack of antecedents could not be due just to the suddenness of its epiphany. This was neither more nor less sudden than the epiphanies of other religions and philosophies which, like Islam, had single historical founders, but whose founders—unlike what is alleged of Muhammad—had a long tradition behind them, as, for instance, Jesus had in the history of Judaism and in the antecedent religion of Israel, and as Gautama had in the previous development of Indian philosophy. The alleged lack of antecedents in Muhammad's case would be inexplicable. The simple and adequate explanation is that this Western picture is an hallucination. In reality there were substantial antecedents to Islam's epiphany and a number of precedents for it, as will be argued in the present chapter. Meanwhile, it is worth pausing to examine how the prevalent Western impression to the contrary arose.

One of the historical phenomena that have created this erroneous impression is the scale, speed, and revolutionariness of Islam's military and political impact on the World within the thirty years beginning with Muhammad's withdrawal from Mecca to Medina in A.D. 622. Within

[1] i.e. Madinat-an-Nabī, meaning 'the city of the Prophet'.
[2] In *The Dynamics of World History*, p. 257.
[3] On p. 16. See also p. 16, footnote 6.
[4] A. L. Kroeber: *The Nature of Culture*, p. 388.

those thirty years the Islamic state incorporated, as has just been noted, the whole of Arabia, the whole of the Sasanian Persian Empire, and the Roman Empire's dominions in Syria and Egypt. These immense political successes are apt to impress modern Western scholars in particular, because modern Western Society is particularly political-minded. The Islamic state conquered vast territories and populations almost at one blow; but, in the subsequent transformation of the conquered peoples' religious, artistic, and intellectual outlook, Islam was no swifter and no more revolutionary than Christianity and Buddhism had been. Subjects can be won more quickly and easily than converts. The conversion of the Islamic state's subjects to Islam was a gradual process.[1] It took at least six centuries, and even then it was not complete. Jewish, Christian, and Zoroastrian minorities have survived in the Islamic World down to this day—partly thanks to the toleration that Muhammad himself enjoined upon Muslims, in the Qur'ān,[2] in their dealings with non-Muslim 'People of the Book' who had submitted to the rule of the Islamic state. Moreover, in so far as Islam won its way, it won it, like the other missionary religions, by unavowedly receiving into itself many of the elements in its converts' previous religions. In this case, as in those, the price of converting was compromise.

Another historical phenomenon that has given Western minds the impression that the advent of Islam brought with it a sharp break in historical continuity is the sudden accompanying elevation of the Arabic language to a dominating position. In the reign of the Caliph 'Abd-al-Malik (*imperabat* A.D. 685–705) Arabic was substituted for Greek as the official language of administration in those dominions of the Islamic state that had formerly belonged to the Roman Empire. But the Arabic language's chief triumph was in the unofficial realm of literature. The sources for the study of Islamic history, from Muhammad's lifetime onwards, are copious, and many of them are of first-rate value from the historian's professional point of view. Muhammad's career, unlike Jesus's, can be followed point by point—and, in some of its chapters, almost day by day—in the full light of history. But these valuable historical records are all in Arabic; and this pulls up short the Western historian who has been following the history of South-West Asia and Egypt in Greek and Latin records over a span of nearly twelve hundred years, beginning with the antecedents of the establishment of the Achaemenian Persian Empire, as recorded in Greek by Herodotus, and coming down to the campaigns of the Roman Emperor Heraclius as recorded in the same language by George the Pisidian (who would have been Herodotus the Carian's neighbour if they had been contemporaries). Then, at the advent of Islam before the end of Heraclius's reign, the Greek-reading Western historian suddenly finds that the language that has served as his key to the history of twelve centuries no longer suffices. This confirms

[1] Accounts of it will be found in T. W. Arnold: *The Preaching of Islam,* 2nd ed. (London 1913, Constable); A. S. Tritton: *The Caliphs and their Non-Muslim Subjects* (London 1930, Milford); L. E. Browne: *The Eclipse of Christianity in Asia* (Cambridge 1933, University Press).
[2] e.g. Surah xxii. 17, quoted in v. 674, footnote 1.

his impression that, at this point, he is confronted with a break in the continuity of history.[1]

This is how it looks to a Western historian, educated in the Greek and Latin languages and literatures, whose point of departure is the Pre-Alexandrine Hellenic World and who views the adjacent Achaemenian Empire and its Hellenic successor-states from the Hellenic angle. He does not realize that this Hellenic point of view gives an inadequate picture of South-West Asian and Egyptian history from first to last; and so, when he is confronted with the manifest indispensability of historical records in the Arabic language for the history of the core of the *Oikoumenê* from the seventh century of the Christian Era onwards, he does not see the significance of this baffling experience. What it signifies is that other languages besides Greek are indispensable for a study of the history of the preceding twelve centuries as well.

Even if the historian confines his attention to the political surface of history, he ought to check the veracity of Herodotus's Greek narrative by comparing it with the Achaemenian emperors' surviving official documents in the Medo-Persian, Elamite, Akkadian, Aramaic, and Egyptian languages and scripts. If he wants to probe down below the political surface to the economic level, he must study the voluminous cuneiform records of private business transactions in the Akkadian language, produced under the Achaemenian and Seleucid regimes, that have been unearthed in Babylonia. The irrigated alluvium of the lower Tigris–Euphrates basin was the economic power-house of each of these empires in turn; and Akkadian, not Greek, is the key language for any study of the economic history of South-West Asia in this age—even for the time when, on the political plane, the Achaemenidae had been supplanted by the Greek-speaking Seleucid dynasty. If the inquirer wants to probe down below the economic level to the religious, then he must read Hebrew, Aramaic, Syriac, Avestan, and Pehlevi—and Pali and Sanskrit too, if he is going to invade India at Demetrius of Bactria's heels. In fact, for any inquirer into Egyptian and South-West Asian history who takes a comprehensive view of history, languages other than Greek are of capital importance throughout, and not merely since the advent of Islam and of the Arabic language in Islam's train. In this perspective the obvious indispensability of Arabic and inadequacy of Greek from the seventh century of the Christian Era onwards will be seen to be no sudden revolutionary new departure. The self-assertion of Arabic merely makes it impossible to continue to turn a blind eye to a situation that has been confronting the inquirer all the time.

Let us suppose that the Roman Empire had not recovered from the

---

[1] J. B. Bury's first edition of *A History of the Later Roman Empire* carried the story down almost to the end of the eighth century of the Christian Era. The second edition breaks off at A.D. 565, the date of the death of the Emperor Justinian, and a few years before the date of the birth of the Prophet Muhammad. After the second edition had been published, Bury told the present writer that he now looked back on the first edition as an act of youthful rashness. He had ventured to deal with the history of the seventh and eighth centuries without having mastered the Arabic language. By the time when he was producing his second edition, he could not face either trying to master Arabic or trying, without having done this, to rewrite the history of those two centuries. So, this time, he had laid down his pen at the latest convenient stopping-place before the date of the beginning of Muhammad's career.

bout of anarchy and disruption into which it fell in A.D. 235. Let us suppose, in fact, that Zenobia, the queen of the North Arabian city-state of Palmyra, had been able to retain the territories that she had acquired, at lightning speed, at the Roman Empire's expense. Her dominions extended, at their widest, over the whole eastern third of the Roman Empire. They stretched north-westward to the Black Sea Straits and south-westward to the Syrtes. Let us suppose, further, that Zenobia had been a Christian, and that she had derived her Christianity from the Mesopotamian Christian kingdom of Osrhoene, and had therefore acquired it in the Syriac language, not in the Greek. And, finally, let us suppose that she had been half a century ahead of Constantine in giving Christianity an official status in her dominions. None of these suppositions is extravagant. History could easily have taken this turn. And, if it had, then Christianity would have made the same impression on Western historians that Islam now makes. It would have seemed to them suddenly and unforeseenly to have changed the face of the World by depriving the Western historian of his linguistic key to an understanding of the World's history. Zenobia's hypothetical Christianity would have enthroned the Syriac language in the Greek language's place, as Muhammad's historical Islam did enthrone Arabic in its place some four hundred years later. This would have created, in Western eyes, the same impression of a revolutionary break; and in this imaginary event, as in the historical event, the impression would have been illusory. All that would then have happened in the third century would have been merely what did happen in the seventh century. A 'pseudomorphosis', in Spengler's usage of the term,[1] would have been convicted of being the camouflage that it always had been in reality. The presence of the ever-present non-Hellenic core of South-West Asian life, beneath the Hellenic veneer, would have been exposed some four hundred years earlier than the actual date at which the veneer was stripped off. But this exposure would not have made a revolutionary break in the continuity of history if it had occurred in the third century, any more than it made one in the seventh century. Islam's alleged lack of antecedents turns out to be nothing more substantial than a Western Hellenist's illusion.

If we look at Pre-Islamic history again, and look, this time, with non-Hellenic eyes, we shall find abundant antecedents and precedents for all the main phenomena that constitute, in combination, the epiphany of Islam.

The non-Arab world was first apprised of the new religion's epiphany by a militant outbreak of Semitic-speaking Nomads from the Arabian Peninsula; but the Arab Völkerwanderung in the seventh century of the Christian Era was not the first eruption of its kind, any more than it was the last. The Arabs themselves had erupted out of Arabia twice before: in the second century B.C., when the Seleucid Empire was losing its grip on the Fertile Crescent, and, before that, in the seventh century B.C., when the Assyrian Empire was beginning to labour under the weight of its self-imposed military burdens. The Aramaean-Chaldaean-Hebrew eruption in the thirteenth century B.C., when the New Empire of Egypt

[1] See Chapter XVIII, Annex, pp. 670–4.

was in decline, is comparable to the Muslim Arab eruption in point of magnitude and vehemence. Round about the beginning of the second millennium B.C. the Amorites had erupted as far afield as their Aramaean successors penetrated. Five or six hundred years earlier the Akkadians had thrust their way out of the desert on to the alluvium, to the north-west of Sumer, and had pressed on, up the Tigris, into the country that they made into Assyria. The Canaanites must have erupted out of Arabia no later than the Akkadians, and their occupation of Syria may have been still earlier.

The vast Islamic empire expanded, within the span of a single genera-tion, out of a tiny nucleus: a single city-state commanding a single oasis. But Muhammad's Yathrib had its predecessors in Zenobia's Palmyra and, on a smaller scale, in Petra and in Hatra. In each of these earlier cases, too, a city-state in an Arabian oasis had generated a notable political power. The Roman Emperor Trajan liquidated the miniature empire of Petra and annexed its territories; but he was defeated in his attempt to capture Hatra. The lines of the Roman invader's unsuccess-ful circumvallation surround the inviolate walls of Hatra to this day. Hatra had been under the protection of the trinity of goddesses who, in Muhammad's day, were the protectresses of Mecca. Their potency was so great that Muhammad almost succumbed to the temptation to stultify his mission by proclaiming them to be daughters of the One True God of the pure religion of Abraham.

Under the Umayyad regime, which centred itself on Syria and chose Damascus for its capital, the Islamic state was, first and foremost, a successor-state of the Roman Empire. In this role it had been anticipated, in the sixth and seventh centuries of the Christian Era, by the princi-pality of the Banu Ghassān, who had guarded the Roman Empire's desert marches, and in the third century by the wide, though short-lived, empire that Zenobia had ruled from Palmyra. The Umayyads (with the single exception of 'Umar II) found Hellenism more to their taste than Islam—as witness the Hellenic decorations of Hishām's palace on the northern outskirts of Jericho. In this philhellenism they had been anticipated by earlier barbarian conquerors of previously Hellenized ground: for instance, the Parthians in Iran and 'Iraq and the Kushans in Bactria and India.

By conquering 'Iraq and Iran as well as Syria and Egypt, the Islamic state had made itself a successor-state of the Sasanian Empire as well as of the Roman Empire. The economic pull of 'Iraq on its Arab con-querors made itself felt when the Umayyad regime was replaced by the 'Abbasid regime, and when the capital of the Islamic state was moved from Damascus to the new city of Baghdad. Under the 'Abbasids the Islamic state took its place in the long series of empires based on 'Iraq's economic resources. The series stretched back through the Sasanian, Parthian, Seleucid, Achaemenian, and Neobabylonian empires to the Empire of Agade, which had given political unity to the Fertile Crescent in the third millennium B.C.

The Islamic state, in the first chapter of its history, was up in arms against the political ascendancy of Hellenism in South-West Asia and

Egypt—an ascendancy that had been upheld there by Roman power since the last century B.C. On the cultural plane, on the other hand, Islam eventually equipped itself for playing its part as a universal religion by drawing on Hellenic intellectual resources.[1] Thus its attitude towards Hellenism was the ambivalent one of attraction towards it on the cultural plane coexisting with hostility towards it on the political plane. But this ambivalence towards Hellenism was not peculiar to Islam. It was the attitude of both Monophysite and Nestorian Christianity at the time when Islam first took the field; and, before that, it had been the attitude of Catholic Christianity until the concordat with the Roman Imperial Government had degraded this into being the 'Imperialist' (Melchite) Church in the eyes of the Roman Empire's disaffected Syrian and Egyptian Christian subjects. Before the days of Constantine and Theodosius, the Catholic Christian Church had been anti-Hellenic and philhellene simultaneously. It had won its converts from Hellenism by presenting itself to them in an Hellenic dress. Islam was following these Christian precedents when, after completing the expulsion of Hellenism from South-West Asia and Egypt on the political plane, it proceeded to provide itself with a theology by having recourse to Hellenic philosophy.

The various aspects of the epiphany and early subsequent history of Islam thus turn out to have antecedents and precedents, like other historical phenomena. More than that, they can be satisfactorily explained. We can see why Muhammad, in his particular generation, was moved to engage in his religious mission. We can see why he was compelled to become a politician as well as a prophet. We can see why the Islamic state, in the first chapter of its history, was able to make its swift and sweeping military conquests. Finally, we can see how, after the establishment of the Islamic world-state, Islam developed into a universal religion of the same order as Christianity and on a par with it.

Muhammad's prophetic mission can be explained as a consequence of the cumulative effect of a gradual but progressive penetration of Arabia by the influences of civilization.[2] This process may have begun before the close of the second millennium B.C., when the domestication of the camel made all but the greatest of the Arabian deserts traversable by Man. Before the end of the last millennium B.C. the Yaman had, as we have seen,[3] been drawn into the field of the Syriac Civilization. In the sixth century B.C. the Neobabylonian Emperor Nabunaid had established an outpost of the Sumero-Akkadian Civilization in the North-West Arabian oasis of Taymā. By Muhammad's time, Judaism and Christianity were radiating their influence into the Arabian Peninsula vigorously from the north-west, the south-west, and the north-east. There were well-established Jewish communities at Khaybar and Yathrib, and Christian communities in the Yaman. In the Arabia of Muhammad's day there was a widespread feeling that it was high time for the Arabs to become 'People of the Book', such as the Jews and the Christians were. Muhammad had equally sincere, though less articulate,

---

[1] See p. 450, with footnote 2, above, and also pp. 471 and 671, footnote 1.
[2] This point has been noticed in iii. 277.   [3] On pp. 393-4.

predecessors in the hanifs, and he had a contemporary and a potential rival in the Prophet Maslamah. If the Hijazi prophet Muhammad had failed, the Najdi prophet Maslamah might have done the equivalent of Muhammad's work; and, if Maslamah, too, had failed, some other prophet would have arisen, in some other part of Arabia, to step into Maslamah's and Muhammad's shoes. So far from springing up 'Minerva-like, full-blown, with the life of one man',[1] Islam, like Christianity, had a long pre-natal history. A normal birth offers an apter simile for the epiphany of Islam than the legendary birth of the goddess Athene. A normal birth is a sudden and dramatic event, but it does not come out of the blue and is therefore not inexplicable.

In the second part of his public career, beginning with his withdrawal from Mecca to Medina, Muhammad successfully played the military and political part for which the Jews, after their loss of their political independence, had cast their expected Messiah.

The Jewish Messiah's designated task was, humanly speaking, a forlorn hope. He was to overthrow a world-empire to which the Jews were subject, and was to establish a Jewish world-empire in its place. It was recognized that the Messiah could succeed only in virtue of his being supported by Yahweh's almighty power. Left to his own human resources he would be foredoomed; and, in fact, as long as the Roman Empire lasted, every Jewish political leader who tried to play the conventional Messiah's part brought a crushing disaster on himself and on his community. The Roman power was invincible and ubiquitous. The mere accusation of aspiring to be the Messiah was enough to procure a death-sentence—as Jesus's Jewish enemies knew when they brought this charge against Him in Pilate's court. As the story is told in the Gospels, the charge against Jesus was groundless. Either He had not claimed to be the Messiah in any sense, or He had made the claim in a non-political and non-militant sense that changed the conventional concept of the Messiah's role out of all recognition. Nevertheless, Jesus was put to death by the Roman authorities. They were taking no chances. In fact, under the regime of the Roman world-state, a prophet was doomed if he was even falsely accused of intending to go into politics and to take up arms. His only hope lay in a policy of strict non-violence, and even this might not save him.

The regime under which Muhammad entered on his prophetic mission was entirely different. He was a citizen of a turbulent city-state. In the Mecca of his day non-violence certainly would not save the life of a prophet who was preaching a doctrine that was objectionable to the local ruling oligarchy. But, unlike the Roman Empire, the Meccan city-state was not ubiquitous. Its jurisdiction was limited to a single oasis. It was practicable to withdraw beyond the reach of the Quraysh's not very long arm; and thus, when Muhammad was offered the political headship of the independent city-state of Medina, he had found his effective retort to the Meccan oligarchy's hostility. Since Muhammad at Medina turned out to be a political genius, his retort, before long, became not merely effective but crushing. His political career need not be considered

[1] Kroeber, quoted on p. 462.

further in this present context, as it has been discussed at some length in a previous volume.[1] It is sufficient here to note that there is nothing inexplicable in it.

Nor is there any mystery about the causes of the early Islamic state's swift and sweeping military successes. The key is to be found in the division of the territories once conquered from the Achaemenidae by Alexander between two rival empires: one of them based on 'Iraq and the other centred on the Mediterranean. This political constellation had been in existence for 700 years by the time when Muhammad's second political successor, the Caliph 'Umar I (*imperabat* A.D. 634–44) overthrew the Sasanian Persian Empire and wrested from the Roman Empire its dominions south-east of Taurus. The two empires had brought these disasters upon themselves by allowing the chronic border-warfare between them to boil up, from a limited competition for the possession of frontier fortresses and provinces, into a life-and-death struggle in which the very existence of both powers was at stake. Most of Muhammad's lifetime (*vivebat circa* A.D. 570–632) was occupied, in the heart of the *Oikoumenê* immediately to the north of Arabia, by two long-drawn-out and devastating Romano-Persian wars (*gerebantur* A.D. 572–91 and 603–28) that ended, as far as the two belligerents' mutual relations were concerned, in nothing more constructive than a re-establishment of the *status quo ante*. The effective consequent change was in the balance of power between the two empires and the Arab barbarians beyond their southern frontiers. Both empires emerged from this double great war exhausted. By contrast, the Arabs emerged notably enriched and instructed. They had earned money by serving as mercenaries on both sides; they had invested much of it in buying up-to-date military equipment; and, most important of all, they had learnt by practice how to use this equipment and how to conduct military operations with large forces on the grand scale. This speeded up and completed a process that had been going on for some centuries past. For religion was not the only element of 'civilization' that had been seeping into Arabia. Military equipment and skill had been seeping in as well, even before the long history of Romano-Persian warfare had mounted to its fatal climax. The most potent new weapon that the Arabs had acquired in the Pre-Islamic Age was the horse,[2] and horsemanship had made the Arabs militarily formidable—as it was to make the Plains Indians of North America when they had acquired the horse from the Spaniards.[3]

Thus, by the time of Muhammad's *hijrah* to Medina, the Arabs already possessed all the requisites for becoming world-conquerors except one, and that was political unity. When Muhammad had given them this it was inevitable that they should erupt and that their eruption should sweep away everything in its path. Few Arabs ever became devotees of Islam for its own sake, and most Arabs strongly objected, at first, to having the political rule of the Islamic state imposed on them. Why should they submit to being ruled by the people of Yathrib in league

---

[1] iii. 466–72.
[2] See L. Caetani: *Studi di Storia Orientale*, vol. i (Milan 1911, Hoepli), p. 346, cited already in viii. 17, footnote 5.   [3] See viii. 637–9.

with a handful of Meccan refugees? The news of Muhammad's death in A.D. 632 was the signal, in Arabia, for a widespread war of secession (*riddah*); and this might have been difficult for Muhammad's political successors to suppress by force of arms alone. The dissident Arabs were reconciled to the rule of the Islamic state by the realization that, under this unified command, they had it in their power to conquer the *Oikoumenê* and plunder it. The misery of the war-stricken Persian and Roman empires, which was so keenly felt by their subjects, represented incredible wealth when appraised by the standards of their starveling Arab conquerors.

In making the Arabs' potential military ascendancy tell by giving them political unity, Muhammad did for them what Philip of Macedon had done for the Hellenes. These had established their military ascendancy over the Achaemenian Persian power as far back as the years 480–479 B.C., when they had so signally defeated Xerxes' attempt to conquer Continental European Greece. The successful march of Cyrus the Younger's 10,000 Hellenic mercenaries from Babylonia to the Black Sea coast of Anatolia in 401–400 B.C., in defiance of the Achaemenian Empire's military power, and the Lacedaemonians' successful campaigns in Western Anatolia in 399–393 B.C., had indicated what might be achieved by a Panhellenic military effort. Indeed, the Spartan King Agesilaus might have anticipated Alexander by sixty years if, in 395 B.C., Athens and Thebes had not joined hands to take the Lacedaemonians in the rear. The Hellenes had to wait until Philip of Macedon had imposed political unity on them in order to reap the harvest of the military ascendancy over the Achaemenian Empire that they had established 145 years before Philip's successor Alexander—the Hellenic 'Umar—crossed the Hellespont.

Kroeber's dictum[1] that 'Islam had no infancy and no real growth' is also irreconcilable with the historical facts. The truth surely is that Islam had an infancy which was unpromising, and was redeemed from this by a growth which was remarkable.

It is true that Islam, as preached by its founder Muhammad, was essentially a 'higher religion'. Muhammad summoned his fellow countrymen the people of Mecca to abandon the worship of their local pantheon, domiciled in the Ka'bah, and to submit themselves to a god who was proclaimed by his Meccan prophet to be the One True God of all men and of the whole Universe. It was this that got Muhammad into trouble with the ruling oligarchy of the Meccan city-state. At the same time, Muhammad's horizon was bounded by the limits of his own nation, as Jesus's horizon was, according to the passages in the Gospel according to St. Matthew[2] in which He is reported to have instructed His emissaries not to visit the gentiles or the Samaritans, but to go rather to 'the lost sheep of the house of Israel'. The Arabs' aspiration to become 'People of the Book', like the Jews and the Christians, was a nationalistic one; and it took a form that is characteristic of barbarians camped on the

---

[1] Quoted on p. 462.
[2] Matt. x. 5–6; xv. 21–28. In Mark vii. 24–30, Jesus is reported to have taken the same line—and this in harsh and wounding language—in His negative first reaction to a Caananite woman's appeal to Him.

fringe of a civilization.[1] The Arabs were sufficiently impressed by the culture of the Roman Empire to hanker after a religion of the kind professed by the Empire's inhabitants; yet at the same time they were sufficiently independent-minded to be unwilling simply to adopt their impressive neighbours' religion as it stood without giving it an Arab national colouring. In the eyes of Arabs of Muhammad's generation, Christianity was the national religion of the Romans and Judaism the national religion of the Jews; and the picture of the One True God that Muhammad presented to his countrymen was, like the Jewish picture of Him, equivocal. Besides being the God of the Universe, He was to be the national god of the Arabs. Islam was to be a revival of the pure religion of Abraham, and this time 'the Chosen People' of Abraham's lineage were to be the Arab offspring of his son Ishmael instead of the Jewish offspring of his son Isaac.

In having this tincture of barbarian nationalism, Islam resembled the Arian form of Christianity which, three centuries earlier, had been adopted by the East German barbarians on the eve of their own invasion of the Roman Empire from the opposite quarter. This element of nationalism in Islam was, of course, greatly reinforced when Muhammad extended the territory of his Medinese state not only over Mecca but over the whole of Arabia. As has been noted already, the Arabs were indifferent to their prophet's religious ideas and ideals, but they appreciated the military power which he had conferred on them by uniting them politically in a Pan-Arabian Islamic Commonwealth, and Islam was carried out of Arabia into the former dominions of the Roman and Sasanian empires as the national religion of the conquering Arab armies.

The conquerors did not much want non-Arab converts. The conquered peoples seemed to them more valuable as surtax-payers than as co-religionists. It was their Zoroastrian and Christian non-Arab subjects who took the Arabs' kingdom by storm. They forced their way into the fold of Islam, deposed the Arabs from their political ascendancy in the Islamic state, and gave Islam itself an organization and a theology[2] which removed, once for all, the ambiguity that, till then, had kept it havering between the two incompatible ideals of nationalism and universality. Thus the non-Arab converts to Muhammad's religion eventually saved for Islam a situation that the founder himself had compromised. But for these converts, it seems probable that Islam would have gone the way that Arian Christianity went. Like the Burgundians, the Visigoths, and the Lombards, the Arabs would have abandoned their barbarian national religion, sooner or later, for the universal religion of their Christian subjects, if these subjects had not, meanwhile, insisted on making of Islam a new higher religion for all men on the pattern of the Christianity that the Christian converts to Islam had formerly professed.

This eventual harvesting of Islam's potentialities as a universal religion was an immense cultural, as well as religious, achievement. It was comparable to what had previously been done for Christianity; and it

---

[1] This point has been made by R. Coulborn in *Toynbee and History*, p. 165. Cp. the present book, v. 230.　　　　　　　　　　[2] See p. 450, with footnotes.

was done by the same people and by the same means. The people whose good offices enabled Islam, as well as Christianity, to grow to its full spiritual and cultural stature were the South-West Asian heirs of the combined Syriac and Hellenic heritages. As we have seen in the preceding chapter,[1] both the Syriac and the Hellenic Civilization's continuity had been broken—the Syriac Civilization's by the impact of Hellenism, and the Hellenic Civilization's by the impact of a Syriac-Hellenic religion, Christianity. The former participants in the two civilizations had lost their consciousness of their distinctive cultures, but they had not lost their cultural fertility. On the contrary, the Syriac and Hellenic cultures, in losing their distinctive identities, had blended into a culture-compost which had an unrivalled nutritive power. The feat of nursing not only one but two higher religions into a maturity at which each of them makes a universal appeal is an achievement that it would be hard to match.

The prevalent depreciation of Islam in the West is a relic of anti-Islamic Christian prejudice. This stubbornly survives even in modern Western minds that feel an obligation, in their intellectual work, to correct the Christian bias in their cultural heritage, and that imagine themselves, in their unfavourable appraisal of Islam, to be acting up to their own high standard of detachment and to be condemning Islam objectively, on its own demerits. Kroeber, for example, has given an interpretation of Islam as an historical phenomenon in the light of an hypothesis of his about the history of the course of civilization in the Old World. Kroeber likens Old-World civilization to a fire that started in the Fertile Crescent and that then spread, as fires are apt to spread, in a progressively widening circle from its point of origin. The flame keeps alight round the circle's ever-advancing circumference, long after it has died away and left nothing but cold grey ashes on the spot which was its original hearth. This hypothesis has some notable merits. The greatest of these is that it fits a number of the historical facts. An almost equal merit is that it rises superior to the one-sided conventional Western prejudice that takes account solely of the westward spread of civilization from Sumer and Egypt through the Mediterranean into Europe, and thence eventually into the Americas, and ignores its contemporaneous spread into India and Eastern Asia. The progress of a movement on its outer edge after it has died down at its original point of departure is a phenomenon that can be observed in a number of situations in non-human nature and also in human affairs. The outward-moving circle of flame has one parallel in the circular wave set in motion by throwing a stone into a pond. The wave continues to travel outwards after the spot where the stone hit the water has become still again. A city, likewise, sometimes continues to grow round its edges after its original core, which was once the heart of its life, has fallen into squalor or even into desolation. And the *Oikoumenê* is, in a sense, one great city: the City of Zeus in which the City of Cecrops is reproduced on the grand scale.[2] This, however, is only a poetic simile; and Kroeber

---

[1] On pp. 446-54.
[2] Marcus Aurelius Antoninus: *Meditations*, Book IV, chap. 23.

himself has warned me[1] that a simile is not the same thing as a demonstration.

It is true, as we have noticed,[2] that, within the span of half a millennium ending in the fourth century of the Christian Era, four civilizations—three of them at home in the heart of the *Oikoumenê* and the fourth, the Hellenic Civilization, also long since established there—dissolved, in the sense that the former participants in them lost their consciousness of continuity with their cultural heritage. It is also true that Islam subsequently established itself in this region in succession to Christianity. Kroeber is, of course, right in saying[3] that 'Islam arose in the very region of the first hearth of all higher civilization: . . . in the Near Eastern area of the Neolithic Revolution, of the first farming and towns and kings and letters.' But he is surely wrong in going on to say[4] that 'it arose at a time when constructive cultural impulses had long since moved out from that hearth'. The loss of consciousness of cultural continuity is not the same thing as a loss of power of cultural creativity. The fusion of the diverse elements of the Syriac and Hellenic civilizations had already provided a fertile compost from which Christianity had sprung; and its fertility now proved great enough to produce a second crop, of comparable value, in the shape of Islam. Have there ever anywhere been 'constructive cultural impulses' that have produced finer fruits than this pair of higher religions with a message for all men?

Islam, in succession to Christianity, came to maturity in the heart of the *Oikoumenê* in an age in which this heart was still beating as vigorously as ever. If Kroeber had been willing to recognize Islam as being the peer of Christianity that it is, he would not have seen it, through jaundiced eyes, as a 'reduced, retractile, civilization, an anti-Hellenic, anti-Sasanian, anti-Christian civilization . . . without art, without much intellectual curiosity or profundity, without many of the aspirations customary in civilizations'.[5] He would not then have been led to explain Islam's imaginary inferiority by making the unwarranted assumption that the region in which Islam came to maturity was by that time a cultural waste land. Whether or not we accept his simile of the outward spread of a fire, leaving a burnt-out centre, as a valid key to the geographical history of civilization in the Old World, it is certain that the fire had not been extinguished in its original hearth either before the conquest of South-West Asia and Egypt by the primitive Muslim Arabs or during the subsequent formative centuries when Islam was being brought to maturity there by local non-Arab converts from among the conquered Christian and Zoroastrian population. Even during the previous age of political division, 'Iraq had been the power-house of the Sasanian Empire, and Syria and Egypt of the Roman Empire. The potency of all three countries was notably enhanced when the Arab conquest reunited them politically for the first time since the break-up of the Achaemenian Empire, nearly a thousand years back. Under the Umayyad and 'Abbasid regimes, South-West Asia and Egypt were still the heart of the *Oikoumenê*, as they had been during the previous three or four thousand years.

---

[1] In *The Nature of Culture*, p. 376, quoted in this volume on p. 38, footnote 2.
[2] On pp. 447–8.   [3] In op. cit., p. 381.   [4] Ibid.   [5] Op. cit., pp. 381–2.

This historic region did eventually fall into adversity and suffer an eclipse from which it is re-emerging in our time. But this did not happen till after Islam had come to maturity there; and Islam was not the cause of it.

The potency of this region was derived, and is derived once again today, from two assets: its local productivity and its geographical location at the centre of the *Oikoumenê*'s network of communications. In the past its staple production was agricultural: the crops raised on its irrigated fields. Today its staple production is mineral: the oil got from below its surface. The region is estimated to contain the major part of the World's oil reserves, as, in the past, it produced the major part of the World's annual cereal harvest. As for this region's geographical role as the central node of the World's communications, the permanent features of the World's geography are so favourable to South-West Asia and Egypt that this region is now recovering its natural position as the mid-point of the *Oikoumenê* less than four hundred years after the date at which the *Oikoumenê* was thrown out of its normal geographical balance by two almost simultaneous revolutionary Western achievements: the discovery of a New World west of the Atlantic and the discovery of the uninterrupted sea-route from the Atlantic coast of Western Europe to Southern and Eastern Asia round the Cape of Good Hope. Since 1869 this roundabout route has been short-circuited by the cutting of the Suez Canal. This has reopened the direct passage for ships between the Indian Ocean and the Mediterranean which existed in the Achaemenian Age after the Emperor Darius I's engineers had cut his canal from Suez to the head of the Nile Delta. The Suez Canal offers the shortest sea-route between the two main concentrations of population in the twentieth-century world: one in Southern and Eastern Asia and the other in Europe and North America; and in our day it has been supplemented by a bundle of air-routes which bunch together where they traverse the land-bridge between Eurasia and Africa.

Thus the heart of the *Oikoumenê* has now surmounted the crisis by which it was overtaken when the fifteenth-century Western maritime adventurers made their momentous geographical discoveries. Thanks to the striking of oil, South-West Asia is now well on the way towards recovering from the previous blow that it had suffered in the thirteenth century of the Christian Era when the Mongols had committed genocide against its population and had also cut the roots of its agricultural productivity by giving the *coup de grâce* to the 4,000-years-old water-control system in 'Iraq.[1] The degree of the devastation that was inflicted by the Mongols on South-West Asia east of Euphrates can be measured by the contrast between present-day agricultural Egypt, which has continued, without a break, to be a going concern since the unification of its water-control system round about 3000 B.C., and present-day agricultural 'Iraq, which even today is only just beginning to recover from the blow dealt to it by the Mongols 700 years ago. The wholesale destruction of human life was still more disastrous than the wrecking of Man's engineering works. Visit Khurāsān, the north-

---

[1] See iv. 42–43.

easternmost province of the present kingdom of Persia, and take your stand in the vast empty space within the four-square walls of the Pre-Mongol city of Tus or the Pre-Mongol city of Nīshāpūr. You will realize that, even after the passage of 700 years, South-West Asia is still prostrate under the blow that it received from the Mongols in the thirteenth century. The thirteenth-century Mongol devastation of South-West Asia, followed by the fifteenth-century West European diversion of the World's sea-routes away from the Levant and the Red Sea, explain, between them, the decline and eclipse of South-West Asia and Egypt in the sixteenth, seventeenth, and eighteenth centuries. This makes the recovery of this region in the nineteenth century and thereafter all the more remarkable and impressive. In the present context the significance of this temporary eclipse and subsequent recovery is that both events have been subsequent to the epiphany and maturation of Islam. And this matter of chronological fact would appear to refute, decisively, Kroeber's imaginative thesis that Islam is Dead Sea fruit grown on waste land.

What is the relation of Islam, as a religion, to the Islamic Civilization that is so prominent a feature in the cultural map of the present-day world? Rushton Coulborn makes the point[1] that 'Islamic Civilization, when it arises, is obviously something new. Its rise was mediated by Islam as a religion.' This dictum is, in my judgement, unexceptionable. I myself have certainly never written anything to the contrary, and would not ever oppose it so long as it is taken as implying no more than it says. I have the impression, however, that Coulborn is intending to imply that the Islamic Civilization came into existence simultaneously with Islam itself, and that in this point its relation is different from that of the Christian civilizations to Christianity. If, in interpreting him in this sense, I have correctly caught his meaning, then he and I disagree. As I see it, the relation of the Islamic Civilization to Islam is the same as that of the Christian civilizations to Christianity. In both cases, as I see them, the religion made its appearance in the World and proceeded to grow to maturity within a social and cultural framework that was older and was also at least partly alien. It was only after this older alien civilization or civilizations had weathered away that the new religion incidentally mothered a new civilization which is legitimately called by its name because it bears its unmistakable stamp.

This construction of the course of events would not, I think, be disputed by any student of the relation between Christianity and the Christian civilizations. It would be recognized that Christianity appeared and matured within the framework of the Hellenic Civilization, and that the Christian civilizations did not begin to come to the surface before the period, running approximately from the latter part of the fourth to the latter part of the seventh century of the Christian Era, when the Hellenic Civilization was dissolving. Christianity in its formative age was the religion of a minority living as strangers and sojourners in a world that was not their own. Islam in its formative age was, as I see it, in the same situation. It came to maturity within the framework of alien

[1] In *Toynbee and History*, p. 163.

civilizations—in this case, not the Hellenic Civilization but the Nestorian Christian, the Monophysite Christian, and the Zoroastrian Iranian. It is true that the Christian minority in the Roman Empire lived in the catacombs, whereas the Muslim minority in the Islamic world-state lived in the camps and the palaces. But this Muslim minority was in the same position as the Christian minority in the essential point that it was living in a world that it had not created and in which it was not at home.

After the epiphany of Islam, as after the epiphany of Christianity, centuries had to pass before the new religion could mother a new civilization; for the necessary pre-condition for that was that the minority should have become the majority. In the circum-Mediterranean world this happened in the course of the three centuries ending in the seventh century of the Christian Era; in South-West Asia and Egypt it happened in the course of the three centuries ending in the thirteenth century of the Christian Era. Before that, the Muslims—including the Arabs' converted non-Arab subjects as well as the Arabs themselves—had been only a minority in the dominions of the Islamic world-state. The Islamic state's Zoroastrian subjects in Iran and in the Oxus–Jaxartes basin had gone over to Islam more quickly, in larger numbers, than its Christian subjects west of Zagros. But the mass-conversions to Islam did not begin to take place in any of the Islamic world-state's dominions till the Islamic state was harried by barbarian invasions. It was the Crusades and the subsequent irruption of the Mongols that moved the mass of the population of South-West Asia and Egypt to rally to Islam as a spiritual force that might perhaps hold society together in a cataclysm in which 'Earth's foundations fled'.

I therefore continue, on reconsideration, to maintain that the Islamic Civilization—or civilizations—arose after the thirteenth century of the Christian Era, when the last remnant of the 'Abbasid world-state had been extinguished by the Mongol war-lord Hūlāgū. In order to locate the place of Islam in history, we have to distinguish clearly between three different things: the Islamic religion that was founded and compromised by the Prophet Muhammad and was then salvaged by his political successors' converted non-Arab subjects; the Islamic state that was founded by the statesman Muhammad and that swiftly grew, like the proverbial grain of mustard-seed, into a tree that overshadowed the Earth;[1] and the Islamic Civilization (or civilizations) that has been a cultural by-product of Islam in the same sense in which the Christian civilizations have been cultural by-products of Christianity. If we do not keep these three different things clearly distinct in our minds, we are likely to go astray in our interpretation of Islam and of its political and cultural by-products.

---

[1] The personal union of absolute political with absolute religious authority in the person of Muhammad died with him. His political successors did not inherit his prerogatives in the field of religion. Decisions about Islamic practice and doctrine on the basis of the Qur'ān and the traditions are reached by a consensus (ijmā') of the learned ('ulamā) in the sacred law. Their role and standing correspond to those of the rabbis in Judaism.

XV. THE HISTORY AND PROSPECTS OF THE JEWS

I. THE RELATIVITY OF THE INTERPRETATION OF JEWISH HISTORY

THE interpretation of Jewish history is a classic illustration of the relativity of an observer's report to his personal relation with his human subject.

The Jews have told their own story from the standpoint of a self-proclaimed 'Chosen People' in whose eyes all other human beings are 'gentiles' (i.e. 'lesser breeds without the law', in Kipling's paraphrase). In the Christian-Muslim half of the present-day world this Jewish standpoint has been accepted by the present-day non-Jewish gentile majority in regard to Jewish history in the Pre-Christian, or, alternatively, the Pre-Muslim, Age.

The Christian Church, for instance, has taken over uncritically the Jewish version of the history of the Jews' predecessors, the peoples of Judah and Israel, as this is presented in the written Torah (in Christian terminology, 'the Old Testament'). Christians, and ex-Christians too, see the Phoenicians, Philistines, Edomites, Moabites, Ammonites, and Damascenes as these are portrayed in the historical books of the Torah; and they see the Seleucid King Antiochus IV and his policy as these are portrayed in the First and Second Books of Maccabees. If the Tyre and Gaza of the last millennium B.C. had living representatives to speak for them today, as Israel and Judah have, they would, no doubt, give a version of the story of their relations with the two highland communities in their hinterland which would hardly be recognizable as being an account of the events that, in the highlanders' version, are familiar to Christians from the Bible. Yet in the established Christian version of this chapter of history the Jews have things all their own way—pending the discovery, by archaeologists, of documents written in the Syriac World, outside Judah and Israel, in the last millennium B.C. that might be of comparable historical value to the documents written in the fourteenth century B.C. that have already been unearthed at Ras ash-Shamrah.

In the established Islamic version of Old-Testament history the Jews have not come off quite so well. Muhammad did follow the lead of the Christian Church in accepting the Jewish thesis that the written Torah is the word of God; but, when the Jews pointed out that some of Muhammad's renderings of Old-Testament stories had got these stories wrong in important particulars, Muhammad accounted for the discrepancy by declaring that the Jews had falsified their own holy scriptures. The Qur'anic version was a restoration of the original, and Islam was 'the pure religion of Abraham'. Thus Muhammad's concession to Jewish claims was partly discounted, even in regard to the age before the new dispensation, by a serious imputation on the Jews' good faith. Yet Muhammad, like the Christian Church, recognized the authority of the written Torah, as being a book inspired by God, in so far as its text might be endorsed by Muhammad as being authentic; and the charge that he made against the Jews did not implicate their forefather Abraham. Like the Jews themselves and like the Christians, Muslims trace their own religious origins back to the revelation that Abraham received from God according to the Jewish tradition. Like Christianity, Islam presupposes Judaism and could never have come into existence if Judaism had not been in existence already.

Thus the Muslims, as well as the Christians, accept, in principle, the Jews' belief in the divine inspiration of the Torah and the consequent belief in the Jews' special status as the recipients of this divine revelation. On the other hand the tables have been turned on the Jews by the Christians and the Muslims in their appraisal of Jewish history since the beginning of the Christian or, alternatively, the Islamic Era.

Christians—and Muslims too, subject to Muhammad's reservation—accept the Jewish account of Jewish history, and of its antecedents in the histories of Judah and Israel, down to the respective beginnings of the Christian and Muslim eras, with the proviso that Judaism was designed, in the Jewish god Yahweh's providence, to be the preparation for Christianity or, alternatively, for Islam, and that the Israelites and their successors the Jews were 'chosen' by God to be the forerunners of His eventual 'Chosen People' the Christians or, alternatively, the Muslims. Upon the advent of Christianity or, alternatively, of Islam, the 'mandate' of Judaism and the Jews 'was exhausted' (to use an apt Chinese formula). Now, in God's own good time, the true 'Chosen People' had arrived on the scene, and the Jews' duty was clear. They ought to have accepted Jesus or, alternatively, Muhammad, at the valuation placed on him in the official doctrine of the Judaic religion of which he was the founder. In declining to accept him on these terms, the Jews were failing to respond to the supreme challenge in their history, and were thereby putting themselves permanently in the wrong and on the shelf. Jewish history and its Israelitish antecedents down to the beginning of Jesus's or, alternatively, Muhammad's ministry still has validity and value as the prelude, arranged by God, to the Christian or, alternatively, to the Muslim, dispensation. Jewish history since one or other of those two climacteric dates is without significance except as a classic example of perversity on the part of a people that, of all peoples, ought to have known better.

It is difficult for anyone brought up in the Christian tradition to shake himself free from the official Christian ideology. He may have discarded Christian doctrine consciously on every point; yet on this particular point he may find that he is still being influenced, subconsciously, by the traditional Christian view in his outlook on Jewish history. Voltaire's outlook is a classic case.[1] I am conscious that my own outlook has been affected in this way. If I had happened to be brought up in the Muslim tradition instead of the Christian one, no doubt my outlook would have been affected correspondingly.

This Christian-Muslim reading of Jewish history is irritating to Jews

---

[1] This is recalled by Rabbi J. B. Agus in *Judaism*, 1956, p. 2. In *The National Jewish Monthly*, November, 1956, Rabbi Agus makes the same point in general terms, with reference to non-orthodox Jews as well as to non-orthodox Christians.

—partly because of the grain of truth that it contains, and partly because of the larger measure of misrepresentation that there is in it.

The grain of truth lies in the fact that the advents of Christianity and Islam, and the subsequent histories of these two religions, are unquestionably two major events in the main course of mankind's history——at least in that half of the *Oikoumenê* that lies to the west of India. Israel, Judah, the Jews, and Judaism did not play major parts in the history of mankind before they gave birth to the two 'deviationist' Judaic world-religions. If Christianity and Islam had never been generated by Judaism's involuntary but undeniable paternity, Judaism would be surviving today in an environment of Hellenic 'paganism', as Zoroastrianism does survive today in an environment of Hindu 'paganism'. We may guess that, in that event, the Jews' position in the World today would have been more like the actual position of the Parsees[1] than like the actual position of the Jews themselves. The Jews would have been more obscure than they now are, but they would also have been more comfortable. The Jews' present-day importance, celebrity, and discomfort all derive from the historic fact that they have involuntarily begotten two Judaic world-religions whose millions of adherents make the preposterous but redoubtable claim to have superseded the Jews, by the Jewish god Yahweh's dispensation, in the role of being this One True God's 'Chosen People'.

The Jews are also genuinely 'a back number' in another sense. Like the Samaritans, they are surviving representatives of a Syriac civilization that otherwise became extinct as long ago as the third or second century B.C., if the disuse of the Aramaic *koinê* may be taken as a criterion of the date at which the Syriac Civilization faded out of existence.[2] The Syriac Civilization as a whole, like its contemporary the Hellenic Civilization, is otherwise 'dead' today except in so far as it still lives in its legacy to the present-day Christian and Islamic civilizations. If it is true—as it seems to be true—that at the western end of the Old World, in contrast to its eastern end, there has been a series of successive 'generations' of civilizations since the species of human society that we call 'civilization' made its first appearance, then it is true that the Jews and Judaism are a relic of a 'generation' that, except for the Samaritans[3] and the Parsees, is otherwise extinct. This is the historical fact that I had in mind when, in volume i of this book, I docketed the Parsees[4] and the Jews (among other present-day communities) with the label 'fossils'. My choice of this particular word may not have been a felicitous one for conveying the historical fact that I wanted to describe. But the fact is a fact, and some name or other for describing it is needed.[5]

At the same time it is, of course, untrue that Jewish history since the advent of Christianity or, alternatively, of Islam is of no account. In refusing to be *gleichgeschaltet* by either of the two 'deviationist' Judaic world-religions, and in surviving as a persistent minority in a Christian

---

[1] See the passage from a work of Rabbi J. B. Agus's, quoted on p. 211, footnote 3.
[2] On this question see pp. 292–3.   [3] See p. 430, footnote 2.
[4] It is a moot question whether the Parsees are to be regarded as surviving representatives of a distinctive Pre-Islamic Iranian culture, or whether we are to hold that this Iranian culture was gradually drawn into the field of the Syriac Civilization in and after the Achaemenian Age (see pp. 431–9 and 460).   [5] See pp. 292–300.

and a Muslim environment, the Jews have made a deep mark on both Christian and Islamic history as living Jews and not merely as dead Jewish forerunners of Christianity and Islam. Thus the Jews have not ceased to count, even in terms of Christian and Islamic history; and, *à fortiori*, they have not ceased to count in terms of their own history. While the Jews' relations with their gentile environment have been notably affected by the advents of Christianity and Islam, these two world-shaking events have had hardly any perceptible effect on the inner life of Jewry or on the evolution of Judaism. In and after the first century of the Christian Era the stream of Jewish religious literature flowed more copiously than ever before. For this period of Jewish religious history we are abundantly documented; and one remarkable feature of this contemporary Jewish documentation is the faintness of the marks that have been made on it by Jesus and by Christianity.

The main source of the impetus that transformed the primitive religion of Israel and Judah into Judaism was the 'traumatic twist' that 'the Jewish psyche received when the Jewish belief in chosen-ness sustained the terrible shock of national disaster and exile'.[1] This shock was administered to the Jews several times over: by Nebuchadnezzar in the second decade of the sixth century B.C., by Antiochus IV in the fourth decade of the second century B.C.; by the Romans in the Romano-Jewish wars of A.D. 66–70 and A.D. 132–5. The Jews' disastrous conflict with the Romans in the first two centuries of the Christian Era had far more effect on the history of Judaism than the advent of Christianity had.[2] It set Judaism hard. It precipitated the closing of the canon of the written Torah, the codification of a commentary on the Torah (the Mishnah), and the production of a commentary (the Gemara) on this commentary, which, together with it, constitutes the Talmud. The period from the time of Herod the Great (*regnabat* 40 B.C.–4 B.C.) to the generation of the Patriarch Jehudah, who codified the Mishnah *circa* A.D. 220, was the age of the Tannaim.[3] Judaism assumed its definitive form during the 150 years beginning with the generation of Rabbi Johanan ben Zakkai, who established his school at Jamnia, with the Romans' leave, in A.D. 70.[4] The canon of the written Torah seems to have been fixed by the Sanhedrin (a non-political body, not to be confused with the pre-war Sanhedrin) that Rabbi Johanan ben Zakkai had set up at Jamnia.[5] The codification of *hălāchōth* (agreed interpretations of the injunctions contained explicitly or implicitly in the written Torah) was started by Rabbi Akiba,[6] who met his death in A.D. 135, and its completion by the Patriarch[7] Jehudah was attained *circa* A.D. 220.[8] The Mishnah was the Pharisees' answer to the disasters of A.D. 70 and A.D. 135.[9] As for the shock administered by Nebuchadnezzar, this had

---

[1] J. L. Talmon in *Commentary*, July, 1957, p. 3.
[2] See R. Travers Herford: *Juda sm in the New Testament Period*, p. 12.
[3] G. F. Moore: *Judaism in the First Centuries of the Christian Era*, vol. i, p. vii.
[4] Ibid.
[5] W. O. E. Oesterley: *The Jews and Judaism during the Greek Period*, p. 45.
[6] R. Travers Herford: *The Pharisees*, p. 73.
[7] Patriarch of the Palestinian Jewish community that survived in Galilee after A.D. 135.
[8] R. Travers Herford: *Christianity in Talmud and Midrash*, p. 17.
[9] R. Travers Herford: *The Pharisees*, p. 192.

inspired Ezekiel, Deutero-Isaiah, and eventually also Ezra. The shock administered by Antiochus IV had inspired the Pharisees. The development of Judaism under the impetus given by these successive shocks was in process for nearly a thousand years (sixth century B.C. to fifth century of the Christian Era). But the advent of Christianity did not administer one of the propelling shocks.

It is 'a mistake to suppose that the rabbis took much interest in Jesus or cared to know much about him'.[1] The Mishnah does not contain the name Jesus or even the disparaging synonyms Ben Stada and Ben Pandira.[2] The rabbinical tradition about Jesus, such as it is, seems to have begun with Rabbi Eliezer ben Horqenos, who was a pupil of Rabbi Johanan ben Zakkai,[3] and whose working life therefore fell in the generation following the Romano-Jewish War of A.D. 66–70. The rabbinical tradition hardly implies knowledge of the Gospels,[4] and 'gospel teaching had no influence upon rabbinic teaching'.[5] 'It is remarkable how very little the Talmud does say about Jesus.'[6] According to the Talmud, Jesus was born out of wedlock. His mother Miriam was a ladies' hairdresser. Her husband was Pappos ben Jehudah. Her paramour was Pandira. Jesus mocked at the words of the wise. He called himself God and said that he would ascend into Heaven. He was tried and executed, by stoning, at Lydda.[7] The guilt—or merit—of having put Jesus to death is ascribed in the Talmud to the Jews, not to the Romans.[8] There is no mention of any claim, on Jesus's part, to be the Messiah.[9]

The Talmud does display some anxiety for fear that Judaism might be undermined from within by an heretical sect labelled 'the Minim', which seems to have been a disparaging nickname for the Jewish Christians.[10] From *circa* A.D. 80 onwards anyone who volunteered, at the sabbath service in a synagogue, to read a passage of the Torah and expound it was required, as a precaution against covert indoctrination of the orthodox by a crypto-Min, to recite the formula, drafted by Rabbi Shemuel ha-Qaton: 'May there be no hope for the Minim.'[11] The rabbis' anxiety about the Minim subsided as the Jewish Christian Church faded out. Considering that this unfortunate community was looked askance at by gentile Christians as well as by orthodox Jews, its prospects had been bleak since the date of Paul's first mission to the gentiles. The rabbinical literature ignores gentile Christianity;[12] and indeed the Jewish religious authorities could feel sure that the Jewish people would be impervious to an heretical form of Judaism when its representatives and advocates were not their fellow Jews, as the Minim were, but were gentiles whose religion would be ruled out of consideration automatically by Post-Exilic

[1] R. Travers Herford: *Christianity in Talmud and Midrash*, p. 359. This book is an authoritative and exhaustive examination of the subject by a distinguished Unitarian scholar. [2] Ibid., p. 351. [3] Ibid., pp. 351–2. [4] Ibid., p. 357. [5] C. G. Montefiore: *Rabbinic Literature and Gospel Teachings*, p. xvii. [6] Herford, op. cit., p. 347. [7] Ibid., p. 348. [8] Ibid., pp. 84 and 86. [9] Ibid., pp. 349 and 380–1. [10] See op. cit., especially pp. 321–41. G. F. Moore notes, in *Judaism in the First Centuries of the Christian Era*, vol. iii, p. 68, that in the talmuds and the midrashim the word 'minim' does not always mean Jewish Christians. The literal meaning of 'minim' is 'species', 'kinds' (i.e. peculiar kinds), and it was a generic term for Jewish heretics. [11] Herford: *Christianity in Talmud and Midrash*, pp. 135 and 388. [12] Ibid., p. 393.

Jewish minds simply by reason of its gentile provenance.[1] In short, neither Jewish nor gentile Christianity made any mark on Judaism.[2]

Thus, if one looks, as one ought to look, at the history of Judaism from inside[3] as well as from outside, it is evidently absurd to imagine that its history has ceased to be significant since the moment of Christianity's advent. During the early centuries of the Christian Era the development of Judaism was still in full swing. The Palestinian Talmud was not completed till the last quarter of the fourth century of the Christian Era, the Babylonian Talmud not till about one hundred years later.[4] This contrast between the historical facts and the conventional Christian and ex-Christian view of the history of the Jews and Judaism shows how difficult it is for anyone brought up with a Christian background to look at Jewish history objectively. An observer with an Islamic background is no less badly placed. An observer with a Jewish background is at an equal disadvantage, since the bias with which he will have to contend will be no less great, though it will, of course, incline him towards the opposite side. Among both Jewish and gentile scholars there have, it is true, been souls that have risen above the prejudices of their ancestral tradition. C. G. Montefiore, J. B. Agus, and G. F. Moore are notable examples.[5] The requisite degree of broadmindedness and generosity is, however, rare in the human race. And, in order to obtain a fully objective and illuminating study of Jewish history, we may have to wait for the appearance of some Hindu or East Asian scholar who has mastered this difficult subject under the spur of a disinterested intellectual curiosity. For the majority of mankind, which lives east of the Sutlej, the Jews and Judaism are not a practical problem, so a scholar from somewhere in this major part of the *Oikoumenê* would not have imbibed any anti-Jewish prejudice from his social and cultural environment—nor any pro-Muslim or pro-Christian

---

[1] The Jews and their predecessors the peoples of Judah and Israel have not, of course, always been proof against gentile religions and ideologies. From the time of their first invasion of Palestine down to the time of the extinction of the Kingdom of Judah, they were constantly attracted by the religion of the Canaanites (see Chapter XIII, *passim*). This was natural, since the culture of the Phoenicians, Jebusites, and other Canaanites was certainly higher than that of the Syriac communities of Hebrew origin in non-religious fields, and was not certainly lower in the religious field until the beginning of the Prophetic movement in Israel and Judah in the eighth century B.C. Judaism has been in danger of corrosion by alien ideologies once again in the Christian and Islamic worlds, since the time when Christianity and Islam themselves began to lose their hold on their adherents. In Western Christendom this began to happen towards the close of the seventeenth century of the Christian Era, and, during the last quarter of a millennium, this Western tendency towards agnosticism, rationalism, and secularization has been affecting, progressively, the whole of the rest of mankind, not excluding the Jews. Between the sixth century B.C. and the eighteenth century of the Christian Era, Judaism was relatively immune against the contagion of alien faiths and ways of life. The big exception, within this long period, was the influence of Zoroastrianism on Judaism during and after the Achaemenian Age (see p. 438).

[2] G. F. Moore: *Judaism in the First Centuries of the Christian Era*, vol. i, p. 92.

[3] 'Toynbee can greatly improve his . . . achievement by making use of the insights of Jewish experience, as indeed he has pledged to do' (Rabbi J. B. Agus in *The National Jewish Monthly*, November, 1956, p. 44).

[4] G. F. Moore: *Judaism in the First Centuries of the Christian Era*, vol. i, p. 4.

[5] R. Travers Herford is as fine a scholar as G. F. Moore, and is also as sympathetic, as well as fair, to the Jews and Judaism as Moore is. At the same time, Herford is not entirely detached in his judgements on the quarrel between the Pharisees and Jesus. When he is dealing with this topic, the reader is aware of another quarrel—that between Unitarianism and Trinitarian Christianity.

prejudice either, since, east of the Sutlej, the two 'deviationist' Judaic world-religions have been aggressive and disturbing spiritual forces by reason of their missionary zeal.

2. THE JEWS' PARAMOUNT AIM AND THE RELIGIOUS AND PSYCHOLOGICAL CONSEQUENCES OF THEIR SUCCESS IN ACHIEVING IT

The Jews may be defined as being the conscious and deliberate heirs and representatives of the people of the Kingdom of Judah, which was extinguished by the Neobabylonian Emperor Nebuchadnezzar in the second decade of the sixth century B.C. Ever since that fearful national disaster the paramount aim of the Judahites deported to Babylon and their Jewish descendants has been to preserve, unbroken, their distinctive national identity. In this they have been brilliantly successful. The Jewish people has managed to survive, as a people, a long series of successive ordeals: the extinction of the Kingdom of Judah and the deportation of the skilled and literate *élite* of its population to Babylon; the attraction, in Babylonia, of the Sumero-Akkadian Civilization, which was superior to the Judahite variety of the Syriac Civilization in everything except its religion and its script; Antiochus IV's attempt to merge Jewry—by force, after persuasion had failed—in an Hellenic Society with a standardized ideology and way of life; the deracination of Palestinian Jewry by the Romans in and after the two great Romano-Jewish wars of A.D. 66–70 and A.D. 132–5; the attraction of the Hellenic Civilization, which was felt even by Palestinian Jews in the third and fourth decades of the second century B.C., and which had a far greater effect on the Jewish diasporá in the cities of the far-flung Hellenic World, particularly in Alexandria-on-Nile; the successive pressures brought to bear on the Jews by Christianity and (more mildly) by Islam to merge themselves in one or other of these two gigantic 'deviationist' Judaic religious communities; the attraction of the Islamic, Byzantine, and Western civilizations. This record is recognized, by friendly and hostile observers alike, as being an extraordinary monument of steadfastness or obstinacy—whichever of the two words the observer may feel inclined to use. The achievement has been possible only because the Jews have always consistently given priority over other aims of theirs to this aim of preserving their distinctive national identity. A Jewish observer has called it 'the stiff-necked Jewish insistence on remaining Jewish under all circumstances'.[1]

One of these other aims has been to return to the country of Judah and to re-establish there a state which should embrace, not only the historic domain of the Kingdom of Judah, but the whole of Eretz Israel, meaning the combined domains of the two kingdoms of Judah and Israel up to the frontiers of the short-lived empire of the two Judahite kings David and Solomon. The aim of re-establishing the state of Judah, at any rate, was a natural corollary of the Jews' paramount aim of preserving their distinctive national identity. Since the invention of agriculture

[1] F. Borkenau in *Commentary*, May, 1955, p. 425.

first rooted the peoples who adopted it to particular patches of the Earth's surface, the possession of a distinctive national identity has, so far, usually been accompanied by the possession of a local national territory. This territorial substructure for the support of a distinctive national identity has, however, been progressively proved not to be indispensable ever since the dawn of civilization brought with it an accelerating improvement in all kinds of means of communication (mental as well as material), and also the establishment of cities, which have been growing in size at an accelerating pace. Looking back on the course of the history of civilization during the last 5,000 years, and paying particular attention to its history in 'the Fertile Crescent', where it made its first appearance, we can see, in retrospect, that communities of a new, non-agricultural, type have been arising. These new-model communities are post-agricultural in their means of livelihood; they live by urban trade and industry; but they resemble the pre-agricultural food-gathering communities in not being bound to some particular patch of the Earth's surface and in being held together socially and culturally by bonds that are not territorial but are cultural and ideological— a distinctive common way of life and common religion. Communities of this new type, capable of preserving their identities in diasporá, made their first appearance, as was to be expected, in the region in which civilization itself made its first appearance. Gradually they have been increasing in numbers and have been spreading, with civilization, over the face of the Earth.[1] The Post-Exilic Jewish diasporá has been one of the most successful of them. The vitality of the Jewish diasporá, and its significance, for mankind as a whole, as being the probable 'wave of the future', is brought out by the contrast between the steady success of the diasporá in surviving—in spite of penalizations, persecutions, and massacres—and the unsatisfactoriness of all attempts up to date, since the Babylonish Captivity, to re-establish a Jewish state on Palestinian soil.

The first of these attempts was made—with the permission and good will of the founder of the Achaemenian Empire, Cyrus—within less than half a century after Nebuchadnezzar had extinguished the Kingdom of Judah and had deported its notables to Babylonia. The latest attempt is being made in our day. It is noteworthy, however, that at all times when it has been open to the Jews in diasporá to emigrate to a Jewish state in Palestine, a great majority of them have invariably preferred to remain in diasporá. This was so in the year 539–538 B.C.; it is so today; and it has always been so all through the intervening twenty-five centuries. At any time between 538 B.C., when Cyrus gave the Babylonian diasporá leave to return, down to, at any rate, the outbreak of the first Romano-Jewish War in A.D. 66, it was open to any member of the Jewish diasporá in Babylonia to return to Palestine. But the number that returned with Zerubbabel in 538 B.C., with Ezra in 458 or 397 B.C., and with Nehemiah in 445 or 384 B.C.,[2] was insignificant compared with the total numbers

---

[1] This has been noticed already on pp. 209–17.

[2] The dates of Nehemiah's and Ezra's respective missions, and their chronological relation to each other, are uncertain, because each mission is dated solely by a regnal year of an Achaemenian Emperor Artaxerxes; and we do not know in either case whether

of the diasporá in Babylonia, which was the diasporá's centre of gravity throughout the Achaemenian, Macedonian, and Roman ages of South-West Asian history. Within the half-century of the Babylonish Captivity, the Jewish exiles had not only created a new way of life and a new set of institutions for themselves in diasporá; they had become so strongly attached to these and so confident that they had discovered effective means for preserving their distinctive national identity in diasporá, that they could not bring themselves to pull up the new roots that they had struck in Babylonian soil, recent though these new roots were. Indeed, so far from the Jewish diasporá in Babylonia re-emigrating *en masse* to Judaea, there was a fresh emigration of Jews from Judaea—this time into the cities, old and new, of the Hellenic World with which the Judaean Jews were brought into contact as a result of the establishment of the Achaemenian Empire's Hellenic successor-states. The Jewish community in Alexandria-on-Nile was merely the most important and conspicuous among a number of new Jewish communities that seeded themselves as far westwards as Rome inclusive. This new Greek-speaking Jewish diasporá in the Hellenic World west of Palestine came to rival, in numbers and importance, the older Aramaic-speaking diasporá in Babylonia. And the emigrants from Judaea into the Hellenic world were, for the most part, not deportees but voluntary settlers.

The present-day Jewish diasporá in the United States, which is the living counterpart, in importance, of the Jewish diasporá in Babylonia from the sixth century B.C. to the thirteenth century of the Christian Era, is reacting in just the same way towards the state of Israel that has been in existence in the former Philistine, Teucrian, and Jebusite districts of Palestine since A.D. 1948. Like their Babylonian predecessors and counterparts, the American Jews today are zealous in fostering a Jewish state in Palestine by contributing money and exerting political influence; but only an insignificant minority of American Jews, and of European Jews in European countries west of Germany, has been showing itself willing to emigrate to Israel. There is also already a perceptible trickle of re-emigration out of Israel into the Western World.

Thus the situation as it was in the Kingdom of Judah before the year 586 B.C. has never been restored in effect, in spite of the repeated efforts—which started within half a century of that date—to re-establish a Jewish community and Jewish state on Palestinian soil. Before 586 B.C. the Judahite community in the World was identical with the population of the Kingdom of Judah. Since then there has never been a Jewish community in Palestine that has been co-extensive with the Jewish community in the World or has even been the most important part of it. The Jewish community re-established in Palestine in and after 539–538 B.C., like its successor in our own day, was a child, protégé, and pensioner—in fact, a by-product—of the Jewish diasporá. Ever since the beginning of the Babylonish Captivity, the diasporá has been Jewry's citadel and

the Artaxerxes in question is Artaxerxes I (*imperabat* 465–424 B.C.) or Artaxerxes II (*imperabat* 404–359 B.C.). So we do not know whether the date of Ezra's mission was 458 B.C. or 397 B.C., or whether the date of Nehemiah's mission was 445 B.C. or 384 B.C. (see G. F. Moore: *Judaism in the First Centuries of the Christian Era*, vol. i, p. 5). Nehemiah may have preceded Ezra.

arsenal.[1] In A.D. 70 and in A.D. 135, as in 586 B.C., the diasporá survived, triumphantly, the destruction of a Jewish community on the soil of Judah. There has been no time since then—not even the eighty years of the Maccabaean Kingdom's sovereign independence (142/1 B.C.–63 B.C.) or the 37 years of Herod the Great's reign (40 B.C.–4 B.C.) by grace of Rome—when a Jewish community in Palestine could have stood on its own feet without financial and diplomatic support from the diasporá. Even in the field of religion the diasporá's role has been dominant. Judaism is a development of the Pre-Exilic religion of Judah that was created in and by the Babylonian diasporá and was imposed by it on the Jewish population in Judaea. The Babylonian Jew Ezra gave Judaism in Palestine the decisive impulse that eventually produced the Pharisaic movement and the rabbinical system.[2] The survival and vitality of the diasporá has been a *tour de force*; but, just on this account, the diasporá has been, and still is, the supreme and characteristic instrument and monument of the Jewish people's persistent will to maintain its distinctive communal identity.

This will to survive as a community anywhere and under any conditions has, since 586 B.C., been paramount over the will to survive as a community on the Palestinian soil once occupied by Judah and Israel. By comparison with survival itself, Zionism has been a secondary Jewish aim. There has also been the aim of converting the gentile world to the worship of Yahweh under the aegis of a world-empire centred on Eretz Israel and ruled by 'the Lord's Anointed': a coming human king of Davidic lineage. This third aim has, hitherto, been half-hearted. The hope of it has been dubious[3] and the pursuit of it has been spasmodic—in contrast to the persistence of the effort to secure the Jewish people's survival. All the same, the expectation of the Messianic Kingdom seems to have been one of the sources of the eventual Jewish belief in the resurrection of the body—a belief that became an obligatory doctrine, and was taken over, as such, from Judaism by Christianity.[4]

[1] The greatness of the diasporá's destiny was foreseen already by Jeremiah. He sent a message to the Jewish deportees in Babylonia urging them to make themselves at home there and to pray to Yahweh for Babylon's welfare (Jer. xxix. 4–7, cited by C. F. Whitley, *The Exilic Age*, p. 52). Ezekiel, too, believed that the future lay with the deportees (ibid., p. 93).

[2] Ezra set himself to make the Torah the governing force in Jewish life. In virtue of this, 'he was in a real sense the true founder of Judaism' (R. Travers Herford: *Judaism in the New Testament Period*, p. 370. Cp. eundem: *The Pharisees*, pp. 56–57).

[3] 'If the World hath indeed been created for our sakes, why do we not enter into possession of our world?' (2(4) Esdras, vi. 56–59, cited by W. O. E. Oesterley: *The Jews and Judaism during the Greek Period*, p. 117).

[4] The question how the belief in the resurrection of the body came to be a cardinal doctrine for Judaism is discussed by G. F. Moore in *Judaism in the First Centuries of the Christian Era*, vol. ii. The traditional Jewish notions about the fate of the dead had been like those of the Hellenic World in its early days, as recorded in the Homeric epic. The ghosts of the dead lead a shadowy existence either in their tombs or in an underworld called Sheol, which is a counterpart of the Hellenic Hades (Moore, op. cit., pp. 289–90). The problem of a human being's fate was slow in catching the attention of a people whose efforts were concentrated on preserving the continuous existence of a community in this world. The expectation of a resurrection is not to be found in the Book of Job (ibid., p. 291); and Ecclesiastes holds that, at death, human beings perish like animals (Eccl. iii. 18–21; ix. 5–6; and, in fact, *passim*). The expectation seems to have made its entry into the Jewish outlook at the time of the resistance to Antiochus IV in the fourth decade of the second century B.C. The Book of Daniel xii. 2–3 expects the resurrection of some Jews, both good and bad, and the Seven Brethren are represented, in

Throughout, the Jews have concentrated on their paramount aim of preserving their distinctive national identity. This focusing of Jewish efforts has been rewarded by success for more than two thousand five hundred years up to date. And this success, in turn, has had revolutionary religious and psychological consequences. It has produced a radical change in the Jews' concept of the character of their national god Yahweh and a radical reinterpretation of the Pre-Exilic literature of Israel and Judah.[1] These two religious changes—especially the change in the concept of the character of Yahweh—have set up a psychological tension in Jewish souls between the nationalism to which they are devoted, heart and soul, and a universalism that has been a by-product of their nationalism—a by-product that has been unintended and undesired but has at the same time been the inescapable price of their maintaining their faith in their nationalism in spite of the trauma inflicted by the experience of losing their political existence and being carried away captive. The tension—which is still unresolved today—is a spiritual struggle between the conflicting claims of two incompatible objects of worship. Which of the two is finally to win the Jews' allegiance? Their worship of their own community, served by and symbolized by their Pre-Exilic ancestors' national god? Or their worship of the One True God—absolute spiritual Reality in Its personal aspect[2]—into whom their national god has been transfigured, in their vision of Him, as a result of the revolutionary change in their concept of Him in the light of their harrowing experiences? 'Decisive in the psychological make-up of the individual is the question whether the group was selected for the sake of universal ideals, or whether those ideals were important because they emerged out of the life of the group.'[3]

If the Jews' worship of Jewry were finally to prevail over their worship of God, then their extraordinary feat of preserving their distinctive national identity in diasporá for 2,500 years would have been unprofitable

2 Maccabees, vi–vii, as looking forward to rising again. This expectation of a bodily resurrection for human beings seems to have been a corollary of the expectation of a Messianic Kingdom. This kingdom—whose coming was equated with 'salvation'—was to be an earthly one (Herford: *Judaism in the New Testament Period*, p. 19); and the righteous dead, especially martyrs for the faith, must rise again in order to participate in it (Herford: *The Pharisees*, p. 173; Moore, op. cit., vol. ii, pp. 312–13). This expectation of a resurrection to life on Earth in the Messianic Kingdom was eventually followed by an expectation of a resurrection to life in Heaven (Herford: *Judaism in the New Testament Period*, p. 116). But its original role was to give the individual Jew a share in the eventual glorious rehabilitation of the Jewish community and state on the soil of Judah (ibid., pp. 112–13).

The belief in the resurrection was an innovation of the Pharisees'. It had no authority in Scripture (ibid., loc. cit.) and it was not accepted by the Sadducees. The Sadducees, however, disappeared, with the Temple, in A.D. 70 (ibid., p. 121), and thereafter the Pharisees had the field to themselves, save for the transient and ineffectual movement of the Minim. According to the orthodox Jewish faith, as this was eventually established by the decisions of Pharisaic rabbis, people who deny that the resurrection is deducible from the Torah are one of three classes that are excluded from the world to come (Moore, op. cit., vol. ii, p. 388).

1 The religion of Israel became Judaism in consequence of the Exile (Moore: *Judaism in the First Centuries of the Christian Era*, vol. i, p. 3; Herford: *Judaism in the New Testament Period*, p. 14). It 'grew out of' the religion of Israel, but was not identical with it (Herford, ibid., p. 20). The change was gradual (ibid.). 'Judaism was continuous throughout its history' (p. 13).

2 'The personality of God was as integral as His unity' (G. F. Moore: *Judaism in the First Centuries of the Christian Era*, vol. i, p. 115).

3 Rabbi J. B. Agus, in *Judaism*, 1956, p. 34.

as far as the Jews themselves were concerned. Self-worship in the first person plural—*nahnīyah* ('nosism') as it is called in Arabic—has been one of the commonest—indeed, most commonplace—of all mankind's religions ever since Man learnt how to mobilize his collective power by means of political organization. This has been the paramount religion of the Egyptiac and Andean worlds; of Umma and Uruk and Ur; of Sparta and Athens and Rome; of Venice and Milan and Florence; of France and England and Germany. If the Jews were finally to put their treasure in this familiar idol, they would be justifying the Christians' and Muslims' judgement on them. The vision of the One True God would have been an involuntary product of Jewry's tribulations, as a pearl is an involuntary product of some irritant that has lodged itself inside the shell of an oyster. The Jewish soul would be a spiritually barren field; and the Christians and Muslims would have been, as they claim to be, the spiritually alert and enlightened seekers after God who had discovered the pearl of great price and had made this neglected treasure their own. This issue has been confronting the Jews for some two thousand five hundred years, since the date when the full vision of the One True God was attained by Deutero-Isaiah. 'Judaism, in one of its aspects, was, and is, a universal religion, while in another aspect it was, and is, a national religion.'[1] The Jews have not yet made their choice between these two incompatible alternatives.

3. THE CHANGE IN THE JEWS' CONCEPT OF THE CHARACTER OF YAHWEH

A radical change in the concept of the character of Yahweh is recorded in the religious literature that the Jews inherited from Israel and Judah and supplemented by their own commentaries on this Pre-Exilic heritage. This literature was precipitated over a period of fourteen hundred years or more, if the oldest strata of the historical books of the Torah are to be dated as early as the tenth century B.C., since the compilation went on till the completion of the Babylonian Talmud in the latter part of the fifth century of the Christian Era.[2] It is not surprising that a radical change should have taken place over a period of this length, in the course of which the worshippers of Yahweh met with a series of momentous experiences and underwent far-reaching changes in the social and cultural conditions of their life. In the accompanying changes in their concept of the character of Yahweh there was not a revolutionary break at any point; and, though the cumulative change in the picture was radical, there were at least two features, and these both important, that remained constant throughout. From the date of our earliest evidence down to the present day, the Israelite, Judahite, and Jewish worshippers of Yahweh have seen him in the form of a person, and they have believed that this divine person demands exact and unquestioning obedience from his human associates. This view of Yahweh is common

[1] R. Travers Herford: *Judaism in the New Testament Period*, p. 89. Cp. p. 96.
[2] G. F. Moore: *Judaism in the First Centuries of the Christian Era*, vol. i, p. 4. The Palestinian Talmud was completed in Galilee in the last quarter of the fourth century of the Christian Era.

to the crudest Israelite and to the most sublime Jewish conceptions of his nature. The Jews did not come to think of him in impersonal terms when they came to identify him with absolute spiritual Reality. The transfiguration of the national war-god of Israel into the One True God of all mankind and the whole Universe left the antique deity's imperious personality intact—in contrast to the depersonalization that overtook Zeus the sky-god of the Hellenes and T'ien the sky-god of the Post-Shang Chinese when he was identified with absolute Reality by the philosophers. Jewish monotheism was not metaphysical. It was moral and therefore personal.[1]

In the evolution of the concept of Yahweh there was this important element of permanence which persisted throughout the radical changes in the rest of the picture of Yahweh's nature. In the course of the formative fourteen or fifteen centuries there was, however, a great divide. The decisive changes took place within a span of not more than two centuries, running from the generation of the prophet Amos in the eighth century B.C. to the generation of Deutero-Isaiah on the eve of the conquest of the Neobabylonian Empire by Cyrus. This 'axis age' in the history of the concept of Yahweh is an exemplification of Aeschylus's insight that 'learning comes through suffering'.[2] This period of rapid and creative change in the outlook of the leading spirits in the religious life of Israel and Judah was also a period in which these two peoples went through three harrowing experiences: the economic and social revolution of the eighth century B.C.; the loss of their political independence and the destruction of their state, which overtook Israel in 722 B.C. and Judah in 586 B.C.; and the deportation of the leading elements in the population which followed in either case—a turn of the screw to which the Israelite diasporá succumbed but which the Jewish diasporá survived. Each of these experiences had its effect on the concept of the character of Yahweh.

Yahweh, as he is presented in the strata of the Torah that are older than the books of the eighth-century prophets, is a national war-god of a familiar type. He is the local god of three communities of Hebrew origin—Israel, Judah, and Edom—and he has his counterparts in Chemosh of Moab, Milcom of Ammon, Athene Poliúchus of Athens, Athana Chalcioecus of Sparta, and for that matter also in those unavowed but zealously worshipped deities Britannia, France, Deutschland and the other collective idols of the Post-Christian West. Yahweh's origin is obscure. It is clear that he was not originally a god of agricultural fertility. Perhaps he may have been the smithy-god of the Midianites, Kenites, or some other Nomad people of the North Arabian desert.[3] His recorded history begins when he becomes the political divinity of Israel. How and when this happened is also obscure. The story of the covenant made between him and Israel at Sinai, which eventually became the orthodox account of the beginning of his association with this people, is not the only account given in the Torah. Alternatively the covenant is said to have been made between Yahweh and

---

[1] G. F. Moore, op. cit., vol. i, pp. 260–1.
[2] 'Pathei mathos' (Aeschylus: *Agamemnon*, ll. 177–8).   [3] See p. 415, footnote 2.

Joshua at Shechem;[1] and at Shechem the god of the covenant may, in truth, have ante-dated the Israelite occupation.[2] In any case, Yahweh comes on to the stage of history as a political god worshipped by three of the Hebrew communities that had lodged themselves in Canaan in or before the thirteenth century B.C.

In the pre-eighth-century books of the Torah, Yahweh is presented as a divinity of a well-known barbaric type. In the traditional account of the making of the covenant between Yahweh and Israel, his *quid pro quo*, in return for Israel's allegiance to him, is to give Israel possession of a land that was neither his to give nor Israel's to take. The Hebrew invaders of Canaan had to lodge themselves there by force of arms, and Yahweh's supreme value to them lay in his military prowess. 'The Lord is a man of war.'[3] 'The Lord strong and mighty, the Lord mighty in battle.'[4] 'Blessed be the Lord my strength, which teacheth my hands to war and my fingers to fight.'[5] This potency of Yahweh's was, however, double-edged. He was as vindictive in punishing his adherents for acts of disobedience as he was effective in giving them military victory at times when they had not incurred his displeasure. The common theme running through the series of incidents in the book of Judges, in the edition in which this has come down to us, is that Yahweh has repeatedly delivered a disobedient Israel into the hands of its enemies, and has then sent the Israelites a rescuer each time that they have repented of their offence. But this primitive Yahweh is worse than vindictive; he is moody, capricious, and impulsive. Many of his acts are so arbitrary as to be unaccountable. He is also physically dangerous to human life, like some blind material force—for instance, a present-day high-tension electrified cable. If this Yahweh had chosen to swoop from Mount Sinai on to Mount Olympus, he would have been a match for the whole war-band of Homeric gods. His character, as depicted at this stage, is, no doubt, a reflection of the temper and outlook then prevalent among his worshippers. If so, the subsequent changes in the picture will be reflections of changes in his worshippers' temper and outlook—spiritual changes that were, themselves, responses to the challenge of harrowing experiences.

The first of these experiences was the economic and social revolution that overtook Israel and Judah in the eighth century B.C. The money economy that had previously established itself in the Phoenician and Philistine cities along the coast of Canaan, and the urban way of life that had been practised there for ages past, now invaded—or reinvaded—the highland cantons in the maritime cities' hinterland. This revolution was comparable to the one that overtook Attica in the next century, when the

---

[1] Joshua xxiv.
[2] See p. 414, footnote 3, and p. 420, footnote 3. On the other hand, Moore holds that the notion of a covenant between Yahweh and Israel is no older than the eighth century B.C., and that it was the introduction of this idea that made the Israelites' and Judahites' relation to Yahweh begin to become different from the neighbouring peoples' relation to their respective gods (*Judaism in the First Centuries of the Christian Era*, vol. i, p. 220).
[3] Exod. xv. 3.   [4] Ps. xxiv. 8.
[5] Ps. cxliv. 1. The dating of the Psalms is still in dispute, but, whatever may have been the date at which the two passages here quoted were written, they represent the picture of Yahweh as it was in the age before Amos and Hosea.

same more sophisticated way of life came in from Ionia and from the commercial cities clustered round the Isthmus of Corinth. In the Syriac World the social consequences of this economic revolution were the same as in the Hellenic. The countryside now had to carry the load of a growing capital city: Samaria in Israel and Jerusalem in Judah. The rich minority of the population, which now gathered in the capital to enjoy its amenities, became richer, partly through usury, while the poor rural minority became poorer. The community was now morally divided, and this raised a question about Yahweh's judgement that had not arisen as long as he had been the war-lord of a community that was held together internally by hostile relations with its neighbours. Now that Yahweh's people was divided against itself on a moral issue, Yahweh must take a line as between one faction and the other; and the eighth-century prophets confidently and eloquently declared Yahweh's judgement in his name. They declared that he stood for justice (as the sun god already stood in Egypt and was to stand in Anatolia, 600 years later, when Aristonicus called the oppressed to arms in Helios' name). The Prophets predicted that, if the oppressors in Israel and Judah did not repent and mend their ways, Yahweh would requite their injustice with a punishment that would involve the community as a whole. At the time, these prophecies fell on deaf ears. The subsequent calamities—the extinction of the state and the deportation of the oppressive notables—recalled the eighth-century prophecies to mind and branded them indelibly on the memories of the conscience-stricken deportees and their descendants. From the time of the Babylonish Captivity onwards, Yahweh, in the Jews' conception of him, was an all-powerful dispenser of justice instead of being an all-powerful tyrant giving rein to his whims.

The eighth century B.C. also saw the beginning of the end of the independence, and indeed of the existence, of the states of the Syriac World. The fourth and last, but also the most virulent, bout of Assyrian militarism was started by King Tiglath-Pileser III (*regnabat* 747–727 B.C.). After he had decisively defeated the united forces of Urartu, Assyria's most formidable rival at the time, and her East Anatolian and North Syrian allies, the whole Syriac World lay at his and his successors' mercy. Israel was obliterated by his immediate successor Sargon in 722 B.C., and the Assyrian sword hung suspended over Judah's head for a century, before Judah, in her turn, suffered Israel's fate in 586 B.C. at the hands of Assyria's Neobabylonian successor-state. Nor was this the end of the story of political disaster. From the date of Tiglath-Pileser III's accession onwards the peoples of Israel and Judah and the Judahites' Jewish heirs found themselves politically impotent in face of a series of overwhelming imperial powers; and, as far as the Jews were concerned, the situation remained the same when one empire gave way to another. The Assyrian Empire was followed successively by the Neobabylonian, the Achaemenian, the Ptolemaic, the Seleucid, the Roman. The imperial regimes varied from time to time in their treatment of the Jews; there were alternating periods of relative leniency and relative oppressiveness; but, throughout the age that saw the progressive change in the Jewish conception of Yahweh, the Jews were always at some empire's mercy—and this not only in Palestine but also in the vast regions, east and west, in which they came to be scattered as a local minority in diasporá.

The reduction of Yahweh's worshippers to a condition of permanent political nullity raised, for them, an agonizing question about the status of their god. In a world of political gods each symbolizing the collective human power of some local community, the gods' fates were implicated in the fates of their local adherents. A war between Israel and Assyria was at the same time a war between the god Yahweh and the god Asshur; and, when Assyria annihilated Israel, the logical inference was that this human military decision also signified that Asshur had overthrown Yahweh. The common-sense conclusion to be drawn from this was that the discomfited god's former worshippers should now transfer their allegiance to the victor god, either abandoning the worship of their own ancestral god altogether or, short of that, continuing to worship him as merely a subordinate member of a pantheon on which the victor god had imposed his supremacy. This was, indeed, the line taken by the defeated and uprooted peoples of Judah's neighbour states: for instance, by the deported Israelites. This was also the reaction of the Judahite refugees in Egypt after the liquidation of the Kingdom of Judah by Nebuchadnezzar. In spite of the prophet Jeremiah's protests they refused to retransfer their allegiance to Yahweh from the Queen of Heaven.[1] Was it not, indeed, mere common sense for the Jews, now that they had felt the full power of Babylon's arm, to become worshippers of Babylon's puissant gods Ishtar and Marduk-Bel?

Here was a crux for worshippers of Yahweh who, in spite of all, could not bear to abandon the worship of their ancestral god. There was, however, one way out of these straits. If Yahweh was not to be written off as having ceased to be mighty in battle, he must be credited with a far greater might and a far longer arm than the defeated Jews' ancestors had dreamed of attributing to him. In the Pre-Exilic Age, Yahweh's kingdom, as his contemporary worshippers had conceived of it, had been confined to the territories of these worshippers' states.[2] The Pre-Exilic peoples of Israel and Judah, including their prophets, had recognized the existence of other gods with political domains of their own in which, presumably, they were not less potent than Yahweh was in his domain.[3] Moab, Ammon, and Tyre, like Israel, Judah, and Edom, might each have been more or less loyal to its own national gods, but worshipping only the god of one's own country is not the same thing as believing that he is the only god in the World.[4] But suppose that one's national god did, in truth, have dominion, not only over one's own nation and national territory, but also over other nations with whom one's own nation had come into disastrous collision. Then one's own nation's defeat and humiliation at foreign hands would leave one's national god's power intact, and would, indeed, be a demonstration that his power was greater than one had

---

[1] Jer. xliv, cited already on p. 428, with footnote 2.
[2] W. O. E. Oesterley: *The Jews and Judaism during the Greek Period*, pp. 124-5. Oesterley mentions Israel and Judah. Edom, too, should be included in the list.
[3] Ibid., p. 94.
[4] G. F. Moore: *Judaism in the First Centuries of the Christian Era*, vol. i, p. 222.

previously imagined. Israel's and Judah's overthrow would have been brought about, not by the Babylonian conqueror's god Marduk-Bel, but by the conquered people's god Yahweh himself. The Babylonian conquerors would then be unintentional and unconscious instruments that had been used by Yahweh for his purpose. Yahweh's omnipotence 'is interlocked with the teleology of history'.[1]

This novel belief in Yahweh's potency beyond the confines of his worshippers' states, which had been forced on these worshippers by the experience of political disaster inflicted by foreign powers, was confirmed and reinforced by the experience of exile. However far the Jews might be deported from the temple at Jerusalem, which had recently become for them the only shrine anywhere in the World where the prescribed ritual worship of Yahweh could be performed legitimately, they still found themselves in Yahweh's presence. When Yahweh had thus proved to be omnipresent[2] as well as almighty,[3] was it any longer conceivable that the gods worshipped by the gentile peoples had any real existence? By the end of the fifty years of compulsory exile under the regime of the Neobabylonian Empire, Deutero-Isaiah had moved on from henotheism—the belief that Yahweh had an exclusive claim on Israel's allegiance—to monotheism: the belief that he was the One True God whose kingdom included all mankind and was coextensive with the Universe itself.[4] But, if it was in truth this almighty god Yahweh himself, not Asshur or Marduk-Bel, who had afflicted Israel and Judah, how could it be that a god who was still the god of Israel and Judah, and who was bound to them by a covenant, had brought himself to inflict these crushing calamities on his own peoples? It was true that they had now recognized that he was a just god, and also true that at least a minority among them had committed injustices which deserved punishment. But the chastisement that they had now received was so disproportionately heavy by comparison with the degree of their offence that it would be a shocking injustice on Yahweh's part if this were the end of the transaction. Therefore it could not be the end. Yahweh must have punished his people, not for his satisfaction, but for their good. He must have punished them in order to give them a chance of repentance; and, if they did repent, he would surely remit their penalty and restore them to their former state of relative well-being. On this interpretation of the motive of Yahweh's acts, he was not only just but was merciful, besides being all-powerful. The classical formulation of this Post-Exilic Jewish theodicy was to be made, centuries later, by a Christian Jewish 'deviationist':

[1] Moore, op. cit., vol. i, p. 375. Rabbi J. B. Agus observes that 'Judaism taught a ready-made *interpretation* of history, but not an objective understanding of it. So profoundly were the Jewish people convinced that the will of God accounted for all events that their interest in the actual events of history was all but extinguished' (*Judaism*, 1956, p. 30).   [2] See Moore, op. cit., vol. i, pp. 370–1.

[3] Both the omnipotence and the omnipresence of Yahweh were proclaimed by Jeremiah (C. F. Whitley: *The Exilic Age*, p. 49). 'Jeremiah was the first of the Hebrew prophets to declare that he could be worshipped wherever he was sought in sincerity of spirit' (ibid., p. 54).

[4] Oesterley, op. cit., pp. 95 and 110–12. C. F. Whitley likewise holds that Deutero-Isaiah was the first of the Prophets to declare that Yahweh was the *sole* true god (*The Exilic Age*, p. 135). But he also holds that Yahweh was clearly a universal god for Ezekiel (ibid., pp. 100–1), and that Amos represents Yahweh as having power outside the frontiers of Israel (ibid., p. 134).

'Whom the Lord loveth he chasteneth, and scourgeth every son whom he receiveth.'[1]

It may be true that, for the Jews, justice, not love, is Yahweh's predominant characteristic.[2] But, in the Jews' vision of him, there is a harmony, not a tension, between the two. 'Justice and mercy were not attributes of a divine being, but the character of a personal god, whom they could not imagine as either unjust or unmerciful.'[3] Mercy and, above and beyond mercy, love were ascribed to him in the eighth century B.C. by the Prophets; and both these qualities were proclaimed with ever-growing insistence and confidence, during the next 1,400 years, in the successive accretions to the corpus of Jewish religious literature.[4] This vision of Yahweh's nature was expressed by thinking of him as being like a father and a mother,[5] and by calling him 'Father in Heaven'. This phrase was coined by the Pharisees,[6] who made their appearance before the end of the second century B.C. It is a familiar rabbinical term.[7] It became an increasingly common form of address,[8] and this always with a personal reference.[9]

This mature Jewish picture of God as our Father in Heaven, misericors et miserator, ar-raḥmān ar-raḥīm, is at the opposite pole from the primitive Israelite picture of a wild, capricious, vindictive Yahweh. 'An ancient civilization was transmuted into a universal religion.'[10] In Jewish minds, under the stress and stimulus of Jewish experiences, the god of Abraham, Isaac, and Jacob has become transfigured in Deutero-Isaiah's vision into the god of Ikhnaton, Jesus, and Muhammad. One consequence of this transfiguration was that this god lost his name—at least in the sense that the utterance of it became tabu in Jewish mouths. To be called by a personal name implies being a representative of a class, from whose other representatives one needs to be distinguished. The name 'Yahweh' implies the names 'Milcom', 'Chemosh', and the rest; and this consecration of their names, through their being put on a par with Yahweh's, implies a recognition of these neighbour gods' reality. When the god of Israel, Judah, and Edom came to be thought of, by Jews, as being the One True God, he also came to be referred to by epithets and periphrases.

The transfiguration also had another consequence which was more momentous. In the Jews' own changed conception of Him, God had become too great, too just, too sublime, too benign for it to be possible to confine Him any longer to His traditional task of serving as the national god of a 'Chosen People'.[11] If He is the creator and lord of the

[1] Heb. xii. 6. This is a reminiscence of Prov. iii. 12.
[2] R. Travers Herford: *The Pharisees*, p. 126. Cp. p. 154.
[3] Moore, op. cit., vol. i, p. 393.
[4] See ibid., pp. 116 and 396–9; C. G. Montefiore: *Rabbinical Literature and Gospel Teachings*, pp. 109 and 312–13.
[5] Moore, op. cit., vol. i, p. 395.
[6] R. Travers Herford: *Judaism in the New Testament Period*, p. 88; idem: *The Pharisees*, p. 151.
[7] Montefiore, op. cit., pp. 125–9. Moore, op. cit., vol. ii, p. 204, notes that it is rabbinical, not apocalyptic.   [8] Moore, op. cit., vol. ii, p. 202.   [9] Ibid., p. 204.
[10] Rabbi J. B. Agus in *Judaism*, vol. 4, No. 4 (Fall, 1955), p. 332.
[11] 'In asserting the oneness of God and His justice, the Israelites made certain that their reach would always out-distance their grasp' (Rabbi J. B. Agus in *Judaism*, 1956, p. 38).

Universe, all His creatures must be His concern. If He is good as well as almighty, He cannot have limited His loving care to a tiny minority of His human creatures and have turned His back on the rest.[1] If the whole World is His and is embraced in His plans, the supreme objective of these plans cannot be the re-establishment of a Jewish state on Palestinian soil. This could be the supreme objective only for a god who was merely a national god, and had therefore lost his kingdom, vocation, and *raison d'être* when the nation on whose worship he had depended had lost its political existence and had been scattered to the four winds. The One True God into whom the god of Israel and Judah had been transfigured could, at will, restore both kingdoms in a trice, and would, no doubt, restore them in His own good time. But, if and when He did perform this provincial act of justice and mercy, it would be incidental to the execution of a universal plan in which such details would be insignificant.

Thus the Jews' theodicy had led them into an impasse. In justifying the ways of Yahweh to Jewry, they had discovered a spiritual treasure of inestimable value for the whole human race. Their god, as He had been transfigured in their hearts and minds as a result of their sufferings, could no longer be their god exclusively;[2] and His transfiguration could not be kept secret from the gentiles, since it was implied in new Jewish forms of worship and was explicitly proclaimed in new Jewish books. How, then, in face of this transfigured godhead, were the Jews to pursue their paramount aim of maintaining the Jewish community's distinctive national identity in a state of exile and political nullity?

There was no possibility of their making a spiritual retreat. It might be tempting, on first thoughts, to reduce the One True God again to the minor dimensions of the national god of Judah that had been His embryo. But this could not be done without at the same time depotentiating Yahweh *redivivus*; for if, after all, the Jews' god was no more than a national god, then he was not even one who was any longer mighty in battle. He was the prostrate adversary of Asshur and Marduk-Bel—at best, defeated; at worst, proved non-existent by the verdict of military history. The only way in which the Jews could save their national god was to lose their national monopoly of him; and, if they were now bound to lose this monopoly, they were faced with a choice between two alternative ways in which this inevitable result might be brought about. Either the Jews themselves might take the initiative in voluntarily sharing their new-found spiritual treasure with the rest of mankind; or they might leave it to the rest of mankind to take the initiative by snatching the treasure out of Jewish hands and running away with it. If the first of these two alternative courses were not taken, the second was bound to be. The treasure brought to light by the Jews was so inestimably valuable that sooner or later, by one means or another, it was sure to become the common treasure of mankind.

This spiritual crux has been a greater challenge to the Jews than the

[1] The rabbis have sought to get over this difficulty by supposing that, at Sinai, the Torah was offered to all mankind but was accepted by Israel alone (Moore, op. cit., vol. i, p. 277).

[2] This point is made by Moore, op. cit., vol. i, pp. 223 and 226.

challenges of loss of independence and deportation to which the change in the Jews' conception of their god's character was a response. There is only one solution for the antinomy[1] between the nationalism which is the Jews' will and the universalism which is an involuntary but inevitable corollary of their nationalism. The Jews must constitute themselves the One True God's missionaries to the rest of mankind,[2] and must make it their paramount aim to convert the World to the vision that has been vouchsafed to the Jews themselves. But the pursuit of this aim by the Jews would require them to unite with their gentile converts in a world-wide religious community of followers of the pure religion of Deutero-Isaiah, and this transformation of a closed national community into an open religious community would run counter to the Jews' hitherto paramount aim of preserving their community's distinctive identity in the form of a nation. The Jews have been racked by this crux for 2,500 years up to date, and they have still to make the choice with which it has confronted them. Happily the way is still open for them. It has not been closed by the advents of Christianity and Islam, as Christians and Muslims severally maintain. For the Jews, these gentile homages to the Jews' transfigured god may be portents and warnings; but they are not more than that; they are not irrevocable cancellations of the Jews' own manifest destiny. This is still intact, for the Jews to embrace, if they will.

4. THE RE-INTERPRETATION OF ISRAEL'S AND JUDAH'S PRE-EXILIC LITERATURE

(i)   *General Effects of the Extinction of the Kingdom of Judah and Deportation of the Jews to Babylonia*

When a community migrates slowly and gradually overland, it is possible for it to bring with it many, or even most, of its ancestral institutions unimpaired, even when its migration eventually carries it a long distance from its starting-point. For instance, the Indo-European-speaking peoples who moved south-eastward right across the Eurasian steppe and found new homes on the Iranian plateau and in India, retained a large fund of ancestral culture in common with those other Indo-European-speaking peoples who made shorter treks in the opposite direction and found new homes in Europe and, from there, in Anatolia. By contrast, a sudden forcible deportation has the same effect as a sea-passage.[3] Only the more easily portable elements of the deportees' culture can be carried with them. Impedimenta have to be left behind, however important they may have been and however painfully the loss of them may be felt. The elements that the deportees manage to take with them are only a selection from a former whole; and this selection has not been chosen by the deportees; it has been imposed on them by necessity. The portable elements of their culture may be casual frag-

---

[1] This antinomy has been noticed already on p. 487.
[2] This point is made by Moore, op. cit., vol. i, pp. 228–9.
[3] For this, see ii. 84–100.

ments. Yet, however casual, they are precious, because they are a salvaged remnant of the deportees' cultural past. Accordingly, they are now treated with greater veneration and solicitude than they ever received before the catastrophe of deportation shattered the integral unity of the culture in which these surviving elements originally inhered. What has survived is now progressively elaborated and developed, until these new accretions come to fill the gaps left by the disruption of the displaced culture's original pattern.

When the Jews were deported from Judah to Babylonia, the most important of the cultural impedimenta that they had to leave behind was the ritual worship of Yahweh in the temple at Jerusalem.[1] The consequent break in their religious history would not have been as great as it was if their deportation had taken place before, instead of after, the synœcism of Judah in the ancient Jebusite city that had been conquered and then been transformed into Judah's capital by David. By the year 586 B.C. the process of centralizing Judah's life in Jerusalem had been going on for 400 years. David had made Jerusalem the capital of the kingdom; Solomon had made its temple the principal shrine for the worship of Yahweh; Josiah had given Yahweh's temple at Jerusalem a monopoly of the cult of him at the expense of the former rural shrines. The extinction of the Kingdom of Judah and the deportation of its notables reversed this long-continuing centripetal movement abruptly and violently. A high proportion of the deported notables were doubtless former residents in Jerusalem. They included priests as well as laymen; and, of the two classes, the priests were the harder hit. As a result of Josiah's innovations, which had made the ritual worship of Yahweh illegitimate anywhere except in his temple at Jerusalem, the deported priests found themselves automatically debarred from performing their professional functions. They therefore, at one stroke, forfeited their religious and social importance within the deported Jewish community. The deportees' determination to preserve their distinctive national identity in exile required, first and foremost, a redoubled loyalty and obedience to their national god; but, in exile, new ways of honouring him had to be improvised; and, in the invention and operation of these new Jewish religious institutions, priests were not privileged any more than they were penalized. They were on a par with the laity.[2] Authority now accrued to individuals, whether priests or laymen, who had the vision to see how to keep the Jews' relation to Yahweh alive in the utterly unforeseen and strange circumstances of the diasporá.

For the creation of new Jewish religious institutions, two materials were at the diasporá's disposal: human beings and books. The human beings had been brought by force to Babylonia, and they had been able to bring their books with them. The new master-institution in which the deported Jews and their Pre-Exilic literature worked together to create something new was the synagogue. This was a weekly meeting on the sabbath day for mutual adult education in the Torah: that is, in Yahweh's

[1] C. F. Whitley underlines Jeremiah's role in cutting Yahweh-worship loose from Jerusalem (*The Exilic Age*, p. 6). Jeremiah condemned not only sacrifice but the Temple (pp. 48–49) and prophesied the Temple's destruction (p. 50).
[2] Moore, op. cit., vol. i, p. 42.

teaching, which the Pre-Exilic literature was held to contain. The synagogues became not merely meetings but meeting-houses with more or less permanent and regular congregations and administrators. The reinterpretation of the Scriptures led, in the second century B.C., to the emergence of the Pharisees: a movement, group, or party which was originally a small minority in the Jewish community and was, in its own estimation, a religious *élite*. The Pharisees devoted their lives to the elucidation of the Torah according to a method of their own; and this Pharisaic method eventually prevailed over all others. It became the only recognized method for the whole of Jewry. Non-Pharisaic renderings of Judaism made their fortunes in the shapes of Christianity and Islam; but they were abandoned or suppressed within the Jewish community. This was the common fate of Judaism as interpreted by the Sadducees (the name given to the priests' party in the Pharisaic Age), the Zealots (the contemporary militant party), and the Galilaean Jewish teacher Jesus. These three interpretations of Judaism differed greatly from each other; but all three alike succumbed to Pharisaism in the competition for winning the Jewish people's adherence.

As for the priests, their traditional authority was already undermined irretrievably by the time (*circa* 520–516 B.C.)[1] when the temple at Jerusalem was rebuilt and the ritual worship of Yahweh was restarted there in what had been the only legitimate practice of it since the time of Josiah. From 516 B.C. to A.D. 70, this ritually correct worship of Yahweh continued to be carried on in the ritually correct place, except for a short break of four or five years (168–164 B.C.) during which the Temple was appropriated by Antiochus IV to the worship of Olympian Zeus. Throughout this period the Jews believed that the Temple ritual was incumbent on them, and they continued dutifully to take part in it and to support it financially. But their spiritual treasure had already been transferred from the Temple to the synagogue and to the Torah; and therefore, throughout this period, the influence of the priesthood steadily declined.

The Book of Deuteronomy, which had been the manifesto of the innovations in Josiah's reign, instructed the people[2] to consult the priests when they needed rulings as to how the Torah was to be interpreted. From Ezra's day onwards the priests lost this key function to the scribes,[3] though Ezra was legislating in and for Judaea at a time when the Temple ritual in Jerusalem was once again a going concern. This enabled the scribes to make themselves independent of the priests.[4] Moreover, these Post-Exilic scribes were not the same as the Pre-Exilic scribes from whom they had taken their name *Sōpherim*. The original scribes had been government officials;[5] their new namesakes were a body of private individuals that was recruited by informal cooptation; and any Jew could be coopted if the fraternity considered that he had the requisite ability in the highly-esteemed new art of re-interpreting the Torah. The priests were the leaders of the opposition to the new scribes' creative but

[1] W. O. E. Oesterley: *The Jews and Judaism during the Greek Period*, p. 199.
[2] Deut. xvii. 9–11.
[3] Oesterley, op. cit., p. 228.
[4] Ibid., p. 229.
[5] Ibid., pp. 227 and 250–1.

audacious concept of an unwritten Torah by which the written Torah was to be interpreted. This was, for the priests, 'an annoying innovation'.[1] But, on this capital question, the priests were overruled and overborne. The Pharisees actually succeeded in forcing on the priests a new redaction of the Temple ritual corresponding to Pharisaic ideas.[2] The Sadducees disappeared with the Temple in A.D. 70.[3] The destruction of the Temple, together with the rest of Jerusalem, in that year was an immense political disaster for Jewry; but, in the history of Judaism as a religion, the cessation of the Temple ritual caused no crisis.[4] By that date the lifeblood of Judaism had long been flowing in other channels.

The priest's loss was the individual's gain. In a situation—and this was the diasporá's situation—in which Jewry's relations with Yahweh could not be maintained through the performance of the priests' professional function, the individual Jew had to be invited, and indeed be conscripted, to step into the breach. Though the Temple ritual at Jerusalem might be in abeyance, it was still possible for Yahweh to be served by his people. The individual could serve him by obeying his commands as these had been revealed by him in the Torah. The god-fearing Jew might, of course, be a priest, but it was in virtue of being simply a Jew, not particularly a priest, that he was called to his new vocation. The personal responsibility of the individual Jew for carrying out Yahweh's teaching, the Torah, was preached during the Babylonish Captivity by Ezekiel,[5] and this idea of Ezekiel's was translated into practice later by the Babylonian Jewish reformer of Judaean Jewry, Ezra.[6] Thus the experience of exile made religion a personal concern for Jews as well as a social one;[7] and, as Judaism became a religion for the individual, the individual became the recipient of God's love.[8] 'Judaism became in the full sense personal religion without ceasing to be national religion.'[9] The relation between God and the individual was stressed by the Pharisees.[10] At the same time, this individualizing of religion in the development of Judaism 'was accomplished beside, not in place of', national and religious solidarity.[11] A distinguished modern Jewish authority on the history of the Jews holds that 'what really matters in the Jewish religion is not the immortality of the individual Jew, but that of the Jewish people'.[12]

(ii) *The Synagogues*

Though there is no surviving record of the origin of the institution of synagogues, it can be inferred that it dates back to the Age of the

[1] Herford: *Judaism in the New Testament Period*, pp. 48–50.
[2] Herford: *The Pharisees*, pp. 47–48.
[3] Herford: *Judaism in the New Testament Period*, p. 121.
[4] Moore, op. cit., vol. i, p. 114.
[5] C. F. Whitley: *The Exilic Age*, pp. 6–7, 99, 109–13.
[6] Herford: *Judaism in the New Testament Period*, pp. 21–22 and 32–33.
[7] Moore, op. cit., vol. i, pp. 224–5.
[8] Ibid., p. 397.
[9] Ibid., p. 121.
[10] Herford: *Judaism in the New Testament Period*, pp. 87–88 and 92.
[11] Moore, op. cit., vol. ii, p. 311.
[12] S. W. Baron: *A Social and Religious History of the Jews*, 2nd ed., vol. i, p. 12.

Babylonish Captivity.[1] It can also be inferred that it was introduced into the Jewish community in Palestine from the diasporá.[2]

'When the synagogue was established there was nothing like it in connexion with any form of religion then known, and there has been nothing like it ever since, except its two descendants the Christian church and the Mohammedan mosque. To have created the synagogue is perhaps the greatest practical achievement of the Jews in all their history.'[3]

'The essence of the synagogue is congregational worship and edification conducted by the congregation through its own members and not by priests on their behalf.'[4]

Nation-wide instruction in religion was something specifically Jewish.[5] In the daily religious life of the Post-Exilic Jews 'the synagogue counted for much more than the Temple did'; and the religion of the synagogue 'suffered no injury through the fall of the Temple'.[6] There was a synagogue within the Temple precincts for perhaps a hundred years before the Temple was destroyed.[7] It may have been planted there in the reign of the philo-Pharisee Hasmonaean queen Alexandra (*regnabat* 75/4–67/6 B.C.).[8] The Pharisees imposed themselves on the Temple, 'but they were at home in the synagogue'.[9] The procedure in the synagogue was not modelled on that in the Temple.[10] In the synagogue service, instruction loomed larger than prayer.[11] The synagogue was used by the Pharisees as their forum for bringing the Torah to the people.[12] Popular religion was a product of the synagogues in the time of Jesus,[13] and it was from the synagogue that Jesus himself obtained his knowledge of scripture.[14]

(iii) *The Pharisees*

The name 'Pharisees' makes its first appearance in the records of Jewish history in the reign of the Hasmonaean king John Hyrcanus (*regnabat* 135–105/4 B.C.),[15] and there is some doubt about the meaning of the word. It is a participle of an Aramaic verb meaning to 'separate'. The 'Pharisees' might be separators or distinguishers of meanings, that is to say interpreters of the Torah,[16] or they might be people who separated themselves from other members of their community whose religious performance fell short, in their eyes, of coming up to the requisite standard of holiness.[17] On this second rendering of the word's meaning, which seems to be the more likely to be the right one, the name 'Pharisees' would signify the same thing as the name 'Kharijites';

---

[1] Herford: *Judaism in the New Testament Period*, p. 23; idem: *The Pharisees*, pp. 89–90.
[2] Oesterley, op. cit., p. 213; Moore, op. cit., vol. i, p. 321.
[3] Herford: *Judaism in the New Testament Period*, p. 26. Cp. Moore, op. cit., vol. i, pp. 114–15 and 281 seqq.
[4] Herford, op. cit., p. 23. Cp. Moore, op. cit., vol. i, pp. 114–15 and 281 seqq.
[5] Moore, op. cit., vol. i, p. 281.
[6] Herford: *Judaism in the New Testament Period*, pp. 28 and 29.
[7] Ibid., pp. 30 and 146.　　　　　　　　　[8] Herford: *The Pharisees*, p. 97.
[9] Ibid., p. 88.　　　[10] Ibid., p. 90.　　　[11] Oesterley, op. cit., p. 214.
[12] Herford: *Judaism in the New Testament Period*, pp. 73 and 134; idem: *The Pharisees*, p. 98.　　　[13] Moore, op. cit., vol. i, p. 518.
[14] Ibid., pp. 288–9.　　　[15] Herford: *The Pharisees*, p. 29.
[16] Moore, op. cit., vol. i, p. 62.　　　[17] Ibid., p. 61.

and the Jewish Pharisees did have the same historical origin that the Muslim Kharijites had.[1] They were a fanatically scrupulous minority who separated themselves, on this account, from the majority of their co-religionists who took their religion in less deadly earnest.[2]

The Pharisees separated themselves, in fact, from almost every other element in the Jewish community. Their earliest quarrel was with the Hasmonaean dynasty and its allies the Sadducees. The precursors of the Pharisees had cooperated with them both during the twenty-six-years-long struggle of Judaean Jewry against the Seleucid power's attempt to Hellenise Judaea (168–142/1 B.C.). But, as soon as the Seleucid Government had acknowledged its defeat, the allied Jewish factions fell out with each other. The purpose for which the rigorists had cooperated with the Hasmonaeans and the Sadducees had not been to set the Hasmonaeans on a throne or to make the Temple safe for the conduct of the ritual worship of Yahweh there according to the Sadducees' traditional practice. Their purpose in taking part in the struggle had been to make Judaea safe for the exact fulfilment of Yahweh's ordinances as revealed in the Torah[3] when this was interpreted according to the method adopted by the new order of scribes that had been instituted by Ezra. After the Seleucid Government's recognition, in 142/1 B.C., of the Hasmonaean House's sovereignty over Judaea, the Pharisees quickly fell out with the Hasmonaean kings John Hyrcanus (*regnabat* 135–105/4 B.C.) and Alexander Jannaeus (*regnabat* 102–76/5 B.C.);[4] and they seem to have become a self-conscious party, with a party name, in the course of this conflict. There was a Pharisaic insurrection against John Hyrcanus,[5] and a riot against Alexander Jannaeus in the Temple at one of the annual celebrations of the Feast of Tabernacles. Six thousand of the demonstrators are said to have been massacred, within the Temple precincts, by Alexander's Pisidian guard.[6] This incident was followed by a six years' civil war in the Hasmonaean Kingdom.[7] The insurgents were not labelled Pharisees;[8] and, indeed, militancy was contrary to Pharisaic principles. But the Pharisees were the beneficiaries of this upheaval. Alexander's widow and successor Alexandra (*regnabat* A.D. 75/4– 67/6) capitulated to them. From that time onwards their position in Jewry was established, and, through all the subsequent military and political vicissitudes of the Jewish community in Palestine, the Pharisees went from strength to strength.

Though the Pharisees had separated themselves from the Hasmonaeans and the Sadducees so emphatically, this does not seem to have been the separation to which they were referring when they took their name. The implied antithesis to the Pharisaic party is not the Sadducee party and not the Hasmonaean dynasty; it is 'the people of the land'

---

[1] Ibid., pp. 61–62, citing Eduard Meyer: *Ursprung und Anfänge des Christentums*, vol. ii (Stuttgart and Berlin 1921, Cotta), p. 284.
[2] Herford: *Judaism in the New Testament Period*, p. 46.
[3] Herford, op. cit., p. 53.
[4] Oesterley, op. cit., p. 37; Herford: *The Pharisees*, pp. 36–39.
[5] Josephus: *The Great Romano-Jewish War*, Book I, chaps. 2, 8, and 67, cited by Moore, op. cit., vol. i, pp. 62–63.
[6] Ibid.
[7] Ibid.   [8] Ibid., p. 64.

(*'am ha-aretz*).[1] The phrase means 'natives', and it had the same opprobrious connotation as this English word in its present usage. It also carried with it several offensive historical reminiscences. It recalled the disgust shown by Ezra and his fellow Babylonian Jewish purists at the laxity of the observance of the Torah in the Palestinian Jewish community of their day. It also recalled the contempt and harshness shown by the Babylonian Jewish diasporá's ancestors, the wealthy urban minority in the Judah of the eighth century B.C., towards the unsophisticated peasantry in the countryside. Finally, it recalled the ruthless expropriation of the previous Canaanite owners of Palestine by the Hebrew barbarian invaders in or before the thirteenth century B.C. Evidence for the Pharisees' hostility to the *'am ha-aretz* is to be found in their writings.[2] Hillel, for instance, pronounced that 'no [member of the] *'am ha-aretz* is religious'.[3] Johanan ben Zakkai exclaimed: 'Galilee! Galilee! Thou hatest the Torah. Before long thou will make common cause with the tax-assessors.'[4] The Pharisees' opposition to the *'am ha-aretz* was due to the Pharisees' passion for the correct observance of the Torah.[5] Defensive precautions were taken by the Pharisees against being involved, through intercourse with the *'am ha-aretz*, in breaches of the Torah.[6]

In the Pharisees' minds the *'am ha-aretz* no doubt included all Jews who did not come up to the Pharisees' own standards. The term would have been applicable, in fact, to the Hasmonaeans and the Sadducees, as well as to the lax and ignorant mass of the common people. The numbers of the *'am ha-aretz* had been increased by the Hasmonaean dynasty's conquests beyond the borders of Judaea. The Samaritans, who were conquered by John Hyrcanus, were proof against the Jewish version of Israel's and Judah's common ancestral religion. John Hyrcanus's destruction of the Samaritans' temple in 128 B.C.[7] merely clinched the Samaritans' loyalty to their own version of the religion of Israel. The citizens of the Hellenic city-states conquered by Alexander Jannaeus preferred death to conversion to Judaism. But the conquered Idumaeans, Galileans,[8] and Ituraeans were forcibly circumcised,[9] and only a small minority of them will have been drawn into the Pharisees' camp by the zeal of the convert. The majority will have swollen the numbers of the *'am ha-aretz*. The Idumaean contingent gave Jewry Herod; the Galilaean contingent gave it Jesus.

Thus the Pharisees were a tiny minority in the Jewish community of their age. Josephus reckons their total numbers at not more than about six thousand;[10] and he was writing of the situation on the eve of the Romano-Jewish War of A.D. 66–70, when Palestinian Jewry included the

---

[1] Herford: *Judaism in the New Testament Period*, pp. 59 and 72; idem: *The Pharisees*, pp. 31–32.
[2] Montefiore op. cit., pp. 6–7.   [3] Moore, op. cit., vol. ii, p. 160.
[4] S. W. Baron: *A Social and Religious History of the Jews*, 2nd ed., vol. i, pp. 278–9.
[5] Montefiore, op. cit., p. 15.   [6] Moore, op. cit., vol. ii, p. 159.
[7] Moore, op. cit., vol. i, pp. 26 and 56.
[8] Idumaea was finally conquered by Aristobulus in 104 B.C. after a first conquest by John Hyrcanus (Moore, op. cit., vol. i, p. 56); Galilee was conquered in 104–102 B.C. (Oesterley, op. cit., p. 37).   [9] Moore, op. cit., vol. i, p. 336.
[10] Herford: *Judaism in the New Testament Period*, p. 60; idem: *The Pharisees*, p. 34.

Idumaeans and Galilaeans as well as the Judaeans, and when the population of the Jewish districts of Palestine had increased as a result of the century of peace and prosperity that the country had been enjoying since the beginning of the reign of Herod the Great (*accessit* 40 B.C.). Moreover, the Pharisees were not only a minority; they were a censorious one; and they frankly displayed their feelings. They had shown their disapproval of the Hasmonaeans when these had been at the height of their power. After the liquidation of the Hasmonaean regime by Pompey in 63 B.C., the Pharisees did not conceal their disapproval of Herod the Great and his successors. They also disapproved of the Zealots, who stood, in the age of Roman ascendancy, for the former Hasmonaean policy of armed resistance to domineering gentile powers.[1] In the Talmud, which is the Pharisees' literary legacy, the Hasmonaeans are ignored and the Zealots are condemned.[2] The Zealots' outlook and temper are reflected in the apocalyptic Jewish literature,[3] and this too —and the apocryphal writings as well—are ignored in the Pharisaic literature.[4]

'The non-Pharisaic literature represents, both on its good and on its bad side, the religious ideas of the large majority of Jews in the period which it covers, while yet it does not represent that which was really vital, creative, and progressive in the Judaism of that period.'[5]

This passage perhaps fully explains the apparent paradox of the Pharisees' eventual triumph. Montefiore raises the question how the rabbis' recorded hostility to the '*am ha-aretz* is compatible with the historical fact that they received popular support.[6] This censorious minority had no coercive power over the masses whom they openly despised.[7] There is some evidence that the hostile feeling was mutual.[8] Yet the Pharisees had great influence over these at least partly hostile masses.[9] Indeed, popular Judaism 'was Pharisaic as far as it went'.[10] 'The people followed the Pharisees.'[11] Present-day Judaism is Pharisaic Judaism.[12] In fact 'Judaism is the monument of the Pharisees.'[13] By contrast, the Hasmonaeans and the Herods, wielding their military and political power, and the Sadducees, wielding their ecclesiastical power,

---

[1] In deploring the militancy of the Zealots, the Pharisees were in agreement with both Herod and Jesus; and this consensus is not surprising. For the Palestinian Jews to challenge Rome in war was criminal folly—as was demonstrated by the outcome of the wars of A.D. 66–70 and A.D. 132–5. The Hasmonaean resistance to the Seleucid Monarchy had been heroic but not foolhardy. The Seleucid power had been an idol whose feet were 'part of clay' (Dan. ii. 33). The Roman power was all of iron. Tacitus (*Historiae*, Book V, chaps. 8–10) draws attention to the Jews' (i.e. the Zealots') miscalculation in imagining that they could deal with the Romans as the Hasmonaeans had dealt with the Seleucidae in the age when the Seleucid power had already been broken by its collision with Rome.   [2] Rabbi J. B. Agus in *Judaism*, 1956, p. 18.

[3] Herford: *Judaism in the New Testament Period*, p. 127; idem: *The Pharisees*, p. 188.

[4] Herford: *Judaism in the New Testament Period*, p. 125.

[5] Ibid., p. 130.   [6] Montefiore, op. cit., p. 11.

[7] Herford: *Judaism in the New Testament Period*, p. 137.

[8] S. W. Baron: *A Social and Religious History of the Jews*, 2nd ed., vol. i, p. 278.

[9] Herford: *Judaism in the New Testament Period*, pp. 77–78.

[10] Ibid., p. 80.

[11] E. Berkovitz: *Judaism: Fossil or Ferment?*, p. 117. Cp. p. 123.

[12] D. W. Riddle: *Jesus and the Pharisees*, p. 3.

[13] Moore, op. cit., vol. ii, p. 193.

did not gain any hold over Jewish hearts; nor did Jesus nor Christianity —not even Jewish Christianity. The Jewish Christians were branded as odious heretics; and even the Sadducees, after they had faded out in A.D. 70, became heretics posthumously on account of their disbelief in the resurrection,[1] after the Pharisees had made the belief in it a *conditio sine quâ non* for being accepted as an orthodox Jew. The Zealots alone were able, in their day, to compete with the Pharisees for the allegiance of the masses;[2] but the Zealots' influence was temporary, the Pharisees' influence was permanent.[3]

What were the reasons for the Pharisees' eventual triumph? In the first place, the Pharisees had a creative aim that answered to the Jewish people's needs, and was within their reach, in the situation in which they found themselves in the Post-Exilic Age. 'Pharisaism was the application of Prophetic teaching to life.'[4] In the second place, the Pharisees had a method for translating the aim into action. In the third place, they were single-minded. They were devoted to their aim and they never flagged in their efforts to put it into effect in accordance with their own prescriptions. Pharisaism won the Jewish people's allegiance both because of the intrinsic spiritual value of its aim and because of the sincerity of the Pharisees in practising what they preached.[5]

Another, though secondary, reason for the Pharisees' success was their pacifism. Their political requirement was negative and modest. They required freedom for themselves to carry out God's commandments, as revealed in His Torah, according to their own method of interpreting the Torah. They would submit to any political regime, Jewish or gentile, that met this minimal demand of theirs.[6] On this condition they were prepared to put up with Herod's government[7] or with the Roman

---

[1] Moore, op. cit., vol. i, p. 86.

[2] Herford: *Judaism in the New Testament Period*, pp. 77–78.   [3] Ibid., p. 82.

[4] Herford: *The Pharisees*, p. 238. The influence of the Prophets on the people's religion was in fact greatest in the Post-Exilic Age (Moore, op. cit., vol. i, p. 15). Ezraic Judaism was bent on putting Prophetic teaching into practice (Herford: *The Pharisees*, pp. 136–7). 'If there had been no Prophets, there would have been no Pharisees, the Prophets would have perished' (ibid., p. 138). Better late than never. Belated recognition and veneration is praiseworthy, not criminal. The Gospels admit the contemporary Pharisees' regard for the Prophets in twisting it into a criminal offence (Matt. xxiii. 29–32; Luke xi. 47).

[5] In the Gospels the Pharisees are denounced as hypocrites (e.g. in Matt. vi. 3–9 and xxiii; Mark xii. 38–40; Luke xi. 39–52). This accusation is unjust, for the Pharisees did not only practise what they preached, they also believed in it. They can perhaps fairly be accused of self-righteousness and self-complacency, and also of formalism. Their formalism was indeed an inevitable consequence of their conception of the nature of the Torah and of the method by which the Torah was to be interpreted. In their belief the Torah was God's teaching, and was therefore to be obeyed precisely, totally, and unquestioningly. They also believed that they had a method of interpreting the Torah by which they could elicit the commandments contained in it. Their whole duty, as they saw it, was to obey these commandments as they were revealed by applying to the Torah the Pharisaic method of interpretation. To draw distinctions between commandments, and to judge that some of these were more important, and therefore more imperative, than others, would have seemed to them, not merely presumptuous, but positively impious. The questionable feature of Pharisaism is its intellectual premises. There can be no doubt that the Pharisees were sincere in acting on them. Hypocrisy is denounced by the rabbis themselves (C. G. Montefiore: *Rabbinical Literature and Gospel Teachings*, pp. 118–19; Herford: *Judaism in the New Testament Period*, p. 55).

[6] Rabbi J. B. Agus points out that the Jews have not only been ready to forgo self-government. They have also been ready to lose their cultural identity as well (e.g. their ancestral language). They have concentrated on preserving their religious identity (*Judaism*, 1956, p. 18).   [7] Moore, op. cit., vol. i, p. 77.

government, though these were, in themselves, no less distasteful to Pharisees than they were to other Jews. The Pharisees tried to keep out of politics,[1] and in principle they were pacifists.[2] 'The whole Zealot movement was contrary to the ground principles of Pharisaism'.[3] For the Pharisees, 'fidelity to their religion and the authority of the interpreters of the Law had completely displaced political loyalty and the sense of civic duty'.[4] 'It was true that', in their view, 'there was and could be only one rightful king over Israel, viz. God; but, until He saw fit to send His messiah to establish His Kingdom, no attempt ought to be made by human action to force His hand.'[5] The right human contribution towards bringing the messianic kingdom into existence was repentance, not violence.[6] Two acts may be cited as being characteristically Pharisaic: the Jewish petition in 63 B.C. to Pompey to abolish the Hasmonaean monarchy,[7] and Rabbi Johanan ben Zakkai's concordat with the Roman military authorities on the eve of the fall of Jerusalem in A.D. 70. Johanan, on his part, agreed to submit to Roman rule; the Romans, on their part, agreed to let him move, unmolested, from Jerusalem to Jamnia, behind the Roman lines, and to establish there his school of rabbinical research.[8]

In maintaining this non-militant political attitude the Pharisees were at one with Jesus and with the Christian Church; and it is no accident that both Pharisaic Judaism and Christianity have survived and that Hasmonaean and Zealot Judaism have perished. This Pharisaic-Christian pacifism was practical common sense in an age in which the historic heart of the *Oikoumenê* was dominated by a series of overwhelmingly powerful and aggressive military empires. But pacifism is also the right policy for a higher religion in all ages and all circumstances, and this for a spiritual reason that is always valid. When the adherents of a higher religion go into politics and take up arms, they thereby stultify their religion and sterilize it—and this the more grievously the more successful they are in achieving the worldly aims into which they have diverted their energies. This truth is illustrated in the histories, not only of Judaism, but of Christianity, Islam, Zoroastrianism, and Sikhism. The Pharisees' pacifism saved Judaism from perishing with the Zealots.

(iv) *The Pharisees' Conception of the Nature of the Jewish Scriptures*

To a sceptical outsider's mind, the Jewish Scriptures are a heterogeneous collection of books, fragments of books, and centos composed

---

[1] Herford: *The Pharisees*, p. 45.
[2] Ibid., p. 190. Cp. *Judaism in the New Testament Period*, pp. 60, 69, 77; Montefiore: *Rabbinic Literature and Gospel Teachings*, pp. 27–30.
[3] Herford: *The Pharisees*, p. 189.   [4] Moore, op. cit., vol. ii, p. 113.
[5] Herford: *Judaism in the New Testament Period*, p. 69.
[6] Ibid., p. 111.   [7] Moore, op. cit., vol. ii, p. 113.
[8] I have been criticized—I think justifiably—by at least two Jewish writers for taking Rabbi Johanan ben Zakkai's concordat with the Romans as a new departure in the history of Judaism and therefore giving Johanan himself too great prominence. E. Berkovits points out that 'he does not represent a new departure in Judaism; he is only one link, though a very important one' (*Judaism: Fossil or Ferment?*, p. 118. Cp. p. 44, footnote 25). M. Samuel points out that Rabbi Johanan needed no conversion; he was in the main stream of Pharisaic tradition (*The Professor and the Fossil*, pp. 86–87).

of fragments. The only thing that all components of the collection have in common is that they are the work of human authors. In genre and subject and, still more, in literary and spiritual value, they differ enormously. The set of books that was eventually made canonical contains mythology, folk-lore, history, law (secular as well as religious), lyric and elegiac poetry, politico-religious prophetic manifestos, additions to these manifestos by anonymous hands in the original authors' names, one problem play (the Book of Job), and, latest in date, one apocalypse (the Book of Daniel). The canonical collection ranges in date over about eight centuries (tenth to second century B.C.). The Pentateuch alone, which was all that was ever accepted as being canonical by the Samaritans,[1] ranges over two or three centuries (not reckoning in the earlier dates of the traditional materials out of which it was composed). The collection, so it appears to the outsider, has no unity. As he sees it, it is certainly not a self-consistent, uniformly authoritative, and all-sufficing divine revelation of what is true and right. This, however, is what the Pharisees saw in it,[2] and the vision possessed them heart and soul. For them their Scriptures were a written revelation of God's teaching (Torah).[3] It was their duty to do what the Torah told them. It was, therefore, also their duty to interpret it right, so far as this could be done by taking unlimited pains. 'Religion, for them, was the realisation, in thought and in act, of all that the Torah revealed, so far as it was given to them to apprehend its meaning.'[4]

'The foundation of Judaism is the belief that religion is revealed.'[5] This belief is, indeed, Judaism's distinctive mark.[6]

'It might be a reasonable religion, but it was in an eminent degree a religion of authority; a revealed religion, which did not ask Man's approval, but demanded obedience to the whole and every part, reason and inclination to the contrary notwithstanding; an exclusive religion which tolerated no divided allegiance.'[7]

The Torah was God's wisdom (*hokmah*).[8] It had been created before the World,[9] and it was unchangeable.[10] It was also deemed to contain an inexhaustible store of still unelicited truth.[11] So, in theory, the possibility of progressive revelation was excluded.[12] Yet even religious beliefs cannot be frozen permanently, however conservative the believers' attitude and intentions may be. A method of unavowedly progressive interpretation of the theoretically unchangeable but at the same time inexhaustible written Torah kept Judaism on the move, and thereby kept it alive.

This way out had to be found and taken because the belief that the

---

[1] Moore, op. cit., vol. i, p. 27.
[2] Ibid., p. 239. Cp. p. 245, footnote 1, and pp. 247–8 and 358.
[3] 'Torah means teaching. . . . Torah does not mean law and never did' (Herford: *Judaism in the New Testament Period*, pp. 30–31. Cp. eundem: *The Pharisees*, p. 54; Moore, op. cit., vol. i, p. 262; Oesterley, op. cit., p. 56).
[4] Herford: *Judaism in the New Testament Period*, p. 47.
[5] Moore, op. cit., vol. i, p. 112.   [6] Ibid., p. 235.   [7] Ibid., p. 324.
[8] Oesterley, op. cit., p. 61; Moore, op. cit., vol. i, pp. 263–5.
[9] Oesterley, op. cit., pp. 61–62.   [10] Moore, op. cit., vol. i, pp. 239 and 269.
[11] Herford: *Christianity in Talmud and Midrash*, p. 10.
[12] Moore, op. cit., vol. i, p. 239.

revelation of God's will was contained in the written Torah had a corollary that was as inescapable as it was awkward. All God's revealed injunctions are, in virtue of their origin, absolutely, and therefore equally, authoritative and obligatory.[1] The belief in verbal inspiration leads to 'an atomistic exegesis'.[2] Every injunction that can be elicited from the text of the written Torah by the agreed method of interpretation stands on its own feet with sovereign authority as one of God's absolute commands. The act of observance is worthless in itself; its intrinsic value and its practical effect are irrelevant; it is valuable solely because it is an act of obedience to God's will.[3] 'A river will carry on its surface sticks and straws and the refuse from its banks; but it is the river which matters, and, without it, the trifles it carries down would never have been noticed.'[4] Accordingly, primitive ritual rules embedded in the older strata of the Pre-Exilic Scriptures were accepted blindly as being God's commands.[5] No incompatibility was felt as between ritual minutiae and ethical principles.[6] 'Conformity to the revealed will of God is the essence of religion.'[7] There is no warrant in Judaism for dissecting the law into a 'ceremonial' and a 'moral' section.[8] For the rabbis, 'right and wrong were ... not defined by the reason and conscience of men ... but by the revealed will of God'.[9] Pre-Exilic 'sin offerings' had been expiations for acts that had no moral significance.[10] 'The specific purifications and expiations of the Law apply almost solely to cases which have intrinsically no moral quality';[11] and, in the Post-Exilic rabbis' eyes, breaches of morally indifferent laws were as sinful as breaches of morals.[12] In the rabbis' view it was possible to sin without knowledge or intention.[13] Sin means a breach of God's law.[14] 'The legal righteousness of the rabbis was, in frequent practice, an odd combination of minute "ceremonial" and outward observances and of the most delicate loving-kindness and the sweetest piety.'[15]

Thus, for the rabbis, 'the Pentateuch was both an inspiration and a bondage'.[16]

'By the terms of their faith, they could not distinguish between one verse and another. . . . Yet the rabbis struggle (unconsciously) in their chains and against their limitations; for all these distinctions between light and heavy commands, all this insistence on "for its own sake", "all for love", all this special stress on "moral" commands such as chastity and love of neighbours and so on, are extra-Pentateuchal; they are read into the text, and are not to be found *in* the text.'[17]

Montefiore draws attention[18] to the extent to which the Rabbis transcended the text of the written Torah. This was made possible by the Pharisaic method of interpreting it.

[1] Ibid., p. 235.   [2] Ibid., p. 248.
[3] Herford: *The Pharisees*, pp. 76–77. Cp. pp. 116–17, 118, 120.
[4] Ibid., p. 69.   [5] Moore, op. cit., vol. ii, pp. 76–77.
[6] Op. cit., vol. i, p. 18.   [7] Op. cit., vol. ii, p. 78.
[8] Ibid., p. 79.   [9] Ibid. Cp. pp. 82 and 89.
[10] Op. cit., vol. i, p. 461.   [11] Ibid., p. 494.
[12] Ibid., p. 462.   [13] Ibid., p. 463.
[14] Ibid., pp. 116–17.   [15] Montefiore, op. cit., p. 198.
[16] Ibid., p. 319.   [17] Ibid. Cp. p. 351.
[18] Ibid., p. 294.

(v) *The Pharisees' Method of interpreting the Written Torah*

The basis of the Pharisaic interpretation of the written Torah was the doctrine that an unwritten Torah, besides the written Torah, had been given to Moses by God; that this had been handed down, by an authentic oral tradition, to the Post-Exilic scribes; that this unwritten Torah, in which the scribes were versed, was as authoritative as the written Torah; and that it could therefore be used legitimately by the scribes as a key for interpreting both the written Torah and the priests' ordinances (*gĕzērōth*) by which the gaps and obscurities in the written Torah had been inadequately supplemented.[1] This audacious new Pharisaic doctrine had been rejected by the Sadducees,[2] but that did not deter the Pharisees from systematically reinterpreting the Torah by means of their revolutionary hermeneutical instrument. The process went on for not less than six hundred years, till it came to an end with the completion of the Babylonian Talmud. 'This conception of the unwritten Torah proved to be the means of saving Judaism from decay.'[3] Scripture unaided by tradition had never been adequate.[4] The new doctrine opened the way for what was, in effect, though not avowedly, a claim on the rabbis' part to be receiving continual inspiration.[5]

'The religious life of the Jewish people was saved by the exaltation of the Torah from being a closed revelation to an open one, from a dead letter to a letter made alive again, from a text long ago set and hardened, whose meaning could never change and which could say nothing new, to a text whose meaning was plastic because freshly interpreted in the light of the growing moral discernment of religious teachers, age after age.'[6]

Thus, in effect, the Post-Exilic scribes had given themselves a free hand. The use that they made of this was to elicit from the text of the written Torah two kinds of sentences: the one kind imperative, the other indicative.[7] A sentence of the imperative kind was called a *hălāchāh* (in the plural, *hălāchōth*). The literal meaning of the word is 'walk'; its technical meaning is a divine command elicited from the written Torah by applying the unwritten Torah to the interpretation of it.[8] The corpus of *halachoth* is what is meant, in the Gospel according to St. Matthew (xv. 2–3), by 'the tradition of the elders'.[9] A sentence of the indicative kind was called a *haggādāh*. It was a statement of matters of fact in such fields as those of theology, ethics, psychology, and metaphysics.[10] A *halachah* was a much more serious matter than a *haggadah* in the rabbis' estimation. It was serious because, if and when it had been ratified by the recognized procedure, obedience to it became absolutely obligatory for

---

[1] For this doctrine of the unwritten Torah, see Oesterley, *The Jews and Judaism during the Greek Period*, p. 58; Herford: *Judaism in the New Testament Period*, pp. 42–43; eundem: *The Pharisees*, p. 63; Moore, op. cit., vol. i, pp. 253–4.
[2] Oesterley, op. cit., pp. 250–1; Herford: *Judaism in the New Testament Period*, p. 46.   [3] Herford, op. cit., p. 44.
[4] Moore, op. cit., vol. i, p. 251.   [5] Herford: *The Pharisees*, pp. 65–66.
[6] Ibid., p. 66. Cp. p. 144.   [7] See Herford: *The Pharisees*, pp. 70–71.
[8] Herford: *Judaism in the New Testament Period*, p. 54.
[9] Ibid.
[10] Ibid., p. 56. Cp. p. 83. Idem: *The Pharisees*, p. 79.

all Jews. The *halachoth*, being binding, must be consistent with each other; the *haggadoth* were not binding and therefore might be mutually contradictory.[1] An accredited teacher could pronounce a *haggadah* on his own individual authority.[2] On the other hand the definition of a *halachah* was the corporate concern of the whole order of rabbis, and it did not become valid unless it had been adopted by a majority vote,[3] or at least by an informal consensus.[4] All *halachoth* were deemed to be implicitly contained in the text of the written Torah.[5] Yet the rabbis sometimes went so far as to set the written Torah aside.[6] 'The ethics of the *halachah* was not identical with the ethics of the Old Testament, and the change from one to the other was deliberately made.'[7] Moreover, the breach of a *halachah* was treated by the rabbis as being a graver offence than disobedience to the Scriptures.[8] An established *halachah* could, however, be modified by subsequent decisions taken in proper form;[9] and thus the corpus of *halachoth* remained plastic until the completion of the Babylonian Talmud. By contrast, the corpus of *haggadoth* did not evolve, and in this it differed from Christian theology.[10] The rabbis' theology remained unsystematic;[11] they did not go in for theological definitions.[12] 'From first to last, they were religious teachers, and neither theologians nor philosophers.'[13]

Herford points out[14] that the Pharisees quarrelled with Jesus because he taught the people 'as one having authority, and not as the scribes'.[15] In other words, he pronounced *halachoth* on his own authority as if they were *haggadoth* and as if he were an accredited rabbi, recognized by the established members of the order. He did not have this status, and, even if he had had it, he would not have been entitled to promulgate *halachoth* of his own unless and until these had been adopted and ratified by a consensus of his colleagues in accordance with the established rabbinical procedure.

'He repudiated the whole system of the *halachah*; and he criticised, and on occasion rejected, the Torah on which the *halachah* was based.[16] . . . What is recorded shows clearly that Jesus had no close acquaintance with the *halachah* which he denounced, and none at all with the theory of it. . . . If he had had such knowledge, he would not have used the case of Corban as a weapon, for the case on that subject was quite other than he supposed.'[17]

---

[1] Herford: *Judaism in the New Testament Period*, p. 57; idem: *The Pharisees*, pp. 81 and 147–8.   [2] Herford: *The Pharisees*, p. 80.
[3] Ibid., pp. 74, 108, 109; *Judaism in the New Testament Period*, p. 54.
[4] There is a parallel to this in Islam. Here, too, rulings become valid through an informal consensus (*ijmā'*) among the doctors of the *Sharī'ah*.
[5] Herford: *The Pharisees*, p. 85.   [6] Moore, op. cit., vol. i, p. 259.
[7] Herford: *The Pharisees*, p. 111.   [8] Moore, op. cit., vol. i, pp. 33–34.
[9] Herford: *The Pharisees*, pp. 110–13.
[10] Herford: *Judaism in the New Testament Period*, p. 84.
[11] Herford: *The Pharisees*, p. 79.
[12] Herford: *Judaism in the New Testament Period*, p. 85.
[13] Ibid., p. 86. Cp. pp. 91–92. Herford makes the point that Christianity allows freedom in moral theology (i.e. in *halachah*) but not in doctrinal theology (i.e. in *haggadah*), whereas in Judaism it is the other way round (*The Pharisees*, p. 105).
[14] In *Judaism in the New Testament Period*, pp. 205–8, and *The Pharisees*, p. 204.
[15] Matt. vii. 29.
[16] Herford: *Judaism in the New Testament Period*, p. 205.
[17] Ibid., p. 208. Cp. *The Pharisees*, pp. 205–7.

It is no wonder that the people 'were astonished at his doctrine',[1] or that the rabbis were not only surprised[2] but were also incensed and alarmed by it. If Jesus had won the people's allegiance, his victory would have spelled the overthrow of the whole system that the scribes had so carefully constructed and were so laboriously putting into effect. Conversely, 'if there had been no Pharisees, the Church would have met with little or no opposition'.[3] The encounter between the Pharisees and Jesus was 'the mutual impact of two irreconcilable conceptions of religion', and 'there was never any attempt at a reconciliation'.[4] The Pharisaic literature does not show any recognition of Jesus's greatness.[5]

The quarrel was the more tragic because, apart from this crucial issue, there was much in common between the two parties. For instance, 'there was a very considerable extent of common ground in the two bodies of teaching. . . . Parallels can be found in the rabbinical literature for perhaps as much as 90 per cent. of the recorded sayings of Jesus.'[6] Neither party borrowed the 'common ground' from the other. 'The most natural and obvious source for the common teaching is the synagogue.'[7] Parables were used in the synagogue teaching.[8] 'Most of what' Jesus 'taught was not original, since he gave for the most part only what was the current teaching of the synagogue.'[9] 'His originality showed itself elsewhere than in the teaching which was common to him and the Pharisees.'[10] Again, there was no quarrel between Jesus and the Pharisees over the issue of nationalism versus universalism, which has been exercising Jewish minds ever since Deutero-Isaiah attained his vision of Yahweh as being the One True God. Though Christianity ceased to be merely a Jewish sect and became a universal religion within a few years of Jesus's death, Jesus himself is represented in the Gospel according to St. Matthew (x. 5–6 and xv. 21–28) as expressly limiting his own mission to Jewry and as excluding the Samaritans and the gentiles from his field of concern; and the harshness of the language here used can have few, if any, parallels in the rabbinical literature.[11]

Nor was there any quarrel over a claim, on Jesus's part, to be the Messiah. There is no mention of such a claim in the rabbinical literature;[12] and 'the claim to be the Messiah was not in itself an offence at all' in the sight of the Jews—though it was in the sight of the Romans.[13] The Jewish Christians' recognition of Jesus as the Messiah did not conflict with Pharisaic orthodoxy.[14] There was no obligatory orthodox doctrine of the Messiah or of the last things.[15] Any Jew could declare himself to be the Messiah at his own peril. The verdict on his claim would be given by

[1] Matt. vii. 28.   [2] Herford: *The Pharisees*, p. 201.   [3] Ibid., p. 213.
[4] Ibid., p. 208. Cp. *Judaism in the New Testament Period*, p. 207.
[5] Herford: *The Pharisees*, p. 212.
[6] Herford: *Judaism in the New Testament Period*, p. 187.
[7] Ibid., p. 192.   [8] Ibid., p. 193.
[9] Ibid., p. 202. Herford notes (ibid., p. 196) that Jesus preached mainly outside the synagogues, and that this was something new.   [10] Ibid., p. 194.
[11] This is pointed out by K. D. Erdmann in *Archiv für Kulturgeschichte*, xxxiii. Band, Heft 2 (1951), p. 294. Moore, op. cit., vol. i, p. 186, notices that Matthew is the most Jewish, as well as the most anti-Pharisaic, of the gospels.
[12] Herford: *Christianity in Talmud and Midrash*, pp. 349 and 380–1; *Judaism in the New Testament Period*, pp. 218–19.
[13] Herford: *Judaism in the New Testament Period*, p. 214.
[14] Moore, op. cit., vol. i, p. 90.   [15] Ibid., p. 162.

history. Some claimants' claims have been recognized by some Jews for shorter or longer periods; but, up to date, no claimant has ever obtained permanent recognition from Jewry as a whole. The most sensational case was Rabbi Akiba's recognition of Bar Cochbah. This rash act proved Akiba fallible, without having done Bar Cochbah any good. Bar Cochbah's insurrection against Roman rule failed; both he and Akiba met their deaths at Roman hands; and in Jewish eyes the event proved that both men had been mistaken on a point of fact—Bar Cochbah in claiming to be the Messiah, and Akiba in endorsing his claim. The outcome must have deterred other eminant rabbis from following Rabbi Akiba's example, but Rabbi Akiba was not condemned for having committed himself.[1] His act and Bar Cochbah's, which in Roman eyes were high treason, were not religious offences in the sight of Rabbi Akiba's fellow doctors of the law. They were unfortunate errors of intellectual judgement.

As for the case of Jesus, Herford holds[2] that there is no evidence that Jesus did claim to be the Messiah, though he evidently thought that he had some kind of divine commission. 'While there was a considerable range of meanings in which the term Messiah could be understood, it is quite evident that Jesus did not identify himself with any of them.'[3] 'In any sense commonly recognized at the time, he was not the Messiah.'[4] It would, indeed, have been a contradiction in terms for the Messiah to declare, as Jesus is said to have declared to Pilate: 'My kingdom is not of this World', with the corollary that his servants would not fight.[5] This pacifism, which put out of court any claim on Jesus's part to be the Messiah in the currently accepted sense, should have commended itself to the Pharisees; for they, too, were pacifists and disapproved of the Zealots just because of the Zealots' militancy.

Thus it would appear that, but for the issue over the *halachah*, the Pharisees and Jesus had no reason for falling out with each other. If this is true, it is a further proof of the importance, in the Pharisees' eyes, of the procedure by which *halachoth* were established.

5. THE ISSUE BETWEEN NATIONALISM AND UNIVERSALISM

Moore truly describes Judaism as being 'the first great missionary religion of the Mediterranean World'.[6] Zoroastrianism and Buddhism were perhaps no later than Judaism in starting on their missionary careers, and Zoroastrianism's mission-field overlapped with Judaism's in South-West Asia. But, at the western end of the Old World, Judaism was certainly the earliest missionary religion in the field. Some of its more notable missionary achievements have been noticed at an earlier point in this volume.[7] It was bound to become a missionary religion when Deutero-Isaiah had seen in the national god of the Jews the One True God of all mankind and the whole Universe. Yet 'the pregnant idea of the mission of Israel found little comprehension or response in

---

[1] Herford: *Judaism in the New Testament Period*, p. 218.   [2] Ibid., p. 213.
[3] Ibid.   [4] Ibid.   [5] John xix. 36.
[6] Op. cit., vol. i, p. 324.   [7] On pp. 85–86.

the centuries that immediately followed'.[1] Two of the products of the Exile—the diasporá and the synagogue—were magnificent potential instruments for converting the World. The diasporá eventually spread westwards along the Mediterranean, as well as eastwards into Iran. Every city of any importance in the Old-World *Oikoumenê* west of India came to contain a local Jewish community, and each of these communities would maintain at least one synagogue. The institution of synagogues had not been invented for missionary purposes; its purpose had been to preserve, in diasporá, the relation between the Jews themselves and their god; but, though this was not the inventors' intention, the synagogue was so attractive that it gathered a circle of gentiles round its Jewish nucleus.[2] When Paul set out to convert the Hellenic World to Christianity, he found, round every Jewish synagogue, an inner circle of gentile proselytes and an outer circle of 'god-fearing' adherents (*sebómenoi*).[3] Judaism had attracted them, yet Christianity captivated them when it appeared on the scene. These gentile converts and semi-converts to Judaism were the first recruits whom the Christian missionaries won for their own faith. Why were Judaism's gentile adherents captured for Christianity so easily? And why, since then, has the western half of the Old World been converted, not to Judaism, but to two 'deviationist' Judaic religions, Christianity and Islam? The answer is that Christianity and Islam each quickly rid itself of the handicap of being a Jewish national religion and an Arab national religion respectively, whereas Judaism has never ceased to be a Jewish national religion, in spite of its having become also a universal religion some two thousand five hundred years ago. 'The Jew is part of a collective destiny, even when he does not know it or is unwilling to share it.'[4] But 'the group distinctiveness of the "peculiar" people is the ever-menacing pitfall for its universal responsibility'.[5]

To convert people to a religion, the missionary must identify himself with them and take them to his bosom on the sole condition that their acceptance of the religion that he has presented to them has been genuine and whole-hearted. The common bond that their conversion has established between the missionary and them should overcome all previous differences of nationality or culture and should place the converts on a footing of complete equality with the messenger whose religion has now become theirs as much as his. The Islamic missionary comes near to living up to this ideal. But the Jewish missionary has hitherto been inhibited from going to this winning length by his overriding anxiety to preserve his community's distinctive identity in the form of a nation. Since Deutero-Isaiah's day the Jews have recognized that God is the father of all men, and not only of Israel.[6] But their recognition of this truth has been prevented from bearing its full fruit by the persistence of a nationalistic conviction that 'the relation of children was only effectively realised by those who belonged to the community of Israel'.[7] The Jews have realized that, since their god is the father of

[1] Moore, op. cit., vol. i, p. 229.   [2] Ibid., p. 324.
[3] See Herford: *Judaism in the New Testament Period*, p. 75.
[4] J. L. Talmon in *Commentary*, July, 1957, p. 4.
[5] E. Berkovitz: *Judaism: Fossil or Ferment?* p. 130.
[6] Herford: *The Pharisees*, pp. 157–8.   [7] Ibid., p. 158.

all men, the conversion of the gentiles is their mission.[1] But this same god, being also theirs, is, in their eyes, Israel's lover; and, if the gentiles ask to share the lover, Israel's reply is: 'You have no part in him.'[2]

This narrow-hearted and ungenerous spirit has led the Jews to offer uninviting alternatives to gentiles who have been attracted towards the religion of Deutero-Isaiah. One alternative was to become a proselyte, but this involved becoming not only a convert to Judaism but also a naturalized member of the Jewish community.[3] According to Philo[4] a proselyte severs all his previous social, as well as religious, ties. The proselyte, if a male, had to submit to circumcision, besides receiving baptism and making a gift to the Temple.[5] It is not surprising that, among the proselytes, women were in a great majority. They were also in a majority among the 'god-fearing' adherents in the outer circle.[6] Gentiles who joined this outer circle were not required, as proselytes were, to take on their shoulders the whole burden of the Torah as interpreted by the Pharisees.[7] But the price of their being let off relatively lightly was that they were kept at arm's length as semi-outsiders: 'second-class citizens' of the Jewish community. It is not surprising that Paul and his fellow Christian missionaries found it easy to draw Judaism's gentile adherents into the fraternity of a rival Judaic religion in which they could still worship Deutero-Isaiah's One True God without being penalized on account of their gentile origin.

In their attitude towards gentiles, Jews today are still the prisoners of the masterful Babylonian Jewish reformer Ezra. His objective was to make the Jews obey the Torah; and, as a necessary means to this end, he took drastic steps to segregate them from their gentile neighbours.[8] 'The general result of his policy was to draw a sharp line of division between Jew and gentile, and to make for the Jewish community a sort of enclosure in the midst of the gentile world.'[9] This was an inevitable effect of enforcing the observance of the Torah as Ezra understood it.[10] But the observance of the Torah as understood by Ezra and by his successors the Pharisees is not an inevitable accompaniment of the religion of Deutero-Isaiah. Ezra raised an issue. He did not settle it. And the debate that he started has been continuing in Jewish hearts and minds ever since.

Montefiore observes that particularism was the rabbis' prevailing mood,[11] and that they were frank in revealing this.[12] 'Yet flashes of universalism break and shine through the darkness':[13] and his comment is that 'somehow the universalist passages of the rabbis seem to me all the more remarkable in view of their prevailing particularism'.[14] In the Modern Age, and above all in the present generation, the debate has become active. In this age, as in the eighth, seventh, and sixth centuries B.C.,[15] the Jews have been meeting with momentous experiences and have been

[1] Herford, *The Pharisees*, op. cit., pp. 158–9.
[2] Moore, op. cit., vol. i, pp. 396–7.   [3] Ibid., pp. 232 and 326–8.
[4] Philo: *De Monarchiâ*, chap. vii, §§ 51–53, cited by Moore, ibid., p. 327.
[5] Moore, op. cit., p. 331.   [6] Ibid., p. 326.
[7] Ibid., p. 325.   [8] Herford: *The Pharisees*, p. 19.
[9] Herford: *Judaism in the New Testament Period*, p. 34.
[10] Ibid., p. 35.   [11] Montefiore, op. cit., p. 69. Cp. p. 81.
[12] Ibid., p. 207.   [13] Ibid., p. 82.
[14] Ibid., p. 107.   [15] See p. 490.

undergoing far-reaching changes in the social and cultural conditions of their life; and it is therefore not surprising that now, once again, their hearts and minds should be on the move.

The first of these great modern changes in the social and cultural conditions of the Jews' life was their 'emancipation' in the Western World in application of the ideas of the French Revolution. Rabbi Agus recalls that, in the Age of Emancipation, Jews in the West have been struggling, in spite of the opposition of Jewish nationalists, to win the status of a religious community, and that this choice has been made, not once, but many times, in many parts of Europe. He cites the line taken by Napoleon's 'sanhedrin' in Paris, which included some distinguished rabbis among its members. This body, representing the Jews of France, renounced the French Jews' previous quasi-national status and also their hope of a return to Eretz Israel. It accepted for them the new status of being 'Jewish Frenchmen'.[1] Rabbi Agus points out[2] that, in the present generation,

'the disappearance of the Jewish "heart-land" in Central Europe, the rise of the state of Israel, and the emergence of American Jewry as the massive centre of the global fellowship of Israel are all decisive factors which imply the opening of a new and completely unprecedented era.'

In other passages Rabbi Agus draws attention to the tenseness of the debate in this new era of Jewish history, and at the same time finds the causes of this tension in human nature and traces its origins back into the Jews' past. Rabbi Agus sees 'the dynamic ideas of history as vertical fields of force between an ideal pole and an instinctive drive'.[3] He puts his finger on the tension between Jewish nationalism and Jewish mono-theism,[4] and on the tension, within Jewish nationalism, between in-stinctive forces of self-assertion and ideal elements of self-transcendance.[5] 'In a religious community, as in an historical nation, we encounter the same tension between self-assertion and self-transcendance.'[6] In Judaism 'there emerged a quadri-polar field of consciousness which was both unprecedented and unparalleled'.[7] 'Each of the four poles of Jewish consciousness—the self-transcendance of religion and its self-satisfied dogmatism, the spiritualization of national feeling and its degeneration into nihilistic chauvinism—could achieve dominance in the soul of the Jew.'[8]

Rabbi Agus's diagnosis can be illustrated from the writings of other contemporary Jewish thinkers. For example, Berkovitz holds that Judaism has no world-wide other-worldly mission.[9] Baron holds that 'the Jewish religion without the "Chosen People" is unthinkable, neither could it, like the other religions, be transplanted from the Jewish to another people'.[10] Berkovitz declares,[11] in Ezra's vein, that 'to accept

---

[1] Rabbi J. B. Agus in *Judaism*, 1956, pp. 20–21.
[2] In *Judaism*, vol. 4, No. 4 (Fall, 1955), p. 319.
[3] *Judaism*, 1956, p. 33.   [4] Ibid., p. 32.
[5] Ibid., p. 33.   [6] Ibid., p. 34.
[7] Ibid., p. 37.   [8] Ibid., p. 38.
[9] E. Berkovitz: *Judaism: Fossil or Ferment?* pp. 124–5.
[10] Baron: op. cit., 2nd ed., vol. i, p. 3.   [11] In op. cit., p. 76.

Judaism without accepting the Mosaic Law is a contradiction in terms'. Eban sees 'the wave of the future' not in the diasporá but in the recently established state of Israel. In his view the present century is signalized by the triumph of national states and is the burial-ground of broader associations.[1] Yet in the same essay[2] the same Jewish writer finds that the characteristics of Judaism are a belief in the possibility of moral choice, a belief in social justice, and a belief in universal peace; and he holds that the Jewish people have conserved their 'union and identity, not for their own sake, but in order to maintain trusteeship over these revolutionary ideals'.[3] Samuel holds[4] that the Jewish people 'is a continuing association of individuals . . . working out an experiment in the relationship to God. . . . When the Messiah will have come, when all peoples will have accepted the faith, the experiment will have been successfully concluded.' The following beautiful and moving passage is part of a Jewish prayer that is prayed by a Jewish congregation today.[5]

'Our guardian, gird us with strength and patience for our holy mission. Grant that all the children of Israel may recognise the goal of Israel's changeful career, so that they may exemplify by their zeal and love for mankind the truth of Israel's watchword: One humanity on earth, even as there is but one God in heaven. Enlighten all that call themselves by thy name with the knowledge that the sanctuary of wood and stone which once crowned Zion's hill was but a gate, through which Israel stepped out into the world to lead mankind nearer unto thee.

'Thou alone knowest when this work of atonement shall be completed; when the day shall dawn in which the light of thy truth shall illumine the whole earth. But that great day of universal reconciliation shall come, as surely as none of thy words return void except it have done that for which thou didst send it.'

The Jewish faith is the vision of the character of the One True God that was caught by the Prophets progressively from Amos to Deutero-Isaiah. The 'experiment' in the relationship to God is 'the application of Prophetic teaching to life' which is Herford's definition of Pharisaism.[6] This is a great spiritual treasure which the Jews have to give to all peoples. But one cannot give a treasure and at the same time keep it to oneself. If the giving of this treasure is the Jews' mission, as it surely is, then this mission requires them, now at last, to make that their paramount aim in place of the incompatible aim that they have always put first, so far, ever since their experience of the Babylonish Captivity. They will have to give up the national form of the Jewish community's distinctive identity in order to become, without reservations, the missionaries of a universal church that will be open, on an equal footing, to anyone, Jew or gentile, who gives his allegiance to Deutero-Isaiah's God and seeks to do His will. In our time the Zionist movement has been travelling in just the opposite direction to this. It has not only clung to, and accentuated, the national form of Jewish communal life. It has also put it back on to a

---

[1] A. Eban in *Toynbee and History*, p. 336.   [2] Ibid., pp. 321–2.
[3] Ibid.   [4] M. Samuel: *The Professor and the Fossil*, p. 176.
[5] *Liberal Jewish Prayer Book*, vol. ii: Services for the Day of Memorial (Rosh Hashanah) and the Day of Atonement (London, 1937, Liberal Jewish Synagogue), pp. 280–1.
[6] Herford: *The Pharisees*, p. 238, quoted already on p. 504.

territorial basis. On the other hand, the contemporary Reform, Conservative, and Liberal movements in the Jewish diasporá have been 'defossilising' their practice of Judaism.[1] They have already travelled far from the Pharisees' interpretation of the Torah and from the undiscriminating obedience to all *halachoth* which this interpretation demands.[2]

It is difficult and painful to renounce aims and practices to which one has remained faithful, at the cost of penalization and persecution, for hundreds of years. But the Jews have at their command a spiritual instrument that, in the past, has enabled them to perform feats as difficult as this. The unwritten Torah was dormant for 1,400 years, from the date of the closing of the Babylonian Talmud till the 'emancipation' of the Jews in the West in the Napoleonic Age. Yet, considering that it proved possible to bring the unwritten Torah to life in Ezra's time, and again in the Age of the Pharisees, it is not surprising that it should also be proving possible to revive it today; and it is an instrument that is equal to the task that has been confronting Jewry by now for 2,500 years. The treasure that the Jews have to give is not the Talmud or the written Torah or the Jewish diasporá or a Jewish national state in Palestine. It is the Prophets' vision of God's character; the relation of human souls to God as the Prophets have seen Him; and the ideals of human conduct that follow from this.

In equipping itself for its universal mission, Judaism might have something to learn from two great Jews whom it has disowned hitherto. It might recall that, at the zenith of the Pharisaic Age, one Pharisee, Paul, was singular in already anticipating the change of outlook that is perceptible among Jews today on a broader front. Paul perceived that the Torah, which had once been a spiritual panoply for the preservation of Judaism, had latterly become a spiritual impediment to the propagation of the Jewish faith, and that therefore the time had come for the Torah to be reinterpreted again. Present-day Jews could recognize in Paul a forerunner of theirs in this field, without having also to accept Paul's belief that Jesus was a divine being. The Jews might also at last lay claim to Jesus, whom they have allowed the Christians to appropriate without any Jewish protest. Jesus was not a Christian; he was a Jew in belief and practice, though, being a Galilaean, he may have been a gentile by descent. There is no evidence that he was not an orthodox Jew. The claims to divinity that are put into his mouth in the Gospels are not evidence of this; they are evidence only of what his Christian adherents in the next generation believed about him. This belief is blasphemous in terms of Judaism; but the blasphemy is Christian: Jesus himself cannot be convicted of it. Jesus was not a Pharisee; but a Jew could be an orthodox Jew without being a Pharisee in Jesus's time, as he can today. On this point, Jesus's Sadducee and Zealot contemporaries were in the same position as Jesus. Moreover, the quarrel between Jesus and the

---

[1] See Rabbi J. B. Agus's comments in the Annex to the present chapter.

[2] 'It has been a disadvantage for Judaism to have for generations, as its second sacred book—for I suppose the Talmud must be more or less so regarded—one which is so long and so composite, so inedited, as it were, and unexpurgated, so full of "high and low", so completely in "undress", as I have often called it, so naïvely and simply compiled' (C. G. Montefiore: *Rabbinic Literature and Gospel Teachings*, pp. 352–3).

Pharisees is progressively losing its meaning as the *halachoth*, after having been kept frozen for so many centuries, are being at last progressively transmuted.[1] To accept Jesus as a Jewish teacher who taught as one having authority does not involve acceptance of the Christian belief in Jesus's divinity.

The Jewish religion is meant for all mankind. So far from its being 'unthinkable' without the 'Chosen People', it cannot fulfil its destiny of becoming a universal religion unless and until the Jews renounce the national form of their distinctive communal identity for the sake of fulfilling their universal religious mission. To accept Judaism without accepting the Mosaic Law is not 'a contradiction in terms', if by 'the Mosaic Law' one means the Torah as reinterpreted by the Pharisees' method. A new Jewish reinterpretation of the Torah—this time as being a symbolic expression of the religious ideals of Judaism—is a necessary condition for Judaism's achievement of its destiny. Judaism's destiny is to be accessible to, and accepted by, the gentiles. It may be true that, without the carapace of the Torah and the Talmud, it is impossible for the Jews to maintain in diasporá their distinctive communal identity in its national form; but there are two ways in which a community's distinctive national identity may disappear: the Israelite way and the Roman. The Ten Tribes lost their national identity through being assimilated by peoples into whose countries they had been deported; the Romans gave up theirs by incorporating in their community the peoples whose countries they had united with their own. The two ways are antithetical in several senses. The Ten Tribes' way is passive, involuntary, and inglorious, and it is natural that the Jews should be on their guard against meeting the fate of their lost kinsmen. On the other hand the Roman way is active, deliberate, and noble, and the renunciation of communal identity in its national form does not involve the loss of communal identity itself when 'an ancient civilization' has been 'transmuted into a universal religion'.[2]

Today the Jews in the diasporá are being told by some Israelis that they are doomed to suffer the fate of the Ten Lost Tribes if they do not emigrate to the present Israeli state. But, in truth, the choices open to the Jews in the diasporá are not confined to these two alternatives. There is a third choice: the Roman choice of incorporating instead of being assimilated. The assimilation of the Jewish diasporá by the surrounding gentile majority is thus not their only alternative to emigration to Israel. Another possibility is that the Jewish diasporá might win converts to a denationalized and defossilized Judaism among the gentile majority around them. What the Romans did on the political plane, the Jews could do on the religious. They could incorporate gentiles in a Jewish religious community by converting them to the religion of Deutero-Isaiah. The greatest of the Prophets up to date, though not necessarily the last of them, would be, not Muhammad, but a Jewish seer who inspired his fellow Jews at last to dedicate themselves to their universal mission wholeheartedly. The World has been waiting for this prophet for 2,500 years.

[1] See Rabbi Agus's comments in loc. cit.   [2] Rabbi Agus, quoted on p. 494.

XVI. THE HISTORY AND PROSPECTS OF THE WEST

THE subject of this chapter is a big one, but the chapter need not be long, since the history and prospects of the West have been discussed at some length in a previous volume.[1] Critics of what I have written about the West there, and in other passages, have dealt, not only with the substance of the subject, but with my views about it. These are of minor interest in themselves, but, since my critics have paid attention to them, and in some cases have apparently misunderstood them, I have dealt briefly with this personal aspect of the subject too in the Annex to Chapter II of the present volume.[2] I therefore need not say much in this chapter about the discussion of my own views.

Unlike the histories of a majority of the civilizations known to us, the history of the West is to-day still an unfinished story. It is therefore hazardous to try to forecast its prospects, even in the form of suggesting a number of alternative possibilities.[3] Even if we were satisfied that the pattern of Western history, up to date, has been more or less the same as that of some other civilization—say, the Hellenic or the Sinic—whose history is over and is therefore known to us from beginning to end, we should have no warrant for forecasting that the future course of Western history will follow Hellenic or Sinic lines, if I am right—as I believe I am—in holding that patterns in the course of human affairs are not predetermined or inevitable, and that therefore past patterns afford no basis for predictions about the future.[4] If this is the truth, we cannot foretell whether or not the Western Civilization is ever going to enter into a universal state, as both the Hellenic and the Sinic did. Still less can we foretell whether, if the future course of Western affairs were to follow the pattern that is a common Helleno-Sinic one up to that point, the West's universal state would be as short-lived as the Hellenic Civilization's was in the western provinces of the Roman Empire, or as long-lived as the Sinic universal state has been.

In the Atomic Age, into which the West—and, with it, the World—has entered in our lifetime, it now looks as if a universal state could not be established again—at any rate not in the standard way, and therefore not in the standard form which that way produced. In the past, universal states have been established as the result of successive wars ending in the overthrow of all great powers except one surviving victor. Even in the age of pre-atomic weapons this way of arriving at political unity was so destructive—psychologically still more than materially—that civilizations which had passed through this harrowing experience usually emerged from it incurably damaged. In the age of atomic weapons no

---

[1] vol. ix, pp. 406–644. [2] On p. 629, footnote 2.
[3] *Ad hominem*, E. Gargan, writing in March, 1955, in *Books on Trial*, finds, not surprisingly, that 'Toynbee, from the start of his work, has rendered judgments on the history of the West which have proved startlingly wrong' (p. 265). In general Gargan is critical of my 'vision of the Western past and future'.
[4] O. Halecki, in *The Intent of Toynbee's History: A Co-operative Appraisal*, has given me credit for having avoided any deterministic interpretation of the history of the West in particular and of mankind in general.

power would reach the final round. There would be no victor; all belligerents alike would be vanquished; and even the first round of atomic warfare might wipe out, not only the belligerent states, but civilization, the human race, and perhaps all life on this planet. It does not follow that mankind cannot and will not attain unity. Now that, for the first time in history, the whole human race has been united on the military plane, the choice confronting us may be one between going all the way to unity or going under. What seems improbable is that a society can ever again be united by force. This seems improbable because the force used in future warfare would be atomic force, and this would annihilate the society, leaving nothing in existence to unite.

Such considerations as these have made me wary of offering predictions—above all about the future of the West. When critics point this out,[1] I take that as commendation and not as censure. And their criticism misses the mark when they go on to accuse me of inconsistency in shrinking from applying to the Western Civilization a pattern of decline and fall that, according to them, I believe to be the inevitable fate of all civilizations.[2] It is true that I should feel rueful if I were convinced that the particular living civilization into which I have been born is bound to break down and disintegrate on the lines on which other civilizations have gone to pieces in the past. It is also true that I think that a pattern of breakdown and disintegration, common to the histories of a number of past civilizations, can be detected when we make a comparative study of them. But I do not believe that this pattern was predetermined or inevitable in any single past case; and therefore, à fortiori, I do not believe that it can be projected into a prediction about the future of a civilization that is still a going concern.[3] I do not believe, as Spengler believes, that there is a fixed pattern to which the history of every civilization is bound to conform. My unwillingness to predict that the Western Civilization will go the way that a number of its predecessors have gone is a consistent application of my conviction that the course of human affairs is not predetermined. It is not a sentimental refusal to apply to the prospects of my own civilization some pattern of breakdown and disintegration that I unavowedly believe to be every civilization's inevitable fate. I have no such cast-iron pattern in my bag of intellectual tools.

As I see it, the fact that the Western Civilization's history is still unfinished not only makes it impossible to predict its future course but also makes it difficult even to discuss the pattern of its past history as far as this has gone up to date. Sir Llewellyn Woodward has pointed out that any number of patterns can be found in history.[4] Even if we manage to see through and discard those that are imaginary, the number of those admitted, by general consensus, to be genuine will still be great. There is room for many patterns; they are not mutually exclusive. The problem

---

[1] e.g. T. J. G. Locher in De Gids, May, 1948, offprint, p. 26; Crane Brinton in The Virginia Quarterly Review, vol. 32, No. 3 (Summer, 1956), pp. 361–75.

[2] See Locher, ibid., p. 27; Geyl in Toynbee and History, pp. 67–68; K. W. Thompson, ibid., p. 216; Spate, ibid., p. 303; B. Prakash in The Modern Review, November, 1953, p. 403; Chr. Hill in The Modern Quarterly, Autumn, 1947, p. 291.

[3] 'Even if we could claim that all past societies have perished, it would not prove that all future ones must' (J. K. Feibleman in T'ien Hsia Monthly, vol. xi, Nos. 1 and 2 (1940), p. 16).   [4] See the passage quoted on p. 168.

raised by their number is that of their relation to each other. When the history of a civilization, or of some greater or lesser historical episode, is complete, it may be practicable, in retrospect, to make out which of the patterns in it is the dominant pattern to which the others are subordinate. But, when the story is still unfinished, the clue is much harder to find. If one looks at a Persian carpet at the stage at which the strip that has already been knotted runs to only a few inches out of an ultimate length of, say, twenty feet, we can perhaps identify the motifs that the total pattern of the finished carpet is going to develop; but we cannot yet single out the master-motif that is going to give form and unity to the whole.

This point may be illustrated from a past chapter of Western history. An observer looking at the Western World at some date early in the fourteenth century of the Christian Era might reasonably have guessed that its master-institution was going to be city-states. At that date the city-states of Northern and Central Italy were masters of the industry and commerce of the Mediterranean. The league of Hansa towns was dominating the Baltic and Scandinavia; the Flemish city-states were a potent force in the economy of England and Northern France. It might well have seemed that the rustic kingdoms, surviving from an earlier phase of the history of the medieval West, were destined to fall entirely under the ascendancy of the pullulating cosmos of city-states, and perhaps eventually to be absorbed into it. An observer acquainted with Hellenic history would recall that this had been the pattern which it had followed; and this might have confirmed his expectation that the pattern of Western history was going to be the same. It would have seemed natural that a later civilization should follow the same course as an older one to which it was affiliated. Yet before the fourteenth century was over the city-states of the medieval Western World had already missed what had seemed, so short a time before, to be their manifest destiny. The War of Chioggia between Venice and Genoa (*gerebatur* A.D. 1378–81) may be taken as the counterpart, in their history, of the Great Atheno-Peloponnesian War of 431–404 B.C., which marked the breakdown of the Hellenic Civilization.[1] Before the close of the fifteenth century it would have been evident to any observer that the key political institution of the Western World was going to be, not city-states, but nation-states conjured out of the old-fashioned feudal kingdoms by an infusion of city-state efficiency and vitality. The lapse of two more centuries had shown that the picture of the West's future which had seemed so convincing at the beginning of the fourteenth century had been an illusion —though a natural and perhaps an inevitable one at that earlier date.

If we think in terms of breakdown and disintegration, we can see, in Western history up to date, several alternative historical patterns, each with its own chronology, any one of which, looked at from some particular point in Western history, might be deemed to mark the breakdown and disintegration of the Western Civilization.

If the medieval Western city-state cosmos could properly be identified—as a fourteenth-century Fleming or Northern Italian might have

[1] See iii. 348.

identified it—with the Western World as a whole, then the date of the
Western Civilization's breakdown would have to be placed in the last
quarter of the fourteenth century,[1] and the chronology of Western history
would correspond almost precisely to the chronology of Hellenic history,
with a time-interval of about eighteen hundred years between the two.
The growth-stage of both civilizations would have lasted for about seven
hundred years (*circa* 1125–425 B.C. in Hellenic history and *circa* A.D. 675–
1375 in Western). The respective breakdowns would have occurred in
the closing decades of the fifth century B.C. and in the closing decades of
the fourteenth century of the Christian Era. The ensuing 'time of
troubles' would have lasted, in either case, for about four hundred years
(431 B.C.–31 B.C. and A.D. 1379–1797). And in either case it would have
been ended by the establishment of a universal state. Augustus's achievement would have had its Western counterpart in Napoleon's; for the
Napoleonic Empire, like the Augustan, brought peace to a broken-down
city-state cosmos by imposing political unity on it.[2] Yet, together with
these striking points of both structural and chronological similarity
between the histories of the Hellenic World and the medieval city-state
cosmos, there are no less striking points of difference; and the non-
Hellenic features in this episode of Western history make it clear that the
breakdown of the Western city-state cosmos was not, after all, tantamount to a breakdown of the Western World as a whole, and that consequently its dissolution was not the end of Western history.

The medieval Western city-states did have one other important experience in common with the Pre-Alexandrine Hellenic city-states and
also with the Pre-Confucian states in China. They came to be surrounded
by a ring of outer states that were on a lower cultural level but of a
higher military calibre; and the parvenu giant powers in this outer ring
competed for the hegemony over Italy and Flanders, as the giant powers
of the Post-Alexandrine Hellenic World competed for the hegemony
over the Aegean and over Sicily.[3] Charles V and Francis I and Henry
VIII are recognizable counterparts of Alexander's diadochi. But here
the two histories take decisively different turns. In the course of
Hellenic history, one of the new great powers of the outer ring, Rome,
succeeded in overthrowing or dominating all its rivals within 263 years
of the beginning of the Hellenic 'time of troubles', if its beginning is to
be dated in the year 431 B.C.; and Rome's thenceforth unchallengeable
power was at Augustus's command when, 137 years after the overthrow
of Macedon at Pydna, his victory at Actium gave him a free hand to
make a political unity of the whole Hellenic World west of Euphrates.
Napoleon had at his disposal the power of France; but France had not
previously succeeded in making herself the sole surviving power in the
Western World; and therefore Napoleon's empire, unlike Augustus's,
was not unchallengeable and did not endure.[4] The Napoleonic Empire's
historical mission—which it accomplished in spite of the shortness of its
duration—was a quite different one from the Augustan Empire's. It was

[1] See iii. 348–50.
[2] See the essay on 'The Napoleonic Empire as a Universal State' in v. 619–42.
[3] See iii. 299–306.   [4] See v. 627–33.

to reabsorb the debris of the medieval Western city-state cosmos into the modern Western World[1] which had been called into existence by a spiritual and intellectual revolution towards the close of the seventeenth century. This final liquidation of the abortive Western city-state cosmos was not a liquidation of the Western Civilization; it was a reinforcement of it.

These considerations indicate that the rise and fall of the medieval Western city-state cosmos has, in truth, been a subordinate episode in Western history, and that its breakdown and disintegration therefore do not spell the breakdown and disintegration of the Western Society as a whole.[2] Yet this conclusion leaves open the possibility that this society as a whole may likewise already have broken down in its turn. One can think of several events in the main course of Western history, each of which might conceivably signify the Western Civilization's breakdown. One such event is the Reformation. This broke the ecclesiastical unity that the West had previously enjoyed under the presidency of the Papacy. The Western Christian ecclesiastical commonwealth had been the master-institution of Western Christendom up to that date. Its destruction through the Reformation might therefore reasonably be held to mark the Western Civilization's breakdown. Alternatively, this might be marked by the outbreak, later on in the sixteenth century, of the Catholic–Protestant Wars of Religion, civil as well as international; for in these wars the Reformation bore its harvest of violence and bitterness. Another alternative date for the breakdown of the Western Civilization would be the *levée en masse* in France in A.D. 1792, which inaugurated a Western age of total war.[3] Another would be the outbreak of the First World War in A.D. 1914, which armed total war with weapons forged, since Carnot's day, by the Industrial Revolution. Another would be A.D. 1945, which saw the dropping of the first atomic bomb.

Each of these alternative dates has serious claims to be regarded as marking the breakdown of the Western Civilization, yet none of these rival claims could be established convincingly by an observer taking his bearings in the year 1961. A recurring past pattern of disintegration emerges from a comparison of the declines and falls of civilizations that have already declined and fallen. A synoptic view of these indicates that, in the past, the usual interval between the breakdown of a civilization and the establishment of its universal state has been approximately four hundred years. The past frequency of an interval of this span is not presumptive evidence that the same chronological pattern is reappearing, or is going to re-appear, in another civilization's still unfinished history. But, with this caveat, it is perhaps legitimate to apply this measure—

---

[1] See v. 633–41.

[2] In previous volumes I have been careful to distinguish between the history of the medieval Western city-state cosmos and the history of the Western Civilization as a whole. The patterns and chronologies of the two histories are not the same. This distinction that I have drawn seems to have been overlooked by K. W. Thompson and by B. Prakash. Thompson supposes that the 'time of troubles' that I have dated 1378–1797 in vi. 326 is there presented by me as being the Western Civilization's (*Toynbee and History*, p. 216). Prakash also takes me to be referring here to the Western Civilization, though only to its western half (*The Modern Review*, November, 1953, p. 402). Actually, I have attributed a 'time of troubles', with these dates, to the Western city-state cosmos only.   [3] See iv. 151–2.

which is the only one that we have—to see how it works out in the West's case. If we apply it to our alternative dates, before our own day, for the possible breakdown of the Western Civilization, the equation of the Reformation with the breakdown would require the establishment of a Western universal state to be a *fait accompli* already by now. It should, in fact, have been established by Germany as a result of the two world wars. But in both world wars Germany suffered defeat, and in the second her defeat was more shattering than it had been in the first. In any case the Western World was certainly not in a universal state in 1961. This was one thing that could be said with assurance about the pattern of Western history up to that date. There had been no Western universal state so far. If we were to take the outbreak of the Wars of Religion, instead of the Reformation, as marking the breakdown, and were to measure our 400-years-long 'time of troubles' from that date, the establishment of a Western universal state would have to be expected in the late nineteen-sixties or the early nineteen-seventies; but this would already be too late for that to be a practical possibility, considering that the atomic weapon was invented in 1945, and that this invention has made the forcible unification of the Western Society or any other society impossible because an attempted unification by means of atomic warfare would annihilate the society itself.

The conclusion seems to be a negative one. We have considered five alternative epochs for the establishment of a Western universal state: the Napoleonic Age, the period covered by the two world wars, a date just before or after 1970, and two more distant future dates: *circa* 2192 (i.e. 1792+400 years) and *circa* 2314 (i.e. 1914+400 years). The first two of these five speculative predictions have already been discredited by the non-occurrence of the expected event at the predicted date; the last three seem to have been put out of court through having been anticipated by the invention of the atomic weapon.

Up to date the Western World has twice eluded, in its Modern Age, the threat of being forcibly united in a universal state; and on each of these two occasions its escape has been due to the same cause. Each time the Western World had expanded, before the attempt was made, to dimensions that made the attempt a forlorn hope. If, in Napoleon's time, the Western World had still been confined to Western Europe, Napoleonic France might have succeeded in forcibly uniting the West by overthrowing the other contemporary West European powers of France's own calibre: the Danubian Hapsburg Monarchy, Great Britain, Prussia. The reason why Napoleon's undertaking proved to be beyond even Napoleonic France's strength was that, by Napoleon's time, France's competition with rival powers had been going on for about three hundred years, and, in the meantime, the Western World had enlarged its borders. On the east, a non-Western power, Russia, had stepped into the Western military and political arena and had thrown a new weight into the balance of power; on the west, Britain had vastly increased her strength by gaining naval command of the oceans and consequently commanding the resources of the huge overseas territories that had been added progressively to the Western World since the closing decades of the fifteenth century. This new overseas extension of the Western World had been developing economically *pari passu* with its growth; and in the Napoleonic Age Britain held the key to it. Napoleon might have succeeded if he had had to deal solely with the Hapsburg Monarchy, Prussia, and a Britain whose resources were no more than those of the British Isles. He was foiled by having also to meet the combination of Russia, with her continental hinterland, and Britain with her overseas hinterland. Germany's failure in the two world wars was due to the same cause as France's failure in the Napoleonic wars. In the course of the hundred years that had elapsed between 1815 and 1914 the opening up and development of North America north of the Rio Grande had raised the war potential of the overseas part of the Western World to a level at which no European power, or combination of European powers, was any longer a match for it.

By the end of the Second World War the expansion of the Western World had gone to extremes on the technological planes of communications and warfare. On these planes the Western system had become, by then, coextensive with the whole habitable and traversable surface of the planet. By the same date a new weapon had been invented that, for the first time in Western history, made it possible for a Western power to unite by force even a Western World that had now become coextensive with the World itself. Since, however, this new weapon was the annihilating atomic one, the condition for its possible use for the old-fashioned purpose of eliminating all competing powers but one was that the user should not merely possess the new weapon but should have a monopoly of it. This condition was fulfilled during the years 1945-9. During those years the atomic weapon was possessed by the United States, and by it alone. If either Germany or Japan had emerged from the Second World War victorious, with the atomic weapon in her hands and with a monopoly of it, we may guess that she would have taken advantage of this unique military opportunity and would have established, by the traditional military method, a universal state that, this time, would have been literally world-wide. The people and administration of the United States did not do this and were not tempted to do it. They would have been horrified if the project had been suggested to them by some American Themistocles. The possibility passed away when the Soviet Union, in its turn, acquired the atomic weapon in 1949. Since then, this weapon has ceased to be a practicable means of imposing political unity on mankind; it has become, instead, a threat to the survival of civilization, of the human race, and of life itself.

Thus the apparent elimination of the possibility of imposing unity by force has made it a matter of life and death for mankind to achieve unity by agreement. The year 1949 opened a new era in human history. Before that date the survival of the human race had been assured ever since the time, part way through the Palaeolithic Age, when mankind had won a decisive and unchallengeable ascendancy over all other forms of life on this planet as well as over inanimate nature. Between that time and the year 1949 Man's crimes and follies could and did wreck civilizations and bring unnecessary and undeserved sufferings upon countless numbers of men, women, and children. But the worst that Man could do with his pre-atomic technology was not enough to enable him to destroy his own race. Genocide, at least, was beyond his power until the atomic weapon had been invented and had been acquired by more states than one in a society that was still partitioned politically among a number of local states and in an age in which states were still in the habit of going to war with each other.

The unprecedented situation arising from the acquisition of the atomic weapon by the Soviet Union as well as by the United States does seem to have made an impression on the minds and imaginations of governments as well as peoples. Between 1949 and 1961 a number of international incidents and crises that, in the past, would have been likely to lead to war were surmounted without a breach of the peace; and the local wars that did flare up in Korea and Vietnam were brought to an end by negotiated settlements on terms that were distasteful to both parties. This indicates that, under the threat of atomic warfare, both the governments and the peoples had become more prudent in their conduct of their relations with their adversaries, and had schooled themselves to exercise an unaccustomed self-restraint. This, in turn, made the continuance of 'co-existence' seem more probable; and mere coexistence, accepted sullenly on both sides as being the less bad of two bad alternatives, was a boon that was not to be despised. It promised to give mankind at least a temporary reprieve; and, in a bad situation, the mere passage of time may bring relief, since human affairs are always on the move and can never be frozen into fixity.

Time could bring relief by altering the balance of power and by shifting people's attention and emotions into new channels. A continuing increase in China's power, for instance, might one day make the Soviet Union and the United States huddle together for mutual protection. (In the recent past they had been drawn together by the menace, to both of them, of the lesser power of Japan.) A continuing rise in West Germany's power might make Czechoslovakia and Poland come to feel that Russia's hegemony was not too high a premium to pay for insurance against the risk of a German *revanche*. West Germany's recovery might also make Russia's existence seem a welcome political and military asset to West European countries that, within living memory, had been victims of German aggression in two world wars. In fact, it seemed probable that, under a continuing regime of coexistence, old feuds would gradually have their edge taken off them by new anxieties, new quarrels, and new enthusiasms. There were encouraging precedents in the history of the coexistence of Protestantism with Catholicism and of Islam with Christianity since the dates at which the Catholic–Protestant and the Christian–Muslim Wars of Religion had petered out. These wars had come to an end because it had become evident to both belligerent parties simultaneously that it was beyond the power of either of them to wipe its adversary off the map. After this recognition, on both sides, of the inevitability of coexistence, the old quarrel between them had gradually become less acrimonious and less absorbing.

These considerations indicated that even a sullen acquiescence, on both sides, in a state of coexistence between the two power-blocs commanded respectively by the United States and by the Soviet Union was all to the good; but this was not a state of human affairs about which mankind could afford to feel complacent. It could not be anything more than a temporary reprieve, and a precarious one at that. Even though no government or people might wish or intend to start an atomic war, one might be started by accident (for instance, by a misunderstanding of orders, or by a sheer loss of nerve, on the part of some junior officer). The power to discharge an atomic weapon might also come within the reach of irresponsible criminals or lunatics as the manufacture of atomic weapons became easier and cheaper and as one state after another succeeded in equipping itself with at least a few of them. Prompt positive action, by international agreement, was therefore imperative.

The first step required was the renunciation of all further tests of new atomic weapons by all states without exception; and a necessary corollary of this was the establishment of an effective system of international control, including inspection, to make sure that all parties were carrying out the self-denying ordinance in good faith. The next step would be an agreement that atomic weapons should not be possessed by any states except the United States and the Soviet Union—with effective arrangements for ensuring that this agreement, too, was carried out. The next step would be that the Soviet Union and the United States themselves should join the no-atomic-weapons club. Some such series of international arrangements might perhaps exorcise the danger of atomic warfare. But there would still remain the problem of regulating the beneficent use of atomic power for human welfare. Whatever might or might not happen in the military field, it seemed certain that there would be a rapid increase in the use of atomic power for constructive peaceful purposes. This probability was, of course, to be welcomed. It opened up the prospect that, for the first time, the amenities of civilization might now be brought within the reach of the whole human race, instead of continuing to be monopolized, as they had been so far, by a small minority of privileged people in the population of a small minority of privileged countries. This boon, however, would have its price. The products of the fission of atoms were not only potent for good or evil; they were also poisonous, for whatever purpose they might be used. Elaborate and costly precautionary measures were needed to preserve the habitat of life on this planet from being contaminated by the poison that the tapping of atomic energy released. Carelessness or callousness about taking the necessary precautions in any one country or province would be a menace to public health all over the World. And this potential menace called for the establishment of a single international authority, with a world-wide jurisdiction, to regulate the peaceful uses of atomic power.[1]

It remained to be seen whether arrangements on the lines sketched above would be made by international agreement, and, if they were achieved, how long the negotiation of them would take. But it was clear that, if and when some such arrangements were brought into operation, the operating authority, or network of authorities, would, in effect, be

[1] See p. 309.

a world government empowered to deal with mankind's most pressing common problem. Unlike the governments of the universal states of the past, this world government would, *ex hypothesi*, have been set up by agreement, instead of being imposed by force. But it would be a world government all the same. If it were agreed that, in the Atomic Age, at least this minimum of world government by mutual consent was the only practical alternative to eventual genocide,[1] this conclusion would raise a searching question. In the second half of the twentieth century of the Christian Era, did mankind possess the resources for creating the revolutionary new institution that had suddenly become necessary if mankind was to save itself from the fatal possibilities inherent in the sudden portentous increase in its command over physical nature?

The resources required were of two kinds—intellectual and moral—and the necessary intellectual resources were manifestly at mankind's disposal in this age in sufficient measure. Human intellectual prowess had tuned up the social technique of organizing co-operative human enterprises, and the subsidiary physical technique of providing the necessary material means of communication, to a pitch at which world government had become a practical administrative possibility. Moral resources were the limiting factor, and these were therefore the crux. Without the modicum of good will in individual souls that would be required for creating the necessary degree of concord between them, co-operation even on the smallest scale would be impracticable;[2] and thus the adequacy or inadequacy of mankind's moral resources would decide whether the vast new material power that had now fallen into human hands was going to be used for good or for evil.

This question had to be asked, in general, about mankind's common human nature; but, in twentieth-century circumstances, it had also to be asked in particular about the habits and outlook induced in human nature by the Western Civilization. It was true that this was only one out of a number of civilizations that had been created by human beings within the past 5,000 years. On the spiritual plane the Western Civilization had not been embraced, so far, by more than a minority of the human race. And, since the Communist Revolution in Russia in 1917, the West had been rapidly losing the technological, military, political, and economic ascendancy over most of the rest of the World which it had enjoyed, before that, since the failure of the 'Osmanlis' second siege of Vienna in 1683. By the year 1961 the West's former ascendancy was manifestly passing away. Yet during the preceding quarter of a

---

1 This thesis was not, of course, generally accepted, though, as I see it, its truth was demonstrated by the considerations set out above. Hans Kohn, for example, holds that I overstress the need for a political unification of the World (*Toynbee and History*, p. 21). In Kohn's view 'a world-state is neither necessary nor desirable' (*Der Monat*, August, 1955, p. 468). If, by a 'world-state', Kohn means one of the traditional type, established by conquest and maintained by force, I hold that, in the Atomic Age, this is, not only unnecessary and undesirable, but impracticable. On the other hand, if Kohn includes, in his usage of the term, a world authority, set up by international agreement, for the control of the use of atomic power, I hold that a world-state in this sense is, for the reasons that I have suggested, the only alternative to mass suicide in the long run.

2 I agree with R. Coulborn that the criterion of progress in history is harmony, and that 'a working measure of agreement upon the objects of life must continue between all men in a civilised society if that society is to continue to grow' (*Phylon*, 1940, offprint, pp. 50 and 56).

millennium this temporary ascendancy of the West had set a stamp on the rest of the World which seemed likely to last long after the West's ascendancy had disappeared.

During its brief period of ascendancy the West had unified the World on the technological plane, and the process of unification could not remain confined to this plane, since technology included military technology, and military technology had now produced the atomic weapon. Technology seems to be difficult to invent but relatively easy to acquire from its inventors by mimesis. An ascendancy based on superiority in technology is therefore a wasting asset. The reason why the West's ascendancy was ebbing away was that the non-Western peoples, beginning with the Russians but not ending with them, had been learning to rival the West in the mastery and use of weapons and other tools of Western origin. But Western technology was not the only element in the Western Civilization that non-Western peoples had been appropriating. Most of them had realized that they could not master Western technology without also mastering Western science.[1] But the Westernizers had not limited their borrowings from the West to Western science and its practical applications. Some of them had also become converts to Western ideologies. The Communist ideology that had been adopted by the Russians and the Chinese, as well as the parliamentary ideology that had been adopted by the Indians, had been made in Britain. (The workshop in which Karl Marx had manufactured Communism had been the British Museum.) Parliamentarism and Communism are political systems, but they are also something more than that. Just as Western technology involves Western science, so Western political systems imply Western moral ideals—conflicting ideals reflected in conflicting systems. Ideologies and ideals cannot be understood or appraised without taking some account of their history. The spiritual history of the West had therefore to be taken into consideration in any twentieth-century estimate of the prospects of the World as a whole.

By the middle decades of the twentieth century the Western Society had passed through a number of revolutions on a number of different planes since it had emerged out of the social and cultural interregnum that had followed the preceding Hellenic Civilization's dissolution. Among all these successive Western revolutions the spiritual revolution during the closing decades of the seventeenth century had been perhaps the most decisive and the most significant up to date.[2] At any rate, this was certainly the revolution that, in the twentieth century, was exerting the greatest continuing influence, not only on the West itself, but on the

---

[1] F. Borkenau maintains that Western technology is the parent of Western science and the child of a Western passion for freedom (*Merkur*, July, 1949, pp. 626 and 632).

[2] I agree with H. Kohn (in *Der Monat*, August, 1955, p. 466) that the Modern World originated, not in fifteenth-century Portugal and Spain, but in seventeenth-century Holland and England (and, I would add, seventeenth-century France as well). Kohn (ibid., p. 467, and in *Toynbee and History*, pp. 356–7 and 359) goes so far as to describe this seventeenth-century spiritual revolution as being the rise of a new civilization bearing the same relation to the preceding Western Christian Civilization that this had borne to the Hellenic. I should be inclined to say rather that it opened a new chapter in Western history, and that it prepared the way for the eventual rise of an oecumenical civilization. Kohn himself says something like this in *The Nation*, 17th February, 1940, p. 257.

rest of the World as well. The seventeenth-century revolution had given the Western Civilization a new form, and, above all, a new spirit, which, for the first time in history, had made the heirs of non-Western civilizations willing to embrace the Western Civilization in exchange for their ancestral heritages. The seventeenth-century Western revolution had thus opened the way for a cultural development of world-wide importance: the Westernization of the World. This, in turn, had opened the way for the transformation of the post-seventeenth-century Western Civilization into a common civilization for the whole human race. This coming oecumenical civilization would necessarily start its career within a Western framework and on a Western basis, by reason of its Western origin; and it seemed likely that this initial Western contribution to it would continue to be important for a long time to come. It also seemed likely, however, that, as time went on, the contributions made by the other pre-oecumenical civilizations would come to be increasingly important.[1] It might be hoped that eventually the ex-Western oecumenical civilization would appropriate and assimilate and harmonize all that was best in all the heritages of all the civilizations that had preceded it.[2]

The seventeenth-century Western revolution that promised to produce such a far-reaching positive result had begun as a negative movement. It had started as a moral reaction against the wickedness, destructiveness, and senselessness of the Catholic–Protestant Wars of Religion, and against the barrenness and inconclusiveness of the accompanying theological controversies that had been fanning political rivalries into military flames. The fathers of the seventeenth-century revolution were not anti-religious, as some of their eighteenth-century successors were. So far from that, one of their objectives was to save religion from being wholly discredited and abandoned. They sought to save it by putting an end to the abuse of it for non-religious purposes. They therefore stood for religious toleration, and, as one means towards this end, they set themselves to divert people's interest from pernicious theological controversy to harmless scientific research and to the useful application of scientific discoveries for the practical purpose of improving technology.

As against my emphasis on the original negativeness of the seventeenth-century Western revolution, Hans Kohn emphasizes the positiveness of the virtues that it developed.[3] On this point I agree with Kohn. I ought to have done more justice to this revolution's positive side. In the light of Kohn's critique I will try to make amends now. Toleration spelled freedom of conscience, and the new respect for this spelled a respect for the rights and dignity of human beings. This brought with it a new standard of social responsibility, social justice, and humane feeling. Noble monuments of this new ideal of human fraternity have been the abolition of the slave-trade and of slavery itself and the legislation for the

[1] 'The dissemination of modern Western civilization over the face of the globe is . . . fraught with the possibility of the rise of new systems of thought and belief which are likely to overshadow and eclipse this very civilization (B. Prakash in *The Modern Review*, November, 1953, p. 402).
[2] Chr. Dawson sees in the past civilizations so many models for the construction of a future oecumenical society (*The Dynamics of World History*, p. 44).
[3] See H. Kohn in *Toynbee and History*, p. 353; *Der Monat*, August, 1955, p. 467.

protection of the poor and weak that has eventually been consolidated in 'the welfare state'. This has had the beneficent positive effect of spreading the amenities of civilization more widely, and that has been made practically possible by the increase in wealth resulting from progress in technology. But Kohn is maintaining that there is something more in the modern Western Civilization than just its technological prowess.[1] The West's technological triumphs have been 'a by-product of the Western freedom of inquiry and the Western sense of personal initiative. They are unthinkable without respect for individual liberty and tolerance of diversity.'[2] Non-Westerners have not always been alive to the spiritual causes of the West's technological success.[3]

Moreover, this success has had an intellectual as well as a moral cause. Intellectually, the progress of Western technology has been due to the application of science to it. And the modern Western cultivation of science, which had started negatively as a diversion from the cult of theology, bred a heightened sense of curiosity and a new spirit of critical inquiry. Neither the Renaissance nor the Reformation had liberated Western minds from their medieval subservience to external authority. The Renaissance had abrogated the intellectual authority of the Christian religion in favour of that of the Greek and Latin classics. The Reformation had substituted the intellectual authority of the text of the Bible and the ecclesiastical authority of the local secular governments (*cuius regio, eius religio*) for the authority of the Catholic Church. Perhaps the most fundamental and radical feature of the seventeenth-century Western revolution was that now, for the first time, Western minds dared consciously and deliberately to think for themselves. In the Battle of the Ancients and Moderns, Westerners made a declaration of their independence from their Hellenic cultural heritage; and this time they did not exchange one mental servitude for another, as their forefathers had done in the Renaissance. Truly 'there is in modern Western Civilization a vital spiritual force which, in the nineteenth and twentieth centuries, has helped to revitalise other civilizations and to enhance their self-awareness'.[4]

It may also be true that I 'underestimate the newness, the greatness, and the originality of the modern West',[5] and this because I lack 'sympathy with the secular ideals which our modern world inherited from

---

[1] Kohn in *The Intent of Toynbee's History: A Cooperative Appraisal*, and in *Die Deutsche Rundschau*, 82. Jahrgang, Heft 3 (March, 1956), p. 262. On the other hand, Pope Pius X, in his address to the Tenth International Congress of Historical Sciences, held in Rome in the autumn of 1955, remarked that what the Western countries are giving to the whole World today is 'modern science and technology' (*Discours de S. S. Pie X au Xème Congrès International des Sciences Historiques* (Cité du Vatican, 1955), p. 21).

[2] Kohn in *The Intent of Toynbee's History: A Cooperative Appraisal*.

[3] Kohn in *Die Deutsche Rundschau*, loc. cit., pp. 262–3.

[4] Kohn in *Toynbee and History*, p. 353. Cp. *Der Monat*, August, 1955, p. 467. This point of Kohn's has also been made by Chr. Dawson. 'The permanent inheritance of Europe, like that of Hellenism, is a spiritual and intellectual one. It has changed the World because it has changed men's minds' (*The Dynamics of World History*, p. 412). Dawson, too, also points out (ibid., p. 411) that the work of modern Western Orientalists and archaeologists has given the non-Western peoples a new understanding of their own past.

[5] Kohn in *Der Monat*, loc. cit., p. 467. Cp. eundem in *Toynbee and History*, pp. 353 and 357, and Geyl, ibid., pp. 363 and 368.

the enlightenment of the eighteenth and the liberalism of the nineteenth centuries'.[1] It may also be true that I am flogging a dead horse in putting the West in its place, as Kohn finds that I am constantly doing.[2] The West, Kohn holds,[3] has already been cured of its hybris. Certainly I am perpetually on guard against the danger of myself succumbing to the insidious vice of 'nosism'. This, no doubt, inclines me to 'lean over backwards'. I am drawn farther in this direction by the effects of a fifteenth-century Italian education in the Greek and Latin classics, since this puts my heart, though not my head, on the side of 'the Ancients' in the Battle of the Books. There may therefore be some justification for Kohn's and Geyl's charge that I depreciate the West unduly. I shall be well advised to take their criticism to heart. At the same time I venture to suggest to them that, in their attitude to the West, they, too, perhaps, lean too far—their inclination being in the opposite direction to mine.

Kohn and Geyl seem to me to flinch from facing the truth that, in the course of the quarter of a millennium that has now passed since the seventeenth-century Western revolution, the modern Western Civilization has displayed not only a bright side but a dark one, and that in our time this dark side has been darker than the darkest stain on the pages of Western history in the Middle Ages or even in the Age of the Wars of Religion. Modern Western technology has now acquired the power to wipe out the human race, simultaneously with the power to bring the amenities of civilization to the whole of it. The advance in humane feeling has been offset by the degeneration of war into an indiscriminate assault on civilians, after it had been reduced in the eighteenth century to a conflict confined to professional combatants and conducted according to agreed rules.[4] The advance in the recognition of the rights and dignity of human beings has been offset by the imposition of the worst tyrannies that the Western Society has ever yet produced.[5] In fact, the history of the Western Civilization during the last quarter of a millennium bears out Shinn's suggestion that 'perhaps . . . the main effect of progress in history is to heighten the possibilities both for achievement and for disaster'.[6]

Geyl maintains[7] that the German National Socialist movement ought not to be debited to the West's account. Kohn likewise maintains[8] that Fascism and Communism are not products of the modern Western

[1] F. H. Underhill in *The Canadian Historical Review*, vol. xxxii, No. 3 (September, 1951), pp. 201–19. Underhill holds that this lack of sympathy disqualifies me 'from making an adequate analysis of the strength and weakness of our civilization'. It is never too late to try to qualify.   [2] *Toynbee and History*, p. 353.
[3] In *Der Monat*, August, 1955, p. 466.   [4] See iv. 141–55.
[5] E. Gargan finds that, on this point, I myself have been guilty of the wilful blindness of which I have just been accusing Geyl and Kohn. He quotes a passage in a volume of mine published in 1928—*The Conduct of British Empire Foreign Relations since the Peace Settlement*, p. 36, footnote 1—in which I forecast that the inter-war phenomenon of dictatorship 'was likely, according to all historical precedents, to be ephemeral'. Gargan adds that 'Toynbee's unwillingness to recognise the phenomenon of modern totalitarianism as a unique development, without historical precedent, has continued through the completion of the ten volumes of *A Study of History*' (*Books on Trial*, March, 1955, p. 266).
[6] R. L. Shinn: *Christianity and the Problem of History*, p. 255.
[7] In *Toynbee and History*, p. 370.
[8] In *Der Monat*, August, 1955, p. 467, and in *The Intent of Toynbee's History: A Cooperative Appraisal*.

Civilization; they are rejections of it—a return to the Middle Ages. This is surely just a refusal to face painful but undeniable facts. If these ideologies that are so abhorrent to modern Western liberals such as Kohn, Geyl, and me are not products of the modern Western Civilization, as our liberalism is, where have they come from? They have not come from Russia or India or China or the Islamic World or a no longer darkest Africa. Hitler was a Sudetenlander; Mussolini was a Romagnol; Marx and Engels were Rhinelanders who settled in England and did their life-work there. The Russians and Chinese would never have invented Communism for themselves. The reason why they are living under Communist regimes today is because Communism was invented in the West and was lying there, ready-made, for non-Westerners to take over. Moreover, the modern ideologies bear the unmistakable stamp of the modern West in some of their most characteristic and most repulsive features: for instance, their cold-bloodedness and their high-powered organization. They do, however, combine cold-bloodedness with fanaticism, in Robespierre's vein. And the second element in this incongruous combination can perhaps properly be described as a return to the spirit of the age of Western history that preceded the seventeenth-century Western revolution.

If Kohn is right on this point, it follows that the modern phase of the Western Civilization must suffer from some inadequacy or deficiency or weakness that has eventually provoked a reaction towards even the vices of a previous phase which the modern phase had temporarily repressed and superseded. And this would mean that a revival of the seventeenth-century and eighteenth-century 'Enlightenment', in which Sumberg sees the West's hope of salvation,[1] will not be enough. There is, indeed, one vital point in which the modern phase of the Western Civilization has remained negative ever since its beginning at the close of the seventeenth century, and that is its attitude towards religion. The liberalism and humanitarianism that have been the positive fruits of the seventeenth-century Western spiritual revolution have derived their spiritual impetus from Christian moral values.[2] But,

'now that liberalism is in eclipse and no longer possesses the power to unite the World, the cosmopolitan culture of the Modern World is like a body without a soul. . . . What has expanded has been: first, Western political and economic power; secondly, Western technology and science; and, thirdly, Western political institutions and social ideals. Christianity has also expanded, but in a far lesser degree.'[3]

It is true that, even in the religious field, the achievement of the modern phase of the Western Civilization has been respectable. It can truly be said that Westerners have never before come so near to acting

[1] T. A. Sumberg in *Social Research*, vol. 14, No. 3 (September, 1947), pp. 267–84, ad fin.

[2] This point is made by Chr. Dawson in *The Dynamics of World History*, p. 410.

[3] Ibid., p. 408. Cp. T. A. Sumberg, loc. cit. I, too, have noted this in *The World and the West*, as B. Prakash points out (*The Modern Review*, November, 1953, p. 403). Prakash also suggests (ibid.) that Christianity, at any rate in its Protestant Western form, has become too closely associated with capitalism to be able to adapt itself to any other economic regime. This seems a hazardous guess, considering how many successive economic regimes Christianity in the West has already outlived.

up to Christian standards of moral conduct as they have in this modern age in which the official tenets of Christianity have been progressively losing their hold on the intellectual allegiance of an ever-growing minority of educated Western men and women.[1] All the same, a quarter of a millennium of religious toleration has, after all, not availed to re-habilitate the West's ancestral religion from the moral discredit brought upon it by the Wars of Religion; and the corrosive effects of this moral discredit have been reinforced by the intellectual scepticism that the triumph of the scientific outlook has brought with it. The tenets of Christianity, and those of other living higher religions too, are incompat-ible, in their traditional form, with the scientific vision of the nature of the Universe. It seems improbable that, in this traditional form, they can ever recapture their former hold on hearts and minds; and, if this were possible, surely it would not be desirable.[2]

The rising gale of scientific discovery has blown away the chaff of traditional religion, and in doing this it has done mankind a service; but it has blown so hard that it has blown away the grain with the husk; and this has been a disservice, since neither science nor the ideologies have grain of their own to offer as a substitute. Their horizons, unlike those of the higher religions, fall far short of the bounds (if there are bounds) of the Universe, and what lies hidden beyond these restricted horizons is the heart of this mysterious and formidable Universe—the very part of it that is of the greatest moment to human beings. Science's horizon is limited by the bounds of Nature, the ideologies' horizon by the bounds of human social life, but the human soul's range cannot be confined within either of these limits. Man is a bread-eating (and rice-eating) social animal; but he is also something more. He is a person, endowed with a conscience and a will, as well as with a self-conscious intellect. This spiritual endowment of his condemns him to a life-long struggle to reconcile himself with the Universe into which he has been born. His inborn instinct is to try to make the Universe revolve round himself; his spiritual task in life is to overcome his self-centredness in order to put himself in harmony with the absolute spiritual Reality that is the true centre of everything in the phenomenal world. This 'flight of the alone to the alone'[3] is the goal of Man's endeavours. His yearning to reach this goal is the only motive strong enough to break through the barrier of self-centredness that stands in the way. Neither science nor the ideologies have anything to say about this spiritual crux.[4] On the other hand, all the

[1] I do not disagree with Chr. Dawson when he says that the social dynamism implicit in Christianity began to assert itself in the West from the time of Saint Francis of Assisi onwards (*The Dynamics of World History*, p. 461). One might carry the initial date back to the time of Saint Benedict, and might say that Saint Francis did for the new urban way of Western life what Saint Benedict had done for its older rural way. But it is also true, I think, that the social implications of Christianity had never before been so widely recognized or so genuinely put into practice in the West as they have been in the secular-minded age that has followed the seventeenth-century Western spiritual revolution.

[2] Kohn notices that I do not expect or desire a return to religion in its traditional form (*Toynbee and History*, p. 354).   [3] Plotinus: *Enneades*, IV. ix. 11.

[4] For this reason, and not because I fight shy of the logical results of my philosophy of history, I think it unlikely that Communism will play in Western history the part that was played in Hellenic history by Christianity (see B. Prakash in *The Modern Review*, November, 1953, p. 402).

higher religions and philosophies are concerned with it. Their visions may be partly delusions; their counsels may be partly misguided; their very concern with the soul's ultimate problem and task may be almost smothered under a heap of irrelevant accretions: ritual observances, social regulations, astronomical theories, and what not. Yet in spite of all their manifest weaknesses the higher religions are the only ways of life, known to Man so far, that do recognise what is the soul's true problem and true quest, and do offer Man some guidance for reaching his spiritual goal.

This means that, however grievously the trustees of the historic higher religions may have abused these religions' mandate, the mandate itself has not been forfeited. It cannot be forfeited unless and until mankind is presented with some new way or ways of life that offer to human souls more effective spiritual help than the historic higher religions can give them. Kohn is unwilling to concede that the Western Civilization is now in decline and that a return to religion is the remedy for this.[1] On this my comment would be that these two theses, both of which Kohn rejects, are not interdependent. The Western Civilization may or may not be in decline in our time; contemporary Westerners are not in a position to diagnose their own civilization's prospects. But, whatever this particular civilization's present prospects may be, a recovery of the essence of religion, if this has been lost, is needed at all times and in all social situations. It is needed because human beings cannot live without it. In order to recover the essence we have to distinguish it and to disengage it from non-essential accretions. This is a task that we undertake at our peril. It is also a task that we dare not shirk on that account. To shirk it is the one course that is undoubtedly more dangerous than to attempt to carry it out. This sifting is a task that can never be accomplished once for all. Each successive generation has to repeat the attempt on its own account. In setting our hand to this perennial human task in our day, we can find some light in modern science; but this glimmer is faint, and may be misleading. Like our predecessors, we have to work in the twilight. We should be fortunate if our gropings were to lead us to the Buddha's approach to Nirvāna or to Deutero-Isaiah's vision of the One True God.[2]

The struggle with self-centredness and the quest for harmony with God are issues between a human soul and God. These personal encounters between God and human beings are religion's true concern; and it is a misuse of religion to try to turn it to account for secular social purposes, even when these are innocent and expedient in themselves. All the same, mankind's collective history does have a bearing on the spiritual demands that are made on individual men and women. It is true that actions, right or wrong, are the acts of individuals and that, through all changes in social circumstances, right and wrong continue to be what they always are. But one social change that seems to have been continuing steadily in one unchanging direction since the beginning of

---

[1] H. Kohn in *Toynbee and History*, p. 351: *Der Monat*, August, 1955, p. 465.
[2] The points made in this paragraph have been considered at greater length in *An Historian's Approach to Religion* (London 1956, Oxford University Press), pp. 261–83.

human history is the cumulative increase in mankind's collective power. This brings with it a cumulative increase in the magnitude of the consequences of doing either wrong or right; and, since doing wrong or right has consequences for other people besides the doer, this social change increases each individual's personal load of moral responsibility.[1] The more portentous the consequences of his acts, the greater the demand upon him to act righteously. In an age in which mankind's collective power has suddenly been increased, for good or evil, a thousand-fold through the tapping of atomic energy, the standard of conduct demanded from ordinary human beings can be no lower than the standard attained in times past by rare saints.

In the Atomic Age cold considerations of mere expediency call for an arduous rise in standards of behaviour. As we have noticed, the peoples and governments had become aware of this, and their awareness was reflected in an increase in the degree of prudence and self-restraint with which international relations had been conducted since the acquisition of the atomic weapon by more than one out of the post-war world's legion of local states. It had been recognized that the price of self-preservation was a mutual acquiescence in co-existence, and the concern for self-preservation had proved strong enough to move mutually hostile peoples, armed with the atomic weapon, to pay this price grudgingly. Yet the calculations of expediency could do no more than postpone the evil day. The negative deterrent provided by mutual fear would have to be replaced by the positive bond of mutual love if the human race was to regain the certitude of survival that, before the fateful years 1945–9, it had been enjoying since some date in the Palaeolithic Age. A critic has reported me correctly as arguing 'that only through a harmonisation of human wills, in a compact freely entered into in the light of divine necessity, can peace prevail among men'.[2] This is, indeed, my belief, but of course it is not my discovery. It is a message handed down to our generation by a golden chain of sages and seers. There is a classical statement of it in Boethius's *Consolations of Philosophy*:[3] the last testament of one of the last custodians of the Hellenic tradition in what had once been the western part of the Roman Empire.

> Hanc rerum seriem ligat
> terras et pelagus regens
> et caelo imperitans, Amor.
> Hic si frena remiserit,
> quidquid nunc amat invicem
> bellum continuo geret,
> et quam nunc socia fide
> pulchris motibus incitant
> certent solvere machinam.
> Hic sancto populos quoque
> iunctos foedere continet,
> hic et coniugii sacrum

---

[1] On this, see E. Gürster: 'Die Atombombe, Schrittmacherin der Welteinigung', in *Die Neue Rundschau*, 13 Heft (Winter, 1949), pp. 134–5.
[2] A. G. Bailey in *Queen's Quarterly*, vol. lxii, No. 1 (Spring, 1955), pp. 100–10.
[3] A. M. S. Boethius: *Philosophiae Consolatio*, Book II, Ode 8.

castis nectit amoribus,
hic fidis etiam sua
dictat iura sodalibus.
O felix hominum genus
si vestros animos Amor,
quo caelum regitur, regat.[1]

XVII. RUSSIA'S PLACE IN HISTORY

A DISCUSSION in 1961 of the history and prospects of the West would have been left hanging in the air if it had not been followed up by a discussion of Russia's place in history. Since the Communist revolution that had trodden on the heels of the Liberal revolution in Russia in 1917, Russia had been challenging the West as it had not been challenged since the recession of the Ottoman Islamic power after the failure of the second Ottoman siege of Vienna in 1683. The Communist Russian challenge to the West was not merely a challenge to the West's former ascendancy over the rest of the Non-Western World; it was also a challenge to Western Liberalism in the name of a Western ideology which had now found a base of operations in a great non-Western country. Under Russian leadership, Communism had set out to compete with Liberalism for the adherence of the non-Western majority of mankind that was not yet committed to either of these two rival Western ways of life. Russian Communism was also challenging Liberalism on its home ground in Western countries. Before 1917 the West had been winning converts all over the World to the ideology of the seventeenth-century Western spiritual revolution. Since 1917 the West had been on the defensive against an ideological counter-offensive. The weapon with which this counter-offensive was being conducted was an ideology of Western origin, but this weapon was now being trained against the West by non-Western hands. These hands were Russian; and this meant that Russia had now come to play a part of capital importance in the decision of the West's destiny.

Considering how overwhelming the West's ascendancy over most of the rest of the World had been during the preceding quarter of a millennium, Communist Russia's feat of turning the tables on the West was impressive. Indeed, in the eyes of anti-Western-minded Asians, Africans, and Indian Americans, looking at history in A.D. 1961, Russia's role in history would probably have seemed to be just this. As they would have seen it, Russia was an example and an inspiration to the rest of the non-Western world because Russia had been the first non-Western country

---

[1]   . . . Love ruling heaven and earth and seas, them in this course doth bind.
And if it once let loose their reins, their friendship turns to war,
Tearing the world whose ordered form their quiet motions bear.
By it all holy laws are made and marriage rites are tied,
By it is faithful friendship joined. How happy mortals were
If that pure love did guide their minds which heavenly spheres doth guide.

(Anonymous translation published in 1609, as revised in H. F. Stewart and E. K. Rand's edition in the Loeb Classical Library, first published in 1918.)

that had had the courage to stand up to the modern West and the ability to beat it at its own game by mastering Western weapons and doing better than their Western originators in the use of them.[1]

Russia's victory in 1957 in the competition between her and the United States for launching the first man-made satellite was, no doubt, hailed all over the Non-Western World as an inspiring symbolic event. It seemed to signify the end of the West's technological superiority, and therefore also the end of the ascendancy which this technological superiority had brought with it. An observer who was acquainted with Russian history would have recalled that Russia's technological competition with the West, which had reached such a dramatic culmination in 1957, had also had a long history. It had started, not in 1917, but in 1689. Lenin had inherited his policy from Peter the Great. And Peter's adoption of the Western technology of his day had been so effective that it had enabled him to defeat decisively one of the great powers of the contemporary Western World, Sweden. His historic victory over Charles XII at Poltava in 1709 had been won within twenty years of the initiation of Peter's Westernizing programme, and within twenty-six years of the historic defeat of the 'Osmanlis under the ramparts of Vienna in 1683. This decisive battle in 1683 had inaugurated a Western ascendancy that had lasted for a quarter of a millennium in the World as a whole. Russia, alone of all the non-Western countries, had succeeded throughout in maintaining her independence. And the decisive battle that had signalized this Russian achievement had been won by Russia near the start. On this interpretation, Russia's role in history was that of serving as the leader in a world-wide resistance movement to the modern West's world-wide aggression.

It would, however, be an inadequate and misleading approach to an examination of Russia's place in history if we were to consider this solely in terms of a technological competition between Russia and the West,[2] and of the effect of this on Western fortunes. It was true that, by 1961, Russia was closely knit up with the West. Communism was a potent Russian import from the West; but, as has been noted, it was far from being the first. The deliberate Westernization of Russian life had been started by Peter the Great 228 years before the Russian Communist revolution, and 1689 was as epoch-making a date in Russian history as 1917. Yet Peter the Great's assertion of his sovereignty and his policy in

---

[1] H. Kohn points out, in *The Intent of Toynbee's History: A Cooperative Appraisal*, that Prussia after 1806 and Japan after 1868 adopted Western technology and Western methods of administration and education, as Russia has done, and that, in these two cases, one of the purposes was to combat contemporary Western Liberal ideas and ideals.

[2] Commenting on a passage in a previous volume of this book (iii. 200–2), B. O'Kennedy remarks that 'it seems an over-simplification to assert that the Soviet experiment is an attempt to turn a nation of peasants into a nation of mechanics, to substitute a new America for the old Russia. Moreover, Professor Toynbee's view of that experiment as a conflict between the ideals of Lenin and the methods of Ford may be a paradoxical confirmation of the ascendancy of Western over Russian civilization, but it fails to explain a great deal that has happened' (*The Irish Times*, 1st March, 1947). I agree.

O'Kennedy's point has also been made apropos of the Westernization, not only of Russia, but of the Non-Western World in general, by I. Neander in *Finanz-Archiv*, Neue Folge, 13 (151/2), pp. 168–78, and in *Grundzüge der Russischen Geschichte* (Darmstadt 1955, Gentner).

1689 was far from being the beginning of Russian history. Seven hundred years before Peter the Great had imposed on Russia the Western Civilization in the modern secular version of it that had just taken shape in his generation, his predecessor Vladimir had imposed on her the Byzantine Civilization in the act of forcibly converting his subjects to Eastern Orthodox Christianity. For nearly two hundred years before that, Russia had been part of the far-flung Scandinavian World, as a result of having been opened up commercially and organized politically by bands of Swedish military adventurers.

The Scandinavian Civilization was abortive; and, after the conversion of the whole Scandinavian World to one or other form of Christianity, the Pre-Christian Scandinavian culture was obliterated. On the other hand the Byzantine Christian Civilization that captivated Russia in and after A.D. 989 made as deep and as enduring a mark on this colonial annex of the Scandinavian World as Western Christianity made on Scandinavia Proper.[1] The modern Western Civilization that was imposed on Russia by Peter the Great and his successors was a veneer. Russia remained Byzantine under the surface. The second bout of Westernization inaugurated by the Communist revolution in 1917 had obviously penetrated deeper down into Russian life than the Petrine revolution, and it had, no doubt, produced a greater disturbance in Russian life's Byzantine depths. Yet, nearly half a century after this latest Westernizing revolution in Russia, the Eastern Orthodox Church was still a powerful force in Russia, and its survival there implied that the Byzantine outlook had survived there too. In 1961 it was not yet possible to guess whether, eventually, the twentieth-century Western Communist ideology would or would not be more successful than the seventeenth-century Western Liberal ideology had been in supplanting the Byzantine Civilization in Russia.[2] All that could be said at that date

[1] See viii. 676–8.

[2] My conception of Russia's Byzantine heritage has been set out in a lecture, originally delivered in Canada, which was afterwards published in *Horizon*, August, 1947, and then in *Civilization on Trial* (New York 1948, Oxford University Press), pp. 164–83. This paper has drawn criticisms from B. Bykhovsky in *New Times*, No. 46 (12th November, 1947), pp. 27–31, and from J. D. Clarkson in an article in *The Russian Review*, vol. 15, No. 3 (July, 1956), pp. 165–72, based on a paper read at the annual meeting of the American Historical Society in Washington, D.C., on 28th December, 1955.

Bykhovsky agrees that Russia did adopt Byzantine culture in the tenth century, but he denies that there is such a thing as a separate Byzantine Civilization. 'Generally known historical facts', he holds, 'incontrovertibly prove . . . the integrality of European (and World) culture' (p. 28). Clarkson sees eye to eye with Bykhovsky on this point. 'Toynbee's fundamental premise that Russia and the West represent two distinct civilizations, set apart by religion', is, Clarkson holds, 'a basic misconception'. I. Neander makes the same point in *Finanz-Archiv*, Neue Folge 13 (1951/2), pp. 168–78, and in *Grundzüge der Russischen Geschichte* (Darmstadt 1955, Gentner), and so does Chr. Hill in *The Modern Quarterly*, Autumn, 1947, p. 306. L. Thorndike, too, upholds the unity of civilization in general terms (*The Journal of Modern History*, vol. vii, No. 3 (September, 1935), pp. 315–17).

Bykhovsky accuses me of falsifying history in order to make of it an engine of ideological controversy. In particular, he castigates me for my 'preposterously absurd and amazingly ignorant identification of the Socialist system established in Russia after the Great October Revolution with the medieval Byzantine state' (p. 29). I do not, of course, identify the two, but I do maintain that the Byzantine Civilization is still alive in Russia below the surface, and that the underlying structure of the Byzantine state can still be discovered beneath the veneer of successive imported Western regimes: first the enlightened autocracy imported from the West by Peter the Great, and then the Communist regime imported by Lenin and his companions. Here, again, however, Bykhovsky

was that the issue had not yet been decided. Meanwhile, this brief recital of familiar historical facts will have indicated that Russia's place in history was not just that of a convert—however important and successful a convert—to the modern Western way of life.

Russia's cultural history, up to date, had followed an unusual course. Since she had made her way into the *Oikoumenê* about eleven hundred years back, she had played a prominent role, cultural as well as political and military, in the World's affairs. Yet so far she had not ever created an original civilization of her own. Three times over within these 1,100 years she had received an alien civilization from abroad: first the Scandinavian, then the Byzantine, and then the Western, and this first in its Liberal and afterwards in its Communist form. On the cultural plane hitherto she had always been a satellite, yet always one of an unusual kind. She had been a satellite that, each time, had more than held its own against the foreign body that had drawn her into its field of attraction. The Scandinavian Civilization was overwhelmed so soon after Russia had been annexed by it that there was no time, in this brief first chapter of Russian history, for Russia to react powerfully on Scandinavia Proper. Russia's association with the Byzantine World and with the West had been longer, and, in each of these two other encounters, the civilization that had attracted Russia had eventually found itself engaged in a tug-o'-war in which the satellite had threatened to reverse the roles of the two parties by usurping the sun's place and reducing the original sun to the subordinate status of a satellite.[1]

and Clarkson see eye to eye. Clarkson says of me that 'he simply does not understand what his friendly critics, Obolensky and Sumner, have written' (see vii. 31–40 and 577–9; viii. 676–8) 'about his notion of a dominating Byzantine political êthos running through Russian history'.

This consensus between a Communist Russian and an American critic is impressive. It is obviously possible that I have over-emphasized the distinctiveness of each of the civilizations in the Syriac-Hellenic family. The sharpness of the dividing line that I have drawn has been noticed by T. R. Fyvel in *The Tribune*, 21st March, 1947, p. 20. It might be more instructive (though I do not think it is) to treat all four Christian civilizations and the Islamic Civilization as being no more than so many variations on one single civilization. My contention may be less convincing than Clarkson's and Bykhovsky's, I concede. But I do not admit that, in making it, I have been influenced by any ideological prejudices. In my view it is no insult either to the Byzantine Civilization or to Russia to label them as being 'non-Western'. On the other hand, I have an impression that this is felt to be an insult by Bykhovsky, Clarkson, and Hill, and possibly by Obolensky and Sumner too; and that their insistence on their thesis that there is no dividing line between Russia and the West is partly inspired by a wish to vindicate Russia's good name, as well as by a dispassionate study of the historical facts. I detect the same feeling in Neander (locc. citt.) and in Spuler (in *Islam*, No. 30 (1952)) when they insist that the Westernization of Russia is not on a par with the Westernization of Asian countries because Russia was already so much closer, culturally, to the West to begin with.

[1] If Russia's cultural history has any counterpart, this is to be found in the cultural history of Iran. Like Russia, Iran received successive alien civilizations from abroad: first the Sumero-Akkadian, then the Syriac, and eventually the Islamic; and, in the last two of her three encounters, Iran—again like Russia—reacted powerfully upon the civilization into whose field she had been drawn. In coalescing with the Syriac Civilization in and after the Achaemenian Age, the Iranian culture was not a passive party. It gave, besides receiving. Its attractiveness is attested by the history of Judaism. An Iranian religion, Zoroastrianism, was the only alien spiritual force that made a mark on Judaism in this age; and this Iranian religion displayed this vitality after Iran had suffered a crushing political disaster in the overthrow of the Achaemenian Empire by Alexander. The overthrow of the Sasanian Empire by the Arabs a thousand years later was a disaster for Iran of comparable magnitude. Yet, this time again, Iran reasserted herself on the cultural plane while she was still politically prostrate. The religious

This reversal of relations had taken place in the Byzantine World before the end of the four and a half centuries that elapsed between the conversion of Russia to Eastern Orthodox Christianity in A.D. 989 and the extinction of the last remnants of the East Roman Empire in 1453–61. In the course of this age the whole of Eastern Orthodox Christendom, Russia included, was successfully attacked and overrun by foreign conquerors on two fronts. The East Roman Empire was assaulted by Western Christians and Turkish Muslims, Russia by Western Christians and Eurasian Nomad Tatars. Both the East Roman nucleus and the Russian annex of the Byzantine World were submerged; but their subsequent fortunes were not the same. The East Roman Empire foundered, and the Greeks, and, with them, the other Orthodox Christian peoples of Anatolia, Transcaucasia, and South-East Europe, remained under Ottoman Turkish rule till the nineteenth century. By contrast, from the fourteenth century onwards, Russia re-emerged, and this time as an effectively centralized state that was capable of holding its own against all comers. Accordingly, after Bulgaria, Serbia, and the East Roman Empire had been erased from the political map, Muscovy lived on as the sole surviving representative of Byzantine Christendom and sole surviving guardian of the Eastern Orthodox Christian faith. The Muscovite branch of the Eastern Orthodox Church repudiated the union with the Roman Church that had been accepted in 1439, at the Council of Florence, by an East Roman Imperial Government that was then in its last agonies. In the next chapter of the Byzantine World's history the Muscovite Government may or may not have taken seriously the theory that, after Constantinople—the Second Rome—had betrayed the Orthodox Christian faith and had been punished for this by being conquered by the 'Osmanlis, faithful Moscow had become the Third Rome.[1] But it seems unquestionable that the experience of being left, from 1461 onwards, as the sole remaining independent champion of Orthodoxy did instil into the Russians a sense of Russia's being a holy country with a unique destiny;[2] and Russia had become this in virtue of having become

conversion of the Iranian people to Islam was accompanied, from the beginning of the 'Abbasid Age onwards, by an Iranianization of Islam on Iranian ground; and this Iranian cultural counter-offensive eventually culminated in the emergence of a distinctive Iranic version of the Islamic Civilization.

[1] This question has been touched upon in vii. 31–40 and 577–9. See the passage there quoted from an unpublished letter of 25th January, 1951, from B. H. Sumner to A. J. Toynbee, and from an unpublished note of 1st June, 1951, by Prince Dmitri Obolensky. See also a paper by Prince Obolensky on 'Russia's Byzantine Heritage' in *Oxford Slavonic Papers*, vol. i (Oxford 1950, Clarendon Press), pp. 37–63. Sumner and Obolensky both hold that the pretension that Moscow was 'the Third Rome' should be taken with a grain of salt. As they see it, it was little more than an academic conceit, which had no great effect either on popular feeling in Russia or on governmental policy.

[2] A suggestion that the Russians have come to regard themselves as being 'the Chosen People' is contested in a letter written to me on 6th March, 1951, by J. Stolnikoff (on this point, see further chapter II, Annex, p. 626, footnote 2). 'Your theory of the "Chosen People",' Stolnikoff writes, 'corresponds only very remotely with the well-established fact of the Russians' freedom from all idea of superiority and disdain in their attitude towards other nations. . . . I suppose that this misunderstanding goes no deeper than a mistaken use of the word "Russian" instead of the word "Sovietic".' I cannot be let off so lightly. I believe that the Russian people's sense of having a special mission dates from A.D. 1453, not just from A.D. 1917. From all accounts, what Stolnikoff says is true of the Russians as individuals in their personal relations with non-Russians; and this is an amiable and admirable Russian tradition. But it is not

the heart and citadel of Orthodox Christendom instead of remaining the outlying province that she had originally been.

This Russian belief in Russia's holiness, orthodoxy, and destiny survived the reception of the modern Western Civilization in Russia in and after the time of Peter the Great. In this Westernizing age it had already asserted itself twice—now clothed, each time, in a Western ideology that, in Russian hands, had been adapted to serve Russian purposes. The nineteenth-century Western Romantic Movement was, in its Western birth-place, no more than a Western family affair. It was the expression of an insistence, on the part of the Germans and other Western peoples, upon the reality and the value of their distinctive national contributions to their common Western Civilization. The movement had been evoked by a French pretension to impose the French national contribution upon the other Western peoples as a standard form for the modern phase of the Western Civilization that had been inaugurated by the seventeenth-century Western cultural revolution. This nineteenth-century Western Romantic Movement inspired the nineteenth-century Russian Slavophiles; but, in taking it over, they gave it a new turn. The Slavophile version of Romanticism was an assertion that the Western Civilization was decadent and that the Russian Civilization was 'the wave of the future'. In the twentieth century the Russian converts to a later Western ideology, Communism, had turned this to the same account. Communism was now 'the wave of the future'; Capitalism was doomed to collapse. Since the West was given over to Capitalism, while Russia had shaken off its toils in the act of embracing the Communist faith, the West was bound to go under and Russia was bound to triumph. Twentieth-century Russian Communism, nineteenth-century Russian Slavophilism, and the fifteenth-century Russian championship of Orthodox Christianity were evidently successive expressions of an identical conviction. This conviction was that Russia had seen the truth and would prosper in virtue of acting on it, while the West had persisted in error and had thereby condemned itself to come to grief.

This Russian belief was not, of course, an original Russian idea. The Russians took it over from their instructors the Byzantine Greeks. In Byzantine Greek eyes the Western Christians were already schismatics, and the Eastern Orthodox Christians were the sole remaining repositories of the true Christian faith. This sense of uniqueness was part of the spoils that the Christian Church had taken from the Jews. It was, in fact, a Jewish pretension that had been purloined from the Jews by gentiles who had become converted to 'deviationist' Judaic religions. In 1961 it could not yet be foreseen whether Russia was going to remain fundamentally Byzantine, or whether she was going to become thoroughly Western in the Communist form of the modern Western Civilization. But, whatever might happen, it seemed certain that, for a long time to come, the Russian spirit and outlook would continue to be Judaic, since this Judaic êthos was common to the Byzantine and the Western tradition. Communism was as patently Judaic in its ideology as

incompatible with a feeling that Russia, as distinguished from individual Russians, has a greater destiny than other countries have.

Eastern Orthodox Christianity was; and, though the modern version of the Western culture, dating from the seventeenth-century spiritual revolution, represented a resolute attempt to purge the Western tradition of its ancestral Judaic fanaticism and intolerance, we have seen that this vein in the Western tradition was not, after all, driven off the field but was merely driven underground, to erupt, in our day, in such ideologies as Communism, Fascism, and National Socialism.

It is thus clear that, within the species of the genus society that we label 'civilizations', the Russian Civilization falls within the same sub-species as the Byzantine, the Western, and the Islamic. Whether we classify it as a variant of the Byzantine or as a variant of the Western or as a separate civilization with a distinctive character of its own, it was undoubtedly part of the crop that had sprung from the blending of the Syriac and Hellenic civilizations in a 'culture-compost'.[1]

If it was true that the world-wide dissemination of the Western Civilization in its modern form had provided the basis and the framework for the formation of an oecumenical civilization, what was Russia's contribution to this coming oecumenical civilization going to be? Perhaps Russia's most important role in this next chapter of mankind's history would be to serve as a medium for the modernization of non-Western peoples that were less far advanced along the path of modernization than Russia herself was.

When we survey the attitudes of the non-Russian peoples who in 1961 were under Russian ascendancy, we find that there were several different categories of them and that these were reacting in different ways.

Russification was being obstinately resisted by subject or satellite or ex-satellite peoples whose cultural background was either Western or Non-Russian Byzantine. The first of these two categories was represented by the Slovenes, Croats, Magyars, Czechoslovaks, Poles, Lithuanians, Letts, and Ests; the second by the Serbs, Rumans, Bulgars, and Georgians. Even the Ukrainians, who are one of three sub-groups within the Russian people itself, were up in arms against being dominated by the Great Russians. These peoples' resistance to Russification was not an anti-Communist movement; it was an anti-Russian movement which antedated the Russian Communist revolution of the year 1917. Under the preceding Imperial Russian regime, Russification had been resisted just as obstinately by the Poles in Congress Poland and by the Finns. Both Congress Poland and Finland were under Russian domination for a hundred years ending in the First World War; yet both countries emerged from this century-long ordeal still un-Russified. The nineteenth-century Georgians, Rumans, and Bulgars also reacted violently against the domination of the Pre-Communist Russians. Though these had represented themselves as 'liberators' from Muslim rulers, these liberated Orthodox Christian peoples became hardly less anti-Russian than the Magyars, a Western people who were re-subjected to Hapsburg rule by invading Russian armies in 1849. The same attitude had been displayed by at least one of the Russians' Muslim subject peoples, the

[1] See pp. 454-61.

Qazan Tatars; and these anti-Russian resistance movements all had the same explanation. The peoples that had resisted Russification were peoples that had felt themselves to be farther advanced than the Russians in civilization. They had therefore been unwilling to receive civilization through a Russian channel. If they were ready to adopt the modern version of the Western Civilization, they wanted to draw this for themselves from its Western fountain-head. They wanted to do that, whichever of the alternative forms of the modern Western Civilization happened to attract them. For example, a Communist Jugoslav, just as much as a Liberal Jugoslav, would want to work out his chosen way of life independently. He would object to having it imposed on him by Russian dictation.

There were, however, other subjects and satellites of Russia who did not feel themselves to be so far advanced in civilization as they felt the Russians to be. The peoples in this category might resent Russian domination and exploitation as hotly as the Jugoslavs, Magyars, and Poles; but they did not feel the same repugnance to receiving modern civilization through a Russian duct. So far from that, they felt that, on the cultural plane, Russia offered them their nearest and most easy access to the Modern World, and that the Russian language was the best vehicle, within their reach, for bringing to them modern knowledge and ideas. Therefore the ablest and most ambitious of their young men and women would be tempted to learn Russian and to complete their education in Moscow or Leningrad. They might feel hostile to Russia politically and might have no inclination towards Russification for its own sake. But they would put up with it as an unpalatable but necessary means towards the end that they had in view; and that was to become first-class citizens of the rising modern oecumenical society. The peoples in this second category included the Turkish-speaking and Finnish-speaking peoples in the Urals (Bashkirs, Voguls, Ostiaks, and the rest), together with the Turkish-speaking and Iranian-speaking peoples of Central Asia (Qazaqs, Uzbegs, Türkmens, Kirghiz, Tajiks) and the Mongol-speaking peoples of Eastern Siberia (the Buriats and the Mongols in Outer Mongolia).

In 1961 this category accounted for no more than a small fraction of the human race, even reckoning in a satellite state like Outer Mongolia, which lay outside the Soviet Union's frontiers. However, the numbers in this category might be expected to increase; for there were vast populations in Asia and Africa, besides the peoples mentioned above, for whom Russification would spell modernization in the form that would be most feasible for them. China, who was not the Soviet Union's satellite, but was her principal Communist ally, was not likely to figure in this list. The Chinese, like the Western and the non-Russian Orthodox Christian peoples, felt themselves to be superior to the Russians in civilization, and the motive that had led them to accept a Communist regime was not a wish to gain entry into the Modern World through a Russian door. The Chinese people's objective was to recover for China her historic cultural and political primacy at the eastern end of the Old-World *Oikoumenê*. But, short of being able to attract China into her cultural field, Russia seemed to have a fair prospect of being able to attract a number of the more backward among the still uncommitted nations.

This prospect suggested that, in the formation of the coming oecumenical society, the Russian culture and language might play, in large tracts of Asia, and possibly of Africa too, the role that was already being played by the Arabic language and culture in Africa, and by the Spanish in the tier of Indian American republics extending from Mexico to Paraguay inclusive. Russification would then be one of several alternative forms of modernization. Its contribution might not be so great as that of the English language or as that of the modern Western Civilization drawn straight from its Western fountain-head; but Russian, like Arabic and Spanish, cultural influence might succeed in pushing its way into regions that were less easily accessible to the modern Western Civilization in its native form.

In the current chapter of history, Russian culture would carry Communism with it; and this ideological concomitant of Russification would either promote the progress of Russification or obstruct it, according to what was the situation at the time in the country in question.

The Communist form of the modern Western Civilization had, so far, seldom or never been the first choice of non-Western peoples that had opted for Westernization in some form or other.[1] Usually their ambition had been to Westernize on Liberal lines—that is, on parliamentary lines on the political plane. It was significant that, in both Russia itself and in China, the eventual Communist revolution had been preceded by an attempt at a Liberal revolution, and had not found its opportunity until this antecedent Liberal revolution had been discredited by having unmistakably miscarried. Russia in 1917 had been in the last throes of a disastrous war, and there the Communist revolution had followed at the Liberal revolution's heels after only a few months' interval. In China the Kuomintang was given a nineteen-years-long run (reckoning from its nation-wide triumph in 1929) before it was convicted of having exhausted its mandate. As for the non-Western peoples who had been under Western rule, their struggles to throw this off had been made in the name of modern Western Liberal principles; and, when they had recovered their political independence, their first impulse, even in cases where their former Western rulers had abdicated only unwillingly and with a bad grace, had been to exercise their new freedom of choice by adopting the Liberal Western way of life, not only on the political plane, but on all planes. In 1961 this could be verified in Southern Vietnam, as well as in India.

This general preference for the Liberal way of life evidently made the association of Communism with Russification a handicap for Russia in her efforts to extend her influence into non-Western countries, beyond her own borders, where she had to deal with countries that were trying to live the Liberal Western way of life and had not, so far, been discouraged by disillusioning experiences. Disillusionment, however, did often follow; and, in a country that had been overtaken by it,

[1] See p. 309.

Communism would be, not a handicap to the entry of Russian influence, but a powerful aid to it.

The experiment of Westernization on Liberal lines was apt to be followed by disillusionment because this experiment was an ambitious one. It was ambitious because the Liberal way of life required and presupposed the existence of able, experienced, and public-spirited citizens in large numbers; and, in most non-Western countries, there was a scarcity of this indispensable human asset. For this reason, parliamentary government had broken down in one after another of these countries when too many of the people who had been entrusted with the working of it had proved incompetent or corrupt or both. The sequel had been a dictatorship, of the kind that, for the same reason, had so often prevailed in the Americas in many of the successor-states of the former Spanish Empire of the Indies. In the Asian and African successor-states of the former Dutch, French, and British colonial empires, many of the dictatorships that followed miscarriages of parliamentary institutions were military. The professional military officers in these countries had been trained in a Western school, and their standards of honesty and public spirit were, in some cases, higher, on the average, than those of the local politicians. On the other hand, these soldiers' experience was limited to their own professional field, and in politics they were novices. The one substantial advantage of dictatorship over parliamentary government in countries in this situation was that the number of able and honest people required for working a dictatorship efficiently was a much smaller one. But this advantage was not a monopoly of the military variety of dictatorship; the Communist variety possessed it too, and it also possessed many other advantages that a military dictatorship lacked.

The Communist ideology was a Christian heresy[1] in the sense that it had singled out several of the elements in Christianity and had concentrated on these to the exclusion of the rest. It had taken from Christianity its social ideals, its intolerance, and its fervour. It was therefore a far more dynamic spiritual force than the conventional sense of professional honour that was the inspiration of public-spirited military dictators. A believing Communist was a dedicated soul, and he could justify his faith by pointing to impressive works. He could point out that the conversion of Russia to Communism had been followed, within forty years, by a technological triumph which might be taken as signifying that Russia had now outstripped the West in the very field in which the West had previously excelled. Russia's example, he could claim, had now demonstrated that, for a poor, uneducated, agricultural people, Communism offered an effective short-cut for catching up with the West in the competition for power; and one of the ambitions of every non-Western country that had felt the weight of the West's former ascendancy was to recover its own traditional position of eminence—historical or legendary. Communism, thus presented, would therefore make a powerful appeal to a non-Western people that had tried, and failed, to catch up with the West by taking the other of the two alternative modern Western roads.

---

[1] This interpretation of Communism has been disputed by Father G. F. Klenk, S.J., in *Stimmen der Zeit*, No. 145 (1949–50), pp. 376–84.

In 1961 mankind was wondering which of these two roads, the Liberal or the Communist, was going to become the high road leading towards a future oecumenical civilization; and at that date the choice between these two alternatives seemed, to many minds, as if it would make all the difference in the world. Yet Communism, as well as Liberalism, was a product and expression of the modern Western Civilization,[1] and the difference between the Liberal and the Communist way of Western life might be expected to diminish progressively with each additional decade of 'coexistence'. The ideological feud that in 1961 was obsessing nearly half the human race might have become no more than an academic issue in the life of an oecumenical society a hundred years later.

XVIII. A RE-SURVEY OF CIVILIZATIONS

IN the course of the first ten volumes of this book I arrived at a list of twenty-three full-blown civilizations, four that were arrested at an early stage in their growth, and five that were abortive. The twenty-three full-blown civilizations on this former list were distributed between a number of different series running, some to three generations of civilizations, some to two, some to one generation only; and, in any series that ran to more than a single generation, the relation of the later civilization or civilizations in this series to its or their immediate predecessor was labelled 'affiliation'. These series were parallel but were not synchronous. The earliest of the Pre-Columbian civilizations in the Americas were perhaps as much as three thousand years later in emerging than the earliest of the civilizations in the Old World. In the Old-World group there was one series, that represented by the Egyptiac Civilization, which ran to a single generation only, yet had a time-span which was of the same order of magnitude as the combined time-spans of the first two generations in the parallel series initiated respectively by the Sumeric, Minoan, Indus, and Shang civilizations.

Thus classified, the list of civilizations worked out as follows:

I. *Full-blown Civilizations*

A. *First Generation, Unrelated to others*
Egyptiac
Andean

B. *First Generation, Unaffiliated to another*
Sumeric
Minoan

---

[1] This point is made by Bykhovsky. 'Marxism-Leninism is not a weapon against Western Civilization—as Mr. Toynbee falsely asserts; it is a weapon against anti-democratic imperialist reaction, which acts as a tremendous break on the development of European and world civilization. The Soviet people treasure every progressive step in the history of the British, French, and every other national culture' (*New Times*, No. 46 (12th November, 1947) ,p. 30). A Western observer can agree with the substance of what Bykhovsky here says, if he can discount Bykhovsky's polemical way of saying it.

Indus[1]
Shang[1]
Mayan

C. *Second Generation, Affiliated to another*

Babylonic (to Sumeric)
Hittite (to Sumeric)
Hellenic (to Minoan)
Syriac (to Minoan)
Indic (to Indus)
Sinic (to Shang)
Yucatec (to Mayan)
Mexic (to Mayan)

D. *Third Generation, Affiliated to another*

Orthodox Christian, main body (to Hellenic)
Orthodox Christian, Russian offshoot (to Hellenic)
Western (to Hellenic)
Arabic Muslim (to Syriac)
Iranic Muslim (to Syriac)
Hindu (to Indic)
Far Eastern, main body (to Sinic)
Far Eastern, Japanese offshoot (to Sinic)

II. *Arrested Civilizations*

Eskimo[2]
Nomadic[3]
'Osmanli[4]
Spartan[5]

III. *Abortive Civilizations*

First Syriac[6]
Far Eastern Christian[7]
Far Western Christian[8]
Scandinavian[9]
Medieval Western City-State Cosmos.[10]

By the time (1958–9) when the present volume was being written, this list had come to need revision. There had been criticisms of the method —or lack of method—by which I had arrived at it.[11] There had also been changes in parts of the picture of the historical facts. These changes had been due to increases in knowledge and understanding, mainly

[1] The Indus and Shang civilizations appear in the list in the form of a genealogical table in vol. vii, opposite p. 772, but not in the lists in vol. i, pp. 131–3. During the twenty years (1934–54) between the dates of publication of vols. i–iii and vols. vii–x, the Indus and Shang cultures had come—as a result of increasing knowledge of them—to look as if they both qualified for being given the status of full-blown civilizations.
[2] See iii. 4–7.   [3] See iii. 7–22.   [4] See iii. 22–50.   [5] See iii. 50–79.
[6] See ii. 388–91.   [7] See ii. 369–85 and 446–52.
[8] See ii. 322–40 and 421–37.   [9] See ii. 340–60 and 434–45.
[10] See iii. 299–306 and v. 619–42.
[11] These have been summarized by Anderle in an unpublished paper.

thanks to new archaeological discoveries and new interpretations of previously known facts. In the light of what my critics have written and what the archaeologists have brought to light since the publication of volumes i–iii of this book, I have reconsidered a number of my previous conclusions already in earlier chapters of this volume. The purpose of the present chapter is to bring together and complete the results of these reconsiderations in the form of a new list of civilizations. The best approach to this will be to examine first the criticisms and then the changes in the archaeologists' picture, with a view to seeing what changes in my list are required.

Most of the criticisms fall under one or other of five heads. The first is a sweeping one. 'Toynbee's list . . . is a peculiar jumble of incompatible and incomparable entities.'[1] My criterion for identifying civilizations is not uniform. In some cases it is material culture, in others religion, in others race.[2] The second line of criticism is that my identifications of civilizations and my demarcations between those that I claim to have identified are subjective.[3] The third is that I have failed to distinguish between major civilizations and those that are 'secondary or peripheral'.[4] The fourth is that my list of 'arrested civilizations' is capricious.[5] The fifth is that my list of abortive civilizations is incomplete.[6] The comprehensive criticism can perhaps be dealt with best by examining each of the others.

The method that I used in identifying the civilizations on my list was to take one instance as a model and apply this to the rest of the field. This method was, I should say, objective in two senses. My model was not an imaginary one; it was an authentic piece of history; and I applied it, I believe, systematically and consistently. At the same time my procedure was, I agree, subjective in some other respects. The model that I used was the history of the Hellenic Civilization and of the Western Civilization's affiliation to the Hellenic through the Christian Church. Evidently the reason why I used this particular model was that I myself happened to be a Westerner who had been educated in the Greek and Latin classics. I should, no doubt, have used another model if I had been either a Chinese, brought up on the Confucian classics, or a Jew brought up on the Torah and the Talmud.[7] Moreover, I was led into misconstruing my model, in at least one important point, by a pre-

    1 P. Bagby: *Culture and History*, p. 177.
    2 W. F. Albright: *From the Stone Age to Christianity*, 2nd ed., pp. 97–98.
    3 K. D. Erdmann in *Archiv für Kulturgeschichte*, xxxiii. Band, Heft 2 (1951), p. 245; A. R. Burn in *History*, February–October 1956, p. 6; R. K. Merton in *The American Journal of Sociology*, vol. xlvii, No. 2 (September, 1941), pp. 205–13; P. Gardiner in *Time and Tide*, 30th October, 1954. Gardiner observes that 'some of the divisions' Toynbee 'makes between temporarily adjoining civilizations seem to be determined by considerations of what course a civilization *must* pursue. . . . In so far as he does this, the conclusions at which he arrives concerning the similar paths followed by different societies . . . merely reflect the method of classification initially employed.' A survey of criticisms of my attempt to identify civilizations is given by Anderle in an unpublished paper.   4 Bagby, op. cit., p. 179.
    5 Bagby, op. cit., p. 180; H. Marrou in *Esprit*, July, 1952, p. 123; A. L. Kroeber: *Style and Civilizations*, pp. 124–5.
    6 Kroeber, ibid. (Kroeber includes, I think, the 'abortive' as well as the 'arrested' civilizations among what he here calls the 'minor' civilizations on my list); R. Coulborn in *Toynbee and History*, p. 163; Bagby, op. cit., pp. 179–80.
    7 See Chapter VI, pp. 170–217.

occupation with Hellenism that was one result of my education in Hellenic literature and history. I thought of the Western Civilization as being affiliated to the Hellenic Civilization exclusively—and this after I had taken note, at an early stage in my inquiry,[1] of the obvious fact that, in Christianity, which was the Western Civilization's historical link with the Hellenic, the Hellenic element was combined with, and dominated by, a Judaic one. I ought to have seen that the Western Civilization was affiliated to both civilizations or—to describe the actual course of historical events more accurately—that it had sprung from soil fertilised by a fusion of the two. This misconstruction of my Hellenic model led me to assume that 'affiliated' civilizations were in all cases affiliated to some single antecedent civilization exclusively; and this led me astray in, for example, my tracing of the affiliation of the Syriac Civilization. I saw this as being affiliated to the Minoan Civilization alone, when in truth it was affiliated to three others as well: the Sumeric, Egyptiac, and Hittite. Multiple affiliations have been at least as common as exclusive affiliations to some single predecessor.[2]

I have tried to correct these errors in earlier chapters of this volume. For instance, I have now checked the results of applying my Hellenic model by applying a Sinic model and a Jewish one as well, and comparing the likenesses and differences of the results.[3] I have recognized the four affiliations of the Syriac Civilization.[4] I have also recognized that the Western Civilization is the product of a Syriac-Hellenic 'culture-compost',[5] and that the same blend of the same two antecedent civilizations has also produced the Orthodox Christian and Islamic civilizations.[6]

There is another subjective element in my original identification and demarcation of civilizations which is more difficult to correct because it has not been imported by me but is inherent in the phenomena themselves.

When I applied, in the rest of the field, the concept of 'affiliation' that I had derived from my picture of the historical relation of the Western Civilization to the Hellenic, I found a number of cases in which the same pattern did, indeed, seem to recur, but this only partially or only faintly. In these cases the question arose whether the evidence for a relative break in continuity was sufficient to warrant the identification of what followed the break as being the history of a new civilization, affiliated to a predecessor in the sense in which the Western Civilization is affiliated to the Hellenic. In spite of the traces of a break, it might, in these cases, be more illuminating to interpret the subsequent period as being continuous with the previous period: in other words, to treat the two periods as being successive chapters in the history of one and the same civilization. In one case—the Egyptiac—I came, in my original survey of civilizations, to the conclusion that here the continuity was more significant than the discontinuity, and that therefore the history of civilization in Egypt before its conversion to Christianity ought to be regarded as being the history of a single continuous civilization and not

---

[1] See i. 40–41 and 57.
[2] This point is made by F. Borkenau in *Merkur*, July, 1949, pp. 633–4, and in *Commentary*, March, 1956, p. 241.　　　　　　　　　　[3] See pp. 186–217.
[4] See pp. 407–10.　　　[5] See pp. 457–8.　　　[6] See pp. 458–9.

as being the history of a series of two civilizations.[1] I took this line in spite of having accepted Breasted's interpretation of the character and history of the worship of Osiris, which, on his interpretation, had some striking features in common with the character and history of Christianity.[2] Now that Breasted's interpretation of the Osirian religion has been discarded by the Egyptologists of the next generation,[3] any previously possible doubts about the continuity of Egyptiac history have been finally dispelled. There were, however, other cases in which the evidence for a break seemed to me to be sufficiently significant to warrant me in identifying what followed the break as being the history of a new civilization, as long as I did this only tentatively and provisionally.[4] These cases that I decided to treat as being doubtful were those of the Orthodox Christian (main body), Arabic Muslim, Iranic Muslim, Hindu, Far Eastern (main body), Babylonic, Yucatec, and Mexic civilizations.

The element of subjectivity, that was inherent in the phenomena here, arose from the fact that there was this string of eight intermediate cases running all the way from the discontinuity between the Hellenic and the Western Civilization at one extreme to the continuity of the Egyptiac Civilization at the other.[5] The intermediate series seemed to present an unbroken chain of gradations, linking the two poles of the gamut. If the history of the Egyptiac Civilization was to be regarded as being continuous, it seemed arbitrary to take the Babylonic Civilization as being a separate representative of the species instead of treating it as a late phase of the Sumeric Civilization. Towards the other end of the scale it seemed arbitrary to treat the Orthodox Christian Civilization as a late phase of the Hellenic if the Western Civilization was to be taken as being a separate representative of the species.[6] I recognized[7] that eventually I should have to come to a decision about the cases that I had left in doubt. The progress of archaeology has decided the cases of my supposed Mexic and Yucatec civilizations for me by making it clear that the civilization of Pre-Columbian Middle America has a continuity and a unity that over-ride the breaks in its course and the distinctiveness of its cultural provinces. I have had to decide the remaining cases myself at my peril, and I have done this in previous chapters of the present volume. I have decided that my supposed Babylonic,[8] Far Eastern (main body),[9] and Hindu[10] civilizations must, on balance, be regarded as being merely later phases of the Sumeric, Sinic, and Indic civilizations respectively. On the other hand, I have decided that my Orthodox Christian (main body) and Islamic civilizations have the same claim as the Western Civilization has to be regarded as being separate civilizations in their own right.[11]

[1] See i. 136–46. [2] See i. 140–5 and the present volume, p. 184.
[3] See p. 95, footnote 1, and pp. 184–5.
[4] See i. 117–18, 133–6, 146, and the present volume, pp. 169–70.
[5] This is a particular instance of a general phenomenon. 'Culture and the events of history are both continuous, over the inhabited Earth as well as in time. Every delimitation is therefore a choice' (A. L. Kroeber: *Style and Civilizations*, p. 154).
[6] Even the West's title to rank as a separate civilization from the Hellenic has been disputed by so eminent an authority as E. R. Curtius (see p. 181, footnote 1).
[7] See i. 117–18 and 133–46. [8] See p. 191.
[9] See pp. 176–80. [10] See pp. 182–4. [11] See pp. 180–2 and 458–9.

While I believe that these conclusions are correct, I recognize that there is an element of subjectivity in them, and I think that the subjectivity here is inherent in the phenomena and is therefore inescapable. It might well seem arbitrary, for example, to allow the claim of my supposed Orthodox Christian Civilization (main body) to be a separate civilization when I am disallowing the claim of my Far Eastern Civilization (main body).

In giving this different treatment to these two cases, I believe I have been right, and that this is demonstrated by the contrast between the respective states of affairs in Orthodox Christendom and in China at the end of the two stories, at a time when both civilizations were on the eve of losing their identities through Westernization. In A.D. 1961 the Eastern Orthodox Church was still the master-institution of the non-Russian Orthodox Christian peoples, whereas the last of the successive avatars of the Roman Empire in the main body of Orthodox Christendom had faded out when the Ottoman Roman Empire had been liquidated in 1922.[1] By contrast, in China by that date Buddhism, which at one time had seemed to have attained the same dominance in Eastern Asia as Christianity in the Byzantine and Western worlds, had long since been appropriated by the indigenous Sinic Civilization.[2] In China in 1961 there were many people still alive who had been born under the regime of the Manchu avatar of the Ch'in (Ts'in)-Han Empire, could remember the Manchu regime's fall, and had been educated in the Confucian classics. This difference between the denouements of the two histories does perhaps warrant a differential treatment of them. Yet, when full allowance has been made for this difference, the resemblance between them remains remarkable. In both cases the life of the civilization in this phase was dominated by the relation between two institutions, one indigenous and secular, the other exotic and religious. In both cases the indigenous secular institution was a resuscitated universal state and the exotic institution was a missionary religion. The resuscitated Chinese and the resuscitated Roman Empire are unmistakable counterparts of each other, and so are Buddhism in China and Christianity in Eastern Orthodox Christendom. These two resemblances in the configurations of the two histories are of such obvious far-reaching historical importance that, even if the difference between the two histories is rightly held to be even more important, it still seems arbitrary to disallow the claim of the supposed Far Eastern Civilization (main body) to independence, while conceding the claim of the supposed Orthodox Christian Civilization. Here, however, I should say, the arbitrariness is inherent in the phenomena and has not been imported by me into the interpretation of them.

The next criticism that I have to examine is that I have treated all the full-blown civilizations as being 'philosophically equivalent' to each other[3] and have not distinguished civilizations that are 'major' from those that are 'secondary or peripheral'. I have hesitated to divide the full-blown civilizations on my list into categories standing for supposed

[1] See p. 193.
[2] See pp. 176–82.
[3] See i. 175–7 and the present volume, p. 170.

differences in importance and value. It would be particularly hazardous to try to estimate the relative value and importance of those civilizations that have been rediscovered by the archaeologists. These are welcome additions to our stock of specimens at our disposal for comparative study. For this purpose they are indispensable. At the same time, our knowledge of them is too scanty and too one-sided to allow us to attempt a valuation of them, since our knowledge is mostly derived from their material remains; and, even in the cases of disinterred civilizations that were literate, and whose documents have been partially recovered and deciphered, these literary remains are fragmentary.[1] It is also hazardous to try to put comparative values on civilizations about which we are less ill-informed. A comparative student's attitude and feeling towards the civilization into which he has been born, and also towards one in whose classical literature he has been educated, can never be the same as his attitude and feeling towards other civilizations with which his relation is less intimate.

Thus any attempt to classify civilizations according to their relative value will open the door wide for the intrusion of subjective judgements.[2] We cannot venture into this field profitably, or even safely, unless we can find some objective criterion. This is not provided by Bagby's proposed distinction between civilizations that are 'secondary and peripheral' and those that are 'major'. But it should be possible to distinguish objectively between civilizations that are 'satellites' of others[3] and civilizations that are independent of any other contemporary civilizations, though they may be affiliated to one or more antecedent civilizations. In distributing the full-blown civilizations between these two categories[4] we should be classifying them according to ascertainable matters of fact—though here we might find ourselves confronted by an unbroken chain of gradations between social units that were separate civilizations, though satellites, and social units that were apparently not civilizations in their own right, but were merely more than usually provincial provinces of a civilization that displayed a number of provincial variants. How, for example, should we classify Elam and Urartu? Were they provinces of the Sumero-Akkadian World or were they satellites of it? And how should we classify the Italy of the last millennium B.C.? Was this a satellite of the Hellenic World or was

---

[1] Literary remains of the Aegean (i.e. Minoan-Helladic-Mycenaean) Civilization have now been deciphered by Michael Ventris, but we still know much too little about this civilization to justify our classifying it, as Bagby does (in op. cit., p. 169), as being in the 'secondary' rather than in the 'major' class.

[2] Bagby's judgement, ibid., that the 'Syro-Phoenician Civilization' (my 'Syriac Civilization') was a secondary one will be contested by many users of the Phoenician alphabet and worshippers of the Jews' god. But a conflict of valuations is inevitably inconclusive.

[3] A satellite civilization would not, of course, necessarily be less important or less valuable than the independent civilization from which it had derived its culture. The Russian and Iranian civilizations, for example, would figure as satellites, but the Russian Civilization could look the Byzantine or the Western in the face without being abashed, and equally the Iranian could hold its own against the Sumero-Akkadian or the Syriac.

[4] Bagby points out, in op. cit., p. 171, that 'all the surviving civilizations, whether major or secondary, have become peripheral to the Western-European within the last two hundred years'. In the same sense the Syriac, Egyptiac, Sumero-Akkadian, and Iranic civilizations became 'peripheral' to the Hellenic in the Post-Alexandrine Age.

it a province of it? In all cases in which we are constrained to draw a dividing line at some point in a continuously graded series, there is inevitably something arbitrary and subjective about our decision, whatever this may be.

The next criticism—that my list of 'arrested civilizations' is capricious —is, I should say, justified. If I had used the phrase 'examples of arrest' instead of 'arrested civilizations', I should have escaped this criticism and still have made the point that I was trying to make in that chapter.[1] As it is, only one of my so-called 'arrested civilizations', the Nomadic, really qualifies for bearing the label 'civilization'; and the Nomadic Civilization is in the 'satellite' class. The 'Osmanlis and the Spartans were communities within societies of the species civilizations; but these two communities were each a fragment of a civilization; neither of them was an entire civilization in itself.[2] As for the Esquimeaux, they are a pre-civilizational society. Their culture is high, but not up to the civilizational level; and, in so far as they are arrested, they are in the situation in which all surviving pre-civilizational societies, of all species,[3] find themselves today.[4] If I had been including societies of all species in my survey, I could have taken the pre-civilizational societies, as a class, as one of my examples of 'arrest'. Alternatively, confining myself to the 'civilizational' species of societies, I could have found examples of 'arrest' within this field that were complete civilizations, not fragments of some civilization, as the 'Osmanlis and the Spartans were. I could have cited all those civilizations that, after entering into a universal state, have been caught in a monotonous round of recurrent avatars of it. But the eventual arrest of the societies in these two categories is not the most significant feature in their histories, and therefore it would be misleading to label them as 'arrested civilizations' simply on account of their having been arrested in the last phase of their careers. The phenomenon of 'arrest' is, I should still say, in itself a significant aspect of human affairs. I should also still say that the four examples that I took as my illustrations of it are all instructive. But, as these examples show, the phenomenon of 'arrest' can be illustrated without introducing a class of 'arrested civilizations' into the classification

[1] iii. 1–111.
[2] W. Gurian puts a fair question when he asks whether Sparta is intelligible apart from the rest of Hellas (*The Review of Politics*, vol. 4, No. 4 (October, 1942), p. 513). The same point is made by J. Vogt in *Saeculum*, No. 2 (1951), pp. 557–74. All the same, a community is on the way to becoming a separate society, with a distinctive civilization of its own, when it has fallen out of step with the rest of its former society. Examples of this can be found in the modern chapter of the history of the Western Civilization. The Castilian and Portuguese-speaking peoples, both in the Iberian Peninsula and in the Americas, took part only partially and half-heartedly in the general Western spiritual revolution towards the end of the seventeenth century. In the nineteenth and twentieth centuries the Prussians did not share in the general change of feeling about the institution of war that began to come over other Western peoples in that age. These other Westerners came more and more to regard war as being a barbarous and criminal anachronism. The Prussians continued to glorify it. These divergences made other Westerners begin to look upon the Iberian peoples as being Don Quixotes, and to look upon the Prussians as being neo-barbarians—redoubtable but at the same time atrocious. The Spartans were the Prussians of the Hellenic World, and from the time when they developed their peculiar institutions they began to be looked at askance by other Hellenes.
[3] Different species of pre-civilizational societies have been noticed on pp. 327–43.
[4] See i. 179.

of societies of this species. I shall therefore now drop this class out of my schedule.

As for my list of abortive civilizations, I agree that this was incomplete. Bagby is right in saying[1] that it was illogical not to have included the Monophysite Christian Civilization in this category when I had included the Nestorian. Here, again, as in compiling a list of 'satellite' civilizations, we need an objective criterion. An abortive civilization might be defined as one whose adherents have tried and failed to perform some particular role which has afterwards been performed successfully by the adherents of some other civilization. When this happens, the first of the two competing civilizations is eclipsed. It either disappears completely or survives as a remnant in holes and corners. For instance, the Nestorian and Monophysite Christian civilizations were two successive attempts to shake off an Hellenic ascendancy over the Christian Church and the Roman Empire. This ascendancy had become an anachronism in the fifth century of the Christian Era, in a world in which, by then, the former Syriac and Hellenic cultures had blended into a 'compost' that had become the common culture of all the former Syriac and Hellenic peoples except the Jews and the Samaritans. However, neither the Nestorians nor the Monophysites proved strong enough to get the better of the Hellenic 'Imperialists' (Melchites). The Nestorians were driven out of the Roman Empire; the Monophysites were driven underground. The enterprise which they had tried and failed to carry out was eventually achieved by the Muslims. In consequence the Syriac-Hellenic 'culture-compost' produced an Islamic Civilization, while the Nestorians and Monophysites have survived only in diasporá or in fastnesses.[2] Wherever we find that one civilization has been supplanted by another, this gives us a clue. Any supplanted civilization is a potential candidate for a place on the list of the civilizations that have been abortive.

We have next to take account of the changes—mainly due to the further progress of archaeological discovery—in our picture of the historical facts.

One such change has been a revision of our former estimate of the relative importance of the different provinces of this or that civilization. There are cases in which some particular province formerly loomed large because we were comparatively well-informed about it. In some of these cases the relative prominence of this once disproportionately

[1] In op. cit., p. 179.
[2] The principal Monophysite diasporás today are the Copts in Egypt and the Armenians, who are now scattered all over the World. The principal surviving Monophysite fastnesses are the Abyssinian plateau, the Tūr ʿAbdin, and the Republic of Erivan at the north-eastern edge of the Armenian plateau. The Nestorians had a fastness in the Hakkiari highlands in Kurdistan till they were uprooted and expelled from there by the Turks during the First World War. The present-day Nestorian diasporá has found a new home in Chicago, and the Patriarch of the Nestorian Church has settled there. In the thirteenth century of the Christian Era the peasantry of ʿIraq were still Nestorian Christians, in so far as they had not become Monophysites, and the Nestorian diasporá was scattered all the way from the east bank of the Tigris to the west coast of the Pacific Ocean across Iran, Transoxania, the Eurasian Steppe, and Northern China; but by then Nestorianism had already lost to Islam its once possible destiny of becoming one of the full-blown civilizations of the Syriac-Hellenic family, on a par with the Orthodox Christian and Western Christian civilizations.

conspicuous province has now diminished because we have become better acquainted with its neighbour provinces and have become more aware of the contribution to its and their common civilizations that they, too, made.

A classical example of a change of perspective produced by the progress of archaeological discovery is the change in our picture of Israel and Judah in the Syriac World. In A.D. 1961 it was less than a hundred years since the archaeological exploration of the Syriac World had begun,[1] and considerably less than that in most of its provinces other than Palestine. Before that the character and history of the Syriac Civilization had been known almost exclusively from one source, and therefore also almost exclusively in terms of the picture that this source presented. This once virtually unique source was the literature of the Israelites and the Jews, and this literature naturally gave Israel and Judah the beau role and put their neighbours in an unfavourable light. This distortion of the truth through the prejudices of one sole surviving literary source is now being progressively rectified by the disinterment of the material remains left by other communities of the Syriac World. When the disinterred artefacts include literary texts, such as the clay tablets, inscribed in the fourteenth century B.C. with Phoenician religious poems, that have been discovered at Ras ash-Shamrah, the rectification of the traditional picture can be considerable. In the case in point we can hardly expect to see the non-Israelite Syriac communities completely rehabilitated, whatever further successes may be in store for archaeological explorers in this field. The surviving literature of the Israelites and the Jews is not only magnificent; it has been entrenched in a position of privilege through having become the holy scriptures of both Judaism and Christianity. We may therefore guess that no amount of relevant new archaeological discoveries could ever reduce 'the People of the Book' in the sight of posterity to their true proportionate stature. All the same, even in this field, the progress of archaeological discovery, as far as it has yet gone, has already changed the traditional picture appreciably.

The changes in the perspective in which we see the Aegean and Middle American worlds seem likely to be more radical. In our former picture of these two worlds, Crete in the one case and the Petén and Usumacinta region in the other enjoyed for a time something of the unique prominence[2] that Israel and Judah have enjoyed, and still enjoy, in our picture of the Syriac World. This led me, in my original list of full-blown civilizations, to use the labels 'Minoan' and 'Mayan' to describe two civilizations that, in the light of subsequent archaeological discoveries, I should now prefer to label 'Aegean' and 'Middle American' respectively.

The disproportionate prominence of the Minoan province of the Aegean Civilization and the Central Mayan province of the Middle American Civilization was not, of course, ever so strongly entrenched as the disproportionate prominence of Israel and Judah in the Syriac World. It lacked the two powerful sanctions of antiquity and superstition.

[1] See ix. 102.   [2] See pp. 365-6 and 407.

The Minoans and the Central Maya had acquired their disproportionate prominence thanks to an accident in the history of archaeological discovery. They happened to have been brought into the light
of modern knowledge earlier than their neighbours; and they were
placed on a pinnacle by the archaeologists who had been dazzled by
their discovery of them. But a king-maker always has it in his power to
dethrone his favourite of yesterday. The archaeologists' temper is apt to
be as ruthless as their progress is swift, and they have latterly been
transferring their favours to other provinces that have been more
recently explored. In the changing archaeological picture of the Aegean
World, the Minoan province in Crete is now being made to dip its flag
to the Helladic province on the mainland. The Mycenaean last phase of
the Aegean Civilization, which followed the fall of Minoan Cnossos and
which extended over Crete, the Archipelago, and the mainland alike,
has also been rising once more in relative repute after a period during
which the brilliance of the Minoan Age of the Aegean Civilization had
temporarily put the subsequent Mycenaean Age out of countenance.
There has been a similar change in the picture of the Middle American
World. Here, as the achievements of a common Middle American
Civilization in the Mayan highlands, on the Mexican plateau, and along
the 'Olméca' sea-board of the Gulf of Mexico have come into view, this
civilization's achievements in the Petén and Usumacinta region have
become relatively less conspicuous. In the Anatolian archaeological
field we may expect to see Khatti and Kizzuwadna and Troy suffer the
same change of fortune as Crete and the Petén if the archaeologists who
have been bringing to light the civilization of Anatolia in the third and
second millennia B.C. follow up their discoveries in the east and the
north-west by disinterring the still buried sites in the south-west. They
have now made a beginning at Beyce Sultan, and their finds here have
already been remarkable and illuminating.

These counter-swings of the pendulum may have gone too far.
Archaeologists are not only apt to be ruthless; they are also apt to be
temperamental and to allow themselves to be unduly swayed by passing
fashions. Yet, even if their recent revisions of the picture may have to
be revised in their turn, it seems likely that a picture in which all the
provinces of a civilization have a place will prove, on the whole, to be
nearer to the truth than a picture in which one province is starred at the
expense of the rest. Changes in the picture in this direction therefore
seem likely to last. The changes of this kind that I have here mentioned
have occurred since the years (1927–34) in which I made my notes for
this book and published the first three volumes. In previous chapters of
the present volume, I have already taken note of the revisions, on my
part, that these changes in the archaeological picture require. In this
chapter I have to make the necessary consequent alterations in my list
of civilizations.

The progress of archaeological discovery has also changed the picture
in another way. It has bridged, or, short of that, has reduced in magnitude, certain breaks that appeared to interrupt the continuity of history
in the picture as it used to be.

We have already noticed the revision, by later archaeologists, of Breasted's interpretation of the Osirian religion as a spiritual force that was both revolutionary and proletarian.[1] This change of interpretation has made the continuity of Egyptiac history look still more closely knit than it looked already. The continuity of history in North China and in Middle America has similarly been underlined by the progress of archaeological discovery. The decipherment of the inscriptions on the 'oracle bones' discovered in North China at Anyang, the latest capital of the Shang, has shown that the script which the Shang were using in the thirteenth century B.C. was identical with the script still in use in China today. In the Shang version of this script, the characters retain, of course, older forms, but the present forms seem to have developed out of the Shang forms without any break in continuity.[2] This discovery brings out the continuity of the history of civilization in China from the Shang Age down to the present day. It is a piece of archaeological evidence that supports the testimony of the ensuing Chou Age's literary tradition. According to this, the Shang people and culture survived the Chou conquest in an asylum in the state of Sung. There was, no doubt, a certain break in continuity between the Shang Age and the Chou Age, and this break was due to the same cause as the more violent break in the Aegean basin between the Aegean Civilization and the subsequent Hellenic Civilization, and in India between the Indus Civilization and the subsequent Indic Civilization. In all these three cases alike, an established civilization suffered the impact of a barbarian Völkerwanderung. There is therefore something arbitrary and subjective in a judgement that puts one of these three cases in a different category from the other two. Yet an assessment of all the relevant facts known to us in each of the three cases does seem to lead to the conclusion that, in the Chinese case, the break of continuity was not great enough to warrant us in classifying the sequel as the history of a new civilization, whereas, in the Indian and Aegean cases, the break was so strongly pronounced that it would be misleading to treat the sequels as being epilogues to the histories of the previous civilizations rather than as being the histories of new civilizations.

In our picture of Middle American history, similarly, the break in continuity at the close of the 'Classic' Age looks less sharp, now that we can view it in the light of recent archaeological discoveries, than it looked when our only sources of information were the legends conveyed in enigmatic pictorial codices or recounted at second hand by Spanish investigators after the Spanish conquest. This literary evidence suggested

---

[1] See p. 550, footnotes 2 and 3, and the references there to earlier passages.
[2] On the other hand, the scripts of the Aegean Civilization and the Indus Civilization passed out of currency when these civilizations disappeared (except for the survival of versions of the Aegean script in a few outlying places, particularly Cyprus). In both the Aegean basin and India there seems to have been a subsequent period, lasting for some centuries, during which the art of writing was unknown, or at least in disuse. When it was revived, this came about through the introduction, from abroad, of a new script that had no historical relation to the last one. An Alexandrian Hellenic scholar of the third or second century B.C., whose mother-tongue was Greek but who wrote this in an alphabet of Phoenician origin, would not have had any better a start than Ventris had for deciphering inscriptions of the Mycenaean Age written in the Greek language in the Minoan 'Linear B' script.

that, down to the end of the Classic Age, civilization in Middle America had been confined to the Central Mayan area (the Petén and Usumacinta region), and that it was only in the Post-classic Age that it radiated from there northwards into Yucatan, north-westwards on to the Mexican plateau, and southwards into the Guatemalan highlands. Seen through this literary lens, Yucatan, for example, looked like new ground that had not been occupied by any civilization before the Post-classic Age, and that was then occupied for the first time by Maya emigrants from the abandoned Central Mayan area, followed by Toltec emigrants from the Mexican plateau. This picture suggested that there had been a Mayan Civilization in the Central Mayan area, and that the disintegration of this had been followed by the rise of two affiliated civilizations, one in Yucatan and the other on the Mexican plateau. This sketch of the configuration of the history of civilization in Middle America has now been proved wrong by changes in the picture that are results of the progress of archaeological discovery. We now know that civilization started as early on the Mexican plateau and in the Guatemalan highlands as in the Central Mayan area, and perhaps still earlier along the 'Olméca' sea-board of the Gulf of Mexico. We also now know that the Central Mayan variant of the Classic phase of the Middle American Civilization spread into Yucatan immediately after it had taken shape at Tikál and Uaxactun. The Post-classic Mayan variant of the Middle American Civilization thus turns out to have been a survival, not a new creation.

These archaeological discoveries lead to the conclusion that, in the history of civilization in Middle America, unity and continuity override discontinuity and diversity. This does not mean that there were no provincial idiosyncracies and no breaks in continuity. One such break was produced by the cumulative effects of the mysterious abandonment of the Classic sites and the subsequent irruption of waves of Chichimec barbarians—first a Toltec wave and later an Aztec one—from the northern hinterland of Middle America on to the Mexican plateau and then on, beyond that, into Yucatan. This particular break in continuity still looks considerable. At the same time, it now no longer looks considerable enough to justify the view that, at this point in Middle American history, an old civilization disappears and two new civilizations arise. On balance, it now seems more instructive to treat the whole of Middle American history as being the history of a single civilization.

We are now in a position to draw up our revised list of civilizations. This works out as follows.

I. *Full-blown Civilizations*

A. *Independent Civilizations*
   Unrelated to Others
   Middle American[1]
   Andean

---

[1] This covers not only the 'Mayan', 'Mexic', and 'Yucatec' civilizations that figure in the original list, but also the Classic phase of Middle American on the Mexican plateau and in Yucatan and in the Guatemalan highlands, which was left out of account in the original list.

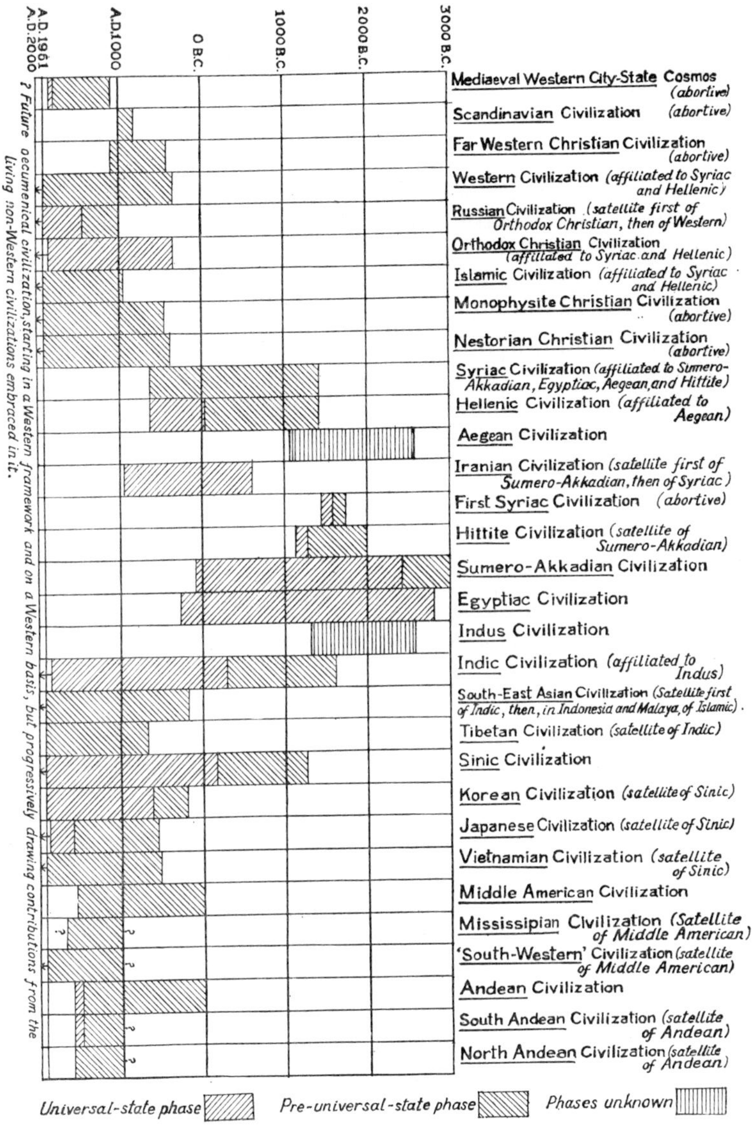

A.D.1961
A.D.2000
A.D.1000
0 B.C.
1000 B.C.
2000 B.C.
3000 B.C.
? Future oecumenical civilization, starting in a Western framework and on a Western basis, but progressively drawing contributions from the living non-Western civilizations embraced in it.
Mediaeval Western City-State Cosmos (abortive)
Scandinavian Civilization (abortive)
Far Western Christian Civilization (abortive)
Western Civilization (affiliated to Syriac and Hellenic)
Russian Civilization (satellite first of Orthodox Christian, then of Western)
Orthodox Christian Civilization (affiliated to Syriac and Hellenic)
Islamic Civilization (affiliated to Syriac and Hellenic)
Monophysite Christian Civilization (abortive)
Nestorian Christian Civilization (abortive)
Syriac Civilization (affiliated to Sumero-Akkadian, Egyptiac, Aegean, and Hittite)
Hellenic Civilization (affiliated to Aegean)
Aegean Civilization
Iranian Civilization (satellite first of Sumero-Akkadian, then of Syriac)
First Syriac Civilization (abortive)
Hittite Civilization (satellite of Sumero-Akkadian)
Sumero-Akkadian Civilization
Egyptiac Civilization
Indus Civilization
Indic Civilization (affiliated to Indus)
South-East Asian Civilization (Satellite first of Indic, then, in Indonesia and Malaya, of Islamic).
Tibetan Civilization (satellite of Indic)
Sinic Civilization
Korean Civilization (satellite of Sinic)
Japanese Civilization (satellite of Sinic)
Vietnamian Civilization (satellite of Sinic)
Middle American Civilization
Mississipian Civilization (Satellite of Middle American)
'South-Western' Civilization (satellite of Middle American)
Andean Civilization
South Andean Civilization (satellite of Andean)
North Andean Civilization (satellite of Andean)
Universal-state phase
Pre-universal-state phase
Phases unknown

Unaffiliated to Others

Sumero-Akkadian[1]
Egyptiac
Aegean[2]
Indus
Sinic[3]

Affiliated to Others (first batch)

Syriac (to Sumero-Akkadian, Egyptiac, Aegean, and Hittite)
Hellenic (to Aegean)
Indic[4] (to Indus)

Affiliated to Others (second batch)

Orthodox Christian ⎫
Western ⎬ (to both Syriac and Hellenic)
Islamic ⎭

B. *Satellite Civilizations*

Mississippian ⎫
'South-Western'[5] ⎬ (of Middle American)

North Andean[6] ⎫
South Andean[7] ⎬ (of Andean)

? Elamite (of Sumero-Akkadian)
Hittite (of Sumero-Akkadian)
? Urartian (of Sumero-Akkadian)
Iranian (first of Sumero-Akkadian, then of Syriac)
Korean ⎫
Japanese ⎬ (of Sinic)
Vietnamian ⎭
?Italic[8] (of Hellenic)

---

[1] This includes the Babylonic as well as the Sumeric Civilization of the original list. The Babylonic last phase of the distinctive civilization of the lower Tigris–Euphrates basin was still Sumeric in its inspiration. Asshurbanipal's library was stocked with texts in the Sumerian language and with glossaries of it. But it would, nevertheless, be misleading to apply the label 'Sumeric' to the civilization current in Assyria and Babylonia in the seventh century B.C., considering that, by that date, the Sumerian language had been 'a dead language' for more than 1,000 years. Since the Age of Hammurabi the Semitic Akkadian language had replaced the Sumerian language as the living vehicle of the Sumeric Civilization. Therefore, Sumero-Akkadian is a more illuminating label than 'Sumeric' for the whole span of a civilization that did not lose its identity till the first century of the Christian Era.

[2] This covers not only the 'Minoan' Civilization of the original list, but also the contemporary 'Helladic' variant of the Aegean Civilization in Continental European Greece, as well as the 'Mycenaean' last phase of both 'Minoan' and 'Helladic'.

[3] This covers not only the 'Sinic' Civilization of the original list, but also the 'Far Eastern (main body)', as well as the pre-Sinic 'Shang' Civilization of vols. vii–x.

[4] This covers not only the 'Indic' Civilization of the original list, but also the 'Hindu' Civilization.

[5] i.e. a Pre-Columbian civilization in what is now the South-West of the United States.   [6] In what are now Ecuador and Colombia.

[7] In what are now Northern Chile and North-Western Argentina.

[8] This would be a civilization common to the Etruscan immigrants into Italy in the last millennium B.C. and the peoples previously established in Italy. The common elements in their civilization (e.g. literacy in the Cumaean alphabet) were of Hellenic origin. The indebtedness of the civilization of Italy in the Hellenic Age to the Hellenic Civilization was so great that it seems more instructive to regard Italy as having been,

South-East Asian (first of Indic, then, in Indonesia and Malaya only, of Islamic)
Tibetan[1] (of Indic)
Russian (first of Orthodox Christian, then of Western)[2]

II. *Abortive Civilizations*

First Syriac[3] (eclipsed by Egyptiac)
Nestorian Christian[4] (eclipsed by Islamic)
Monophysite Christian (eclipsed by Islamic)
Far Western Christian[5] (eclipsed by Western)
Scandinavian[5] (eclipsed by Western)
Medieval Western City-State Cosmos (eclipsed by Modern Western)

The accompanying chart[6] displays the time-spans of all the civilizations included in this revised list, except for those possible satellite civilizations whose claims to rank as separate civilizations seem dubious.[7]

in this age, a province of the Hellenic World rather than a satellite of it. The Hellenic Civilization did acquire satellites, but not till the Post-Alexandrine age. In that age the Sumero-Akkadian, Egyptiac, and Syriac civilizations became satellites of the Hellenic Civilization before they lost their identities. As a consequence of having drawn the Syriac Civilization into its field, the Hellenic Civilization lost its own identity in an Hellenic-Syriac cultural amalgam.

1 Including the Mongol and Calmuck converts to the Tibetan form of Mahayana Buddhism.

2 The Russian Civilization was not the only one that had been drawn into the field of the Western Civilization since the closing decades of the seventeenth century. Two of the non-Russian Orthodox Christian peoples—the Greeks and the Serbs—began to Westernize as early as the Russians. Since then, one non-Western society after another had followed in the Russians' wake. Indeed, in 1961 it might have been hard to find any living non-Western society, either of the civilizational or of the pre-civilizational kind, that had not become a satellite of the Western Civilization in some degree. This relation between them and the West might, however, turn out to have been only a passing phase, to judge by what happened after the Syriac Civilization had been drawn into the field of the Hellenic. In the light of this historical precedent it seemed possible that the civilizations of the West and its satellites would blend into a new oecumenical civilization drawing contributions from all of them.   3 See ii. 388–91.

4 This is, as Bagby points out in op. cit., p. 179, the abortive civilization labelled 'Far Eastern Christian' in my original list.

5 In an unpublished paper on my work, under the title 'Betrachtungen über Arnold J. Toynbees Deutung des Menschheitsgeschehens', O. Höver questions whether I am right in classifying the Far Western Christian and the Scandinavian Civilization as having been abortive. He points out that both civilizations had a long history behind them. I agree, but, as I see it, Ireland before the fifth century of the Christian Era and Scandinavia before the ninth century were still in the pre-civilizational stage. See also eundem: 'Buchführung und Bilanz der Weltgeschichte in neuer Sicht: Zu A. Toynbees Deutung des Frühzeitlichen Menschengeschehens', in *Zeitschrift für Religions- und Geistesgeschichte*, Jahrgang 2, Heft 3 (1949/50), pp. 247–59.

6 On p. 559.

7 In each case the pre-universal-state phase of the civilization, if there was such a phase (and in most cases there was), has been marked in a different stipple from the universal-state phase, if the civilization in question ever entered into that phase. For this purpose the universal-state phase has been taken as including all successive avatars of the original universal state, in cases in which this was reconstituted either once, or more than once, after a temporary lapse, or repeated temporary lapses, into political disunity. In cases (e.g. those of the Aegean Civilization and the Indus Civilization) in which we do not know whether the society did or did not ever enter into the universal-state phase, this civilization's total time-span has been marked uniformly in a different stipple again.

In cases of affiliation the interregnum between the submergence of the antecedent civilization and the emergence of the affiliated civilization has been included in the time-spans of both civilizations, instead of being excluded from both. This has been

XIX. THE NEXT LEDGE

IN earlier volumes of this book[1] I have compared the situation of mankind in the present age to a climber's pitch. Below us lies the ledge that our pre-human ancestors reached in the act of becoming human. In the Age of the Civilizations mankind has been making a number of attempts to scale the cliff-face that towers up from the ledge reached by Primitive Man. The next ledge above, unlike the ledge immediately below, is invisible to climbers who are striving to reach it. All that they know is that they feel compelled to risk their necks in the hope of gaining this next ledge and in the faith that the endeavour is worth while.

This simile is a myth in the Platonic usage of the word.[2] Frankfort has pointed out[3] that I have not arrived at it empirically: that is to say, not by induction from observed phenomena. The same point has been made, not *ad hominem* but in general terms, by Erdmann.[4] The problem of 'Historismus' cannot, Erdmann contends, be solved by the progress of the social sciences. The *Geisteswissenschaften* (studies in the field of human affairs) are merely the anterooms of history; and Ernst Troeltsch recognized, as Erdmann here recalls, that 'Historismus' is 'a problem that points to something beyond itself (*ein über sich hinausweisendes Problem*)'. In this phrase Troeltsch is indicating the point at which Plato, whenever he reaches it, resorts to a myth deliberately. Myths are unenlightening if they do not transcend experience, and unwarrantable if they contradict it. My myth of the climber's pitch is, I should say, in accord with mankind's experience in the Age of the Civilizations. The civilizations themselves are movements; they are purposeful movements aiming at an objective; and they are not the only movements of the kind in the span of human history that is within our ken. They were preceded by a series of earlier new departures in which mankind's pace gradually accelerated and its impetus slowly gathered momentum. Moreover, within less than two thousand five hundred years of the date of the emergence of the earliest of the civilizations, the earliest of the

done in order to make it clear that the time-spans of the two civilizations overlapped below the surface.

The time-spans of the five Christian and Islamic civilizations have been reckoned as starting from the date at which Islam and each of the four main Christian sects began to make mass-conversions. The starting-dates of the Christian and Islamic civilizations have, of course, to be distinguished clearly from the starting-dates of the two religions Christianity and Islam themselves. During the first three or four centuries of these two religions' existence, which were their formative centuries, their adherents amounted numerically to no more than a diasporá scattered among a majority that professed other religions; and the religion of a minority cannot provide the framework or basis for a civilization. The eventual mass-conversions made the emergence of Christian and Islamic civilizations possible for the first time. The Islamic diasporá became a ruling minority within twenty years of the Hijrah, whereas the Christian diasporá remained a subject minority until not much less than three hundred years after the Crucifixion. But this political difference is not to the point. The religion of a ruling minority is no more capable than the religion of a subject minority is of serving as the matrix of a new civilization. In the age in which the Umayyad and 'Abbasid Caliphate was at its zenith, there was an Islamic political power but not yet an Islamic society constituting a civilization.

[1] i. 192–4; iii. 2–3.　　　　　　　　　　　　　　　[2] See pp. 250–2.
[3] H. Frankfort in *The Birth of Civilization in the Near East*, pp. 25–26.
[4] K. D. Erdmann in *Archiv für Kulturgeschichte*, xxxiii. Band, Heft 2 (1951), pp. 181–2.

higher religions appeared and, in appearing, stepped up the impetus to a still higher degree. After the World had suffered the shock of the First World War, Smuts remarked[1] that 'the tents have been struck and the great caravan of humanity is once more on the march'. This was true of the generation of which it was said; but it is no less true of all previous generations of which there is any surviving record.

Though the goal of mankind's continuous and increasing endeavours is still hidden below our horizon, we know, nevertheless, what it is. We can discern it, without having to divine the future, by looking inwards; for mankind's goal is written large in the constitution of human nature. What changed our pre-human ancestors into human beings like ourselves was the acquisition of consciousness and will.[2] These two spiritual faculties are human nature's distinguishing marks; and their character is ambivalent. They are both a treasure that gives us hope and a burden that puts us in peril. Their emergence in Man has split the unity of the Universe, and broken its harmony, for every conscious, wilful, human soul. The price of human knowledge and freedom is an intellectual and a moral relativity. Each of us sees the Universe divided between himself and all the rest of it; and each of us seeks to make himself the centre round which all the rest shall revolve. This constitution of human nature sets human nature's goal. Its goal is to transcend the intellectual and moral limitations that its relativity imposes on it. Its intellectual goal is to see the Universe as it is in the sight of God, instead of seeing it with the distorted vision of one of God's self-centred creatures. Human nature's moral goal is to make the self's will coincide with God's will, instead of pursuing self-regarding purposes of its own.

Few, if any, human souls have been entirely unaware of this goal or entirely indifferent to it. The saints have dedicated themselves to the pursuit of it, and some saints have come within a hair's breadth of attaining it—as it has seemed to spectators of ordinary spiritual stature, though never to the spiritual athletes themselves. The value of the goal lies in the goal itself; and therefore the goal cannot be attained unless it is pursued for its own sake. But, since the wages of sin is death,[3] and this truth is continually being attested by experience, there has always been a utilitarian incentive, as well as a disinterested motive, for conduct that, when disinterested, is righteous. In our day this utilitarian consideration has become pressing, owing to a sudden immense increase in the power that knowledge and freedom have been accumulating in human hands. The human power that has increased is not a human soul's power over itself. There is no evidence of any increase in that within the time over which our records extend. So far as

[1] J. C. Smuts: *The League of Nations: A Practical Suggestion* (London 1918, Hodder & Stoughton), p. 71.
[2] The reality of human freedom is recognized by people who differ widely from each other in their account of it. 'The rationalists will . . . admit, probably, that, within certain biological limits, Man is free. This freedom, however, is not, to them, the freedom of "the law of God", nor is it evidence of the intervention of anything supernatural in human affairs. This freedom is a biologica phenomenon, purely and simply' (M. Savelle in *The Pacific Historical Review*, vol. xxv, No. 1 (February, 1956), pp. 56–67).
[3] Rom. vi. 23.

one can guess, human beings are no better, and saints are no more frequent, in the present-day world than they will have been in, let us say, the Lower Palaeolithic Age. The power that has been accumulating and increasing is collective power over both human souls and non-human nature. Now that mankind's collective power is within sight of becoming able to extinguish all human life, and perhaps all life of any kind on the face of the planet, the works of righteousness are being demanded of us urgently, not only for their own sake, but by our concern for self-preservation.

For approaching this objective we might seem to have a choice between two roads: one rough and narrow, the other smooth and broad. The hard way of doing the works of righteousness is to be righteous. It is hard, but it is unquestionably open, since it is the way that is followed by the saints. The easy way would be to be 'conditioned' to be incapable of choosing to do anything else. This is the way of the social insects on Earth—or of the angels in Heaven if we prefer to speak the language of Christian mythology. Till within living memory this bee-like or angelic way of doing righteous acts willy-nilly was not open to the human race. The possibility of 'conditioning' human souls, like the possibility of genocide, has appeared above Man's horizon within our own life-time. When Aldous Huxley's *Brave New World* was published in 1932, the notion of 'brain-washing' was still little more than an anti-Utopian flight of fancy. By 1961 it had become part of mankind's ever-growing repertory of accomplishments. Considering that these two portentous new crimes—genocide and 'conditioning'—had become feasible simultaneously, mankind might be strongly tempted to seek security against genocide by acquiescing in 'conditioning'. If it were a question of choosing between the two evils, it would be difficult for human beings to decide that the self-annihilation of their own race was the lesser evil of the two. To be 'conditioned' would be likely to seem a less terrible option than to be extinguished; and, even if 'conditioning' were not commended by presenting itself as the only practical alternative to extinction,[1] it would have an attraction in itself for beings saddled with the burden of consciousness and will. This burden, inherent in human nature, is a grievous one. We are born with it on our backs; and it condemns us to serve a life-sentence of tension and struggle. If we could get rid of it, we could relax and rest. And, if the power to get rid of it has now at last come within our reach, why should we not avail ourselves of it? The burden has been imposed on us without our leave being asked. What obligation have we to go on putting up with it when once we have learnt how to relieve ourselves of it? The attraction of 'conditioning' is akin to the attraction of drugs and intoxicants.

[1] It can also commend itself insidiously by masquerading as its own antithesis: self-determination. F. A. Hayek makes the point that the demand for conscious control or direction of social purposes means, in effect, a demand for giving some single mind and will the control over all others. It means this, in Hayek's view, because '"conscious" and "deliberate" are terms which have meaning only when applied to individuals' (*The Counter-Revolution of Science*, p. 87). There is, however, surely the alternative possibility that a conscious and deliberate control may be exercised jointly by a number of minds and wills achieving and maintaining agreement with each other. If this were not possible, there could be no such thing as human society. For this, unlike insect society, is not a product of automatic instinctive behaviour.

One specious argument in favour of submitting to being 'conditioned' would be that, after all, this would not be an entirely new departure. Should we be doing anything more novel or more questionable than just carrying to its logical conclusion a human practice that must be as old as, or older than, mankind itself? Human society may be inconceivable without conscious and deliberate agreement, but it is also hardly conceivable without the bond of habit; and, if it is true that our pre-human ancestors could hardly have managed to become human beings without having been social animals already,[1] habit must always have been one of the key-institutions of human life. Our habits are inculcated by our education. This, taken in the broad sense, is a life-long social drill. It teaches us to perform by mimesis, without reasoning why, all kinds of acts that we should never have dreamed of if we had been left to ourselves.[2] Between drilling and 'conditioning' is there any great gulf? Could not 'conditioning' be fairly described as being social drill that is made infallibly effective by being given a final twist to clinch it?

This argument is rebutted by a series of counter-considerations. It may be true that human beings have not been able to maintain society without having recourse to mimesis and inculcating it by social drill. But the road leading to sociality by mimesis is a short cut; and the fact that it may have been difficult to avoid taking it cannot blind us to the further fact that mimesis has been one of society's dangerous weaknesses.[3] Mimesis is dangerous for the reason for which it is convenient. It partially anaesthetizes our human faculties of thinking and choosing, and this can dislocate a human society by paralysing human nature. If mimesis can work this havoc, 'conditioning' must be baneful *à fortiori*. For the difference between 'conditioning' and social drill is one of those differences of degree that amount to differences in kind.

Most of the social drill that has made the wheels of society go round has, at most times and places, been largely spontaneous and unorganized. Even where it has been applied consciously and deliberately, as, for instance, in commercial advertising, in religious indoctrination and ritual, and in the literal military drilling of the Spartan or the Prussian parade-ground, it has not had the power to produce an irreversible change in human nature. The cake of custom, formed by social drill, can be broken, and, when it is, human nature emerges intact. To break it in defiance of strong public feeling in its favour requires, no doubt, the courage and resoluteness of a hero; but the saints and the martyrs have successfully risen to the occasion; and ordinary human beings have found it easy to break the cake when they have escaped from the social environment in which it has been formed. The Spartan abroad was notoriously prone to react against his Lycurgean training by going to extremes of licentiousness; and thousands of Germans who have emigrated to the United States after having been put through the mill of the Prussian Army have become admirable citizens of a democratic community. By contrast, the objective of 'conditioning' is to deprive human beings permanently of their capacity to think and to will, and, since this

[1] See i. 173.   [2] See i. 191–2 and iii. 245–8 and 373.   [3] See iv. 119–33.

is the capacity that makes us human, for good or for evil, 'conditioning' is an attempt to destroy human nature itself. Perhaps we do not yet know enough about its results, up to date, to be able to tell whether or not its aim is actually attainable. We do know, however, that this has been the aim of its practitioners in our time; and we also know that the new science of psychology has equipped them with devilish devices which, in the past, were not at the drill-sergeant's, priest's, or advertiser's disposal.

Therefore we should stop and think, not just twice but many times, before we decide to commit ourselves to this psychological technique. This may look like a heaven-sent engine for hoisting us on to the ledge above us before the new military technique of genocide has had time to annihilate us. Yet the ledge on which the technique of 'conditioning' would deposit us would turn out not to be the one above our last ledge. That last ledge was the ledge that we reached in the act of becoming human. We should now find ourselves on the ledge below that: the ledge reached by our ancestors when they became pre-human animals: the ledge, in fact, on which the social insects are still marooned. Instead of having taken a quick step up, we should have taken two quick steps down. The psychological machine that we had mistaken for an elevator would have proved to be a dejector.

A student of the social insects has thrown out an interesting suggestion.[1] The stupendous altruistic social acts that are performed willy-nilly by the social insects as we know them may have been originally performed, by these 'conditioned' creatures' remote ancestors, as acts of free choice, guided by rational thought. In Hingston's mind this idea was perhaps no more than a *jeu d'esprit*; but a myth about a non-human order of living beings may throw light on mankind's past, as well as on our possible future. If it is true that our ancestors had become social animals before they became human beings endowed with consciousness and will, these pre-human social animals must have been 'conditioned' to perform their social functions, as the non-human social animals—bees, ants, and termites—still are. The act that turned our ancestors into human beings must have been a victorious revolt against their hereditary spiritual bondage. It must, in fact, have been a successful assertion of a previously undreamed-of freedom to think and to choose; and these are the faculties that we now recognize as being the distinctive characteristics of human nature.

And what about the mythical history of the angels? Christian mythology represents the angels as doing God's will willy-nilly, like the social insects. But it also tells the story of a war in Heaven, when Satan rebelled against God and Satan's fellow angels took sides either with God or with the rebel. This story presupposes that, at the time of Satan's rebellion, angels possessed the freedom of choice that is possessed by human beings. Are these two pieces of angelology to be reconciled by supposing that the loyal angels were rewarded by being made immune, thenceforth, against the possibility of committing Satan's sin? If their

[1] R. W. G. Hingston: *Problems of Instinct and Intelligence* (London 1928, Arnold), p. 268, quoted in iii. 108.

nature was indeed changed in this way, was that truly a reward? Would it not be nearer the truth to call it a preventive penalization? Regarded from a human standpoint, it would look like a spiritual mutilation that deprived the loyal angels of their greatest previous spiritual treasure. And, if the fallen angels preserved their anthropoid spiritual freedom, did not this more than compensate them for having been cast down from Heaven into the Abyss? Are not these free fallen angels in Hell on a spiritually higher ledge than their fellows who have remained in Heaven at the price of being 'conditioned'? Anyway, free angels, even though fallen, are nearer akin, spiritually, to us human beings than 'conditioned' angels are. Self-respecting human beings will assuredly endorse Zaehner's dictum[1] that 'Man is not an angel, and, in seeking to be one, he deprives himself of something that is essential to his being'.

The freedom of the human self is a curse inasmuch as it is the source of spiritual evil in Man, but at the same time it is an inestimable treasure inasmuch as it is also the only source, in Man, of spiritual good. We recognize its value for us when we find ourselves under threat of being deprived of it. To be 'conditioned' is a fatal evil in itself, even if our 'unconditioned' fellow human being who is 'conditioning' us is doing this in all good faith, not in order to serve his own self-centred ends, but in order to make our wills compulsorily conform to God's will as our human 'conditioner' sees it.[2] God's will cannot be done by human beings at some other human being's dictation. Each of us has to try to discover for himself, through his own travail and at his own peril, what God's will for him is. And, since Man is a social being, each individual's peril and travail is also peril and travail for his fellow men. This is the inalienable privilege and penalty of being human.[3] We can escape it only by giving up being human, and human nature revolts against attempts to constrain it to make this renunciation. In the past, would-be tyrants have often been baffled by encountering something intractable in their intended victims. Fortunately for mankind, human nature is more mulish than it is sheep-like. This has been a saving human quality; but, until our day, our mulish human nature has never had to face the new psychological weapon that a present-day tyrant wields. In this new situation we may have to fight with all our strength to defend and pre-serve the freedom of our personalities which is our human birthright. We hold this precious gift not as owners but as trustees. Our free selves are ours to be used by us, not for self-centred purposes of our own, but

[1] R. C. Zaehner: *At Sundry Times* (London 1958, Faber), p. 168.
[2] Actually, a 'conditioner' who is sincerely trying to 'condition' his fellow human beings to do God's will must have a self-contradictory notion of what God's will is. The 'conditioner' himself will be 'unconditioned' *ex hypothesi*. If he himself were not still in possession of his native human consciousness and will, he would be unable either to set himself his objective of 'conditioning' his fellow human beings or to work towards it. But he cannot reasonably suppose that God wills him and his fellow human creatures to be different from each other in kind. What is good for one must be good for the rest where what is in question is the fundamental structure of human nature. Therefore, on the 'conditioner's' own premises, God must will the 'conditioner' to be 'conditioned' like his intended victims, and must therefore will him to be incapable of carrying out his self-conferred mission; or, alternatively, God must will the 'conditioner's' intended vic-tims, as well as the 'conditioner' himself, to be 'unconditioned', and must therefore disap-prove of the 'conditioner's' aim.
[3] See E. Gürster in *Die Neue Rundschau*, 13. Heft (Winter, 1949), pp. 140 and 141.

in God's service. The angels' and the social insects' involuntary way is not the way for human beings.

If this is our decision, it commits us to the other alternative. Human beings will have to try to follow the way of the saints; and this is hard indeed. A human being who enters on it is involving himself in a perpetual struggle and exposing himself to perpetual danger;[1] and, even at the price of this tribulation, the seeker's goal will never be reached to the seeker's satisfaction. It cannot be, because a human being who rises to sainthood does not undergo a spiritual mutation. He does not become a creature of another species.[2] The distinctive characteristics of human nature are the freedom of the human consciousness and the human will; and this freedom is a saint's, as well as an ordinary human being's, spiritual instrument. The goal of a saint's endeavour is, not to sterilize his spiritual freedom, but to put it to work in God's service. This service is perfect freedom if it is perfectly performed; but the saint will be painfully aware of the gulf—invisible to ordinary human eyes— between his achievement and his ideal of perfection. As Berkovitz has well said,[3] there is perfection neither in this world nor in any other, but only in God; and this means that a human soul's—even a saint's soul's—fight with self-centredness will be unceasing.

If this is the truth, it tells us that the next ledge, if we succeed in reaching it, will not be a resting-place. Rest cannot be procured for human beings in this world by means of institutions, even if these are admirably designed for meeting the needs of the time, and even if they are accepted whole-heartedly and operated in good faith.

'Whatever may be achieved, in the nearer or more distant future, in the way of institutions, organisations, federations, it will remain true that nothing achieved in history can be made permanently secure. There is no such thing as a human organisation that can be established "securely" through being made weather-proof against the all-disintegrating action of time.'[4]

'The culture-cycle as a whole might be described as an alternation between rigid traditionalism and tendencies to disruption and chaos. And history knows of no resting-point in this up-and-down.'[5]

Rest would also not be one of the rewards of a spiritual effort that succeeded in transfiguring human society into a communion of saints. Even in a saintly society the victory over self-centredness, collective and individual, would never be complete, and the effort would therefore have to be unremitting. This means that the next ledge will be the scene of a spiritual struggle that will not be less intense than the struggle

---

[1] See i. 277–99 and iii. 373.

[2] In iii. 232, I quoted, and endorsed, a passage in Bergson's *Les Deux Sources de la Morale et de la Religion* in which Bergson seems to suggest that to become a saint means to become something like a 'superman'. If this is Bergson's meaning here, I find, on second thoughts, that I do not agree with him over this, if, by 'superman', one means an ex-human creature that has become immune to the human failing of making a wrong choice. This immunity could be acquired only at the cost of forfeiting the capacity to make choices of any kind, wrong or right.

[3] E. Berkovitz: *Judaism: Fossil or Ferment?*, pp. 125–6.

[4] E. Gürster in *Die Neue Rundschau*, 13. Heft (Winter, 1949), pp. 141–2.

[5] F. Borkenau in *Commentary*, March, 1956, p. 244.

to climb, from ledge to ledge, up the face of the cliff. Moreover, this conclusion about the conditions that await us on the next ledge above us
raises a question about the ledge immediately below us. Perhaps this,
too, was not, in truth, the resting-place that, so far, I have taken it to
have been. Miss Oakeley reminds us[1] that 'we must not ignore the
gigantic effort of "Primitive" Man in rising from the sub-human to the
human'. This effort is one that I had taken into account: it is the effort
of climbing the precipice next below ours. But the successful performance of this feat may not, after all, have been followed by an age of
torpor. Christopher Dawson points out that, even where a culture is
apparently static, a continuous effort is required for the task of merely
keeping the culture in that condition.[2] Dawson's observation would, no
doubt, be confirmed from personal experience if we could call as wit-
nesses the elders responsible for the management of any one of the most
primitive human societies still extant; and, in the age of the Egyptiac
or the Sinic universal state, a Pharaonic or Confucian civil servant
would assuredly have given the same testimony. Like the physicist, the
anthropologist recognizes that what looks, to an uninitiated eye, as if
it were a motionless solid body is in reality a swirling legion of invisible
dancers, each dancing with all its might for dear life.

The last word here may be left for a poet to speak. George Herbert
has perceived[3] that, when God at first made Man, rest was not included
among the gifts with which He endowed him. The poet has also divined
that this gift was withheld for a purpose. God's intent towards Man, as
Herbert sees it, was that,

> if goodness lead him not, yet weariness
> may toss him to My breast.

The intrinsic imperfection of human nature does, indeed, both require
and provide a spur. Yet struggle and danger—Man's two inseparable
companions on his journey through this world—are no more than means
to an end; and they are not the only means of advancing towards the
goal of human endeavours that Man has at his disposal. The best means
is identical with the end itself. This end is goodness; and, though human
goodness never attains perfection, not even in the soul of the greatest
saint, Man travels best when his imperfect goodness leads him.

If this is our conclusion, what, if any, practical bearing does it have
on the urgent question of our time? What are we to do to save ourselves,
here and now, in the alarming situation in which the human race now
finds itself? Try to become saints? And this with the foreknowledge
that, however far we may succeed in advancing towards this ambitious
spiritual goal, we shall never succeed in reaching it, and, meanwhile,
shall never win release from danger, struggle, and weariness? If we
agree that this spiritual endeavour is the only alternative to self-
annihilation *en masse* now that we possess the atomic weapon, is not that
merely an indirect way of saying that mass-suicide is now mankind's

---

[1] H. D. Oakeley in *Philosophy*, vol. xi, No. 42 (April, 1936), p. 190.
[2] Chr. Dawson: *The Dynamics of World History*, pp. 451–2.
[3] George Herbert: *The Pulley*.

inevitable fate? Is the suggested alternative really a practical proposition? What percentage of the thousands of millions of human beings who have lived and died so far has ever dreamed of aiming at sainthood? Can one imagine *l'homme moyen sensuel* devoting himself to an aim that calls for this degree of sacrifice, and that, even at that cost, is impossible to achieve more than approximately and imperfectly? Even if you could convince him that this is now his only alternative to self-destruction, and even if he were to do his best, is it conceivable that he would be capable of doing even the minimum necessary for saving the situation?

One answer to these questions is that the very thing that makes the pursuit of saintliness look like a thankless task is something that also makes it a practicable one. The task seems thankless because it cannot be achieved perfectly, and the reason why it cannot is because the aspirant to sainthood does not cease to be a human being. Unlike the imaginary superman, the saint is not an ex-human being who has turned into another kind of creature through some mysterious mutation that is none of his own doing. He is a human being who has raised himself above the average level of human goodness; and, if he believes, and is right in believing, that he could not have risen without the help of God's grace, this is a further indication that the saint himself is no more than a human creature. Sainthood, thus described, is a well-attested historical phenomenon, and the human beings who have risen to this higher spiritual altitude have done so in different degrees. What some human beings have achieved in some degree must be a practicable objective for others; if grace has been offered to some souls, it will have been offered to all, whatever Augustine and Calvin may say; and any measure of success in approaching sainthood will have spiritual value. It is not a case of being asked to attempt the impossible or of being faced with a choice between all or nothing. The road towards sainthood is, in fact, an open one on which even the worst and weakest human being can set foot, though this open road stretches away towards an ever-receding spiritual horizon.

One of the first steps on the road is to acquire some sense of responsibility and to act on this by restraining one's own self-centred impulses. All sane adult human beings are responsible-minded to some minimum degree. Indeed, this is one of the definitions of what sanity means. One field in which ordinary human beings in the mass have managed to behave more or less responsibly is the handling of tools. In making his tools progressively more effective, Man has also made the misuse of them progressively more dangerous. In harnessing atomic energy he has now acquired a tool which is so potent that, if used as a weapon, it might destroy, not merely a hostile army or people or merely the users themselves, but the whole human race. This new power has challenged the holders of it not to misuse it; and, since the dropping of the bombs on Japan in 1945, there have been indications that the holders of atomic power have been conscious of the new and awful responsibility that their possession of this power entails. The invention of the atomic weapon has made future resort to war a crime against the human race. And it is noteworthy that, since the end of the Second World

War, the World's most powerful nations and governments have shown an uncustomary self-restraint on some critical occasions. They have given priority to their sense of responsibility for avoiding a world-war that would be fought, this time, with atomic weapons, and they have subordinated, to this paramount concern, their national *amour propre* and ambitions and even their ideological convictions.

On the road towards sainthood, this budding sense of obligation not to exterminate the human race is, no doubt, only a feeble and far-off step. The attitude is negative and the motive is largely self-regarding, since it is obvious that atomic war-makers could not exterminate their fellow men without exterminating themselves together with the rest. At the same time this step marks a notable breach with the habit of going to war, which is coeval with civilization. It is encouraging evidence of human nature's power to respond to the challenge of a revolutionary change of circumstances. It is also of great immediate practical importance, because it keeps mankind's foot in the door that opens into the future, and so promises to give time for Man's sense of responsibility towards mankind as a whole to take a more positive form.

If the first step on Man's road towards sainthood is the renunciation of Man's traditional role of being his brother's murderer, the second step would be an acceptance of Man's new role of being his brother's keeper; and, happily, this sense of responsibility for the positive welfare of Man's fellow human beings has already declared itself. It is, indeed, one of the fruits of the seventeenth-century Western spiritual revolution. We have noticed, in another context,[1] that, in the post-seventeenth-century Western World, the progressive recession of belief in Christianity's traditional doctrines has been accompanied by a progressive advance in the practice of Christianity's moral precepts; and that, although this advance has been opposed, in the West itself, by the reactionary ideologies that have raised their heads there in our generation,[2] the ideals of Howard and Wilberforce have, so far, not been driven off the field by the counter-ideals of Mussolini and Hitler, but have, on the contrary, been disseminated, in company with other elements of the modern Western Civilization, among the non-Western majority of the human race. As landmarks[3] in the advance of this modern humanitarianism, we may single out the abolition of the slave-trade and of slavery itself, the abolition of barbarous forms of punishment, the humanization of the treatment of prisoners and lunatics, the establishment of old-age pensions and national health services, and, in general, the narrowing of the gulf between a poor majority's and a rich minority's conditions of life. This advance towards greater social justice through an increase in human kindness has been taking place in two fields simultaneously: as between different classes in a single country and also as between different countries in a world that is now in process of being unified morally and socially as well as technologically and militarily. The relatively rich minority of the human race has now recognized that it has an obligation to make material sacrifices in order to assist the relatively poor majority to raise its standard of living on both the material

[1] See pp. 532–3.   [2] See pp. 528–9 and 531–2.   [3] See pp. 529–30.

and the spiritual plane. Peoples that are still exercising political control over other peoples have now come, thanks to an American lead, to expect to pay for this political privilege instead of any longer expecting to draw the traditional profits of empire.

These practical steps towards the vindication of fundamental and universal human rights leave us still far away from the achievement of a communion of saints. Yet this conscious and deliberate advance towards brotherhood in a community embracing the whole human race is surely even farther removed from the involuntary sociality of the bee-hive and the ant-heap.

II ANNEX

Ad Hominem

I. ACKNOWLEDGEMENTS AND THANKS TO MY CRITICS

THE possible value of self-examination as an aid to the study of human affairs has been discussed in Chapter II. I there suggested that this might be a promising means for trying to mitigate the distorting effects of the human student's relativity to his cultural milieu and his personality. This suggestion is not original: it is made in passages that I have quoted from books and articles[1] that had already been published at the time when I was writing this chapter. Nor, I think, is it a controversial suggestion. At any rate, I have not come across any opposition to it. Disagreement begins when we put the question whether the self-analyst should make his findings public. No doubt, if he found sympathy and response, showing his cards might bring him valuable help in his undertaking. The significance of some of the evidence about himself that he put on the table—without, perhaps, having fully understood its significance himself—might be transparent to some of his readers, even if they were not professional psychologists. He would, however, be laying himself open to the cutting comment that, for his readers, his conscientious—or self-important—self-revelation was boring because it was superfluous. They did not need any commentary from him to enable them to size up and discount 'the personal factor' in his work; this leapt to the eye; he had already revealed himself, unintentionally and unconsciously.

I can illustrate this point *ad hominem* from some comments on the first ten volumes of this book. The presentation of history there given has been criticized as being 'personal'[2] and 'subjective'.[3] Of course, all

---

[1] See p. 60, footnote 2.

[2] 'A Personal View of History' was the heading of Bagby's review of volumes vii–x of this book in *The Times Literary Supplement* (reprinted in *Toynbee and History*). Kohn calls the book 'an intensely personal document'; 'a profession of faith' (ibid., p. 351); and he uses the same phrases in an article, headed 'Toynbees Glaubensbekenntnis', in *Der Monat* (Berlin, August, 1955), p. 465. Leddy, too, sees in it 'a highly personal work' (*The Phoenix*, vol. 11, No. 4 (1957), p. 140). Altree finds in the book 'a normative system based on a very private interpretation of the course of human destiny' (*Toynbee and History*, p. 271). Hourani comments that, while the book is 'in a sense conventional, for all its air of originality, in a more profound way it is deeply personal' (*The Dublin Review*, vol. 229, No. 470 (December, 1955), p. 387). R. K. Merton observes that 'Toynbee's transcendental theology enacted upon the stage of human history is a matter of private faith, not historical sociology' (*The American Journal of Sociology*, vol. xlvii, No. 2 (September, 1941), pp. 205–13). C. W. Weinberger remarks that 'the magnitude of the endeavour seems almost to have overwhelmed the author into putting far too much of his personal self into it' (*San Francisco Chronicle*, 17th October, 1954). R. H. Tawney notes that 'the book does not, in' his 'judgment, lose, but gains, from the note of personal conviction which runs through its pages, and from the occasional confessions of faith in which conviction finds its voice' (*International Affairs*, November, 1939, p. 806). This consensus shows that in these volumes 'the personal factor' must be transparent.

[3] Sir Ernest Barker in *Toynbee and History*, p. 92. M. Savelle speaks of my 'extreme subjectivity'. 'Modern historians will find it impossible to accept "intuitive truth" as evidence of anything beyond the individual experience of the person whose intuitive experience it is' (*The Pacific Historical Review*, vol. xxv, No. 1 (February, 1956), pp. 55–67). T. R. Fyvel finds that 'on almost every page one can trace what appears

interpretations, and indeed all would-be objective statements of fact, are inevitably 'subjective' and 'personal' in the sense of the argument in Chapter II of this volume. They are all inescapably relative to the inquirer's own fundamental presuppositions. But my critics evidently mean something more than this, and their meaning is brought out by Sir Ernest Barker when he says of me that 'he has not discounted himself enough'.[1] These criticisms—which are, I am sure, deserved—imply that the critics have already been able to do the discounting for themselves, without needing aid from the author. It is therefore not surprising that, when I opened the bag of tools with which I had done the job, the critics should have 'thanked me for nothing'. The autobiographical information included in my 'acknowledgements and thanks'[2] was evidently distasteful to Sir Ernest Barker,[3] and it has given Trevor-Roper an opening for making some amusing play with it.[4]

Having learnt my lesson 'in the hard way', I have tried to profit by it in the present volume by taking a new path that has been opened up for me by my critics. I have left the initiative to them, and have taken up the topics on which their comments have converged. Since the purpose of publishing books and reviewing them is, not to defend and attack personal positions, but to co-operate in working for the advancement of knowledge and understanding, I have concentrated, in the main body of this volume, on topics which seem likely to be of some general interest, and I have set as many as possible of my critics' comments, and my reflections on these, in this impersonal context. But this procedure has left, still unacknowledged, a considerable body of criticism that is concerned with 'the personal factor' in my book; and this has put me in a dilemma. If I follow my critics on to this ground, I expose myself again to being censured or ridiculed for setting foot on it. If I keep off it, I am ignoring a large part of my critics' work. I am sincerely grateful to my critics, even including the small minority of them who have seemed to me to show traces of personal animus or even of an intention to do me personal damage. These, among the rest, have at any rate done me the

---

[to be] a purely subjective approach to historical events and characters' (*The Tribune*, 21st March, 1947, p. 21). M. S. Bates feels that 'at times the subjectivism is oppressive' (*Christianity and Crisis*, vol. 15, No. 4 (21st March, 1955), pp. 27–30 and 32). In C. B. Joynt's eyes, 'such history is private, purely subjective history. Vast sections . . . are solipsistic in content' (*The Australasian Journal of Philosophy*, vol. 34, No. 3 (December, 1956), p. 201). A milder statement of the same judgement is that 'our author may not be as dispassionate and objective as he thinks he is' (A. N. Holcombe in *The American Political Science Review*, vol. xlix, No. 4 (December, 1955), p. 1151).

[1] Sir Ernest Barker in *Toynbee and History*, p. 92.   [2] See vol. x, pp. 213–42.

[3] While criticizing me for not being more reticent, Barker suggests an interpretation of my motives which, besides being kindly, is correct. Mumford, in *Toynbee and History*, p. 141, also recognizes that my purpose was an impersonal one and not a wish to exhibit my personality. A. N. Holcombe finds that 'the author's candid intellectual autobiography, which explains how he came to set less store by politics and more by religion', is 'one of the most attractive features of the work' (*The American Political Science Review*, vol. xlix, No. 4 (December, 1955), pp. 1151–4). I have the impression, however, that, in passing this favourable judgement, Holcombe is in a minority among my critics.

Blackmur finds that the whole book is an intellectual autobiography, and that, in this sense, one of the three orders of apprehension that are to be found in it is the personal one, the other two being the documentary and the religious (*Kenyon Review*, Summer, 1955, pp. 357–70).

[4] H. Trevor-Roper in *Encounter*, June, 1957. On the article as a whole, no comment.

service of spending some of their working time on giving their minds to my book, and the result has been a boon for me. Their pummellings have given me a mental massage that has loosened the joints and muscles of my mind and has set it moving on a new course. The least that I can do in return is to debate with them when they call on me to reply, as Geyl has been calling almost plaintively. I have therefore decided to take Geyl for the spokesman of the jury, and to do my critics the courtesy of giving them a reply, even when the questions that they raise are concerned with my personal outlook. I have put this more personal part of the debate in this annex, and, here too, I have concentrated, as far as I have been able, on topics that might be of some general interest, such as, for example, the effects of a classical education. Precautions, however, are no guarantee of security when one is venturing into a mine-field.

2. EFFECTS OF A CLASSICAL EDUCATION

(i) *Fortunate Effects*

In a review of previous volumes of this book Hourani has commented[1] that 'the very elements of which his theory is built are the commonplaces of an English classical education'. I agree with this comment, if I may supplement it by reminding the reader that this kind of education was not an English invention or peculiarity. The form current in England, during the years 1896 to 1911, when I was receiving my classical education there, had been established, between four and five hundred years back, in Italy. At the turn of the nineteenth and twentieth centuries this was still the standard form of higher education not only in England but throughout the Western World, including Western countries outside Europe. And at the same date an education in some 'classical' language and literature, though not, of course, in those that ranked as classical in the West, was also still the standard form of higher education in Eastern Asia, India, Persia, Turkey, and the Arab countries, as well as among the Jewish diasporá in what was then the 'Jewish Pale' of the Russian Empire. In fact, it still held the field in every one of the civilizations then in existence.[2] It had also been the standard form of higher education in civilizations that were then no longer in existence: for instance, the Sumero-Akkadian in its Babylonic phase and the Egyptiac.

A 'classical' education may be defined as one in which the staple discipline is an initiation into some culture that is older than the present-day culture of the society in which this form of higher education is the established one. While being distinct from the present-day culture, the

---

[1] In loc. cit., p. 386.
[2] In Russia one of the effective forms of the process of 'Westernization' since the time of Peter the Great had been the introduction of a 'classical' education in the Greek and Latin languages and literature. The Greek language and literature had not been imposed on Russia by the Greek Orthodox Christian missionaries who had converted her to Christianity, and there had not been a renaissance of Greek culture there corresponding to the renaissance of Latin and Greek culture in the West. The Byzantine Greeks' abstention from the practice of 'cultural imperialism' is noteworthy, considering that they were enthusiasts for the classical literature of their Hellenic predecessors. The Greek classics were the staple of Byzantine higher education.

'classical' culture in which present-day higher education is given will have some historical relation with it. It will be the past culture of the same society in some earlier phase of its history, or it will be the culture of some earlier society to which the present-day society is 'affiliated' in the sense in which the Western Civilization may be said to be affiliated to the Hellenic. The medium in which an education in a 'classical' culture is given is usually that of language and literature. A knowledge of languages, and copies of the texts of books written in them, have often survived the other elements—states, laws, architecture, and so on—of the culture in which these languages and this literature were once current; and a literature, even if only fragments of it survive, can give a glimpse (though this may sometimes be a deceptive glimpse) into the rest of the life of the vanished society in which this literature was created.

The language in which the 'classical' literature is conveyed need not be a 'dead' language. A twentieth-century Persian peasant who knows a quantity of 'classical' Persian poetry by heart finds this easy because the language of Firdawsi, Sa'di, and Hafiz is not so very different from the peasant's own present-day mother-tongue. Even where the 'classical' language is one that has passed out of every-day use, or has never been used for every-day purposes at any date, it may not be 'dead' in the strict sense of being completely out of currency. In the Western World, for instance, the Latin language has had an unbroken history—going back to the time when it was one of the two official languages of the Roman Empire—as the liturgical language of the Roman Catholic Church; and even in every-day usage it still lives in the current form of English in Latin phrases—'ad hominem', 'dramatis personae', 'ceteris paribus', 'mutatis mutandis', 'pari passu', 'ipso facto', 'sine die', 'vice versa', 'pro' and 'con.', 'nem. con.', 'i.e.', 'e.g.', 'viz.' (i.e. videlicet), 'etcetera'—which are embedded there like flints in chalk.

At what value is the 'classical' kind of education to be appraised? Evidently it cannot just be taken for granted that it is valuable as well as venerable, simply because it has held the field so long and so widely. In retrospect we can see that its reign has been due partly to the inertia that accounts for so much in human affairs, and partly to cultural breakdowns resulting in 'intermediate periods' or 'interregna' or 'dark ages', after which the subsequent culture has been rightly felt to be inferior to the relics of a culture that had been prevalent before the catastrophe. In our own day we are seeing this kind of education being rapidly ousted from its traditional, once sacrosanct, position by a new kind that has for its staples a scientific knowledge of non-human nature and a technological 'know-how' for making natural processes serve human purposes. This is happening not only in the West, where modern science and technology originated, but in the rest of the World, where, today, the mastering of up-to-date Western technology and science is a crucial part of a process of 'Westernization' that has now come to be almost world-wide.

No doubt it is conceivable that the new oecumenical civilization that is now taking shape within a Western framework might bring on itself a catastrophe comparable in magnitude, scale for scale, with the catastrophes that other civilizations have brought on themselves in the past, and it is also conceivable that, in that imaginary future situation, the present-day education in science and technology might, in its turn, become 'classical': that is to say, might become petrified in a pre-third-world-war form. This, however, seems improbable, because—in contrast to the 'timelessness' of great literature, which is its weakness as well as its strength—it is the strength, as well as the weakness, of science that it is cumulative. The piety towards the past, which is one of the virtues of 'humane studies',[1] stands condemned as a vice in science's intellectual and ethical code. For scientists it is an obligatory ambition that they should strive to supersede their own past achievements, and it is a point of honour for them that they should ruthlessly discard all findings that have been invalidated by science's subsequent advance. Therefore, if science survives, it seems likely still to keep on the move; and, therefore, again, it seems likely that, if the traditional kind of 'classical' education were to be ousted completely, it would not, in any circumstances, be replaced by a scientific equivalent.

If this forecast carries conviction, it makes an appraisal of 'classical' education a matter of great practical, as well as theoretical, interest in our day. This has, as we have seen, been virtually the only form of higher education since the civilizations of earlier generations came to be consecrated as 'classical' as a consolation prize for their failure to survive. If it were true that we are now within sight of seeing this traditional form of higher education driven off the field, this would mean that we are now at an epoch-making point in educational history, and this would make it seem prudent to 'stop, look, and listen', and not just forge ahead blindly.

What, then, is to be mankind's verdict on the traditional 'classical' kind of higher education? Individual judgements on this issue, as on others, are subject to the sway of relativity, and therefore differ as widely as the fundamental presuppositions by which they are governed. My own judgement, in this case, is implicit in my feelings about the 'classical' education that I myself received. My generation was almost the last in England to be given an education in the Greek and Latin languages and literature that remained faithful to the strictest fifteenth-century Italian standards. The aim was not merely to make us read Greek and Latin more fluently than French or German, and to have as great a familiarity with Greek and Latin literature as with English; it was to give us the ability to write Greek and Latin prose, and verse as well, with ever greater virtuosity. The ideal was to produce counterfeits of the original literature that a Greek or Latin author, in each *genre*, might have mistaken for authentic pieces if he could have been raised from the dead to read our productions. We were under no illusions about the possibility of attaining this ideal objective. The more skilful one became, by practice, in playing this literary game, the more sharply one became aware that one's most plausible *tours de force* would have seemed the most exquisitely absurd to an old master of Greek or Latin style, just

---

[1] See A. J. P. Taylor's phrase quoted in footnote 4 to p. 66.

because the lapses that would show our productions up, as being the fakes that they were, would be ridiculous minutiae.

As I describe the education that was given to me, it may sound like something fantastic to someone who has never had it, or even to someone who has had it only in an attenuated form. Perhaps the strangest thing about it is that, if I had been a Chinese child of my age, instead of being an English one, I should have come in for a classical education that would have been almost identical down to such details as being taught to write essays in the 'classical' language and 'classical' style. At opposite ends of the Old World, and also all the way across it between these extremities, societies engaged on second or third attempts at the enterprise of civilization had arrived independently at this queer system of education, and, after arriving at it, had persisted in it for hundreds of years. If 'classical' education has been one of Mankind's follies, it has, at any rate, not been a rare one.

I myself do not think that it has been a folly. I am aware of its shortcomings, and, *ad hominem*, of consequent effects on my own outlook and work that have been unfortunate. This unfortunate side of the effects has been pointed out by some of my critics and is discussed at a later point in this annex. Yet, when I try to strike as just a balance as I can between 'pros' and 'cons', I find myself now, as ever, counting it as a piece of supreme good fortune that, being born, as I was, in England, I happened to be born there just early enough to come in for this education in an uncompromisingly complete version of it. I feel no wistful regrets that I finished receiving my formal education just too soon to benefit by any of the new kinds of higher education that have been gaining ground in England since then. The judgement implicit in these feelings is piquantly different from the judgements of some of my younger contemporaries: for example, Philip Bagby. In a critique of me and my work[1] he sums up by pronouncing that

'we can only think it unfortunate that his education, like that of so many historians, was exclusively humanistic; he has been deprived of the tools he needed for his self-appointed task.'

I will now give my reasons for holding that a 'classical' education—in 'classical' Greek, Latin, Arabic, Persian, Sanskrit, Chinese, or whichever of the consecrated languages it may be—is a rather valuable tool for the task on which Bagby and I have both been engaged. In Chapter I I have already made the point that no tool can ever be good for all purposes and that every tool has its own peculiar weaknesses. I shall be going on to say what I think the weaknesses of a 'classical' education are. I am aware of intrinsic weaknesses in it that come to light when one uses it—even if one does not push the use of it, as I may sometimes have pushed it, beyond the limits of its effectiveness.

The sovereign virtue that I find in a 'classical' education is that the subject of it is human affairs. The synonym 'humanistic', which Bagby uses in the passage just quoted, gives an accurate description of a 'classical' education's field. Of course, this is not the only possible kind

---

[1] In *Culture and History*, pp. 177–82.

of education in human affairs. 'Modern', as well as 'ancient', affairs can be made the staple for a formal 'humane' education; and by far the most important education in human affairs that a human being ever receives is not given in any formal course at all; it comes from the life-long experience of rubbing shoulders with one's fellows that a social animal, such as Man is, is bound to have. However, even this universal and never-ceasing practical education in 'the humanities' does not and cannot limit its temporal horizon to affairs that are contemporary in the strict sense. For phenomena present themselves to our human minds as if they were on the move, and human phenomena, like others, are not intelligible to us unless we apprehend them in their time-perspective. This applies to all minds, including those—and they are still a majority —that receive no formal education at all. In their practical education in human affairs they win their stereoscopic vision by seeing through the eyes of their parents and grandparents as well as through those of their brothers and sisters. So a 'classical' education shares with every other kind of 'humane' education the two merits of being a study of Man and being an historical study of him. And it is surely true that Man is 'the proper study of mankind'.

This study is 'proper' in the sense of being indispensable, whatever else our studies may or may not include. The study of Man is indispensable because, since at least as long ago as half-way through the Palaeolithic Age, Man has been the most awkward and dangerous presence in mankind's universe. Moreover, if this has been true for the last few hundred thousand years, the 'survival value' of taking this truth to heart, and of acting on it in education and in all other human activities, has been increasing *pari passu* with the increase in mankind's command over non-human nature; and this command has been increasing at an accelerating pace which, in our day, has reached a momentary climax in science's and technology's joint feat of splitting atoms. Man has never before been so dangerous to himself as he has now become in consequence of this latest of his discoveries in the field of the study of non-human nature; yet this is also the moment at which mankind is giving more and more room to a new kind of education in technology and science at the expense of education in the 'humanities'. In these circumstances, surely, we ought to think long and hard before we allow any form of 'humane' education, not excluding the traditional forms, to be crowded out.

As between the different possible forms of an education in the study of Man, the 'classical' form has one advantage over the 'modern' form that is an intrinsic advantage and a permanent one, but is also particularly valuable in the age into which we have now entered.

The human race has now condemned itself, by its technological prowess, to having to choose between committing universal genocide and learning to live as one family. The crucial difficulty, for us today, of learning to live as one family is manifest. We have suddenly all been brought into point-blank range of each other for military, political, and economic purposes by the recent unprecedented advance in technology that has been made in the West; but we are still divided from each other by being partakers in a number of different local cultures. The differences between these local cultures are still sharp, and sharp cultural differences breed mutual misunderstanding, fear, and hostility. Fortunately, all mankind seems to be moving towards a future common cultural standing-ground through a world-wide process of 'modernization' (a euphemism for cultural standardization on a pattern of Western origin). But the pace of cultural change is much slower than the pace of technological change; and, while technological change seems to know no limits to its capacity for acceleration, the pace of cultural change seems to have limits set to it by the limits of the pace at which the human psyche is capable of adapting itself to changes in its environment. Therefore the time-lag of cultural change behind technological change, which has always been great, seems likely to grow greater.

This lengthening time-interval is a dangerous time-zone for mankind to traverse. It is the period during which we shall be capable, as we now already are, of annihilating ourselves, without yet having become capable of getting on with each other (or, as we say in our contemporary political jargon, 'coexisting'). One of the chief obstacles to our treating each other tolerantly, sympathetically, and considerately is the illusion, which we find it hard to overcome, that our own particular relative values and standards are universal and absolute. Any means at our disposal for dispelling this dangerous illusion, even partially, therefore has an unusually high value for mankind at the present day. And a 'classical' education is an effective means for dispelling the illusion, partially at least, inasmuch as a 'classical' education teaches one to appreciate and revere a culture that is not one's own.

This is a first step towards becoming aware of the relativity of one's outlook to one's social milieu and one's personality; and an awakening to this truth sets one's feet on the path towards intellectual and moral salvation. Learning to admire what one recognizes as being admirable in an alien culture opens one's eyes to the blemishes in one's own culture, and this makes one receptive to the sense of humility which is the necessary condition for achieving even the smallest measure of insight and discretion. The mere fact that the culture in which one is being educated is not one's own is enough in itself to teach one this lesson. But the lesson is also taught explicitly in the literatures of the earlier civilizations that have been canonized by subsequent civilizations as 'classics'. These literatures, like all literatures, reflect and convey something of the experience of the societies in which they were created. The participants in the civilizations of the first two generations lived to have the tragic but illuminating and regenerating experience of seeing their high hopes brought to naught by their own perverse acts. In the 'classical' literatures a student of them will catch the note of learning through suffering,[1] and will feel the awe inspired by the spectacle of the sinner's fateful progress from success through pride to catastrophe.[2] This wisdom is

---

[1] See further, pp. 609 and 617.

[2] Several critics have pointed out that the Hellenic doctrine of nemesis has been one of the formative ideas in the working out of my view of history. K. D. Erdmann finds that, for me, history is the tragedy of civilization (*Archiv für Kulturgeschichte*, xxxiii. Band, Heft 2 (1951), p. 190). R. V. Chase finds that 'Toynbee has given us a new interpretation of the noblest concept of the Western mind: the idea that Man's life is a

enshrined in the Chinese 'classics', and it is also deeply embedded in the cultural background of the Western World. It is the common foundation of the otherwise different outlooks of classical Greek and Latin literature, the Old Testament,[1] and the New Testament.[2]

Thus a 'classical' education gives one a standing-ground from which one can look at one's own civilization from outside, and so see it with new eyes. A classically educated modern Westerner can see the Western World with the eyes of those fifteenth-century scholars who recovered for the West a first-hand knowledge of the Hellenic culture, as far as this could be found embalmed in Greek and Latin literature.[3] Seen from this 'classical' standpoint, our familiar Western World undergoes a metamorphosis that is startling but instructive.

The only way of appraising a civilization is to measure it against at least one other representative of its own species. So long as a Western observer stays standing inside his own society's charmed circle, the Western World will appear to him to be coextensive with the World, and the Western Civilization to be identical with Civilization. Viewed from the Hellenist's observation-peak in the different world that can be conjured up in a Western mind that has been educated in the Greek and Latin classics, the self-expatriated Westerner's own world now looms less large and looks less grand. Its appearance on the scene strikes him as being, at best, an epilogue that makes an anti-climax. At worst it seems an impertinence or even an outrage. He and his Western forebears now appear to him as the Greeks' and Romans' *diadochi* and *epigoni*. Can we disown our descent from the barbarians who slunk in like hyaenas to feast on the dead giant's carrion corpse? So can our vaunted Western Civilization be anything better than a vain repetition

tragedy' (*The American Scholar*, vol. 16, No. 3 (Summer, 1947), pp. 268–82). As T. A. Sumberg sees it, 'it is clear that Toynbee's Protean volumes contain not one but two theories of historical development. The first and earlier in appearance is the naturalistic one: Man makes his own history in a world not made for him, but in which a favourable outcome of Environment-Man transactions makes for his prosperity; this prosperity, however, is always in a delicate balance under constantly changing conditions. This naturalistic view sometimes takes on the classical aspects of a Greek tragedy; every society is born with a taint which always results in its death, however desperately the fated victim struggles. But this view is increasingly driven off the stage by the traditional Christian eschatological conceptions' (*Social Research*, vol. 14, No. 3 (September, 1947), pp. 267–84). Sumberg is, I think, mistaken in holding that the characteristic plot of a Greek tragedy is an exposition of a philosophy of determinism. While catastrophe may be the almost unescapable nemesis of hybris, hybris is not the inevitable reaction to success. An alternative reaction to it is humility, and humility does not attract the thunderbolt. If I am right on this point, then Sumberg will be wrong in drawing so sharp an antithesis as he does draw between the Hellenic and the Christian view of life.

In M. C. Swabey's view, 'the presence of nemesis in an historical work marks its philosophical character' (*The Judgment of History*, p. 193).

[1] See p. 623, footnote 1. Rabbi J. B. Agus recalls, in *Judaism*, vol. 4, No. 4 (Fall, 1955), pp. 330–1, that a belief in the spiritual fruitfulness of suffering is part of the core of the Jewish religion.

[2] I myself believe that this is a true insight, and that it gets to the heart of the problem that Man presents to himself. But this is, of course, a controversial issue. My insistence on 'the nemesis of creativity' strikes Geyl as being excessive (*Toynbee and History*, p. 17). Taylor notices, with disapproval, that, in my eyes, 'the worst sin is to believe that Man made himself' (ibid., p. 117).

[3] It would be still more illuminating if we could see our Western Civilization with the eyes, not of our own Italian Hellenists, but of the Hellenes themselves; but this is, of course, impossible, since the first shoots of the Western Civilization did not appear above the ground till at least three hundred years after the stubble of the previous crop had withered away in what had been the Roman Empire's western provinces.

of the glorious Hellenic cycle? As for the transplanted Western observer's mother-tongue, this and the other languages of the present-day European peoples grate on an ear that has been attuned to the music of Latin and Greek. In fact, the Western Civilization shrivels to dimensions that are, if anything, smaller than life but that, all the same, are perhaps nearer to life-size than the grandiose mirage that deceives the eye so long as it is viewing its native civilization from within, in 'splendid isolation'.

Besides making it possible for a Westerner to look at the West from an historical vantage-point in the past, a Greek 'classical' education will also enable him to look at it from a geographical vantage-point outside the West's own territorial domain. It is hardly possible to study Hellenic literature and history without becoming mentally familiar with the geographical setting in which the drama was acted; and, if a classically educated Westerner eventually finds an opportunity to visit the coasts and islands of the Aegean, he will discover, perhaps rather to his surprise, that here, beyond the bounds of his own Western World, present-day human affairs can be no less interesting or less instructive than those famous long-since-past affairs that have drawn him hither so far away from home. In the Aegean he will encounter, not only the physical remains of the defunct Hellenic Civilization, but living human participants in two other civilizations, the Byzantine and the Islamic, which are still going concerns and which, like the Hellenic Civilization, are distinct and separate representatives of this species of society from the civilization in which the visitor himself has been brought up. It is true that the Western Civilization has been impinging on the Byzantine and on the Islamic since the seventeenth and the eighteenth centuries respectively. Yet, under the surface, both still retain their original distinctive characters, and the participants in each of them look at the present-day world, including the West, from a non-Western point of view.

Travelling in Greece in 1911-12 for the purpose of increasing my knowledge and understanding of the Hellenic Civilization by gaining a first-hand acquaintance with what was once its homeland, I received my first lessons on the subject of contemporary international politics, and received them from instructors who did not look at the contemporary world from a Western point of view. In speculating about the date at which the coming war between the Western Powers was going to break out, Greek peasants in 1912 were not concerned about the fortunes of the prospective Western belligerents. What interested them, and interested them intensely, was the bearing of this eagerly expected civil war in the West upon the prospects, for Greece, of acquiring Macedonia. For them the paramount interest in international politics was whether there was to be a fulfilment of Greek national aspirations. The question of the destiny of the Western World was, for them, incidental and subordinate to Greek interests. Thus, on Greek soil in the last stage of my classical education, I learnt, unexpectedly, a double lesson about the contemporary world in which I myself was living. I learnt that there was such a thing as international politics (a subject about which I had heard little or nothing at Oxford in the years 1907-11); and I learnt simultaneously to look at this newly discovered province of human affairs from a non-Western standpoint. These two lessons, together, educated me for a subsequent professional career in this field of study, and their value for me has proved inexhaustible. Listening in 1957 to discussions in Arab countries about the bearing on Arab national aspirations of 'the Cold War' between the Soviet Union and the United States, I remembered those discussions in Greek villages to which I had once listened, now nearly half a century back; and I realized that the Arabs were as indifferent to the destinies of Russia and the West today as the Greeks had been on the eve of the First World War.

These would seem to be ways in which a classical education can be valuable to a student of human affairs. It can help, in some measure, to correct the distorting effects, on his vision, of the relativity of his point of view to his own cultural milieu. Of course, it is beyond the power of even the most thorough-going 'classical' education to prise the recipient of it right out of his native setting and replant him in an artificially acquired one;[1] and, even if the process of transplantation could be carried through completely, the changeling would not have got rid of the human mind's inescapable handicap. He would now find himself under the sway of his relativity to his new cultural milieu. A change of cultural milieu cannot exorcise the relativity to which an observer, everywhere and at all times, will find himself subject.

Actually, the half-and-half position of straddling between two worlds —his native world and his acquired 'classical' one—gives the classically educated observer what is, perhaps, the most favourable opportunity possible for overcoming the limitations set by relativity to some degree.[2]

---

[1] Geyl points out that I am inside the West, whatever I may think or say (*Toynbee and History*, p. 367). F. Neilson finds that the relativity of my point of view to the time that happens to be the present for me gets in the light of my observation of the past (*The American Journal of Economics and Sociology*, Supplement to vol. 14, No. 3 (April, 1955), p. 5. Cp. p. 19). I 'shall not escape the charge of patriotic prejudice and the taint of national outlook' (ibid., p. 74). On this question, see further pp. 606–20.

[2] This straddling position does give the observer something like a binocular vision, but Trinkaus points out that I, at any rate, have still remained the prisoner of my relativity to my Western and Hellenic standpoints. As he sees it, I force the rest of history into the configuration that I fancy I have found in Hellenic and Western history. And, when I try to answer the questions that confront the West today by reference to the histories of other civilizations, these points of reference are not really external to the West, since I see the histories of these other civilizations in terms of Western and Hellenic history. 'Therefore, in spite of all his protests against the Western attitude of contempt for "natives" and for other civilizations, Toynbee remains, at a deeper level, enclosed within his conception of the Western way of life' (C. Trinkaus in *Science and Society*, vol. xii, No. 1 (New York, 1948), pp. 224–5). The same point is made by Frankfort. 'Toynbee's images betray an evolutionistic as well as a moral bias. . . . Toynbee merely projects postulates which fulfil an emotional need in the West into human groups whose values lie elsewhere. . . . Why should we characterise civilisations which have achieved a deep and lasting harmony (like those of the Zuni or certain Polynesians) as "arrested civilizations"? . . . Why should these chimaeras ["the road ahead"; "the cliff above"] disturb the satisfaction of people who have attained the double integration of individual and society, and society and nature? . . . Toynbee . . . remains completely under the spell of a nineteenth-century Western outlook. His evolutionary bias, his empiricism, and his treatment of civilizations as "specimens of a species" are all of a piece' (H. Frankfort: *The Birth of Civilization in the Near East*, pp. 24 and 26).

It has also been pointed out that I have likewise remained the prisoner of my Christian upbringing. In *Toynbee and History*, p. 345, Father L. Walker pronounces that my 'own beliefs are almost all entirely Christian in inspiration', and that a belief in charity in matters of religion is the only inspiration that I have derived from 'the Orient'. Against this judgement, I file two pleas. The first is a sophistical one: Christianity, as well as the

This is a valuable advantage; for the achievement of at least a minimum measure of detachment from the toils of relativity is, I am convinced, a necessary condition for making any serious study of human affairs for any purpose.[1] But, besides having this general utility, a classical education puts in one's hands an excellent tool for the particular purpose of trying to make a comparative study of civilizations; and this is the first step, and a big one, towards arriving at a comprehensive morphology of human affairs. Since, for Westerners, 'the classics' means the Greek and Latin literature that was one of the expressions of the Hellenic culture, the Hellenic Civilization is the obvious 'jumping-off ground' for a Western inquirer who has a comparative study of civilizations in view; and it is no accident that it has been put to this use by one after another of the Western explorers in this field, beginning, now more than two hundred years ago, with the pioneer Giambattista Vico, the most original and imaginative of any so far.

An acquaintance with the culture and history of the Hellenic Civilization is a promising tool in a Westerner's hands if he is trying to make a comparative study of civilizations, for the same reason that it is a promising one if he is trying to counteract the relativity of his outlook and standards to his native Western cultural milieu. In both mental operations the illuminating procedure is the drawing of a comparison between societies that seem to be distinct and different in character and 'style' from each other, yet, at the same time, seem to be representatives of one and the same species. As an instrument for study, the Hellenic Civilization has a second point in its favour besides the primary point of not being the Western student's native society. Unlike the Western Civilization the Hellenic is no longer in existence. So the whole of its history is known to us, more or less, from beginning to end; and, if it is a drama, and if this drama has a plot, we shall not be debarred from unravelling the plot by being unable to witness the performance of the closing acts. In our interpretation we may, of course, go astray; there will probably be more interpretations than one in the field, and judgements between them are unlikely to be definitive. But at any rate the whole story is on record, for us to make of it what we can. By contrast, the drama of the Western Civilization is still being played. We do not know what ending it is going to have. We do not even know that it is going to come to an end, if I am right in my contention[2] that, unlike organisms, institutions have no inexorable maximum span of duration. Nor do we know how the acts of this Western drama that have already been played by our time will look, in retrospect, to Western and non-Western eyes at successive dates in the future. In fact, there are so many open questions

charitable Indian religions and philosophies, came from 'the Orient' in the ordinary meaning of the term. My second plea is a serious one. If I have learnt from 'the Orient' the lesson of charity, that is a great lesson to have learnt from this source (vide Saint Paul on this subject). I myself should say that the most unfortunate single effect on my outlook that has come from my having remained a prisoner of my Christian upbringing is that I have hitherto seen Judaism almost entirely through Christian eyes (see p. 596, with footnotes 3–6, and p. 597, with footnote 1).

[1] This conviction of mine, too, is controversial. Geyl, for instance, feels that Toynbee's 'ostentation of detachment from his own heritage' is 'prideful', 'sinful', and 'ridiculous' (Toynbee and History, p. 368).

[2] See pp. 268–9.

about a specimen that is incomplete that its usefulness for purposes of study is restricted. The completeness of the Hellenic specimen of the species 'civilizations' is one of this specimen's most valuable properties.

Its value can be measured by the importance of the contribution to an understanding of human affairs that Vico was able to make by using the Hellenic Civilization as his key. It is true that he was a man of genius. Still, he had a knowledge of only two civilizations at his command, his own and the Hellenic, and, of these two, one, his own, was an incomplete specimen, as we have just noticed. Yet, by comparing this with the Hellenic, he succeeded in bringing to light the cyclic rhythm in the course of history in the Age of the Civilizations. One may not accept the thesis that this cyclic movement is the whole movement. One may hold, as I hold in company with many other inquirers, that the cyclic movement does not account for all the phenomena. But it would be hard to demonstrate that, short of accounting for everything, it is not at least a very important element in human affairs. And a comparison between two terms, one of which was the history of the Hellenic Civilization, was the operation by which Vico arrived at his illuminating results.

Since Vico's time the number of the specimens at the disposal of a Westerner for making a comparative study of civilizations has been considerably increased—partly through progress in Western knowledge of the cultures and histories of the surviving non-Western civilizations, and partly through the wonderful achievements of Western archaeologists in disinterring the material relics of defunct civilizations whose former existence had been almost or even quite forgotten. This increase in the quantity of relevant phenomena within a Western inquirer's knowledge has raised a number of new questions. How many specimens of the species 'civilizations' have now come within the observer's field of vision? On what criterion are we to establish which of these newly discovered entities is entitled to rank as a civilization? On what criterion, again, are we to demarcate them from each other? If a Western inquirer is exercised by these questions, his knowledge of the Hellenic Civilization places in his hand an exploratory—or, in the logicians' language, 'heuristic'—tool. He can take the Hellenic Civilization as a provisional 'model' of what a complete specimen of the species 'civilizations' might be expected to be. Since the species is a hypothetical construction based on the observation that the Hellenic and the Western Society exhibit an impressive number of common features, it follows, *ex hypothesi*, that any other society that resembles one or other or both of these prototypes, to the extent, more or less, of their resemblance to each other, can be recognized as being an additional specimen, and, in consequence, also an additional indication of the usefulness of the exploratory hypothesis.

Of course, the number of specimens identified and accredited in this way will not necessarily exhaust the list. The Hellenic Civilization is a key that will not unlock all doors, and other tools can and should be used as alternatives where the Hellenic tool fails to do the job. In the earlier volumes of this book I myself have used the Hellenic key to the uttermost of its capacity and, as I have now come to think, beyond it. I have also neglected to try other keys where the Hellenic key has obviously not fitted the lock. These were faults, I confess, and in Chapter VI of this volume I have tried to take a first step towards correcting them. But a method is not discredited by a practitioner's faulty use of it. A 'model'[1] is a most effective tool if it is used skilfully and discriminatingly; and the Hellenic Civilization, which is the model readiest to the hand of a Western collector of other specimens of the same species, has been used recently, not only by me, in the present book, but by Spengler before and by Bagby since. Bagby uses as his model the completed history of the Hellenic Civilization, supplemented by the still continuing history of the Western;[2] and with this 'heuristic' instrument he identifies a pattern of the Hellenic-Western type in other civilizations. He finds this pattern strongly pronounced in the history of his Chinese and Indian civilizations,[3] and detects traces of it in most of the other civilizations[4] on his list of nine specimens of the species.

The Hellenic and Western pair of specimens can also be put to the further use of throwing light on the nature of the relations between civilizations; and this is a necessary part of any comprehensive study of human affairs. For civilizations are not in truth the windowless Leibnizian monads—each going its own way without influencing, or being influenced by, any of the others—that Spengler holds them to be. Encounters between civilizations that are contemporary with each other, and historical relations between civilizations of different dates, are as prominent and important features of human history in the Age of the Civilizations as the likenesses and differences between civilizations regarded as being so many specimens of one species. While a comparative study of the histories and 'styles' of civilizations can take its start in a comparison of the Western Civilization with the Hellenic, a study of the historical relations between civilizations of different dates can take its start in an examination of the historical relation in which the same two civilizations stand to each other. At the beginning of this book, I took the historical relation between the Western and the Hellenic Civilization as a 'model' for the historical inquiry, and the likenesses and differences between them as a 'model' for the comparative one. Looking back at my use of the historical 'model', I now think that I made the same mistake with it that I made with the typological 'model' for comparative study: I overworked it. But I still think that it is good for some work—good, in fact, for the important work of studying the historical relation between civilizations of different dates.

These considerations confirm my belief that a knowledge of the Hellenic Civilization is a valuable tool in a Western inquirer's hands for exploring two of the principal fields that have to be explored in a comprehensive study of human affairs. This tool's value has, in fact, received recognition in the practical form of employment. It has been employed, for instance, by three inquirers whom I have mentioned—Vico, Spengler, and Bagby—besides myself. Its employment by Vico and by me might not seem to have much significance if it had not also been employed by the other two. Vico and I both had the same fifteenth-century Italian classical education, and our use of the Hellenic Civilization, up to the hilt, might be dismissed with the cutting remark that this was, after all, the only tool that these two poor creatures had.[1] But this is not true of either Spengler or Bagby. Neither of these two inquirers, I believe, was brought up almost exclusively on the Greek and Latin classics, as Vico and I were. Spengler was a mathematician; Bagby puts his trust in anthropology. All the same, they, too, have both made use of the Hellenic Civilization, and, more than that, have used it, as Vico and I have, as their key-tool. That must surely mean that it is a tool of obvious value, and this, again, must mean that a classical education is something worth having.

(ii) *Unfortunate Effects*

(a) *Effects on my Writing of English*

I have, I hope, now convincingly made my point that a classical education has much to be said for it, and this both in general and for the particular purpose of trying to make a comprehensive study of human affairs. Since, however, this happens to be the kind of education that I myself have received, I must not blow its trumpet without also dwelling on some of the unfortunate effects that it has had for me. I am aware of these unfortunate effects—partly thanks to my critics' strictures on them. These reflect, of course, on me, and not on the classical kind of education; for many people have been drilled in this as thoroughly as I have been without taking the harm from it that I have taken.

For example, I have allowed my classical education in the Greek and Latin languages to have an unfortunate effect on the style in which I write my English mother-tongue. I often fall into writing English clumsily. A number of critics have castigated this in sharper words,[2]

---

[1] If I needed consolation for the hard words that Bagby uses in his critique of my work, I should find it in his treatment of Vico. 'In 1725 . . . Giambattista Vico, a half-educated Neapolitan literary hack, published the first version of his *Scienza Nuova*, which prefigures in a confused and ungrammatical manner many aspects of nineteenth-century historical thought' (P. Bagby: *Culture and History*, p. 12). If one is put in the stocks, it is indeed consoling to find oneself neck-and-neck with Vico there. This makes it an honour to be treated to the punishment. Companionship in the stocks becomes fellowship in a distinguished academy.

[2] See, for example, Sir Ernest Barker in *Toynbee and History*, pp. 93 and 97; P. Bagby, ibid., p. 109; A. J. P. Taylor, ibid., p. 116; H. Kohn, ibid., p. 351, and in *Der Monat*, August, 1955, p. 465 (Kohn kindly uses the gentle words 'old-fashioned' and 'ornamental'); J. F. Leddy in *The Phoenix*, vol. 11, No. 4 (1957), p. 140; A. Hourani in *The Dublin Review*, vol. 229, No. 470 (December, 1955), p. 388; F. Neilson in *The American Journal of Economics and Sociology*, Supplement to vol. 14, No. 3 (April, 1955), p. 48; C. B. Joynt in *The Australasian Journal of Philosophy*, vol. 34, No. 3 (December, 1956), p. 193; J. M. T. in *The Oxford Magazine*, 28th October, 1954; C. Poore in *The New York Times*, 17th October, 1954; W. O. Ault in *The Journal of Bible and Religion*, April, 1955, pp. 119–23.

Unfavourable judgements are partially offset by others. For instance, in *The Times Literary Supplement* of 17th August, 1956, a writer who comes down on the unfavourable side does also find some points in favour of my way of writing; and this is actually praised by some critics: e.g. F. J. Teggart in a letter to me of 8th January, 1936; F. L. Schuman in *The Nation*, 6th November, 1954; G. Mann in *Der Monat*, Jahrgang 1, Heft 4 (January, 1949), pp. 34–40; M. Savelle in *The Pacific Historical Review*, vol. xxv, No. 1 (February, 1956), pp. 55–67; T. A. Sumberg in *Social Research*, vol. 14, No. 3 (September, 1947), pp. 267–84; P. M .Sweezy in *The Nation*, 19th October, 1946; W. F.

and one of them, Sir Ernest Barker, has also given the correct diagnosis of the malady. He traces it to the effects of my classical education. I write English, he justly says, in a Ciceronian style, as if it were a foreign language. The stuff calls for a literary surgeon's knife to 'break up and rewrite the long rolling cryptic sentences' and cut out 'the ornate alias',[1] to chasten the metaphors, to prune the analogies.[2] The reviewer in *The Oxford Magazine* wittily remarks that I have 'never felt obliged to use one word if two would do'. The writer in *The Times Literary Supplement* who kindly credits me with a 'mastery over words' expressed 'in a clear prose of the most pliable steel', also justly debits me with 'another style . . . encumbered by its own wealth, like a man who loads himself with souvenirs from every resort he ever visited'.

'There are times [this writer finds] when the long sentences—every adjective and adverb inserted, all loopholes stopped up, and nothing left to the imagination—would clog the mind even if they were not further burdened with cumbrous Latinisations.'

Barker points out that this particular unfortunate result of a classical education is not universal and is therefore not inevitable. He cites his own case as an instance. He has had the same classical education that I have had, without succumbing to this malady; and this is true. If one's automatic reaction to an inoculation is excessive, that is one's own lookout. If one's error is only partly involuntary, and is partly the result of an irrational prejudice, one is still more to blame. But the question of culpability is beside the point. The point is that language is not a private plaything. It is a means of communication or nothing. A writer must write in the language that is current among the public that he wishes to reach; and, in writing this language, he must follow the usual practice of his and his readers' day. He writes in order to be read, and, in his encounter with his reader, the reader has the last word. At any moment the reader can stop reading if he wishes, but the writer can never stop wishing to have readers. If he were to become indifferent to his book's being read, this would make nonsense of his whole activity, and he would have done better if he had never put pen to paper. So, if he falls into writing in a style which is alien to the genius of his linguistic medium, or which, short of that, is noticeably discordant with ordinary current usage, he stands to lose more by his personal peculiarity than

---

Albright in *The Evening Sun* of Baltimore, 14th October, 1954, and in *From the Stone Age to Christianity*, 2nd ed., p. 97; F. H. Underhill in *The Canadian Historical Review*, vol. xxxii, No. 3 (September, 1951), pp. 201–19.
     I am very grateful to these favourable critics—the more so because I am not one of them myself.
     G. Mann observes, in *Der Monat*, Jahrgang 1, Heft 4 (January, 1949), pp. 34–40, that it is the literary qualities of my work—e.g. a gift for describing, illustrating, and quoting aptly—that have won an entry for my ideas among 'the broad masses'. Mann remarks that what seems to the masses to be a merit is decidedly a defect in the eyes of the scientific world. In Mann's own opinion my method is, in truth, not altogether satisfactory from a scientific point of view. E. Fiess, in *Toynbee and History*, pp. 381–2, credits me with 'ability to use words evocatively', but notes that 'an unwitting simplification may thus creep in'. Fiess examines judiciously the case for and against my long sentences, my key words, and the allusiveness of my style.
     [1] Sir Ernest Barker in *Toynbee and History*, p. 93.
     [2] Ibid., p. 97.

his reader does. The reader who finds his style difficult, or just irritating, has an easy remedy. He can put the book down and pick up another written in a more congenial style by a different author. But the price that the irritating author may have to pay for having indulged his literary eccentricity is to frustrate himself by defeating his own purposes. He will certainly reduce the number of his readers.

Here is an effect of a classical education that has been an unfortunate one for me. My Latinizing way of writing English is not, of course, deliberate. It is the unintended result of many hours spent, at an impressionable age, on writing Latin prose. But, as far as I have become conscious of this fault, I have, I think, been partly inhibited from correcting it by a distaste for the vernacular languages of the Western World which is also the result of a classical education. This is partly a classical scholar's irrational prejudice. I have been educated into seeing in French a vulgar deformation of Latin, and in English a barbarous substitute for it. But I also have a rational ground for finding these Western vernaculars inferior to Latin and Attic Greek, and also to Pre-Atatürk Ottoman Turkish (of which I have a smattering).

The grammar and the syntax of these three languages work together not only to allow, but to demand, a style that leaves the reader in no doubt about the logical connexion between the words and phrases in which the writer is addressing him. A writer employing such logical linguistic media as these can and should bring out clearly the distinction between subordinate clauses and the main clause on which they logically depend. And, if it is Latin or Attic Greek that he is writing, he also can and should link sentence to sentence by conjunctions expressing precise and finely differentiated logical relations. If one has been brought up on languages of this kind, and on the highly articulated structural style that comes natural to him when he writes in them, he will feel that the Western vernaculars, and the style in which, nowadays, they are usually written, are inferior inasmuch as they throw upon the reader the work of establishing the logical relations that it is the writer's business to indicate. And it is true that the natural style in these languages, in contrast to Attic Greek and Latin, is an uncoordinated series of short indicative sentences, linked together, if at all, by conjunctions with only vague and ambiguous logical connotations. It is also true, however, that this staccato style is not just a symptom of degeneracy and perversity. It, too, has its reason. Its first objective is simplicity, and it achieves this at the price of sacrificing logical clarity. The classically educated reader and writer are apt to overlook this valuable virtue of the loose-jointed vernacular style's obvious defects. On the other hand, a master of the vernacular style finds the integrated classical style clumsy even when the medium is an integrated language, and he finds it grotesque when a contemporary employs it, as I have done, in writing one of the current vernaculars.

Considering how much of the literature of the Western Civilization was written in Latin down to the fifteenth century, it is not surprising that the early modern writers in the vernaculars should have continued to employ the classical style, inappropriate though this was to their new linguistic medium. But the impossibility of writing English satisfactorily in this style has been demonstrated, once for all, by the contrast between Milton's magnificent failure as a writer of prose and Dryden's adroit success. Dryden was not gifted with Milton's genius, but he had the sense to realize what could and could not be done with the English language, and to adapt his own style to the medium in which he and Milton both had to work. Subsequent writers of English have no excuse for not heeding this warning example. Where Milton failed, how can they expect to succeed? We have to take our linguistic medium as we find it. To apply the point *ad hominem*, the accident of my birthplace and cultural milieu has given me the English language for my mother-tongue; and it is my good fortune that this language, which I have never had to learn artificially, happens to be today the mother-tongue of many nations besides my own, and also to be a lingua franca of almost world-wide currency. So I must write in English, and therefore should try to write it in the style that is demanded by the language's genius and is prescribed by current usage.

I have found this difficult because I have had a classical education in Greek and Latin. Having been educated in this way, I should feel more at home if Greek and Latin were the media of communication between me and my public. It is a reflection on a classical education, as well as on one particular recipient of it, that it should have educated me into putting myself out of tune with my mother-tongue and, in consequence, also, to some extent, with the public among whom I hope to find readers.

(b) Effects on the Range of my Knowledge

In a criticism of me for my treatment of Judaism, Berkovitz remarks[1] that 'the friendliest thing one may say about him is that he is an ignoramus'. This may be friendly, but unfortunately it is not illuminating, because a state of general ignorance is not particularly distinctive either of me or of anyone else in the present-day world. Here and now, in fact, everybody is an ignoramus if his personal range of knowledge is measured against the total pool of knowledge on which he could draw if he had the capacity.[2] The pertinent question is how far his particular educational equipment falls short of what is required for the particular enterprise on which he is engaged. *Ad hominem* the question is how far my own equipment falls short of what is required for trying to make a comprehensive study of the morphology of human affairs.[3] It goes without

---

[1] E. Berkovitz: *Judaism: Fossil or Ferment?*, p. 42.
[2] See Chapter IV, pp. 105–6.
[3] A catalogue of points in which he finds me ignorant is given by the late Professor D. M. Robinson in *The Intent of Toynbee's History: A Cooperative Appraisal*. A number of Robinson's shots hit the mark, but the percentage of misses is high enough to make it necessary for me to ask readers of this passage not to take Robinson's statements on trust without verifying them for themselves. They can do this by consulting my wife's admirable indexes to this book, without having to read the text.

For instance, Robinson says that 'Sparta is in the main sadly ignored' (op. cit.). Yet in volume iii there is a chapter on Sparta that runs to 29 pages (iii. 50–79). In my wife's index to vols. i–iii the entry 'Sparta' occupies more than 11 inches of a column; in her index to vols. iv–vi the corresponding entry occupies more than three and a half inches, with cross-references to Agis IV (two inches) and Cleomenes III

saying, of course, that, if the study is to be comprehensive, it must be panoramic, not microscopic, in its mental scale. A comprehensive study of the morphology of human affairs in detail has come, for the reasons considered in Chapter IV, to be an enterprise quite beyond the powers of any individual mind today. Nothing short of a third world war fought with atomic weapons could conceivably reduce our present vast common store of knowledge to the manageable proportions that would make relative omniscience possible, once again, for some future Bede or Alcuin in a re-barbarized Post-Western World.

Looking, from this point of view, at my own range of knowledge, I am ruefully aware that my classical education has left me almost entirely ignorant of modern Western discoveries, from the seventeenth century onwards, in the fields of mathematics and physical science. This is indeed a big blank. Yet I do not think that my education, in leaving this great gap in my knowledge, has thereby crippled me for attempting my particular enterprise. It is true that this personal ignorance about some of the characteristic achievements of the Western Civilization in its modern age is a serious handicap to an understanding of the Western Society's modern genius.[1] But, after all, the Western Civilization is only one of a number of specimens of the species of society that it represents; and, as we have seen,[2] it is an imperfect specimen in the sense that its history is still unfinished. At a pinch, therefore, we could dispense with this Western specimen in making a comparative study of civilizations. At any rate, an ignorance of even an important aspect of the Western Civilization is not fatal for inquiring into the morphology of the civilizations as a class. The intellectual equipment that is indispensable for this enterprise is a knowledge of at least the salient features of as many as possible of the known civilizations

(three and a half inches). In the index to vols. vii–x the corresponding entry occupies nearly two and a half inches.

Other inaccuracies in Robinson's catalogue are noted in the present volume, on p. 599, footnote 1, and p. 600, footnote 1.

In self-defence, I have to point these inaccuracies out, though I feel rueful about having to do this when Robinson is no longer in this world to stand up for himself. His misses illustrate the same general point as his hits. The point is that no human mind is impeccable, not even the mind of the finest scholar—and Robinson was a very fine one.

[1] This point is made by J. K. Feibleman in *T'ien Hsia Monthly*, vol. xi, Nos. 1 and 2 (1940), p. 155. Chr. Hill notes that I tend to 'treat as of secondary importance the sort of progress which is reflected in technique and economic production, and to regard all civilizations as "philosophically contemporaneous". He [Toynbee] approaches "Western Christendom" of the last 1000 years as a single civilisation: the technical and economic transformation of mediaeval society by the rise of capitalism is regarded as of secondary importance' (*The Modern Quarterly*, Autumn, 1947, p. 293). F. H. Underhill traces this outlook of mine back to the effect on me of a classical education. 'While Toynbee's mastery of the Oxford "Greats" [i.e. *Literae Humaniores*] discipline gave him great advantages as a student of world history, it also made him liable to certain shortcomings. "Greats" is a purely literary discipline; the students learn little about Greek science and nothing about modern science. More than one critic has remarked on Toynbee's blindness to what science has achieved in our modern world and to the difference that this makes between us and all other civilizations. . . . Toynbee seems to me to brush aside much too easily any adequate consideration of the relation between technological progress and the growth of a civilization' (*The Canadian Historical Review*, vol. xxxii, No. 3 (September, 1951), pp. 201–19). References to some of the critics whom Underhill has in mind will be found on p. 600, footnote 2.

F. Borkenau discerns a turn of the tide of public feeling in the West against technology, as one of the reactions to the invention of the atomic weapon (*Merkur*, July, 1949, p. 625). [2] On pp. 584–5.

that have already run their course. This is the province of knowledge on which I have concentrated my efforts since the end of my formal education in the Greek and Latin languages and literature.

This formal education, which I was given intensively over a period of fifteen years, has equipped me with a certain knowledge and understanding of one civilization, the Hellenic. It has also set me a standard to aim at in trying, under my own steam, to continue my education and to extend its range during these last fifty years.[1] In a busy working life, in which the first call on one's energies is the need to earn a living for one's family and for oneself, the governing factor in one's course of adult self-education is one's choice of priorities in laying out the use of a limited amount of spare working-time. The choice that one makes is not, of course, entirely planned and deliberate. It is partly determined by intellectual interests and preferences for which one can give no rational explanation. As far, however, as I have worked on a deliberate plan, I have given priority to trying to learn as much as possible about as many as possible of the other societies, living or 'dead', of the species of which the Hellenic Society has been the prototype for me.[2]

A study of the Hellenic Civilization leads one on, of itself, as I have noticed in this chapter already,[3] to a study of two living civilizations, the Byzantine and the Islamic. A knowledge of Attic Greek, in the form in which it became the lingua franca (*koinê*) of the whole Hellenic World, makes accessible the medieval Byzantine literature in this language, and also makes it easy to pick up a knowledge of Modern Greek in its colloquial form and, still more, in its rather artificial literary one. As for Arabic, Persian, and Turkish, it has been my ambition, from an early age, to make myself as much at home in these three leading languages of the Islamic World as I am in Attic Greek and in Latin. But I have not found time to achieve this ambition so far; and, in this book, I have had to deal with the Islamic Civilization as best I could with only a smattering of Arabic and Ottoman Turkish and not even that minimum acquaintance with Modern Persian. Of these three languages, I have given the lowest priority to Persian for the same reason that has made me try to learn something about the Byzantine Civilization in Russia without having learnt Russian, and something about the civilizations of India without having learnt Sanskrit. Persian, Russian, and Sanskrit are languages of the Indo-European family to which Greek, Latin, English, and nearly all the living vernaculars of the Western World, besides English, belong. So, for a classically educated Englishman, the

---

[1] A. N. Holcombe notices (in *The American Political Science Review*, vol. xlix, No. 4 (December, 1955), pp. 1151–4) that I have not succeeded in teaching myself as much about any other civilization as I was taught about the Hellenic at school and at the university.

[2] Bagby, who divides his list of civilizations into a 'major' and a 'secondary' class, remarks, in *Culture and History*, p. 179, that I mention no more than two or three of his 'secondary' civilizations, and he wonders whether I am ignorant of the existence of the rest or have included them as parts of other civilizations on my list. The second of these two alternatives that he allows me hits the truth. My list of civilizations does not coincide with Bagby's list. But, whereas Bagby seems to be struck by the points in which the two lists disagree, I am struck by the points in which they correspond with each other. In revising my own list in this volume, I have introduced a 'satellite' class of civilizations. 'Satellite' seems to me to be a less subjective notion than 'secondary' (see pp. 551–3).

[3] On pp. 582–3.

acquisition of yet another Indo-European language does not hold any great promise of widening his linguistic horizon. By contrast, even the slight acquaintance with Arabic and Turkish that I have gained has been, for me, an invaluable asset because it has given me a glimpse of two non-Indo-European linguistic worlds, the Semitic and the Ural-Altaic, in which the structure of the languages, and to some extent also the psychology that this structure reflects, are different from anything within the experience of someone whose mother-tongue is an Indo-European one and who has not broken out of the wide bounds of the Indo-European family.

Thanks to the marvellous work done by Western archaeologists in Egypt, South-West Asia, and the Aegean since the French invasion of Egypt in A.D. 1798, a knowledge of the Hellenic Civilization now leads, not only forwards in time to a study of the Byzantine and Islamic civilizations, but also backwards to a rediscovery of temporarily forgotten civilizations in the Hellenic Civilization's historical background. The Minoan-Helladic-Mycenaean Civilization in the Aegean, which is the Hellenic Civilization's direct predecessor, has been rediscovered almost within my lifetime. The most recent outstanding achievement in this exciting series—Ventris's decipherment of the Minoan linear script 'B' and demonstration that the language conveyed in it is Greek— was made in 1952. This resurrection of the Pre-Hellenic past in the Hellenic Civilization's homeland is bound to be enthralling for a contemporary Hellenist, especially if he is interested in the Hellenic Civilization as being a prototype of one kind of society, and is on the look-out for other representatives of this. He is also bound to be interested in the Minoan-Helladic-Mycenaean Civilization's older, and earlier rediscovered, contemporaries in Egypt and 'Iraq (labelled 'Egyptiac' and 'Sumero-Akkadian' in my revised list of civilizations), and its younger contemporary in Anatolia (the 'Hittite' Civilization). In 1911–12 I was in Greece for ten months as a student of the British School at Athens. It is true that I spent all my time during that stay in walking about the country. I have never taken part in an archaeological excavation or learnt, by practising it, the archaeologist's swiftly developing technique. I have not mastered any of the temporarily forgotten scripts, languages, and literatures that the archaeologists have rediscovered and deciphered.[1] But, at second-hand, I have been an eager student of the additions that the archaeologists have made to our fund of knowledge. In pursuing civilizations backward in time beyond the point at which literary records begin, an inquirer ascends a trail that has been blazed for him by the archaeologists, and by them alone, in the huge dark forest of oblivion. An archaeologically uninstructed explorer of the comparative study of civilizations could not do without the precious additional specimens that the archaeologists have added to his collection.[2]

---

[1] Eduard Meyer was perhaps the last historian who was able, at least in some measure, to deal at first hand with original texts in Ancient Egyptian and in Akkadian, as well as in Greek and Latin. Meyer's example proves that this intellectual feat is possible, but I have found it beyond my strength.

[2] Bagby truly says that the distinction between history and archaeology 'is essentially one of technique rather than subject-matter; the historian digs in the archives and the

My own feeling towards the archaeologists is one of gratitude as well as admiration.[1]

The conventional single-track diagram of history makes it all lead up to the observer's own time and place, and the Western variant of this scheme arrives at its own self-centred goal by making a succession of arbitrary side-steps in a westward direction: from 'Iraq and Egypt to the Aegean; from the Aegean to Italy; from Italy to Transalpine Western Europe; and thence to the Americas in the Post-Columbian Age. A Western explorer of the comparative study of civilizations has therefore to lean over eastwards in order to correct his own society's westward *penchant*. If he fails to make this readjustment of the conventional Western stance, he will be turning a blind eye to one half of the *Oikoumenê*; and this wilful blindness will halve, for him, the number of the civilizations that should have been within his ken. Since the rise of the civilizations of the earliest generation, some five thousand years ago, in the waist of the Old World, where the Red Sea and the Persian Gulf of the Indian Ocean all but touch the Mediterranean inlet of the Atlantic, civilization has fanned out symmetrically in both directions, eastward as well as westward. I have therefore made an effort to gain some foothold in the history and archaeology of the eastern wing of the *Oikoumenê*: that is, India, Eastern Asia, and Pre-Columbian Nuclear America, east of the Pacific. In this area I have deliberately neglected Sanskrit, have looked longingly at Pali (the vehicle of the Hinayana Buddhist scriptures), and have not dared to dream of memorizing Chinese characters. And in this area, too, I have been greatly beholden to the archaeologists, as far as an amateur can profit by their work. Here, again, within my own lifetime, they have lengthened the range of our vision of the past in India and in China by disinterring relics of the Indus Culture and the Shang Culture. As for the civilizations of the Andes and Middle America, with their satellites in what are now Colombia, Northern Chile, North-Western Argentina, and the south-western and south-east-central sections of the United States, we are indebted to the archaeologists for the whole of our knowledge, except for Spanish records of the phases during and immediately preceding the Spanish Conquest.

The two major Pre-Columbian civilizations in the Americas are, of course, particularly valuable for a comparative study of civilizations because of their separateness from the civilizations of the Old World. Whatever may be the final verdict on the alleged Pre-Columbian contacts, made perhaps from both directions, between the civilizations of the

archaeologist in the soil, but both are concerned with what happened to large groups of men and what they did in the past' (*Culture and History*, p. 28).

[1] Laurence Stone says (in *Toynbee and History*, p. 112) that in this book I have used little archaeological material dating from later than 1920. This may be partially true of vols. i–iii, which were started in 1930 and published in 1934. But it is certainly not true of vols. vii–x, which were published in 1954. Most of my references to articles in archaeological journals are, naturally, to be found in annexes in which I deal in detail with particular topics. If Stone had looked at the Annex on the Achaemenian Empire in vii. 580–689, or at the piece on chronology in x. 167–212, he would have found that here I have cited papers published up to the moment before I went to press, and that, while writing these pieces, I have been in personal communication with specialists who were working on the subjects at the time.

two hemispheres, it seems already to be established that these contacts were not factors of first-class importance in the history of either group. In essentials each of the two groups went through the processes of genesis, growth, breakdown, and disintegration independently of the other.[1]

I have also tried to learn something about the Nomadic Civilization, which has lived in a symbiosis with the sedentary civilizations of the Old World from its rise, early in the second millennium B.C., down to its virtual suppression within the last two centuries. My main effort in my course of self-education has, in fact, been put into a study of Man's attempts, within the last 5,000 years, to rise above the level of pre-civilizational culture. Besides trying to make a panoramic study of as many specimens of the species 'civilization' as I could identify and handle, I have tried to do the same with the philosophies and the 'higher religions' that have made their appearance in and since the last millennium B.C., during the time when the civilizations of the second generation were disintegrating. This may read like a recital of efforts to extend my knowledge over a range that would be more or less commensurate with the enterprise on which I have embarked. But, for me, it is a reminder of how far I have fallen short of my aim. I have not attained, in any non-Hellenic field, anything like the standard of knowledge and understanding that has been given to me in the Hellenic field by my old-fashioned Western 'classical' education. In my knowledge of the non-Hellenic civilizations and the higher religions there are appalling gaps. And my knowledge of the aeons of history before these last 5,000 years is little better than sheer ignorance. A recital of some blank patches that are conspicuous to me will bring out some of my limitations. There will, no doubt, be others to which I am blind but which are no less conspicuous to my critics.

In my study of civilizations and higher religions I am acutely conscious of three dim spots and of one general shortcoming.

One of these dim spots is my neglect of the civilization in which I myself have been brought up. This neglect has been partly deliberate, and for this I have had three reasons. The first reason (mentioned already) is that the Western Civilization is an imperfect specimen of its species because its history is still unfinished. Then, as far as I do want to know about the Western Civilization, I feel that I can imbibe this knowledge through my pores, since, after all, this is the cultural atmosphere in which I live and move. My classical education has not made me immune to my Western cultural environment. It has not been as effective as all that. My third reason for deliberately neglecting the West is that the historical and sociological information about the West is voluminous out of all proportion to its value for a comparative study of civilizations. The bulk of it consists of details that, for my purpose, are not very significant or illuminating. If I were to plunge into this ocean of non-significant detail I might find myself unable to get my head above water again for the rest of my working life. These seem to me to be three rational grounds for treating the West rather cavalierly if one

[1] See Chapters X and XI, pp. 357–75.

is trying to make a comprehensive study of the morphology of human affairs. But I have also to confess to an irrational reaction to which I refer again at a later point in this chapter.[1] The West's self-adulation in modern times—since about the end of the seventeenth century—provokes me into depreciating the West emotionally some degrees below my rational appraisal of its peculiar defects and peculiar merits.

A second dim spot, of which I am aware, is my neglect of Israel, Judah, the Jews, and Judaism. I have neglected these out of proportion to their true importance. Judaism is one of half-a-dozen living higher religions, and two of the others, Christianity and Islam, are, in origin, denationalized versions of it.[2] When Jewish critics accuse me of seeing Judaism, not through Jewish eyes, but through those of the Christian Church, supplemented by Eduard Meyer's,[3] I have to plead guilty to the charge. Though my personal religious beliefs are, in some points, nearer to Judaism[4] than they are to orthodox Christianity, it is true that I have tended to see Judaism through Christian eyes in the sense that I have seen it, in the conventional Christian perspective, as a prelude to Christianity, and as one which rejected its manifest destiny when it repudiated the new religious insight or revelation to which it had been leading up.[5] A Christian or Muslim gentile ought, of course, to try to correct his sectarian prejudice by trying to reverse his stand and to look at his own religion through Jewish eyes. After this deflating exercise, he might find himself in a condition to look at Judaism through Jewish eyes as a phenomenon in itself, and one that would still have had the supreme value that it does have, even supposing that Christianity and Islam had never come into existence.

I am ignorant of the Rabbinical Jewish literature and of the Jewish philosophy that flourished in an early Islamic and a medieval Western cultural environment.[6] I know the Pharisees, not through their own writings, but through the denunciations of them in the Gospels (de-

---

[1] On pp. 626–30.　　　　　　　　　　　　　　　[2] See pp. 87–88 and 511–17.
[3] 'A man whose only sources on Judaism are the New Testament and Eduard Meyer' (E. Berkovitz: *Judaism: Fossil or Ferment?*, p. 41).

[4] I am particularly grateful to Rabbi J. B. Agus for his testimony on this point. 'Seen in the light of the essential ideas of Judaism, his philosophy of history', Rabbi Agus says, referring to mine, 'is in line with the genuine impetus of the Hebrew prophets and of the master-builders of the Talmud. . . . In the most profound and real sense, Toynbee's main theses are faithful to the spirit of our Holy Scriptures and to the spiritual genius of Judaism' (Rabbi J. B. Agus in *Judaism*, vol. 4, No. 4 (Fall, 1955), pp. 219 and 329).

[5] 'All readers of Toynbee's work are impressed by the strong Christian bias. . . . Though he repudiates fundamentalism with the utmost scorn, he clings to the dogmatic view that the emergence of Christianity has rendered Judaism superfluous' (Agus in loc. cit., p. 319. Cp. Berkovitz, op. cit., pp. 10 and 13; M. Samuel: *The Professor and the Fossil*, pp. 72 and 104–5). In another place (*The National Jewish Monthly*, November, 1956, pp. 43–44) Rabbi Agus points out that, 'similarly, we who are non-Orthodox and therefore also non-fundamentalist, operate with the symbols and mode of thought of the Jewish tradition'. 'Failure to take account of the categories of thought of the non-Jewish World is one of the enduring factors in Jewish history, resulting in tragedies that were manifestly avoidable' (*Judaism*, Winter, 1956, p. 45). Agus's conclusion is an admirable one. 'Identity of approach is out of the question, but we can learn from one another if we continue to converse agreeably and with mutual respect. . . . There is . . . need for a continuous conversation to be carried on between the representatives of the two traditions, for their mutual benefit and enlightenment' (*The National Jewish Monthly*, November, 1956, pp. 43–44).

[6] Samuel points out, in op. cit., pp. 22–23, that I do not mention the Talmud, the Mishnah, the Midrashim, or any Jewish philosopher—not even Spinoza.

nunciations that are echoes of a family quarrel within the bosom of the Jewish fraternity).[1] Worst of all, I have never learnt even a smattering of Hebrew. Since childhood, Hebrew has left me cold, whereas I have had a passionate desire to learn Arabic. This partiality is evidently irrational; for a knowledge of either of these two Semitic languages would have had the same liberating effect on a mind imprisoned in an Indo-European mother-tongue, and both languages alike open the door to a first-hand acquaintance with a great literature. A Jewish critic might jump to the conclusion that this coldness towards the Hebrew language was the effect of anti-Semitic or anti-Zionist feelings. But it dates back in me to a time before Zionism had become practical politics, and, though I am opposed to Zionism (identifying it, as I do, with Western nationalism and colonialism),[2] I have never felt any inclination to be anti-Semitic.[3] There have always been more Jews than Arabs in my circle of friends— as was indeed to be expected, considering that my home has not been in Dar-al-Islam, and that in Christendom there is no Muslim diasporá comparable to the Jewish. So I cannot account for my acquiescence in this particular dim spot, but I am none the less conscious of its being there.

My third dim spot in my study of civilizations is South-East Asia, continental and insular. This region has not been the birthplace of any independent civilization; but the Indian, Chinese, and Islamic civilizations have all radiated into it and have all undergone modifications there as a result of the experiences of displacement and of contact with the indigenous cultures and with each other. The South-East Asian modifications of the Indian and Chinese civilizations are perhaps sufficiently differentiated from the originals to warrant a classification of them as separate civilizations of the satellite kind.[4] I am only now beginning to enter this South-East Asian field. Except for having made the sea-passage through the Straits of Malacca in 1929, I did not find an opportunity of visiting either Indonesia or continental South-East Asia till 1956. As a matter of fact it might have been difficult to obtain anything like a true picture of South-East Asian history and culture at an earlier date than now; for South-East Asia, like Nuclear America, is an area in which the progress of archaeological discovery has only lately reached a point at which the picture revealed by it is beginning to come into focus.

[1] The following points about the Pharisees are made, among others, by Berkovitz in op. cit. The Pharisees were the Jewish community's 'creative minority' (p. 116). 'They were lay teachers and lay preachers' (p. 117). 'Some of the publicans might well have followed Jesus; the people followed the Pharisees' (p. 117). 'The Pharisees' greatest achievement was that their people followed them' (p. 123). Before the appearance of Christianity, the Pharisees had solved the problem of the spirit and the letter (p. 117). The concept of the fatherhood of God is a Pharisee insight (pp. 58–60). *Ad hominem*, Toynbee is a Pharisee without knowing it (p. 73).
   Samuel, in op. cit., makes the point that 'the Pharisees were the heirs of the Prophets' (p. 88). He asks: 'Why does Professor Toynbee take the denunciations of the Gospels literally, and those of the Prophets metaphorically?' (pp. 92–93).
   Klausner's recognition that all the logia attributed to Jesus appear in the rabbinical literature too has been cited in footnote 2 to p. 87.   [2] See pp. 627–8.
   [3] I am particularly grateful to Rabbi J. B. Agus for testifying that I am 'most certainly not' an anti-Semite (*The Jewish National Monthly*, November, 1956, p. 43).
   [4] See p. 552 and the chart on p. 559.

The general shortcoming in my study of the civilizations is, I should judge, a more serious weakness than any particular dim spot. In my attempt to explore their morphology I have taken too little note of some of the threads that weave the ever-changing pattern of a culture, and I have therefore made little contribution, so far, towards helping to bring to light either the distinctive cultural patterns or 'styles' of particular civilizations[1] or the common pattern, if there is one, on which the individual patterns of particular cultures, and the specific pattern of each of the species of culture, are so many variations.

My first concern has been to explore the uniformities that come to light when one takes a synoptic view of the histories of a number of different civilizations,[2] and this primary aim—abetted, no doubt, by unconscious and unintentional partialities in the distribution of my interests and values—has led me to concentrate my attention on two, above all, of the several provinces of human activity and experience:

---

[1] A. L. Kroeber comments, in *Style and Civilizations*, p. 120: 'The culture itself, as something substantive, is hardly examined by Toynbee except incidentally; its specific quality is scarcely portrayed; least of all is it viewed as a style or possible assemblage of styles' (cp. ibid., p. 158). Toynbee 'did not really try to classify civilizations as cultures' (ibid., p. 125). 'His "civilizations" are societies, not cultures' (ibid., p. 126). 'The distinctive and differential qualities of his civilizations are largely missed or ignored' (ibid., p. 127). In Kroeber's view, the medium in which the style of an entire culture is expressed is usually psychological.

Kroeber also comments, in *The Nature of Culture*, pp. 330–1, that my delineation of cultures is based too much on events, too little on quality. I agree with the second of the two points made by Kroeber in this last cited passage, but not with the first. I do not think that, in human affairs, there is really an antithesis between 'quality' and 'events'. It is of the essence of human affairs that they are perpetually on the move. T. J. G. Locher is interpreting my view correctly when he says that my theory of growth is 'dynamic-ethical', not 'biological-static' (*De Gids*, May, 1948, offprint, p. 16). So, as I see it, the style of a civilization cannot be viewed realistically if it is not viewed as something that is changing all the time under our eyes. A. R. Burn makes the point that, 'to a great extent, societies can change as one unit', and that, consequently, 'their changes are, to this extent, *not* amenable to the statistical methods of prediction, employed by insurance companies, which Toynbee stresses. There is a field of study here', he adds, 'to which one would like to see much attention devoted in any future *Study of History*' (*History*, February–October, 1956, p. 13).

David Thomson comments that, in my work, 'civilizations are judged primarily in terms of their survival value and longevity, and hardly at all in terms of their quality or the height of their achievement' (*The Spectator*, 17th January, 1947). H. Werner finds that I am 'not a physiognomist' (*kein physiognomiker*); I have not got beyond mere description. I do not go into any structural problems. I do not make any attempt at a self-contained 'holistic' (*ganzheitliche*) interpretation of cultural phenomena. At the most I have a doctrine of culture-phases, but have no doctrine of culture-morphology. In short I have come to grief over the task of constructing a genuine morphology (*Deutsche Vierteljahrsschrift für Literaturwissenschaft und Geistesgeschichte*, No. 29 (1955), pp. 543–5). F. Borkenau finds that I do not make any serious attempt 'to discuss the specific characteristics of the various civilizations' (*Commentary*, March, 1956, pp. 240–1). In Trinkaus's view, 'Toynbee shrinks from a real analysis of social relations based on historical data' (*Science and Society*, vol. xxii, No. 1 (New York 1948), p. 229). I do not shrink from this; I just have not got round to it yet. I have a programme that has been keeping me on the run. But, whatever may be the cause of my being behindhand in this field, there seems to be a consensus that, here, Spengler is a long way ahead of me (see p. 601, footnote 1).

[2] In Trinkaus's view, as expounded in loc. cit., pp. 235–6, 'an alternative procedure . . . is to analyse the inner structure of a given civilization, or a sample one, in order to find the contrasts with other civilizations rather than similarities'. If one had analysed the structural and dynamic interrelations of the elements of a civilization in a number of different cases, one might then be able to arrive at 'a rank-ordering of their comparative value and sequential role in Man's development. The criterion employed would be the degree of realisation of the human potential in the widest number of men within the society.'

namely, changes in social structure[1] and changes in religious attitude. These two topics are, of course, both important, and they lie at opposite extremes of the cultural gamut. Social structure is the most external element in a human being's life; religion is the most intimate. The gamut, however, includes other notes besides these two, and the music of cultural life is a symphony in which all notes play some part. An eye for changes in social structure leads one to dwell on politics and war; an eye for changes in religious attitude leads one to dwell on psychological phenomena and spiritual experiences. I have dwelt on these two elements in culture[2] perhaps out of proportion to the attention that I

---

[1] F. Engel-Janosi points out, in *Wissenschaft und Weltbild*, 2. Jahrgang, Heft 4 (October, 1949), p. 270, that my kind of history approaches sociology. Other critics, however, have censured me for not having studied sociology and not having used the sociologists' method. H. E. Barnes finds that I do 'not possess the indispensable command of the techniques and subject matter of cultural anthropology, historical sociology, and social history' (*An Introduction to the History of Sociology*, p. 729) and that 'there is no indication that he is familiar with American sociological literature' (ibid., p. 724). D. G. Macrae finds that I have neglected or dealt very unsatisfactorily with the history of social organization (*The Literary Guide*, January, 1955, p. 14). Mumford notices my 'failure to recognise the important pioneer work, on parallel lines', of Sir Patrick Geddes. 'Toynbee never arrives at a theory of the city, such as Geddes brilliantly developed.' 'Toynbee unfortunately takes refuge mainly in a political and economic explanation of the rise of civilisations' (*The New Republic*, 27th November, 1935, p. 65). P. A. Sorokin (in *Toynbee and History*, pp. 178 and 189–90) points out my ignorance of sociological works, and suggests that, if I had studied Tarde on mimesis, I could have saved space and have avoided errors. My ignorance of Tarde's work is noticed by E. F. J. Zahn, too (in *Toynbee und das Problem der Geschichte*, p. 20). R. K. Merton detects that I have not read Pareto (*The American Journal of Sociology*, vol. xlvii, No. 2 (September, 1941), pp. 205–13). D. M. Robinson says that Toynbee 'neglects sociology, not even mentioning Durkheim, Max Weber, Boas, or Cole' (*The Intent of Toynbee's History: A Cooperative Appraisal*). If, before committing himself to this statement, Robinson had checked it by consulting my wife's index to vols. i–iii of this book, he would have found references there to both Cole and Boas. I not only cite them but quote passages from works of theirs. My two quotations from works of Cole's in these first three volumes contain statements of a point of capital importance for the study of human affairs: the point that societies are not organisms.

Postan's verdict on me is that, 'until he writes a work of sociology, he will not be able to rid himself of his vague images or to meet the challenge of his fruitful ones' (*The Sociological Review*, vol. xxviii, p. 63). In Postan's eyes the virtue of the sociological method is that it is microscopic. I have done some of this watchmaker's work in some of the annexes to the present book, and have found it fascinating. But it gives no help towards solving the crucial current problem in the study of human affairs, which is, as I see it, the problem of quantity. For this reason, and also because, in practice, though not in principle, present-day Western sociologists confine themselves almost entirely to the microscopic study of tiny patches of contemporary Western social texture, and treat this, not historically, but as still life, I agree with Bagby, as I have said above in Chapter IV, in holding that the sociologists' work is not of much use for our purpose. On the other hand, I also agree with Bagby that in neglecting the anthropologists' method I have deprived myself of a valuable tool. When he pronounces that this has been fatal to my work, I suspect that he may be exaggerating. The anthropologists' method is, after all, only one of a number of tools in the workman's bag. But, of course, the value of one's own work is a question on which one's own judgement is worth little more than zero.

[2] Bagby censures 'the incredible poverty' of my subject matter. According to him, it is confined almost entirely to political and military affairs (*Toynbee and History*, p. 104). In the same article, however, he criticizes me (ibid., p. 107) for having given too prominent and, worse still, too independent a place to religion, and complains elsewhere (in *Culture and History*, p. 6) that, before Bagby's own advent, 'an Englishman or an American who seeks to understand history must choose between Collingwood's unregulated intuitions and Toynbee's religious fantasies'. It seems inconsistent to prosecute on a charge of single-track-mindedness twice over, each time on a different count. But, if Bagby had said that I had paid too much attention to the *two* topics of religion and politics (including war), at the cost of unduly neglecting other human activities, his comment would have been fair and instructive.

have given to others: for instance, the fine arts,[1] science and technology,[2] and economics.[3] The consequent deficiency in my work can be measured by contrasting it with a feature of Spengler's work that—to my mind and, I believe, in the judgement of most other students of him as well—is one of Spengler's most brilliant achievements.

[1] D. M. Robinson notes against me that 'he neglects art, without which no man can really understand history' (*The Intent of Toynbee's History: A Cooperative Appraisal*). J. K. Feibleman remarks that, in my work, the arts and sciences of peace are ignored, and that the failure to comprehend the place of these in history is one of my two major shortcomings—the second of them being my attempt to found my system on transcendental religion (*T'ien Hsia Monthly*, vol. xi, Nos. 1 and 2 (1940), pp. 22 and 152). Sorokin (in *Toynbee and History*, p. 179) finds me inadequate on art and science (as well as on philosophy, law, and all history except Hellenic). D. M. Robinson censures me for neglecting 'the fields of archaeology, numismatics, ceramics, glyptics, sculpture, and architecture', as well as sociology (*The Intent of Toynbee's History: A Cooperative Appraisal*). For sociology see the present chapter, p. 599, footnote 1. As for archaeology, Robinson is answered in the following passage of W. H. McNeill's contribution to the same cooperative appraisal. 'The scope and content of *A Study of History* is dependent on the work done by archaeologists, much of it within the present century. If the goodly company of the archaeologists had not discovered and studied Sumerian, Babylonian, Assyrian, Minoan, Mycenaean, Hittite, Indus, Shang, and Mayan civilizations, Toynbee could not have conceived history as he did. In this most elementary sense, his book is a product of our age' (*The Intent of Toynbee's History: A Cooperative Appraisal*). T. J. G. Locher makes Robinson's criticism in *De Gids*, May, 1948, offprint, p. 9, in gracious terms. Why, he asks, does an artistic personality draw so little on the history of art for his study? I plead guilty to this charge.

[2] This point has been touched upon already on p. 591, in footnote 1. J. Romein remarks (in *Toynbee and History*, pp. 348–9) that I depreciate the value and significance of rational science and technology. E. Fiess remarks (ibid., p. 383) that I depreciate the value and significance of scientific method by perversely identifying it with mere technology; and the same charge is made by Feibleman (in *T'ien Hsia Monthly*, loc. cit.). P. A. Sorokin is right in pointing out that, in my belief, there is no correlation between progress and recession in technology and progress and recession in culture. In Sorokin's view this is, at the least, an exaggeration of the truth, if it is not a sheer fallacy (Sorokin in *Toynbee and History*, pp. 180 and 185).

John Strachey, in an unpublished critique, observes that I grossly neglect Man's need to conquer his material environment, and therefore gravely underestimate the importance of technology. 'All his highest values—"etherialisation" and "self-determination" —are quite impossible of achievement without a higher technique than 99 per cent of the World has even yet realised.' E. Fiess (in *Toynbee and History*, p. 383) finds, in my interpretation of history, a strange depreciation of the importance of material progress. Cp. J. Madaule (in *Diogenes*, No. 13 (Spring, 1956), p. 42), and T. J. G. Locher in *De Gids*, May, 1948, offprint, p. 22. Lewis Mumford (in *Diogenes*, No. 13 (Spring, 1956), p. 18) finds that I ignore the positive conditions for the growth of civilization, e.g. the importance of the acquisition of storeable foodstuffs. Lynn Thorndike criticizes me for neglecting material and technical advance (*The Journal of Modern History*, vol. vii, No. 3 (September, 1935), p. 317). A. H. Hanson castigates my 'extraordinary ignorance' of the materialist interpretation of history, and strongly objects to my describing the technical achievements of the civilizations that I label 'arrested' as being a reversion to animalism (*Science and Society*, No. 13, 1949, pp. 118–35). In the particular case of the Nomads, Owen Lattimore points out, in *The Atlantic Monthly*, April, 1948, pp. 104–5, that 'the transition from marginal farming to the breeding of livestock has not usually been the result of the "challenge" of climatic desiccation. Rather, it has been the result sometimes of the discovery and sometimes of the imitation of a new technique'. P. M. Sweezy had already made this point in *The Nation*, 19th October, 1946, on the authority of Lattimore's masterly book *Inner Asian Frontiers of China*.

[3] Crane Brinton notes that I believe that we ought to re-transfer our spiritual treasure from economics to religion (*The Virginia Quarterly Review*, vol. 32, No. 3 (Summer, 1956), pp. 361–75). R. H. Tawney has the impression that I am not much interested in the economic aspects of social growth and decay (*International Affairs*, November, 1939, p. 800). Allan Nevins puts his finger on my 'general inadequacy in treating the economic factors of history' (*The New York World-Telegram and Sun*, 7th December, 1934). Strachey, a propos of my eulogy of Pope Gregory the Great in vol. iv, pp. 184–5, for having built 'upon a religious rock and not upon economic sands', remarks that, while it is true that one needs to have an ideology, it is no less true that one needs to have an economy as well. F. Neilson (in *The American Journal of Economics and Sociology*, supplement to vol. 14, No. 3 (April, 1955), p. 3) remarks that my work lacks the economic foundations that are provided by Plato in *The Republic*.

Spengler's first concern in approaching a civilization is to divine its distinctive 'style' or character. In this particular civilization, what is the dominant activity? How do the other activities relate themselves to this one? What is the dominant activity, and the corresponding configuration of culture, in that other civilization over there? What does the dominance of different activities in different cultures tell us about the qualitative differences between those cultures? Spengler may have been rather less well versed in the details of history than I, for instance, may be. But he had the insight of genius, and his diagnoses of the distinctive characters of different civilizations are the field in which his genius most clearly displays itself.[1] These diagnoses may stand or may fall. It is quite likely that some of them will be rejected by an eventual consensus of Spengler's successors. Spengler himself arrived at his results largely by intuition, and in arriving at them he challenged other inquirers, endowed with different temperaments and different mental gifts, to follow in his tracks and to confirm or confute his findings by methodical investigations.

By good fortune, a promising method was being worked out at the very time when Spengler was thinking, writing, and publishing. It was being worked out, not in the sociologists' and historians' study of the civilizations, but in the anthropologists' study of the pre-civilizational societies. While the historians were ignoring the patterns in human affairs and the sociologists were poring over minute patches of them, the anthropologists of the 'cultural' school were learning to look at a culture as a whole and to trace out its 'configurations': Kroeber's felicitous word. Kroeber himself has taken a first step, and a long one, towards extending the application of the cultural anthropologists' outlook and method from the study of pre-civilizational societies to the study of civilizations. Dawson is on the same road.[2] Bagby started to follow Kroeber's lead, and was proposing to make a systematic study of the morphology of civilizations on anthropological lines.[3]

Thus the stimulus of Spengler's gift of insight has prompted other inquirers to bring to bear, in Spengler's field, a scientific intellectual tool by which Spengler's own findings can be tested and perhaps surpassed. Anthropological method is indeed a key that promises to unlock doors when it is applied to the study of civilizations. Since no particular

[1] By comparison with Spengler's presentation of history, M. E. Lauer finds that mine gives, not an inside view, but one seen from outside (*von aussen her*) (*Blätter für Anthroposophie*, January, 1952). To G. Masur's mind, I have not conjured up any arresting picture of civilizations as self-contained unities or 'wholes' (*Ganzheiten*), comparable to Spengler's 'Apollinean' or 'Faustian' culture (the *Historische Zeitschrift*, Band 177 (1954), pp. 521–2). G. E. von Grunebaum finds that, unlike Spengler, I fail to characterize my collective agents from within by an exposition of their existential outlook and problems (*The Intent of Toynbee's History: A Cooperative Appraisal*). Other judgements on my work on the same lines have been cited on p. 598, footnote 1. Christopher Dawson, however, finds not only me, but Spengler too, guilty of not taking account of the complexity of the elements of culture that make up a civilization (*The Dynamics of World History*, p. 423). Sorokin dismisses, as being 'misleading and inaccurate', 'the Spenglerian–Toynbee ascription of some specific perennial tendency to this or that civilization, regardless of the period of its history' (*Toynbee and History*, p. 186, quoted already on p. 288).

[2] See, for instance, what he writes in *Toynbee and History*, p. 138.

[3] See *Culture and History*, pp. 7–9 and 18–21. Unhappily, these plans have been cut short by Bagby's untimely death.

key ever turns out to be a master-key, there will, no doubt, be some doors that will prove recalcitrant to this one.[1] The anthropological method of studying a culture has been devised for dealing with pre-civilizational cultures, and in these, as we have noticed, the degree of integration is high. In its application to societies of the species 'civilizations' the anthropological method might be less fruitful; and it might even be stultifying if we were to seek to apply it automatically to the unprecedented cultural situation that has been produced by the epiphany of the higher religions.[2] These, as we have seen, have broken away from the traditional association of religion with other cultural activities and have asserted their independence as representatives of a new species of society. Still, the anthropological method seems likely to produce valuable results for the study of the Age of the Civilizations down to this point at any rate. If it helps us to explore the cultural configurations of the civilizations of the first and second generations, it will have proved to be a tool of great value. From now onwards I shall pick this tool up and try it myself. 'Better late than never.'

I might have picked it up earlier, and therefore have found better opportunities for taking advantage of it,[3] if I had paid more attention than I have to the study of the pre-civilizational societies.[4] My neglect of these is, I should guess, the most serious single one of the many deficiencies in my equipment for making a study of human affairs. It is not just that a better acquaintance with communities in the pre-civilizational stage would also have made me better acquainted with the anthropologists and with their method of work. The pre-civilizational societies have an intrinsic importance and value of their own,[5] and this for several reasons.

[1] Bagby appears to believe that the cultural anthropologists' approach is not just *a* key, but is *the* key, to success in a study of the civilizations. Spengler, he remarks, 'in spite of his wild exaggerations and his reliance on intuition, did have a concept of culture which approaches the anthropological one and used it far more systematically and with far more respect for the evidence than his successor' [i.e. myself] (*Culture and History*, p. 181). Bagby has certainly used his anthropological key with good effect and would, I am sure, have won further successes with it. But everyone is inclined to overestimate the value of his own favourite tool. My favourite one has been the use of the Hellenic Civilization as a 'model', and I am conscious that I have fallen into the mistake of trying to apply this 'model' beyond its proper limits and of neglecting to experiment with alternatives. Bagby has been criticized by a reviewer in *The Times Literary Supplement*, 3rd October, 1958, for succumbing to 'the tendency to see cultural anthropology, not so much as a useful ancillary tool for the historian, as a panacea for all historiographical ills and, finally, an overall substitute for history'.

[2] This has been argued on pp. 81–85.

[3] Other critics, besides Bagby, have censured me for not having done this. C. Trinkaus finds that, while I do apply the method of anthropology to history, I do this only very superficially (*Science and Society*, vol. xii, No. 1 (1948), p. 221). R. K. Merton detects (in loc. cit.) that I have not read Durkheim, and he pronounces that, in my account of the diffusion of culture, my 'unfamiliarity with detailed analytical studies of diffusion is painfully evident'.

[4] See pp. 150–3. O. Höver criticizes my treatment of both the Palaeolithic and the Neolithic Age in a paper in typescript. See also the same writer's 'Buchführung und Bilanz der Weltgeschichte: Zu A. Toynbees Deutung des Frühzeitlichen Menschengeschehens', in the *Zeitschrift für Religions- und Geistesgeschichte*, Jahrgang 2, Heft 3 (1949/50), pp. 247–59. I have tried to make some amends for my relative neglect of the pre-civilizational cultures by dealing with them—all too briefly and ignorantly—in Chapter IX of the present volume.

[5] Christopher Dawson justly charges both Spengler and me with under-estimating the importance of both the primitives and the barbarians (*Toynbee and History*, pp. 137 and 139; *The Dynamics of World History*, p. 422).

In the first place, the pre-civilizational societies represent one out of three species of human society—and this the oldest and by far the longest-lived so far. One cannot see the other two—civilizations and churches—in their true historical perspective unless one is able to see them against the background of pre-civilizational culture. In the second place, it is too crude a classification to distribute all societies, other than churches, between just two species. The line that I have drawn between 'primitive societies' and 'civilizations' is too sharp.[1] In the course of the years during which I have been writing this book the progress of archaeological discovery has made it more and more clear that the Old-World group of civilizations and the New-World group each rises, like a cluster of pyramids, from a platform which, itself, already stands above ground level. Between the civilizations of the earliest generation and the primitive societies in those civilizations' historical background there intervenes the transitional stage of culture—labelled 'Neolithic' in the Old World and 'Formative' in the New World—that has been discussed in Chapter IX of this volume. And, in the background of this transitional stage, there is no undifferentiated primitive phase. Behind the Neolithic looms the Mesolithic, behind this the Upper Palaeolithic, and the Lower Palaeolithic behind that. At the earliest moment at which we catch our first glimpse of Man on Earth, we find him not only on the move but already moving at an accelerating pace. This crescendo of acceleration is continuing today. In our generation it is perhaps the most difficult and dangerous of all the current problems of the human race. We cannot plot the curve of this movement, not to speak of trying to explain it, unless we look at it as a whole. A study of human affairs must be comprehensive if it is to have any hope of becoming intelligible, and no study will be comprehensive if the pre-civilizational societies are left out of the picture.

Nor, in this comprehensive picture, are the pre-civilizational societies merely part of the furniture of the past. They are still represented in the living contemporary world.[2] And here their most important representatives are not the extant pre-civilizational societies still surviving as separate social entities in the interstices between the civilizations. These have been played upon by the radiation of the civilizations ever since the first civilizations made their appearance some five thousand years ago. This radiation has been increasing in intensity, and its disintegrating effects have been cumulative. Most of the surviving pre-civilizational societies are now within sight of dissolution, and the human beings who have participated in them are being caught in the meshes of the world-wide civilization that is taking shape within a Western framework. The most important, and by far the most numerous, representatives of pre-civilizational culture today are the peasants who have been living their own lives, unassimilated, under the surface of the civilizations ever since these came into existence.[3] This peasantry still accounts, today, for nearly three-quarters of the living generation of mankind, and they are

---

[1] See pp. 150–3, with the references on p. 150, in footnote 6, to critics who have made this point.
[2] P. A. Sorokin, in *Toynbee and History*, p. 184, makes this point in more general terms.   [3] See Mumford in *Diogenes*, No. 13 (Spring, 1956), p. 14.

still in the 'Formative' or 'Neolithic' stage in their state of mind and even in their way of life. This has remained substantially what it was, in spite of successive changes in technical equipment—from stone tools to stone and copper side by side, and from copper, via bronze, to iron and steel.[1] It is only in our day that this hitherto Neolithic-minded peasant majority of the human race is beginning to obtain some share in the amenities of the civilization whose burden it has been carrying on its shoulders for these last five thousand years.

It may be that the peasantry, in now taking the kingdom of civilization by storm, is unwittingly pushing its way into a slaughter-house. The revolutionary possibility of bringing the benefits of civilization within reach of all men has been conjured up by an acceleration of the advance of technology at an unprecedented rate during the last 200 years. This technological revolution has been a Western achievement, and it has now placed in the hands of the Western peoples and their accomplished Russian pupils new weapons potent enough for committing genocide. If the technocrat civilizations were to use this tremendous power for their own destruction, their exceptional progress in technology would be seen, in retrospect, to have been one of those cultural developments that make their ingenious authors unfit to survive; and then the Earth would be inherited, if it were still habitable, by the societies that had been saved from genocide by their comparative technological backwardness. With an eye to this possible event, it seems advisable that students of human affairs today should pay considerable attention to the most primitive societies now surviving in the most secluded natural fastnesses in the Southern Hemisphere. If the technocrat civilizations were to eliminate themselves without making the entire surface of this planet uninhabitable for human beings, human history might be carried on, and the Earth might eventually be repopulated, by those remnants of primitive peoples that are now living, on sufferance, in the interior of Sumatra and Borneo and Australia.

These are strong grounds for taking the study of pre-civilizational societies seriously if one is seriously concerned with the study of human affairs. But, behind and beyond anthropology, further fields of inquiry open up. There is geography in the sense of a study of Man in his interaction with his non-human environment. There is biology in the sense of a study of the physical structure and development of life. Beyond and behind geography and biology there is geology, bringing with it a perspective in which Man looks like a maggot, and life like a virus lately defacing the surface of a once aseptic planet. And behind and beyond geology there is astronomy, bringing with it another perspective again—one, this time, in which our planet looks like a mote, and our geology like a fleeting wisp of cloud. This regress of studies carries the inquirer back into the past behind the genesis of Man and the genesis of life; yet it is as relevant to the study of human affairs as the study of the pre-civilizational societies is to the study of the civilizations and the churches. Kroeber points out[2] that biology, geology, and astronomy are historical, not scientific, inquiries. He also observes[3] that

---

[1] See pp. 151–2.   [2] In *The Nature of Culture*, pp. 54, 70, 80, 123.   [3] Ibid., p. 73.

science and history differ, not in their field of inquiry, but in the nature of their approach, and that the historical approach can be applied to all phenomena of every kind. This observation is surely correct, and, at one stroke, it wipes out all those conventional 'inter-disciplinary' demarcation lines that might have offered an inquirer into human affairs a prospect of setting some limit to his expanding mental universe. A classically educated inquirer will find this levelling of traditional barriers formidable. I myself have been denounced, with justice, as a naïvely ignorant amateur trespasser, even in the more or less human province of geography.[1] When I have met with such a trouncing at so short a distance from home, how shall I dare to run the gauntlet of the biologists, geologists, and astronomers?

Worse still, the would-be student of human affairs has to pursue his foolhardy quest right through the flaming ramparts of the physical cosmos into the boundless mental spaces of philosophy.[2] Naturally I have been denounced as being no better a philosopher than I am a geographer,[3] but here my classical education has left me in a better posture for self-defence. In 1909–11, when I was reading *Literas Humaniores* at Oxford, I got one foot in between the door-post and the door of the philosopher's closet; and I have just managed to keep it there since then. So this door cannot be slammed and bolted in my face. I can peep into the closet when I choose, and I have done so in this volume.

Such glimpses are, no doubt, all to the good. At the same time this survey of the range of my knowledge will have shown how inadequate it is for the enterprise on which I have embarked. 'The book *is* his education.'[4] What is the verdict? Through the rumble of criticism, my ear seems to catch two rather different voices. One voice is saying: 'He has failed to achieve it. Of course he has. It cannot be done.' The other voice is saying: 'He has failed to achieve it. Of course he has. He has not the tools or the wits. But it *can* be done. I am doing it myself.' Of the two, the conceited voice sounds less forbidding than the defeatist one for the prospects of progress in the pursuit of the quest for knowledge. Conceitedness, of course, can unintentionally defeat itself. It is a parasite on ability, and it may strangle it. But the defeatist attitude gives ability no chance at all. And the study of human affairs cannot advance if ability will not venture into this perilous field.

---

[1] See O. H. K. Spate in *Toynbee and History*, p. 287; in *The Geographical Journal*, vol. cxviii, Part 4 (December, 1952), pp. 409–11; and, in fact, *passim*.

[2] See Lucretius: *De Rerum Natura*, Book I, ll. 72–77.

[3] Like Spengler, Toynbee has not any philosophical system to give his scheme some rational objectivity (H. J. Morgenthau in *Toynbee and History*, p. 196). 'Toynbee crosses certain logical gaps on shaky bridges' (R. V. Chase in *The American Scholar*, vol. 16, No. 3 (Summer, 1947), pp. 268–82). His work is not philosophy; it is 'philosophy of history'. And what is that? Methodology? Metaphysics? Logic? (K. W. Thompson in *Toynbee and History*, pp. 200–1). 'Toynbee's *A Study of History* is, strictly speaking, not a philosophy of history. Modern philosophy of history, as represented among others by thinkers like Dilthey, Croce, Ortega y Gasset, or in England by R. G. Collingwood, has been chiefly concerned with the questions of historical knowledge itself' (Hajo Holborn in *The Saturday Review of Literature*, 31st May, 1947, p. 12). Toynbee is unfamiliar with philosophy and uncomplimentary to it (J. K. Feibleman in *T'ien Hsia Monthly*, vol. xi, Nos. 1 and 2 (1940), pp. 17 and 148–50). 'Little interested in philosophy' (W. Gurian in *The Review of Politics*, vol. 4, No. 4 (October, 1942), p. 511). 'Toynbee ist kein philosophisch-kritische Geist' (Zahn, op. cit., p. 45).

[4] A. Hourani in *The Dublin Review*, vol. 229, No. 470 (December, 1955), p. 386.

3. EFFECTS OF HAVING BEEN BORN IN 1889 AND IN ENGLAND

'Genuine concern with problems [*Problematik*] always springs from roots in the life of the contemporary world and is implicated in the play of real contemporary opposing forces. It never hovers, free as air, withdrawn from the World and out of touch with Reality.'[1]

Anyone in any country affected by the First World War who was alive and grown-up at the time of its outbreak is likely to have felt that this was an epoch-making event. Someone who was just grown-up, and whose country was England, will have been particularly sensitive to this feeling. Like his elders, he could look back, with a grown-up participant's eyes, on the life of a period that had now been abruptly and unexpectedly brought to an end; and, for English people, this period had been running, without any dramatic break, for almost twice as long as for the people of most other countries. For the English, August 1914 spelled the sudden end of a period of peace that they had been enjoying by then for all but a hundred years, since the last shot fired at the Battle of Waterloo. The breaches in this English century of peace had been minor disturbances that had not interrupted the even tenor of England's life. On the other hand, in most other parts of the World there had been a decisive break, for good or evil, about half-way through that century's course. France had suffered the débâcle and the *Commune* in the years 1870–1. The same years had seen the completion of the political unification of Italy and of Germany. For Italy this revolutionary change had taken twelve years (1859–70) and for Germany eight (1864–71). Canada, too, had attained political unity in a self-governing federation in 1867. The United States' unity had been preserved, but its internal balance of power had been at the same time revolutionized, in the Civil War of 1861–5, the greatest, bloodiest, and most devastating war of any in the World between 1815 and 1914. In Russia a new age had opened with the liberation of the serfs in 1861 and the accompanying reforms of other institutions. India had been through the shattering experience of the Mutiny of 1857, and China through the shattering experience of her war with Great Britain and France in 1858–60, which finally brought home to her a realization of her impotence in face of Western military power. These upheavals all round England had either left her untouched or had failed to touch her to the quick. And this exemption from the World's common lot in the eighteen-sixties and seventies made the shock of 1914 particularly severe for her. Having been born in England in 1889, I felt this shock in its full force, and it must have been affecting my outlook and my work continuously and profoundly ever since.

I certainly caught the Victorian Age by its tail, only to see it immediately slip out of my hands. This experience of mine is, of course, nothing individual or unique. It is common to all surviving representatives of my generation. All the same, it has attracted the attention of several of my critics. To Holcombe's eyes I display 'a large measure of the attitudes and spirit of a late Victorian Englishman'.[2] In Toynbee,

[1] E. F. J. Zahn: *Toynbee und das Problem der Geschichte*, p. 7.
[2] A. N. Holcombe in *The American Political Science Review*, vol. xlix, No. 4, p. 1151.

Kohn signals to the German public, we are back in Gladstone's world. Toynbee is 'one of the last representatives of the Western humanistic culture'.[1] In this description, Kohn carries me back, in Gladstone's company, to the world of Giambattista Vico and of Poggio Bracciolini. His placing of me is, I believe, correct,[2] and it throws into relief the greatness of the break which an Englishman, brought up in this traditional culture, experienced in 1914. No doubt this explains why I strike at least three of my contemporaries[3] as being out of tune with the age in which I have been living and working ever since: the new age that opened at the outbreak of the First World War. Neilson pronounces that 'thought today runs in other channels'. Savelle sums up, more judicially, that

'it is conceivable that Arnold Toynbee may prove to be the prophet of a new era in the intellectual and spiritual life of mankind. . . .[4] On the other hand, *A Study of History* may prove to be an anachronism, a book, essentially backward-looking, that seeks to rationalise the failures of religion into the terms of an indomitable and unquenchable faith. . . . In this case the *Meisterwerk* must become but the most eloquent of all the voices of those who are still living in an age of faith that is past, who are not at home, and who, therefore, are not happy, in the atomic relativistic universe revealed by science—a universe of which they are integral parts but which knows them not.'

The impression made on these critics is noteworthy because two of them, at any rate, were older than I am, yet they evidently did not feel that they themselves had been affected in the same way. Is this estrangement from the present an advantage or a handicap for a student of human

---

[1] H. Kohn in *Der Monat*, August, 1955, p. 465. The word that I have translated 'culture' is *Bildung*, which means so much more than *Erziehung* or than 'education'.

[2] If it is correct, then Crossman has got me wrong. In *The New Statesman*, 8th March, 1947, Crossman reported that I have 'a medieval mind' and am a secular Thomist. Crossman's characterization of me and Kohn's are incompatible, and I think it is Crossman's that has gone astray. To be any kind of a Thomist, one must dote on Aristotle, and I have never succeeded in appreciating '*the* philosopher', as he was, *par excellence*, for Saint Thomas Aquinas.

[3] Sir Ernest Barker in *Toynbee and History*, p. 94; F. Neilson in *The American Journal of Economics and Sociology*, Supplement to vol. 14, No. 3 (April, 1955), p. 1.; M. Savelle in *The Pacific Historical Review*, vol. xxv, No. 1 (February, 1956), p. 67.

[4] Short of being hailed as 'the prophet of a new era', I have been recognized by some critics as being, for evil or good or neither, a characteristic representative of my own generation. Holcombe, for instance, reports that, besides being a Late Victorian Englishman, I am 'a genuine citizen of our world'. M. Watnick, in *The Antioch Review*, No. 7 (Winter, 1947–8), pp. 587–602, finds that, 'whatever else it may be, Toynbee's theory of history is a superb guide to the temper of our times' in a manifestation of this that Watnick himself deplores. 'We are witnessing today a recrudescence of an extreme anti-rationalism, a transcendental escapism, and a general impatience with rigorous scientific method.' And Toynbee's general attitude is 'in perfect accord with the prevailing "failure of nerve". . . . If our technical age has written history in its own image, the theologian-historian Toynbee has rewritten it with a highly sensitive awareness of a different image.'
  In an article entitled 'Hedendaagsche Augustinisme' in *Historie en Metahistorie*, H. Baudet suggests that in both Spengler's work and mine one can see the reciprocal action on each other of an author and the age in which he is living (pp. 44–45). Like Spengler (Baudet finds), I have had some influence on my contemporaries. In both cases Baudet attributes this effect to the forcefulness of a 'primary vision' that is simple and therefore easily comprehensible, rather than to the enveloping mass of information and argument. 'The panoramic prognosis to which it . . . leads, answers to the needs of the present age' (p. 46. Cp. p. 61). 'Toynbee's *Study of History* plays the role of the latest theodicy thrown up by the history of Western Christendom' (ibid., p. 61).

affairs? Bagby,[1] perhaps ironically, puts the question whether it is 'better to be a displaced Victorian or a disillusioned child of the times'. Spate takes it for granted that I am a disillusioned Victorian besides being a displaced one. He suggests[2] that a liberal humanism which has lost its self-assurance is slippery ground for the building of a big structure. If Spate is right about this, his own plight must be much the same as mine. But is he right? I do not think he is.

For a student of human affairs on the 'panoramic' scale, the experience of being catapulted out of the Gladstonian Age of Western history into the Hitlerian Age must surely have been professionally valuable in at least two ways. To even partially detached from the age into which one happens to have been born must liberate one's mind, at least in some measure, from the warping and blinding effects of its relativity to its immediate social milieu. In fact, a pilgrim and sojourner in the Hitlerian Age will have profited by his abiding memory of a Gladstonian childhood and early manhood. This memory will have reinforced the enduring effect of a classical education in giving him a modicum of mental detachment,[3] and this is a priceless treasure for a student of human affairs. In the second place, the jolt received in August 1914 will have made it impossible, for the rest of one's life, to forget that human affairs are perpetually on the move; and a consciousness of this is a priceless treasure for anyone who is trying to study human affairs from the historian's particular angle of vision.

As a child I was brought up with a great-uncle whose lifetime almost spanned the English century of peace. He had been born in 1820, five years after the date of the Battle of Waterloo, and he died in 1909, five years before the date of the outbreak of the First World War. Externally, his lifetime was as eventful as it could well have been. It had seen a transformation of the material conditions of life in England and, to a lesser extent, in other parts of the World. My great-uncle himself had been born and brought up on a farm in Lincolnshire, had gone to sea and risen to the command of an East Indiaman, and had ended his working life as an official in the newly established Meteorological Office in London. Yet, in spite of the external changes in his private station as well as in his cultural environment, my great-uncle's life had not been eventful psychologically. His experience of life had left him, I believe, unaware that life is not stable. If he had been an historian or a sociologist, he would have been unlucky in his generation. And, conversely, I believe that I have been lucky, professionally, in mine. In August 1914 I was twenty-five years old, and the lesson impressed on me in that month has remained with me ever since.

I have now lived through two world wars and have seen the second of these culminate in the invention and use of atomic weapons. We have since invented rockets capable of delivering far more destructive bombs from any point on the surface of this planet to any other point. It has been noticed by my critics that this experience, which has been the

[1] In *Toynbee and History*, p. 110.   [2] Ibid., p. 287.
[3] Holcombe is perhaps reporting that this has been the effect of these experiences on me when he concludes, in loc. cit., that 'Toynbee is not only a late Victorian Englishman but also a timeless cosmopolitan'.

consequence of the date at which I was born, has coloured my attitude towards a number of issues; and these are issues that concern, not only the present age, but the whole of human history. I hate war, and at the same time I am fascinated by the study of it,[1] and give a very great deal of attention to it.[2] At the same time, too, I am reluctant to admit that the use of force has had decisive effects on the course of human history.[3] In general, I minimize the effects of material factors of all kinds, economic and technological[4] as well as military, and I magnify the effects of spiritual factors.[5] In particular, I glorify suffering, and dwell on the creative spiritual effects that suffering has sometimes had.[6] These attitudes of mine, applied to politics, have made me hostile to any form of nationalism at any time and place.[7] In the world of my own day I condemn not only the Fascist Italian and Nazi German extremes

[1] J. K. Feibleman, in *T'ien Hsia Monthly*, vol. xi, Nos. 1 and 2 (1940), p. 144. This combination of hating war with being intensely interested in it is, I think, what has made both Sir Ernest Barker (in *Toynbee and History*, p. 94) and Bagby (ibid., p. 105) accuse me of 'ambivalence'. [2] Bagby, ibid., p. 104.

[3] This is noticed—and criticized—by, for example, Pieter Geyl in *Toynbee and History*, p. 57; K. W. Thompson, ibid., p. 218; J. K. Feibleman in loc. cit., p. 142; T. J. G. Locher in *De Gids*, May, 1948, offprint, p. 22; K. D. Erdmann in *Archiv für Kulturgeschichte*, xxiii. Band, Heft 2 (1951), p. 217; H. Baudet in *Historie en Metahistorie*, pp. 54 and 57; G. Masur in the *Historische Zeitschrift*, Band 177 (1954), pp. 521–2; P. Kecskemeti in *The Modern Review*, vol. 1, No. 4 (June, 1947), pp. 308–13; H. D. Oakeley in *Philosophy*, April, 1936, p. 193; E. I. Watkin in *The Tablet*, 12th August, 1939; H. Holborn in *The Saturday Review of Literature*, 31st May, 1947; reviewers in *The Listener*, 19th October, 1939, and in *The Glasgow Herald*, 2nd August, 1939; and O. Höver in a paper in typescript.
These critics judge that I have tried to push my point farther than is warranted by the evidence of history. Force *has* been signally effective on a number of notable occasions. The classic example that they cite is the conquest of Middle America and Peru by the Spaniards: e.g. Geyl in op. cit., pp. 55–56; K. W. Thompson in op. cit., pp. 218–19; Erdmann in op. cit., p. 218; Watkin in loc. cit.; Holborn in loc. cit.; and the reviewer in *The Glasgow Herald*. Erdmann also appeals to Hellenic history, and cites, as some of the causes of the decline and fall of the Hellenic Civilization, the impact on the Hellenic World of such external powers as the Persians and the Carthaginians and, at a later stage, the barbarians and the Christians. Watkin points out that, according to my own account, the Far Western Christian Civilization of 'the Celtic Fringe' succumbed to the superior force of the contemporary Roman Christendom, and that even the more formidable Scandinavian Civilization eventually capitulated to this. Other critics contest my inclination to depreciate the effectiveness of force in more general terms. Borkenau and Masur, for instance, point out that 'creative minorities' do not, as a matter of fact, ever rely exclusively on 'charm' as their means of retaining their leadership. Oakeley points out that geographical expansion is often impossible without the use of force, and that, 'in the early days of a people's development, expansion to some extent seems a necessary movement'.
[4] See p. 591, footnote 1, and p. 600, footnote 2.
[5] The Rev. E. R. Hardy Jr. judges that, 'from a Christian point of view, the trouble with' my ' "true religion" ' is that it is 'too purely spiritual' (*The Intent of Toynbee's History: A Cooperative Appraisal*). Pieter Geyl exclaims, in *Debates with Historians*, p. 142: 'This exclusive spiritualism is more than I can swallow.' C. B. Joynt criticizes me for taking 'a strongly dualistic view of the mind-body relation' (*Australasian Journal of Philosophy*, vol. 34, No. 3 (December, 1956), p. 195).
[6] 'In a sense it would be even true to say that the prophet's [Deutero-Isaiah's] "suffering servant" is the key to the understanding of Mr. Toynbee's *Study*' (E. Berkovitz: *Judaism: Fossil or Ferment?*, p. 36). F. Engel-Janosi notices that, in my attitude, there is an accent on suffering (*Wissenschaft und Weltbild*, 2. Jahrgang, Heft 4 (October, 1949), p. 269). Sorokin opposes this attitude of mine (in *Toynbee and History*, pp. 188–9). I have declared this attitude at a previous point in this chapter (on pp. 580–1), as well as in many other contexts.
[7] Geyl judges that I unduly depreciate the importance of national units (*Toynbee and History*, p. 71) and that I do not do justice to the part played by local national life and culture within the framework of the Western Civilization (ibid., p. 70). Renier (ibid., p. 75) convicts me of being illiberal in my criticism of historians who write history within national frameworks.

of nationalism, but also British, French, and Dutch colonialism and the spirit that has led the United States and the Soviet Union into a competition for world-dominion at the risk of committing genocide and making the surface of this planet uninhabitable. I have a passion for unity,[1] and deplore the division of the World into sovereign independent local states.

I agree that I do have these feelings and attitudes, and that I have them partly as a result of my reactions to the public events through which I happen to have lived. These two admissions do not, in themselves, tell either for or against the effects that my experience has had on me. It may have darkened and confused my vision, or it may have made me see clearer than, perhaps, I might have seen if I had happened to live in a less catastrophic age. The help or hindrance, for a study of human affairs, that I have derived from my generation's experience is something that cannot be judged *a priori* or *en bloc*. Each point ought to be considered on its merits.

I do hate war and this for the familiar reasons that have made most people hate it for most of the time since this sinister institution was first established. War is an impersonal use of collective human force for the purpose of imposing the will of the rulers and people of one state on those of another. It is impossible to make war without having a political organization and an economic surplus; so war can hardly be older than civilization. In any case, since the rise of civilization, war has been one of its two chief scandals and scourges—the other being the system of social and economic inequality and injustice which expresses itself in class distinctions and which finds its extreme form in the institution of slavery. War is hateful—this is almost too trite to repeat—because it is wicked, because it causes suffering, and because it works havoc. The psychological havoc that it works—its *karma*, in the language of Indian philosophy—is both more devastating in its effects and more difficult to undo than the material damage that it inflicts. On the evidence of history, war has been the immediate cause of most of the breakdowns and disintegrations of civilizations of which we have a record. Today, since the invention of atomic weapons, war has become capable of destroying, not only mankind's civilizations, but mankind itself. It has not become, because it could not become, more wicked than it always has been. But it has now become not only wicked but senseless, since weapons have now reached a potency that will obliterate the traditional distinction between victors and vanquished. Atomic weapons will bring not only defeat but annihilation on all belligerents alike.

Watkin suggests[2] that my consciousness of the present potentialities

---

[1] Sir Ernest Barker in *Toynbee and History*, pp. 94–95. There are, of course, two different ways in which this passion can declare itself. One may be eager for practical concord and fraternity, and one may be eager for a unitary vision of human affairs and of all other phenomena. These two forms of the passion are not incompatible. I plead guilty to the second as well as to the first. The first accounts for my animus against the concept of 'Europe' versus the World, which is noticed by Richard Pares in *The English Historical Review*, vol. lxxi, No. 279 (April, 1956), p. 269. In the matter of seeking for unity of vision, W. Gurian notices, in *The Review of Politics*, October, 1942, p. 511, that I have 'a passion for synthesis'. Christopher Dawson notices, in *Toynbee and History*, p. 136, that I am moved by the Hellenic quest for a synoptic vision and by the Hebrew quest for a theodicy. See also p. 9, footnote 1.

[2] In *The Tablet*, 12th August, 1939, p. 204.

of war may have coloured retrospectively my estimate of the actual effects of war in the past.

'In this vision and probable forecast we fear he is right. But it has, we think, led him to an inconsistent and hesitant view of the part actually played by war in human civilizations. At times he distinguishes between justifiable and unjustifiable war, between wars which preserve a growing civilization from barbarians without, and anarchy within, the pale, and wars of militarist aggression. For example, he seems to approve of Timur Lenk's (Tamburlaine's) wars against the Mongol Nomads, and to condemn only the wars waged by his mad ambition against the Persians, Turks, and Indians. But at other times—as, for instance, when he describes and condemns the palette whereon Narmer (Menes) depicts the war by which he united Egypt—he seems to condemn war indiscriminately. This confusion—in which he projects and enlarges the perception that national wars under present conditions must spell ruin for our civilization into an indiscriminate pacifism which condemns war throughout history—has, we think, damaged his historical picture. For it is abundantly clear that civilization could not have arisen and developed without the employment of war, however destructive its unbridled indulgence proved later.'

Watkin's analysis is acute; and I agree that one must try to distinguish between the different purposes for which wars have been fought, and the different degrees of the material and spiritual devastation that they have inflicted. This is a necessary step towards arriving—if that is possible—at a more or less dispassionate and objective appreciation of the role of war in history. As Watkin points out, I have been feeling my way towards drawing distinctions of these kinds, without having succeeded, so far, in drawing them clearly. On reconsideration, I find myself still holding that all wars are wrong, whatever may be their purposes and their consequences. But I agree that, in the past, the choice between going to war and not going to war has sometimes been a choice between two evils. If the evil in not going to war is greater than the evil in going to war—and this not just for the party that is having to make the choice, but for society as a whole—then, I suppose, going to war would be morally justifiable. Yet a war that, on these grounds, might rank as a 'just' war, according to the definition of this in Christian theology, would not, on that account, be a war that worked no havoc. A war always works havoc, even when one of the belligerents is not morally to blame for having started it. Moreover, it is part of the nature of war, once started, to get out of hand; and many belligerents who have made war 'justly' at the start have drifted into the commission of injustice before the end of the story. Watkin's contention that 'civilization could not have arisen and developed without the employment of war' is, I should say, non-proven, and is perhaps intrinsically impossible either to demonstrate or to refute. If it were accepted, the implications for the destiny of civilization would be grim. We should be confronted with the tragic fact that the price of civilization had been the imposition on mankind of a fatal load of *karma*; and we should have to face the tragic prospect that this *karma*—in the shape of an institution that is both evil and uncontrollable—is likely, sooner or later, to destroy, not only civilization, but also Man its maker.

In diagnosing my attitude towards war as being 'ambivalent', my critics imply, I think, that my interest in the study of war shows that, while I hate it on one level of my psyche, I love it on another. If this is the implication, I do not admit that the diagnosis is correct. For, while it is true that one cannot love a thing without being interested in it, this does not prove the truth of the converse proposition that one cannot be interested in a thing without loving it. This is, in fact, disproved by familiar cases. An intelligence officer, for instance, is absorbingly interested in 'the enemy'. A surgeon or physiologist who is fighting cancer is absorbingly interested in cancerous growths. But in both these cases the feeling that inspires this interest is, not a love for one's opponent, but a desire to conquer him. For me, as for most other human beings, war is an enemy of the human race and a cancer preying upon human society and destroying the most valuable elements in human culture. The first step towards conquering a dangerous enemy or keeping at bay a dangerous disease is to take the danger seriously. This is one of the elementary rules of self-defence. The most fatal of all possible reactions to an opponent is to try to get rid of him by ignoring his existence. This is, surely, childishly irrational, and, if so, any student of human affairs in the Age of the Civilizations up to date ought to give far more attention to war than to all the arts of peace put together. It is an unhappy but undeniable truth that, during these last 5,000 years, mankind has spent on war by far the greater part of the hitherto meagre surplus, over and above our provision for the bare necessities of life, that we have succeeded in wresting from non-human nature. A derisorily small fraction of this tiny surplus has been spent on the arts of peace—and, till within living memory, most of this fraction has been misappropriated to the unjust purpose of providing the amenities of civilization for a privileged minority.

On these considerations I maintain that my combination of hatred with interest in my attitude towards war does not convict me of psychological 'ambivalence' but does acquit me of trying to hide my head in the sands. On the other hand, I acknowledge that I have been guilty of some 'wishful thinking' in pushing my denial of the efficacity of the use of force as far as I have pushed it. If one believes, as I do, that war has had an important effect on the course of human affairs, it is inconsistent to maintain that the use of force has not been efficacious. On this point I accept two of Feibleman's *dicta*. 'An event', he says,[1] 'is never actual without some gentleness, nor possible without some violence.' Some measure of force is inherent in all organizations, and all of them are also ephemeral.[2] In other words, force is efficacious to no lesser an extent than the institutions in which it is an ingredient. If force has not proved efficacious in the long run, this is because all known human institutions have had short runs up to date measured by the age of the human race. I have argued, however,[3] that human institutions, unlike human lives, have no inexorable maximum span of duration, but are

[1] In loc. cit., p. 144.   [2] Ibid., pp. 142–3.   [3] See pp. 268–9.

capable, in principle, of lasting for an indefinite length of time when once they have been brought into existence. If I am right in thinking this, then I am bound to concede that the effects of the use of force might continue to make themselves felt *in saecula saeculorum*.

Pares suggests[1] that I do not fully believe my own thesis that no civilization has ever perished through the violent impact, from outside, of some alien human force. On reconsideration, I find myself still unable to cite a single case of the breakdown and disintegration of a civilization in which I think it is certain that this was the work of some external agency. In all cases in which our knowledge of the course of events is sufficient to enable us to diagnose the causes of breakdown and disintegration with any assurance, I believe now, as before, that the verdict suggested by the evidence is one of suicide,[2] not one of murder. But I also admit that, if I left it at that, I should not have given a full or a completely final answer to Pares' probing question. For one thing, the evidence, as I interpret it, does not only show that the civilizations that have come to grief have miscarried as a result of the operation of internal causes; it also shows that, at least in the later stages of the subsequent process of disintegration, external agencies—in the shape of barbarians, higher religions, or alien civilizations—have sped the disintegrating civilization on its course towards final dissolution or have at any rate administered the final *coup de grâce*. In the classical case of the two Pre-Columbian civilizations in the New World it is obvious that the Spanish invaders dealt these civilizations the final blow, even if this was only the last in a series in which the first had been self-inflicted.

The Middle American and the Andean Society did, I believe, each break down at least four hundred years before the Spaniards arrived in the Americas from the other side of the Atlantic. In the history of each of these civilizations the 'Classic' phase, in which it is evident that the civilization was prospering and progressing, seems to have broken down at the turn of the tenth and eleventh centuries of the Christian Era.[3] In the Andean World this breakdown is represented, in the archaeological evidence, by the advent of the Tiahuanacoid horizon; in the Middle American World it is represented by the sack of Teotihuacán and by the desertion of the lowland Maya 'ceremonial centres' in what is now Northern Guatemala. In taking this evidence as an indication of a breakdown in my sense of the term,[4] I am perhaps on fairly strong ground, as I can appeal here, in support of my interpretation, to a consensus of the archaeologists working in this field. But I also have to admit that my concept of social and cultural breakdown is contested by many, perhaps by a majority, of my fellow historians, and I also have to

[1] In loc. cit., p. 267.
[2] R. L. Shinn remarks that this conclusion is made easy for me by my belief in original sin, and that, in some cases, destruction seems to be a disproportionately heavy penalty for the fault that I diagnose (*Christianity and the Problem of History*, p. 228).
[3] The absolute dating of Middle American history in terms of the Christian Era is still in dispute, though there is no disagreement about the relative dating of the successive phases of Middle American culture that have been brought to light by archaeological discoveries. The datings given here are those of the Martinez–Goodman–Thompson correlations. Spinden sets back the chronology by 260 years, and his correlation seems to be supported by recent carbon-14 tests.   [4] See pp. 300–5.

ask myself what, as far as I can guess, would have been likely to happen supposing that military adventurers from the Far West of the Old World had succeeded in crossing the Atlantic in the generation of the Cid or in the generation of Tāriq instead of being kept waiting until the generation of Cortés. If Tāriq had ferried his expeditionary force across the straits of Dakar instead of the straits of Gibraltar, it would have reached Middle America and the Andean World in the eighth century of the Christian Era. According to either of the two present tentative correlations of Middle American chronology with the Christian Era, the invaders from the Old World would then have found the indigenous civilizations of the New World still in what would have been their 'growth stage' in my terminology. Can I guarantee to Richard Pares that, in these circumstances, the invaders would have been repulsed?

Evidently, in the light of what actually happened 400 years later, it would be unwarrantable to pronounce dogmatically that the indigenous civilizations of the New World would undoubtedly have held their own against invaders from the Old World if these had made their appearance before the New-World civilizations had broken down internally. I may be right in holding that one of the reasons for their failure to hold their own against the Spaniards in the sixteenth century was their own unhappy condition at that time. Middle America was then in the throes of being forcibly united by the particularly brutal and sadistic militarism of the Aztecs. The Andean World had just been forcibly united by the militarism of the Incas; and, though the Inca regime was comparatively benevolent, the effects of the antecedent Inca conquest, and of the warfare between local powers before that, had been destructive and exhausting. At the same time it would be arbitrary to ignore another, entirely different, factor which was also one of the obvious causes of the indigenous American civilizations' overthrow by the sixteenth-century Spanish conquerors. The Aztecs were hopelessly outmatched by the Spaniards in military equipment. The Andean World had only recently entered the Bronze Age, and Middle America was still in the Neolithic Age, whereas even the Far West of the Old World had been in the Iron Age for about two thousand years by this time.[1] If the invasion of the New World from the Old World across the Atlantic had taken place 800 years before its actual date, the magnitude of the disparity between the two parties in their military equipment would have been of the same order as it was in the sixteenth century.

Thus the balance was tilted continuously, as well as heavily, to the indigenous American civilizations' disadvantage in the military sphere. Might this disadvantage have been offset if the peoples of Nuclear America had been subjected to their ordeal of being attacked by far better armed invaders from the Old World at a date when the social and cultural situation in Nuclear America was more propitious? The possibility that, in this case, the Andean peoples, at any rate, might have

---

[1] In *The Glasgow Herald*, 2nd August, 1939, a reviewer comments: 'It was Spanish steel and gunpowder that overthrew the Andean Civilization of the Incas, and a comparable technical superiority may slay our civilization.'

held their own is suggested by the actual course of events there after the Spaniards' arrival. The mass of the population submitted docilely to their new conquerors, and we may guess that this was largely because the preceding Inca conquest and domination had conditioned them to submissiveness in advance. Thus the social and cultural conditions then prevailing in the Andean World reinforced the adverse effect of the Incaic armies' military weakness in face of Old-World armaments; and the two adverse factors in combination told heavily in favour of the Old-World invaders. The Incas themselves, however, had not been affected by the docility in which they had successfully schooled their subjects for the benefit, as it turned out, of their Spanish supplanters. And a remnant of them had the spirit to stand up to the terrible experience of being suddenly and unexpectedly overthrown by invaders, out of the blue, equipped with overwhelmingly superior weapons.

When they found themselves thus ousted from their established position as the unchallenged masters of a great empire, the survivors of the Incas were not cowed. They withdrew into the forest-clad tropical eastern slopes of the Andes; and, though they were hardly more at home in this *montaña* than the Spaniards were, they took full advantage of the difficulties of the terrain and managed here to keep the Spaniards at bay for a whole generation. Moreover, before their resistance was overcome, they had begun to master the use of the Spaniards' outlandish weapons. And, farther afield, beyond the extreme southern and northern fringes of Nuclear America, one of the most effective of the Spanish weapons, the horse, was adopted with such success by indigenous barbarians—the Araucanians in Central Chile and the Plains Indians in the Rio Grande and Mississippi basins—that these were able to hold out against the cumulative pressure of conquest and colonization from the Old World for more than three hundred years after the date at which the Spaniards had first set foot on continental American ground. It is significant that both the Araucanians and the Plains Indians had previously been beyond the range of the indigenous American civilizations and had been unaffected by their breakdown and disintegration. The Araucanians had resisted the Incas as successfully as they afterwards resisted the Incas' Spanish successors; the Plains Indians had never crossed the Aztecs' path.

The historical evidence does suggest that, if the Old-World invasion of the New World across the Atlantic had occurred at a date at which the civilizations of the New World were still healthy and flourishing, this auspicious social and cultural factor might indeed have gone some way towards offsetting the Old-World invaders' superiority in military equipment. But obviously it is impossible to guarantee that it would have offset this formidable advantage sufficiently to have enabled the peoples of Nuclear America to beat the invaders off and to go on making their own history independently.

Moreover, we have to take account of four now extinct Old-World civilizations—the Minoan, the Hittite, the Indus, and the Shang—whose histories, like those of the two now extinct indigenous civilizations of the New World, have been brought to light by archaeological research. In these four Old-World cases, as in the two New-World cases, we know that the final blow was delivered by invaders from outside and that in each case it was a shattering one; but we do not know enough about the previous histories of any of the four to be able to tell whether or not it had suffered a previous internal 'breakdown' such as the two indigenous American civilizations seem to have suffered at the stage which is marked, in the archaeological record, by the ending of the 'Classic' phase of their culture. In the history of the Hittite Civilization we have the record of a great war between the two principal powers in the Hittite World, Khatti and Arzawa, at some date in the latter part of the fourteenth century B.C., and it seems possible that this war, in which Arzawa was overthrown, may have left Khatti, too, permanently weakened. There is evidence, in the record, that from that time onwards the Khatti Empire began to have increasing difficulty in holding its own against rebels at home and raiders from abroad. At the same time there was another drain on Khatti's resources—her long-drawn-out and inconclusive series of wars with Egypt over Syria—and here the source of weakness was a conflict with a power that was external to the Hittite World. In any case, the barbarian Völkerwanderung that overthrew the Khatti Empire and destroyed its capital city Khattušaš (Boghazqal'eh) round about the turn of the thirteenth and twelfth centuries B.C. was an external force of sufficient magnitude to have wrecked the Hittite Civilization, even if this had not already wrecked itself before this final catastrophe overtook it.

On reconsideration, then, I agree that force has sometimes played a decisive part in human affairs, and I also agree that the force which has been the immediate cause of the destruction of civilizations may sometimes have been an external force and not a domestic one. I still cannot think of any case in which it can be demonstrated that the force which dealt a civilization its mortal wound was an external one, while I can think of several cases in which it is evident that the mortal wound was self-inflicted, and in which the stricken civilization did not become a prey to external forces until it was already moribund. Cases in point are, I should say, the histories of the Hellenic Civilization and the two indigenous civilizations of the New World. At the same time I agree that it is non-proven that a civilization has never been destroyed by blows from outside without any previous suicidal acts of its own.

As for the charge that I have unduly depreciated the importance, in human affairs, of material factors of all kinds, non-military as well as military, I have acknowledged the justice of this already in discussing the unfortunate effects that a classical education has had for me.[1] Here, I am afraid, my reaction to public events in my own lifetime has reinforced the influence of my education; and, together, they have led me to under-estimate the power of both matter and force over the course of human affairs.

I shall try, from now onwards, to see these two ugly but potent and important factors in something more like their true proportions. But proportions are, by their very nature, relative, and, in admitting that

[1] See p. 600, with footnotes 2 and 3.

matter and force count for more than I have hitherto been willing to allow, I am not conceding that matter has the same power as spirit, or force the same power as love. No doubt the mental dichotomy of Reality into love versus power or into spirit versus matter is a misrepresentation; but, if the argument in the first chapter of this volume[1] is valid, the distortion of Reality that is involved in all such mental articulations of it is the inevitable price of human consciousness and thought; and, in so far as we have to distinguish spirit from matter, and love from force, in thinking about human affairs, I still maintain that spirit, and particularly the creative spiritual effect of suffering for the sake of love, is the distinctive and significant feature of human nature.

The power of creative suffering must be evident to anyone of my age; for the generation into which I happen to have been born has not only been Hitler's generation in the West and Stalin's in Russia; it has also been Gandhi's in India; and it can already be forecast with some confidence that Gandhi's effect on human history is going to be greater and more lasting than either Stalin's or Hitler's. But a recognition of the truth that spiritual power speaks the last word in human affairs is not any one particular generation's monopoly. It is the lesson of human experience at all times and places; and anyone, at any time and place, can learn it, not only from his personal experience, but from the stored and transmitted experience of his society's cultural heritage. A Westerner of my age who has been brought up as a Christian or a Jew and has been given a classical education will have had this lesson borne in upon him from many quarters,[2] in addition to his personal experience in his own lifetime. I myself was first made conscious of the creative power of suffering by the Athenian poet Aeschylus in the chorus in his *Agamemnon* in which he speculates on the nature and purpose of Reality seen in the personal form of a supreme god. I followed up the lesson in the *Prometheus*, and then realized that, all the time, it had been staring me in the face in the figure of 'the Suffering Servant' in Deutero-Isaiah and in the figure of Christ in the New Testament. When I afterwards carried my self-education beyond the eastern bounds of the Syriac and Hellenic worlds, I found that Prometheus and the Suffering Servant and Christ had Indian counterparts in the Buddha and in the bodhisattvas that had been imagined in the Buddha's likeness. If I wanted to describe, in epitome, the nature and the motive of a bodhisattva's act of self-sacrifice, I could do it by quoting Saint Paul's description of Christ's act of self-sacrifice in his Epistle to the Philippians.[3]

I have still to reconsider the effect of the events in my lifetime on my political outlook. I admit that the experience of my generation has made me hate nationalism and deplore the division of the World into sovereign independent local states.[4] But here I do not admit that my reaction to

[1] See pp. 8–13.   [2] See pp. 580–1.   [3] Phil. ii. 6–8.
[4] My hatred of nationalism has been noted by H. Baudet in *Historie en Metahistorie*, p. 51. My opposition to parochialism in all its forms has been approved by Rabbi J. B. Agus in *Judaism*, Fall, 1955, p. 325. On the other hand, A. N. Holcombe holds that 'Toynbee's hatred of the Nazi version of the sovereign national state leads him to what seems to be an unbalanced condemnation of modern nationalism in all its forms' (*The American Political Science Review*, vol. xlix, No. 4 (December, 1955), pp. 1151–4).

my generation's experience has led me astray. Unrestricted local sovereignty and intemperate local patriotism are, surely, threatening at this moment to bring destruction on our present-day society, and perhaps on mankind itself. These are not only obvious dangers; they are also obvious anachronisms in a world in which the progress of techno-logy has given human operations a planetary range and has at the same time armed the governments of local states with genocidal weapons. But one did not need to wait to be born in A.D. 1889 in order to become aware of the war-head of destructive power that local sovereignty and local patriotism carry with them. This has been manifest since the Sumeric Civilization broke down as the result of a crescendo of fratricidal wars between its local city-states, and the Sumerians brought that catastrophe on themselves not much less than four thousand five hundred years ago. A classically educated Westerner could learn the same lesson from his knowledge of the history of the Hellenic Civilization; a classically educated Chinese could learn it from his knowledge of the history of the Sinic World in the age of the Contending States. When my older con-temporary, Sir Ernest Barker, declares, and repeats, that he believes in national states and in national churches,[1] I feel that he is strangely over-looking or ignoring what look to me like unmistakable signs of the times.

On the other hand, when Sir Ernest goes on to say that the proper aim in politics is a harmony between 'national' and 'universal',[2] I heartily agree with him. Where national states have claimed absolute sovereignty and have demanded unqualified loyalty from their respective subjects, the result hitherto has, I believe, invariably been a crescendo of warfare that has eventually wrecked the civilization in which this anarchy has been tolerated. On the other hand, where local variety and autonomy have been completely suppressed for the benefit of a standardized culture and a centralized government in a unitary empire coextensive with the whole domain of a civilization, I believe that the social and cultural consequences have been unfortunate in these circumstances too. The Roman Empire prospered under the principate, when it was administered as a commonwealth of still autonomous, but no longer sovereign, city-states; it decayed with the decay of local autonomy and with the transformation of the world-government from an instrument for keeping the peace into an agency for the centralized bureaucratic ad-ministration of local as well as common affairs. The history of the Chinese Empire tells the same tale. The Ch'in imperial regime, which put an end to the intolerable anarchy of the Contending States, went, in reaction against this, to a hardly more tolerable opposite extreme of centraliza-tion and bureaucracy. In consequence it was overthrown by internal in-surrections within a few years of its founder's death. By contrast, the founder of the succeeding Han imperial regime, Liu P'ang, made a compromise between centralism and local autonomy on lines that were subsequently followed independently by Augustus at the other end of the Old World. In consequence the Chinese Empire, in the form in which

G. Masur maintains that 'nations have been the torch-bearers—of the Western Civiliza-tion, at any rate' (the *Historische Zeitschrift*, Band 177 (1954), pp. 521–2).

[1] Sir Ernest Barker in *Toynbee and History*, pp. 96 and 101.
[2] Ibid., p. 101.

Liu P'ang refounded it, lasted thereafter, on and off, for more than twenty-one centuries.

In the light of the success of Liu P'ang's and Augustus's policy, I agree with Sir Ernest Barker that a harmony between 'national' and 'universal' is the proper objective of statesmanship. But I do not know whether he would agree with me in holding that, if the harmony is to be effective and enduring, the authority of the 'universal', and the loyalty paid to it, must be paramount. This was one of the conditions of the compromise that was worked out by Liu P'ang and by Augustus, and this was, I should say, the secret of the success of the regime inaugurated by each of them. *A fortiori*, in our world-wide society in the present Atomic Age we shall not have assured the survival of the human race until we have established a world-government and have made the present national governments subordinate to it.[1] Of course, even in an age of world-wide communications, local administration, in a hierarchy of different geographical scales, will continue to be necessary. In the world-wide society into which we are now moving, national units will have the same part to play that the states have in a federation, and the counties or departments in a unitary national state. National loyalties in such fields as literature, art, and sport can continue to enrich our common human life without being the menace to the human race's existence that national loyalties are today when we are still indulging in them in the fields of politics and war. But, in an age when political nationalism has come to be a threat to the human race's survival, our paramount loyalty must be transferred from our local nation to mankind as a whole. To commit genocide in the name of local patriotism would be senseless besides being criminal; for, in perpetrating the destruction of the human race, one would be ensuring the destruction of one's own nation among the rest. In an age in which genocide has become a possibility, the only way of making sense of local loyalty is to subordinate it to a world-wide loyalty. This, and nothing short of this, will ensure the survival of each local nation; for this can now be ensured only by ensuring the survival of mankind.[2]

[1] This would be my answer to T. E. Sumberg's pertinent criticism that I have said nothing about the character of the political order that is to succeed national states if these are to be deprived of their sovereignty (*Social Research*, vol. 14, No. 3 (September, 1947), pp. 267–84).

[2] Perhaps this paragraph meets a point that has been put to me by Sir Geoffrey Vickers in a letter of 1st February, 1943.

'The intense cultivation of the nation-state is an instinctive attempt to supply a double need.

'For the first time, large communities have the power, and know they have the power, to create their own conditions. For this a machine is needed of size and scope altogether new—a machine capable of redistributing income, determining the use of land and property, enforcing standards of health, conditioning the adult, and educating the young. For a very large community, the state alone can provide such machinery; but, in doing so, it is assuming a wholly new function.

'Further, for such an enterprise a sentiment is needed, embracing the whole group, sufficiently strong and enduring to make the individual put *Gemeines* before *Eigenes* and tomorrow before today—at least to the extent needed in order to agree upon and to carry out these long-term efforts at collective self-creation. The sentiments must centre on the community which is the subject and the object of this collective effort. . . .

'The existing state machines are facts; they are incomparably the most powerful existing social machines. The sentiments of existing nations are facts. They are much the strongest existing collective sentiments, and are rooted in the realities of historical,

This is my belief. I believe it on the evidence as I see it; and I find this evidence both in the events of my own lifetime and in the previous course of history as far as I know it. But I do not just believe this as an intellectual proposition; I also most eagerly hope that, in our time, mankind is going to take the revolutionary new departure that our un-precedented new situation demands of us. I hope this because I believe that, if mankind cannot now bring itself at last to live as one family, the penalty, in our new situation, must be genocide sooner or later. And I wish, with all my heart, that the human race may survive, because I believe that Man has been given the capacity to see God, and I believe that this is the *summum bonum* towards which all creation groans and travails. Pieter Geyl says of me[1] that 'his dream is the unity of mankind in the love of God. Or rather, his dream is to participate in that loving vision and see its approach and realisation.' I am grateful to Geyl for the insight with which he has perceived what I feel, and for the sympathy with which he has described it. Obviously I am not the best judge of whether or not he is right in holding that the dream with which he credits me has overwhelmed my interest in particular phenomena and has made my thinking 'unhistorical'.[2] If this has been the price of my 'vision' it has been a high one; yet, whatever the price, 'I will not cease from mental strife'.

4. EFFECTS OF BEING WHAT ONE IS

(i) *Irreverence towards Pretensions to Uniqueness*

'What one is' might be expected, on first thoughts, to be the most easily identifiable of all things when the analyst is oneself. But it is notoriously difficult to disentangle 'nature' from 'nurture'; and I cannot feel sure, in my own case, that my irreverence towards pretensions to uniqueness is wholly the product of one of Nature's dice-throws in her game of genes. I may have inherited a tendency towards this attitude from unknown and perhaps remote ancestors, and I may have been led to develop it by influences that have been part of my informal education. I am a Londoner born and bred, and have lived and worked in London except for two years (1913–15) during which I was a don at Oxford. Since early childhood I have been constantly riding in London omni-buses and listening with delight to the conductors' running commentary on the human condition and the nature of the Universe. Perhaps I have caught some of my irreverence from the London bus-conductors,

social, and physical continuity. Are not these the only bases, rudimentary though they are, for a new advance?'

I agree that they can be invaluable bases for a new advance towards an increase in welfare—particularly for the poverty-stricken three-quarters of mankind. But, if they are to serve this constructive purpose, they must not be the *only* bases. In an age of guided intercontinental missiles with atomic war-heads, national states will produce, not welfare, but genocide, if they are allowed to remain the only units of social organiza-tion and only focuses of loyalty. In order to turn them into welfare agencies we have to deprive them of their traditional sovereignty and subordinate them, both legally and emotionally, to a higher authority. This world-authority would be the servant of the whole human race, and its first duty would be to help the race to provide for its own self-preservation.

[1] In *Toynbee and History*, p. 361.   [2] Geyl, ibid.

perhaps some of it from the London sparrows. Anyway, whether it is inborn in me or has seeped into me from my life-long cockney environment, I am conscious of the effects that it has had on my outlook.

I am convinced that irreverence, where irreverence is due, is one of the cardinal virtues. Even with my qualification 'where due', this conviction is, of course, a highly controversial one; and, without it, I myself should feel that, so far from being a virtue, irreverence would be a vice, and a very odious one. To be a virtue, irreverence must be discriminating: for there are other virtues, met with outside ourselves in our experience—above all, self-sacrifice for the sake of love—which are touchstones of our characters. They cry out to us to revere them; and, if we are irresponsive, we stand condemned. I am thinking, for example, of the passage in Saint Paul's Epistle to the Philippians in which he celebrates the great deed of loving self-sacrifice that is the Buddha's deed and the bodhisattvas' as well as Christ's.[1] I should feel that I had committed a grievous sin if ever I found myself reacting irreverently towards such deeds as this, or towards any lesser manifestations of spiritual greatness. The spiritual presence in the Universe that is greater than Man manifests itself to Man in more forms than one: in the 'myths' in which our human imagination penetrates perhaps farthest into the mystery of the Universe, as well as in the 'facts' presented in the records of the past or experienced at first hand in the present. In the face of this spiritual presence in any of its manifestations, irreverence would be impious and despicable. But, if one reveres this elusive yet ubiquitous essence of spiritual Reality, one is bound to reject all pretensions to uniqueness, whether these are put forward in Man's name or in God's. In the face of such pretensions, irreverence has, I am convinced, a salutary part to play. It can save us from the error of falling down and worshipping idols.

This sharp distinction that I make between idols and Reality, and between the irreverence and the reverence that are due respectively to each, has been overlooked, I think, by Stecchini in a critique of a previous volume of the present book.

'An examination [Stecchini says] of Toynbee's early writings, produced when he was merely a specialist in Greek history, reveals his surprising dislike of the characteristic values of Greek civilization. In this narrower context, there is laid bare the self-destructive bent of his thought: he feels ever compelled to subvert that which he avowedly stands for. The key to Toynbee's animus against the Jews is in that contradiction.'[2]

What I do feel ever compelled to subvert is not 'that which I avowedly stand for'; it is anything which seems to me to be an idol. And this horror of idolatry has been implanted in me by the heritage from Judaism in Christianity—a heritage that is made much of in the Protestant form of Christianity in which I was brought up. This Judaic iconoclasm of mine makes me reject, with particular vehemence, the claims to uniqueness that are made by the Judaic religions. Fitzsimons notes[3] that I 'rebelled

[1] See p. 617.
[2] L. C. Stecchini in *Midstream*, Autumn, 1956, pp. 84–91.
[3] In *The Review of Politics*, vol. 19, No. 4 (October, 1957), pp. 544–53.

against the exclusivism and complacency of the Victorian world. . . . He suffers', Fitzsimons says of me, 'from an unwillingness to believe that there can be an exclusive truth.'[1] My intransigence over this issue has been accurately noted in a critique of my work by Berkovitz. 'One of its basic principles', he writes,[2] 'indicates that there is nothing unique about either Judaism or Jewry, as there is nothing unique about anything else in human history.'

There is, of course, an epistemological sense, examined in Chapter I, in which every phenomenon is unique. When the intellect has acquired knowledge of a phenomenon by analysing and classifying all the features, shared by it with other phenomena, that the intellect is able to discern, there always remains an unexhausted, and perhaps inexhaustible, residue that is provisionally unique by definition, because it is still unclassified. But this unknown unique residue is not in the phenomenon itself. A phenomenon is, by definition, something that is perceptible to a human mind. The unique residue in each phenomenon is indistinguishable from the Reality beyond all phenomena; and the uniqueness of Reality precludes any phenomenon from being unique essentially and intrinsically. At the most, a phenomenon can be unique only momentarily and, so to speak, 'operationally': that is to say, if it is serving as a temporary vehicle or instrument for an act of creation.[3] To this extent only, I agree that, 'if history reveals a purpose, there are people who are the instruments of this purpose'.[4] In respect of this case in which the momentary vehicles of creation are human souls, the distinction between provisional uniqueness and intrinsic uniqueness has been finely drawn by Rabbi Agus:

'The quality of "uniqueness" is altogether legitimate in the vertical dimension of ideas and culture, for then the achievements of one group are held out as the potential possessions of all groups. But "uniqueness" as an innate quality of being is exclusive in character, invidious in intent, invariably offensive.'[5]

It is the pretensions to uniqueness in the second of these two senses that move me to irreverence.

For a Westerner brought up in the Christian tradition, the Jews' claim to be 'the Chosen People' is the classical case of a pretension to

---

[1] This outlook of mine is called by Fitzsimons 'Toynbee's charitable universalism'. This is a charitable description of it; and it is indeed true that my outlook is derived from the bright as well as from the dark facet of the Jewish vision of God's character that Christianity has inherited. A God who is the loving father of all His creatures cannot have left the majority of them outside His fold; He cannot have concentrated His love and care on some 'chosen' minority. If the same God is also jealous of His status as the One True God of the whole Universe, He will have laid upon every one of His creatures the commandment 'thou shalt have no other Gods before me'. Jealousy and love are an incongruous pair of attributes, considering that a love which is genuine and pure is incompatible with any self-regarding feelings. But, if it were conceivable that God could be both jealous and loving, these two veins of feeling would work together on one issue. They would conspire to make the Judaic God intolerant of any claim to uniqueness except His own.

[2] E. Berkovitz: *Judaism: Fossil or Ferment?*, p. 17, note 52.

[3] The language in this sentence may (I am aware) be read as implying that creation is the act of a person, and even one of a human-like kind. I do not mean to imply this, but I cannot find any less anthropomorphic words in the anthropocentric vocabulary of human language.   [4] Stecchini, ibid.

[5] Rabbi J. B. Agus in *Judaism*, Fall, 1955, p. 328.

uniqueness of the objectionable kind; but this is, of course, only one example of a common human aberration; and the aberration is a common one because its source is Man's besetting sin of self-centredness. I acknowledge, without misgiving or apology, that I tilt against pretensions to uniqueness wherever I encounter them. I react against them the most vigorously when they are put forward on behalf of some group or institution with which I happen to be associated, and for which I am therefore partially responsible to some infinitesimal extent. In the case in point, for instance, I feel more concern about pretensions to uniqueness on behalf of Jewry, Judaism, and Christianity than I feel about the corresponding pretensions on behalf of Islam. I do not find Islamic pretensions any less preposterous than I find Christian or Jewish pretensions. But, as my ancestral religious tradition happens to be the Christian one, and the Christian tradition has Jewish but not Islamic antecedents, I feel more responsible when such claims are made by Christians and Jews than when they are made by Muslims. Similarly, as my ancestral Christian tradition happens to be the Protestant one, and as I have not become a Catholic, I feel more responsible for Protestant pretensions than for Catholic pretensions. But I do combat pretensions to uniqueness abroad as well as at home. I combat them wherever I find them. In combating them I try, however, to distinguish between the pretension that I reject and other features in the institution or group or individual on whose behalf the pretension is made. An unacceptable pretension may be found in company with characteristics and achievements that call for love and admiration; and it is possible to love and admire something or somebody unreservedly without imagining that it or he or she is admirable or lovable uniquely.

I will now illustrate my attitude by giving a short catalogue of pretensions that I reject.

I reject the pretension to be 'a Chosen People' in whatever people's name it is made. The Jews, 'the British Israelites', the British 'sahibs' and Hindu Brahmans in India, the Japanese, my fellow Balliol men at Oxford, my fellow Teutons the German Nazis, all seem to me to have been chosen by no one except themselves. And, if that is the truth, it disposes of their claim, since every human institution, group, and individual is unique in its own estimation. When Joshua's and Sampson's Israelites ask me to acknowledge their uniqueness, I retort by looking at them through Canaanite and Philistine eyes. These are, after all, the eyes through which we should be seeing the Israelites today if the Books of the Law and the Prophets had come down to us in the version current in Sidon or Gath instead of our possessing them, as we do, only in the version current in Israel and Judah. As I see it, the mental dichotomy of mankind into Jews and gentiles, sheep and goats, is an illusion generated by the universal human malady of self-centredness.[1] Kipling's

---

[1] Jewish and Christian apologists sometimes try to mitigate the invidiousness of the pretension that the Jews are a chosen people by pointing out that, while the validity of the claim may be questionable, the consequence of its having been made is beyond dispute. The spiritual privilege, if it has indeed been conferred, has entailed a practical martyrdom. 'To be the chosen people of God' has been 'a temporal misfortune' for the Jews of the Mosaic dispensation (R. C. Zaehner: *At Sundry Times*, p. 177). 'If it was an

Recessional is eloquent and moving, but 'lesser breeds without the law' is a line in it that makes me smile, for here the sensitive poet is protruding the British Israelite's cloven hoof.

I reject the pretension of Christianity to be a unique revelation of the truth about Reality and a unique means of grace and salvation.[1] I reject the Christian Church's argument that it is unique in virtue of the uniqueness of Christ and of His incarnation. What Jesus thought and said about Himself cannot, I believe, be recovered from the words written of Him and put into His mouth in the New Testament. But, whatever Jesus may or may not have believed about Himself, we have to consider whether it seems to us credible that a God who, in Christianity's Judaic vision of Him, is another name for love, and who is believed to have demonstrated His love for Man by becoming incarnate in a human being, will have done this self-sacrificing deed of 'emptying Himself' at one time and place and one only.

Which is the more consonant with the Christian belief that God is love? The other Christian belief in the uniqueness of Christ's incarnation? Or the Hindu belief that Vishnu has subjected himself to more avatars than one,[2] and the Buddhist belief that more sentient beings

honour and a privilege to have been so chosen, it was full of danger, and exposed the bearer of it to the ill-will and jealousy of his fellow men. In this way the difficulty was got over of combining a religion meant for all mankind, and to which they were invited, with a religion confined in actual fact to one single nation' (R. Travers Herford: *Judaism in the New Testament Period*, p. 97). 'The Covenant grants no privileges but is the source of greater demands and heightened responsibility' (E. Berkovits: *Judaism: Fossil or Ferment?*, p. 67). 'A divine destiny reluctantly assumed, everlastingly repudiated, everlastingly reclaimed' (M. Samuel: *The Professor and the Fossil*, p. 106). 'The concept of Israel's choice is one of humility not of arrogance. The selection is a burden, not a grace' (A. Eban in *Toynbee and History*, p. 327).

I find this apologia unconvincing. I agree that the role of 'Chosen People' has been 'everlastingly reclaimed' by the Jews, but I do not know of any evidence that it was 'reluctantly assumed' in the first instance. The Jews are not the only people who have been willing to offer up costly sacrifices on the altar of their collective self-centredness. But self-centredness remains the sin that it is, however high a price one may be willing to pay for the psychological satisfaction that one obtains from committing it. I agree with Rabbi J. B. Agus (in *Judaism*, 1956, p. 34) in deprecating the sense of self-importance and the pride that are apt to be engendered by a belief that one has been 'chosen' by God—whether God's choice is believed to have been signified by one's birth or by confession and observance or by conversion.

While the suffering that the Jews have brought on themselves through this self-centredness is not meritorious in them, any more than it is in anyone else, it certainly is a merit, and a great one, in the Jews that they learnt the spiritual lesson that can be found in suffering, but, more often than not, is missed. 'Judaism . . . taught the possibility of transmuting pain into spiritual greatness' (Rabbi J. B. Agus in *Judaism*, Fall, 1955, p. 330). It is also a great merit of the Jews that, from the time of the Prophets onwards, there have always been Israelite, and subsequently Jewish, critics of 'the Chosen People's' claim to uniqueness. See, for example, Agus ibid., pp. 325–8. 'It is not the Jews that are unique, but the Torah as the Word of God and the Jews as the bearers of the Torah' (ibid., p. 326).

As for Antisemitism, this is a left-handed admission of the validity of the Jews' claim to uniqueness. 'Antisemitism, singling out the Jew as the demonic force in history, is manifestly the doctrine of "chosenness" with inverse valence. . . . There was a causal historical connexion between the Jew and the peculiar brand of hatred that was directed toward him' (Rabbi J. B. Agus in *Judaism*, 1956, p. 40).

[1] Edward Gargan—no doubt among many others—criticizes me for this in *Books on Trial*, March, 1955.

[2] The contrast between the uniqueness of Christ's incarnation according to Christian belief and the repeatedness of Vishnu's incarnations according to Hindu belief has been cited by Christopher Dawson (*The Dynamics of World History*, p. 236) as presumptive evidence in favour of the Christian belief's being the truth. Here, of course, Dawson is reproducing one of the traditional arguments of Christian apologists. But it is surely an

than one have taken the bodhisattva's tremendous vow to forgo his own self-liberation until he shall have shepherded all his fellow beings into the fold that he himself will have forborne till then to enter? Which, again, is the more consonant with the Christian conception of God's character? The Christian belief that there is only one revelation of the truth and one road to salvation? Or the belief, common to Hinduism and to the Pre-Christian religions of the Hellenic World, that the heart of the mystery of the Universe must be approachable by more roads than one? This Christian-hearted belief was expressed, in a letter to Saint Ambrose, by Quintus Aurelius Symmachus, the last non-Christian spokesman for religious liberty against an intolerant Christian Roman Government. If I am told that I cannot claim to be a Christian unless I take Ambrose's side against Symmachus's, I can only reply that, if so, I am not a Christian but a Symmachan,[1] or, in present-day terms, a Hindu.[2]

I also reject the pretension of Communism to be a unique discovery of the truth about Reality—at least in the province of human affairs—and a unique means of putting right what is wrong with human society, particularly in its 'capitalist' form. I am not blind to the importance of the social side of human life or to the shortcomings of all known social systems up to date. I do not know of any human society in which drastic social reform has not been overdue at every stage of its history. For this reason I do not believe that society under a Communist regime is, or is ever likely to be, the last word in social organization. I do not believe in the Jewish-Christian myth of the Millennium in its Communist version —the eventual 'withering' of the state—any more than I believe in it in its original Jewish-Christian context. We can, and I hope shall, humanize and civilize traditional methods of government and administration almost out of recognition; but I cannot foresee the complete elimination of the use of coercion in public affairs, because I cannot foresee a transformation of human nature that is going to deprive human beings of their freedom to do wrong and of their wish to do it on occasion. Individual human beings are the realities of human life, as I see it; and their problems are the fundamental human problems. Communism, it

argument in a circle. Uniqueness is deemed by Christians to be intrinsically superior to recurrence *because* they believe in the uniqueness of Christ's incarnation. On the other hand, recurrence is deemed to be superior to uniqueness by Hellenic philosophers, because they believe that what is general is superior to what is particular. Christian apologists have ignored this Hellenic argument; they have not refuted it.

[1] The Rev. E. R. Hardy Jr. says: 'I am not sure that Toynbee is really as much on Symmachus's side as he thinks he is. . . . I really think he is closer to Ambrose than to Symmachus' (*The Intent of Toynbee's History: A Cooperative Appraisal*). I confess to being a bit shaken by this judgement, since I have a great respect for Dr. Hardy's acumen.

[2] Albert Hourani is stating my beliefs correctly when he says that Toynbee 'wishes for a truth that excludes nothing'; that it seems to me wicked in the adherents of any religion if they make an exclusive claim for their own particular faith; and that on this point the principal target of my censure is the Christian Church. He is, of course, also correct in declaring that, if one rejects the Incarnation, one is rejecting Christianity (see *The Dublin Review*, vol. 229, No. 470 (December, 1955), pp. 393–5). In Christopher Dawson's eyes the philosophical equivalence of all the higher religions is a still more questionable notion of mine than the philosophical equivalence of all the civilizations (*Toynbee and History*, p. 134). In *The Observer*, 17th October, 1954, Dawson makes the impressive point that it is difficult to treat the higher religions as equivalent units, 'since religious values cannot be measured by empirical sociological criteria'.

seems to me, does not attempt to grapple with the problems of an individual human person, or to offer him or her the personal help that each of us needs for battling with the inescapable sufferings and trials that overtake us in the course of our individual lives. In this important negative point, Communism resembles Fascism, National Socialism, and the other Post-Christian Western ideologies in the present-day World,[1] and differs from the traditional higher religions of both the Judaic and the Indian group. This is, I should say, a radical defect in Communism. It would put Communism out of court for me even if I believed—as I do not—that Communism's prescription for social reform was absolutely —not just relatively—right; that it was practicably attainable; and that, in the process of attaining it, the end justified the use of violent and oppressive means. Communism claims to be a prescription for something more than just a necessary and beneficial social reform; it claims to provide a comprehensive way of life. I should still reject this larger pretension, even if I accepted the smaller one.

A gentile Westerner bears more responsibility for Communism than he bears for Christianity. The Christian religion and church had taken their classical shape several centuries before the first shoots of the Western Civilization made themselves visible above ground. Communism, on the other hand, was incubated in the bosom of the modern Western World. Its founders, Marx and Engels, were born and brought up in the Rhineland, and they spent the best part of their working lives in England—Marx in London, reading and writing in the British Museum, and Engels in Manchester, managing a factory. As a Westerner and an Englishman, I should feel more responsible for Communism today than I do feel, if, within my lifetime, the Russians[2] and the Chinese had not run away with it—as the sailor ran away with 'the bottle imp' in Robert Louis Stevenson's thrilling story with that title.

I reject the pretension of the Western Civilization to be a unique representative of the species: the only civilization truly worthy of the name. When I ask my fellow Westerners what the West stands for, and am told, as I usually am, that it stands for justice, freedom, and humanity, I ask if there is any civilization on record—not excluding those once represented by the Assyrians and the Aztecs—that has not also claimed to stand for the self-same virtues. Surely these are virtues to which all

---

[1] Edward Gargan criticizes me, in *Books on Trial*, March, 1955, for my 'unwillingness to recognise the phenomenon of modern totalitarianism as a unique development, without historical precedent'.

[2] The Russians have run away with Communism, but there is no evidence that they have fallen into the error of imagining that they have become 'the Chosen People' in virtue of having embraced an ideology that they—or their rulers in their name—now accept as being the one true faith. This is not the first time that there has been a national conversion in Russian history. Russia became a Christian country more than nine hundred years before she became a Communist one; and in the past the Russians, or some of them, have regarded their country as being 'Holy Russia', and regarded Moscow as being 'the Third Rome', because they believed themselves to be the only surviving Christian people that was still truly Orthodox. But this conviction did not lead the Russians into looking down upon other peoples and treating these with contempt; and there is no reason to suppose that the replacement of Eastern Orthodox Christianity by Communism as the national faith of Russia has infected the Russian people with a sense of superiority from which they were previously free. This point has been put to me in a letter of 6th March, 1951, from J. Stolnikoff which has been cited already on p. 540, footnote 2.

human beings feel themselves constrained to pay homage, but to which no human beings have ever succeeded in living up. If I am asked whether I do not consider that the West has lived up to them, a catalogue of Western atrocities flashes through my mind faster than the revolutions of an unreeling film: the Crusades, the Spanish Inquisition, the Spanish conquest of Peru, the Catholic-Protestant Wars of Religion, the English slave-trade, plantation slavery in the Old South of the United States, present-day racial discrimination there and in Kenya, in Central Africa, and in South Africa, two world wars in one lifetime, the cold-blooded genocide of Jews by Nazis, the French war of repression against the national resistance movement in Algeria.

Two Jewish scholars, Talmon and Berkovitz, have analysed my attitude correctly. Talmon finds that my irritation at the Jews, like my opposition to a Europocentric presentation of history, comes from a sense of guilt towards the Western colonial powers' subject peoples. In my eyes the West is a perpetual aggressor. I trace the West's arrogance back to the Jewish notion of a 'Chosen People'. And there is, Talmon agrees, 'a distinctive Jewish ingredient at the very core of Western civilization'.[1] Berkovitz pronounces that, in my eyes, Nazi Germany's guilt is the West's. 'His loathing of the [Nazi] "caricature" of the West', Berkovitz says of me, 'is really a form of "self-contempt"'; and my hostility towards Zionism—which I associate with Nazism—is an externalization of this agonizing feeling. 'The unbridled vehemence of Toynbee's condemnation of Zionism is out of all proportion to the guilt on the Zionist side. Accusing Zionism of "Nazism" reveals the measure of Toynbee's condemnation of "Nazism" in his own West.'[2] This analysis is acute, and I think there is some truth in it. On reconsideration, I do not find that I have changed my view of Zionism. I think that, in the Zionist movement, Western Jews have assimilated gentile Western Civilization in the most unfortunate possible form. They have assimilated the West's nationalism[3] and colonialism. The seizure of the houses, lands, and property of the 900,000 Palestinian Arabs who are now refugees is on a moral level with the worst crimes and injustices committed, during the last four or five centuries, by gentile West European conquerors and colonists overseas. This is still my judgement on the Zionist movement's record in Palestine since it first began to resort to violence there.[4] At the same time, on second thoughts, I do think it may be true that the vehemence of my condemnation of Zionism has been out of proportion to the magnitude of Zionism's guilt; and I also think that, if I have exaggerated, the psychological explanation of this exaggeration that has been suggested by Berkovitz may be the right one. In

[1] J. L. Talmon in *Commentary*, July, 1957, pp. 5–7.

[2] E. Berkovitz: *Judaism: Fossil or Ferment?*, pp. 108–12.

[3] Geyl points out (in *Toynbee and History*, p. 361) that this aspect of Zionism accounts for my opposition to it.

[4] I also want to say, in the same breath, that I admire the objectivity, concern for righteousness, and civic courage of other Jews who have protested publicly against the injustices, wrongs, and cruelties committed by Israelis against Arabs. As a classic example, I will cite Rabbi Agus's judgement, given in *Judaism*, Fall, 1955, pp. 322–4. Since the days of the Prophets it has been one of the glories of the Israelites, and the Jews after them, that they have been the foremost denouncers of their own sins.

the German Nazis, as in the English 'Black-and-Tans', I see the detestable dark side of the countenance of the Western Civilization in which I myself am an involuntary participant, and in the Jewish Zionists I see disciples of the Nazis. The Jews are, of course, not the only persecuted people that has reacted to persecution by doing as it has been done by; and, of course too, the Jews who have reacted in this tragically perverse way are only one section of Jewry. Yet the spectacle of any Jews, however few, following in the Nazis' footsteps is enough to drive a sensitive gentile or Jewish spectator almost to despair. Of all peoples in the World, the Jews have had the longest and the harshest experience of what it means to be victims of injustice and cruelty. That any Jews should inflict on a third party some of the very wrongs that Jews have suffered at Western hands is a portent that makes one wonder whether there may not be something irredeemably evil, not in Jewish human nature in particular, nor again just in Western human nature, but in the human nature common to all men.

At this, Zionists may exclaim in protest: 'Are our misdeeds really as bad as those of our gentile Western neighbours?' And gentile Westerners may exclaim: 'Are our misdeeds really as bad as those of the Aztecs and the Assyrians?' My answer to such protests would be that, in my eyes, a synoptic view of the histories of the civilizations gives the impression that all of them were philosophically equivalent.[1] I do not think that the Western Civilization's record has been below the average,[2] but I find no evidence that it has been above it, and certainly no evidence that it is unique in its virtues any more than in its vices. I also note, with fear and trembling, that the West's record is still incomplete, and, in the Atomic Age into which I have now lived, my apprehension increases as I watch the Recording Angel's 'moving finger' indefatigably going on writing. Talmon is mistaken in thinking[3] that I have 'missed a truth of awful import, a mystery of tragic grandeur—the ambivalence with which the whole of the Western achievement is charged from the start'.

If one rejects the Western Civilization's general pretension to uniqueness, one will also be critical of any particular pretensions to uniqueness that one finds this civilization making in particular provinces of its domain or in particular fields of its activity.

As I myself happen to have been born and brought up an Englishman,

---

[1] This impression of mine is noted and contested by Dawson in *Toynbee and History*, pp. 130–1. In *The Observer*, 17th October, 1954, Dawson concedes that 'it is possible to treat the civilizations as equivalent units on the ground of their limitations in time and space'. D. Thomson finds that my argument in favour of the 'philosophical contemporaneity' of civilizations is 'specious' (*The Spectator*, 17th January, 1947). Sweezy brands it as 'a disastrous doctrine' (*The Nation*, 19th October, 1946, p. 442).

[2] I do not accept Geyl's assertions that I have no regard for the Western Civilization (*Toynbee and History*, p. 363) and that I ignore its merits in the modern chapter of its history (ibid., p. 368). I do not agree with his contention that the Nazi movement ought not to be debited to the West's account (ibid., p. 370). If the Nazis were not Westerners, what were they? They were not Jews or Russians or Arabs. They were Germans, and the whole of Germany had been part and parcel of Western Christendom for the last 1,100 years before the date of Hitler's *Sendung*. If German Western Christians or ex-Christians could do, and did do, what the Nazis did, no other Western Christians or ex-Christians can now be sure that, in similar circumstances, they might not find themselves doing the same. The Nazi movement is a modern Western phenomenon that should have pricked the bubble of modern Western self-complacency.

[3] See *Commentary*, July, 1957, p. 9.

I am alive to my own countrymen's pretension to be *crême de la crême*. The self-same sense of superiority that all Westerners feel towards other human beings is felt by English Westerners towards other Westerners as well. In an Englishman's presence a Frenchman knows what being in a Frenchman's presence feels like to, let us say, an Algerian.[1] This English sense of superiority is, of course, a delusion and a ridiculous one. I was on the point of writing that I had not succumbed to it, when I was pulled up short by a sudden misgiving. I myself am an Englishman, after all, and, on this point, all Englishmen are probably incorrigible, however strenuously they may practise the wholesome exercise of leaning over backwards.[2]

[1] 'Some Brahmans are as white as Frenchmen.' These ingenuous words were published, in my lifetime, by a distinguished Englishman who was my older contemporary. In the present-day Anglo-Saxon language the adjective 'white' does not, of course, mean 'white' when the missing substantive is 'human skin'. It means 'exhibiting an abnormal deficiency of pigmentation'. In recent times this slight physical peculiarity has been taken, by some of those who suffer from it, as being a token of racial superiority, because peoples suffering from it have been enjoying a temporary ascendancy in the World. The passage quoted above reveals two assumptions in the mind of its English author. He takes it for granted that the deficiency is less conspicuous in Frenchmen's skins than it is in his English fellow countrymen's (he cannot ever have visited Normandy); and he also takes it for granted that, in a Brahman's skin, the deficiency is a good mark—even if it comes up only to the French and not to the English standard. He does not realize that, in the Brahman, this peculiarity is a birthmark of his ancestors' barbaric origin. It stamps him as an authentic unassimilated descendant of the Aryan Nomads who invaded India from Central Asia some time during the later centuries of the second millennium B.C.

[2] In 'leaning over backwards' it is easy to lean farther than one intends. Sir Llewellyn Woodward has noticed that in vols. i–iii of this book 'there is a certain petulance, at times even a lack of balance, in the treatment of the modern Western Civilization. This petulance can be understood', he concedes, 'at a time when fantastic nonsense is talked about "Nordic Man"; nevertheless, it is out of place', he suggests, 'in a philosophical study' (*The Spectator*, 6th July, 1934). This judgement seems to me to hit the mark exactly, and in the present volume I have had it in mind all the time, and have been trying to bring my attitude towards our Western Civilization into the balance that Woodward rightly recommends. I am as irreverent as ever towards Western pretensions that seem to me to be excessive. But irreverence can be good-tempered, and ought to be. When it is petulant, it defeats its purpose, which is to combat extravagances by ridiculing them. I plead guilty to occasional petulance, and also to not always being able to resist a childish temptation to pull provocative tails. I also acknowledge, without any sense of guilt, that, as a result of taking a classical education seriously, I have become psychologically detached to some extent from the Western Civilization in which I happen to have been born and brought up. But, when all these elements in my attitude towards the West are added together, they do not convict me of being anti-Western, or anything like it.

I might have let this go without saying it if I had not been denounced as a traitor to the West by at least two of my critics. Father G. F. Klenk, S.J., who calls me 'a deserter' (in *Stimmen der Zeit*, 1949/50, p. 145), makes amends, it is true, by bracketing me, in this role, with Thomas Mann. G. F. Hudson (in *The Twentieth Century*, November, 1954, pp. 403–12), quoting a statement of mine that I have spent 'two decades trying to read the map of history from a non-Western angle of vision', correctly presumes that I would not admit that this angle of vision was an *anti*-Western one. Hudson himself, however, attributes to me the view that the worst that could happen to the West would be no more than it deserved. 'Professor Toynbee . . . is profoundly alienated in spirit from the civilization that he has had the misfortune to inherit. His heart is in an earlier age of that civilization—the medieval—and he disapproves fundamentally of the course its development has taken since the latter half of the seventeenth century. He shares Mr. T. S. Eliot's antipathy for "decent godless people". . . . It is this that explains his obvious relish in "taking it out of" modern Western Man, and his *Schadenfreude* at the spectacle of the latter's recent tribulations.'

I am grateful to Hudson for bracketing me with T. S. Eliot. It is as great a distinction as it is to be bracketed with Thomas Mann. But his indictment is just brilliant nonsense. I have a substantial stake in the West's future: eleven grandchildren. How could it be supposed that I am licking my lips over the possibility that they may be wiped out of existence? There is nothing that I want more than that the West should survive. But,

Fortunately I have been pushed backwards in reaction against the pull of modern Western nationalism in the field of formal education. One of the virtues of the old-fashioned 'classical' education was that it taught one to put one's treasure in something outside the immediate here and now. The objective of a post-classical non-scientific education in the West is to soak the student's mind in the language, literature, history, and manners of his own country, on the assumption that this is a valuable training for citizenship in a democratic national state. At Oxford one day in the year 1910, when the end of my formal classical education was in sight, I picked up the current syllabus of the Oxford School of Modern History to consider whether, after taking my final classical examination at the University in *literis humanioribus*, I should spend the next year at Oxford reading modern history or spend it in Greece walking about the countryside. A brief glance at that syllabus was decisive. The quantity of English history that was prescribed in it as obligatory was enough to knock me over backwards—the more so when I found that what was not specifically English in the prescribed history course was still almost exclusively West European. Accustomed, as I had become by then, to roaming freely in the great open spaces of Hellenic history, with its vistas opening on to the still broader realms of the history of mankind and the history of the Universe, I felt as if I was being invited to put my head into a stuffy little closet that had not had an airing for years. I had been thrilled by English history at the age of four, when my mother had told the story to me in instalments, night by night, while she was putting me to bed. But my mother had made it thrilling by making it do for me what Hellenic history had been doing at a later stage. The prospect of studying English history in accordance with the specifications of the Oxford syllabus was unattractive to me; so I went to Greece, and have been thankful, ever since, that this was the alternative for which I then opted. Sir Ernest Barker is right in reporting[1] that I do not know English history and do not love it.

to survive, it must save itself. And I believe that irreverence such as mine is the most salutary attitude for Westerners to take towards their civilization in its present crisis. For the last two or three centuries the West has been enjoying an ascendancy over the non-Western majority of mankind. In our time this abnormal and unwholesome position of ours has become untenable. Our problem is how to climb down to a normal level of equality without having a great fall. Salvation for us Westerners today lies, I feel sure, in taking to heart the parable of the mote and the beam. A great fall is in store for us if we harden our hearts by nursing a pretension to uniqueness which is, as it always has been, irreconcilable with reality. In the present state of the West the attitude that, in a Westerner, is high treason is not irreverence towards our civilization, but adulation of it.

[1] In *Toynbee and History*, pp. 98–99. In this context Sir Ernest mentions that he has looked up the entries 'Egypt' and 'England' in my wife's index to volumes vii–x of the present book, and has ascertained, by applying a tape-measure, that 'England' occupies as much as one-sixth of the amount of space that is occupied by 'Egypt'. This remarkable figure just shows how difficult it is to rectify the distorting effects of one's relativity to one's cultural milieu. I really do not think that it would be possible to try harder or more sincerely than I have tried to get over the bias implanted in me by the accident that I am a Westerner and an English one. Yet here I stand hopelessly convicted by an eminent fellow Englishman and fellow historian of having given a disproportionately large space to my own country in a study that was intended to deal with human history generally and impartially.

To give one-sixth as much space to England as to Egypt is fantastic, and nothing but my being an Englishman can account for my having gone to that length. It is fantastic because the proper proportion would be, not one-sixth, but something nearer to one-sixtieth. Compared to Egypt, what is England, after all? Egypt has played a central part

He might have added that, for the same reason, I have no love for the barbarians. The nineteenth-century Englishman's self-esteem led him to extend his high estimate of himself to his Teutonic barbarian ancestors. J. R. Green and other English historians of his school fancied that they had traced back to primitive Teutonic institutions the origins of modern Western democracy. This hare that the disgruntled French aristocrat de Gobineau had started, and that the English had then chased, was pursued more laboriously by Continental Teutonic *Germanisten*, till in our day it has been run to death by Professor Hauer under Hitler's auspices. The one unquestionable service that the Nazis have rendered to scholarship is the unintended one of making the legend of a Teutonic barbarian golden age untenable by making it ludicrous.

I have always been embarrassed by this Anglo-German conspiracy with a French aristocrat to idealize our common barbarian ancestors. It has seemed to me to be just stuff and nonsense,[1] and the feel of the barbarian blood in my veins has made me shudder. No wonder, for I have the misfortune to have a double dose of it. When the Jewish Prophet Ezekiel wanted to shake the complacency of his fellow exiles, he gave them a reminder that 'your mother was a Hittite and your father was a wandering Aramaean'.[2] The corresponding confession that I have to make is an even more painful one. My mother was a Mercian and my father was a trespassing Dane. My great-grandfather was a farmer at Swineshead in the Lincolnshire fens, and the name of the village commemorates the historical fact that this part of Britain has been swamped by a Teutonic barbarian invasion not once only, but twice, since the withdrawal of the Roman garrison. Sveyn must have been a Danish invader who carved his hide out of land that previous Anglian invaders had stolen, in their time, from British subjects of the Roman Empire. Samuel declares that I envy the Jews;[3] and it is true that, if it were possible to change one's lineage, as it is to change one's name, I might find myself tempted to barter my Anglo-Danish birthright for a Jewish,

in human history for the last 5,000 years at least. For the first 3,500 of those 5,000 years she was the seat of an entire civilization—and this one of the two first civilizations to make their appearance. During the last 1,500 years, it is true, Egypt has been only part of the domain of a civilization that has occupied a wider area. Yet in her Christian period Egypt gave monasticism to the entire Christian World, and in her Islamic period she served as a citadel for the whole of Islam from the beginning of the Crusades until the end of the Mongol Völkerwanderung. It would be hardly an exaggeration to say that Islam owes its survival today to the service that Egypt did for it in an age in which it came very near to being wiped out. In recent times again, Egypt has been the first country in the Arab World to modernize itself by adopting the Western form of civilization. This is why Egypt is the leading Arab country now.

What has England to show for herself in comparison with Egypt's record? England has never been the seat of an independent self-contained civilization. She has always taken over the civilization of the adjoining part of the Continent. She has never played a part of first-class importance in the World as a whole except during the quarter of a millennium including, but also ending in, the Second World War. And, even during the period of her greatness, she was still never more than one out of half-a-dozen Western 'great powers', and several dozen Western national states.

Sir Ernest's tape-measurement is indeed illuminating.

[1] Two of my Teutonic critics, H. A. L. Fisher and K. D. Erdmann, think that, in previous volumes of this book, I have underestimated the amount and value of the Teutonic barbarians' contribution to the Western Civilization (Erdmann in *Archiv für Kulturgeschichte*, xxxiii. Band, Heft 2 (1951), p. 242; Fisher in *The Nineteenth Century and After*, December, 1934, p. 669).   [2] Ezek. xvi. 45.

[3] M. Samuel: *The Professor and the Fossil*, p. 138.

Arab, Greek, Italian, Dravidian, or Chinese one. I hope I should resist the temptation if it were feasible for me to be exposed to it; for its attractiveness to me would do me no credit. I should be seeking the childish satisfaction of pulling Nordic Man's tail, and the snobbish satisfaction of grafting myself on to the family tree of people who came into the swim of civilization two or three millennia earlier than the Englishman's reputed progenitors, stallion Hengist and mare Horsa.

Here I am confessing a preference for a longer over a shorter cultural pedigree, but not a preference for any particular racial 'points' over any other set (I use the word 'points' in the dog-fancier's sense). I reject all pretensions to spiritual superiority on the score of physical race, whatever may be the human breed on whose behalf these pretensions are being put forward. I do not know of there being any evidence for any correlation between physical and spiritual characteristics. The pretension is, I believe, as unscientific as it certainly is offensive.[1] The worst offenders today seem to be the surviving descendants of the Sanskrit-speaking barbarian invaders of the domain of the Indus Culture and the Teutonic-speaking barbarian invaders of the domain of the Roman Empire. Happily, in both India and the Western World, traditional discriminatory practices are arousing feelings of guilt and shame among an increasing number of people in the racially privileged strata of society, and in India and the United States, at least, the upholders of racial discrimination are now fighting what looks as if it were going to be a losing battle. In Kenya some of them, to their credit, are beginning to reconsider their point of view. But they are holding out defiantly in South Africa and in Central Africa; and in England—whose Teutonic-speaking inhabitants have hitherto prided themselves on being relatively free from racial prejudice at home, though not in India—a small immigration of British subjects of African race has been enough to provoke ugly manifestations of race-feeling. At the moment at which I was writing these words, Notting Hill and Nottingham were in the news, side by side with Little Rock and Johannesberg. Race-feeling seems, indeed, to be a characteristic vice of the Teutonic-speaking peoples, whether their homes happen to be in Europe or overseas, and whether they happen to talk Teuton in the High Dutch, Low Dutch, or English dialect of the language. On this issue, at any rate, Romance-speaking Westerners and Muslims have a less humiliating record.

Race-feeling is an unfortunate expression of a sense of self-importance; and the Western peoples that have been indulging in it have been showing up, in this unflattering caricature, an unfortunate vein in the spirit of the modern West as a whole. The modern West has plumed itself particularly on its achievements in the fields of technology, science, economics, and general command over the material element in non-human nature. Moreover, it has persuaded the rest of mankind to adopt these modern Western standards—alien though they are to the traditional standards set for civilization in most other attempts at it, including

---

[1] I have, however, been criticized by Lynn Thorndike (in *The Journal of Modern History*, September, 1935, pp. 315–17) for minimizing untenably 'the unmistakable evidence of physical inheritance'.

the pre-modern Western one. The present Atomic Age is at the same time the Age of Westernization. Not only the Russians but the Asians and Africans are now rushing to take the kingdom of Western materialism by storm; and they are regarding their success or failure in reaching this exotic objective as being the measure of their success or failure in life. This spectacle, too, moves me to irreverence; and this has provoked me, as I realize, into writing off these 'boosted' Western achievements at what may prove to have been a lower valuation than is their due. Of course, no valuation could be low enough if mankind is going to seize the opportunity for committing genocide that the modern West's inventions have placed in our hands. But, if we manage to restrain ourselves from committing this suicidal crime and folly, we shall have in our hands, for the first time in history, the material means of making the benefits of civilization accessible to all men. And, if the fruits of modern Western science and technology are eventually used for this beneficent purpose, our successors may yet learn to bless the modern West in retrospect.

I also reject the pretensions which are, I think, made explicitly or implicitly by some present-day Western scholars. Here again, I feel misgivings; for, in venturing to criticize my kind, I am implying that I am entitled to dissociate myself from them. This is obviously hazardous, since I am a present-day Western scholar myself, and the mote that I spy in the eye of some of my colleagues may therefore be a beam in my own eye without my being aware of its presence there. All the same, I am going to stick out my neck, and utter two criticisms at my peril. My first criticism is that scholars of the school that I here have in mind are inclined to put all their faith and all their works too into specialization. My second criticism is that they are inclined to overrate the importance of their own contributions to the advancement of knowledge, and to underrate the importance of the heritage that they have taken over from their predecessors.

On the question of specialization I do not dispute the argument that, in the present-day world, the accumulated and still fast accumulating store of knowledge is so great by comparison with the capacity of one mind in one lifetime that specialization has become an indispensable intellectual tool. But being indispensable is not the same thing as being all-sufficient; and the target of my criticism is an apparent unwillingness to recognize that specialization alone is not enough to give us the knowledge and understanding that we are seeking. The farther that specialization is carried, the more of the meaning of the phenomena is left unplumbed in the unexplored gaps between the specialists' deep but narrowly constricted borings. This method leaves critical questions not only unanswered but unasked. And they will remain unasked if the microscopic approach is not supplemented by a panoramic one.[1] Without

---

[1] See pp. 132–5. O. F. Anderle observes, in an unpublished paper, that the specialists are apt to assume that a panoramic view of history means just a collection of specialist views. He points out that this is a fallacy. W. H. Walsh points out (in *Toynbee and History*, p. 127) that it is philosophically naïve to imagine that, if only one accumulates a large enough amount of historical knowledge, this, in itself, will give a clue to the meaning of the historical phenomena. He attributes this *naïveté* to me. I think he would have

a combination of the two, there can be no stereoscopic vision. Turning a blind eye to the panoramic view is not one of my own sins, I should guess. And some of my severest critics would, I am sure, nod assent if I said the same thing in other words and confessed that a refusal to generalize was not one of my virtues. I should be happy if I felt sure that I was also free from the second of the two sins that I have just been attributing to some of the other practitioners of my profession.

In studying the work of some present-day scholars I have seen them succumbing to an illusion that is not, I should say, to their credit. When one or other of them makes a discovery that alters by, say, two per cent. the picture of the phenomena that he has inherited from eminent predecessors, he is apt to get the true proportions confused, or even transposed. He will feel, think, and write as if ninety-eight per cent. of the picture in its new look had been contributed by his own discovery, leaving a beggarly two per cent. to his eminent predecessors' credit. This is an intellectual illusion which is morally revealing, for it is the nemesis of a pair of moral failings—conceitedness and impiety. If the scholar had kept himself free from these failings he might have saved himself from succumbing to the illusion. If one has truly achieved a two-per-cent. improvement in knowledge and understanding, that is an achievement with which one could and should rest content. It is also an achievement which one could never have made at all if the ninety-eight per cent. had not been achieved already, thanks to the labours of predecessors in an endless regress. When one is standing on the shoulders of someone taller than oneself, it is a mistake to proclaim that one has forded the river on one's own feet and that Saint Christopher's contribution to the achievement has been a negligible one.

This comic illusion and the serious moral failings that permit it to arise do not figure in the catalogue of scholars' traditional faults. Traditionally they have been inclined to err in the opposite direction. In the Western World, for a thousand years ending in the seventeenth century, the characteristic mistake made by scholars was to pay too great deference to past authority. It was, no doubt, a bright day in the history of Western scholarship, science, and thought when Western minds began to dare to think for themselves. But the light would begin to fade if independence of mind were to degenerate into the vain conceit of fancying oneself to be Alpha and Omega. The most likely result of this hallucination would be a drop to Gamma Minus. This is, I fear, one of the dangers to which modern Western scholarship is exposing itself. The hallucination that is putting scholarship in jeopardy is the scholar's version of the pretension to uniqueness; and that, I believe, is the archsin of the modern Western World. If I am convicted of being one of the offenders,[1] I hope I shall lean over backwards, in revulsion from myself, till my head touches my heels.

When I am provoked by the self-complacency of present-day scholar-

been nearer the mark if he had attributed it to the specialists. My view is actually the opposite. I believe that history does not disclose its meaning if one does not go out in search of a meaning. I also believe that the right way to search for this is to frame hypotheses and to try these hypotheses out. This is anathema to some of the specialists.

[1] Charges against me on this count are cited on p. 638, footnote 2.

ship, I find myself wanting to restart the 'Ancients'' seventeenth-century battle against the 'Moderns'.[1] Nevertheless, Sir Ernest Barker is right when he says of me[2] that 'he dislikes renaissances' and is 'more a critic than a disciple' of the Hellenic Civilization. I dislike renaissances because their record shows, I think, that, on balance, they have done more to stifle than to stimulate creativity in the societies in which they have been conjured up. So, in the case of the Italian renaissance of Hellenism, to which I myself owe so much, my head gets the better of my heart and sets me firmly on the side of the 'Moderns' against the 'Ancients' in their seventeenth-century settlement of accounts. As for my critical attitude towards Hellenism, I am provoked into it, not so much by the Hellenes themselves, as by their uncritical Western disciples.

When Western Hellenists pay the Hellenes the left-handed compliment of bracketing them with themselves as children of light in contrast with benighted 'Orientals', I rebel against this move to make the Hellenes partners in the West's self-conferred uniqueness.[3] I then find myself siding with Darius against the Ionians and with Xerxes against the Hellenic Alliance. I call Xenophon and Alexander to witness that, when they came to know the Persians personally, they were deeply impressed by the sterling qualities of character that they found in them. Might it not, then, perhaps have been better for the Hellenes if unity and peace had been imposed on them by the Persians in the fifth century B.C.? This would have spared the Hellenes those four and a half centuries of tribulation that they brought upon themselves between the Emperor Darius's generation and the Emperor Augustus's.

I also rebel against the uncritical docility with which Western Hellenists have swallowed whole the Athenian account of Hellenic history.

---

[1] In one of O. H. K. Spate's critiques of my work (in *Toynbee and History*, pp. 296–7) I am mildly taken to task for having studied, and quoted at some length, the treatise on *Effects of Differences in Atmosphere, Water, and Location* in the *Corpus Hippocrateum*. How perverse, when I have shown such abysmal ignorance of the work of modern Western geographers! The implication is that the results of the study of geography in the Hellenic World in the fifth century B.C. have been put out of date by the work of Western geographers in the twentieth century of the Christian Era. So why waste one's time on this antiquated stuff, when there is such a wealth of up-to-date stuff to be mastered? This attitude is, it seems to me, revealing. It discloses the mental climate in which some present-day scholars work. As far as I can see, there is no reason to suppose that a Coan geographer of the fifth century B.C. is not just as worth studying and quoting today as, say, a living French one. The only conceivable ground for thinking otherwise would be an irrational conviction that present-day Western scholarship is something unique. Yet Heaven knows how it is going to stand comparison with Hellenic scholarship when the two come up for reappraisal by posterity, say, 5,000 years from now. No doubt, in the study of geography, the lapse of twenty-four centuries has brought with it a considerable net increase in the stock of information on which an inquirer can draw; but there is no evidence that this passage of time has been accompanied by any advance in human intelligence. The capacity of human minds to think about the relation between human beings and their non-human environment was not inferior in the fifth century B.C. to what it is today, and the stock of information accessible by that date was already sufficient for this purpose.

[2] In *Toynbee and History*, p. 92. My critical attitude towards Hellenism has been noticed by L. C. Stecchini in *Midstream*, Autumn, 1956, pp. 84–91, in a passage cited in the present chapter on p. 621. It has also been noticed by E. E. Y. Hales in *History To-day*, May, 1955, p. 322.

[3] This is the answer to Hales' question, in loc. cit: 'Why does the work of this scholar, nurtured in Hellenism, display so marked an anti-Greek bias?' He suggests that I am critical of Hellenism because I am critical of the Western Civilization to which Hellenism has made so large a contribution. But this would leave my critical attitude towards the Western Civilization still unexplained. I have tried to explain this on pp. 626–9.

We should surely be able to appreciate and admire Athenian literature, architecture, and art as they deserve without allowing the ambivalent Greek word *kalós* to hoax us into agreeing that what is beautiful is therefore also good. In this issue between Hellene and Hellene I am on the anti-Athenian side. I look askance at Attica from the Boeotian side of Mount Cithaeron. And, when I stand on the acropolis of Athens, I can never forget that the money with which those incomparable buildings and sculptures were paid for was not the Athenians' own and was not theirs to spend on Athenian public monuments. It was taken from contributions, intended for expenditure on common defence, which came out of the pockets of Athens' 'allies'; and the Athenians had the power to 'convert' these funds to an illegitimate use because they had reduced these nominal 'allies' to subjection by force of arms. As I mount from the Propylaea towards the Parthenon, the names Thasos, Naxos, Samos, Mytilene, Melos run through my head. And, when Hellenists lament the fall of Athens at the end of the Great Atheno-Peloponnesian War, I recall that Athens' antagonists and Athens' subjects were just as truly Hellenes as the Athenians were, and that, for them, the demolition of the Long Walls spelled liberation for the Hellenic World from the yoke of 'a tyrant city'.

In reacting against Athens in particular and against Hellenism in general, I am also exercising my human right of self-defence. Considering that my formal education has been an Hellenic one deriving from the renaissance of Hellenism in fifteenth-century Italy, I should be a lost soul if I allowed myself to be completely captivated by the double spell of Hellenism and Hellenism's Italian renaissance. I must react against this if I am not to succumb to it. But, in thus fighting for my intellectual independence, I am at the same time showing black ingratitude. I am remorsefully aware that my debt to the Italian renaissance and to Hellenism is immeasurable. The only extenuating circumstance that I can plead is that, after I have thoroughly seen through them both, and have thought and written the worst about them, I find myself still loving and admiring them as much as ever.

Sir Ernest also demurs[1] to my calling institutions[2] 'slums'. I think they really do deserve the name, considering the contrast that they present, in point of moral standards, to human relations of the intimate kind. Sir Ernest attended many more committee meetings in his life than I ever have; and I am sure that, as a committeeman, he recognized an experience of which I am conscious. As committeemen we accept, and even propose, enormities that we would never commit as human beings. On committees we behave more callously, meanly, and irresponsibly than we behave as individuals; and, in this ugly feature, committees are characteristic of all institutions.[3] This seems an inevitable consequence of the nature of institutions and of their purpose. Institutions are contrivances for establishing and maintaining co-operation between human beings beyond the range within which co-operation arises spontaneously

---

[1] In *Toynbee and History*, p. 96.
[2] A definition of the term 'institutions' has been offered on pp. 268-71.
[3] See p. 270.

from direct personal intercourse. Institutions are indispensable for civilization because the maximum number of human beings with which any one of us can be in a personal relation is small compared with the minimum number that must be induced or constrained to co-operate for technological, economic, political, and religious purposes if co-operation is to be on a large enough scale to produce the surplus of time and energy that is civilization's mainspring.[1] But this indispensable institutional co-operation inevitably has its price. By definition, institutional relations are impersonal relations; and, as soon as human relations become impersonal, they lose the principal safeguards of which personal relations have the benefit within their narrow circle. So long as one is in personal touch with another human being, one may love him; and 'it's love that makes the World go round'. Alternatively, of course, one may hate him; but, even if one does hate someone with whom one is in personal touch, one can never completely repudiate one's responsibility towards him, or completely bring oneself to treat him as if he were not human, so long as one's personal contact with him continues. Domestic slaves, for example, have never been treated so badly as slaves on plantations, down mines, or in factories.[2] Social life on the institutional level lacks the saving grace that a personal relation carries with it; and in this sense institutions are truly slums, I should say.

Of course slums can be cleaned or even cleared; and this is one of the calls to a holy life that have been made upon human nature by the higher religions. This is the meaning, in social terms, of their gospel of the brotherhood of Man. All men, they proclaim, are brothers in virtue of a spiritual bond which, in their view, links each human soul with an absolute spiritual Reality. The Absolute makes this bond possible by presenting Itself to Man in the likeness of a personality. Different glimpses of the supreme Reality in this aspect of Its nature are caught from different angles. It may be seen as a god who feels and acts like a father towards the beings who owe their existence to Him as their creator. Or it may be seen as a being who loves His fellow beings so much that He sacrifices Himself for their sake. He may sacrifice Himself, as Christ does in Saint Paul's paean in praise of Him, by emptying Himself of power and glory; or He may sacrifice Himself, as a bodhisattva does in a Mahayanian Buddhist's conception, by forbearing to empty Himself of the pains and sorrows of sensuous life. In both conceptions the sacrifice is thought of as going to the uttermost extreme; and, in both, one part of its redemptive purpose is to redeem human beings from their institutional slum-life.

However, Sir Ernest feels that, for describing institutions, 'slums' is too offensive a label. So, in deference to him, I herewith withdraw it, and substitute the innocuous label 'public utilities'. So long as institutions are conducted as 'public utilities' bona fide—are conducted, that is to say, impersonally and unemotionally—it would be captious to quarrel with them on principle, though it would also be unrealistic ever to relax the eternal vigilance which alone can prevent even the best regulated institutions from generating unintended inhuman effects. Unfortunately,

---

[1] This point has been made on p. 270.   [2] See p. 308, footnote 2.

human nature is not content to be impersonal, even in spheres of life in which impersonalness is in place. Our irrepressible self-centredness is always seeking for new worlds to conquer, and the institutional world offers an irresistibly inviting opportunity for aggrandizement to self-centredness in the formidable collective form in which the first person swells from the singular number into the plural. Time and again, institutions have been captured by collective self-centredness and have been used by it to serve its anti-social and anti-human ends. In the specious name of loyalty to institutions the happiness, welfare, and life of millions of men, women, and children have been sacrificed again and again—and this without the victims' leave being asked, when they have not been induced to throw themselves voluntarily under the wheels of Juggernaut's car. If Sir Ernest does not take care, he will lure me into asking him to agree with me that, if we are not to call institutions 'slums', we shall have to call them 'molochs'. When the votaries of an institution proclaim that it is something unique and that it must be idolized accordingly, they are serving a warning on us that they have converted a public utility into a public nuisance.

I cannot conclude this chapter without touching on the direst of all the many forms of the pretension to uniqueness that the saving virtue of irreverence has to combat. Self-centredness reveals itself nakedly in the arch-sin of pride;[1] and human pride culminates in the assumption that Man is the highest spiritual reality that exists. Irreverence in the face of hybris is a reaction that is not just my personal idiosyncrasy. The Hellenic and the Jewish attitude to life agree in reacting to hybris with abhorrence. The lesson that hybris leads inexorably and deservedly to catastrophe is proclaimed unceasingly in the New Testament as well as in the Old Testament and in the corpus of Hellenic poetry. If I myself stand convicted of hybris, as some of my critics hold that I do,[2] I acknowledge that I am a fair target for the retributive thunderbolt.

[1] See pp. 580–1.

[2] See p. 634. Mumford charges me with the sin of pride for fancying that, in my scheme for the comparative study of civilizations, I have a complete explanation of human affairs in my bag. I do not, he objects, make enough allowance for what is non-repetitive and unique (*Diogenes*, Spring, 1956, p. 25). E. E. Y. Hales' judgement is that 'it is misleading to say that he is misleading in treating his views about the births of civilizations as though they were laws arrived at by empirical analysis, and he is even more misleading in writing about the present and the future in the same sort of terms. This is where he himself yields to that same sin of *hybris* of which he is so conscious in history' (*History Today*, May, 1955, p. 322). T. R. Fyvel observes that, 'throughout the *Study*, Mr. Toynbee inveighs against the sense of *hubris*, of excessive pride, God-like ambition, which he attributes to a whole succession of characters in history. But to attempt a secular interpretation of history which should show the finality of the present crisis, which should tally with Professor Toynbee's Christian outlook, and which should show what is Britain's correct foreign policy today—wasn't there', Fyvel asks, 'a touch of *hubris* about the undertaking?' (*The Tribune*, 21st March, 1947). M. A. Fitzsimons finds that, 'in view of the boldness of his enterprise, the modesty of his description of it is not convincing. After all, Toynbee has tried—with success, so he believes—to read the design of God. Yet he refuses to accept the literal and exclusive truth of the teaching of a particular higher religion' (*The Review of Politics*, vol. 19, No. 4 (October, 1957), pp. 544–53). C. B. Joynt is the most severe. 'Toynbee really pretends to give an estimate of the total significance of the historical process, thus supplying indirect evidence of the dangers of the *hubris* he castigates so strongly. For to give an estimate of the total significance of the historical process is to pretend to the attributes of a transcendent mind. Pride could hardly carry anyone further than that' (*The Australasian Journal of Philosophy*, vol. 34, No. 3 (December, 1956), p. 202).

In considering these charges I find myself drawing distinctions between them. I do

Hybris is a sin that is not peculiar to human beings. It is the besetting sin of everything that has life in it, and a living god is not made immune against it by his divinity. When God empties Himself of His power and glory for His creatures' sake, He moves us, by the magnetic attraction of His love, to respond to Him with an answering love and with the added gratitude and adoration that the divine-human encounter evokes in the infinitely weaker of the two parties to it when the infinitely stronger party lays His strength aside. But God, when seen by Man in Man's own likeness, can present a malefic vision as well as a beatific one. If it pleases Him to take tyrannous advantage of His almighty power, instead of self-sacrificingly divesting Himself of it, He may thunder at Israel from Sinai or browbeat Job from the whirlwind or make Arjuna's hair stand on end at the horror of his gnashing teeth and flaming jaws, or lower gloomily, like Blake's Urizen, over a prostrate human race.

If God presents Himself, or is presented, in this odious epiphany as a superhuman *miles gloriosus*, irreverence is surely Man's proper reaction, and defiance his proper retort. In the last scene in the Book of Job the human hero is presented in as unflattering a posture as the divine villain of the piece. He penitently grovels in dust and ashes under the menace of a divine omnipotence that is aggressively unrepentant and unabashed. It would have become Job better if, instead, he had replied in kind like Ajax. If he had, then, no doubt, he would have forfeited his consolation prizes, and perhaps his life as well; but he would have saved his human dignity. How could he bring himself to accept a second batch of children as an adequate compensation for the first batch that Yahweh had given Satan permission to do to death? Human souls are not standardized interchangeable commodities like coins or crocks. The human reply that wins my respect and allegiance is not Job's; it is Epicurus's.

> Humana ante oculos foede cum vita iaceret
> in terris oppressa gravi sub religione
> quae caput a caeli regionibus ostendebat
> horribili super aspectu mortalibus instans,
> primum Graius homo mortalis tollere contra
> est oculos ausus primusque obsistere contra;

not think it is presumptuous to try to take a comprehensive view of human affairs. There are, I think (as I have argued in Chapter V), some questions that can be asked only in these comprehensive terms and that nevertheless need asking—not least in the present chapter of human history. What would be hybris here would be to imagine that one's own particular attempt at a comprehensive view was complete and definitive, and that one's own questions and own answers to these were the last word. It would also be hybris to imagine that, if a human mind could give an account of human affairs which really was the last word in terms of human reason, this achievement would be Alpha and Omega. Even if human reason were to go as far as it is capable of going, and this without falling into error at any point, it would still have to reckon with the unfathomable residue of Reality that it would have failed to catch in the meshes of its analytic and classificatory mental net.

In the original plan of my work I was perhaps guilty of the hybris that Mumford imputes to me. I have admitted this at an earlier point in the present volume (see p. 85, footnote 1) and have pleaded in extenuation that I changed my plan when, in trying to carry it out, I discovered its limitations. I then went over from a rationalist approach to a 'trans-rationalist' one. This is, to my mind, the necessary consequence of taking Mumford's criticism to heart and acting on it. But to judge by his accompanying criticism of me on the score of excessive other-worldliness, this return of mine towards religion is not the reorientation that he was intending to recommend.

> quem neque fama deum nec fulmina nec minitanti
> murmure compressit coelum, sed eo magis acrem
> irritat animi virtutem.[1]

This is the limit to which human audacity can go. The devout poet, in the fervour of his anti-religious faith, feels sure that the saviour-philosopher has won a decisive victory, not only for himself, but also for all his fellow men. 'Ergo vivida vis animi pervicit.'[2] Others may not share Lucretius's confidence in the invincibility of the human mind's moral and intellectual prowess. But, when God is presented to me in the unedifying counter-transfiguration in which Arjuna is reported to have beheld Him for an instant, I take my stand at Epicurus's side.

(ii) *Disregard for Scholarly Caution*[3]

Caution is, in the abstract, a morally neutral attitude; but, in the abstract, it is also a meaningless term. It is an attitude that implies engagement in action of some kind; and, according to what kind it is, caution is either a virtue or a vice. In a surgeon, pilot, driver, or signalman, disregard for caution would, of course, be a crime. A practitioner of any of these professions has other peoples' lives in his hands to save or lose; and, if he were to throw lives away through being incautious, that would be unpardonable. In professions such as these a mistake, once made, may be irreparable; and it may have irreparable consequences, too, for the other people concerned. A scholar, however, is not in this grim position. Mistakes made by him will not put any life in jeopardy, not even his own. And his mistakes are certain to be repaired for him before he has time to repair them himself. They will be repaired by his critics. These will swoop down on his published work like kites, and with kites' eyes for the weak points in it. So the scholar has nothing to lose, either for other people or for himself, except his own personal reputation for scholarliness.

A reputation for scholarliness is expendable, and it is a scholar's duty to risk it. If the scholar adopts the surgeon's, pilot's, driver's, and signalman's cautionary maxim 'safety first', caution, in him, will be a vice. It will be a vice, in him, for two reasons. In a scholar, who has nothing but his reputation to lose, caution will be a self-regarding attitude; and scholarship is, or should be, an impersonal co-operative enterprise. In the second place, this self-regarding attitude will be inimical to the fulfilment of what is scholarship's purpose. Its purpose is the advancement of knowledge and understanding, and this is best served by an attitude that is undiplomatic.

---

[1] Lucretius: *De Rerum Natura*, Book I, ll. 62–70. 'When human life was lying conspicuously and shamefully prostrate, crushed under the weight of Religion, which was displaying its head from the heavens above and was lowering over mortals with a fearful countenance, a Greek human hero was the first to look the monster in the face, and the first to resist her. Nothing could cow him: not the gods' prestige, not thunderbolts nor heaven with its menacing rumble. These threats stimulated his piercing mind to deeds of all the greater prowess.'

[2] Op. cit., Book I, l. 72. 'Therefore the vital force of his mind won through' (I cannot find English words to reproduce the alliteration of the Latin).

[3] 'Over-cautiousness is not one of Toynbee's defects' (The Rev. E. R. Hardy Jr. in *The Intent of Toynbee's History: A Cooperative Appraisal*).

Intellectual progress is achieved by the 'heuristic' method[1] of trial and error and the dialectical method of thesis and antithesis, exposition and criticism.[2] Its procedure is a continual debate, and this is perpetually producing results of two sorts: provisional answers to some of the questions that have already been subjects of discussion, and approaches to new questions that the course of the discussion has brought to light. An answer is never more than provisional, even when there is a momentary consensus in its favour. At any time it may be upset by fresh advances in understanding or in knowledge, and then the old question will become a new one again.[3] As for the new questions, they may eventually be answered provisionally or may be judged to be unanswerable in their original terms, and therefore perhaps to have been wrongly formulated. So long as this intellectual activity continues, fresh advances in understanding and knowledge may be made; but activity is

---

[1] See pp. 41–45.

[2] Several critics have recognized that the dialectical method is the method that I follow. Sir Maurice Powicke, for instance, says of my work that 'it will endure, not because it will or should win general agreement, but because it is the best existing discussion—not an explanation to be accepted or rejected' (*The Manchester Guardian*, 29th September, 1939).

At least four critics (John Strachey, Owen Lattimore, Lewis Mumford, and A. R. Burn) have pointed out that I am at one with Marx and Engels in seeing in the dialectical process not only the most fruitful method of gaining increases in knowledge and understanding, but also one of the fundamental rhythms in the movement of human affairs, and perhaps in the movement of the whole phenomenal universe. I acknowledge this intellectual affinity, and can see how it has come about. Though I am Marx's and Engels' junior by several generations and have a high respect for their intellectual powers as far as I am acquainted with their work, I have to confess that I am as ill-read in them as I am in Tarde, Pareto, Durkheim, Geddes, and other outstanding intellectual lights of whom I have been convicted by my critics of being ignorant. I did not get my vision of a dialectical universe from Marx and Engels; I got it from a source to which their philosophy, too, can be traced back. In fact, I got it from the Old Testament. This is, of course, one of the fountain-heads of Western thought, and the theme that runs through, and binds together, this otherwise rather heterogeneous collection of Israelite and Jewish books is a constantly recurring dialectic of encounters between a series of human beings and God.

Strachey has drawn attention, in an unpublished critique of my work, to this Biblical pre-established harmony of mine with Marx and Engels (and, of course, also with other Biblical-minded thinkers). Lattimore, in *The Atlantic Monthly*, April, 1948, p. 105, notices that 'to a surprising extent many of Toynbee's intellectual devices for measuring both growth and disintegration, such as the dominant minority, the internal and external proletariat, withdrawal-and-return, the impact of new forces on old institutions, "schism in the soul", or alternative active and passive substitutes for old ways of behaviour, and in general his concept of the relation between society and the individual, are markedly dialectical—quite as dialectical as Marxism, though his trend towards religious mysticism is utterly un-Marxist.'

Mumford observes, in *The New Republic*, 27th November, 1935, p. 64, that 'Toynbee is conscious of some inner rhythm that may abet the process [of change]. . . . In granting the possibility of such a rhythm, Toynbee is on the side of Marx and against most of the empirical historians. Surprisingly, Toynbee does not mention Hegel, Marx, or Engels, or, for that matter, Emerson, in connexion with this rhythmic interpretation, although he openly derives part of his terminology from Marx. But the fact is that Marx . . . is Toynbee's true spiritual progenitor.'

Burn suggests, in *History*, February–October, 1956, p. 12, that Toynbee 'never appears to have realised, even now, . . . that in Marxism his formula of "challenge and response" is anticipated and made the basis of a very fruitful historical theory, that of the "dialectical" interplay of individual wills with social, and especially economic, circumstances'. I do not know what evidence Burn thinks he has for accusing me of this particular piece of ignorance. This time I do not plead guilty.

[3] 'The relation of history and the human mind would . . . appear to be dialectical in the sense that they constantly act and react upon one another, producing fresh insights into the relations between facts' (C. B. Joynt in *The Australasian Journal of Philosophy*, December, 1956, p. 198).

dependent on atmosphere. The psychological atmosphere in which intellectual activity flourishes is one, not of cautious reserve, but of eagerness to explore the possibilities of unknown ground and readiness to take whatever risks may be entailed. In fact, the virtue that makes a good scholar is the opposite of the virtue that makes a good diplomatist or a good practitioner of one of the dangerous trades. It is more like the virtue that is required for business enterprise.

This last comparison should put the scholar on his guard against some of the vices that dog his virtue's heels. In the economic field an entrepreneur will be giving himself no chance of winning successes if he shrinks from taking risks; but he will also be courting failure if the risks that he takes are ill-considered. The more adventurous he dares to be, the more important it becomes for him to be careful and precise, and, above all, to exercise good judgement. This is an example that the scholar should take to heart. His duty to disregard caution is not a licence for bad judgement, superficiality, and inaccuracy. It is true that, if he does display these faults, this will double or treble the fire-power of the criticism that he will draw; and to draw criticism is his objective in putting a case, if it is true that the procedure of scholarship is the give-and-take of a debate. But, in provoking by sinning, he will be causing a wasteful expenditure of ammunition on unprofitable targets. And to sin deliberately, in order that criticism may abound, is as wrong-headed as it is to do this in order that grace may. It is also more wanton, since criticism, unlike grace, is sure to abound anyway; its economics are, indeed, those of abundance.

So a scholar must not expect that, if he shows a dutiful and valiant disregard for caution, this will earn him a free pardon for bad judgement and low standards of workmanship. These faults will still be the grave faults that they are. He is unlikely to be free from them altogether. In so far as he falls into them, perhaps he may hope to be half forgiven if he makes atonement by exercising a virtue that, in a scholar, is an even greater one than adventurousness.

In deliberately disregarding caution a scholar is not merely exposing himself to criticism; he is inviting it; and in doing so he is implicitly taking upon himself a moral obligation to respond in a constructive way to this criticism when it comes. If he succeeds in doing this, his initial disregard for caution may justify itself in retrospect. If he breaks down at this point, he will be convicted of having taken a course that he could not stay. So it is a counsel of enlightened self-interest, as well as a point of honour, for him to try to rise to the occasion. His implicit obligation, in the face of his critics, is a difficult and exacting one. However sharp the stings and stabs may be, he must not let them cut him to the heart. He must not wince and shrivel up. He must not turn surly and mulish. He will be his own worst enemy—a far worse one than the most malicious critic imaginable—if he mutters: 'what I have written I have written' and then spends the rest of his working life in trying to defend his past positions just because he happens to have adopted them once upon a time. The constructive response to criticism lies in profiting by it for the impersonal purpose of promoting the advancement of understanding and knowledge. One must take the criticism to heart as a stimulus for thinking again. One must consider whether the encounter between theses and antitheses may not open the way for making some provisional syntheses and for propounding some new problems.

This enterprise calls, in its turn, for certain psychological attitudes and qualities: in the first place, for good humour, but still more, perhaps, for a sanguine temperament and for an insatiable zest. Other peoples' critiques of one's work make (*experto crede*) a low intellectual diet. When they are numerous and voluminous, the long task of studying them has the depressing effect of taking daily doses of weed-killer. The killing of the weeds is a salutary operation, however disagreeable it may be. But one would be paying for this benefit too dearly if one allowed the poison to kill the vegetables too. One would be allowing one's cabbage-patch to be reduced to a desert. A scholar who has made himself a target for criticism can guard himself against letting it have this devastating effect if he can manage to regard his critics as being his benefactors, even when they do not mean to be, and as being his fellow workers in the common cause of the advancement of understanding and knowledge, even when this is not their immediate aim. Private intellectual enterprise, unlike private economic enterprise, lives by co-operation, not by competition.

I will now put some of my critics in the witness-box. Their evidence may throw light on the questions how far I myself have lived up to the virtues that I have just been demanding in a scholar, and how far I have been guilty of the vices that I have been condemning in him.

Several critics have pronounced that my work is a contribution towards keeping thought moving, whatever else it may be or not be. Some critics describe it as being stimulating,[1] others as being provocative.[2] Discounting the differences between these critics' approaches, I think they are saying the same thing in different words.[3] Spate, for instance, allows[4] that orthodox-minded scholars will find in my work 'an irritant stimulus to re-thinking their own postulates'. Leddy sees in me[5] 'the Oxford don seeking to stimulate rather than to instruct'.[6] Taylor finds[7] that 'the stimulus is to criticism and contradiction, not to acceptance'. Dyason describes my work as 'a spur and a warning'.[8] Anderle[9] weighs some 'pros' and 'cons':

'Much of what Toynbee has set out to do will certainly prove to be impracticable, and the system as a whole will hardly maintain itself in its present form. However, unless all appearances are deceptive, a great deal

---

[1] e.g. R. K. Merton in *The American Journal of Sociology*, vol. xlvii, No. 2 (September, 1941), p. 213, and P. Geyl in *Toynbee and History*, p. 65. 'Could we but lay aside his system', Geyl here remarks, 'we could find in his analyses and parallels, in his interpretations and even in his terminology, so much to stimulate thought and to activate the imagination!'   [2] e.g. E. E. Y. Hales in *History Today*, May, 1955, p. 323.
[3] Both words are used by A. N. Holcombe in *The American Political Science Review*, December, 1955, p. 1151.   [4] In *Toynbee and History*, p. 304.
[5] In *The Phoenix*, vol. 11, No. 4 (1957), p. 140.
[6] Something has gone wrong here. It is true that I have been an Oxford don, but I was one for little more than two years, and those as long ago as 1913–15.
[7] In *Toynbee and History*, p. 121.
[8] E. C. Dyason in *The Australian Outlook*, March, 1949, p. 59.
[9] In an unpublished paper.

of it will turn out to be fruitful as well as stimulating (*anregend*). . . . No theory is definitive. Every theory is provisional only. A theory will have yielded the best performance of which it is capable if it has kept going the flow of research. Toynbee's *Study* does more than that: it opens up an entirely new view of history.'

Taylor concedes[1] that I have asked some of the right questions, even though I have almost invariably given the wrong answers to them. Postan finds[2] that I have 'all the questions in the world to ask, but no patch on which even a single satisfactory answer can be raised'. Zahn points out[3] that 'comprehension (*Erkenntnis*) sometimes consists in just a correct understanding (*Verstehen*) of questions that are unanswerable'.

Höver finds[4] that I have introduced a new scale of values; Schuman[5] that the completion of the first ten volumes of the present book 'opens a wholly new chapter in Man's endless quest to comprehend the meaning of human experience'; Holborn[6] that it 'opens entirely new vistas of history'; a reviewer in *The Economist*[7] that it 'has opened doors which were previously closed'. Mumford finds[8] that the questions that I ask open up new ground; and, in another critique,[9] his conclusion is: 'This *Study of History*, then, is not a terminus, but a starting point, from which the roads radiate in many directions.'

Mumford's conclusion is not Bagby's. Bagby pronounces[10] that

'Toynbee has done a great disservice to the comparative study of civilizations and tended to bring discredit on the whole enterprise by undertaking his investigations in so ill-conceived and unscientific a manner. He represents, even in comparison with Spengler, a step backwards towards the pre-scientific moralising philosophy of history; as the apocalyptic visions in the later volumes show, he is primarily a prophet—a prophet disguised as a "modern Western student of history".'

Here we are back in a controversy that has been touched on in this volume in Chapter III. What is to be made of ethics and religion in a study of human affairs? Is it possible to find common intellectual ground between rationalists and people who hold that there are things which cannot be ignored by any student of human affairs yet which also cannot be dealt with adequately if one tries to do it with the human reason's tools solely? As I have discussed these questions already, I need not reopen them here.[11]

---

[1] In *Toynbee and History*, p. 121.
[2] In *The Sociological Review*, vol. xxviii (1936), p. 63.
[3] In *Toynbee und das Problem der Geschichte*, p. 13.
[4] Otto Höver in a typescript paper, of which he kindly sent me a copy, with the title: 'Betrachtungen über Arnold J. Toynbees Deutung des Menschengeschens'. See also the same writer's 'Buchführung und Bilanz der Weltgeschichte in Neuer Sicht: zu A. Toynbees Deutung des Frühzeitlichen Menschengeschehens', in the *Zeitschrift für Religions- und Geistesgeschichte*, Jahrgang 2, Heft 3 (1949/50), pp. 247–59.
[5] F. L. Schuman in *The Nation*, 6th November, 1954.
[6] H. Holborn in *The Saturday Review of Literature*, 31st May, 1947, p. 29.
[7] *The Economist*, 6th November, 1954.   [8] In *Toynbee and History*, p. 141.
[9] In *Diogenes*, No. 13 (Spring, 1956), p. 28.
[10] In *Culture and History*, p. 181.
[11] Soon after I had written these words the sad news of Bagby's death at the age of forty on 20th September, 1958, was announced in *The Times* on the same day (3rd October, 1958) on which a review of his book *Culture and History* was published in *The*

Other critics have anticipated me, as was to be expected, in convicting
me of faults that, in the present chapter, I have just been condemning in
myself and in any other scholar who may have been guilty of them.
Anderle, for instance, who certainly has no bias against me or my work,
judges[1] that my critics are right in holding that my work does not come
up to certain scholarly standards, and he justly adds that I cannot be
exempted from being judged by these standards. I have been guilty, for
instance, of inconsistencies, and of outright contradictions.[2] In a paper
on the historical validity of my approach to the universal churches[3] the
Reverend E. R. Hardy Jr. finds that my knowledge in this field is largely
on the handbook level, only in some places on the level of the scholar
who consults original sources, and only in the case of Christianity on the
level of the practising believer. Den Boer pronounces[4] that 'Toynbee
constructs and . . . does it haphazardly'. And Weil makes the same
criticism in more gracious language.[5] 'At times', as Weil puts it, 'the
constructive artist in him triumphs . . . over the carefully weighing
historian.' He concludes[6] that my terms fail to provide a stable framework for the motley events of history. To Gurian's eyes[7] 'the fundamental concepts appear as very thin', and 'they are means of subjective
classification'. Shinn finds that my work 'is least convincing in its
systematization'.[8] 'Never', in Hook's experience, 'has such an imposing
architectonic synthesis rested on such spindly theoretical foundations.'[9]
'Doubts arise' in Burn's mind when he 'comes to consider the plan and
execution of the work as a whole'.[10] A reviewer in *The Listener*[11] finds the
length and the relative irrelevance of some of my annexes aggravating in
'an already dangerously elaborated and burdened work'. Ralph suggests[12]
that 'perhaps the enduring value of the *Study* will be found not in his
schema . . . but in his defence of liberal human values and his incisive
observations in passing'. In Tawney's judgement[13] 'the frame is less
important than the picture, and the plan of the book than the discussion

Times Literary Supplement. This has been a great and unexpected loss for the systematic
study of human affairs. Bagby had a very clear mind as well as a very able one, and, in
the years that would have lain before him in the normal expectation of life, he might
have achieved the further results of which his published prolegomena gave promise.
I have a much higher opinion of his work than he had of mine. If I had died at Bagby's
age, I should have left behind me nothing of the present book beyond my manuscript
notes for the first ten volumes.   [1] In op. cit.
   [2] In the same unpublished paper, Anderle gives a list of contradictions pointed out by
other critics, especially Hampl and Gurian. These cannot be condoned, and they would
be even more reprehensible than they are if, in the writing of this book, I had had the
benefit of the 'well-organized filing cabinets and industrious research staffs' with which
W. Gurian credits me twice in five pages (see *The Review of Politics*, vol. 4, No. 4,
pp. 509 and 514). W. F. Albright, too, assumes that I have been provided with 'a
staff of research assistants and secretaries' (*From The Stone Age to Christianity*, 2nd ed.,
p. 96). These ministering legions of mine are creatures of Gurian's and Albright's
imagination.
   [3] In *The Intent of Toynbee's History: A Cooperative Appraisal.*
   [4] In *Toynbee and History*, p. 223.
   [5] Ibid., p. 282.   [6] Ibid., p. 286.
   [7] See *The Review of Politics*, vol. 4, No. 4 (October, 1942), p. 511.
   [8] R. L. Shinn: *Christianity and the Problem of History*, p. 241.
   [9] A. S. Hook in *The Partisan Review*, June, 1948, p. 691.
   [10] A. R. Burn in *History*, February–October, 1956, p. 1.
   [11] *The Listener*, 19th October, 1939.
   [12] P. L. Ralph in *The Saturday Review*, 16th October, 1954, p. 20.
   [13] R. H. Tawney in *International Affairs*, November, 1939, p. 801.

which fills it'. Kohn, too, finds[1] that my treatment of details is a more important feature of my work than the general framework in which I try to place them. On the other hand, O. Lattimore[2] and K. W. Thompson[3] say, in identical words, that the 'architectural design' is much better than the 'building material'. When these criticisms are put together, both the content and the form of my work come out badly.

Other strictures are still more searching. Spate[4] castigates my thought for a recklessness that is exhibited in my use of analogy.[5] As Samuel sees me,[6] 'he pursues any promising hint, no matter where it leads'. I should guess that this is what Kaufmann, too, has in mind when he says of me[7] that he 'lacks the conscience of the sound historian'. This is serious, if it is true of me, as Sir Ernest Barker thinks it is,[8] that his 'judgment is not equal to his knowledge'. Barker's opinion on this important point is supported by an identical one of Gurian's, who wonders at finding in himself 'this strange combination of respect for the immense erudition of the author and regret for the absence of balance in his judgment'.[9] Macrae does not believe that the wealth of information that I have harvested from the past 'is in any way equalled by the understanding that' I attempt 'to give of human destiny'.[10] My case begins to look almost hopeless if Vogt and Hourani are right in convicting me of arbitrariness and dogmatism too.[11] However, Guerard finds[12] that, 'in his boldest attempts, the British scholar'—i.e. Toynbee, in contrast to Spengler—'remains an empiricist, a Baconian'. Engel-Janosi, too, points out that I reject Spengler's determinism, and he finds that, by comparison with this great man, at any rate, I am tentative in my attitude.[13] Anderle, too, comes to my rescue here. He points out[14] that most of my critics have ignored my own explicit recognition that all historical work is always provisional, never definitive.

In recognizing this I have anticipated Caillois' forecast that my work will be superseded.[15] This judgement of his is shown by the context not to be intended to be condemnatory. Anyway, I concur in it enthusiastically, and venture to add that, as I see it, the quicker my work is superseded, the more successful it will have proved to be, since this will have given the measure of the stimulating—or provocative—effect that it will have had; and success, for a work of scholarship, has, to my mind, to be gauged in these terms. If Spate is right in scheduling it[16] as a house built on the sands, my comment on this is that, before the flood comes down

---

[1] In *Toynbee and History*, p. 358.
[2] Owen Lattimore in *The Atlantic Monthly*, April, 1948, p. 105.
[3] In *The Political Science Quarterly*, September, 1956, p. 367.
[4] In *Toynbee and History*, p. 303.
[5] This criticism has been cited already in a discussion of the uses of analogy on pp. 30–41.
[6] M. Samuel: *The Professor and the Fossil*, p. 138.
[7] In *Toynbee and History*, p. 306.   [8] See ibid., p. 92.
[9] W. Gurian in *The Review of Politics*, October, 1942, p. 508.
[10] D. G. Macrae in *The Literary Guide*, January, 1955.
[11] Vogt in *Saeculum*, No. 2 (1951), pp. 557–74; Hourani in loc. cit., p. 388.
[12] A. L. Guerard in *The Herald-Tribune*, 28th October, 1934.
[13] F. Engel-Janosi in *Wissenschaft und Weltbild*, 2. Jahrgang, Heft 4 (October, 1949), pp. 267 and 265.   [14] In op. cit.
[15] R. Caillois in *Diogenes*, Spring, 1956, p. 1.
[16] In *Toynbee and History*, p. 304.

and the temporary structure falls, the rebuilding programme will already have become overdue. When the spate has come and gone, the site will be clear for the erection of a rather more up-to-date temporary structure in place of mine—pending the next flood, the next clearance, the next rebuilding, and so on in *saecula saeculorum*. If Morgenthau is right in calling my work an 'Icarean effort',[1] my comment is that Icarus's crash was a tragedy, if it was one, for nobody but himself. When Icarus crashed, his more competent father Daedalus made a happy landing. And, in consequence, the experience of flying is today within the reach of any man, woman, or child, provided that the necessary money is forthcoming for buying the ticket. Today anyone can fly thanks to the adventurousness of the pioneers. Also, even today, travelling by air is still something of an adventure for the passenger; for though he can be sure that the pilot will put safety first, he cannot, even so, be quite sure that he is going to come down alive, when once he is up aloft.

Other critics who share Spate's and Morgenthau's opinion that I have come to grief have suggested two explanations: I have tried to straddle the whole of history; and I have tried to straddle both history and 'metahistory'[2] and have jumbled them up.

E. R. Curtius has done me the honour of saying that in this book 'we are given the whole of history. For the first time, the survey is a complete one.'[3] With the same generosity, Hans Kohn says of me that a sense of unity will be my contribution[4] and that 'he is perhaps the first to attempt to write the history of the human race in the genuine meaning of the phrase'.[5] E. E. Y. Hales says that my work 'surveys the entire field more widely than it has ever before been surveyed'.[6] In Hales' view this is where my interpretation of history 'has the advantage over all others'. On the other hand, Kohn says[7] of my work, in the context of the passage just quoted, that, 'in its fundamental conception, it is an attempt at the impossible, and for this reason it miscarries'. The same point is made by H. Marrou. 'To write', he says,[8] 'a universal history and, *a fortiori*, to think, as Toynbee does, about the totality of universal history, is an undertaking that runs up against a technical impossibility.' (Marrou shows himself as generous as Curtius and Kohn in adding the comment: 'Toynbee a trop osé, mais l'audace. . . .')[9] M. Postan suggests[10] that, if I had been a social scientist, I would never have attempted, as I have, 'to solve the problems of civilization and society by a frontal attack on the massed evidence of all the historical societies'. T. J. G. Locher observes[11] that

'our age is asking for a total vision, now that the World has grown together into so close a unity. This superhuman task is the one at which Toynbee has tried his hand—and, in my judgment, he has miscarried in things of cardinal importance.'

1 In *Toynbee and History*, p. 199.
2 The meaning of this word has been examined on pp. 227–9.
3 E. R. Curtius in *Merkur*, 2. Jahrgang, 4. Heft [Heft 10] (1948), p. 528.
4 *Toynbee and History*, p. 359.   5 H. Kohn in *Der Monat*, August 1955, p. 469.
6 *History Today*, May, 1955, p. 323.   7 In *Der Monat*, pag. cit.
8 In *Esprit*, July, 1952, p. 121.   9 Ibid., p. 122.
10 In *The Sociological Review*, vol. xxviii (1936), pp. 62–63.
11 In *De Gids*, May, 1948, offprint, p. 30, quoted already on p. 141.

It will be seen that the point made by Locher in the first sentence of this passage is the one that I have made in this volume in Chapter V.[1] In the new state of human affairs into which we have been moving in our time, a comprehensive study of human affairs is being asked for because it has become a crying need, and the intelligent public, all over the World, has become alive to this. If that is the truth, then it cannot be wrong to try to meet this need. Any scholar who ventures out on this enterprise will at least be showing public spirit, however he fares. If my own venture is judged to have miscarried, this is a trivial mishap. No one stands to lose by my failure except myself, and the way remains clear for any number of others to have their try and, it is to be hoped, to fare better. If we are faced here by nothing more serious than one man's failure—due just to his personal inadequacy for carrying out a big task—there is no reason for concern. But what if Kohn and Marrou are right? What if this is an enterprise that it is intrinsically impossible to achieve, so that my failure is not just my funeral but is also a warning that nobody else can be any more successful?

If this is the true situation, it is one that is both tragic and comic. It is tragic, if true, that the vision for which our age is asking should be unattainable. 'Where there is no vision, the people perish.' And we are now aware that today mankind is in danger of perishing by committing genocide if we cannot learn at last to live as one family. We shall hardly be able to make this revolution in human life without the inspiration of a new vision. And, if a new vision is unattainable, this is assuredly tragic. But it is also comic, if true, that we should be debarred from winning the understanding that we need by the abundance of the knowledge that we have at our disposal. This sounds too paradoxical to make sense. Yet this is, in effect, what Kohn and Marrou are saying. There is now, they are telling us, such a plethora of potential knowledge in our library stacks and in our filing cabinets that it has ceased to be possible to have in our heads any comprehension of its purport. The abundance in our larder condemns us to starve. So we must resign ourselves to drifting towards catastrophe without a hope of being able to take bearings or steer a course. How fortunate, compared to us, were our predecessors in the time of Dante and, still more, no doubt, in the time of Bede. Their understanding was not clouded, as ours is, by a surfeit of information. They could see a vision, and so could find their way in this mysterious universe in which we, their too well-informed successors, are now blindly floundering.

When I am asked to believe this, I find that my credulity is not equal to it. Human minds in the present-day world show no signs of being any less capable of coping with the perennial human situation than they were in the Western Middle Ages or in the Age of Neanderthal Man. I have no doubt that we shall discover how to administer the economics of abundance on the intellectual plane as well as on the material one. If the enterprise at which I have been trying my hand has miscarried, I cannot be acquitted on the plea that this was a superhuman undertaking and a technical impossibility. The failure is mine, and the blame for it is on my head. I do not pretend that I have solved the problem, but I also do not agree that it is impossible that it should ever be solved.[1]

This brings me to the second explanation of the miscarriage that my critics report. I have tried to deal with metahistory as well as history, and I have confused these two different levels of understanding. Here there are two separate indictments which have to be kept distinct, because it is possible to be found guilty on the first count without being found guilty on the second. In fact, I plead guilty on the first, while on the second I plead not guilty.

I have extended my field of inquiry from history to metahistory consciously and deliberately. I have noted in Chapter II that I began my work in this book by trying to give an intelligible comprehensive account of history—since the emergence of the species of human culture that we call 'civilization'—in the form of a comparative study of all the known societies of this species that either are, or once have been, engaged on this enterprise. In the course of my inquiry, however, I came to the conclusion that the histories of the 'higher religions' could not be made intelligible within this conceptual framework, and that I must therefore make the experiment of reversing my previous plan of operations. I must see whether I could obtain a more intelligible picture of history by explaining civilizations in terms of higher religions than I had obtained by trying to explain these in terms of civilizations. I had already taken note of this new departure at the point in the book at which I was making it,[2] and a number of my critics have also put their finger on this inconsistency in my procedure and on the implicit rift in my system of thought.[3]

Hourani observes, in reviewing the four volumes of the book which were published in 1954, that 'in the last few years Toynbee's view of history and of the Universe has changed radically'. 'On the one hand, "civilization" is seen as something ultimate.' Alternatively, the goal is sainthood.[4] Anderle observes[5] that, unlike Spengler, I have a rift in my system, and that there are signs in my work of a tension of will and an inner conflict. As he sees it, I have missed fire in an attempt to produce an empirical-scientific morphology of civilizations to take the place of Spengler's artistic-intuitive one. In my eyes (Anderle correctly reports) Spengler's determinism is his Achilles' heel, and I have made the assumption that Man *must* be free, without realizing how gravely biased this point of departure is.

'One cannot construct a self-contained "holistic" (*ganzheitliche*) morphology of civilizations and at the same time interpret the civilizations as open processes. Toynbee was not willing either to renounce the first of these two objectives or to sacrifice the second. This makes a rift in his system and makes it untenable as a whole.'

---

[1] The problem of quantity in the study of human affairs has been discussed in this volume in Chapter IV. [2] See vii. 420–3.
[3] See the references on p. 27, footnote 2. See also p. 94, footnote 1, and p. 100, footnote 3.
[4] A. Hourani in *The Dublin Review*, vol. 229, No. 470 (December, 1955), pp. 387–8 and 384–5. [5] O. F. Anderle in op. cit.

I acknowledge this rift, but I do not agree that it makes my system untenable. On the contrary, I believe that it would have become untenable if I had tried to escape the rift by making believe that the net of human reason has no holes in it. My system, in showing a rift, corresponds, I believe, to an inescapable dichotomy, in any human mind's vision of Reality, between uniformities that are intelligible and irregularities that are inexplicable because, for all that we can tell, they are unique. If we tidy up our mental panorama by drawing a veil over either of these two elements in it on the plea that we cannot admit their coexistence because we cannot see how they can be mutually compatible, we shall be deferring to logic at the cost of giving the lie to experience.

The rift that Anderle has found in my system has been noticed by other critics too. Indeed, they find that the 'openness' of my mental horizon extends not only to a belief in the freedom of human wills, but also to a belief in a spiritual presence beyond the phenomena which involves me in a trans-rational extension of my rational approach to the study of human affairs. Savelle, for instance, comments[1] on my work that,

'when he treats of historic civilizations upon the basis of empirical sources (especially in volumes i–vi), his history writing and his empiricism are brilliantly successful. It can be said, indeed, that his demonstration of natural law in human history—resting, as it does, upon historical evidence —is very substantially grounded and would be difficult to refute. But in his treatment of the "Soul" and the "One True God" he makes a leap of faith that a historian insisting upon empirical evidence cannot follow. That there is poetry in history, of course, can be agreed. But that there is a poetic licence for the historian to soar far beyond his empirically verifiable data for the enjoyment of a wholly subjective "beatific vision", the empirical historian could never admit.'

Sumberg attributes the rift in my work to a failure of nerve which he, as well as Watnick,[2] imputes to me.

'It seems fair [Sumberg says] to conjecture that [Toynbee] became frightened of the vision he was developing in the earlier portions of his work, a vision of Man's endless and repetitive suffering to no purpose. . . . He was driven, therefore, to bring Jesus on the stage as the *deus ex machina* of the drama.'[3]

Voegelin observes[4] that, in the present book, from volume vii onwards, the history of religion becomes, for me, history proper, and that I now no longer take civilizations as being the intelligible fields of study. He correctly remarks that 'the plan, as it was conceived on the first existential level, was retained to cover the studies on the last existential level', and he makes the justified criticism that 'neither has the plan of the first level been completed, nor has the last level found an organisational level of its own'.[5]

---

[1] In *The Pacific Historical Review*, February, 1956, pp. 55–67.
[2] See p. 607, footnote 4.
[3] *Social Research*, vol. 14, No. 3 (September, 1947), pp. 267–84.
[4] In *The Intent of Toynbee's History: A Cooperative Appraisal.*
[5] Voegelin does me the honour of suggesting that vols. vii–x of my book stand to

It will be seen that Voegelin criticizes me not, as Anderle does, for having changed my plan of operations, but for having failed, so far, to construct the new intellectual framework that the new plan requires for its execution. This is a charge to which I plead guilty. In volumes vii–x of this book I did try to carry out the new plan within the original framework. This was a mistake in procedure, and in the present volume I am trying to take at least the first step towards correcting it. I am grateful to Voegelin for his constructive criticism, and still more grateful to him for approving of my unwillingness to remain the prisoner of a self-contained system of ideas of my own making, when once I had become convinced that, within the limits of this system, I should not find myself able to do justice to some of the most important of the phenomena that I was studying. After pointing out that the definitions which I successively propose have a way of each superseding its predecessors, Voegelin insists that 'under no circumstances must they be pitted against each other by a logic of the external world which ignores the logic of existence'.

The openness of my mental horizon, which Voegelin notices and commends, has also been noticed by Baudet. In my view, he points out, history is an open road, in contrast to Saint Augustine's view that its course is predetermined.[1] This is, I think, what Erdmann has in mind when he suggests[2] that the unity of my book is like the unity of an expedition or a pilgrimage.

vols. i–vi in the relation in which Saint Augustine's *De Civitate Dei* stands to Orosius's *Historia contra Paganos*. H. E. Barnes calls me 'Orosius and Augustine in modern dress' (*An Introduction to the History of Sociology*, pp. 717–36). Brinton notes that 'Saint Augustine's *City of God*, supplemented by the work of Orosius, supplied for a medieval Christian the psychological equivalent of the time series, charts, and the like which the modern mind demands. Some of Toynbee's most suggestive work', he adds, 'has been done in this field. Many of his phrases—"challenge-and-response", "creative minority", "mimesis", "rout-and-rally", "Herodianism or Zealotism", "knock-out-blow"—can help, used carefully, to do the work of the mere historian' (*The Virginian Quarterly Review*, Summer, 1956, pp. 361–75).

I have been associated with Saint Augustine by other critics too: for instance, H. Baudet: 'Hedendaagsch Augustinisme' in *Historie en Metahistorie*; M. Savelle in *The Pacific Historical Review*, February, 1956, p. 55; T. A. Sumberg in *Social Research*, vol. 14, No. 3 (September, 1947), pp. 267–84; C. B. Joynt in *The Australasian Journal of Philosophy*, December, 1956, p. 202; Sir Llewellyn Woodward in *The Spectator*, 18th August, 1939; L. Mumford in *Diogenes*, Spring, 1956, p. 21; J. H. Nichols in *The Journal of Religion*, No. 28 (1948), pp. 99–119; H. Kuhn in *The Journal of Philosophy*, 21st August, 1947, p. 499; G. M. Bryan in *Social Forces*, 26 (March, 1948), pp. 288–92; E. I. Watkin in *The Tablet*, 12th August, 1939; F. J. Teggart in a letter to me of 8th January, 1936.

Being paired with a giant is a formidable honour for a pygmy. He comes off badly in all situations. When the giant is estimated at his true stature, the pygmy's inferiority invites uncomplimentary comparisons—though, as the pygmy sees it, these might perhaps have gone without saying. Baudet finds it worth mentioning (in op. cit., pp. 50 and 61) that Augustine is greater, more heroic, more naïve, and more logical than I am in my 'Augustinism without God or Devil'. Brinton notes (in loc. cit.) that, unlike Augustine, I have 'no firm armature of accepted theology', and that I seem 'at times to attempt the really shocking combination of Saint Augustine and Pelagius'. Nichols also demurs to my Pelagianism, and pronounces that, on this point, I come off badly by comparison with Saint Augustine. When, however, the giant is given a box on the ear, I suffer from the repercussions. Sir Llewellyn Woodward, for example, after suggesting (in *The Spectator*, 11th August, 1938) that my work might have some 'therapeutic value because it is written, like the *De Civitate Dei*, under the strain of immediate social catastrophe', hastens to remind his readers and me that 'Saint Augustine's work is, in the last analysis, a great masterpiece of special pleading'.

[1] H. Baudet: 'Hedendaagsch Augustinisme' in *Historie en Metahistorie*, pp. 48 and 49.
[2] K. D. Erdmann in *Archiv für Kulturgeschichte*, xxxiii. Band, Heft 2, p. 189.

'The goal of the journey and the serial order of the stations on the way to it maintain their positions, but it is not possible to predict what discoveries and insights the journey may reveal.'

Mumford is, I believe, saying the same thing in non-metaphorical language when he remarks that Toynbee's questions 'cannot be answered in terms of the metaphysical and sociological framework that he has used';[1] and that 'the salvation towards which this . . . study points lies outside the field of history'.[2]

Mumford's observation is pursued farther by Erdmann in an analytical examination of four key concepts of mine: challenge-and-response; withdrawal-and-return, loss of self-determination, and transfiguration. Erdmann finds that all four of them have originated in the mental world of 'salvational history' (*Heilsgeschichte*).

'The four concepts have a "salvational" nucleus round which the historical material concentrates, in the way in which the introduction, from outside, of an isomorphic crystal makes it possible for a mass of matter that is ripe for crystallisation to come together in clear shapes. Through those four crystals [of Toynbee's], metahistory becomes visible in and beyond history. The Hellenic Civilization's property of serving as a transparent medium through which the primordial phenomenon (*das Urphänomen*) of culture itself becomes visible, is, as we have recognised, one of the presuppositions of Toynbee's thought. This experience now repeats itself on a larger scale. History itself now acquires the property of serving as a transparent medium for giving visibility to "salvational history".'[3]

Christopher Dawson, in an essay on the problem of metahistory,[4] writes[5] that 'the case of Toynbee is a difficult one, because he is at the same time an historian, a sociologist of comparative culture, and a metahistorian'. Morgenthau finds that I look to religion to give me a superempirical standard, because, like Spengler, I have no philosophical system to give my construction of history some rational objectivity;[6] and Erdmann observes[7] that I try to combine Wells' view of the movement of history as non-recurrent and Spengler's view of it as cyclical by bringing the supernatural back into the picture. 'The tension between the natural and the supernatural order gives room for the world of freedom that reveals itself in history.'[8] In my view, Erdmann suggests, 'the destiny (*Schicksal*) of the civilizations . . . is the subject matter of universal history, but its proper theme is the development of religion'.[9] Progress, as it appears in my construction of history, is a protean phenomenon. It presents itself in the Age of Primitive Life as evolution, in the Age of Civilization as 'salvational history' (*Heilsgeschichte*), in the age following the Age of Civilization as eschatology.[10] If this construction

---

[1] L. Mumford in *Toynbee and History*, p. 146.
[2] L. Mumford in *Diogenes*, Spring, 1956, p. 11.
[3] K. D. Erdmann in *Archiv für Kulturgeschichte*, xxxiii. Band, Heft 2, p. 247.
[4] Reprinted in *The Dynamics of World History*, pp. 287–93.
[5] Ibid. p. 292.
[6] H. J. Morgenthau in *Toynbee and History*, p. 196.
[7] In loc. cit., p. 235.
[8] Ibid.
[9] Ibid., p. 234.
[10] Ibid., pp. 236-7.

of mine had to be represented in some visual symbolism, my apocalyptic beast would have to be given a fish's tail, a man's body, and a saint's head.[1] On this humorous flight of fancy my own comment would be: 'Well, if the creature that I have drawn is indeed a chimaera, how true my drawing is to life as life's image is refracted through the human mind's cracked lens.'

Erdmann is not alone in convicting me of writing 'salvational history' (*Heilsgeschichte*). Baudet describes my work as 'a kind of doctrine of salvation' (*een soort heilsleer*).[2] And a number of other writers have made the same observation in more general terms. Holcombe remarks[3] that 'what, in fact, Toynbee has finally given us is a religious interpretation of history'. Stecchini observes[4] that 'Toynbee, who constantly stresses the importance of having a philosophy of history, knows well that philosophy of history is a form of theology'. Coulborn, too, says[5] that I am a theologian masked as a philosopher. Joynt finds[6] in my work 'a subtle blend of sound history and a great deal of theology' (though, in noting that 'metaphysics is not history', he seems to credit me with being a philosopher as well as a theologian). David Thomson finds[7] that I am 'something of a mystic', and the same charge is made against me by L. S. Woolf.[8] Sweezy finds[9] that, in sharp contrast to Wells, I am 'at bottom a mystic who believes that Man is inherently incapable of shaping his own development and that therefore the only way to make life meaningful is to abandon the effort and embrace religion'.

Other critics see in my work not merely a religious interpretation of history but a 'theodicy': that is to say, an attempt to justify the ways of God to Man. Barnes classifies it[10] as being '"a theodicy" rather than straightforward history or scientific sociology'. It is called a theodicy by Leddy,[11] Walsh,[12] and Baudet,[13] and 'an undisguised theodicy' by Watnick.[14] B. D. Wolfe[15] calls it—with some irony—'a masterpiece of Christian historical apologetics and exegesis'. R. Coulborn finds[16] that my theodicy 'is too neat to be true'.

Other critics—Hughes and Coulborn, for instance—see a conflict in me between the believer and the scholar—a conflict without a decision, in Coulborn's view, since he reports that the scholar has not been driven off the field.[17] Kohn suggests[18] that the scholar, as a scholar, cannot

[1] *Archiv für Kulturgeschichte*, xxxiii. Band, Heft 2, p. 237.
[2] H. Baudet: 'Hedendaagsch Augustinisme' in *Historie en Metahistorie*, p. 48.
[3] A. N. Holcombe in *The American Political Science Review*, vol. xlix, No. 4 (December, 1955), pp. 1151–4.
[4] L. C. Stecchini in *Midstream*, Autumn, 1956, pp. 84–91.
[5] R. Coulborn in *Phylon*, 1940, offprint, p. 4.
[6] C. B. Joynt in *The Australasian Journal of Philosophy*, December, 1956, pp. 200 and 202. [7] In *The News Chronicle*, 14th October, 1954.
[8] In *The New Statesman and Nation*, 23rd September, 1939.
[9] P. M. Sweezy in *The Nation*, 19th October, 1946.
[10] H. E. Barnes in *An Introduction to the History of Sociology*, p. 719.
[11] J. F. Leddy in *The Phoenix*, vol. 11 (1957), No. 4, pp. 141–2.
[12] W. H. Walsh in *Toynbee and History*, pp. 126–7.
[13] H. Baudet in op. cit., p. 61.
[14] M. Watnick in *The Antioch Review*, No. 7 (Winter, 1947–8), pp. 587–602.
[15] B. D. Wolfe in *The American Mercury*, No. 64 (1947), p. 756.
[16] In *Toynbee and History*, pp. 156–7.
[17] R. Coulborn, ibid., pp. 148–9; H. S. Hughes: *Oswald Spengler: A Critical Estimate*, pp. 41 and 140. Hughes notes that Vico, too, was pulled in contrary directions by his critical faculty and by his Christian convictions.
[18] H. Kohn in *Toynbee and History*, pp. 353–4.

accept the Jewish and Christian belief, taken on faith, that history is God's path.

This conflict, if demonstrable, might, I suppose, be taken as psychological evidence of an unresolved contradiction that other critics find in my thinking. Mumford and Sumberg see this as a contradiction between a thisworldliness and an Augustinian otherworldliness;[1] Löwith[2] as one between a cyclic classical and a purposeful and meaningful Christian tradition; Masur[3] as one between 'Kulturkreisidee' and 'Theodiceegedanke'; Weil[4] as one between 'the principles on which' my 'scheme of the development of civilization is based and' my 'personal judgment of historical phenomena'. Anderle interprets Weil's words[5] as meaning, in more precise terms, a contradiction between the 'empirical-historical' and the '*a priori* absolute aspect' and comments:

'The case shows clearly that one cannot dispense with the need to draw a tidy boundary-line between the two realms. This is required in the interests of both science and religion, since each of these can attain its highest point only by keeping within its own sphere.'

Werner says that I have mixed up history and 'salvational history' (*Heilsgeschichte*)[6] and that, in my work, 'historical reflexion and "salvational" (*Heilsgeschichtliche*) expectation have not been brought into any convincing relation with each other'.[7] Erdmann observes that

' "challenge and response" do not find their explanation in terms of research into historical causation. The interpretation that they offer is in terms of the Christian doctrine about the nature of Man (*Christliche Anthropologie*). History and metahistory—the inquiry into causes and the inquiry into meaning—operate on different levels of comprehension (*Erkenntnis*). One is bound to admit that Toynbee has not been tidy in drawing the distinction between the two. Evidently, for the purpose that he has in view, he does not feel any pressing need for this. Ought one to regret that he has not gone to work with greater philosophical precision? Instead, let us rejoice that someone has had the courage to cope, in a fulness of measure nowhere else achieved, with the mass of material presented by history on the world-scale (*den Weltstoff*), and to fit it all together into one picture.'[8]

These last sentences are generous to me. For all of us who have embarked on the same enterprise, they give warning, at the same time, of the enterprise's formidable magnitude. The crux of it, however, is not this intellectual problem of coping with an unprecedented amount of information. If necessity is the mother of invention, we may look forward to seeing human minds find ways and means of achieving this;

---

[1] L. Mumford in *Diogenes*, Spring, 1956, p. 21; T. A. Sumberg in *Social Research*, vol. 14, No. 3 (September, 1947), pp. 267–74.
[2] K. Löwith: *Meaning in History*, pp. 12–13.
[3] G. Masur in the *Historische Zeitschrift*, Band 177 (1954), pp. 521–2.
[4] In *Toynbee and History*, p. 285.
[5] In op. cit.
[6] H. Werner: 'Spengler und Toynbee' in *Deutsche Vierteljahrsschrift für Literaturwissenschaft und Geistesgeschichte*, 29. Jahrgang, xxix. Band, p. 531.
[7] Ibid., p. 533.
[8] K. D. Erdmann in *Archiv für Kulturgeschichte*, xxxiii. Band, Heft 2 (1951), pp. 206–7.

and, happily, the truth of this inspiriting proverb is attested by the record of mankind's past. The crux is an issue that cannot be settled by one of those provisional agreements that sometimes result from intellectual debate. It is the issue between rationalism and trans-rationalism, discussed in this volume in Chapter III.

Rationalists hold that the clarity of the mind's intellectual vision is obscured, and the findings of its logical reason are adulterated and, at the worst, obliterated, if we allow our thinking to be contaminated by non-rational mental attitudes and processes. Rationalists may dismiss these as fantasies, or they may concede that they have some status in a mental domain of their own. A rationalist is less concerned to ascertain their status than he is to insulate the intellect from them and from their, in his view, intellectually pernicious influence. On the other side, trans-rationalists hold that the intellect has not the capacity to achieve its objective unaided. The intellect's objective, they agree with the rationalists, is to find explanations of the phenomena with which a human being is confronted. But they contend that the explanations arrived at by intellectual processes alone are unsatisfying, even intellectually, and are also inadequate for the practical conduct of human life. In their view those trans-rational mental attitudes and processes in which the rationalist sees the intellect's ruin are, in truth, the intellect's salvation. In the trans-rationalist's view, therefore, it is disastrous, even intellectually, to try to insulate the intellect from the other faculties of the human soul. Our aim, they hold, should be just the opposite. We should aim at a symphony between the intellect and the soul's trans-rational faculties. To try to dissociate them is unnatural; to keep them in their natural harmony is the key to finding our way in the mysterious universe into which we are born.

This perennial controversy is being conducted with unusual bitterness in the present-day world. My own work stands within the arena of this conflict; and this, I believe, partly accounts for the strength of the disapproval and dislike that it has aroused in some of its rationalist critics, and for the sharpness of the opposition between their judgements and some others.

Some critics maintain that the contradiction that they find in my thought has not only not been resolved by me but is one that does not admit of any solution. And they hold, as Anderle holds, that the different lines of inquiry that, in their judgement, I have jumbled up cannot be brought into any relation with each other. In my work, as Joynt sees it,

'categories which are the result of empirical generalisations, such as the balance of power and business cycles, are treated *on the same level of meaning* and as if they were derived *in exactly the same way* as "the laws of God". . . . Toynbee has attempted to blend two kinds of knowledge: religious and historical. The epistemology of the latter is empirical and it cannot be successfully joined to the former. What Toynbee has written is really much closer to theology than history.'[1]

Walsh holds[2] that, in seeking a theodicy, I have ceased to be an historian;

---

[1] C. B. Joynt in *The Australasian Journal of Philosophy*, December, 1956, p. 200.
[2] W. H. Walsh in *Toynbee and History*, pp. 126–7.

and Stone[1] that I am not justified in claiming to be an historian considering that what I produce is metaphysical stuff. Woodward makes the
same point with what seems to me to be greater discernment:

'The answer to the question "why" would appear to lie outside the
scope of history. In a sense Professor Toynbee realises, by turning to
mythology, that he is looking in history for something he will never find;
but the answers from mythology are really only guesses at the question
"how", and guesses which are not so near to the point as the patient work
of modern specialists. The answer appears as far off as ever.'[2]

Mumford finds[3] that my 'supernaturalism' is 'a radical defect' in my
philosophy; Feibleman[4] that an attempt to found my system on transcendental philosophy is one of two major defects in my work. In Nevins'
expectation,[5] 'countless readers will . . . view Toynbee's heavy emphasis
on religion, as the one element in the human march through time which
really justifies it, as another fundamental flaw'. Joynt puts on the judge's
black cap.

'If this kind of practice is to be pursued, then historians might as well
shut up shop and all take holy orders. . . . One can but conclude that this
curious marriage of metaphysics and history has not succeeded and should
end in a divorce.'[6]

Kuhn gives me a splendid funeral.

'As Hegel before him, so Toynbee undertakes to rewrite Saint Augustine's principal work by interpreting the City of Man as the City of God *in
statu nascendi*. In both cases the result is a magnificent failure.'[7]

Happily for me, other critics seem to see my practice in a different
light. Brinton, for instance, suggests[8] that

'much of the quarrel between Toynbee and the historians is . . . in a purely
rational sense unnecessary, since . . . they are not attempting the same
task. . . .
'What is Toynbee's *Study of History*? It is not a theological system, not
a prophetic work in the specific sense that word has in the Judaeo-
Christian tradition, though it has something in common with these. . . . It
is surely a theodicy; but, if we think of Milton or Leibnitz, of Joseph de
Maistre, or even of the author of the Book of Job, it is a vague and imprecise theodicy. Indeed, at times so great is Toynbee's insistence on the
freedom of the human spirit, his work sounds more like an "anthropo-
dicy". It is most certainly a philosophy of history, . . . [but it] belongs in
fact to a kind of sub-species within the species, a sub-species clearly
marked by its own characteristics. Toynbee's work is best called a "City
of God".
'By a "City of God" we understand an eschatological system in which

[1] L. Stone in *Toynbee and History*, p. 111.
[2] E. L. Woodward in *The Spectator*, 6th July, 1934, p. 21.
[3] L. Mumford in *The Pacific Spectator*, No. 1 (1947), pp. 391–8.
[4] J. K. Feibleman in *T'ien Hsia Monthly*, vol. xi, Nos. 1 and 2 (1940), p. 152.
[5] A. Nevins in *The New York World-Telegram and Sun*, 7th December, 1954.
[6] Joynt in *The Australasian Journal of Philosophy*, December, 1956, pp. 200 and 202.
[7] H. Kuhn in *The Journal of Philosophy*, 28th August, 1947, p. 499.
[8] Crane Brinton in *The Virginia Quarterly Review*, Summer, 1956, pp. 361–75.

evidence taken from the historical record . . . is used to transcend history. . . . For the empiricist, a "City of God", though it uses empirical evidence to arrive at conclusions, does so by adding something—shall we say the yeast?—that alters the empirical evidence in a way the empiricist himself thinks *his* mind does not alter it, a way he does not like. Shall we say modestly that the empiricist prefers the unleavened loaf?'

I will close by quoting two anonymous appraisals of the book.

'The story of Mankind is not usefully written as one of perpetual frustration[1] and the unendingly unsuccessful quest for the earthly kingdom. In his sixth volume,[2] indeed, Dr. Toynbee comes very near to recognising that human history is the story of individual souls in a transcendental setting, and that the lowly role of societies and civilizations is to provide the stage for acts of moral choice, and that the only essential stage properties are dilemmas and temptations; and, so viewed, the scene disclosed to the historian is essentially satisfactory and good.'[3]

'Two main problems are his [Dr. Toynbee's] special concern: what characteristic and typical patterns, if any, have civilizations followed in their development; and what dynamic forces have produced both the patterns and the development as a whole? At one level Dr. Toynbee is thus a student of what may be called the sociology of history; at another and far deeper level he is a seeker after, and an expounder of, what to him (and to many others) is the ultimate meaning.'[4]

The passages last quoted bring out the sharpness of the religious cleavage, in the World today, between the rationalists and the 'many others' of whom my unknown reviewer and I are two representatives. This is a battle in which I myself am a combatant and in which my work is, in a minor way, contested ground. Since I am so deeply implicated, I am evidently in no position to try to deliver judgement on the issue at stake. The verdict—or perhaps a succession of differing verdicts—will be rendered, if it is ever rendered, by posterity.

---

[1] Cp. Aldous Huxley: 'History as the Experience of Frustration' in *The Magazine of the Year*, vol. i, No. 7 (September, 1947), pp. 106–12.—A. J. T.

[2] This passage occurs in a review of vols. iv–vi. The reviewer might, I should guess, have said the same of vols. vii–x if these had been published at the time.—A. J. T.

[3] *The Listener*, 19th October, 1939.

[4] *The Economist*, 6th November, 1954.

IV ANNEX

Is there any Master-activity in Human Affairs?

HUMAN activities are numerous and various. There is technology: the invention, manufacture, and use of tools. There is economics: the winning of a livelihood for human beings from Nature, and the distribution of the product among the people who are competing for it. There is politics: the handling of the power that accumulates as a result of co-operation between people in large numbers. There is art: the expression of Man's appreciation of the beauty of the Universe in which he finds himself. There is study: the satisfaction of Man's curiosity about the Universe. There is religion: Man's impulse to get into touch, and into harmony, with an absolute spiritual Reality, whose presence behind the phenomena makes itself felt in the experience of many, perhaps most, human beings. Then there is recreation: the use that people make of the spare time that their work leaves them. There is education: not in just the formal sense of the word, but in the broader sense in which education means the transmission of the whole cultural heritage of the present generation and its predecessors to the rising generation and its successors. These are some of the main human activities. The list is a crude one, and it will not have covered the whole range of these activities; but it will perhaps have covered enough to show that human activities are remarkable for their variety.

In spite of this variety, the different activities are so closely interconnected that it is impossible to deal with any one of them without also having to take account of at least one or two of the others.

For instance, education is concerned with all the rest, in as much as it is concerned with handing on the whole of the cultural heritage, including ways of recreation.

Technology, it is obvious, cannot be insulated from economics, because tools are the means by which we win our livelihood from Nature. But, unfortunately, technology cannot be insulated from politics either, because some of the tools that technology makes are weapons, and weapons are used by human beings not only against non-human living creatures; they are used against other human beings as well; and war is one of the products of political power. Wars can be waged only by people living in communities that have achieved some degree of political organisation.

Economics, again, cannot be insulated from politics. The distribution of the product of economic activity is largely determined by the play of political power; and political power itself depends on economic resources. In order to be able to make war, a government needs to have at its command the economic sinews of war. It is not enough to have subjects who are willing to fight.

Politicians interest themselves in all activities that have some bearing on power. They are interested in religion if they can harness their subjects' religious feelings to serve their policy. Despotic governments in our time have been interested in education as a means of influencing the rising generation of their subjects at an impressionable age. In the year 1961 all governments were interested in technological and scientific education as a generator of political power. The government of the Roman Empire was interested in recreation as a means of keeping the populace of the capital city in a good humour and diverting its attention from politics.

Art, it is evident, cannot be insulated from technology. It is impossible to define the points at which the so-called 'useful' arts and crafts end and the so-called 'fine' arts begin. Indeed, if art ceases to be useful—that is to say, if it ceases to satisfy some real human need—the life goes out of it. Of course, the need served by art may be a spiritual need. Art has often served religion and been inspired by it.

Study is closely akin to art; it is not without reason that we bracket together 'the arts and sciences'. Study shares with art and religion the virtue of being 'disinterested'. Like them, it is not pursued for economic or political motives. But, in the modern Western World since the close of the seventeenth century, the study of non-human Nature has been linked up with technology. This alliance has given both technology and science an unprecedented impetus; and in our time technology, inspired by science, has become the key to political power.

Recreation is bound up with economics: its cost is a charge on the livelihood that we win from Nature. In the Roman Empire the whole population had to pay for the 'bread and circuses' doled out to the populace of Rome, and afterwards to the populace of Constantinople. Recreation is also closely connected with education: in a child's life there is not that sharp line that there is in a grown-up person's between work and play. Recreation also fuses with art and study and technology. Students and artists, and craftsmen too, share with children the happiness of finding recreation in their work. And works of art give mankind in general its highest kind of recreation.

Thus human activities are not only very various; they are also very intimately inter-connected. At the same time they cannot be reduced to a unity by treating some single one of them as if it were paramount over all the rest. 'Quantitative measurements . . . will not help us to decide whether the political, the economic, or the religious point of view is more important for a general understanding of history.'[1] In fact, there is no master-activity: history is multi-dimensional.[2] 'General history must work with a number of factors rather than with only one',[3] and we must use multi-dimensional blocks as our units of analysis.[3] This is what is demanded of a student of human affairs by the structure of the phenomena that he is studying. But this demand on him makes his subject a formidably complicated one. For this reason, ever since the earliest attempts at understanding, interpreting, and recording human history, students of it have constantly been tempted to distort their picture of it by trying to simplify it. The would-be simplifier's obvious recourse is to single out some one of Man's various activities and to treat this as Man's

---

[1] M. R. Cohen: *The Meaning of Human History*, p. 226.
[2] Ibid., p. 225.   [3] Ibid., p. 228.

master-activity—subordinating all the others to it or even leaving them out of the picture altogether. This procedure is as ineffectual as it is high-handed. Some illustrations of it will bring out its weakness.

The oldest candidate for the role of master-activity is politics. Until only the other day, the conventional way of writing history was to give a chronicle of reigns, wars, battles, and military and political revolutions. E. A. Freeman, a nineteenth-century English historian, pronounced that 'history is past politics, and politics present history'.[1] Since that time, our picture of human affairs has become broader and ampler, and historians have paid deference to this change of outlook by interspersing their political narrative with paragraphs, or even whole chapters, on the progress of art or religion or technology. Few, however, so far, have attempted to write comprehensive narratives, taking account of all human activities and bringing out the interplay between them all the way through. Sir George Trevelyan has done this with brilliant success, but there are not many like him.

Why has the treatment of politics as the master-activity persisted so long? And why is it dying so hard?

One obvious reason why it is dying hard is that it makes the writing of history a fairly simple task compared with Trevelyan's method of keeping a number of different human activities in view simultaneously and all the time. The reason why the political approach to history has persisted so long is that it has behind it a greater weight of tradition than any other approach.

Political history is the history of pooled human power; and the earliest historians were rulers who wielded the power, not only to make military conquests, but to have these recorded. One of the oldest historical documents known to us is 'the palette of Narmer', on which a king of Upper Egypt, who had conquered Lower Egypt and had thus unified Egypt politically, had a record made of his achievement. This record is a pictorial one, in bas-relief. It was made round about the year 3000 B.C. at the very dawn, if not before the dawn, of the art of writing in Egypt. From 'Iraq we have a similar record—also in bas-relief, but with an explanatory inscription—of the Akkadian King Naramsin's invasion of the highlands to the east of the lower basin of the Tigris and Euphrates. Naramsin's record is six or seven hundred years later in date than Narmer's. We have much fuller records, dating from the twelfth century B.C. onwards, made by kings of Assyria. These Assyrian records, too, are military and political in their contents. But it is significant that, in form though not in fact, these are records, not of war and politics, but of technology, art, and religion. Some of these long Assyrian military and political records are given the form of appendixes to a brief record of the founding or restoration of a temple. Others take the form of predictions about future military and political events by a god, in

---

[1] In a memoir of J. R. Seeley, G. W. Prothero notes that, 'though he did not coin the phrase "History is past politics, and politics present history", it is perhaps more strictly applicable to his view of history than to that of its author' (Prothero in Seeley: *The Growth of British Policy* (Cambridge 1895, University Press, 2 vols.), vol. i, p. xii).
    Prothero here assumes that the authorship of this dictum is a matter of common knowledge. Such evidence as I have found all points to Freeman.

answer to an inquiry on the king's part. These *soi-disant* predictions are really narratives of events that have already happened. It looks as if the kings of Assyria had suspected that architectural, artistic, and religious activities might really be the master-activities, but had been unable to resist the temptation to swamp their records of these comparatively disinterested and enlightened proceedings under an egotistic and boastful record of their military and political achievements.

The expansion of political history into general history has not been accomplished satisfactorily by the rather superficial device of interrupting a political narrative here and there and interpolating a chapter on one of the non-political human activities. This failure of the political school of history to reform itself effectively has opened the way for a revolutionary attack on it. Marx and Engels have set out to depose politics from its traditional place of honour in the presentation of history, and to enthrone economics in its stead. Marx has won general acceptance for his thesis that reigns and wars are not the master-key to the interpretation of history, but not for his further thesis that this master-key is to be found in economics. Marx's and Engels' theses were neither so crude nor so dogmatic as they have been represented as being by admirers as well as by opponents. Their thesis that economics is the key to history was hedged about with a number of qualifications and caveats. These bear witness to Marx's and Engels' intellectual ability. Still, in substance, Marx's doctrine is that the method of production of Man's means of livelihood, together with the system by which the means of production are controlled, governs and determines most other things in human life. The key to power is an economic key, not a political one; the key to an understanding of human affairs is to understand economics. Many people who are not ideological followers of Marx hold these Marxian views today.

In his outlook Marx was a child of his age, as even a genius is bound to be.[1] In the West in the middle decades of the nineteenth century, at least three things were happening which suggested that the most important of all human activities was economics. Westerners had just become aware of economics as being a distinct and important human activity; and this was an exciting new discovery. The discovery had been made as a result of two contemporary revolutions: a technological revolution by which muscle-power had been replaced by water-power and steam-power as the driving-force for machines; and an organizational revolution by which small-scale manufacture (in the literal sense of the word) had been replaced by large-scale production conducted by capitalists employing workers for wages. The third thing in the contemporary scene that drew attention to economics was the sufferings, during the first stage of the Industrial Revolution, of the new class of industrial wage-earners that this revolution had called into existence.

Unquestionably Marx was right in holding that economics was important, and also in holding that something drastic ought to be done to relieve the industrial workers' sufferings. All the World can agree with Marx on these two points without also having to agree with him

[1] See pp. 125–7.

that his remedy for the nineteenth-century industrial workers' sufferings was the best one, or that economics is not merely important, but all-important. The answer to the thesis that economics is all-important is: 'Man doth not live by bread only.'[1] If the thesis that politics is Man's master-activity will not work—and Marx has done us all a service in showing that it will not—the similar thesis that economics is Man's master-activity will not work either.

As a matter of fact, when people's economic interests and their political feelings have pulled different ways, people have usually given rein to their political feelings and have let their economic interests go hang. This subordination of economics to politics could be illustrated by any number of historical examples. Here two will suffice. In the Danubian Hapsburg Monarchy before the First World War the port of Trieste possessed a hinterland that ensured its prosperity. Yet the Italian majority in the population of Trieste longed for the break-up of the Monarchy, on whose existence their livelihood depended, because of their political ambition, as Italians by nationality, to see Trieste annexed to Italy. In Palestine, after the First World War, the British, who had taken a mandate for administering the country, hoped that the Arab population would be reconciled to the influx of Jewish immigrants by the prospect that this would bring with it increases in land values and rises in wages. But the Arabs' minds did not work in that way. The prospect that preoccupied them was a political one. Jewish immigration threatened to reduce the Palestinian Arabs to the status of a subject minority. In their minds this political menace entirely outweighed the prospect of economic gains. These two examples are characteristic, and their significance is clear. If it is true that politics is not all-important, it must be true, *a fortiori*, that economics is not.

What other human activities, besides economics and politics, have been, or seem likely to be, put forward as candidates for the role of master-activity? Recreation, art, and study have never, so far, been in the running; and education seems unlikely to be, in spite of the fact that education commands the doorway to the future. There are, however, two other obvious candidates: technology and religion.

Technology is almost bound to look like Man's master-activity in the eyes of a student of the so-called Prehistoric Age of mankind's career. In this age human societies had not yet managed to produce a surplus over and above the requirements of bare subsistence. They were therefore unable to maintain a leisured minority. They were therefore illiterate, since the art of writing requires a leisured minority to invent and practise it. They have therefore left no written records. And therefore Man's tools are almost the only surviving evidences of Man's development, and even of his existence, for the first half million or million years of mankind's history. Compared with the abundance of the tools that have survived from the Palaeolithic Age, the fragments of human skeletons of the same antiquity have, so far, been rare finds. And perhaps even the oldest human bones so far found are young compared with the oldest tools in our museums.

[1] Deut. viii. 3, quoted in Matt. iv. 4 and Luke iv. 4.

Accordingly, the prehistorian is inclined to see Man as *homo faber* ('Man the technician') rather than as *homo sapiens* ('Man the possessor of a consciousness and a will'). Or perhaps the prehistorian would say that the invention and use of tools was the means by which Man educated himself into becoming intelligent and purposeful. We may agree that a process of self-education through technology may have speeded up Man's exercise of his intelligence. Man must, however, have been immensely intelligent already before he could dream of inventing his first tool. This first of his many inventions is, after all, his most brilliant technological achievement for all time. It already contained, in germ, such later feats as the splitting of the atom and the launching of artificial satellites to circle round the Earth and to lasso the Moon. When once Man had chipped his first flint, these derivative inventions were already on their way. But what would our picture of early Palaeolithic Man look like if, instead of having no evidence of him except his tools and a few of his bones, we had as wide a knowledge of all his activities as we have for our study of his descendants within the last 5,000 years? Even for the study of later Palaeolithic Man, perhaps 10,000 to 50,000 years ago, we have not only tools and bones but also paintings on the walls of the caves in which he lived; and these paintings open up vistas on fields of life that are blanks in our picture of these relatively recent men's predecessors. Later Palaeolithic Man's paintings tell us a great deal about his artistic skill and sense, and they even allow us to infer something about the character of his religion. If we had the same amount and variety of knowledge about early Palaeolithic Man, would his tools loom so large in our picture of him as they loom now in the absence of any other evidences of his doings? In other words, would prehistorians be as much inclined as they are now to think of technology as being Man's master-activity?

'Man doth not live by bread only, but by every word that proceedeth out of the mouth of the Lord doth Man live.'[1] Here is the voice of religion making its claim to be Man's master-activity; and, of all the competing claims, this is surely the strongest. Its strength, however, lies in the fact that religion is not on a par with the other activities on our list. Religion is Man's attempt to get into touch with an absolute spiritual Reality behind the phenomena of the Universe, and, having made contact with It, to live in harmony with It. This activity is all-pervading. It comprehends all the others. Moreover, it is Man's life-line. When once a creature has acquired, as Man has, a conscious intellect and a free will, this creature must either seek and find God or destroy itself. 'Where there is no vision, the people perish.'[2] Religion, then, would be Man's master-activity if there were such a thing. But religion's claim can be vindicated only by being put in terms that transcend it. Religion is Man's master-activity only in the sense that religion embraces all Man's other activities in itself.

[1] Deut. viii. 3.   [2] Prov. xxix. 18.

VII ANNEX

Comment by Rabbi J. B. Agus on Professor Toynbee's Use of the Term 'Fossil' with Reference to the Jewish Community

I

THE connotation of the term 'fossil', which is repugnant to Jews, derives from the scale of values which is current in this, the century of Darwinism. In the pre-Darwinian world marks of antiquity were highly prized. Josephus in his *Contra Apionem* strives to prove the great antiquity of the Jewish people. To be put in the category of a 'coelacanthus', a living species of fish, belonging to a phylon of creation that is otherwise extinct, was always a point of pride for Jewish writers. The Jewish poet-philosopher, Jehudah Halevi, went so far as to describe the Jewish community as a 'body, without a head and a heart. Nay, even more, not even a skeleton, but scattered bones, like the bones which Ezekiel saw. . . .' But in Jehudah Halevi's view these bones were still better than the other religious communities, which in his view were like man-made dolls (*The Kusuri*, II, 29, 30).

In the realm of ideas and cultural values the 'test of time' is a measure of validity and worth; in the world of evolving species, resistance to change is the primary sin, leading to the penalty of fossilization and ultimately extinction.

Religious societies pre-eminently and national units generally are both value-centred and survival-centred. The philosopher of history is justified in applying biological categories to societies only in so far as they are survival-centred. Universal values, reflecting facets of truth, beauty, goodness, or holiness, are essentially imperishable.

Is then the Jewish community primarily survival-centred, or is it primarily value-centred? Professor Toynbee bases his analysis on the first assumption. He attributes the articulation of Judaism into a set of rites and observances and its creation of a complex communal structure to the 'will to live' of a harassed community. In this reasoning, Professor Toynbee is at one with all nationalist Jewish historians—in particular with Achad Ha'am and Simon Dubnow.

Nevertheless, this view is definitely one-sided. The continuous stream of Jewish literature demonstrates the value-centredness and idea-centredness of Jewish leadership. Admittedly, in the actual press of daily events, it is not feasible for people to distinguish between the needs of their group and its ideals. But, in so far as literature reflects the inner life of a community, the dominance of religious beliefs and values is clear. Those who did not share the values and beliefs of the community became participants in the prevailing faith.

The collective interests of the Jewish community by no means coincided with the collective ideals of the Jews. Throughout Medieval Europe, Jews were admitted into the ranks of the nobility when they joined the Christian Church. The followers of Jacob Frank in eighteenth-century Poland achieved this rank, though their number was well in excess of 15,000. The self-image of the Jewish people included at all times the belief of being utterly committed to the service of the One God. The ethnic 'will to live' was a function and a corollary of the religious 'will to be true', not vice versa. Nationalist Jewish historians were impelled to reverse this relationship in keeping with a materialistic and biological bias. But their endeavours are utterly unconvincing. For the religious motivation of Jewish life is unmistakable, and religion is the domain of ultimate ends, not of manipulated means.

II

A subsidiary implication of the term 'fossil' is the judgement that vital energy is concentrated altogether upon the struggle for survival, ignoring the goals of survival, and that this undue emphasis makes the group overly defensive and armour-conscious.

No one who studies Jewish history can deny that the self-segregating impetus was at diverse times all-powerful. On the other hand, as Herbert Spencer pointed out, in every living society the things which make life possible are likely to take precedence over the things that life makes possible. This is particularly true in times of extreme emergency. Thus, the ethnic factor predominated in Jewish consciousness during periods of persecution.

As to this conflict of motivations within the Jewish soul, we may recognize it as the perennial issue between the rationalistic and the romantic schools of Jewish thought. To the rationalists, the ideas and ideals of Judaism were primary, and the Jews were only their temporary custodians waiting for the light of truth to dawn on all men. To the romanticists, the Jewish people in themselves were of supreme value, awaiting their vindication and the confounding of their enemies 'in the end of days'.

Because Jewish life and thought were not monolithic in the first century of our era even, as they certainly are not today, we cannot apply any one category to the entire community. Behold the Hellenistic Jews at the time of Philo and Jesus, who were universalistic and humanistic, glorying in the title 'citizens of the World'. Their disappearances from the stage of history was due more to external factors than to the lack of spiritual vigor.

It is, therefore, advisable to shun the use of the noun 'fossil' and speak instead of processes—a process of 'fossilization' as one tendency and a process of spiritualization as the other movement in the opposite direction.

XIII ANNEX

Comments by Rabbi J. B. Agus on the Notion of Uniqueness

I FULLY concur with the assertion of Professor Toynbee that the career of the Jew in history is not 'unique', in an ultimate sense. Nothing is so universal among nations as the claim of uniqueness. The romantic philosophers of Russia and Poland, of Germany and Italy, asserted the uniqueness of their respective 'national souls'.

The history of the Jews is unique in the same sense as are the histories of all human groups—i.e. as a compound reflecting diverse historical forces, not as an element, standing apart, defying analysis and *sui generis*.

But, inasmuch as nations and religions are generally placed in different categories, it is important to recognize the intimate bond of unity between the two domains in Judaism, though one or another aspect might predominate at any one time.

The 'non-uniqueness' of Jewry implies also the non-exceptional status of the Jewish diasporá. Along with all religious and cultural minorities, they should learn to maintain a healthy balance between their communal identity and the universal values of mankind. In this way they serve as vanguards of the evolving society of our emergent One World, which can only be of a pluralistic character.

XV ANNEX

Comments by Rabbi J. B. Agus on the Continuity of the Prophetic Element in Judaism

PROFESSOR TOYNBEE calls for the renunciation by the diasporá Jews of their 'communal identity' and for the repudiation of the Torah, so that they be free to convert mankind to the religion of the Prophets. This call emerges from his analysis of the role played by the Law and the national structure in the Greco-Roman world of antiquity.

The issue is stated in stark and rigid terms, as if the situation today was no different than in the first century. Neither the Law nor the national body is today a high and impassable barrier.[1]

For more than a century the Reform and Conservative movements have been preaching that the *halachoth* were instruments of piety, not its substance. Transmuted into rites and ceremonies which enhance the drama of worship, the residual *halachoth* cannot possibly hinder the dissemination of the faith. And the nature of the Jewish 'communal identity' has also undergone a fundamental transformation. The ancient 'natural' community has been replaced by a plethora of voluntary organizations, with the Synagogue occupying the central place. There is no organization embracing all Jews, and, by the same token, no Jew can possibly belong to all Jewish organizations. In their turn the diverse organizations of Jewry are integrated into the total pattern of the voluntary associational life of the overall community.

The transformation of the Law and the transformation of the communal system were brought about in part by external factors and in part by the continued operation of the Prophetic strand within the Jewish tradition.

The Jewish community of America is presently an 'open society'— i.e. individuals are free not only to choose whether or not to belong, but also to determine the terms and extent of their affiliation. However, those contemporary movements which aim at the imposition of a totalitarian unity upon the Jewish community, converting it into a 'close society' of an ethnic character, are properly subject to Professor Toynbee's critique.

It is at this point that the dialogue between Judaism and Christianity approaches a crisis of mutual misunderstanding. To Christians, Jesus and Paul represent the acme of the Prophetic message—the one in transcending the Law, the other in transcending the national community. But, in the Jewish tradition, as Professor Toynbee and Herford point out, the Prophetic tradition was channeled through the Mishnah and Talmud, without any reference to Jesus and Paul. Within the Talmud the Prophetic tradition is continued as an undercurrent, with the priestly mentality predominating. And, alongside the Talmud, there was the philosophic tradition which was articulated so brilliantly by

[1] I have now revised my original draft of the last section of Chapter XV in the light of Rabbi Agus's comments in the present Annex.—A. J. T.

Philo. Coursing through subterranean channels, it emerged again in the tenth century, reaching a splendid climax in Maimonides. Through the lonely, titanic figure of Spinoza, philosophical Judaism helped to prepare the ground for the philosophy of the Enlightenment. The modern movements of Reform, Conservativism, and, I might add, Liberal Orthodoxy, are indeed continuations of the philosophical current in Jewish thought, and Jewish philosophy is essentially a continuation of the Prophetic current within the stream of Judaism.

But what is the essence of the Prophetic heritage, and what does conversion to the 'religion of Deutero-Isaiah' really mean?

The classical Prophets maintained that religion is a dynamic balance of two insights—that which is afforded by tradition and mystical experience, on the one hand, and that which is derived from the twin lights of intelligence and conscience, on the other hand. Subjective piety and loyalty were blended in their vision with objective reflection and ethical fervor. They transcended ritualism by the rational emphasis on inwardness; they transcended blind ethnicism by the ethical emphasis on the values of universal humanity. And, in transcending both ritualism and ethnicism, they created that dynamic equilibrium between faith and reason which is genuine religion, and that creative synthesis of loyalties that is humanistic, idealistic nationalism. The religious philosophers were the true heirs of the Prophets, in that they too saw religion as a living blend of subjective feeling and objective reflection.

From this analysis the implications of Prophetic religion for our day are clear. Not to reject the 'communal identity' into which we are born, but to transcend its limitations and narrow horizons, so that our national group might serve the larger cause of mankind. Not to repudiate the pattern of observances in one's religion, but to transcend their exclusiveness and absoluteness, that they might serve as fitting instruments of universal religion.

Hence, a mission for the Jews—yes, but not for Jews only. Precisely the same mission applies to those Christians and Moslems who, like the Prophets, recognize two sources of religion, subjective faith and objective reasoning. The liberals of all faiths assume a common domain of ethical values and rational principles. At the same time they may well employ the rituals and loyalties of their respective groups in their efforts to attain deeper levels of insight for themselves and for the communities to which they belong.

The liberals who would be heirs of the Prophets dare not secede from their respective communities, nor can they in conscience break with the ceremonial-organizational patterns of their respective faiths. The Prophets stayed with their people, spoke their language, and infused their volcanic fire into the actual cultural-social structure of their day. If they had not done so, they would have worked in a vacuum.

The great need of humanity today is to overcome the peril of 'the idolization of the temporary self'. This can be achieved by the application of the Golden Rule to groups as well as to individuals. The Golden Rule of ethics is actually the application of the objective approach to human relations. Yet absolute objectivity, making no allowance for the sanctum sanctorum of the human heart, can be as totalitarian in its tyranny as absolute subjectivity. People must learn to guard the inner mystery of their being, refining it in art, articulating and cultivating it in the observances of religion, even while they pursue the objective pathway to Reality. Along both the inner and outer pathways to the mystery of being, the road ahead is infinite. By the same token, all human groups must not pursue the goal of objectivity so exclusively as to abolish their respective traditions. For then we should be left with blank, grey uniformity. Rather, like the Hebrew Prophets, they should seek to maintain a creative confrontation of their subjective tradition with the broad light of objective research and reflection.

Neither the policy of assimilating others by conversion nor the prospect of total dissolution in the grey ocean of humanity is in keeping with the intent of a Golden Rule for cultural and religious groups. Let us recall Immanuel Kant's formulation of this rule: 'Act so that your action may be a standard of action for all.' Manifestly, imperialism in the domain of the spirit may be as irksome as in the domain of politics. But in all healthy human relations a balance is maintained between self-assertion and self-surrender. All groups can contribute to the general welfare by integrating their subjective tradition into the objective structure of all-human values.

Conversion of the 'religion of Deutero-Isaiah' is to a 'church invisible', transcending denominational lines, and rising far beyond the parochial symbols of any one faith.

Spengler's Concept of 'Pseudomorphosis'

SPENGLER'S concept of 'pseudomorphosis' ('Deceptive Cultural Formation') is one of the most illuminating of his intuitions. It throws light, for instance, on the relation between a satellite civilization and the society into whose field it has been drawn.

In essence the idea is a simple one. When two civilizations are interacting with each other, their meeting may be on an unequal footing.[1] At the moment one of the two may be the more powerful, the other the more creative. In this situation the more creative civilization will be constrained to conform outwardly to the more powerful civilization's cultural configuration, like a hermit crab who fits himself into a shell that is not his own. But an observer would be allowing himself to be misled if here he were to take appearances at their face value. He must look below the surface, study what underlies it, and take due note of the difference between the two. 'The hands are the hands of Esau',[2] but only because they have been disguised in order to deceive. 'The voice is Jacob's voice.' That is authentic, and it is therefore telltale, provided that the listener is not bent upon being deceived.

Spengler uses the concept of 'pseudomorphosis' in his attempt to elucidate the configuration of the history of civilization in the Old World, west of India, since the beginning of the Christian Era. The eastward and southward expansion of the Hellenic Civilization, in and after the generation of Alexander the Great, had laid an Hellenic veneer —political, intellectual, and aesthetic—over South-West Asia and Egypt. Consequently, as Spengler sees it, his hypothetical 'Magian Civilization'—which, according to him, arose in this region at about the beginning of the Christian Era—was compelled to camouflage itself, during the first few centuries of its existence, by presenting itself in an Hellenic guise. It does not reveal itself in its true colours till a later stage, when it has mustered sufficient strength to break through the Hellenic veneer; but a student's discerning eye can divine its presence, below the surface, from the very beginning of the subterranean first chapter of its history.[3] Though Spengler thus introduces 'pseudo-

---

[1] In contacts between two or more civilizations that are contemporary with each other, this seems to be the usual situation (see viii. 464–6).

[2] Gen. xxvii. 22.

[3] F. H. Underhill, in *The Canadian Historical Review*, vol. xxxvi, No. 3 (September, 1955), p. 255, has applied Spengler's notion of the 'pseudomorphosis' of a hypothetical 'Magian Civilization' to interpret my *Weltanschauung*.

'Many critics have commented on how deeply Toynbee seems to be alienated from his own society. . . . I think a case could be made, using Spenglerian language, for the thesis that he is a Magian soul, born out of due time. In spite of his belief about himself that the Hellenic Civilization is his spiritual home, he is not really an Apollinian man. His spiritual home is in that part of the World beyond the Hellespont, in the society that produced the mystical magical "higher" religions which were eventually to defeat Hellenism. It is the historical development of this part of the World that fascinates him most; he devotes more of his pages to it than to any other area. I have a feeling that some day a psychologist who is interested in history will turn up and proceed to demonstrate that Toynbee's whole adult life has been spent in a long struggle by his subconscious

morphosis' and the 'Magian Civilization' in association with each other, we may reject his hypothetical 'Magian Civilization' without having to reject his concept of 'pseudomorphosis' as well. These two ideas of his do not stand or fall together, and the idea of 'pseudomorphosis' can be applied in alternative attempts to interpret the cultural history of the western half of the Old World during these last two millennia.

Two points, in particular, are unacceptable in Spengler's picture of his 'Magian Civilization'. He assumes that it was something entirely new, and he also assumes that it had nothing genuinely in common with the Hellenic Civilization whose outward form it was compelled to adopt during its subterranean formative age. This is not the picture that meets our eye when we look at the new configurations of culture that have actually made their appearance in the western half of the Old-World *Oikoumenê* since the beginning of the Christian Era. These authentic historical configurations are, as we know, two higher religions, Christianity and Islam, and five civilizations: four of them Christian and the fifth Islamic. None of these are new in the absolute sense of having inherited nothing from the past; and none of them is non-Hellenic in the sense of having no vein of Hellenism in its essence. These two religions and five civilizations have all sprung from ground fertilized by a blend between the debris of the Hellenic culture and the debris of the Syriac: a Syriac-Hellenic 'culture-compost', as I have labelled it. In the formative age of Christianity there was, nevertheless, a 'pseudomorphosis' in Spengler's sense. Christian art and Christian theology, for instance, did express themselves in Hellenic forms in which they did not find themselves completely at home. At the same time there was a genuine Hellenic ingredient in the very heart of Christianity, and this not only in the Eastern Orthodox and Western Catholic versions of it, but also in the Nestorian and Monophysite Christian resistance movements to 'Melchite' ecclesiastical and political domination. Part, at least, of this Hellenic ingredient was eventually communicated by Nestorian and Monophysite Christianity to Islam.[1]

Magian self to overcome the Hellenic education imposed on his conscious English self at school and college.'

I find Underhill's analysis of me convincing. Before I began to be educated in Hellenism, I had been inoculated with Christianity, and the earlier influence usually proves to be the stronger. I have always sympathized with the Christians against the Hellenes in the Roman Imperial Age, and with the Persians against the Hellenes in Xerxes' day, as well as in Alexander's. Standing on the platform at Persepolis has been, for me, a more memorable experience than standing on the acropolis at Athens. My eyes inform me that the Parthenon frieze is a masterpiece and that the Persepolitan friezes are conventional and clumsy. Yet, in me, this obviously far inferior art strikes a more responsive chord.

This schism in my psyche, on which Underhill has put his finger, would not be worth mentioning if it were just an idiosyncrasy of mine. I fancy, though, that, in being thus inwardly divided in my spiritual sympathies and allegiances, I am typical of all the people who have been brought up in one or other of the civilizations of the Syriac-Hellenic family (as I call it in my jargon). These divided feelings can be traced back to Alexander himself. In the act of overthrowing the empire that the Persians had built, he became personally acquainted with the Persians, and their virtues impressed and attracted him so much that he half regretted the damage that he had done and had half a mind to try to repair it. The Syriac and the Hellenic ingredients in the 'culture-compost' from which the Christian and Islamic civilizations have sprung have failed to make a perfect blend, and the unresolved discord has been communicated to the crops grown on this fertile soil.

[1] Islamic theology has been worked out, on a pattern set by Christian theology, in terms of Hellenic philosophy; and this has led, in the cultural history of the Islamic Civilization, as it has in the cultural history of the Christian civilizations, to a renaissance

In consequence, Islam, too, is a member of the family of Syriac-Hellenic societies.

In the history of the encounter between the Syriac and Hellenic civilizations—an encounter from which the Syriac-Hellenic societies eventually sprang—the fusion that produced a 'culture-compost' had been preceded by a stage in which the Syriac Civilization had been the Hellenic Civilization's satellite. In the relation between a satellite and the civilization into whose field it has been drawn, 'pseudomorphosis' has come into play in a number of other cases as well.

For example, when the Iranian culture was drawn into the field of the Syriac Civilization in the course of the Achaemenian age, one of the eventual results was a 'pseudomorphosis' on the linguistic plane in the shape of the Pehlevi language. In Pehlevi, some words are written alphabetically in the Aramaic *koinê*, but they are read as ideograms standing for the corresponding words in Middle Persian.[1] On this linguistic plane, in a later chapter of history, the Arabic language succeeded in penetrating into New Persian more deeply.[2] But at this price the submerged Iranian culture succeeded, in its turn, in giving New Persian the status of a literary language that was able to hold its own against Arabic in the Perso-Turkish half of the Islamic World. Since an early stage in the decline of the 'Abbasid Caliphate, the Islamic World has been articulated into two distinct cultural zones: an Iranic zone and an Arabic one. Since the sixteenth century of the Christian Era, Iran has reasserted its distinctive communal identity on the religious plane as well. In acquiescing in Shah Isma'il's imposition of the Imami Shi'ite version of Islam on his new subjects, the Persians acquired a distinctive national religion of their own for the first time since their conversion to Islam from Zoroastrianism after the overthrow of the Sasanian regime.[3]

of Hellenic philosophy itself and, with it, of Hellenic science (see p. 450, footnote 2). There is, however, one Hellenic element in Christianity—and this at Christianity's core—which Islam has not taken over, but has, on the contrary, repudiated; and this is the deification of Jesus and the consequent conception of the Godhead as being a trinity. Muhammad and, following him, Islam have given Jesus the highest rank that it is possible to give Him without recognizing Him as being divine or as being the last and greatest of the prophets. According to Islamic doctrine, Jesus is the last and greatest of the prophets save for Muhammad, and miracles are ascribed to Him which Muhammad does not claim for himself. Muhammad adopted from the Monophysite Christian neighbours of the Arabia of his day the belief—branded by Orthodox Christians as docetism—that the Passion was an illusion, and that the figure nailed to the Cross was a substitute or a phantom, not Jesus Himself (see Qur'ān, iv. 156 (Fluegel's numbering)). It is remarkable that Muhammad should have made this Monophysite Christian belief his own, since the Monophysites had been led to it by their thesis that Christ's nature was exclusively divine, and by their agreement with the Jews and Greeks (1 Cor. i. 23) in holding that it was inconceivable that a divine being should have suffered death and, moreover, should have suffered it in a form devised as a punishment for criminal human beings. It might look as if Muhammad had seen, in Jesus, a superhuman being. In Muhammad's belief Jesus is supported by the spirit of holiness, or is himself a spirit from God (Qur'ān, ii. 81, iv. 169, v. 109, xxi. 91). Nevertheless, Muhammad reacted, just as strongly as the Jews, against the Christian claim that Jesus is God. In Muslim eyes the deification of Jesus is *shirk* (see L. Gardet and M.-M. Anawati: *Introduction à la Théologie Musulmane* (Paris 1943, Vrin), p. 438): a blasphemous association of one of God's creatures with God Himself; the doctrine of the Trinity is polytheism.

Thus the vein of Hellenism goes less deep in Islam than it goes in Christianity, but at the same time it is present in Islam too. See also pp. 451, with footnote 1, 467, and 471.
[1] See pp. 433-4.   [2] See ibid.
[3] The Arab Muslim conquerors' Zoroastrian subjects seem to have been converted to Islam more readily and rapidly than their Christian subjects. In the light of this, it is

Since the fifteenth century of the Christian Era, Islam has captured Indonesia. In this case the conversion has been accomplished by peaceful missionary enterprise, not by force of arms, and therefore has not provoked the militant opposition that it did arouse among Hindus in India. Nevertheless, Islam in Indonesia has not succeeded in supplanting, below the surface, the Indian culture—Hindu and Buddhist—which had been paramount in Indonesia for more than a thousand years before Islam's arrival there. A present-day Indonesian Muslim reminds himself of his Hindu cultural heritage by assuming a Sanskrit name in conjunction with his Arabic one; and he celebrates the Prophet Muhammad's birthday (the *Mawlid*) by entertaining himself with puppet-plays in which the characters are the heroes of the Mahabharata. Here we can watch the Indian culture, which the Indonesians have never ceased to cherish, breaking through an Islamic veneer. The Islamic surface of present-day Indonesian culture is, in fact, a 'pseudomorphosis'. But so, too, was the Indian culture which preceded Islam in Indonesia and the Malay Peninsula and which, in the Hinayanian Buddhist version of it, is still paramount on the South-East Asian mainland in Burma, Thailand, and Cambodia. In South-East Asia the dissemination of Indian culture, like the later dissemination of Islam in the insular and peninsular parts of the region, was a peaceful process. But the Indian Civilization in South-East Asia experienced the same fortune that Islam experienced there later. The Indian Civilization, too, failed to supplant the previously prevailing local cultures. Below the surface these continued to hold their own. In South-East Asia the exotic forms of Indian architecture, art, and religion have been adapted to express a native South-East Asian content.[1]

An example of 'pseudomorphosis' on an oecumenical scale is presented by the Western surface of the present-day world as a whole. The first non-Western societies to be Westernized were the Middle American and the Andean. By now, they have been nominally Western and Christian for more than four hundred years. Yet today, in the highlands of Guatemala and on the Las Casas plateau in the adjoining corner of Mexico, one can see Christian churches being used for the celebration of Pre-Christian rites by an unsophisticated peasantry. In Mexico City one can see the motifs and the spirit of the same Pre-Christian religion being resuscitated by sophisticated painters and sculptors trained in a Western school and using a Western technique. In the minds of these artists themselves this is conscious and deliberate archaism. But the artificially resuscitated Pre-Columbian religious art has a compelling power of its own. In souls less sophisticated than those of its resuscitators it might reactivate the ancient feelings and beliefs of which it is a potent symbol. In Mexico, as in Indonesia, we seem to be witnessing the bankruptcy of a 'pseudomorphosis'. The underlying reality is breaking through the veneer. In the history of the Westernization of Russia we can read the same story. Since the generation of Peter the Great, Russian

the more remarkable that Iran should have preserved its cultural individuality so tenaciously under an Arabic and Islamic surface.
[1] See D. G. E. Hall: *A History of South-East Asia* (London 1955, Macmillan), *passim*.

novelists, philosophers, and ideologists have been conforming outwardly to Western conventions, but, in Russian hands, the Western mould has yielded unmistakably Russian products.[1] If the Westernization of the World calls into existence an oecumenical civilization, we may expect to see this new world-wide culture start on a Western basis; but, in the light of such precedents as those just cited, we may also expect to see the non-Western elements below the surface eventually break through the Western crust. Spengler's concept of 'pseudomorphosis' thus seems likely to be illuminating for the new chapter of history on which mankind is entering in our day.

[1] See p. 538.

BIBLIOGRAPHY

A. WORKS OF GENERAL INTEREST[1]

1. THE GENERAL STUDY OF HUMAN AFFAIRS

(i) *The Theory of Knowledge in its Application to the Study of Human Affairs*

BRAITHWAITE, R. B.: *Scientific Explanation: A Study of the Function of Theory, Probability, and Law in Science*, Cambridge, 1953, University Press.

BUCHDAHL, G.: 'The Inductive Process and Inductive Inference' in *The Australasian Journal of Philosophy*, vol. 24, No. 3, Glebe, N.S.W., December, 1956, pp. 164–81.

COATES, W. H.: 'Relativism and the Use of Hypothesis in History' in *The Journal of Modern History*, vol. xxi, No. 1, Chicago, March, 1949, pp. 23–27.

DEUTSCH, K. W.: 'Mechanism, Organism, and Society: Some Models in Natural and Social Science' in *Philosophy of Science*, vol. 18, No. 3, Baltimore, July, 1951, pp. 230–52.

DRAY, W.: *Laws and Explanation in History*, Oxford, 1957, University Press.

HAYEK, F. A.: *The Counter-Revolution of Science: Studies on the Abuse of Reason*, Glencoe, Ill., 1952, The Free Press; London, Allen & Unwin.

INGE, DEAN W. R.: 'The Place of Myth in Philosophy' in *Philosophy*, vol. xi, No. 42, London, April, 1936, pp. 131–45.

JOSEPH, H. W. B.: *An Introduction to Logic*, 2nd ed., Oxford, 1916, Clarendon Press.

JOYNT, C. B., and RESCHER, N.: 'On Explanation in History' in *Mind*, New Series, vol. lxviii, No. 271, Edinburgh, July, 1959, pp. 383–8.

KLUCKHOHN, CLYDE: 'Ethical Relativity' in *The Journal of Philosophy*, vol. lii, No. 23, Lancaster, Pa., 10th November, 1955, pp. 663–77.

MONRO, P. H.: 'Are Moral Problems Genuine?' in *Mind*, New Series, vol. lxv, Edinburgh, April, 1956, pp. 166–83.

OAKELEY, HILDA D.: 'Philosophic History and Prophecy' in *Philosophy*, vol. xi, No. 42, London, April, 1936, pp. 186–94.

POPPER, K. R.: *The Poverty of Historicism*, London, 1957, Routledge & Kegan Paul.

RESCHER, NICHOLAS: 'Reasoned Justification of Moral Judgments' in *The Journal of Philosophy*, vol. lv, No. 6, Lancaster, Pa., 13th March, 1958, pp. 248–55.

—— and JOYNT, C. B.: 'Evidence in History and in the Law' in *The Journal of Philosophy*, vol. lvi, No. 13, Lancaster, Pa., 18th June, 1959, pp. 561–78.

SOCIAL SCIENCE RESEARCH COUNCIL'S COMMITTEE ON HISTORIOGRAPHY: *Report*, New York, 1954.

SWABEY, M. C.: *The Judgment of History*, New York, 1954, Philosophical Library.

[1] Some of these contain incidental critiques of A. J. Toynbee's work.

(ii) *The Morphology of History and Metahistory*

BAGBY, PHILIP: *Culture and History: Prolegomena to the Comparative Study of Civilizations*, London, 1958, Longmans.

BARNES, H. E. (ed.): *An Introduction to the History of Sociology*, Chicago, 1948, University of Chicago Press.

BORKENAU, F.: 'Technik und Fortschritt' in *Merkur*, 111. Jahrgang, 7. Heft, Baden-Baden, July, 1949, pp. 625–37.

BULLOCK, ALAN: 'The Historian's Purpose: History and Metahistory' in *History Today*, vol. i, No. 2, London, February, 1951, pp. 5–11.

CLARK, G. N.: 'The Origin of the Cambridge Modern History' in *The Cambridge Historical Journal*, vol. viii, No. 2, 1945, pp. 57–64.

COHEN, M. R.: *The Meaning of Human History*, La Salle, 1947, Open Court Publishing Company.

COULBORN, R.: 'The Meaning of History' in *Ethics*, vol. lv, No. 1, Chicago, October, 1944, pp. 46–62.

CURTIUS, ERNST ROBERT: 'Europäische Literatur und Lateinisches Mittelalter' in *Merkur*, 1. Jahrgang, 4. Heft [Heft 4], Baden-Baden, 1947, pp. 481–96.

D'ARCY, FATHER M. C., S.J.: *The Sense of History, Secular and Sacred*, London, 1959, Faber.

DAWSON, CHRISTOPHER: *The Dynamics of World History*, ed. by J. J. Mulloy, London, 1957, Sheed & Ward.

ERDMANN, K. D.: 'Das Problem des Historismus in der Neueren Englischen Geschichtswissenschaft' in the *Historische Zeitschrift*, Band 170, Munich, 1950, pp. 73–88.

GÜRSTER, E.: 'Die Atombombe, Schrittmacherin der Welteinigung?' in *Die Neue Rundschau*, 13. Heft, Amsterdam, Winter, 1949, pp. 125–43.

HARBISON, ELMORE HARRIS: 'The Problem of the Christian Historian' in *Theology Today*, vol. v, Princeton, October, 1948, pp. 388–405.

HOFER, W.: *Geschichte zwischen Philosophie und Politik*, Basel, 1946, Verlag für Recht und Gesellschaft.

HUGHES, H. STUART: *Oswald Spengler: A Critical Estimate*, New York, 1952, Scribners.

IBN KHALDŪN: *Muqaddimah*, translated from the Arabic by F. Rosenthal, London, 1958, Routledge & Kegan Paul, 3 vols.

KOPPERS, W.: 'Der Historische Gedanke in Ethnologie und Prähistorie' in *Kultur und Sprache*, Vienna, 1952, Herold, pp. 11–65.

KROEBER, A. L.: *The Nature of Culture*, Chicago, 1952, University of Chicago Press.

—— 'Stimulus Diffusion' in *The American Anthropologist*, New Series, vol. 42, No. 1, Menasha, Wisc., January–March, 1940, pp. 1–20; reprinted in *The Nature of Culture*, Chicago, 1952, University of Chicago Press, pp. 344–57.

—— *Style and Civilizations*, Ithaca, N.Y., 1957, Cornell University Press.

LÖWITH, KARL: *Meaning in History: The Theological Implications of the Philosophy of History*, Chicago, 1949, University of Chicago Press.

MARITAIN, JACQUES: *On the Philosophy of History*, London, 1959, Bles.

MILNE, E. A.: *Modern Cosmology and the Christian Idea of God*, Oxford, 1952, Clarendon Press.

PRAKASH, BUDDHA: 'The Hindu Philosophy of History' in *The Journal of the History of Ideas*, vol. xvi, No. 4, New York, October, 1955, pp. 494–505.

RICHARDSON, D. B.: 'The Philosophy of History and the Stability of Civilizations' in *The Thomist*, vol. xx, No. 2, Baltimore, April, 1957, pp. 158–90.
SHINN, R. L.: *Christianity and the Problem of History*, New York, 1953, Scribners.
SPENGLER, OSWALD: *Der Untergang des Abendlandes*, Munich, 1919–22, Beck, 2 vols.: i, Gestalt und Wirklichkeit; ii, Welthistorische Perspektiven.
TEILHARD DE CHARDIN, S.J., FATHER PIERRE: *Le Phénomène Humain*, Paris, 1955, Éditions du Seuil; English translation by Bernard Wall: *The Phenomenon of Man*, London, 1959, Collins.
VOGT, JOSEPH: *Gesetz und Handlungsfreiheit in der Geschichte: Studien zur Historischen Wiederholung*, Stuttgart, 1955, Kohlhammer.
ZAEHNER, R. C.: *At Sundry Times: An Essay in the Comparison of Religions*, London, 1958, Faber.

(iii) *The Relation between Man and His Environment*

MONTEFIORE, A. C., and WILLIAMS, W. M.: 'Determinism and Possibilism' in *Geographical Studies*, vol. 2, No. 1, London, 1955, Birkbeck College, pp. 1–11.
SPATE, O. H. K.: 'How Determined is Possibilism?' in *Geographical Studies*, vol. iv, No. 1, London, 1957, pp. 3–12.
SPROUT, H. and M.: *Man-Milieu Relationship Hypothesis in the Context of International Politics*, Princeton, 1956, Princeton University Center of International Studies.

2. THE PRELUDE TO THE RISE OF CIVILIZATION IN SUMER AND EGYPT

BAUMGARTEL, E. J.: *The Cultures of Prehistoric Egypt*, London, 1955, Cumberlege.
BRAIDWOOD, R. J.: *The Near East and the Foundations of Civilization*, Eugene, 1952, Oregon State System of Higher Education.
CHILDE, V. G.: *Man Makes Himself*, London, 1936, Watts.
—— *What Happened in History*, Harmondsworth, 1942, Penguin.
COON, C. S.: *The History of Man from the First Human to Primitive Culture and Beyond*, London, 1955, Cape.
COULBORN, RUSHTON: *The Origin of Civilized Societies*, Princeton, 1959, Princeton University Press.
FRANKFORT, H.: *The Birth of Civilization in the Near East*, London, 1951, Williams & Norgate.
GLUECK, NELSON: *The River Jordan*, London, 1946, Lutterworth Press.
KENYON, KATHLEEN: *Digging up Jericho*, London, 1957, Benn.
LLOYD, SETON: *Early Anatolia: The Archaeology of Asia Minor before the Greeks*, Harmondsworth, 1956, Pelican.
REDFIELD, R.: *The Primitive World and its Transformations*, Ithaca, N.Y., 1953, Cornell University Press.

3. THE RISE OF CIVILIZATION IN CHINA

CREEL, H. G.: *Studies in Early Chinese Culture: First Series*, Baltimore, 1937, Waverley Press.
—— *The Birth of China*, New York, 1937, Reynal and Hitchcock.
LI CHI: *The Beginnings of Chinese Civilization*, Seattle, 1957, University of Washington Press.

678   BIBLIOGRAPHY

NEEDHAM, JOSEPH: *Science and Civilization in China*, Cambridge, vol. i, 1954; vol. ii, 1956; vol. iii, 1959, University Press.
ROXBY, P. M.: 'The Major Regions of China' in *Geography: The Quarterly Journal of the Geographical Association*, vol. 23, Manchester, 1938, pp. 9–14.
—— 'The Terrain of Early Chinese Civilization' in *Geography: The Quarterly Journal of the Geographical Association*, vol. 23, Manchester, 1938, pp. 225–36.

4. THE CONFIGURATION OF CHINESE HISTORY

ALTREE, WAYNE: 'Toynbee's Treatment of Chinese History' in *Saeculum*, Band vi, Heft 1, Freiburg-im-Breisgau, 1955, pp. 10–34; revised version in *Toynbee and History*, pp. 243–72.
CAMERON, M. E.: 'A Bisection of Chinese History' in *The Pacific Historical Review*, vol. viii, No. 4, Berkeley, Cal., December, 1939, pp. 401–12.
CHI, CH'AO-TING: *Key Economic Areas in Chinese History as Revealed in the Development of Public Works for Water-Control*, London, 1936, Allen & Unwin.
FRANKE, H.: 'Orientalistik: i. Teil: Sinologie' in *Wissenschaftliche Forschungsberichte*, Band 19, Bern, 1953, Francke.
KIRBY, E. S.: *Economic History of China*, London, 1954, Allen & Unwin.
WATSON, B.: *Ssu-ma Ch'ien: Grand Historian of China*, New York, 1958, Columbia University Press.
WRIGHT, A. F.: 'Buddhism and Chinese Culture: Phases of Interaction' in *The Journal of Asian Studies*, vol. xvii, No. 1, Ann Arbor, Mich., November, 1957, pp. 17–42.
—— *Buddhism in Chinese History*, Stanford, 1959, Stanford University Press.
—— 'The Formation of Sui Ideology, 581–604' in FAIRBANK, J. K. (ed.): *Chinese Thought and Institutions*, Chicago, 1957, University of Chicago Press, pp. 71–104 and 352–63.
—— 'The Study of Chinese Civilization': roneo presented to the Seminar on the Comparative Study of Civilizations at the Center for Advanced Study in the Behavioral Sciences, Stanford, Cal., March, 1958.

5. THE PRE-COLUMBIAN CIVILIZATIONS OF THE AMERICAS

BENNETT, W. C. (ed.): 'A Reappraisal of Peruvian Archaeology' in *Memoirs of the Society for American Archaeology*, No. 4 (supplement to *American Antiquity*, vol. xiii, No. 4, Part 2, April, 1948), Menasha, Wisc., 1948, pp. 1–121.
—— and BIRD, J. R.: *Andean Culture History*, American Museum of Natural History, Handbook Series, No. 15, New York, 1949.
BERNAL, IGNACIO: *Mesoamérica: Período Indígena*, México, 1953, Instituto Panamericano de Geografía e Historia.
BORHEGYI, S. F. DE: 'The Development of Folk and Complex Cultures in the Southern Mayan Area' in *American Antiquity*, vol. xxi, No. 4, Menasha, Wisc., April, 1956, pp. 343–56.
BUSHNELL, G. H. S.: *Peru*, London, 1958, Thames & Hudson.
FRAU, S. C.: *Las Civilizaciones Prehispánicas de América*, Buenos Aires, 1955, Editorial Sudamericana.
MASON, J. A.: *The Ancient Civilizations of Peru*, Harmondsworth, 1957, Pelican.

STEWARD, J. H. (ed.): *Handbook of South American Indians, vol. 2: The Andean Civilizations*, Washington, D.C., 1946, U.S. Government Printing Office.

VARII AUCTORES (KIDDER, V.; THOMPSON, E. S.; SHOOK, E. M.; STONE, D.; CARRERA, A. G.; DARDÓN, H. C.; VELA, D.; CHINCHILLA, C. S.; BORHEGYI, S. F. DE): *Arqueología Guatemalteca*, Guatemala, 1957, Ministerio de Educación Pública.

WAUCHOPE, R.: 'Implications of Radioactive Dates from Middle and South America' in Publication No. 18 of the Middle American Research Institute of Tulane University, New Orleans, 1954, pp. 17–40.

WILLEY, G. R.: 'Estimated Correlations and Dating of South and Central American Culture Sequences' in *American Antiquity*, vol. 23, No. 4, Part 2, Menasha, Wisc., April, 1958, pp. 353–78.

—— *Prehistoric Settlement Patterns in the Virú Valley, Peru*, Smithsonian Institution, Bureau of American Ethnology, Bulletin 158, Washington, D.C., 1953, U.S. Government Printing Office.

—— 'The Intermediate Area of Nuclear America: Its Prehistoric Relationships to Middle America and Peru': typescript of paper read to the Thirty-Third International Congress of Americanists, held at San José, Costa Rica, July, 1958.

—— 'The Interrelated Rise of the Native Cultures of Middle and South America' in *The Seventy-Fifth Anniversary Volume of the Anthropological Society of Washington*, Washington, D.C., 1955, pp. 28–45.

—— 'The Prehistoric Civilizations of Nuclear America' in *The American Anthropologist*, New Series, vol. 57, No. 3, Part 1, Menasha, Wisc., June, 1955, pp. 571–93.

—— 'The Structure of Ancient Maya Society: Evidence from the Southern Lowlands' in *The American Anthropologist*, New Series, vol. 58, No. 5, Menasha, Wisc., October, 1956, pp. 777–82.

—— and PHILLIPS, P.: 'Method and Theory in American Archaeology, II: Historical-Developmental Interpretation' in *The American Anthropologist*, New Series, vol. 57, No. 4, Menasha, Wisc., August, 1955, pp. 723–819.

—— —— *Method and Theory in American Archaeology*, Chicago, 1958, University of Chicago Press.

6. PRE-COLUMBIAN CONTACTS BETWEEN THE AMERICAS AND THE OLD WORLD

DIXON, R. B.: 'The Problem of the Sweet Potato in Polynesia' in *The American Anthropologist*, New Series, vol. 34, No. 1, Menasha, Wisc., January–March, 1932, pp. 40–56.

HEINE-GELDERN, R.: 'Some Problems of Migration in the Pacific' in *Kultur und Sprache*, Vienna, 1952, Herold, pp. 313–62.

HORNELL, J.: 'Was there Pre-Columbian Contact between the Peoples of Oceania and South America?' in *The Journal of the Polynesian Society*, vol. 54, Wellington, N.Z., 1945, pp. 167–91.

SHARP, A.: *Ancient Voyagers in the Pacific*, London, 1956, Polynesian Society; Harmondsworth, 1957, Penguin.

7. THE SYRIAC CIVILIZATION (INCLUDING ISRAEL AND JUDAH)

ALBRIGHT, W. F.: *Archaeology and the Religion of Israel*, 4th ed., Baltimore, 1956, Johns Hopkins University Press.

ALBRIGHT, W. F. *From the Stone Age to Christianity*, 2nd ed., Baltimore, 1957, Johns Hopkins University Press.
—— *The Archaeology of Palestine*, Harmondsworth, 1949, Penguin.
DUPONT-SOMMER, A.: *Les Araméens*, Paris, 1949, Maisonneuve.
HENNING, W. B.: *Zoroaster*, London, 1951, Cumberlege.
ROBINSON, T. H.: *A History of Israel*, vol. i: 'From the Exodus to the Fall of Jerusalem, 586 B.C.', Oxford, 1932, Clarendon Press (in OESTERLEY, W. O. E., and ROBINSON, T. H.: *A History of Israel*, 2 vols.).
ROWLEY, H. H.: *From Joseph to Joshua: Biblical Traditions in the Light of Archaeology*, London, 1950, Cumberlege.

8. THE JEWS SINCE 586 B.C.

AGUS, RABBI J. B.: 'Towards a Philosophy of Jewish History' in *Judaism: A Quarterly Journal of Jewish Life and Thought*, New York, Spring, Summer, Fall, Winter, 1956.
BARON, S. W.: *A Social and Religious History of the Jews*, 2nd ed., vol. i: 'Ancient Times': Part I, New York, 1952, Columbia University Press.
HERFORD, R. TRAVERS: *Christianity in Talmud and Midrash*, London, 1903, Williams & Norgate.
—— *Judaism in the New Testament Period*, London, 1928, Lindsey Press.
—— *The Pharisees*, London, 1924, Allen & Unwin.
MONTEFIORE, C. G.: *Rabbinic Literature and Gospel Teachings*, London, 1930, Macmillan.
MOORE, G. F.: *Judaism in the First Centuries of the Christian Era: The Age of the Tannaim*, Cambridge, Mass., 1927–30, Harvard University Press, 3 vols.
OESTERLEY, W. O. E.: *A History of Israel*, vol. ii: 'From the Fall of Jerusalem, 586 B.C., to the Bar-Kokhba Revolt, A.D. 135', Oxford, 1932, Clarendon Press (in OESTERLEY, W. O. E., and ROBINSON, T. H.: *A History of Israel*, 2 vols.).
—— *The Jews and Judaism during the Greek Period: The Background of Christianity*, London, 1941, S.P.C.K.
RIDDLE, D. W.: *Jesus and the Pharisees: A Study in Christian Tradition*, Chicago, 1928, University of Chicago Press.
TALMON, J. L.: 'Uniqueness and Universality of Jewish History' in *Commentary*, vol. 24, No. 1, New York, July, 1957, pp. 1–14.
WHITLEY, C. F.: *The Exilic Age*, London, 1957, Longmans.

B. CRITIQUES OF A. J. TOYNBEE'S WORK[1]

AGUS, RABBI J. B.: 'Is Toynbee an Anti-Semite?' in *The National Jewish Monthly*, Washington, D.C., November, 1956, pp. 32 and 40–44.
—— 'Toynbee and Judaism' in *Judaism: A Quarterly Journal of Jewish Life and Thought*, vol. 4, No. 4, New York, Fall, 1955, pp. 319–32.
ALBRIGHT, W. F.: review of *A Study of History*, vols. vii–x, in *The Evening Sun*, Baltimore, Maryland, 14th October, 1954.
ANDERLE, OTHMAR F.: *Das Universalhistorische System Arnold Joseph Toynbees*, Frankfurt-am-Main and Vienna, 1955, Humboldt-Verlag.
ANDERLE, OTHMAR F.: 'Die Toynbee-Kritik: Das Universalhistorische

---

[1] This is not an attempt at a complete bibliography. With a few exceptions, it is limited to works actually quoted or cited in the present volume.

System Arnold J. Toynbees im Urteil der Wissenschaft' in *Saeculum*, Band. ix, Heft 2, Freiburg-im-Breisgau, 1958, pp. 189–259.
—— unpublished paper.
ANONYMOUS: review of *A Study of History*, vols. iv–vi, in *The Glasgow Herald*, 2nd August, 1939.
—— review of *A Study of History*, vols. i–iii, in *The Japan Chronicle*, 29th July, 1934.
—— review of *A Study of History*, vols. iv–vi, in *The Listener*, London, 19th October, 1939.
—— 'The Sense of the Past' in *The Times Literary Supplement*, No. 2842, London, 17th August, 1956, p. x.
AULT, W. O.: 'Toynbee's Study of History' in *Journal of Bible and Religion*, Walcott, N.Y., April, 1955, National Association of Biblical Instructors, pp. 119–23.
BAGBY, PHILIP: 'A Personal View of History' in *The Times Literary Supplement*, No. 2751, London, 22nd October, 1954, pp. 665–6; reprinted in *Toynbee and History*, pp. 103–10.
BAILEY, A. G.: 'The Impact of Toynbee' in *Queen's Quarterly*, vol. lxii, No. 1, Kingston, Ontario, Spring, 1955, pp. 100–10.
BARKER, SIR ERNEST: 'Dr. Toynbee's Study of History' in *International Affairs*, vol. 31, London, 1955, pp. 5–16; reprinted in *Toynbee and History*, pp. 89–102.
BARNES, HARRY ELMER: 'Arnold Joseph Toynbee: Orosius and Augustine in Modern Dress' in *An Introduction to the History of Sociology*, ed. by H. E. Barnes (Chicago, 1948, University of Chicago Press), pp. 717–36.
BARRACLOUGH, GEOFFREY: 'The Prospects of the Western World' in *The Listener*, London, 14th October, 1954, p. 639; reprinted in *Toynbee and History*, pp. 118–21.
BATES, M. SEARLE: 'Toynbee as Historian' in *Christianity and Crisis*, vol. 15, No. 4, 21st March, 1955, pp. 27–30 and 32.
BAUDET, H.: 'Hedendaagsch Augustinisme' in *Historie en Metahistorie*, 'Robert Fruin' Lustrumbundel, Leiden, 1952, University Press, pp. 43–63.
BAZÁN, RAFAEL GUEVARA: typescript letters from Lima, 10th March, 1955, and 17th January, 1956.
BEARD, CHARLES A.: review of *A Study of History*, vols. i–iii, in *The American Historical Review*, vol. xl, No. 2, New York, January, 1935, pp. 307–9.
BECKER, H.: review of *A Study of History*, vols. i–vi, in *The Annals of the American Academy of Political and Social Science*, vol. 210, Philadelphia, July, 1940, pp. 159–62.
BERKOVITZ, E.: *Judaism: Fossil or Ferment?*, New York, 1956, Philosophical Library.
BIRKS, G. A.: 'Toynbee and his Critics' in *Philosophy*, vol. xxv, No. 95, London, October, 1950, pp. 336–40.
—— typescript letter from Leeds, 23rd January, 1949.
BISHKO, JULIAN: review of *A Study of History*, vols. vii–x, in *The Richmond News*, Richmond, Virginia, 21st October, 1954.
BLACKMUR, R. P.: 'Reflections of Toynbee' in *The Kenyon Review*, vol. xvii, No. 3, Gambier, Ohio, Summer, 1955, pp. 357–70.
BORKENAU, F.: 'Toynbee and the Culture Cycle' in *Commentary*, vol. 21, No. 3, New York, March, 1956, pp. 239–49.
—— 'Toynbee's Judgment on the Jews' in *Commentary*, vol. 19, No. 5, New York, May, 1955, pp. 421–7.

BRINTON, CRANE: 'Toynbee's City of God' in *The Virginia Quarterly Review*, vol. 32, No. 3, Charlottesville, Summer, 1956, pp. 361–75.

BRYAN, G. McLEOD: 'The Kingdom of God Concept in Sorokin and Toynbee' in *Social Forces*, vol. 26, No. 3, Baltimore, March, 1948, pp. 288–92.

BURN, A. R.: 'The Comparative Study of Civilizations: Toynbee's Study of History' in *History*, vol. xli, Nos. 141/143, London, February–October, 1956, pp. 1–15.

BYKHOVSKY, B.: 'Professor Toynbee presents "East" and "West"' in *New Times*, No. 46, Moscow, 12th November, 1947, pp. 27–31.

CAILLOIS, ROGER: Foreword to 'The Contribution of Arnold Toynbee' in *Diogenes*, No. 13, Chicago, Spring, 1956, University of Chicago Press, pp. 2–4.

CAMERON MERIBETH E.: 'A Rehandling of Japanese History' in *The Far Eastern Quarterly*, vol. i, No. 2, New York, February, 1942, pp. 150–60.

CATLIN, GEORGE: 'Toynbee's Study of History' in *The Political Science Quarterly*, vol. 70, No. 1, New York, March, 1955, pp. 107–12; reprinted in *Toynbee and History*, pp. 167–71.

CHASE, RICHARD V.: 'History versus the City of God' in *The Partisan Review*, vol. 11, No. 1, New York, Winter, 1944, pp. 45–55.

—— 'Toynbee: The Historian as Artist' in *The American Scholar*, vol. 16, No. 3, New York, Summer, 1947, pp. 268–82.

CHAUDHURI, NIRAD C.: typescript letters from Calcutta, 15th July and 27th August, 1936, enclosing typescript papers on 'The Character of "Hindu Society"', 'The Apparentation and Affiliation of Societies in India', 'The Relativity of Historical Thought'.

CHRISTIAN, JAMES L.: letter from Quincy, Mass., 10th April, 1957, enclosing outline of dissertation on 'Toynbee's Concept of Man'.

Christian Register, The, vol. 134, No. 4, Boston, Mass., April, 1955, pp. 9–19 and 26: articles on A. J. Toynbee's work by Hans Kohn and Pieter Geyl.

CLARK, R. T.: review of *A Study of History*, vols. i–vi, in *The Nineteenth Century and After*, vol. 130, No. 777, London, November, 1941, pp. 295–300.

CLARKSON, JESSE D.: 'Toynbee on Slavic and Russian History', a paper delivered at the annual meeting of the American Historical Society in Washington, D.C., 28th December, 1955, published in *The Russian Review*, vol. 15, No. 3, Hanover, N.H., July, 1956, pp. 165–72.

COULBORN, RUSHTON: 'Fact and Fiction in Toynbee's Study of History' in *Ethics*, vol. lxvi, No. 4, Chicago, July, 1956; reprinted in *Toynbee and History*, pp. 148–66.

—— 'The Individual and the Growth of Civilizations: An Answer to Arnold Toynbee and Henri Bergson' in *Phylon*, vol. i, Atlanta, Georgia, 1940, pp. 69–89, 136–48, 243–64 (offprint, 58 pp.).

CREEDY, F.: typescript letter of 2nd May, 1955, enclosing typescript paper on 'Toynbee and Anthropology'.

CROSSMAN, R. H. S.: 'The Mystic World of Arnold Toynbee' in *The New Statesman and Nation*, London, 8th March, 1947; and in *The New Republic*, vol. cxviii, New York, 14th July, 1947, pp. 24–26.

CURTIUS, ERNST ROBERT: 'Toynbees Geschichtslehre' in *Merkur*, 2. Jahrgang, 4. Heft [Heft 10], Baden-Baden, 1948, pp. 507–29.

DAWSON, CHRISTOPHER,: 'Toynbee's Odyssey of the West' in *The Commonweal*, vol. 61, No. 3, New York, 22nd October, 1954, pp. 62–67.

—— review of *A Study of History*, vols. vii–x, in *The Observer*, London, 17th October, 1954.

DAWSON, CHRISTOPHER: 'Toynbee's Study of History: The Place of Civilizations in History' in *International Affairs*, vol. 31, London, 1955, pp. 149–58; reprinted in *Toynbee and History*, pp. 129–39.

DEN BOER, W.: 'Toynbee and Classical History: Historiography and Myth' in Dutch in *De Gids*, iiie Jahrgang, Deel 4, No. 10, Amsterdam, October, 1948, pp. 12–40; in English in *Toynbee and History*, pp. 221–42.

Diogenes, No. 13, Chicago, Spring, 1956, University of Chicago Press: 'The Contribution of Arnold Toynbee.'

DOWLING, J. W.: 'Relative Archaism: A New Fallacy and Mr. Toynbee' in *The Journal of Philosophy*, vol. xliii, No. 16, New York, 1st August, 1946, pp. 421–35.

DREES, LUDWIG: *Die Botschaft Toynbees an die Abendländische Welt*, Stuttgart, 1952, Kohlhammer.

DYASON, E. C.: 'Three Roads to Thule: Toynbee, Mannheim, and Northrop' in *The Australian Outlook*, vol. 3, No. 1, Sydney, March, 1949, pp. 46–61.

EBAN, ABBA: 'The Toynbee Heresy' in *Toynbee and History*, pp. 320–37.

ENGEL-JANOSI, F.: 'Das Historische Weltbild Arnold J. Toynbees' in *Wissenschaft und Weltbild*, 2. Jahrgang, Heft 4, Vienna, October, 1949, pp. 261–71.

—— 'Toynbee and the Tradition of Universal History' in *The Intent of Toynbee's History: A Cooperative Appraisal*.

ERDMANN, K. D.: 'Toynbee: Eine Zwischenbilanz' in *Archiv für Kulturgeschichte*, xxxiii. Band, Heft 2, Marburg/Lahn, 1951, Simons, pp. 174–250.

FEBVRE, L.: review of *A Study of History*, vols. i–iii, in *Revue de la Métaphysique et de Morale*, vol. 43 (1936), pp. 573–602.

FEIBLEMAN, J. K.: 'Toynbee's Theory of History' in *T'ien Hsia Monthly*, vol. ix, No. 1, pp. 9–29, and No. 2, pp. 140–73 (1940), Ann Arbor, 1941, Edwards.

FIESS, EDWARD: 'Toynbee as Poet' in *The Journal of the History of Ideas*, vol. 16, No. 2, New York, April, 1955, pp. 275–80; reprinted in *Toynbee and History*, pp. 378–84.

FISHER, H. A. L.: 'A Universal Historian' in *The Nineteenth Century and After*, London, December, 1934, pp. 662–73.

FITZSIMONS, M. A.: 'Toynbee's Approach to the History and Character of the United States' in *The Intent of Toynbee's History: A Cooperative Appraisal*.

—— 'Toynbee's Summa: Discussions and Problems' in *The Review of Politics*, vol. 19, No. 4, Notre Dame, Ind., October, 1957, pp. 544–53.

FOUCHÉ, LEO: 'Causes and Consequences of the Great Trek' [in the light of the notion of challenge-and-response] in *The Star*, Johannesburg, 12th December, 1936.

FRANKFORT, HENRI: letter published in *The Observer*, London, 31st January, 1954.

FYVEL, T. R.: review of D. C. Somervell's Abridgement of *A Study of History*, vols. i–vi, in *The Tribune*, London, 21st March, 1947, pp. 20–21.

GARDINER, PATRICK: review of *A Study of History*, vols. vii–x, in *Time and Tide*, London, 30th October, 1954, pp. 1454 and 1456.

GARGAN, EDWARD T. (ed.): *The Intent of Toynbee's History: A Cooperative Appraisal* [papers presented at a conference at Loyola University Chicago, September, 1955], in course of publication.

—— *The Intent of Toynbee's History: A Cooperative Appraisal*, Introduction.

GARGAN, EDWARD T.: 'The Meaning of Toynbee's History' in *Books on Trial*, vol. xiii, No. 5, March, 1955, pp. 221–2 and 265–7.

GEYL, PIETER: *Debates with Historians*, The Hague, 1955, Nijhoff; Groningen, 1955, Wolters; New York, 1956, Philosophical Library.

—— 'Toynbee as Prophet' in *Debates with Historians*, New York, 1956, Philosophical Library, pp. 158–78; reprinted in *Toynbee and History*, pp. 360–77.

—— 'Toynbee's System of Civilizations', in Dutch in *Jaarverslag*, 1946; and in *Tochten en Toernooien*, 1950; in English in *The Journal of the History of Ideas*, New York, 1948; in *The Pattern of the Past*, Boston, 1949, Beacon Press, pp. 3–72; and in *Toynbee and History*, pp. 39–72.

—— TOYNBEE, A. J., SOROKIN, P. A.: *The Pattern of the Past: Can We Determine It?* Boston, 1949, Beacon Press.

GREGORY, T. S.: 'The Meaning of History: Mr. Toynbee's Approach' in *The Dublin Review*, vol. 220, No. 440, London, Spring, 1947, pp. 74–87.

GRUNEBAUM, G. E. VON: 'Toynbee's Concept of Islamic Civilization' in *The Intent of Toynbee's History: A Cooperative Appraisal.*

GUERARD, A. L.: review of *A Study of History*, vols. i–iii, in *The New York Herald-Tribune*, 28th October, 1934.

GURIAN, W.: 'Toynbee's Time-Machine' in *The Review of Politics*, vol. 4, No. 4, Notre Dame, Ind., October, 1942, pp. 508–14.

HALECKI, OSKAR: 'The Validity of Toynbee's Conception of the Prospects of Western Civilization' in *The Intent of Toynbee's History: A Cooperative Appraisal.*

HALES, E. E. Y.: 'Arnold Toynbee's Study of History' in *History Today*, London, April, 1955, pp. 236–43; May, 1955, pp. 317–23.

HALÉVY, DANIEL: 'A. J. Toynbee et son Étude d'Histoire' in *La Revue* (*Littérature, Histoire, Arts, et Sciences*) *des Deux Mondes*, 3rd year, No. 17, Paris, 1st September, 1950, pp. 38–42.

HAMPL, F.: 'Grundsätzliches zum Werke Arnold J. Toynbees' in the *Historische Zeitschrift*, Band 173, Heft 3, Munich, 1952, pp. 449–66.

HANDLIN, OSCAR: 'Toynbee's Pied Piper-made History', review of D. C. Somervell's Abridgement of *A Study of History*, vols. i–vi, in *The Partisan Review*, vol. 14, No. 4, New York, July–August, 1947, pp. 371–9.

HANSON, A. H.: 'History and Mr. Toynbee' in *Science and Society*, No. 13, New York, 1949, pp. 118–35.

HARDY, THE REV. E. R., Jr.: 'The Historical Validity of Toynbee's Approach to Universal Churches' in *The Intent of Toynbee's History: A Cooperative Appraisal.*

HEINE-GELDERN, R.: in 'The Contribution of Arnold Toynbee' in *Diogenes*, No. 13, Chicago, Spring, 1956, University of Chicago Press, pp. 82–97.

HICKS, GRANVILLE: 'Toynbee's Study of History Concludes with the Future still a Question Mark' in *The New Leader*, vol. 37, No. 42, New York, 18th October, 1954, pp. 22–23.

HILL, CHRISTOPHER: 'Time and Mr. Toynbee' in *The Modern Quarterly*, New Series, vol. 2, No. 4, London, Autumn, 1947, pp. 290–307.

HOLBORN, HAJO: review of D. C. Somervell's Abridgement of *A Study of History*, vols. i–vi, in *The Saturday Review of Literature*, vol. xxx, No. 22, New York, 31st May, 1947, pp. 11–12 and 29.

HOLCOMBE, ARTHUR N.: review of *A Study of History*, vols. vii–x, in *The American Political Science Review*, vol. xlix, No. 4, Washington, D.C., December, 1955, pp. 1151–4.

HOOK, SIDNEY: 'Mr. Toynbee's City of God' in *The Partisan Review*, vol. 15, No. 6, New York, June, 1948, pp. 691–9.

HÖPKER, W.: 'Arnold J. Toynbee als Christlicher Denker' in *Zeitwende*, Munich, August, 1949, pp. 131–7.

HOURANI, ALBERT: 'Toynbee's Vision of History' in *The Dublin Review*, vol. 229, No. 470, London, December, 1955, pp. 375–401.

HÖVER, OTTO: 'Betrachtungen über Arnold J. Toynbee's Deutung des Menschheitsgeschehens': typescript paper.

—— 'Buchführung und Bilanz der Weltgeschichte in Neuer Sicht: zu A. Toynbees Deutung der Frühzeitlichen Menschengeschehens' in the *Zeitschrift für Religions- und Geistesgeschichte*, Jahrgang 2, Heft 3, Marburg, 1949–50, pp. 247–59.

HUDSON, G. F.: 'Toynbee versus Gibbon' in *The Twentieth Century*, vol. 156, No. 933, London, November, 1954, pp. 403–12.

HUXLEY, ALDOUS: 'History as the Experience of Frustration' in *The Magazine of the Year*, vol. 1, No. 7, New York, September, 1947, pp. 106–12.

Intent, The, of Toynbee's History: A Cooperative Appraisal [papers presented at a conference at Loyola University Chicago, 1955], ed. by Edward T. Gargan, in course of publication.

JAYATILLEKE, K. N.: 'A Recent Criticism of Buddhism' in *The University of Ceylon Review*, vol. xv, Nos. 3 and 4, Colombo, July–October, 1957, pp. 135–50.

JEFTANOVIC, NENAD: typescript letter from The Fletcher School of Law and Diplomacy, Medford, Mass., 26th July, 1957.

JOYNT, G. B.: 'Toynbee and the Problem of Historical Knowledge' in *Australasian Journal of Philosophy*, vol. 34, No. 3, Glebe, N.S.W., December, 1956, pp. 193–202.

KAUFMANN, WALTER: 'Toynbee and Super-History' in *The Partisan Review*, vol. 22, No. 4, New York, Fall, 1955, pp. 531–41; reprinted in *Toynbee and History*, pp. 305–15.

KECSKEMETI, PAUL: 'Timeless History' in *The Modern Review*, vol. 1, No. 4, New York, June, 1947, American Labor Conference on International Affairs, pp. 308–13.

KIRK, RUSSELL: 'The Truth of Western Civilization' in *Sheed and Ward's Own Trumpet*, New York, Christmas, 1954, p. 5.

KLENK, FATHER G. FRIEDRICH, S.J.: 'Geschichte als Anruf und Antwort der Freiheit' in *Stimmen der Zeit*, No. 145, Freiburg, 1949/50, pp. 376–84.

KNIGHT, RAY: letters from Eastbourne, 7th, 29th, 30th July, 1936, on the use of parables and myths.

KOHN, HANS: 'Faith and Vision of a Universal World' in *The Christian Register*, vol. 134, No. 4, Boston, Mass., April, 1955, pp. 9–12; reprinted in *Toynbee and History*, pp. 351–9.

—— review of *A Study of History*, vols. iv–vi, in *The Nation*, New York, 17th February, 1940, pp. 256–7.

—— 'Toynbee and Russia' in *The Intent of Toynbee's History: A Cooperative Appraisal*.

—— 'Toynbees Glaubensbekenntnis' in *Der Monat*, 7. Jahrgang, Heft 83, Berlin, August, 1955, pp. 464–9.

KROEBER, A. L.: review of *A Study of History*, vols. i–vi, in *The American Anthropologist*, New Series, vol. 45, No. 2, Menasha, Wisc., April–June, 1943, pp. 294–9.

KUHN, H.: review of D. C. Somervell's Abridgement of *A Study of History*, vols. i–vi, in *The Journal of Philosophy*, vol. xliv, No. 18, New York, 28th August, 1947, pp. 485–99.

LATTIMORE, OWEN: 'Spengler and Toynbee' in *The Atlantic Monthly*, vol. 181, No. 4, Boston, Mass., April, 1948, pp. 104–5.
LAUER, HANS ERHARD: 'Weltgeschichte und Gegenwart in der Schau Arnold Toynbees' in *Blätter für Anthroposophie*, 4. Jahrgang, No. 1, Basel, January, 1952, pp. 14–18.
LEAN, TANGYE: 'A Study of Toynbee' in *Horizon*, London, January, 1947, pp. 24–55; reprinted in *Toynbee and History*, pp. 12–38.
LEDDY, J. F.: 'Toynbee and the History of Rome' in *The Phoenix: The Journal of the Classical Association of Canada*, vol. 11, No. 4, Toronto, 1957, University of Toronto Press, pp. 139–52.
LEFÉBVRE, G.: review of *A Study of History*, vols. i–vi, in *La Revue Historique*, Paris, January–March, 1949, pp. 109–13.
LOCHER, THEODORE J. G.: 'Toynbee's Antwoord' in *De Gids*, iiie Jg., Deel 2, No. 5, Amsterdam, May, 1948, pp. 99–128 (offprint, 30 pp.).
McNEILL, WILLIAM H.: 'Some Basic Assumptions of Toynbee's Study of History' in *The Intent of Toynbee's History: A Cooperative Appraisal*.
MACRAE, DONALD G.: 'Journey into Night' in *The Literary Guide*, vol. 70, No. 1, London, January, 1955, pp. 13–15.
MADAULE, JACQUES: in 'The Contribution of Arnold Toynbee' in *Diogenes*, No. 13, Spring, 1956, pp. 32–44.
MANN, GOLO: 'Arnold Toynbee und die Weltgeschichte' in *Der Monat*, 1. Jahrgang, Heft 4, Berlin, January, 1949, pp. 34–40.
—— review of the German translation of D. C. Somervell's Abridgement of *A Study of History*, vols. i–vi, in the *Frankfurter Rundschau*, No. 229, 1st October, 1949, p. 6.
MARROU, HENRI: 'D'une Théorie de la Civilisation à la Théologie de l'Histoire' in *Esprit*, 20e Année, No. 7 [No. 192], Paris, July, 1952, pp. 112–29.
MARVIN, F. S.: review of *A Study of History*, vols. i–iii, in *The Hibbert Journal*, London, July, 1935, pp. 622–5.
MASON, H. L.: *Toynbee's Approach to World Politics*, New Orleans, 1958, Tulane University; The Hague, 1958, Martinus Nijhoff.
MASUR, GERHARD: 'Arnold Toynbees Philosophie der Geschichte' in the *Historische Zeitschrift*, Band 174, Munich, 1952, pp. 269–86.
—— review of Pieter Geyl's *From Ranke to Toynbee* (Northampton, Mass., 1952, Smith College Studies in History) in the *Historische Zeitschrift*, Band 177, Munich, 1954, pp. 521–2.
MERTON, ROBERT K.: review of *A Study of History*, vols. iv–vi, in *The American Journal of Sociology*, vol. xlvii, No. 2, Chicago, September, 1941, pp. 205–13.
MICHELL, H.: 'Herr Spengler and Mr. Toynbee' in *Transactions of the Royal Society of Canada*, vol. xlii, Series III, June, 1949, Section Two, pp. 103–13; reprinted in *Toynbee and History*, pp. 77–88.
MONTAGU, M. F. ASHLEY (ed.): *Toynbee and History: Critical Essays and Reviews*, Boston, 1956, Porter Sargent.
MORGENTHAU, H. J.: 'Toynbee and the Historical Imagination' in *Encounter*, vol. iv, No. 3 [No. 18], London, March, 1955, pp. 70–76; reprinted in *Toynbee and History*, pp. 191–9.
MUMFORD, LEWIS: 'Civilized History' in *The New Republic*, New York, 27th November, 1935, pp. 63–66.
—— in 'The Contribution of Arnold Toynbee' in *Diogenes*, No. 13, Spring, 1956, pp. 11–28.

MUMFORD, LEWIS: 'The Napoleon of Notting Hill' in *The New Republic*, vol. 131, New York, 8th November, 1954, pp. 15–18; reprinted in *Toynbee and History*, pp. 140–7.
—— 'Transfiguration or Renewal' in *The Pacific Spectator*, vol. 1, No. 4, Stanford University, Cal., Autumn, 1947, pp. 391–8.
NEILSON, F.: 'Toynbee's A Study of History' in *The American Journal of Economics and Sociology*, vol. 6, No. 4, Lancaster, Penna., July, 1947, pp. 451–72.
—— 'Arnold J. Toynbee: A Study of History' in *The American Journal of Economics and Sociology*, Supplement to vol. 14, No. 3, Lancaster, Penna., April, 1955, pp. 1–77.
NEVINS, ALLAN: 'Toynbee climbs a Majestic Peak' in *The New York World-Telegram and Sun*, 7th December, 1954.
NICHOLS, JAMES HASTINGS: 'Die Weltgeschichtliche Aufgabe der Religion nach Toynbees Geschichtsphilosophie' in *Studium Generale*, Jahrgang 4, Heft 3, Berlin, March, 1951, pp. 175–82.
—— 'Religion in Toynbee's History' in *The Journal of Religion*, No. 28, Chicago, 1948, pp. 99–119.
OBOLENSKY, PRINCE DMITRI: 'Russia's Byzantine Heritage' in *Oxford Slavonic Papers*, vol. i, Oxford, 1950, Clarendon Press.
—— unpublished note of 1st June, 1951, on the concept of 'Moscow the Third Rome'.
O'KENNEDY, BRIAN: review of *A Study of History* in *The Irish Times*, Dublin, 1st March, 1957.
PARES, RICHARD: review of *A Study of History* in *The English Historical Review*, vol. lxxi, No. 279, London, April, 1956, pp. 256–72.
POORE, CHARLES: review of *A Study of History*, vols. vii–x, in *The New York Times*, 17th October, 1954.
POSTAN, MICHAEL: 'Professor Toynbee's Study of History' in *The Sociological Review*, vol. xxviii, London, 1936, Le Play House Press, pp. 50–63.
POWICKE, SIR F. MAURICE: review of *A Study of History*, vols. iv–vi, in *The Manchester Guardian*, 29th September, 1939.
PRAKASH, BUDDHA: 'Toynbee: His Philosophy of History and Treatment of Modern Civilization' in *The Modern Review*, vol. lxxxiv, No. 5, Calcutta, November, 1953, pp. 401–3.
RALPH, PHILIP LEE: 'Toynbee's Call to Faith', review of *A Study of History*, vols. vii–x, in *The Saturday Review*, vol. xxxvii, No. 42, New York, 16th October, 1954, pp. 18–20.
RENIER, G. J.: 'Toynbee's A Study of History' in G. J. RENIER: *History: Its Purpose and Method*, Boston, 1950, Beacon Press, pp. 215–19; reprinted in *Toynbee and History*, pp. 73–76.
RENOU, L.: in 'The Contribution of Arnold Toynbee' in *Diogenes*, No. 13, Spring, 1956, pp. 70–79.
ROBIN, F. E.: 'The Professor and the Fossil' in *Committee Reporter*, vol. 12, No. 6, New York, October–November, 1955, pp. 1 and 7–8; reprinted in *Toynbee and History*, pp. 316–19.
ROBINSON, D. M.: 'The Historical Validity of Toynbee's Approach to the Greco-Roman World' in *The Intent of Toynbee's History: A Cooperative Appraisal*.
ROMEIN, JAN: 'Reason or Religion: An Old Dispute Renewed' in *Toynbee and History*, pp. 347–50.
SAMUEL, MAURICE: *The Professor and the Fossil*, New York, 1956, Knopf.
SAMUEL, VISCOUNT: review of *A Study of History*, vols. i–iii, in *John o'London's Weekly*, 5th January, 1935.

SAVELLE, MAX: 'The Philosophy of the General: Toynbee versus the Naturalists' in *The Pacific Historical Review*, vol. xxv, No. 1, Berkeley, Cal., February, 1956, pp. 55–67.

SCHUMAN, FREDERICK L.: 'The Paradoxes of Dr. Toynbee', review of *A Study of History*, vols. vii–x, in *The Nation*, vol. 179, No. 19, New York, 6th November, 1954, pp. 405–7.

SOROKIN, PITIRIM A.: 'Toynbee's Philosophy of History' in *The Journal of Modern History*, vol. xii, No. 3, Chicago, September, 1940, pp. 374–87; reprinted in *The Pattern of the Past*, Boston, 1949, Beacon Press, pp. 95–126; and in *Toynbee and History*, pp. 172–87.

—— 'Toynbee's Study of History: The Last Four Volumes' in *The Annals of the American Academy of Political and Social Sciences*, vol. 299, Philadelphia, May, 1955, pp. 144–6; reprinted in *Toynbee and History*, pp. 187–90.

SPATE, O. H. K.: 'Reflections on Toynbee's Study of History: A Geographer's View' in *Historical Studies: Australia and New Zealand*, vol. 5, No. 20, Melbourne, May, 1953, University of Melbourne, pp. 324–37; reprinted in *Toynbee and History*, pp. 287–304.

—— 'Toynbee and Huntington: A Study in Determinism' in *The Geographical Journal*, vol. cxviii, Part 4, London, December, 1952, pp. 406–28.

STECCHINI, LIVIO C.: 'Arnold Toynbee: Neo-Barbarian' in *Midstream: A Quarterly Jewish Review*, vol. ii, No. 4, New York, Autumn, 1956, pp. 84–91.

STOLNIKOFF, JEAN: manuscript letter from Antoing, Hainault, 6th March, 1951, maintaining that the Russians do not feel themselves to be 'a chosen people'.

STONE, LAURENCE: 'Historical Consequences and Happy Families' in *The Spectator*, London, 29th October, 1954, pp. 526–8; reprinted in *Toynbee and History*, pp. 111–14.

STRACHEY, JOHN: critique of A.J.T.'s views on religion; challenge and response in Africa; industrialism; chronology; the relation of A.J.T.'s theory to Marxist theory and dialectic; A.J.T.'s and Marx's theory of the class-conflict: typescript.

—— manuscript letter from Lambourne Old Rectory, 3rd August, 1950.

SUMBERG: THEODORE A.: 'Toynbee and the Decline of Western Civilization' in *Social Research*, vol. 14, No. 3, New York, September, 1947, pp. 267–84.

SUMNER, B. H.: unpublished letter of 25th January, 1951, on the concept of 'Moscow the Third Rome'.

SWEEZY, PAUL M.: 'Signs of the Times' in *The Nation*, New York, 19th October, 1946, pp. 440 and 442–4.

TAWNEY, R. H.: review of *A Study of History*, vols. iv–vi, in *International Affairs*, London, November, 1939, pp. 798–806.

TAYLOR, A. J. P.: 'Much Learning . . .' in *The New Statesman and Nation*, London, 16th October, 1954, pp. 479–80; reprinted in *Toynbee and History*, pp. 115–17.

TEGGART, F. J.: letter from Department of Social Institutions, University of California, Berkeley, Cal., 8th January, 1936, referring to a review by him of *A Study of History*, vols. i–iii.

THOMPSON, KENNETH W.: in 'The Contribution of Arnold Toynbee' in *Diogenes*, No. 13, Spring, 1956, pp. 53–67.

—— 'Toynbee and the Theory of International Politics' in *The Political Science Quarterly*, vol. lxxi, No. 3, New York, September, 1956, Academy of Political Science, pp. 365–86.

THOMPSON, KENNETH W.: 'Toynbee and World Politics: Democracy and Foreign Policy' in *The Review of Politics*, vol. 18, No. 4, Notre Dame, Ind., October, 1956, pp. 418–43.

—— 'Toynbee's Approach to History Reviewed' in *Ethics*, vol. lxv, No. 4, Chicago, July, 1955, pp. 287–303; reprinted in *Toynbee and History*, pp. 200–20.

THOMSON, DAVID: review of D. C. Somervell's Abridgement of *A Study of History*, vols. i–vi, in *The Spectator*, vol. 178, No. 6186, London, 17th January, 1947, pp. 81–82.

—— review of *A Study of History*, vols. vii–x, in *The News Chronicle*, London, 14th October, 1954.

THORNDIKE, LYNN: review of *A Study of History*, vols. i–iii, in *The Journal of Modern History*, vol. vii, No. 3, Chicago, September, 1935, pp. 315–17.

TINGSTEN, HERBERT: 'Science or Mysticism' in *Dagens Nyheter*, Stockholm, 16th January, 1949.

TORMODSEN, J. A., and WASBERG, GUNNAR CHRISTIE: 'Arnold J. Toynbee og A Study of History' in *Samtiden*, vol. 58, hefte 2, Oslo, 1949, pp. 647–60.

Toynbee and History: Critical Essays and Reviews, ed. by M. F. Ashley Montagu, Boston, 1956, Porter Sargent.

TREVOR-ROPER, HUGH: 'Arnold Toynbee's Millennium' in *Encounter*, [vol. 8, No. 6], No. 45, London, June, 1957, pp. 14–28.

—— 'Testing the Toynbee System' in *The Sunday Times*, London, 17th October, 1954; reprinted in *Toynbee and History*, pp. 122–4.

TRINKAUS, CHARLES: 'Toynbee against History' in *Science and Society*, vol. xii, No. 1, New York, 1948, pp. 218–39.

UNDERHILL, FRANK H.: 'Arnold Toynbee, Metahistorian' in *The Canadian Historical Review*, vol. xxxii, No. 3, Toronto, September, 1951, pp. 201–19.

—— 'The Toynbee of the 1950s' in *The Canadian Historical Review*, vol. xxxvi, No. 3, Toronto, September, 1955, pp. 222–35.

VICKERS, SIR GEOFFREY: manuscript letter from London, 1st February, 1943.

VOEGELIN, ERICH: 'Toynbee's History as a Search for Truth' in *The Intent of Toynbee's History: A Cooperative Appraisal*.

VOGT, JOSEPH: 'Die Antike Kultur in Toynbees Geschichtslehre' in *Saeculum*, Band ii, Heft 4, Freiburg-im-Breisgau, 1951, pp. 557–74.

WALKER, FATHER LINUS, O.P.: 'Toynbee and Religion: A Catholic View' in *The Thomist*, vol. 18, No. 2, Baltimore, April, 1955, pp. 292–9; reprinted in *Toynbee and History*, pp. 338–46.

WALSH, W. H.: 'The End of a Great Work' in *The Times*, London, 14th October, 1954, p. 9; reprinted in *Toynbee and History*, pp. 125–8.

WARWICK, A. SHERWOOD: review of *A Study of History*, vols. vii–x, in *The Louisville Courier-Journal*, 14th November, 1954.

WATNICK, MORRIS: 'Toynbee's Nine Books of History against the Pagans' in *The Antioch Review*, No. 7, Yellow Springs, Ohio, Winter, 1947–8, pp. 587–602.

WEIL, G.: 'Arnold Toynbee's Conception of the Future of Islam' in *Middle Eastern Affairs*, vol. 2, No. 1, New York, January, 1951, pp. 3–17; reprinted in *Toynbee and History*, pp. 273–86.

WEINBERGER, CASPAR WILLARD: review of *A Study of History*, vols. vii–x, in *The San Francisco Chronicle*, 17th October, 1954.

WERNER, H.: 'Spengler und Toynbee' in *Deutsche Vierteljahrsschrift für Literaturwissenschaft und Geistesgeschichte*, 29. Jahrgang, xxix. Band, Stuttgart, 1955, Metzler, pp. 528–54.

WOLFE, BERTRAM D.: 'Dissenting Opinion on Toynbee' in *The American Mercury*, vol. 64, No. 282, New York, June, 1947, pp. 748–55.

WOODWARD, C. VANN: 'Toynbee and Metahistory' in *The American Scholar*, vol. 27, No. 3, New York, Summer, 1958, pp. 384–92.

WOODWARD, SIR E. LLEWELLYN: review of *A Study of History*, vols. i–iii, in *The Spectator*, London, 6th July, 1934, p. 21.

—— review of *A Study of History*, vols. iv–vi, in *The Spectator*, London, 18th August, 1939.

WOOLF, LEONARD: review of *A Study of History*, vols. iv–vi, in *The New Statesman and Nation*, London, 23rd September, 1939.

ZAHN, E. F. J.: *Toynbee und das Problem der Geschichte*, Köln and Opladen, 1954, Westdeutscher Verlag.

INDEX

In the cross-references in this index, references in small capitals (e.g. ARAB
CALIPHATE at the end of the heading 'Abbasid Caliphate) are to other main
headings, while references in ordinary type are to subdivisions of the same main
heading.